Westbrook Maine Cemeteries

Plus the Surrounding Towns of Cumberland, Falmouth, Gorham, Portland and Windham

Compiled by
Karen Sherman Ketover

HERITAGE BOOKS
2019

HERITAGE BOOKS
AN IMPRINT OF HERITAGE BOOKS, INC.

Books, CDs, and more—Worldwide

For our listing of thousands of titles see our website at
www.HeritageBooks.com

Published 2019 by
HERITAGE BOOKS, INC.
Publishing Division
5810 Ruatan Street
Berwyn Heights, Md. 20740

Copyright © 1996 Karen Sherman Ketover

Heritage Books by the author:

Fabius M. Ray's Story of Westbrook [Maine]

Sullivan County, Tennessee Cemeteries

Westbrook, Maine Cemeteries; Plus the Surrounding Towns of Cumberland, Falmouth, Gorham, Portland & Windham

All rights reserved. No part of this book may be reproduced or transmitted in any form or by any means, electronic or mechanical, including photocopying, recording or by any information storage and retrieval system without written permission from the author, except for the inclusion of brief quotations in a review.

International Standard Book Numbers
Paperbound: 978-0-7884-0401-6
Clothbound: 978-0-7884-8235-9

First of all I want to thank my husband Jay for all his support during this project. I couldn't have done it without him. He spent countless week-ends over the past 2 1/2 years driving all over searching for cemeteries. He hiked through the weeds and the woods looking for lost gravestones. He has read off thousands of names and death dates while I wrote them down. He also photographed many old stones and a general overview of the cemeteries. I couldn't have asked for better help than Jay gave me.

Many thanks to those who gave me lists and directions for many cemeteries I would never have found. Thank you to my friend Patricia Larrabee who helped me track down lost burials at Woodlawn Cemetery. Also to Arthur Gordan, Ken Karby and Eleanor Conant Saunders. To Bob Blais of Blais Funeral Home for helping me secure a copy of St.Hyacinth's burials, to Brenda Caldwell, Gorham Town Clerk and to all those people we stopped and asked, "Where are we!". Lastly, to the City of Westbrook, a grateful thank you for keeping very good records for the past 108 years.

This is my second book on cemeteries and I tried very hard not to make errors. I'd forgotten how tired one gets after 5 or 6 hours standing in the sun or rain, trying to write while swatting black flies. Some stones are impossible to read, I gave it my best guess. I used turn of the century newspaper articles, obituaries and town histories to fill in some of the blanks that were left by questionable stones. This doesn't insure accuracy, but maybe it will help.

Each cemetery list notes what was done at that cemetery. Whether I checked it stone by stone or if it was a list given to me or I simply couldn't find the cemetery.

Here are some abbreviations that I used:

inf/o	infant of	s/o	son of
bu:	burial date	d/o	dauther of
s.b.	stillborn	ch/o	child of
cem.	cemetery	w/o	wife of
rem.	removed	h/o	husband of
?	couldn't be sure	XX	no first name
unm.	unmarried	XXXX	no date
y	years	[G.S.]	gravestone
m	months	R.S.	Revolutionary Soldier
h	hours	C.W.	Civil War Soldier
{O}	obituaries		

Westbrook was originally a part of the township now known as "Ancient Falmouth," as first laid out Falmouth embraced the territory now included with the boundaries of Falmouth, Westbrook, Deering, Cape Elizabeth and Portland, together with a large number of islands in Casco Bay. The work of dismemberment began with the incorporation of Cape Elizabeth in 1765. July 4, 1786, "the Neck," as it had been called previous to that time, was constituted a separate town by the name of Portland, which received a city charter in 1832. But, notwithstanding, these encroachments of the General Court upon its ancient boundaries Falmouth was still a large town; so large, in fact, that in the year 1813 it underwent a division a third time, being severed very nearly in twain; the western portion taking the name of Stroudwater while the eastern part was permitted to retain the ancient name, as it does to the present day. By permission of the General Court the name of Stroudwater was dropped, after a year, and that of Westbrook assumed by the new town in honor of Col. Thomas Westbrook who had formerly resided, and was supposed to be buried within its limits.

As thus constituted the town of Westbrook took, at once, a prominent rank among the towns of the "old Commonwealth;" and from that time forth, under the parent state no less than since the separation of Maine from Massachusetts, its position among sister towns has been steadfastly maintained. After its incorporation in 1813, more than half a century of uninterrupted prosperity ensued; but finally, in 1869, it was felt by the majority of the inhabitants of that portion of the town contiguous to Portland that their interests would be better subserved by a further division, and the incorporation of still another town from the territory of old Falmouth. This feeling led to the "division contest" still fresh in the memories of most readers of these columns, the result of which was that the present large and wealthy town of Deering began its corporate existence on the 21st day of March, A.D.,1871.

The town thus ushered into being was named in honor of Mr. James Deering, long a respected citizen of Westbrook, but better known as one of the merchant princes of Portland during the first half of the present century. His private residence was the fine mansion home within the town which bears his name, a little way out from Portland on the Saccarappa road.

-- taken in part from the *Westbrook Chronicle*, Feb.16,1883.

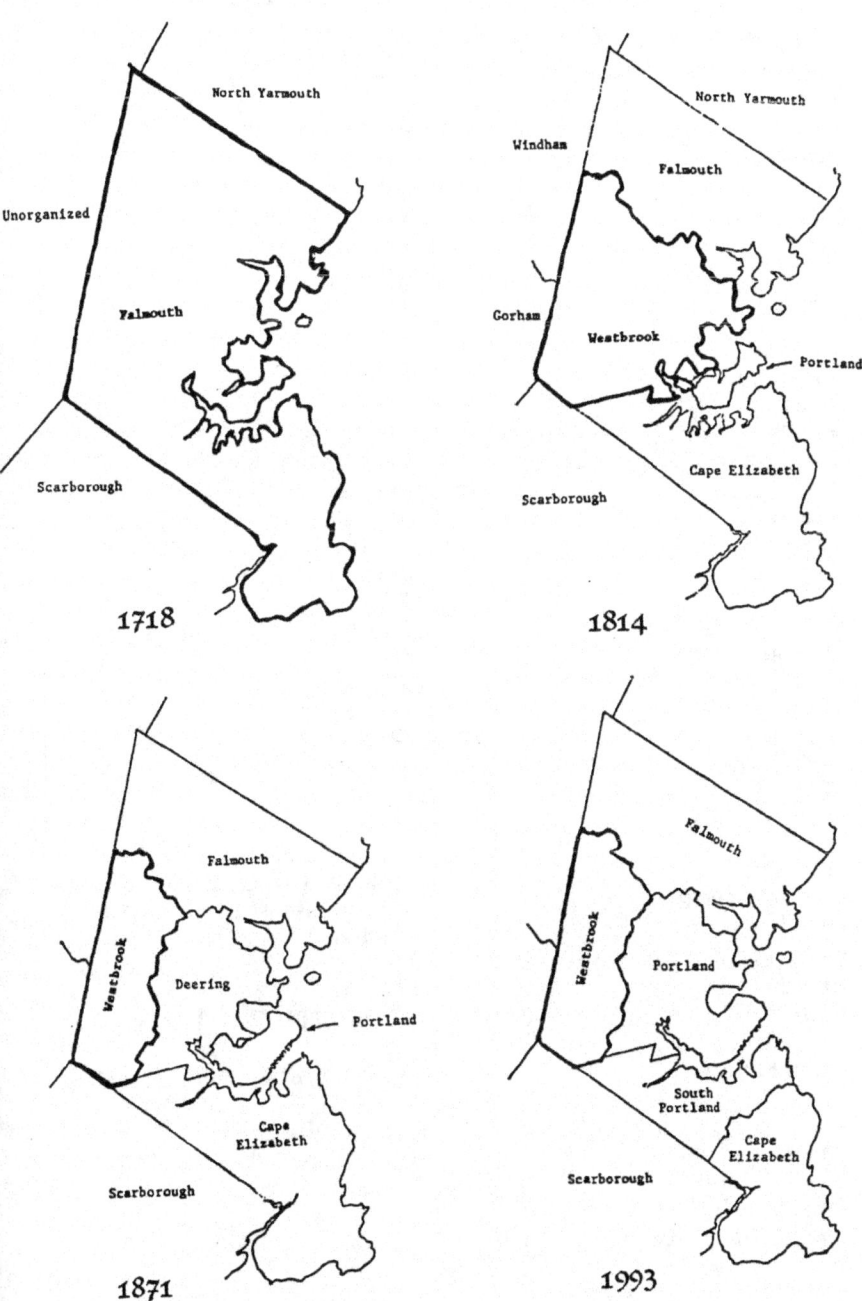

In 1814 Westbrook separates from Falmouth.
Deering separates from Westbrook in 1871.

FALMOUTH

Falmouth Memorial Library had many old lists of cemeteries. I located all I could and checked all those stones. A few of them I just couldn't find.

Blanchard	5
Crabtree-Hobbs	16
Field	3
Foreside Community Church	17
Huston	152
Leighton	3
Leighton	5
Leighton Tomb	239
Leighton-Staples	239
Lord	3
Marston	4
Marston	5
McGregor	3
Merrill	5
Merrill-Knight	3
Packard	15
Pine Grove	8
Pleasant Hill	1
Quaker	16
Unknown	16
Watts	5
West Falmouth	17

CUMBERLAND

I did the last 4 stone by stone and they are current through 1994.

Allen Family	363
Farris	33
Foreside Community Church, part in Falmouth	17
Morrison Hill Church	23
West Cumberland United Methodist Church	25

WINDHAM

Windham reportedly has 28 cemeteries, I checked 16 stone by stone. The other lists were given to me and weren't checked.

Arlington	87
Austin	72
Brown	36
Chase	53
Chute	40
Dolley	49
Elder	70
Friends	74
Goold	44
Hanson	70
John Akers Knight	41
Knight	41
Knight	71
Loveitt	37
Mayberry	44
McIntosh	70
Morrell	72
Mugford	39
Old Anderson	39
Old Quaker	76
Old Smith	77
Purinton	51
Smith	58
Stevens	69
Stevens Farm	99
Unnamed Craigie Road	41
Varney Pasture	39
Windham Hill	83

SOUTH PORTLAND

Smith Street Cemetery	413

This was done stone by stone and is current through 1994.

PORTLAND

Portland's old cemeteries were given to me by the Evergreen Cemetery Office. The only ones I checked stone by stone were Stroudwater, Grand Trunk and Summit Street.

Bailey	107
Bailey's Hill	112
Evergreen	138
Friend's	109
Frost	109
George Street	100
Grand Trunk	110
Maplewood	111
Stroudwater	100
Summit Street	100
Unnamed	112
Wilson Monument	100
Pine Grove	119
Pine Grove Cemetery Assoc.	112

WESTBROOK

Westbrook city cemeteries are current through 1994. St. Hyacinth Church Cemetery is 75% checked. Their burial records are grossly incomplete. Winter set in and I was unable to complete checking stone by stone.

Alms House/City Farm	152
Cobb	148
Conant	145
Gowen Family	146
Grant Family	239
Hale	145
Hardy	145
Highland Lake	148
Highland Lake Church	147
Jameson	151
Johnson	146
Knight	145
Larrabee	147
Lord	147
Lunt	147
Proctor	239
Saccarappa	240
St. Hyacinth	268
Veterans at Saccarappa	240a
Westbrook, Col.	146
Woodlawn	153

GORHAM

Gorham cemeteries as noted were generously given to me by Brenda Caldwell, Gorham Town Clerk. The private cemetery associations denied having any burial records. I was going to do them stone by stone but decided to let them keep their secrets and only included those given to me by Mrs. Caldwell. I filled in what blanks I could using McLellan's *History of Gorham*.

Clay	338
Dyer Family	343
Eastern	364
Farmer	322
Fort Hill	339
Hamblen Family	344
Hillside	329
Huston Family	363
Nonesuch	340
North Gorham	322
North Street	355
Sapling Hill	340
Shaws Mill	363
Smith	355
South Gorham	344
South Street	319
Swett	342
West Gorham	353
White Rock	352
Surname Index	418

I am always updating my files on these and other cemeteries that I have located. Any queries may be sent, with a self-addressed, stamped envelope, to

Karen Sherman Ketover
P.O. Box 1307
Westbrook, ME 04098

✤ **PLEASANT HILL** ✤
Also known as the Batchelder
Cemetery. Off Cleeve's Farm Road.
Rev. War, War of 1812 & Civil War
Veterans are buried here.

ADAMS
Henry Herbert,May 22,1858,2y,
  s/o Chas. & Louisa.
Lizzie P. Noyes,1861-1901,w/o Willis.
Rufus H.,Apr.2,1860,35y,h/o Mary.
Willis G.,1859-1901.
Willis,G.,1879-1910,s/o W.G.& Lizzie.
ALLEN
Almon S.,1848-1908.
Erixine C.,Mar.27,1857,31y,
  w/o Almon.
ANDERSON
Henry W.,1868-1908.
BACHELDER
Susanna,July 18,1841,78y,w/o Jos.
BATCHELDER
Elbridge L.,May 10,1861,37y.
Eliza D.Merrill,Dec.6,1856,21y,
  w/o S.P.
John,Dec.21,1818,29y.
Mary,Jan.26,1872,70y,s/o Samuel.
Mary Jane,Mar.19,1850,20y,
  only d/o Samuel & Mary.
Samuel L.,Dec.23,1851,54y.
BARBER
Ellen F.,1863-1904,w/o Harold.
BARBOUR
Clarence O.,Dec.14,1853,4y,
  s/o Smith & Emily.
Elizabeth,Sept.5,1882,60y
Emily,Apr.1,1856,43y,w/o Barbour.
Harry,1866-1888.
Smith,Dec.17,1811-May 26,1895.
CHAMBERLAIN
Mary A.,June 8,1889,74y,
  w/o Nathaniel.
CLOUDMAN
Mary,Sept.1,1898,w/o Louis O.
COBB
Angerline S.,Apr.21,1850,6y,
  d/o Daniel & Eliza S.
Dorcus,May 29,1874,75y,w/o Issac.
Hannah H.,Nov.1,1867,88y.
Isaac,July 29,1865,81y.
Nelson B.,Nov.4,1842,11y,s/o D. & E.
COLLEY
Ada E.,Knight,1858-1899,w/o Henry.
Arthur R.,188X-1935.
Charles W.,Feb.1,1858,7y.
Frank J.,1880-1935,s/o H. & Ada.
Henry,1860-1902.

Ina,Jan.1864,1y.
Joseph G.,Sept.5,1864,54y.
Mahala A.,Dec.13,1863,20y.
Sarah A.,Apr.12,1854,38y.
Sarah S.,Apr.18,1856,10y.
William,Dec.7,1841,9m,s/o J.G.& S.A.
CRITCHETT
John,June 1,1813,36y,
  killed on the Chesapeake.
Susan,Sept.11,1850,69y,wid/o John.
DOBBIN
Daniel,July 3,1889,82y.
James,Jr.,July 4,1837,42y.
James,Mar.7,1751-Aug.24,1853,
  S.C. Mil. Rev.War.
Joseph,Oct.10,1825,99y.
Sarah W.,May 14,1896,78y.
DOUGHTY
Sarah G.,Aug.5,1875,34y,w/o Alvin S.
FOGG
Sara E. Gammon,Dec.12,1876,24y,
  w/o George H.
FOSTER
Everlener,May 15,1859,25y,w/o Geo.
GAMMON
Delia M.,1811-1891,w/o Peter.
Xlen Augusta,Nov.17,1859,11y.
XX Lucilia,Sept.24,1860,26y.
Julia Adelaide,Nov.1,1859,15y.
Peter,1808-1899.
HUSTON
Charlotte,Aug.25,1851,75y.
Gowen,May 15,1848?,69y.
Ingraham E.,Dec.11,1877,66y.
Mary L.,Sept.13,1851,67y.
Paul,Jan.13,1855,80y.
JONES
Abigail Knight,May 3,1827,52y,
  w/o Butter.
KNIGHT
Abbie B.,Apr.29,1879,67y,w/o Isaac.
Abbie F.,Mar.16,1862,19y.
Ann,Mar.28,1889,75y,w/o Samuel.
Annie L.,Jan.1878-June 24,1879,
  d/o W.H.&M.E.
Betsey,May 1934,63y,w/o Nathan'l.
Charles,Capt.,Aug.1,1869,78y.
Charlotte,June 12,1810,42y,
  2nd w/o Stephen.
Cyrena,Aug.1,1861,43y,w/o Jos.
Edward W.,Dec.1803-Aug.10,1831.
Eliza J.,Sept.29,1855,27y.
Eliza,Feb.9,1828,35y,w/o Alexand.
Ella D.Baker,1860-XXXX,w/o Wm.E.
Ephraim,1776-1857.
Ezra E.,1834-1898.

Frederick,Oct.15,1848,27y,
 s/o Alexander & Eliza.
Idellette ?,May 1854,7m,d/o S.M.& A.
Jacob,Jan.27,1843,86y.
Jacob,Jr.,Apr.12,1816,32y.
Jane,1781-1856,w/o Ephraim.
John M.,Capt.,Sept.10,1842,45y.
John,Capt.,Apr.1818-Sept.15,1849.
Joseph,Mar.11,1885,72y.
Lucinda Thompson,1841-1909,
 w/o Ezra.
Margaret,Sept.5,1853,28y,w/o Reuben.
Mary E.Bucknam,1828-1908,
 w/o Amos.
Mary,Apr.23,1843,85y,w/o Jacob.
Mary,Mar.26,1867,81y,w/o Zebul.
Nancy,Nov.5,1854,30y,wid/o Fred.
Nathaniel,Jan.5,1868,96y.
Oliver,Dea.,Aug.26,1849,77y.
--araxa,May 4,1858,w/o Oliver.
Paulina,Jan.1849,8m,d/o S.M.& Ann.
Pheobe G.,Mar.5,1850,32y,
 w/o Reuben.
Priscilla,Aug.17,1822,79y,w/o George.
Rachel,Apr.14,1846,67y,w/o Jacob,Jr.
Reuben,Aug.13,1877,63y,h/o Sarah A.
Samuel,Nov.26,1855,76y.
Samuel M.,May 17,1871,62y.
Sarah A. Whitney,1825-1901.
Stephen,Oct.10,1825,99y.
Sumner A.,May 23,1854,20y,
 s/o Samuel M. & Ann.
William E.,1858-1908.
William G.,Mar.27,1849,4m,
 s/o Joseph & Cyrena.
Zebulon,Oct.31,1848,64y.
LORD
Bethany K.,Sept.17,1851,22y.
James,Jan.21,1877,95.
James,Sept.17,1888,78y.
Lucy,Apr.1,1862,74y,w/o James.
Pheebe G,July 16,1824-Jan.9,1905
MARIAH
Ann,Sept.15,1853,16y.
MARSTON
David,Nov.8,1852,80y.
Mary W.,Aug.7,1888,75y,w/o David.
MERRILL
Laura F.M.,Jan.30,1858,17y,
 d/o Paul E. & Sophia A.
Sarah S.,Oct.8,1849,3y,
 d/o Adam & Eveline S.
Sophia A.,Feb.17,1853,33y,w/o Paul.
MORSE
Elizabeth,Aug.31,1868,97y,
 w/o Jonathan.
Ephraim,May 5,1832,68y.

Jonathan,Feb.25,1824,50y.
Rachel,Oct.7,1846,75y,w/o Eph.
PETERSON
Elen M., Kattie G., Willie H.,Jonnie,
 4 ch/o John H. & Maria S., no dates.
SHUTE
John H.J.,Sept.25,1845,22y.
SKILLIN
Almon,Oct.6,1847,18y,s/o Edw. & Han.
Edward,Mar.24,1868,73y.
Hannah,July 12,1803-
 June 30,1879,w/o Edward.
Leonora,Nov.1,1846,12y,
 d/o Edward& Hannah.
Royal Lincoln,Dec.31,1827,2m,
 s/o Edward & Hannah.
SMITH
Anthony,Mar.10,1863,51y.
SWETT
Charles M.,Feb.8,1851,3d,s/o C.S.
Clara A.,June1853,10w,d/o Wm.& E.
John F.,Apr.26,1846,s/o Wm.& C. P.
Moses,Sept.4,1848,83y.
TURNER
Caroline Susan Knight,July 27,1828,
 22y,w/o Ebenezer & d/o Sam.& Mary.
WAITE
Amasa,Oct.28,1847,66y.
Betsey,Apr.1801-Jan.1877,w/o Amasa.
Edward L.,Nov.23,1866-
 Dec.23,1883,s/o H.L.& E.J.
Ella F.,Dec.2,1870-Sept.30,1892,
 d/o H.L.&E.J.
Elmer H.,Nov.7,1776-July 9,1777.
Fannie,May 1871,2y,d/o H.L.& E.J.
Henry L.,Nov.8,1838-Aug.28,1912.
Jane,June 24,1834,52y,w/o Amasa.
Susan,Aug.8,1844,70y.
William B.,Jan.22,1877,70y.
WEYMOUTH
Freddie L.,Jan.11,1863,18m,
 s/o Wm.& S.L.
Solomon B.,Sept.14,1859,30y.
WILDER
Albion,Dec.15,1831-Nov.1,1884.
James M.,1837-1888.
John E.,Jan.31,1863,40y,
 s/o J. & Laura S.
John,Jan.28,1847,56y,h/o Laura S.
Laura S.,Sept.25,1797-July 14,1879.
Martin,Apr.26,1854,41y.
Susan K.,Jan.30,1885,28y,
 d/o John & Laura.
WYMAN
Mary Ann,July 2,1838,31y.

✤ **MERRILL-KNIGHT** ✤
On easterly bank of the Presumpscot River in a thick grove of trees, off Allen Ave. Ext. Abandoned and barely readiable in 1896. Didn't locate.

KNIGHT
Deborah,July 1,1801,38y, w/o Stephen.
MERRILL
Abigail,Nov.7,1806,82y,s/o Jas.
James,Maj.,Nov.17,1806,78y.

✤ **FIELD CEMETERY** ✤
98 Field Road, Falmouth.
Checked stone by stone.

ADAMS
Andrew J.,Dec.22,1832-Feb.26,1905.
Cordelia J.,Oct.23,1832-May 16,1864,w/o A.J.
Mary J.Murdock,Aug.16,1844-July 12,1915,w/o Andrew J.
Mary,Sept.29,1850,75y,w/o Sam.
Samuel,Jan.11,1853,84y.
FIELD
Elizabeth,June 16,1811,38y, w/o Hanson.
FOSTER
Lizzie M.,Mar.16,1859,23y, w/o James H.
Separated from this cemetery was two stones in a stand of pine trees behind it, one is readiable.
FIELD
Maria S.,Dec.9,1859,31y,w/o Charles.

✤ **LEIGHTON CEMETERY** ✤
84 Brook Road rear, Falmouth.

HICKS
Nathaniel,May 7,1856,83y.
Sarah,Aug.18,1858,85y,w/o Nath'l.
LEIGHTON
Alfred L.,1847-1905.
Asa,Sept.30,1873,72y.
Betsey Jane Moody,1830-1907, w/o Hale.
David,Dec.18,1767-Dec.10,1825.
Edward Gilman,July 31,1793-Feb.22,1850.
Elisa,Oct.11,1857,45y,w/o Asa.
Ephraim,June 14,1798-May 21,1878.
Hale,1828-1906.
Hannah D.,Hicks,Apr.9,1793-Sept.30,1824,w/o Edward G.
Hannah H.,1829-1905,w/o Alfred.

Hannah,Dec.27,1878,72y, w/o Ephraim.
Horace,Mar.24,1878,25y,s/o Hale & B.J.
Jane,Feb.3,1864,62y,w/o Edw. G.
Lucy Baker,Feb.5,1767Apr.15,1837, w/o David.
Mary,Sept.3,1832,26y,w/o Asa.
Samuel S.,Mar.11,1857,23y, s/o A.L.& H.H.
Silas,Sept.1771-Jan.28,1856.
Sophia,May 2,1849,46y,w/o Ephraim.
Ursula,Dec.24,1796-Mar.8,1879.
Josiah L.,B.Apr.1792,s/o Jed. & E.
Susan,XXXX.

✤ **LORD CEMTERY** ✤
Lowell Farm Road, Falmouth.
Checked stone by stone.

LORD
John,Sept.25,1856,78y.
Eunice.1811-1902, d/o John & A.
Abigail,Mar.16,1821,90y,w/o John.
PRIDE
Joseph,June 8,1886,84y.

✤ **McGREGOR CEMETERY** ✤
90 Falmouth Road, Falmouth.
Well maintained, checked all stones.

BUTTERFIELD
Abigail,Jan.27,1819, d/o Jonathan & Prudence.
David McGregore,Feb.4,1819, s/o Jonathan & Prudence.
FOSTER
Hannah G.,1799-1884.
HICKS
Joseph P.,Nov.11,1846,16y,s/o L.& S.
Lemuel,Aug.24,1870,75y,h/o Salome.
Salome Merrill,Mar.28,1862,64y
McGREGOR
David,Rev.,b.Londonderry,NH, Mar.21,1771-Oct.19,1845,74y.
Rebecca,Dec.14,1788-July 2,1852, 64y,w/o David.
MERRILL
Abby Ellen,Dec.23,1848,12m, d/o S.M.& E. A.
Abigail,Apr.19,1829,w/o Bennair
Abigail,Oct.26,1862,77y,wid/o Jacob.
Achsah,Dec.27,1836,35y,w/o Jas. A.
Asenath,Oct.28,1822,28y,w/o Giles.
Augustus E.N.,Nov.28,1855,9y.
Benaiah,Apr.19,1819,23y,s/o B. & A.
Bennair,Apr.2,1831,62y.
Caleb S.,Oct.5,1849,24y.

3

Charity N.,Apr.18,1876,85y,
 w/o Jeremiah.
Charity,June 27,1858,37y,
 d/o Giles & Asenath.
Charlotte D.,Feb.15,1850,60y,
 w/o Robt. A.,d/o Bennair & Abigail.
Edward,Nov.20,1818,6y,s/o B.& A.
Elizabeth,July 16,1815,58y,
 w/o Jacob.
Emma Ellis,July 1817,12y,
 d/o R.A. & S.A.
Estella F.,Oct.11,1850,10m,
 d/o W.N.& Lydia T.
Fennick D.,1821,6y,s/o Giles & A.
Frank,June1849,18m,s/o W.N.& L.T.
George P.,Sept.24,1850,32y.
Giles,Col.,July 1849,61y,War 1812.
Henry A.,Dec.12,1854,22y.
Jacob,Mar.1835,80y,Rev. Soldier.
James,Dec.28,1854,93y.
Jeremiah,Oct.13,1865,79y.
John B.,Jan.25,1853,17y.
Josiah,Nov.2,1820,18y,s/o B. & A.
Mary E.,Sept.8,1851,3y.
Mary J.,Feb.26,1857,50y,w/o Leonard.
Mary Pettingal,Dec.12,1818,12y,
Mary,Jan.29,1807,21y,d/o Jas.& Mary.
Matilda,Apr.13,1820,20y,
 d/o R.A.& S.A.
Robert Adams,Apr.23,1853,79y,
 s/o Giles & Asenath.
Saline,July 3,1847,82y,w/o Jas.
Samuel M.,Oct.12,1849.
Sarah A.,July 1,1818,44y,w/o Robt. A.
Sarah S.,Oct.8,1849,3y,
 d/o Adam & Eveline.
Sarah,Oct.13,1882,79y.
William N.,Oct.4,1850,25y.

MILTIMORE
Dorcus,Sept.10,1830,30y,
 w/o Rev. William.
Elizabeth Williams,b.Windham,NH-
 d.Mar.5,1826,w/o Rev.William,
 d/o Simon.
Mary Merrill,Mar.31,1811,4y,
 d/o Wm.& E.W.

PETTINGILL
Benjamin,Apr.8,1837,76y.
Daniel,Nov.13,1812,14y,s/o Ben & M.
Mary,Nov.24,1806,43y,w/o Benj.

POPE
John,May 4,1829,67y.
Louisa,Jan.11,1804/64,69y.
Mary,May 28,1829,63y,w/o John.

SWETT
James,Capt.,1846.

WEBBER
Clarissa,Mar.20,1815,31y,
 w/o Capt. Aaron.

✦ **MARSTON CEMETERY** ✦
202 Falmouth Road, Falmouth.
Checked all stones.

BLANCHARD
Alfred M.,Oct.1847,4y, s/o E.C.& S.
Isabella F.,June 24,1859,20y,d/o E.C.

COLLEY
Lucy J Davis,Sept.5,1849,27y,
 w/o Joseph. G.

MARSTON
Alfred B.,May 29,1884,76y.
Benjamin M.,Mar.24,1861,54y.
Bethia A.,Oct.23,1908,95y,w/o Peter N.
Cornelia M.,May 5,1858,22y,
 d/o B.M.& M.C.
Elsie M.,1851-1934.
Francenia M.,Dec.25,1839,5y,
 d/o B.M.& M.C.
Francis,Oct.1839,5d,s/o P.N.& B.A.
Joseph S.,June 16,1864,23y,
 s/o P.N.& B.A.
Hannah Matilda,Mar.19,1850,13y,
 d/o P.N.& B.A.
Harriet A. Haskell,1835-1901,
 w/o Seward B.
Horace C.,1842-1880.
Mary A.,Nov.14,1881,69y,w/o Alfr. B.
Mary C.,1812-1876,w/o Benj.M.
Peter,Jan.30,1861,82y.
Peter N.,Dea.,June 14,1891,80y.
Salome,Oct.1,1858,76y.
Seward B.,1829-1914.

MERRILL
Ann R. Miller,Feb.6,1892,63y,
 w/o Benjamin F.
Benjamin F.,Sept.29,1868,63y.
Charles D.,Nov.4,1839-Sept.3,1862.
Frances E.,July 18,1879,50y,
 w/o Theo.H.
Henry M.,Sept.3,1847,16m,
 s/o B.F.& M.L.
Julia E.,Apr.1865,16y,d/o B.F.& A.R.
Mary S.,July 7,1844,16y,
 d/o B.F.& M.L.
Mercy Ann,Oct.1848,1m,
 d/o B.F.& M.L.
Mercy L.,Sept.12,1848,43y,
 w/o Benjamin F.
Paul E.,Capt.,Mar.7,1854.
Sarah,Apr.5,1776,26y,w/o Moses,
 d/o Nathaniel Carll.
Theodore H.,Oct.12,1859,31y.

PATRICK
Almira,Sept.28,1871,75y.
Clara M.,Oct.13,1858,44y.
PRINCE
Eliza,Apr.5,1869,74y,w/o Reuben.
Reuben,Capt.,Feb.8,1856,63y.
RICHARDS
Aphia,July 12,1865,75y,w/o Samuel.
Eunice,Jan.24,1847,14y,
 d/o Samuel & Aphia.
Hannah,1820-1899.
Samuel,May 30,1861,78y.
YOUNG
 ch/o D.U. & C.:
Almira S.,Sept.10,1850,4y,
Henry S.,Apr.7,1858,4y.
Mary H.,Jan.17,1851,9y.

✣ **WATTS FAMILY CEMETERY** ✣
Near 135 Field Road, Falmouth.
This all we found buried in the weeds.

WATTS
Hannah,May 25,1879,84y,
 d/o Samuel & Damarius.
foot stone: M.W.

✣ **MERRILL GRAVEYARD** ✣
185 Woodville Road. Most stones are too worn to read, all were checked.

ADAMS
Dorcas,Oct.13,1781-1804,w/o Moses,Jr.
Isaac Deering,Mar.11,1817,2y,
 s/o Isaac & Pricilla.
DONNELL
William S.,Jan.1,1838,62y.
ILSLEY
Betsy,Sept.13,1804,22y,w/o Nath'l.
Dorcus,1862,38y?, w/o Nathaniel.
George F.,Mar.29,1822,
 s/o Nathaniel & Judith.
Nathaniel,Sept.13,1804, ?.
Woodbury,1804.
LOCKE
Susanna,Nov.22,1822,w/o Abijah.
MERRILL
Apphia,1843,80y.
Deering,Jan.29,1840,35y.
Dorcus,Jan.22,1862,68y,
 w/o Nathan.
Elizabeth,Dec.11,1807,42y,
 w/o Nathan.
Elizabeth,June 7,1823,25y,
 d/o Nathan & Elizabeth.
Elizabeth,1801,13y,
 d/o Silas & Hannah.

Hannah,Mar.19,1839,85y,
 w/o Humphrey.
Hannah,Jan.1826,79y,w/o Silas.
Humphrey,Jan.24,1825,76y, R.S.
Isaac,Jan.9,1830.
Israel,1848,88y.
Israel,Jan.20,1825,25y,
 s/o Nathan & Elizabeth.
Luther,Apr.1823,32y,drowned,
 s/o Silas.
Mary,Dec.4,1863,84y.
Myra,Nov.30,1810,14y,
 d/o Nathan & Elizabeth.
Nathan,Feb.10,1826,65y.
Nathan,Jr.,Mar.24,1826,24y,
 s/o Nathan & Elizabeth.
Olive,Oct.31,1820,27y,
 d/o Nathan & Elizabeth.
Silas,Sept.26,1808,64y.
MITCHELL
Deering,1810.
NOYES
Elizabeth,Dec.2,1803,w/o Samuel.
Samuel P.,Mar.2/27,1803/9,51y.
SAWYER
Bertha A.,1846,
 d/o Simon & Almira Jane.

✣ **LEIGHTON FAMILY** ✣
413 Blackstrap Road, Falmouth.

LEIGHTON
Dorothy Hall,1733-c.1777,w/o George.
Eunice Gerrish,Oct.3,1755-
 Oct.1821,w/o Jedediah.
George,1727-XXXX.
Jedediah,1757-1851.
Josiah L.,B.Apr.14,1792,s/o Jed. & E.
Susan,XXXX.

✣ **BLANCHARD CEMETERY** ✣
215-225 Winn Road,Falmouth.Active.
Did not update or check this list.

ADAMS
Benjamin W.,1824-1903.
Bradley J.,1830-1908.
Edwin R.,July 4,1880,53y.
Frances Ellen,Nov.24,1866,3y,
 d/o B.W.& S.B.
Isaac,Mar.11,1852,77y.
Isaac,Mar.11,1817,2y,
 s/o Isaac & Priscilla.
Ongelina,Sept.13,1858,26y,d/o I. & P.
Priscilla,Sept.21,1867,78y,w/o Isaac.
Sarah B.,June 11,1881,50y,w/o Benj.
Sarah P.,1838-XXXX,w/o Bradley J.

ALLEN
Abbie Stocker,1835-XXXX.
Ann Winslow,Oct.30,1892,95y.
Daniel,Oct.15,1839,44y,h/o Ann W.
Idella Stocker,1857-XXXX,
  d/o J. & Abbie.
Josiah,1831-1909,h/o Abbie.
ANDERSON
John,June 5,1816,72y.
James A.,June 1842,9m,s/o J.& L.
James M.,May 22,1867,56y.
Lydia,Aug.11,1878,64y,w/o Jas. M.
Martha,Dec.20,1836,9Xy, w/o John.
Nancy R. Murry,1792-1854.
Robert,1783-1817,h/o Nancy R.
ASQUITH
Frank,1904-1911.
Joseph W.,1840-1914.
BACHELDER
Nellie E.,1878-1914,w/o Fred.
BAILEY
Isaac W.,Jan.9,1856,23m,
  s/o Chas.& Abigail.
BLANCHARD
Bela,Feb.5,1893,79y.
Frank B.,May 28,1851-Dec.1908
Salome P.,Oct.7,1883,68y,w/o Bela.
BRINK
A. Margrathe,1852-1891,w/o Jacob.
Jacob H.,1839-1912.
John W.,1886-1910.
Margaret,1888-1891.
Sarah L.,1884-1911.
CALDER
Jennie M.Purrington,Aug.2,1866-
  Dec.14,1905,w/o H.L.
DUNBAR
Annie S.,Jan.18,1869-July 2,1886.
DUNHAM
Dorothy M.Adams,July 2,1883,
  64y,w/o Sewall B.
Elizabeth S.,Mar.3,1872,54y,
  w/o John.
Hannah,Nov.17,180X,28y,w/o Jos.
Isaac,July 26,1881,36y.
John A.,Aug.14,1876,64y.
Joseph T.,Feb.16,1843,1y,
  s/o S.B. & D.M.
Joseph,Oct.21,1835,61y.
Rebecca M.C.,Aug.25,1839,26y,
  w/o Enos.
FIELD
Albina I.,Sept.10,1848-
  Apr.21,1876,ch/o Wm. & B.M.
Barbara M.,July 13,1806-
  Dec.9,1893,w/o William.
Eben C.,Sept.4,1806-May 20,1881.

Marzellia,May 30,1835-May 1,1853,
  d/o Wm. & B.M.
Ruth,Jan.13,1832,56y,
  w/o Capt.Alpheus.
Sarah,Nov.24,1822-Oct.29,1893,
  w/o Eben C.
William Henry,1839-XXXX.
William,May 13,1806-Jan.14,1893.
GALLISON
Sarah,1834-1905.
GURNEY
Ann Eliza,Jan.31,1867,38y,w/o John P.
HADLOCK
Lydia,1818-1849,d/o Wm.& Sarah.
Sarah Leighton,1780-1849.
Susan,1805-1877,d/o Wm. & Sarah.
William,1781-1863,h/o Sarah.
HALL
Anneliza,1826-1829.
Granville,1823-1896.
Huldah Winslow,1788-1866.
Jeremiah,1788-1868,h/o Huldah.
Jeremiah,1878-1878,s/o G. & M.
Lois,1833-1892.
Miranda Field,1841-1899,
  w/o Granville.
HUSTON
Charles P.,1847-1913?.
Effie May O'Brien,Aug.6,1875-
  July 3,1897,w/o Stephen G.
Eliza J.,Jan.13,1888,70y,w/o Stephen.
Ella,1859-XXXX,w/o Chas.P.
Erven T.,Mar.26,1837,5m,
  s/o William & S.
Freddie,Apr.6,1875-July 28,1876,
  s/o W. & M.E.
Joseph,1812-1894,s/o W. & M.E.
Julia A. Gallison,1912,87y,w/o Merrill.
Maria,1823-1857,w/o Joseph.
Merrill,Jan.15,1892,68y.
Rebecca J.,Nov.6,1851,22y,
  d/o Wm.& Susan.
Stephen,Jr.1899,?,78y.
Susan,Feb.24,1867,66y,w/o Wm.
Walter H.,Jan.12,1892,33y.
William,Mar.6,1859,67y.
LEIGHTON
Mary Roberts,1846-XXXX,w/o R.M.
Rufus M.,1839-1917.
Susan A.,1853-1914,w/o Wm.H.
William H.,1847-1901.
LINCOLN
John W.,1843-1915.
Julia A.,1844-1917,w/o John W.
LORD
Annie C.,1889-1909,w/o Merton C.
Crawford H.,Sept.1861-Oct.1,1902.

LUFKIN
J. Howard,Mar.4,1886,29y.
John O.,Apr.15,1864,51y,h/o Rachel
Rachel H.,June 24,1868,49y.
LUND
Jorgen S.,May 23,1829-Mar.26,1903.
Mariane Olsen,Apr.7,1827,w/o Jorgen.
MERRILL
Abbie G.,Jan.6,1907,77y,w/o Geo.F.
Clarissa,July 11,1842,50y,
 w/o Oliver.
Daniel,Feb.21,1824,75y.
Daniel,Apr.30,1883,85y,h/o Dorcus.
Dorcus,Mar.7,1837,39y.
Elizabeth,May 11,1876,92y.
George F.,Oct.13,1880,54y.
James,Feb.2,1851,in France,s/o Jas.
Mary,July 5,1843,88y,w/o Daniel.
Oliver,Feb.15,1868,83y.
William H.,July 1836,10m,s/o Jas.
MORRISON
Ernest L.,1882-1906,
 s/o J.P. & Georgianna.
John P.,1838-1895.
MOUNTFORT
Caroline,1821-1903.
Frank H.,Jan.8,1860-Feb.10,1906.
George,July 10,1878,82y.
Henry,Feb.15,1798-Aug.1,1872.
John T.,Jan.29,1887,54y.
Lois,Sept.29,1872,76y,w/o George.
Lorenzo,1828-1878.
Louisa Atkins,1824-1897,w/o J.T.
Martha I.,May 3,1803-Nov.24,1835,
 w/o Henry.
Mary,Nov.1821,21m,d/o Geo. & L.
MURRY
Angie,1828-1899,d/o C. & M.
Cotton,1798-1860.
Jane,May 20,1835,26y,w/o Sam.
Joy R.,Dec.27,1841,31y.
Lucy,Mar.17,1847,77y,w/o Jas.
M., 1798-1868,w/o Cotton.
Mary Russell,1827-1874,d/o C. & M.
Nancy R.,1792-1854.
NEWBEGIN
Comfort,June 2,1840,35y,w/o Robert.
Robert,May 13,1866,65y.
NOYES
Susan J.,Sept.24,1877?,27y,
 w/o Charles D.
O'BRIEN
Benjamin F.,May 8,1896,35y.
PURRINGTON
Alice Lois,June 19,1838.
Humphrey,June 5,1833-Apr.14,1866.

Stella A.,Oct.13,1858-June 10,1912,
 d/o H.P.& A.L.
RICHARDS
Curtis C.,1813-1893,h/o Martha.
Martha Anderson,1817-1904.
Nancy Ella,1852-1863,d/o C.C.& M.A.
Olive S.,1828-1910.
SHOLES
Sarah,Oct.8,1900,87y,w/o Zephaniah.
Zephaniah,Sept.30,1889,76y.
SOULE
Howard A.,Feb.2,1845-Feb.9,1885.
STEWART
John M.,Aug.18,1899,64y.
STOCKER
George W.,1789-1867.
Peace Allen,1794-1876,w/o G.W.
TERRISON
Anne,June 17,1911,74y.
Herman,Jan.15,1896-Dec.24,1916.
Hermine,July 17,1911,74y.
Teddie T.,Dec.10,1902-Mar.6,1910.
WATTS
Gertrude,June1882,6w,d/o J. & M.E.
John K.,1839-1912.
Mary E.,1842-XXXX,w/o John K.
WHITEHOUSE
Abbie F.,Feb.11,1853,3m,
 d/o B.W. & J.P.
Elizabeth Ellen,Mar.17,1844,
 d/o B.W.& J.P.
Elizabeth J.,Apr.25,1839,24y,
 w/o Capt.Benj.
Jeddiah Porter,Feb.2,1846,3y,
 s/o B.W. & J.P.
Joann P.,Oct.15,1853,33y,
 w/o Capt.Benj.
Josiah L.,1839-1906.
Sarah W.,Oct.29,1832,7m,
 d/o Isaac & Betsey.
WINSLOW
Elizabeth,Nov.22,1836,75y,w/o Thos.
Fred K.,1853-1895.
Mary F.,1835-1915,w/o Albert.

✤ **MARSTON FAMILY** ✤
Near 235 Gray Road.
Checked all stones.

MARSTON
Alexander G.,Jan.5,1905,83y.
Ann,Feb.13,1865,82y,w/o Benj.
Benjamin,Sept.16,1843,69y.
Dorcas E.,June 9,1862,d/o A.G. & R.B.
Rosetta B.,Dec.25,1893,55y,w/o A.G.

✤ **PINE GROVE CEMETERY** ✤
Rte. 88, Falmouth Foreside.
Active, did not check or update.

ALLEN
George M.,Aug.24,1849,1y,s/o G.W.
George W.,1822-1901,h/o Lydia.
Josie M.,1856-1886,d/o G.W. & L.
Lydia R. Lambert,1826-1907
Maria,Dec.13,1868,70y,w/o Wm.
Priscilla,1833-1894,w/o Andw W.
William,Nov.29,1871,76y.
ANDERSON
Catherine,May 9,1851-
 June 30,1891,w/o H.P.
Clara E. Jordan,1852-1928.
Wilber A.,1858-1888.
BATCHELDER
Josiah,Dr.,XXXX.
BOWIE
Lucy J.,July 1882,25y,w/o Manchester.
Manchester,1850-1889.
Merton L.,Oct.1881,8m,s/o M.& L.J.
Oresa,Apr.3,1883,25y,
 d/o Nath'l & Caroline.
BROWN
Pheobe,1839-1896,w/o Wm.R.
Sarah L.,June 26,1845-
 Aug.11,1886,d/o Abner & Sally.
BRUNS
Karen S.,Mar.12,1895,43y,
 w/o Niels I.N.
BUCKMAN
Arthur,Capt.,1819-1886.
Eliza,1813-1857.
Frank B.,XXXX,s/o Arthur & Eliza.
Georgia E.,1876-1889,d/o C.H.& M.E.
Hattie R.,Mar.24,1858-
 Dec.17,1887,w/o George M.
Herbert J.,Feb.25,1877,25y.
Lucy T.,1861-1891,w/o Capt.C.H.
Mary Ella,Nov.18,1881,35y,
 w/o Capt. C.H.
Welden N.,May 12,1882,2y.
BUCKNAM
Almira,XXXX,w/o Capt. John.
Anna Jan.23,1776,61y,w/o Capt.Wm.
Betsey B.,July 26,1791,40y,
 2nd w/o Samuel.
Eliza,Aug.26,1852,62y,s/o Ezra T.
Elizabeth,Aug.25,1869,77y,w/o John.
Ezra T.,May 10,1858,73y.
Ezra,1823-1892.
Hannah Dunbar,Dec.20,1856,85y,
 3rd w/o Samuel.
Isreal,Aug.10,1848,41y.
John,Capt.,Dec.13,1848,71y.

John,Oct.1,1865,73y.
Mary,Aug.24,1857,20y.
Mary Ann,May 30,1848,37y.
Nancy,July 11,1844,75y.
Samuel,Apr.5,1814,62y,h/o Sarah.
Sarah Cummings,Feb.2,1785,36y.
Walter R.,XXXX,s/o Ezra & Matilda.
William,Capt.,Jan.14,1776,67y.
CALLENDER
George Henry,Apr.2,1833,10m,
 s/o George H. & Elizabeth P.
Isabelle,Jan.9,1843,24y,w/o W.B.
CHENERY
Angeline,Feb.22,1831,23y.
Deborah L.,July 6,1845,18y,
 d/o John & Susan.
John,May 7,1841,64y.
John,1811-1879.
Mary D.,Apr.29,1873,53y,w/o John.
Moses,Aug.3,1853,30y.
Susan,Nov.4,1861,78y.
CLEVELAND
Alpheus,Mar.26,1780,23y.
CLARK
Huldah,Feb.20,1780,27y,w/o Wm.,
 d/o Jon.& Rebecca.
CLOUGH
Annie,May 31,1881,37y,w/o Fred.
Frederic A.,1839-1897.
Hattie,Nov.22,1885,29y,w/o Fred.
COBB
Bethiah Silsby,Feb.3,1834,47y,
 w/o David.
COLLEY
Curtis,Feb.17,1898,84y.
Elizabeth M.,1812-1893.
Ellen Rand,XXXX,w/o Samuel N.
Ida Dorcus,1882-1911,d/o S.N.& E.
John S.,1826-1893.
Mary J.,July 24,1891,69y,w/o Curtis.
Ruth,XXXX,3w,d/o Curtis & M.J.
Samuel N.,XXXX.
Walter P.,1859-1893,s/o L.S.& S.A.
CRAM
Georgianna W.,Mar.15,1845-
 Sept.5,1846,d/o Green & Harriet.
Green,1811-1857.
Harriet B.,1820-1905,w/o Green.
CROSS
Anna M.,Nov.9,1898-Jan.24,1900,
 d/o J.E.& Jennie.
CUMMINGS
Frank W.,Feb.27,1876,23y.
DAVIS
Apphia I.,Apr.10,1807-Feb.6,1886,
 w/o John Y.
Edward,Nov.17,1856,76y.

John Augustine,Mar.25,1835-
Sept.11,1853,s/o John Y. & A.I.
John Y.,Sept.1804-Apr.11,1836.
Rowland,Sept.14,1791,64y.
Rowland,Capt.,Oct.25,1824,69y.
Susannah,Oct.14,1854,71y,w/o Edw.
DIXON
Mary Ella,Nov.28,1852-
Nov.2,1886,w/o John B.
DUNBAR
Annie S.,Apr.25,1872,17y,
d/o Peter & Hannah S.
Hannah S.,Apr.18,1813-Jan.13,1891.
Peter,1807-1889,h/o Hannah S.
DUNLAP
Benjamin,May 4,1808-Jan.20,1886.
Charles F.,June 2,1845-May 13,1913.
Edward P.,June 14,1838-Nov.10,1863
Edwin,June 14-17,1838.
Harriet M.,Nov.18,1833-Mar.16,1857
Nancy W.,Mar.26,1809-May 4,1831,
w/o Benjamin.
Samuel F.,Jan.4,1831-June 18,1852.
EBBESON
Peter,July 3,1888,59y.
FIELD
Alice, XXXX, 6m.
Seward L.,June 9,1897,63y.
Sophia A.,Nov.14,1869,36y,w/o S. L.
FISHER
William W.,1835-1902.
FLYNN
Annie,1858-1909,w/o Augustus.
Augustus,1845-XXXX.
FROST
Whitley J.,Mar.15,1839-Aug.30,1901.
FULTON
Kezzie D.,June 29,1836-
Oct.25,1870,w/o J.E.
GOW
Josephine Bowie,Mar.22,1882,
27y,w/o James.
Pearl A.,June1883,1y,d/o J.A. & J.B.
JURGENSON
Lorenz,Sept.24,1829-Oct.7,1905.
Mette Maria,July 1,1842-
Dec.16,1912,w/o Lorenz.
HALL
Annie B.,1857-1892,w/o Geo. L.
Benjamin,1824-1903.
Charlie,Dec.1864,6m,s/o F. F.& M.E.
Emma,Aug.1867,15m,s/o F.F.&M.E.
Frank H.,1886-1890,s/o G.L.& A.B.
Frederick F.,1824-1898.
Mary E.,Merill,1837-1914,w/o Fred. F.
Mary,1830-1882,w/o Benj.
Moses,Capt.,July 3,1824,40y.

HAMBLEN
Edith H.1869-1907,d/o W.& Irene.
Irene Lunt,1827-1904,w/o Wm.
William,1828-1903.
HANSON
Christiana M.,1856-1904,w/o John B.
Hilda M.,b.1880,in Norway-1905,
d/o Jans & Annie E.
Lizzie,Apr.10,1868,25y,w/o T.E.
HICKS
Joseph P.,Jan.18,1830-Nov.11,1846.
Lemuel,Aug.11,1795-Aug.24,1870.
Matilda J.,Feb.21,1824-Dec.14,1898.
HIGGINS
Abbie M.,Feb.7,1839-June 6,1903.
Joanna,Aug.19,1865,88y.
HINKS
Fred W.,Oct.14,1880-
Sept.21,1881,s/o B.A. & A.C.
Henry Philip,Aug.22,1893,
s/o Henry C. & Minnie.
HOBBS
Charles P.,1821-1846.
Daniel, Dea.,June 5,1860,68y.
Elizabeth J. Marston,1820-1895,
w/o Daniel.
Elizabeth,Apr.1847,4m,d/o C.P.& E.
Lucretia P.,Aug.9,1882,83y,w/o Daniel.
Mary Ann,Mar.1827,14m,d/o D.& L.
Willam P.,Sept.19,1859,29y.
HODSDON
Andrew,Sept.29,1865,83y.
baby,Aug.5,1854,1y,ch/o E. & E.E.P.
Celia Emeline,July 17,1850,5y,
d/o Ezekiel & Elizabeth E.P.
Eliza E.P.,July 26,1819-
Jan.17,1879,w/o Ezekial.
Sarah,June 5,1868,84y,w/o Andw.
Willie Prince,Aug.7,1854,3y,drowned,
grandson/o Noyes & Hannah Prince.
HUSTON
Adeline,1855-1904.
Dorcas A.,1821-1883.
Etta J.,1876-1879,d/o Har. P & A.L.
Etta A.,1850-1872,d/o Robt. & D.A.
Harlan P.,1849-1907.
Henry F.,1845-1849.
Robert,1820-1896.
Willie,1860-1862,s/o Rob. & Dorc.
JACKSON
Susan,Oct.10,1871,86y,w/o Stephen.
JENSON
Marie,Apr.20,1831-May 18,1904.
JOHNSON
John,Capt.,Apr.24,1873,88y.
Joanna B.,May 20,1853,36y,
d/o John & Susan.

Susan,Sept.18,1865,73y,w/o John.
JONES
Albert,XXXX,21y.
Butler,Feb.17,1829,55y.
Carrie P.,July 29,1872,11y.
Elizabeth F. Lafferty,1829-1872.
Frances,Capt.,Sept.26,1831,20y.
Jabez,Mar.12,1824,84y.
Mary,Oct.3,1784,37y,w/o Jabez.
Mary,Apr.14,1767,63y,w/o Nathaniel.
Moses,June 17,1750,22y,
  s/o Nathaniel & Mary.
Nathaniel,Capt.,1745,71y.
Robert P.,1828-1894,h/o Elizabeth F.
JORDAN
Lillian,1866-1898.
KELLEY
Albert Henry,Apr.13,1839,11m &
Darius,Feb.9,1843,5m,
  2 sons/o Ralph & Eliza.
KIMBALL
Ann M.Gray,1832-XXXX,w/o Horace.
Horace P.,1831-1904.
KNIGHT
Algernon,1847-XXXX.
Alonzo,1833-1918,h/o Mary Catherine.
Annie L.,1878-1897.
Apphia B.,Aug.31,1799-July 26,1845.
Arnette,Oct.10,1847,2y,
  d/o Osgood & Emily.
Carrie B.,1880-1918.
Charles H.,Aug.1856,11m,s/o O.& E.
Eliza A.,1851-1914.
Ella G.M.,Jan.5,1874-Nov.18,1897,
  w/o Edward F.
Eugene,Sept.29,1861,2y,
  s/o Amos & Mary E.
Georgianna M.,Dec.10,1849,21m,
  d/o O. & E.
Herbert E.,1876-XXXX.
Isaac M.,1849-1919.
Joshua K.,May 8,1799-Dec.31,1834.
Leonard,1803-1880,h/o Mary Jane.
Mary E.,1854-XXXX.
Mary Catherine Merrill,1848-XXXX.
Mary Jane Davis,1806-1857.
William H.,1851-XXXX.
LAMONT
Hulda A.,1847-1909,w/o Chas. D.
LAWSON
Helene,1891/97 ?,d/o C. & C.
LEIGHTON
Abbie S., July 15,1874,21y,
  d/o Geo. W. & Ruth C.
Edward A.,Aug.6,1882,15y,
  s/o Amos & Sarah P.
George W.,May 19,1897,79y.

Herbert G.,July 22,1873,16y,
  s/o Geo. W.& Ruth C.
Howard W.,Nov.28,1876,24y,
  s/o Amos & Sarah P.
Levi E.,1824-1893,h/o Martha A.
Lydia E.,1856-1903,d/o L.E.& M.A.
Martha A. Staples,1831-1903.
Olive,1862-1892,w/o Geo. W.
Ruth C.,Apr.5,1877,52y,w/o Geo.W.
LIBBY
Edith Pearl,Mar.31,1897,6m,
  d/o W.P.& K.P.
LITTLEJOHN
Mary J.,1852-1909.
LOCKE
Deborah N.,Apr.8,1823-
  Dec.31,1893,w/o Miles L.
Deborah,Oct.20,1879,88y.
Elizabeth,July 19,1824-Apr.9,1896.
2 inf/o N.G.&S.,1854 & 1857.
Joanna,May 23,1899,92y,
  w/o Capt. Ebenezer.
Margaret J.Merrill,Aug.14,1835-
  Feb.16,1908.
Matilda P.,Jan.16,1863,20y.
Miles L.,May 17,1818-Feb.1,1888.
Nathaniel,Dec.8,1758,28y.
Nathaniel G.,Dec.9,1873,61y.
Orville E.,June 13,1876,19y.
Sarah,Mar.21,1880,59y,w/o N.G.
Walter W.,Nov.15,1829-Nov.16,1889.
LORD
Benjamin,1792-Oct.24,1872.
Eunice,Jan.5,1838-Feb.11,1909.
Huldah B.,Mar.28,1866,59y,w/o Benj.
James W.,Nov.16,1914.
LORING
Ella M.,Apr.15,1901,51y,w/o Howard.
Howard C.,Capt.,Nov.11,1905,57y.
LOWELL
Bradford,July 18,1871,24y.
LUNT
Daniel,1802-1884,h/o Eliza Dunbar
Elias,Apr.1826-May 9,1863.
Eliza Dunbar,1806-1900.
Ernest A.,1868-1901,s/o J.M.& E.H.
Osgood,1842-1882,s/o Dan. & Eliza.
William C.,Capt.,1855-1912.
MARSTON
David,June 1807-May 1894.
Hellen G.,June 26,1863,d/o D. & L.A.
Louisa Ann,1811-May 1892,w/o David.
MASON
David,Feb.22,1871,37y.
MATHEWS
Edward,XXXX,h/o Emily M.
Emily M. Brown,1838-1913.

MELCHER
Aaron,Feb.1,1845,72y.
Amos B.,June 30,1877,63y.
Bell P.,1848-1905.
M.Caroline,1818-1902,w/o Amos B.
Phoebe,Feb.2,1834,52y,w/o Aaron.
MERRILL
Abigail Y.,May 23,1885,73y,
 w/o Deering.
Albert J.,1882-1887,s/o A.J.&A.W.
Albert J.,1806-1898.
Alfred,1827-XXXX.
Austen,Sept.1896,3y,d/o H.J.&M.F.
Bertie M.,Mar.1884,20y,s/o J.K.&F.E.
Clarissa,Nov.13,1867,95y,w/o Reuben.
Daniel P.,Jan.2,1845,25y,
 s/o Samuel & Lucretia.
Davis N.,1824-1841,at sea,
 s/o Josh & Emily.
Deering,Jan.29,1840,35y.
Dolly,Mar.12,1839,50y.
Edward W.,July 16,1840,18y,
 s/o Joseph & L.N.
Edward,1830-1886.
Elden E.,1847-1887,s/o N.E.& S.M.
Elizabeth E.,1855-1858.
Emily J.,1825-1895,w/o Jacob.
Emily,1799-1884,w/o Joshua,{1879}.
Emma A.,1828-1862,d/o Josh.& Emily
Emma,Jan.29,1861,75y.
Ephraim,Dea.,Nov.29,1855,78y.
Ernest G.,1867-1868,d/o M.L.& M.A.
Eunice,Mar.28,1817,34y,w/o Stephen.
Eunice,1807-1863,w/o Greely.
Fenwick,1821-1893.
Florentine,1836-1836,
 d/o Greely & Eunice.
Frances,1825-1901,w/o J.K.
Frances,Dec.18,1887,91y,w/o Reuben.
Frederic H.,1855-1856.
George Henry,Aug.1,1828,4y,
 s/o Joseph & Abigail.
Greely,1805-1864.
Hannah Minerva Cooper,1830-1901,
 w/o Jas.Edw.
Harlan P.,1841-1904.
Hattie T.,1869-1884,d/o M.L.& M.A.
Helen M.Hodgkins,1843-XXXX,
 w/o Harlan.
Hellen,Mar.1892,9m,d/o H.J.&M.F.
Henry A.,Apr.26,1876,21y,in Cuba,
 s/o J.K.&F.E.
Horace,Jan.16,1840,18y,
 s/o Joseph & Lucy.
Humphrey,Dec.22,1852,70y.
Jacob,1821-1880.
James Edward,1828-1912.
Jane,1829-1905,w/o Alfred.
Joseph E.,Sept.27,1853,3y,s/o E.P.& M.
Joseph K.,Aug.11,1826-Sept.13,1882.
Joseph William,July 21,1831-
 Dec.15,1891,h/o Julia P.N.
Joseph,Dec.1,1862,37y,s/o Jos.& Lucy.
Joseph,May 15,1825,34y.
Joshua H.,May 7,1868,61y.
Joshua,1796-1879.
Joshua,Nov.10,1837,79y.
Julia A.,1825-1902,w/o Fenwick.
Julia P.N.,July 22,1841-Jan.30,1875.
Julia,Sept.14,1864,4y,w/o J.J.&E.J.
Lucretia,Oct.2,1862,65y,w/o Sam'l.
Luther M.,Nov.7,1850,24y,
 s/o Samuel & Lucretia.
Mabel,May,23,1870,3w,d/o Edw.
Marian Stevens,1808-1877,w/o Albert.
Martha A.,1846-XXXX,w/o Martin L.
Martin L.,1844-1877.
Mary Susanna,1812-1906.
Mary, Apr.24,1806-Oct.28,1881,
 w/o Edward P.
Mary,June 22,1845,82y,
 w/o Dea. Joshua.
Nathaniel E.,1821-1906.
Nathaniel,Mar.18,1798-Dec.24,1880.
Phinelie,1837-1856,
 ch/o Greely & Eunice.
Priscilla,Dec.9,1831,47y.
Reuben,July 29,1818,53y.
Reuben,Nov.25,1890,95y.
Salome,July 4,1836,51y,w/o Humphrey.
Salome,Aug.27,1797-Mar.28,1882,
 w/o Lemuel.
Samuel,Sept.26,1862,76y.
Sarah C.,Jan.18,1804-July 28,1876.
Sarah,1824-1907.
Sarah,Apr.13,1813,68y,
 wid/o Capt. Stephen.
Stephen I.,Aug.9,1876,65y.
Stephen,Capt.,Aug.27,1803,61y.
Stephen,Jr.,July 7,1824,55y.
Susan M.,1821-1887,w/o Nath'l E.
Theophilus,Mar.1840-Feb.4,1860.
Wendell C.,Aug.15,1850,10m,
 only s/o Jos. & Frances.
William Y.,May 20,1828,4y,
 s/o Moses & Margaret J.
Zachariah,Aug.30,1868,85y.
MILLER
Christiana M.I.,1887-1890,
 d/o Andw & Elsie.
Jens C.,1878-1890,s/o A. & Elsie.
Richard A.,1907-1908,
 s/o Lauritz N.& Annie M.

MOODY
Benjamin,Jan.6,1805,66y.
Benjamin,Dr.,Dec.4,1839,32y.
Caleb,Capt.,Oct.6,1854,29y.
Eben,Capt.,Apr.4,1871,61y.
Glendy,Jan.1,1821-Feb.7,1883.
Hannah,Oct.14,1851,wid/o Jonathan.
Jael,June 9,1795,45y,w/o Benjam.
James,Capt.,July 28,1837,26y,
 in Surinam,S.A.
Jonathan,Capt.Apr.16,1835,62y.
Jonathan,Jr.,Mar.24,1824, in NY,23y.
Jonathan,Nov.29,1845,19y,drowned.
Joseph,May 4,1840,17y,at Amsterdam.
Judith,Apr.3,1816,45y,w/o Jon.
Mary,Mar.12,1824,17y.
Philip,Dec.29,1862,in CA.,28y.
Rachel,Oct.30,1841,25y.
Salome,June 17,1877,67y,w/o Eben.
Samuel,Jan.9,1829,26y,s/o Jon.
Samuel,Capt.,Mar.25,1858,73y.
Silas M.,June 10,1850,21y.
NORTON
Benjamin R.,Capt.,1828-1878.
Charles B.,Capt.,1861-1898,at sea,
 s/o B.R.& V.B.
Harriet A.,1830-1900.
John F.,1825-1866.
Vienna B.,1825-1892,w/o Benj.R.
NOYES
Abigail,May 28,1866,80y,w/o Nath'l.
Amos W.,1830-1887.
Ann B.,Mar.15,1882,57y.
Benjamin,1809-1860.
Bucknam,Jan.22,1804-July 19,1879.
Charles W.,July 10,1853-May 29,1900.
Charles R.,Nov.15,1850,18y,
 s/o Bucknam & Susan.
Charity,Apr.25,1790,27y,w/o John.
Cyrus,Mar.23,1806-Aug.24,1891.
Dora M.,Nov.28,1895,34y,w/o Harry K.
Edward, Oct.19,1868,68y.
Eliza A.L.,1820-1911,w/o Benj.
George E.,Mar.26,1868,17y,
 s/o John & Harriet.
Frank,July 12,1835-June 23,1882.
Harriet Merrill,1809-1856,w/o John.
John M.,Aug.6,1869,24y.
John,1809-1895.
Joseph H.,Apr.14,1865,35y.
Josiah,Dec.3,1819,61y.
Lucy A.,Apr.28,1870,35y.
Lucy N.,Jan.15,1894,74y,w/o Edw.
Margaret A.Delano,July 27,1812-
 Mar.8,1900, w/o Cyrus.
Margaret E.,Dec.23,1862,3y,
 d/o Edw.& Lucy C.

Merrill,Oct.24,1879,85y.
Nathan D.,Nov.13,1875,47y.
Nathan,Capt.,Aug.30,1848,62y.
Nathanial,Capt.,July 2,1770,89y.
Nathaniel,1826-1845,
 s/o Reuben & Susan.
Priscilla,May 31,1767,81y,w/o Nath'l.
Rachel,May 15,1818,47y,w/o Silas.
Reuben M.,1817-1833,
 s/o Reuben & Susan.
Reuben,1789-1840.
Robert,Dec.7,1869,69y.
Rosie A.C.,Sept.18,1858-XXXX,
 w/o Chas.W.
Samuel M.,1816-18X4,s/o R. & S.
Susan M.,1794-1866,w/o Reuben.
Susan S. Lord,Apr.30,Apr.9,1902,
 w/o Frank.
Susan,Jan.13,1808-Dec.28,1876,
 w/o Bucknam.
Susannah,May 28,1861,92y,
 w/o Josiah.
PAGE
Maria F.,May 23,1856-Aug.29,1889.
PAIGE
Cecelia,Dec.1,1870,1y,C.E.&M.J.
Charles E.,Mar.26,1871,25y.
Flora C.,May 1871,6m,s/o C.E.& M.J.
PATRICK
Charlotte,Nov.12,1866,71y.
PECK
Lydia W. Blake,Mar.9,1816-
 Feb.24,1884,w/o H.N.
PETERSON
Bertha,1844-1913,w/o H.P.
H.P.Lysgaard,1846-1900.
PETTINGILL
Ann Buckman,1801-1887,w/o Benj.
Benjamin,1796-1870.
John M.,1829-1895.
Mary A.,1832-1873,d/o Ben. & Ann.
PHILLIPS
Charles,1874-1876,s/o John & Mary.
POOL
Job.,Feb.4,1843,79y.
Mary,May 29,1853,84y,w/o Job.
POTE
Anna,Mar.10,1781,26y,w/o Increase.
Charles,Capt.,Nov.4,1870,61y.
Eliza D.,Aug.20,1851,34y,w/o Chas.
Increase,Capt.,1760.
Jane Grant,Aug.17,1786,64y,
 w/o Capt.Greenfield Pote.
Mary,Apr.30,1788,w/o Gameliel.
PRINCE
Amos N.& Daniel,XXXX,
 ch/o Noyes & Hannah.

Ann,1799-1883,w/o Jacob.
Edward S.,Apr.16,1889,55y.
Fannie M.,1859-1908.
George Loring,June 10,1828,14m,
  s/o Samuel & Jane.
Hannah,Sept.1,1840,53y,w/o Noyes.
Jacob,1799-1835.
Jane Y.,May 17,1856,50y,w/o Samuel.
Mary,Mar.25,1881,85y,w/o Capt. Wm.
Mary Estelle,b. & d. June 16,1897.
Nellie M.,1845-1900,w/o Neal J.
Noyes,Capt.,Jan.4,1830,43y,at sea.
Pamela B.Knight,1837-1915,w/o Edw.
Reuben,1835-1894.
Samuel,Capt.,Nov.6,1865,67y.
Samuel Wallace,Jan.30,1861,22y,
  s/o Samuel & Jane.
Thomas,Feb.184X,24y,lost at sea,
  s/o Noyes &Hannah.
Timothy D.,Aug.7,1854,35y,
  drowned,s/o Noyes & Hannah.
William P.M.,Sept.6,1852,23y,
  s/o Noyes & Hannah.
William D.,Sept.23,1853,22y,
  s/o Wm.& Mary.
William,Capt.Apr.29,1795-
  June 1,1864.
PUMROY
Alexander,Oct.1837,29y,lost at sea.
Almira,Dec.21,1839,25y,w/o Alexander.
Areanna,June 8,1837-Sept.6,1879,
  d/o Alexander & Almira.
RAMSDELL
Sophronie E.,June 1,1868,8y,
  d/o E.H.& D.A.
RICE
Charity M.,Apr.8,1837,28y,
  w/o Nicholas.
RICHARDS
Caroline,June 26,1898,73y,
  w/o William N.
Clarence,Feb.1860,1m,s/o Wm. & C.
Hannah,1817-1900,w/o Josiah.
Ida Ellingwood,Jan.1859,2y,d/o Wm.
John Edw.,June1840,15y,s/o Wm.
Josiah,1806-1890.
Mary H.,Apr.10,1811-Dec.6,1890.
Mehetable,Nov.9,1864,80y,w/o Wm.
William N.,Sept.25,1892,73y.
William,Apr.20,1840,61y.
RICHARDSON
Polly,June 28,1853,61y,wid/o John.
RICKER
John W.,Capt.,1821-1891.
Robert W.,1837-1908.
Sarah Lurvey,1819-1908,w/o John W.

ROBBINS
Annie E.,June 13,1851-Dec.4,1913.
George H.,XXXX,h/o Annie E.
Grace H.,1821-1892.
James E.,1854-1872.
Nelson,1807-1884.
William,1852-1872.
ROBINSON
Edward F.,XXXX,h/o Jennie F.
Jennie F.Mayberry,1859-1910.
Lloyd,1896-1898,s/o E.F.& J.F.
Susie J.,1897-1897,d/o J. G.& C. C.
Warren G.,1903-1904,d/o J G.& C.
ROSE
Alice C. Stone,Mar.28,1884,26y,
  w/o W.M.,d/o H.M. & C.L.
SAWYER
Abigail,Mar.10,1848,82y,w/o John.
G.Wilbert,Apr.23,1891-Jan.6,1894.
Jerusha,Mar.18,1773-May 10,1856,
  w/o Asa.
John,Oct.1802,1y,s/o John & A.
John,Dec.6,1842,82y.
Leslie A.,Mar.19,1887-Oct.1897.
Nabby,Jan.1800,4y,d/o J. & Abigail.
Susanna,Jan.1800,6y,d/o John & A.
SHAW
Anne Dana Barrows,1837-1898,
  w/o Judson.
Catherine,1818-1908,w/o Jas. T.
James M.,1850-1904.
James T.,1818-1859.
Judson Wade,1833-1905.
Lillie F.,1859-1864.
Medora A.,1848-XXXX.
SMALL
Daniel F.,1839-1904,h/o Diantha.
Diantha P. Brown,1836-XXXX.
SMITH
Ethel L.,Aug.1870,3w,d/o F.J.& E.L.
Lydia M.,Aug.1870,19y,w/o F.J.J.
SOULE
William H.,Jan.26,1863-
  June 20,1887,s/o A. & E.A.
ST.CLAIR
Charles J.,Nov.1884.
STONE
Alice Miriam,Jan.10,1856,18m,
  d/o H.M. & C.L.
Catherine L., Blake,Apr.11,1826-
  May 19,1905,w/o Henry M.
Cynthia,July 30,1867,78y,
  w/o Samuel.
Henry M.,Jan.31,1823-Mar.5,1902.
Samuel,Rev.,Aug.20,1874,86y.
Sarah McIntire,1819-1874,
  lost at sea,w/o William C.

Selma P.,1870-1876,d/o O. & S.P.
Selma P.,1850-1871,w/o Oscar.
William C.,Capt.,1818-1874,at sea.
STROUT
Ethel P.,Mar.28,1913,1y.
STURDIVANT
Hannah,May 8,1871,67y.
SWETT
Abby U.C. Norton,1843-1902,
  w/o Walter K.
Abigail,1799-1880.
Ada M.,1857-1861,
  d/o Simon & Margaret.
Annie,1866,27y,w/o R.H.
Chester L.,Nov.19,1862,2y.
Damietta M. Norton,1836-1904.
Eliza,1806-1894,w/o Joshua.
Elliot Walter,June 23,1893,20y,
  s/o W.K.& A.U.C.
Frank M.,1832-XXXX.
George W.,1845-1848,
  s/o Simon & Margaret S.
Joshua,1797-1873.
Leander N.,1834-1913,h/o Damietta.
Margaret S.,1814-1876,w/o Simon M.
Mary A.,1833-1904,w/o Frank M.
Moses,Feb.20,1883,85y.
Samuel,1798-1854.
Sarah,Oct.26,1886,83y,w/o Moses.
Simon M.,1812-1876.
W.Curtis,Feb.20,1874,41y.
Walter K.,Capt.,1839-XXXX.
THRASHER
Joseph,Mar.8,1801,51y.
Susannah,Apr.7,1805,53y,wid/o Jos.
THURLOW
Alice May,Nov.1895,8m,d/o W.I.& I.F.
TITCOMB
Ascenath Merrill,Aug.15,1824-
  Oct.7,1907,w/o Elbridge.
Elbridge,Jan.23,1883,61y.
William,Dec.13,1803-Apr.1,1806,
  w/o William,Jr.
TUKESBURY
Erwin N.,M.D.,Aug.27,1872,59y.
  3 sons/o Erwin N. & M.G.:
Alfred Foster,Oct.15,1863,21y.
Charles D.,Mar.1840-Sept.1884.
Fremont Foster,Jan.3,1859,2y.
TURNER
Charles H.,1853-1875.
Edward,July 16,1855,s/o G.W.& E.K.
Eliza K.,Oct.14,1855,36y,w/o G.W.
Emma,Sept.24,1825,18m,
  d/o Capt. George & Mary Anne.
Frederic A.,1856-1856.
G.W.,Feb.4,1900,78y.

George,Capt.,Sept.9,1848,52y.
George,Mar.1848,9m,s/o G.W.&E.K.
Henry M.,1828-1888.
infant,May 1832,d/o Geo. & Mary A.
Josephine,Dec.1852,9m,d/o G.W.&E.K.
Mary,Nov.7,1798-Mar.21,1875,
  w/o Capt. George.
Martha Ellen,1833-1900,w/o Henry M.
Mary Hall,Sept.20,1840,11m,
  d/o Geo. & Mary Anne.
Seward M.,Sept.22,1833,4m,
  s/o Geo. & Mary Anne.
WAITE
Ralph Starling,May 4,1892,2y,
  s/o W.M.& A.S.
WARD
3 ch/o of Dexter W. & Lucinda C.:
Alonzo Waterman,1858-1891,
Caroline Dana,1859-1861,
Dexter Gray,Mar.10,1874,10d.
Dexter Waterman,1827-1889.
Lucinda Cram,1836-1911,w/o D.W.
WASHBURN
Ammi S.,Sept.5,1850-Apr.9,1900.
WEBSTER
Fannie H.,1830-1906.
Otis J.,1834-1904.
WELCH
Annie E.,1882-1906,
  d/o J.A.& Myrtella.
Isaac,Dec.21,1872,65y.
Mary I.,Mar.17,1844,34y,w/o Isaac.
Roxanna F.,1868,36y,w/o Jos.A.
WHITE
A.,1827-1891.
Charlotte,Sept.28,1864,w/o A.,
  & d/o John.
WHITMAN
Annie Ward,1857-1913,w/o Clark.
Clark B.,XXXX.
WIGGINS
Abbie M.,Feb.7,1839-June 6,1903.
WILDER
Adelaide Knight,1852-1921.
Lincoln,1850-1919.
WILLIAMS
Albert,Feb.15,1869,22y.
Albert,1851-1852.
Anna,1848-1849.
Caleb S.,Feb.27,1850,28y,s/o Eben.
Caleb S.,Aug.23,1821,20y,s/o Eben.
Ebenezer,Capt.,Mar.18,1857,84y.
Ebenezer,Rev.,June 13,1738-
  Feb.25,1799.
Ebenezer,Mar.25,1861,53y,
  s/o Ebenezer & Sarah.
Edmund J.,1853-1876.

Elmira L.,July 6,1898,64y,
w/o Capt.John.
Gustavus,Dea.,1864-1881.
Isabel,1856-1878.
James F.,1856-1879.
James S.,Capt.,Sept.25,1804-
Dec.15,1878.
Jennette,Oct.27,1880,62y,
d/o Eben.& Sarah.
Joan,June 20,1831,11y,d/o E. & S.
John,Capt.,Nov.2,1871,53y.
Mary E.,May 24,1820-
Dec.31,1880,w/o Capt. J.E.
Mary E.,1866-1898.
Mary,Feb.24,1814,71y,w/o Rev.Eben.
Minnie A.,1862-1899.
Samuel,May 29,1815-July 9,1895.
Sarah A.,Feb.1831,17y,
d/o Ebenezer & Sarah.
Sarah,June 20,1853,73y,
w/o Capt. Ebenezer.
Wealthy,1825-1910,w/o William.
William,1812.
William W.,1859-1877.
WILSON
Elizabeth Maude,Aug.27,1906-
Apr.27,1907,d/o Malcom & Alice M.
John,1836-1901.
Rosa Skillins,1836-1908,w/o John.
WINSLOW
Charles E.,1844-1893.
WYMAN
Edwin B.,Sept.22,1887,39y.
Mary Addie,Feb.14,1886,38y,
w/o Edward B.
YORK
A.G.,Capt.,1818-XXXX.
Abigail,Sept.1,1860,82y.
Edward L.,Dec.26,1839-July 26,1858.
Edward,Oct.23,1828,18y,
s/o Samuel G.& Abigail.
Ella J.,June 5,1850-Aug.16,1856.
George D.,Apr.7,1842-Nov.20,1912.
Hannah Sweetisr,1818-XXXX,at sea.
Jane,June 12,1810,53y,w/o Jos.
John W.,1811-1833.
John,Nov.4,1889,73y.
Joseph U.,Feb.7,1825,24y.
Joseph,Aug.15,1807-Nov.7,1892.
Joseph,Capt.,July 1,1841,92y.
Joseph,Oct.18,1760,33y.
Mary A.,Jan.9,1848-Aug.16,1856.
Mary,Apr.3,1821,40y,w/o Capt.Wm.
Mary,Mar.20,1822-Jan.3,1896,
w/o Capt. Samuel.
Mary Susan,Sept.24,1823,1y,
d/o Wm.& Susan.

Samuel,May 19,1863,85y.
Samuel,Capt.,Oct.12,1803-
May 14,1893.
Susan H.,June 11,1894,85y.
Susan P.,Apr.5,1824,34y,2nd w/o Wm.
William,Capt.,July 12,1824,45y.

✧ **PACKARD CEMETERY** ✧
124 Brook Street, Falmouth.
This was completed stone by stone.

AASKOV
Amelia C.,1870-1950.
Harry H.,1881-1956.
Karen C.,1856-1891.
Peter P.,1854-1923.
ABBOTT
John S.,1833-1912.
Josephine Hardy,1836-1896,w/o John S
Lemuel W.,Feb.22,1866,27y.
Mary Ann,Dec.6,1873,71y,w/o Col.M.
M.,Col.,Apr.24,1868,68y.
Samuel W.,Feb.22,1866,27y.
ALLEN
Reuben,Dec.16,1854,45y.
BLANCHARD
Emily F.,1856-1932,w/o Chas.G.
BRACKETT
Adrianna,1848-XXXX,w/o Lionel.
Grace L.,1872-1932,w/o Geo.T.
Lionel P.,1827-1901.
DeCRENY
Sarah W.,1838-1923.
DONNELL
Arzelia,Nov.2,1838,2m.
Benj.,Mar.10,1865,56y.
Charlotte L.,Dec.18,1845,25y,
w/o Benjamin.
inf/o Benj. & Charlotte,July 1840.
Joshua P.,June 21,1839,25y.
Joshua P.,Aug.21,1842,14m.
Octavia L.,1825-1901,w/o Benj.
GRAHAM
George T.,1871-1947.
Hannah Bell,1867-1937.
HARDY
Ann, 1814-1893,w/o Oliver.
Elenor M.,Jan.2,1859,22y.
George F.,July 8,1863, 19y.
Oliver,1811-1890.
HOBBS
Rachel,Mar.7,1894,61y,w/o Daniel P.
LEIGHTON
Abigail,Apr.18,1855,63y,w/o Silas.
Addison G.,1831-1905.
Angie,July 12,1875.
Clemenia R.,1829-1872,w/o G.B.

Daniel,May 26,1872,82y.
Emma D.,Apr.3,1847,41y,w/o Jeddiah.
Eugene F.,Aug.9,1877,15y,
 s/o A.G. & S.W.
Franklin,Oct.10,1869,42y,
 s/o Daniel & Mary.
George W.,Aug.23,1862,13y.
Granville B.,1826-1881.
Hatevil,Sept.16,1849,42y.
Isaac,Capt.,July 4,1862,79y.
James E.,Oct.14,1856,33y.
Jane,Oct.8,1868,w/o Joseph.
Jeddiah,Mar.2,1892,83y.
Mary,Feb.17,1850,w/o Daniel.
Mary,Sept.29,1859,33y.
Minerva S.,Aug.28,1863,73y,
 w/o Isaac.
Ora L.,Nov.27,1898,29y, s/o A.G.&
 S.W., lost on the Steamer Portland.
Silas, Esq.,June 7,1878, 87y.

LIBBY
Angelina A.,1916-XXXX.
Charles E.,1866.
Charles G.,1858-1909.
Charles H., 1878-1961.
Harriet M.,1881-1956, w/o C.H.
Lester H.,1889-1951.
Malcolm R.,1923-1957.
Mary Ann,Aug.15,1867,38y.

LINNEKEN
Eva V. Libby,1900-1935,w/o R.A.

NICHOLS
Catherine,Mar.8,1856,39y,w/o D.
Danforth,Feb.6,1861,56y.

OLSEN
Charles,Jan.23,1916,46y.

PACKARD
Nathaniel,Feb.22,1869,72y.

PEARSON
Edwin,Aug.6,1879,74y.
Edwin F.,1880-1942.
Hattie A.,1877-1963.
Lucy C.,1835-1900, w/o T.J.
Prudencia C.,Feb.12,1871,67y.
Thomas J.,1832-1914.

ROBERTS
Anna,1798-1858,w/o G.C.
Granville C.,1799-1862.

SCHOLL
John,1814-1865,h/o Ottilia.
Ottilia Hippel,1822-1903.
Philip L.,1845-1926, w/o J.& O.
Wilhelmina M.,1853-1937,d/o J.& O.

SHERMAN
Adrianna F.,1848-1922,w/o Lionel.

SHERWOOD
Maude F.,1887-1947,w/o Lester H.

STARBIRD
Carrie, Feb.4,1865,3y,d/o E.H.& O.
infant,Mar.1860,7m,d/o E.H.& O.

WALDEN
John G.,June 26,1888,h/o Lucy L.
Lucy Leighton,Aug.5,1897.
No last names-illegible.
Henrietta, can't read, d/o ??.
Jane,d.1857,d/o James & Jane ??.

✣ **CRABTREE-HOBBS** ✣
Near Leighton's Crossing,West
Falmouth. Couldn't locate.

CRABTREE
Hannah,Dec.1,1862,85y,w/o Wm.
John L.,Nov.22,1856,36y.
Sarah,Aug.23,1788-Aug.26,1873.
William,Aug.28,1843,83y.

HOBBS
Eleanor,Nov.19,1833,74y,w/o Jon
Jonathan,Mar.9,1836,86y.
Mary,Oct.28,1808,48y,w/o Jon.

✣ **QUAKER CEMETERY** ✣
29 Blackstrap Road, Falmouth.
The Quaker Church stood on this
spot in 1740. Couldn't locate.

KNIGHT
Charles,Sept.17,1886,75y.
Mary G.,Oct.10,1857,43y,w/o Chas.
Bacchus L.,Sept.11,1864,17y.

LOWELL
Miriam K.,May 24,1876,80y.

SNELL
Mary H. Knight,Aug.25,1894,53y,
 w/o George W.

WINSLOW
Benjamin,Aug.7,1780-
 Apr.22,1843,62y,h/o Lois.
Jane,Apr.23,1817-Nov.25,1847.
Lois,July 26,1862,69y.

✣ **UNKNOWN CEMETERY** ✣
On the road from Pride's Corner to
Mountfort Hill. Couldn't locate.

BRACKETT
Elizabeth Merrill,June2,1860,
 77y,w/o Reuben.
Esther P.,June 2,1885,69y.
Mary Ann,Oct.2,1884,67y.
Reuben,June 21,1848,69y.

PRIDE
Harriet B.,1815-1830,d/o P.& M.
Mary Baker,1787-1865,w/o Peter.

Peter,1789-1838.
THOMBS
Ezra,1812-1895.

✦ WEST FALMOUTH ✦
Location unknown. Reported to have been destroyed.

ADAMS
Isreal B.,June 22,1874,62y.
BRACKETT
Charles W.F.,Jan..19,1867,42y.
Teresa,Jan.2,1866,67y,
 wid/o Dr. Samuel.
FIELD
Amos,Jr.,Capt.,Apr.10,1842,39y.
Lois J.,July 21,1838,3y,d/o A.& H.
GALLISON
Henry,Mar.20,1822,3m,s/o H. & S.
Henry,May 14,1874,78y.
John,June 24,1833,13m,s/o H. & S.
Sarah,Dec.19,1860,64y,w/o Henry.
HALL
Abby,Nov.23,1892,88y,w/o Henry.
Andrew,Aug.23,1831,81y.
Elizabeth C.,July 7,1832,34y.
George,Nov.20,1862,73y.
Henry,Dea.,Oct.12,1874,79y.
Huldah,July 25,1841,47y,w/o Henry.
Jane,Dec.30,1826,70y,w/o Andrew.
Jefferson A.,Jan.11,1827,6m,
 s/o G.& E.C.
Mary P.,Mar.8,1878,74y,w/o George.
Mary R.,Mar.12,1883,53y,w/o Benj.
Thomas T.,Nov.11,1858,29y,
 s/o G.& E.C.
HILL
Laura,Sept.25,1852,d/o O.J.& C.P.
HOBBS
Jeremiah,May 8,1879,82y.
Joan G.,Dec.3,1871,69y,w/o Jeremiah.
Josiah,Col.,Oct.29,1849,87y,Rev.S.
Mary,Jan.13,1852,83y,w/o Josiah.
LUNT
Edwin S.,Sept.22,1846,22m,
 s/o Benj.& Ann A.
MERRILL
Charles E.,AUg.16,1859,24y.
Eliza C.,Mar.28,1875,81y.
Elizabeth,Mar.30,1828,51y.
Esther,Apr.2,1880,87y.
Esther,Apr.30,1841,72y.
Freddie H.,Sept.6,1856,19m,
 s/o F.& J.A.
Frederic,Apr.13,1856,30y.
James,Maj.Gen.,Dec.15,1820,63y
Josiah,Mar.19,1871,77y.

Hannah I.,Nov.25,1863,59y,w/o Hugh.
Henry M.,Dec.14,1861,39y,
 s/o J. & E.C.
Hugh P.,Mar.9,1879,77y.
Lizzie E.,Feb.1858,3m,d/o F. & J.A.
Mary E.,Dec.29,1842,16y,
 d/o Peter & Esther.
Ozias,June 9,1855,84y.
Peter,Feb.3,1876,79y.
NEWMAN
George M.,Jan.28,1876,12y.
Helen M.,Nov.8,1872,53y,w/o Joseph.
Joseph,Feb.14,1887,75y.
NOYES
Harriet,Aug.28,1856,47y,w/o John.
PARSONS
Lizzie F.,Aug.7,1853,26t.
SANBORN
Benjamin,Dr.,Feb.27,1846,45y,
 s/o William & L.A.
Emily A.,Aug.25,1850,d/o Wm.& L.A.
Frederic,June 17,1849,in Michigan,
 s/o Wm. & L.A.
Lucy Ann,Oct.19,1819,15y,
 d/o Wm. & L.A.
Nancy Merrill,June 5,1864,81y,
 in Mich.,w/o William.
William,Dr.,Mar.13,1847,78y.
SWETT
Adams,Aug.29,1848,58y.
Elizabeth,Jan.3,1840,40y,s/o Samuel.
Samuel,Apr.16,1873,79y.
TRUE
Elizabeth V.,Oct.23,1841,1y,
 d/o Lyman C. & Mary H.
Nathaniel,July 29,1843,59y.
WINCH
Ellen M.,July 30,1876,33y,w/o Ezra.

✦ FORESIDE COMMUNITY
CHURCH CEMETERY ✦
340 Foreside Road,Falmouth and part is in Cumberland. Nice cemetery. Completed stone by stone.

ALLEN
Ann Maria,Dec.29,1845,8y,d/o S. & R.
Ephraim,July 7,1834,50y.
James,1848-1907.
Joseph,1849,76y.
Rachel Sturdivant,Oct.4,1815-
 Apr.4,1907,w/o Stephen.
Rosamond,Sept.1854,4m,d/o S. & R.
Stephen,Rev.,Mar.10,1810-July 3,1888.
ANDERSON
Alvanus E.,1853-XXXX.

ATHERTON
Peter,1856 ?.
William A.Dec.20,1863,27y.
BEEM
Charlotte M. Alden,1871-1960,
  w/o Franklin K.
Franklin K.,1857-1929.
Marjorie,1903,26y,d/o F.K.& C.M.A.
Priscilla Alden,1896-1924,
  d/o F.K.& C.
BLANCHARD
Emily E.,1857-1900.
John D.,Dec.10,1810,71y.
Joseph T.,1848-1931.
Lydia S.,Apr.28,1841,70y,w/o John D.
Priscilla Mountfort Thompson,
  Mar.3,1827-Jan.22,1916,w/o Wm. W.
William W.,Mar.11,1815-Sept.1,1881.
William M.,1900-1900.
BRACKETT
Esther M.,1905-1968,
  d/o R.G. & M.C.M.
Harriet L.,1855-1862.
Harriet R.,1824-1906.
Mary C. Morrill,1867-1956,w/o R.G.
Philip E.,1899-1962,s/o R.G. & M.C.
Philip R.,1863-1891.
Reuben G.,1859-1908.
Samuel M.,1820-1895.
BROWN
Clarence H.,1868,11y,
  s/o Thomas & Elizabeth F.
Daniel,1868,22y.
Elizabeth N.,1886,36y,w/o Thomas.
Ellen F.,1868,50y.
Estella M.,1903-1983,w/o Philip E.
Orman S.,1933-1990.
Philip E.,1903-1981.
Thomas,May 13,1902,87y.
Warren S.,1904-1967,
  h/o Mary Kamendulis.
BRUCE
Ada L.,1865,5y,d/o F. & M.
Charles,sunken stone,s/o F. & M.
Frederic,1825-1912.
Maria,1835-1905,w/o Frederic.
BUCKNAM
Emeline,Nov.30,1840,13m,
  d/o Jospeh & Margaret.
Joseph,Capt.,1804-1885.
Margaret,1806-1892,w/o Joseph.
William E.,1849-1884,s/o J. & M.
BUXTON
Abigail,Dec.6,1811,18y,
  d/o Wm. & Deborah.
Edward F.,1871,30y.
Hannah,Nov.28,1878,82y.

Maria G.,1846-1880,d/o Wm. & Mary.
Mary A.,Dec.17,1814-Jan.14,1883,
  w/o Wm.Jr.
William,Mar.25,1845,82y.
William,Jr.,Dec.22,1797-Dec.22,1848.
CAHILL
Leslie P.,1914-1973,
  h/o Doris Smallwood.
CEDEBJER
Carl G.,1895-1982.
Edna S.,1897-XXXX,w/o Carl G.
CHASE
Angelina Gerrish,1842-1914.
Annie T.,1868-1945.
Arthur G.,1882-1955.
Carolyn G. Livingston,1891-1982.
Daniel D.,1880-1972,h/o C.G.L.
Fred E,1875-1945,h/o Neva S.S.
Neva S. Soule,1875-1959.
CHENEY
Rebecca,July 28,1838,63y,w/o Solomon.
CHENERY
Ebenezer,Sept.18,1801-Oct.21,1859.
Susan Poland,Oct.10,1810-
  Oct.25,1868,w/o Ebenezer.
CLARK
Eliza A.,Jan.28,1882,w/o M.C.
Matthew C.,1816-Jan.23,1882.
COE
Mazelle Rumery,1930-1988,
  w/o Robert S.
COLESWORTHY
Anna,May 25,1851,76y,w/o D.P.
Daniel P.,July 9,1852,75y.
Marie Antoinette,Jan.12,1842,4y,
  d/o S.H. & Olive.
COLLINS
Elizabeth Amanda,Feb.28,1823,
  d/o Joseph & Hannah.
Hannah,Nov.21,1820,69y.
Hannah,May 21,1787-Feb.4,1865.
Hannah,Feb.8,1815,d/o Jos. & Han.
inf/ch/of J. & H., May 28,1816.
Joseph,Aug.30,1779,in Roxbury,MA-
  July 29,1863,h/o Hannah {1865}.
CRAM
Emilie Soule Chase,1913-1989,
  w/o Robert L.
DECOSTER
Horace A.,Aug.6,1876,30y,
Lucy A.,Mar.23,1867,49y,
  w/o Alexander.
DOUGHTY
Isabella,1851 ?,11m, &
Lucinda,Mar.25,1815,10m,
  d/o George & Lucinda.

DRINKWATER
Elizabeth A.,May 22,1863,56y,
  w/o William
Hannah,Nov.13,1824,22y,w/o Reuben.
Mary,May 2,1823,36y,w/o Retire.
Mary,May 6,1818,6md/o R. & M.
Retiar/Retire,Dec.27,1863,74y.
Retire,Sept.8,1823,s/o R. & Mary.
William P.,Capt.,Aug.12,1849,44y.
  children/o Wm.P. & Elizabeth A:
Cyrus S.,1839-1887.
Hannah E.,Jan.25,1871,39y.
Harrison W.,1835-1837.
Mary A.B.,May 5,1869,61y.
Mary M. Tyler,1842-1845.
DURAN
Elisha S.,1887,78y.
Eunice,1888,78y,w/o Elisha S.
Julia C.,1896,44y,d/o E.S. & E.
EDWARDS
Etta F.,1881,22y,w/o Silas C.
FESSENDEN
Hannah,1837-1858.
GILLELAN
David Taylor,1872-1948.
Helen Norton,1880-1956,w/o David.
GOODRICH
Cary Eugene,Nov.21,1857-
  Nov.1,1883,w/o Levi J.
GOODENOW
Charles,1873,42y.
Darius,1861,25y,s/o Benj. & Sarah.
Sarah S.,1866,58y,w/o Benjamin.
Willie,1851,18y,s/o Benj. & Sarah.
GOULD
Ephraim S.,Jan.30,1846,21y,
  s/o Samuel & Ann.
GREELEY
Anna M.,1875,66y,w/o Ira.
Ira,1894,86y.
  sons/o Ira & Anna M.:
Alfred N.,1840,7m.
Charles H.,1848,14m
Joseph H.,Mar.5,1877,40y.
Orrin A.,1871,22y.
HALL
Emma York,1855-1922,w/o Milton.
Frank York,1875-1925,
  s/o Milton W.& Emma Y.
Milton W.,1900,51y.
William P.,1901,80y.
HAMLIN
Anne Wilson,1861-1833,w/o Simon M.
HAMILTON
Dennis Brackett,1857-1949,h/o Ellen.
Ellen Southworth Blanchard,
  1851-1934.

HARRIS
Emeline,1838,4y,s/o John & R.
John,1883,83y.
Joseph,1828-1905.
Julia A.,1850,20y,d/o John & R.
Martha P.,1900,62y.
Mary Ellen,1839-1920,w/o Jos.
Mary Jane,1847,15y,d/o John & R.
Rosannah,1855,47y,w/o John.
HITCHINGS
Samuel K.,1857-1887.
HOPKINSON
Priscilla Hamilton,1887-1972.
Ralph Stimson,1889-1959.
Stephen Southworth,1927-1990.
HORR
Annie L.,1888-1933.
Everett E.,1891-1942.
Ida B.,1894-1942.
Jennie H.,1862-1934.
Joseph J.,1867-1951.
Levi C.,1866-1951.
HUGHES
Elizabeth B.,1908-1991,w/o H.T.
Harold T.,1989-1959.
Louise Mary,1923-1978,w/o Wm.
William Brown,1928-1992.
JACOBS
E. Eugene III,1920-1980.
JONES
Henrietta P.,Apr.14,1818-May 16,1883.
Joseph,Aug.2,1848,1y.
Lelia,Sept.21,1852,5d.
William Y.,Apr.17,1813-Sept.15,1883.
KENNEDY
Sarah A.,Oct.4,1888,64y,w/o Michael.
KILBORN
Mary,1904-1911,d/o Jos. & Mary.
Mary Liscomb,1876-19XX.
KNAPP
Elizabeth,Sept.27,1865,39y,w/o Ziba.
KNIGHT
Michael,Jan.9,1833,63y.
Susan,May 15,1849,79y,w/o Michael.
William,May 4,1826,24y.
LAWRENCE
Dorcus,1879,70y,w/o William.
Edward,1837,s/o Wm.& Dorcus.
William,Oct.1837,26y.
LEEPER
Arline Currier,1906-1990.
LESLIE
Maria W.,1839-1897.
LITTLEJOHN
Mary Sawyer,1819-1885.
Nathan,1816-1893,h/o Mary.
  children/o Nathan & Mary:

Annie W.,1856-1873.
Eugenia E.,1844,8m.
Mary Elizabeth,1846-1850.
LOCKE
John M.,May 24,1883,76y.
Phebe P.,Sept.29,1858,46y,w/o John.
Warren C.,Mar.23,1890,39y.
LOWE
Annie A. Sturdivant,1849-1918.
Marcellus,Capt.,1844-1881.
Sumner S.,1879-1960.
Virginia C. Sands,1879-1957,
  w/o Sumner S.
LYNCH
Barbara W.,1915-1982,w/o John.
John,1911-1980.
MARINER
Moses,Aug.31,1832,90y.
MASON
Edith M. Lowe,1874-1950,w/o Fred.
Fred,1874-1964.
John,Oct.22,1824,63y.
John,Jr.,July 11,1804,20y.
Lucy,Mar.25,1854,96y,w/o Capt.John.
Nathaniel,Apr.1810,21y.
Reuben,Apr.19,1816,29y.
MAYO
Fred A.,June 24,1883,7y.
McLELLAN
David,1885-1905.
MERRILL
Asa,1826-1905.
Catherine N.,Jan.10,1823,10d.
Cornelia B. Farwell,1837-1921.
John,Aug.3,1881,81y.
Rebecca J.,May 20,1854,20y.
Sally Chenery,Mar.13,1882,81y.
Sarah,July 9,1847,17y.
METCALF
Sophronia H.,1866,28y,w/o Nathan H.
MILLIKEN
Alexander,1771-1853.
Michal B.,1811-1877,w/o Alex.
Rachel J.,1839-1893.
MITCHELL
Louise F.,1842-1916.
MOODY
Eliza,July 18,1846,38y,w/o Joshua.
Joshua,Capt.,Nov.10,1859,46y.
MORRISON
Amelia Poland,Nov.8,1861,32y,
  w/o Geo.C.,d/o Charles & Eunice.
MURPHY
Elizabeth Kilborn,1911-1953.
NELSON
Andrew,Jan.8,1860,65y.
Betsey,Sept.1,1874,82y.

NEWBEGIN
Edward Henry,1870-1906,h/o E.W.K.
Edward King,1903-1947,
  s/o E.H & E.W.
Elizabeth Woodbury King,1867-1921.
NEWMAN
George S.,July1841-July 1873,
  in Alaska.
Joseph,Feb.1837-Apr.1853,
  Mariel,Cuba.
Lucy,Dec.1849,15y,d/o Sam'l & Louisa.
NICKERSON
Charles L.,1866-1929.
Charles W.,1837-1912.
Edward J.,1889-1964.
Effie J.,1877-1963,w/o Walter F.
Ethel M.,1875-1944,w/o Frank D.
Frank D.,1879-1975.
Frank Ernest, infant,XXXX.
Herschel M.,1905-1956.
Isa A.,1868-1942,w/o Chas. L.
John W.,Sr.,1917-1984.
Linwood Ashe,1934-1937.
Louise,1908-1991.
Sarah E. Kennedy,1843-1920.
Viola I.,1892-1946.
Walter F.,Nov.18,1876-1961.
NORTON
Alice Maude Sturdivant,1857-1944,
  w/o Edmund R.
Almira S.,1888,53y,w/o Henry K.
Almira Atherton,1812-1898,
  w/o Shubael.
Edmund R.,1854-1937.
Eugene S.,1848-1919,h/o D.G.S.
Deborah G. Sturdivant,1851-1912.
Harold G.,1878-1950,h/o Helene.
Helene Maddocks,1883-1976.
Henry K.,Capt.,1921,88y.
Herschel W.,1861,5y,s/o H.K. & A.S.
Louis H.,1870-1955.
Myra J.,1909,19y.
Shubael D.,Capt.,June 12,1876,67y.
Sophronia,1862,59y,
  w/o Rev. Bennett N.
Walter S.,1881-1882,s/o E.S. & D.G.
NOYES
Hannah,Oct.7,1854,79y,w/o Nehemiah.
OLSON
C. Walter,1885-1978.
Mary Fredericka,1854-1939.
Ragnhild E.,1894-XXXX,w/o C. Walter.
PALMER
Janet Lowe,1917-1986,
  d/o Sumner & Virginia.

PARTRIDGE
Margaret Chase,1866-1950,
w/o Walter.
Walter,1864-1939.
PETEE
James,Jan.1817-Aug.1832,
s/o John & Jane.
PETERSON
Anna K.,w/o Hans P.
Dora C.,1890-1896.
Hans P.,1849-1909.
Katrina M.,1862-1939,w/o Hans P.
Maria C.,1865-1889,w/o Hans P.
PIERCE
Andrew,Mar.12,1846,33y.
POLAND
Abigail W.,Feb.28,1841,9y,
d/o James & Eliza.
Charles T.,May 28,1828,5y,
s/o Charles & Lucy.
Charles,Oct.20,1795-Dec.19,1867.
Eliza,Apr.7,1850,55y,w/o Jas.
Eunice,Mar.9,1794-June 29,1864,
w/o Charles.
James,Capt.,Oct.27,1862,69y.
Josiah S.,Oct.7,1810,23y.
Mary Ann,Apr.7,1838,2y.
Sarah,Dec.13,1870,65y,w/o James.
POTE
Charles,1842,66y.
Esther,July 1871 ?,87y.
Mary,1843,23y,d/o Chas. & Esther.
  sons/o Samuel & Sarah:
Charles,Dec.7,1843.
Jeremiah,July 7,1821,26y.
William,Mar.27,1819,28y,at sea.
PRINCE
Ammy,Nov.1,1842,79y,h/o Desire.
Betsey,Feb.9,1793-Apr.11,1875,
  w/o George.
Charles,1822-1853,s/o Chas. & B.
Desire,Sept.19,1838,82y.
George,Aug.14,1788-Jan.8,1864.
George,Jr.,1829-1857,s/o G. & B.
Harriet,1817-1893.
Leach D.,1827-1866,s/o Geo. & B.
Sabina H.,Aug.22,1794-Jan.9,1871.
RACKLEY
Eugene M.,1912-1934.
RANKS
Martha Cox,1864,39y,w/o Rev.S.
REDDING
Catherine B.,June 23,1849,31y,
  d/o John.
John,Capt.,Sept.18,1820,30y,in Cuba.
RIGGS
Alice J.Merrill,1868-1955,w/o L.W.

Annie C.,1862-1864,d/o L.W.& A.J.
Asa, XXXX.
Hattie L.,1865-1865,d/o L.W. & A.J.
Louis W.,1862-1929.
RUMERY/RUMROY
Alexander,Oct.1837,29y,at sea,
  s/o Richard & Joann.
Alice M. Sturdivant,1906-1983.
Joanna,Aug.28,1841,61y,
  wid/o Richard.
Dwight A.,1904-1988,h/o Alice M.
Nathaniel L.Y.,Jan.9,1828,
  23y,drowned.
Richard,Sept.11,1839,68y.
SARDY
Frances Isadora,Oct.24,1840,5m,
  d/o John B. & Hannah.
SAMPSON
Maudie A.,1884-XXXX.
Schuyler Sargent,1912-1957.
Walter C.,1874-1958.
SCALES
Rebecca,July 16,1831,67y,w/o Wm.
William,Feb.5,1844,80y.
SEAVEY
Jane,Mar.13,1843,37y,w/o Marichand,
  d/o Joseph & Hannah Collins.
SHAW
Dorothy MacDonald,1897-1934.
John M.,Jr.,1904-1989.
John M.,Sr.,1866-1938.
Minnie E.,1872-1952,w/o John M.,Sr.
Pearl B.,1904-1972,w/o John M.,Jr.
SIMMONS
Charlotte,Dec.1834,24y,w/o Willard S.
SIMONTON
Eben,1858-1943.
Wilhemina O.,1857-1941,w/o Eben.
SMALLWOOD
Della L.,1889-1988.
ST.CLAIR
Gertrude,1842-1935.
Herbert S.,1860-1912.
Hollis,1810-1897.
Jane S. Merrill,Aug.3,1921,85y,
  w/o Hollis.
Jane,1817-1871,w/o Hollis.
STARLING
Eliza A. Davis,1822-1901,w/o Jos.
George Lewis,1882-1953.
Joseph,Capt.,1823-1904.
Josephine Oliver,1848-1939.
Josiah B.,1858-1928.
Sarah L.,1853-1928,w/o J.B.
  3 s/o J.B. & S.L.:
Hobart E.,1890-1891,Sewell D.,1887-1887, & William M.,1884-1904.

STEWART
Charles A.,Jr.,1906-1990.
Louise K.,1910-1978.
STOWELL
Eugene,1859-1887,h/o Laura.
Frank L.,1861-1898,s/o L.J.& M.J.
John E.,1865-1891,s/o L.J.& M.J.
Laura Graffam,1862-1888.
Luther J.,1825-1878.
Mary J. Day,1829-1883.
STURDIVANT
Albert G.,1844-1921.
Alice,1873-1954,w/o Greeley.
Alice Cushing,Dec.1865,20y,
d/o Ephraim & Mary T.
Allen G.,Capt.,Apr.30,1843,33y.
Alvan,Mar.21,1876,65y.
Amelia Ann,June 27,1848,28y,
w/o Cyrus.
Amelia F.,1841,6w.,d/o Cyrus & A.A.
Anna Sirois,1885-1924,2nd w/o Oscar.
Annie T. Judge,1852-Sept.29,1888,
w/o Oscar R.
Annie F.S.Stone,1867-1947.
Augustus,1848,9w,s/o Eph. & Mary.
Blanche E.,Mar.26,1854,15m,
d/o Henry & Delia A.
Betsey York,Dec.8,1905,89y.
Charles C.,Capt.,Oct.1840-
Sept.5,1867
Charles V.,1909-1984,s/o Percy C.
Cleopatra,Aug.29,1878,4y.
Cyrus Henry,Mar.27,1816,9m,
s/o Cyrus & Amelia Ann.
David,Nov.30,1809,68y.
David,June 20,1887,72y,h/o Betsey.
Deborah,Oct.20,1856,71y.
Dolly S.T.,Jan.21,1843,33y,
w/o Ephraim.
Dolly S.,Jan.21,1843,d/o Eph.& D.S.T.
Edward B,Oct.1,1861,12y.
Eleanor Davis,1911-1991,w/o Chas. V.
Eliza H. Chipman,1847-1919,w/o A. G
Eliza L.,Nov.18,1852,39y,w/o Allen G.
Elizabeth Sawyer,Feb.7,1820-
Apr.10,1882,w/o Jospeh S.
Elizabeth,18XX-XXXX,d/o Eph. & M.T.
Elizabeth,May 1,1855-Nov.24,1922.
Ephraim,1782-1868.
Gardner Francis,July 28,1907-
Sept.29,1918,s/o Gardner & Ida L.
Gardner L.,Dr.,Mar.1873-Mar.13,1929.
Gardner M.,Sept.5,1851,32y.
Greeley,Sept.16,1857,80y.
Greeley,1861-1937,s/o Jos. & Eliz.
Hannah,Dec.14,1847,69y.

Harriet J.,Oct.1886-June 12,1887,
d/o Oscar R.& Annie T.
Helen Jordan,1900-1934,w/o Sam.
Howard M.,1844-1918.
Ida L. Palmer,Nov.3,1873-
Apr.3,1955,w/o Gardner L.
infant,Mar.25,1883,ch/o O.R.& A.T.
James M.,1848-1907.
James,Capt.,Aug.3,1858,46y.
Jane P.,July 2,1878,64y,w/o Alvan.
Jane,Mar.23,1826,79y,w/o David.
Joseph S.,1805-1888.
Joseph U.,Apr.20,1862,25y.
Joseph,Jan.11,1849,76y.
Joseph,XXXX.
Josephine S. Pulsifer,1915-1986,
d/o Greeley & Alice.
Lydia R.,May 26,1876,61y,w/o Jas.
Lyman P.,Mar.26,1850-July 13,1902.
Maria A.,May 7,1887,46y.
Maria,Sept.27,1848-Jan.8,1894,
w/o William {1910}.
Mary L. Vining,1874-1960,w/o P.G.
Mary R.,1856-1940,w/o James M.
Mary S.Howerton,1898-1988,
d/o Greeley & Alice.
Mary,July 30,1890,77y,2nd w/o Eph.
May Louise,Feb.8,1864,9y,d/o H. & D.
Oscar R.,1847-1939.
Percy G.,1859-1944.
Persis G.,1848-XXXX,s/o Eph. & M.T.
Philip D.,1859-1921.
Rachel,1834,50y,w/o Ephraim.
Samuel P.,1900-1968.
Sumner,1850-1931,s/o Eph. & Mary T.
Ward,1841,11m,s/o Eph. & Dolly.
Will T.,May 9,1875-June 29,1903,
w/o Wm. & Maria.
William A.,Nov.16,1862,22y.
William,Dec.12,1843-Oct.3,1910.
TAPLIN
James G.,1935-1977.
TAYLOR
Ann Marshall,1904-1992.
Edna S. Bennett,1876-1971.
George E.,May 5,1879,64y.
Hannah,Jan.11,1865,89y,
w/o Rev. Joseph.
Lucy Ann,Aug.18,1843,21y,w/o Geo.
Prescott H.,Capt.,1871-1937.
THOMPSON
Carolyn Sturdivant,1907-1967,
w/o Forrest E.
Ella G.,1847-1926.
Forrest E.,1907-1987.
Francis H.,Sept.1840-1919
Joseph E.,1871-1906,s/o Francis.

Margaret,1851-1930.
Marietta Starling,1850-1929,
w/o Francis H.
TITCOMB
Abigail,Apr.1,1857,73y,w/o Benj.
Abigail,Sept.21,1841,21y,d/o B. & A.
Anna,Nov.1,1840,60y,w/o Capt.Wm.
Benjamin,Nov.5,1859,76y.
3 sons/o Benjamin & Abigail: at sea:
Benjamin,Jr.,May 20,1833,20y,
Ebenezer W.,Aug.6,1831,20y, &
Stephen T,May 5,1840,23y.
Elizabeth C.,Sept.7,1844,26y,d/o Geo.
Elizabeth Tompson,1867,66y,
w/o Samuel.
Elizabeth Tukey,1760-1844,w/o Wm.
George,Capt.,Apr.1,1825,36y.
Jane,Nov.21,1847,56y,w/o Geo.
Mary Ann,Mar.25,1808-Sept.26,1815,
d/o Wm.,Jr. & Ann.
Samuel,Capt.,1854,58y,in Cuba.
Sophronia,Oct.9,1815,2y.
William,Dec.24,1837,31y,
s/o Capt. Wm.& Anna.
William,1758-1833,Rev. War.
William,Jr.,Dec.31,1837,31y.
TOMPSON
Mary Andrus,1752-XXXX,
mar. Joseph Blanchard,1768,
mar. Joseph Tompson,1799.
TREEN
Desire S.P.,Nov.25,1863,71y.
UNDERWOOD
David,Dec.21,1830,69y.
John,1818,27y,in Havana,Cuba.
Joseph,Capt.,Jan.23,1846,93y.
Lois D.,1876,34y,w/o John.
Mary,Mar.11,1795,36y,w/o Jos.
VIGUE
John H.,1912-1978.
WALLS
Pamela C.,1845-1910,w/o Thomas.
Thomas W.,Capt.,1845-1883.
WATERHOUSE
Margaret E.,May 17,1858,30y,
w/o Joseph S.
WEBSTER
Hannah,June 16,1817,69y,
wid/o Ebenezer.
WHITMORE
Isabel,1852-1927,w/o S.C.
Margaret C. Luques,1892-XXXX,
w/o Ray.
Ray S.,1888-1942,s/o S.C.& I.
S. Luques,1915-1964.
Swanton C.,1852-1935.

WHITNEY
Alma M. Brackett,July 24,1857-
June 22,1906,w/o Fairfield.
WILBER
Charles,Mar.23,1846.
WILBUR
Allen S.Y.,Dec.1859,2y,s/o A.& M.
Mary York,Nov.4,1807-Jan.1,1862,
w/o Addison.
WOODMAN
Arthur B.,Dr.,1902-1973.
Charlotte E. Gibson,1910-1970.
YORK
Betsey B.,1859,w/o William.
Clara H.,1853-1921.
Deborah,1819-1881,d/o Wm.& B.B.
Edward M.,Sept.27,1857,10y,
s/o John C. & Judith R.
Frank L.,1873,24y,s/o W.P. & U.
George W.,1848,21y,s/o Jos.& Mary.
Joseph,1860,67y.
Judith R.,1855,33y,w/o John C.
Margaret E.,1842,19y,d/o Jos.& M.
Martha S. Titcomb,Feb.16,1799-
Nov.4,1886,w/o Robert C.
Mary Pote,1871,78y,w/o Jos.
Polly,Apr.5,1818,57y,w/o Wm.
Reuben C.,July 15,1792-Apr.26,1884.
Sarah R.,1841-1935.
Sarah Jane,1843,25y,d/o Jos. & M.
Sarah,Feb.1844,77y,w/o Joseph.
Ursala,1825-1896,w/o William P.
William Ring,Jan.16,1848,90y.
William S.,Sept.1833,42y.

✦ **MORRISON HILL CHURCH** ✦
Gray Road, Cumberland. Also known
as the Universalist Church.
Completed stone by stone.

BEAN
Ann M.,Jan.20,1852,7m,
d/o Horace & Ann.
BRACKETT
Enda,Apr.28,1857,69y,w/o Moses.
Moses D.,Dec.21,1871,45y.
COBB
Freddie H.,1873-1951.
Jane A.,1854-1895.
EMERY
Carrie B. Hall,1881-1947,w/o G.W.
George W.,1886-1963.
Howard H.,908-1927,s/o G.W. & C.B.
FLINT
Cora A.,1866-1888,d/o L. & E.C.
Emily C. Cobb,1851-1918,w/o Leonard.
Leonard,1842-1905.

Louisa,1876-1880,d/o L. & E.C.
HALL
Edward T.,Oct.24,1914,68y.
Florence May,Nov.6,1910,34y,
　d/o E.& L.
George Frank,June 7,1915,43y.
infant,Apr.1874,14y,s/o E.T. & L.
Lorana,Aug.20,1902,62y,w/o Edw.T.
HAM
George A.,Capt.,1849-1917.
Herbert A.,1875-1887,s/o Geo. & L.
Lizzie M.,1850-1906,w/o Geo. A.
HASKELL
Elizabeth,Oct.27,1884,59y,w/o Moses.
Moses,Apr.6,1882,70y.
HICKS
Charles,Aug.12,1822-Jan.22,1907.
Cyrus,Nov.14,1876,78y,h/o Hanah.
George H.,June 16,1852,8y,
　s/o Thos.& Hannah.
Hannah,June 2,1880,78y.
Retair D.,Nov.9,1859-
　Aug.15,1864,s/o C.& R.D.
Roxanna D.,Sept.8,1822-
　Apr.21,1889,w/o Charles.
HOYT
Joseph A.,1876-1945.
Mildred,1893-XXXX.
HULIT
Eben,1822-1894.
Herman M.,1864-1954.
Hattie L.,June 15,1904,32y,
　d/o J.& P.S.
John,Sept.30,1906,80y.
Mary W.,1861-1952.
Nellie H.,1862-1925,w/o John.
P. Seymour,1867-1951.
Phoebe W.,1832-1913,w/o Eben.
HUMPHREY
Ada,July 1859,4y,d/o Hiram & A.
Aurelia,Apr.10,1906,81y,w/o Hiram.
Augustus,Mar.1849,5w,s/o H. & A.
Mary E.,July 1859,2y,d/o H. & A.
Melville A.,Sept.1859,14y,s/o H.& A.
LEIGHTON
Abigail,Mar.31,1870,86y,w/o Geo.
Abigail,Apr.17,1816,2y,
　d/o George & Abigail.
Albert,Jr.,Sept.12,1865,36y.
Cynthia,Sept.4,1878,55y,w/o Robt.
Cynthia Ellen,Sept.20,1847,3m.
Cyrus C.,1837-1901.
Edward J.,1872-1947.
Ellen E.,1851-1927,w/o Robt.N.
Ernest J.,1881-1896,s/o Robt.& Ellen.
Ezekiel,Apr.30,1873,75y.
Fannie S.,1918-1988.

Frances J.E.,Apr.14,1849,5w.
George,Mar.28,1866,78y.
Hannah,July 1857,9y,d/o E.& L.A.
Lillian V.,1891-1969,w/o Edw.J.
Lucy A.,Aug.10,1906,89y.
Margaret B.,1842-1916,w/o Cyrus.
Millissa,Aug.18,1858,8m.
Paletiah,Jan.31,1817,64y.
Robert N.,1846-1902.
Robert,Oct.3,1861,53y.
Rufus,Oct.13,1825,10m,
　s/o George & Abigail.
Stephen H.L.,May 8,1847,12y.
Willis J.,Feb.12,1853,5m.
LIBBY
Ella Mountfort,1890-1965,w/o Fred.
Fred Roy,1884-1962.
Lelia M.,1913-1993.
LORD
Ida May,Nov.26,1859,3y.
Jane H.,Nov.1,1863,28y,w/o Chas.A.
LUFKIN
Osman W.,1870-1926.
Vesta M.,1881-XXXX,w/o Osman W.
MORRISON
Angie C.,1880-XXXX,w/o Ezra.
Ezra W.,1857-1926.
Florence A.,Oct.22,1860,5m,
　d/o I.W. & M.B.
Isaac W.,1828-1904.
Martha H.,1823-1861?,w/o Rufus.
Mary B.,1832-1902,w/o I.W.
Rufus,1823-1879.
Sarah W.,1828-1864,2nd w/o Rufus.
children of Rufus & Martha:
Cynthia,1860-1861.
Eunice J.,1847-1849.
Ezra M.,1853-1856.
Joseph P.,1848-1888.
Lucien,1858-1922.
Rufus B.,1855-1916.
Susan J.,1850-1880.
MOUNTFORT
Horace B.,Dec.30,1896,26y.
Richard,1825-1911,h/o Loemma.
Lizzie Huston,1869-1947,w/o Willis L.
Loemma Whitney,1825-1910.
Willis L.,1856-1917.
NEWELL
Frank E.,1879-1920,h/o Lena.
Lena Mountfort,1890-1984.
PRIDE
Adam B.,May 31,1851,49y.
Daniel H.,July 31m,1841,9y,
　s/o A.B.& J.H.
Hannah,Dec.15,1847,74y,
　w/o Thomas.

Jane H.,Mar.3,1875,71y.
Joseph,July 10,1845,53y.
Martha M.,Jan.15,1837,10m,
  d/o Benj.,Jr.,& Lavina.
Susan M.,Mar.18,1849,23y.
Susan,Mar.26,1846,44y,wid/o Jos.
Thomas,May 30,1845,80y.
RIDEOUT
Benjamin,Mar.28,1860,57y.
Lavina P.,Sept.7,1867,70y,w/o Benj.
SNELL
Joseph,June 29,1865,62y.
Sarah H.,June 16,1861,58y,w/o Jos.
TAME
Inez P.,Jan.9,188X-May 23,1962.
John,1879-1953.
Lizzie O.,1872-1926.
THURSTON
Cynthia J.,1862-1928,w/o Willis A.
Ella V./J.,1892-1990,w/o Walter.
Walton M.,1886-1961.
Willis A.,1857-1918.
WASHBURN
Charles A.,Oct.1843,4y,s/o Otis & R.
Freeland,1859,2m,
  s/o Lorenzo S. & Mary.
Otis,June 4,1859,57y.
Rachel S.,Oct.27,1859,71y,w/o Otis.
WHITNEY
Alexander,Oct.15,1871,83y.
Andrew J.,May 3,1906,75y.
Barbara,Mar.19,1870,77y,w/o Alex.
Benjamin,Aug.8,1861,31y.
Eliza,Sept.26,1849,44y,w/o Phineas.
Humphrey,Feb.16,1867,80y.
James,Mar.22,1877,86y.
Jane,Dec.9,1876,33y,w/o Benj.
John M.,June 7,1855,22y.
Lucy,May 24,1894,80y.
Mary Alice,1867,1y,d/o Benj. & Jane.
Perez,May 12,1853,58y.
Phineas,Sept.17,1877,79y.
Polly,Oct.27,1856,55y,w/o Perez.
Sally,Jan.22,1886,97y,w/o Humphrey.
WILSON
Frances W. Emery,1911-1991,
  w/o Roderic P.
Lloyd,1928-1935,s/o Roderic & F.W.E.
WINCH
Edwin,1843-1907.
Harriet R.,1844-1925,w/o Edwin.
Louisa,XXXX.
Newell,XXXX.
Rachel Shay,1810-1882,w/o Samuel.
Samuel,1804-1882.
Winnie J.,June 19,1877,4y,
  d/o Sam.& Rachel.

❖ **WEST CUMBERLAND UNITED METHODIST CHURCH** ❖
50 Blackstrap Road.
Also known as the Poplar Ridge Cemetery. Completed stone by stone.

ABBOTT
Adelaide E.,1875-1913,d/o R.L.& H.E.
Alfred L.,1866-1890,s/o R.L. & H.E.
Augustus S.,Aug.18,1905,68y,
  s/o George & Lydia J.
George,Mar.24,1886,74y.
Hannah E.,1846-1927.
Inez M.,1882-1960,d/o Royal & H.
Lydia J.,Dec.27,1859,61y,w/o George.
Mary M.,1878-1949,d/o Royal & H.
Royal L.,1842-1917.
ADAMS
Arlene H.,1914-1974.
Edward P.,1889-1964.
Harry W.,1881-1967,bro/o Edw.
ALDRICH
Albion C.,1870-1928.
ALLEN
Comfort,1796-1864,w/o Joshua.
Daniel, Co.,G.,12th ME Inf.
David,1820-1896.
Hannah,Sept.10,1916,61y,w/o Jacob.
Jacob,Sept.10,1843,80y.
Joshua,Feb.19,1860,74y.
Lucinda,1814-1899,w/o David.
Lydia,May 14,1826,32y,w/o Josh.
Martha J.,1845-1864.
Paul W.,1947-1950.
BABB
Edith Winslow,1884-1978.
George H.,1882-1933,h/o Edith.
BABBIDGE
Lydia M. Allen,1850-1923.
Perez,1841-1914,h/o Lydia.
BAGLEY
Calvin A.,1904-1988.
Ruth B.,1917-1972.
BAKER
Elisha,Apr.30,1821,84y.
Temperance,Apr.3,1852,97y,w/o E.
BALK
Vivian M.,1912-1988.
BICKFORD
Margaret Pringle,1890-1974.
BLACK
Augustus D.,1863-1955.
Charles B.,1823-1896,h/o Huldah.
Emma M.,1869-1949.
Gedion,1850-1864.
Huldah Libby,1818-1892.
Isaiah A.,Nov.15,1859,2y,s/o C.R.& H.

Jane,Sept.2,1872,32y.
Josiah,May 26,1881,87y.
Mary E.,Apr.24,1862,1y,d/o J. & J.
Mary J.,Dec.19,1869,36y,d/o J. & Jane.
Milton,Feb.24,1879-Mar.23,1904,
  adopted s/o Chas.R. & Huldah.
BLAKE
Alma C.,1896-1980.
Bertha A.,1867-1943,w/o Fred M.
Charles,1857-1905,s/o M.G.& S.A.
Ella F.,1855-1858,d/o M.G.& E.F.
Fred M.,1859-1951.
Leroy C.,1888-1893,s/o F.M.& B.A.
Maurice Parker,1897-1963.
Moses G.,1834-1901.
Raimond M.,1895-1913,s/o F.M. & B.A.
Sarah A.,1825-1917,w/o Moses G.
BOWDEN
Edith Reed,1910-1947 & inf.
BOWIE
Russell E.,1915-1990,h/o Vivian.
BREIL
John P.,1872-1953.
Lydia M. Westerberg,1899-1975.
Walter A.,1880-1967.
BRILLINGHAM
Joann D. Brown,1934-1989,
  d/o Alden & Madalyn.
BROWN
Alden S.,1912-1989.
Alice M.,1891-1964,w/o Thos. N.
Harry A.,1917-1961,h/o Kathlen H
Madalyn M.,1915-XXXX,w/o Alden S.
Thomas N.,1890-1974.
BUSHWAY
Wilfred W.,1892-1960,h/o Geneva.
BUXTON
Hazel Wilson,1892-1918,w/o W.R.
Lucretia E. Laughton,1903-XXXX,
  2nd w/o Wilbur R.
Warren H.,1925-1947,s/o W.R. & L.E.
Wilbur R.,1890-1962.
CARRIER
Arthur J.,1921-1977,h/o Aubine H.
CENTER
Charles H.,1872,20y.
CLEAVES
Ellen,May 3,1846,84y,w/o Wm.
William,June 25,1841,86y.
CLEMENT
Blanche C.,1885-1947,w/o P.C.
Philip C.,1885-1958.
CLIFFORD
Antoinette E. Ayer,1844-1940,
  w/o Charles E.
Edward C.,1878-1936.
Franklin M.,1875-1955.

Nathan S.,1872-1958.
COPP
Albert J.,June 21,1877,27y.
Annie C.,1896-1965.
Benjamin F.,Feb.15,1873,64y.
Bernice Etta,1893-1894,d/o J.F.& M.E.
Eric M.,1943-1943.
Howell R.,1918-1965.
John F.,1843-1927,h/o Mary Etta.
Lizzie,1884-1976.
Mary E.,Apr.24,1875,30y.
Mary Etta Black,1853-1901.
Mary J.,Mar.18,1885,70y,w/o Benj. F.
Milton,1922-1992.
Sandra L.,1945-1976.
CROCKER
Arthur M.,1876-1932.
Eva S. Black,1877-1917.
CROCKETT
Alfred K.,Jr.,1909-1970.
Elizabeth R. Perkins,1909-1986,
  w/o Alfred K.,Jr.
CURNEIL
Frank W.,1912-1985,h/o Ruth C.
DAVIS
James,1882-1965.
DOUGHTY
Miriam,June 1817,20m,d/o H. & S.
Sarah,Feb.2,1822,25y.
Winslow,Mar.25,1819,18m,
  s/o Hezekiah & Sarah.
DUNN
B. Ruth,1909-1952, w/o Geo. M.
George M.,1910-1975.
Karen A.,1954-1969.
DYER
Julia A.,Dec.5,1851,5y,
  only ch/o Robert & Ruth.
Ruth Ann,Jan.5,1865,38y,w/o Robt.
Sarah Morrill,1861-1943,
  d/o Levi H. & Prudence E.
Susan,Feb.19,1870,44y,w/o Robt.
ELLIOTT
3 ch/o William & Miranda C.:
Charles A.,Sept.1847,1y, &
Charles J.,Aug.1844,1y, &
Helen W.,Oct.2,1847,7y.
infant,Apr.3,1858,1m,d/o J.R.& C.
Miranda C.,Nov.9,1879,74y,w/o Wm.
Nellie L.,Oct.26,1857,2y,d/o J.R.& C.
Onsville G.,Jan.22,1883,22y.
William,Capt.,Feb.26,1878,76y.
FARMER
Tillie Leighton,Apr.11,1890-
  Sept.26,1965.
FARWELL
Mary A.,Nov.17,1909,84y,w/o Samuel.

FIELD
Albert A.,1834-1910.
Charles H.,1865-1948,s/o A.A.& M.A.
Floyd M.,1890-1892,s/o C.H.& L.F.
Hiram L.,Oct.3,1911,70y.
Huldah Ann,Nov.16,1839,8y,
 d/o Hiram L., & Lepha.
Jean M.,1874-1941.
Joshua,Dec.9,1846,37y.
Lizzie F.,1871-1939,w/o Charles H.
Margaret A.,1834-1907,w/o Albert O.
Polly S.,July 21,1852,30y,wid/o Jas.
Robert W.1894-1945.
Verna F.,1901-1970.
Zachariah,Feb.11,1879,74y.
FOSTER
Arthur R.,XXXX.
Nellie E. Russell,XXXX, w/o Arthur.
FRANK
Arlene M. Bowie, 1939-1987.
David W.,1960-1975.
Luella,Dec.21,1871,6y,adopted
 d/o Granville & Sarah A.
Roscoe D.,1928-1994,h/o June Pickens
Sarah Augusta Buzzell,Feb.7,1872,
 24y,w/o Granville, d/o Silas & Hana C
Willis F.,1922-1985.
FRY
Betsey,June 21,1849,57y,w/o Jon.
GERRISH
Malinda,Nov.26,1815-Oct.31,1897,
 w/o Stephen.
Susan,Dec.26,1837,42y,w/o Stephen.
GIBBS
Roscoe,Co.1,1st ME Inf.,Sp.Am.War.
GRAHAM
Martha E.,1832-1896.
William,1828-1909.
GREGG
Dorothy York,1889-1913,w/o Fred S.
GUNN
Alice G.,1912-1976,w/o M.A.
Murray A.,1904-1977.
GURNEY
James H.,Aug.3,1875,39y.
GUSTIN
Charles D.,1870-1926,h/o Grace.
Grace M. Russell,1875-1955.
HALL
Adam L.,Sept.4,1846,8y,s/o Wm.S.& E.
Emeline Leighton,Mar.1,1864,45y,
 w/o William S.
Lot,May 19,1857,75y.
Sarah Titcomb,Apr.29,1836,53y,
 w/o Lot.
HANSEN
Martin W.,1917-1979,h/o Hazel M.

HARMON
Harry E.,1897-1963.
Ina D.,1914-1991,w/o H.E.
HARVEY
Elizabeth Adams,1869-1948.
HAWKES
Bradford S.,1912-1981,h/o Ethel.
Hattie F. Reed,1888-1963.
Lenville L.,1909-1984,h/o Audrey M.
Waldo E.,1885-1955.
HICKS
Albion Wilson,1828-1906.
Alfred,July 10,1890,68y.
Abigail,Feb.21,1834,47y,w/o Sam.
Dolly,July 11,1844,18y,
 d/o Samuel & Abigail.
Eddie F.,Mar.3,1866,6y,s/o A.W.& E.
Eliza A. Huston,1831-1906,w/o Albion.
Elizabeth L. Leighton,1821-1904,
 w/o Joseph.
George,Sept.21,1879,99y.
Hannah,Nov.27,1857,72y,w/o Geo.
inf.,Apr.3,1854,d/o Alfred & Lois.
John H.,1847-1887.
John,July 13,1846,30y.
Joseph,1819-1880.
Lois,Oct.15,1897,73y,w/o Alfred.
Lydia,Feb.28,1848,77y,wid/o James.
Nancy A.,Aug.30,1868,16y,
 d/o A.W.& E.A.
Samuel W.,Dec.23,1859,5y,s/o A. & E.
HILL
Samuel L.,1838-1926.
Victoria E. Huston,1842-1906,
 w/o S. L.,d/o Maurice.
HOLMES
Lillian M. Briel,1873-1920.
Charles M.,Jan.10,1868-Oct.27,1911,
 h/o Lillian
HULIT
Emma F.,Apr.1862,11m,d/o J. & L.P.
Hannah E.,Feb.26,1871,86y,w/o Jon.
Harriet E.,Mar.1862,3y,d/o J. & L.P.
Jonathan,Capt.,Mar.17,1854,81y.
Loemma P.,Jan.1,1862,28y,w/o John.
Nellie F.,1882-1958.
Wilbur N.,1874-1961.
HUSTON
Benjamin S.,1840-1905.
Bertha,Feb.17,1876,5y,
 d/o Melville & Miranda E.
Elbridge B.,May 23,1847-
 June 26,1914,s/o Maurice & Jane.
Elmer I.,1871-1948.
Grace Ross,1877-1954,w/o E.I.
infant,XX,d/o Melville O.& Miranda E.

Jane L. Frank,June 6,1818-
June 13,1909,w/o Maurice.
Julia L.,1841-1933.
M.Louisa,Oct.8,1868,22y,
  d/o Isaac & Margaret.
Maurice,Apr.7,1807-Apr.14,1890.
Nancy F. Thompson,Aug.16,1840-
June 5,1919, d/o Maurice & Jane.
HUTCHINS
Charles J.,1926-1992.
INGERSOL
Emma L.,1867-1942.
Lewis M.,1861-1897.
KING
Elbridge G.,Jan.1,1844,29y.
KINNEY
Morris L.,1919-1974,h/o Priscilla S.
LANDERSHEIM
Katharina F.,1903-1992.
LATHAM
Betsey M.,1807-1888,w/o Nath'l B.
Elias,Oct.25,1863,20y.
James F.,1832-1891.
Joshua,Nov.20,1859,19y,
  s/o NathanielB. & B.
Nathaniel B.,1807-1888.
LAUGHTON
Elizabeth,1872-1948,w/o Warren.
Warren, 1871-1958.
LEAVITT
Carroll A.,1916-1945.
Clarence F.,1910-1987,h/o Lucy A.
Edith Morrell,1920,XXXX.
LEIGHTON
Abigail K.,1811-1902.
Adam,Mar.5,1866,54y.
Addie M.Winslow,1862-XXXX,
  w/o James M.
Alfred,Mar.9,1839,18y,
  s/o Robert & Tabitha.
Andrew,1829-1890.
Andrew,Capt.,June 16,1830,68y.
Anna M.,Aug.15,1884,54y,w/o Sewell P.
Anna,1864-XXXX.
Annie M.,Aug.15,1884,54y,w/o Sewall.
Ansel W.,1873-1934.
Augusta,1823-1891,w/o Chas. J.
Benjamin W.,1850-1922.
Celia H.,1855-1902.
Celia,Apr.4,1850,18m,d/o Robt.& Lucy.
Charles E.,1868-1943.
Charles H.,1826-1909.
Charles J.,1820-1883.
Christianna L.,July 14,1844,22y,
  d/o James & Prudence.
Daniel E.,Feb.28,1899,68y.
Daniel,Sept.26,1840,45y.
Daniel,Sept.6,1860,73y.
Deborah M.,Apr.11,1870,52y,
  w/o Nicholas.
Diana Gilbert,1829-1898,w/o Enos,
  lost at sea on Streamer Portland.
Elias F.,1834-1912.
Elizabeth,Oct.3,1859,42y,w/o Sam.
Elizabeth C.,July 7,1844-
  Oct.18,1845,d/o Nich. & Deborah.
Elizabeth L.Carter,1849-1923,
  w/o Joseph P.
Emma W.,Aug.1862,6m,d/o J.N.& H.
Emma,1862-1863,
  d/o Charles J. & Augusta.
Enos,1828-1905.
Enos,1829-1893.
Ezekiel,Jan.6,1872,77y.
Flora A.,1860-1921.
Frank N.,1857-1901.
George O.,July 21,1848,8y,
  s/o Moses & Hannah.
George P.,1852-1920.
Grace E.,1875-XXXX,w/o Horace.
Gertrude M. Stimson,1881-1932.
Hannah F.,1838-1915.
Hannah,June 7,1878,w/o Daniel.
Hannah,1827-1899,w/o James N.
Hannah,Feb.28,1899,87y,w/o Daniel.
Hannah,Oct.23,1886,85y,
  w/o Moses {1876}.
Harriet G.,1851-1887,
  d/o Lorenzo & Lucy.
Helen,1838-1859.
Henry,1841-1909.
Henry,Aug.1,1846-Apr.18,1847,
  s/o Nicholas & Deborah.
Horace,1849-1920.
Hugh,1796-1868.
infant,1858-1858,
  s/o Chas. J & Augusta.
infant,May 23-24,1843,
  s/o Nicholas & Deborah.
Isaac S.,Jan.30,1866,57y.
James J.,1860-1930.
James N.,1826-1917.
James,Apr.12,1844,47y.
Joann,Nov.30,1811,3y,d/o R. & T.
Joel,Dec.28,1884,77y.
Jonathan,Oct.13,1865,42y.
Joseph P.,1849-1886.
Julia Ann,Dec.21,1898,82y,w/o Adam.
Loemma,Apr.5,1827,28y,w/o Moses.
Lorenzo H.,1821-1902.
Louise R.,Mar.25,1881,67y,w/o Joel.
Lucinda R.,June 14,1861,10y,
  d/o Joel & L.R.
Lucy G.,Dec.28,1902,75y,w/o Robt.

Lucy Russell,1828-1900,
  w/o Lorenzo H.
Marcellus,1844-1903.
Margaret E.,Apr.3,1844,14m,
  d/o James & Prudence.
Margaret,1850-1863,
  d/o Chas.J.& Augusta.
Mariam, XXXX,w/o Isaac S.
Mary A.,Sept.28,1877,77y,w/o Wm.
Mary C.,May 31,1878,80y,
  w/o Ezekiel.
Mary E.,1856-1920,w/o Wm.W.
Mary Marston Noyes,1781-
  Apr.17,1866,w/o Jedediah.
Mary,Oct.1853,3m,d/o Jon. & Mary.
Mary Weymouth,Feb.9,1845,81y,
  wid/o Capt. Andrew.
Miriam Huston,1803-1886,w/o Hugh.
Moses W.,June 30,1884,66y.
Moses W.,Sept.8,1863,2y,
  s/o Moses & Hannah.
Moses,June 12,1876,82y.
Nancy A.,1836-1911,w/o Chas. H.
Nellie Phinney,1852-1924,w/o Henry.
Nicholas,Nov.5,1873,73y.
Oran,1838-1868.
Osroe,June 11,1855,10y,
  ch/o Joel & L.R.
Patience N.,1826-1892.
Patience,May 12,1827,35y,w/o Wm.
Peter,June 28,1848,63y.
Prudence,Oct.25,1874,73y,w/o Jas.
Rachel,Oct.7,1865,77y,w/o Peter.
Ralph C.,1866-1937.
Rebbeca J.,1847-1925,w/o Daniel,
  {1899}
Robert W.,Mar.1857,2y,s/o R. & L.
Robert,Mar.7,1851,72y.
Robert,May 15,1893,72y.
Sadie Wyman,XXXX,w/o Scott.
Sarah A.,Aug.2,1867,22y,w/o Pat. H.
Sarah,XXXX,2m,d/o Patrick & Sarah.
Scott,Aug.1847-Jan.1898.
Sewell P.,June 26,1886,64y.
Sophronia,1835-1921.
Tabitha Fowler,Feb.17,1860,79y,
  w/o Robert.
Willey,Sept.18,1857,3y,
  s/o Robt. & Lucy.
William A.,1840-1860.
William W.,1846-1918.
William,1813-1902.
William,Oct.3,1840,52y.
William,Sept.23,1861,19y.
Willis H.,1860-1938.
LELAND
Walter E.,1916-1966,h/o Doris Morrill.

LEWIS
Alice L.,1884-1966.
Ernest T.,1880-1957.
LIBBY
Edward,1853-1911.
Eunice L.,1861-1957,w/o Edw.
  their children:
Asa J.,1890-1891,
baby,1879-1879,
Elsie J.,1895-1896,
Harry K.,1888-1916.
Mary E. Leighton,1866-1920,w/o Wm.
William W.,1846-1918.
LINNEKEN
Erving Lloyd,1903-1972.
LOGAN
William J.,1903-1968,h/o Doris Shaw.
LOWE
Abigail Winslow,Sept.4,1898,
  85y,w/o George H.
George A.,June 23,1863,22y,
  s/o George H.
George H.,Mar.25,1876,68y.
Joseph A.,Sept.27,1879,30y,s/o G.& A.
LUFKIN
Edna H.,XXXX,w/o Winslow.
Gracie,XXXX.
Inez M.,1875-1896,d/o W.H.& E.H.
Winslow H.,1844-1925.
LYFORD
Clara B.,1881-1962,w/o Fred C.
Fred C.,1865-1934.
MAGUIRE
Alice Crane,1878-1971.
Joseph Everett,1874-1937.
MAIN
Alice J. Chase,1864-1942,w/o Elvin M.
Elvin M.,1864-1935.
Lyman Emerson,1894-1965.
Maude G. Lockhart,1898-1975,
  w/o Lyman.
MALONE
Lewis H.,1918-1966.
Lucy C.,1887-1973,w/o Olen.
Olen,1879-1958.
MALING
Abigail,Feb.10,1814,56y.
MANSISE
Cornelius W.,Jan.27,1885,45y.
Miranda F.,July 10,1930,90y,
  w/o Cornelius W.
MARSTON
Harriet,Mar.3,1823,19y.
Mary,Nov.12,1821,21y.
McLAUGHLIN
Elmer,1866-1911.
Emily C.,1871-1955,w/o Elmer.

McLELLAN
Abigial S.Winslow,1877-1963,
  d/o A.F.& M.A.
MEADER
Marion K.,1923-XXXX.
Melvin G.,1922-1981.
MOORE
Eva M. Crocker,1898-1953.
Roy O.,1891-XXXX,h/o Eva M.
MORRILL
Abbie A.,June 25,1884,38y.
Albion W.,Aug.13,1861,18y,
  s/o Josiah & Sarah.
Andrew,Dec.1800,2y,s/o Jos. & E.G.
Angelina,1842-1927,w/o Josiah.
Ann E.,Sept.25,1842,8y,
  d/o Isaiah & Eunice.
Annie E. Black,1866-1941,w/o Irvin.
Beverly A.,1931-1940.
Caroline A.Clark,1850-1921,w/o F.H.
Catherine S.,1847-1905,w/o Clifford R.
Charles H.,1830-1912.
Clifford R.,1844-1893.
Dianne,1944-1945.
Elizabeth G.,Mar.1,1824,53y,
  w/o John.
Elizabeth J.,XXXX,w/o Charles H.
Elizabeth G.,Mar.1,1824,53y,
  w/o John,Jr.
Ervin L.,1916-1961,h/o Mary.
Ervin,1855-1930.
Francis S.,Oct.10,1850,12y,
  s/o Isaiah & Eunice.
Frederic H.,1859-1926.
George W.,1848.
Gladys M.,1896-1948.
Irvin,1855-1930.
Isaiah,June 20,1853,46y.
John,Jr.,Nov.12,1804,38y.
Josiah,July 8,1871,67y.
Josiah,1837-1916.
L.S.,XXXX,4m.
Levi H.,1832-1913.
Linwood C.,1894-1976.
Prudence E. Clough,1837-1905,
  w/o Levi H.
Reuben S.,July 16,1841,45y.
Sarah Hicks,Feb.3,1894,87y,
  w/o Josaih {1871}.
Stanley E.,1947-1983.
Willis,Oct.6,1859,s/o C.H.& Eliza.J.
Winthrop,Aug.29,1835,40y,
  s/o Jos. & E.G.
Winthrop E.,Sept.19,1837,
  s/o Isaiah & E.
MORRISON
Andrew P.,1847-1892.

Clara E.,1853-1884.
Ephraim,1791-1871.
Ephraim,1835-1913.
James H.,1839-1859.
James,1813-1855.
John,1789-1870.
Mary Pettingill,1818-1888,
  w/o James {1855}.
MOUNTFORT
Alton O.,1889-1970.
Bertie D.,June1886-Apr.1894,
  adopted s/o Alb. S. & Harriet E.
Caroline M.,1874-1958,w/o Geo.
Charles R.,1868-1955.
D.H.,XXXX,Co.D.,25th Maine Inf.
Edward C.,Nov.17,1859,9y,
  s/o G. & H.F.
Evelina D.,Feb.3,1884,42y,w/o D.H.
George E.,1876-1973.
Greenleaf,Oct.9,1872,71y.
Hannah T.,Feb.22,1875,66y,
  w/o Greenleaf.
Hollis R.,Lieut.,1836-1925.
James W.,1842-1914.
Jerusha,July 2,1850,85y,w/o John.
John,Feb.28,1855,87y.
Lorinda,1838-1928, w/o Otis A.
Martha L.,1876-1954,w/o Walter H.
Maude Bailey,1896-1987,w/o Alton O.
Nancy R.,1809-1889,w/o Sam'l.
Oliver B.,1846-1916.
Otis A.,1836-1898.
Roxanna A.,1938-1884,w/o Hollis.
Samuel,1803-1887.
Viola S.,1874-1938,w/o Charles
Walter H.,1873-1953.
NORTON
Alice E. Wilson,1862-1937.
Byron A.,1863-1948.
Carrie E. Pride,1866-1941.
Dwight Whitney,1932-1989.
Harold W.,1896-1980.
Ina W.,1896-1983.
inf. s/o Willard & Alice E.,
  Mar.30,1894,11d.
Josie M.,1883-1953, w/o Milton.
Milton C.,1833-XXXX.
Otis R.,1925-1963.
Willard S.,1867-1936.
NOYES
Marston,XXXX,83y.
O'BRIEN
Annie L.,1864-1938,w/o S.C.
Maria C.,Jan.1916-May 5,1920.
Stephen C.,1847-1928.
PEARSON
Jonathan,Aug.23,1841,75y.

Mehitable,Aug.25,1840,72y.
Paulina,July 18,1836,30y,
w/o Col. Isaac O.
PETERSON
Catherine Lawson,1857-1931.
Dora V.,1889-1967,w/o Howard.
Hans M.,1851-1941,h/o Catherine.
Howard W.,1896-1947.
Lucy B.,1893-1930,w/o Peter M
Marjorie R.,1925-1925,d/o P.M. & L.
PETTINGILL
John,1789-1870,h/o Mercy.
Mercy,July 30,1830,37y.
PIKE
Herbert,1896-1946.
PLIMPTON
Eleanora C.,May 6,1858,25y,
w/o Charles R.
PURRINGTON
Evelina,May 12,1900,77y,w/o Geo. H.
George H.,Sept.6,1888,86y.
Harriet,Dec.2,1856,45y,w/o George H.
Simeon,June 14,1845,39y.
PURVIS
Adam,Jan.15,1878,78y.
Ruthie T.,Aug.9,1876,76y,w/o Adam.
QUIRION
Joseph C.,1928-1981.
RAMSEY
Ezra,1835-1928,h/o Sarah J.
Fred O.,1871-1930.
Forest,1879-1954.
Sarah J. Low,1838-1923.
REED
Walter Plummer,1913-1961.
RIDEOUT
Ruth,Sept.23,1852,82y,w/o Wm.
William,Jan.23,1831,R.S.
ROBERTS
Abbie,1848-1910,w/o Richard.
Bertha L.,1903-1990.
Gardner M.,1906-1984.
Minnie,1881-1949.
Orestes, 1878-1939.
Richard, XXXX.
ROCHE
Elmer L.,1911-1976.
RUSSELL
Alton R.,1909-XXXX.
Augusta W.,1835-1884,w/o Eli.
Charles P.,1861-1929,s/o Eli & A.W.
Edith B.,1864-1868,d/o Eli & A.W.
Eli,1832-1899.
Grace A.,1868-1947,d/o Eli & A.
Hale W.,1872-1940,s/o Eli & A.
Hilda,1902-1958,w/o Alton R.
Joseph,Mar.2,1848,65y.

Mary S.1835-1904,w/o Silas.
Minnie Gertrude,Aug.11,1872,
2y,d/o Silas & Mary S.
Priscilla,Feb.18,1877,84y,w/o Joseph.
Sarah W.,July 20,1896,74y.
Silas,1834-1904.
Willie W.,1853-1869,s/o Eli & A.W.
SEAVEY
Frank W.,1869-1953.
Mildred B. Clough,1876-1960.
SENECAL
Henry D.,1982,s/o Louis & Judy.
SHAW
Angeline,Feb.1m,1857,21y,d/o J. & H.
Benjamin H.,Feb.14,1859,26y,
s/o Jas.& H.
Benjamin W.,1861-1930.
Charles L.,1872-1951.
Cyrus W.,1828-1905.
Daniel,1830-1895.
Edgar E.,1872-1906,s/o D. & E.E
Elizabeth E.,1835-1927,w/o Daniel.
Emily Sloat,1911-1961,w/o Wesley H.
Ethel A.,1909-1983.
Flora B.,1858-1915,d/o Daniel & E.E.
Hannah,June 10,1880,76y,w/o James.
Harold W.,1892-1932.
Ida E.,1876-1952.
Ida G.,1861-1928.
James,June 22,1886,88y.
Leora L.,1883-1983.
Leslie L.,1908-1989,h/o Janet L
Lewis C.,1874-1936.
Mary Leighton,1875-1940.
Oscar E.,1867-1948.
Raymond E.,1908-1980.
Robert E.,1931-1983.
Sarah J.,1834-1905,w/o Cyrus W.
Winfred S.,1870-1949.
Zelia M.,1887-1969.
SKILLIN
Alexander,1869-1958.
Benjamin,Aug.4,1840,h/o Mary.
Mary,June 28,1850,81y.
Susie W.,1869-1939,w/o Alex.
SLOAT
Arthur H.,1922-1981.
Bert F.,1897-1970.
Effie Giberson,1891-1969.
Helen M.,1909-1975.
Herbert G.,1893-1960.
inf/o D.E.& S.E.,1960, 61 & 63.
John M.,1899-1981.
Laura E.,1858-1944.
Randall J.,1964-1966.
Verna J.,1900-1966,w/o John M

SMALL
Benjamin,1845-1925,h/o V.O.H.
Benjamin,1876-XXXX.
Vianna O. Huston,1844-1925.
SNELL
Ada C.,Feb.18,1863,8y,d/o G.W.& F.J
Freddy W.,Oct.4,1862,3y, s/o G. & F.
Frances J.,Aug.17,1861,27y,w/o Geo.
George W.,Nov.17,1890,56y.
Mary E.,1840-1928,w/o Wm.H.
William H.,1836-1925.
SOULE
George E.,Aug.4,1876-
Sept.9,1876,s/o John & Lucinda.
SPRINGFIELD
Jaretta Main,1920-1986.
STEVENS
Mary Russell,1877-1942,
w/o Grenville.
STINSON
Chauncey N.,1896-1969,
h/o Flora M. Robbins.
STODDARD
Gordon P.,1935-1990.
THOMES
Mary S.,1863,25y, adpt. d/o
Moses & Sarah.
Moses,1885,70y,h/o Sarah A.
Sarah A. Whitney,1907,88y.
THORESEN
Kristine,1865-1916,w/o T.P.
Sara E.,1832-1921.
Thorvald P.,1858-1920.
TILLSON
inf. son, 1934.
Kenneth W.,1912-1933.
TRUE
Inez B. Grandbois,1916-1982.
Robert Clayton,1911-1957.
ULLRICH
Alexander A.,1924-1985.
VERRILL
Amy,XXXX,d/o W. & L.R.
Elmer,1881-1950.
Etta,1885-1956.
Lucinda Russell,1862-1890,
w/o Wadsworth.
Silas, XXXX.
WAIG
Howard K.,1907-1965,h/o Josephine.
WALTON
Charles A.,Feb.6,1879,26y.
Charles William,Aug.26,1893,
15y, s/o C.W. & F.
Franie,XXXX,w/o C.A.
WARNER
Eliot M.,1932-1992.

WASHBURN
Ellen M.,1861-1868,d/o S.W.& E.E.
Eunice E.,1841-1915,w/o Sid.W.
Herman,1878-1880,s/o S.W.& E.E.
Sidney W.,1837-1886.
WEST
Addie Maynard,1849-1931.
Anna Katherine,1884-1964,w/o Percy.
Granville,1827-1907.
James E.,1909-1919,s/o P.F.& A.K.
James L.,1836-1911.
John,1796-1877.
Percy F.,1884-1968.
Sarah L.,1797-1881,w/o John.
Vaughan A.,1875-1924.
WHITNEY
Benjamin,Oct.25,1837,45y.
Deborah,Aug.31,1834,71y,w/o James.
Patience,May 11,1867,67y,
w/o Benjamin.
William,July 13,1827,7m,s/o Benj.& P
WILSON
Abbie A.,Mar.6,1923,84y,w/o Daniel.
Albion,Oct.12,1827,6y,
s/o Levi & Sarah.
Alice W.,1895-1966.
Almira,Jan.27,1817-Feb.8,1905.
Ann M.,1843-1922,w/o Nathan. L.
Armie,Oct.1861,17m,s/o N.B. & L.P.
Belle L.,1889-1966,w/o Frank C.
Belva L.,1891-1984.
Caroline,Sept.24,1831,18y,d/o C. & L.
Carrie E. Harding,1858-1931,w/o F.H.
Carrie E.,1855-1917.
Charles N.,Mar.8,1853,29y.
Cornelius,1830-1898.
Cyrus,July 14,1873,83y.
Daniel E.,Feb.28,1899,68y.
Daniel,May 14,1891,51y.
Edgar Neal,2nd,1925-1926.
Elbridge,Jan.20,1879,60y.
Elizabeth,Dec.2,1869,76y,w/o Nath'l.
Emily S.,1852-1882.
Ethel B.,1888-1977,w/o Willis E.
Ethel,1882-1893.
Eva W.,1872-1955.
Frank C.,1879-1960.
Frank H.,1857-1913.
George N.,1851-1926.
George W.,Aug.3,1847,12y,
s/o Joel & Julia.
Guy C.,1874-1949.
Hattie M.,1867-1902.
Henry M.,1884-1970.
Herman M.,1865-1932.
Howard,1887-1948.
Ichabod,Nov.17,1827,75y.

James H.,1927-1987.
Joanna,Nov.7,1815,5y,
 d/o Levi & Sarah.
Joel, Nov.14,1839,32y.
Joseph E.,1877-1957.
Joseph,1821-1901.
Julia C.,1839-1904,w/o Cornelius.
Julia L.,1875-1966,w/o Guy.
Julia,Nov.14,1839,32y,w/o Joel.
Leonard,1817-1901.
Lepha,Sept.1828,15m,d/o J. & S.
Levi,Aug.11,1864,80y.
Loemma P.,1831-1924.
Lois,Apr.6,1877,82y,w/o Cyrus.
Lorenzo H.,1837-1918.
Lucy,July 13,1829,41y.
Luther,Dec.6,1827,4y,
 s/o Nathaniel & Elizabeth.
Mabel I.,1904-XXXX.
Mahala C.,1831-1905,w/o Wm.H.
Marsha Ann,1936-1938.
Melville M.,1902-1971.
Mildred F.,1877-1967,w/o Jos. E.
Nancy,1816-1892,w/o Leonard.
Nathaniel B.,1827-1896.
Nathaniel L.,1832-1920.
Nathaniel, Aug.31,1870,73y.
Nathaniel,May 4,1841,77y.
Olive R. Carlton,1895-1968.
Phyllis S.,1905-1976,w/o Stan.
Randall H.,1880-1943,h/o Olive R.
Rebecca J.,Feb.17,1847-
 Oct.3,1925,w/o Daniel E.
Ruth,Sept.9,1834,78y,w/o Ichabod.
Sarah E. Shaw,1839-1895,
 w/o Nathaniel L.
Sarah F.,1856-1949,w/o Lorenzo.
Sarah,Oct.15,1835,68y,w/o Nathan.
Sarah,Oct.6,1867,88y.
Sarah,Sept.21,1853,68y,w/o Levi.
Stanley F.,1904-XXXX.
Stella M.,1889-1978.
Vernon E.,1893-1976.
Willard,1886-1924.
William F.,Nov.10,1859,8y,
 s/o Charles N. & Maria A.
William H.,1825-1896.
Willis Emery,1890-1966.
Windfield,1915-1957.
children/of Cornelius & Julia C.:
Mary I.,1869-1962.
Myra,1877-1961.
William W.,1872-1940.
Zelia,1863-1938.
WINSLOW
Abby H.,May 23,1851,19y,d/o A. & A.
Adam,June 20,1867,72y.

Adam F.,1836-1906.
Adelaide V.,1845-1868,d/o C.W.& S.E.
Anne,Nov.17,1877,80y,w/o Adam.
Charles W.,1817-1881.
Elizabeth A.T.,1866-1882,
 d/o A.F.& M.A.
Elizabeth,Jan.4,1843,66y,w/o James.
Ethylin,1867-1869.
George W.,Nov.1865,8m,s/o A. & S.
Hannah,1840-1888,w/o Jason H.
Hezekiah,Capt.,Dec.21,1838,75y.
Jason H.,1838-1869.
Lois H.,1847-1871,d/o C.W.& S.E.
Lydia,Feb.20,1878,77y,
 d/o James & Elizabeth.
Mary Abbie,1839-1903,w/o Adam F.
Mary F.,Oct.19,1860,21y,
 d/o Adam & A.
Phoebe,May 17,1832,68y,
 w/o Hezekiah
Sarah E.,1819-1871,w/o Charles W.
William F.,1873-1884,s/o A.F.& M.A.
WISEWELL
Alice J.,Oct.1860,1y,d/o C.A.D.& M.A.
Mary A.,Sept.19,1862,1y,
 d/o Charles A.D.& Selina.
YORK
George,Feb.2,1889-Oct.3,1918.

✧ **FARRIS CEMETERY** ✧
Bruce Hill Road & Blanchard Road,
Cumberland. Completed stone by
stone.

ABBOTT
Harland,1872-1916.
Martha C.,1862-1950.
ANDERSON
Anna M.,1865-1953.
Arthur B.,1908-1993.
Casper,1865-1940.
Phyllis M.,1908-1975.
Richard J.C.,1932-1983.
BEALS
Edward L.,1909-1983.
Maud A. Barstow,1907-1969.
BLANCHARD
Abigail,Oct.22,1852,38y,w/o Eben.
Almira,Dec.11,1859,53y.
Apphia,Mar.7,1841,42y,w/o Cyrus.
Charles H.,1829-1903.
Cyrus,1817,22y,s/o Cyrus & Apph.
Eben,Mar.24,1848,32y.
Hannah S.,May 21,1879,78y.
Maranda Nutting,1827-1915,
 w/o Charles H.
Sarah,Mar.28,1848,44y.

BRIDGE
Maud A. Kinney,1934-1965.
BURNELL
Irwin,1906-1991.
Ruth E., 1910-1993.
BURNHAM
George,1841-1915.
Lillian M.,1886-1918,d/o G. & M.
Mary M.,1860-1926,w/o George.
CHANDLER
Flora M. Knight,1904-1979.
Francis Gustin,1913-1949,w/o Walter.
Walter R.,1907-1968.
CHASE
Francena D.,1917-1974,w/o G.E.
Gad E.,1912-1979.
CLOUGH
Abigail,18XX.
Elbridge R.,1840-1910.
Franklin B.,Feb.19,1869,19y,
s/o Samuel B. & Fanny.
Harriet E. Rideout,184-1925,
w/o Elbridge R.
J.B.,Capt.,May 3,1850,26y.
Jane B.,June 20,1857,40y.
Levi,1798-1872.
Melville,1843-1857,s/o L.& P.
Priscilla,1807-1863,w/o Levi.
Sarah,1832-1863,d/o L. & P.
XX,Dec.22,1858,87y.
XX,Nov.13,1830,21y.
EKBERG
John H.,1907-1983,h/o Floise H.
EVANS
Dorothy J.,1906-1979.
Gordon W.,1907-1985.
FARNSWORTH
Ernest E.,1905-1992.
FARRIS
Alexander H.,1819-1879.
Dorothy,1903.
Hannah F.,1823-1902.
FARWELL
Anna M. Beals,1884-1975,
d/o N.D. & H.M.
Arthur,1878-1942.
Emma,1876-1944,w/o Frank.
Frank A.,Jr.,1915-1989,h/o Grace S.J.
Frank,1875-1953.
Harriet M. Farris,1848-1932,w/o N.D.
Jeanette,1920-1967.
Lois,1923-1935.
Myra,1887-1973.
Neal D.,1844-1916.
Walter,1871-1900,s/o N.D. & H.M.
Walter,1901-1901.
Walter,1917-1979.

FICKETT
Richard E.,1923-1992.
FRANK
Alvin,1822-1912.
George A.,Feb.11,1871-Jan.10,1884.
Laura A.,Dec.13,1876,15y.
Sarah A.,1832-1911,w/o Alvin.
GARDNER
Hannah R.,1884,79y.
Joel B.,May 7,1847,37y,s/o O. & M.
Martin V.,Jan.13,1860,21y.
Miriam M.,May 3,1873,29y.
William O.,Feb.15,1844,10y.
GREELEY
Asa,Aug.28,1874,63y.
Elizabeth B.,Apr.9,1893,81y.
Ruth,Feb.18,1874,63y,w/o Asa.
Thomas,Feb.1876,71y.
GURNEY
Bela B.,Mar.12,1861,29y.
Emily J.,Sept.16,1859,14y.
Lemuel,Capt.,Nov.1,1849,46y.
HANSEN
Anders,1852-1918.
Blanche C.,1886-1967.
George W.,Sr.,1913-1976.
Golda Eloise,1912-1912,
d/o Augustus & Clara E.
Marie,1848-1923,w/o Anders.
HARRIS
Eunice,1808-1889,w/o Jeriah.
Harriet Ford,1840 ?,39y,w/o Oznia.
Jeriah,1797-1885.
Mary Ann,1839-1880,d/o J. & E.
Miriam H. Haskell,July 12,1863,
85y,w/o Ozni.
Ozni,Dec.25,1843,78y.
Oznia,Jan.15,1871,71y.
HETHCOAT
Joan C.,1930-1980,w/o Richard.
HICKS
Andriana,Jan.15,1871,28y,
d/o John & Betsy B.
Anson N.,1845-1926.
Elvira B.,1841-1915.
Ernest L.,1875-1960.
Nellie C.,1888-1970.
HYNES
Charles W.,1884-1927.
Ella J.,1865-1947.
Goldie V.,1906-1986,w/o N.T.
Norwood T.,1906-1939.
Susie I.,1869-1947.
William E.,1862-1946.
JACOBS
Clinton E.,1889-1940.
Dana E.,1923-1925,s/o C.E.& G.A.

Grace A. Burnham,1893-1929.
KINNEY
Curtis L.,III,1935-1946.
Wesley Alger,1889-1965.
Wesley A.,Sr.,1896-1965.
LeGROW
Alfred C.,1945-1975.
Lester R.,1910-1980.
Mona L.,1915-1985.
MASON
Abbie M.,1870-1947.
Alberta P.,1894-1963,w/o Carl.
Carl L.,1893-1968.
Charles B.,1872-1949.
MERRILL
Abel,1777-1871.
Cyrus H.,1848-1872.
Danie,XXXX.
Daniel S.,1818-1893,h/o Elmira.
Elmira P. Clough,1822-1887.
Louran E.,1804-1888.
NORCROSS
Charles,Nov.8,1889,35y.
Leroy P.,1879-1932.
Lucetta A.,May 19,1889,35y,
w/o Chase
OLIVER
Florence B.,1899-1981.
Fred B.,1898-1992.
PETERSON
Annie B. Sawyer,1872-1945.
Christian,1866-1936,h/o Annie B.
Ernest T.,1904-1988.
Gladys M. Witham,1894-1957.
John H.,1896-1979.
PRIDE
Charles Aloen ?,1898,56y,s/o J. & M.
Frederick,Dec.21,1862,20y,
s/o John & Mary.
Horace S.,1850-1889.
John,Mar.23,1871,53y.
Lemuel T.,1852-1903.
Mary,Apr.27,1895,75y.
Nathan,June 13,1886,37y.
PRINCE
Annie D. Libby,1888-1979.
Clarence H.,1850-1920.
Ella M. Blanchard,1959-1914.
Frederick,1858-1860.
George H.,1881-1962.
Henry A.,1853-1860.
James A.,1819-1872.
Sophronia Gray,1827-1914,w/o Wm.L.
Synthia E.,1854,4m.
Willard,1855,2m.
William Gray,1853-1889.
William Leighton,1825-1887.

RIDEOUT
B.T., XXXX, Co.E.,17th ME Inf.
Elias,Feb.26,1872,65y.
Elizabeth S.,Aug.20,1870,68y.
Jane,Jan.21,1863,56y,w/o Elias.
Joshua M.,Nov.21,1876,73y.
Mary S.,Jan.31,1853,41y,w/o Nicholas.
Nicholas,Feb.7,1795-Oct.18,1873.
Reuben K.,Oct.27,1862,19y,
s/o Joshua W.& Elizabeth S.
Susan Jane,Sept.4,1874,9y,
d/o Josh. & Eliza.
William,1839-1898.
SCOTT
Evelyn E.,1894-1970.
Lester C.,1896-1973.
Nedra,1936-1960,d/o L.C. & E.E.
SHAW
A.Caroline,1843-1886,w/o N.M.
4 infants/o Seward & Abigail:
Abby Susan,Dec.9,1840,8y,
Abby Susan,July 29,1842,7m,
Harriet Elen,Jan.19,1844,6m,
infant,Feb.23,1832,1m.
E. Bryant,1823-1896.
Mary M.,1822-1907,w/o E.B.
Nelson M.,1836-1921.
children/o N.M. & A.C.:
Alice S. Bradford,1868-1944.
Angie M.,1873-1895.
Emma D.,1871-1955.
Ethel C.,1875-1922.
Herbert,1868-1905.
STUDLEY
no information.
SULLIVAN
William G., Nov.19,1952.
TAYLOR
Anna M.,1909-1988.
John E.,1913-1976.
John E.,1936-1993.
Lane O.,1940-1982.,h/o Johanna.
THOITS
Mary A.,1856-1915,w/o Wm.H.
William H.,1854-1912.
THURSTON
Heather R.,1982-1982.
WALKER
Clarence E.,1885-1956.
Margaret L. Hynes,1885-1951.
WATSON
Fannie L.,1881-1969,w/o G.F.
George F.,1878-1955.
WHITCOMB
Lucy B.,1804-1888.
Lucy Jane,June 10,1888,83y.

WILSON
Addie,1879-1930.
WINSLOW
Joseph,1873,74y.
Mary P.,Feb.18,1878,70y,w/o Jos.
WITHAM
Frank G.,19863-1947.
Lelia M. Smith,1864-1927,w/o F.G.
Leon W.,1892-1915.

✤ **BROWN CEMETERY** ✤
9 Chute Road. Windham.
Completed stone by stone.

ANDREW
Abraham,Apr.19,1795,9y,
 s/o John & Elizabeth.
John,Aug.8,1791,47y.
Nancy Green,Mar.7,1832,48y,
 w/o Jonathan.
BODGE
Albert C.,Nov.16,1840,1y,
 s/o Josiah & Isabella.
Betsey M.,May 25,1876,78y,
 w/o John.
Emilia J.,Mar.20,1816,10m,
 d/o Thomas,Jr.,& Abigail.
Eunice C.,1833-1886,d/o John & B.M.
John,Sept.1,1873,79y.
Lindley J.,Apr.8,1864,2y, only
 ch/o John J. & Martha Webb.
BROWN
Emeline Smith,July 29,1848,
 31y,w/o Ezra.
Emeline,Nov.13,1843,11m,
 d/o Ezra & Emeline.
Ezra,June 20,1809-Oct.9,1858,
 s/o Wm. & Hannah Elder.
Hannah Elder,Mar.21,1849,65y,
 w/o William.
Keziah H.,Sept.5,1811-July 8,1883.
Lois C., 1854?, stone sunk.
Mary A.,June 5,1860,19y,
 d/o Ezra & Emeline.
William,Esq.,Aug.22,1782-Dec.16,
 1851,s/o Ezra & Mary Boobier.
CASH
Abbie A.,1852-1902,w/o F.A.
Allie F.,1880-1903, &
Eva P. Robinson,1887-1920,
 2 d/o F.A & A.A.
Frederick A.,1853-19XX.
Jacob,Aug.23,1891,68y.
Melville,Feb.21,1851,2y,
 s/o Jacob & Mary.

CHESLEY
Enoch,Dec.8,1850,72y,
 s/o Joseph & Abigail.
CRAGUE
Jane B. Elder,1817-Aug.23,1900,
 w/o Peter.
Peter,Apr.23,1873,61y.
CRAM
Caleb S.,Feb.2,1870,64y.
Levi Thomas,Jan.16,1837,9m,
 s/o John & Mehitable.
EMERY
Alice A. Webb,Sept.25,1835-
 Jan.2,1871,w/o Charles F.
David A.,Feb.11,1864,17y,
 s/o David & Eunice F.
Eunice Maria,Jan.24,1869,3y,
 only ch/o Chas. & Alice.
FRENCH
George W.,1847-1918.
Mary E.,1845-1915,w/o Geo.W.
GALLISON
Abigail,Apr.14,1836,78y.
John,Sept.6,1840,86y,h/o Abig.
John W.,July 16,1848,28y,
 s/o John & Susan.
John,Jr.,June 22,1864,84y.
Sarah C.,Oct.20,1811,2y,
 d/o John & Susan.
Susan,July 25,1845,53y,
 w/o John (1864).
William,stone sunk,s/o J. & Susan.
GRAFFAM
Sarah,Sept.23,1820,5m,
 d/o Wm. & Hannah.
HANSON
Fidelia Wight,Aug.9,1814-
 May 12,1860,w/o Wm.P.
William P.,July 14,1811- Aug.29,1879.
HAWKES
Mary,Oct.17,1865,77y,w/o David.
JOHNSON
Rebecca E. Webb,1847-1930,
 w/o Mathew.
LITTLE
Eliza,1804-1886,w/o Moses.
Mary E.,Sept.6,1828-
 Sept.14,1851,d/o Moses & Eliza
Moses,Jr.,Mar.5,1810-
 Sept.12,1843,s/o Paul & Mary.
MILLIONS
Mehitable,Jan.21,1837,66y,w/o Thos.
RAND
Mary T.,1865-1941.
REA
Caleb,Col.,Sept.11,1849.

Caleb,Dr.,Dec.29,1796,40y,
　s/o Daniel.
Sarah White,Jan.22,1836,78y,
　w/o Caleb.
WEBB
Caroline Mayberry,May 1,1810-
　Dec.25,1900,w/o Josiah,1870.
Edward M.,Sept.12,1833-
　July 11,1853.
F. Marshall,1842-1905.
John,June 17,1799-
　Sept.23,1877,s/o Josiah & Reb.
Jordan,1857-1870,
　s/o Josiah & Caroline.
Josiah,May 12,1765-Sept.8,1849,
　s/o James & Elizabeth.
Josiah,Jan.9,1797-Sept.1,1870,
　s/o Josiah & Rebecca Elder.
Martha M.,Jan.9,1808-
　May 22,1883,w/o John.
Mary,Dec.29,1792-Oct.25,1857
　d/o Josiah & Rebecca E.
Moses L.,July 29,1844-
　July 1,1845,s/o John & Martha
Rebecca Elder,Aug.27,1764-
　Oct.6,1838,w/o Josiah(1849).
Rebecca E.,Apr.6,1828-
　Sept.16,1846,d/o John & Martha
Susan E.,Sept.24,1846-Sept.6,1847.
WHITTIER
Ezra H.,1866-1892,s/o H. & H.
Hannah E. Brown,1826-
　Sept.20,1890,w/o Hazen.
Hannah J.,1859-1859,d/o H. & H
Hazen H.,Nov.1829-Apr.1884.
Mary Ella,1857-1894,d/o Hazen
William B.,1862-1890,s/o H.H. & H..

✦ **LOVEITT CEMETERY** ✦
Also called Gambo Cemetery.
494 River Road, Windham. All
gravestones were checked.

ATKINSON
Edwin W.,1836-1894.
Guy,1873-1873.
Sarah Goold,1841-1925.
BICKFORD
Ainsworth L.,1887-1889.
Anne E.,1841-1888.
Arvid R.,1862-1925.
Melvina B.,Oct.27,1860,16m,
　d/o Leveitt T. & Jamie E.
Nellie R.,Dec.10,1861,9m,
　d/o Leveitt T. & Jamie E.
Thomas,Sept.24,1851,47y.

CARTONI
Neal,1912-1953.
DAY
Jacob T.,1837-1906h/o Sarah.
Sarah F. Loveitt,1848-1907.
DOLLEY
Huldah,1818-1856,w/o John.
John,1816-1892.
Joseph E.,Aug.29,1863,11w,
　s/o John & Nancy B.
Louise,1868-1918.
Lucius W.,Sept.28,1893,40y.
Nancy B. Loveitt,1822-1906,
　1st w/o Robert Loveitt,
　2nd w/o John Dolley.
GOOLD
Olivier Ames,1843-1905.
HANSON
Ader F.,June 3,1859,10m,
　d/o Edmund & Rachel.
Edmund,1808-1884,
　s/o Ezekiel & Mary.
Newall P.,Feb.4,1902,62y.
Rachel Smith,1813-1897,w/o Edm.
HOOPER
Benjamin,1803-Apr.14,1870,
　s/o Wm. & Elizabeth Vickery.
Charles F.,1834-1899,s/o B. & L.G.
Clinton B.,Feb.23,1908,67y,
　s/o B. & L.G.
Lizzie H.,Sept.22,1860,1y,
　d/o Charles & Mary.
Lucy Griffin,Mar.2,1879,80y,
　2nd w/o Benjamin.
Mary J.Dolley,1839-1910,w/o Chas.F
LEAVITT (on gravestone)
Benjamin,Feb.6,1781-Jan.1857,
　s/o Jonathan & Mariam.
Betsey Files,1788-June 25,1859,
　w/o Benjamin.
Flora,1839-June 7,1863,w/o Wm. H.
Frank,1859-1944.
James K.P.,Oct.14,1865,20y,
　s/o Charles & Nancy.
James,Mar.16,1783-Mar.4,1867,
　s/o Jon & Mariam,
　Had 4 wives:
　1st. Margaret Mitchel
　2nd. Charlotte Gallison,m.1816.
　3rd. Mrs. Mary Hooper.
　4th Mrs. ? Libby.
Lillian,1864-1951.
Mary Hooper,Nov.2,1854,58y,
　3rd w/o James.
Willie,1863-1864,
　s/o William & Flora Thompson.

LIBBY
Marjorie B.,1918-1989.
LORD
Elwell S.,1905-1926.
Lutie W.,1874-1950,w/o S.E.
Sherman E.,1865-1947.
Sherman J.,1893-1941.
LOVEITT
Charles,June 12,1811-May 29,1850,
  s/o Robt. & Sally.
Deborah,Oct.15,1774-June 8,1851,
  d/o Jon & Mariam.
Gardner,July 6,1821-May 10,1853,
  s/o Jonathan & Lucy.
Hiram C.,Apr.14,1817-Apr.30,1904,
  s/o Jonathan & Lucy.
Jonathan,Sept.1743-Mar.1819.
Jonathan,Aug.19,1776-Apr.16,1848,
  s/o Jonathan & Mariam.
Lucy Cobbey,Sept.29,1784
  Oct.14,1862,w/o Jonathan (1848).
Mariam Mitchel,Mar.31,1748-
  Aug.14,1826,w/o Jonathan.
Nancy Gallison,May 6,1823-
  Apr.13,1905,w/o Hiram C.
Sally Chute,1785-Mar.25,1848,
  w/o Robert.
Thomas C.,July 22,1809-
  June 2,1837,s/o Robt. & Sally.
LOVIS
Charles H.,Oct.6,1854-Jan.15,1931.
Lucy E. Loveitt,Aug.31,1859-
  May 27,1944,w/o Charles H.
MAXFIELD
Maude Atkinson,1875-1903,w/o W.B.
Walter B.,1870-1898.
MAYNARD
Annie C.,1861-1941.
Albert W.,1881-1942.
Ethel M.,1877-1920.
Margaret E.,1905-XXXX.
MORTON
Abigail,Dec.22,1858,51y,w/o Ransom.
NELSON
Mary E.,Apr.11,1837-Oct.25,1925.
Thomas,Sept.21,1842-Mar.8,1913.
O'BRIEN
Mary L.,1880-1946,
  d/o Lucius & Louise Dolley.
RAND
Elizabeth,Mar.1856,75y,w/o Rolland.
Elizabeth,Jan.26,1828,15y,
  d/o Rolland & Elizabeth.
Isabella,Mar.31,1840,19y,d/o R. & E.
Rolland,Jan.18,1846,75y.
William,Apr.21,1815,5y,s/o R. & E.

ROBINSON
Eliza D.,1814-1885.
Sullivan,1814-1884.
THAYER
Charles,Oct.22,1886,26y,
  s/o Edward & Almeda.
Emma J. Dolley,Dec.27,1861-
  Jan.2,1963,w/o Charles and w/o
  Wilbur Stanton,Mar.10,1857-
  Sept.3,1914,buried in Hiram,ME.
THOMPSON
Flora Leavitt,Oct.5,1889,70y,
  w/o Daniel.
WALKER
Abbie A.,June 17,1864,18y,
  w/o Edwin H.
Alfreda,1851-1928,
  d/o Charles & Elizabeth.
Mary M. Lamb,1846-1927,w/o Oliver.
Oliver H.,1837-1908.
WEBB
Margret A.,1846-1913.
Stephen S.,1845-1915.
WILLIAMS
James,Mar.28,1859,7m,
  s/o John & Isabella.
XX,
Grover C.,stone unreadable.

A small plaque off to the side:
In memory of the 45 men who lost their
lives in the Gambo Power Mill explosion
1828-1901.

I obtained the list of dead from
scrapbook articles c.1910:

"Between July 19,1828, when
the first explosion occurred, and
Feb.7,1901, the powder mills at
Gambo have had 25 explosions causing
the death of 45 men. There have been
several others in which no one was
injured.

Following is the list of dates when
one or more lost their lives: July 19,
1828, Josiah Clark, Hanson Irish,
Major Maines, William Moses, James
Green, Noah Babb and Daniel Moses;
Oct.17,1835, Charles Humphrey;
Sept.2,1847, Greenleaf Bachelder;
July 18,1849, Dennis Hatch;
Oct.1,1850, Leander White;
Sept.22,1851, Thomas Bickford;
Oct.12,1855, Luther Robinson, Edwin
Hardy, John Swett, Franklin Hawkes,

Samuel Phinney, George Whipple and James Whipple; May 6, 1856, Alfred R. Allen; Oct.4,1856. George White, Oliver Gerry, Peter Ritchie; Jan.15,1859, David C. Jones; July 9, 1861, Chas. Carmichael; July 7,1862, Augustus H. Little; Albert Glidden, Mary Varney; Nov.15,1863, Haggart Freeman; Feb.22,1869, Charles Charlow; July 2,1869, Benjamin Hawkes; Aug.6,1870, Frank Jordan; Nov.15,1871, John Densmore; Oct.27,1879, C.P. Stokes, Clinton Mayberry; Jan.31,1884, Reuben Kenney; May 11,1886, Clarence Clay, Henry Hooper; Nov.15,1888, Walter Childs, Edwin Williams; Dec.3,1888, William Bamblet, May 9,1898, Walter Maxfield, Frank Guptill, Feb.7,1902,Thomas A. Field, John Ross.

✤ **MUGFORD FAMILY** ✤
483 River Rd.,Windham.
Many unmarked field stones and broken stones, all stones checked.

BRAGDON
Harriet J.,July 28,1855,36y.
Samuel R.,1818-1895,1st w. Harriet.
Sarah M.,Sept.1845,12w,d/o S.& H.
JONES
David R.,1859,31y.
Herbert J.,Apr.29,1878,18m, s/o Edward.
MUGFORD
Lois Graffam,Feb.10,1820,58y, w/o Robt.,d/o Caleb & Lois Bennett.
Robert Jr.,Dec.30,1755-Feb.14,1835, s/o Robert & Mary Evans.
YORK
Mary,Apr.27,1822,27y.

✤ **VARNEY PASTURE** ✤
No location, Windham.

BAKER
Ichobod,1842.
ELDER
Keziah,1786.
William ,Jr.,1786.

✤ **OLD ANDERSON** ✤
Also called Hunnewell Cemetery.
near 434 River Road, Windham.
Checked all stones.

ANDERSON
Abraham,Dec.25,1768,63y.
Ann,Dec.1,1802,85y,w/o Abraham.
CRAGUE
Ann,Jan.23,1834,33y.
Benjamin,Feb.20,1802-Apr.18,1875,73y.
Elicia,Sept.6,1834,66y,w/o John.
Hannah V.,Mar.9,1845,46y,w/o Josiah.
Hugh,Oct.24,1768-May 3,1842.
James,Dec.8,1872,77y.
John,Jan.29,1764-Sept.30,1840, s/o Hugh & Eliz.
Mary,Sept.6,1823,26y,w/o John.Jr.
Phebe,Sept.10,1857.
Rebecca,Sept.9,1874,77y,s/o James.
Thomas,Dec.11,1875,64y.
GOODELL
John,1850.
HUNNEWELL
Anna Mitchell,Sept.6,1835,44y, w/o Zerubabel.
Elijah,Mar.19,1815,67y, s/o Zerubabel & Hannah.
Elijah,Sept.16,1836,20y, s/o Zerubbabel & Anna.
Hannah Cobb Swett,Apr.24,1791, 80y,wid/o John Swett, 2nd w/o Zerubabel.
Rebecca Locke,Feb.12,1830,83y, w/o Elijah.
Zerubabel,1784-XXXX, s/o Elijah & Rebecca.
Zerubbabel,Apr.15,1714-Aug.23, 1803,s/o Roger & Mary Adams.
PAINE
Hannah,Nov.21,1806,76y.

Out behind the old Anderson homestead just beyond this cemetery a monument stands alone, and it reads:
"This farm was settled by Dea. Abrm. Anderson 1738."
on the other side:
"Abraham Anderson and Lucy Smith married April 13,1788 died 1844.
Monument erected to their memory by their son John."

✤ **CHUTE CEMETERY** ✤
On Chute Road, Windham.
All stones checked and photographed.

The first of 2 large monuments on the left:
(panel 1) This monument is erected to the memory of George Washington Chute whose body lies near it's foundation on the north-west side. He was born on this farm May 4,1805 and here is lived all his life and here he died a bachelor Nov.18,1882 aged 77 years.
(panel 2) This family burial lot walled in and prepared by George W. Chute in 1845. He also enclosed the adjoining public burial ground and in March 1882 he presented it unconditionally to the town of Windham which was accepted the same day by a vote.
(panel 3) Josiah Chute who is buried near was the son of Curtis Chute and the father of George W. Chute. He was orderly sergeant and clerk of the company commanded by Capt. Thomas Mayberry of Windham,in the regiment of Massachusetts forces under Col. Francis, in the war of the Revolution. Sergeant Chute was wounded in the shoulder by a musket ball at the battle of Hub-bardstown July 7,1777 and was honorably discharged at the close of his term of 3 yrs. service Jan.1,1779. He died in 1834 age 75 years.

monument on right side states:
(panel 1) This cenataph was erected to the memory of Capt. Thomas Chute the first settler of New Marble-head, now Windham. He was born in London, England in 1690 and came to Marblehead, Mass., previous to 1725. He was one of the origianl grantees, and one of the committee for the location of the new township, in 1735, and drew home-lot #12.
(panel 2) Thomas Chute had 2 daughters, with an only son Curtis Chute,who lived with the father. He, (with another) was killed by lightening at Falmouth June 5,1767, while he was one of the selectman of Windham.
(panel 3) By direction in the will of George W. Chute, this monument was erected in 1884, by William Goold, executor.

(panel 4) The record of the First Church in Falmouth, now Portland says October 1738 Thomas Chute, Mary his wife and Abagail,their daughter, being regularly dismissed from the Church in Marblehead were admitted to the church here. There they remained two years, while Mr. Chute, in summer, was preparing a home for his family on the river end of his lot in the wilderness. He removed here, and was the first clerk of the new town, and afterwards one of the board of selectmen. He died in 1770, aged 80 years. The place of his burial is unknown.

Other gravestones in enclosure:
CHUTE
Catherine Clement,Dec.13,1877, 77y,w/o Josiah,Jr.
George Washington,May 4,1805- Nov.18,1882.
Josiah,Oct.2,1834,75y.
Mary,Nov.19,1843,80y,w/o Josiah.
COBB
Arabella D.,May 18,1853- Nov.17,1853,d/o F.M. & M.G.
Francis M.,1827-1876.
Mary G.,1831-1900,w/o Francis
Walter F.,Oct.27,1855- May 1,1876,s/o F.M. & Mary G.
KINGSBURY
George,June 30,1892,71y.
Susan,Mar.9,1889,w/o George.
SWETT
Emily,1812-June 18,1848,35y.
John,Nov.23,1845,87y, s/o John & Sarah.
Mary Hunnewell,1779- May 5,1863,w/o John.
William C.,Mar.31,1883,60y, s/o John & Mary.

In a small, separate enclosure to the right of this one:
COBB
Heman W.,1824-1900.
Sarah A. Bagdon,1830-1904, w/o Heman.

"A few short years of will past,
And we shall reach the shore,
Where death-divided friends,at last,
Shall meet to part no more."

✤ **JOHN AKERS KNIGHT** ✤
Dutton Hill Road, Windham.
ALLEN
Elias B.,1842.
Jeremiah H.,1842.
BAKER
Elizabeth,1829,w/o Josiah.
Josiah,1829.
HAMBLET
George W.,Apr.20,1865,4y,
  s/o Daniel & Elizabeth Knight.
HAWKES
William,1878.
HAWKS
Ebenezer,1836.
Eliaz,1825,s/o Ebenezer.
Rebecca,1819,w/o Ebenezer.
JACKSON
Aurilla Rosina Knight,1830-
  1863,w/o Elvin,d/o Moses & R.
KNIGHT
Eliza Doughty,June 5,1807-
  May 20,1837,1st w/o Stephen.
Eliza Elkins,July 3,1895,82y,
  2nd w/o Stephen.
Greenlief Horace,1824-1847,
  s/o Moses & Rebecca.
Moses,May 27,1887,89y, s/o John
  Akers & Keziah Morril.
Olive Cushman,1836-1877,
  d/o Moses & Rebecca.
Rebecca Huston,Sept.18,1878,
  73y,w/o Moses.
Sarah J.,Mar.24,1865,22y,
  d/o Stephen & 2nd w. Eliza Elkins
Stephen Huston,Aug.-Sept.1839,
  s/o Moses & Rebecca.
MAXWELL
Auvilla H.,1860,d/o Jacob.
Betsy,Feb.21,1858,49y,w/o Jacob.
Elizabeth,1817,14y,d/o Jacob.
Jacob,1860.
John G.,Jan.1850,18m,s/o Jacob.
John O.,1845,11m,s/o Jacob.
Malvina F.,1849,4y,d/o Jacob.
McDONALD
Betsey,1847,w/o Isucic.
MORRELL
Ann,1843,w/o Thomas.
Thomas,1850.

Riopel Funeral Home
ROLAND G. RIOPEL, Proprietor
(Air Conditioned) (1963)
Funeral Director and Embalmer
AMBULANCE SERVICE ANYWHERE
8 PLEASANT ST.　Tel. 854-8171　WESTBROOK

✤ **BURYING GROUND** ✤
Off Craigie Road,Windham.
Not located.
COBB
Catherine L.,1853,w/o John.
John,1847.
HAWKES
Cynthia,1848,d/o I. & Rebecca.
George,1828,s/o Isaiah & Rebecca
Gilbert,1860, 1st wife Cynthia.
Isaiah,1792-1858,
  s/o James & Margaret Estes.
Louisa C.,1821-1897,d/o I. & R.
Rebecca Cobb,1794-1831,
  1st w/o Isaiah.

✤ **KNIGHT BURIAL GROUND** ✤
30 Pope Road,Windham.
Completed stone by stone.
ALLEN
Mary E.,1855,40y,w/o Jonathan.
ANDREWS
Albert H.,1887,75y.
ANTHOINE
Ann E.,1860,13y,d/o Nichol. & Sophia.
Anna Pattangall,Apr.3,1764-
  Dec.24,1849,w/o Nicholas.
Caroline G.,1849,4y,
  d/o John & Mary Ann.
Carolyn M. Hawkes,1859-1926,
  w/o Charles.
Charles H.,1849-1924.
John,May 9,1794-Feb.2,1860.
Martha D. Gowen,1853-1930,
  w/o True.
Mary Ann Gilman,1815-1869,
  w/o John.
Moses P.,1916.
Nicholas,1876.
Nicholas,1798-1834.
Sophia A.,1817-1876,w/o Nich.
True M.,1851-1934,s/o Nicholas,Jr.
  & Sophie Merrill Athoine.
ATWATER
Alma A.,1879-1958,w/o Jos. G.
Joseph G.,1868-1951.
BAILEY
Levi,June 1804-July 25,1884.
Levi,Jr.,1839-1884,
  h/o Elizabeth Whitney.
Mary,Jan.1864,52y,w/o Levi,
  d/o Jon.& Mary Cobb Sawyer.
Mary Annie,1870,d/o Levi.
BOODY
Cornelia Green,1888,76y,w/o Sewell.

Edmund,1859,20y,
 s/o Sewell & Cornelia.
Martha J.,1892,43y,d/o Sewell.
Sewell,1873.
BRACKETT
Rebecca Roberts,1871,70y,
 w/o Zachariah,d/o Joshua & Eliz.
BROWN
Sarah Lowell,1841,64y,w/o Ezra
COBB
Betsey,1874,87y,w/o Nathaniel.
Daniel,1827-1894.
Edith M.,1886-1889,d/o Uriah
Flora Ella,1860-1918,d/o Danl.
Florence M.,1860,d/o Daniel.
James D.,1872-1920.
Laura A.,1847-XXXX,w/o Uriah.
Louisa,1812-1904.
Louisa H.,1867,d/o Ephraim.
Lucinda Libby,1886,w/o Samuel.
Lucy Ellen,1843,d/o Ephraim.
Matilda P. Morrill,1833-1905,
 w/o Daniel.
Nathaniel,1825,43y.
Samuel,1896.
Uriah,1840-1902.
Willard P.,1881-1883,s/o U.C.
CREELMAN
Gordan W.,1892-XXXX,h/o H.R.A.
Helen R. Anthoine,1888-1933.
June Elizabeth,1930-1944.
CURTIS
Sylvia P.,1916.
DOLLEY
David J.,1878-1927.
E.J.,1867.
Ebenezer,1824-1891.
Ellen M.,1845-1931,w/o Eben.
George W.,1881-1938.
Lawrence N.,Sr.,1901-1977,
 s/o David & Mabel.
Mabel L.,1877-1942.
Margaret A.,1987.
Margaret W.,1920-1987.
Mark A.,1954-1957.
Patia,1882-1901,d/o E. & E.M.
Raymond L.,1944-1944.
Rena May,1917,18y,d/o David J.
Roland J.,1914-1992.
Ronald J.,1992,s/o David.
Ronald J.,1914.
Warren,1874-1942.
FIELD
Colby J.,1862,3y,d/o J. & M.
James,June 2,1881,68y.
Margaret,June 8,1892,64y,w/o James.

HALL
Amos,Nov.27,1832,37y.
Ann S.,1857,w/o Benaiah.
Fanny Hanson,1796-1827,w/o Amos.
Lucius W.,1836,14y,s/o David.
Lydia P.,1845,w/o David S.
HANSON
Albert Trickey,1852,15m,
 s/o Jason & Isabella McIntosh.
Ann Elliott,Dec.1,1805-
 Jan.11,1884,w/o Joshua.
Anna Elliott,1853,w/o Ichabod.
Annie,1884,10y,d/o Geo.E. & E.
Annie,1854-1864,d/o Geo.& E.
Beniah,1801-1825,24ys/o Ezek.
Converse,1864,d/o J.G.
Ezekiel,Nov.6,1767-Feb.1848.
Ferdinand,1842,19m,
 s/o Jason & Isabelle.
George,1821,13y,s/o Moses.
George F.,Jr.,1853-1857,
 s/o Geo. F. & Eliza Bodge.
George F.,1830-1855,
 s/o Joshua & Sally.
Hannah Gowen,Oct.24,1787-
 Mar.21,1841,1st w/o Thomas.
Ichobod Jr.,1761-May 28,1853,
 s/o Ichobod & Abigail Hayes.
James Gowen,Apr.23,1816-
 May 28,1873,s/o Thos & Hanna.
Jason,1845-1881,
 s/o Josiah & Sally Hill.
Joshua,Nov.18,1803-Nov.30,
 1880,s/o Ichobod & Anna Elliott.
Marcia Bishop,1818-1906,
 w/o Jas G., d/o Geo. & Nancy.
Mary Plummer,1776-1868,
 w/o Ezekiel.
Mary Ann,1834,21y,d/o Moses.
Mary F.,1864,16y,d/o Josh. & S.
Moses,1858,28y.
Sarah,1804.
Sarah,1832,w/o Moses.
Sarah Hill,1884,77y,w/o Joshua.
Stephen Converse,1855-1856,
 s/o Geo. F. & Eliza.
Stephen Converse,1831-1834,
 s/o Joshua & Sally.
Thomas,Mar.25,1787-
 Jan.28,1872,s/o Ichobod,Jr.
HAWKES
Amos,1815-1886,
 s/o Benjamin & Ruth
Anna Hawkes,1820,45y,w/o David.
Benjamin,1859,87y,
 s/o Amos & Deborah.
David,1839,69y.

David F.,1856,53y.
Edna Gowen,1824-1901,w/o Amos.
Edwin,1869.
Edwin A.,1869,10y,
  s/o David & Louisa.
Ellen W.,1864,18y,d/o David.
Frances A.C. Knight,1828-1866,
  w/o Joshua R.,d/o Robt.& Eunice.
Franklin,1855-1857.
Joshua R.,1828-1902.
Louisa,1818-1889,w/o David F.
Louisa Bel,1864,6y,d/o D. & L.
Mary F.,1847,7y,d/o David & L..
Oliver,1857,27y,s/o Ben. & Ruth
Patience,1837-1905.
Ruanna,1864,d/o Amos & Edna.
Ruth Roberts,Oct.10,1867,80y,
  w/o Benjamin.
Sarah M.,1828-1894,
  d/o Benjamin & Ruth.

HUSSEY
Caroline A.,1877,44y,d/o John.
Catherine,1851,80y,w/o John.
John D.,1855,86y.
John,Jr.,1881,80y.
Joseph,1832,18m,s/o J.& S.
Lucinda P.,1874,44y,d/o J. & S.
Moses C.,1832,12y,s/o Daniel & Lydia.
Sarah,1869,w/o John,Jr.

JAMES
David,1874.

JONES
Annie,1864,d/o Charles.
Betsey A.,1853,25y,w/o Charles,
  d/o John & Sally Hanson.
David,Mar.11,1874,41y.

JORDAN
Mary,1875,71y,w/o Peter.
Peter,1873,74y.

KNIGHT
Alfred,1887,34y,s/o Mark & E.J.
Ann,1831,42y.
Charles C.,1834,21y.
Emily J.Hobbs,1887,75y.
Eugene E.,1869,3m.
Henry,1856,8y,s/o Mark & E.J.
Jonathan,1837,78y.
Jonathan,1759-1840,
  s/o Mark & Mary Johnson.
Mark,1806-1892,h/o Emily J.
Mary A.,1869,33y,w/o Joseph.
Mary,1866,22y,d/o Mark & E.J.
Orrin B.,1863,2y,s/o Joseph H.
Rufus W.,1856,10y,s/o M.& E.J.
Sarah W.,1839,78y,
  w/o Jonathan (1837).

LIBBY
Abram I.,1867-1938.
Ella J.,1936,w/o A.I.
Russell,1933.

LORD
Caroline,1862,27y,
  d/o Edmund & Sarah.
George,Capt.,1890,43y.
Jane Y.,1886,68y,w/o Stephen.
Stephen,1862,51y.

LOUGHRAN
Cora B. Dolley,1887-1923.
William P.,XXXX.

LOWELL
Abbie,1844-1919,d/o U. & M.J.
Abigail Gallison,1840,57y,w/o John B.
Abner,1821,3y,s/o John & Abig.
Betsey Hawkes,Oct.21,1848,46y.
Caroline,1891,67y,w/o Edw. J.
Charles N.,1897,39y,
  s/o Nathaniel & M.P.
Clara Bickford,1894,61y.
Cyrus Hamilton,1837,2y,
  s/o Daniel & B.
Cyrus,1806-1829,s/o John & Abigail.
Daniel B.,Nov.25,1865,75y.
Darius,1887,73y.
Emily,1848-1895,d/o Urban
George Willis,1856-1864,
  s/o Urban & Mary.
Hamilton Smith,Capt.,1866,24y.
John B.,Sept.22,1859,85y.
John Fletcher,1851-1864,
  s/o Urbain & M.J.B.
Joshua,Nov.221839,39y,
  s/o Abner & Ludia Purrington.
Lindley,1849,2y,s/o Nathan & M.
Louisa Hawkes,1869,31y,d/o Daniel.
Lucy H.,1865,51y,1st w/o Darius.
Mary J. Blake,1818-1897,w/o Urban.
Mary P.,1891,73y,w/o Nathanl.
Nathaniel,1889,70y.
Oliver Hawkes,1863,33y,at Gettysburg
Sarah Mayberry,1749-1838,w/o Josh.
Urban,1816-1890.

MASON
Sarah W.,1874,45y,w/o George.

MERRICK
Margaret,1876,17y,w/o Wm.

MOLZEN
Anna L.,Jan.14, 1903.
Ernest C.,1899-1969.
Geneva Woodman,1908-1982.
Melvin H.,1904-XXXX,h/o G.W.

MOODY
Charles B.,1919.

NEWELL
George A.,1847-1930.
Mary E.,1839-1903,w/o Geo. A.
POWERS
Betsey,1795-1821.
Ichabod H.,1851,30y.
PRIDE
Rachel A.,1826-1865,2nd w/o Ryerson.
Ryerson,1810-1889.
RENDALL
Ellen M.,1834,22y,w/o E.B.
ROBERTS
Betsey,1843,67y,w/o Joshua.
Joshua,1803,33y.
SAWYER
Andrew J.,1865.
SMITH
Frank L.,1833.
Sarah L.,1833,33y.
SOULE
Rufus,Capt.,1874,68y.
WALDEN
Lydia,1837,44y,w/o Nathaniel.
Nathaniel,1870.
WATERHOUSE
Albert L.,1874-1958.
Elizabeth,1875-1944.
George H.,1885-XXXX.
Margaret J.,1876-1953.
Minnie E.,1896-1978.
Rebecca Watson,1852-1929.
William,183901929,h/o Rebeca.
WOODMAN
Baby,1898.
George N.,1871-1943.
James O.,1845-1896.
S. Alice,1876-1948,w/o George.
WRIGHT
Ann Jane,1872.
YOUNG
Betsey,1863,82y,w/o William.
William,1861,91y.

✣ **GOOLD CEMETERY** ✣
Nash & Windham Center Rd.,
Windham.

BARTON
Dorothy Eliott,Feb.12,1842,87y,
w/o Ebenezer.
Ebenezer,Apr.15,1785,35y.
BROWN
Alice F.,1857,d/o J.B.
John,Jr.,1890.
Miriam,Jan.25,1820-Sept.8,1859,
w/o John,Jr.

COOK
Betsey,1861.
GOOLD
Benjamin,1863,58y,h/o Mary
Ann Sargent,s/o Nathan,(1823).
Betsey Gowen, Oct.22,1866,85y,
w/o Nathan,d/o Jas.& Edna Knight
Betsey Shane,1882,93y,w/o Ezra
Edna Louise,1879, d/o Wm. &
Louise Hitchings Goold.
Ellen,1850-1924,d/o Wm. & Nabby.
Ezra,1789-1818,s/o Benjamin.
Ida Isabelle,1855,d/o Nat. & M.J.
John,1803-1806,s/o Nathan.
Mariam Swett,1805,33y,
1st w/o Nathan.
Mary Ellen Kimball,1873,48y,
1st w/o Nathan (1897).
Mary J. Follansbee Smith,
XXXX, 2nd w/o Nathan (1897).
Naby Tukey Clark,1816-1897,
s/o Wm.,d/o Seth & N.T.Clark.
Nathan,Apr.10,1778-1823,h/o Betsey.
Nathan,Dec.19,1821-Sept.9,1897,
s/o Nathan & B.
William,Apr.13,1809- May 22,1890,
s/o Nathan & Betsey.
HARDING
George H.,1904.
Margaret Ellen,1943.
Mary E.,1881.
Warren,1871.
JAQUIS
John G.,1895.
JONES
Dorothy,1860,d/o Eben.
MORRIS
Caroline,1879,d/o Wm.W.
MORTON
Anne E.,1874,d/o Wm.
Stephen T.,1863.
William F.,1864.
William White,1868.
PRIDE
Nancy Gowen,1828-1884,w/o Sam'l F.
Samuel Freeman,1829-XXXX.

✣ **MAYBERRY CEMETERY** ✣
29 Park Road, Windham.
This was done stone by stone.

ALLEN
Albert H.,1874-1912.
Charles T.,1859-1914.
Charles W.,1887-1964.
Donald E.,1910-1988.
Earle J.,1906-1972.

Edith H.,1887-1972,w/o Chas.W
Edward C.,1836-1925.
Elizabeth J.,1911-1987,w/o Harold C.
George E.,1865-1944.
Grace G.,1877-1936w/o Donald.
Harold C.,1912-1989
Josephine M., XXXX.
Lorraine M.,1935-1994,w/o Philip H.
Marguerite,1972.
Marguerite M.,1906-1993,w/o Earle J.
Martha A.,1863-1914.
Mary S.,1918,w/o Edw.C.
Olive G.,1910-1971.
Roscoe G.,1872-1941.
ATWOOD
Elizabeth B.,XXXX,w/o Stanley H.
Stanley H.,1922-1975.
BATCHELDER
Llewellyn W.,1893-1963.
Zilla M.,1889-1963.
BELL
Fred A.,1918-1964,h/o Edith.
Johnna C.,1952-1976,d/o Fred.
BLAKE
Hannah Elkins,1850-1878,
w/o Walter P.
Walter A.,1878-1879,s,/o W.P. & H.E.
BOWDEN
Dorothy S.,1902-1986.
BROWN
Andrew J.,1924-1979.
Betty Thomas,Nov.29,1863,84y,
w/o Joseph.
Ira,1871,61y,s/o Jos. & Betty.
Isaiah,1844,25y,s/o Joseph.
Joseph,Sept.29,1828,68y.
Lucille J.,1925-1984,w/o A.J.
Mabel M.,1902-1972,w/o Wallace.
Peter,1822,7y,s/o Joseph.
Robert W.,1926-1968.
Sally,1840,19y,d/o Joseph.
Samuel,1821,16y,s/o Joseph.
Wallace L.,1896-1953.
BRUTON
John D.,1925-1971,
h/o Phyllis R. Mayberry.
CAMPBELL
Nicole,1988.
Melinda,1988,d/o Frank.
CARROLL
Michael P.,1975-1988.
CASTELLA
Sarah,Feb.20,1868,15m,
d/o George & Helen Rackliff.
CHASE
Amelia Maye,1929-1991,
w/o Raymond L.

Mary E. Wilson,1894-1983,
w/o Raymond L.,Sr.
Raymond L.,Sr.,1891-1977.
CHRISTIAN
Wilfred J.,Sr.,1904-1960.
Dorothy E. Marsh,XXXX,w/o Wilfred J.
COLBY
Henry,1825-1900,h/o Miranda.
Miranda C.,1834-1905.
COTTON
Leslie,1889-1962.
Mildred,1891-1975,w/o Leslie.
CROMMIE
Robert E.,1914-1988.
CURTIS
Cheryl A.,XXXX,w/o Lawrence,Jr.
Geraldine M.,1909-1953.
Jeannette,1910-1988,w/o L. W.,Sr.
Lawrence W.,1907-1984.
Lawrence,Jr.,1944-1987.
DOUGLASS
Mary E. Colby,1861-1913,w/o Thos. M.
Thomas M.,1859-1926.
DREW
Beatrice W.,1905-1972,w/o Herbert.
Herbert A.,Sr.,1908-1985.
DROST
George E.,1929-1993.
ELDER
Clarence E.,1872,21y, adopted
s/o Joseph & Lydia.
Dorcus,1860,34y,w/o Isaiah.
Joseph,1821-1898.
Lydia C.,1812-1886,w/o Joseph.
Melissa E.,1860,4y,d/o Isaiah.
ELKINS
Caroline M. Legrow,1817-1865,
w/o Wm.,Jr.
Geneva Ruth,1910,1y,d/o Owen O.
Georgia A.,1853-1945,w/o I.C.
Hannah M.,1844,29y.
Isaiah C.,1849-1924.
Mary,1826,26y.
Owen O.,1882-1935.
Rebecca,1859.
Ruth Elva,1917-1952,d/o Owen & S.E.
Sarah J.,1856-1876,d/o Wm.
Susannah,1820,45y,w/o Wm.
Susie E. Davis,1888-1940,w/o Owen.
William Jr.,1804-1871.
William,1846,73y.
William,1871,h/o Caroline.
ESPEAIGNETTE
Edith F.,1922-1979,w/o Fred W.
ESTES
Annie G.,1852-1933,w/o Daniel.
Daniel W.,1854-1943.

Nellie M.,1882-1971.
FIELD
Alwilda,1889-1936.
James E.,1882-1956.
FOSTER
Wilfred Morris,1930-1984.
GILMAN
Stanley C.,1914-1986,h/o Theresa L.
GRADY
W. Michael,1949-1978.
GRANT
Barry E.,1923-1983,h/o Emma Tenny.
Eugenia F.,1889-1969,w/o Ray W.
Kenneth J. II,1944-1984,
  s/o Barry & Emma.
Ralph W.,1911-1974,
  h/o Mildred Meggison.
Ray W.,1889-1975.
Susan J.,1964-1964,d/o R.W. & M.M.
GRAVES
Jonnie E.,XXXX,2m,s/o J. & Nellie
HANSLEY
Sarah E. Small,1884,61y,
  d/o Samuel & Lucy.
HANSON
Rutherford,1898-1987.
HARRIMAN
Arthur G.III,1909-1987,
  h/o Elizabeth B. Burgess.
HASKELL
M. Victoria Baker,1851-1902,
  w/o Oliver D.
Ada,1858-1927.
Ann M.,1843-1926.
Anna B.,1806-1829.
Casadana,1853-1944.
Charity,1808-1839,w/o O.P.
Daniel,1768-1845.
Daniel M.,1813-1838.
Ella M.,1847-1935.
Emma Allen,1867-1967.
Esther E.,1845-1919.
Everline,1810-1887.
Hattie J.Spencer,1859-1918,
  w/o Samuel V.
Herman P.,1887-1960.
Kemis L.,1965.
Lizzie W.,1883,9y,d/o S. & M.M.
Martha M.Webb,1851-1898,
  w/o Samuel V.
Mary,1770-1863,w/o Daniel (1770)
Nancy G.,1819-1901,w/o O.P.
Oliver D.,1856-1921.
Oliver M.,1851-1851,
  s/o Oliver & Nancy.
Oliver P.,1808-1893.
Oville V.,1887-1971.

Rachel M.,1849-1905.
Samuel V.,1888-1908.
Sarah J.,1842-1904.
Wirt Chester,1883,5m.
HAWKES
David R.,Capt.,1889-1903.
Edwin E.,1856-1924,s/o D.R. & S.J.
Sarah J.,1829-1911,w/o David.
HAYES
Dallas G.,1905-1001,w/o W.H.
Walter H.,1906-1971.
HIBBARD
Clark D.,1833-1888.
Rachel,1879-1934,d/o C.D.& R.A
Ruby A.,1835-1916,w/o Clark.
HIGGINS
Charles,1902-1971,h/o Eleanor.
Harry,Sr,1900-1971,h/o Owens
Harry L.,Jr.,1930-1953.
HOWARD
Joseph H.,XXXX,Canadian Soldier.
HUNT
Carrie,1858-19XX.
Robart A.,1990,s/o Stephen R.
INGALLS
Florence B. Mayberry,1898-1990,
  w/o Nelson.
Nelson P.,1895-1984.
IRISH
Charles F.,1859-1932.
Eliza H. Mayberry,1858-1953,
  w/o Charles F.
JACOB
Louis P.,1914-1976, h/o Mona C.
JORDAN
Howard L.,1903-1978.
R. Bernice,1907-1982,w/o H.L.
JOSLIN
Violet M.,1917-1987.
KEENAN
Allan Michael,1971-1991.
KIRK
Mahlon R.,1931-1994,h/o Joan Brown.
KNOUSE
Boyd E.1912-1975.
Clara C.,1911-1992,w/o Boyd E.
LAMB
Dorothy E.,1911-1969,w/o W.R.
Peter Wm.,Sr.,1943-1991.
William R.,1909-1969.
LANDRY
Brian Keith,1961-1985.
LARRIVEE
Eugene J.,1923-1982.
Marilyn I.,1925-1994.
LEIGHTON
Roland R.,1951-1982.

Stanley F.,1903-1985,h/o Inez
LOPES
Anna,1903-1981.
John,1903-1991.
LOWELL
Geroge W.,Jr.,1931-1979,
  h/o Charlotte R.
LUCEY
Cornelius V.,1914-1968.
MAINS
Linwood C.,1930-1994.
Sandra J.,1959-1987.
MANNETTE
Michael F.,1968-1988,s/o John.
Thomas F.,1918-1992,h/o Priscilla.
MAYBERRY
Abigail,1832,65y,2nd w/o Wm.
Adelaide C. Loveitt,1843-1900,
  w/o Wm.F.
Almeda E.,1848-1939,
  d/o Richard & M.J.
Andrew,1778-1864,
  s/o Wm. & Jane Miller.
Asa L.,1880,68y,
  s/o Andrew & Margaret.
Carla Allen,1866-1925,w/o Frank N.
Charity A.,Jan.15,1855,15y,
  d/o Robert & Pamela.
Clark,1827-1836,s/o Josh. & E.
Clyde S.,1913-1941.
E. Clinton,1849-1879,
  s/o Samuel & Jane.
Edmond D.,1832-1910,
  s/o Josiah & Eliza.
Eliza H.,1858-1953,
  d/o Josiah & Martha.
Eliza Swett,1795-1834,
  2nd w/o Josiah.
Ellen A.,1847-1918,
  d/o Samuel & Jane Todd.
Ellen R.,1912-1912 & baby.
Ernest D.,1868-1937.
Etta J.,1863-1946,w/o Ernest.
Eunice,1879,58y,w/o Joseph.
Eunice Miller,1782-1815,
  1st w/o Josiah.
Frank N.,1858-1948,
  s/o Richard & M.J.
Fred E.,1865-1951,s/o R.& M.J.
Grace V.,1894-1956,w/o Wilbur
Helen Morton,1827-1882,
  2nd w/o Samuel.
Ida E.,1860-1879,d/o Josh.& M.
James L.,1843,23y,s/o And.& M.
Jane S. Todd,1854,32y,
  1st w/o Samuel.
Joseph,1888,63y,s/o Thos.&M.
Joshua S.,1822-1905.
Josiah,1783-1870,
  s/o Wm.& Jane Miller.
Julia A.,1865-1922,w/o Royal T.
Leroy M.,1894-1974.
Lester F.,1891-1956.
Lillian G.,1900-1994,w/o Lester F.
Lyman F.,Aug.20,1869,18y,
  s/o Asa & Sarah.
Mabel Young,1870-1907,w/o M.E.
Margaret Trott,1790-1872,w/o Andw.
Marion E.,1901-1982,w/o Leroy M.
Martha Allen,1834-1921,
  2nd w/o Joshua.
Mary Senter,1790-1846,
  3rd w/o Josiah.
Mary,1820,50y,1st w/o Wm.
Mary Trott,1881,83y,w/o Thos.
Mary A.,1851-1937.
Mary E.D.,Sept.27,1855,13y,
  d/o Robert & Pamela.
Mary J. Trott,1821-1900,w/o Richard.
Melbourne E.,1864-1935,
  s/o Edmund & Sarah A.
Minnie E.,1879-1869,
  d/o Joshua & Martha.
Olive Ann,1855-1866,d/o Josh. & Pam.
Olive P. Emery,1833-1855,
  1st w/o Joshua.
Pamela A. Webb,1891,79y,w/o Robert.
Rebecca Elkins,1798-1859,
  4th w/o Joshua.
Richard,1814-1897,s/o Josh. & Eunice.
Richard L.,1878-1919.
Robert,1854,44y,s/o J. & E.
Royal T.,1853-1915,s/o Sam'l & Jane.
Rubie,1871-1879,
  d/o Joshua & Martha.
Samuel,1812-1837.
Samuel,1811-1889.
Samuel,1811,37y.
Sarah,1879,69y,w/o Asa.
Sarah,1806-1883,d/o Wm.& M.
Sarah A. Knight,1835-1894,w/o Edm.
Sarah Pattengall,1858,82yw/o Sam'l.
Stephen,1825-1912.
Thomas,1878,82y.
Warren E.,1930-1952.
Wilbur L.,1889-1949.
William,1834,65y.
William F.,1828-1910.
McKNIGHT
Esley J.,1904-1990.
McMILLIN
Robert G.,1950-1990,
  h/o Dolores Audet.

McNEIL
Jessica Lee,1969-1989,d/o John.
MEG-QUIER
Mable R.,1898,39y,w/o O.E.
Ruby,1893,4m,d/o O.E.& M.R.
MELANSON
Beatrice S.,1898-1981.
MERRILL
Jonathan F.,1831-1919.
MILLS
Elroy M.,1933-1987.
MORRILL
Carrie M. Elkins,1860-1882, w/o Henry G.
MORSE
George Ivory,1873-1953.
Geraldine Grant,1932-1984.
Isabel,1881-1968,2nd w/o George.
Mabel May,1875-1919,w/o George I.
MORTON
Wallace I.,II,1958-1969.
NEWCOMB
Nicholas,1994-1994.
PARKER
Forrest Walter,1909-1960.
PERRON
Jennifer L.,1984.
PETERSON
Doris M. Allen,1912-1961,h/o Guy C.
PORELL
Reginald A.,1923-1990.
POTTER
Willis,1941-1992,h/o Polly.
PRICE
baby girl,1988,d/o Lewis D.
QUINT
Erica Jean,1969-1970.
RACKLIFF
Andrew M.,1863,61y.
Eunice H.,1892,70y,w/o Andw M.
Sarah C.,1868,d/o A.M. & E.
RANDALL
Herman F.,1910-1975,h/o Elsie.
RICH
Edith L.,XXXX.
Howard L.,1910-1980,Edith L.
RICHARD
Mark D.,1966-1989.
RILEY
Ronald C.,Sr.,1934-1992, h/o Patricia A.
ROLLINS
Flora M.,1856,3m,d/o John R.
John R.,1891,66y.
John R.,1861,18m,s/o John R.
Lucinda M.,1891,65y,w/o John.

SAWYER
Christine L.,1898-1962.
SCOTT
Emma E.,1855-1934,w/o T.J.
Thomas J.,1857-19XX.
SELLERS
Claire R.,1937-1991.
SENTER
Mary Anderson,Dec.3,1846,56y, d/o Edward & Mary.
Noah J.,Dec.17,1837,h/o Mary.
SMALL
baby,1994.
Charles L.,Sr.,1923-1993.
Clyde S.,1941.
David Otis,1813-1880.
Dorothy,1791-1879, w/o Frances.
Ellen R.,1912.
Ernest B.,1873-1941.
Frances,1785-1865.
Grace V.,1956.
John G.,1860,30y.
Lillian J.,1875-1955,w/o Ernest B.
Lucy,1818-1888,w/o David Otis.
Lucy,XXXX,78y,w/o Samuel.
Lydia A.,1885,52y.
Mary G.,1856,33y.
Orrin W.,1899,56y.
Samuel,1876,85y.
SMITH
Cathleen D. Grady,1951-1992,w/o Geo
Emma May,1885-1969.
STROUT
Virginia S.,1914-1992.
SWEETLAND
Evelyn M.,1919-1993,w/o Robert E.
SYLVESTER
Lillian E.,1887-1964,w/o William Z.
William Z.,1877-1968.
TAPLEY
Kathleen W.,1929-1990,w/o N.
Norman Allen,Sr.,1923-1988.
TIBBETS
Doris M.,1924-1977,w/o Robt.
Robert A.,1916-1990.
VERRILL
Arthur G.,1906-1953,h/o L.E.N.
Lillian E. Norton,1904-1994.
VINAL
Alvin O.,1852-1938.
Eliza F. Hawkes,1858-1953,w/o Alvin.
WALL
Larry R.,1948-1956,s/o Marjorie L.
WARREN
Daniel P.,1960-1968.
Hollie W.,1918-1980.
Holly M.,1964-1968.

WEBB
Cheryl J.,1947-1987.
Ralph Peabody,1920-1979,
  h/o Amelia H.
WHITE
Harold C.,1912-1991.
Helen F.,1912-1989,w/o H.C.
WILLIAMS
Richard H.,1935-1990,
  h/o Jean M. Gilman.
Talbert F.,Jr.,1956-1956.
WINSLOW
Edna N. Blanchard,1900-1984,
  w/o Ralph L.
Ralph L.,1895-1992.
WOODWORTH
Doris F. Tarr,1907-1986,w/o G.W.C.
George W.C.,1906-1988.
YORK
Alfred Isaiah,1921-1945.
Ernest K.,1886-1959.
Ethel Caroline,1883-1961,w/o E. K.
YOUNG
Alton P.,1911-1983,h/o Ella F.
Atwood W.,1880-1969.
Blanche E.,1883-1965,w/o A.W.
Gertrude May 1909-1910,
  d/o A.W. & B.E.
XX ?
Nana,1887-1970.

✤ **DOLLEY CEMETERY** ✤
189 Varney Mill Road,Windham.
Completed stone by stone.

ALLEN
Abagail,1851,61y,1st w/o Reuben.
Albert W.,1890-1969.
Amanda P.,1857-1951,w/o H.J.
Elbridge,1816-1890.
Eliza A.,1814-1889,
  w/o Elbridge & w/o Otis.
Ellen J. Brooks,1851-1923,
  w/o Fred W.
Frank H.,1857-1936.
Fred W.,1854-1940.
Hannah,1790-1853,1st w/o Jacob.
Hannah,1876,69y,2nd w/o Reuben.
Hannah S.,1811-1879,2nd w/o Jacob.
Harvey J.,1857-1923.
Jacob,1796-1879.
Jeremiah,1843-1862.
Joseph C.,1883-1904.
Lester W.,1879-1952.
Lucy A. Bauer,1859-1940,w/o Frank H.
Otis,1811-1861.
Reuben,1873,83y.

ANDERSON
George F.,1916-1959.
BAILEY
Mary O.,1843-1912,w/o Wm.B.
BAUER
Georgie B.,1866,9m,s/o H.E.&M.
Isabell,1857-1901.
Mary D.,1873,37y,w/o Henry E.
BERRY
David L.,1959-1986.
Eliza,1807-1894,w/o Thomas.
Sarah E.,1827-1911,w/o Wm.E.
Thomas,1792-1879.
William E.,1826-1908.
BORTELL
Arthur E.,Sr.,1936-1993,h/o Lucy M.
BOWDEN
Doris K.,1913-1992.
Douglas L.,1942-1986.
Roger W.,1916-1986.
BRITT
Virginia D.,1917-1994.
BROOKS
Rhoda S.,1887,74y,w/o Step. P.
BROWN
Althea A.,1923-1988,w/o Ralph E.
Carl R.,1941-1992,s/o R.& A.
BURNELL
David W.,1965-1985.
BUSH
Eugene Thomas,1925-1985,
  h/o Claudette E.,
CALKINS
Frank A.,XXXX.
CARLL
Eugene M.,1887-1939.
CARR
Ruth E.,1920-1972.
CECERRA
Marino,1911-1991,
  h/o Elsie Rankin Friend.
CELLAMORE
Frank H.,1921-1988,h/o Catherine M.
DOHERTY
Elmer F.,1918-1988,h/o Audrey L.
DOLLEY
Charles W.,1854-XXXX.
Edward,XXXX.
Esther M.,1781-1877,w/o Jos.
Joseph E.,1781-1855.
Samuel M.,XXXX.
Sophronia,1881-1982,w/o Wm.M.
Sylvia,XXXX.
William M.,1828-1871.
DOLLOFF
Charles E.,1903-1985,h/o Lillian I.

ELLIS
Richard A.,1955-1977.
EWING
Michael S.,1961-1984.
FAULKNER
Sylvester D.,1874-1903.
FORBES
Frank R.,1911-1978.
George S.,1909-1956.
Janet W.,1844-1930.
John C.,1915-1971.
Muriel P.,1922-1992,w/o John C.
Richard L.,1878-1956.
Selma S.,1885-1954.
Walter A.,1990.
FOSTER
Morrison H.,1917-1984,h/o Evelyn M.
GALLOP
Tom,1941-1991.
GRAFFAM
Charles B.,1864,6m,
s/o Joseph & Patience.
GROVER
Robert,1929-1991,h/o Carolyn Buxton.
HALE
Nicole Ruth,1985,d/o Robert W.
HARRIS
Blanche Fern,1926-1990,w/o Wayne R.
Wayne R.,1920-1991.
HENNESSY
Nancy J. Lamere,1944-1987,
w/o Charles K.
HERRING
Hattie E.,1920-1965.
HOOPER
Melissa Ann,1981-1990,
d/o Allen & Sherry.
IRISH
Emma J. Allen,1891-1976,
w/o Joshua S.
Joshua S.,1884-1940.
Joseph,1921-1921,s/o Joshua S.
JACOB/S
Doris M.,1934-1990,w/o Abraham.
Abraham,1929-1989.
Abraham,Jr.,1949-1984.
Trish L.,1985-1985.
JEWETT
Gwendolyne,1913-1992,w/o Philip S.
KEENE
Leon B.,1904-1991,h/o Grace E.
KINNEY
Ernest,1905-1967.
LAILER
Mildred M.,1901-1985,w/o Thomas L.
Thomas L.,1898-1990.

LAMB
Carroll P.,1910-1974,
h/o Marjorie W. Legrow.
Eliza A. Dolley,1813-1905,w/o Sallas.
Hattie J.,1855-1863,d/o Sallas
Joseph W.,1834-1869.
Melinda,1842,4y,d/o Sallas.
Sallas,1814-1887.
Sallas,Jr.,1850-1863.
LANDRY
Albert O.,1924-1991.
LEGROW
Cordelia B.,1838-1858.
Jane,1797-1853,w/o Joseph.
Joseph,1798-1859.
Langdon,1828-1865.
LIBBY
Elizabeth W.,1899-1972,w/o Geo. A.
Flossie D.,1882-1933.
George A.,1899-1972.
MANCHESTER
Ann Maria,1859,16y,d/o Wm & Betsey.
Benjamin R.,1832-1909.
Betsey E.,1879,57y,1st w/o Wm.
Charles H.W.,1874,23y,s/o Wm. & B.
Edward,XXXX.
Ellen F. Small,1838-1916,
2nd w/o William.
Elvira A. Hale,1843-1909,w/o Benj.
Martha,1796-1883,w/o Stephen.
Stephen,1795-1890.
William,1820-1898.
MANK
Charles E.,1906-1992,h/o Grace M.
McNAMARA
Margaret E.,1913-1993.
MESSIER
Gertrude Clara Daicy,1896-1962,
w/o Louis.
MINERVINO
Michael,1915-1986,h/o Phyllis C.,
MORONG
Paul E.,1901-1978,h/o Mildred R.
MORRELL
Ai, 1869,68y.
Mary A.,1833,4y,d/o Ai.
Mary A.M.,1838,2y,d/o Ai.
Rebecca,1803-1888.
Rebecca J.,1841,2y,d/o Ai & Rebecca.
Rebecca J.,1855,11y.
MORTON
Herbert R.,1872-1934.
Etta S.,1877-1968.
PARKINSON
Alice,1818-1900.
PARRY
Dorothy L.,1906-1985,h/o Richard L.

PENDLETON
Forrest E.,1901-1979,h/o Alice D.
PETTINGILL
Irma M.,1986.
PRATT
Virginia M.,1907-1994,w/o Warren T.
PROCTOR
Ida May,1859,11m,d/o H. & Patience.
SKILLIN
Patience D.,1846-1889,w/o John F.
SMALL
Cynthia I.,1950-1991.
SMITHSON
Carolin C.,XXXX,w/o Ross V.
Ida B.,1878-1970,w/o James R.
James R.,1869-1948.
Marion A.,1915-1984,w/o Robert E.
Robert E.,1914-1987.
Ross V.,1919-1980.
SPRAGUE
Kenneth E.,1961-1988.
STACEY
Philip H.,1909-1988.
Ruth Hull,1909-1991,w/o Philip H.
STROUT
Ellen M.,1847-1873,w/o Nathan
Nathan A.,1836-1904.
THOMPSON
Carrie L.,1885-1974.
TURNER
Mary L.,1887-1980,1st w/o Saben A.
Saben A.,1888-1967.
VARNEY
Ellen M.,1830-1857.
WILLIAMS
Laura A.,1936-1988,w/o Frederick.

✤ **PURINTON CEMETERY** ✤
Route 202, Windham.
Checked stone by stone.

ALLEN
Alvin,1834,22y,s/o Andw.& Anna
Andrew,1864,77y.
Anne,1875,83y,w/o Andrew.
Betsey E. Hawkes,1829-1905,
w/o Wm.H.
Elizabeth,1856,35y,w/o Emery.
Hannah,1836,22y,d/o Andrew.
William H.,1829-1912.
BAKER
Benjamin M.,1899,81y,s/o Elias
& Margaret Morrill Baker.
Benjamin,1865,72y.
Charlotte L.,1868,36y, 2nd w/o Wm.
Cyrus A.,1854,26y, s/o Wm.
Elias L.,1854,7y,s/o Benj. & Hannah.

Elias,1872,77y.
Eliza A.,1866,62y,1st w/o Wm.
Eliza Jane,1885,15y,d/o Wm.
Eugene,1862-1929.
Hannah A. Baker,1882,63y,w/o Ben M.
Hannah M.,1851,16y,d/o Wm.
John,1854,16y,s/o Wm.
Josiah,1843,12y,s/o B.& Mary.
Lizzie,1863,6y,d/o Benj. M.
Margaret,1889,96y,w/o Elias.
Mary Allen,1858,61y,w/o Benj.
Sarah E.,1849,3y,d/o Wm.
William A.,1850,18y,s/o W.& E.
William,1873,72y.
CHANDLER
Lydia Ellen,1868,28y,w/o J.B.,
d/o William & Mary Maxfield.
inf/o J.B.& L.E.,1868.
CROCKETT
Julia P.,1895,w/o J.E.
ELLIOTT
Alvin A.,1895,59y,h/o Apphia Legrow.
Alvin A.,1896-1901,s/o C.M.& N.F.
Aphia L.,1905,67y,w/o Alvin A.
Charles B.,1840-1910.
Charles M.,1867-1918.
Charlotte,1808-1865,2nd w/o John.
Hannah,1767-1836,w/o Jedediah.
Huldah,1803-1845,w/o John.
Jedediah,1760-1844.
John,1796-1881.
Mahlon F.,1882-1883.
Mary J.,1828-1853.
Nettie M.,1872-1936.
Orin L.,1900,25y.
FOSTER
Joseph P.,1843-1876.
GILMAN
Alan L.,1962-1982.
Alice S.,1892-1964.
Betty Ann,1935-1936.
GLANTZ
Andrew G.,1913-1984,h/o Georgie.
Andrew G.,1885-1904,s/o J.P. & H.A.
Annie R.,1869-1925,Aug.
Auguestus P.,1874-1937.
Hannah A.,1849-1940,w/o J.P.
John P.,1842-1903.
John S.,1869-1904,s/o J.P.& H.H.
GRAHAM
Scott,c.1991, approx.20y.
HAINES
Benjamin,?, broken stone.
Levina,1881,86y,w/o Benj.
Sarah Jane,1852,
d/o Benj.& Lovina.
Susanna,1870,85y,w/o Timothy.

Timothy,1871,86y.
HALL
Edward,1854,29y.
Rosilla B.,1858,w/o Edward.
HARMON
Alvin A.,1837,2y,s/o John G.
Ann Jenett,1852,10y,
 d/o John G.& Mary Ann.
Frances Ella,1851,1y,
 d/o Daniel & Sarah E.
James S.,1854,s/o Daniel.
James Stanley,1851,6m,
 s/o Daniel & Sarah E.
HAWKES
Abagail,1810-1872,w/o Joseph.
Hattie P.,1860,2y,d/o Jeremiah.
Jeremiah,1863,48y.
Joseph,1800-1872.
Lucretta,1848-1934,w/o Moses M.
Lydia M.,1854,6y,d/o Jeremiah.
Mary Ann,1887,72y,w/o Jeremiah.
Moses M.,XXXX,Maine Infantry.
HUFF
Bertha E.,1933-1935,d/o Mel.E.
Geneva A.,1987.
Melvin Everett,1896-1969.
Melvin J.,1928-1928,s/o Mel.E.
HUSTON
Elisha P.,1825,2y,s/o M.&S.H.
Moses,1830,38y.
Sarah H.,1876,78y,w/o Moses.
KEMP
Esther A. Elder,1813-1881.
John E.,1819-1900,h/o E.A.E.
LEGROW
Adelaide T.,1846-1927.
Anna,1862,63y,w/o Benjamin.
Asa,1804-1867.
Benjamin,1859,59y.
Caroline,1965,w/o Herbert.
Charles C.,1908-1975,
 h/o Gladys P. Clarke.
Clement M.,1842-1886.
Eben,1819-1889.
Edward M.,1868,23y,s/o Lewis.
Emogene F.,1858-1930.
Ephraim,1869,67y.
Eugene,1850,3d,s/o Asa & M.A.
Eunice,1842,16m,d/o A. & Mary.
Eunice,1810-1841,w/o Asa.
George Ward,1868,2y,
 s/o Eben & Lizzie.
Hannah Field,1846,72y,w/o Jos.
Herbert,1859-1936.
Jacob M.,1842-1915.
Joseph,1839,70y.
Lewis,XXXX.

Lizzie B.,1828-1893,w/o Eben.
Lucinda,1855-1856,d/o Rufus.
Lydia,1816-1905,w/o Rufus.
Lydia P.,1887,83y,w/o Ephraim.
Mary Ann,1819-1901.
Mary Jane,XXXX,w/o Lewis.
Rufus,1850,inf/o Rufus.
Rufus,1807-1893.
Samuel E.,1868,12y,s/o Eben.
Stephen A.,1866-1867,s/o H.& S
Susie F.,1868,15y,d/o Eben.
Virgie,1868,4y, s/o Eben.
LEIGHTON
Joseph,1838,33y.
Sarah M.,1827,inf/o Joseph & Eunice.
LIBBY
Andrew,1855,84y.
Anna B.,1865,6y,d/o E.H.
Ebenezer H.,1822-1868.
Edwin M.,1853-1874,s/o Ebenezer.
Elias,1869,72y.
Elizabeth,1878,83y,w/o Elias.
Elmira A.,1855-1879,d/o E.H.
Marietta P.,1831-1876,w/o Ebenez. H.
Rebecca H.,1837,2m,d/o Elias.
Sarah,1855,84y,s/o Andrew.
Sumner F.,1859,2y,s/o E.H.&M.P
MAXFIELD
Albert,1836-1923,s/o Wm. & Mary.
Franklin,Dec.30,1898,s/o Wm. & M.
Mary Waterhouse,1798-1880,w/o Wm.
William,1798-1885,
 s/o Eliakim & Rebecca Mann.
MAXWELL
Francis M.,1903,71y.
Mary A.,1881,44y,w/o F. M.
MORRELL
Alfreda A.,1842-1904,w/o John.
John,1834-1904.
PALMER
Alice H,1887-1965,w/o Chas.A.
Charles A.,1890-XXXX.
Vernon L.,1908-1909,s/o C.A.
William E.,1910-11,s/o Chas.A.
PARTRIDGE
Albion K.,1821-1902.
Mary E.,1863-1884,d/o Albion.
Sarah P.,1831-1909.
Walter,1871-1930.
PURINTON
Abijah,1850.
Barsheba,1853,90y,w/o Abijah.
Elisha,1869,76y.
Eunice,1885,82y,w/o Elisha.
Harry,1885,1y.
Joseph E.,1845-1910.
Lizzie L.,1857,d/o Richard.

Lucy M.,1809-1886.
Mary,1838,32y,w/o Richard.
Melissa Houston,1848-1899,
 w/o Joseph E.
Rebecca,1839,32y,w/o Elisha.
Richard,1867,68y.
Sarah,1825,26y,w/o Elisha.
SEELEY
James W.,1911,69y.
SILLA
Mary H.,1871,71y.
William,1882,82y.
SMALL
Abigail,1866,53y,w/o Gilbert.
Gilbert,1880,68y.
Sophia Frank,1829-1898,w/o Gilbert.
TUKEY
Anna L.,1856,d/o Wm.& Sarah.
Edgar,1858,s/o J.L.& M.L.
Martha A.B.,1862,23y,w/o Joseph L.
Sarah,1873,58y,w/o Wm.
VARNEY
Herbert G.,1857,10m,
 s/o Lindley H. & Martha.
WILLEY
Hattie M. Dinsmore,1854-1933,
 1st h. Joseph Foster,
 2nd w/o George.
Clifford E.,1890-1905.

✧ **CHASE CEMETERY** ✧
94 Highland Cliff Road.,Windham.
Completed stone by stone.

ALDRICH
Edna F.Bubar,1908-1993.
Floyd B.,1901-1962.
ALLEN
Nellie Pratt,1856-1928,w/o John.
ATKINSON
Evelyn L.,1930-1984,w/o Hiram.
AUSTIN
Ella H. Woodman,1870-1920,
 w/o Llewlyn E.
Llewlyn E.,1865-1954.
BACHELDER (on gravestone)
Hiram T.,1839-1896,
 s/o Liba & Rebecca.
BACON
Annie M.,1883-1959,d/o Clara C
BAILEY
Anna C.,Mar.29,1889,54y,w/o Dr.C.W.
BAKER
Rosie,1930-1982.
BANKS
Thelma J.,1901-1926 in India,
 d/o Hiram & Zelia Hawkes.

BATCHELDER
Cynthia J.,1842-May 1,1868,
 d/o Liba & Rebecca.
Fred F.,1860-1889,s/o W.A. & M.H.
Frederick,Sept.28,1846,3y,
 s/o Liba & Rebecca.
Liba,Oct.23,1870,63y.
Lizzie,July 8,1834-
 July 22,1899,d/o Liba & R.
Mary E.,1841-1909,
 w/o Hiram T.Bachelder.
Rebecca Smith,May 1893,84y,
 w/o Liba,d/o Hezekiah & Sally.
Sophronia,Oct.30,1859,14y.
BEAL
Roger D.,Jan.20,1950-Jan.20,1963.
BICKFORD
Eunice H.,Aug.7,1872,29y,w/o Geo.
BLAKE
Arthur J.,Jan.1896-Apr.1980.
Elsie M. Ham,Feb.6,1895-
 Nov.7,1963,w/o Arthur J.
Luella A.,June 19,1883-Dec.5,1962.
BODGE
Abigail Thrasher,1809-
 1892,w/o Thomas (1890)
Andrew,Jan.20,1810-Oct.30,1899,
 s/o Thos. & Betsey,h/o Sally Manson.
Benjamin,Aug.21,1831,75y,
 1st w. Susannah Hunnewell
 2nd w. Elizabeth Gammon,
 Rev.War Soldier
Betsey Mayberry,Nov.7,1860,84y,
 w/o Thomas.
Charles A.,1870-1907,
 s/o Edwin & Esther.
Charles H.,Nov.29,1863,25y,
 Rev.War Soldier.
Edwin A.,1835-1901,
 s/o Josiah & Isabelle.
Ermina M.,1867-1952,w/o Charles A.
Esther A. Harmon,1811-1896,
 2nd w/o John A.
Esther E. Haskell,1845-1919,
 w/o Edwin A.
Eunice F. Means Emery,1817-
 1902,2nd w/o Josiah.
*Freddie,1860-1875,s/o Edw & Mary.
*George A.,Apr.8,1858-July 15,1864,
 s/o Edwn & Mry.
*Isabella Richards,61y,
 Feb.10,1864,1st w/o Josiah.
John A.,Rev.,1814-1902.
*Josiah,Dec.191886,82y,
 s/o Thos. & Betsey.
*Mary Hanson,Oct.10,1839-
 May 28,1864, w/o Edwin A.

Sarah M.,May 30,1893,82y,w/o Andrw.
Thomas,1781-Aug.6,1856,
  s/o Benjamin & Susannah.
Thomas,1812-1890,
  s/o Thos. & Betsey.
William,1820-Oct.21,1843,
  twin bro/o Eunice.
* Removed Nov.1902 from grave-
  yard on Josiah Bodge farm.
BROWN
Dana R.,Mar.1950-July 1972.
Madeline,May 22,1906-Dec.14,1986.
Shirley M.,Jan.1929-Oct.1980.
Suzanne,1947-1986.
BUBAR
Lee F.,1887-1949,
  father/o Edna F. Aldrich.
BUTTS
Russell E.,1950-1961.
BUZEN
Frederick G.,June 9,1914-Nov.17,1987
Helen B. Balt Long,May 9,1912-
  June 13,1985.
CASWELL
Charles W.,1852-1913.
Edgar H.,1881-1895,s/o C.W. & H.E.P.
Harriet E. Pride,1858-1929,w/o C.W.
CHASE
Hiram,1804-1888,h/o M.J.S.
Mary J. Smith,1811-1885.
CLARK
Eugene E.,Sept.20,1950-Dec.29,1993.
Frances A. Baker,1911-1977.
Maurice C.,Sr.,1912-1987.
Winfield R.,Aug.18,1923-Oct.9,1993.
COBB
Ann S. Hale,Jan.17,1831-
  June 28,1904,w/o Charles A.
Annie Luella,1861-1877,
  d/o J.A. & M.J.
Benjamin J.,1883-1977.
Charles A.,Aug.31,1826-
  June 23,1905.
Charles H.,1886-1921.
Charlotte F.,1895-1980.
Elias,Aug.27,1890,94y.
Eluire,1806-1867,w/o Wm. S.
Ephraim,1808-1875.
Frank E.,1838-1925.
Fred T.,1867-1936.
Helen L. Spear,1874-1937,w/o Nelson.
Ione F.,1864-1951,w/o Nathaniel H.
J. Alonzo,Dec.26,1834-Jan.26,1901.
John A.,1835-1919.
Lida S. Jackman,1876-1962,w/o Fred.
Loviza H.,July 1,1867,20y,
  d/o Ephraim & Sarah.

Lucy Ellen,Nov.28,1842,14m.
Lucy M.,Sept.20,1860,27y,
  d/o Wm. S. & Eunice.
Laurence D.,1895-1978.
Martha E. Frank,1848-1829,
  w/o Frank E.
Melissa J. Smith,1835-1929,
  w/o John A.
Nathaniel H.,1862-1944.
Nelson B.,1864-1948.
Ruth I.,1897-1899,d/o A. & S.
Sarah M.,1817-1900,w/o Ephraim.
Sarah M.,1899-XXXX.
Susan,Aug.23,1863,57y,w/o Elias.
Walter N.,1892-1962,h/o Reba Varney.
William S.,1811-1895.
CURTIS
Burleigh E.,1922-1944.
Leslie E.,1894-1989,h/o L.M.B.
Lillian M. Ball,1895-1985.
DAVIS
Doris M.,Mar.3,1933-Aug.24,1989.
Hebert W.,1926-1989.
Nancy J.,1940-1990.
Richard E.,Sept.11,1933-Aug.18,1988.
DEARBORN
Harry M.,Jan.24,1914-
  Mar.29,1971,h/o Margret Pratt
DICKINSON
Frances I.,1913-1990,w/o Lester C.
DOLE
Mary Elizabeth,1850-1937,w/o Wm. B.
Phebe C.,1835-1909,w/o Sam.T.
Samuel T.,1831-1912.
William B.,Jan.4,1887,32y.
DUNBAR
Hadassah,1847-1932,w/o Jas.
DYER
Doris,1914-1977.
Edgar,1880-1941,h/o Mildred.
Kenneth,1911-1991.
Mildred Hawkes,1887-1916.
Viola S.,1896-1985.
ELLIOTT
Belva,1909-1991,w/o Robert.
EMERSON
Roger L.,Jan.11,1954-Sept.15,1992,
  h/o Patricia A.
ENNIS
Eunice E.,Jan.26,1891-Sept.26,1953,
  w/o Joseph L.
Joseph L.,Aug.19,1888-July 23,1953.
ESTES
Emily Hawkes,1897-1969,w/o Leroy.
Erlion R.,1928-1935,s/o Leroy & Emily.
Leroy S.,1887-1954.

FOGG
Albert H.,1871-1918.
Georgie I. Spear,1877-1955.
FOSTER
Mabel S.,July 7,1891-Dec.6,1984.
FOWLER
Frank Anthony,Sr.,
 Oct.27,1926-Dec.29,1990.
FRANK
Ebenezer,Aug.1,1880,76y.
Louisa,Apr.13,1883,76y,w/o Ebenezer.
FROST
Rolene L.,Mar.23,1955-May 24,1993.
GOODWIN
Donald W.,1912-1994.
Ethelyn H.,June 26,1927-
 Oct.16,1988,w/o Douglas J.,Sr.
Robert F.,1926-1975.
GRANT
George A.,1933-1958,h/o Bertha L.
George B.,1882-1963.
Josephine V.,1902-1991,w/o George B.
GRAY
Hoyt B.,1915-1992,h/o V. Adele Owen.
HAMILTON
Amanda L.,Mar.30,1981, inf.
HANSCOME
Sally Jayne,Apr.11,1938-
 Feb.22,1939,d/o Harold &
 Marjorie, sis/o Helen & Steven.
HARDING
Stanley W.,Feb.4,1930-
 Feb.18,1992,h/o Persis Hall.
HARMON
Nancy A.,Dec.7,1942-
 Oct.26,1974,w/o Alfred J.
HAWKES
Anna A.,1859-1917.
Bertha Marian Hunnewell,
 Sept.22,1891-Apr.30,1973,
 w/o John C.
Caroline Rogers,1901-1984,
 w/o Herbert H.
Charles W.,1873-1935.
Clarence E.,1902-1960.
Clifford A.,1904-1969,h/o Helen M.
Cyrus A.,1893-1954.
Dorcus,1800-1896,w/o Ebenezar.
Ebenezar,1785-1853.
Elenor L.,1915,newb.
 d/o Cyrus & Myrtle.
Elmer,1855-1926.
Elmira Cobb,1853-1926,w/o Wm L.
Emily J.,June 28,1880,58y,w/o Cyrus.
Ernest A.,1879-1931.
Eunice C.,1823-1844.
George,1828-1915.

Gertrude I.,1900-1980,w/o Lincoln E.
Hazel M. Manchester,
 Aug.25,1894-XXXX,w/o Howard.
Harriet Woodman,1878-1927,
 w/o Elmer.
Helen L.,1908-1979.
Herbert H.,1899-1983,
 s/o Elmer & Harriet.
Hiram C.,1861-1935.
Howard G.,Oct.28,1894-May 15,1970.
John Carroll,Aug.23,1891-
 July 24,1969.
Joshua L.,1836-1894.
Lillian S. Godfrey,1873-1897,
 1st w/o Charles W.
Lincoln E.,1901-1948.
Lizzie M. Cobb,1875-1915,
 2nd w/o Charles W.
Mary L.,1880-1918,w/o Ern. A.
Merle W.,1916-197X,
 d/o Cyrus & Myrtle.
Myrtle L. Austin,1898-19XX,
 w/o Cyrus A.
Nancy B.,1832-1915,w/o Geo.
Peter & Family, no information.
Rachel C.,Sept.4,1890,81y.
Rachel S.,1906-1984.
William L.,1852-1933.
Wyman Eveleth,Aug.9,1898-
 Dec.20,1983,h/o Eliza B.
Zelia F. Cobb,1865-1958,w/o Hiram.
twin girls,1958,
 d/o Harry & Marjorie E.
HOOPER
Harold A.,1900-1988.
Velma M.,1898-1987,w/o H. A.
IRISH
Charles G.,1847-1916.
Charlotte E. Caswell,
 Mar.9,1879-June 24,1937,w/o Frank.
Elverdo,1873-1947.
Frank E.,1840-1915.
Frank P.,June 24,1878-Dec.21,1946.
Isaac,Nov.25,1884,83y.
John W.,Dec.11,1903-Dec.5,1981,
 s/o Frank & Charlte
Lois Stevens,Apr.24,1868,60y,
 w/o Isaac.
Manley L.,Sept.7,1928-Sept.10,1989.
Marian E. Hawkes,Sept.4,1902-
 Dec.2,1992,w/o John.
Mary J,1830-1917,w/o Frank E
Mary L.,1847-1921,w/o Geo. F.
JAMESON
Emma A. Weeks,1895-1974.
Lee L.,1903-1979,h/o E.A.W.

JIMINO
Louis J.,July 3,1934-Sept.2, 1994, d/o Nancy A. Coogins.
JOHNSON
Bessie M. McLellan,Aug.23, 1889-Dec.24,1983, w/o Edw. H.
Edward H.,Aug.16,1886-Mar.23,1951.
Warren E.,Jan.22,1938-Mar.3,1938, s/o Merton & Catherine.
KEELER
H. Louise Alden,1896-1971.
Horatio M.,1867-1915.
Leonora E.,1871-1963,w/o H.M.
Parker M.,1894-1968,h/o H.L.A
KELLEY
Agnes M.,Aug.4,1917-Jan.10,1994, w/o Frederick E.
KINGHORN
Stanley T.,July 8,1912-Dec.13,1980,h/o Gladys Pratt.
KNUDSEN
Arthur C.,Feb.4,1895-Apr.2,1972.
Eva L. Verrill,Mar.27,1905-Oct.25,1979,w/o A. C.
LAMB
Susan T.,Jan.31,1889,77y.
William C.,May 31,1885,72y.
LEIGHTON
Allen P.,Dec.18,1877-July 12,1952.
Andrew,1806-1831,h/o M.H.
Annie Hall,1906-1979, w/o L. Burnham.
Benjamin T.,1845-1897.
Charlotte L. Harmon,1847-1931,w/o Benjamin T.
Clifford R.,1901-1902, s/o Henry & Emma.
Donald E.,1927-1976, h/o Shirley Weeks.
Edna J.,1877-1964,w/o Melvin.
Emma A.,1866-1905,w/o H. P.
Henry P.,1873-1957.
L. Burnham,1904-1993.
Margaret Hawkes,1813-1883.
Melvin,1880-1960.
Susie,b&d.1902,d/o H & Emma.
LIBBY
Edna M.,1895-1977.
LOWELL
Emma M.,Dec.13,1912-Apr.12,1985,w/o Clair.
LYNCH
Doris M.,1922-1985,w/o Stan.
MARINELLI
Joseph P.,June 28,1905-Dec.4,1987,h/o Lucille Woodis.

MASON
Cora G.,Apr.17,1920-Aug.9,1991, w/o Weston T.,Sr.
MAYNARD
Mildred Grant,1922-1990, w/o Albert James.
McELROY
Richard P.,Jan.19,1950-Feb.3,1989,h/o Susan E.
McLELLAN
Fred H.,1887-1970.
Helen D.,1898-1975,w/o F.H.
McMACKIN
Lyndon A.,1907-1968.
MEGGISON
Gladys M.,Sept.26,1891-May 7,1983.
MERMELSTEIN
Kathi,Sept.24,1944-Oct.10,1989.
MILLETT
Lineous M.,1883-1944.
Nettie M.,1879-1967,w/o L.M.
Philip M.,1913-1987,h/o Dorothy.
MILLS
Jennie Edwards,1881-1916, d/o Abner & Mareitta Smith.
MITCHELL
Jon S.,1964, infant.
MONTGOMERY
James,1847-1915.
MORRILL
Annie E.,Apr.1,1878,1y,d/o H.H.& A.E.
Catherine A.,1908-1908.
Israel,1817-XXXX.
Katie E.,1848-1899,w/o H.T.
Kenneth P.,1910-1970.
Leroy S.,1874-1919.
Lizzie P.,1823-1904,w/o Israel.
Lydia A.,1882-1956.
Margaret A.,Dec.13,1913,65y.
Rebecca L.,July 20,1878,5y, d/o H.H.& A.E.
NELSON
Florence L.,1884-1969.
PACKARD
Marion,1893-1975.
PANE
Ellen E.,1848-1884.
PENDER
Clinton R.,1922-1923,s/o E.E. & P.L.B.
Everitt E.,1893-1993,h/o P.L.B.
Pearl L. Ball,1898-1987.
PENDEXTER
George R.,1873-1943.
Jessie M.,1913-1991,w/o O.G.
Mabel G.,1880-1957,w/o Geo. R.
Orrin G.,1907-1964.
Walter H.,1915-1933.

PETERSON
Basil Royce,Aug.20,1913-
Dec.6,1987,h/o Phyllis Dyer.
PINE
Perle,1904-1991.
PLUMMER
Earl R.,Aug.12,1926-Sept.18,1993.
PRATT
Abbie A.,1860-1906.
C. Laurence,1899-1920.
Charles W.,1851-1915.
Cora E.,1868-1950,w/o Robinson.
Eva J.,1892-1978.
Grace Weeks,1893-1992.
Ida May,Oct.23,1893-
Dec.22,1893,d/o John & Mary S
J.Edgar,1907-1970.
James R.,Rev.,1887-1968.
John E.,Jan.26,1862-Feb.26,1940.
Lauretta G.,1909-1934,
d/o Robinson & C.E.
Lyman W.,1888-1907.
Mary E.,1888-1891,
d/o Robinson & C.E.
Martilla J.,May 2,1867-
Oct.13,1923,w/o John E.
Mary S.,Feb.12,1868-
Nov.14,1895,w/o John E.
Robinson,1858-1930.
PRIDE
Rachel M.,1850-1888,w/o Wm.H.
Thomas,XXXX,3m,s/o Rachel & Wm.
RAYNES
Annie,1799-Dec.1,1878.
REYNOLDS
Bertha A.,1888-1967.
Everett C.,1874-1951.
Vera M.,1919-1987.
RILEY
Osborn J.,1883-1946.
ROBBINS
Iris M.,1916-1994,m.1935,Roger E.
ROGERS
Howard O.,1905-1989.
RUSSELL
Peter J.,Dec.7,1950-Apr.9,1988.
RUTHERFORD
Betty Ann, Sept.26,1958-Dec.5,1963.
Laurif E.,July 31,1912-Mar.16,1975.
Udavilla M.,Oct.26,1914-XXXX,
w/o Laurif.
SAWYER
Annie C. Jorgensen,
June 1,1884-Feb.2,1953.
Annie Smith,
Feb.23,1844-Oct.16,1914.
Arthur,1916, s/o Frank & Annie.

Cecil L.,July 28,1909-May 19,1984,
h/o Dorothy.
Dennis J.,Apr.6,1835-Aug.12,1912,
h/o Annie Smith.
Eugene J.,1865-1943,h/o M.E.D.
Francis E.,1830-1911.
Frank S.,1875-1951.
Guy E.,July 11,1911-Sept.17,
1958,h/o Charlotte Rolfe.
Lovina N.,1878-1950.
Mary A.,1833-1908,w/o F. E.
Mary E. Davis,1869-1919.
Paul E.,1941-1944.
William A.,1873-1952.
SEDGLEY
Stephen A.,1865-1929.
SHAW
Alevilda Cobb,1868-1929,w/o Daniel.
Daniel W.,1866-1923.
Doris A. Sawyer,
Mar.14,1928-July 17,1989.
Jason C.,1834-1924.
L. Augusta,1881-1960.
Lincoln K.,1911-1956,
adopted s/o Reuben A.
Lizzie Maude,1875-1878,
d/o Jason & Minerva.
Minerva L.,1838-1922,w/o Jason.
Reuben A.,1873-1945.
SHEA
Laura F.,1857-1944,w/o Nathaniel.
SHEIL
Ruth A.,Nov.30,1932-Mar.25,1983.
SMITH
Abner Thomas,1842-1910.
George Henry,1846-1905,
s/o Wm. & Sarah Hawkes.
George Tyng,Oct.22,1833-
July 14,1910.
Ida M. Batchelder,1855-1916,
w/o Simon A.
Marietta E. Littlefield,1853-1913,
w/o Abner.
Oressa D. Lamb,Oct.4,1833-
May 10,1909,w/o George.
Simon A.,1850-1935.
Susan C.,1819-1914.
Susan H.,Jan.5,1898,91y,w/o Thomas.
Thomas,Feb.2,1885,81y.
William M.,1822-1917,h/o S.C.
SPILLER
Cora M.,1905-1985,w/o Geo. M.
Pauline C.,1921-1985,w/o Ralph H.,Sr.
SPINNEY
Frank J.,Oct.27,1912-Jan.2,1991,
h/o Christine.

SPEAR
George F.,1848-1923.
Sarah J.,Mar.29,1891,67y,w/o Wm.F.
William F.,May 2,1896,75y.
STEEVES
Chelsey Nicole,Apr.7,1992,
  d/o Tammy & David.
STEVENS
Annie R.,1865-1883.
Clarence,1892-1960.
Ella J.,1869-1915.
George H. Elder,1863-1922.
Mary S. Cobb,1860-XXXX,w/o Geo.H.E.
Rebecca A.,1827-1907,w/o Wm.
William,1825-1892.
William,Jr.,1857-1915.
Winnie B.,1875-1892.
SWENDSEN
Russell F.,1919-1985,h/o Mary G.
SUTHERLAND
Elizabeth F. Carter,
  July 7,1888-Mar.3,1968.
Frank,Sr.,Aug.3,1887-Oct.28,1979.
SZOSTAK
Barbara J.,1953-1954.
William V.,Feb.5,1918-Feb.6,1965.
TELLE
Matthew Allen,Mar.1991,newb.
TOWNSEND
Barbara A.,Aug.18,1937-
  Sept.14,1981,w/o Cecil.
Cecil W.,Feb.22,1932-Aug.30,1994.
VERRILL
Clyde I. Gribbin,Mar.21,1901-
  May 6,1982,w/o Leroy P.
Fred S.,Dec.5,1895-Jan.9,1978,
  h/o Ethel.
Linden Earl,Jan.20,1922-
  Jan.16, 1964,h/o Winafred D. Spiller.
VIOLETTE
Mary J.,Mar.27,1919-Oct.27,1988,
  d/o Mabel Foster.
WALES
Madeline,1914-1981.
Ralston M.,1910-1970.
WARD
Cyrus K.,Rev.,1835-1902.
WARK
A. Ralph,1891-1973.
WEEKS
Lewis,1863-1942.
Lincoln W.,1901-1971,
  h/o Gladys Rogers.
Nellie Emma Shea,1865-
  1932,w/o Lewis.
Stephen W.,1957-1965,
  s/o Ralph & Jean.

WENTWORTH
Aurilla H.,1868-1918,w/o L.A.
Leslie A.,1875-1949.
WESCOTT
Carroll L.,1893-1937.
John L.,1864-1957.
Lillian M.,1873-1958,w/o J.L.
WEST
Emma M.,1858-1938,
  1st w/o Frederick W.
Francis Douglas,1914-1977.
Frederick W.,1857-1919.
John,1853-1903.
Lillian W.,1890-1976,
  2nd w/o Frederick W.
Mary F.,1850-1917,w/o John.
WITHAM
Charles N.,1857-1942.
Clara C.,1856-1940.
WOODIS
A. Eliot,1909-1968.
Alta L.,1917-1938,w/o A. Eliot.
XX, Cora Bell,Jan.23,1869,3y.
XX, Georgie,XXXX,infant.
XX, Bobby,1927-1928.

✧ **SMITH CEMETERY** ✧
513 Route 202, Windham.
Checked approx. 75% of stones.

ABBOTT
Herbert,1878-1959.
Nellie,1872-1972.
ADAMS
Edmund Lester,1865-1879,
  s/o I.D. & Z.A.
Edna,1964.
Laura E.,1970.
Renold E.,1962.
Zilpha A.Boothby,1908.
ALEWINE
James T.,1968.
ALLEN
Alfred R.,May 6,1856,92y.
Alice Hall,1860-1933.
Alvin,1879-1959.
Aubrey S.,1880-1966.
Cynthia S.,1849,1y,d/o Alfred R.
Dorothy L.,XXXX.
Flora B.,1898-1975.
Florence I.,1869-1958.
Frances E.,1837-1912,w/o Thos.
Georgina C.,1887-1954,w/o Aubrey S.
inf/o L.W. & M.R.,1950.
James F.,1919-1945.
Jesse M.,1959.
L. Wayne,1927-1992.

Lawrence H.,1894-1950.
Myrtle H.,1888-1950.
Nathan J.,1857-1944.
Paul W.,1921-1925.
Philip W.,1887-1943.
Salome Libby,1902,w/o Alfred R.
Susie M.,1883-1961.
Thomas,1830-1910.
ANDREW
George Irving,1895-1960.
Gertrude B.,1894-1975.
ANDREWS
Ernest J.,1964.
Ruth A.,XXXX,w/o Ernest J.
ANTHOINE
Blanche L.,1891-1849.
Charles Neal,1959.
Clifford T.,1893-1988.
Florence B.,1987,w/o Charles N.
Howard W.,1882-1960.
ATHERTON
Annie L. Burns,1888-1944.
Charles P.,1892-1970,h/o A.L.B
Clifford N.,1886-1953.
Elsie L.,1888-1967,w/o Cliff. N.
Florence M.,1967,w/o Charles P.
Frank D.,1858-1947.
Geneva M.,1893-1967,w/o Geo.
George W.,1890-1959.
Lucinda Lamb,1861-1985,w/o Frank.
AUGER
Helen E.,1978.
AUSTIN
Philip L.,1992.
BABB
George W.,1905-1982.
BAKER
Clarence C.,1919.
BARDEN
Beverly Ann Taylor,1936-1992,
  w/o Robert J.
BARTELL
Wellington L.,1989.
BAUER
Lottie,Apr.9,1859,21y,
  d/o George & Isabelle.
BEANE
Lillian M.,1870-1920.
BEERS
Irving F.,1976.
BELYEA
Eulalie W.,1985.
Percy H.,1957.
BENNETT
Laurence P.,1967.
Nellie P.,XXXX,w/o Laurence.

BERRY
Martha C.,1910-1961,w/o Marshall.
BESSLEY
Ada L. Towle,1876-1938,w/o E.J
Edna M.,1899-1936.
Edward J.,1874-XXXX.
BISHOP
George H.,1887-1964.
Lena M.,1900-1962,w/o Geo.H.
Teresa M.,1960-1960.
BLACK
David A.,Jr.,1993-1993.
Gardner E.,1898-1969,h/o Goldie S.
Marylou,1950-1955.
Patricia M.,1949-1949.
Tresa M.,1973.
BODGE
Clinton T.,1854-1923.
Elizabeth Jones,1857-1919,w/o C.T.
BOLSTER
Adalaide L.,1851-1928.
David O.,1847-1928.
BORTELL
Winfred C.,XXXX.
Lillian M.,XXXX.
Willington L.,1989.
BOTHWICK
Dorothy L.,1906-1993.
Harry L.,1898-1965.
Earle P.,1983.
BRACKETT
Edith Lucy,1970.
BRADY
Vanessa A.,1978,d/o Thomas.
BRANSON
Nora Baker,1913-1975,w/o Sidney R.
BROOME
Miranda Davis,1987.
BROWN
Murray E.,1979.
Thelma L.,w/o Murray E.
BURRELL
Sarah H.,June 13,1888,79y,w/o Sam'l.
BUSTIN
Leslie T.,XXXX.
CAMPBELL
Ella L.,w/o George.
Mildred Edna,1925-1991
CHANDLER
C. Alvan,XXXX.
Grace,XXXX,w/o C. Alvan.
W. David,1943,s/o C. Alvan.
CHARPENTIER
Hector G.,1892-1970.
Natalie A.,1892-1988,w/o H.G.
CHENEY
Arnold B.,1980.

Maxine F.,1986.
CHELSEY
Robert George,1980.
CLARK
Agnes N.,1988,w/o Christoph. J.
Chris J.,XXXX.
COBB
Alta E.,1897-1974.
Arthur E.,1890-1967.
Callie E.,1871-1949,w/o Willis I.
Carol A.,1966.
Carrie E.,1940,w/o Wm.L.
Carrie L.,1867-1945,w/o Ed. C.
Clyde,1990.
David W.,XXXX.
Edwin C.,1865-1931.
Elias H.,1870-1879.
Ellis,1877-1915.
Ernest,1875-1947.
Hannah E.,1849-1929,w/o Isaac.
Isaac,1846-1896.
Jane H.,XXXX.
Jennie L.,1873-1953,w/o Ellis.
Jesse L.,1955.
Lewis H.,1926-1994,h/o Alice L.
Lillian,1868-1914.
Lizzie,1871-XXXX.
Lois Jenny,1953.
Mallie G.,1942-1963.
Mary L.1866-1868.
Nancy,1830-1897.
Nathaniel,1825-1901.
Wilie,1867-1869.
Willis L.,1866-1924.
COLCORD
Edwin A.,1971.
COLE
Elmira P.,1826-1852.
Mildred L.,1899-1953.
CROCKETT
Maria Liusa,1980,d/o Wm.E.
Stephen,XXXX.
CROSS
Hilda J.,1971.
John M.,1961.
CUMMINGS
James E.,1988.
CURRIE
Aleda R.,1967,w/o Donald
Donald W.,1980.
CURRIER
Blanch R.,1974.
DAILEY
F. Louise,1907-1985,w/o H. D.
Hazen,1907-1975.
DAVIS
Louise A.,1912-1988.

DAY
Gerald,1916-1971.
Viola M.,1921-1977,w/o Gerald.
DEGRASSE
Benjamin,1871-1959.
Ira R.,1889-1969.
DESHON
Iola B.,1993,w/o Maxwell A.
Maxwell A.,1986.
DOLBY
Jean B.,1988,w/o Robert.
Kimberly Ann,1920-1973,d/o Timothy.
DOUGLAS
Albion H.,1949-1965,s/o L.J.& R.E.P.
Dorothy B.,1975,w/o Robert.
Robert E.,1980.
Lewis J.,1909-1963.
DOW
Stephen A.,1888-1956.
Zelinda H.,1838-1975.
DUMONT
Allen C.,1986.
DUNHAM
Arthur W.,1972.
Mamie M.,1978.
DUNLAP
Bertham,1887-1892,d/o F.B.
Flora B.,1865-1946.
Gladys L.,1897-1969.
Howard L.,1893-1966.
James L.,1863-1936.
DUNTON
James R.,1972.
DURANT
Agnes L.,1872-1962,w/o Benj.
Benjamin H.,1867-1943.
Eliza J.,1908-1981.
Nina H.,1895-1974.
Richard,1934-1935.
DYER
Asenath B.,1986,w/o Howard.
Charles H.,1916-1986,h/o Audrey.
Eva B.,1977.
Howard F.,1966.
Mildred I.,1916,w/o Edgar.
William W.,1948.
ELDER
Callie E.,1843-1914.
Harriet,1870-1925.
Joseph,1840-1909.
Lydia,1805-1876.
ELLIOT
Edith P.,1876-1977,w/o Orin L.
EMMONS
Jean Harris,1986.
ESTES
Emily M.,1925-1970,w/o Eugene.

EVANS
John,1902-1917.
FARR
Leslie Dean,1933.
FELLOWS
James,1847-1899.
John T.,1820-1900.
Sarah,1821-1897.
FICKETT
Caren Jo,1985,w/o Richard A.
Jason R.,1973.
FIELD
Annah,Feb.23,1765-Feb.10,1857,
w/o William.
Beatrice Bernier,1884-1902.
Catherine,1820-1900,w/o Eben.
Charles H.,Oct.28,1842-
Aug.6,1859,s/o E. & C.
Charles W.W.,1892-1918.
Charlie,Oct.3,1859-May 14,1863,
s/o E. & C.
Ebenezer,1808-1877.
Emily D. Lamb,1857-1946,w/o Wm. F.
William F.,1840-1893.
William,May 9,1763-June 3,1836.
FIORILLO
Maxine,1986.
FISH
Annabelle H.,1973.
FOGG
Catharine K.,Feb.2,1867,69y,
w/o Josiah.
Eliza,Nov.19,1873,71y.
Hannah,July 29,1856.
James,Aug.21,1825,56y.
Josiah,Jan.31,1870,70y.
Sally,May 20,1849,72y.
Sarah V.A.,Apr.9,1817,6y,d/o Josiah.
FORD
Barbara E.,1990.
FOSS
Emily J.,1858-XXXX,w/o M.D.
Mosley D.,1856-1963.
FOSTER
Cedric A.,1906-1982.
Irma F.,1911-1986,w/o C. A.
Jennie S.,1871-1939,w/o W.K.
William K.,1877-1962.
FOWLES
Bertha M.,1888-1971.
Herman L.,1890-1960.
FOYE
Elsie M.,1968,w/o Leslie
FRANK
James Melvin,1968.
FRYE
Clarence H.,1988.

FULLER
George C.,1994.
GALLAGHER
Elizabeth,1865-1923.
GALLANT
Florence Pecoraro,Oct.1994,
w/o Lawrence.
GAMMON
Matilda Hill,1835-1916
Orison,1832-1895.
GAUDET
Glenda Mae,1986,w/o James O.
GIBBIN
Dwight V.,1991.
GILLIAM
Jacqueline D.,1987.
GILMAN
Alan L.,1962-1982.
Alice S.,1892-1964.
Betty Ann,1935-1936.
Glendon L.,1988,h/o Virginia M.
GILPATRICK
Annie Devine,1886-1923,w/o Frank S.
Frank S.,1852-1919.
GLEASON
Isa F.,1889-1969,w/o W. F.
Wallace F.,1890-1955.
GORRIVAN
Joseph H.,1889-1956.
GOWEN
Caroline W.,1833-1857.
GRAHAM
Scott, c.1991, approx. 20y.
GRAY
Sheridan D.,1992.
GREENLAW
Alphonzo I.,1966.
Carrie A.M.,1877-1959.
Carroll J.,1973.
Clifford,1875-1947.
Earl L.,1953.
Ernest C.,1911.
Gloria M.,1981.
Harold J.,1952.
John,1890.
Kimbly Jo.,XXXX
Leslie,1871-1943.
Lucy E.,1873-1953,w/o Leslie.
Philip M.,1977.
Sarah A.1915,w/o John.
Stephen D.,1986.
Violet,1973.
Winifred H.,1963,w/o Harold.
GRIBBEN
Dwight V.,1920-1991,h/o Erla.
GRIFFIN
Frank N.,1888-1954.

Rose B.,1892-1981.
GUPTILL
Floribel G.,1883-1964,w/o P.F.
Perley F.,1881-1958.
HACKETT
David S.,1823-1871.
Miriam M.,1830-1905,w/o D.S.
HADDOCK
Phyllis E.,1986,w/o Walter R.
HAFNER
Charles R.,1979.
HAGEN
Louis W.,1901-1965,h/o Beatrice A.
HALL
Agnes,1878-1944,w/o Walter B.
Charles L.,1862-1939.
Charles W.,1842-1920.
Ellen F.,1846-1920,w/o Chas.W.
John M.,1975.
Kenneth Alan,1938.
Lillian F.,1917-1917,d/o Walter.
Mary A.,1834-1919.
Valentine G.,1836-1889
Walter B.,1874-1949.
HANSCOM
Uriah,1804-1839.
Winfield Huntley,1874-1941.
HANSEN
Albert C.,Sr.,1898-1980.
Caroline H.,1875-1958,w/o E. T.
Jennie A.,1904-1967,w/o Al. C.
Emil T.,1865-1926.
HANSON
Fred S.,1873-1879,s/o Geo. B.
George B.,1846-1929.
Mary E.,1850-1927,w/o Geo. B.
HARMON
Esther W.,1891-1958.
Orland C.,1886-1968.
HARNDEN
Elizabeth A.,1984,w/o Durward.
HARRIS
Clifford A.,1987.
Mary J.,1845-1917,w/o Silas H.
Thomas C.,1982.
HASKELL
Bessie M.,1897-1937,w/o W. E.
Charles A.,1836-1921.
Fred L.,1865-1936.
Hannah A.,1838-1918,w/o C.A.
Harriet H.,1991,w/o Ora.
Jessie A.,1860-1920,w/o Fred L.
Ora,1978.
Sidney H.,1899.
Walter E.,1889-1972.
Winifred H.,1895-1954.

HATCH
Carlena F.,1992.
Everett M.,1962.
Marion Shaw,1970,w/o Everett.
HATT
Cecil M.,1969.
David C.,1965.
Marie Della,1987.
Marie,1987,w/o Cecil.
Mary A.,1973.
William C.,1970.
HAWKES
Ada H.,1980.
Albion K.,1857-1901,s/o Peter & Mary.
Alley,1809-1890.
Alley E.,1885-1970.
Ann Louisa,1822-1909,w/o Alley.
Annie L.,1850-1928,w/o Fred S.
Charles M.,July 8,1860,26y,
 s/o Thomas & Lovisa.
Charlotte,Oct.28,1842,31y,w/o Alley.
Dorothy,1892-1970,w/o Alley.
E. Ethel,1883-1973.
Edna F.,1894-1979.
Eleanor,1970.
Elmer H.,1879-1955.
Frances M.,Sept.14,1846,11y,
 s/o Thomas & Lovisa.
Frank N.,1933.
Fred S.,1850-1919.
George H.,1851-1948.
Hulda M.,1974,w/o Wm.C.
James,May 21,1857,84y.
Lottie,1864-1936.
Lovisa,Dec.10,1893,86y,w/o Thomas.
Lydia M. Varney,1845-1932.
Margaret L.,1887-1900.
Mary A.,Jan.26,1906,52y.
Percy M.,1971.
Philip W.,1886-1965.
Rebecca,Dec.12,1856,80y,w/o James.
Richard N.,1992.
Thomas,1808-1861,53y,
 s/o Benjamin & Ruth..
Willie A.,July 23,1863,17y,
 s/o Alley & A.L.
William C.,1964.
William M.,1976.
HAYDEN
Edith B. Perkins,1915-1982.
HAYDT
Clyde K.,1989.
HILL
Alice B.,1971.
Bertha,1885-1975.
Charles H.,1923-1994.
Charles W.,1940-1940.

Drusella M.,1888,8y,d/o H.H.&F.
Drusilla R.,1851,10y,d/o H.H.&F
Edith M.,1961,w/o Herbert.
Frances M.,1810-1901,w/o Henry.
George E.,1848-1917.
Gladys T.,1915-1985,w/o C.H.
Henry H.,Mar.20,1874,67y.
Henry H.,1907-1962.
Herbert F.,1968.
Henry H.,1962.
Ida M.,1851-1917,w/o Geo.
Mildred H.,1982.
HOBB
Wesley G.,Jr.,1968.
Carrie E.,1874.
HOBSON
Hebert,Sr.,1986,h/o Marjorie.
HODGDON
Howard W.,1947.
Marion S.,1975,w/o Howard.
HORR
Edwin L.,1978.
Harry B.,1876-1918.
Ian L. Libby,1887-1961.
HOWLEY
Luella M.,1834-1984,w/o W.T.
William T.,1892-1949.
HOYT
Edith M.,1876.
Raymond C.,1971.
HUNT
Jay C.,1888-1957.
Mabel S.,1882-1963.
HUSSEY
Julia H.,1861-1939.
Walter C.,1859-1942.
JACKSON
Clifford L.,1961.
Evelyn K.,1986,w/o Willard.
Robert W.1967,h/o Pauline E.
Willard W.,1962.
JACQUIS
Martha M.,1923,w/o Walter S.
JAQUIS
Hannah,1818-1881,w/o Henry.
Harvey A.,1908.
Henry,1813-1889.
John,1807-1895.
Lucinda A.,1883-1969.
Mary,1965.
Walter S.,1924.
JEAN
Medora N.,1965.
JEFFORDS
Edith W.,1913,w/o Harry B.
Harry B.,1973.
Harry B.,1980.

JOHNSON
Frances M.,July 12,1888,49y.
Frank D.,1869-1914.
Heather Lynn,1974.
JONES
Abbie R.,1836-Feb.26,1910,
  1st w/o Joseph.
Amos H.,1834-1861.
Charles,1825-1889.
Charles W.,1840-1877.
Emily,1831-1896,w/o Chas.
Horace N.,1859-1883.
Joseph T.,1837-1920.
Ormon Albert,1870-1880,
  only ch/o Jos.T. & Abbie.
JORDAN
Alphonso,1848-1923.
Ellen,1821-1906,w/o William.
Harriet M.,1850-1916,w/o Alp.
Isaac R.,1846-1922.
Susan B. Field,1842-1919,
  2nd w/o Isaac B.
William,1819-1868.
William,1876-1956.
JORGENSEN
Herbert P.1983.
John H.,1895-1950.
Linda C.,1975,w/o Charles Wm.
Marie B.,1860-1938,w/o N. P.
Niles C.,1887-1967.
Niles P.,1860-1942.
KALLOCK
Almanzer,1841-1916.
Hannah,1881,w/o Henry.
Henry,1889.
Margaret,184X-1919,w/o Almanzer.
Sarah A. Jaquis,1850-1886,
  w/o Almanzer.
KATON
Alice J.,1868-1943.
baby,1900.
KEMP
Etta M.,1860-1939,w/o John A.
George H.,1863-1908.
John A.,1852-1927.
Lucretia Allen,1834-1915,w/o Sam'l R.
Maria A.,1862-1892.
Melvin M.,1889-1974.
Melvin W.,1858-1922.
Samuel R.,1831-1903.
KENT
John Patrick,1908-1985.
KIMBALL
Kenneth,1904-1953.
Mildred M.,1908-1975,w/o Ken.
Ricky D.,1962,s/o Joey E.

KING
Joseph L.,May 25,1857,58y.
Linda,1989.
KNIGHT
Elwood F.,1943.
Guy B.,1963,h/o Gladys W.
LAFFIN
Archie C.,1958.
Caroline P.,1961.
LAMB
Annie Rogers,1860-1940.
Ella F.,1867-1928,w/o Eugene.
Eugene B.,1950.
Helen G.,1990,w/o Walter W.
Lincoln W.,1886-1886.
Mabel E.,1946.
Walter W.,Sr.,1991.
Willard,1850-1925,h/o Annie R
LARRABEE
Angeline,1832-1896.
LARRIVEE
Jerry J.,1980.
Jerry J.,JR.,1986.
LARSEN
Martin,1838-1911.
LEGROW
Bertha W.,1965.
Clement M.,1902,s/o John.
John O.,1957.
LENNAN
Lewellyn H.,1912.
LEONARD
Delano D.,1983.
Olive L.,1982,w/o Delano.
LIBBY
Abbie G.,1976,w/o Philip O.
Anna R. Black,1848-1923,w/o Richard.
Bela P.,1829-1897.
David A.,1989.
Dwight L.,Sr.,1980.
Elsie M.,1968. Everett E.,1992.
Ernest W.,1896-1960.
Everett W.,1890-1978.
George E.,1920-1988,h/o Beulah
Ina H.,1961.
Inez E.,1931-1975.
Lillian M.,1901-1993,w/o Ernest W.
Lucius P.,1854-1939.
Mary E.,1844-1912,w/o Sam.
Mary S.,1830-1898.
Melvina M.,1860-1946,w/o Lucius P.
Norma A.,1905-1977,w/o E. E.
Osmon,1883-1952.
Richard L.,1842-1919.
Robert E.,1945-1945.
Samuel,1838-1920.
Sumner B.,1860-1928.

Willis R.,1887-1960.
LITTLE
Elmer M.,1912-1985.
Grace W.,1912-1967.
LOMBARD
Robert L.,1984.
LORD
Nathan D.,1977.
Rene P.,1991,w/o Harlie.
LOVETT
Jasper H.,1892-1956,h/o Thelma.
LOWELL
Augusta P.,1827-1884,w/o Ed J.
Dana P.,1856-1929.
Edward J.,1820-1905.
Gertrude B.,1889-1908,
  d/o D.P. & N.F.
Grace,1881-1937,w/o Ralph R.
Nettie F.,1858-1942,w/o Dana.
Olive S.,Apr.3,1857,21y,w/o Oliver.
Ralph M.,1992.
LUNT
Carroll,1919-1976.
Florence M.,1897-1967.
Oscar H.,1866-1945.
MacDONALD
Annie C.,1877-1955,w/o Sinc. A.
Barbara Haynes,1934-1990,
  w/o F. Allen.
Donald S.,1917-1993.
Frank E.,1902-1982,
  h/o Louise A. Baker.
John S.,1916-1952.
Malcolm E.,1880-1958.
Phyllis A.,1917-1968,w/o Robt.
Robert B.,1920-1980.
Robert C.,1912-1983.
Roderick M.,1895-1929.
Sinclair A.,1873-1951.
MAHONEY
Ethel L.,1983.
MAINS
Barbara J.,1969,w/o Allan.
John L.,1963.
Winfred F.,1921.
MANCHESTER
Gilbert S.,1958.
LaForest,1987.
Stephen,1717-1807, 1st w.
  Grace Farrow, died c.1745,26y.
  3rd w. Mary Bailey, May 15,1815,88y.
MANN
Emma B.,1851-1927,w/o J. J.
Jacob J.,1927.
MARTIN
Myona,1939-1939.

MAYBERRY
Betsey,Aug.11,1874,71y,w/o Ezekiel.
Ellen,1986.
Howard S.,1978.
Ezekiel,June 28,1841,46y.
Lucy A.,Jan.20,1872,41y,w/o Richd W.
Minnie M.,1870,2m,d/o R.W.& L.
Nellie,1986,w/o Howard S.
Richard W.,Jan.11,1875,42y.
McGINTY
Amanda R.,1892-1971.
Mertie E.,1921-1942.
McLELLAN
Bertha,1889-1942.
Charles L.,1877-1953.
Horace J.,1905-1991.
Marion E.,1837-1945.
Thelma M.,1910-1969,w/o H.J.
MEEHAN
Abram,1948.
Florence L.,1972.
Lester H.,1970.
Mary,1962.
Roland,1970.
Russell,1993.
Sophronia B.,1960.
MERRILL
Abbie P. Hawkes,1881-1965.
Alice M.,1882-1920,w/o Chas H.
Alphonso S.,1835-1921.
Charles H.,1875-1964.
Josephine Field,1848-1962,
 w/o Alphonso.
Katherine P.,1865-1955,2nd w/o Chas.
MICHAUD
Amanda Lee,1986,d/o Gregory.
MIELE
Janet L.,1925-1961.
Josephine S.,1899-1951.
Pasquale E.,1887-1966.
MOORE
Almond O.,1982.
Charles R.,1854-1925.
Deborah,1952.
Dora M.,1892-1892,d/o Chas. R.
Emma E. Witham,1859-1926,
 w/o Charles R.
Emma S.,1901-1901.
Ernest M.,1959.
Harry M.,1905-1912.
Herman T.,1897-1898,s/o Charles.
Irving L.,1884-1884,s/o Chas.
Kevin E.,1973,s/o Richard.
Walter S.,1899-1954.
MOREAU
Addie Wyman,1986,w/o Ira Wyman.

MORRELL
Andrew J.,Dec.26,1880,47y.
Annie B.,1876-1958.
Calvin G.,1920-1974,
 h/o Grace Greenlaw.
Elroy F.,1914-1967,
 h/o Mary Weston,s/o E.F.& E.M.
Elroy F.,1876-1942,s/o J.K.& I.
Eva Martis,1884-1942,w/o El F.
Frances A.,1838,8m,d/o Thos.& L.
Hannah B.,Apr.14,1869,54y.
Isabel Field,1850-1942,w/o James K.
James K.,1846-1916.
Katie I.,1879-1885,d/o J.K.& I.
Lott M.,1873-1964.
Lydia A.,Jan.1892,83y,w/o Thos.
Sarah K.,Jan.25,1896,60y,w/o And J.
Thomas,Sept.20,1881,75y.
MORRIS
Edith Libby,1947-1993,d/o Geo.
MORSE
Preston E.,1993.
Stephen,1981.
NASH
Charles,1839-1864.
Clara A.,1956.
Edward,1841-1901.
Father ?, 1807-1887.
H.H.-N.,1777-1866.
Mary J.,1917,w/o Silas.
Mother ?,1804-1879.
Nathan,1834-1864.
Sarah,1835-1895.
NEELEY
Edith F.,1964,w/o Joseph.
Joseph,1955.
NELSON
Bessie M. Varney,1895-1936.
Lester M.,1878-1956,h/o Bessie.
Patrick,1993,s/o Robert.
NOONAN
James F.,1947-1971.
OCONNEL
Edith,1971.
PALMER
Roland W.,1954.
PARSONS
J. Dana,1905-1993.
Edna W. Haggett,1899-1985,w/o J. D.
Helen W.,1874-1932,w/o Seth.
Seth D.,1877-1953.
PARTRIDGE
Alice M.,1875-1952,w/o Jos. H.
John,1902-1917.
Joseph H.,1867-1953.
PECORARO
Geanerean,1975.

PERRY
Mabel A.,1895-1967.
PETTO
Joseph,1964.
PLUMMER
Beatrice J.,1899-1940.
Carrabelle J.,1874-1926,
w/o Ernest.
Ernest,1872-1941.
Grace M.,1876-1940.
POST
Herbert F.,1894-1965.
POTTER
Kathleen V.,1971,w/o Oswald D.
PRATT
Cora M.,1945,w/o Euba.
Euba C.,1945.
PRIDE
Alvin A.,1830-1914.
Annie,1872-1872.
Dorcas,1798-1869,w/o Lemuel.
Jason N.,1842-1938,h/o Julia.
Julia Hanson,1844-1907,39y.
Lemuel,1786-1862.
Mary J.,1828-1852.
Nathan,1824-1848.
PRIOR
Charles F.,XXXX.
Susan C.,XXXX.
PROCTOR
Edmund M.,1808-1868.
Edmund M.,1857-1861.
Nancy T.,1841-1918.
Sally,1795-1866.
Sarah,1814-1889,w/o Edmund.
Sophronia L.,1839-1857,d/o Edmund.
W. Scott,1848-1896.
PULIERIS
Ella,1983,w/o Janis.
Gunars,1981.
Janis,1980.
QUINLAN
David L.,1932-1983.
Roger,1933-1976.
William C.,Jr.,1949-1923.
REED
Edmund E.,1896-1931.
Mabel E.,1900-1928,w/o E.E.
REYNOLDS
Dorothy H.,XXXX,w/o Edwin.
Edwin L.,1976.
RIESER
Thelma,1903-1982.
RIVERS
Franklin H.,1979.
Nellie G.,1973,w/o Franklin.

ROBBINS
Durward E.,XXXX.
Leontines,XXXX.
ROBERTS
Jane Field,1826-1859,
d/o William & Annah.
John L.,Jr.,1989.
ROLILLARD
F. Coleman,1987,h/o Alberta M.
ROBINSON
Charles E.,1968.
Robin Lee,1963.
ROGERS
Albert B.,1991.
Albert T.,1912.
Alice B.,1870-1954.
Alyn Dale,1955.
Andrew J.,1881-1944.
Annie C.,186X-1896,w/o Marsh.
Beatrice F.,XXXX,w/o Lawrence.
Cora M.,1877-1961.
Hazel E.,1992,w/o Percival.
Lawrence B.,1984.
Linwood A.,1871-1949.
Livilla P.,1903,w/o Albert T.
Lyndon K.,1907-1954,
h/o Doris Atherton.
Marshall H.,186X-1938.
Maude R.,1889-1926.
Maurice L.,1978.
Myona M.,1939.
Myrtle Mann,1880-1957,w/o Walter.
Percival A.,1983.
Walter S.,1879-1949.
ROWE
Charles A.,1913-1986,h/o Dorothy J.
Denis Abijah,1977,h/o Joyce R.
RYALL
Fred W.,1971.
Joan P.,1964.
Mary E.,1976.
SANBORN
Charles W.,XXXX.
Helen M.,1978.
SAWYER
Alfreda I.,1937.
Allen F.,1992.
Chester E.,1874-1932.
Chester F.,1980.
Charles L.,1871-1915.
Clyde M.,1981.
Cora M.,1871-1947.
Dorothy C.,XXXX,w/o George S.
Ferdinand,1868-1960.
George S.,Jr.,XXXX.
George S.,Sr.,1974.
George W.,1918.

Guy E.,1958.
Hall C.,1992.
Hazel J.,1981.
Katie A.,1868-1938.
Marcia E.,1876-1906.
Solange S.,1972.
SAYWARD
Allen B.,1971.
John H.,1869-1917.
Kate F.,1872-1942,w/o John H.
Stella M.,1896-1897,d/o J.H.
Sherman A.,1920-1920.
SCOTT
John F.,1954-1954,s/o John W.
Margery Wilson,1916-1959,
  w/o John W.
SEAVEY
Alonzo H.,1869-1936.
Alonzo R.,1989.
Clyde,1903-1966.
Dorothy E.,XXXX.
Estelle M.,1983.
Eva E. Hanscom,1880-1971.
Helen H.,1903-1980,w/o Clyde.
Ruth,1956.
SENTER
Albina C.,1852-1938.
John G.,1849-1928.
Nellie F.,1878-1936.
Susie E.,1879-1941.
SHAW
Alta Mae,1969.
Doris L.,1981.
John H.,1975.
Nathaniel,1964.
Richard,XXXX.
SMALLEY
Ida D.,1887-1976.
Hazel I.,XXXX.
Martin P.,XXXX.
SMITH
Abigail,Sept.7,1849,27y,w/o Thomas.
Angie G.,1989.
Anna H. Pierce,1848-1935,w/o Wilbur.
Gladys Anita,1924-1991,w/o Derwood.
Harold A.,1963.
Mary Elder,1794-Jan.26,1863.
Silas H.,1949,5m,s/o T.H. & Ab.
Wilber G.,1848-1934.
William,Major,1802-July 4,1886,
  s/o Hezekiah & Sally.
STAPLES
Algie V.,XXXX.
Harris A.,1964.
STEEVES
Carolyn L.,1991,w/o Donald M.
Donald M.,1987.

Lena M.,1971,w/o Russell P.
Russell P.,1978.
STEVENS
Hannah M.,1810-1859,w/o Isaac.
STILES
Beverly K.,1980.
Dana C.,1932-1975.
Keith L.,Sr.,1930-1981,h/o Mary E.
STIMPSON
Julia V.,1959.
Walter E.,1987.
STINSON
Katherine,1857-1924.
STONE
4 ch/o Sullivan, 1891.
Eli,1911,27y.
Eliza J.,1858-1917,w/o Sul.S.
Elwin H.,1890-1953.
Everett A.,1888-1959.
Frances A.,1921,81y,w/o Eli.
Jennie I.,1901-1985.
Lena M.,1868-1955,w/o Orrin.
Orrin F.,1868-1953.
Sullivan S.,1847-1930.
STRIKER
Ruth Q.,1902-1980.
STULTS
Albert I.,1970.
Lillian E.,1983.
STURGIS
James,1825-1879.
Louisa C.,1822-1903,w/o Jas.
SWAN
Charles D.,1937.
Florence H.,1978,w/o John C.
TAYLOR
Carroll E.,1892-1949.
Chester B.,1983.
Charles A.,1909-1953.
Edwina E.,1977.
Glendon L.,1988.
Lucy A.,1912-1963.
Marie B.,1898-1981.
THAYER
Douglas Leon,1847-1971.
THOMES
Herbert S.,1975,h/o Margaret M.
THOMPSON
Clara R.,1850-1922,w/o Wm. A.
Frances,1993,w/o Gerald.
Gerald F.,1993.
Martha J.,1872-1930.
Paul E.,1914-1992,
  h/o Dorothea,d.1910.
William A.,1847-1919.
TIMMONS
Annie M. Douglas,1875-1960.

Arthur E.,1904.
Christine H.,XXXX.
Ernest S.,1968.
Flora D.,XXXX,w/o Wilbur G.
Grace J.,1951.
Harold C.,1988.
John C.,1882-1969.
Kimball,1994.
Marion L.,1971,
Raymond E.,Sr.,1989.
Robert D.,XXXX.
Robert D.,1958.
Robert E.,1918,s/o Robt. D.
Wilbur G.,1979.
TOMS
Marion L.,XXXX.
Melissa,1969.
Robert N.,1947.
TORREY
Lois Winslow,1837-1853,w/o Dr. H.D.
TOWLE
Helen L.,1973.
Loring R.,XXXX
TOWNSEND
Ernest D.,1977.
TRIPP
Ann L.,1989.
TROTT
Frank E.,Mar.14,1875,30y.
TUKEY
Abby Louise,May 26,1807,41y,
 d/o Joshua & Lydia K.
Caroline Webb,1851-1911,w/o Daniel.
Daniel Rogers,1841-1912,
 s/o Joshua & Lydia K.
Harriet Frances,1847-1882,
 d/o Joshua & Lydia K.
Joshua,1814-1888, 2nd w.
 Lewen Sturgess Swett.
Lydia Kennard,1872,56y,
 1st w/o Joshua.
Melissa Jane,1849-1882,
 d/o Joshua & Lydia K.
Olive Smith,1891,39y.
VARNEY
Adelia L.,1853-1923,
 2nd w/o Edwin.
Augusta E.,1960,11y,d/o Otis & J
Bertha Allen,1897-1970,w/o Carl H.
Beryl O.,XXXX,w/o Harold W.
Bessie F.,1974,d/o Elton.
Carl H.,1892-1982,s/o Sumner.
Cecil F.,1966.
Charles L.,1843-1921.
Charles S.,1941.
Charles W.,1993.
Cyrus B.,1839-1925.

Doris A.,1978,w/o Elton.
Edgar W.,1896-1970.
Edward Lowell,1842-1864.
Edwin,1854-1930.
Elizabeth,June 1,1841,54y,w/o Thos.
Elton C.,1971.
Eva M. Nugent,1887-1982,w/o Leroy.
Everett G.,1931-1986.
Harold W.,1972.
Henry L.,1855-1951.
Jane Lowell,1815-1867.
Jane T.,Feb.1888,75y,w/o Otis.
Joel,1809-1879.
L. Mildred Taylor,1809,w/o Carl.
Laura Bangs,1842-1916,w/o Cyrus B.
Leroy R.,1884-1954.
Lizzie Cole,1844-1884,w/o Nehemiah.
Lora A.,1815-1875,w/o Nehem.
Lucy Ann,1957.
Martha A.,1848-1899,w/o Edwn.
Mary A.,1852-1885,w/o Chas. L.
Mary E.,1976,w/o Cecil.
Mary K. Brown,1853-1948,
 w/o Sumner.
Maud Manchester,1882-1920,
 w/o Wilbur.
Melissa J.,1852,3y,d/o Wm.& H.
Myrtle,XXXX,w/o Edgar.
Nehmiah L.,1813-1865.
Otis,June 10,1891,76y.
Silas,Apr.21,1841,16y.
Sumner B.,1857-1947.
Thomas,Aug.2,1868,76y.
Walter C.,1872-1955.
Wilbur,1876-1880.
VAUGHN
Ernest H.,1882-1954.
William C.,1912-1958.
WAITE
Anthony J.,1908-1990,
 s/o Joshua & Hannah Barrett.
George,1990.
WALKER
Albert S.,1972.
Harvey E.,1894-1977.
James E.,1976.
Lillian E.,1989.
Maude,1882-1956,w/o Harvey.
Mildred B.,1989,w/o Albert S.
WARNER
Ruth T.,1922-1987.
William D.,1903-1981.
WEBBER
John J.,1886-1967.
WEDGE
Melvin J.,1859-1931,h/o Louise

WENTWORTH
Edna S.,1929-1936.
WESCOTT
Joseph,Dec.11,1864,44y.
Lydia D.,Apr.1870,48y,w/o Jos.
Robert S.,1908-1986.
WHIDDEN
Barbara D.,XXXX,w/o Beryle D.
Beryle D.,1977.
WHITE
Florence A.,1915-1994,
  w/o Albert R.,Jr.
John Mc.,1937.
Willard F.,1988.
WILLEY
Harold E.,1876-1955.
Harriet V.,1878-1955.
Kenneth G.,1912-1926.
Allan O.,XXXX.
WILLIAMS
Gordon G.,XXXX.
John G.,1988.
Katherine H.,XXXX,w/o Gordon.
Margaret,1982.
WILSON
Bertha M.,1979,w/o Wm. M.
William M.,1981.
WING
James L.,1975.
WINSLOW
Leland R.,1985.
Virginia E.,XXXX.
WOODS
Floria M.,1981,w/o George S.
Minnie E.,1908-1970.
Willis G.,1906-1973.
WORITNY
Charlotte A.,1986,w/o George.
George,1965.
WORREY
Eugene A.,1976.
Marilyn C.,XXXX.
WYMAN
Addie Varney,1902-1986,w/o Ira W.
Beverly,1928-1990,w/o Ira,Jr.
Ira W.,1898-1953.
Tracy F.,1932-1932,d/o Ira W.
YATES
Freeman,1818-1864.
Mary,1818-1895,w/o Freeman.
YORK
E. Leslie,1898-1967.
Herbert L.,1872-1952.
Marcia E.,1876-1930,w/o H. L.

✤ **STEVENS CEMETERY** ✤
Franklin Stevens Road,Windham.

MAXWELL
Moses,1891.
Sarah,XXXX.
NEWCOMB
Hannah,1872.
SANBORN
Fred P.,1947.
Jessie,19XX,w/o Fred P.
STAPLES
David,1882.
George F.,1842.
Horace L.,1842.
John W.,1842.
Lydia,1881.
Lydia M.,1861.
Maria,1942.
William B.,1843.
STEVENS
Adelaide A.,1843-1909,
  d/o Franklin & Salome.
Anne Millions,XXXX,w/o Richard.
David,1796-1839.
Eliza,1836-1849,
  d/o Jonathan & Thankful.
Ella A.,1879.
Franklin,1814-1886,
  s/o Nathaniel & Molly.
Freddie,1863,s/o Isaac.
Hannah,1778-1849,
  d/o Jonathan & Mehitable.
Isaac,1869.
John,Nov.27,1841,h/o Lydia
Jordan, s/o Richard & Anne
Jonathan,Nov.27,1849,
  h/o Thankful, s/o Jon. & Martha.
John,Sr.,Dec.18,1786,80y.
Martha Millions,1763-1849,
  2nd w/o Jonathan.
Mehitable Mackentire,Nov.29,
  1780,1st w/o Jonathan.
Molly Cobb,1883,96y,w/o Nath'l.
Nathaniel,Mar.3,1858,
  s/o Chase & Rebecca.
Richard,bapt. 1765,
  s/o J.Jr.& Hannah Wescott.
Salome B. Hall,1890,w/o Franklin.
Sarah,1827-1849,
  d/o Jonathan & Thankful.
Thankful Newcomb,1794-1869,
  w/o Jonathan S.
THURLOW
Anna,1853,w/o Isaac.
Isaac,XXXX.

VARNEY
Alpheus L.,1951.
Anna G.,1876.
Ezekiel,1890.
George L.,1959.
Ida May Balsor,Sept.9,1905,43y,
 w/o Frank H.,d/o Andw & Johanna.
James E.,1888.
Johnson,1918.
Levi,1885.
Margaret J.,1873
Martha E.,1914,w/o Wm.H.
Mary Ann,1892.
Nettie,1912,w/o Johnson.
Olice L.,1876,d/o James E.
Samuel G.,1968.
William H.,1914.
WATERHOUSE
Eliza Stevens,Sept.23,1824,
 19y,w/o Samuel.
William P.,Sept.23,1825,
 s/o Samuel & Eliza S.

✤ **HANSEN BURIAL GROUND** ✤
No location. Windham.

HANSON
Catherine Hanscom,Aug.12,1838,72y,
 w/o Ezra.
Cyrus,Apr.23,1840,2y,only ch/o Steph.
Ezra,Aug.30,1843,77y,
 s/o Ichobod & Abigail Hayes.
Hannah Frank,May 29,1838,25y,
 2nd w/o Stephen.
Hannah Kilborn,June10,1873,75y,
 wid/o Stephen.
May C. Putney,June 30,1831,23y,
 1st w/o Stephen.
Stephen,Oct.6,1790-Dec.25,1872,
 s/o Ezra & Cather.

✤ **ELDER CEMETERY** ✤
River Rd.,near Westbrook line.
Not located.

ELDER
Abbie A.,XXXX,d/o Josiah & Jane.
Hiram,1887/1909 ?,s/o J. & J.
Jane Stone,1883, w/o Josiah.
Josiah,1805-1883,s/o Silas &
 Abigail Chesley Elder.
Maria S.,1901,d/o J. & J.
Marshall,1831-1913,s/o J. & J.
Sarah J.,1887,d/o J. & J.
Willie, XXXX.

✤ **McINTOSH CEMETERY** ✤
38 Falmouth Road,Windham.

ANTHOINE
Elroy M.,1867,s/o W.H.
Henry C.,1868,s/o W.H.
Orrilla J.,1868,w/o W.H.
AUSTIN
Charles L.,1854.
Addie,Mar.9,1901,40y.
Ella A.,1977.
Esther,1854.
Greenlief F.,1931.
Hannah,Aug.1901,76y.
Jonah,1894.
Minerva A.,1915,w/o Jonah.
Randall K.,1956.
Randall W.,1937.
Sofronia E.,1927,w/o Randall W.
Stephen,Jan.20,1888,74y.
Thomas M.,XXXX.
Willard,Sept.7,1890,27y.
BROOKS
John K.,1839.
CLARK
Lucy A.,1901.
Lucy Jane,1949,3y.
COBB
Elias H.,1879,9y.
DEERING
Betsey,June 21,1897,77y.
Charles,Feb.11,1898,71y.
ELDER
Lois,Apr.26,1891,60y.
Mariam F.,1842.
Rhea,Mar.7,1874,77y.
ELWELL
Ella May,1907.
FRANK
Angelia,1845,d/o Rufus.
Lewis,1859.
Nancy,1878,w/o William.
FRYE
Eliot C.,1977,s/o Nathaniel.
Elizabeth H.,1850,d/o Nathaniel.
Elmira R.,1852,w/o Nathaniel.
Susan,1892,w/o Nathaniel G.
HAGGMAN
Clifford J.,1922.
HANSON
Charles A.,1911.
Oliver,1831-1894.
Sarah J.,1912,w/o Oliver.
INGERSOLL
Abram A.,1852.
Daniel,XXXX.
Daniel A.,1926.

Mary S.,1857.
Olive L.,1896,w/o Abram A.
S. Angelia,1934.
KEMP
Eunice,1788-1875,w/o Ebenez.
LIBBY
3 ch/o Samuel.
Almira,July 31,1881,51y.
Ann,Jan.7,1882,72y,w/o Peter.
Annie A.,1904.
Arthur,June 22,1880,69y.
Asa,1883.
Betsey,Aug.12,1894,62y.
Cora,Dec.6,1874,16y.
Cora Z.,1875.
Elias H.,1840-1862,in VA,
 s/o James & Mary.
Eliza Cash,1931,w/o Joseph.
Elizabeth,Feb.10,1883,45y.
Elmira Field,1881,w/o Lorenzo.
Elnora,1852-1878,/o James & Mary.
Eva,XXXX,d/o Joseph.
Florra E.,1860,d/o Isaac.
Frank F.,1915.
Gideon,Sept.1870,39y,
Gideon,Jr.,1791-1870.
Harriet E.,Nov.19,1881,25y.
Harris B.,1867.
Herbert E.,1875.
Isaac,Sept.26,1884,89y.
Isaac H.,XXXX.
James,1904.
James D.,1855-1864,s/o Jas & Mary.
James W.,1895.
Jane Prince,1877,w/o Gideon.
Joseph,1838 ?- XXXX.
Julia,18XX,w/o Frank F.
Keziah,1883,w/o Samuel P.
Lorenzo D.,1904.
Margaret,Apr.22,1898,63y.
Martha E.,1859,d/o Asa.
Mary,1897,w/o James.
Nancy,Sept.9,1885,w/o Arthur.
Newil,1819,s/o Asa.
Perley,XXXX,s/o Joseph.
Saloma A.,1854,d/o Asa.
Samuel P.,1813-1866,
 s/o Gideon & Jane.
Sarah,Nov.28,1883,w/o Daniel.
Syvanus P.,18151,s/o Asa.
William,Jr.,1858.
LITTLEFIELD
Elias,Aug.25,1877.
Rachel,Feb.12,1872,w/o Elias.
LOWELL
Abby,1840,w/o Stephen.
Albert,1863.

McINTOSH
Charles F.,1851,s/o James.
Eunice Stuart,1871,83y,w/o Jas.
James,1846,62y.
Patia,1847,d/o James.
MERRILL
Byron,1875,s/o Harris.
Cora G.,1878,d/o Harris.
Fannie E.,1879,w/o Harris.
Harris,1885.
Hellen M.,1902.
Leonard R.,1882.
Lillian,1862.
Lois Baker,1877,w/o Nathaniel.
Lorana,1848,d/o Nathaniel.
Nathaniel,1865.
Willard R.,1899.
STEWART
James L.,XXXX.
William,1877.
STUART
Jeremiah,1886.
Lucy,1894,w/o Jeremiah.
Peter,XXXX,s/o Jeremiah.
THOITS
Sarah,Dec.1877,22y,w/o Geo. A.
TUERO
Sarah,1865,w/o C.T.
VARNEY
Nehemiah,1862.
Stephen,1851.
WHITNEY
Louisa,1852,w/o Obadiah H.

✧ **KNIGHT CEMETERY** ✧
135 Brand & Knight Rd.,Windham.
Completed stone by stone.

ALLEN
Grace V.,1879-1918.
BRACKETT
Hannah L.,1848-1913.
CANNELL
Everett H.,Sr.,1898-1960,h/o Frances.
Everett H.,Jr.,1927-1991.
Francis Boothby,1904-1957.
Perley L.,1920-1979.
DOLLEY
Daniel K.,Mar.7,1863,
 s/o Samuel & Hannah H.
FENTON
Huldah Jane,Sept.29,1859,
 d/o Samuel & Hannah Dolley.
GREENLAW
Paul R.,1929-1989,h/o Mary Ann.
HUNT
Arvilla S.,1865-1944.

Elliot S.,1931-1935,s/o Philip.
Lloyd T.,1905-1906.
Philip A.,1903-1968.
KNIGHT
Bryon L.,1883-1911.
Elijah,Sept.1855.
Elizabeth,Oct.6,1859,84y,w/o Elijah.
Ella S.,1874-1960.
Emily Coolbroth,1842-1905,w/o Wm.
Emily D. Stevens,1823-1861,w/o Wm.
Howard Scott,1896-1975.
Marjorie E.,1901-1983,w/o Howard.
Sarah,Feb.17,1832,33y,w/o Reuben.
Scott W.,1870-1898.
William,1836-1916.
LAMB
3 ch/o William & Mary:
Mary,1852-1861,
Leander,1845-1863,
Ida May,1866-1874.
Eliza R.,1823-1914,w/o Wm. B.
Emma J. Parker,1877-1961,
w/o Wilbur A.
Emmeline Whtiney,1841-1926,
w/o William A.
Flora M.,1869-1949.
Frank E.,1863-1955.
Hannah M.,Dec.23,1871,84y,
w/o Richard.
Mary,1785-1871,w/o William.
Paul W.,1914-1954.
Richard,May 4,1863,86y.
Sarah S.,May 26,1863,8y.
Wilbur A.,1882-1951.
William,1788-1869.
William A.,1820-1902.
William B.,1823-1891.
LIBBY
Arthur W.,1896-1972.
LORD
Howard C.,1906-1939.
MANCHESTER
Aaron,1827-1898.
Harriet F.,1829-XXXX,w/o Aaron
Stephen,1859,10m,s/o A. & H.F.
Stephen,Apr.22,1865,2y,
s/o Greenlief & Octavia.
MILES
Abbie C.,1869-1956.
MUNROE
Robert A.,1927-1978,h/o Joan.
Timothy,1967-1967.
ROBERTS
Maynard M.,1922-1984.
SANDERS
Abbie L.,1846-1932,w/o John B.
Amelia A.,1889-1963w/o W.F.

John B.,1847-1911.
Walter F.,1878-1957.
SMITH
Bernard Irvin,1924-1987.
Charles A.,1899-1952.
Charles A.,1974-1922.
Frank A.,1861-1940.
Lewis H.,1853-1931,h/o Mary.
Mary Lombard,1841-1923.
WEEMAN
Frank W.,1884.
WETHERBEE
Charles E.,1933.
Lucy P.,1963,w/o Charles E.

✤ **AUSTIN CEMETERY** ✤
Nash Road,Windham. Not located.

AUSTIN
Edgar E.,1943.
Eliza King,1864,w/o William.
Jonah,1824.
Leander,1855,18y,s/o W.& E.K.
Pauline Brown,XXXX.
Raymond H.,Sr.,1993.
Raymond King,1972.
Sarah,1819,30y,d/o Jonah.
Sarah E.,1926.
Sarah Foote,1837,2nd w/o Jonah.
William,1876.
William King,1902.

✤ **MORRELL CEMETERY** ✤
514a Route 202, Windham.
This cemetery was done stone by stone.

AKERS
Benjamin F.,1828-1859,s/o J. M. & C.
Charles M.,1841-1891,s/o J. M. & C.
Comfort,1802-1883,w/o John.
George A.,1830-1854,s/o J.M.
John,1800-1882.
Mary C.,1832-1918,d/o J.M.& C
William H.,1835-1905,s/o J.M.
BAKER
Amanda A. Cobb,May 11,1886,58y,
w/o William.
COBB
Arnelia M.,Oct.26,1868,
d/o Wm.& Lepha.
Harriet M.,Mar.16,1845,25y,d/o Wm.
Lepha,May 8,1861,w/o William.
William,1869,84y.
COFFIN
Almira F.,1852-1869.
DANIELS
Mary E.,Oct.16,1859,24y,w/o Isaiah.

ELDER
Alemeda Louvisa,1843-1860,
  d/o Richard.
Charles,July 14,1847,80y.
Ellen Maria,1848-1851,
  d/o Richard & Roxcillana.
Isaac,1840-1846,s/o R.J. & Rox.
Mary Louvisa,1843-1878,
  d/o Richard J. & Rox.
Richard J.,1807-1877.
Roxcillana,1810-1866,w/o Richard.
Stephen W.,1841-1842,s/o R.J.
FARWELL
Alice Read,1870-1912.
Easter I.,1898-1951.
Frank W.,1892-1929.
FIELD
Callie S.,June 21,1861,d/o J. & R.A.
George R.,1879,12y,s/o J.&R.A.
Ida L.,May 1869,12y,d/o J. & R.A
Jeremiah,1833-1908.
Ruth A.,1834-1911,w/o Jeremiah.
Willard,1871-1905.
FOSTER
Emma M.,1869-1929,w/o Geo.
George B.,1875-1953.
FOYE
Ethel M.,1890-1952.
GILMAN
William H.,1817-1837.
GUPTIL
Catherine H.,1852-1879.
HALL
Daniel K.,1869-1918.
Effie E.,1872-1953.
HUNEWELL
Ervin C.,Jr.,1909-1925.
Spencer E.,1907-1929,
  s/o Ervin C.& Grace Spencer.
HUNEWILL
Ann W.,1840-1929,w/o John.
Ervin E.,8173-1860,
  s/o John & Ann.
Hanson E.,1856-XXXX,s/o J.& A.
James J.,1864-1920,s/o J. & A.
John,1770-1861.
John R.,1867-XXXX,s/o J. & A.
John W.,1834-1898.
Mary Foster,1796-1855,w/o John.
Mary L.,1860-1863,d/o J. & A.
HUNT
Thelma Watson,Oct.1994,89y.
KIMBALL
Alice M. Greenlaw,1862-1905.
Dorothy H.,1909-1981.
Edward J.,1860-1926,h/o A.M.G.
Joseph G.,1892-1958.

LEGROW
Hannah,Feb.24,1831,32y,w/o Amos.
LIBBY
Laura E.,1838-1861,w/o Elbridge.
LOVEITT
Albion L.,1863-1937.
Louisa H.,1869-1948,d/o A.L. & L.H.
Madeline Louise,1901-1903,
  d/o Albion & Louisa.
LOWELL
Alden G.,1827-June 7,1878,
  s/o Ed. & Sally Estes.
Carrie Jane,1868-1932.
Clarence Frederick,1857-1924.
Ellen J.,1829-1869,1st w/o A.G.
McLELLAN
Jordan,1838-1921.
R. Guy,1874-1889,s/o J. & C.J.
Cynthia J.,1838-1894,w/o Jordan.
Eliza,1837-1921,2nd w/o Jord.
Stephen J.,1865,s/o Jordan.
MORRELL
Annie L.,1879-1946,w/o Eugene.
Annie L.,1844-1924,w/o Cornel.
C. Susie,1875-1875,d/o Jac.& D.
Clifford E.,1906-1969.
Cornelius N.,1837-1918.
Dexter J.,1850-1916.
Delphina,1842-1925,w/o Jacob.
Elizabeth,1886,w/o Jacob B.
Eugene L.,1877-1959.
Fannie S.,1908-XXXX.
Jacob,Capt.,1798-1871.
Jacob B.,1839-1895.
Jacob N.,1845-1911.
Jane W.,1807-1882,w/o Jacob.
Lizzie M.,1840-1896,w/o Jacob B.
Lovisa,Aug.17,1852,17y,
  d/o Stephen & Lydia.
Louisa A.,1834-1900,w/o Wm G.
Lydia,Aug.1872,66y,w/o Stephen
Maybel,1903-1928,d/o E.M.& A.
Margaret B.,1831-1850,d/o Jacob.
Maude,1874-1890,d/o J.B. & L.
Philip S.,1913-1981,h/o Arline
Stephen,Feb.11,1887,83y.
William G.,1839-1912.
MOSES
E.,1835-1915.
F.O.,XXXX.
H.G.,XXXX.
R.L.,XXXX.
READ
Augustus,1834-1908.
George R.,1832-1887.
Lizzie J.,1833-1931,w/o August
Sarah Abbie,1849-1929,w/o Geo.

Walter Howard,1872-1961.
RIDEOUT
Joann H.,May 1869,70y,w/o Wm
SAWYER
Aseneith H.,1829-1895,w/o Wm
Bertha R.,1871-1951.
Esther F.,1900-1902.
Howard L.,1864-1919.
Nathan,1870,2y,s/o William.
Sarah J.,1834-1860,w/o Dennis
William F.,1832-1925.
SAYWARD
Albert N.,1850-1921.
Eldridge,1811-1898.
Harlon,1887-1988,s/o A.L. & M.
Henry,1843-1869,s/o Elbridge.
Horace,1890-1941.
Martha J. Wescott.1858-1941,
w/o Albert N.
Mary H.,1812-1897,w/o Elbridg
STAPLES
Clark H.,Nov.14,1862,40y.
Hall,Nov.13,1873,68y.
Harriet A.,1836-1893.
James C.,1875-1903.
Louisa H.,Nov.18,1865,58y,w/o Hall.
Mildred L.,Feb.23,1867,
d/o Stephen & Harriet.
Stephen H.,1829-1888.
SWETT
Albion O.,1855,19y.
Calista Abbott,1856-1923,w/o John N.
John Nelson,1839-1914.
THAYER
Martha L. Morrell,1849-1933,
w/o Edward F.
TUKEY
Louann,1814-1899.
VARNEY
Hiram,1806-1842.
Mark S.,1862,s/o Hiram.
Sumner C.,1846-1855,s/o Hiram.
Susan G.,1805-1874,w/o Hiram.
WALKER
Abbie E.,1843-1908,w/o Edwin.
Edwin H.,1844-1911.
WALLACE
Irvine E.,1893-Oct.1,1918.
Lorenzo D.,1893.
Mary Ann,1906,w/o Lorenzo.

GEO. T. SPRINGER & CO.,

Undertakers, Embalmers and
Funeral Directors.
Newly appointed rooms at
116 Main St.,   WESTBROOK, ME.
(1894)

✤ **FRIENDS CEMETERY** ✤
Route 202,Windham.
Completed stone by stone.

ALDRICH
Elizabeth Stanley,1896-1941.
Loyal B.,XXXX, h/o Elizabeth S.
ALLEN
Cyrus Kennard,1832-1908,
s/o Joel & Joanna.
Eliza E.,1843-1858,d/o Nathan.
Fred C.,1868-1945.
Henry W.,Aug.15,1830-XXXX,
s/o Nathan & Mary Estes.
Isaiah P.,1914.
Jennie C.,1890-1944,w/o Fred.
Jeremiah Hacker,1849-1850,
s/o Josiah.
Josiah S.,1818-1894, s/o
Ebenezer & Elizabeth Southwick.
Mary Estes,1885,81y,w/o Nathan.
Mary Read Hacker,1820-1883,
w/o Josiah S.
Melinda R.,1918,w/o Isaiah P.
Nathan,1857,57y.
Phebe,1892.
Sybil,1880.
William,1851-1852,s/o Josiah.
CHUTE
Joseph C.,1886,62y.
Sarah S.,1893,66y,w/o Joseph C.
COBB
Martha L.,1892.
COLLINS
Anna W.,1877,85y,w/o John.
Evelina M.,1827-1910.
COOK
Abbie J.,1822-1918.
Albert E.,1923.
Amy D.,1840-1903,w/o Edw. C.
Callie R.,1894,w/o A.E.
Catherine Hamblen,1893,
1st w/o Valentine.
Elijah,1818-1911.
Emily A.,1821-1908,w/o Wm H.
Eunice Grant,1864,74y,1st w/o Jos.
George H.,Feb.18,1854-
Jan.31,1896,s/o Elij. & Abigail.
George H.,1869,s/o Elijah.
Huldah,1874,w/o Lemuel.
James M.,1843-1866.
Joseph,1890,88y.
Lydia Hocker,1829-1859,w/o William.
Martha L. Cobb,1844-1892.
Valentine M.,1863,47y,
s/o Daniel,Jr. & Jane Whitney.
William H.,1828-1891.

DAVIS
Raymond C.,1987.
DEVERY
Bertha A.,1844-1955.
Charles E.,1869-1951.
DOLLEY
Amelia,1849-1867,d/o Jos.& E.
Catherine,1880.
Deborah,1836-1899.
Esther,1806-1871,w/o Joseph.
Esther,1890.
Hannah Bailey,1782-1865,
 w/o Jeremiah.
Hannah Dolley,1917,w/o J.T.
Jeremiah,Apr.1777-June1863.
Joseph,1806-1889.
Patience,1892.
Timothy,1897.
HACKETT
Oliver,1885,73y.
HALL
Alice A.,1867-1959.
Anna F.,1831-1920,w/o J. Hacker.
J. Hacker,1838-1908.
Emma,XXXX,d/o J.Hacker & Anna.
Sara F.,1871-1961.
HANSON
Cynthia Robinson,1869,62y,
 1st w/o Amos.
Nathan,1876,44y.
HAWKES
Levi,1780-1866,s/o Amos Jr. & Lydia.
Rhoda,1793-1859.
Thankful,1803-1875,d/o A. Jr. & L.
HOAG
Moses,1804-1879.
Sara Fry,1807-1899,w/o Moses.
HODGE
Annie Robinson,1857-1892.
HOWE
Elizabeth T.,1963.
HUSSEY
Patience,XXXX,78y.
JACKSON
Edith E.,1959,w/o Fred C.
Fred C.,1919.
JONES
Abbie Lord,1930,w/o Daniel C.
Charles L.,1915,s/o Herbert L.
Charles W.,1933.
Daniel C.,1833-1891,
 s/o Lemuel & Huldah.
Elisha,1798-1874,s/o Edw & Mary.
Elma R.,1860-61,d/o I. & Emily.
Emily Read,1903/8,w/o Isaiah.
George L.,1933,s/o D.C. & Abbie.

Herbert L.,1874-1908,
 s/o Lindley H. & Maria.
Isaiah,1912.
Lemuel,Jr.,1853. ?.
Lena M.,1882-1899.
Lindley H.,1843-1912,
 s/o Lemuel & Huldah.
Maria Jepson,1844-1917,w/o Lindley.
Nellie H.,1866-1948.
Sarah Hawkes,June 20,1857,
 1st w/o Elisha.
KENNARD
Timothy,1880.
LIBBY
Charles A.,1879-1954.
Edith G.,XXXX,w/o Charles A.
LOWELL
James,1789-1884,
 s/o John & Mary Chapman.
Mercy/Mary Hawkes,1862,65y,
 w/o James.
LUNDBERG
Alice L.,1959.
George E.,1910.
MARSTON
Jacob,1871,78y.
Lois,1868,76y,w/o Jacob.
MAXFIELD
Nancy E.,1866,10m,
 d/o Rufus & Mary Ann.
MOORE
Maria Kennard,Oct.8,1895,72y,
 w/o Leonard H.
MORTON
Julia M.,1887,w/o Frank J.
NICHOLS
Charles,1811-1887,
 s/o Samuel & Dorcus.
Charles A.,1842-1908,s/o C.A. & E.O.
Earl Everett,1895,
 inf/o Chas. A. & Ellen M.
Emily F. Sawyer,1842-1888,w/o Chas.
Ellen M. Cook,1860-1959,w/o Chas. A.
Esther Owen,1808-1892,w/o C.
OLESEN
Carolyn F.,1934-1944.
John H.,1896-1953.
Ruth F.,1902-1993.
POPE
Alice Marie,1860-1929.
Eliza,1842-1864,d/o I. & S.W.
Ellen P.,1854-1950,
 d/o Robert & Jullette.
Etta K.,1860-1892.
Hannah,1822-1863,d/o Nathan.
Isaiah,1805-1872,h/o Sarah W. Cook,
 s/o Nathan & Phebe.

Jane,1812-1868,d/o Nath. & P.
Joseph,1817-1891,s/o N. & P.A.
Jullette Kennard,Jan.4,1876,
 w/o Robert,d/o Elijah & Lucy.
Lucy M.,1851-1875,
 d/o Robert & Jullette.
Lydia A.,1840-1864,
 d/o Isaiah & Sarah.
Lydia Mayfield,1906,w/o Nathan.
Maria Cook,1806-1888,w/o Oliver.
Mary,1806-1892,d/o Rob. & M.
Mary M.,1849-1879,d/o I.&S.W.
Nathan,1819-1894,s/o Nat. & P.
Nathan Oliver,1850-1924.
Oliver,1807-1883,s/o Nathan & Phebe.
Phebe,1799-1883.
Phebe,1844-1932.
Robert,1808-1876,s/o Robt. & Mary.
Sarah W.,1850,w/o Isaiah.
READ
Mariam R.,1840,d/o Noah.
Nathan,1884,73y.
Nathan,1878,83y.
Rufus,1864,24y.
Ruth Horton,1886,89y,w/o Nathan.
Sarah M.,1896.
REED
Noah,Apr.1,1844, Rev. Soldier.
REEVES
Katherine S.,1959,w/o Walter.
Walter,1978.
ROBINSON
Anna,1804-1876,d/o Stp. & M.
Charles G.,1868,74y,s/o Elijah.
Elijah,1868,s/o Reuben & Lydia.
Elizabeth,1894,2y,d/o Tim & S.
Ellen P.,1841-1869,
 d/o Oliver & Sarah O. Taber.
Emma,May 1867,75y,w/o John.
Ermina Freeman,1877,58y,w/o Elijah.
Hattie,1889,72y,w/o J.W.
Henry,1820-1883.
Huldah,1868,77y,
 s/o Stephen & Content Alley.
John,1864.
John W.,1812-1876,s/o Reuben.
Lane,1870,w/o Timothy.
Lydia Varney,1820-1886,w/o Henry.
Mary Robinson.,Aug.1869,85y,
 w/o Stephen (1868).
Oliver,1812-1890,s/o Tim & S.
Otis,1814-1884,s/o John & Emma.
Sarah Winslow,Nov.24,1870,
 92y,w/o Timothy.
Stephen,Dec.11,1868,87y.
Stephen,1819-1865.

Timothy,Feb.8,1865,
 s/o Stephen & Content.
SMITH
Timothy F.,1958-1960.
SNOW
Annie, Mary & Lucy;
 3 d/o A.B.,XXXX.
Augustus B.,1832-1907.
Fred A.,1863-1927.
Lucy A.,1832-1909,w/o Augustus B.
SYLVESTER
Frank M.,1880,20y.
Zadlock,Oct.29,1908,84y,
 s/o Zadlock & Mary Jordan.
VARNEY
Peace,1881,w/o Timothy.
Timothy,1892.
WARREN
Virginia A.,1912-1944.
WEBB
Ellen F.,1935,w/o Stephen H.
Emma,1845-1911.
Mary E.,1953,w/o Paul.
Mary J.,1831-1906.
Nathan,1868,35y.
Noah,1870,31y.
Olive S.,1888-1900.
Stephen,Feb.9,1872,77y.
Stephen H.,1920.
Tabitha Robinson,1804-1887,
 w/o Stephen.
WINSLOW
George E.,1866-1899.
Hannah S.,1862,w/o James.
James,1877.
Louisa E.,Oct.13,1891,58y.
Margaret J.,1845-1930.
Oliver,1828-1915,h/o M.J.
WRIGHT
June W.,1993,d/o Edward.

✣ **OLD QUAKER BURIAL GROUND**
Route 202, Windham.
Only remaining stones in 1994 *.
Many burials were obtained from old
Quaker records and newspaper articles.

ALLEN
Nathan,1800-July 22,1857,
 h/o Mary Estes,s/o Ebenezer &
 Charity Pope Allen.
COBB
Elmira,1852,w/o Isaac.
* Phebe,Apr.27,1854,84y,w/o William.
* William,Feb.12,1844,75y.
COOK
Daniel,1800-Feb.22,1732.

GOOLD
Daniel,July 1780-Mar.1798,
s/o Benjamin & Phebe Noble.
HAMILTON
* Hannah,Mar.10,1847,73y,w/o John.
HANSON
Jonathan,1877.
HASKELL
Oliver P.,1893.
HAWKES
Charlotte,1842,1st w/o Alley.
*Elijah W.,Oct.9,1856,36y.
*Herbert W.,Mar.11,1853,
s/o W.W. & M.H.
James Jr.,May 21,1857,84y,
s/o James & Elizabeth Crague.
Rebecca Robinson,Dec.12,1853,
80y,w/o James.
JONES
Lemuel,Jr.,1853,44y,
h/o Huldah Cook,bu: Friends Cem.
KENNARD
Lydia,1768-1859,w/o Abijah.
LIBBY
*Daniel,June 15,1854,54y.
MAYBERRY
Eunice,1879,w/o Joseph.
Joseph,1888.
POPE
*Elijah,Dr.,Jan.21,1856,40y.
Nathan,Jan.20,1859,83y,
s/o Elijah & Phebe Winslow.
*Phebe Allen,Nov.2,1849,71y,
w/o Nathan.
Sarah Whitney,July 5,1850,
w/o Isaiah,d/o Daniel & Jane C.
PURINTON
Abijah,1848.
Hannah,1847,w/o Abijah.
ROBINSON
John,Aug.21,1800.
Salome Kennard,1767-1853,
w/o Timothy.
Tabitha Winslow,Apr.30,1822,
w/o John.
Timothy,Apr.17,1767-
June 5,1851,s/o John & Tabitha
SWETT
* Albion Ormond,1837-1853,
s/o David P. & Louann.
VARNEY
Abijah,1773-1858,
s/o Timothy & Joanna.
WINSLOW
* Anna,June 30,1853,73y.
Louisa E.,1891.

✣ **OLD SMITH BURYING GROUND**
434 River Road, Windham. Also called
the Smith Anderson Cemetery.
According to Samuel T. Dole in 1899,
the first person buried at the Smith
Cemetery was Grace Farrow
Manchester, wife of Stephen, her
brother and a child. Also mentioned
were her father John Farrow and his
wife. In Rev. John Wight's record book,
he recorded the following dates.
All in unmarked graves:

ANDERSON
Abraham,Oct.22,1748,1y,
s/o Abraham & Bathshua.
Bathshua,Nov.13,1945,13y,
d/o Abraham & Bathshua.
Bathshua,July 4,1751,w/o Abraham.
Isaac,Mar.7,1746/7,
s/o Abraham & Bathshua.
FARROW
Abigail,1753,d/o John & Hannah.
HUNNEWELL
Roger,Nov.12,1747,7y,
s/o Zerubabel & Hannah.
KNIGHT
Hannah,Mar.2,1746/7,36y,w/o Wm.
MANCHESTER
Gershom,Mar.15,1749/50,62y,
2nd w. Mary Farrow,Oct.7,1744,
s/o Stephen & Mary,
MAYBERRY
John,Aug.27,1748,5m, &
William,Apr.26,1745,
2 s/o Thomas & Bethia.
STARBIRD
Elizabeth,May 17,1749,
d/o Nathaniel & Elizabeth.
STARLING
Miriam,Sept.4,1751,7m,
d/o Joseph & Mary.
TRIPP
Othniel, Nov.20,1744,
s/o Othniel & Hannah.
WEBB
Joshua,Nov.3,1749,5y,
s/o Samuel & Bethia.
WIGHT
Elijah, Oct.24,1745,2m,
s/o John & Deliverance.
WINSHIP
Ephraim,Aug.27,1751,
s/o Ephraim & Mehitable.
Mehitable,Apr.17,1750,44y,w/o Ephr.

Also the following gravestones from a list that was given to me. Many gravestones were missed. I checked about 50% of the stones, but did not complete this cemetery.

ADJUTANT
Ann S.,1881,w/o John F.
Elias F.,1921.
Etta E.,1888,w/o Elias F.
John F.,1900,69y.
ANDERSON
Abraham,Sept.3,1844,86y.
Ann Williams Jameson,1804-1879, w/o John.
Chester R.,1933.
Edward,Oct.30,1801-1867.
Edward F.,1827-1904, s/o Peter S.& Susan B.
Edward W.,1828-1861, s/o John & Ann.
Elizabeth W.,1811-1893, d/o Peter & Ann.
Frances A. Perley,1870, w/o Edward, (1861).
inf/o Abraham & Lucy,Aug.1791.
John,1791,7m,s/o Abrah. & Lucy
John,1782-1853,s/o Abraham & Lucy.
John Farwell,1823-1887, s/o John & Ann.
Louisa Berry,1804-1881, w/o John (1867)
Lucretia C.,1820-1901, d/o Peter S. & Susan.
Lucy,May 1821,25y,w/o John.
Lucy Smith,1769-1844,w/o Abraham.
Lucy F.,1822-1902,d/o P. & S.
Marcia F.,1903.
Marcia W.,1898,w/o John.
Mehitable H. Cole,1883,47y, w/o Edward F.
Nora K.,1945,w/o Chester R.
Olive Ann,1824-1843,d/o P.& S.
Peter S.,1789-1867,s/o Abr.&L.
Peter,Nov.9,1775,s/o Peter Thacher.
Rebecca,Apr.19,1782 ?, d/o Peter Thacher.
Susan Bodge,1780-1876,w/o Peter S.
Susan M.,1931,d/o Edward F.
Susan M.,1831-1849,d/o P.& S.
William,July17XX,3m,s/o Ab.&L.
BABB
Elias M.,Dec.7,1855,50y.
Irene,Dec.1856,16y,d/o Elias.
Sarah E.,1909.
Sarah L.Hawkes,Feb.21,1806-Nov.21,1854,w/o Elias M.

Ann Maria,1880,w/o George.
BACHELDER
Ann Maria,Apr.20,1880,42y,w/o Geo.
Eva,July 2,1880,13y.
George,Dec.11,1895,78y.
Mary A.,1909,2nd w/o George R.
BACON
Albert,1844-1847,s/o John.
Eunice K.,1809-1892,w/o John.
John,1809-1892.
John A.,1834-1843,s/o John.
BAILEY
Charles W.,M.D.,1907.
Charles H.,1857.
Jesse C.,1885.
BARKER
Ann W.,May 21,1850,w/o Chas.
Charles,Mar.21,1822,50y.
BERRY
Henry,Mar.14,1846,44y.
Joshua,Oct.13,1847,80y.
Olive Wilson,May 6,1815,46y, w/o Joshua.
BICKFORD
Abby,Apr.20,1856,11y.
Caroline F.,1894,w/o Wm.
Harry Hayes,Jan.5,1892,14y.
inf/o Wm. & L.A.H.,Sept.2,1850.
John,Dec.31,1891,17y.
Lucy H.,July 17,1880,57y.
William,1893,76y,h/o Lucy H.
BRACKETT
Elizabeth,Sept.1881,w/o Jerem.
Jeremiah,Dec.27,1869,74y.
Martha A.,1900,w/o Thomas.
Thomas,1816-1885.
Thomas F.,1841-1852.
BRAGDON
Caroline G.,1899,w/o Levi.
Levi,1907.
Philip S.,Feb.14,1890,21y.
Samuel,Jan.8,1895,76y.
BROWN
Ezra,Mar.21,1826,76y.
Sarah,Dec.2,1798,41y,w/o Ezra.
BURNHAM
John,Mar.1,1796,27y.
CASH
James R.,Mar.27,1865,18y.
Mary,Nov.1849,29y,w/o Jas. P.
CASWELL
Edgar H.,June 24,1895,13y.
Henry W.,July 2,1898,28d.
CLAY
Ella,1875,d/o Willis.
Frank R.,1960.
Herbert,1923.

Marion E.,1926,d/o Frank R.
Mary A.,1908,w/o Willis.
William,1907.
CLOUDMAN
Abraham A.,Oct.11,1897.
Elizabeth,1877,75y,w/o Nathan.
Nathan,June 17,1869,69y.
CLOUTMAN
Mary,Dec.21,1821,77y,d/o Edw.
COBB
Harriet H.,1886,69y,w/o Lewis.
Jeannette,Sept.1875,25y,
  d/o Lewis & Harriet.
Lewis,1808-1887.
COBBY
Abigail Witham,Feb.1,1812,64y,
  w/o John.
Eleanor,Mar.31,1810,101y.
Eunice,Oct.12,1839,60y.
Francis J.,1849,32y,d/o Jos.& Rebecca.
John,1749-1821,s/o Eleanor.
Joseph,1782-Apr.21,1837.
Rebecca,Aug.30,1863,80y,w/o Joseph.
CODMAN
Richard,Sept.9,1833,72y.
Susan H.,Sept.26,1842,62y,w/o Rich.
CORDWELL
Mary,1832-1856,w/o Stephen A.
DAVIS
Edward H.,Apr.30,1871,32y.
Matthew A.,1876.
DOLE
Apphia,1793-1815,d/o S. & M.
Daniel W.,1807-1876,
  s/o Oliver & Elizabeth.
Eliza A. Boody,Mar.18,1832,24y,
  1st w/o Daniel W.
Elizabeth Mayberry,1833,w/o Oliver.
Freddie,Mar.28,1856,10 days,
  s/o Richard & Rox.
Jennie,1856-1863,d/o Richard.
Mehitable Mayberry,
  1766-1843,w/o Samuel.
Mary W. Hasty,1815-1872,
  2nd w/o Daniel W.
Oliver,1798-1838,s/o Sam. & M
Richard,Aug.1765-Oct.18,1864,
  s/o D.W. & E.A.
Roxilla M. Chute,1901,w/o Rich.
Samuel,Oct.18,1844,79y.
DOUGLASS
Edmund,Aug.8,1892,73y.
Eliza Mayberry,July 2,1886,
  67y,2nd w/o Edmund.
Eunice Boody,May 30,1851,
  41y,1st w/o Edmund.

ELDER
Abigail Chesley,June 3,1853,
  82y,w/o Silas.
Caleb,1813-1885,s/o Silas & A.
Caroline,1824-1845,
  d/o Reuben & Sally.
Dorcas,1803-1833,d/o S. & A.
Edward,1820-1855,s/o R. & S.
Irving,1929.
John,May 15,1828,76y,
  s/o Wm. & Mary.
Lois,1801-1874,d/o S. & A.
Lydia M.,Jan.31,1866,29y,
  w/o Albert L.
Marie N.,1925.
Mary Akers,1783,58y,w/o Wm.
Mary M.,1865-1942.
Peter,1794-1859,s/o Silas & A.
Rebecca Graffam,1759-1829,w/o John.
Reuben,1793-1839,s/o S. & A.,
  h/o Sally Crague.
Silas,Sept.16,1841,72y,
  s/o William & Mary.
Warren S.,1908-1984.
William,Aug.8,1767,58y.
William,Sr.,Oct.20,1799,74y,s/o Sam'l.
ELLIOTT
Angie M.,Oct.30,1892-
  May 1892,w/o Frank.
FOSS
Jane Trott,1811-1876.
FREEMAN
Alice E.,1865,d/o S.W.& C.H.
Ann M.,Mar.25,1847,3y,d/o Benjamin.
Anna M.,1939,w/o Stephen.
Benjamin,1818-1890,s/o Josiah & B.
Betsey Webb,1750-1873,w/o Josiah.
Caroline H. Walker,1865,
  2nd w/o Stephen W.
Charity A. Bodge,1818-1842,
  1st w/o Stephen W.
Charles H.,1939.
Ella M.,1851-1865,d/o S.W.& C.
Erving W.,1847-1849,s/o S.W.
John A.,Jan.28,1890,66y,h/o Minerva.
John M.,XXXX.
Josiah,1791-1868.
Martha A. Ingersol,1823-1863,
  w/o Benjamin.
Minerva Small,Mar.23,1889.
Patia D.,1933,w/o Charles H.
Rose Elva,July 4,1852,14m.
Stephen W.,Aug.26,1897,80y.
William B.,1860.
GLENDENNING
Mary F.,1929.
Charles Raymond,1901.

Mary T.,1942.
Reginald R.,1944.
Susan W.,1888,w/o Charles R.
GOODELL
Charles Raymond,1832-1901.
Louisa Anderson,1871-1952,
  w/o Myron.
Mary Thurston,1863-1942.
Myron Alexander,1865-1939.
Reginald Rusden,1869-1944.
Susan Watson,1835-1888,w/o Charles.
GRAFFAM
Bathsheba,1774-Dec.30,1837.
Caleb,Capt.,Nov.11,1784,73y.
Enoch,Aug.28,1827.
Hannah,Sept.11,1764,43y.
Lois,Jan.12,1804,43y.
Lois,May 21,1798,19y,d/o Peter.
GRANGER
Caroline,Apr.14,1831,d/o Geo.
George,Jan.11,1846,45y.
Polly,July 25,1841,34y.
GRANT
Alfreda,1950.
Clara,1943.
Daniel H.,1862.
Eunice A.,1903,w/o Francis.
Francis H.,1924.
Hannah Hardy,1873,56y,w/o Jas.
Harlan S.,XXXX.
James,June 3,1874,66y.
Reginald,1879.
GRAY
Eleanor B.,1978.
HALL
J. Porter,Feb.17,1881,63y.
Sarah J.,Nov.11,1861,42y,w/o J.P.
HARDY
Betsy Hawkes,Feb.26,1810-
  1863,w/o Lewis,d/o Jos. & Reb.
HARRIS
Alfreda,1857-1857,d/o Francis.
Betsey,Aug.12,1853,63y,w/o Levi.
Charles E.,XXXX.
Francis,1819-1888.
Levi,Aug.23,1871,81y.
Mary B.,1815-1879.
HAWKES
Abner Lowell,Dec.21,1819-1841,
  s/o Jos. & Rebecca.
Caroline S.,1879,w/o Hamilton.
Charles J.,Mar.11,1864,15y,
  s/o Samuel.
Ebenezer,1726-1805.
Ebenezer,May 14,1817-July 1,1882.
Eliza,1887,w/o Samuel.

Ellen Wilson,1824-1881,
  w/o Ebenezer (1882).
Hamilton,1912.
Joseph,1768-1837,
  s/o Ebenezer & Sarah Griffin.
Joseph Jr.,Apr.4,1812-
  Jan.19,1844,h/o Eunice Bodge,
  s/o Jos. & Rebecca Lowell.
Lloyd D.,1880-1881,
  s/o Wesley & Sadie W.
Mary,1850-1880,w/o W.L.
Rebecca Lowell,1780-1838,
  w/o Joseph (1837),
  d/o Joshua & Sarah.
Samuel,1896.
Sarah Griffin,1730-1805,
  w/o Ebenezer (1805).
HAWXWELL
James,1915.
HUNNEWELL
Anna S.,1883.
Bessie M.,1895.
Charles F.,1918.
Charles H.,1912.
Edwin,1890.
Helena R.,1949.
Margaret S.,1909.
Mary I.,1901.
INGERSOLL
Martha,Jan.6,1860,63y,w/o Peter.
Peter,May 27,1846,51y.
IRWIN
Annie E. Webb,1903.
George W.,1896,s/o John.
JACKSON
H. Annie,1922,w/o Henry B.
Henry B.,1828.
Thadeus L.,1896,s/o Henry B.
JACOBSON
Geneva M.,1909,d/o Peter.
Grace L.,1975.
Jerania W.,1906.
Peter,1953.
JAMESON
Ann,June 3,1847,69y,
  w/o Capt. Samuel.
JENSEN
Anna K.,1901,w/o Peter A.
Peter A.,1907.
JOHNSON
Miriam A.,1916,w/o Edwin R.
JORDAN
Carrie L.,1935,w/o William C.
Gerald B.,1927.
J. Melville,1946.
Marjorie A.,Feb.17,1898,15y.

KNIGHT
3 d/o Lorenzo & M.E.:
Alfreda A.,Oct.29,1876,20y.
Mary Etta,June 26,1854,1y.
Orinda,Feb.8,1879,11y.
Lorenzo D.,1833-1893.
Mary Ann,1906,w/o Lorenzo.
LANCASTER
Lucy,1932.
LARRY
Bessie May 1986.
Ethel A.,1965.
Sarah E.,1945.
William A.,1917.
LORD
Anne,1919,w/o Charles W.
Anne,1978.
Charles Wm.,1917.
Elinor L.,1967,w/o John.
Florence,XXXX,w/o John Jr.
Florence U.,1993.
John,1939.
John,Jr.,XXXX.
Rebecca C.,1970,w/o Robert H.
Robert H.W.,1934.
LORENZEN
H. Thomas,1942.
Caroline,1924.
Lorenz,1898.
Martin,1889.
MABER
Samuel,Nov.16,1811,37y.
MAYBERRY
Alvin,Aug.22,1883,76y.
Caroline B.,Aug.25,1843,21y,
  d/o John.
Caroline W.,1849,d/o Daniel.
Charity,Apr.23,1855,75y.
Charlotte J.,Dec.4,1850,37y,
  w/o Daniel.
Daniel,1882.
Hannah,1860,w/o Daniel.
James,Apr.17,1840,73y.
James,Oct.3,1856,67y.
Jane,Nov.25,1851,82y.
John,1818.
John,Apr.1,1841,78y.
John,June 3,1876,91y.
Nathaniel,1839,s/o Daniel.
Rebecca,May 14,1847,87y.
Rebecca R.,Aug.11,1888,80y,w/o Alvin.
Sally,Mar.21,1864,73y,w/o James.
Sally,July 22,1869,86y.
Samuel Mabury,Nov.16,1811,37y.
Thomas,June 27,1805.
William,1829.

McCULLOUGH
Hattie,May 19,1884,21y.
George A.,1856,s/o John I.
Isabel,Nov.6,1867,23y,2nd w/o John.
John,XXXX.
Susan J.T.Smith,Sept.9,1865,44y,
  w/o John.
McMILLAN
Viola B.,1893.
MERRILL
Adelaid,1866,d/o J.F.
Hannah B.,May 27,1865,30y,w/o J.F.
MERSEREAU
Hannah W.,1938.
MILLER
Ann Cloudman,1829-1909.
Elinor Lord,1983,w/o Joseph L.
Jason,1833-1882,h/o Ann C.
Joseph L.,1978.
MITCHELL
Hannah,Apr.11,1890,60y.
Rufus E.,1900,h/o Hannah.
MONTGOMERY
Edgar R.,1919.
Frederick,1898,1y,s/o Edgar R.
Lavina E.,1900,w/o Edgar R.
PADDON
Betsy,Mar.15,1870,94y,w/o John.
PAINE
Hannah,Nov.24,1806,76y.
PARKER
Louisa A.,1952,w/o Myron.
Myron A.,1939.
PHILPOT
Alice T.,1982,w/o John E.
Cyrus,1964.
John E.,1967.
Maigaiet Q.,1915,w/o Cyrus.
PRIDE
Eliza W.,June 22,1866,65y,
  w/o Alexander.
QUIMBY
Rebecca,Jan.9,1850,47y,w/o Simeon.
RIGGS
Jeremiah,Sept.10,1869,74y.
Lydia,Oct.5,1857,59y,w/o Jeremiah.
SAWYER
Edgar F.,1858-1885.
Eunice E.,Oct.18,1849,1y.
Eunice R.,Nov.28,1898,70y,w/o Wm. F.
Zelia F.,Sept.2,1860,8y.
SCHREIBER
Edna H.,1947.
SEABURY
Hannahet,1905,w/o Wm. A.
William A.,XXXX.

SEAMANS
Vera,May 10,1898,6y.
SHAW
Clara L.,Mar.21,1881-Mar.13,1885,
 d/o Nathaniel L.
Daniel,Mar.19,1878,82y.
Daniel B.,1926.
Frank L.,1860,s/o Nathaniel.
Jesse,1877,s/o D.B.
John A.,June 13,1863,s/o Nathaniel.
Lavinia,May 4,1870,70y,w/o Daniel.
Reuben A.,June 11,1860,7y,
 s/o Nathaniel.
SIEWERTSEN
Christian,c.1900.
SMITH
Adaline Y.,May 24,1845,1y,d/o Lewis.
Alvilla,Apr.25,1865,18y,d/o Lewis.
Andrew R.,1831-1885.
Edward Tyng,1826-1909,
 s/o Thomas & Eliza.
Eliza Chamberlain,1801-1888,
 w/o Thomas.
Eliza F.,1908,w/o Andrew R.
Eliza Marston,1906,84y,w/o Edw. T.
Elizabeth Wendell,Oct.16,1799,57y,
 w/o Peter.
Elizabeth P.,July 9,1865,47y,
 w/o Lewis.
Frederick,1796-1877.
Harriet W.,Feb.16,1863.
Hezekiah,July 15,1824,70y.
J. Baxter,Aug.11,1865,28y.
Jane Hunt Loring,Apr.20,1824,70y,
 2nd w/o Peter.
Loranah,1898.
Lucy,1918.
Martha,1798-1881,w/o Frederick.
Martha E.,1865,6y,d/o Lewis.
Mary Ann,1823-1867,d/o Thos L. & E.
Peter Thacher,Oct.26,1826,95y.
Rebecca,1783-1808,d/o Peter.
Sally,Jan.3,1854,88y,
 w/o Hezekiah,d/o Peter & Eliza.
Sarah A.,1900.
Thomas,1770-1802,s/o P. & E.
Thomas L.,1797-1882,
 s/o Thomas. & Polly.
Wendell T.,1835-1864,
 s/o Thomas & Eliza.
Willie H.,Sept.25,1864,1y.
SPRING
Marcia W.,1901.
STANLEY
Laura M.,1927.
STAPLES
Abbie F.,1923,w/o Isaiah F.

Clara E.,XXXX,w/o Vaughn.
Ellen,1903.
Fred M.,1964.
Isaiah F.,1928.
Judith Ann,1945.
Linda M.,1966,d/o Fred R.
Mabel S.,1968,w/o Fred M.
Patricia Ann,1936.
Rose A.,1948.
Vaughn B.,XXXX.
STEVENS
Betsey,1897,w/o Mark H.
Charles H.,Feb.3,1892,27y.
Edward,Apr.19,1870,25y.
Freddie H.,1870,4m,s/o Edward.
Helen W.,XXXX.
Isaac,1913.
Mark H.Sept.11,1879,64y.
Mary B.,1902,w/o Isaac.
Willie F.,XXXX.
SWENSEN
Clifton,1913.
Julia,1937.
SWETT
James W.,Oct.20,1883,43y.
TROTT
Elizabeth S.,Sept.4,1905,87y,
 d/o John & Martha Stevens.
John,1786-1832,s/o Thos. & Sarah.
John,Jr.,1826-1828.
Martha Millions Stevens,
 1791-1881,2nd w/o John.
Sarah Knapp,1740-1837,w/o Thomas.
Sarah,1814-1887.
Thomas,Capt.,1731-1821,
 s/o John & Lydia.
William,1831-1832,
 s/o John & Martha.
TRUE
Alice B.,Apr.7,1897,74y,w/o Edward S.
Edward S.,Dec.21,1891,70y.
WALKER
Samuel,Feb.26,1841,22y.
WARK
Anna M.,July 21,1898,2y,d/o James A.
Florence C.,1915,w/o James A.
George J.,1970.
James A.,1911.
WATSON
Susan R.,Oct.19,1843,w/o Edw.
WEBB
Annie M.,1897.
Hannahette,1840,16y,d/o Steph.
John,Nov.30,1896,78y.
John F.,1900.
Lucy Ann,Apr.16,1886,64y,w/o John.
Mary,July 13,1889,92y,w/o Stephen.

Stephen,May 13,1868,76y.
WEBER
Alfred,1965.
Annie M.,1942,w/o August F.
August F.,1934.
Frederick A.,May 2,1898,5m,
  s/o August F.
Isabelle,XXXX,d/o August F.
Perry J.,1893,s/o August F.
WESCOTT
Daniel M.,1903.
Louisa M.,Nov.16,1894,63y,
  w/o Daniel.
WIER
Polly Barker Smith,Jan.12,1846,75y,
  w/o Robert, 1st h. Thomas Smith.
Robert,Aug.30,1835,60y.
WIGHT
Elijah,Aug.5,1742-Oct.24,1744,
  s/o John & Mary Pond.
John,May 8,1753,55y.
WILSON
Mabel A.,1991.
Olive F.,1915.
WINSHIP
Sally,1840.
WINLSOW
Mary,Feb.16,1848,37y,w/o Jas.

✥ **WINDHAM HILL** ✥
142 Windham Center Road.
Incomplete list.

AIKENS
Cora Harlow,1960.
Emily P.,1988.
Frederick A.,1948.
Frederick H.,1955.
Helen G.,1986,w/o Frederick.
James E.,1936.
ANDERSON
Abraham,1779-1859,
  s/o Edw.& Mary Mayberry.
Anna,1863,w/o Abraham.
Charles,1868,s/o Charles.
Charles,1886.
Clara B.,1989,w/o Clifford J.
Clifford J.,1958.
Dorcus Ann,1820,d/o Abraham.
Edward,1804,51y,s/o A.& Anna.
Frank L.,1919.
George & wife,XXXX.
George,Jr.,wife & 2 ch.,XXXX.
George A.,1820,s/o Abraham.
Leon M.,1957.
Lilias G.,1895,d/o Frank.
Lucretia R.,1970,w/o Leon M.

Mary,1850.
Mary,1846,w/o Edward.
Richard,1776-1802,s/o Edward.
Richard,1850.
Thomas,1796-1832,s/o Edw.& M
ANTHOINE
Amos,1870.
Daniel W.,1862.
George N.,1905.
Lucy Hall,1880,w/o Amos.
Mary W.,1882,d/o Amos.
William Hall,1833,s/o Amos.
BEAL
Bertram,XXXX.
Elva B.,1977,1st w/o Bertram.
Garfield L.,1978.
Helen G.,XXXX,2nd w/o Bertram.
Morris Alanson,1933.
BENNETT
Edward,1885.
Sally,1852,w/o /Edward.
BOLTON
Anna H.,1766-1836,
  d/o Thos.& Mary Crague.
BRADBURY
Alice M.,1884,d/o Cotton.
Cotton M.,1917.
Ella L.,1893,w/o Cotton.
Frank,1947.
Fred,XXXX.
James,M.D.,Apr.28,1772-Feb.7,1844.
James C.,1905.
Jennie M.,1901.
Susan D.,1877,w/o Cotton.
BROMLEY
G. Horace,1968.
Irene L.,1975,d/o G. Horace.
Lelia R.,1944,w/o Lewis.
Lewis O.,1937.
Lucy H.,1975,w/o G. Horace.
Raymond E.,1910.
BROWN
John,Dec.10,1875,92y.
Mary N.,1847,d/o John.
Relief,1872,d/o John.
Thankful,June 16,1855,62y,w/o John.
COBB
Alice & Mary,XXXX,d/o John C.
Charlotte M.,1911,w/o Isaac.
Hattie Amelia,1900,d/o Iassac.
Isaac,1876.
COLE
XX, d/o Raymond,1957.
DAVIS
Christianna,1837,w/o Geo. W.
Eliza C.,1889,w/o Geo. W.
George W.,1883.

Harriet G.,1916.
DAY
Everett A.,1961.
Mielikki S.,1994,w/o Everett.
DODGE
Olive F.,1941.
DOUGHTY
Eveline F.,1890,w/o Joseph W.
Joseph W.,1908.
DUBOIS
Laura A.,1950.
William E.,1955.
DUNHAM
Emma E.,1944.
ELWELL
A. Lewis,1888.
EMERY
Elijah E.,XXXX,no stone.
Mariam,1876,w/o E.E.
ESTY
Dorothy L.,1948.
Frances Cole,XXXX,w/o Harold.
EVELETH
John,Sept.17,1859.
Rebecca Merrill,1872,w/o John.
FELKER
Jane E.,1865.
FREEMAN
Samuel,1842.
FROST
Edward B.,1851.
GOODRICH
Abbie C.,1918.
HALE
B.F.,1849.
HALL
Alfreda H.,1920,d/o Wm.F.
Caroline,1848.
Emily Jane,XXXX,w/o Webb.
Hannah,1857,w/o James.
James,1879.
Levina,1916,w/o Wm.F.
William,Oct.6,1813,
  s/o Daniel & Lorena Winslow.
William Frederick,July 10,1911,90y.
HANSON
Eleanor,1803-04,d/o Wm.& M.
Fannie E.,1888,w/o T.E.
Hannah,1795-98,d/o Wm. & M.
Hannah,1800-05,d/o Wm. & M.
Isaac,1798-1805,s/o Wm.& M.
John,Jan.17-27,1805,s/o W.&M
Matilda Elder,1818.
Samuel,1737-1813,
  h/o Hannah Jenkins.
William,1786-1805,s/o W & M.

William,Oct.29,1814,
  s/o Samuel & Hannah..
HARDING
Ellen E.,1854,d/o Geo.
George K.,1842,39y.
HARRIS
Rebecca,XXXX.
HASKELL
Margaret M.,1854,w/o Wm.
William,1840.
HAWKES
Lottie D.,1881,w/o Loren.
HEBELER
David H.,1957.
HINDLE
Ellen A.,1988.
HODSDON
Betsey,1845,w/o Ephriam.
Ephraim,1843.
Joshua,1808.
Julia,1846.
HOUGHTON
Henry L.,1846,s/o Henry.
Melinda,1834,w/o Henry.
HUSSEY
S.H.,1894.
Georgia A.,1889,w/o Ulmer P.
Elmer P.,1911.
William f.,1894.
IRWIN
Clark T.,Sr.,1988.
JOHNSON
Ann Tate,1778-1852.
Charles,1865,88y,h/o Ann Tate,
  s/o Jas. & Elizabeth Porterfield.
Charles Pope,1814-1888,
  s/o Charles & Ann.
Elizabeth,1939.
Ella & Lewis,XXXX,ch/o Samuel.
Elmer E.,1959.
Frank H.,1905.
Grace B.,1977,w/o Elmer E.
Harriet Robers Berry,1815-1903,
  w/o Charles P.
Lucenda A.,1892,w/o Samuel.
Samuel Tate,1819-1887,1st w.
  Olive Coombs,2nd w. Lucinda
  Trull,s/o Charles & Ann.
William C.,1966.
JORDAN
Abba,XXXX,w/o Albert.
Albus R.,1868.
Ann,1841,d/o Peter.
Carrie A.,1956,w/o Wm.C.
Ellen,XXXX,no stone.
Hannah,Jan.31,1840,79y,w/o John.
John,Oct.28,1845,71y.

Madeline R.,1907,d/o Wm. C.
Martha B.,1903.
William C.,1944.
KELLOGG
Gardner,1826.
KINGMAN
William,Jr.,1854.
LEONARD
Abraham,XXXX,no stone.
Albert,1880.
Austin,XXXX,no stone.
Eliza A.,1890,w/o Albert.
Elmira,XXXX,no stone.
Elvira A.,19XX.
Georgeanna,XXXX,d/o Austin.
Juliette,1855,d/o Albert.
Leonora,1858,w/o Austin.
Sara A.,1912,d/o Albert.
William A.,1829,s/o Albert.
LIBBY
Mary A.,1848,w/o Phineas.
LITTLE
Abba H.,1881.
Augustus H.,1862,at Gambo,
 s/o Paul & Sarah.
Catherine B.,1904.
Hannah Horton,1888,w/o Moses.
Henry A.,1827,s/o Moses.
Moses,1866,s/o Paul & Sarah N.
Moses H.,1916.
Paul,Apr.1,1740-Feb.11,1818.
Sarah,1797.
Sarah,1817.
Sarah N.,1848,d/o Moses.
William P.F.,1845,s/o Moses.
LORENZEN
Alfred,1959.
Elsie B.,XXXX,w/o Alfred.
LOWELL
Gladys B.,1962.
Josie W.,1959.
Lewis F.,1960.
Shirley J.,1935.
MAINS
Anna,1856.
David,1900.
David,1835.
Dorcas,1840.
Hiram H.,1845.
Major,1828.
MARCH
Alcin,XXXX,s/o Benjamin.
Benjamin,XXXX,no stone.
Jane,XXXX,w/o Benjamin.
Lucy Jane,Oct.12,1841,15y,
 d/o Benjamin & Jane.
Maria,XXXX,no stone.

MASON
Esther,1883,w/o Roger.
Martha J.,1899.
Roger P.,1900.
MAYBERRY
Alfreda,1847,d/o Enoch.
Elizabeth,1849,w/o Enoch.
Enoch,1846.
Mary F.,1859,w/o John O.
McDONALD
Nathan,1842,s/o Charles.
MERRILL
Betsey,Sept.1,1821,26y.
Dorcas,Oct.29,1829,47y.
Elizabeth,Nov.23,1822,20m.,
 d/o Thomas & Dorcus.
Thomas,July 25,1826,63y,h/o Dorcus.
MORRELL
Dorcas,1840,w/o Jacob.
Hannah,1811,w/o Jacob.
Jacob,1836.
Susan,1819,d/o Jacob.
MORSE
George S.,1911.
Martha A.,1921.
PARSONS
According to one S.M.Watson's
articles he stated: "On a long tablet
lying upon stone posts was inscribed
the following, viz:-
Thomas Parsons, proprietor of
Parsonfield, had 10 sons and 9
daughters.
Joseph,1762-1839. His wives,
Lydia Lord,1769-1799.
Abigail Adams,1774-1842.
 1st Children:
Nancy, 1786-1828.
Joseph,1788-1790.
Lydia,1790-XXXX.
Mary,1792-XXXX.
Joseph,1794-1815.
Sarah,1796-XXXX.
Pamelia,1798-1843.
 2nd Children:
Hannah,1801-1839.
Catherine,1803-1831.
Martha P.,1805-1832.
Charles G.,1807-1864.
Maranda A.,1809-XXXX.
Susan,1811-1844.
Susannah,1813-1844.
Joseph A.,1815-XXXX.
Frances U.,1818-XXXX. "
other PARSONS burials:
Alice Jane,1901,w/o Chas. G.
Charles A.,1858.

Clarissa Ann,Dec.5,1850,43y,
  w/o Dr. Charles G.,
  d/o Dr. J. Bradbury.
J. Addison,1886.
Joseph,1762-1839.
Mary E.,1891.
Nancy,1885,w/o J.B.
Sarah,1872.
Thomas B.,Feb.15,1789-Oct.23,1870.
PEASE
Alonzo,Apr.25,1845,13y,
  s/o Dr. Nathaniel & Martha P.
PENNELL
Ann Maria,1870,w/o Albert P.
PLAISTED
Maude I.,1968,w/o Harris.
PORTER
Anna C.,1923.
PRATT
Mary A.,1931,w/o Geo.T.
PURINTON
Anna H.,1833,d/o Chas. E.
Edwin C.,1842,s/o Chas. E.
QUIMBY
Clive V.,1952.
Ethel,1981,w/o Clive V.
RAND
Annie E.,1926,w/o James T.
James T.,1909.
RICE
Hattie S.,XXXX,d/o Sawyer.
ROBINSON
Lillian F.,1977,w/o Robert.
Robert E.,1980.
ROGERS
Ann Lizzie,1853,d/o Wm.
Caroline H.,1843,d/o Wm.
Catherine,1878,w/o Daniel.
Daniel,Apr.28,1853,49y.
Elizabeth,1836,d/o Daniel.
Georgia S.,1853,d/o Wm.
John,Jan.1,1817,80y.
Joshua,1849.
Lorana,Mar.4,1850,77y.
Mary Ann,1836,d/o Daniel.
SAUL
Evelyn J.,1921.
SENTER
Alfonzo,1931.
Ann E.,1849.
Asa,1868.
Caroline,1898.
Catherine,1873,w/o Greenlief.
Charles P.,1917.
Edward A.,1813,s/o Noah J.
Eliza Webb,1920,w/o Alfonzo.
Elizabeth,1892,w/o Geo. A.
Etta W.,1894,w/o Geo. G.
Ganney F.,1879,w/o Asa.
George A.,1981.
George H.,1908.
Greenlief,1890.
Henrietta,1879.
Henry F.,1886.
Isabella,1897.
Laura F.,1898.
Martha T.,1912.
Mellie M.,1895.
Susan A.,1905,w/o Henry F.
William F.,1846,s/o Asa.
SHAW
Ella G.,1967.
SMITH
Alonzo,1862.
Corneila A.,1899,w/o James E.
Frances A.,1914.
Harry A.,1927.
Henry,1781.
James E.,1920.
Jane E.,1864,w/o Henry.
Mary Ellen,1835,d/o Wm.
Melissa,1882.
STEVENS
Leon W.,1978.
Winfred,XXXX,w/o Leon W.
STEWART
Deliverance,1822,w/o John.
TAYLOR
Lewis A.,1850,s/o Lewis.
THOMPSON
Julia A.,1884,d/o Levi.
Lemuel,1900.
Mary J.,1872,w/o Lemuel.
TONER
Mary Edith,1916.
TUERO
Annie S.,XXXX.
TUKEY
Samuel,Jan.13,1852,73y.
USHER
Frances,1883.
VARNEY
3 ch/o Elijah,XXXX.
Abigail,1848,w/o Elijah.
Caroline C.,1901,d/o Ezekiel.
Elijah,XXXX.
Eliza C.,1869.
Ezekiel,1800-1888,
  s/o Daniel & Peace Morrill.
Florence G.,1922,w/o Thomas.
Irma B.,1967,w/o Lewis G.
Leona B.,1880,d/o Thomas.
Lewis G.,1959.
Mary G.,XXXX,w/o Elijah.

Susan S.,1918.
Thomas,1923.
WALTON
James P.,1938.
Jessie M.,1946,w/o James P.
WEBB
Abby J.,1858,d/o Wm. W.
Elmer E.1869,s/o Wm. W.
Florence M.,1888.
Jason,1877.
Lavina Boody,1879,67y,
w/o Jason,1st h. Geo. K. Harding.
Lorrie,XXXX,w/o Albert P.
WHITE
Alice,1812,60y,w/o Peter.
Ann,XXXX,d/o Peter.
Huldah,1865,w/o Peter.
*Mark,Capt.,Aug.29,1832,51y.
*Nathaniel,Jan.31,1853,55y.
*Peter,June 2,1804,56y,Rev.S.
Peter,1849.
*Soloman,June 12,1817,25y.
Soloman,Col.,Feb.3,1841,24y,
s/o Capt.Mark & Mary.
*removed from the White Family
Burial Ground near White's Bridge
in Standish.
WHITEHEAD
Miriam M.,1978,w/o Robert C.
Robert C.,1953.
WIGGIN
Arthur H.,1945.
Cora E.,1895,w/o Arthur H.
Ralph W.,1894.
WINTERS
Clara S.,1896,w/o Jos. H.
Joseph H.,1927.
WISWELL
Catherine J.,June 24,1881,67y,
2nd w/o Rev. Luther.
Ellen K.,1881,d/o Luther.
Luther,Jan.9,1801-1885.
Mary F.,1866,d/o Luther.
Mary F.,1858,d/o Luther.
Sophronia K.,Jan.8,1860,54y,
1st w/o Rev. Luther.

✦ **ARLINGTON CEMETERY** ✦
Route 302, Windham.
Not checked or updated.

ALDEN
Harry S.,1944.
Ila L.,1956.
ALDRICH
Oscar,1978.

ALEXANDER
Athelene H.,1993,w/o Carl.
ALLEN
Alma E.,1966,w/o Milton.
Edward T.,1976.
Milton F.,1972.
Weltha G.,1973,w/o Edward T.
AMATO
Francis J.,1918,h/o Waneta E.
AMES
Carroll E.,1967.
Charlotte Mason,1943,w/o C.E.
Erma W.,1961.
Ida E. Mayo,1918.
William A.,1919.
ANDERSON
Angie,1875,w/o William.
William,1887.
ANZELC
Anton w.,1986.
Susan Helen,1978.
ARNTZ
Harold E.,1922.
Olive B.,1981.
ARSENAULT
Rudolph A.,1988.
ATHERTON
Flora I.,1954,w/o Frank.
ATKINSON
Lawrence H.,1970.
Oland I.,1969.
BABB
John,1846.
John C.,1874.
BADGER
Dale L.,1985.
BAILEY
Maud L. Eklof,1923.
William B.,1909.
BAKER
Abbie A.,1884,w/o E.L.
Cassius P.,1911.
David P.,1860,38y.
Elias Leander,1924.
Elizabeth L.,1909,w/o Loring.
Emily J.,1881,w/o D.P.
Hattie May,1967,d/o E.L.
Loring,1882.
Ralph W.,1857,s/o D.P.
BANGS
Alice G.,1968,w/o Irving C.
BEDIGAN
Ann M.,1979,w/o Harry.
Harry H.,1974.
BELL
Lois,1859,d/o G.G.

BENOIT
Helen G.,1981,w/o Ernest.
BLACK
Mary,1911,w/o Abel.
BLAKE
Mary L.,1990.
BODGE
Deborah D.,1923,w/o Edgar.
Edgar M.,1933.
Gertrude A.,1944.
BOLUS
Richard G.,1972.
Ruth L.,1979.
BOODY
Edmund,1852.
Eliza L.,1901,w/o Henry H.
Ella M.,1880,w/o Frederick C.
Henry H.,1877.
Howard H.,1943.
Louise,1866.
Lydia,1872,w/o Edmund.
Lydia M.,1846,d/o Edmund.
Mary C.,1926.
BOUCHER
Daniel J.,1971.
David C.,1972.
BOUDREAU
Marie C.,1990.
Moise J.,1966.
BOUSQUET
Germaine L.,1971.
BRAGDON
Mary Jane,1987.
Thomas J.,1908.
BRAZIER
Joseph,1885.
Mary S.,1892,w/o Joseph.
BROWN
Dorothy M.,1989.
Gloria E.,1965
Harriet J.,1922,w/o Ira.
Ira,1904.
Irene,1977,w/o Henry.
Locada,1947.
Otis S.,1896.
Vernon,1966.
BRUME
Burleigh E.,1959.
Nettie M.,1988,w/o Burleigh.
BRUNI
Josephine,1975.
BRUNS
Thomas P.,1971.
BUCKLAND
Alfred E.,1974.
BURCHILL
A. Elizabeth,1975.

BURKE
Charlotte M.,1900,
w/o Ernest,Sr.
Ernest J.,Sr.,1992.
BURNHAM
George E.,1993.
BURNS
Admah G.,1961.
Thomas P.,1979.
BUSH
John Ralph,1954.
BUSHLEY
Robert A.,1974.
BUTLER
Donald W.,1982.
Edward L.,Jr.,1993.
Robert Scott,1920.
CALDER
Chester T.,1975.
Gwenivere L.,1979,w/o Chester.
CARLE
Kenneth,1980.
CARLTON
David E.,1971.
CARON
Leonard E.,1983.
CARTLAND
Roscoe,1986.
Margaret E.,1986,w/o Roscoe.
CASEY
Kenneth G.,1979.
CHAFFIN
Orrin,1853.
Cornelia,1935.
Dorohty Green,1894.
Emma A.,1901,w/o Orrin.
Mary G.,1871,w/o Orrin P.
Robert,1880.
CHAISSON
John,1980.
John Lem,1980.
Olive M.,1987.
CHANDLER
Stanley O.,1979.
Virginia C.,1980,w/o Geo.E.
CHAPLIN
Albert N.,1868,s/o Richard.
Charles W.,1932.
Clifford H.,Sr.,1980.
Cora R. Cash,1943,w/o Chas.W.
Dana L.,1944,s/o Cliiford.
Everett M.,1918,s/o Clifford.
George L.,1929.
Ida M.,1862,d/o Richard M.
Jeanette M.,1977,w/o Clifford.
Lucy M.,1910.
Millard E.,1916.

Nettie M.,1977,w/o Clifford.
Richard,1888.
CHASE
Thaddeus S.,1867.
CHRISTIE
Norman L.,1988.
CHUTE
Annie B.,1904,w/o Wilson.
CLARK
David O.,1983.
James Cragin,1979.
Josiah,1855.
Lucy,1852,w/o Josiah.
CLEMENTS
Alma I.,1991,w/o Dana N.
Dana N.,1988.
CLEMONS
Corizan L.,1994.
COBB
Albion E.,1914.
Albion E.,Jr.,1887,s/o Albion.
Flora M.,1949,w/o Albion E.
COLBY
Charles H.,1937.
Jennie O.,1943,w/o Chas. H.
CONNOR
Theodore F.,1959.
COOK
Charles H.,1922.
Ellen C.,1903,w/o Chas.H.
Lessie B.,1889,d/o Chas.H.
CRAM
Abbie M.,1947.
Daniel,1927.
Emeline,1900,w/o Erastus.
Emily,1977.
Erastus,1893.
Gertrude A.,1883.
Harris W.,1979.
Josie B.,1885,w/o Daniel W.
Laura J.,1953,w/o Daniel.
Lizzie Bell,1859,d/o Erastus.
William H.,1949.
CROCKER
Anita,1994.
CROCKETT
Roger H.,1989.
Charlotte I.,1889,w/o J.E.
CROMMIE
Geraldine M.,1979,w/o Edward.
CROTO
Alice I.,1984.
CULLETON
Midlred E.,1940,w/o Wm.N.
CUMMINGS
Muriel Ellen,1991.

CUNNINGHAM
Charlotte B.,1988,w/o Maurice.
Maurice F.,1977.
CURIT
Gertrude E.,1987,w/o Harvey S.
Harland,1993.
Harvey S.,1988.
Lillian F.,1944,w/o Harland.
CUSHING
Jennie E.,1965.
Raymond G.,1958.
CUSHMAN
Barbara A.,1992,w/o Vinal.
Vinal C.,1972.
DAVIS
Albert S.,1927.
Elizabeth A.,1962.
Leory E.,Jr.,1979.
Rosanna G.,1927,w/o Albert S.
DAY
Durwood John,1955.
DEVINE
Walter W.,1960.
DEXTER
Hattie A.,1843.
DIETZ
Walter T.,1973.
DONAHUE
Jerry B.,1981.
Patrick B.,1970,s/o Jerry B.
DOYLE
Harry E.,1929.
Lizzie M.,1895,w/o H.E.
DUNSMORE
Stella A.,1971.
DYER
Philip A.,1959.
EDES
George C.,1948.
EDWARDS
Isaac,1902.
Mary A.,1937,w/o Royal N.
Melvin W.,1934.
Nancy,1897,w/o Isaac.
Royal,1935.
Royal L.,1961.
Wheelock,1962.
EKLOF
Oswald r.,1904.
ELDER
Beverly L.,1989,w/o James S.
Lydia M.,1976.
ELLINWOOD
Delmar C.,1953.
Lillian,1965.
EMERSON
Frank A.,1954.

Lester R.,1993.
Ruth I.,1953,w/o Frank.
EMERY
Rebekah A.,1895.
FECTEAU
George P.,1980,h/o Ida A.
FERGUSON
Mary A.,1964.
FERNALD
Lilla W.,1993,w/o Chas. W.
FITZGERALD
Ralph H.,1949.
FLAHERTY
Virginia,1984.
FLEMING
Hamilton J.,1980.
FLYE
Serena M.,1976,w/o W. J.
Walter J.,1919.
FORTIN
Winona,1916,d/o Leon J.
FOSTER
Lizzie R.,1905,w/o Wm.
William W.,1903.
FREEMAN
Abie A.,1923,w/o Leonard.
Alice M.,1949.
Almon L.,1926.
Beatrice O.,1966.
*Clara,May 10,1863,5y,
   d/o Samuel & Sarah.
G. Warren,1858.
Leonard K.,1967.
Leonard S.,1931.
Lucy L.,1914,w/o Geo. W.
Mary F.,1910,w/o Samuel R.
*Nancy,May 12,1863,13y,
   d/o Samuel & Sarah.
Samuel R.,1912.
*Samuel,Dec.5,1892,80y.
*Sarah,Apr.20,1892,79y,
   w/o Samuel.
*Sargent S.,Nov.1,1861,23y,
   s/o Samuel & Sarah.
* reportedly removed from the
Freeman family graveyard near
White's Bridge, Windham.
GARFIELD
Leo D.,1992,h/o H. Sue.
GATES
Elisha A.,1926.
GAUDET
Colin L.,1947.
GERDES
Joseph,1952.
GERRY
David,1929.

Ella C.,1931,w/o David.
Lulie M.,1958.
GILSON
Nellie N.,1920,w/o F. Emerson.
F. Emerson,1918.
GOODWIN
ALfred E.,1982.
Lillian M.,1969.
GORDON
Adelbert P.,1969,h/o Mary E.
Alice Smith,1983,w/o Alphonso.
Alphonso E.,1972.
Basil B.,1985.
Clara B.,1981.
George A.,1914.
William A.,Sr.,1969.
GRAFFAM
Laurie M.,1976.
Philip,Jr.,1978.
Philip,Sr.,1972.
GRAHAM
Beulah L.,1969.
Wilford D.,Sr.,1969.
GRAVES
Clayton R.,1968.
Isabelle M.,1982,w/o Clayton.
GRAY
Clifton E.,1978.
GREEN
Alfred D.,1972.
Marie C.,1993,w/o Alfred.
GREENE
Mary A.,1879,w/o Rufus.
Rufus,1889.
Thomas W.,1980.
GRIFFIN
Olga A.,1972.
GUILMAN
Shirley J.,11982,w/o Robert.
HAGBERG
Aldana M.,1915,w/o Chas.E.
Charles E.,1898.
HAMMOND
Augusta B.,1928,w/o John A.
John A.,1916.
Vernon H.,1874.
HANSON
Elmer L.,1976.
Lawrence M.,1948.
Mildred L.,1979,w/o Elmer.
HARMON
Abbie M.,1929,w/o Samuel.
Ann,1863,w/o Wm.
Florence G.,1987.
Jane R.,1843,d/o Wm.
John,1852,s/o Samuel.
Jordan,1856.

Lewis R.,1853.
Ray A.,1970.
Sally,1846,w/o Samuel.
Samuel,1912.
William,1869.
HARRIMAN
Abbie W.,1896,w/o Wm.
HARRIS
Margaret,1981,w/o Frank E.
HART
Francis H.,1979.
Margaret W.,1972,w/o Francis.
William,1944.
HARVEY
Alice M.,1971.
HASKELL
Lawrence D.,1955.
Marion C.,1974.,w/o Lawrence.
Robert W.,1974.
HATHAWAY
Richard,1857.
HAWKES
Charles O.,1897.
Lillian S.,1947.
Sarah J.,1918.
HEAL
Roland J.,1959.
HERRICK
Arhtur L.,1972.
Emma E.,1899,d/o Wesley C.
Eugene E.,1939.
Hildred S.,1987.
John W.,1886.,s/o Wesley C.
Martha P.,1916.
Melissa A.,1916,w/o Wesley C.
Wesley C.,1925.
HERSEY
June T.,1987.
Robert H.,1989.
HIGGINS
Arnold R.,1985.
Hazel E.,1988,w/o Arnold R.
HILL
Arthur H.,1972.
Josie M.,1964.
HINKSON
George L.,1989.
HODSDON
John B.,1883.
Nancy Yates,1886,w/o John B.
HOOPER
Beryl P.,1905.
Charles F.,1937.
Mary A.,1888.
HOWARD
Mary J.,1987.

HUNT
Columbus,1833.
Hiram,1895.
Mary Ann,1847,w/o Moses.
Mary W.,1902,w/o Columbus.
Moses,1849.
Samuel L.,1843,s/o C.& M.W.
Sarah A.,1848.
HUTCHINSON
Lawrence H.,1895.
Louise J.,1993,w/o L.H.
IRISH
Agnes Ella ,1989,w/o Albert.
JACQUES
Anna L.,1965.
Fred W.,1947.
JAYNES
Leonard H.,1932.
JEPSON
Ada F.,1982,d/o Edw.W.
Clara E.,1951,w/o Edw.W.
Edward,1951.
James H.,1923.
Mary W.,1912,w/o James H.
JOHNSON
Alan S.,1992,s/o Sanders R.
Elbridge,1924.
Leslie H.,Jr.,1970.
Mattie D.,1994,w/o Sanders R.
Mercy A.,1923,w/o Elbridge.
Sanders R.,1992.
JONES
Allen H.,1964.
Charles F.,1988.
Laura E.,1971.
JORDAN
Lucretia A.,1912.
Albert W.,1937.
Almon,1903.
Augustus,1885.
Betsey S.,1903,w/o Jos.B.
Charles,1878.
Christina P.,1955,w/o Freeman.
Clara,1890,w/o Geo.
Daniel R.,1935.
Fred B.,1946.
Fred B.,1983.
Fred Sumner,1884.
Freeman E.,1952.
George F.,1901.
Helen A.,1956.
Jane,1896.
John B.,1897.
Joseph B.,1896.
Joshua A.,1853.
Laura E.,1945,w/o Albert W.
Malcolm,1960.

Mary A.,1879,w/o Jos.B.
Minnie G.,1867,d/o Jos.B.
Oliver S.,1861,w/o Jos. B.
Perley D.,1962.
Phillip E.,1962.
Phyllis W.,1982,w/o Perley D.
Ralph H.,Sr.,1975.
Vergie N.,1975,w/o Ralph Sr.
William,1880.
JOY
Alice G.,1992.
Ellis B.,1982,w/o Ellis B.
KECK
Lorie Ann,1972.
Stephanie Sue.1972.
KENNARD
H.Dorothy,1977,w/o Philip E.
Albert,1902,81y,
  s/o Wm. & Charity Winslow.
Charity,1857,w/o Wm.
Edna L.,1943,w/o Frank.
Frank E.,1960.
Hulda,1914,w/o Russell.
Jennis S.,1926,w/o Edw.A.
Louise M.,1961.
Russell,1872.
Sarah Manchester,1891,w/o Albert.
William,1861.
KENNIE
James W.,1975.
Edith H.,1984,w/o Jas. W.
Philip J.,1923.
KENNISTON
Wilbert H.,1970.
KILBORN
Goldie,1893,d/o R.C.
KIMBALL
Robert C.,1985,h/o Roberta E.
KINCAID
D. Wilmont,1957.
Sophie M.,1959.
KNIGHT
Charles A.,1852.
Hannah K.,1901.
KEONIG
Constance M.,1983,w/o Frank H.
KOLJONEN
Saimi E.,1980.
LAILER
Annie C.,1990.
LAKIN
Eleanor,1982,w/o Ernest.
Violetta M.,1917.
LAMB
Alexander M.,1867.
Alice M. Rice,1906,w/o Ralph.
Ferdinand M.,1921.

Georgie K.,1903,d/o Ralph.
Harriet E.,1912,w/o Sylvanus.
Hattie,1865,d/o Sylvanus.
Louise C.,1917.
Mary E.,1931.
Nathaniel S.,1847,s/o Alexander.
Sylvanus B.,1917.
LANE
Emily,1943,w.o Wm.H.
John M.,1943.
William H.,1944.
LANGILLE
Irving G.,1986.
LARHETTE
Edwin S.,1977.
LAWRENCE
Donald E.,Jr.,1962,s/o Lawrence.
Harold A.,1987.
Lizzie B.,1926,w/o Warner B.
Mureall B.,1975.
Virginia M.,1978,w/o Wm. H.
LEAVITT
Alice G.,1924,w/o Ed.L.
Edward L.,1947.
LEEMAN
Jean T.,1966,w/o R.H.
LEGERE
Ellen V.,1964.
LEGROW
Clifford C.,1966,s/o Frederick.
Frederick E.,1905.
Lorana E.,1925.
Margaret,1953.
LEIGHTON
Belma E.,1964.
Edwin W.,1948.
Madeline E.,1934.
Minnie B.,1937,w/o Edw.W.
LEWIS
Harold L.,1967.
Ralph G.,1969.
Timothy,1959.
LIBBY
Alfred L.,1884,s/o James E.
Arthur,1865.
Calvin,1882.
Charlotte G.,1981.
Charles D.,1967.
Daniel,1894.
Dorothy E.,1913.
Edwin,1897.
Eliza,1901,w/o Lewis.
Florence A.,1984,w/o Wm.F.
Florence M.,1901.
George A.,1907.
Gertrude E.,1913.
Hazel A.,1916,w/o Perley M.

James F.,1973.
Leila May,1882,d/o James.
Lewis,1893.
Lewis,Jr.,1897.
Lydia Grant,1891,w/o Edwin.
Perley M.,1916.
Prescott D.,1915.
Robert E.,1918.
Ruth M.,1986.
Sherman,1897.
Stanley,1968.
Stephen H.,1863,s/o Lewis.
William Francis,1989.
William H.,1973.
LOGUE
 Evelyn K.,1994,w/o Eugene H.
LOMBARD
 A. Blanche,1962,w/o Leon F.
 Emma R.,1938,w/o John.
 Fred,1920.
 Henry,1895.
 Iva E.,1978,w/o Harry L.
 John M.,1939.
 John W.,1899.
 Leon F.,1945.
 Lucy E.,1843,w/o John W.
 William K.,1850,s/o John.
LONG
 Stella D.,1941.
LORD
 Edith M.,1955,w/o Wilbur.
 Wilbur,1945.
LORING
 Pauline S.,1972.
 Richard W.,1994.
LOWELL
 Henry W.,1972.
 Reginald A.,1952.
MacGARTH
 Robert S.,1989.
MacKENZIE
 Donald G.,1987.
MacLEOD
 Clarence R.,1990.
MACOMBER
 Doris,1991.
MAINES
 Bertha M.,1918,w/o Chas.
 Charles H.,1907.
 Clyde L.,1972.
 Earle C.,1953.
 Edna C.,1980,w/o E.Clifford.
 Henry,1935.
 Margaret,1937.
MAINS
 Adelbert L.,1961.
 Beatrice M.,1980,w/o Clyde.

Benjamin,1908.
Calvin E.,1927.
Clyde L.,1972.
Dana,1886,s/o Josiah.
Dorothy G.,1971.
Earl C.,1953.
Ella,1915.
Ellen H.,1906,w/o John K.
George D.,1890.
Harry L.,1987.
Harry R.,1983.
Henry B.,1919.
Irving L.,1933.
John K.,1900.
Johnnie R.,1889,s/o I.L.
Julia,1913,w/o Calvin E.
Kenneth M.,1981.
Margaret J.,1894,w/o H.B.
Sophronia,1884,w/o Benjamin.
Tracy B.,1920.
MANCHESTER
 2 ch/o Daniel,185X.
 Albert W.,1891.
 Alice A.,1878,w/o A, Moses.
 Almond S.,1953.
 Bertha,1903.
 Dora M.,1898,w/o Frank L.
 Eben C.,1859.
 Emily J.,1869,d/o Nahum.
 Emma G.,1925.
 Ephriam,1876.
 Florence,1966.
 Gershom,1853.
 Huldha,1866.
 Ida F.,1906.
 John,1879.
 Josiah C.,1855.
 Lawrence,1985.
 Lizzie B.,1859.
 Lydia D.,1888,w/o Nahum.
 Marion H.,1958.
 Mary,1871,w/o Ephraim.
 Michael A.,1969.
 Myrtle,1987.
 Naham,1890.
 Nahum,1881.
 Royal B.,1924.
 Ruth K.,1871,w/o Jacob.
 Seward M.,1904.
 Warren S.,1940.
MANN
 Amos,1925.
 Annie M.,1926.
 Charles L.,1944.
 Everett W.,1990.
 Lizzie E.,1948,w/o Willie S.
 Lois G.,1888,w/o Chas.L.

Mary G.,1945.
Oliver A.,1932.
Willie S.,1941.
MARSHALL
Thomas T.,1967.
MASON
Albert,1930.
Clara A.,1937,w/o Albert.
Fred,1912.
MAXFIELD
Ann Mary,1911,w/o Rufus A.
Rufus A.,1890.
MAXWELL
Abia,1865,w/o E.J.
MAYBERRY
Charles L.,1872,s/o Orpha.
Emily A.,1915.
Emma F.,1908.
Eunice M.,1881,w/o Josiah W.
Fern M.,1983.
Ida C.,1936.
Jasper E.,1990.
John G.,1905.
Josiah W.,1886.
Lewis C.,1979.
Marion E.,1977,w/o Jasper E.
Mary E.,1929.
Orpha B.,1945,w/o Sydney A.
Sydney A.,1922.
MAYO
Abbie H.,1882,d/o E.H.
Abbie S.,1890,w/o E.H.
Eben H.,1892.
Flora J.,1932,w/o Geo. C.
Frank R.,1918.
Freddie,1880,s/o Geo. C.
George C.,1919.
Harry B.,1905.
Melissa,1916,w/o Frank R.
Willie,1882,s/o Geo. c.
McCATHERIN
Harry W.,1982.
McDEVITT
James H.,JR.,1976.
James H.,Sr.,1988.
McDONALD
Mary Ann,1852.
Edward H.,1984.
Edwin A.1966.
Eli,1854.
Emma D.,1897,w/o Thomas.
Flora J.,1879.
Hannah P.,1870,w/o Thomas W.
James,1836.
Nellie,1981,w/o Edwin A.
Phoebe,1870,w/o Edw. H.
Rachel,1868,w/o James.

Thomas,1884.
McGOLDRICK
John C.,1977.
John R.,1987.
Rita H.,1974,w/o John R.
McINTOSH
Eben,1844.
Fredinand,1843,s/o Eben.
Isabella,1844,d/o Eben.
Sarah M.,1882,w/o Eben.
McLUCAS
Mary E.,1979.
McPHEE
Lois E.,1973.
McPHERSON
Lillian A.,1942.
MEYER
Violet L.,1992,w/o Herman A.
MILLER
Nellie B.,1933,w/o Wm. H.
William H.,1928.
MILLS
Melvin W.,1970.
MITCHELL
Hattie R.,1943.
Perley E.,1926.
MOFFETT
Florence,1982.
MOODY
Ronald A.,1976.
MOREY
Robert C.,1993.
MORRELL
Alfreda A.,1987.
Calvin,1886.
Everett E.,1988.
Guy C.,1875.
Kenneth M.,1969.
Ralph V.,1874,s/o Calvin.
Tosabelle,1980.
MORRILL
Annie E.,1931,w/o Frank H.
Charles H.,1870.
Charles H.W.,1888.
Frank H.,1946.
Mary A.,1901,w/o Charles H.
Rosabelle Shaw,1980,w/o Alfred.
Rupert E.,1983.
MORRISON
Frederick,1968.
MORSE
Donald,1968.
Ernest,Sr.,1990.
Theodore,1988.
MORTON
Caleb,1896.
Helen D.,1871,d/o Robert.

Nancy,1888,w/o Caleb.
Robert,1869.
MOSES
Clifford L.,1955.
Marcia G.,1956.
MOTLEY
William,1845.
MOYER
Mabel Edes,1980.
MUNDY
Delores L.,1977.
NASON
Albert,1845.
Abraham,1875.
Abraham,1848.
Albion T.,1890.
Alphonzo,1833,s/o Eben.
Annie I.,1994,w/o Walter.
Charlotte J.,1939,w/o Leroy B.
Eliakim W.,1900.
Eliza M.,1893,w/o Samuel L.
Ellen L.,1883,d/o J.S.
James,1881.
Leory B.,1919.
Louisa P.,1849,d/o James.
Lucinda L.,1894,w/o Eliakim.
Lucy P.,1879,w/o James.
Lydia L.,1841,d/o Abraham.
Lydia L.,1833,w/o Abraham.
Rosalia J.,1872.
Samuel L.,1882.
Walter A.,1988.
Wescott,1833,s/o Abraham.
Willis B.,1896,s/o Leroy.
William H.,1889.
NELSON
George K.,1975.
Louise M.,1935,w/o Michael.
Michael K.,1983.
NEWCOMB
Harriet H.,1894,w/o Levi S.
Harry S.,1911.
Levi S.,1914.
Vernold P.,1969.
NICHOLS
Anne G.,1964,1st w/o Ernest.
Ernest G.,1978.
Floyd G.,1963.
Paul A.,1980.
NOONE
John,1975.
NOWAK
Margarete,1964,w/o Karl W.
O'BRION
William E.,1987.
PAGE
Addie W.,1891,w/o Irving C.

Alice G.,1968,w/o Irving C.
Annie E.,1965.
Bertha M.,1897.
Betsey D.,1852,w/o Samuel.
Clyde I.,1932.
Dorothy L.,1910.
Hartley D.,1985.
Inez C.,1948.
Irving C.,1968.
Irving C.,Jr.,1941.
Irving S.,1903.
Joseph M.,1982,s/o Dennis.
Lucy,1840,w/o Samuel.
Margurite,1963,w/o Irving Jr.
Mary,1966,w/o Walter.
Mary R.,1920,w/o William.
Mary W.,1903,w/o Stephen.
Samuel,1848.
Stephen D.,1945,s/o Clyde I.
Stephen D.,1912.
Walter A.,1946.
William G.,1909,s/o Wm.
PALMER
John C.,1922.
PARKER
Carrie M.,1920,w/o Cyrus T.
Cyrus T.,1910.
Edith A.,1890.
Oscar W.,1946.
PAUL
Mervin L.,1907.
PAYNE
Marilyn J.,1981.
PEARSON
Helen M.,1979,w/o John H.
John H.,1976.
PEARY
Clifford C.,1982.
Roberta,1982,w/o C.C.
PEAVEY
Edna T.,1973.
Frederick R.,1959.
PERKINS
Calvin,1919.
Florence R.,1938.
Mildred E.,1992,w/o Ralph,Sr.
Myrtle H.,1982.
Ralph L.,1970.
William A.,1987.
PERRY
Mary B.,1982.
PHILPOT
Arthur W.,1973.
Harry B.,1954.
Mildred A.,1967.
PHINNEY
Carleton E.,1953.

Charles M.,1963.
PICKERING
Irene B.,1981.
PITT
Caroline L.,1962,w/o Harry.
Harry V.,1959.
PLACE
Lizzie,1904,w/o Asa G.
PLUMMER
Alice M.,1936,w/o Fred W.
D. William,1968.
Daniel E.,1942.
Earl P.,1993.
Eudora E.,1941,w/o D.W.
Franklin H.,1982.
Fred P.,1950.
Fred W.,1962.
Harry M.,1986.
Leona S.,1965.
Marguerite,1963,w/o Harry M.
Pearl,1950,w/o Fred.
Robert A.,1947.
Sander L.,1947.
POLAND
John,Jr.,1981.
Phyllis P.,1993,w/o John,Jr.
PORTERFIELD
Elizabeth,1852.
James,1851.
POTTER
Elden W.,1991.
Walter A.,1994.
POWERS
Dorothy M.,1977,w/o Melville.
Melville W.,1978.
PRAY
Kathleen M.,1969,w/o Dean.
PRIDE
Frank O.,1858.
Frank O.,1927.
Frank T.,1928.
Jessie M.,1971,w/o Leon H.
Leon H.,1939.
Mary F.,1883,w/o Frank T.
Oressa B.,1976,w/o Frank O.
Porter,1951.
Sarah A.,1907,w/o Frank O.
PRINCE
Annie M.,1898,d/o Benjamin.
Benjamin N.,1864.
Esther A.,1911.
Watson N.,1915.
PROCTOR
Abbie W.,1902.
Betsey,1878,w/o Ebenezer.
Beulah M.,1956,w/o Clarence.
Clarence W.,1937.

Daniel,1902.
Don P.,1965.
Ebenezer R.,1827.
Frank L.,1910.
Fred W.,1894.
George A.,1886.
Haslam,1894.
Marion B.,1969.
Pateince E.,1894,w/o Haslam.
Rebecca A.1928,w/o Fred W.
Viola S.,1901,w/o Geo. A.
PULKKINEN
Lahya J.,1983.
RACKLEY
Alvah H.,1993.
RAND
Lester,1898.
Susan G.,1915,w/o Lester.
REED
Donald F.,1980.
Pearl H.,1993,w/o Donald F.
REYNOLDS
Manley D.,1974.
Marcia,1985.
Marie S.,1983.
RHOADES
Charles W.,1983.
RICE
Adlinda G.,1874,w/o Ashley F.
Louine V.,1967,w/o Chester.
RICHARDS
Alfred J.,1992.
Lydia M.,1856,d/o Samuel.
Mary A.,1898,w/o Samuel.
Samuel,1885.
RICHARDSON
Roland,1977,h/o Helen M.
RIDLON
Earland S.,1967.
ROBERTSON
Leslie J.,1968.
Benjamin B.,1967.
Margaret H.,1972.
Maude E.,1979.
RODGERS
Mary R.,1884.
ROGERS
Abiah F.,1880,w/o John.
Charles,1892.
Charles B.,1862.
Clara M.,1903,w/o Cyrus L.
Cyrus L.,1908.
Dora Shaw,1921,w/o Frank.
Elizabeth M.,1892.
Elva L.,1980.
Frank O.,1938.
Jennie G.,1994,w/o Maurice L.

John R.,1822.
L. Ella,1912.
Margaret T.,1965.
Mary L.,1890,w/o Wm.H.
Maynard G.,Sr.,1967.
Orin N.,1855.
Rebecca,1910,w/o Charles.
Regina M.,1951.
Reginald,1951.
Sally Ann,1986,w/o Arkie.
Sarah E.,1883,w/o Wm.
William,1865.
William H.,1926.
ROLFE
Charles L.,1993.
ROMER
Dorothy L.,1989.
ROTH
E.Corrine,1952,w/o Geo.
SANBORN
Louise A.,1987.
SAWYER
Christopher E.,1987.
Kimberly J.,1980,d/o Donald.
SCANDALIOS
George M.,1968.
SCHELLINGER
Lewis,1983.
SEELEY
Katie H.,1919,w/o Frank J.
SENTER
3 ch/o George G.,188X.
Etta W.,1894,w/o Geo. G.
George G.,1887.
SHAW
Almond,1863.
Ann E.,1917,w/o Winthrop M.
Benjamin F.,1912,w/o Edmond.
Bethiah,1897,w/o Edmond.
Catherine H.,1897,w/o Wm.
Charles G.,1979.
Clara W.,1919.
Edmund,1875.
Etta Louise,1983.
Eunice P.,1908,w/o Samuel Y.
Ida E.,1971,w/o Milton E.
John Y.,1864.
Lewis,1889.
Lewis E.,1947.
Merle B.,1977.
Milton E.,1972.
Pearlice M.,1969,w/o Lewis E.
Roxanna,1889,w/o Enoch.
Russell S.,1981.
Samuel Y.,1863.
Susie,1930.
Willie I.,1865,s/o W.& C.H.

Winthrop M.,1925.
William,1890.
SHERWOOD
LLoyd B.,1970.
SIMMONS
Charles A.,1930.
M. Gertrude,1938.
SINCLAIR
Barbara L.,1981,w/o Blaisdell.
Blaisdell E.,1981.
SKILLIN
Cephas W.,1909.
Clara E.,1921,w/o Cephas.
Edward W.,1950.
Isabelle C.,1950.
John F.,1904.
Lester B.,1961.
Rose,1936,w/o Walter.
SKILLINGS
Kenneth C.,1983.
SKINNER
Araminta A.,1923.
SMALL
Phyllis,1985.
Walter H.,Sr.,1980.
SMITH
Abby H.,1925,w/o John F.
Alice M.,1905.
Andrew F.,1901.
Arthur R.,1914,s/o Chas.H.
Charles H.,1897.
Clarence F.,1982.
Cornelia M.,1931.
Eunice L.,1893.
Henry B.,1899.
Irene F.,1914.
John F.,1914.
Kathryn M.,1968.
Lizzie J.,1933.
Lydia C.,1952.
Marion,1951.
Mayetta,1933.
R. Russell,1918,s/o Ralph.
Robert A.,1969.
Rosanna,1908,w/o Henry B.
Roy E.,1971.
SNOW
Stephen A.,1974,s/o Jeffrey.
SOMES
Betsey,1872,w/o John G.
John G.,1850.
SPIERS
Abbie E.,1895,w/o John.
Ida M.,1939,w/o John S.
John S.,1909.
SPOFFORD
Augustus N.,1987.

SPOSEDO
Clara,1929,w/o Elihue.
Elihue,1907.
Eunice,1886,w/o Wm.
Frank P.,1917.
Lizzie A.,1923.
William G.,1933.
William,1908.
SPRAGUE
Fulton,1951.
STANDLEY
Ethel M.,1979,w/o Frederick.
Frederick W.,1965.
Frances S.,1873.
Lucinda P.,1908.
William W.,1900.
STANTON
Eunice B.,1988,w/o Richard.
Richard I.,1952.
STAPLES
George W.,1979.
STEIN
Lena L.,1918.
Letitia L.,1988.
3 ch/o Daniel,185X.
STEVENS
3 ch/o Daniel & Ann:
Alfred M.,Oct.5,1850,14m.
Caroline D.,Apr.17,1850,2y,
George W.,Dec.19,1844,3y,
STROUT
Cynthia,1886.
Edwin W.,1913.
Emma,1942.
Jerusha,1896,w/o Samuel.
Joseph H.,1975.
Samuel D.,1911.
William W.,1875.
STUART
Clinton,1977.
SWAN
Annie,1888.
Lydia A.,1907,w/o Orren.
May,1894.
Orren,1899.
TABER
George W.,1966.
TAIT
Earl J.,1981.
Jessica Ann,1977,d/o Terry.
TALFER
Gabrielle,1991.
TANDBERG
Mildred L.,1952.
Trygve,1963.
TAYLOR
Eliza A.,1894,w/o James.
Fannie L.,1929.
James,1889.
John H.,1978.
Katie I.,1945,w/o Lester E.
Lester E.,1931.
Nettie,1884,d/o James.
Ralph G.,1942.
TEEL
Clarence J.,1945.
THIBIDEAU
George,1957.
THOMAS
Clara E.,1987,w/o Vernley R.
Leslie A.,1988.
Vernley R.,1988.
Vernley Ray.,1970.
THOMPSON
Eltron H.,1961.
Florence S.,1970,
Jennie M.,1930,w/o Joseph.
Joseph H.,1927.
Leslie A.,1970.
Leslie,Jr.,1988.
TIBBETTS
Leon H.,1952.
Muriel E.,1969.
TOBIE
Hannah E.,1840.
Julia E.,1855.
Levi,1886.
Lucretia A.,1919.
Lydia G.,1887,w/o Levi.
TRUE
Frank G.,1964.
Michael H.,1956,s/o Harry G.
Vivian P.,1956.
TRUMBALL
George W.,1882.
TURKINGTON
Brenda H.,1994,w/o Bruce S.
Bruce,1974.
Florence,1974.
Samuel,1956.
TURNER
Cecil Ray.1985.
Clarence O.,1902,s/o R.N.
Doris Lord,1983.
UPTON
David S.,1972.
VARNEY
Effie E.,1883,w/o Albert W.
Frank A.,1883.
Lewis B.,1970.
Lizzie M.,1972.
VENTRESCA
Angelo J.,1982.

VINCENT
Dorothy J.,1970,w/o Merle.
VOSMUS
Royal J.,1993.
WAKEFIELD
Jason,1892.
Jason,1864.
Marie L.,1978,w/o Ray A.
Martha,1922.
Ray A.,1967.
Sarah,1896,w/o Jason.
WALSH
Leslie C.,1994,s/o Walter.
WEBB
David,1976.
WENTWORTH
Anna M.,1901,w/o Benjamin F.
Antoinette M.,1838.
Benjamin F.,1894.
Frances M.,1901.
Royal W.,1890.
William N.,1955.
WESCOTT
Bernice C.,1993,w/o Geo.S.
Bessie F.,1980,w/o Raymond E.
Ella H.,1907,w/o L.E.
WHITNEY
Almon J.,1956.
Frank B.,1950.
Philip R.,1954.
WIDGER
Kimberly J.,1973.
WILBUR
Ronald L.,1978.
WILEY
Eunice Yates,1993,w/o Francis N.
WILLIAMS
Florence L.,1972.
WINSHIP
George C.,1935.
Harry H.,Sr.,1956.
Lottie L.,1992,w/o Harry H.
WINSLOW
Arthur R.,1979.
Dora,1983.
Gladys,1930.
Rubia P.,1994,w/o Arthur A.
WOLSTENHULME
John,Sr.,1977.
Lillioan,1973,w/o John,Jr.
WOODBURY
Frank O.,1963.
WORTH
Earl M.,1974.
WORTHING
Albion M.,1880.

WRIGHT
3 ch/o Gregory H.
Gregory,1976.
YATES
Francis N.,1972.
John E.,1977.
Pearl I.1964,w/o John E.
YORK
Beatrice A.,1949,w/o Dana C.
Dana C.,1945.
YOUNG
George G.,1879.
Wayne,1948.

✣ STEVENS FARM BURIAL GROUND ✣

Montgomery Road, Windham. According to the information given to me this cemetery has been totally destroyed over the years, the gravestones were reportedly stolen. The following are known to be interred here:

NEWCOMB
Hannah,Oct.28,1872,83y.
STEVENS
Anne Millions,XXXX,w/o Richard.
David,1839,43y,s/o Jonathan &
 Martha Millions.
Eliza,Sept.1849,d/o Jon. & T.
Freddie,May 19,1863,3m,
 s/o Isaac & Mary B. Hawkes.
Hannah,Oct.1849,71y,
 died insane,d/o Jon. & Mehitable.
John,Mar.6,1841,48y,s/o Rich. & Anne.
Jonathan,Oct.27,1849.
Jonathan,Sr.,alive in 1807,
 settled this farm & chose spot for
 this family burial place.
Martha Millions,Oct.1849,86y,
 2nd w/o Jonathan,Sr.
Mehitable Macintire, Nov.29,
 1780,1st w/o Jonathan Sr.
Richard,XXXX,s/o John,Jr.& Hannah
 Wescott.
Sarah,Sept.1849,d/o Jon. & T.
Thankful Newcomb,Feb.20,1869,
 74y,w/o Jonathan.
THURLOW
Anna Stevens,spring 1853,70y,
 wid/o Isaac.
Isaac,XXXX.
WATERHOUSE
Eliza Stevens,Sept.23,1824,19y,
 w/o Samuel.
William P.,Sept.23,1825,11m,
 s/o Samuel & Eliza.

✧ GEORGE STREET ✧
George Street, Portland.
Records from Evergreen Cemetery.

BEELS/BEALS
Mary, July 3,1855,85y,w/o Joseph.
BERRY
Josiah,Feb.12,1815,79y,h/o Thankful.
Thankful, Nov.28,1821,78y.
HIGGINS
Elisha,Mar.9,1836,86y.
Mary, Sept.10,1834,80y,w/o Elisha.
SAWYER
Isaac,Oct.29,1818,68y.
STEVENS
Charlotte,Aug.9,1785-Dec.7,1860,
  wid/o Benj.
Benjamin, Nov.25,1850,72y.
Josiah,May 7,1800,unmarked grave.
Mercy, Oct.23,1809,31y,w/o Joseph
Susan,Jan.21,1847,66y.
Susanna,Aug.1,1830,87y,
  wid/o Joshua.
??- SR Percy PCY SR 1779.
  LCY SR 1782.

✧ WILSON MONUMENT ✧
Allen Avenue between Ray Street
and Cobb Road, Portland.

WILSON
Anna Huston, XXXX, w/o Nathan.
Gowen,Feb.25,1825,40y.
John March,Dec.30,1798-
  Sept.18,1884.
Nathaniel,Major,Oct.28,1819,78y
Polly, Aug.1,1811,10y,
  d/o Nathaniel & Anna.
Sarah,Mar.6,1821,39y,w/o Gowen.

✧ SUMMIT STREET ✧
Summit St., off Allen Ave. Ext.,
Portland. 1 monument, 2 grave-
markers, 2 small stones.

HAMBLIN
G.D., no dates.
M.M., no dates.
Royal H., no dates.
WALLACE
Sidie A., no dates.

"This is the debt to justice due,
That we have paid & so must you."

✧ STROUDWATER BURYING GROUND ✧
1318 Westbrook St., Portland.
Completed stone by stone.
The burying ground was established in 1727 and the earliest stone is or was dated 1738. "The cemetery lot comprises about an acre of land, extending from the road connecting the village of Stroudwater with the village of Saccarappa, back westerly to the Stroudwater river. The earliest reference made to the place in manuscript record thus far found is in the year 1744, in a mortgage deed, made by the Smalls who occupied the farm next northerly, and now known by the name of Quinby farm, in favor of General Samuel Waldo. A part of the lot is ill adapted to the use for which it was given to the parish in 1787 by one of the heirs of the Waldos, and like other places of its character many interred there, particularly the early settlers of the place, have no distinguishing marks."
---Leonard B.Chapman,
Aug.24,1895, The Deering News.

ADAMS
James,Feb.1,1798,20y,
  s/o Capt. Ebenezer & Lydia.
BARKER
Abigail Gorham,June 29,1790,
  40y, 1st w/o Jeremiah.
Eunice,Nov.10,1799,29y,
  3rd w/o Jeremiah.
Jeremiah,Dr., Mar.31,1752,
  in Barnstable died in Gorham,
  Oct.4,1835. Had 5 wives, a R.S.
Susanna Garrett,June 3,1794,
  25y,2nd w/o Jeremiah.
BARTLETT
Caleb,Aug.13,1820,63y.
Caleb, Sept.1823,45y, St.Domingo,
  s/o Charles &Eleanor.
Charles R.,Nov.7,1839,1y,
  s/o Chas. & Eleanor E.
Charles,July 11,1849,56y,
  War of 1812.
Charles,May 20,1843,9m,
  s/o Chas.. & Eleanor E.
Charles,Oct.10,1845,1y,s/o Wm.& S.
Eleanor E.,Dec.7,1846,38y,w/o Chas
Elizabeth,Apr.23,1840,81y, w/o Caleb.
Elizabeth,Mar.26,1836,22y,d/o R.& M

Flavel,June 12,1849,20d,
  s/o Wm. & Susan.
Frank M. Aug.14,1846,7m,s/o C.& E.
George,Dec.1826,34y, on passage
  to Cuba, s/o Caleb & Elizabeth.
Holmes,Nov.9,1854,56y.
Isaac,Sept.1799,19y, St.Domingo,
  s/o C.& E.E.
Isaac,1812,s/o Robert & Mary.
Mary Small,Oct.28,1812,35y.
Robert,Jan.19,1827,44y,h/o Mary S.
Susan,June 26,1849,38y,w/o Wm.
BATES
Ella M.,XXXX.
BOND
Dennis,Oct.26,1834,22y,
  New Orleans, s/o E. & S.
Elijah,Dec.31,1835,67y.
Elijah, Jr.,Feb.2,1851,43y, s/o E. & S.
Jonas,Dec.17,1857,52y,s/o E. & S.
Leonard,Apr.22,1859,50y,s/o E.&S.
Sarah,June 25,1846,w/o Elijah.
Sarah,Dec.30,1881,78y.
BREWER
Dexter,Capt.,Sept.6,1850,55y.
Jane Frost,June 30,1833,37y.
BROAD
Almira,Mar.10,1797-Sept.10,1867,
  d/o Thaddeus.
Almira Ann (Auntie),1820-1903,
  d/o Amos & Abigial.
Edward B.,June 7,1872,52y,
  s/o Epharim & Elizabeth.
Elizabeth Greene,May 20,1865,
  78y, w/o Ephraim.
Ephraim,Mar.23,1774-Sept.1,1856,
  s/o Thaddeus, War of 1812.
Ephraim,Aug.20,1817-XXXX,
  h/o Mary Skillin.
Eunice,Dec.28,1775-Sept.10,1856,
  d/o Thaddeus.
George B.,Feb.22,1859,47y.
Harriot,Apr.21,1804,23y,
  d/o Ephraim & Abigail.
Joseph,Mar.11,1782-Dec.1,1854,72y,
  s/o Thaddeus,War of 1812
Lucy Skillings,Jan.9,1837,84y,
  wid/o Thaddeus
Silas,Apr.8,1795-Mar.19,1873,
  s/o Thaddeus,War of 1812.
Thaddeus,Dec.12,1744-June 9,1824.
Thaddeus,Jr.,Dec.3,1777-
  May 28,1807.
Thomas,Aug.15,1791-Oct.17,1865,
  s/o Thaddeus,War of 1812.
William,Mar.3,1772-Aug.6,1849,
  77y,War of 1812.

William F.,Sept.3,1859,35y.
BROWNE
Lydia Howard,Oct.13,1805,
  in Falmouth,49y,w/o Thomas.
Thomas T.,Rev., May 17,1734-
  Oct.17,1797,s/o Rev.John.
BRUNS
Marie,1825-1899, w/o Jef S.
CHAMBERLAIN
Abigail,Feb.21,1816,36y,w/o Jos.
Joseph,Oct.16,1810-Sept.6,1811,
  s/o Jos. & Abigail.
Martha,June 11,1809-May 26,1811,
  d/o Joseph & Abigail.
CHAPMAN
Alfred,June 6,1894,54y.
Lydia Starbird,b.Mar.6,1768-
  XXXX,w/o Shadrach.
Mary,1838,d/o S.& L.S.
Shadrach,b.Mar.6,1764.-XXXX.
CHESLEY
Albert,Aug.7,1837,33y.
Almira Dyer,Jan.15,1854,57y,
  2nd w/o Charles.
Alpheus,Mar.8,1851,22y,
  s/o Charles & Almira.
Catherine,Oct.16,1825,20y,
  1st w/o Charles.
Charles, Apr.28,1874,76y.
Edward Oct.4,1838,22y.
Edwin O.,Sept.21,1857,24y,
  s/o Charles & Almira.
Ellen B.,May 4,1844,34y.
Mary Ann Broad,May 9,1867,59y,
  3rd w/o Charles,d/o Ephraim.
Octavia D.,Sept.9,1867,24y,d/o C.& A.
CLARK
Jane F.,Feb.4,1819,6y,
  d/o Peter T. & Eleanor.
COOMBS
Christine H.,1899-1982.
Frank M.,1895-1940.
COPPS
Abigail,July 3,1852,60y,w/o Joseph.
CUMMINGS
  Children of Francis J. & Mary Jane:
Andrew Jackson,July 30,1833,2y.
Charles Maxfield,Apr.28,1836,2y
Charles Winslow,Apr.25,1841,8m
Frances Caroline,Jan.2,1836,10m
Frances Caroline,June19,1833,4y
George Andrew,May 14,1830,1m
Marietta Frances,Jan.25,1854,15y.
Martha Ella,July 6,1846,5m.
Mary Eliza Shaw,Jan.5,1848,5y.
Francis J.& Mary Jane also buried
  here, in umarked graves.

DALTON
Huldah,1814,2nd w/o Samuel &
3 children who died previously.
Mary B.,1809,1st w/o Samuel.
Samuel,Apr.27,1821,50y.
DILL
Cyprus L.,1828-1900.
DOLE
Anne Partridge,Dec.21,1839-
July 9,1887, d/o Dan. & Mary H.
Catherine,Sept.15,1898,87y.
Daniel,Capt.,Mar.30,1803,86y.
Daniel,Jr.,1757-Feb.23,1815.
Daniel,1813-1900,h/o Mary.
Helen M.,Aug.29,1849,8y,
d/o Daniel & Mary.
Helen R.,Sept.9,1850-July 4,1888,
d/o Daniel & Mary.
Katherine,Jan.10,1861,76y,
1st w/o Daniel (d.1815).
Louisa F.,1848-1924,d/o D.&M.H.
Mary H.,1821-1900.
Moses,May 20,1766-Sept.4,1788,
s/o Capt. Daniel & Sarah.
Sarah Pearson,July 11,1784,61y,
w/o Daniel.
DURGIN
Nora,Jan.18,1870-Nov.15,1950.
EPES
Abigail Frost,Aug.26,1744-
Mar.10,1826,wid/o Daniel,d/o Chas.
FARWELL
Hazel M. Vail,1900-1928,w/o Warren.
Norman,1927-1989.
Warren E.,1893-1988.
FICKETT
Abbie A. Chaplin,1847-1920,
w/o Franklin.
Asa,Feb.14,1769-Sept.6,1835.
Charles, 1845-1919.
Cora,1866-1949,w/o Geo.E.
Dorcas Plummer,Dec.11,1819,55y,
1st w/o Asa.
Eliza Edwards,Feb.22,1866,79y,
2nd w/o Asa.
Elizabeth Larraby,Jan.20,1901,
91y,w/o Nahum.
Franklin, Aug.12,1884,41y.
George E.,1868-1901.
Jeanette S.,June 17,1809-
Apr.13,1890, d/o Asa & Dorcas.
Mary E.,1850-1912,w/o Chas.
Nahum,June 17,1809-
Nov.25,1866,s/o Asa & Dorcus.
FITZGERALD
Thomas,Capt.,Sept.11,1803,53y.

FOGG
Clifford,1890-1962.
Grace E. Vail,1898-1960,w/o Cliff.
Netta Louise,1928-1928.
FOYE
William,July 31,1849,62y.
William E.,Sept.17,1848,16y,
s/o Wm. & S.F.
FRASTER
Elizabeth,Apr.2,1843,29y.
Mary M.,May 20,1825,7m,
both d/o Seth & Hannah.
FROST
Andrew Pepperell,Oct.1752-
May 24,1805.
Andrew P.,Dec.14,1845,54y.
Charles,Nov.5,1746-Jan.8,1747,
s/o Chas. & Joanna.
Charles,Aug.27,1710-Jan.4,1756.
Eleanor Slemons,Oct.6,1795,
37y,w/o Andrew P.,d/o Wm.
Frederick H.,1902-1973.
Helen C.,1903-1989,w/o Fred.
Jane,Aug.20,1750-June 23,1792,
42y,d/o Chas.
Joanna,Sept.23,1739-Nov.6,1739,
6w,d/o Chas.& Joanna
Joanna Jackson,Jan.7,1796,80y,
wid/o Charles{1756}.
William,Aug.20,1748-Jan.23,1791,
s/o Charles.
William,Aug.5,1816,27y.
GOODWIN
Elmer Sidney,Oct.29,1873,21y,
s/o Edw. & Cassandra.
George S.,Aug.7,1851,13m,
s/o Edw. & Cassandra.
Lucy E.,Mar.21,1855,5m,
d/o Edward & Cassandra.
Lucy Maria,Nov.28,18XX.
Mary M.,Aug.5,18XX,22m.
GRAY
Eliza Waldron,1843-1925.
HAMILTON
Silas,Capt.,June 2,1821,46y.
HANCOCK
Charles E.,May 6,1844,4y,
s/o John & Hannah.
HANSCOME
Charlotte A.,1842-1897,
bu. in Gorham, w/o Humphry.
HANSON
Olive Stevens, XXXX.
HASKELL
Henry Noyes,1847-1909.
Leonora C. Stinson & infant son,
1870, w/o Henry.

HAWES
Andrew,1836-1928.
Annie M.Libby,1851-1920,w/o A.
4 children of Martin & Mary Ann:
  Edmund,June 17,1842,3y,
  Henrietta, Sept.16,1843,3y,
  Horatio,Feb.20,1850,9y,drowned.
  Moses Q.,June 29,1859,16y,
    s/o Martin & Mary Ann.
Martin,July 13,1855,47y.
Mary Ann Quinby,1812-Dec.13,1883,
  w/o Martin.
HERRICK
Phebe,Nov.20,1838,74y.
HILL
Catherine Slemons,1860-1945.
HINDS
Sophinetta,June 14,1853,28y,
  1st w/o Daniel,d/o Samuel Morton.
Warren,Oct.28,1848,11m,
  s/o Daniel & Sophinett.
HOLMES
Erastus,Oct.17,1808,2y,
Israel,Aug.15,1805,1y,
  both s/o William & Lydia.
HORN
Susan,Sept.6,1862,73y.
HOWARD
Stephen,1835-1898.
HUNT
no other information.
HUTCHINS
Fred R.,1871-1956.
Lillian,1875-1935,w/o Fred R.
JACKSON
Abigail,1714-1813,w/o Thomas {1819}.
Ella S. Cummings,1857-1933,
  w/o Thomas W.
Louisa Jordan,1826-1913,
  w/o Thomas {1892}.
Louise C.,1891-1893.
Mary,1782-1842,w/o Thomas {1854}.
Thomas,1736-1819.
Thomas,1783-1854.
Thomas,1824-1892.
Thomas W.,1856-1914.
Warren,1894-1907.
JACOBS
Elias,June 18,1858,33y.
Elias M.,Aug.5,1850,14m,
  s/o Elias & Ellen.
Ellen Fickett,July 30,1875,
  53y, w/o Elias.
George B.,1854-1927.
George F.,Feb.24,1877-Aug.7,1878,
  s/o Geo.B. & M.L.
Mary L.Libby,1856-1932,w/o G.B.

Raymond P.,July 24,1887-
June 15,1901,s/o Geo. & Mary.
JOHNSON
Abby J.,Sept.11,1843,9m,
  d/o Isaac & Abby.
Abigail H.,Mar.15,1852,42y,
  w/o Isaac.
Alexander,May 13,1840,63y,
  s/o John & Eleanor.
Dorcus,Dec.8,1822-Apr.10,1906.
Eleanor Lamb,Nov.15,1740-
  May 20,1820, w/o John.
George,Nov.7,1820-Jan.3,1897.
Isaac,Jan.13,1875,73y.
John,May 14,1737-May 28,1833.
John H.,1864-1942.
John Lamb,May 1784-May 25,1844.
Miriam, Apr.7,1853,86y,w/o Randall.
Nellie R.,1865-1947,w/o J.H.
Randall,May 26,1848,81y.
Sarah, June 3,1876,83y,w/o Alexander
William,May 18,1796,25y,
  s/o John & Eleanor.
JONES
Elizabeth,May 23,1852,60y.
George S.,Capt.,May 26,1848,49y
John,Aug.22,1837,80y.
Lucy,Oct.23,1827,60y,w/o John.
JORDAN
Susan,Aug.28,1840,50y,w/o John.
KENNIE
Ronald D.,Dec.13,1947-Nov.22,1967.
KLINGER
Catherine,1881-1954.
LEE
Fred A.,1859-1917.
LEWIS
Archelaus,Maj.,Jan.2,1834,81y,
  War of 1812.
Charles,Nov.15,1825,37y,
  s/o Archelaus & Elizabeth.
Elizabeth Browne,Sept.13,1804,37y,
  w/o 2nd Archelaus,d/o Parson Browne.
Frances Angier McClink & infant,
  Nov.5,1815,41y,w/o Archelaus.
John Cotton,Sept.15,1800,1y,s/o A.& E
Rebeckah,Feb.18,1753-Dec.17,1788,
  36y,1st w/o Archelaus.
Thomas Brown, Nov.1804,10m,
  s/o Archelaus & Elizabeth.
Thomas,Rev.,Oct.18,1797,64y.
Thomas,Sept.1,1797,4y,
  s/o Archelaus & Elizabeth.
LIBBY
Almon,Rev.,Oct.10,1816-Nov.1,1895.
Almon Cyrus,Dec.24,1848-
  Feb.27,1938.

Charles E.,1844-1904.
Charles S.,Nov.2,1854-May 12,1896.
Ella Slemons,1851-1930,w/o Chas. E.
Hannah Hall,Jan.20,1819-
  Feb.23,1895,w/o Almon.
Harriet Foss,1884-1969,
  w/o Lucien Percy.
Isaac,Feb.15,1818-May 12,1885.
Lucien Percy,1877-1951.
Mahala,Dec.11,1831-May 10,1898,
  w/o Isaac.
Mary Tate,Mar.10,1838,63y, w/o Wm.
Sylvia,Aug.19,1916-Oct.4,1918,
  d/o Lucien P. & Harriet F.
LOBDELL
Almon,Rev.,Oct.10,1816-Nov.1,1895.
Charlotte,Feb.27,1840,47y,
  w/o Isaac {1832}.
Hannah H. Hall,Jan.20,1819-
  Feb.23,1895,w/o Almon.
Isaac,Jan.26,1802,87y.
Isaac,Capt.,Jr.June 18,1806,51y.
Isaac,Jr.,July 31,1832,44y.
twins: Edward,Oct.27-30,1799
  & Charles,Oct.27,1799-
  Aug.9,1801,s/o Isaac & Mary.
MASON
Daniel,Oct.9,1817,60y.
Edwin,Nov.29,1834-Nov.14,1864.
Eunice N.Winship,Mar.19,1868,
  51y, w/o Samuel.
Elizabeth H.,Feb.17,1838-
  May 15,1878.
Nancy,Dec.31,1814,20y.
Samuel,Feb.4,1837,54y.
Samuel,Oct.3,1818-June 2,1871,
  h/o Eunice.
MAXFIELD
Adelaide B.,Oct.2,1862,18y,
  d/o Charles & Julia.
Andrew Jackson,July 30,1833,2y.
Charles,Feb.23,1804-Mar.7,1897.
Charles,Apr.28,1836,2d.
Charles,Sept.7,1857, 19y,
  s/o Charles & Julia.
Clifford D.,1885-1935.
Daniel,Feb.27,1812,42y.
Edna Cummings,Feb.13,1893-
  Aug.7,1969.
Emily F.M.,Nov.11,1842-
  Jan.3,1937,d/o Charles & J.A.
Frances Caroline,Jan.2,18XX,9m.
Frances Caroline,June 19,1833,4y.
George Andrew,May 14,1830,1m.
Harold Foster,Oct.21,1892-
  Oct.26,1948.
Horatio,1851-1949.

Isabella,Apr.25,1852,93y,w/o William.
Julia Ann,Aug.13,1808-Oct.12,1874,
  w/o Charles.
Julia M.,May 2,1831-Feb.14,1914,
  d/o Chas.&Julia.
Lansia,XXXX, inf/o Chas.&J.A.
Louisa S.,Sept.19,1848-
  June 16,1892, d/o Chas.& J.A.
Lydia Bailey,Sept.24,1861,85y,
  wid/o Daniel.
Marion L.,1888-1917,
  d/o Horatio & Mary Alice Dole.
Mary Alice Dole,1853-1922,
  w/o Horatio.
T.Maude Bartley,1891-1969
William, May 1,1840,80y.
McMAHON
William,Dec.31,1803,66y.
MEANS
infant granddaughters of James,XXXX.
James,Oct.15,1832,79y, R.S.
Mary,Nov.27,1831,77y.
Mary,Mar.18,1788-Mar.16,1837,48y.
MERRILL
Eunice D. Quinby,Apr.2,1880,
  55y, w/o John, d/o Moses & Jane.
MILLIKEN
John M.,Jr.,Oct.9,1875,86y,h/o Susan.
Susan Fickett,Nov.14,1858,66y.
MITCHELL
Ann,Apr.30,1840,65y,w/o Peleg.
Anna R.,Aug.22,1864,42y,
  w/o Dr. Augustus.
Augustus,July 13,1807,1y,
  s/o Peleg & Ann.
Lucius,Sept.6,1805,1y,s/o P.&A.
Peleg,Apr.2,1859,83y,War of 1812.
Rosa Apr.7,1855,12y,
  d/o Dr.Augustus & Anna R.
Victor Eugene,Jan.2,1859,13y,
  s/o A. & A.R.
MOON
Metta L.,May 26,1926-May 8,1968.
MORTON
Albert,1847-1914.
Anna Maria Chapman,1818-1899,
  w/o George W.
George W.,1813-1887.
Susan Ellen McDonald,1894-1912,
  w/o Albert.
NAYLOR
Marion Jackson,1895-1922,
  w/o William R.
Marjorie-Ella, XXXX.
OSGOOD
Caroline A.,June 27,1863,44y,
  w/o Elbridge A.

Clemence C.,Apr.13,1849,3y,
 d/o Elbridge G. & Caroline A.
George R.,Oct.18,1844,7m,
 s/o E.G.& C.A.
PARKER
Abba C.,Dec.6,1859,12y,d/o J.&A.
Abigail,Nov.15,1867,62y,w/o Jas.
Herbert Whitney,Nov.5,1896-
 Nov.23,1897.
Horace,1826-1890.
James,1801-1885.
Joseph C.,1827-1897.
Julia Hicks,1833-1917,w/o Jos.C
Mae (infant),June 3,1903.
Martha A.,Oct.12,1864,34y,
 d/o James & Abigail.
Mary S.,1837-1885.
PARTRIDGE
Anne,Sept.15,1839,87y.
James,1801-1885.
Rhoda,Oct.6,1834,79y.
PATRIDGE
Jesse,Capt.,Dec.21,1795,53y.
PIERCE
Charles,July 23,1777,MA-
 Oct.26,1827.
Margaret Porterfield,Apr.2,1853,
 71y,w/o Charles.
PORTERFIELD
Elizabeth,Oct.12,1844,98y,w/o Wm.
James,Sept.9,1826,50y,War of 1812.
Polly,Apr.3,1854,74y.
Thomas,Mar.23,1813,7y,in Waterford.
William,Aug.16,1788,45y,War of 1812.
QUINBY
Almira F.,Oct.1909,81y,d/o M.& A
Andrew T.,Aug.17,1811,9m,
 s/o Moses & Anne.
Andrew T.,June 9,1834,18y,
 s/o Moses & Anne.
Anne,Apr 2,1859,70y, w/o Moses.
Eunice Freeman,Jan.19,1762-
 Dec.12,1790 & inf. son,w/o John.
Fred, M.D.,Feb.18,1853-
 Feb.3,1894,s/o Thomas & Jane.
George,Sept.21,1790,16m,
 s/o John & Eunice.
Jane E.,Mar.22,1819-Mar.3,1903,
 w/o Thomas.
John, Capt.,May 12,1758-
 Sept.27,1806.
Joseph,Apr.14,1776,61y,
 bu: at Saccarappa Cemetery.
Lucretia D.,Dec.25,1861,21y,
 only d/o Thomas & Jane E.,
Mary Haskell,Apr.22,1722-
 Apr.12,1815,wid/o Jos.

Mary,Aug.17,1828,11y,
 d/o Levi & Mary.
Moses,May 6,1857,71y.
Thomas,Dec.15,1813-June 18,1885,
 h/o Jane E.
Thomas,M.D.,May 10,1855-
 June 30,1946,h/o Justine Schaller,
 s/o Thos.& Jane Brewer Quinby.
REMICK
Benjamin,c.1862 and his wife,
 c.1848,both unmarked graves.
RICHARDS
Annie M.L.,1871-1956.
Melville F.,1882-1938.
RIGGS
Anna,June 17,1821,87y, w/o Jerem.
Jeremiah,Dr.,Dec.1800,70y.
ROBINSON
Bertha S.,1888-1973.
John A.R.,1893-1959.
ROUNDS
James,Nov.1826.
RYALL
Frank H.,1864-1864.
Jane L.,1841-1857.
Joseph C.,1865-1879.
Mary Ann,1841-1871.
Rebecca M.,1837-1868.
Sarah C.,1837-1862.
Sarah J.,1863-1863.
William,1832-1912.
SCOLLEY
Janette T.,Dec.25,1837,21y,
 d/o Thos. & Sophia.
Thomas,June 28,1837,34y.
William,1866-1930.
SLEMONS
Catherine Hill,1860-1945.
George,Aug.29,1817-1898,
 s/o Wm. & Abigail.
Lydia Margaret,1824-1897,
 w/o George,d/o Shad. Chapman.
Oliver,Nov.20,1825-Jan.22,1850,
 s/o Wm.& Abigail Quinby Slemons.
Robert,Apr.2,1823,76y.
Sarah,May 2,1826,31y.
Sarah,Jan15,1848,81y,w/o Robt.
SLOAN
Adam,of Scotland,Nov.8,1824,76y.
SMITH
Thomas,Nov.7,1845,26y,
 s/o Tyng & Hannah.
SPARROW
Abba C.,Feb.4,1858,27y.
Eleanor Porterfield,Nov.17,1773-
 Aug.5,1865,2nd w/o Jonathan.
Elizabeth E.,Jan.1,1852,25y.

Hannah,Feb.10,1799,25y,
   1st w/o Jonathan.
Isaac,July 12,1835,38y.
Jonathan,Dec.25,1768-Aug.20,1843.
Maria,June 1,1803-July 29,1885.
Phebe,Dec.5,1798,2y,d/o J. & H.
Thos. J.,Mar.4,1805-Dec.22,1870.
STEVENS
Charles Bartlett, XXXX.
Dora G.,1854-1896,1st w/o John.
Fred J.,1884-1910, s/o John & Jul.
John F.,1860-1909.
Julia G.,1868-1946,w/o John.
Lillian M.N. Ames, XXXX,
   w/o Michael. President/National
   Women's Christian Temperance Union
Lucy Maria,Nov.28,1843,4y,
   d/o Leonard & Hannah.
Mary M.,Aug.1850,22m,d/o L.& H.
Michael,1833-1915.
Nancy Chapman,Nov.18,1791-
   Sept.24,1874, d/o Shaddack,
   2nd w/o Tristram C.
Sophia,Apr.3,1878,85y,
   w/o Daniel,d/o Mary Peaks.
Tristram Coffin,Nov.6,1779-
   Sept.3,1870.
STIMSON
Susannah,July 19,1809,47y.
TATE
Catherine,Sept.6,1818,38y,
   d/o Robt. & Martha.
Dora F.,Apr.24,1858,
   d/o John S. & Julia.
Eleanor,Nov.20,1784,38y,w/o Wm.
Elizabeth,July 26,1769,29y,
   w/o Capt.Samuel.
George,1794,93y.
George,Oct.31,1847,75y,
   s/o Robert & Martha.
John S.,no dates,3y, s/o J.S. & Julia.
John S.,Mar.5,1861,38y.
Mary,1770,60y, w/o George.
Martha Slemons,Apr.3,1822,71y,
   wid/o Robert.
Robert, Capt.,Jan.3,1751-
   June 24,1804, at Berbice.
Samuel,Nov.22,1776,3y,s/o W.&E
Samuel Oct.9,1817,60y,s/o W.&E.
THOMAS
Children of Nathaniel & Maria:
Edward S.,Sept.18,1835,4y.
John F.,Oct.18,XXXX.
John G.,Sept.20,1834,3m.
Mary,June 1834,33y,in Boston.
Susan P.,June 17,1834,4y.
Susan F.,Feb.15,1836,1y.

THOMES
Benjamin,Nov.22,1809,45y.
Charity,May 14,1823,72y, wid/o Benj.
Job,Jan.10,1827,41y.
Nathaniel,July 8,1862,67y.
Phebe,Aug.23,1830,42y,
   friend & companion of Samuel.
THUNBORG
Mary W.Pierce,May 30,1813-
   Sept.12,1887,74y,w/o Olof N.
Olof N.,Sept.24,1867,35y.
Wilhelmina M.,Apr.7,1858,2y,
   d/o Olof N. & Mary S./W.
TINKHAM
George S.,Mar.8 -May 20,1911.
Gladys C.,Aug.13,1890-June 29,1960.
Henry S.,Feb.1,1915.
Robert S.,Mar.30,1888-Sept.6,1934.
TITCOMB
Andrew,Nov.19,1818,65y.
Louisa,1823-1905.
Mary, Aug.30,1796,37y,w/o Andw.
Rebecca,May 5,1808,58y,
   2nd w/o Andrew.
Sarah,Aug.25,1783-May 5,1840.
TRICKEY
David,1741-Sept.5,1814,War of 1812.
Mary Hobbs,Aug.7,1799,54y,
   w/o David.
William,July 8,1825,38y,War of 1812.
VAIL
Addie E.,Nov.29,1872-June 13,1896,
   d/o C.N. & Celia H.
Charles N.,Mar.26,1833-Aug.16,1904.
Elsie M.,1897-1897.
George Herbert,1865-1920.
Harriet C. Sawyer,1869-1943,
   w/o George Herbert.
Nellie M.,Oct.8,1866-June 11,1911,
   d/o C.N. & C.H.
WALKER
Archibald,Dec.28,1835,58y.
Hannah,1813-1895.
Jane C.,1816-1895,w/o Stephen.
Patience,Oct.15,1825,42y,
   w/o Archibald,also their children.
WARD
George J.,Nov.24,1864,8y,
William H.,Mar.16,1856,1y,
   both s/o John & Sarah.
WATERHOUSE
Alpheus,Sept.15,1805-July 3,1863,
   s/o Robt. & Elizabeth.
Amos W.,Oct.10,1855,37y.
Elizabeth (Polly) Fickett,
   Aug.13,1829,56y,w/o Robert.
Celia,1805-1876,w/o Alpheus.

Celia Frances,July 5, 1845-
Aug.17,1850,d/o Alpheus & Celia L.
Frances Augusta,Jan.16,1860,
24y,w/o Amos.
Frederick,Aug.13,1837.
Robert,Nov.15,1769-Aug.7,1808,
s/o William.
WEBB
James,Col.,1753-Sept.6,1825.
Nancy Cony,Jan.5,1808,1st w/o Jas.
Mary Thomes Peaks, June 24,1841,
72y, 2nd wid/o James.

Additional information on persons buried here was found in Leonard B.Chapman's articles from the turn of the century.

✧ **BAILEY CEMETERY** ✧
1612 Forest Ave., Portland.
Records from Evergreen Cemetery.

BABB
Marcenar A.,Nov.24,1870,23y,
d/o Warren & Mary E.
BAILEY
Abbie W.,1823-1908,w/o Lafayette.
Alexander,Nov.8,1790-June 8, 1882.
Alexander,Jr.,1820-1875.
Benjamin, 1764-Aug.16,1844.
Catherine,May 18,1842,30y,
w/o Samuel K.,
d/o Josiah & Sally Stevens.
Children of Alex. & Mariam: Frank, Walter,Netta, & Lester,no dates.
Clarence W.,1850-1923.
Edna May, Feb.2,1893,13d,
d/o E.G. & E.
Elizabeth Stevens, Apr.8,1813 -
Jan.12,1894,
d/o Nath'l & Abigail Stevens.
Fred M.,1878-1899.
Georgianna Leighton,1861-1911,
s/o Clarence.
John,Apr.12,1796-Aug.4,1870.
Lafayette,1825-1852.
Mariam T. Doughty,1825-1912,
w/o Alex.Jr.
Mary A. Haggett, Aug.8,1849,
22y, w/o Peter B.
Mary Brackett,Sept.14,1760-
Oct.16,1823,1st w/o Benjamin.
Olive Brackett, July 22,1872,74y,
w/o John.
Peter Brackett, Nov.1822-1855.
Sally,June 9,1796-Aug.9,1883,
w/o Alexander.

Samuel K., Apr.1,1863,55y.
Stillman G.,Nov.24,1862,23y,
d. in East New York,
s/o Samuel K. & Catherine
BLAKE
James,July 27,1843,89y.
John, July 27,1848,89y.
Sarah,Oct.11,1828,81y,w/o John.
BRACKETT
Abigail Read,1789-1846,w/o Zachar.
Jeremiah C.,Sept.10,1809-
Jan.17,1883.
Jerrietta C.,Jan.18,1855-
Jan.7,1913,d/o J.C. & Sophronia.
Leonard, XXXX, s/o Z. & A.
Sophronia Ellen Knight,
Sept.22,1821-Sept.22,1856,
w/o Jeremiah C.
Zachariah B.,1786-1840.
BRISCO
Sally Rose,Aug.1,1822,50y,w/o Thos.
BUCK
Martha A.,1836-1904, w/o T.P.
Theodore P.,1832-1911.
BUTLER
Eliza Frances, May 2,1847,5y,
d/o Frances & Eliza.
CLARK
Lucy Ellen,Jan.19,1851,6m,
d/o Bela & Louisa.
COLLINS
Clifford N.,1891-1918.
Gertrude M. Lunt,XXXX,w/o C.N.
DYKE
Arthur W.,1889-1890.
Sumner W.,1874-1899.
FRENCH
Isabella, Aug.2,1839, 3y,
d/o Joseph & Catherine.
Joseph,Dec.20,1847,37y.
GAMMON
Sarah W,Jan.9,1852,45y,w/o Stephen.
GRANT
Daughters of Wm. & Sarah:
Cordelia E.,Dec.4,1851,16y.
Frances A.,Nov.3,1851,19y.
HALL
Helene,July 21,1839,37y,w/o Philo.
HASKELL
Lydia,Apr.6,1802-Feb.6,1895.
HICKS
James,Jan.13,1866,70y.
James W.,Feb.25,1828,3m,
s/o James & Sophia.
HOWARD
Abizer,Feb.20,1834,70y.
Abizer,Feb.16,1846,53y.

Anna,Nov.29,1844,51y,w/o Abizer.
Sally,Apr.28,1848,82y,w/o Abizer.
JEPSON
Albert,1857-1916.
KENNEY
Mary, Aug.29,1840,64y,w/o Wm.
Nevella, Sept.6,1844,3y,d/o S.& S.
Samuel,Apr.7,1830,2y,s/o S.& S.
Stetson, Aug.18,1889,86y.
Susan, Nov.28,1867, 59y,w/o Stets.
William,Nov.7,1846,74y.
KNIGHT
Amos, Esq.,June 21,1849,68y.
LIBBY
Octavia,May 24,1829-1905,w/o S.F
Samuel F.,1829-1876.
LUNT
Abbie,1865-1902, d/o J. & S.
Abigail,May 3,1865,75y.
Addie L. Wakefield,1858-1902,
  w/o Neal.
Ellen, Oct.24,1869,69y.
Eunice M., July 23,1848,44y,w/o Saml.
Harriet E.,Dec.24,1905, 52y,
  d/o Samuel & Louisa.
Louisa, Oct.6,1900, 87y, w/o S.H.
Neal D.,1854-1919.
Samuel H.,Apr.5,1864,57y.
Susan,1840-1906, w/o James.
MANSFIELD
Samuel, Apr.16,1857,36y.
MARSTON
Rebecca B.,Apr.27,1869,61y.
MERRILL
Louisa Small,Apr.17,1844,22y,
  w/o Moses & d/o Charles Howard.
MURRAY
Catherine S., Aug.29,1846,10m,
  d/o Joel & Mary.
NASON
Simeon,Jan.6,1847,32y. father/o:
Louisa F.,Nov.12,1849 &
Mary S., Aug.23,1859,18y.
Thomas Oct.17,1864,45y,
  h/o Frances A., & father/o:
Laura B., Aug.26,1854, 8m &
Sumner,Aug.2,1853, 11m.
NEWMAN
Ebenezer,Jan.11,1836,58y
Mary,Nov.15,1838,59y,w/o Eben.
NORTH
Abigail,Jan.30,1825,34y,w/o Elisha.
Harriet W., Sept.19,1848,1y,
  d/o S.& M.A.
Martha,Oct.20,1834,51y,w/o Elijah.
Mary A.W.,Feb.4,1861,39y,w/o Sam'l.

Mary Emma,Nov.4,1863,6y,
  d/o Samuel & Mary A.W.
Samuel,Oct.6,1862,45y.
NUTTER
Anthony,Oct.17,1859,61y.
Caroline,Mar.29,1842,18y,d/o A. & M.
Mariam, Aug.31,1861,65y,w/o A.
PAINE
Dorcas, July 6,1831,84y,wid/o J.
Jonathan, Capt.,Nov.6,1824,84y.
PHELPS
Edna M.,May 25,1895-June 19,
  1896, inf/o Alfred J. & Lalia.
Thomas,1867-1890,
  s/o W. & A. of Cape Breton.
PRIDE
Ansel,Mar.25,1877,74y.
Betsey, XXXX, w/o Nathan.
Charlotte,1798-1866,w/o Thos.
Charlotte E.,1835-1914.
Ellen A.,Feb.12,1850,2y,d/o F.& S
Frederic, Aug.22,1872,65y.
Hannah,Feb 3,1887,74y,w/o Jas.
Harriet,Feb.15,1845,49y,w/o Sam.
Helena, Apr.28,1843,17y,
  d/o Samuel & Harriet.
James,Mar.25,1879,69y.
Joseph,Dec.4,1843,88y.
Joseph H.,1822-1902.
Mary, Mar.30,1842,79y,w/o Jos.
Leonard,1844-1864.
Nathan, Mar.8,1844,81y.
Samuel K.,Sept.17,1854,62y.
Sophia,Dec.12,1881,66y,w/o Fred.
Thomas,1792-1864.
Thomas B.,1826-1868.
Zebulon K.,1830-1916.
READ
Dorothy Blake,1764-1835, w/o Jon.
Jonathan,1752-1835.
RICKER
children of Samuel & Mary:
Estella M.,May 27,1880,11y &
Ida E.,June 3,1880,16y.
SAWYER
Children of George & Sarah:
Eddie J.,Jan.17,1866,11m &
Mary F.,June 12,1862,5m.
SMALL
Alonzo B.,Sept.10,1847,2y.
Charles Howard,1815-1866,
  s/o William & Sarah.
STAPLES
S.A., XXXX.
STEVENS
Abigail,Dec.4,1849,67y.
F.W., XXXX.

Isaac Sawyer,Sept.17,1748-
Oct.23,1820.
John B.,July 28,1826,12y,
only s/o Josiah & Sally.
Josiah,Dec.24,1818,34y
Nathaniel,Mar.21,1780-
June 1,1853,73y,h/o Abigail.
Sarah Brackett,Oct.18,1749-
Feb.28,1830,wid/o Isaac S.
THAYER
Ellen M., Aug.20,1837,1y,
d/o Hiram & Mariah.
THORN
Harriet F.,Dec.18,1835,5y,
d/o Job & Ann.
WAGG
Bertha L.,Dec.24,1875-
Apr.15,1878, d/o E.K.& A.S.
Edward K.,May 29,1892,36y.
Isabelle G.,May 14,1880-
Aug.14,1897, d/o E.K.& A.S.
WEBB
Elizabeth, Aug.10,1732-Apr.1827,
wid/o John.
WOODFORD
Chauncey,Mar.1,1774-
Aug.24,1841,68y.
Isaac,Mar.22,1837,30y.
Lucy,June 27,1854,73y,w/o Chauncey,
d/o Capt.Isaac Sawyer Stevens.

✧ **FROST CEMETERY** ✧
1 mile NE of Allen's Corner.
10 unmarked graves in 1896. 1
memorial stone:

FROST
George,Jan.6,1785-Aug.13,1865.

✧ **FRIEND'S CEMETERY** ✧
Behind the Friend's Meeting House
1837 Forest Ave., Portland.

BAILEY
Eliza P. Knight,1849-XXXX,w/o F.E.
Ferdinand E.,1847-1920.
Linnie D.,July 18,1893,12y,
d/o F.E. & Elisha P.
CARTLAND
Almira,1822-1894.
Lucy E.,May 17,1873,12y.
Stephen, 1822-1894.
COBB
Dorothy,1893, d/o C.E. & H.H.
DOLE
L. Maria Goddard,1850-XXXX.
William D.,1846-1915,h/o L.M.G.

FRYE
Lavinia,Feb 6,1861,in Vassalborough,
63y,w/o Ebenezer.
GALLISON
Harriet E.,Apr.23,1881,60y.
HACKER
Charlie,Aug.23,1864, 2m,
s/o I.N. & L.M.
Howard H.,1895-1896,s/o A.J.& I.F.
Ida F. Dawes,1871-1896, w/o A.J.
Isaiah N.,1826-1916.
L. Maria,1834-1918, w/o I.N.
William I.,1870-1920.
HANSON
Almira S.,May 24,1889,70y,w/o Tim.
Timothy,June 19,1887,78y.
HAWES
Ellen Maria,1813-1901,w/o Jos.
Joseph,1806-1885.
HAWKES
Alice W. Smith, Sept.11,1835 -
Feb.13,1920, w/o Ezra Jr.
Ann L.,July 12,1841-Aug.13, 1858.
Eugene,1883-1947.
Ezra,1792-1879.
Ezra, Jr.,Mar.22,1834, China -
Apr.27,1901.
Hannah,1797-1871,w/o Ezra.
Joseph John G., Sept.9,1838-
Jan.9,1909.
Lucy Nichols,XXXX,w/o Winslow
Lydia R., XXXX, w/o Joseph.
Mary Bailey,1882-1963,w/o Eugene.
Winslow,1830-1910.
HUNT
Mary Alma,1860-1921.
JONES
Caleb, Oct.14,1876,79y.
Caroline,Oct.27,1827-Mar.29,1912.
David,1833-1917.
Franklin, Aug.3,1855,23y,
s/o Caleb & Lydia.
Frederick,1846-1900.
Lydia H.,Jan.5,1889,90y,w/o Caleb.
Martha P., June 10,1853,26y,
d/o C. & L.
Minnetta A.,Nov.8,1850-
Jan.24,1880,w/o Frederick.
Sarah M., 1831-1901.
Sophronia E.,Jan.29,1845-
Mar.12,1905.
LEIGHTON
Ernest,Apr.13,1882, 2y,
s/o Oliver H. & Hannah A.
LOWELL
Abner,1848-XXXX.
Mary B.B.,1851-1922,w/o Abner.

MAYBERRY
Eliza F. Oct.10,1906,70y,w/o Rich.
MINOT
Henry M.,July 28,1804-Feb.22,1868.
Jane C.,Aug.22,1809-
 Feb.22,1887, w/o H.M.
John, Nov.4,1780-Feb.24,1870.
Nettie W.,June 29,1879,34y, w/o A.F.
MODOC
Frank, June 6,1886,45y,
 An Indian Chief of the Modoc
 Tribe, an Indian Territory &
 a friend Minister, died in the
 full triumph of Christian faith.
MOORE
T. Albert 1842-1903
Martha R.,1844-1909,w/o T.A.
PARKER
Mary,Apr.24,1882,35y,w/o Isaac W.
PEASLEE
Amos,Dec.19,1891,82y,h/o M.A.F.
Mary A.F.,Feb.22,1868,54y.
PRIDE
Ellen S.,Sept.21,1838-Sept.24,1849,
 d/o Wm. & E.M.
William, July 15,1813-Oct.24,1842.
PURINGTON
Anne,Nov.7,1860,92y, w/o Wm.
William,Apr.15,1851.
RICH
Eunice J.,July 1,1871,82y.
ROGERS
Hannah,Oct.20,1863,43y.
WINSLOW
Josiah,Jan.23,1880,88y.
Hannah Hacker,1823-1917,
 w/o Stephen R.
Lydia, Apr.29,1871,w/o Josiah.
Stephen R.,1823-1899.

✢ **GRAND TRUNK CEMETERY** ✢
Presumpscott Street, Portland.
6 (*) legible markers remain out of
approx. 95 markers as of the end of
1994. At least 10 persons were buried
with no markers. Records from
Evergreen Cemetery Office.

BARBOUR
Frances Jane,July 4,1846,15y,
 d/o George & Emma.
John,Aug.27,1869,67y.
Mary A.,Oct.7,1855,27y,d/o J.&M.
BLAKE
Emeline,May 15,1847,19y,
 d/o Samuel & Martha H.
Lucy, May 26,1807,w/o Wm.

Samuel,Feb.11,1846,52y.
Samuel G.,Sept.26,1825,3y,
 s/o Samuel & Martha H.
Sarah,June 18,1843,67y,w/o Wm.
BOOTHBY
Eva Ella,Jan.9,1852,2y, d/o S. & F.I.
*Frances I.,1815-1893,w/o Silas.
Silas,1814-1867.
DAVIS
Simon,Mar.17,1810,44y.
GALVIN
Harriot,Sept.21,1805,5y,
 d/o Timothy & Joanna.
Timothy,Feb.2,1766,Ireland -1836.
GRAVES
Andrew,Nov.28,1860, 86y.
Crispus,Mar.15,1879,63y.
Susannah,Dec.4,1793,48y,w/o Crispus.
Tabitha, Sept.7,1849,67y,w/o And.
JOHNSON
Jonas,1782,Pelham,NH-
 Dec.2,1837,55y.
LUNT
Jane,Sept.12,1834,80y, w/o Jos.
Mrs.Joseph,Sept.15,1804,47y.
MERRILL
Joseph,Apr.8,1823,65y.
MOSELY
Ann,Feb.24,1856,57y,w/o James.
*James,Dec.9,1892,56y.
SAWYER
Anthony,June 21,1804,69y.
Crispus, Aug.24,1873,69y.
Dorcus,Dec.15,1856,55y,w/o Jos.
Joseph M.,June 1,1875,79y.
Joseph Merrill,Sept.27,1835,2y,
 s/o Joseph M.& Dorcus.
Susanna,Feb.6,1805,40y,
 w/o Capt. Thomas.
Tabitha,Dec.6,1857,89y,w/o Wm.
*Thomas,Jr.,Dec.15,1785-Apr.21,1807
William,May 14,1825,62y.
SMALL
Warren, XXXX.
SMITH
Francis,June 4,1840,49y.
WILCOX
*Agnes,Apr.2,1864,44y,w/o Geo.

"A few short years of will past,
And we shall reach the shore,
Where death-divided friends,at last,
Shall meet to part no more."

✦ **MAPLEWOOD CEMETERY** ✦
"Allen's Corner Graveyard"
Fobes Street, Portland. Records from
Evergreen Cemetery Office.

BISHOP
Adeline,Oct.21,1806-Dec.1,1830,
 d/o George &Nancy.
Catherine, Aug.1,1820,75y.
George & Edward,May 2,1825-
 Apr.20,1827,twin s/o G.&N.
George,Jan.21,1787-June 9,1861.
Julia Ann,Mar.11,1821-
 Sept.12,1842,d/o Geo. &N.
Mary,Apr.19,1819,74y.
Mary,Oct.7,1812-June 23,1856,
 d/o George &Nancy.
Nancy,Feb.14,1788-July 5,1872,
 84y,w/o George.
BROWN
Susan M.,Nov.19,1896,80y.
COBB
Abigail,Oct.3,1810,79y,w/o Jas.
Abigail, Mar.21,1845,47y.
Alexander,Oct.3,1841,31y.
Amos,Nov.3,1809,13y,s/o Jon. & Hope.
Chipman,May 12,1837,72y.
Elizabeth,Jan.23,1828,10y,
 d/o Alex & Love.
Eunice,Jan.15,1840,35y.
Hope, Nov.27,1809,58y,w/o Jon.
Hope,XXXX,65y,w/o Jonathan.
James,Nov.10,1769,47y.
James,Feb.4,1793,
 s/o Jonathan & Hope.
James, Jr.,Oct.16,1836,87y.
Jane,Jan.31,1858,93y,w/o Chipman
Jonathan,Feb.27,1833,72y.
Jonathan,Oct.5,1842,34y.
Mary Stewart,XXXX,w/o Jonathan.
William,1794-1866.
DAVIDSON
William,May 5,1822,43y.
DOLE
James S.,Oct.6,1873,54y.
John,Oct.31,1853,67y.
John,1830-1895.
Sarah E.,Oct.22,1865,64y,w/o John.
Sarah S.,Dec.16,1838,11y,
 d/o John & Sarah.
William H.,1835-1917.
DOUGHTY
Hannah,July 26,1838,84y,w/o Jos.
John, Aug.1828,26y.
Joseph, Sept.3,1838,84y.
FLETCHER
Charles R.,Sept.9,1841-Nov.11,1890.

HARPER
Deborah, May 25,1813,31y,w/o James.
Henry, Nov.8,1830,22y.
HOLMES
Elbridge,May 24,1853,43y.
Polly, Oct.21,1820,39y,
 w/o Capt. Bartlett Holmes.
HUSTON
Eunice,Apr.4,1820,48y,w/o John.
John, Capt.,Sept.11,1817,53y.
Sally, Feb.18,1855,84y.
Thomas, Sept.15,1840,57y.
LUCE
Addie,Nov.1,1895,d/o Alb. & Adeline.
McDONALD
Catherine,Oct.15,1842,34y,w/o Eli.
MUGFORD
Frankie A.,Oct.1,1866,2y,
 s/o Augustus W.& Mary J.
Izette S.,June 1,1872,3y,
 d/o Augustus W. & Mary J.
Mary J.,Nov.19,1887,47y,
 w/o Augustus.
SMALL
James A.,Mar.20,1864,5y, and
Hattie J., Mar.27,1864, 5y,
 twins of Joseph & A.M.S. Small.
John D.,Oct.28,1856,1y,
 s/o Joseph & A.M.S.
TORREY
Albina,Apr.23,1837,11y,d/o J. & M.
Mary, July 10,1853,56y,w/o Jas.
James, May 2,1872,82y.
WILSON
Angeline W.,Oct.1,1812-
 July 4,1903, d/o Henry & Mary.
Elmira L.,Feb.9,1827-May 25,1902,
 d/o Henry & Mary Bailey Wilson.
George,June 21,1847,24y,
 s/o Amos & Sibbel.
Henry L.,July 12,1823-Nov.5,1880,
 s/o Henry & Mary.
John S., Aug.5,1852,26y.
Mary A.B., Dec.25,1815-Feb.6,1896,
 d/o Henry & Mary .
WINSLOW
Flora,XXX,d/o Andrew Scott Winslow.

CHARLES LEBARGE,
Furnishing Undertaker,
Coffins, Caskets and Robes. . . .
 . . . Flowers and Wreaths a Specialty.
Also—House Painter and Paper Hanger.
Work done by Day or by Contract at Reasonable Rates.
FITCH STREET. WESTBROOK.

❖ **BAILEY'S HILL CEMETERY** ❖
Mitchell's Hill, now Edwards St., Portland. Benjamin Bailey left 3 1/2 acres of land to his 2 daughters, Dorothy & Sally. 1/4 was for a burying ground, "some bodies already have been buried". In 1841 a fence was built around it. 4 known burials:

BRADLEY
Sarah Crocker,Apr.27,1821,41y, 1st w/o Rev. Caleb Bradley.
HALL
Mary Riggs, XXXX,w/o Thomas.
KING
William,May 14,1820-May 9,1846.
RICE
Mary,Aug.19,1826 or 1866, 21y.

After the establishment of Evergreen & Pine Grove Cemeteries, the engraved stones were removed to one of them. In 1898, 2 were still left, Mary Rice and Mary Riggs. I shall assume these were finally removed. Every so often since the turn of the century someone wants to level the tomb.
---From L.B. Chapman articles.

❖ **UNNAMED CEMETERY** ❖
Near 1125 Washington Ave.,Portland.

KNIGHT
Hannah,May 10,1794,39y,w/o Sam.
Jeremiah,Apr.15,1789,17y, s/o Samuel & Hannah.
Samuel,Feb.24,1820,66y, s/o Capt.Samuel & Mary (Knight) Knight & gr/s of Henry Knight.
Simeon,May 28,1809,22y, s/o Samuel & Hannah.
Rebecca,Feb.23,1846,84y,w/o Sam.
MORSE
Lewis,Mar.21,1825,17m, only s/o Stephen & Mary B.
Mary B.,May 25,1825,22y, w/o Capt.Stephen.
SAWYER
Asa,June 27,1858,81y,s/o Anthony.
Benjamin,Dec.13,1825,56y.
Caroline,1820-1891.
Eunice,Sept.9,1820,29y, d/o Benj. & Rebecca Sawyer.
Fanny,Dec.27,1827,31y, d/o Richard & Abigail.
Lewis Bean,Jan.24,1858,60y, s/o Benj. & Rebecca.

Nancy Y.,July 16,1824,21y.
Rebecca,Oct.3,1852,76y, w/o Benj.,d/o Adam & Betsey Knight Barbour.
Sarah,Jan.1,1851,71y,w/o Asa, d/o Samuel Knight.
WHITTEN
Thomas S.,Aug.29,1826,18y.

❖ **PINE GROVE CEMETERY ASSOCIATION** ❖
Taken from "Grandpa's Scrapbook", The Deering News,July 27,1895. Series of articles written by Leonard B. Chapman.

The records of the clerk of Pine Grove Cemetery Association are all contained in what was once a blank book, 7x8 inches square and 1/2 in. thick. It was opened to the purpose for which it was used Oct.12,1841, closed Feb.12,1894, a period of over a half a century. Walter B. Goodrich filled the place until his death, a period of 27 years; then Frank G. Stevens held the position 16 years, who was followed by Walter F. Goodrich one year (1885); then came William Jordan who served until 1893, making in the meantime but five pages of records.

The commencement is as follows:
To George Bishop, Esquire, one of the Justices of the Peace, within and for the County of Cumberland:
We, the subscribers, inhabitants of the town of Westbrook, feeling desirous of incorporating ourselves as a body politic for the purpose of purchasing land and suitably preparing the same for a burying ground, do hereby request you issue a warrant for the calling of a meeting of said subscribers to be holden at the Seminary in said Westbrook, on the eighteenth day of October next, at two o'clock in the afternoon, to act on the following articles, to wit:
1st. To choose a moderator.
2nd. To choose a clerk.
3rd. To choose a collector and treasurer.
4th. To raise money for the purpose of purchasing a lot of land, and suitably fencing the same and preparing it for a burying ground.

5th. To act on any other matter that may be deemed legal and proper relating to said burying ground.
Westbrook, Me. Sept.27,1841.

S.B.Stevens
Levi Morrill
Freeman Porter
Rev.Zenas Thompson
Oliver Buckley
Gerry Cook
Walter B. Goodrich
Samuel Jordan
C.S.Buckley
Simeon Hersey
Elisha Higgins
E.D.Woodford
Alfred Stevens
John Read
Rufus Dunham
A.G.Fobes
Rufus Morrill
Jeremiah Butler
Nathan L. Woodbury
Joseph Cox
John R. True.
Westbrook Seminary,
Oct.18,1841.

Agreeable to above warrant and notification the proprietors met, when the meeting was called to order by S.B.Stevens, who, having read the warrant and notice, proceeded to ballot for and choose:
S.B.Stevens-Moderator.
A.G. Fobes-Clerk.
Walter B. Goodrich-Collector and Treasurer.
The clerk was then sworn by the moderator.
Voted-To adjourn to meet at this place at 4 o'clock in this afternoon.
At the adjourned meeting it was voted to raise $250 and assess the amount upon the several members of the corporation in equal proportions to defray the expenses of purchasing land, building fences and other necessary attendant expenses.
Voted-That this association assume the name of Pine Grove Cemetery.
Voted-That we empower W.B. Goodrich, the collector and treasurer, to confer with and purchase of Oliver Buckley a lot of land laying in the rear of and adjoining the westerly side of the land belonging to the Westbrook Seminary, and receive a deed thereof in behalf of the pro-prietors of the Pine Grove Cemetery.
Voted-That Oliver Buckley, Samuel Jordan, Levi Morrill, Alfred Stevens and Jeremiah Beale be a committee to contract for and cause to be constructed a suitable fence around the contemplated land now to be purchased.
Voted-That S.B.Stevens,(Rev.) Zenas Thompson and Samuel Jordan be a committee to arrange, lay out and lot off the above named land when purchased.
Upon a fly leaf in the clerk's book is written as follows: "Deed of land purchased for cemetery recorded in Cumberland Registry, Book 177, page 134. Consideration $100." Then appears the following:
Description
Beginning at a post in the northerly corner of the Seminary lot, thence north,66 degrees west, 22 rods to a stake;thence south, 26 degrees 30 minutes west 21 rods to a stake; thence south, 63 degrees and 30 minutes east, 22 rods to a post; thence north 26 degrees 30 minutes east, 23 rods to first bounds mentioned, containing three acres and four square rods.
May 21, at 4 o'clock p.m., 1842, a meeting of the proprietors of the cemetery company was holden at the Seminary when it was:
Voted-That the plan reported by the committee chosen "to arrange, lay out and lot off" the Pine Grove Cemetery lot be accepted and the land layed out agreeable thereto.
Voted-That each and every proprietor meet at the Pine Grove Cemetery on Saturday the 28th instant, (May 28, 1842) at 8 o'clock in the morning, and to labor all day, or be assessed the sum of $1 as an equivalent therefor, and that these meetings be continued each succeeding Saturday under the superintendance, or to employ some other person, out of the proprieotors, to take his place as the same, until a sum not exceeding $100 equally and several assessed shall be expended.
May 28,1842,5 o'clock P.M.
Voted-That we authorize W.B. Goodrich to contract for sixty-four

granite posts 24 inches long, 6 inches square, the top flat and severally numbered on top with black paint.
Westbrook Seminary,
June 12,1842, 5 o'clcok P.M.
Voted-To raise a committee of three to draft a code of by-laws for the govern-ment and better regulation of this association to be presented for their consideration at the next meeting, and Nathan L. Woodbury, Walter B. Goodrich and John Read were chosen said committee.

Voted-That the committee whose duty was to "arrange, lay out and lot off the cemetery lot" be requested to number the several lots upon the plan.

Voted-To make a disposition of the lots to the several proprietors at the next meeting of the same.

June 25, 1 o'clock P.M.

Voted-To accept the report of the committee to whom was assigned the duty of numbering the plan, and that the plan as numbered by the committee be placed upon file and a draft of same be drawn on the clerk's book of records of the association.

Voted-That the choice of one lot to each proprietor be sold forthwith to the highest bidder, and that the chairman, Mr. Gerry Cook, be the auctioneer.

Following is a transcript of the record:
First choice to N.L.Woodbury, $1.50 for No.17; 2, LeviMorrill, $2.50, 16; 3rd Jeremiah Beedle, $2.50, 49; 4, Gerry Cook,$2.00, 24; 5, Samuel Jordan,$1.50, 9; 6, Free-man Porter, $1.00,10; 7, Charles S.Buckley,$1.00, 7; 8, John Read, .75,8; 9,W.B.Goodrich, .50, 47; 10, Rufus Morrill, .50,23; 11, E.D.Woodford, .50, 62; 12, John K. True, .25, 31; 13, Simeon Hersey, .25, 22; 14, Elisha Higgins, .25, 57; 15, Rufus Dunham, .25, 59; 16, (Rev.) Zenos Thompson, .25, 29; 17, Alfred Stevens, .13, 41; 18 Joseph Cox, .6, 2; 19, S.B.Stevens, .14, 50; 20, A.G. Fobes, .14,48.   Total,$15.97.

Voted-That any one of the proprietors may exchange his for any one of the unsold lots within one week from this day, by giving notice thereof to the secretary of the number he may have selected.

Voted-That Messrs. Levi Morrill, Dunham and True be a committee to nominate a president and five others that shall constitute a board of directors and also a secretary.

The committee reported as follows:
President-Nathan S. Woodbury
Vice President-John Read
Samuel B. Stevens,
Samuel Jordan,
Rufus Morrill,
John K. True,
Walter B. Goodrich,as Directors.
A.G.Fobes,Secretary.

Voted-To reconsider the vote where-by No. 13 was appropriated for a stranger's lot and substitute No. 30.

Voted-To see the surplus wood cut from the cemetery lot, forthwith which was auctioned off to Charles S. Buckley for $5.   Voted-To adjourn.

By-Laws of the Pine Grove Cemetery, Adapted 1842.

Article 1.-The annual meeting of the association shall be holden at the Seminary in Westbrook on the last Saturday in June annually.

Article 2.-The officers of the association shall consist of a president, vice-president, treasurer and secretary, who shall be chosen at the annual meeting and shall hold their officer for one year,or until others shall be chosen in their places, the chairman of the board of directors shall be the treasurer.

Article 3.-The president shall preside at all meeting of the association, and in his absence the vice president shall preside. The secretary shall call all meetings of the association by giving personal notice, or leaving written notice at their usual places of abode of each of the proprietors and shall keep a record of all doings of the association.

Article 4.-The directors shall have the general supervision and control of the affairs of the association.

Article 5.-In case of death or resignation of any of the officers the directors shall have a right to fill vacancies and the officer or officers elected by them shall hold their offices until the next annual meeting.

Article 6.-No person shall have a right to cut any tree or trees, standing upon his lot until he shall have obtained permission of the directors so to do.

Article 7.-Any proprietor wishing to make improvements on his lot shall first obtain permission from the board of directors which shall be in writing stating what improvements are to be made, and said permit shall be signed by the president and secretary.

Artilce 8.-No proprietor shall be permitted to use his lot for any other purpose except to bury his deceased relatives or friends or to ornament and improve it as he may be permitted by the board of directors.

Article 9.-The directors shall have power and authority to sell and convey by deed in their own name, for and in behalf of the proprietors, any lot or lots, which may at any time remain unsold, in said Pine Grove Cemetery, to such persons as they may deem proper, but if said directors shall disagree as to the propriety of selling to any applicant, they shall lay the application of such person before the proprietors at their annual meeting next for action and then proceed as said proprietors shall direct.

Article 10.-No person shall be entitled to a deed or to occupy or improve any lot in said Pine Grove Cemetery until he shall have paid for the same.

Article 11.-The treasurer shall keep a full account of all monies received by him and the manner in which it shall have been expended, and at the annual meeting shall lay before the proprietors a true account of the same, and he shall be responsible to said proprietors for all monies received and shall pay over to his successor in office all monies which shall remain in his hands.

Article 12.-It shall be the duty of the directors to commence and prosecute to a final decision in law every person who shall injure, destroy or disfigure any of the property of said Pine Grove Cemetery.

Article 13.-It shall be the duty of the secretary to call a special meeting of the proprietors of said Pine Grove Cemetery at the written request of any five of said proprietors, setting forth the purpose of said meeting and the time of holding the same.

Article 14.-The foregoing articles may be altered or amended at any annual meeting of the proprietors by a majority of the original proprietors of said Pine Grove Cemetery or their heirs or assigns.

Voted-To accept and adopt the foregoing as the standing by-laws of the Pine Grove Cemetery.

----At the same meeting at which the by-laws were adopted it was-

Voted-That a committee of three be appointed to select one lot to be appropriated for the burial of strangers, also one lot for ministers of all denominations.

Voted-that Samuel Jordan, S.B. Stevens and Rufus Morrill be a committee, who, having attended to their duty, reported that they had selected lot No.21 for strangers and No.28 for ministers.

Voted-That the same committee select a lot to be appropriated to Westbrook Seminary and lot No.13 was selected and dedicated.

Voted-That the vote whereby lot No.21 was appropriated for a strangers' lot be reconsider and lot No.30 be substituted.

Voted-To sell the surplus wood cut on the cemetery lot be sold forthwith at auction, which was struck off to Charles Buckley for $5.

Nothing appears on the record worthy of note until 1843 when it was-

Voted-That the original proprietors be severally a committee to dispose of one lot each for the sum of $12.

From 1843 until 1848 there are no entries in the secretary's book, when it was-

Voted-That Samuel B.Stevens, Freeman Porter and Rufus Dunham be authorized to spend $100 for painting fence, setting trees, etc.

In 1850 an attempt was made to change article 9 of the by-laws but the attempt failed. At that time there was $41.49 in the treasury.

In 1851 there was $55.49 in the treasury, and there was due the association $64.

Voted-That lots No.28 and 13 appropriated for the seminary and ministers be sold, they not having been occupied.

Voted-That George Libby, Samuel Jordan and Benj. W. Ballard be a committee to build a receiving tomb.

Voted-To spend $25 for the purpose of the tomb and procurement of a hearse house if necessary after the subscription is expended.

Voted-That Oliver Buckley, the owner of land on the western side of the cemetery be permitted to bring into the cemetery as much land on that side of the cemetery as he pleases as the directors of the cemetery may agree to.

In 1851 officers were elected as follows:
   Alfred Stevens-Pres.
   Walter B.Goodrich-Sec.
   William Eldrdge-Vice Pres.
   Alfred Stevens,
   Samuel Jordan,
   F.Porter,
   George Libby,
   John Reed, as Directors.

There was then in the treasury $106.58.

Eight votes were passed that were recorded, some of which I here present.

That Geo. Libby be paid for building the tomb and hearse house.

That Messr. Reed and Libby be a committee to remove the fence and place it out on line between the cemetery and William Kenney's and make what new fence is necessary.

That the request of the sewing circle in relation to furnishing dressing for setting trees and shrubs on the main avenue to referred to the directors.

That the directors be authorized to lay out the land which is to be enclosed by the removal of the fence to Kenney's line as they see fit, and affix such prices on the lots as they may think proper. (The small lots on the side of the plane here annexed show the comparative size of the addition.)

That the vote whereby No.21 was appropriated for a stranger's lot be reconsidered and the same offered for sale.

That the bodies deposited on lot No.21 be removed to lot No.79

That Messrs. George Libby and Freeman Porter be a committee to procure a hearse.

That the owners of lots be allowed to place stones as they see fit.

In 1853, there was $76.96 in the treasury and there was $108 due for lots sold;and it was voted to loan what money was not in use.

In 1854, a hearse was purchased of Mr. John Sawyer and $150 paid for the same.

At this procure the right of way through Evergreen Cemetery owned by Portland to Pine Grove Cemetery, "provided we take away our fence and give then privilege to draw water from our well."

In 1855,it was voted to purchase two shares in the Atlantic & St. Lawrence R.R.Co. at $80 each. The next year there was a balance of $129.81 in the treasury.

In 1857, permission was granted by a vote of the Portland city government to allow the Pine Grove Cemetery Association to pass through Evergreen Cemetery, and a unanimous vote was passed to remove the fence between the two lots.

The old fence was sold to the highest bidder who was E.B.Fobes at 25 cents per rod, "there being 43 rod." $155.03 in the treasury.

When and by whom the well was constructed the clerk's records do not show, but at the meeting of the association holden July 9,1883, it was voted "to accept Mr.Geyer's offer of $200 for the 'Well lot,'" -the well, I presume, having been filled.

In 1858 Elisha Higgins was chosen president who held the place until 1865, when Freeman Porter was chosen his successor.

In 1859 there was $208.62 in the treasury, and in 1860 there was $215.08 when it was voted to collect the Town order, also the interest on all other demands and deposit the amount in the Portland Savings Bank.

Voted-That any one who may be allowed to take the hearse, besides the sexton,besides the sexton, shall return the same in as good condition as when taken.

Voted-That E.B.Forbes be allowed the privilege to make a carriage gateway in the fence on the northerly side of the cemetery and against the second carriage avenue from the Seminary grounds.

In 1861 there was $211.65 in the hands of the treasurer, "not including all the back interest."

In 1862 there was $229.04 in the treasury, deposited in the Savings Bank.

Voted-That the treasurer be authorized to pay the Ladies Sewing Circle the amount they paid to John R. Sawyer from their funds for hearse runners.

The amount paid for taking care of the grounds was $5 annually-this was for walks-not lots.

In 1863 cash in Savings bank $229.35; cash on hand $82; note $16.59.

The sexton reported he had received $2 for use of hearse, and E.B.Forbes was continued in the office on an annual salary of $5 which included care of the grounds.

In 1864 the question of taking into the enclosure a piece of Mr.Forbes' was brought up, and Walter B. Goodrich, Geo. Libby and Wm. Eldridge were appointed a committee to confer with him, and Aug.13,1864 the committee reported, which report was accompanied with a plan, and the motion of Mr. Geo. Libby to accept Mr. Forbes' proposition, on motion of Hon. Samuel Jordan, was laid on the table, and a committee was chosen to ascertain what Mr. Forbes would take for his land, "with right of way from Plains road to cemetery." The committee consisted of Sam'l Jordan, Chandler Rackleff and N.K.Sawyer. This committee reported that Mr. Forbes would sell the whole lot for $1100, or the 60 lots at $20 each, and wait for his pay until the lots were sold. The meeting thought the price too high.

Total amount of cash in treasury $270.05.

Voted-That the gate opened to the cemetery by Mr. Forbes be permanently closed till otherwise ordered by the proprietors.

1866, Whole number of burials during the year, 4. Albert Jones was sexton.

In 1867 Voted-That an assessment of fifty cents be put upon each lot owner for the purpose of clearing up the grounds to be collected by Albert Jones. $318.28 in the treasury.

In 1869,Voted-To inquire into the expediency of building a new receiving tomb, but when it was ascertained $1,500 would be required the matter was dropped.

In 1872, Voted-That Samuel Jordan, N.K.Sawyer and Granville M. Stevens be a committee to confer with E.B.Forbes with the view of uniting the two yards and obtaining a permanent passageway through his property. Voted-To close the Seminary entrance, and to sell the lot used for an entrance from the Seminary grounds.

Voted-That lot No.55, now standing in the name of Miss Harriet R. Francis be changed to A.S.Alden at request of H.R.Francis.

In 1872, one Gavit made a plan for a receiving tomb to cost $1,500 and a committee was chosen to solicit subscriptions, but nothing came of the movement.

In 1874, a committee consisting of Francis Purrington, Alfred Stevens and E.B.Sawyer was chosen to confer with E.B.Forbes with regard to removing division fence between the two lots.

Voted-To close all gates and passageways in connection with the Seminary grounds.

From this time forward, a period of six years no officers were chosen, a quorum not being present at meetings, until July 17,1880, the following named persons were chosen:
Pres.-E.B.Forbes
Vice Pres.-George Mead Stevens
Sec.-Frank G. Stevens
Treas.-Alfred Stevens
Directors-Rufus Dunham, Rufus Morrill,Alfred Stevens, Walter F. Goodrich, Granville M. Stevens.

In 1883, there was $390 in the treasury, and in 1885 $432.67.

In 1886, the second article in the call for the annual meeting reads:
To hear the report of the secretary as to deeding the said cemetery to the

city of Portland to become a part of Evergreen Cemetery but no quorum was present. The treasurer reported $718.18 in the treasury.

In 1887 there was no attendance of members at the annual meeting.

In 1888, no attendance, $1,367.48 in treasury.

Deering,Me.,Feb.12,1894.

At the meeting of the surviving officers of Pine Grove Cemetery Association held this day at the residence of Granville M. Stevens for the purpose of filling vacancies in the Board of officers occasioned by death, there being present Messrs. Walter F. Goodrich, George Mead Stevens, and Rufus Morrill the following named persons were unanimously elected.

Pres.-James N. Read in place of Rufus Dunham,dec'd.
Sec.-Frederick Dunham in place of William Jordan, dec'd.
Director-Joseph S. Dunham in place of Rufus Dunham, dec'd.
Chairman-Walter R. Goodrich.

And here the old book of records was closed it being full.

On the fly leaf in the back of the book is a record which I here present in full. "1861-List of names of proprietors in Pine Grove Cemetery."

No. of Lot.
1. Robert Allen & Hunt
2. E. Cox.
3. Wm. & Geo. M. Stevens.
4. Wm. Scammon.
5. Wm. Thorn & James Johnson.
6. Albert Bennett.
7. Charles Buckley.
8. John Read.
9. Samuel Jordan.
10. Freeman Porter.
11. J. Kemp & A. Jones.
12. S. Jordan & Hiram Dow.
13. Geo. Wilson & ---.
14. Edward Newman.
15. Almon Leach.
16. Levi Morrill.
17. N.L.Woodbury.
18. Hancock & Henry.
19. E.B.Fobes.
20. Jonathan Smith.
21. J. Sargent.
22. Hersey & Saunders.
23. Rufus Morrill.
24. Gerry Cook & W. Polleys.
25. W. Small.
26. Dr. Henry Hunt.
27. Hiram Howard.
28. Capt. T. Seal.
29. J.A.Thompson.
30. A. Sweetser.
31. N.K.Sawyer.
32. Mrs. Boody.
33. J.F. Moses.
34. Stevens & Pierce.
35. Wm. Jordan.
36. Leonard O. Raynolds.
37. Wm. Eldridge & Walker.
38. A. Dyer & Kimball.
39. Frederick Sawyer.
40. John Newman.
41. Alfred Stevens.
42. Oliver Buckley.
43. B. Larabee.
44. Adams.
45. D. Davis.
46. W. Hanson.
47. Walter B. Goodrich.
48. Albert Forbes.
49. J. Bedell.
50. Sarah B. Stevens.
51. Chandler Rackleff.
52. David Thompson.
53. Geo. Libby.
54. Thos. J. Riggs.
55. Isabell Alden.
56. J. Bedell.
57. Elisha Higgins.
58. Mrs. Woodford.
59. Rufus Dunham.
60. John Dunham.
61. Hood & Stevens.
62. Daniel Choat.
63. Charles & Eben Sawyer.
64. Amos Greenleaf & John Homes.
65. John Larabee.
66. Henry Blake.
67. Capt. Chase & Mrs. Larabee.
68. Aaron Winlsow.
69. J. Swett.
70. Lothrop Libby.
71. James Dyer.
72. John Chase.
73. Joshua Lunt.
74. B.W.Ballard.
75. Daniel Anderson.
76. Johnson & Lobdell.
77. Jason Wilson.
78. Mrs. Gurney.
79. Strangers.

This closes our notes on Pine Grove Cemetery Association.

Pine Grove Cemetery

(Cemetery plan diagram showing plots arranged along Main Avenue—11-2 Rods Wide, with Seminary Grounds on left and 21 Rods on right, 22 Rods across top. Copy of Original Plan Numbered by Committee.)

Plots listed include:
- Top row: 61. Henry Stevens | 60. John Dunham | 52. George Libby | 58. David Thompson | 45. Daniel Davis | 44. Adams | 57. Wm. Eldridge | 56. L. O. Reynolds
- 62. Daniel Choat | 59. Rufus Dunham | 54. T. J. Riggs | 51. Chandler Rackliff | 46. Wm. H. Hanson | 43. B. Larrabee | 38. Alfred Dyer | 35. Wm. Jordan
- 63. C. & E. Sawyer | 58. E. D. Woodfords | 55. H. Francis | 50. Saml. B. Stevens | 47. Walter B. Goodrich | 42. Oliver Buckley | 39. Fred'k Sawyer | 34. Albion Libby
- 64. Amos Greenleaf | 57. Elisha Higgins | 56. Jeremiah Bedell | 49. Jeremiah Bedell | 48. A. G. Fobes | 41. Alfred Stevens | 40. John Newman | J. F. Moses

Gate.

- No. 1. Robert Allen | 2. John Beed | 9. Saml. Jordan | 16. Levi Morrill | 17. N. L. Woodbury | 24. Gerry Cook | 25. Wm. H. Small | 32. Mrs. Boody
- 2. J. Cox | 7. C. S. Buckley | 10. Freeman Porter | 15. Almon Leach | 18. Henney & Hancock | 23. Rufus Morrill | 26. Dr. Henry Hunt | 31. John R. ... as
- 3. Wm. Stevens | 6. Albert Bennett | 11. Jeremiah H. Kemp | 14. Edward Newman | 19. F. Hall | 22. Simeon Hersey | 27. Hiram Howard | 30. A. F. Sweetsir
- 4. Wm. Scammon | 5. W. J. Thorn | 12. S. J. Jordan, H. H. Dow | 13. George Wilson | 20. Jonathan Smith | 21. Sargent & Hubbard | 28. Levi Q. Pierce | 29. J. A. Thompson

Bottom row: Strangers 77 | Tomb | Mrs. Garner 73 | Jason Wilson 77 | Johanna & Lobdell 76 | Daniel Anderson 75 | E. W. Ballard 74 | Joshua Fant 73 | John Chase 72 | Jonas Dyer 71 | S. Libby 70 | John Swett 69 | Arron Winslow 68 | Chase 67 | Henry Blake 86 | John Larrabee 65

Pine Grove Cemetery

✤ **PINE GROVE CEMETERY** ✤
Inside Evergreen Cemetery, Portland.
Interments from Cemetery Office.

ABBOTT
Edna F.,Jan.1,1905,47y.
Rebecca A.,Mar.13,1918,87y.
ADAMS
Cornelius,Feb.11,1814,32y.
Eva,1865-1920.
Franklin,1895-1912.
George Willis,1854-1927.
Linda Swett,1859-Oct.26,1933.
Rebecca,June 27,1850,63y.
ALCOTT
Elmer C.,1882-June 2,1969.
Nellie P. Avery,1886-Dec.23, 1948.
ALDEN
Adeline Blake,1832-1907.
Alpheus S.,1829-1897.
Elizabeth E.Stevens,1829-1909.
George Forest,Jan.8,1865-1912.
Henry, XXXX.
Isabel,Jan.1,1832,16y.
Isabell, XXXX.
Isabell B. Frances,May 15,1862, 65y, w/o Jesse Dunbar Alden.
Jesse Dunbar,May 21,1835,45y.
Jesse Franklin,1835-1882,Boston.

John Q. Adams,Apr.12,1828,8m.
Nellie V., 1870-1938.
Susan Dunbar,May 13,1842,18y.
Walter, XXXX.
ALLEN
Averlin B.,June 16,1832-Sept.21,1908.
Carrie Esther Benton,1870-Nov.1960.
Charles H.,Dec.10,1828-May 1,1896.
Clarence Henry,1886-Aug.16,1956.
Harriet R.,Aug10,1856-Apr.23,1932.
John H.,Jan.13,1953.
Margaret, Oct.19,1907.
Martha Stevens,1874-June 1959.
AMES
Sadie E.(Sarah),1855-1938.
ANDERSON
Edward A.,1830-1913.
Frederick W.,Aug.31,1909,54y.
Henry, Nov.10,1859-Dec.3,1860.
Mabel, July 17,1947,74y.
Marietta T.,Dec.28,1922,71y.
Mary B. Proctor,1834-1886.
Mary I., Apr.18,1904-Apr.2,1993.
Sarah F.,Mar.19,1900,70y.
Thomas,Feb.15,1898,63y.
William,Oct.30,1896.
ARMSTRONG
Cecil,1888-May 28,1904.
Julia (Julianna),1853-1901.

Robert,June 14,1920,74y.
Winifred G.,1878-1902.
ARSENAULT
Mary E.,June 27,1921,6d.
ATKINS
Joseph W.,June 30,1887,44y.
Lucy A.,July 29,1819-July 7,1886.
Nathaniel,Apr.13,1814-Apr.7,1885
AUSTIN
Addie,XXXX.
William M.,1888 -XXXX.
AYMAR
John H./R.,1842-1913.
Mary,1860-1933.
Mary F.,1840-1881.
Maud F.,1874-Dec.25,1954.
BABBIDGE
Carrie Louise Dingley,1879 -
Oct.22,1958.
Sumner W.,1869-1948.
BABCOCK
Abigail G.(Abbie),Mar.3,1822-
Feb.21,1907.
BACHELDER
Anne,Jan.18,1916,90y.
Lyman A., Jan.20,1902,66y.
Roderick A.,Feb.13,1905,40y,
 rem. to Evergreen in 1906.
Samuel P.,Dec 5,1824-June 18,1881.
Virginia H.,Feb.2,1938,83y.
BAILEY
Abbie D.,Aug.22,1880,26y,
 rem.to Highland Lake, May 1906.
Albion,XXXX.
Alice F.,May 18,1898,35y.
Almon,XXXX.
Elizabeth,May 25,1914.
Elizabeth S.,1835-1902.
George S.,1811-1859.
Georgia L.,Feb. 27,1885,1y,
 rem. to Highland Lake 1906.
Rena Louise,Dec.23,1902,2y.
Sarah W.,1812-1865.
Sewall B.,1837-Oct.27,1926.
BALDWIN
Carlton W., Sr.,Sept.29,1988,87y.
BALLARD
Arthur, XXXX.
B.W., XXXX.
Benjamin W.,Jan.8,1863,50y.
Carrie May,May 29,1858-
Sept.28,1865.
Charmanitta, Nov.4,1944,55y.
Edward H.,Oct.24,1920,74y.
George H.,1828-1893.
Harry S.,1869-1928.
Henrietta M. Boody,1869-1940.

M.A., XXXX.
Mary A., Apr.17,1855,43y
Mildred Stevens,Mar.8,1965,58y.
Nancy E.,June 25,1934,85y.
Sarah B. Stevens,1828-1904.
BANKS
Elias F.,1855-1909.
Helen M. Eldridge,1858-1915.
Irene H.,May 22,1970,37y,d/o Sarah E.
Sarah E.,Apr.9,1880-Nov.17,1917.
BARBOUR
Eva A.,May 8,1872-Dec.5,1905.
BARROWS
Gertrude Gurney,Feb.21,XX85.
BEAN
Hattie,1816-1884.
Leonard O.,1820-1895.
BEDELL
Aaron, Sept.26,1844, 5y.
Aaron L.,Oct.17,1844,7w.
Abbie,1813-1819.
Addington D.,Dec.6,1842-Oct.25,1921.
Albion L.,Jan.24,1880,28y.
Alvah H.,June 28,1861,24y.
Charles O.,Nov.28,1836-Apr.13,1838.
Edward A.,Feb.14,1847,4y.
Elizabeth,May 27,1891,86y.
Granville M.,Nov.23,1876,26y.
J. Frank,Jan.19,1875,29y.
Jeremiah,Apr.24,1809-Oct.26,1849.
John,Jan.20,1813-June 10,1888.
Mary D.,Sept.11,1874.
Nancy P.,May 14,1852,24y.
Zenas G., Jan.8,1871,37y.
BENNETT
Adda, Nov.20,1856,11y.
Albert Francis, Sept.3,1847,1y.
Albert P.,1820-1888.
Frances Elizabeth B.,1841-1906.
George Washington,1835-Sept.1903.
Maria J.,1918-1893.
Mary Ann Eastman,July 21,1889,84y.
BERG
Charles H.,Aug.13,1935.
BERRY
May F. Rackleff,1867-1930.
BICKNELL
Sarah A.,1841-1917.
Walter F.,1837-1911.
BISHOP
George, Jr.,1825-1907.
BLAKE
Alexander,1821-1889.
Charles H.,1840-1901.
Charles W.,1860-May 7,1950.
Frederick C.,1974.
George,1835-1909.

Harriet E. Ballard,1839-1903.
Helen O. Weeks,1869-1913.
Henry, Apr.20,1869,80y.
Martha J. Newman,1842-1901.
Nancy,1793-1873.
BLANCHARD
Alice May,June 10,1908,28y.
Harriette, June 6,1938,34y.
Selwyn,Dec.14,1951,51y.
BODGE
Anna L.,Dec.3,1933,76y.
Francis O.J.,1835-1923.
Martha E. Howard,1833-1915, w/o Franklin.
Wilfred Pearl,1890-1891.
William H.H.,1853-1895.
BOLTON
Ai, Apr.8,1867,31y.
Elvira, Feb.11,1862,21y.
BONNEY
Mary Emily, Oct.16,1855,20y.
BOODY
Erwin H.,1881-1946.
Mary C., Dec.30,1975,93y.
Frank H.H.,1880-1913.
George Dana,Mar.9,1863,17y, in VA., w/o H.B. & A.M.
Henry B.,Dec.31,1880,63y.
Henry F.,840-1905.
Henry H., 1789-1853.
Lucy,1844-1921.
Mary B. 1796-1866.
Mary C.,1774-1863.
BOOTHBY
Almira C.,1854-1867.
Mary Anna,1861-1918.
Mary C. Jones,1822-1907.
William,1817-1899.
Willis D.,1858-1864.
BOWEN
Harriet D.,Dec.15,1951,53y.
BRACKETT
Alton C.,Mar.15,1827-July 20,1893.
Hattie E.,Oct.27,1866,10y.
Horatio S.,May 3,1916,81y.
Sarah Ann, Apr.14,1820-Nov.21,1897.
BRADLEY
Caleb, Rev.,June 2,1861,89y.
Charles A.,1813-1895.
Frances Ellen,Apr.8,1858,31y.
Leonard W. Mar.24,1866,48y.
Louisa Shaw,May 1877,30y.
Ruth N. Adams,1809-1868.
Sarah Crocker,Apr.27,1821,41y.
BREWER
Florence D.1856-1930.
Henrique M., June 8,1855,16m.

Henry M.,1821-1908.
Malvina D.,1821-1907.
Mary E. Smith,1857-1942.
Thomas L.,1855-1920.
BROWN
Christine M.,May 7,1959,76y.
Clara K. Cross,May 2,1889,37y.
Lydia H., Apr.12,1936,78y.
BRYANT
Caroline Tucker,1844-1860.
David Tucker,1835-1835.
Elizabeth Adams,1833-1860.
Mary Louisa,1841-1918.
Susan Rebecca,1837-1858.
Susan Warren Tucker,1807-1871.
Timothy,1807-1864.
BUCK
Aurelia J.,1812-1903.
BUCKLEY
Addline B.Woodford,1827-1902.
Carrie A.,1844-1902.
Charles M.,1835-1903.
Edward M.,1825-1913.
Edward W.,Oct.23,1824,8y.
F.R.,XXXX.
Frank M.,1846-1888.
Frederick H.,Apr.8,1844,4m.
L.J.,XXXX.
Laura J.,XXXX.
Martha,Sept.15,1839,78y, w/o Soloman.
Martha A.,XXXX.
Oliver,1782-1872,h/o Sally.
Oliver H.,Apr.27,1897,58y.
Orrin,Feb. 9,1852,38y.
R.E., XXXX.
Ralph E.,Sept.5,1851,7m.
Sally Buckley,1789-1828.
BURCHILL
Ernest, Jan.3,1915,1hr.
BURNHAM
Ann Emery,Apr.23,1838-Jan.8,1915.
Emeline Bailey,1829-1911.
Leonard C.,1831-1904.
Lizzie J.,1849-1912.
Lydia Libby,1823-1903.
Thomas S.,May 21,1834-Nov.19,1900.
William M.,1824-1904.
Sophronia H.,Mar.30,1892,76y.
Thomas H.,Nov.27,1880,66y.
CALDWELL
Helen Willoughly,Oct.22,1956,69y
CAMPBELL
Cecil E.,Aug.12,1892,1y.
Eunice,Sept.14,1900,39y.
Nellie L.,1858-1936.
Walter E.,1856-1917.

CARTER
Daniel,Oct.25,1833-Apr.27,1908.
Edward O.,Oct.21,1865-Nov.26,1865.
Lucy K.,Mar.31,1825-Mar.16,1913
CARY
Katrina Steinman, June 11,1853-
June 5,1932.
CHADSEY
Benjamin,1826-1901.
Fred Dudley, Jan.5,1859-Mar.2,1901.
John Fenwick, Sept.18,1851-
Mar.30,1894.
Maria H. Blethen,1834-1888,
rem. from North Yarmouth 1896.
Mary A. Howard,1820-1910.
CHAMBERLAIN
James K.,1867-1942.
John A.,1916.
Lucy A.,1877-Dec.12,1954.
CHAMBERS
William,May 30,1923,49y.
CHARRON
Martha Bodge,Feb.14,1954,57y.
CHAS
Charles C., Nov.26,1870,37y.
CHASE
Augustus L. Oct.18,1813-Oct.3,1837.
Benjamin P.,June 22,1836,25y.
Henry G.,July 4,1847.
Isaac, Sept.9,1843,29y.
Isaac N.,1844-1893.
Isacanna,1844-1923.
John, Mar.1,1875,62y.
Jonathan,Mar.23,1881,91y.
Joshua E.,July 20,1811-Oct.15,1861.
Leonard,1809-1884.
Lodeemy,Feb.14,1859.
Simon F.,Feb.17,1903,76y.
Susan F.,1817-1877.
Tirzah,Jan.28,1877,83y.
Willie H.,1880-1881.
CHENERY
Barbara E.,1813-1889.
Charlie A., Sept.23,1850-Nov.10,1852.
Daniel D.,1841-1926.
Eben,June 17,1844-Sept.16,1863.
Edward,1808-1891.
Fred D.,Dec.27,1871-May 17,1887.
Hattie J.,Dec.25,1863,18y.
Helen F.,Jan.2,1932,88y.
Henrietta P.Dow,1843-1904.
John J., Sept.16,1816-Nov. 18,1878.
Joseph,1770-1817.
Joseph,Aug.4,1803-Mar.22,1883.
Margaret W., Aug.30,1857,46y.
Marrietta, Dec.17,1840-July 11,1864.

Mary E. Woodford, July 16,1821-
Nov.15,1899.
Mary T.,June 12,1805-Oct.25,1893
Rebecca,1774-1863.
William,May 25, 1917,
rem. from Evergreen.
William,1838-1898.
William H.,Oct.28,1933,67y.
CHILDS
Lucy P.,Nov.11,1840-Nov.15,1881.
CHOATE
Caroline,Sept.12,1889,81y.
CHRISTIE
Clarence L.,1956.
Marion A.,1974, 86y.
CHUBBUCK
George D.,1833-1866.
Sarah L. Larrabee,1839-1913.
CILLEY
Agnes M.,1897-1899.
Albert A.,1855-1925.
Arthur A.,1885-1940.
Ella M.,Jan.16,1955,97y.
Elva L.,May 5,1970,89y,w/o Geo.
George Granville,Nov.28,1955,72y.
Laura Annie,1892-1895.
Nellie M.,1890-1895.
CLAPP
Emma Isadore Moses,1860-1938.
George Gregory,1858-1934.
CLARK
Bela S.,1817-1881.
Charles H.,1830-1882.
Elizabeth N.,1826-1866.
Granville E.,1860,2m.
Harriet J. Hawkes,1867-1957.
Harry E.,1868,3y.
John Addison, Dec.14,1853-
Nov.7,1908.
Louisa F. Pride,1821-1903.
Lucy B.,1866,3w.
Oscar L.,Feb.11,1895-Jan.5,1887.
CLARKE
Clara A.,1868-1950.
Clesson J.,1870-1929.
Florence Mabel,Apr.2,1982,88y.
CLEMENT
Thalia L.,Apr.1,1930,62y.
CLOUGH
Benjamin,1762-1838.
Harrison L.,Sept.25,1936,19y.
Harrison Linwood,1884-1918.
Polly,1770-1850.
COBB
child,June 1,1921,5hrs.
child,June 1,1921,1hr.
Benjamin S.,1821-1901.

Charles,1838-1914.
Dorcas D. Leighton,1838-1914.
Enoch B.,Dec.18,1871,40y.
George K.,May 15,1900,71y.
Henrietta Ellis,1846-1868.
Leonice B.,1840-1918.
Martha A.,Sept.11,1875,40y.
Orin,1842-1917.
Otis,1799-1877.
Ruth Knight,1804-1880.
COLBY
Helen W.J.,Feb.18,1941,94y.
COLE
Sophia E.,Sept.20,1930,79y.
COLLEY
Charles B.,1864-Oct.18,1954.
Charlotte Ellen Lowell,1831-1915.
Deering,1818-1902.
Laura E. Nov.25,1862-June 14,1864.
Mabel D. Simmons,1875-1957.
CONARY
A.Judson,Nov.27,1926,76y.
Laura S.,1850-1902.
COOK
Ada L.,Feb.2,1935,84y.
2 s.b. babies,1 in 1959,1 in 1968.
Cornelius H.,XXXX.
Edwin O.,XXXX.
Edwin O.,XXXX.
(M.) Etta,1850-1902.
John H.,1847-1909.
Mary E.,1841-1908.
COOKSON
inf/o Wm.W.,Jan.7,1897,5d.
William W.,Nov.18,1900,2m.
COOMBS
Nellie Gertrude,Jan.12,XX60,94y.
COREY
Katrina F. May 5,1932,78y.
COSTELLO
Esther,May 6,1892.
COTTON
Africa P.,1825-1896.
George C., Apr.11,1929,70y.
Jennie,May 10,1925,67y.
Sarah,1828-1893.
COX
Charlotte,Aug.14,1852,58y, wid/o Joseph.
Charlotte S.,July 7,1843,4y.
Harriet R.,May 3,1847,26y,w/o Enoch.
Jane S.,July 21,1843,9m.
Joseph,Mar.28,1843,50y.
CRAM
Allen A. Purington,1853-1931.
Bertha Greenhalgh,1870-1941.
Frank H.,May 3,1922,62y.

George M.,1858-1916.
Harry L.,1871-1944.
Hattie E.,May 13,1897,44y.
Hattie L.,Feb 22,1934,85y.
Jennie L.Leighton, June 5,1834-Jan.8,1919,w/o Orlando B. Cram.
Julia Christine Jackson,1871-1946.
Mary Jane, Nov.15,1950,81y.
Nettie,May 15,XX70.
Orlando B.,Mar.13,1833-Jan.1,1906.
CRANDALL
Dorothy J.,Aug.16,1993,79y.
Harold R.,Oct.24,1987.
CRIBB
Henrietta, Apr.1,1937,73Y.
CROSS
Charles E., M.D.,Nov.24,1887,33y.
Colin E.,Feb.13,1855,37y.
Louisa,Feb.11,1855,3m.
CURTIS
Eva Hazel,June 23,1889-Aug.7,1899.
J.H., XXXX.
M.J.H., XXXX.
Martha Ann Hersey, 1829-1895.
Milford A., 1858-1901.
Samuel, 1824-1901.
DANIELS
Katherine C.,Oct.27,1927,28y.
DARKER
Alvah R.,Nov.20,1927,14y.
DARLING
infant,Jan.19,1913, s.b.
Laura L.,Sept.9,1909,3m.
DAVIS
Charles K.,1837-1910.
Charlott S., Apr.17,1882,61y.
Christopher S.,Feb.26,1873,76y.
Clara C.,June 22,1875,61y.
Daniel S.,1812-1894.
Fanny, June 7,1873,73y.
Frank W.,Dec.15,1903,20y.
George,1826,1y.
Herbert, June 21,1886.
Irene E. Stevens (Irvena), Oct.22,1886, 40y.
Louisa B.,Nov.17,1888,30y.
Margaret B.A.,Dec.19,1869,42y.
Mary,Oct.26,1850,36y.
Mary A.,1855-1912.
Stella,Mar.1,1859,84y.
DAY
James F.,1848-1885.
Maria F. Howard,1827-1873.
DEARBORN
Ernest W.,Mar.10,1886,5y.
Harold A.,Nov.15,1888,6y.

DeGRASSE
Oscar F.,May 5,1921-June 1,1973.
DENNIS
Della H.,Aug.5,1916,73y.
John C.,Jan 3,1919,75y.
DeWITT
Henry R.,1819-Dec.15,1884,rem. from West Cumberland,Nov.2,1896.
Sarah J.,1828-1904
DeCORMIER
Alice M.,May 26,1974.
DIMICK
Mae L.,May 18,XX63,76y.
DINGLEY
Albert,1852-1928.
Elizabeth Ann Huston,1852-1910.
DOW
Henrietta P.,Oct 3,1840,5y.
Hiram H.,Oct.15,1893,88y.
Henry Pearson,Sept.12,1860,20y.
Jonathan,Aug.11,1855,23y.
Roscoe,XXXX.
DRESSER
infant, Mar19,1898,s.b.
Lawrence E.,Jan.16,1897,6y.
DUNHAM
Annie M. Davey,1854-1926.
Arthur,XXXX.
Beatrice,1898-1898.
Charles A.,1852-1911.
Charles S.,Sept.2,1851,3y.
Edward F., June 20,1910,31y.
Emeline C. Sept.17,1841,1y.
Emeline S.,Dec.28,1840,29y.
Emma A.,1868-1958.
Emma B. Sargent,1826-Sept.1910.
Ethel Sargent,Mar.4,1885-Oct.1,1900.
Frances E.,Nov.23,1820-Mar.14,1887.
Frederick, 1854-June 1,1938.
Grace, XXXX.
Hannah Emery,1785-1872.
Harriet G.,Feb.14,1929,48y.
Harriet R.,Mar.27,1939,86y.
Harry S.,Oct.18,1933, 57y.
Horace W., Feb. 8,1928,67y.
John,Dec.23,1845,63y.
John,May 18,1819-June 9,1889.
John F.,1856-XXXX.
John L.,Jan.23,1926,69y.
Joseph S.,1852-1909.
Lyman, XXXX.
Lyman, Dec.22,1845,7y.
Rufus,1815-1893.
DYER
Albert W.,June 5,1878-Feb.18,1914.
Alford, Dec.27,1887,76y.
Alford Lyman,Sept.18,1848,10y.

Alford Delano,May 16,1861,3y.
Ann Rebecca, May 11,1885,66y.
Blanche S. (Henrietta B.), 1874-Oct. 3, 1948.
Charles M., Nov.15,1841-Jan.18,1904.
Ellen L.,June 30,1852-July 11,1934.
James,May 6,1874,74y.
James H.,Jan.4,1871,37y.
Lucy W. Cushing,Apr.13,1805-Dec.22,1897.
Lydia,Dec.26,1878,97y.
Martha,Dec.16,1861,31y.
Miriam L.,Aug.20,1890,74y.
William K., Aug.14,1848,4y.
EDWARD
child, May 26,1921,s.b.
ELDEN
Nellie D.,Apr.13,1844,8y.
ELDER
Edwin Smith, Rev.,1837-1906.
Ellen Dana,1876-1883.
Fabius E.,1860-1935.
Sarah Ellen,1836-1930.
ELDRIDGE
Addie,1855-1856.
Alvah G.,1853-1922.
Betsy Ann, Apr.2,1852,17y.
Charles,1857-1873.
Delia A.Warren,1856-1921.
Ellen E. Newman,1833-1904.
Helen C., Sept.6,1893-Nov.24,1891.
J.Rutilus,Nov.23,1832,1y.
John Walker, Apr.3,1852,43y.
Johnnie,1866-1867.
Leon W.,Oct.12,XX82,85y.
Levi Gilman,1831-1899.
Mellvina, Feb.1,1840,3y.
Ralph H.,Jan.2,1913,34y.
Rhoda N.,Dec.22,1854,50y.
William Wallace,Aug.11,1844,13y.
William,Oct.6,1885,75y.
ELLIOT
Mary E., Sept.10,1863,24y.
ELMER
Theresa N.,Oct.9,1850,4m.
EMERY
Eben,May 3,1923,75y.
Horace/Harris,Aug.8,1884,70y.
Mary F.,Oct.12,1867,41y.
Mary L.,Oct.8,1871,21y.
Sophia E.,June 14,1912,61y.
ESTABROOKS
Edith Pearl Flood,1799-Jan.18,1857.
EUSTIS
Ida V., Dec 5, 1925,52y.
FERRIS
Doris O'Sullivan,Mar.15,XX83,88y.

Ezra,July 5,1965,84y.
FIELDING
Agnes Archibald,1855-1938.
Annie B. Shaw,1863-1923.
Charles,1863-1946.
Ruth,Sept.30,1896-Jan.22,1897.
Sarah E.,June 10,1917,78y.
Thomas H.,1858-1922.
FLINT
Dorothy J.,XXXX.
Roger W.,Feb.18,1992,90y.
FLUENT
Frances O.,Mar.7,1885,65y.
Hannah Larrabee,1832-1911.
John M.,Dec.1,1881,59y.
Marie L.,May 6,1853,27y.
Rufus,1824-1892.
FOGG
Ernestine,1850-1902.
George H.,Feb.13,1931,50y.
FORBES
Alpheus,Mar.1852.
Ann D. Burr,Oct.2,1899.
Charles S.,Oct.29,1865.
Elizur,Dec.29,1884.
Helen A.,Jan.5,1934,93y.
Lester, XXXX, infant.
Lester H., July 1892.
Martha Goodrich,Jan.14,1885.
Minnie F.,Feb.16,1861,26y,
  w/o Andrew J.
FOWLER
Abbie L. Shirley,1839-1900.
Cara,Mar.24,1858-Apr.20,1864.
Eddie,May 10,1860-Apr.17,1864.
Frances Ellen Thompson,
  Feb.24,1837-June 23,1918.
Frank,1837-1902.
Harry,1867-1939.
Henry Jones,Dec.28,1833-
  Jan.25,1907.
Winifred Bryant,1868-1939.
FOY/FOYE
Anna B.,Dec.30,1918,57y.
Annie Estella,Aug.23,1863,8m.
Annie Graham,1845-1901.
Charles W.,Jan.29,1914,81y.
Grace L.,1878-1949.
John W.,1874-1930.
GARDINER
Florence N.,Apr.6,1927.
GIVEN
Charles S.,July 15,1892, s.b.
GLENCROSS
Sara, Feb.16,1884-July 27,1976.
GODDARD
Rose Clementine,June 4,1951,66y.

GOING
Walter S.,Nov.8,1921,41y.
GOODHUE
Anna Proctor,1870-1948.
Ralph Fessenden,1866-Nov.24,1954.
GOODRICH
Caroline,1830-1923,
  d/o Walter B.& Maria F.
Maria Frances,May 29,1891,86y,
  w/o Walter B.
Walter B.,Aug.4,1869,67y.
Walter F.,1834-Jan.1908,
  s/o W.B. & M.F.
GOODWIN
Lois E.,1981,74y.
William Lee,1900-1961.
GOOLD
Eddie J.,Sept.16,1865,4m.
Ella A. Hamblet, 1851-1928.
Emeline,1840-1913.
Mary, Sept.21,1887,86y.
Mary E.,Oct.13,1865,22y.
Samuel G.,June 1,1839,1y.
William,June 1,1868,73y.
William N.,1844-1902.
GOULD
Elizabeth Noyes,June 1873-Feb.1920.
Harry R., June 19,1942,70y.
GOWER
Eunice Leighton,Oct.1873,70y.
Harriet N.,Mar.17,1909,73y.
Jason,Nov.16,1907, 66y,
  s/o Capt. Joshua & Eunice Gower.
Joshua, Col.,Mar 9,1874,71y.
GRAFFAM
Alta Z.,1857-1871.
Annie E.,1859-1887.
Benjamin,1830-May 8,1895,65y.
Lizzie S.,1855-1887.
Mary,1830-1888.
GREEN
Henry N.,1832-1901.
Martah E. Cobb,1831-1918.
GREENLEAF
Joseph, Dec.26,1851,75y.
Sally, Nov.10,1855,69y.
GROWS
Lucy E.,Mar.22,1854-Oct.18,1882.
GURNEY
Allie,June 6,1875,8y.
Charles Edwin,1847-1889.
Charles Edwin,1874-1945.
Jennie Hunnewell,1846-1892.
HACKETT
Tirash E.,Sept.10,1855,39y.
HAGBERG
Alice M.,1881-XXXX.

Oscar Leland,1882-1946.
HAINES
Isiah W.,1817-1892.
John, May 1,1816,1y.
Mary J., Sept.4,1815,1y.
Phebe W. Doughty,1821-Apr.26,1910.
HALL
Adelaide B. Newman,1835-1912.
Alvin, Capt.,Jan.26,1903,81y,
s/o Greenfield & Sarah Prince Hall.
Alvin B.,May 13,1861-1884.
Alvin Ohio Kerring,1860-XXXX.
Ann E. Read,1818-1867.
Appleton,May 29,1818-Jan.2,1840.
Byron A.,1831-1907.
Charles B.,1827-1909.
Clara C., Jan.25,1924,62y.
Florence Iva,Jan.23,1959,81y.
George Franklin,1829-1904.
George H.,Jan.22,1931,66y.
Harriet Augusta Sawyer,1831-1915.
Julia A.,Apr.25,1897,71y.
Julia May, Jan.25,1883-1884.
Mary A.,1866-1946.
Mary A. Crockett,1835-1915.
Nancy,1845-1851.
Nellie F.,1861-1938.
Nellie S., Apr.16,1862-1884.
Sarah Bailey,1825-1894.
Walter,Nov.8,1893,2d.
Walter R.,1861-1898.
William M.,1815-1891.
HALLETT
Emma C. Mar.11,1945,80y.
John E.,Jan.23,1922,69y.
HANCOCK
Lydia H.,Aug.19,1798-Mar.30,1878.
Sarah, Feb.2,1842,77y.
HANSON
Alonzo,1839-1916.
Clarence E.,1873-1911.
Elizabeth M. Sawyer,1841-1916.
Harriett F.,1838-1841.
Lee Parker,May 28,1898,3y.
Marvin S.,May 18,1898,1y.
Mary W. Davis,Oct.19,1849,30y.
Mildred D.,Apr.20,1900,1y.
Olive Delia Diman,1892-1941.
William S.,1865-XXXX.
HARRIS
B. Irene, May 4,1980,51y.
HASKELL
Eugene R.,1888-1922.
Harriet E.,Feb.5,1824-Jan.31,1888.
Sewell B.,Mar.15,1901,78y.
HATCH
Harriet M.,Oct.2,1916,82y.

Juliet S.,Mar.8,1867,13y.
HAWKES
child,Oct.31,1914, s.b.
D. Winslow,1838-July 1910.
Martha E.,1841-1929.
HERRICK
Alice R.,Mar.30,1926,46y.
HERSEY
Esther J.,June 13,1834-Oct.29,1907.
Hannah S.,Feb.12,1803-May 10,1881.
Sarah A. Myra, Nov.21,1833-Feb.13,1892.
Samuel S.,Nov.17,1831-Dec.3,1912
Simeon,Mar.10,1805-July 14,1885
Stillman, May 12,1837-Aug.19,1838.
HIGGINS
Elisha, Feb.9,1823-May 26,1892.
Elisha, Nov.27,1868,88y.
Francis,Oct.5,1820-July 11,1910.
Gracie,Sept.19,1868,3m.
Henry E.,Aug.8,1865,2y.
Junia S.,May 4,1852,11m.
Lizzie,July 30,1877,45y.
Lucy, Oct.26,1857,70y.
Martha,Sept.2,1856,29y.
Mary Jane,Feb.10,1818,23y.
Olive D.,Mar.14,1826-June 4,1884.
Sarah A.,July 21,1859,32y.
Susie W.,June 24,1878-Feb.23,1918.
HILL
Guy E.,1877-Oct.1966.
Henry A.,1849-1925.
Louisa C. Mellen,1852-1883.
Lucy M. Cribb,1875-1940.
Mary Susan Small,1822-1905.
Octavius A.,1824-Nov.1909.
HINDS
Alan Stuart,1917-May 1,1953.
Albert Henry,1874-1946.
Albert Henry,1911-1961.
Grace LIbby,1876-1946.
HITCHINGS
Susan S., Aug.16,1850,32y.
HOADLEY
William Thomas,Oct 4,1951,70y.
HOEGG
Betsey,June 1788-June 1864.
Daniel H.,May 1783-May 1853.
Daniel Warren,June 27,1910,82y.
Isa, Feb.1861-Feb.1865.
Maria F.,Jan.1835-Jan.1865.
HOLMES
Christopher,Apr.17XX-May 186X,92y.
James R.,Feb.1,1893,87y.
John B. May 13,1897,85y.
Judith Morrell,Dec.27,1852,77y.
Lucy, Apr.6,1886,81y.

Lucy E.,May 22,1862,16y.
Mary,XXXX.
Theodosia,Jan.3,1879,75y.
HOLSTON
William Motley,Dec.30,1903,1y,
 s/o Leonard.
HOOD
Daniel, Oct.1877,74y.
Georgina P.,Apr.15,1835-Dec.31,1908.
Harriet E.,Dec.16,1826,25y.
Julia Warren,Oct.19,1839-
 May 8,1895.
Mary, Apr.8,1861,87y.
Pamela M.,Aug.15,1861,65y.
Susan,June 12,1852,56y.
Warren S., Sept.11,1831,1y.
HOPKINS
Anne E. Nute,June 6,1819-
 Apr.21,1835.
Charles M.,Feb.17,1885,1y.
Emily J.D., July 11,1860,15y.
George, Sept.22,1847,41y.
George Walter,1886-May 6,1956.
Ida G.P.,1878-1960.
Sarah J., Mar.3,1885,77y.
HORNE
Martha C.,Mar.12,1892,81y.
HOWARD
Albert S.,Feb.22,1902,60y.
Alma F.,July 24,1929,58y.
Augustus S.,1843-1919.
Ethel L., Sept.13,1917,7m.
George,Dec.10,1850,20y.
Gracie, Mar.18,1882,11m.
Hiram H.,Dec 7,1889,83y.
Joseph E.,Oct.29,1929,50y.
Lenora McDonald,May 10,1873,
 63y, w/o Hiram.
Lenora, Oct.15,1913.
Nancy A.M.,June 26,1926,77y.
Ormanda M.,Aug.28 1896,5m.
Pearlie Vista,Nov.9,1897,12y.
Percy W.,June 26,1898,24y.
Simeon,1791-1870.
Tryphosa Bowker,1790-1861.
Walter T.,Sept.7,1936,64y.
HOWELL
Mary Smith Jerris,1851-1925.
HUDSON
Emily F. Elbridge,1860-1938.
George H.,1859-1933.
Harry W.,1880-1921.
Theodora B.,1843-1920.
Winfield T.,1871-1897.
Jane Plummer,1801-1855.
HUNNEWELL
William,1805-1881.

HUNT
Alice R. 1859-Mar. 27,1922.
Allston Frost, Dr.,1863-Apr.24,1958.
Bethian S.,1816-1886.
Carrie,XXXX.
Ella J.,1857-1893.
Emeline, Mar.1,1907,83y,
 rem. from tomb in Evergreen.
Emma,XXXX.
Henry J.,Apr.17,1853-Oct.12,1918.
Henry N.,June 18,1957,68y.
J., Dr. Feb.3,1778, in London,NH-
 Aug.16,1846.
John Edward, Jan.1,1941,22y.
John M.,1815-1880.
Mary,XXXX.
Walter L.,1879-1880.
HUNTINGTON
Alice M.,Dec.28,1910,44y.
Alpheus,1820-1905.
Frederick W.,Jan.23,1919,62y.
Irene M.,1890-1905.
Lucy A. Jack,1827-1908.
HUSTON
Ansel A., Aug.2,1836-June 28,1902.
Elbridge H.,1833-1919.
Fannie A. Boothby,Nov.12,1840-
 Feb.9,1898.
Jane Augusta,1869-1946.
Joann (Johan),Mar.7,1884,69y.
M.Malvina, Oct.28,1839-Apr.17,1887.
ILSLEY
Ellen E.,Nov.26,1888,56y.
Henry W.,Dec.26,1856-Nov.26,1929.
Stephen E. Oct.2,1886,49y.
INGRAHAM
Edward K. May 13,1882,53y.
JACKSON
Abigail S.,1824-1913.
George W.,1859-1862.
Henry S.,1820-1872.
JACOBS
Ralph W.,Feb.28,1886.
JARRETT
Alice Jarrett Herrick,1880-1926.
Stephen M.,1876-1918.
JERRIS
Ellen G. Larrabee,Feb.12,1832-
 July 28,1907.
Frederick Larrabee,
 Dec.21,1869-Mar.7,1918.
Harriette, Jan.25,1942,75y.
William H., Nov.20,1819-May 31,1885.
JOHNSON
Alice L.,1873-1906.
Betsy F. Tupper,1861-1897,rem. from
 Black Point,Scarboro,Oct.9,1902.

Betsey S.,Sept.27,1867,48y.
Charles S.,1899-Feb.3,1900.
Ellen M.,1831-1907.
Emma L.,1848-1909.
Esther,June 22,1833,3y.
Eunice A.,Jan.27,1862,13y.
Frank,Sept.8,1852,2y.
George,Aug.25,1860,3y.
George W.,1843-1898.
James, Nov.26,1870,68y.
James W.,June 23,1833,1y.
John,1829-1889.
John H.,Dec.30,1859,22y.
Jonathan,Feb.6,1822-Apr.26,1877.
Marie,June 18,1833,5y.
Rebecca J.,1825-1892.
Richard M.,Oct.20,1866,4y.
Ruth,July 14,1856,46y.
Ruth Amanda,Sept.20,1848,1y.
JOHNSTONE
Frank L.,1895-1918.
Georgiana Dana,1863-1947.
JONES
Albert,Oct.15,1813-May 15,1873.
Harriet J.,1813-1910.
John L.,July 3,1930,16d.
John Larrabee,Mar.12,1880-Apr.1959.
Sarah Howe,July 18,1787-Aug.22,1881
William Henry, Jr.,Sept.23,1952.
JORDAN
Alice E. Burr, May 8, 1969, 58y,
  w/o Edward C.,Jr
Anna A.,1861-1907.
Edward C.,Mar.17,1846-Sept.15,1935.
Edward N.,Sept.24,1862,26y.
Eliza Woodford,1815-Mar.26,1851,
  wid/o Joseph.
Elsie L. Boody,Jan.7,1880-
  Feb.15,1974.
Elvira Thayer,1821-1901.
Eunice A. Seal, Feb.4,1808-
  May 23,1863.
Fannie Sumner,Sept.20,1861,9y.
Henry I.,Jan.31,1844-Oct.16,1870.
Henry Irving,Dec.27,1877-Jan.1,1950.
Horace M., Dec.10,1833-May 6,1926.
infant, Nov.25,1910, s.b.
Jane W. Pearson,1815-1884.
Laura,Nov.1,1971,82y,w/o Sam. W.
Marcia Bradbury,Feb.6,1855-
  Sept.20,1923.
Samuel,June 6,1805-Dec.14,1880.
Samuel J.,Mar.14,1852,3y.
Samuel J.,July 10,1861,43y.
Samuel W.,Dec.30,1878-July 19,1924.
William,1813-1893.
William P.,July 27,1838,27y.

KEMP
Caroline Jones,1825-1850.
Jeremiah H.,1823-1901.
Junius,1849-1850.
KENNEY
Henry,May 15,1858,3y.
John S.,Jan.29,1827.
Josiah S.,Aug.10,18XX,23y.
Lucinda May 12,1889,87y.
Ruth A. Field,1834-1915.
William,June 20,1865,69y.
William H.,1824-1881.
KENT
Lawrence Edward,Jan.24,1912-
  Nov.11,1979.
Lloyd I.,Jr.,Aug.27,1909-Oct.21,1990.
Lloyd I.,Sr.,1885-June 10,1968.
Lucy Estelle, Apr 4,1889-Aug.28,1977.
Marion M., Sept.20,1915-Feb.25,1978.
KIMBALL
Allie,Nov.29,1849,12y.
Annie,May 15,1867,11y.
Charles C.,July 1,1839,6y.
Clara C.,Oct.11,1852,17y.
Clarissa D. Colby, Aug.30,1830,30y.
Edmund, Aug.10,1859-Jan.17,1890.
Frank,Dec.14,1849,2y.
John C.,May 12,1830,5m.
Sarah D.,Mar.20,1879,78y.
Sarah H.,Aug.21,1867,41y.
William,Mar.24,1868,72y.
William C.,Dec 2,1867,46y.
Willie,Aug.10,1858,2m.
KNAUT
Mabel Stevens,1870-1903.
KNIGHT
Alice,1891-Sept.22,1977.
Asa,Oct.10,1857,84y.
Chester C.,Aug.25,1983,70y.
Clifford J.,1887-Nov.13,1970.
Etta Margot Fielding,1870-1946.
Frances S.,Oct.10,1860,79y.
Helen M.,1915-July 15,1980.
Jane T.,May 8,1884,77y.
Joshua,Feb.7,1853,47y.
Willard W.,1874-1943.
KNOWLES
Annie Hunnewell Small,1867-1960.
LARRABEE
child/o George, May 15,1889.
Adelaide,May 1841-June 30,1842.
Benjamin, Nov.1828-Sept.18,1832.
Benjamin,Jan.28,1801-Oct.4,1867.
Benjamin,1878-1908.
Benjamin,1836-1915.
David,1830-1902.
Ellen M.,June 30,1824,43y.

Eunice W. Fluent,1827-1895.
Frederic D.,1841-1921.
Harriet F.,Oct.20,1835-Feb.8,1874.
Henry,1845-1921.
John,1805-1882.
Joshua B.,Sept.3,1856,28y,
Katherine B., Sept.7,1839-
June 4,1886.
Louisa A.,Dec.1837-Nov.12,1840.
Marion C. LeGrow,1854-1929.
Ruth Bassett Choate,XXXX.
Samuel,1853-1920.
Sarah L.,1812-May 20,1897.
Sophronia Goold, Apr.16,1808-
July 25,1842.
Sophronia L.,Dec.1833-Nov.1837.
William L.,1826-1913.
LATHAM
Charles F.,1868-1923.
George,May 11,1893.
Sarah J.,Feb.26,1838-Oct.4,1904.
LAWRENCE
Margaret,1865-Feb.20,1956.
LEACH
Almon,1817-1886.
Clara M.,1824-1870.
LEAVITT
Alice D.,Jan.22,1950,87y.
Annie C.P.,Feb.16,1884,26y.
Ernest A.,1880-1882.
Miner H.L.,Aug.21,1942,79y.
LEIGHTON
Abbiel M. Wheeler,182X-1896.
Alpheus S.,1855-Feb. 5,1937.
Andrew H.,1822-1903.
Carl M.,1897-1925.
Cora A. Varney,1867-1935.
Elizabeth Hall,Feb.27,1870-
Apr.20,1941.
Emily Jane Small,1817-1908.
Hattie,XXXX.
Herbert,XXXX.
Icabod W.,1811-1907.
Jennie Hadley Bean,1854-1923.
Jerome C.,Jan.10,1864-Oct.19,1930.
Laura,Mar.1,1892-Apr.7,1892.
Louise,Mar.1,1892-Mar.26,1892.
Marshall P.,1879-1920.
Walter E.,Apr.2,1859,2y.
William L.,1864-1944.
LIBBY
Abram,Mar.2,1808-May 21,1855.
Betsey, Apr.20,1848,78y,w/o David.
David, Apr.26,1818,48y.
Fanny,Apr. 9,1879,74y,w/o George.
Flora,Feb.25,1873,3w.
Frances,May 29,1882,72y.

George,Mar.14,1827,74y.
George,June 13,1852,3y,
adopted s/o George & Fanny.
George,Dec.22,1878,78y.
George,1881-Oct.23,1951,70y.
Hannah E.,July 15,1802-July 13,1883.
Hattie Mae Cobb,1877-Dec.21,1963.
Howard,Aug.15,1871,6m.
John S.,Oct.15,1863,8m.
Malinda V.,Sept.19,1837,1y.
Mary Frances,Sept.26,1861,27y.
Mary H., Nov.14,1904,75y.
Nancy B.Stevens,1818-Mar.18,1854,
w/o Storer.
Noah,Jan.20,1852,1y.
Oscar S.,Aug.10,1867,17y,
s/o Storer & Nancy.
Oscar F.,May 14,1928,59y,
adopted s/o Storer & Nancy.
Priscilla P.,June 21,1848,21y.,
d/o George & Fanny.
Rosina H.,Dec.7,1840,88y.
Ruth Ella,Nov.2,1889,4y.
Storer, Sept.13,1887, 68y.,
s/o Storer & Nancy.
LITTLE
Anna E. Pelton,1860-1932.
George D.,1850-1921.
George H.,1880-1913.
infant,Dec.26,1915,prem.
Mary Louise,1849-1936.
LORD
Samuel,1853-1918.
Samuel,July 30,1884, s.b.
LOVELL
John L.,1819-May 10,1879, rem.
from No. Yarmouth May 27,1896.
LOW
Annie L. Buck,1858-Dec.1,1934.
Frank H.,1851-1907.
Robert,Nov.3,1884.
LOWELL
Ada J.,1850-1927.
Barbara L.,1922-1923.
Cyrus,1899-XXXX.
Eliza, Jan.22,1886,82y.
Emma F. Burnett,1873-1943.
George H., Sr.,1864-1960.
Harriet L.,Mar.23,1873,33y.
Hiram, Feb.29,1872,67y.
Justina F.,1886-1887.
Mabel F.,1898-XXXX.
Oliver A.,1855-1920.
Sarah E.,June 14,1870,36y.
LUCAS
Celestia E. Gilman,
June 22,1840-Oct.25,1912.

Everett A.,Apr.14,1878-Apr.3,1879.
Ida A.,Oct.20,1944,86y.
James,Oct.10,1836-June 11,1894.
Mary E., Aug.6,1867-1868.
Robert Mar.14 - July 14,1876.
Robert, May 19,1928,82y.
Sarah L.,May 24 - Nov.28,1871.
William B.,June 8,1886,1y.
LUNT
Caroline W.,1821-1888.
Joshua,1815-1895.
LYDSTONE
Olive,Mar.20,1914.
LYNCH
Joanna B.,Aug.22,1882,82y.
McDONALD
Adaline B.,1838-1918.
Nancy Bishop,Feb.29,1840.
McGARTH
Addie P.,1884-1908.
James, Jan.3,1908, prem.
Richard S.,Oct.5,1906,2m.
McINTIRE
Annette,Oct. 1906.
Eveline,June 28,1896,71y.
Joseph,1847-1904.
Mary J. Misenor,1852-1919.
Mary R.,May 28,1903,83y.
Nancy H.,1907.
McINTOSH
Charles E.,1875-Dec.16,1916,
1st policeman in Portland to be shot.
Dora B.,1876-1924.
Doris A.,1903-1905.
McKEEN
Jennie M. Cilley,1878-1958.
Leroy E.,1968,87y.
McKENNEY
Florence M. Jackson,1864-1930.
McLEAN
Mabel Annie,1876-Oct.25,1933.
McPHERSON
Elizabeth J.,Mar.4,1861,34y.
MACE
Mildred L.,June 6,1922,30y.
MAGILL
Grace, Apr.1971.
Jessee B.,Jan.23,1964,87y.
MANSFIELD
Angie R.,1846-1935.
child, Nov.2,1875-Mar.29,1877.
MARKS
Chapman David,Mar.26,1960,81y.
MARSDEN
William,1867-1940.

MARSHALL
Ella E. Tucker,June 26,1908-
June 7,1977.
MARSTON
Albion F.,Oct.16,1948.
Charles B.,1852-1854.
Charles M.,1855-1880.
Emma B.,1929-XXXX.
Harris D.,1857-1877.
Henry M.,1827-1877.
Mary W.,1829-1910.
MARTIN
Anna M. Boody,Apr.1,1866,66y,
H.B. Boody - 1st husb.
MASON
Cora Woodman,Oct.15,1953,87y.
MATHEWS
Mercy,June 6,1812-Nov.14,1886.
Thomas R.,Mar.30,1820-Feb.23,1887.
MAXFIELD
Ella F. Stevens,1858-1937.
Herbert N.,1880-1941.
MAXWELL
Adelia,1865-1887.
Annie Small,Apr.14,1965,56y.
Clement P.,1818-1897.
Esther,Sept.18,1863,70y.
Floella,1869-1955.
George C.,1892-1903.
Helen Esther,1846-1924.
Henry Clinton,1849-1886.
Howell C.,1859-Jan.1908,
s/o C.P. & Mary Reckford Maxwell.
infant,Jan.1,1895.
John,Mar.17,1898,3w.
John, buried July 11, XX85.
Mary A.,1827-1903.
Maxwell,Park Benjamin,1861-1886.
Sharon Elizabeth,Jan.2,1945,16d.
MELCHER
Bertha Newcomb,1867-1920.
Donald F.,Nov.12,1938.
George M.,1817-1878.
Harry H.,1865-1922.
Mary E. Varnum,1842-1900.
MERRILL
Adelbert H.,Oct.11,1976,79y.
Adelbert, Mrs., 1964.
Annie Donnethorne,1862-1943.
Charles V.,1853-1935.
Charlotte L., July 28,1839-
Oct.11,1877.
Earl B.,1866-1924.
Eddie,1878-1886.
Edmund P.,Oct.18,1837-Jan.31,1883.
Elizabeth A.,1871-XXXX.

Glynn E.,1891-1911.
Howard O.,1860-1929.
infant,July 6,1917,prem.
Jessie M.,1893-1935.
Lyman P.,Dec.19,1882,50y.
Mary A. Hale,Apr.4,1906,71y.
Myrtie A., Aug.10,1879,2y.
Percy, July 1879,6y.
Percy B.,1890-1945.
Ronaldo L.,Aug.26,1879,20y.
Susie M. Cobb,1846-1913.
MISENOR
Albert,1864-1882.
Mary K.,Sept.1,1885,9d.
Reuben H.,1867-1903.
Susan E.,1826-1896.
MOODY
Charles H.,1819-1852.
MOORE
Carrie Maria Black,1878-Apr. 16,1953.
Emmie F. Gay,1852-1930.
Luke,1810-1890.
Luke Laberton,1849-1925.
Mary Atherton,1806-1894.
Mary Isabell,1843-1899.
Theresa Jane,1840-1899.
William Edward,Jan 4,1957,69y.
MORRILL
Adelaide S.,Apr.5,1852-Feb.18,1881.
Bessie,Apr.29,1878-May 20,1881.
Charles Edwin,May 14,1841-Feb.16,1891.
Charlotte W. Safford,1868-1919.
Edmund N.,1869-1943.
Edward W., Oct.10,1828,9m.
Edward W.,Feb.12,1833,19m.
Elizabeth B. Allen,1827-1896.
Ella M.,July 3,1844-Jan.13,1868.
Harriet J. Quincy, Nov.22,1889,73y.
Harriet Jane, Sept.13,1839-Oct.26,1886.
Levi,Dec.31,1868,66y.
Levi,Oct.6,1872-Apr.19,1901.
Lizzie A.B.,Dec.16,1835-Sept.6,1868.
Mary S.,Mar.24,1863-July 1,1890.
Mary Webb, Apr.16,1834,39y.
Rena H.,Dec.29,1853-Sept.12,1882.
Rufus, Aug.8,1860,64y.
Rufus, Jr.,1836-1917.
Sally Webb,Jan.8,1891,88y.
Sarah Sawyer,1867-1945.
Stephen,Nov.30,1827,4y.
Stephen Aug.12,1853,24y.
Susan B.,Feb.13,1826-Mar.15,1911.
MORRIS
Francis Turman,Oct.13,1991,72y.

MORSE
Percy,Feb.13,1919,48y.
MOSES
Annie Estella,1858-1949.
Aldora Paine,1852-1932.
Charles O.,July 27,1884,2w.
George W.,1851-1931.
Hellen F.,XXXX.
Herbert F.,Aug.1,1863,8y.
Joshua Freeman,1822-1901.
Margaret E.,XXXX,4y.
Mary Gray,1865-1943.
Sarah E. Gray,1822-Oct.3,1904.
Sarah Gay,May 2,1943,78y.
MOSHER
Paul Woodman,Sept.1870-Mar.1872.
MOUNTFORD
Harry Elwood,Apr.9,1877-Nov.11,1905
Mary L. Stevens,1869-Aug.11,1950.
MURDOCK
Clara Stevens,1855-1924.
James Henry,Sept.6,1849-Jan.25,1882
NEAL
Eunice,May 11,1887,76y.
NEWCOMB
Elisha, Co.,Aug.28,1794-Oct.15,1883.
Sybil C.,Apr.29,1798-Mar.19,1885.
Clara A.,Jan.12,1874,25y.
Edward,Dec.13,1892,76y.
Helen Augusta,1858-1862.
John,May 26,1885,81y.
Melville,Feb.22,1847,10y.
Mercy Hamilton,Nov.30,1899,93y.
NEWTON
Pervis W.,1890-1964.
NICHOLS
Etta M., Apr.7,1885,33y.
NICKOLS
Zadioc D., Corp.,May 20,1903.
NOYES
David Franklin,1817-1906.
Emily Smith,1833-Oct.24,1895.
Georgiana, Aug.6,1924,85y.
Jane T./L.,Dec.6,1887,79y.
NUTE
Elisabeth Morrell,Aug.7,1790-May 10,1878.
John T.,Dec.17,1787-Dec.27,1857.
NUTTING
Ida L. Leighton,Nov.26,1875,26y.
OAKSMITH
Frances Woodbury, Oct.8,1831-Apr.17,1914.
O'BRIEN
John H., Jr.,Feb. 21,XX82,70y.
OGDEN
Anna Bennett,1839-1921.

Charles Talcott,1839-1911.
Marguerite,1877-May 16,1953.
Philip H.,1869-1943.
OLIVER
Sally,1789-1828.
ORTON
Agnes E.,1875-1932.
PACKARD
Mary, Dec 25, XX42,78y.
PARTRIDGE
Frank L.,June 3,1907,54y.
Frank L.,Mrs., Feb.23,1890.
William,Nov.22,1887,28y.
PEARSON
Direxa,July 8,1835,53y.
M. Alice,Nov.17,1884,44y.
Mary P.,Apr.11,1874,60y.
Samuel,Nov.18,1856,73y.
Samuel, 3rd, Aug.22,1871,19y.
Samuel, 2nd, Nov 29,1877,61y.
PELTON
Annie Agnes,July 2, XX91,96y.
Annie L., Oct.23,1886,1y.
Bertha Mary, Aug.9,1884,4m.
Fermer W.,May 27,1955,76y.
James,1832-1903.
Joseph E.,Sept.14,1896,3m.
Joseph Sylvester,Aug.9,1947,83y.
Mary A.,Oct.6,1930,68y.
Rebecca J. Harriman Stone, 1833-1912.
Virginia, Jan.4,1907, s.b.
Willard D.,Mar.16,1894,11m.
PENFOLD
Ralph B.,Sept.26,1925,39y.
PENNEY
Leonard,May 20,1885,73y.
Rhapsena,May 25,1886,82y.
PETERSON
Charles H.,Mar.31,1978,97y.
Charles W., Sept.9,1885, s.b.
Charles W.H., July 6,1856-June 30,1928.
Elizabeth N.,July 21,1917,1m.
Everett,Oct.10,1918,21m.
Maud A.,Sept.19,1887,5y.
Melissa Foster,May 6,1964.
Osca, Sept.9,1885.
PIERCE
Cordelia Stevens,July 15,1904, 82y, w/o Levi.
Emeline I./T. Sept.13,1846-June 27,1884.
Florence May, Feb.13,1852-Dec.30,1872.
Levi Q., Apr.29,1858,42y.

POLLEY
Eva May,Sept.2,1852,3m.
Mary,Jan.3,1846,51y.
Mary Jane,Nov.7,1843,3m.
Sarah K.,Aug.20,1861,38y.
William,Apr.7,1832,61y.
POLLEYS
Woodbury H., Capt.,1817-Nov.12,1885,68y.
POLLOCK
Anna D.,May 5,1845-Apr.17,1920.
Adelaide A.,1841-1917.
Fred A.,Mar.16,1843-Apr.8,1924.
G.Frederick,Oct.3,1879-Dec.12,1956.
George W.,1810-1888.
George W.R.,July 18,1839-May 3,1893.
Jennie M./Jane W.,May 23,1846-Jan.8,1900.
Jessie H.,1882-1888.
Lilliam M.,Nov.28, XX85,95y.
Marie L. Boothby, Apr.4,1940.
Sarah,1820-1887.
PORTER
Freeman,July 9,1808-Mar.14,1887
Little Oliver May,May - Dec.1828.
Martha M., Jan.24,1903,62y.
Mary Ann,June 2,1808-June 1,1899.
Samuel B., Apr.16,1840-Sept.2,1868.
Theresa E., June 28,1836-Jan.19,1846.
William Partridge, Oct. 2,1800-Sept.28,1829.
POWERS
Henrietta W., Oct.24,1927,73y.
PRATT
child of George A.June16,1901,s.b.
Alanson S.,Sept.13,1889,24y, rem. from Everett, MA,Dec.1897.
Aratus E.,Apr.30,1895,69y.
Blanche M.,1872-1922.
Grace M.,Oct.8,1922,50y.
Judidiah A.,Mar.25,1914,73y.
PRIDE
Frances Helen,1844-1922.
Frances O.J.S.,1838-1911.
Henry G.,1874-1882.
Leonard Eugene,1870-Nov.26,1962, 92y.
Orman J., Oct. 25, 1979, 97y.
PRINCE
Charles H.,Sept.15,1863-1884.
PROCTOR
Bethsheba,1799-1864.
Charles,1792-1869.
PURINTON
Abby W. Oct.27,1861,48y.

Anna M.,Nov 1,1894,51y.
Francis,Oct.12,1881,74y.
QUINBY
Albion N. Aug.18,1915,79y.
Emily F. Jordan,1836-1901.
Jane L.,Feb.9,1881,53y.
QUINN
Edward Robert,Feb.24,1948,prem.
Inez H., Dec.6,1970.
RACKLEFF
Angelina,July 28,1835,2y.
Chandler,Capt.,Feb.25,1872,78y.
Chandler, Jr.,1813-1857.
Charles A.,1836-1907.
Cordelia, Feb.8,1849,16y.
Edith C. Soule,1862-1909.
Edward C.,1842-1847.
Edward F.,1848-1849.
Ella F. Higgins,1817-1876.
Ellen Dunscomb,1852-1884.
Grace V. Read,1866-1919.
Harriet,July 10,1850,56y.
Henry A.,1865 -XXXX.
Susan H., Jan.18,1874,66y.
Theodosia McKenney,1812-1903.
RADCLIFF
Arthur,XXXX,7w.
Capt.,June 11,1862,43y.
RAMSEY
The 3 below delivered to Robert Ramsey for shipment to Bath.
Ada M.,Sept 9,1875,14m.
Fred M.,Apr.19,1878,8m.
John H.,May 2, 897,45y.
Oliver W., Jr.,July 27,1897,6m.
Robert Thomas, Apr.18,1939,81y.
RAND
Annie E.,Mar.21,1926,72y.
RAYMOND
James, May 2,1888,75y, rem. to Westbrook May 14,1895.
Marion M.,Sept.12,1884,10m.
READ
Eunice Hodson,1792-1832.
Harriet B.,1818-1886.
James Neal,1820-Feb.1912.
Jane Woodford,1807-1882.
John,1793-1889.
John H.,1828-1918.
Mary A. Dow,1830-1911.
Nancy,1836-1844.
Nancy Horton,1792-1889.
Noah,1830-1909.
Rebecca Stevens,1823-1854.
Ruby M.,1840-1909.

RECORD
Cynthia M., Sept.15,1848-Oct.27,1908.
Irene Stevesn, Oct.6,1819-Aug.7,1898.
Lewis Leonard,Rev., Sept.1,1816-Dec.7,1871.
Lewis Miner, Nov. 20, 1855-July 17,1875, s/o L.L. & I.S.
Willie, Jan.24-Oct. 5,1861, s/o L.L. & I.S.
REMPHER
Lizzie M., Aug.8,1906,49y.
REYNOLDS
Alice A.,1851-1930.
Edith Cram,June 30,1954,57y.
Ellen M. Stevens,1817-1898.
Leonard O.,1814-1882.
Martha Ellen,1842-1911.
Richard H., Aug.3,1977,39y.
Sidney James,June 11,1965,77y.
RICCI
infant, Dec.19,1960, prem.
RICHARDSON
Ada C. Mar.25,1869 6y.
RIGGS
Charles I.,1855-1917.
Hannah,1788-1849.
Lilliam M.,1857-1910.
Lydia B.,1818-1868.
Thomas,1786-1853.
Thomas J.,1816-1887.
RILEY
Willard W., Apr.19,1898,33y.
ROBBINS
Elizabeth Ann Rogers, Aug.12,1852-Jan.23,1933.
Floyd Rogers, Feb.13,1881-July 4,1900.
Frederic E.C., July 23,1852-Jan.2,1921.
ROBERTS
Alice, XXXX.
Carrie M.,1862-1901.
Cora B.,1875-Mar.25,1954.
Eben E.,1838-1886.
Emeline S.,Nov.24,1864,29y.
Frank F.,1864-1935.
infant,Jan.7,1900, s.b.
Jennie,1885-1877.
Lenora H.,1836-1918.
Moses G.,1826-1899.
Rebecca P.,1828-1926.
Sarah E. Howard,1833-1920.
Thomas T.,Dec.8,1861,32y.
Vella I.,XXXX,3y.
Walter, XXXX,2y.

Wendall H.,1865-1889.
William F.,1833-1911.
Willie A.,Sept.16,1873-July 22, 1894.
ROBINSON
Jeanette S.,1974.
ROGERS
Caroline F.,May 30,1838,1y.
Isaac,Dec 28,1855 56y.
Mary A.,Dec.28,1835,6m.
Mary H.,Sept.20,1833,1y.
Mercy B.,Dec.22,1885,82y.
ROSS
Mary B.,May 29,1829-July 2,1912.
Simon, Sept.13,1824-Dec.21,1883.
ROWE
Augusta L. Chase,1838-1907.
George W.,1826-1915.
Henry H., June 17,1885,39y.
Henry T., Apr.18,1878 -XXXX.
Joseph B., Jan.13,1871,8y.
Julia A., Nov.27,1878,52y.
Lutie A., Jan.27,1875,2y.
RUSSELL
Addie S., Sept.18,1938,88y.
Laura S.,Sept.29,1886-Nov.29,1963.
RYDER
Mary Ann Coombs,1851-1942.
Moses Allen,1842-1920.
SAMPSON
Clinton R., Aug.10, XX82,88y.
Clinton T.,1928-1975,47y.
Edward K.,July 2,1835-Jan.1,1908.
Horace Lincoln,1869-1907.
Horace Record,1896-1899.
James Arthur,XXXX.
Laura A.,Apr.23,1834-Oct.29,1880
Laura Ellen Ryder,1871-1949.
SANBORN
Anna May, Aug.11,XXXX-
   Sept.10,1934.
Earl D.,1902-1965.
Geraldine L.,1924-1925.
Julia H. Odencrantz,Nov.28,1985, 82y.
Ruth Helen,1823-1949.
Scharlotice A., Apr.15,1925,s.b.
SANDS
Cyrus Fenderson,1830-1907.
Leuna M.,1878-1950.
Mary Aberdeen Mathews,1846-1932.
SARGENT
Leo M.,1878-Dec.28,1963,85y.
Ruth L.,Oct.26,1972,84y.
SAUNDERS
Esther T.,May 1778-May 1873.
Jane S., Oct.1815-Jan.1904.
Samuel, Feb.1776-July 1855.
Thomas T., Sept.1804-Oct.1878.

SAWYER
Albert Francis, 1868-1937.
Alfred S.,1847-1873.
Alice M.,XXXX.
Augusta Stevens,1800-1889.
Caroline D., Sept.26,1860.
Charles A.,Dec.21,1916,2y.
Charles E.,1845-1873.
Charles S.,1817-1873.
Dorcus Ellen,1837-1910.
Edward, Oct.15,1845-Nov.10,1847.
Eben B.,Apr.7,1884,76y.
Eliza, Jan.26,1839.
Elizabeth C., Nov.29,1905,70y.
Elizabeth Noyes,Mar.17,1855,86y.
Enoch Coz,1798,37y.
Francis M.,1826-1894.
Frank, June 21,1848-Nov.22,1860.
Fred E.,June 11,1851-Jan.26,1928.
Frederick,1809-1858.
Hannah, Sept.27,1870.
Harriet E. Merrill,1810-1900.
Harris Eastman,July 5,1911,43y.
Herbert,1869-1895.
Hiram,1802-1893.
infant,Aug. 2,1904,s.b.,ch/o Albert W.
John R.,Feb.22,1889,76y.
Jonathan N.,June 11,1838,75y.
Julia A.,1824-1896.
Lewis, Jan.23,1847,45y.
Lucy A.H. Buck,1839-1910.
Lucy Ann C.,Feb.6,1849,37y.
Mary A.,1821-1849.
Mary A.,Nov.14,1852.
Mary Elizabeth Lanigan,1868-1927.
May Bell (Mary B.),1876-1893.
Nathaniel K.,1822-1904,
   1st w. S.A.Morrill,2nd w. H.Bell.
Phebe H.,1829-1904.
Rosella D.,Jan.1,1849-Oct.16,1937.
Sarah,XXXX.
Sarah,Jan.21,1821,53y, w/o Jonath.
Sarah A.,1822-1872.
William,Oct 25,1857-Oct. 20,18XX.
William F.,Mar.13,1848-July 22,1880.
William K.,1840-1912/3.
SCAMMAN
Ada C., Aug.13, 1852,10y.
Adah E. Chase,1818-1910.
Charles Everett,1895-Feb.8,1896.
Charles F.,1857-1902.
Thalia Corbett Clement,1867-1930.
Tirzah C.,1845-1902.
William M.,1814-1905.
Willie W., Oct.11,1859,9y.
SCHMITZ
Nellie Burnham, 1875-Aug.1966.

William,1868-Nov.15,1962.
SCOTT
Eunice,June 6,1906,2d.
SCRIBNER
Bertha I., Apr.24,1968.
Clarence E., Nov.9,1941,74y.
Helen M. Bailey,1847-1891.
Helen M., Nov. 21,1900,4y.
Horatio G.,1843-1908.
Rena L. Bailey,1900-1902.
SEAL
Ann, Apr.14,1820,10y.
Ann,June 21,1861,83y.
Augusta R. Thayer,1828-1852.
Ava Blanche Carmen,1872-1939.
Edith E.,Jan.21,1886,21y.
Edith M.,Sept.11,1884 5m.
Edith M.,1872-1930.
Elizabeth E. Grows,1867-1919.
George A., Apr.17,1923,62y.
George F.,1831-July 1913.
George F.,Oct.18,1962,5y.
Harold Frost,1887-Oct.26,1962.
Herbert B.,1863-1946.
Mary Louise Ballard,1836-1911.
Queenie H.,1893-Aug. 3,1975.
Thomas,Dec.9,1857,85y.
Thomas, Jr., Apr.7,1860,46y.
William Frost, June 20 1818-Jan.29,1888.
SEAVEY
Marcian, Dr., 1804-1886.
SHEEHAN
Mary,1934.
Olive,1894-June 12, 1955.
SHEPPARD
Georgie A. McDonald, July 22,1852-Jan.23,1880.
Harriet T., 1829-1903.
Joseph W., Capt.,1850-1912.
Richard, Capt.,1822-1900.
SHINN
Albert,Dec.6,1885-Dec.16,1885.
Barbara,1913-Apr.20,1976.
Edward Leroy, Apr.5,1877-Feb.5,1939.
Maria S. Burnell,July 7,1847-Aug.7,1934.
Marjorie V., Dec. 9, XX80,91y.
Paul Haywood, DMD., Apr.29,1879-Apr.10,1931.
Quillen Hamilton, Rev., Jan.1,1845-Sept.6,1907.
SHIRLEY
Elizabeth L.,1840-1925.
Mary J.,Apr.4,1810-Apr.23,1886.
Soloman T.,May 18,1808-Feb.11,1878.

SKILLINGS
Susan A., Feb.11,1921,76y.
SMALL
Atkins,Nov.7,1784-May 3,1859,74y.
Benjamin, Apr.10,1850, m.
Carrie Amanda Lowe,1844-1918.
Clarence L.,1895-XXXX.
Emma,Jan.4,1850-Feb.11,1878.
Frank A.,1896-1904.
Fred L.,1865-XXXX.
Jennie Walsh,1868-1916.
Lucinda P.,May 18,1846,5y, d/o William & Sarah.
Martha,Oct.30,1788-1874.
Reuben L.,1866-1917.
Sarah Howard, Dec.24,1895, 81y,w/o Wm.H.
William H.,Sept.24,1813-Nov.11,1903.
William H.,Jr.,Sept.14,1847-1923, s/o Wm. & Sarah.
SMITH
Edwina, Oct.4,1820,2m.
Elizabeth,1795-1877.
Emeline M.,Jan.13,1832-Oct.29,1908.
Hattie E.,Oct.5,1926,77y.
Jonathan,1794-1881.
Judith Knight May 2,1869,71y.
Julia A. Washburn,1851-1936.
Laurence C.,Dec.24,1834-Dec.22,1915.
Leonard B.,Dec.20,1893.
Lucy J.,June 2,1826-Aug.1,1904.
Moses, Aug.14,1843,59y.
Nathan A.,Nov.8,1831,11m.
Robert B.,1835-1914.
SOULE
Daniel B.,1834-1906.
Minnieola A.,1865-1936.
Virginia H.,1838-1920.
SPENCER
Mary M.,1888-Sept.1,1975,87y.
Oscar Perley,1888-May 13,1965,77y.
STARBIRD
Alfred L.,Nov.10,1923,71y.
STEINMAN
Burgetta C.,Dec.17,1937,59y.
John Albert,1874-1896.
John H.,Aug.30,1846-Mar.25,1886
Mary A.,1849-1924.
Rosina M.,Nov.29,1884-Feb.11,1886.
STEVENS
Albert H.,July 21,1869,5y.
Alberta A.,May 9,1949,77y.
Alfred, Sept.3,1801-Sept.9,1884.
Alfred A.,1836-1923.
Alfred Pablo,June 9,1958,84y.
Alice T.,Oct.8,1926,39y.
Alton E.,Apr.6,1894,3y.

Alton E.,1861-1952.
Alvertina S. Buckley,
 Feb.20,1844-Aug.14,1900.
Annie, Feb.20,1963,86y.
Annie Irene,XXXX.
Augusta, Sept.4,1904.
Betsey, Nov.13,1838,66y.
Carl W., Apr.10,1894,4y.
Caroline W./H.,1865-1948.
Charles M.,1864-1864.
Charlotte W.,1840-1935.
Clark,July 10,1838-July 30,1902.
Edward Clifton, Oct.21,1844-
 Mar.26,1919.
Elizabeth M. Jackson,1877-1945.
Emeline, July 28,1856,22y,w/o O.B.
Emily R.S.,1834-1902.
Emma,XXXX.
Frank Eugene, Apr.23,1855,2y.
Frank G.,Dec.25,1840-Feb.15,1913.
Frederick Jevons,1866-Apr.18,1908.
George Byron,1839-1926.
George M.,1816-1902.
George W.I.,1871-Dec.10,1956.
Georgiana,Apr 23,1905.
Gertrude E.,1890-1953.
Grace J., Sept.2,1885,10m.
Graham, 1867-1867.
Graham Chase,July 18,1926,48y.
Grenville, Mar.31,1910,77y.
Hannah E. Chase,1821-1903.
Harriet K. Francis,Oct.14,1887,92y.
Harriet H., May 21,1829,28y.
Harriet Sawyer,1817-1865.
Harry C. Mar.23,1905,35y.
Helen Pike,1868-1932.
Henry F., Oct.20,1906,50y.
Jean S. Graham,1843-1921.
John A.,June 16,1911,68y.
Jonathan, May 18,1818,54y.
Jotham,1819-1859.
Levi B.,1811-1889.
Lilla Cathleen,Dec.12,1899,1y.
Lovina,Feb.13,1834-Mar.21,1889.
M.P., XXXX.
Maria D. Moses,Mar.30,1843-
 Feb.13,1889, w/o E.C.
Marion,July 1966.
Mary A. Aug.4,1876,75y.
Mary J. Huston,1829-1910.
Maud T.,July 18,1889,22y.
Miriam B. Berry,Dec.18,1865,87y.
Nancy G. Buckley,Feb.22,1806-
 Dec.21,1903.
Nellie I.,1860-1922.
Olliena Dunham,Mar.15,1894,47y.

Orin B.,Lt.,May 16,1861,34y,
 in Fredericksburg, VA.
Philip H.,1869-Sept.13,1958.
Ruth Emma,Dec. 20, 1868, 3y.
Sally, Apr.1,1863,75y, w/o Wm.
Samuel B.,July 24,1848,49y.
Samuel Henry,1827-1910.
Sarah B., Nov.11,1799-July 6,1890.
Sarah Maria,1832-1916.
Thomas C.,Mar.18,1853,2y.
Thomas C.,Nov.3,1869,72y.
William,Jan.3,1862,76y.
William A.,1862-1862.
William Pitt,Oct.8,1928.
Z.B.,XXXX.
Zachariah B., May 17,1856,78y.
STONE
Betsey,June 23,1822-May 13,1874
Eben,Dr.,July 9,1817-Apr.14,1880
Elizabeth H.,1840-1922.
Nancy Adelaide,Nov.6,1846,5m.
Nancy M.,May 14,1846,27y.
William H.,1839-1893.
Willie,Nov.1,1863,6y.
SWALLOW
Barbara Gay, Apr.13,1969,12y.
SWEETSER
Algernon Cox, Apr.20,1838,10m.
Mary Jane B.,Dec.8,1851,16m.
SWEET
Ferdinand M.,1830-1908.
George S.,July 9,1892,54y.
Irene F.Kenney,1832-Sept.26,1908
John W.,1811-1864.
Nancy L.,1815-1882.
SYLVESTER
George E.,Aug.2,1899,11m.
George O. Mar.9,1907,1m.
TAYLOR
Arthur,Aug.4,1897,infant.
Arthur M.,Mar.13,1886,4y.
Arthur W.,May 2,1925,
 rem.to Woodlawn.
TENNEY
John P.,Capt.,May 8,1906.
Louisa E.,Nov.26,1900.
THOMPSON
David,1810-1883.
Fred B.,Apr.22,1862-Feb.16,1919.
George E.,1840-1913.
Louisa,1812-1867.
Louise Hayes,1842-1926.
Mabel F. Huston,Nov.8,1866-
 Nov.5,1907.
Priscilla,Sept.15,1835-July 14,1843.
THORN
Helen Louise,XXXX,13m.

Jane, XXXX,4m.
Jane S.,Dec.6,1856,32y.
Mary C., July 13,1832,10y.
THORNE
William J.,Sept.2,1889,79y.
TIBBETTS
Alice M.,1875-1919.
Arthur P.,1907-1907.
Bernice M.,Jan.1967.
Carroll B.,1911-1911.
Doris L.,May 22,1971.
Charles S.,Nov.20,1917,s.b.
Charles S.,1866-1943.
Hazel,Dec.10,1905,6y.
Laura,1901-1901.
Ralph S.,1905-Apr.18,1990.
Wilbur C.,1913-1914.
William Luther,Feb.15,1919-Jan.15,1943.
TOMPKINS
Louise A. Turner,1845-1933.
TORREY
David,1821-1888.
Harriet F. Jordan,1822-1901.
TROY
Auverne E.,Feb.13,1935,40y.
TRYON
Abbie, Apr.21,1899,84y.
TUCKER
Charles Henry,May 17,1849,6y.
Charles William,Feb.18,1857,2y.
David,July 13,1874,57y.
Hattie M. Vose,June 7,1876,55y.
Hattie Maria,Jan.23,1862,6m.
Mary Elizabeth,May 28,1959,79y.
TUKESBURY
Lillian R.,1879-1900.
Mary A.,1852-1909.
Roger L.,1877-1878.
TUTTLE
Abbie H. Bedell,1838-1908.
True, Sept.4,1834-Aug.2,1892.
TWOMBLY
George A.,July 7,1856,30y.
VORIS
Aletha Isabel,1875-July 30,1958.
VOSE
Lulie M.,Sept.18,1872,31y.
WAKEFIELD
Elizabeth A.,Nov.11,1904,75y.
William,1816-1884.
WALKER
Annie R.,1855-1895.
Arthur K.,1844-1920.
Artie W.,XXXX.
Calvin S.,1855-Jan.1898,s/o Henry
Charles B.,1864-1872.

Edward S.,1857-1930, s/o H.B.& Zelia Lunt Walker.
Edward Sherbourne,1875-Aug.26,1962.
Ernest,1866-1872.
Geneva Eva Cilley,1880-1905.
Grace H.,Mar 24,1906,18m.
H.Percy,1859-1907.
Harriet A. Clark,1846-1920.
Henrietta B.,1864-1937.
Henry B.,1819-1900.
Isabel M. Wilson,1849-1919.
Joseph F.,Jan.6,1917,69y.
Laurence,Mar.1,1914,39y.
Lyman H.,1849-1938.
Mary J. Hawkes,1871-1942.
Ora A.,Aug.9,1908,6y.
Ralph, XXXX.
Sarah K. Bodge,1812-1881.
Sidonia B.,Dec.23,1932,51y, rem. to Evergreen, Dec.1936.
William P.,1807-1892.
Winfred Howard,1881-June 7,1961.
Zelia A. Lunt,1825-1899.
WALLACE
Charles O.,Apr.26,1899,58y.
Lida A., Aug.14,1920.
Maria M.,Sept.9,1885.
Ray C., Aug.7,1900 5m.
WALTON
Florence N.,Nov.30,1860-Jan.31,1943.
Joseph B.,Nov.11,1849-Nov.7,1932
WATERMAN
Willie,Nov.22,1850,1y.
WELD
Martha E. Blake,1827-1910.
WESTON
Eliza Elden,Mar.30,1816-Feb. 26,1892.
James P.,DD., July 14,1815 - Dec.31.1888.
WEYMOUTH
Catherine M.,1859-1887.
WHITE
Albert R.,1881-Mar.27,1952,70y.
Grace Leighton,1888-May 8,1968.
Sarah, May 11,1851,89y.
WHITEHOUSE
Jane O.,Feb.6,1888,92y.
WIGGINS
Luther E.,June 21,1852,12y.
Melvina R.,June 29,1855,13y.
WILLARD
Elsie Winslow,1875-Apr.1911, w/o Dr. Lawrence E.
Lawrence E.,1874.

WILSON
Adam W.,1854-1919.
Annie L.,1844-1914.
Charles L.,1858-1906.
Elmer E., Oct.15,1896,
  rem. to Evergreen May 1924.
Emma J.,1844-1920.
Fannie E.,1842-1902.
George,1815-1884.
George, Jr., July 27,1915-
  Sept.20,1915.
George, 1881-Sept.27,1961.
Isabell W.,1848-1851.
Jason,1810-1860.
Leighton, Jan.31,1920, s.b.
Lois P.,1820-1887.
Lucy Barbour,1881-Nov.4,1957.
Marcia B.,1845-1910.
Mary Ann,1813-1896.
Orrin,1815-1853.
Phebe Winslow,1822-1860.
Rufus,Dec.12,1924,85y.
Wallace H.,1850-1918.
Zelia F.,1847-1859.
WINSLOW
Aaron,July 27,1854,75y.
Edward C.,Feb.24,1886,64y.
Eunice Hunewell,1837-1914.
Frederick,1835-1923.
Fred L., Oct.10,1965,76y.
Lousia Hamlin,1821-1887.
Henrietta Louise O'Brion,1955.
Sarah B. Seavey,1815-Nov.16,1899.
Sarah Deane, Feb.2,1864,75y.
WITHAM
Abigail,1800-1894.
WOODBURY
A. Amelia,Mar.8,1824-Apr.14,1868
George W.,1829-1894.
Hannah Esther, Oct.12,1802-
  Jan.11,1876.
Mary Edwards,1837-1928.
Nathan L.,Jan.3,1798-Oct. 2,1880.
WOODFORD
Charles D., June 3,1818-Sept.13,1818.
E.D., Apr.5,1849,67y.
Hannah B.,July 20,1885,77y.
Harriet, Apr.3 -July 23,1813.
Isiah,July 12,1819,40y.
Lucinda J.,1858-1936.
Margaret, Sept.4,1858.
Mary, Sept.6-8,1808.
Mary Ann, Dec.25,1816-Feb.26,1817.
Mary Frances,Dec.20,1789-
  Oct.21,1871.
WOODMAN
Amanda F.,Mar.19,1853,25y.

Anna C. Cutler,July 21,1854-
  Apr.18,1925.
Barbara E. Bisbee, 1917-1947.
Edna S., Nov.8,1904,15y.
Eulleatta, Mar.26,1942,77y.
Harold W., Oct.2, XX81,88y.
Jonathan Mar.3,1934,70y.
Lucy H.,1837-1915.
Mary E. Weston,Jan.25,1849-
  Dec.27,1888.
Nathan A.,Nov.3,1923,70y.
Nathan M.,1831-1886.
Ralph Moore,June 19,1965,80y.
Walter,Aug.30,1852-Sept.4,1928.
WRIGHT
Ann Jane,Feb.21,1872,60y, rem. from
  Knight Cemetery,Windham,Oct.1897.
Maria E. Grant Feb.27,1902,72y.
Thomas, 1810-Oct.31,1883,rem. from
  Knight Cemetery,Windham,Aug.1897
WYER
Annie G.,Nov.28,1963,78y.
WYETH
Flora Maud,May 20,1886,10y.
George W.P.,1844-1914.
Minnie F., Feb. 25,1874,3w.
Sarah J.A.,1850-June 25,1915,
  w/o George W.P. Wyeth.
Winnifred May, Sept.22,1880,1y.
YORK
Atta May (Alta), Oct.21,1936,69y.
Miriam F.,Jan.13,1905,42y.
Miriam S. Ballard,1828-1893.
William F.,Mar.12,1928,68y.

✧ **EVERGREEN CEMETERY** ✧
672 Stevens Ave.,Portland.
Began in 1852 due to space limitations of the 2 existing cemeteries, with 55 acres. Later purchases expanded this cemetery to over 370 acres. Approximately 60,000 people are buried here, unfortunately the records for the early burials (c.1852-c.1870's) have been lost. I transcribed a small portion of the gravestones prior to 1875. Most burials records can be found at the Evergreen Office.
Forest City Cemetery was laid out in 1858 for more inexpensive burials and Mt. Cavalry Cemetery was built for the Catholics.

ADAMS
John O.,Oct.9,1833,16y.
AKERS
Eleanor W.,1827-1881.
BACON
Asenath,Dec.19,1788-
Feb.16,1847, w/o Nathaniel.
Nathaniel,July 13,1786-Feb.25,1869.
Parsons,Apr.14,1853,29y.
John Mason,Aug.15,1878,65y.
Margaret,Dec.13,1887,68y,
w/o John Mason.
BARTOL
Anna Given,May 14,1788-
Dec.18,1863,w/o George.
George,Aug.8,1779-Apr.6,1855.
BATEMAN
John,Sept.22,1827-Sept.24,1898.
Lucy Jane,Dec.8,1828-Feb.9,1860,
w/o John.
Mary,Mar.16,1843-Apr.4,1870,
w/o John.
BEALE
Cynthia Colby,Sept.5,1885,79y,
w/o Samuel N.
Martha Ann,July 1,1844,40y,
w/o Samuel N.
Samuel N.,May 10,1803-Sept.10,1869.
BECKETT
Abigail,July 4,1788-June 11,1873.
Charles E.,Sept.9,1866,54y.
CALDWELL
Merritt,Nov.29,1806-June 6,1848.
CARPENTER
Seth G.,1819-1844.
CHURCHILL
Eunice S. Dyer,Nov.17,1838,
23y,w/o Thomas.
Thomas,June 15,1838,24y, at sea.
CLARKE
Marcia H.,Oct.22,1871,33y,
d/o R.L.& Marcia Robinson.
CLIFFORD
Cordelia R.,Sept.22,1863,39y.
Hannah Ayer,1811-1892.
Nathan J.,Jan.12,1832-
Aug.16,1869,h/o Hannah Ayer.
CORNING
Clarence Hamilton,1834-1879.
COVELL
Phebe J.,July 23,1900,84y,w/o Stan.
Stanley,Aug.2,1867,56y.
COX
Adeline Preble,Sept.1,1805-
Aug.19,1883,w/o John Cox,
d/o Capt.Enoch & Salley Preble.

John,Feb.13,1795-Jan.,25,1871,
s/o John & Susan Greenleaf Cox.
Thankful Harris,Oct.19,1798-
July 11,1833,
d/o Jeremiah & Thankful Gore.
CRAM (TOMB)
Harry Kittridge,July 2,1853-
Apr.23,1854 ,
s/o N.O. & Mary R.B.K.Cram.
J. Abbie Hodgkins,1847-1932.
Julia Hodgkins,Feb.2,1866-
July 13,1940.
Julia A. Hodgkins,Jan.28,1894-
Mar.8,1915,w/o Nathaniel.
Margaret Hodgkins,b. Apr.26,1868.
Mary R.B.Kittridge,b.Epping,N.H.,
May 10,1815-May 12,1861.
Nathaniel O.,Mar.9,1813-
Mar.16,1894,h/o Mary R.B.
Octavia Kittridge,Aug.16,1851-
Aug.15,1862,d/o N.O. & M.R.B.
Octavia Lambard,July 9,1864-
Mar.15,1930.
COUSES, ch/o Dr.Wm.P. & Susan H.:
Mary Balch & Robert Wheaton II,
Oct.3-10,1912.
CUMMINGS
Anne Clifford,Jan.19,1830-
Nov.14,1899,w/o Enoch.
Enoch Lincoln,May 23,1827-
Jan.21,1858.
CUSHMAN
Alvan,Aug.5,1859,72y,h/o Nancy.
Anna W.,Jan.1861,20y,d/o A.& N.
Charles Henry,Dec.15,1866,5y,
s/o J.S.& M.E.
John S.,Rev.,Jan.20,1870,36y.
L.W.,1849,19y.
Nancy Smith,Jan.24,1864,66y.
Rosamond,Feb.5,1811-Oct.6,1887,
w/o Merritt.
Sarah E.W.,May 5,1852,22y,
eldest d/o Alvan & Nancy.
Susan E. Hasty,Aug.6,1833-
July 22,1883,w/o George H.
DANA
Louisa,Apr.21,1855,20y,d/o Jas & M.
DAVIS
Isaiah H.,Mar.21,1878,69y.
DEAKE
Abigail G.,Aug.30,1843,59y.
Benjamin,Aug.7,1854,74y.
Charles,Oct.2,1811-Dec.16,1873.
Ella Christine,Dec.22,1917,
in Paris, d/o Charles & Olive.
Olive Y.,Aug.30,1819-Apr.6,1872,
w/o Charles.

DEANE
Annie S.Morse,Sept.28,1827-
Sept.1,1880,w/o Henry P.
Henry P.,Oct.9,1823-Mar.25,1873.
Willie,1850-1872,s/o H.P.& A.S.
DRESSER
Alfred M.,Sept.10,1870,63y.
Martha A.,1813-1889,w/o Alfred.
DROWNE
Elizabeth E.Studivant,Jan.31,1822-
Nov.27,1891,w/o Joseph.
Joseph,Jan.31,1808-Jan.23,1897.
DUNCAN
Mary, XXXX,2y.
Mary, XXXX,4y.
DYER
Amanda P.,1817-1841.
Betsey,Dec.29,1858,92y,w/o Ezekial.
Elizabeth,July 23,1862,72y,
w/o Lemuel.
Ezekial,June 25,1849,86y.
Lemuel,Jan.24,1847,61y.
EAXON
Eunice G.,May 7,1865,59y,w/o Wm H.
EMERSON
Sarah,May 13,1863,54y.
Stephen,Mar.14,1807-May 26,1869,
h/o Sarah.
FESSENDEN
Deborah Chandler,June 11,1792-
Dec.5,1873,w/o Samuel.
Samuel,July 16,1784-Mar.19,1869
William Pitt,1806-1869.
FRATES
Antoine,Aug.17,1867,87y.
Mary,Dec.14,1859,81y,w/o Antoine.
GILMAN
Charlotte Jenks,Mar.14,1858,61y.
Ellen M.,Feb.16,1864,40y.
Nathaniel J.,Mar.5,1867,48y.
Samuel,Mar.25,1852,62y,h/o C.J.
Susan,Aug.25,1865,38y,w/o N.J.
GORE
Jeremiah,Jan.12,1762-Oct.12,1836.
Thankful Harris,Dec.26,1765-
May 26,1856,w/o Jeremiah.
GRAY
Edward,Dec.29,1851,48y.
GREEN
Benjamin,Oct.29,1836,43y.
Benjamin F.,July 30,1855,31y,
died in Trieste.
GREGG
Eliza J. Miltimore,1810-1869.
Silas Dinsmore,1806-1853,
lost at sea,h/o Eliza J.

GRISWOLD
Clara Susan,1848,2y.
Nelly J.,Feb.9,1858,48y,w/o Virgil.
Virgil,Sept.8,1867,60y.
HALE
Ella Marie,Oct.7,1853-Apr.5,1896.
Joseph,Feb.5,1820,42y.
Joseph,Oct.1,1815-Mar.31,1869.
Sarah B.Stetson,Sept.9,1815-
Mar.8,1893,w/o Joseph.
HALL
Huldah H.,Dec.3,1876,77y.
Paul,Feb.8,1867,68y,h/o H.H.
HAMILTON
John,Capt.,1796-1847.
Sarah W.,1795-1858,w/o John.
4 ch/o John & Sarah:
John E.,1836-1863,
Emma M.,1830-1879,
Amelia A.,1836-1863 &
Albina S.,1828-1879.
HAMMOND
Abby B.,Feb.7,1818-Mar.4,1874.
Sophie T.,Nov.1819-Jan.1894.
Thankful,Mar.11,1785-June 21,1866,
w/o Thomas.
Thomas,June 28,1786-Apr.1,1871.
Thomas,Jr.,Nov.5,1806-Feb.29,1868.
William,1816-1880,h/o Abby B.
HANSON
Eliza Ann,Apr.13,1829-
June 19,1859,d/o Sam. & Statira
Persis E.Greeley,May 20,1815-
June 10,1883,w/o Samuel.
Philip Greeley,Mar.30,1849-
June 18,1853, s/o Sam. & Persis.
Samuel,Nov.14,1788-Aug.25,1862.
Samuel,Feb.22,1847-Dec.28,1905.
Statira Morton,Aug.12,1836,39y,
w/o Samuel.
Veranus C.,May 14,1871,58y.
HARRIS
Augustus Louville,Jan.26,1828,
3m, s/o John & Thankful.
Charles M.,1814-1886,s/o J. & T.
John,Dec.8,1853,67y.
HARTSHORN
Albert H.,July 3,1859,22y,s/o J.M.& L.
Hannah L.,Oct.17,1900,64y.
Jesse M.,Mar.13,1889,74y.
Lucy A.,Mar.25,1871,60y,w/o J. M.
HEYWOOD
Foster,July 27,1845,46y.
HILL
George A.,1819-1865.
Sarah Alice,1860-1878.

HOLBROOK
Alfred,2nd., Aug.10,1872,28y.
INGRAHAM
Octavius C.,Mar.1843-May12,1964.
JACKSON
Harriet S. Elliott,1839-1879,
  2nd w/o Isaac.
Harriet S. Hartshorn,1820-1876
  & her 3 infants, w/o Isaac.
Isaac,1818-1882.
JEWETT (one monument)
George,1795-1883.
Hannah L. Tucker,1861-1933,
  w/o William S.
Joseph, Deacon,July 15,1796,47y.
Joseph L.,Apr.7,1845,19y,
  s/o Joseph & Mary.
Joseph S.,Oct.5,1870,82y,
  s/o Joseph & Ruth.
Mary J.,July 17,1894,
  d/o Joseph & Mary.
Mary Parker,Aug.26,1863,66y,
  w/o Joseph S.
Ruth,May 7,1848,92y,w/o Joseph.
Sarah,Aug.29,1875,90y,
  d/o Joseph & Ruth.
William S.,1844-1899.
ch/o Joseph & Ruth:
Hannah,Sept.29,1803,13y,
James C.,Dec.9,1822,12y.
Luther,July 31,1866,63y.
William,Apr.4,1863,82y.
KIDDER
James Drummind,June 1,1869,67y.
Holwell,Mar.26,1865,27y.
Kate Drummond,Sept.17,1871,25y.
Marianne Holwell,June 1,1808-
  Aug.11,1893,w/o James.
KNIGHT
Willis M.,May 8,1877,20y.
LEIGHTON
Caroline P. Trundy,Jan.21,1855,
  31y,w/o Leonard,d/o Wm. & Harriet
Emma J.,July 27,1875,21y,
  d/o George F.& Hannah
LEWIS
Susan,Apr.7,1861,75y,
  wid/o Capt.Anthony
Lewis, late w/o William Thompson.
LITTLE
Frances M.,June 29,1858,52y.
Hall J.,Sept.30,1864,61y.
Rebekah,Sept.23,1847,71y,
  w/o Stephen.
Stephen,Mar.22,1852,78y.
McDOWELL
Rachel Ann,1836-1854.

William,1838-1967.
MARTIN
John,Sept.2,1855,35y.
Mary Morrill,Mar.24,1831-
  Feb.13,1889.
MAXWELL
James,Feb.14,1850,39y.
Martha,July 17,1838,26y,w/o Jas.
MEGQUIRE
John L.,Jan.3,1840,45y.
Serena D.,Aug.24,1871.
MERRILL
Martha,June 14,1852,82y.
MORSE
Jane,Aug.10,1809-June 21,1896.
Jonathan Kimball,Aug.24,1802-
  June 20,1860.
NEWTON
Jane Dow,May 19,1871,79y,w/o G.J.
Gideon J.,Rev.,Feb.17,1859,71y.
PARRIS
Albion Keith,Jan.19,1788-
  Feb.11,1867.
Samuel,Sept.10,1847,92y,Rev.Sol.
Sarah,Aug.1,1836,77y,w/o Samuel.
PARKER
Nathaniel,May 19,1853,26y.
PARSONS
Nancy P.,1799-1873,wid/o Peter.
PATTEN
Celia,July 18,1858,73y.
George W.,Aug.3,1853,35y.
Stephen,May 15,1764-Feb.17,1854,
  h/o Celia.
Susan H.,Aug.12,1857,45y.
PAYSON
Ann Louisa Shipman,Nov.1848.
Carlone S.,1815-1816.
Charles Henry,1816-1819.
Edward,D.D.,b.NH,July 25,1783-
  Oct.22,1826,h/o Ann Louisa.
PEARSON
George H.,June 27,1849,20y.
Jacob J.,Nov.23,1858,26y.
PENNELL
Charles,Jan.21,1865,31y.
PETERS
Horatio Quincy,1816-1858.
Miriam Todd,1814-1890,
  w/o Horatio.
PHINNEY
Betsey H.Heyford,1822-1866.
Edmund,1818-1884,h/o Betsey H.
Jane Meade Hight,1829-1918,w/o Ed.
6 inf/o E. & B.H., XXXX.
PLUMMER
A.J.,Sept.8,1838,30y.

2 d/o A.J.&Rebecca E.:
Elsie J.,July 16,1885,55y,
Francis A.,Dec.16,1836,4y,
Rebecca E.,May 2,1854,50y.
PREBLE
Enoch,Capt.,July 2,1763-
Sept.28,1842,s/o Jedediah.
George Henry,Feb.25,1816-Mar.1,1885
Henry Oxnard,Jan.1,1847-
May 21,1871,24y,s/o Geo. H.& Susan.
Mehetable,Aug.20,1805,77y,
w/o Jedidiah.
Sally,Sept.22,1748-June 20,1818,
w/o Enoch,d/o Dea. Thomas Cross.
Susan Zabiah,Aug.1,1820-
July 22,1875,d/o John & Thankful H.
Cox, w/o Comm. G.H. Preble for 30y.
PRINCE
Edward C.,Nov.26,1849,28y.
Hannah B.,Jan.3,1869,36y.
Hugh,Jan.1,1840,51y.
Molly,Apr.18,1860,73y.
William H.,Apr.1888,70y.
RICE
Nehemiah C.,Dec.1802-July 1881.
Phebe Tyler,May 1804-Aug.1860,
w/o Nehemiah.
RICHARDS
Caroline A. Nelson,1817-XXXX &
her children, w/o Joshua A.
Joshua A.,1814-1852.
ROBERTS
Mary S.,1786 in Durham-1860,76y
ROBINSON
Charles W.,Aug.23,1848,2y,s/o R.L.
William H.,June 9,1861,18y,
oldest s/o R.L. & Marcia.
ROSS
William,1811-1875,h/o Sarah.
SAMPSON
Jane R.,Nov.3,1854,34y,w/o Micah.
SANBORN
Lyman,Nov.20,1813-Feb.19,1874.
Phebe J. Leavitt,Sept.8,1833-
Feb.27,1873, w/o Lyman.
SAWYER
Eliza,July 17,1874,75y.
Hannah C.,July 11,1868,19y,
w/o Daniel W.
SMITH
Frances Ormond Jonathan,1806-1876.
SPLAR (?)
Caroline P.,Aug.28,1861,20y,w/o Leve.
STARR
Daniel,Mar.27,1795,in Cornwallis,
Nova Scotia-d.Nov.13,1868, NY.

Sarah Alice,July 29,1802,
in Wolfville,Nova Scotia -
Oct.9,1870,w/o Daniel.
STEVENS
D.Henry,July 10,1871,32y.
Daniel,Aug.12,1813-Feb.6,1867.
Maude,June 12,1877,33y,w/o Wm. K.
May Alice,Sept.1871.
Sarah Kimball,Jan.22,1812-
Nov.8,1896,w/o D.
STETSON
Almira,July 18,1870,84y,w/o James P.
Ede K.,Oct.18,1850,50y,2nd w/o Jas P
George,Apr.2,1849,14y.
James P.,Jan.26,1857,84y.
James P.,Jr.,Mar.1811.
Margaret,Sept.28,1825,45y,w/o Jas. P.
STORER
George Lord, b.&d.1825,s/o J. & M.
John,1796-1867,from Sanford
John Lewis,1828-1843,s/o J.& M.
Meribah Hobbs,1797-1860,w/o John.
STROUT
Eben,1802-1880.
Hannah C.,1800-1873,w/o Eben.
STURDIVANT
Addison C.,Sept.17,1824-Aug.27,1864.
Ephrima G.,Feb.27,1817-
Sept.20,1818,s/o Isaac & Olive.
Isaac,Mar.4,1784-Dec.18,1827.
Mary T.,Feb.14,1812-Oct.6,1827,
d/o Isaac & Olive.
Olive,Mar.31,1790-Oct.18,1827.
SUMNER
Eben,Aug.15,1856,82y.
Eben E.,Oct.11,1837,27y.
Elizabeth T.,Aug.2,1886,82y,w/o Eben.
Henrieta,Jan.30,1865,83y,w/o Eben.
John L.,Dec.24,1846,30y.
Mary C.,Sept.25,1866,48y,
d/o Eben & Henrietta.
TANNER
Christopher S.,Oct.23,1878,16y.
Robert,Jr.,Apr.24,1872,18y,
s/o Robert & Sarah.
Sarah,Aug.15,1874,46y,w/o Robert.
Sarah Ann,Nov.28,1873,18y.
3 inf/o Robert & Sarah, no dates.
TAPPAN
Sarah,Mar.31,1872,89y,w/o John.
TATE
George,1796-1842.
THAYER
Lydia E.,Nov.20,1871,81y.
Solomon,Dec.22,1857,68y,h/o Lydia
THOMSON
Edward P.,Feb.17,1853,34y.

TODD
John,Feb.21,1854,75y.
TROWBRIDGE
Charles,Feb.26,1869,63y.
Eunice,Oct.26,1852,76y,w/o John.
John,Maj.,Nov.14,1835,60y.
Sarah H.,1807-1897,w/o Charles.
UNDERWOOD
Abby,1805-1874.
Benjamin,1798-1866.
WATSON
Barron C.,Nov.15,1823-Oct.30,1894.
John Fanning,Oct.9,1857-May 5,1859, s/o Barron C.
Julia Whitman,June 27,1866,37y, & s.b. infant,w/o Barron C. Watson.
William McKinstry,Apr.21,1856-Feb.19,1857,s/o B.C.
WHITNEY
Charles H.,1828-1885.
Charlotte Cook,1803-1850,w/o Nath'l.
Frederick,1831-1870.
Hannah Porter,1826-1854,w/o C.H.
Nathaniel,1800-1838.
Nathaniel,1842-1854.

WILLIAMS
Bella F., date buried in ground.
Betsey,July 16,1793-Jan.21,1872.
Charles L.,b.Mar.1,1841-XXXX.
Ida Florence Freind,Dec.16,1845-Jan.28,1886, w/o Charles L.
Isabella,Mar.21,1845,40y,w/o Levi.
Julia A.,Dec.31,1872,70y,w/o Levi.
Levi,May 13,1865,69y.
WILLIS
Frederick,1856,14y.
Julia Whitman,Apr.21,1872,70y.
William,1845,20y,s/o Wm.& Julia.
William,Feb.17,1870,75y,h/o Julia.
WINSLOW
Anna,Aug.28,1844,70y.
David,Feb.1,1859,83y.
Esther,Sept.1858,25y.
James,Dec.7,1867,67y.
Patience B.,Nov.20,1878,84y.
WITHAM
Albion,1826-1863.
YEATON
John,July 20,1884,78y,h/o Susan.
Susan N.,Jan.10,1875,61y.

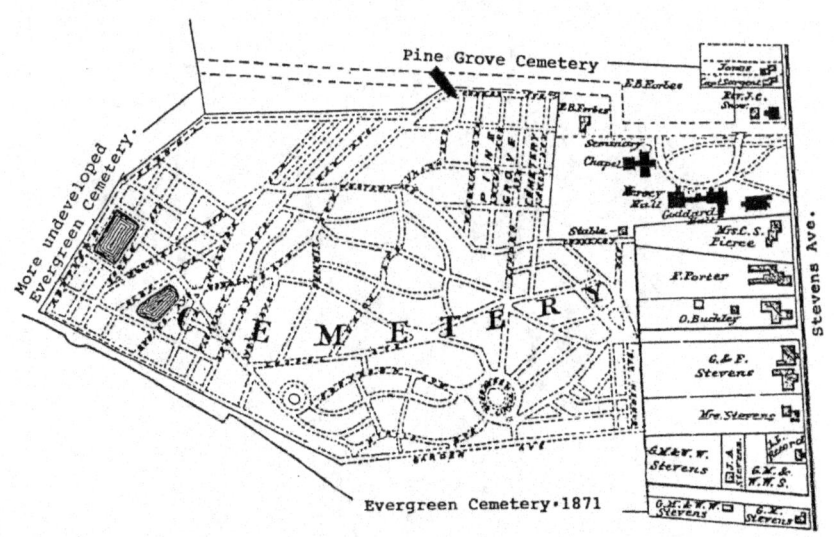

Evergreen Cemetery・1871

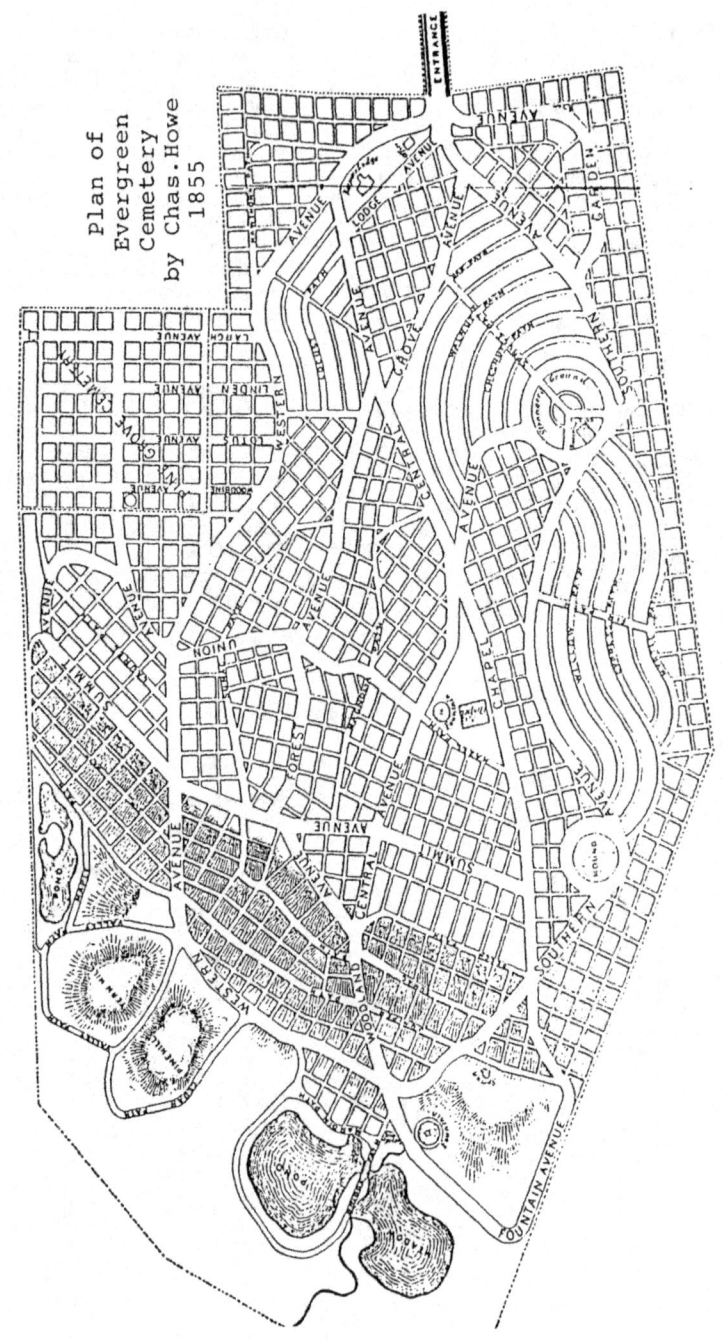

Plan of Evergreen Cemetery by Chas. Howe 1855

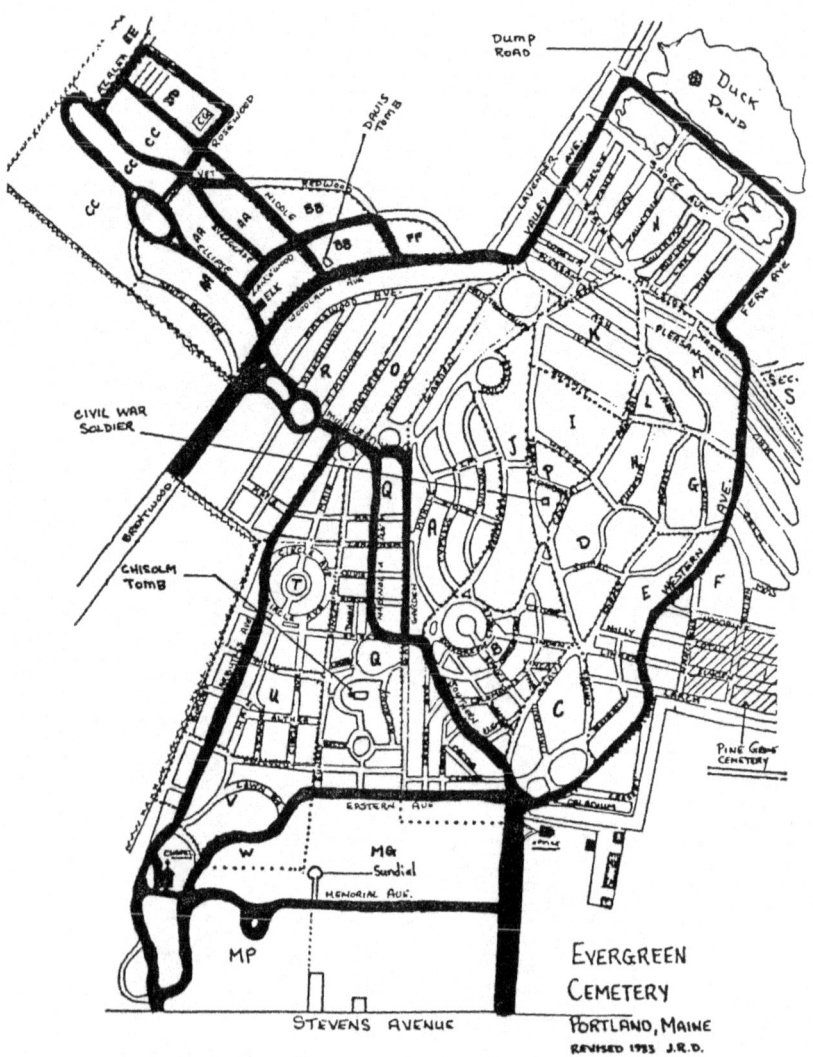

✤ **HARDY CEMETERY** ✤
138 Hardy Road, Westbrook.
Destroyed, stones upturned
by falling trees and neglected.
* removed to Highland Lake Cem.,
headstones were left behind.

HARDY
*Albion,May 1827,23y,
  s/o Amos & Anna.
*Amos,1806-1859.
*Anna,Feb.1867,w/o Amos.
Daniel, Oct.19,1851,76y.
Daniel, Sept.29,1826,3y,
  s/o Daniel & Hanna.
Francis,Mar.14,1844,24y,
  s/o Daniel & Hanna.
Hanna,Nov.22,1858,79y,w/o Dan'l.

✤ **CONANT CEMETERY** ✤
Conant Street, Westbrook.
In 1938 5 government headstones
were set on graves of Revolutionary
Soldiers.

BABB
Daniel, Sept.2,1872.
BIXBY
William, d. ?, War 1812.
CONANT
Ann, Sept.21,1844,w/o Daniel.
Eva G.Laidhaw,1895-1992,w/o Percy.
Joseph,Nov.9,1701-Jan.2,1765,
  and his wife,no information.
Percy,1890-1976.
Samuel, d. ?, War of 1812.
Samuel & Hannah Worcester,
  his wife, bro/o Joseph.
FREEMAN
Enoch,Sept.14,1750-
  Dec.4,1832,s/o Enoch & Mary.
Enoch,Feb.27,1814,81y,s/o Enoch.
Mary,July 21,1796-
  July15,1844,d/o Enoch & M.
Mehitable Cushing,
  Feb.27,1844,84y,w/o Enoch.
Nathaniel,stone broken,can't read,
  War of 1812
Sally, Oct.27,1797-Sept.7,1815,
  d/o Enoch & Mehitable.
HAWES
Joseph, Oct. 1770 in Dorchester,MA-
  Dec.2,1806.
QUINBY
George Washington,1813.

SAUNDERS
Donald,Jan.10,1994,80y,
  h/o Eleanor Conant.
WEBB
Frances,1826 ?, Mass. Militia.
James, can't read.
Jonathan, Nov.25,1755 in Gorham-
  Apr.8,1810.
WISE
Elizebeth Pearson, Feb.1722-
  Jan.25,1799, wid/o Dr. Joseph,
  2nd d/o Moses P. of Falmouth.

✤ **KNIGHT CEMETERY** ✤
360 Duck Pond Road.
In fair condition, several have been
removed to Woodlawn Cemetery.

BROWN
Harriet E.,Aug.16,1909,w/o Lewis P
COBB
Dorcas,July 7,1825,39y,w/o Jas,Jr.
GARREY
Mark, Nov.2,1845, 21y,
  s/o Daniel & Martha.
KNIGHT
Amos, Dec.15,1863,79y
Caroline,Dec.2,1889,84y,w/o Levi.
Charles C.,1820-1890.
David,Feb.29,1868,73y.
Frank,Nov.30,1872,74y.
Joanna,Jan.7,1867,68y,w/o Amos.
Leonard,July 2,1842,4d,
  s/o Levi & Caroline.
Levi,Nov.22,1869,77y.
Louisa F.,Aug.19,1839,10y,
  d/o Amos & Joanna.
Mary,Jan.5,1868,71y,w/o David.
Thomas,Jan.21,1839, 58y.

✤ **HALE CEMETERY** ✤
222 Duck Pond Road, Westbrook.
Hale reportedly built here after
they were burnt out of Portland
(Falmouth) by Mowatt in 1776.

HALE
Alpheus,May 21,1817-Mar.5,1898.
George, July 13, 1850, 57y.
George R.,1821-1862.
Josephine Mallard,1858-1883.
Leon, XXXX,h/o Josephine.
Martha,Jan.23,1797-Aug.9,1883.

✦ **WESTBROOK GRAVESITE** ✦
Knight Farm, County Road,
Westbrook. Site located in 1976.

WESTBROOK
Thomas, Col., 1674-1744.

✦ **JOHNSON CEMETERY** ✦
630 County Road,Westbrook.

GARDNER
Eliza L.,Dec.16,1867,65y,w/o Charles.
JOHNSON
Elizabeth, June 4,1838,29y ?,w/o Wm.
Richard,Apr.24,1816 ?,80y.
XXXX,1838, s/o XX.
KNIGHT
Ann,June 15,1817,40y,w/o Geo.
Betsey,June 9,1839,19y,
d/o George & Mary.
Charles H.,June 10,1865-Oct.19,1865.
Clara F.,Sept.5,1856,4y,
d/o Nathaniel & Martha K.
Eunice J.,Oct.6,1825-Jan.12,1889.
George,Feb.18,1837,59y.
Hattie A.,July 14,1863-
Aug.1,1864,d/o Henry & Sarah.
Henry,Sept.1,1824-Nov.13,1866.
Hezekiah,June 13,1827-Oct.21,1879.
John,Dec.3,1857,76y.
John E.,May 18,1850-Jan.23,1869,
s/o Henry & Sarah.
Mary,Feb.11,1870,w/o George.
Sarah J.,Apr.22,1830-Feb.12,1867,
w/o Henry.
Warren C.,Feb.5,1852-
Nov.20,1881,s/o Henry & Sarah.
LIBBY
Mary J.,Mar.12,1808-
Feb.22,1850,w/o Elbridge G.
MORSE
Alonzo,Aug.23,1876,50y.
Sarah S.,Nov.19,1870,49y,w/o A.
PARKER
Charles H.,Feb.21,1883.
James,1803-1884.
Sarah Green,1802-1892,w/o Jas.
Rebecca, B., can't read.
WESTERBERG
Erika Matilda,1875-1913.
XXXX
Eunice, can't read dates,
d/o Paul & Abigail.

✦ **GOWEN FAMILY CEMETERY** ✦
611 Duck Pond Road, Westbrook.
Burials from 1780 to 1934.

BARBOUR
David,1783-1834,
neph/o Edna Knight Gowen.
Joseph,1811-1893,s/oD. &Mary.
Mary Brackett, 1784-1836,
w/o David, d/o Wm.
Ruth Lord,1823-1897,w/o Jos.
GORDON
Hannah Knight,1837-1896,
w/o John,Jr., d/o John Knight.
Howard,1871-1901,
s/o John,Jr. & Hannah K.
Ida Babbidge,1871-1931,w/o Howard.
John, Jr.,1835-1903.
Mary A. Knight,1825-1892,
sis/o Hannah,2nd w/o John H.,Sr.
GOWEN
Adeline,1828-1872,d/o Peter & Nancy.
Anna Anthoine, June 29,1800-
Dec.31,1851, w/o Moses,
d/o Nicholas,Jr. & Anne.
Deborah Winslow Hawkes,
Nov. 1797-Feb. 25, 1886,
w/o Levi, d/o Amos Hawkes I.
Edna Knight, 1756-1814,
1st w/o James I.
Hannah Pride,1784-1866,
w/o Jas. II, d/o Henry, Sr. &
Anna Brackett Pride.
infant,d/o Moses & Anne,XXXX.
James I., 1754, Kittery.-1822.
James II,June 1785-Apr.1852,
s/o James I. & Edna.
Levi,June 28,1790-
Nov.4,1851,2nd s/o Jas. I & Edna.
Levi,Jr,1837-1838,s/o L.&D
Levi,1855 -1903,s/o Wm. & Mary Ann.
Lucy Staples Leighton,1760-1838,
1st w/o Hatevil Leighton,
2nd w/o James I.
Mary Ann Pride,1823-1908,
1st w/o William, d/o H.Pride,Jr.
Mary, died young,unmarked grave.
Moses,May 22,1792-Mar.18,1826,
s/o James I. & Edna.
Nancy Wakefield,1807-1886,
w/o Peter,d/o Gibeon Wakefield.
Nathaniel Wakefield,1836-
Mar.5,1920, s/o Peter & Nancy.
Peter,Jan.1802-Aug.1874,
s/o James I. & Edna.
Sarah Foster,Dec.1845-June14,1872,
1st w/o Nathaniel.

Stephen,died young,unmarked grave.
William, 1823-1871, s/o Levi.
KNIGHT
Caroline Hill,1797-1873,w/o John.
John,1791-1849.
Samuel,1839-1862,drowned in
Duck Pond, s/o John & Caroline.
LEIGHTON
Ebenezer,1782-1869,s/o Jas I. & Lucy.
Hannah Hawkes,1786-1878,
w/o Ebenezer, d/o A. Hawkes II.
Holman,1822-1882,s/o Eben & Han.
PRIDE
Anna Brackett,1764-1838,
w/o Henry,Sr.,d/o Thos.Brackett.
George,1864-1934,s/o Sam & Nancy
Henry, Jr.,1795-1852,
s/o Henry, Sr. & Anna.
Henry, Sr.,1757-1836,s/o Capt.Jos.
Martha Allen,1810-1848,
1st w/o Ryerson,s/o H. Pride, Sr.
Martha Leighton,1801-1874,w/o H.,Jr.
Nancy,1790-1848, d/o H.,Sr.& A.
Nancy Gowen,1828-1884,
w/o Sam. F.,d/o Jas. II & Hannah.
Samuel Freeman,1829-1909,
s/o Peter.
STAPLES
Joseph,1829-1914, bro/o Steph.
Stephen,1826-1916.
Susan Gowen,1831-Jan.22,1922,
w/o Stephen, d/o Peter & Nancy G.

✦ **LUNT CEMETERY** ✦
355 Bridgton Road (Rt.302),
behind St. Edmunds. Neglected.
2 headstones,1 foot stone. 4 stone
corners of enclosure left.

LUNT
George W.,1794-1871.
Harriet Baker,1793-1858.
WALKER
Mary Ann Lunt,Mar.6,1857,27y,
w/o Henry B., d/o George W.

✦ **HIGHLAND LAKE
CONGREGATIONAL CHURCH
CEMETERY** ✦
1303 Bridgton Road, Westbrook.

HAVEN
Andrew, Capt., Aug.6,1829 -
Aug.18,1889, at sea.
Ann Woodbury, Mar.17,1854, 26y,
w/o Andrew.

Cornelia P.,Nov.3,1852,7m, d/o A.& A.
PRIDE
Alexander,1802-1880.
Cornelius B.,1823-1901.
Emeline Woodbury,1821-1896,w/o C.B
Jane M., July 19,1834,30y.
Jane,1834,4m, d/o of Jane M.
Mary E.,1826-1911, 3rd w/o Alex.
SMALL
Julia A,Nov.19,1808-Jan.25,1865,
wid/o Daniel of Raymond.
WOODBURY
Ann Plummer,1852,67y,
w/o Ebenezer,d/o Robert Plummer.
Ebenezer, Capt.,Nov.24,1778-Dec.2,1855.
Jane,Dec.6,1848,34y,d/o Ebenezer.
Elizabeth,XXXX.
John,XXXX.
Rueben,Sept.28,1847,9m,s/o J.& E.
Sarah,Jan.16,1851,30y,d/o Ebenez.

✦ **LARRABEE CEMETERY** ✦
Liza Harmon Road, behind Larrabee
Heights Complex, Westbrook.

COBBEY
John,July 10,1776-June 25,1800,
s/o John & Abigail.
LARRABEE
Benjamin, July 8,1832, 64y.
Jane Cobbey, Apr.15,1778-
Apr. 25, 1824, w/o Benjamin.
Sarah Lamb,Oct.29,1847,56y,
2nd w/o Benjamin.
TRICKEY
Emma, Sept.XXXX, 5m,
d/o Henry & Abigail.

✦ **LORD CEMETERY** ✦
680 Duck Pond Road, Westbrook.
Fair condition, needs attention.

LORD
Charles A.,1830-XXXX.
Loring, Oct.30,1885,16y, s/o C.A.& L.P
Lucy P.,Oct.4,1847,30y, w/o Chas.
Lydia,Dec.7,1755-Oct.23,1844,
w/o Nathaniel.
Nathan, May 2,1867, 81y.
Nathaniel,June 19,1747-Apr.17,1826.
Priscilla, 1791-XXXX.
Samuel,1795-1884.
Susan Barbour,1792-1871,w/o Samuel

LOVEJOY
Harriet M., Apr.3,1826-Oct.13,1896.
WESCOTT
Anne H., Apr.25,1863,13m,
d/o J.R. & F.E.
Frances E. Lord,1828-Dec.1883,
w/o James. R.
James R.,1833-Mar.15,1874,
s/o Wm, grand/s of Isaac.

✣ **COBB CEMETERY** ✣
551 Methodist Road,Westbrook.
2 enclosures. Maintained.

First enclosure:
COBB
Amos A.,Sept.1,1832,2y,s/o A.&N.
Asa,1794-1875.
Eva A.,July 8,1860,2y,
only d/o Charles W., & Mary.
Mary E.,Mar.9,1858, 23y.
Nancy Dole,1796-1865, w/o Asa.
Willis I.,Mar.7,1858,13m,
s/o Solomon & Abby.
Second enclosure:
1 wooden white painted cross.

✣ **HIGHLAND LAKE CEMETERY**
Rt. 302, behind the Woodbury Farm.
Active and maintained cemetery.
Highland Lake Cemetery Association
transferred the cemetery to the City
of Westbrook in 1942. Interments
obtained from Cemetery records.

ABBOTT
John B.,Feb.20,1973,69y.
Phyllis B.,June 6,1981,69y.
ADAMS
Dora M.,Feb.23,1987,83y.
Wilbur E.,Oct.12,1970,77y.
ALLEN
Harriet J. Parker,1838-1906.
Harry D.,Feb.20,1928,47y.
Harry G.,Mar.14,1991,78y.
Herbert A.,Apr.20,1965,83y.
Linna M.,Nov.1,1971,76y.
Mabel G., Jan. 28,1964,89y.
Rodman,1830-1907.
William H.,1861-1897,
s/o Rodman & Harriet J.
AUBE
infant, Aug.13,1960, s.b.
ANTHOINE
Doris Adeline, Sept.15,1892-
Apr. 14, 1970.

Edith W.K.Putnam, Dec.3,1879-
Nov.16,1948, w/o Wm.J.
M. Adelaide, Oct. 26,1845-
July 9,1892, w/o J.G.
William Jordan, Nov.4,1866-
Jan. 28,1958.
BABBIDGE
Herbert D.,1871-1956.
Susie A.,1872-1902, w/o H.D.
BAILEY
Abbie D. Babb, Aug.22,1880-1906,
w/o G.F.
Avis L.,May 25,1966,70y.
Edna P.,Dec.12,1993.
George F.,Feb. 28,1847-Mar.27,1921.
George L., Mar.31,1883-Feb.27,1885
James A., Aug.2,1886-Nov.25,1905.
Lulie A. Gowen, Oct.17,1857-
Aug.16,1913, w/o George F.
Percival O.,Feb.10,1965,69y.
BEAN
Alberta E., Nov.13,1957,83y.
BLANCHARD
Lila M., Nov.15,1944, 42y.
Lloyd T., Aug.7,1960, 65y.
Mary B.,July 20,1966, 82y.
BOULLIE
Clifford L.,Nov.4,1964,73y.
Emvilla E.,May 11,1971,68y.
BOWDEN
Marion B., Apr.16,1974,66y.
BOYD
Charles W.,May 6,1944,61y.
BRACKETT
Annette M.,May 1,1978, 78y.
Marshall E.,May 22,1987,89y.
BRAGDON
Arabelle, Nov.7,1964,85y.
BROWN
Augustus E.,May 12,1943,81y.
Emma E.,Dec.22,1959,92y.
Harriet, May 10,1888,88y.
Walter V.,July 5,1939,41y.
BURNHAM
Charles E., Nov.28,1947,63y.
George E., July 20,1943,71y.
Goldie, May 7,1943,47y.
Henry W., Nov.18,1974,62y.
Lennie P., Aug.30,1954,79y.
Martha E., July 20,1970,57y.
BURTON
Charles S.,Mar.5,1970,85y.
Estella F.,Apr.30,1962,71y.
Richard E.,Dec.20,1976,53y.
CAMPBELL
John A.,July 19,1982,88y.
Pearl I.,Nov.5,1982,84y.

CARROLL
Cornelia L.,1860-1944.
CHANDLER
Gladys M.,Dec.3,1980,82y.
Neel W.,June 14,1980,80y.
CLARK
Inez L.,May 23,1926,34y.
COBB
James H., Nov.15,1898,81y.
CRANTON
C.Elizabeth,Oct.16,1927,75y.
Lila B., Nov.13,1928,67y.
DEARBORN
Alice A.,Dec.20,1946,80y.
Herbert L.,Mar.11,1979,75y.
Ivory W.,Feb.12,1953,87y.
Wesley C.,Aug.24,1943,22y.
DREW
Mary E.,Oct.25,1863,25y.
EAGER
James B.,Nov.16,1973,70y.
FAYE
Delbert A.,Nov.26,1974,71y.
FIELDING
Harry, Apr.17,1886-May 29,1928.
Neta J. Bailey, Mar.29,1888-
Mar. 6,1952, w/o H.F.
FOWLER
John A., Apr.11,1939,77y.
John E.,Mar.9,1966,75y.
Mary E.,Mar.9,1943,81y.
FRANK
Almon L.,1843-1907.
Charles, July 2,1969,72y.
Marion, Sept. 27,1975,76y.
GANEAU
Augustus J.,May 30,1991,70y.
GERRY
Lowell M., Aug. 4,1856,30y.
GIVEN
Dorothy E.,June 19,1987,79y.
GORDAN
Arthur C.,Sr.,Apr.28,1983,86y.
Eva M., July 31,1988, 90y.
Grace G., 1928, 50y.
John A.,Nov.20,1951,82y.
John L., Apr.28,1983,73y.
Marion, Nov.28,1981,73y.
Rhoda E.,Jan.11,1988,52y.
GOWEN
Carrie L.,1859-1864.
Clara A.,1834-1913.
Henry J.,June 22,1987,90y.
Ida P. Shenault,1857-1920,w/o Jas.
infant, Apr.8,1958, s.b.
Isabelle W.,Feb.14,1992,87y.
James,1855-1930.

James H.,1822-1920.
Lulie A., Aug.16,1913,56y.
William A.,1868-1890.
William A.,May 14,1899,31y.
GREEN
Viola Blanche,1897-1986.
Dorothy E.,1921-1922.
HALE
Eugene E., Dec.22,1984,77y.
Leon C., May 9,1990, 85y.
HARDY
Albion,1857,23y.
Amos,1806-1859.
Annie Knight,1867,64y.
Annie L., Jan.28,1930,63y.
Eliza M. Gowen,1877-1965,w/o
Ernest.
Ernest F.,1873-1956.
Fanny R. Frank,1840-1930,w/o Jas.L.
James L.,1839-1915.
Margaret,1836, 3y.
HARMON
Hazel W.,Oct.21,1975,70y.
HAWKES
Ada L.,1869-1956.
Amos E.,Jan.13,1984,80y.
Amos W.,1886.
Clara E. Jordan,1856-1942,w/o W.H.
Dorothy M.,1895-1981,w/o Harold.
Edna M., 1896.
Fannie A. Rogers,1934, 61y.
Franklin, Apr.19,1979,21y.
George O.,1864-1922.
Harold D.,1892-1933.
Inez L. Clark,1891-1926,w/o M.W.
Isaiah,1869-1945.
James F.,1855-1920.
Julie M.,1854-1934.
Leon W.,1885.
Linwood A.,1894.
Maurice W.,1888-1922.
Sarah B.,1930,85y.
Walter H.,1857-1918.
HAWKINS
Abigail,1884-1924.
Nelson,1881-1942.
HERRICK
Arnold E.,Jan.7,1975,80y.
Lina M.,Feb.9,1994,97y.
HUNTLEY
Maurice E.,Dec.31,1945,28y.
Ruth L., Apr.24,1985,65y.
HUSTON
Clarence S,1895-1900,s/o F.S.& E.F
Eliza A.,July 6,1843- Aug. 2,1887.
Elizabeth F. Waite,1872-1938.
Frederick E.,1902-1904,s/o F.S.& E.F.

Frederick S.,1864-1914,h/o Elizabeth
Philip J.,1906-1907,s/o F.S. & E.F.
William M., Mar.28,1843-
Apr.9,1895,h/o Eliza.
JAMESON
Alice M., Apr.10,1939,61y.
Georgia M.,1886-1953.
George W.,1832-1902.
Julia A.,Apr.26,1872,37y,w/o Geo.
Orrin C.,1881-1955.
Sarah F.,1842-1906.
JOHNSON
Arthur H.,May 2,1956,72y.
JORDAN
Charles E., Jr.,Aug.13,1973,9y.
Clara G./E.,May 26,1942, 86y.
Margaret W.,1849-1911.
Mary A.,1817-1892, w/o W.H.
William H., Dec.16,1907.
KAUFMAN
Charles,May 25,1944.
KING
Wilfred J.,Sr.,Jan.25,1991,78y.
Wilfred J., II, Aug.9,1991,44y.
KNIGHT
Albion,1834-1857.
Dwinal,1847-1916.
Ellen M.,1842-1923
Fred D.,1888-1964.
Helen A.,1858-1919,w/o Dwinal.
infant,July 20,1953, s.b.
Margaret,1833-1836.
Maude A.,1891-1956.
Thomas,1841-1891.
LEIGHTON
Harold J.,Nov.27,1922,2y.
LESTER
Sarah J.,1831-1907.
LOWELL
George F.,1872-1925.
Georgianna Lord,1836-1922
Harriet E./T., 1875-1953.
Hattie L.,1868-1944.
James S.,1867-1936.
Lillian E.,1874-1904,d/o W.R. & G.
William, July 9,1901,59y.
MACOMBER
Carrie, Aug.10,1931,59y.
Mabel, Aug.31,1942,43y.
Martha L., Jan.14,1977,77y.
Walter H., Nov.14,1967,70y.
MANCHESTER
Neta B.,May 6,1952.
MANK
Marion G.,May 16,1984,84y.
MURCH
Mamie,1884,71y.

NASH
Charles N.,Dec.11,1990,75y.
NOYES
Gertrude A.,Nov.1,1966,83y.
OVINGTON
B.Laura,Mar.31,1992.
PARSLEY
Fannie R.,Dec.1,1954,80y.
PAYNE
Mary A.,June 22,1963,93y.
PHELPS
Alfred J., Apr.12,1962,56y.
Alfred J.,Sept. 29,1927,65y.
Thomas G.,May 2,1951,53y.
Thomas G.,Jr.,1940,18y.
POTTLE
George E.,May 24,1993,72y.
Harry, Apr.17,1958, 68y.
Mae L.,Jan.28,1977, 80y.
PRIDE
Alpheus,Dec.2,1819-Apr.17,1901.
Effie M.,1870-1939.
George A.,1861-1893.
Guy S.,1892-1947.
Isadora F.,Mar.8,1953,80y.
James H., 1869-1937.
Mary A., 1858-1947.
Mary E.,1826-1911, w/o Alex.
Mary J.,Sept.1828-Dec.1906, w/o Alpheus.
Ulysses R.,1864-1922.
William Henry, 1828-1919.
RUSSELL
Arthur A.,1907-1989.
Claris H.,1917- XXXX.
SAWYER
Alba L.,May 19,1978,62y.
Jennie,1869-1922, w/o John.
John, 1853-1924.
Ralph C., July 20,1968, 55y.
Sarah E. Kilborn, 1876,50y.
Sumner P.,1818-1899.
SHAW
Florence A., Nov.29,1983,80y.
SHENUALT
Adeline C. Reckford,1836-1908, w/o Wm.H.
Daniel H.,July 7,1859-July 5,1929.
Helen M.,June 27,1866-Mar.3,1931.
William H.,1830-1908.
SILVER
Lottie L.,1881-1976.
SIMMONDS
Annie M.,1845-1918.
John F.,May 24,1938, 88y.
SMALL
Asa,1787-1865.

Cornelius A.,1827-1919.
Frank S.,1865-1894.
George L.,Sept. 26,1962,67y.
Henry T.,July 7,1941,47y.
Jeremiah,XXXX.
Jerusha,XXXX, w/o Jeremiah.
John K.,1872-1915.
Johnson K.,1834-1911.
Johnson K.,Mar.2,1915,42y.
Nancy D.,1834-1905,w/o Corn. A.
Patience K.,1792-1840,w/o Asa.
Peter, XXXX.
Sadie E.,1873-1962,w/o John K.
Sarah, Aug.19,1986,91y.
Walter E.,Sr.,Aug.11,1975, 51y.
SPILLER
William D.,Jan.4,1933,67y.
SWAN/SWAIN
Emma L. Bunker,1866-1933,w/o M.N.
Milton N.,1867-1961.
TAYLOR/TAILOR
Alice F.,1870-1947, w/o F.A.
Frederick A.,1879-1927.
TEBBETTS
Isadora,1873-1953.
THOMAS
Charles A.,1866-1944.
Charles O.,1832-1917.
Doris A., May 4,1970, 77y.
Harrietta A., July 6,1914,74y.
Harrison Cleveland,
   Mar.17,1891-XXXX.
VAN VLIET
Ruby L.,Mar.7,1958, 62y.
Ruth,July 18,1992, 66y.
William, Sept.16,1969, 77y.
WALDRON
Adeline,Feb.5,1975,82y.
WALKER
Alalia L.,1878-1951,w/o H.S.
Beverley A.,1930-1930.
H. Allan,1905-1909.
Herbert S.,1880-1968.
Ora A.,1902-1908.
WESCOTT
George W.,1859-1923.
Mary E.,1850-1932,w/o Geo. W.
WIGHTMAN
Harrietta A.,1839-1914,w/o C.O.
WILDES
Dorothy,Aug.29,1915,6m.
Ethel M.,Nov.13,1916,2m.
Harold C.,Sept.19,1961,59y.
Jess B.,Dec.15,1964,86y.
Lerena M.,Feb. 6,1919,37y.
Lorana,Feb.18,1919,12d.
Lorenzo,Feb.16,1919,10d.

Margaret T.,Jan.12,1929,2y.
Phyllis H.,July 11,1986,80y.
WILIES
David A.,July 31,1919,7y.
WOODBURY
Abigail, Sept.9,1802,3y,
   d/o Joshua & Margaret.
Alvin,1879,68y.
Alvin D.,1894, 1y.
Alvin D.,July 14,1899,87y.
Alvin D.,1927,71y.
Anna, Sept.14,1802,1y,
   d/o Joshua & Margaret.
Annie Oct.26,1939,86y.
Daniel,1870,56y.
Daniel,1931,76y.
Emeline,Sept.16,1867,44y,w/o Daniel.
Joseph,Mar.26,1861,55y.
Joshua, July 1826,67y,
   only s/o Peter of Cape Eliz.
Joshua, July 4,1803-May 31,1853.
Lloyd L.,Feb.10,1967,79y.
Louwice E.,Sept.29,1986,76y.
Lowell H.,July 11,1944,55y.
Lowell, Jr.,Feb.12,1915,3y.
Malilada G.,1895, 81y.
Margaret Strout,Mar.19,1835,56y,
   w/o Joshua.
Nathan L.,Dec.19,1914,54y.
Wenoma H.,Dec.15,1965,75y.

✣ **JAMESON CEMETERY** ✣
Off Rte. 302, behind the Pride's Corner
Fire Station in the woods.
Badly neglected, stones tipped, all
stones were readable, except 2.

CHASE
Alice Cornelia,Aug.15,1859,2m.
Ina Eloise,Aug.28,1859,2y.
HODGKINS
Mary Webb ,Nov.1,1837,60y,
   2nd hus. Ebenezer.
JAMESON
Bethany Webb Knight,Nov.18,1886,
   94y,2nd w/o Charles.
Charles,Oct.10,1877,74y.
Charles N.,Aug.15,1858,6m &
Julia,Aug.30,1858,5m, ch/o
   John H. & Hannah M.
John H.,Mar.17,1887,51y.
John H.,Apr.19,1882,22y.
Hannah M. Ayer,Apr.12,XXXX.
Ruth Webb,Apr.24,1858,60y,
   1st w/o Charles.

KNIGHT
John W. & Emma S., XXXX,
  ch/o Benjamin & Bethany.
Sarah W.,May 17,1838,22y,
  d/o Benjamin.
MARTIN
Julia O. Jameson,Mar.17,1879,20y,
  w/o Jeremiah M.,d/o Chas.& Ruth.

✦ **ALMS HOUSE/CITY FARM** ✦
Saco Street. Closed in 1949.

This facility was closed in 1949.
Persons listed here were not located
in any city cemetery, but did die or
were supplied a funeral from the Alms
House. Many more died while in
residence here, most were not named
in the City Reports, just a count of
deaths per year.

Alore,child,1871.
Averill,Mrs.,1864.
Babb,Miss,1885.
Bergeron, child,1891
Blake,J.,1871.
Boynton, Andrew,1902, 64y.
Brown,A.,1891.
Carroll, child,1876.
Chapman,C.,1881.
Chicohnee,1871.
Cobb, ch/o I., 1862.
Coburn,Mr.,1866.
Coburn,Mrs.,1862.
Coyne, Mary, Feb.17,1912.
Craig,Mrs.,1872.
Cutter, Annie E.,Aug.10,1899.
Daniels, Charles, Sept.19,1905.
Dillingham,Mrs.,1885.
Duke,Mrs.,1871.
Dyer, Lucinda, 1910.
Fields,Ruth,1861.
Freeman,Jane,1885.
Furnell,C.,1890.
Garland,Mr.,1879.
Gilbert,Mrs.,1889.
Gordan,Mrs.,1862.
Goyet,Mrs.,1881.
Harrington,1869.
Hill, Mrs., 1892.
Hubbard,George,1885.
Huckins, Mary, Feb.25,1908.
Hunt, Lewis, Mar.4,1912.
Johnson,Margaret,1861.
Jordan,child,1863.
Lemontague,Mrs.,1890.
Libby, ch/o Ezra,1876.

Libby, George,1910.
Libby,Nettie,1878.
Lord,W.S.,1890.
Lowell, Mabel, 1899, 26y.
Lowell,Nancy,1876.
Mackey,child,1862.
Mahoney,1869.
Mason,child,1890.
Maw,C.F.,1862.
McCollough,S.,1862.
McLellan, child,1891.
Merrill, Mrs., 1892.
Moffitt, child,1856.
Moffitt, Sept. 9,1912.
Newcomb, Freedom, May 27,1912.
Perry, Philip, 1904, inf/o Paul.
Porter,Mrs.,1866.
Potter, Mrs.,1872.
Ricker, girl,1889.
Riley,Peter,1871,killed on R.R.
Sawyer,Thomas,1865.
Stiles,Mary,1883.
Theot,S.,1871.
Thorne,Mr.,1890.
Towle,J.,1883.
Wallace, Eliza, Feb.10,1901.
Wallace,child,1863.
Wallace,George,1883.
Wallace,T.,1862.
Webb,B.,1883.
Wentworth,child,1889.
Winslow, W.,1891.

✦ **HUSTON FAMILY CEMETERY** ✦
96 Mast Rd.,Falmouth.
Reported to have 30 graves here.

HUSTON
Abba W.,1855-1856, d/o Stephen &
  Joan Woodbury.
Elizabeth,1836,70y,w/o Stephen.
Emerson,Aug.25,1873,24y.
Isaac,1806-1858.
Margaret Field,1810-1880,w/o Isaac.
Stephen,1823,58y,h/o Elizabeth.
Stephen,1812-1903.
2 ch/o Stephen & Elizabeth:
  Charles,Isaac & Benjamin.
William & his wife are buried here in
  an unmarked graves.
O'NEILL
Catherine,Dec.27,1884,58y,
  housekeeper & companion to
  Stephen (1903).

✣ **WOODLAWN CEMETERY** ✣
380 Stroudwater Street, Westbrook.
In 1885 land was purchased for
a city cemetery and was opened
in 1886. Information was obtained
from city records and is current.

AASKOV
Augusta C.,Feb.3,1941,78y.
Christine J.,Apr.29,1975,80y.
Clifford M.,June 21,1928,4d.
infant, Apr.15,1927, s.b.
J. Clifford,Dec.5,1985,90y.
John P.,May 9,1940,77y.
ABBOTT
Alma Boynton,Mar.4,1931,84y.
A. Elliott,Jan.19, 1978,63y.
Amos H.,Dec.10,1948,73y.
Davis Norton, Mar.11,1930,87y.
John M.,Jan.3,1966,86y.
Josephine E., Aug. 21,1950,73y.
Maude M.,June 16,1954,79y.
Mildred L.,Sept.6,1959,75y.
Pauline W.,Feb.8,1991,92y.
ADAIR
Alexander,Nov.21,1975,94y.
Alexander,Jr.,July 23,1947,41y.
Florence E.,Apr.8,1953,68y.
infant,June 9,1924, s.b.
ADAMS
Alice M.,Mar.191972,55y.
Annah,Aug.12,1929,67y.
Arabelle H.,Sept.6,1927,20y.
C. Dylan, May 14,1992, s.b.
Charles A., Jan.26,1987,76y.
Dorothy M., June 10, 1954, 66y.
Ernest C., July 5, 1941, 53y.
Forest Eugene,Sept. 28,1918,23y.
Frederick O.,Mar.15,1930,38y.
George F.,Nov.2,1932, 62y.
Harold Leon,Jan.18,1953,36y.
Harry F.,Jan.18,1969,82y.
Harry O.,Dec.17,1966,87y.
Harvey E.,Dec.21,1918,37y,
  removed from Gray,ME,1922.
John F.,Jan.26,1918,55y.
John H.,Aug.23,1949,69y.
Kathleen,Dec.22,1983,63y.
Lillian G.,Apr.22,1976,91y.
Louise,XXXX,12y.
Maude A.,June 5,1994.
Martha W.,Dec.21,1946,74y.
Myron L.,Jan.11,1932,31y.
Nina B.,Feb.6,1946,58y.
Oren E.,Mar.22,1949,45y.
Robert F.,Jr.,July 12,1957,3m.
Robin J.,Sept.16,1961,14d.

Stephen E., Apr.5,1934,83y.
ADDE
Mildred V., Aug.18,1979.
ADDITON
Edith M.,bu: Oct.9,1950,70y.
Frederick G.,Jan.24,1945,94y.
Lydia Susan,Nov.15,1925,71y.
Rosebelle,June 6,1968.
ADKINS
Jennie M.,July 17,1950.
AHERNS
Hattie S.,July 29,1985,83y.
Herman E.,June 29,1967,60y.
AHO
Arnos E.,May 21,1962.
ALBEE
Bird M.,June 29,1965,87y.
ALCORN
Bernice W.,Feb.17,1960,93y.
Harlan G., Oct.14,1957,67y.
Irene A.,June 15,1988,83y.
William H.,Jan.1,1919,67y.
ALDEN
Alice Gertrude,Jan.1,1938,71y.
Fred L.,Oct.14,1929,69y.
ALEXANDER
Cecil,Nov.22,1949,64y.
Edith O.,Feb.14,1989,91y.
ALLAN
Arthur E.,Nov.11,1934,73y.
Marshall J.,Jan.9,1965,77y.
Maude T.,June 5,1964,90y.
Myron,Nov.4,1934.
Ralph,June 7,1942,43y.
Rebecca B.,Dec.12,1916,47y.
Robert Howe,Jan.26,1918,11m.
Sheila F.,Feb.5,1963,19y.
Vernon R.,Jan.23,1955,36y.
Virginia Evelyn, Aug.29,1918,20y.
William H.,Aug. 27,1913,66y.
Winnifred Edwards,Jan.8,1944,54y.
ALLEN
Abbie May Laverty,Jan.12,1907,
  37y, w/o E.
Andrew M.,Mar.24,1963,80y.
Annie B.,1839-1913.
April,Feb.6,1963,1y.
Bertha,1876,6y,d/o L.&Annie.
Bertha M.,Feb.14,1910,20y.
Bessie M.,Oct.4,1968,81y.
Cary,Feb.6,1963,8m.
Clarence M.,Feb.6,1963,22y.
Dora M.L.,Jan.22,1957,86y.
Edgar M.,1876,4y,s/o L.&A.
Edna F.,Jan.23,1923,30y.
Effie L.,Feb.7,1969,67y.
Elizabeth B.,Nov.23,1971,48y.

Eva B.,July 9,1949,70y.
Florence L.,Jan.18,1956,48y.
Frances A., Apr.15,1967,84y.
Frank, Aug.12,1951,84y.
Frank H.,June 30,1946,50y.
Frank H.,May 4,1933,76y.
Grace V. Lamb, Sept.14,1918,
  39y, removed to Knight Cem.
  in North Windham,1945.
Hazel L.,Dec.17,1991,79y.
Hortense M.,Jan.28,1944,81y.
infant,Feb.24,1924,5d.
Jeremiah, July 14,1919,51y.
Kathleen M.,Mar. 5,1970,55y.
Kenneth M.,Oct.19,1947,25y.
Leander V.,Dec.20,1917,74y.
Lester J.,Nov.16,1920,26y.
Lillie A.,Mar.7,1937,84y.
Lizzie G.,Feb.6,1935,90y.
Mark E. Mar.2,1935,65y.
AMES
Charles T., Aug.1,1926,76y.
Donna Lee,Mar.17,1956,13y.
Evie S.,1852-1892,w/o C.T.
Hanson G.,1879-1881,s/o C.T.
infant,May 11,1957,4hrs.
Theodore J.,Dec.11,1993,73y.
ANAGNESTEPOULES
Aposteles V.,July 19,1973,75y.
ANDERSEN
A.Abbott, July 18,1940,70y.
A.P.,1876-1914.
Alfred Oliver,Mar.21,1944,64y.
Anders H.,bu:Jan.2,1951,92y.
Andrew,Nov.22,1914,64y.
Annie M.,May 24,1961,67y.
Arthur H.,Apr.14,1948,53y.
Arthur W.,Jan.16,1972,78y.
Beatrice E.,May 18,1985,87y.
Bertha B.,Jan.29,1936,59y.
Carl,Jan.25,1990,85y.
Caroline,1848-1905.
Caroline B.,Dec.4,1907,45y.
Carrie B.,1862-1907.
Carroll W.,Jr,Dec.25,1984,63y.
Carroll W.,Sr,Jan.18,1981,86y.
David E.,May 22,1960,66y.
David L.,Nov.21,1977,84y.
Dorothy F.,Dec.6,1983,74y.
Edward,Mar.3,1938,81y.
Edward N.,Nov.29,1976,70y.
Eline,Aug.7,1949,82y.
Elizabeth M.,Feb.22,1963,75y.
Ella C./V.,Oct. 21,1936,66y.
Elmer D. Sept.9,1918,22y.
Emma A.,Aug.21,1940,67y.
Georgianna H.,July 4,1986,61y.

Harold C.,Apr.2,1982,83y.
Harriett L.,Dec.20,1962,83y.
Harry W.,Sept.5,1960,77y.
Helen G.,Mar.17,1968,77y.
infant,May 10,1945, s.b.
infant, Nov. 27,1945, s.b.
Isabel F.,Jan.7,1982,84y.
Jens Peter,Nov.9,1932,75y.
John R.,Mar.13,1943,53y.
June Phyllis,July 12,1932, s.b.
Keith A., July 4,1976, 57y.
Laura P.,Oct. 30,1985,88y.
Maren T., Aug. 31,1944,86y.
Marjorie L.,Apr.24,1974,60y.
Mildred,May 8,1919,40y, w/o Dr. Geo.
Nina Elizabeth,June 8,1923,13d.
Philip C.,Mar.25,1973,66y.
Sadie E.,Feb15,1940,48y.
Soren Peter,Dec.9,1952,83y.
Walter T.,July 16,1928,56y.
William,Aug.25,1882,63y.
ANDREN
Helen A.,Mar.29,1983,88y.
Oscar R.,Feb.11,1960,70y.
Oscar R.,Jr,Mar.22,1942,26y.
ANDREWS
Annie J.,Aug.8,1956,38y.
Arthur E.,Apr.18,1941,89y.
Augusta H.,Sept.7,1931,8y.
Barbara L.,Mar.17,1956,13y.
Charles R., Nov.15,1957,82y.
Charlotte B., Aug.4,1916,62y,
  w/o Arthur.
Charlotte,Mar.11,1935,63y.
Ellenett,1835-1902,w/o Geo.H.
Elmer D., Jan.2,1921, s/o Edw.
Franklin F.,Feb.6,1928,80y.
George H.,Apr.29,1903,58y.
Gertrude M.,Aug.17,1959,65y.
Gracie,1876-1860.
Harland E.,Oct.8,1989,87y.
Harold O.,Dec.15,1985,82y.
Harrison R.,June 5,1972,79y.
Henry O.,July 3,1950,72y.
Howard Mansfield,Feb.27,1944,68y.
Irene M.,Feb. 6,1971,60y.
Janet B.,Sept.8,1993,67y.
Jennie G.,July 20,1952,85y.
Joan Elizabeth,Sept.24,1993,53y.
Leslie E.,Mar.17,1956,38y.
Lottie O.,Feb.18,1964,81y.
Marian G.,Dec.20,1960,82y.
Mary C.,Aug.10,1960,82y.
Ola M.,Feb.24,1978,83y.
Richard A.,Mar.17,1956,9y.
Ruby Y.,Nov.1,1957,67y.
Sarah Louisa,Feb.12,1928,48y.

Silas S.,June 7,1928,84y.
Stanley E.,Jr,May 21,1974,26y.
Stephen,May 1,1984,16y.
Thomas E.,Nov.17,1940,58y.
Velma May,Nov.30,1925,1y.
Virginia E.,Jan.13,1978,67y.
Vivian E.,Mar.17,1956,38y.
Walter C.,Sept.30,1954,56y.
William L.,May 28,1914,24y.
ANNIS
Horace H.,bu.June 23,1941,81y.
Lizzie B.,bu.May 7,1927.
William C.,May 27,1957,48y.
ANTHOINE
Ambrose L.,Oct.12,1935, 70y.
Joseph H.,Mar.18,1930,86y.
Marian A.,Sept.6,1968,85y.
Marinda E.,bu: Oct.21,1936,80y.
ANTHONY
Barbara Jane,Oct.8,1930,s.b.
APPLEBY
Francis E.,Feb.9,1956,55y.
Irwin F.,Jan.7,1934,10y.
Sara J.,Mar.6,1984,81y.
ARCHAMBEAU
Winnifred,Sept.28,1965,39y.
ARENOVSKY
Julia Mae,Nov.16,1917,55y.
Simon,Nov.8,1916,60y,h/o Julie.
AREY
Ethel M.,Apr.14,1987,89y.
Herbert B.,May 2,1964,64y.
Jennie S.,July 17,1903.
Leon A.,Feb.19,1983,52y.
ARMSTRONG
Eva L.,Jan.9,1963,83y.
Richard N., Apr.25,1940,65y.
ARSENAULT
Arthur J.,Aug.1994,69y.
infant, Apr.22,1917, s.b.
infant, Dec.10,1957, 5hrs.
infant, Mar.23,962, s.b.
infant, Mar.15,1962, s.b.
Stephen J., Aug.1,1961,55y.
ASHBY
Tamra C.,Apr.12,1983,s.b.
ASHLEY
John L.,July 10,1974,62y.
ASKER
Emil,Feb19,1978,82y.
Frances E.,Feb.20,1955,61y.
Glenna E.,Aug.13,1959,58y.
ATHAS
Costas V.,Aug.2,1932,42y.
George C.,Jan.17,1918, 6m.
Mary T.,Mar.22,1980,87y
Rosemary C.,Dec.18,1989,60y.

ATHEARN
Sara P.,June 12,1970.
ATWATER
Komach C.,Apr.1,1984,88y.
AUBE
C. Edward,May 6,1992,89y.
Vera S.,Apr.26,1975,74y.
AUBIN
Alfred A.,Jan.21,1942,48y.
AULD
Eva M., Mar.24,1960,75y.
William B., Jan.23,1954,69y.
AUSTIN
Cora Martin,Sept.8,1991,86y.
Fanny,1828-May 10,1900,w/o Simeon.
Sadie J.,June 28,1955,84y.
AXELSON
Andress,Mar.21,1980,67y.
August M.,June 14,1945,71y.
B.G.H.,1811-1911,sis/o Edw.
Borthelde,Feb. 2,1911,29y.
Caroline E.,Aug10,1973,82y.
Charles P., Aug.24,1955,65y.
child,Dec.2,1921.
Dorothy Emily,July 5,1916,2d.
Edward,Nov.5,1802-Mar.16,1840.
Edward, Apr.23,1959,64y.
Elfred H.,Sept.7,1925,53y.
Ella M.,Sept.1,1984,92y.
Emily B.,Jan.3,1920,w/o August M.
Emma B.,Dec.31,1919.
Fanny,May 10,1900,73y.
Jens,Dec.1,1956,56y.
Johanna Frederikke,July 17,1907, 65y,w/o Edward.
John,Jr.,Nov.29,1994,69y.
Marie A.,Mar.5,1984,76y.
AYER
A. Howard, Aug.4,1913,54y.
Albion P.1823-1895.
Byron P.1848-1851,s/o A.P.& E.C.
Eunice C.,June 24,1912,88y.
Freddie,1857-1857.
Howard G.1853-1858,s/o A.P.& E.C.
Minnie M.,1857-1858.
Sarah Luella,Nov.9,1940,85y.
BABB
Ada C.,May 17,1944,77y.
Alice J.,Mar.3,1966,92y.
Charlotte,1835-1902.
Cyrus F.,1832-1855,s/o B.& H.
Earle H.,Mar.15,1953,67y.
Elijah L.,1830-1848,s/o B.& H.
Ella Goff,bu:Dec.27,1928,80y.
Elmer M.,Jan.8,1960,64y.
Emma Francis,Apr.15,1929,64y.
Emma K.,May 1,1963,80y.

Francis J.,July 15,1912,16d.
Fred Webster,Sept.23,1942,78y.
George W.,bu:Apr.8,1927,37y.
Harlan P.,Feb.14,1934,71y.
Harold A., Sept.22,1948,67y.
Harriette L.,Aug.21,1952,87y.
Isaac,Feb.12,1942,88y.
Henry S.,1836-Oct.15,1892.
James,1808-1901.
James C.,1838-1850.
Jennie S.,1841-July 5,1917,w/o Hen.S.
Jesse E.,1807-1839.
John,1840-1869.
John,Capt.,1862,80y.
Lemuel G.,Sept19,1945,63y.
Lois,1849-1849.
Lois W.,1811-1899,w/o Jas.
Louisa,1843-1874.
Lucy G.,Apr.10,1954.
Luther P.,1869-1876.
Margaret M.,Jan.1,1949,55y.
Mary Eudora,May 6,1947,58y.
Melissa, Apr. 22,1914,81y.
Mildred I., Apr. 23,1975,87y.
Nora A.,May 1,1938,63y.
Orin, rem. from Saccarappa
 Cemetery, Aug.20,1914.
Rebekah,1848,70y.
Ruth W.Jan.6,1912,78y,wid/o Wm.
Stella K.,Jan. 8,1975,88y.
Wilfred F.,Mar.22,1932,79y.
William A.,Feb.25,1899,70y.
BABBIDGE
Annie May,Dec.9,1929,39y.
Ardis S.,July 14,1971,78y.
Arthur H. Sept.19,1964,72y.
Eliza, Sept.26,1906,70y.
Ernest M.,Mar.1,1969,79y.
Ida May, Feb.4,1933,67y.
James W.,Dec.24,1916,58y.
Julia N., Nov.30,1983,90y.
Leon A.,Oct.17,1953,51y.
Martha E.,Mar.9,1974,77y.
Perley L.,Mar.19,1956,81y.
Roland M.,July 20,1964,41y.
Susan B.,bu: Nov.19,1928.
William W.,Mar.25,1953,33y.
BACHELDER
Archelus,May 23,1926,78y.
Edward Merrill,July 1,1940,15y.
Edward W.,Dec.20,1962, 83y.
Edwin M.,Oct.9,1936,69y.
Flora C.,Jan.16,1938,82y.
Franklin P.,Feb.27,1945,
 in action in Germany.
Greenleaf E.,Jan.7,1917,69y.
Hattie M. Feb.24,1935,52y.

Jennie M.,Oct.8,1951,83y.
Levi,Jan.3,1919, 69y.
Lizzie,1878-1896.
Mabel H.,Oct.22,1959, 72y.
Marie E.,Nov.25,1912, 67y.
Pearl P.,Jan.11,1989, 101y.
Percival Angus,June 12,1930,46y.
Rachel MacL.,1854-1888.
Ralph W.,May 6,1963, 62y.
Walter M., Aug.24,1964, 69y.
BACHOFEN
Marie L.,May 7,1961,88y.
Theodore J.,June 29,1955,88y.
BACON
Eunice Etta, Oct.23,1930,83y.
J.Wesley,Nov.14,1907,58y.
Verona,Nov.8,1928,80y.
BAGDAHN
Karoline P.,Oct.1,1917,26y.
BAHNERT
George C.L.,Nov.12,1933,60y.
BAILEY
Almeda,1850-1852.
Almeda R.,1827-1888,w/o Benj.F.
Benjamin F.,Nov.6,1900,79y.
Bridget M., Aug.12,1989, 22y.
Byron N., Feb. 23,1928,77y.
Cecil F., Feb.23,1967,71y.
Charles W.,1845-Dec.15, 1907.
Clara,1846-1893.
Dale Reed, Sept.22,1946,20min.
Edna P.,Dec.12,1993,66y.
Emma L.,bu:July 5,1941,73y.
Eva,Sept.20,1893,Apr.9,1907.
Ezra F.,Apr.26,1920,90y.
Florence, 1855-Sept.3,1898.
George M.,Aug.7,1948.
Georgia,Aug.13,1947,74y.
Hazel H.,Jan.25,1977,78y.
Isaac A.,Mar.26, 1919,52y.
Jennie E.,1845-1907.
John M.,May 10, 1927,67y.
Lida H.,Nov.12,1947,90y.
Lucy A.,Jan. 27,1905,66y.
Myron K.,Mar.15,1974, 65y.
Ralph F.,Jan.12,1976, 68y.
Sarah C.,Mar.19,1915, 51y.
Sarah S.,Oct.24,1947,79y.
Sena N., Feb.5,1989,77y.
Wayne Robert, Nov.2,1930,11y.
BAIRD
Ruth A., Aug.14,1986,72y.
BAKER
Agnes,Jan.22,1920,85y.
Allen F.,Aug.16,1930,1m.
Annie B.,July 2,1965,89y.
Boyston,Jan.14,1920,ch/o Chas. A.

Gladys, Aug.27,1893,5m.
Harry L., Oct.13,1951,79y.
John, May 5,1900,67y.
Roy E.,Oct. 8,1970,73y.
BALL
Elizabeth C.,Nov.13,1952,77y.
John, Nov.12,1928,67y.
BALLARD
Blanche,May 10,1968,77y.
Charles A.,Nov.21,1962,76y.
Sadie G., Apr.25,1932,51y.
BAMBERG
Alice,Jan.28,1975,90y.
Frank, bu:June 26,1940,60y.
BANCROFT
Charles M.,June 11,1935,89y.
Charles W., Jan.28,1968,87y.
Edward, bu:Aug.8,1927,52y.
Edwina M., Jan.11,1961,84y.
Elizabeth M., Jan.16,1918,71y.
Elizabeth R.,Dec.26,1990,91y.
Elva F.,Mar.25,1946,58y.
infant, Nov.6,1902,18d.
Jacob Alexander,July 11,1953,78y.
Robert A.,Sept.11,1971,63y.
William A., Mar.24,1936,24y.
BANKS
Elizabeth E.,May 30,1971,88y.
infant,Mar.28,1922, s.b.
John K.,1883-1893.
Thelma P.,Feb. 29,1948,41y.
William,July 5,1949, 64y.
William H.,Jan.2,1985,78y.
BARBOUR
Adelaide E., Apr.1,1992,77y.
Alvin A., Sept.14,1957,82y.
Alvin Richard,Feb.14,1947,1m.
Augustus J. May 14,1903.
Caroline, Nov.21,1925,75y.
Edith T., Apr.1,1980,58y.
Edward A.,Dec.26,1954,36y.
Edwin H.,1874,s/o Oliver & Caroline
Edwin R.,no date,23y,rem.
  from Saccarappa Cem.1914.
Ellen M., Aug.7,1921,74y,
  wid/o Lorenzo.
Esther G., Apr 21,1985,78y.
Floyd H., May 19,1962,35y.
Forest E.,Nov.14,1901,19y.
Forest Lloyd,Mar.23,1922,1y.
George L.,bu: Aug.14,1967,43y.
Grace S., Apr.24,1968,74y.
Grover C.,Nov.22,1905,19y.
Grover C.,July 15,1989,67y.
Harry N.,Nov.12,1938,58y.
Harry W,Jr,Mar.24,1918,2d.
Herbert D.,May 27,1933,54y.

infant, Aug.11,1927, prem.
infant, May 10,1948, prem.
Lorenzo,Dec.25,1908,68y, s/o
  Hiram & Emma Winslow Barbour.
Martha L.,May 14,1972,92y.
Myrtle C.,Mar.7,1980,74y.
Oliver,June 19,1914,65y.
Philip H.,Nov.28,1985,69y.
Sadie M.,Dec.21,1954,70y.
Thomas W.,Mar.18,1979,68y.
BARKER
Carrie D., Nov.8,1918,61y.
Charles E.,Nov.21,1923,72y.
Edward J.,Apr.3,1934,47y.
Edwin J.,July 27,1991,64y.
Olive M., Apr.8,1962,72y.
BARNES
Edward,bu:June 20,1948,66y.
Edwin,1898.
Hattie S.,Nov.3,1931,66y.
Howard E.,Jan.16,1977,75y.
Levinnie G.,Nov.19,1970,66y.
Marilyn J., Apr.4,1927, newb.
Mary, Aug.3,1903,58y,wid/o Jas.
Maude E. Apr.29,1963,86y.
BARNEY
Donald C.,Mar.25,1971,69y.
BARRETT
Cora I.,June 14,1934,73y.
Felix M., M.D.,Apr.27,1920,59y.
John, Sept.14,1973,87y.
BARROWS
Adrian W., Feb.27,1990,64y.
Donald E., Oct.27,1968,5y.
Edna L., Aug.15,1986,59y.
Eunice E., Nov.3,1975,77y.
infant, July 27,1942, s.b.
John C., 1920, rem. from Smith
  Anderson Cemetery, 1921.
John H., Mar. 31,1960, 53y.
John Howard, Mar.30,1922,47y.
Madalyn B., Dec.11,1991,82y.
Mary J.,July 27,1954,86y.
Robert E., Sept.20,1986,52y.
Stanley Burton, Mar.1,1931,7m.
twin girls, Sept.17,1955,14 hrs.
Willis Emery,1921,8m,s/o W.& E.
Willis J., Apr.27,1971,75y.
BARRY
Robert R.,June 27,1990,64y.
BARTER
Clyde, Nov.18,1964,30y.
Eleanor H., Apr.11,1974,64y.
Philip M.,Jr.,Jan.25,1947,22y.
Robert E., Apr.11,1985,86y.
BARTON
George H., Aug.9,1977,74y.

Ione L., Mar.10,1988,85y.
BASSETT
Charles E., Dec.11,1932,49y,
rem. from Waterville 1961
Katherine A., Nov.11,1960,76y.
Margaret, Mar.24,1988,70y.
BASTON
Lucinda G.,Dec.6,1925,90y.
Winfred, Aug.2,1903,39y.
BATCHELDER
Charles A., Sept.18,1979,65y.
Erna E.H. Sept.9.1990,71y.
Grinlief E.,Jan.4,1917,69y.
Helen J.,June 20,1994,71y.
Lena D.,May 14,1982,96y.
Percy E.,Jan.2,1988,71y.
Perley D.,Dec.24,1943 57y.
Ralph W.,May 4,1963,62y.
BAXTER
George,June 1,1924,33y.
BAYLISS
Evelyn W., Aug.2,1975,67y.
BEAL/BEALE
Arline,Mar.21,1992,71y.
Emerson H.,Dec.15,1974,62y.
Jennifer M., Sept.30,1950,2y.
Judson, Oct.18,1901,47y.
Roscoe E.,Dec.22,1973,75y.
Russell M.,June 2,1990,68y.
BEAN
Charles E.,Jan. 2,1990,83y.
infant, Feb.19,1958,24d.
BEARCE
Daniel M.,Jan.6,1924,69y.
Ellen O., Aug.12,1942,84y.
BEATTY
Florence L.,Dec.5,1965,61y.
Thomas A.,Apr.30,1953,49y.
Thomas L.,Dec.8,1946,70y.
BEAULEC
Bertha E., Jan.28,1977,92y.
BEAUMIER
Hazel, June16,1993,84y.
Joseph F.,Mar.18,1991,81y.
BEAVER
Mary P. Oct.31,1972,51y.
BEESLEY
Agnes S.,Aug.27,1952,75y.
Albert F.,bu:Nov.16,1926,1y.
Amelia,Dec.10,1900,3y.
Annie C.,June 29,1994,87y.
Charles A.,June 4,1943,64y.
Charles H.,Mar.30,1973,71y.
Floyd, Mar.30,1926,2m.
George M.,Aug.6,1969.
Harold W.,Jan.27,1944,36y.
Ida, Nov.1,1974,92y.

infant,bu: July 1941.
Sadie E.,Jan.31,1928,27y.
Walter, Apr.10,1969, 63y.
BEGIN
Mary Jean,Feb.4,1984,44y.
BELL
Abigail C.,May 21,1914,19y.
Evelyn B.,Oct.19,1985, 94y.
Fred A.,Jan.19,1964,45y,rem. to
Mayberry Cem.,Windham 1976.
Harlan L.,Aug. 8,1958,67y.
Hugh S.,Apr.26,1934,76y.
John H.,Mar.1,1973,85y.
Louisa H.,Oct.4,1914,16m.
Louise M., July 5,1960,69y.
Mary, Apr.1,1938,79y.
William S.,Oct.17,1987,97y.
BENNETT
Agnes Y.,May 30,1950,91y.
Alice, XXXX,9m,rem. from North
Cemetery, Gorham,Oct.13,1933.
Arthur,Jan.9,1934, 37y.
Donna E.,Oct.8,1957, 3y.
Edith M.,June 25,1953,57y.
Eva F.,Jan.21,1955,63y.
Flora K.,Mar.22,1962,82y.
Florence E.,May 26,1932,76y.
George R.,Mar.15,1937,74y.
Guy R.,May 10,1970,80y.
Harold C.,Oct.7,1956,61y.
Morris,Dec.1981 in NY,72y.
Nelson C.,Oct.30,1951,75y.
Roland S.,July 23,1982,56y.
Ruth W.,July 27,1957, 70y.
Willard C.,Aug.15,1942,56y.
BERNIER
Evelyn M.,Sept.11,1993,79y.
Evelyn S.,Feb.11,1966,50y.
Mabel F., Jan.16,1970, 55y.
Rudolphe J.,Nov.23,1978,60y.
Steven D.,Nov.21,1989,24y.
BERRY
Albert W.,May 21,1939,48y.
Arlene E.,Nov.13,1967,20y.
child, Jan.17,1917,s.b.
Charles H.,Sept.28,1922,50y.
Charles H.,Mar.30,1973,71y.
Earl C.,Sept.26,1920,26y.
Edna M.,Nov.22,1979.
Edward F.,Feb 27,1945,63y.
Eleanor M.,Apr.21,1975,57y.
Everett W.,1898-1898.
Floyd M., Mar.30,1926,2m.
Frank C., July 19,1969,73y.
George M.,Aug.6,1969.
Harold W.,Jan.27,1944,36y.
Harris B.,Dec.8,1943,83y.

Harry B.,Sept.15,1901,1y.
Hattie H.,Mar.20,1940,79y.
Ida E.,Nov.1,1974, 92y.
infant,June 9,1942.
James,1864-1901.
Jennie M.,Dec. 27,1973,81y.
Kenneth E., Apr.20,1959,43y.
Laura Mary, Aug. 25,1932,28y.
Lena M., Dec.14,1990,84y.
Leola G., Aug. 24,1990,71y.
Leroy Irving, Aug.13,1924,2y.
Lewis J.,Sept.20,1981,76y.
Lizzie M.,Dec.10,1965,88y.
Lottie M.,Mar.11,1987,83y.
Manning S.,Feb.25,1986,93y.
Martin D.,Jan.5,1935, 62y.
Mary Louise,Oct.27,1915,11m.
Mary S.,July 10,1936,65y.
Mertie F., Apr.14,1899, 1y.
Nellie, Aug.31,1943, 58y.
Norman E.,June 14,1983,11d.
Perley E.,Feb.20,1967,80y.
Ralph M.,Dec.24,1938,34y.
Reynold"Bud",Apr.24,1991,46y.
Roscoe D.,Nov.18,1939,75y.
Sadie E.,Jan.31,1928,27y.
Sumner C.,May 20, 1950, 3y.
Tena B., May 25,1947,77y.
Violette A. Parker,Feb.14,1909,
  w/o William.
Walter, Apr.10,1969 63y.
William H.,Mar.8,1921,61y.
BERRYMENT
Annie, Sept. 2,1895,3m.
Anthony, July 2,1909,73y.
James A., May 22,1935,43y.
Lydia M., Feb. 25,1986,94y.
Ruth J.,1888,35y,w/o A.
BETTNEY
Leonard K.,Mar.20,1984,45y.
Louise E.,May 3,1984,73y.
BEVERAGE
Ethel Dec.29,1950,70y.
Harrison O.,Sept.20,1943,65y.
BILLINGS
Frank A.,June 3,1983,79y.
Meta M.,May 31,1984.
BILLINGTON
Eldora I.,Feb.5,1981,92y.
Ray,Aug. 21,1963,73y.
BILODEAU
Charles C.,M.D.,Dec.5,1951,41y.
Ethel C.,Dec.24,1948,68y.
infant,Nov. 21,1974, s.b.
J.Frank, Oct.19,1951,77y.
Richard J.,Jr,Jan.6,1974, inf.
Stanley R.,bu:Nov.29,1971,s.b.

BIRD
Dennis G.,Feb.28,1959,2d.
BISBEE
Harriett M.,Nov.17,1902,23y.
BISHOP
Agnes Powers,Feb.21,1954,79y.
Beatrice, June 1932,51y.
Harvey H.,Rev.,May 30,1939,62y.
Harvey J.,Dec.29,1932,94y.
Ida J., Dec.13,1959,93y.
Joseph W.,May 27,1952,76y.
Mary E.,Jan.26,1941,78y.
Naomi Martin,May 11,1924,82y.
Willard F.,Dec.3,1955,90y.
BIXBY
infant,Sept.20,1931, s.b.
Bernice W.,May 13,1958,64y.
Leo H.,Nov.4,1944,54y.
BLACK
Adeline A., Oct. 2,1914, 72y.
Calvin, bu:Dec.19,1941,69y.
Carrie Pride, Oct.18 1939,83y.
Charles, Mar.3,1965,73y.
Charlotte E.,Mar.5,1972,83y.
Ellen M., June 6,1900,43y.
Elliot F., Apr.5,1918,39y.
Elmira Barker,1825-1909.
Eugene L.,1871-1872.
Frank P., Oct.10,1944,91y.
infant,June 24,1944, s.b.
Isiah,1876-1882.
Mahlon C., May 4,1913,68y,
  h/o Adeline Dolley.
Mary E.,Aug.12,1994,23y.
Michael C.,Mar.4,1979,17y.
Milton,1875-1875.
Roscoe W.,1878-1879.
Willis R.,1855-1881.
BLACKWOOD
Alma A.,Nov.24,1930,68y.
Isaac N.,July 27,1910,51y.
BLAISDELL
Wallace J.,Oct.30,1986,66y.
BLAKE
Andrew J.,Feb.23,1927,63y.
Arlita M.,May 15,1905,2m,
  d/o Bert S. & Edna A.Lewis,
Bertrand S. Jan.25,1952,67y.
Clara D.,Feb.13,1980,82y.
Edna A., Aug.10,1943.
Everett A.,Jan.2,1949,50y.
Joseph,Mar.29,1953,82y.
Isabelle L., Apr.27,1935,33y.
L.Ruth,June 5,1992,67y.
Lemine D.,July 3,1923,52y.
Lewis,Mar.23,1904,48y.
Margaret L.,Jan. 21,1930.

Marion A.,Apr. 6,1907,6m.
Mary F.,Nov.10,1940,67y.
Mary M.,June 27,1957, 86y.
Milmoy/Millmay,Oct.25,1911,
23y,d/o Osman L. & Rose K.
Osman L.,Feb.22,1934,84y.
Perley E.,Dec.28,1974.
Rose K., Aug. 8,1943,81y.
Russell E., June 16,1970,49y.
Ruth L.,June 5,1992,67y.
Sarah L., Apr.29,1912,93y.
BLANCHARD
Agnes M.,Feb.12,1935,59y.
Anna C.,Dec.18,1955,91y.
Augustus B., Apr.2,1950, 77y.
Burleigh E.,May 24,1922,16y.
Charlene Altina, Apr.17,1947,7m.
Jennie A.,June 1,1896,19y,w/o A.B.
Vern S.,Mar.12,1951,54y.
BLANCHET
J. Alphonso"Sam",Jan.26,1990,87y.
Pauline E.,May 14,1975,72y.
BLASLAND
Ethel M.,May 4,1967,73y.
Georgia L.,June 7,1920,54y.
Gladys,bu:Dec.14,1965,75y.
Kit R.,Dec.13,1908,49y,
h/o Georgia Royal.
Raymond H.,June 22,1956,62y.
BLENIS
Alden S.,May 4,1951,82y.
Annie B.,Jan.18,1946,74y.
BLEMIS
Hilma F.,Jan.7,1922,12y.
Kermit,Oct.13,1919,13y.
Levera May,Jan.27,1919,26y,
d/o A.S. & Annie.
BLENKHORN
Roland B.,July 22,1984,67y.
BLIVEN
Carrie O.,Jan.30,1962,80y.
BODGE
Elbridge S.,Mar.1923,83y.
Elizabeth A. Day, Aug.16,1908,64y.
Emma R.,bu:Dec.21,1932,63y.
Ernest A.,July 15,1929,61y.
Fred Allen,Feb.24,1943,73y.
Helen C.,Nov.12,1960,62y.
Wilbur G.,Nov.21,1958,66y.
BOE
Ruby Eunice,May 3,1916,1y.
BOFF
Mildred J.,Jan. 1,1982,86y.
BOGDAHN
Jens P.,Jan.14,1976,84y.
Jensine M.,Dec.15,1981,88y.
Karoline, Sept.28,1917,26y.

BOHNSEN
Arthur W., Apr.12,1958,70y.
Christine M.,Feb.14,1918,61y.
Ethel A.,Dec.15,1985,92y.
John C.,Dr.,May 26,1965,87y.
Leda,Jan.10,1938,42y.
BOISSONNEAU
Alphonse L., Aug.7,1978,69y.
Elizabeth F.,Jan.20,1980,64y.
Rose M., Apr.14,1946,50y.
BOLDUC
Sabrina C.,Nov.5,1957,6m.
BOLLES
Dorothy B.,June 7,1977,65y.
BONDARKO
Evelyn M.,Dec.21,1983,51y.
Steven W.,June 16,1986,59y.
BONNELL
Bruce Lund, Apr.4,1948,5y.
Harold C., Apr.18,1988,81y.
BOODY
Deborah Gowen,Jan.10,1919,61y.
John G., July 29,1939, 83y.
BOOMER
Florence S.,May 8,1909,10y.
Henry,May 24,1951,87y.
Jane H.,Sept.23,1975,87y.
Stephen H.,Dec.23,1989,95y.
Susan S.,June 5,1933,72y.
BOOTH
Armine V.,Dec.21,1929,69y.
Elworth L.,Feb.25,1965,82y.
Eva Florence,Dec.5,1953,77y.
Evelyn E.,Nov. 5,1988,80y.
Harry F.,June 19,1910,3m.
Roscoe C.,May 22,1936,75y.
BOOTHBY
Ada C., Aug.29,1937,65y.
Evelyn R.,Mar.11,1975,86y.
Everett E.,Dec.28,1976,78y.
Everett O.,Oct.29,1973,81y.
Grace S.,Apr.11,1958,82y.
Isaac M.,Jan.24,1954,84y.
Lydia B.,Nov.29,1962,60y.
Myron J.,Jan.23,1969,59y.
Richard C.,Jan.24,1936,67y.
Robert C.,July 21,1970.
BOULIER
Donald W.,June 21,1990,26y.
Donald T.W.,June 27,1990,2y.
BOULLIE
John E.,June 2,1988,22y.
BOURDAGE
Ernest, Aug. 4,1932,3d.
BOURE
Joseph L.,Jan.14,1979,15d.

BOUTELLE
infant,Dec.10,1941,newb.
BOUTHILLETTE
Donat P.,Nov.3,1976,65y.
Gladys,Jan.14,1979,75y.
BOWERS
Mary Michael,Apr.30,1943,9hrs.
BOWES
Verle Vernon, no date,46y,
rem. from L.A.,CA.,Sept.1968.
BOYCE
Annie C.,Feb.23,1939,76y.
Arnold T.,Apr.27,1931,22y.
Charles A.,June 5,1948,56y.
Frank A.,June 3,1921,64y.
Grace Trask, Oct.14,1949, 6y.
Harold F.,Aug.30,1895,5m.
Lester,Mar.19,1904,14y.
Manola G.,Nov.26,1989,93y.
BOYD
Agnes, Apr.3,1892,36y,w/o Jas. H.
Annie Fleming,1848-Nov.9,1918, w/o Samuel.
Christian,July 19,1892,3y.
Eliza,can't read, infant.
Elizabeth,1889-1898,d/o S.& A.
Ethel,July 25, 1892,9y.
Harriet C.,1856-1908,w/o Jas. H.
James H.,1850-Aug.12,1942.
Martha C.,1893,14y,d/o J.H.& A.
Samuel,Oct.18,1888,43y,
Thomas,July 19,1892,5y.
BOYLE
Arthur L.,bu:Nov.30,1942,63y.
BOYNTON
Angelina,Jan.4,1989,97y.
Charles A.,Jan.14,1920,9m.
Charles M.,Feb.21,1933,59y.
Ella May,June 9,1922,48y.
Harry W.,July 7,1942,48y.
Jennie,Feb.28,1987,91y.
Leon M., July 16,1976,85y.
Willard J.,Oct.26,1948,51y.
BRACE
Arthur,Nov.10,1961,67y.
BRACKETT
Anthony G.L.,Dr.,Aug.5,1986,76y.
Carl,Feb.11,1972,85y.
Catherine C., Apr.1,1918,62y.
Clarice M.,Jan.26,1950,33y.
Dana A., Apr.22,1922,68y.
Edith M., Sept.1963,75y.
Ellie R.,Dec.21,1900,17y.
Elsie Verne,Oct.3,1955,73y.
Emil J.,Mar.7,1923,67y.
Ettie,Jan.26,1920,73y,wid/o Geo.H.
George E., July 11,1932,75y.
Hattie E., Aug.2,1947,87y.
James R., Sept.9,1970,43y.
Jesse V., Mar.14,1937,52y.
Katherine B.,Apr.4,1918,62y.
Lois,Jan.23,1905,15y.
Malcomb, Apr.5,1915.
Martha V.,Oct.16,1990,72y.
Mary L., Apr.18,1944,88y.
Mary M.,June 24,1973,27y.
Nellie, Sept. 30,1909,w/o Clifford.
T. Wilson,1907.
BRACY
Deborah L.,Feb.25,1950,1m.
BRADBURY
Doris Helen,June 7,1923,2d.
Edgar,Mar.17,1941,77y.
Martha J.,Mar.2,1917,62y.
Martha Swan,Mar.5,1917,62y.
Nellie A.,Apr.1,1923,61y.
Nellie C.,Mar.29,1927,24y.
BRADGON
Alma E.,Dec.5,1946,71y.
Augusta P.,Aug.20,1906,71y.
Claudia Eve,June 13,1951,1d.
Clifford S.,Jan.18,1956,85y.
Dorothy F.,Jan.24,1979,73y.
Eleanor N.,Oct.22,1965,55y.
Ellen L.,Sept.14,1961,85y.
Florence W.,Mar.5,1957,81y.
George L.,Aug.27,1949,24y.
George O.,Aug.13,1914,48y.
Gladys E.,Aug.28,1987,73y.
Harold L.,Jan.18,1970,69y.
Hazel E.,Dec.1,1985,89y.
Helen D.,Jan.8,1982,86y.
Jacob S.,Aug.15,1922,90y.
James F.,Jan.22,1949,72y.
Julia S.,Oct.23,1924,73y.
Kenneth W.,June 5,1966,63y.
Lewis H.,Oct.12,1943,63y.
Lillian Gertrude,May 14,1919,27y.
Lillian M., Sept.22,1978,66y.
Marietta B.,Dec.25,1983.
Mary E.,Jan.15,1936,70y.
Mary S.,Apr.12,1941,57y.
Minnie E.,Nov.19,1955,86y.
Nellie,Sept.30,1909,w/o Clifford
Philip O.,Aug.15,1993,83y.
Ralph H., Apr.3,1981,67y.
Ralph M., Aug.15,1977,80y.
Stanley F.,Aug.9,1993.
Victoria H.,June 19,1983,82y.
Walter L."Shiner"May 11,1988,78y.
William, Aug.3,1914,57y.
William A.,Jan.18,1965,96y.
BRADLEY
Edward Bernier,Sept.17,1943,23d.

BRALEY
Norma Irene,Feb.28,1933,3d.
Percy L.,Feb.12,1991,83y.
Rose, Oct.14,1981,77y.
BRANNIGAN
Bertha L.,Mar.9,1958,67y.
Martin A.,Mar.21,1957,77y.
BRASSARD
Alice A.,Jan.22,1988,57y.
Lawrence,Aug.1,1932,52y.
BRAZIER
George E.,Jr.,Apr.8,1974,53y.
BREEDLOVE
Ruth M.,Oct.3,1984,67y.
BREEN
Mary Elizabeth,Feb.8,1930,1y.
William H.,June 17,1946,50y.
BRIDGES
George W.,Apr.21,1910,30y,
h/o Josie Black.
infant,Jan.21,1942,5d.
infant, Sept.27, 1954, prem.
Josephine M., Aug.28,1959,83y.
Llewellyn B., Oct.14,1985,75y.
BRIDGHAM
Wade,Dec 5,1923,1d.
BRIGHTMAN
Jennie M.,Dec.8,1971,86y.
Lewis A.,Apr.7,1925, 15y.
Omer W.,Aug.27,1942,73y.
BRIX
Anna M.,Nov.23,1943,70y.
Harold P.,Sept.21,1983,80y.
J.Christian,Mar.1,1966,65y.
Marcia I.,Feb.25,1940,35y.
BROCK
James Albert,July 12,1932,52y.
Mattie, Aug.22,1939,60y.
BROCKELBANK
Richard C.,Dec.13,1968,33y.
BROOKS
Bertha P.,June 7,1974,105y.
Edward S.,Jan.2,1934,87y.
Harry D.,Mar.18,1948,79y.
infant, July 23,1953.
Mary Josephine, Apr.13,1925,77y.
Reynold H., Sept.21,1983,86y.
BROWN
Alice S.,Oct.10,1949,72y.
Anna W.,Jan.3,1943,73y.
Arlene M., Apr.30,1987,70y.
Arthur H.,Dec.20,1963,73y.
Charles F., Aug.13,1973,61y.
Charles F.,May 27,1987.
Charles Fred,Nov.23,1898,65y.
Clifford English,Apr.14,1942,1y.
Edwin L.,June 7,1944,74y.

Effie P.,Jan.15,1981,96y.
Eleanor M.,Nov.30,1961,87y.
Ernest Clifford,Jan.25,1908,20y,
s/o Ernest.
Esther E.,Dec.5,1944,67y.
Fannie G.,May 26,1991,69y.
Fielda M.,July 30,1916,1y.
Freda May,Aug.1,1916,1y.
Frederick B.,May 23,1980,89y.
George E.,Apr.18,1923,64y.
Gertrude A.,Aug.31,1963,82y.
Gladys B.,Apr.16,1988,87y.
Imogene E.,Mar.3,1937,90y.
infant, July 23,1953.
James L.,Dec.19,1921,53y.
Joseph C.,1830-1895.
Lillian Ida,Sept.28,1918,51y.
Mary, May 31,1905,73y.
Nancy E.,Feb.4,1961,88y.
Nathaniel A.,Feb.18,1920,70y.
Neil,Sept.26,1994,73y.
Perl B., Feb.17,1952,77y.
Phillip W.,July 17,1955,50y.
Rosetta,May 23,1947,92y.
Sarah A.,1820-1886.
Shirley E.,Nov.17,1976,72y.
Shirley R.,Dec.10,1994,61y.
Tena,1860-1882.
Theodore S.,Mar.6,1945,74y.
William H. Mar.4,1940,48y.
BROWNE
Alan L.,Nov.20,1981,30y.
George A.,June 14,1987,27y.
Victor A.,Sept.10,1973,51y.
BROWNLEE
David L.,June 12,1988,77y.
Delma S.,Sept.23,1987,75y.
Janice,Feb.20,1936,6m.
Paul C.,Jan.18,1981,57y.
BRUECK
Frederick,Dec.9,1991,82y.
Marie B.,Mar.30,1994
BRUNS
Blanch V.,May 1,1966,72y.
BRUSH
John F.,Mar.27,1994,78y.
BRYANT
Addie S.,1849-July 1901.
Annie M.,Oct.18,1943,81y.
Etta Crowley,Oct.19,1955,63y.
Evelyn L.,Nov.8,1961,89y.
Harold W.,Feb.1,1964,67y.
infant, Aug.1978, s.b.
Jane S.,June 24,1982 61y.
John W.,Aug.8,1956,86y.
Ralph C.,Nov.24,1979,91y.
Ralph C.,May 11,1949,20y.

BRYDEN
Harriet R.,1889-1890,d/o R.& A.
John W.,Oct.15,1950,72y.
Robert,Feb.20,1910,56y.
BRYSON
Alexander C.,Aug.7,1974,89y.
Donald, Jan.28,1910,31y.
Margaret,Feb.16,1908,32y.
Mary A.,May 28,1974,87y.
Robert, Mar.3,1922,87y.
Richard A.,Nov.1,1990,66y.
Ruth, Aug.28,1894,22d.
William N.,Aug.26,1929,47y.
BUCHARD
Albert,bu:May 15,1928,57y.
BUCK
Blair M.,Sept.26,1967,35y.
BUCKLEY
George A.,Nov.8,1964,86y.
George W.,Nov.23,1973,57y.
infant,Dec.9,1956,9hrs.
infant,July 29,1957,prem.
infant,Mar.18,1958, s.b..
infant,Feb.25,1959,13hrs.
Murial L.,Feb.10,1981,65y.
BUGBEE
Helen,Apr.14,1921,36y.
LeRoy,May 6,1904,2y.
BUNNELL
Alice W., 3m.,rem. from
  Saccarappa Cem.Nov.18,1924.
Annie Mayberry,Mar.12,1943,61y.
Bessie E.,June 22,1947,54y.
Frederick J.,Nov.8,1953,79y.
Helen M.,Oct.17,1924,21y.
Joseph W.,Nov.18,1952,83y.
Mabel I.,June 1917,40y,rem.
  from Saccarappa Cem.Nov.1924.
Margaret,Jan.26,1900,6m.
no name, removed from
  Saccarappa Cem.Nov.18,1924.
Philip P.,Dec.21,1942,34y.
Thelma,Mar.29,1925,6hrs.
William R.,Nov.22,1947,54y.
BUNYAN
Edward J.,Nov.3,1907,28y.
BURDWOOD
infant, Nov.11,1946, 2d.
BURGESS
Abbie H.,May 28,1903,23y.
Benjamin S.,Jan.17,1943,65y.
Clarence W.,June 26,1947,54y.
Evelyn B.,Sept.3,1968,74y.
Ruth D.,May 3,1925,78y.
BURGH
Agnes Tosh,Sept.24,1923,83y.
Elizabeth J., Apr.3,1942,67y.

George H.,1875-1896.
Henry T.,1883-1894.
James,1863-1895.
James, Aug.25,1898,2m.
John,May 4,1912,72y.
John, Jr.,1867-Sept. 6,1896.
Joseph M.,Sept.6,1928,55y.
BURGIN
David Eugene,Nov.4,1918,33y.
BURKE
Arthur M.,Jan.31,1966,72y.
Ethel L.,Mar.16,1981,86y.
BURNELL
Angelia Thatcher,Dec.19,1902,
  62y, w/o Nathaniel A.
Charles B.,Feb.23,1927,46y.
Clarence W.,Aug.10,1970,70y.
Doris,June 18,1981,86y.
Emma W.,Jan.30,1960,93y.
Eva M.,1877,4m,d/o N.A.&A.T.
Eva M.,Jan.2,1978,51y.
Frank C.,Apr.19,1994,73y.
Frank J.,Aug.1,1946,67y.
Frank Clifford,Jr.,Jan.1944,2m.
Fred A.,Dec.13,1934,63y.
Gerald,May 10,1970,48y.
Gene Arlen,Jan. 29,1944,2m.
James Arthur,Feb.18,1948,7m.
John Phinney, Mar.7,1947,84y.
Joseph Walter,Jan.7,1972,67y.
Lena M.,Mar.10,1904,2m.
Lottie A.,May 13,1929,62y.
Margaret D.,July 14,1970,86y.
Nathaniel A.,Jan.10,1918,79y.
Pauline M., Apr.20,1943,3y.
Perley E.,Nov. 2,1968,56y.
Ruth T.,Oct.2,1976,79y.
Shirley Jane,July 18,1947,8m.
Stanley R.,Mar.30,1978,41y.
BURNHAM
Abbie Elizab.,July 31,1931,74y.
Blanch B.,Feb. 2,1964.
Clyde E.,Sr.,Aug.15,1978,82y.
Ella M.,May 1,1945,69y.
Fred B.,Jan.6,1933,50y.
Gertrude E.,Apr.4,1942,65y.
John Harris,June 1,1931,74y.
J.J.,June 22,1893,32y.
John,Feb.11,1899,67y.
Lewis R.,Sept.22,1985,52y.
Mary A.,Sept.11,1939,93y.
BURNS
Abbie Louise,Mar.5,1937,87y.
Arline L.,June 1,1925,20y.
Edward A.,Aug.27,1986,73y.
Elizabeth H.,July 2,1953,72y.
Frank P.,Apr.15,1922,39y.

Grace A.,Nov.2,1980,94y.
Harry B.,Apr.9, 1943,63y.
Louise H.,Feb.27,1945,60y.
Mary O'Hagen,Feb.24,1954,79y.
Patrick, Feb.13,1931,61y.
Philip R.,Oct.4,1966,80y.
Robert M.,M.D.,Jan.14,1991,78y.
Thurston S.,Oct.1,1922,71y.
Vernon R.,Oct.18,1958,57y.
BURPEE
C. Herbert,June 9,1963,74y.
Evangelyn L.,July 20,1970,82y.
J.Richard,Jan.26,1974,52y.
BURROUGHS
Adeline Roy,Sept.4,1954,88y.
Albert H.,M.D.,Sept.13,1918,75y.
Fanny,XXXX, w/o Dr. A.H.,rem.
  from Buckfield May 16,1919.
BURROWS
Annie M.,Feb.19,1942,47y.
Irene, Apr.3,1927,s.b.
Joseph D.,July 21,1954,60y.
Joseph D.,Jr.,May 10,1923,8m.
Louise M.,Jan.6,1967,68y.
Margaret Ruth, removed from
  Gorham Cemetery May 1923.
Mary D.,Feb.15,1971,85y.
Philip W.,Jr.,Jan.29,1953,16y.
Philip W.,Sr.,Oct.12,1985,70y.
Robert S., Sept.19,1963,69y.
Roy Herbert,June 7,1926,2m.
Roy H.,Aug.7,1956,69y.
BURTON
Annie B.,Aug.28,1919, 49y.
Hilda V.,June 17,1981,60y.
J. Floyd,June17,1965,60y.
Jennie, Aug.31,1919,49y.
John F., Jr.,Sept.3,1969,44y.
John T. Oct.22,1920,51y.
Naomi E.,Dec.16,1964,58y.
BUSBY
Richard J.,Mar.3,1977,57y.
BUTLER
Charles C.,Sept.4,1974,66y.
Margaret C.,Mar.30,1977,67y.
BUTTERFIELD
Raymond,July 11,1984,53y.
BUTTS
Walter A.,Sept.1,1954,37y,
  rem. to Forest City,Portland.
BUZZELL
Fred P.C.,Dec.7,1951.
Paul M.,Aug.12,1979,64y.
Ruth C.,July 29,1977,86y.
Wilbur J.,May 8,1965,56y.
BYE
infant,June 5,1952, s.b.

CABANA
Wilfred,Oct.4,1976,44y.
CABRAL
Miriam N.,July 4,1992,68y,
  d/o Nina Adams.
CACCIA
Ellen B.,Jan.24,1946,62y.
Walter,Nov.22,1971.
CAIRNS
Christine,bu:May 20,1936,24y.
Christopher D.,Sept.14,1958,58y.
infant,Sept.13,1934,1d.
infant,June 22,1924,prem.
James D.,Oct.13,1948,59y.
Joseph,June 18,1932,70y.
Margaret, bu:June 24,1932.
Rachel D.,bu: Dec.20,1941,80y.
Thomas H.,Jr.,June 2,1934,1hr.
CALLAHAN
Bertha M., Oct.22,1949,64y.
CALLAMORE
Allan M.,Mar.24,1970.
CALNAN
Bessie P.,Oct.31,1934,71y.
Brent M.,Feb.17,1977,5y.
CAMERON
Bessie P. Roberts,1863-1934,w/o Edm.
Edmund,1859-Mar.13,1914.
CAMIRE
Raymond A.,Mar.11,1989,63y.
Leo,July 30,1988,72y.
CAMPBELL
Annas,1831-1913.
Annie1850- May 12,1937.
Caroline,Feb.26,1922,36y.
Charles,1872-1875.
Edwin,Dec.15,1940,70y.
George Percy, Dec.16,1987,79y.
infant, Sept.15,1945,s.b.
John F.,Mar.30,1907,1y.
Lillian F., Apr.6,1906,2y.
Margaret C.,June 13,1976,63y.
Mary M.,May 22,1963,76y.
Paul K.,Oct.22,1975,65y.
Thomas,1849-1896.
Walter A.,Dec.27,1971,57y.
CANFIELD
Grace S.,May 31,1946,79y.
CANNELL
Addie M.,Nov.8,1952,78y.
Albert,Jan.20,1846-Sept.12,1922.
Alice L.,Mar.3,1931,54y.
Laura E.Morton,Mar.2,1905,53y.
Lydia Hall Davis,Nov.25,1839-
  May 28,1910,w/o Albert.
Philip, 1899.
Royal B.,Feb.6,1958,83y.

Samuel A.,July 6,1926,78y.
CANNING
Andrew C.,Mar.18,1975,92y.
Bertha C. Oct.14,1955,71y.
Charles A.,Sept.3,1982,76y.
Clifford R.,Apr.13,1974,68y.
James W.,1857-1907.
Sarah J. Livingstone,1860-1902, w/o James W.
CAPE
Edna J.,Oct.27,1975,87y.
William H.,Feb.27,1953,67y.
William, Jr.,July 11,1931,15m.
CARLSON
child, Oct.6,1917, s.b.
John Albert,July 31,1916, ch/o John & Mary.
CARMICHAEL
Ellery D.,Feb.5,1979,48y.
CARON
Agnes E.,July 23,1972,56y.
Edward J.,Oct.18,1990,77y.
infant,bu: Aug.30,1971, s.b.
Joseph, Mrs.,June 11,1938.
CARPENTER
Darrell C.,Sept.3,1916,4m.
CARR
Archie B.,Sept.14,1919,42y, rem. from Oak Hill Cem. May 14,1947.
Arthur A.,Dec.18,1964,67y.
Edwin B., Sr.,Nov.26,1978,80y.
Henry, Apr.16,1912,60y.
Herbert H.,May 10,1948,67y.
Minnie L.,Mar.24,1988,88y.
Rose T.,Mar.12,1985,88y.
Viola F.,June 3,1986,89y.
Walter S., Apr.21,1961,61y.
Winnifred M.,Feb.1,1968,88y.
CARRAS
Harry L.,Oct.24,1988,66y.
infant, Feb.27,1953, prem.
CARROLL
Freida M.,Sept.30,1967,63y.
George, Nov.20,1974,74y.
CARTER
infant, Aug.31,1975, s.b.
infant, Oct.7,1976,s.b.
Thomas C.,July 17,1988,73y.
CARTLAND
Abbie D.,Jan.27,1929,65y.
John,1820-1902.
Mariam, Apr.13,1948,97y.
Nancy,1823-1912,w/o John.
CARTRET
Annie G.,Sept 6,1947,69y.
Chester E.,Jan.25,1926,35y.
Edward A.,Dec.18,1952,88y.

Laura A.,July 20,1919,54y,w/o E.A.
CARVER
Emily M.,Aug.19,1984,83y.
F. Bernard,Mar.4,1971,90y.
Fred E., Sept.1,1948,86y.
Georgia T.,Feb.9,1968,87y.
Howard I.,June 2,1976,60y.
Jennie M.,Aug.5,1977,93y.
Mildred M.,May 27,1991,83y.
Perley W.,Sr.,Mar.30,1975,68y.
Scott A.,Feb.12,1962,1m.
Volly B.,Feb.15,1974,70y.
CARY
Fred A.,June 16,1992,81y.
Olive M.,Feb.27,1992,80y.
CASEY
Albert L.,June 15,1993,75y.
Annie Wilson,July 12,1930,66y.
Margaret G., Oct. 1,1976, 59y.
Mildred W., Nov.17,1937, 49y.
Richard Warren,Aug13,1917,2m.
S. Belle, Apr.8,1935,32y.
Wilbur R.,Rev,Sept.27,1970,73y.
William N.,Feb.17,1926,72y.
CASH
Alma L.,Mar.3,1965,49y.
Celia,Nov.13,1908,34y,w/o Jas Wm.
Clara E.,Feb.3,1964, s.b.
Clara E., Jan.11,1963,62y.
Clinton, Mar.30,1951,77y.
James William, Jan. 8,1940,65y.
Jenness E., Apr.25,1933,31y.
Linwood G., Aug.27,1991,76y.
Lucy Patrick,July 13,1933,82y.
Maude E.,Mar.18,1944,67y.
Orlando,Jan.3,1906,64y.
Vernon Ellsworth,Feb.1,1958,27y.
Winfield A., Nov.16,1966,74y.
CASSANOS
Harry D.,Sept.17,1918,7d.
CASSIA
Ellen,bu: May 9,1946.
CASTLE
Lisa A.,July 3,1975,16y.
CATER
Edward W.,May 15,1925,18y.
Martha F.,Oct. 2,1933,49y.
CATES
G. Myrtle,Mar.10,1956,57y.
CATLIN
Bryon W.,Sept.2,1984, 94y.
Bryon W.,Jr.,Apr.12,1989,74y.
Hazel L.,Mar.3,1986,91y.
CHADBOURNE
Charles E.,S/Sgt.,May 7,1943,19y.
Darlene R.,Apr.12,1945,8hrs.
Donald E.,Feb.8,1945 in Germ.,19y.

Donald L.,Nov.13,1965,19y.
Ernest C.,July 13,1972,88y.
Frederick E.,May 13,1957,35y.
Lillian E.,Sept.17, 1979,84y.
Theodore James,Mar.5,1944,1d.
Walter G.,Apr.4,1980,68y.
CHADBURN
infant,Dec.5,1946, s.b.
William H.,May 31,1985,62y.
CHADWICK
Alma L.,July 29,1982,68y.
Clarence R.,May 28,1981,82y.
CHAMARD
Louis J.,Jr.,Nov.14,1994,65y.
CHAMBERS
Addie Graffam,Apr.16,1940,69y.
William,June 17,1951,75y.
CHAMPAINE
John L.,Feb.13,1952,73y.
Vera M.,Oct. 6,1964,75y.
CHANDLER
Abbie Cobb,Feb.16,1933,76y.
Albert H.,Dec.20,1953,76y.
Albert Louis,Feb.5,1924,72y.
Mabel Reed,Nov.5,1953,73y.
Ralph,1889,4y,s/o A.& A.B.
CHAPLIN
Albert A.,Feb.1,1969,86y.
Frank A.,Nov.12,1959,79y.
Harry E.,Feb.21,1971,82y.
Luella B.,Apr.23,1934,69y.
Maggie N.,Dec.5,1969,86y.
Mildred I.,Mar.19,1974,83y.
Millard, Sr., Nov.27,1991,73y.
Mortimer W.,Mar. 6,1976,63y.
Ora L.,Dec.5,1982,97y.
Roy W.,Dec.14,1925,42y.
Willis B.,Feb.14,1919,62y.
CHAPMAN
Addie M.,Nov.11,1960,65y.
Annie S.,July 10,1973,95y.
Ernest W.,July 29,1959,79y.
Gladys G.,July 27,1974,71y.
Janet A.,Dec.2,1973,82y.
Mason M.,Dec.31,1931,57y.
Moses M.,Aug.22,1905,72y.
Napoleon B.,May 10,1940,74y.
Nathan C.,Mar.9,1990,85y.
CHARMARD
Dominique E.,Mar.26,1965,56y.
Evelyn C.,Feb 25,1966,57y.
Frances H.,Jan.5,1989,82y.
CHASE
Albert E.,Feb.28,1952,81y.
Alice M.,July 26,1955,83y.
Annie M.,Aug.20,1950,83y.
Calanthy L.,June 14,1973,83y.

Carroll W.,Nov.3,1952,68y.
Della R.,Dec.14,1926,40y.
Edna W.,May 1,1923,33y.
Elmer L.,June 8,1940,26y.
Eunice G.,Oct.16,1966,77y.
Frank A,Sr,bu:Nov.13,1944,83y
Frank A.,July 12,1958,69y.
Harry B.,Sr.,Feb.8,1980,91y.
Isabelle M.,July 14,1938,76y.
John S., Nov.13,1931.
Judson A.,Feb.18,1956,88y.
Lizzie M.,June 16,1962,88y.
Mabel E. Ward,Oct.20,1928,58y.
Mildred E.,Dec.24,1974,83y.
Perley M., June 11,1964,58y.
Robert E.,May 24,1982,68y.
Selden A.,Mar.28,1956,68y.
CHENEY
E. Claire, Oct.21,1972,80y.
Florence G.,Jan.15,1977,80y.
Harold N.,May 31,1975,86y.
CHESLEY
Albert A.,Oct.28,1934,97y.
Albert H., Dec.26,1970, 84y.
Anne, Nov.30,1943,1d.
Delia,bu:June 19,1930,80y.
infant, Jan.23,1942,8d.
infant,bu:Dec.5,1941, s.b.
Malcolm,Jr.,Sept.11,1962,29y.
Malcolm,Sr.,July 13,1961,70y.
Mary F.,Mar.28,1962,66y.
CHICK
Clyde B., Aug.16,1984,84y.
Frederick B.,July 5,1987,87y.
Joseph Floyd, Apr.9,1910,9d.
CHICKO
Josephine R.,Mar.20,1979.
CHIN
Harry,June 30,1930,49y.
CHIPMAN
Hanno, Sr.,May 6,1970,63y.
Hanno R.,Jr.,June 20,1993,68y
Leland M., Jan.22,1935,53y.
Minnie R.,Mar.12,1935,51y.
Visula D.,Feb.19,1911,1m.
CHRISTENSEN
Albert M.,May 20,1953,65y.
Alfred E.,Jan.20,1968,74y
Florence M., Apr.9,1974,92y.
Fred A.,May 14,1955,79y.
Freda E.,July 1,1963,94y.
Harry H.,Aug. 1,1956,42y.
Ingard,June 13,1917,18y.
John,Dec.31,1972, 83y.
John A.,Oct.19,1969,48y.
Jorgen,June 12,1946,65y.
Kenneth L.,Oct.11,1985,42y.

Kjeld,bu:Jan.19,1943,76y.
Linda J.,May 20,1937,46y.
Maren F.,Apr.6,1990,92y.
Maren P.,Nov.11,1969,86y.
Niels Holgar C.,May 31,1954,68y.
O. Dagmar,Feb.26,1965,78y.
Rudolph,Dec 9,1925, s.b.
Ruth A., Apr.10,1948,31y.
Selma, Apr.28,1960,76y.
Shirley J.,Nov.1,1993,72y.
CHRISTE
Mabel D.,Aug.21,1970,88y.
Philip G.,Oct.7,1994,93y.
CHUTE
Adelbert C.,Mar.10,1913,65y, d/o Capt.James & Mary Hoyt.
Adelbert C.,June 15,1944,39y.
Edith,1876-1876,d/o A.C.&L.M.
Herbert E.,Aug.20,1941,67y.
Lizzie Jordan,Mar.31,1942,86y.
Sadie G.,Nov.4,1942,70y.
Verona,Feb.14,1903,6y, d/o Herb.
CILLEY
Lawrence N.,Jan.6,1980.
Madelyn L.,1973, in Florida.
CLAPPER
Ernest H.,Apr.2,1967,80y.
Inez M.,Sept.1,1978,87y.
CLARK/CLARKE
Albert J.,May 10,1980.
Alta Keith,bu:June 24,1936,41y.
Charles S.,bu: Apr.8,1935.
Edward Norton,Apr.6,1939.
Eleanor,Dec.10,1979,86y.
Elizabeth Jones,Jan.21,1921,25y.
Esmeralda B.,Jan.19,1985,84y.
Floyd,Dec.12,1921.
Frank Arlington,Apr.20,1932,29y
Haddon B.,Nov.13,1971,76y.
infant,Mar. 22,1944, newb.
infant,Mar.30,1925, s.b.
infant,bu:Sept.5,1951,11hrs.
Jennie L.,July 4,1917,54y.
Leonard F.,Apr.13,1930, 55y.
Ora M.,Jan.12,1966, 77y.
Phyllis B.,XXXX, 3m.
Richard L.,May 19,1927,16d.
Ruth S., Nov.14,1963, 70y.
Warren B., Oct.28,1987, 68y.
Wilbur D., Sr.,Oct.11,1976,77y.
Winifred L.,Mar.29,1993,82y.
CLARKE
John,Jan. 2,1928, 33y.
Lee C.,July 29,1942,53y.
Leonard E.,June 8,1984,78y.
Lester M.,Mar.9,1990,79y.
Marion S.,Oct.2,1984,74y.

Millie S.,July 8,1986,98y.
CLAUSSEN
Claus G.,Nov.1,1967,95y.
Dora J.,Nov.26,1907,1y.
CLAY
Alonzo,Mar.8,1910,57y.
Bessie, XXXX,1y, rem. from Gorham Cem.,1914.
Cora E.,Feb.12,1952,84y.
Grace, XXXX,1y, rem. from Gorham Cem.,1914.
Inez H.,Mar.10,1954,70y.
James,Dec.20,1934,85y.
Lottie,Jan. 22,1922,66y.
Mary C. Butler,Feb.10,1919, 74y, w/o Alonzo.
CLEEVES
Inez P., bu:July 6,1936, 2y.
infant, bu:July 20,1937, s.b.
Patricia J.,Dec.3,1934,4m.
CLEMENT
J. Elliott, Oct.27,1948,51y.
CLISH
Thomas F.,Mar.4,1955,56y.
Vesta H.,Nov.21,1956,62y.
CLOUDMAN
A.G.,May 15,1842-Feb.21,1909.
Annie Waterhouse,Dec.11,1948,97y.
Annie E. Bodge,Feb.21,1909, 66y, w/o Frances.
Andrew C.,Apr.13,1936,72y.
Charles M.,Oct.31,1932, 82y.
Charlotte F.,Nov.5,1966, 83y.
Eliza H.,Jan.21,1893,73y.
F.Harold,Dec.5,1967,74y.
Fannie F. Cordwell,Aug.4,1922,59y.
Frances A.,Apr.15,1926,86y.
Frances H.,June 1939,rem.from Fla.
Herbert, Apr.17,1918,30y.
John,July 27,1815-June 30,1894.
Margaret P.,Feb.25,1948,72y.
Myra, Aug.18,1940,56y.
Percy H.,Dec.3,1870-Aug.20,1889.
CLOUGH
Martha L.,July 2,1975,73y.
CLOUTIER
Donald J.,June 13,1980,65y.
infant,May 24,1972, s.b.
COALFLEET
Owen, Mar.6,1960,85y.
COBB
A.C., Mrs.,Feb.21,1909,66y.
Adelaide A.,Sept.12,1939,79y.
Agnes M.,Feb.8,1943,60y.
Annette C.,1840July 9,1910.
Annie L.,Dec.28,1918,76y.
Annie Stoddard,Sept.29,1918,77y

Apphia D.,Jan.9,1935,53y.
Catherine B.,Mar.7,1913,62y.
Charles M.,May 14,1945,79y.
Clement M.,July 6,1949,62y.
Edgar A.,Mar.9,1936,89y.
Edgar L.,Sept.19,1919.
Edward L.,Oct.13,1963,75y.
Elisa,1884-1888,
  d/o J.E& H.E.Naylor Cobb.
Ernest A.,May 8,1956,83y.
Florence D.,Feb.23,1961,52y.
Gardiner H.,Jan.27,1922,66y.
George C.,Dec.25,1956,74y.
George L.,Apr.6,1961,64y.
Guy O.,Aug.8,1973,81y.
George M.,May 9,1914,54y.
Henrietta, Jan.28,1945,78y.
Henry S.,Jan.31,1953, 78y.
Herbert L.,1864-1889,s/o J.G.& L.A.
Herbert, July 10,1915,62y.
infant,Sept.20,1919,s.b.,ch/oL.F.
Jennie A.,June 13,1915,50y.
Jennie F., Apr.30,1946,79y.
John S.,Mar.31,1954,74y.
Joseph E.,Apr.6,1911,63y.
Joseph G.,Apr.6,1915,80y.
Julia L., June 6,1961,91y.
Leander B.,Dec.5,1919,56y.
LeRoy O.,Dr.,1872-Feb.1909,
  s/o Oliver A.
Lorenzo T.,Sept.1,1956,71y.
Louise M.,May 30,1975,84y.
Lydia A.,1836-1862,w/o J.G.
Martha L.,Feb.4,1976,72y.
Mary E., Oct.23,1935, 84y.
Maude A.,May 15,1968,89y.
Moses K.,Dec.26,1911.
Oliver A.,Feb.7,1920,81y.
Robert L.,Jan.15,1985,66y.
Russell Maxfield,Feb.24,1919,2m.
Sarah, Apr.9,1962,61y.
Walter P.,Mar.31,1916,40y.
Winifred,Sept.29,1918.
COCHRANE
Robert J.,July 19,1976,67y.
COFFIN
Albion F.,XXXX,53y,rem.from
  Greenwood Cem.Biddeford1928.
Ernest R.,Jan.28,1960,63y.
Florence A.,Apr.16,1943,61y.
Phillip A.,infant,XXXX,rem.
  Greenwood Cem.,Biddeford,1928.
Statira J.,Mar.31,1974,60y.
Sylvia,XXXX,39y,rem. from
  Greenwood Cem.,Biddeford 1928.
COLBURN
Flossie A.,May 7,1976,66y.

COLBY
Anna N.,Dec.20,1983,88y.
COLE
Addie,Jan.8,1944,76y.
Addiebelle L.,Oct.5,1957,77y.
Annie M.,Feb.14,1964,80y.
Charles C.,May 12,1941,77y.
Earle H.,1889-1889.
Ernestine E.,Mar.30,1961,58y.
Everett F.,Nov.25,1958,73y.
Harold F.,Jr.,Sept.13,1945,15y.
Harold F.,Sr.,Oct.4,1983,79y.
Harry R., Nov.29,1945,58y.
Herman H.,May 11,1918,26y.
Ivory, rem. from Brownsville,
  ME in1929.
Kenneth M.,Dec.12,1979,76y.
Marilyn H.,May 10,1948,17y.
Melvina R.,May 28,1951,94y.
Merton,1894-1895.
Myrtle M.,Jan.2,1981,88y.
Nathan R.,1891-1905.
Oliver F.,Nov.25,1960,82y.
Rachel,July 15,1895,77y.
Raymond B.,Jan.4,1974,45y.
Ruth B.,July 15,1954.
COLEMAN
Emily F.,June 19,1936,81y.
Harry M.,bu:1929.
Lareine E.,Mar.18,1970,84y.
COLLEY
Lucy E.,Feb.11,1929,68y.
Margaret B.,Feb.12,1949,52y.
COLLINS
Carol Ann, Apr.1,1942,7m.
Carroll C.,Sept.14,1937,14y.
Clayton F.,Cpl.,Sept.4,1944
  in Burma,21y.
Fern C.,June 12,1965,60y.
Frank C., Oct.23,1992.
George T.,Oct.16,1994,85y.
Harry D.,May 6,1958,74y.
R. Milton,Jan.23,1970,58y.
Susie S.,June 5,1986,101y.
COLLIS
infant, Oct.24,1932, prem.
COLPRITT
infant, May 21,1948,s.b.
CONANT
Alice, July 9,1905,8d.
Charles Dale,Dec.18,1923,18d.
Ella M., Apr.9,1987,83y.
Elmira S.,1844-1880.
Eugene L.,Sept.30,1946,47y.
Eugene W.,Jan.22,1965,90y.
George W.,Jan.13,1945,76y.

Grace M.,June 27,1915,35y,w/o Eugen.
children, Sept.6,1926.
infant, Oct.9,1920, s.b.
infant, Apr.16,1919,s.b.
John W.,Feb.1893,53y,h/o Hattie B.
Lucy A., Oct.13,1955,76y.
Lynne, July 7,1974,81y.
Mabel N.,Oct. 26,1944,40y.
Manola E.,July 30,1976,77y.
Mark W.,Aug.2,1977,77y.
Maurice A.,Jan.7,1987,58y.
Merle L.,Apr.26,1961,55y.
Philip V.,Aug.19,1959,67y.
Sarah Lizzie,July 2,1926,74y.
Walter, June 6, 1901,7m.
Zelma A.,Aug.10,1914,9m.
CONDON
William A., Sept. 25,1894,29y.
Wilmar A.,1885-1894.
CONKLIN
George F., Sr., Apr.6,1972,83y.
Hazel E.,Dec.12,1966,74y.
Marie G., Aug.4,1968,41y.
CONNELL
Catherine E., Mar.29,1910,3d.
James,1887-1895.
CONNER
Arthur,May 20,1935,55y.
Charles M.,Mar.16,1979,65y.
Elizabeth M., Aug.13,1931,96y.
Emma J.,Nov.16,1955,68y.
infant,July 4,1944,prem.
Jeannette L.,Mar.25,1992,76y.
Lillian G.,May 14,1973,59y.
Marion E.,June 12,1983,66y.
Mary E., Aug.8,1970,86y.
Milton H.,Jan.12,1992,80y.
CONNORS
Charles, July 30,1898,45y.
COOK
Alice M.,July 13, 1963,72y.
Eli R.,Dec.18,1960, 80y.
Elmi M.,Oct.31,1949,69y.
Frederick R.,Sept.14,1927,9y.
Irene V.,Nov.27,1984,86y.
Laura M.,rem. from Saccarappa Cemetery Apr.30,1927.
Leslie Randolph,Nov.22,1918,13y.
Philip D.,May 25,1952, 64y.
Victoria Lillian,July 1,1925,4y.
COOKE
Helen M.,Feb.29,1976,80y.
COOLBROTH
Alice,1793-1862,w/o John.
John W.,1791-1823.
Lucy, Apr.17,1894,74y.

COOLFLEET
Owen, Mar.6,1960,85y.
COOLONG
George,July 12,1985,84y.
COOMBS
Clara,1854-1857.
Ella,1855-1857.
Emma,1852-1854.
J.M.,1825-1917.
Jetye Beth,Feb.8,1917,91y.
Milton W.,Sept.11,1945,68y.
N.C.,Judge,1818-1897.
Rena M.,1950,56y.
COOPER
Arthur B.,Mar.14,1980,61y.
Charles A.,May 16,1916,70y.
COPELAND
Rachael S.,Jan.29,1975,59y.
COPPOCK
Edward, Sept.25,1941,81y.
James, Sept.1,1920,56y.
Sarah Dodd,Feb.7,1917,56y.
CORBETT
Amelia, Aug.5,1930,66y.
Charles H.,Oct.2,1934,58y.
Harry J.,Jan.3,1984,83y.
CORBIN
Yvone M., Apr.13,1993,72y.
CORDWELL
A.A., Apr.15,1913,58y.
Ella Francis, Aug.29,1931,78y.
Stephen E.,Jan.14,1948,78y.
Winnifred M., Apr.8,1932,64y.
CORKERY
infant,July 2,1960,1hr.
infant,May 10,1959,7hrs.
infant,Oct.3,1956,7hrs.
Herbert T.,Dec.15,1971,75y.
Merrill L.,Mar.22,1988,64y.
Mildred I.,Jan.23,1990,86y.
CORO
Hilda, Sept.8,1922,4y.
COSTA
Lettie L., Sept.24,1970,92y.
COTE
Ellen M.,Oct.4,1992,90y.
Roland P.,June 23,1945,41y.
Theodore J.,Nov.8,1986,84y.
COTTON
Blanch L.,Sept.6,1961,76y.
Carroll H.,June 18,1929,60y.
Charles Sumner,Nov.9,1932,66y.
Edmund C.,May 4,1976,85y.
Eugenia,Mar.22,1963,86y.
H. Elizabeth,Feb.22,1926,80y.
Helen,Sept.27,1931,63y.

Howard,Sept.29,1904,60y.
J. Howard,Jan.30,1973,65y.
Jane M.,Feb.9,1941,71y.
Jennie M.,Nov.18,1969,81y.
John Bryce,Apr.17,1944,2d.
Lester C.,Nov.11,1918,3m.
Linwood S.,Sept.8,1969,63y.
Maria A.,Jan.17,1921,47y.
Ralph Hayden,Jan.1,1931,45y.
William,Oct.18,1935,63y.
COURNDYER
Dennis,June 20,1994,32y.
COUSENS/COUSINS
Alice M.,May 20,1968,84y.
Anna F. Dec.31,1976,85y.
Effie M., Apr.16,1940,60y.
Harry Winfield,Sept.8,1952,76y.
Lawrence Earle,Sept.25,1914,5m.
Martha M.,bu:Oct.5,1924,82y.
Oscar Lincoln,May 9,1919,57y.
Ralph W.,Oct.23,1941,59y.
Sarah Louise,June 3,1948,86y.
Susie L.,Apr.19,1922,35y.
W.S., Feb.27,1920,72y.
COWAN
James,Oct.21,1892,3m.
Katie,1881-1889.
Lizzie,Oct.29,1892,1m.
COX
Cecil S.,July 6,1960,70y.
Elizabeth Anne,Feb.17,1931,83y.
Ethel F., Apr.25,1968,91y.
CRABTREE
infant,Oct.1,1942,5hrs.
CRAFT
Eleanor C., July 29,1989,72y.
Harold R.,Mar.17,1985,69y.
CRAGIN
Beulah M.,Jan.16,1978,84y.
Edith E., Sept.14,1970,55y.
Frank G.,May 17,1978,84y.
Mary K.,May 3,1973,50y.
CRAIGIE
Addie L.,Apr.30,1918,28y.
Bryce J.,Jan.2,1935,12y.
Hazel H.,Oct.28,1966,66y.
infant, Apr.25,1918,s.b.
Isabelle,July 13,1928,69y.
CRAGUE
Annie R., Apr.9,1975,93y.
Florence Lillian,Apr.10,1932,38y.
George H.,Feb.14,1932,42y.
Martha E.,Sept.26,1988,94y.
Walter B.,June 16,1956,64y.
William J.,May 6,1963,52y.
CRAM
Caroline S.,Apr.10,1965,93y.
Carroll C.,Dec.13,1984,80y.
Elliott S.,Jan.3,1969,61y.
Frank B.,Mar.11,1953,52y.
Helen S.,June 21,1945,58y.
Leander E.,Apr.7,1966,72y.
Walter D.,bu:Sept.20,1942,38y.
CRANDALL
Robert G.,Dec.4,1990,52y.
CRAWFORD
Cecile O.,Oct.26,1992,62y.
Edna Ruth, Oct.21,1918,5m.
Jessie M., June 27,1985,75y.
Lawrence M.,May 29,1921,27y.
Mabel P.,Mar.23,1950,59y.
Stewart A.,June 22,1960,72y.
CRAWLEY
Ruth, Nov.19,1918,69y.
CRESSY
Daniel, Aug. 6,1914,66y.
Evelyn O.,Dec.11,1989,81y.
George Franklin,Nov.27,1956,81y.
Lorana Smith,June 30,1921,78y.
Mabelle L.,June 2,1934,53y.
Willard D.,Dr.,Dec.17,1980,76y.
CROCKER
Bessie J., Apr.6,1935,58y.
CROCKETT
Elma V.,Dec.4,1915,11m.
Hilda M., May 23,1946,1d.
Nina G.,Feb.7,1960,77y.
Viola Gertrude Perham,
 Oct.7,1918,18y.
CROOKER
Bessie J.,Apr.6,1935,58y.
E. Ray,May 2,1961,63y.
Ronello J.,June 18,1921,47y.
CROSBY
Calvin "Joe",Nov.24,1986,81y.
Dorothy A.,May 27,1985,82y.
Irene L.,Dec.14,1989,80y.
Lillian,Jan.7,1962,90y.
Mary L.,Sept.20,1984,61y.
Thomas S. Sr.,Apr.7,1986,86y.
Willie E.,Jan.2,1938,65y.
CROSS
Clyde A.,Sept.4,1990,81y.
Emma T.,Nov.10,1975,75y.
CROWE
Albert G.,Dec.30,1958,28y.
Arthur M.,Nov.26,1979,85y.
Beverly A.,June 23,1984,46y.
Frank M.,Dec.28,1985,77y.
infant, Apr.14,1928, s.b.
Louise O.,Sept.13,1981,85y.
Mary M.,May 7,1990,63y.
CROWLEY
Benjamin R.,July 23,1976,79y.

Cora L.,Nov.23,1960,75y.
John H.,Jan.27,1965,74y.
Ruth E.,Nov.16,1918,14y.
Windred,Apr.9,1900,37y.
CROZIER
Amy S.,June 5,1944,70y.
James W.,June 14,1962,90y.
Sarah M.,Feb.3,1904,27y.
CUMBERLAND
Kenneth E., Sr.,Aug.3,1976.
CUMMINGS
Adelbert B.,Oct.15,1940,65y.
Agnes W.,Apr.25,1964,80y.
Bertha L.,Oct.8,1954,50y.
child, Mar.24,1892,2y.
Chester H.,June 28,1967,73y.
Chester L.,Dec.3,1986,78y.
Elizabeth,1875-1875,d/o F.A.& J.S.
Ernest F.,Apr.16,1963,66y.
Ethel R.,Dec.25,1978,84y.
Eugene I.,Jan.7,1936,68y.
Frank W.,July 30,1935,67y.
Fred A.,1853-1890,
John A.,Dec.17,1963,80y.
Lillian A.,Nov.2,1943,69y.
Lizzie M.,Apr.16,1944,69y.
Mabel H.,May 13,1953,79y.
Margaret H.,Dec.19,1948,76y.
Martha,Feb.21,1897.
Melroy E.,Nov.2,1964,73y.
Stanton C.,Jan.22,1939,28y.
Wallace W.,Mar.24,1926,25y.
William, Nov.26,1956,80y.
CUNNINGHAM
Edna W.,Sept.29,1963,49y.
CURIT
Alpha T.,Nov.12,1960,80y.
Elsie E.,Apr.4,1959,65y.
CURRAN
Jeannette E.,Aug.14,1952,30y.
CURRIER
Janice,Feb.22,1987,70y.
John H.,July 30,1947,59y.
Mary E.,Mar.21,1960,63y.
Stanley L.,July 13,1966,51y.
Stella M.,Feb.7,1978.
CURRY
Celia M.,Apr.2,1983,95y.
Phebe J.W.,1835-1858,w/o E.H.
CURTIS
Blanche V.,May 12,1972,92y.
Charles E.,Apr.2,1961,86y.
Chester C.,Nov.12,1965,55y.
Earle W.,June 3,1970,72y.
Grace L.,Dec.21,1990.
Helen R.,June 12,1938,26y.
Mildred L.,May 30,1971.

Scott & James,May 16,1970,1d.
CUSHING
George L.,Sept.24,1959,64y.
infant,Jan.2,1947.
Susan M.,Mar.4,1987,94y.
CUTTER
Addie S.,Nov.24,1943,89y.
B. Clifford,Mar.14,1934,48y.
Gladys M.,Mar.2,1914,22y.
John F.,Apr.10,1901,59y.
Katherine W. Turner,
    Oct.19,1917,77y.
Maude Helen,Jan.17,1956,60y.
William W.,Sept.24,1915,64y.
CYR
Alice L.,June 13,1966,59y.
DAISEY
Joseph E.,Oct.9,1979,46y.
DAHMS
Lawrence P."Babe",Feb.13,1993,60y.
DALEY
Donald H.,Nov.11,1980,77y.
Dora, Aug.23,1991,92y.
Elizabeth S.,Jan.1,1975,78y.
James E., Jr.,Jan.21,1976,81y.
Rebecca J.,Mar.16,1964,82y.
Robert G.,Nov.14,1947,3d.
William J.,Apr.10,1970,75y.
DALL
infant,bu:Nov.9,1942,s.b.
Mary I.,Mar.12,1969,46y.
DALLEN
Margaret M.,June 2,1986,90y.
Ward W.,May 4,1986,84y.
DAMON
Elizabeth F.,Mar.15,1961,53y.
Herbert W.,Mar.1,1976,52y.
Kathleen E.,Oct.16,1994,38y.
DANA
Charlotte Emery,Oct.23,1915,1y.
Ellen L.,Aug.24,1894,39y.
Ethel M.,Feb.18,1952,75y.
Florence H.,Feb.2,1972,93y.
Frank J.,Sept.9,1924,80y.
Howard H.,Oct.29,1981,67y.
Howard, Jr.,Oct.23,1966,13hrs.
Louisa W.,May 26,1952,82y.
Luther,Aug.29,1966,85y.
Marion P.,Sept.8,1985,97y.
Mary B.,Oct.19,1954,71y.
Mary L.H.,July 24,1919,70y.
Philip,Feb.7,1954,79y.
Philip Jr.,July 1,1986,76y.
Woodbury K.,May 18,1924,83y.
DANFORTH
Lillian E.,Feb.23,1935,64y.

DANIE
Antonio,Mar.7,1990,79y.
Ruth M.,Aug.23,1994,81y.
DANIELS
infant,bu:Sept.30,1975, s.b.
infant,May 4,1956,prem.
Louis A.,Jr.,Dec.8,1988,74y.
Rose A.,Oct.8,1968,55y.
Victor F.,Feb.19,1960,42y.
DARKIS
Henry B.,Oct.9,1984,78y.
Jeanette,May 30,1973,46y.
DARLING
Leroy R.,July 28,1986,56y.
Winona A.,Apr.5,1994,75y.
DAUPHINEE
Alfred F.,Apr.6,1985,64y.
DAVENPORT
Burt G.,Oct.6,1966,51y.
Eliza D.,May 26,1918,92y.
Marcella G.,May 16,1976.
DAVIDSON
Eliza,May 28,1918,92y.
Mata S.,Sept.26,1991,85y.
DAVIS
Adella H.,Apr.17,1942,84y.
Albert,Dec.2,1942,82y.
Albert O.,Feb.10,1982,79y.
Alonzo W.,Oct.17,1935,80y.
Amos,July 13,1919,64y,rem. from White Rock Cemetery, 1919.
Amos Carroll,Nov.12,1928,s.b.
Appia D. Cobb,July 17,1919,91y, w/o Amos.
Arthur E.,Mar.12,1985,82y.
Barrett V.,Dec.17,1960,57y.
Charles, Sept.5,1953,95y.
child, July 16,1900,6m.
Clara W.,July 18,1964,84y.
Elizabeth M.,Mar.9,1993,86y.
Emma J.,July 4,1938,75y.
Ethel J.,Nov.27,1956,70y.
Francis M.,Mar.5,1962,46y.
Frederick A.,Jan.1,1968,79y.
Frederick C.,XXXX.
Gertrude R.,Aug.10,1976,72y.
Hazel M.,Apr.7,1979,87y.
Ida Birmingham, Feb.15,1916, 54y, native of Watertown,NY.
Irene A.,July 7,1994,89y.
Jessie G.,Aug.3,1994,89y.
Jessie S.,Dec.2,1907,58y,w/o Thos.
John H.,Oct.21,1968,57y.
John J.,Jan.5,1954,74y.
Kenneth M.,Sept.8,1983,80y.
Lizzie Gray,May 28,1913,w/o Chas.
Lorenzo F.,Nov.5,1926,70y.

Lyman W.,Apr.12,1966,85y.
Lyndol W.,Feb.4,1931,2m.
Mabel P.,Nov.24,1947,59y.
Magnus C.,Nov.14,1962,84y.
Margaret,Feb.6,1990,82y.
Mildred Iona,Sept.15,1930,6y.
Mildred V.,Apr.19,1977,66y.
Nathan, June 27,1922,60y.
Nellie R.,May 17,1977,76y.
Nelson R.,July 16,1942,65y.
Norman S.,July 3,1976,57y.
Parson P.,Oct.13,1939,75y.
Paul A.,Apr.26,1966,62y.
Pearl A.,Sept.5,1974,60y.
Phebe C., Apr.15,1934,73y.
Sarah M., Aug.4,1936,59y.
T.Lawrence, Nov.27,1985,80y.
Thomas, Jan.24,1931,81y.
Warren C.,June 27,1994,86u.
Wendell B.,June 9,1990,70y.
Willis, Apr.12,1948,53y.
DAY
Adella May,Apr.21,1938,70y.
Ansel, Apr.3,1968,75y.
Augusta,Aug.14,1908,61y.
David E.,Feb.13,1975,74y.
Effie L.,Dec.25,1954,51y.
Emma,bu:Feb.5,1937,76y.
Frank B.,Dec.21,1969,95y.
Helen C.,Feb.5,1979,58y.
Herbert, Mar.27,1916.
infant,Sept. 23,1949,1d.
infant,Sept.24,1947, s.b.
Isadore T.,Feb.12,1957,79y.
Martha C.,Dec.10,1959,67y.
Richard R.,Feb.6,1985,38y.
Roland A.,Sept.3,1985,64y.
True W.,Sr.,Dec.21,1990,77y.
DEAKIN
Howard H.,Feb.1,1964,67y.
Mabel,Dec.19 1978,81y.
DEAN
Abbie,Feb.17,1936,75y.
Relatives of Abbie Dean,rem. from Saccarappa Cem. in 1920.
DeBECK
Alman E.,Mar.14,1933,62y.
Charles E.,Feb.26,1970,91y.
Elizabeth,Dec.22,1918,80y.
Ellen,Feb.15,1917,72y.
George W.,June 2,1916,74y.
Grace E.,June 7,1944,55y.
Leonard H.,1872-1898.
Leonard M., Apr.22,1899,24y.
Robert, Aug.23,1911,67y.
Robert W.,June 4,1928.

DECKER
Elfreda L.,Aug.24,1951,46y.
Esther J.,Oct.3,1922,75y.
DeCOSTA/DeCOSTE
Charles E.,Oct.8,1950,62y.
Lucrete M.,Dec.5,1968,83y.
Mary G.,Jan.26,1964,73y.
DELCOURT
Kerin J.,bu:Nov.14,1962,6w.
infant,bu:Dec.27,1963,s.b.
DeLONG
Stephen W.,Feb.18,1965,80y.
DELORME
George T.,bu:Nov.30,1950,32y.
DEMERS
Laurette F.,Nov.21,1985,63y.
DENNISON
Gregory,May 22,1970,23y.
Myriane E.,May 12,1991,72y.
DENSMORE
Donald B.,Dec.14,1993,77y.
DERAGON
Joseph T.,Mar.9,1979,90y.
Josephine M., Oct. 21,1978.
DeRICE
infant,May 10,1946,prem.
DeROCHE
Terri Lee,Dec.23,1958,4m.
DeROCHER
Robert J.,III,Jan.22,1990,2d.
DeROSIER
Joseph W.,II,Oct.26,1985,19y.
DEWEY
Virginia W.,Mar.4,1983,80y.
DEXTER
Clementine P.,Jan.24,1983,82y.
George W.,Dec.5,1973,75y.
DiBIASE
infant,May 14,1968,s.b.
DICKEY
Florence,May 27,1929,50y.
William C.,June 30,1938,65y.
DIFFIN
Gary L.,Feb.24,1971,23y.
Leo E.,Oct.15,1987,61y.
DILL
Albert E.,Sept.6,1944,72y.
Lawrence A.,Dec.25,1976,40y.
Sadie E.,Nov.25,1955,75y.
DINEEN
George J., May 6,1966,69y.
Iver L., Sept.1,1973,78y.
DINSMORE
Alice S., Sept.10,1957,78y.
Charles H.,Nov.11,1935,79y.
Clara M., July 21,1981,85y.
Eleanor M.,Nov.20,1958,44y.

Francis A.,Nov.7,1972,77y.
Isabelle M.,Mar.1,1951,89y.
Jane,rem.from Saccrppa Cem.1934.
Margaret Elizab.,June 6,1943,43y.
N. Albertus,Jan.22,1939,74y.
Nellie E.,Jan.18,1950,77y.
William A., Sept.25,1934,64y.
DION
Edward R.,Jan.3,1972,63y.
Eva I.,Mar.11,1965,59y.
DIX
Ernestine E.,Dec.7,1975,56y.
DOAK
Sylvia H.,Apr.21,1994,60y.
DOBSON
Charles L., Apr.11,1973,68y.
DOLLOFF
infant, Oct.20,1947,s.b.
DONOVAN
Raymond E.,Mar.1,1989,77y.
DORITY
Mary A., Jan.6,1974 61y.
DOUCETTE
Dorothy F.,Nov.12,1960,48y.
Eda V.,Oct.17,1945,53y.
Howard R., Aug.22,1955,30y.
infant,May 29,1924,s.b.
James F.,Dec.21,1976,92y.
John J.,Sept.29,1957,80y.
Maurita K.,Oct.29,1974,23y.
Robert E.,Dec.19,1935,1d.
Ruth,Oct.11,1991.
Winifred B.,Jan.5,1974,86y.
DOUGHERTY
Bessie, Oct.16,1937,65y.
Harry W.,July 25,1947,49y.
Ivernia C.,Jan.25,1970,67y.
James, Mar.4,1918,58y.
William H.,Feb.16,1969,41y.
DOUGHTY
Eugene L.,Oct. 27,1964, 48y.
infant, Nov.17,1975, s.b.
Pearl Madeline,Jan.21,1992,95y.
DOUGLAS
Andrew B.,May 5,1967,39y.
Annie L.,Oct.25,1926,56y.
Charles E.,Oct.15,1952,67y.
Charles W.,Oct15,1956,82y.
Duncan D.,Dec.18,1975,45y.
Edmund,1819-1892.
Edna L., Sept.29,1956,77y.
Effie W.,Nov.20,1954,72y.
Eliza,1819-1886,w/o Edm.
Elizabeth,1918,52y.
Elizabeth F.,Mar.13,1952,76y.
Elisha, Mar.5,1907,82y.
Emma W.,Nov.21,1933,67y.

Eunice,1816-1857,w/oEdm.
Genie L.,July 30,1977,92y.
Gloria G.,May 25,1938,1m.
Harry L.,Apr.14,1956,65y.
Henry B.,Mar.23,1936,77y.
infant,Jan.6,1925, s.b.
Irvin H., Aug.10,1959,80y.
Jennie,1839-1897,w/o Henry B.
Lawrence D.,Dec.19,1989,75y.
Lewis C.,June 20,1960,63y.
Mabel P.,July 22,1954,49y.
Marion L.,Mar.3,1970,78y.
Ralph M.,June 20,1945,58y.
Thornton P.,July 19,1930,20y.
DOW
Elizabeth C.,Dec.31,1992,78y.
Hale M., Apr.11,1959,70y.
Henrietta H.,Nov.2,1962,72y.
DOWLING
George W., Apr.1,1965,81y.
Geraldine L.,Nov.19,1974,63y.
Harriet C., Mar.2,1947,63y.
Raymond M., Nov.11,1978,60y.
DOWNS
Frances P.,bu:Dec.31,1966,67y.
Frederick L., Aug. 2,1949,55y.
DOYLE
Estella M., Sept. 6,1941,52y.
DRESSER
Doris E.,1903-1904.
Dorothy H.,Sept.9,1900,3m.
Edna Louise, 3y, rem. from
Saccarappa Cemetery 1926.
Ernest L.,Dec.21,1928,56y.
Harriet R.,1871-1908.
Hattie Raymond, Apr.19,1908,36y, w/o Ernest L.
Reliance A., June 16,1919,82y, w/o Stephen.
Rhoda A., Feb.10,1929,82y.
Stephen M., Dec.14,1928,89y.
DRINKWATER
Edgar E.,Mar.28,1974,66y.
Everett,Oct.21,1921,3d.
Forrest E.,Mar.15,1918,5m.
Gilbert A.,Feb.3,1927,3d.
Mary Lincoln,Jan.15,1919,38y.
Norma Ruth, Oct.9,1921,7m.
Ralph E., Apr.19,1927,3m.
DRISCOLL
Cornelius,Jan.7,1916,58y.
Mary,Jan.17,1916,60y.
DRISKO
Agnes E.,Mar.25,1967,84y.
Amanda W.,July 14,1904,84y.
Perl W.,Apr.17,1952,75y.
Rhodell W.,Aug.24,1915,60y.

DRUIN
Mary Lucy, Feb.25,1952.
Ellen,Nov.11,1919,34y,w/o Moses.
DUBAY
Deanna Wallace,July 18,1992,55y.
DUCHAINE
Albert J., Mar.16,1958,57y.
Donald W.,July 4,1987,26y.
DUCHAINEAU
Paul J.E.,Mar.25,1955,38y.
DUCHESNE
Eugene J.,Oct.5,1973,67y.
DUCLOS
Violet K.,Aug.3,1979,61y.
DUDLEY
Charles,Dec.21,1945,72y.
DUE
Andres,May 1,1930,80y.
Frederick Andrw.,Sept.21,1918,18y.
Gladys A.,Sept.14,1910,2y.
Maren,Nov.31,1921,71y.
Minnie S.,Sept. 2,1926,48y.
Niels N.,July 6,1959,82y.
Ralph H.,Aug.22,1914,1y.
Raymond,Sept.27,1972,60y.
DUFFILL
Jane Dale, Aug.29,1926,87y.
DUGAS
Leonard R.,Mar.13,1965,36y.
Roger Marshall,May 1,1988,22y.
DUNBAR
Dorothy C.,Oct.23,1976,79y.
Frank M.,Dec.16,1952,64y.
Steven A.,Jan.13, 1982,31y.
Thaddeus W.,July 7,1961,72y.
DUNCAN
James E.,Mar.31,1987,65y.
DUNFIELD
Emily W.,May 2,1952,80y.
Fred M.,Oct.31,1937,40y.
DUNLAP
Avis C.,Oct.17,1944,66y.
Louis A.,Aug.5,1980,78y.
Maurice A., Apr.23,1952.
DUNN
Agnes N.,Oct.26,1982,93y.
Alice,Feb.12,1948,69y.
Alfred H.,June 21,1967,55y.
Ellen Frances, Nov.9,1919,34y.
Everett E.,Feb.21,1964,88y.
George C.,Sept.26,1913,67y.
George W., Oct.16,1942,10y.
Grace E., Apr.7,1898,51y.
Henry,Nov.10,1910,39y,s/o Geo. C.
Moses T.,July 11,1962,79y.
Raymond W.,Dec.26,1981,73y.

DUNNELL
George E.,Sept.22,1921,76y.
Harriet F.B.,Sept.3,1901,77y,w/o Jos.
Joseph,Jan.21,1898,81y.
DUNTON
Benjamin,Aug.10,1951,60y.
Florence B.,Jan.23,1956,58y.
DURAN
Emma F.,Oct.3,1925,69y.
Willis H.,Jan.2,1925,69y.
DURANT
Hilda May,Sept.5,1937,7m.
Juanita H.,June 6,1931,33y.
DURELL/DURRELL
Calvin E.,June 19,1961,82y.
Edgar A.,June 5,1931,75y.
Elijah A.,Apr.27,1910,75y.
Frances E.,June 2,1910,75y, w/o Elijah A.
Mabel F,Apr.2,1920,52y,w/o Edgar.
Sadie B.,Feb.23,1945,63y.
DWYER
Addie S.,June 15,1975, 78y.
DYER
Albert, July 22,1993,76y.
Albion E.,Mar.21,1973,82y.
Celanire M.,Sept.23,1944,40y.
Charles H.,Apr.20,1931,89y.
Clifford M.,Oct.19,1964,71y.
Doris M.,Mar.4,1977,75y.
George O.,Dec.19,1907,6y.
James,Feb.28,1992,45y.
Lulu R.,Feb.6,1957,69y.
Mary E., Apr.4,1914,76y.
Mary E. Lamb,bu: Aug.28,1937.
Mary S.,Mar.8,1959,56y.
Mederick C.,S/Sgt.,Feb.7,1945, 31y, in the Philippines.
Millard,Jan.20,1944,65y.
Morton M.,Dec.30,1970,83y.
Scott A.,July 24,1959,12d.
William E.,June 9,1963,76y.
DYSON
Edward,Sept.11,1926.
Eva F., Aug.25,1943,52y.
EALY
Ruth D., Apr.22,1972,85y.
Wm. Everett,July 15,1960,69y.
EARL
Everett S.,Dec.7,1972,51y.
EATON
Joseph B.,Oct.17,1940,82y.
Nellie N.,Oct.22,1945,86y.
EASTMAN
Barbara K.,Jan.16,1966,37y.
Clark B.,Apr.18,1940,66y.
Etta E.,Feb.27,1927,62y.
Maud E.,Apr.27,1943,67y.
Moses C., May 3,1936,69y.
EASTUP
Leroy D.,Apr.2,1913,1y.
EDDY
Hiram E.,Mar.1,1929,78y.
EDGERLY
August,bu:Oct.24,1925,65y.
Charles B.,Aug.28,1934.
Clifford T.,Apr.8,1980,65y.
Edward L.,Oct.26,1970,89y.
Ella M.,June 13,1966,82y.
Emery I.,Nov.4,1940,30y.
Frank,Oct. 8,1918,26y.
Frank L.,Mar.6,1962,79y.
G. Lee, Oct.26,1980,88y.
Granvill Hicks,Mar.1,1927,64y.
Harriet R.,June 28,1932,86y.
Hattie M., Apr.3,1918,29y.
Howard E.,May 1,1945,1m.
Hugh B. Jr.,Nov.1981.
Ida G.,June 2,1953,80y.
Ina A.,Jan.9,1923, 37y.
Lewis W.,Apr.24,1912,77y.
Levi,June 29,1921,64y.
Marietta G.,July 5,1966,77y.
Mary E.,Jan.26,1932,72y.
Nellie M.,May 31,1899,39y.
Ruth A.,Feb.26,1922,45y.
Thomas L.,Feb.22,1950,11y.
EDWARDS
Bertha L.,1884-1977.
Charles B.,1864-1934.
Frank McLellan,June 9,1872.
Isabel,June 9,1870.
John F., Apr.22,1991.
Lizzie M.Brown,1836-Mar.28,1875 ,w/o Lewis Warren.
Martha J.1864-1895,w/o Chas. B.
Minnie I.,July 27,1993,89y.
ELDER
Charles S.,Feb.11,1929,78y.
George A.,1846-1875.
infant,June 8,1947,s.b.
infant,Oct.18,1942,s.b.
Jane S.,Sept.28,1912,68y.
John D.,Sept.2,1914,67y.
Mary, Apr.8,1907,55y.
Mehitible Sands,1814-1877,w/o Sol. L.
Percy S.,Jan.1,1937,62y.
Solomon L.,1813-1873.
ELDRIDGE
Francis A., June 18,1991,74y.
Ralph, H. Jan.2,1913,rem.from Pine Grove Cem.,Portland,1945.
ELKINS
Cora L., Oct.25,1956,88y.

Harry B.,bu: Apr.24,1922,56y.
Hazel A.,Jan.9,1978,84y.
Lester H., Sept.19,1971,76y.
Leone E., bu:Dec.31,1921.
Mother,1844-1938.
Father,1842-1910.
ELLIOTT
Henry L.,1883-1890.
infant, Sept.21,1993,1d.
Josiah W.,June 5,1927,66y.
Minnie G.,Dec.29,1985,99y.
Rachel M.Crichton,1861-1893,
 w/o Josiah.
Seth E.,Aug.23,1958,73y.
Susie A.Leavitt,1871-May 28,1941,
 w/o Josiah W.
ELOARTOKA
Adam, Oct.26,1916,25y.
ELWELL
Annie, Nov.5,1916.
Annie M.,Mar.9,1927,45y.
Annie Mabel, July 29,1937,65y.
Beatrice H.,Dec.27,1972,51y.
Benjamin D., Jan.10, 1929, 89y.
Berte D.,Apr.24,1973.
Carrie V.,bu:May 2,1936,75y.
Charles F.,Apr.5,1942,40y.
Charles O.,Oct.14,1943.
Charles P.,Mar.6,1929,65y.
Clara, Oct.25,1906.
Edward, Dec. 31,1896,14d.
Eliose E.,Feb.10,1986,90y.
Emily J.,1847-Jan.12,1900,w/o Wm M
Eudora,bu:Nov.19,1941,75y.
Frances Ellen,Dec.26,1915,76y.
Frank W.,Sept.28,1947,79y.
Frederick L.,Apr.10,1956,86y.
Gertie,1872-1873,d/o Martha E.
Hezekiah,1842-July 9,1925,
 Civil War 1861-1866.
Ida G.,Mar.15,1924,51y.
Irene E.,Nov.30,1978,85y.
James Wm.,Sept.26,1944,2m.
Jeannette M.,May 19,1992,64y.
Leon C.,June 24,1963,76y.
Leonora Pearl,June 26,1920,6y.
Lloyd,Apr.4,1994,73y.
Mabel A.,Apr.11,1958,76y.
Martah E.,Mar.21,1841-1908,
 w/o Benjamin D.
Mary A.,July 11,1900,53y.
Mary H.,Feb.1,1927,84y.
Mildred G.,May 6,1941,48y.
Olivia L.Feb. 3,1918,68y.
Percy H.,Oct. 21, 1953, 84y.
Preston J.,Apr. 21, 1903, 65y.
Sarah L.,1846-1893,w/o Hezekiah.

Simon W.,Oct.21,1914, 69y.
Stephen L.,Jan.11,1929,53y.
Thurman, Nov.11,1959,71y.
Thurman R."Bud"Feb. 27,1992,73y.
Washburn C.,June 19,1916,78y.
William J.,1872-1908.
William M.,1846-1897.
EMERSON
Elsworth L., Apr.8,1918,7m.
EMERY
Alice W.,Oct.18,1960, 67y.
Charles A.,Sept.8,1969,63y.
Edith B.,Dec.11,1982,77y.
Edward Barker, Apr.12,1940,6m.
Eleanor D., Apr. 11, 1990, 83y.
Ellen Hayden,July 19,1936,85y.
Everett W.,Oct.9,1979,64y.
Frank,bu:May 10,1928,70y.
Erland James,Dec.22,1942,17y.
Leonard H.,Oct.22,1964,85y.
Lillian B.,Dec.22,1968,91y.
Marjory V.,Sept.1,1987,71y.
Maurice D.,Dec.12,199373y.
Perley L.,Oct.14,1956,38y.
Philip H.,Aug.21,1983,73y.
Ruby M.,July 9,1972,46y.
Sarah E.,Aug.16,1980,78y.
Selden W.,May 31,1993,83y.
Susan J.,Mar.3,1945,7d.
Teresa M., Jan.7,1974, s.b.
EMMONS
Elizabeth Hinds,June 3,1894,
 84y,rem. from Saccarappa 1917.
Frederick A.,June 12,1903,69y,
 rem. from Saccarappa 1917.
Richard C., Apr.1,1987,63y.
William A.,1805-1849.
ERKELENS
Ruth P.,Jan.21,1963,67y.
ERSKINE
Herbert E.,June 15,1983,71y.
ESTES
A. Marion, May 10,1992,80y.
Bertha E.,May 7, 1946, 57y.
Brenda L.,June 29, 1955, 4d.
Edward Thomas,May 15,1945,1y.
Elwood M.,Mar.19,1993,65y.
Ernest S., Apr.30,1958, 68y.
Ernest Waldo,Jan.21,1919,1y.
Ernest W.,& Ruth E.,XXXX,s.b.,
 rem. from Saccarappa Cem.1941.
infant,June 30,1934,3hrs.
infant,Jan.23,1966, s.b.
James S.,Feb.19,1962,11y.
John W., Sr.,Feb.10,1984,73y.
Marion H.,May 10,1992,80y.
Merton E.,Feb.19,1991,81y.

Muriel, Sept.30,1925, s.b.
Richard Melvin, Dec.6,1940, 7m.
Ruth Edwina, May 24,1925,4y.
ESTY/ESTEY
Clyde S.,Jan.12,1968,62y.
Etta E.,Nov.14,1915,49y.
Etta L., Apr.18,1981,76y.
Fred W.,Feb.25,1952,80y.
Gladys,Oct.4,1982,84y.
Guy M.,Feb.1,1952,55y.
Hiram J.,Mar.20,1909,65y.
Hiram W.,Feb.7,1976,82y.
Horace B.,Apr.26,1974,75y.
Irma S.,Aug.17,1991,78y.
Joyce M.,June 10,1985,47y.
Kenneth L.,Sept.14,1978,76y.
Laura D.,Jan.26,1991,83y.
Lizzie Maude,Nov.30,1949,71y.
Valerie J.,Oct.20,1955,28y.
EVANS
Adelaide D.,May 8,1954,68y.
Alfred H.,Aug.8,1970,81y.
Bina L.,Nov.10,1968,80y.
Clyde W.,May 16,1973,67y.
George N.,Mar.14,1960,78y.
Harriet E.,Dec.28,1973,86y.
FABRICIUS
Marijane H.,Dec.1,1947,86y.
Martin,Mar.30,1930,60y.
FAIRBANKS
Frank E.,July 6,1951,87y.
Roselie B.,Aug.29, 939,66y.
FAIRSERVICE
Blanche M.,Feb.12,1921,42y.
James A.,Oct.31,1958,80y.
FALT
Aimsley Mardell,Sept.13,1927,60y.
Christina K.,May 16,1935,59y.
FARLEY
Alfred D.,Apr.19,1949,55y.
Beverly J.,Nov.8,1986,71y.
Edith May,1896-1897.
Elsie L.,Mar.24,1989,83y.
Helen S.,Nov.15,1972,71y.
Isabelle,Feb.21,1955,85y.
Janet L.,Feb.23,1994,78y.
Philip E.,Feb.28,1989,85y.
Ray D.,June 10,1956,56y.
William C.,Jan.29,1960,92y.
Winton H.,July 2,1985,78y.
FARNSWORTH
Harry G., Apr.6,1909, s.b.
Herbert E., Jr.,Mar.10,1941,32y.
Nellie, May 24,1922, 65y.
Percy W.,May 6,1895,4d.
FARQUARHASEN
Joanna M.,Aug.7,1940,81y.

Peter, Feb.25,1914,58y.
FARR
Alice M.,Sept.10,1980, 91y.
Alma, Mar.17,1906, 2d.
Arthur C.,Dec. 2,1965,73y.
Arthur R.,Mar.22,1994,76y.
Elizabeth E.,Feb.19,1979,84y.
Evelyn E.,Nov.19,1961,73y.
Frank P.,bu:Oct. 13,1940,4m.
Frank Percy,Jr.,Oct.23,1931,4m.
Mary C.,1855-1908.
Percy F.,Jan.28,1961,71y.
Percy L.,Apr.25,1970,82y.
FARRAR
Julian H.,Apr.16,1928,65y.
Nellie G.,May 17,1942,77y.
FARWELL
Donald F.,June 19,1979,38y.
Earlon,Oct.3,1991,61y.
Evelyn B.,Jan.24,1986,83y.
Leigh M.,Dec.1,1982,69y.
Lloyd V.,Mar.17,1963,54y.
Jennie May,Oct.8,1903,2y.
Richard J., Feb.4,1939,1m.
William E.,Jan. 5,1976,76y.
William E.,Feb.5,1940,70y.
FAULKNER
Andrew,Aug.4,1934,56y.
Lucille,Sept.21,1989,61y.
Margaret C.,Jan.9,1989,70y.
Margaret E.,Dec.13,1958,72y.
Robert,Oct.13,1938,59y.
Robert L.,June 26,1983,51y.
FAWCETT
Walter W.,May 5,1975,65y.
FECTEAU
Michael G.,May 14,1985,47y.
FEENER
Aubrey, Nov.16,1961,68y.
FELLOWS
Flora M., Feb.12,1927,65y.
FENLESON
Clifton W.,Jr.,Sept.6,1928,10y.
Clifton W.,June 17,1963,73y.
Winfield S.,June 10,1958,94y.
FERNALD
Albert,Feb.20,1948,91y.
Edith Holmes,Nov.18,1947,83y.
Edward K.,1913,53y.
Harold E.,July 20,1993,91y.
Harry N.,1880-1882.
infant, May 8,1953, s.b.
Lottie K., Apr.15,1894,38y.
Marion F.,Oct.30,1967,80y.
Mary E.,June 11,1906,58y.
Mary H.,Oct.7,1976,77y.
Winfield R.,Jr.,Nov.15,1986,67y.

FERREN
Emily H.,Oct.15,1984,77y.
Frank Leslie,Dec.27,1932,58y.
Susan S.,Feb.6,1943,60y.
Vinal L.,May 11,1973,63y.
FERRIS
Emily M.,Sept.17,1971,53y.
infant,Oct.26,1944, prem.
Oakley L.,Sept.5,1962,48y.
FICK
Mamie B.,Jan.25,1954,71y.
Oscar A.,Mar.22,1965,84y.
FIELD
Elizabeth M.,May 7,1929,53y.
Esther M.,Aug.19,1956,44y.
George L.,Jan.2,1935,73y.
Leonard A.,Feb.18,1952,71y.
Minnie B.,Aug.27,1959,93y.
Rodney L.,Nov.30,1956,43y.
FIFIELD
Marietta G.,June 3,1953,82y.
FILES
Etta O.,May 1,1939,80y.
Fred W.,Mar.8,1928,72y.
Harry W.,Oct.18,1985,87y.
Marion S.,Sept.17,1970,70y.
Mary H.,Apr.22,1952,67y.
Ralph H.,Feb.3,1931,45y.
Walton N.,Nov.9,1937,79y.
FILIAULT
Origene L.,Feb.1,1988,73y.
FINAL
Norman E.,Sr.,Mar.30,1991,55y.
FINNERTY
Trevor F.,June 20,1985,78y.
FINNEY
Cecilia M.L.,Jan.30,1984,88y.
Earl G.,Mar.1,1975,74y.
Irvin H.,May 20,1979,80y.
Jennie A.,Dec.1,1994,96y.
FINNERTY
Elan E.,Mar.20,1994,81y.
FISH
Ada M.,May 31,1957,44y.
infant,July 26,1944,s.b.
infant,Sept.7,1942,prem.
Jack E.,Jan.9,1936,23y.
Warren G.,July 2,1965,80y.
FISHER
Lloyd Ronald,Jan.23,1918,8m.
FISK
George M.,Dec.25,1925,29y.
John J.,May 25,1927,74y.
Lillian Norton, Apr.3,1944,80y.
FITTS
Viola Day, Apr.15,1939,53y.

FITZ
Glendon C.,Nov.9,1975,61y.
Olive B.,July 9,1981,66y.
Robert A.,Jan.1,1983,41y.
FITZGERALD
Charles H.,July 30,1961,73y.
Fred W.,Nov.13,1994,83y.
Myra E.,Apr.27,1963,72y.
FLETCHER
Lois Sanborn, Apr.10,1948,54y.
Robert M.,Nov.28,1978,44y.
Roy Emery,Feb.10,1956,78y.
FLICK
Gordon F.,Sr., Apr.8,1977,64y.
Jennie V.,Jan.5,1968,55y.
Mary A.,July 28,1953,50y.
Samuel P.,bu:Feb.26,1962,58y.
Sandra A.,Jan.31,1979,35y.
FLINT
Jane Ellen,Jan.3,1989,51y.
FLYE
Herbert B.,Oct.12,1916,5m.
FOBES
Mary,Jan.7,1925,69y.
FOGG
Anna Janet,Mar.26,1926,7d.
Charles Edgar,May 14,1993,70y
Charles Lennox, Aug. 20,1926,63y.
Edward M.,Mar.4,1893,50y.
Freeman,1870-1905.
G. Annie,May 3,1942,92y.
George S,July 14,1838-Oct.4,1887.
Gladys,Aug.25,1904,8y.
Harriette,Apr.12,1918,80y.
Harriet Jordan,Oct.21,1930.
Harriet L.,May 24,1918,36y.
Harvey S.,July 8,1968,65y.
Helen,bu:Aug.17,1928,41y.
Irvin E.,Oct.30,1945,70y.
Myrtle M.,Apr.8,1971,72y.
Rose F.,May 20,1961,85y.
Sherman W.,May 19,1929,4d.
Wilma W.,June 7,1957,61y.
FOLEY
Christine T.,Feb.4,1981,61y.
Louella M., Jan.7,1955,58y.
FOOTE
Ralph C.,Sept.10,1970,7m.
FORD
Bethina,Aug.1,1925,76y.
FORREST
Ann,Feb.15,1893,62y.
Bella,Feb.21,1941,80y.
Frank E.,1872-1890,s/o J.E.&J.A.
James,Aug.16,1900,70y.
Jane,1867-1911.d/o Jas.& Ann Lee.
John E.,1844-1895,s/o J.E.&J.A.

Louisa Bushby,Oct.6,1932,57y.
FOSS
Ambrose,July 8,1935,92y.
Carrie M.,Apr.28,1975,88y.
Ellen H.,July 8,1921,73y.
infant,Jan.28,1948, s.b.
Margaret H.,Sept.20,1892,5m.
Melverda J.,Apr.23,1936,56y.
Minnie A.,1871-1907,w/o Lester.
Roger A.,Oct.1,1919,75y.
Roger K.,July 1933,40y.
Walter E.,Oct.3,1918,31y.
William T.,bu:Nov.3,1969,15y.
FOSTER
Albert R.,May 5,1976, 68y.
Angelia, Apr.11,1986,83y.
Annie D.,May 20,1907,71y.
Arlene D.,Sept.26,1969,68y.
Beulah B.,July 11,1993,83y.
Charles Edward, May 8,1925,8y.
Charlotte, Aug.19,1916,77y.
Chesley W.,Oct.2,1940,32y.
Edgar H.,July 8,1922,11y.
Edward H.,Jan.29,1927,57y.
Ethel B.,May 30,1968,75y.
George C.,Jan.21,1903,70y.
Henry W.,May 8,1937,79y.
James C.,Nov.17,1937,71y.
Jennie E.,Apr.22,1940,81y.
Jessie Lewis,Apr.2,1990,94y.
John C.,Aug.29,1944,57y.
Lloyd W.,Apr.11,1970,51y.
Mabel W.,Aug.25,1970,84y.
Mary Walker,Nov.27,1928,40y.
Nellie Dresser,Dec.11,1953,78y.
Perley H.,Apr.20,1967,82y.
Sidney, Apr.21,1904,23y.
Thomas A.,III,Apr.11,1957,19y.
Wilbur A.,Jan.30,1974,60y.
William Q.,Dec.1,1955,64y.
FOURNIER
Edna,Jan.10,1994,75y.
Evelyn A.,Apr.15,1987,80y.
Marcell J.,Nov.20,1968,67y.
William P., May 12,1979,85y.
FOYE
Evelyn M.,June 28,1965,52y.
infant,Dec.10,1939,s.b.
infant,May 25,1941,1d.
Peter J.,May 30,1927,60y.
Thomas H.,Dec.12,1979,61y.
FOYETTE
Zephrian,Mar.26,1916,45y.
Zephrian, Mrs.,Oct.4,1915.
FRANK
Abbie C.,Sept.30,1946,76y.
A. Maude,Mar.16,1951,66y.

Bernard C.,Apr.29,1981,51y.
Bertha I.,Feb.10,1963,72y.
Carrie S.,Feb.14,1953,87y.
Charles W.,Nov.19,1933,66y.
Clayton H., Feb.28,1964,58y.
Clayton H."Ted",Aug.29,1991,54y.
Clinton M.,1890-1890.
Henry B.,Dec.19,1949,68y.
infant, Mar.15, 1965, s.b.
John R.,1891-1891.
Luther A.,Mar.1,1931,70y.
Walter E.,Feb.16,1958,70y.
FRASER
David C.,July 23,1953,72y.
Gertrude F.,Nov.7,1942,57y.
FREDERICK
Evelyn L.,Aug.30,1944,60y.
Howard M.,Oct.7,1939,59y.
FREEMAN
Alice L.,May 23,1909,2m.
Dorothy,Jan.31,1970,73y.
Maggie,Apr.6,1929,41y.
FRENCH
Alice Sawyer,bu:Nov.30,1937,64y.
Aulena M.,June 8,1931,67y.
Florence A.,Feb.13,1937,24y.
George Allen,May 27,1931.
Guy O.,June 15,1954,64y.
Marcia E.,Apr.15,1945, 65y.
Raymond S.,Aug.15,1919,10y.
Rose C.,Mar.22,1947,68y.
William,Jan.31,1933,57y.
FROST
Donald M.,Jan.28,1980.
Florence E.,Feb.21,1969,77y.
Maynard F.,Mar.14,1949,66y.
Russell M.,May 27,1974,38y.
FRYE
Mary J.,Apr.10,1956,6d.
FULLER
Beatrice E.,Mar.19,1985,84y.
Frank W.,Aug.15,1958,70y.
Harriet E.,June 19,1934,78y.
infant, Oct.1,1954, s.b.
Maurice W.,Feb.23,1980,88y.
Martie M., Apr.21,1972,74y.
FULLERTON
John A.,Feb.19,1978,69y.
GAFFNEY
Annie J.,Oct.14,1962,70y.
John Francis,Apr.20,1954,71y.
GAGNON
Alfred J.,Oct.7,1979,80y.
GALE
Kenneth B.,Mar.6,1994,75y.
GALLANT
Mrs.,Feb.10,1903,42y.

Cecile,Nov.24,1985,67y.
George J.,May 14,1986,84y.
infant,Sept.9,1980, s.b.
John P.,Jan.11,1962,85y.
Joseph Cyrus,June 1,1923,45y.
Katie E.,Aug.19,1966,84y.
Mildred,Apr.26,1918,1y.
Ruth C.,Mar.10,1988,74y.
Stephen E.,Sept.26,1956,44y.
Sylvia C.,Oct.21,1957,49y.
GALLOP
Edgar H.,Feb.19,1936,1d.
GAMMON
Ethyle,Jan.27,1937,71y.
GARDINER
C.Rhodes,Mar.19,1983,79y.
Dora C.,May 29,1984,81y.
GARLAND
Alma T.,Feb.13,1990,78y.
Charles T.,Oct.21,1937,72y.
Frances Ellen,Jan. 30,1917,75y, w/o Washington.
infant, Apr. 8, 1938, s.b.
Janes A.,July 10,1969,92y.
Leon F.,Nov.3,1967,70y.
Ralph W.,Jan.29,1979,73y.
Sadie F.,June 30,1959,91y.
Thomas E.,Aug.291969,6wks.
Washington,1827-1903.
GARNER
Boyd M.,Aug.22,1958,63y.
Ida M.,Sept.13,1977,79y.
GARVEY
William F.,Feb.7,1979,56y.
GASSETT
Ernest E.,Jan.16,1957,67y.
Glenna G.,June 5,1948,58y.
GATHERCOLE
Earl,Dec.9,1986,27y.
GAY
Althea E.,Sept.6,1993,92y.
Amedee J.,Mar.10,1945,43y.
Isabelle, Apr.2,1911,72y.
GAYTON
Freida E.,June 21,1987,78y.
George W.,Oct.11,1970,64y.
GEER
Alice,May 25,1973,78y.
Arthur K.,Sept.21,1944,44y.
George I.,Jan.20,1945,60y.
George L.,Jan.14,1920,62y.
infant,Mar.10,1928.
infant,Nov.14,1946, s.b.
infant,Sept.1,1948, s.b.
Jennie M.,Jan.20,1961,76y.
Kate A.,Dec.2,1916,53y.
Richard Dana,Jan.19,1947,4d.

GELINAS
Eugene A.,Apr.8,1990,87y.
GEMMELL
Arthur J.,Apr.2,1967,78y.
Charles,Jan.20,1916,55y.
E., Mar.31,1915,59y.
Susie B.,May 23,1968,67y.
GEORGE
Ada Shaw,Oct.30,1918,62y.
Frank R.,Feb.21,1932,46y.
GEREY
Maria,Mar.3,1917,47y.
GERRISH
Herbert W., Sept.13,1932,52y.
GERRY
Archiel,Aug.19,1937,46y.
GETCHELL
Amanda G.,July 7,1899,27y.
GIDDY
Ella D.,bu:Oct.5,1940,72y.
Frank W.,Apr.25,1912,39y.
GILBERT
Addie F.,May 3,1947,88y.
Jetson,Feb.13,1911,59y.
Leslie F.,Mar.27,1957,69y.
Roy L.,Mar.4,1946,67y.
GILDART
Sarah K.,1839-1901.
GILMAN
Alice Louise, Aug.22,1918,16y.
Alma S.,Nov.24,1990,87y.
Ann E., Apr.2,1992,46y.
Charles H., Oct.29,1946,62y.
Clara A.,Aug.1,1958.
Dana E.,Sept.17,1971,76y.
Edna B.,Aug.5,1941,45y.
Edna Florence,June 10,1916,27y.
Edward, May 12,1921,62y.
George H.,Dec.24,1969.
infant,Oct.13,1927,s.b.
infant,June 28,1964,2d.
Iola W.,May 5,1979,76y.
John A.,Sept.28,1966,84y.
Mary Ann,May 1,1934,75y.
Norman S.,June 28,1905,5y.
Verne Francis,1889-1906.
William C.,Mar.17,1957,6y.
William G.,1857-1897, h/o Mary E.Richard.
Willie,July 19,1898,12y.
GILMORE
Temperance F.,Mar.16,1932,84y.
GILPATRICK
Daniel O.,July 31,1930,50y.
Frances T.,Feb.14,1972,84y.
Helen L.,May 30,1991,74y.
Jennie S.,Mar.13,1915,72y.

Joseph H.,Jan.14,1924,49y.
GILPIN
George,Dec.31,1929,71y.
GIRARD
Dorothy L.,Aug.6,1966,62y.
Julia,Nov.26,1965,45y.
William,Jan.27,1977,75y.
GLEASON
Charles E., Nov.28,1915,65y.
GLIDDEN
Edna M.,Sept.25,1986,86y.
Frank H.,Dec.3,1955,57y.
Joyce I.,Feb.16,1927,16d.
GODDARD
Charles E.,Aug.14,1945,70y.
George M.,Sept.6,1894,21y.
William,Aug.6,1895,59y.
GOFF
Alton,May 17,1892,42y.
Carrie A.,July 20,1936,61y.
Carroll,Apr.22,1893,5y,s/o F.&M.
Edna B.,Feb.11,1986,92y.
Eugene W.,Sept.14,1924,64y.
Fred O.,May 23,1918.
Hazel,b.&d. 1892,d/o Fred & Minnie.
Hazel,Apr.3,1917,22y.
Hazel,Feb.10,1912.
Ida M.,Sept.5,1940,66y.
infant,Feb.8,1927.
Julia A.,Jan.11,1914,60y.
Katherine W.,May 25,1983,83y.
Lendell M.,Nov.1,1956,65y.
Marcia Gray,Mar.9,1942,51y.
Mary M.,Feb.5,1929,64y.
Millard F.,Oct.30,1955,58y,
  rem. to Yarmouth, July 1983.
Minnie F.,Aug.16,1916,48y.
Stanley E.,July 11,1933,39y.
Stanley E.,Feb.25,1980,62y.
Wilbur L.,Feb.5,1981.
GOLDEN
Florence W., Apr.26,1971,79y.
James,July 3,1975,92y.
James A.,Nov.26,1974, 54y.
Rita A.,Oct.20,1978,54y.
GOLDER
Bernard C.,Feb.12,1970,65y.
Beth Anne,July 23,1968,2y.
Mary G.,Apr.21,1952,68y.
Willa A.,Sept.24,1973,60y.
Willie F.,Mar.3,1956,73y.
GOODALL
Clarissa L.,Mar.28,1936,67y.
Esther,1822-1857.
George,1847-Dec.19,1906.
John A.,1853-Sept.5,1895.
John W.,1819-1854.

Richard,Oct.2,1928,79y.
Thomas J.,1850-1882.
GOODNOUGH
Anna G.,May 29,1965,77y.
Glenn M.,Apr.4,1974,58y.
Melvin L.,Aug.8,1956,82y.
GOODNOW
Eva M.,Dec.9,1964,77y.
GOODRIDGE
Alice M.,1884-1904.
Clarence W.,July 24,1953,66y.
Ella D.,Apr.28,1941,80y.
Erland,can't read stone.
Florence,can't read stone.
Florence L.,Jan.31,1978,84y.
George M.,Oct.6,1938,85y.
Joshua H.,Aug.10,1962,75y.
Rizpah M.,Jan.15,1951,62y.
GOODWIN
Alice E.,May 30,1955.
Ella E.,Nov.20,1936,79y.
F. Maurice,Sept.25,1937,32y.
F. Maurice,Nov.2,1937,s.b.
Frank W.,Oct.8,1936,61y.
Harriet L.,Feb.22,1967,76y.
Richard,Jan.20,1904,75y.
GOOGINS
Carola F.,Dec.19,1960,60y.
Freeman J.,Feb.11,1981,81y.
Harriet R.,Feb.4,1988,93y.
GORDON
Dorothy M.,Sept.21,1971,69y.
E. May,Oct.3,1949,71y.
Elihu T.,July 20,1929,52y.
Etta K.,Oct.17,1950,67y.
George L.,Apr.21,1961,78y.
Joseph S.,Feb.1,1947,69y.
Marie A. Apr.24,1904,9m.
Oscar T.,Oct.14,1947,67y.
Philip H.,Aug.5,1954,53y.
Theodore J.,July 22,1961,50y.
GORRIE
Amanda B.,June 2,1915,61y.
Andrew E.,Dec.27,1988,77y.
Annie, Aug.29,1966,80y.
Bertha M.,Aug.31,1964,78y.
Ernest A.,Jan.17,1952,68y.
Ernest F.,Feb.8,1985,64y.
Everett O.,June 30,1971,83y.
F. Burland,Jan.10,1961,80y.
Lawrence E.,Nov.17,1991.
Leroy T.,Nov.25,1969,91y.
Lester A.,Nov.1,1955,70y.
Lottie B.,July 24,1969,82y.
Louise S.,Jan.10,1993,78y,
Robert T.,June 26,1963,51y.
Richard A.,Mar.23,1955,42y.

Thomas, Apr.21,1923,83y.
Tristram A.,Nov.13,1919,29y.
William T.,Mar.1,1983,68y.
Winfred B.,July 30,1961,78y.
GOSS
Harold H.,Sept.6,1900,9m.
no name,Oct.4,1901.
GOWEN
Adelbert L.,Dec.17,1993,84y.
Clarence K.,Jan.20,1981.
infant, Apr.16,1924,1d.
James,1891-1892.
John G., Jr.,Aug.3,1929,7y.
John Z., Sept.23,1950,72y.
Laura E.,Feb.2,1965,80y.
Lizzie,1888-1892.
Reta L.,Jan.4,1968,45y.
GOWER
Mary E.,Oct.14,1919,66y.
GRACE
Francis G., Feb.7,1924,78y.
Leon M.,Apr.8,1923,27y.
Marion B.,June 18,1994,97y.
GRADY
Julia S.,May 26,1970,89y.
GRAFFAM
Albert,May 28,1921,78y.
Algie K.,Jan.6,1983,63y.
Alice G.,June 3,1967,82y.
Annie,Nov.2,1923,71y.
Annie M.,Nov.28,1971,85y.
Cecil L.,Mar.12,1975,68y.
Dana W.,May 4,1960,81y.
Daniel,Apr.29,1902,70y.
Eben L.,May 25,1923,59y.
Edith E.,Nov.4,1927,42y.
Ellsworth E.,May 2,1982,81y.
Elmer E.,July 10,1935,73y.
Frank,May 9,1963,87y.
Frank H., Apr.20,1920,66y.
Fred, Apr.11,1914,58y.
J.A.,1839-1919.
Joanna B.,Mar.22,1898,65y.
Joseph A.,Aug.21,1919,80y.
Lizzie S.,1855-1887,w/o Fred.
Mary,Jan.17,1982,81y.
Nellie E.,Aug.28,1899,43y.
Nellie J.,Nov.22,1988,79y.
Nora B.,July 16,1916,40y.
Phyllis M.,Sept.21,1908,7m.
Robert,1837-1906.
Sarah E., rem. from Evergreen Cemetery,Oct.8,1914.
Walter S.,July 16,1910,46y.
GRAHAM
Barbara M.,Nov.1,1930,4m.
Cecilia,Oct.9,1989,65y.
Charles B.,Oct.20,1935,74y.
Charles C.,Sept.7,1917,78y.
Cora B.,Oct.26,1982,82y.
Dorothy E.,May 20,1949,41y.
Earl M.,Sept.1,1970,69y.
Elden A.,June 23,1945,70y.
Elizabeth E.,Nov.7,1957,81y.
Ellen,Aug.22,1941,69y.
George C.,bu:Nov.21,1937,69y.
Harriet J. Perry,May 16,1917,74y, w/o Charles.
infant,Mar.8,1965,s.b.
James W.,Oct.11,1946,74y.
James W.,XXXX.
James W.,XXXX.
Joseph H.,Dec.20,1953,76y.
King F.,Sept.24,1935,66y.
Laura E.,Apr.15,1921,72y,w/o Peter S.
Madeline,Feb.14,1985,84y.
Malcolm H.,Mar.6,1953,44y.
Mary Ellen,Dec.7,1925,72y.
Mary F.,Jan.13,1941,68y.
Merle E.,Oct.29,1964,77y.
Peter S.,Feb.16,1925,78y.
Philip M.,Jan.16,1953,38y.
Rose B.,Dec.10,1952,84y.
Ruth Virginia, Apr.1,1921,6y.
William Alvin, July 20,1932,60y.
GRANT
Benjamin M.,Aug.28,1976.
Bernice P.,Apr.29,1974,80y.
Charles F.,Dec.22,1946,56y.
Clara J.,Jan. 8,1934,80y.
Clara M.,Oct.2,1925,59y.
Effie A.,Dec.14,1989,85y.
Everett J.,July 1,1991,92y.
Eva J.,June 6,1967,53y.
Fairfield,June 30,1938,86y.
Frances L.,Mar.15,1987,60y.
Gilman B.,Nov. 2,1926,70y.
Grace J.,Oct.13,1982,66y.
Harlan S.,Apr.20,1965,85y.
Harry W.,Feb.14,1956,74y.
Ida M.,Feb.19,1934,72y.
Isadore B.,Aug.24,1930,49y.
Lillian H.,Sept.1,1988,75y.
Louis,Feb.24,1992,68y.
Louise R.,Aug.24,1977,81y.
Mildred O.,Oct.29,1959,77y.
Mina,Feb.24,1975,83y.
Philip B.,Mar.17,1991,78y.
Ray P.,Jan.18,1980,86y.
Rufus H.,Sept.3,1926,74y.
Smith A.,Oct.10,1977,76y.
Stanley K.,June 28,1973,66y.
Thelma L.,Aug.30,1988,77y.

GRAVES
Elizabeth B.,Mar.14,1955,85y.
James,bu:Mar.3,1943.
Raymond E.,Nov.26,1976,57y.
GRAY
Albert Leroy,Mar.14,1943,49y.
Alvah,1853-1863.
Amy F.,Nov.24,1961,93y.
Arthur,1822-1884.
Arthur E.,Sept.24,1943,84y.
Bertha G.,July 24,1945,50y.
David, Sept.30,1985,30y.
Ella May,July 1920,59y.
Ella M.,Feb.3,1931,72y.
Ethel I.,May 21,1962,82y.
George B.,Apr.28,1917,54y.
Mary E.,Nov.26,1938,69y.
Margaret Wyer,1822-1909,w/o Arthur.
Minot D.,XXXX,69y.
Windsor,1851-1863.
GREELEY
Jannette H.,Aug.31,1952,93y. William F.,Mar.11,1921,68y.
GREEN
Charles E.,Aug.25,1963,69y.
Genevieve,22y, rem. from Saccarappa Cem. June 1927.
Gertrude,Feb.13,1983,66y.
Harold E.,Oct.8,1956,56y.
Irene L.,Sept.25,1972,74y.
Jennie M.,Nov.24,1919,3d.
Lillian M.,Jan.22,1991,94y.
T.Linwood,Mar.6,1914,2d.
GREENE
Adelbert E.,June 23,1928,72y.
Charles R.,May 17,1992.
Dorothy A.,Feb.11,1956,42y.
infant,July 7,1910, s.b.
Jennie May, Oct.21,1926,37y.
M. Helen,Jan.14,1972,70y.
Mary, Aug.23,1953,90y.
Norman E.,Sept.9,1966,74y.
Peter T.,Dec.4,1974,37y.
R. Charles,Jr.,May 17,1992.
Thomas L.,Feb.25,1941,57y.
Virginia B.,Apr.14,1939,26y.
GREENLAW
Alphonso E.,May 29,1958,93y.
Dana S.,Apr.1,1972,72y.
Frank,Jan.1,1939,72y.
Hilda B.,Dec.27,1989,90y.
Joseph G.,May 26,1907,76y.
Kate A.,Mar.26,1918,48y.
Marcia,1877-1880,d/o J.C.& M.E.
Mary E.,Oct.22,1909,75y.
Philip B.,Apr.24,1969,72y.

GREENLEAF
Cora Ethel,Mar.30,1927,14y.
Deborah R.,July 19,1966,16y.
Frank D.,Sept.12,1918,31y.
Nine Belle, Sept.14,1918,12y.
GREENOUGH
Ada E.,Nov.1,1934,64y.
Margaret L.,July 11,1916,65y.
GREENWOOD
Ernest L.,May 11,1990,86y.
Louise L.,Apr.17,1994,87y.
GREEP
infant, Apr.12,1953,15hrs.
GRENDELL
Thelma E.,Mar.24,1961,43y.
GRENIER
Nettie E.,Feb.14,1953,49y.
Wilfred,Nov.23,1984.
GRIER
Robert, Sept.6,1893,50y.
GRIFFIN
Charles E.,Jan.27,1930,76y.
Lewis H.,Dec.9,1989,53y.
Lizzy Hussey, Apr.9,1941,86y.
Ruth E.,June 16, 1989, 68y.
William H.,Aug.20,1966,44y.
GRIFFITHS
Albert E.,June 5,1953,52y.
Edna P.,Sept.3,1967,67y.
Eleanor E.,Mar.21,1993,77y.
Florence H.,May 18,1923,27y.
Henry J.,Feb.14,1962,68y.
Lillian M.,July 13,1986,87y.
GRIGGS
Henry Kimball,1820-Dec.11,1907.
Mary Elizabeth,Oct.23,1934,84y.
Sarah Blair,1825-1912.
GRIMES
Syrena,May 3,1919,85y.
GROSE
George E.,Feb.5,1918,35d.
GROVER
Bernard L.,Apr.1,1978,59y.
Elizabeth F.,Aug.2,1973,53y.
N.B., Mar.28,1897,63y.
GUERNSEY
George R., Mar.1,1976,60y.
Katherine M.,Oct.7,1971,69y.
GUIMOND
Aime J., Nov.7,1976,78y.
Lavina M.,June 10,1984,82y.
GUINARD
Leo F.,Jr.,Apr.3,1986,23y.
GUNN
Kenneth R.,June 29,1969,59y.
GUPTILL
Lizzie W.,July 12,1922,65y.

Lottie Josephine, Apr.23,1943,4y.
Lyman, Sept. 23,1906,59y.
GURNEY
Cleve M.,May 6,1982,73y.
Dorothy F.,Feb.14,1981,73y.
GUSHGA
Joseph,Jan.2,1946,55y (?).
GUSTIN
George Edward,bu:Aug.19,1927.
GUTHRIE
Carol E.,July 19,1966,5y.
GUYER
Emma B.,Nov.7,1929,33y.
HAASE
Louisa S.,Mar.17,1929,80y.
William F.,Dec.11,1925,73y.
HACKETT
Carroll E.,Nov.20,1940,76y.
Edna M.,Dec.19,1975,75y.
Gertrude,June 28,1934,68y.
Gertrude M.,Apr.5,1966,73y.
Ralph E.,July 9,1967,75y.
Urban C.,Nov.20,1969,72y.
HADDOCK
Bertha,Feb.23,1951,82y.
Edith I.,Aug.15,1954,62y.
Walter,Apr.26,1970,88y.
HADLOCK
Annie E.,1842-1906.
Ella W.,1865,11m.
George S.,Mar.30,1914,72y.
James Wm.,Nov.10,1940,72y.
May S.,Dec.26,1951,80y.
James & Louisa,XXXX.
HAENESEL
William D.,Oct.10,1975,56y.
HAGAN
E. Margaret,May 23,1942,52y.
Elizabeth D.,June 20,1974,83y.
Jason McClintock,July 1915,27y.
HAGERMAN
Owen A.,Oct.28,1955,34y.
Roger O. Oct.15,1943,2m.
HAGUE
Frank T.,Nov.2,1969,67y.
Lawrence A. Aug.30,1982,62y.
HAHN
Joan Marie, July 5,1952,s.b.
Lottie May, Feb. 5,1953,78y.
William,Dec.19,1963,90y.
HALE
Annie M.,May 21,1939,64y.
Charles A.,Mar.9,1952,62y.
Dennis R.,Oct.21,1987,32y.
Edward H.,Aug. 6,1916,65y.
Everett A.,Mar.16,1899,8m.
infant,June 14,1925, s.b.

infant,Jan.5,1957, s.b.
Jennie K.,Apr.9,1964,73y.
Lillian M.,June 21,1930,61y.
Lloyd M.,June 25,1925,6y.
Margaret M.,Aug.22,1927,s.b.
Margaret M.,July 7,1941,47y.
Merton P.,Dec.16,1973,81y.
Mildred E.,Sept.26,1900,5y.
Nathaniel,1897,78y, rem.from
  Knights Private Cem. in Pride's
  Corner Oct. 5, 1921.
Nellie C.,May 20,1946,25y.
Nellie H.,Dec.19,1915,55y.
Richard N.,June 16,1959,22y.
Robert,July 2,1924, s.b.
HALL
Andrew M.,Nov.11,1905,73y.
Anna D.,Mar.15,1955,93y.
Bertha J.,May 9,1933,59y.
Charles, Feb.8,1937,44y.
Charles E., Mar.9,1963,62y.
Earl S.,M.D.,Aug.19,1955,64y.
Ernest C.,Feb.12,1993,99y.
Edward W.,June 15,1961,49y.
Eliza, Feb.21,1911.
Emma E.,July 28,1978,74y.
Flora E.,Mar.6,1975,83y.
Johanne F.P.,Mar.30,1988,88y.
John F.,Apr.4,1921,62y.
John L.B.,May 30,1921,70y.
Lizzie R., Sept. 21,1900, rem.
  from Saccarappa Cem. 1921.
Mabelle L.,Sept. 4,1982,86y.
Margaret W.,Mar.17,1984,85y.
Mary E.,Sept.13,1929,72y.
Mary Melvina, Sept.17,1932,87y.
Mildred, May 5, 1926, 34y.
William L., Apr.24,1911,40y.
HALLORAN
Betty C., May 7,1927.
HALLOWELL
Arline, Apr.24,1925,prem.
Bert D.,June 29,1912,22y.
Beverly,Mar.15,1926,1d.
Charles H.,Oct.27,1965,88y.
Clyde S.,May 10,1928,27y.
Elmer E.,May 26,1966,67y.
Evangeline M.,Jan.26,1963, 87y.
George E.,Jan.21,1935,at birth.
George Henry, July 29,1931,65y.
Hazel J.,Dec 21,1977,68y.
Herbert E.,Aug.27,1990,84y.
Howard,May 28,1916,46y.
infant,Sept.4,1940,aborted.
Louella H.,June 25,1977,77y.
Louisa H.,July 19,1916,80y.
Mary W.,July 14,1942,74y.

Samuel S.,Oct.23,1907,75y.
Stanwood,Nov.1,1936, s.b.
HAM
Sarah D.,Aug.7,1967,83y.
HAMBLEN
Beatrice D.,Mar.9,1964,48y.
HAMEL
Alphonse,Jan.7,1965,74y.
HAMILTON
Ada M.,Feb.5,1956,86y.
Ambrose,Capt.,1827-1889.
Benjamin H.,Jan.12,1979,86y.
Bertha Stall Harris,
   June 17,1993,99y
Dexter K.,Mar.25,1944,75y.
Elvyra Mae, Apr. 5,1959,
   rem. from Gray Cem. 1961.
Eva B.,Nov.5,1967,97y.
George B.,Mar.14,1960,95y.
Hannah E.,Dec.20,1917,84y.
Harold C.,July 9,1980,92y.
infant,July 5,1918, s.b.
infant, June 1,1953.
Julia F.,Dec.15,1930.
Margaret S.,Mar.13,1974,66y.
Mary I., Aug.4,1938,75y.
Maynard C.,May 18,1959,46y.
Millard M.,Oct.7,1964,37y.
Muriel L.,Aug.13,1958,64y.
Olga M., Aug.12,1985,93y.
Philip W.,Dec.9,1993,93y.
Ray E.,May 28,1914,5m.
Robert W.,Nov.29,1961,88y.
Sall Harris,June 17,1992,99y.
Theresa R.,June 5,1931,67y,
   w/o William D.
William D., Mar.11,1954,76y.
William F.,1854-1906.
Wilmot J.,1858-1911.
HAMLIN
Sarah Jean,Oct.5,1988,1d.
HAMM
Ida B.,July 25,1959,76y.
HANDY
Annie M.,Oct.17,1960,86y.
Fred A.,Feb.3,1945,73y.
HANES
Elva M.,Jan.10,1919,33y.
HANLON
Patrick J.,Feb.26,1983,66y.
HANSCOM
Caroline M., Oct.18,1933,57y.
Dora Parker,Dec.3,1935,78y.
Henry J.,Mar.16,1920,59y.
Lucinda H.,May 18,1944,76y.
HANSCOME
Florence E.,July 13,1938,79y.

HANSEN
Andres P.,Nov.11,1958,75y.
Ann J.,Jan.13,1960,66y.
Anna K.,June 10,1951,73y.
Forest L.,1898-1904.
Franz M., Apr.24,1986,67y.
H. Nyholm, Feb.3,1968,81y.
Hans,May 2,1936,62y.
Hans H.,Dec.12,1927,5y.
Hans M.,Feb.6,1929,52y.
Harold E. Sept.8,1932,17y.
Helen K.,July 5,1928,2d.
Ida A.,May 29,1979,71y.
Jacob K.,July 15,1937,62y.
Kathleen M., Apr.26,1988,71y.
Laura,May 19,1924,50y.
Lena, Oct.11,1961,72y.
Lillian M.,May 3,1989,79y.
Lulu M.,1873-1904.
Marie P.,May 5,1959,84y.
Martin,Dec.15,1979,84y.
Philip A.,June 9,1991,64y.
Veranus,XXXX, 69y, rem.
   from South Windham 1914.
Yens,May 5,1900,1d.
HANSON
Addie, May 25, 1915, 65y.
Christy E.,Aug.11,1993,85y.
Cornelius F., Sept. 2,1941,23y.
Edna Augusta, May 22,1922,18y.
Emily,1840-1898.
Emma V., Jan.14,1930,28y.
Jane C., July 17,1953,78y.
Marius,Apr.25,1993,80y.
Morris Raymond,Apr.25,1914,1y.
Verranus C., June 4,1939,64y.
William Henry,Jan.2,1845-Dec.3,1913.
HARDING
Ida C.,July 24,1965,89y.
HARDY
S. David, bu:Jan.3,1969,5y.
HARLOW
Edward P.,Dec.3,1925,54y.
Gertrude E.,Oct.22,1968,88y.
HARMON
Abbie D.,Mar.2,1939,81y.
Alvin T.,Apr.3,1923,71y.
Amanda,Jan.15,1981,92y.
Arthur R.,Feb.1,1959,82y.
Bernice K.,Nov.6,1964,83y.
Charles W.,Oct 8,1971,58y.
Elias,Aug.15,1920,74y.
Ella M.,Jan.2,1972,77y.
infant,Sept.16,1919,1d.
Jasper J., Apr.20,1963,82y.
Lizzie,1826-1899,w/o Elias.
Raymond A.,bu:Oct.6,1941,s.b.

HARRIGAN
Katherine E., Apr.27,1960,88y.
Michael J., June 9, 1959, 83y.
HARRIMAN
Alphonso D.,Dec.11,1952,76y.
Arlene E.,Jan. 27,1976,64y.
Arthur G.,May 30,1922,42y.
Donald H.,Jan.17,1965,65y.
Francis E.,July 21,1917,41y.
Hattie May, Apr.19,1945,70y.
Horatio Nelson,Dec.20,1952,79y,
Laura J.,Nov.8,1918,77y.
Lawrence Willis,Nov.1,1931,11y.
Lewis T.,June 24,1946,74y.
Lillian May,bu:Nov.29,1942,63y.
Lyman M.,May 7,1942,69y.
Mabel L.,Apr.8,1958,82y.
Marion Louise,Apr.26,1900,3m.
no name, Apr.3,1897, prem.
no name, Aug.28,1895,7m.
Paris Edwin, Oct.21,1918,19y.
Philemon, Feb. 3,1925,77y.
Roland,Jan.12,1977,69y.
Shirley L.,Feb.24,1934,2m.
Wilbur E., Apr.7,1957,85y.
William E., Oct.28,1988,85y.
HARRINGTON
Prescott T.,May 18,1942,35y.
HARRIS
Donald H.,Jan.17,1965,65y.
Doris M.,Dec.13,1926,23y.
Edmund, Sept.21,1956,56y.
infant,Nov.27,1926,prem.
infant,Dec.1,1949,1d.
Kevin L.,June 20,1963,2m.
Laurel R.,June 24,1973,67y.
Margaret C.,Jan.28,1980,74y.
Philip A.,Jan.11,1929,4y.
Viola J., Oct.21,1988,60y.
HARRISON
Danny L., Apr.22,1984, 38y.
George J.,Oct.29,1886,23y.
HART
Bryon S.,July 5,1967,57y.
Heman, Oct.3,1993,86y.
Una, June 6,1972,56y.
Madeline A.,July 7,1952,45y.
Mary F.,Feb.5,1987,78y.
Virginia D.,Aug.11,1980,72y.
HARTFORD
E'llora F."Lola",May 3,1993,72y.
Herbert B., Aug.24,1980,59y.
HARTHORN
Archibald A., Jan.27,1937,75y.
Ina M., Mar.10,1949,88y.
HARTLEY
Martha B.,June 26,1975,85y.

William,Sept.12,1944,53y.
HARVEY
Annie S.,Sept.4,1941,72y.
Charles A.,July 27,1937,87y.
Elizabeth,Oct.12,1899,69y.
Joseph Newton,Mar.16,1926.
HARVIE
Mary Small, Jan 26,1930,35y.
HASELTON
Benj. Edwin,Dec.27,1932,43y.
Fannie E.,Apr.15,1927,60y.
John H.,Dec.20,1926,71y.
HASKELL
Benjamin,Apr.1765,18m,s/o B.& L;
Benjamin,Dr.,Oct.14,1785,60y;
Lydia Freeman,May 20,1798,61y,
 w/o Benjamin;
Lydia Parker,June 7,1782,7y,
 d/o Benj. & Lydia;
William Freeman,XXXX,
 s/o Benjemin & Lydia;
The above were removed from the
Pike Street Lot in 1905.
Bertha G.,Mar.2,1965,86y.
Blanche P.,Jan.31,1960,87y.
Byron E.,Dec.4,1943,69y.
Cora I.,Nov. 23,1947,89y.
Donald B.,May 31,1977,61y.
Earl W., July 20,1979,64y.
Edith, July 21,1965,78y.
Edwin J.,Nov.6,1930,80y.
Frances W.,Mar.7,1966,84y.
Frank, July 24,1896,58y.
Fred P., Apr.20, 1961,75y.
Geneva P.,Sept.1,1965,75y.
George E.,Feb.19,1989,76y.
George E.,Sept.4,1923,54y.
Harriett A.,Sept.29,1961,75y.
Marjorie Coolidge,Sept.13,1915,2y.
Mildred V.,Mar.31,1967,78y.
Philip C.,May 3,1915,37y.
Rebecca Jewett,Mar.24, 1926,77y.
Roger,Feb.5,1939,58y.
Statie E.,June 19,1946,9y.
Walter F.,Aug.11,1943,71y.
Violet B.,Sept.21,1988,59y.
HATCH
Elliot L.,Sept.23,1949,81y.
Etta Z.,Oct.26,1949,90y.
Katherine V.,Apr.11,1902,2y.
HATHAWAY
Edith M., Apr.16,1975,77y.
George H.,Jan.1,1924,38y.
HAWES
Ella C.,Jan.8,1942,88y.
Ellie K.,Feb.10,1964,77y.
Henry H.B., Apr.10,1932,80y.

HAWKES
Abner L.,Nov.2,1921,79y.
Agnes B.,July 20,1972,70y.
Albion H.,bu:Dec.8,1902,45y.
Alice A., Aug.9,1908,40y.
Anetta S.,Mar.14,1959,94y.
Anne, Feb.9,1930,1d.
Arthur Everett,Sept.16,1905,16y.
Arol P., Sept.27,1971,71y.
Arol P.,Jr.,May 18,1930,3y.
Berland H.,Sept.4,1982,83y.
Bertie,1889-1892.
Catherine S.,July 12,1973,86y.
Christina B.,May 1,1990,89y.
Clara M., Sept.12,1933, 81y.
David, Apr.24,1936,s.b.
Edwin David,Jan.22,1928,50y.
E. Leroy,Aug.15,1944,67y.
Elmira,Jan.1922,87y.
Emily J.,bu: Apr.28,1936,78y.
Emily W.,Nov.26,1975,87y.
Ernest,1884-1884.
Ernest A.,Dec.5,1960,40y.
Eva May,1896-1896.
Everett A.,Pfc.,Mar.15,1948,in action.
Ferdinand W.,Feb.25,1975,84y.
George W.,Mar.30,1907,63y.
Gertrude M.,Feb.14,1953, 80y.
Hebert L.,Aug.23,1893,3y.
Herbert A.,Sept.20,1920,51y.
Helen,Feb.9,1930,1d.
Helen E.,Jan.26,1937,72y.
Horace,1869-1895.
Horace P.,Feb.5,1962,65y.
Ina E.,July 23,1989,90y.
infant,July 8,1967, s.b.
infant,Mar.1,1964, s.b.
infant,Mar.14,1928,3d.
James A.,June 11,1940,72y.
Josephine N.,Nov.6,1968,100y.
Joshua L.,1814-1878.
Kenneth M.,Oct.23,1993,86y.
Lilla M.,Sept.6,1993,87y.
Lawrence W.,June 28,1987,64y.
Marietta,Sept.3,1932,82y.
Marrett A.,Feb.8,1954,51y.
Mary W.,Dec.25,1934,86y.
Maude Pike,Oct.29,1944,69y.
Maurice, Aug.17,1972,72y.
Melville E.,July 7,1928,74y.
Myra Jane, Apr.1,1921,62y.
Myrtilla W.,Nov.15,1989,82y.
Neander, Oct.30,1931,81y.
Nettie M., Apr.18,1969,89y.
Rena, Mar.17,1901,19y.
Rosa B.,Sept.8,1906,38y.
Sadie W.,June 19,1946,89y.
Sandra P.,Nov.1,1977,39y.
Sara E.,Jan.18,1988,83y.
Sarah K.,1861-1908,w/oJoshua L.
Smith, Jan.20,1929,67y.
Victoria A.,Mar.5,1938,68y.
Wesley M., Oct.31,1914,64y.
William T.,July 27,1944,76y.
Zelia S.,1860-1863,d/o J.L.&S.K.
HAY
Alice W.,Oct.14,1981,85y.
Cora G.,Jan.18,1989,90y.
Edwin P.,can't read stone.
Grace B.,1901.
Harriet Blanche, Nov.4,1874,
 5m, rem. from Nova Scotia 1924.
Harry F.G.,Jan.3,1968,90y.
Harry G., Sept.16,1990,59y
James Wm., Aug.28,1880, 15y,
 rem. from Nova Scotia, 1924.
Marion S., July 5,1938, 54y.
Richard C.,May 28,1978,51y.
Walter F.W.,M.D.,Dec.27,1944,47y.
Walter F.W.,Jr.,May 16,1977,54y.
Wyman S., 1902, 8y, rem.
 from Nova Scotia 1924.
Wyman Whittmore, June 5,1893,
 10y, rem. from Nova Scotia1924.
HAYES
Charles D.,June 17,1953,68y.
Edith H.,1882-1886,d//o J.F.& H.A.
John F.,Mar.11,1921,66y.
HAYWARD
Timothy J.,June 26,1961, s.b.
HAZELTON
Annie, Mar.27,1904,25y.
Florence E., Mar.8,1918,52y.
Fred W., Aug.16,1912,45y.
Gardner, Apr.18,1912,72y.
Joseph H., Feb.22,1908,68y.
Mary E., Feb.7,1933,88y.
Pauline, Feb.28,1908,64y.
William C., Apr.18,1916,51y.
HAZLETT
Alton E., Sept.10,1976,74y.
Jean N., Dec. 24, 1975,29y.
HEATH
Alfred Lyman, May 20,1931,23y.
Bertha M.,Jan.10,1976,85y.
Erving W.,Feb.25,1988,80y.
Patricia Vivian, Aug.29,1945,11y.
HEBENSTREIT
Sidney M., Nov.16,1978,81y.
HEBERT
Benjamin,July 15,1974,88y.
Emma L.,July 5,1964,72y.
Matile,Mar.20,1913,85y.
Warren F.,Aug.21,1993,79y.

HEEL
Matway, Sept.19,1967,75y.
Olga,Mar.19,1992,96y.
HELMING
Lilburn M.,Nov.2,1961,61y.
HELMOLD
Clinton C., Aug.3,1966,96y.
Kendell C., Jan.18,1975,46y.
HEMINGWAY
Raymond C., Mar.23,1969,49y.
HENDERSON
Agnes,Apr.3,1922,81y.
Agnes M.,Nov.5,1921,47y.
Andrew B.,June 7,1938,65y.
Cora S., Sept.14,1963,88y.
Eva M.,Dec.16,1965,86y.
George Warren,Mar.24,1918,6d.
James D.,June 29,1954,71y.
John Gibson,Jan.15,1951,86y.
John P.,Jan.4,1968,56y.
Josephine D.,Apr.19,1975,86y.
Lucinda M.,Oct.21,1911,25y.
Ruth L.,July 4,1921,8y.
Thomas M., Mar.1962,95y.
HENDRICKSON
Antony L.,July 20,1942,60y.
Charles,1880-1906.
Constance,Nov.15,1985,76y.
Esther,July 10,1912,3m.
Georgianna C.,Mar.26,1947,64y,
rem. to Rochester,N.H.,1976.
Gladys M.,Mar.13,1969,71y.
Henry L.,June 26,1948,70y.
Henry N.,Feb.1,1941,68y.
John, Jan.12,1934.
Joseph C.,June 20,1958,56y.
Karl T.,June 26,1986,76y.
Leafy,Nov.15,1909,28y.
Lewis A., Oct.9,1977,60y.
Lorenz P.,June 26,1928,80y.
Marie F.,Dec.7,1930,76y.
Nellie H.M.,1893-1901.
Nicholena,May.1923,73y.
Thomas T.,Aug.12,1921,45y.
Wayland C.,Apr.29,1969,66y.
HENRY
Ada E.,Oct.8,1899,9y.
George W.,Apr.6,1917,59y.
Jennie G.,Oct.9,1942,82y.
HERMAN
Frances Lillian,1908-1909.
George Edward,June 5,1931,75y.
George F.,Apr.12,1933,57y.
Hattie M.,bu:Dec.1959,78y.
Hebert E.,Nov.15,1902,70y.
Lillian N.,Aug.1,1938,83y.
Soloman A.,Apr.30,1951,66y.

HERRICK
Clifford E.,Jr.,Nov.20,1985,60y.
Hazel B.,July 2,1956,61y.
Lina M.,Feb.9,1994,97y.
Linwood W., Apr.17,1962,72y.
Mary, June 21,1932,72y.
Roland G., Mar.30,1970.
Susan Agnes,Jan.30,1951,62y.
HERSEY
Lucia,July 18,1956,47y.
HEWES
Henry W.,Apr.21,1949,69y.
HEY
Frances E., Apr.20,1964,82y.
Thomas H.,Feb.7,1960,81y.
HICKEY
Harold W.,Apr.28,1991,68y.
HICKS
Charles J.,Nov.22,1947,64y.
Florence N.,July 2,1935,73y.
Harold E.,June 23,1940,53y.
infant,July 21,1943,11hrs.
Irving E.,Apr.19,1927,68y.
HIGGINS
Alice H., Aug.10,1979,12y.
Arnold D.,Dec.31,1986,67y.
Clarence B.,Feb.16,1952,79y.
Ella J.,Jan.25,1921,66y.
Ellen B.,July 16,1975,67y.
Frances B.,June 27,1940,64y.
Fred K., Aug.31,1978,74y.
Harry K.,Jan.3,1962,79y.
Hazel H.,Nov.11,1918,18y.
John A.,Oct.4,1908,54y.
Joseph, Aug.10,1979,7y.
June M., Sept.7,1959,76y.
Lulu M.,Jan.15,1993,69y.
Merrilee A.,Aug.10,1979,15y.
Prentiss R.,Nov.16,1950,52y.
Rosemary H.,Aug.10,1979,32y.
Sarah J.,1889,1y.
Thelma G.,Sept.30,1960,64y.
Virgil M.,Feb.20,1966,59y.
Virginia M., Dec.30,1959,42y.
HILL
Ensfield A.,Sept.3,1991,72y.
Eva M.,Oct.18,1993,92y.
Leonard E.,Feb.5,1933,12y.
Loton M.,Feb.10,1946,72y.
Nellie E.,Jan.7,1950,57y.
Ralph E.,Oct.29,1971,72y.
Willard S.,Feb.5,1933,6y.
William S.,Apr.14,1937,64y.
HILLOCK
Ariel W.,May 21,1977,73y.
Cynthia J.,Feb.18,1980.
Hazel,bu: July 22,1930,2m.

infant,bu:Apr.26,1967.
Richard D.,Aug.4,1945,4y.
HILLS
Lewis L.,M.D.,June 9,1956,79y,
Louis L.,Jr.,June 26,1972,47y.
Mary R.,Nov.19,1913, 34y.
Ruth T.,July 28,1972.
HILTON
Daniel Adams,Oct.4,1993,16m.
Roger,1856-June 1,1892.
HOBSON
Edwin J.,Feb.16,1913,74y.
Ella D.,Aug.3,1930,73y.
Margaret, Oct.2,1922, s.b.
Marie H. Nute,1840-1891,w/o Ed.J.
HODGKINS
Charles E.,Mar.9,1916,84y.
Charles H.,Feb.24,1990,93y.
Charles R.,Mar.10,1976,52y.
Earl L.,Aug.29,1956,54y
Hannah G.,May 18,1921,81y.
Henry E.,Apr.29,1939,67y.
Laura A.,Dec.17,1893,61y.
Olive F.,Apr.18,1954,82y.
Ruth E.,May 3,1971,73y.
HOFFMAN
Timothy S.,Jr.,May 8,1993,15w.
HOGAN
Lewis J.,June 3,1940,57y.
HOLLIS
Wendall W.,July 6,1910,71y.
HOLM
Edward T.,Sept.19,1954,50y.
Florence M.,Aug.28,1968,85y.
Hans H., May 3,1955,89y.
Lydia R.,Oct.15,1898,58y.
Margaret D.,Feb.23,1947,75y.
Maria,Feb.10,1906,70y.
Peter C.,Nov.24,1914,78y.
Vernie C.,Feb.16,1916,29y.
William Edward,Nov.3,1929,52y.
William L.,Feb.26,1920,86y.
HOLSTON
Clyde W.,Mar.20,1918,23y.
Cora L.,Sept.3,1941,75y.
Ella M.,June 4,1961,88y.
Frances E., Apr.4,1980,62y.
Ida M.,May 15,1933,81y.
Leonard C.,Nov.7,1956,83y.
Reuben C.,Dec.15,1923, 68y.
William H.,Sept.21,1925,81y.
HOLT
Archie M., Apr.21,1954,75y.
Clifford I.,Dec.3,1972,75y.
infant,Jan.7,1916, s.b.
infant,Feb.18,1918, s.b.
Lewellyn A., Aug.1,1942,26y.

Lewis R., Aug.14,1908,6m.
Nellie May,Feb.25,1923,37y.
Racheal,Dec.5,1903,35y.
Robert I.,July 28,1921,39y.
William, May 24,1904,11y.
William J., May 11,1980.
Winifred M., Feb.10,1960,70y.
HOOD
Annie M.,June 4,1978,85y.
Charles A.,bu:Sept.2,1935,75y.
Clarence E.,Jan.27,1916,1m.
Clarence,Feb.15,1929, prem.
infant, Aug. 25,1912, s.b.
Lilas M.,Sept.26,1945,68y.
HOOKER
Ellen C.,Jan.21,1924,77y.
HOOPER
A.Scott, Feb.28,1935.
Blanche G.,June 12,1973,75y.
Charles E.,May 14,1916,69y.
Earle J.,Aug.12,1957,75y.
Edward H.,Oct.20,1916,58y.
Elizabeth May,Mar.18,1920,43y.
Florence M.,May 8,1973,83y.
Florence M.,Oct.29,1955,76y.
Helen,May 24,1937,89y.
Herbert E.,Sept.28,1927,51y.
Lot N.,Feb.13,1916,65y.
Sarah I.,Nov.25,1949,93y.
Statie E.,Apr.14,1917,60y.
Stella F.,Oct.8,1943,79y.
Stuart H.,Nov.4,1917,65y.
Willie A.,1881-1890.
HOPKINS
Bertha F.,June 12,1967,94y.
Cynthia M.,Feb.14,1973,73y.
Elmira A.,July 18,1905,62y.
James R.,Aug.11,1898,68y.
Melvin L.,Apr.15,1945,78y.
Mildred E.,May 6,1970,68y.
Oris L.,June 25,1950,58y.
S. Ormand,July 14,1973,73y.
Sadie A.,Jan.11,1915,22y.
HOPKINSON
Mary J.,Mar.27,1961,89y.
Stephen F., Apr.20,1951,89y.
HORR
Harry, rem. from Saccarappa
  Cem. in Nov.1919.
Mary E., Nov.16,1906,73y.
S. Luella,Dec.29,1928,82y.
Sarah Augusta,1844-1906.
HOWARD
Annie L., Nov. 20,1945, 48y.
Florence M.,May 14,1991,80y.
Rupert A.,Apr.23,1982,72y.
Virgil E.,July 23,1982,51y.

HOWE
Almira E.,1832-1860,w/o Robert.
Charles L.,1863-1881,s/o R. & A.E.
Lizzie J.,1850-July 28,1895,
  w/o Robert L.
Lennie F,1875-1881,s/o R.L.& M.A.
Maggie A.,1846-1877,w/o Robert L.
Nanette Cora,Sept.25,1930,73y.
Robert E.,1868-1889,s/o Robt.& Almir.
Robert,1832-Feb.3,1913.
HOY
Glenda R.,Dr.,Dec.24,1987,93y.
H. Victor, Dr.,Nov.29,1960,66y.
HOYT
Dorothy E.,Apr.17,1977,63y.
Gladys C.,Mar.15,1983,75y.
Reginald,June 1,1984,78y.
HUBBARD
Maureen Jensen,July 30,1994,51y.
HUDSON
Charles E.,Mar.23,1964,74y.
Deltha M.,July 7,1982,61y.
Earl W.,Sept.12,1965,73y.
Earl W.,Jr.,Feb.23,1992,70y.
Ella I.,Feb.12,1963,70y.
Georgia S.,Feb.19,1935,70y.
Herbert S.,Mar.10,1937,71y.
infant, bu:Jan.22,1936, s.b.
Lillian E.,June 17,1962,62y.
Marie Lillian,Oct.25,1932,11y.
Margaret S.,July 16,1965,72y.
Ralph S.,Feb.8,1942,47y.
Richard P., Aug.1,1979,38y.
HUESTON
Barbara,Aug,1923,63y.
Frances L.,Apr.13,1975,74y.
George Douglas,Oct.14,1918,24y.
Gladys C.,Sept.20,1920,24y.
James H.,July 7,1925,60y.
HUFF
Helen G.,Dec.6,1987,81y.
Ralph I.,May 20,1966,61y.
HUGHES
Clarence A.,Aug.14,1969,66y.
John J.,Nov.20,1974,46y.
HULBERT
Sadie M.,Apr.23,1949,62y.
HULIT
Eben L.,Apr.9,1920,23y.
Edwin M.,Sept.4,1931,75y.
Harriet W.,Nov.26,1939,76y.
O. Clyde,Dec.16,1987,82y.
HUNNEWELL
Winnifred B.,June 27,1958,66y.

HUNNIWELL
Hannah,July 26,1753,33y,
  w/o Zerubabel,rem. from the
  Haskell Lot in 1905.
HUNT
Annie B.,Aug.19,1961,85y.
Avis M.,Feb.12,1983,45y.
Carl R.,Feb.9,1920,37y.
Charles H.,Apr.14,1924,80y.
Dolly W.,1818-1900.
Elizabeth D.,bu:1910,63y.
Franklin C.,bu:1877,7y.
George F.,Nov.21,1923,84y.
H.A.,1858-1901.
Hazel B.,bu:May 13,1974.
Herbert A., Sept.21,1899,40y.
infants,1891 & 1892.
Ione M., Jan.8,1945,80y.
Madeline C.,Sept.23,1989,93y.
Mary E.,Oct.30,1898,1d.
Sadie S.Jordan,Jan.22,1891w/o H.A.
Susan A.,1847-June 24,1893.
Warren L.,Aug.1,1920,55y.
William H.,Oct.20,1925,37y.
HUNTER
Albert L.,Jan.1,1943,70y.
Ezekiel,Feb.20,1916,55y.
Mary L.,May 16,1952,69y.
Pearl MacLean,June 10,1953,61y.
Robert, May 23,1937,81y.
Sarah C.,May 29,1918,61y.
William J.,Jan.8,1927,75y.
HUNTLEY
Blanch, Jan.14,1992,91y.
Charles Foster,May 11,1927,1y.
Karl O., Oct.26,1954,59y.
HURD
Alton B., Mar.11,1968,53y.
Charles A., Apr.22,1937,73y.
Martha L., Feb.4,1946,76y.
Philip W., May 7,1956,57y.
HURLEY
Eva, Jan.17,1925,48y.
HUSE
Clarence C.,Jan.29,1945,51y.
Elma C., Jan.28,1968,69y.
Joseph L.,Oct.12,1969,7y.
HUSSEY
Albert L.,Sept.20,1980,61y.
Arvilla M.,May 21,1948,66y.
Benjamin,Feb.13,1892,78y.
Esther,Sept.11,1898,73y.
John H.,Dec.25,1931,84y.
HUSSEY
Phyllis M.,July 15,1994,72y.
HUSSY
Emogene, May 31,1914,64y.

HUSTON
Addie Q.,June 9,1959,89y.
Lewis Porter,Nov.15,1942,73y.
HUTCHINS
Hannah Babb,1806-1897.
Henry M.,Apr.8,1938,77y.
Lillian J.,Nov.20,1941,75y.
HUTCHINSON
Charles E.,July 18,1924,3d.
Louise F.,Oct.22,1971,72y.
Louise L.,May 18,1950,60y.
Ralph H.,Dr.,June 8,1979,89y.
HUTTO
Charles C.,Sr.,Aug.2,1981,63y.
HYDE
Nellie C.,Nov.14,1966,78y.
INGERSOLL
Alice S.,July 12,1948,83y.
Mary L.,Nov.11,1975,80y.
Samuel B.,Jan.18,1937,77y.
INGRAHAM
Gertrude E., Apr.12,1968,75y.
Henry W.,Sr.,Mar.14,1953,62y.
Martha E., Apr.1893.
Martha E.,1840-1896.
William H.,1818-1894.
William W.,Sept.1894.
IRISH
Georgie H. Prince,1840-1879,w/o Wm.
J. Addie, Oct.15,1956,85y.
Martha H.,July 12,1917,77y.
William H.,1843-1901.
IRVING
Erma L.,Feb.23,1961,65y.
Walter,Sr.,Aug.5,1992.
IVERSON
Anna K., Apr.15, 1908,79y.
JACKSON
Almore K., Apr 7,1928,55y.
David K.,Dec.17, 1921,79y.
Ella J.,Nov.3,1918,70y.
Fernando L.,Oct.22,1936,66y.
Harry B.,Feb.27,1982,61y.
Howard B.,Aug.21,1960,56y.
infant,Oct.9,1926, prem.
Incar J.,June 2,1909,68y.
Irene,Jan.24,1945,75y.
Lillian A.,Dec.6,1931,60y.
JACOBSEN
Hans B./P., May 3,1958,85y.
Jeanette M., Feb. 22,1965,85y.
Kenneth, Oct.29,1975,47y.
Peter C.,June 15,1910,71y.
JACQUES
Raynold A.,July 19,1982,53y.
JAMES
Augustus J., May 17, 1928, 47y.
Carol A., June 4, 1954, 17y.
Raymond C., May 8,1981,70y.
Ronald Gary,Nov.12,1948,7m.
Winifred L.,Aug. 4,1964, 79y.
JAQUES
Alice W.,Mar.6,1986,84y.
Harold K.,Dec.4,1962,71y.
Nettie L.,June 7,1950,90y.
JARMAN
Audrey M., Mar.18,1971,36y.
JARRY
Barbara R.,June 28,1974,42y.
Clement,May 25,1968,67y.
Yvonne,May 19,1968.
JEFFERDS
Augustus E.,Oct.29,1898,50y.
Cora, Oct.4,1902,19y.
Ella, Apr.29,1928,80y.
George A.,Jan.27,1954,66y.
Harry A.,Oct.17,1984,61y.
JENKINS
David,Feb.14,1953,75y.
Edith E.,Nov.23,1960,82y.
Sarah J.,Mar.6,1925,66y.
JENKS
Howard A.,Nov.21,1963,66y.
JENNETTE
S.,1853-1892.
JENNINGS
Aubrey E.,Feb.2,1981,56y.
JENNISON
Elizabeth Hannah,Sept.14,1943,68y
Hugh L.,Dec.7,1952,78y.
JENSEN
Alfrieda E.,Feb.22,1948,72y.
Anders,Aug.11,1935,72y.
Andrews,Aug.20,1939,71y.
Annie C.,Aug.16,1966,76y.
Arthur M.,Aug.30,1928,21y.
Carl B.,Feb.7,1976,70y.
Cecelia M.C.,Nov.24,1934,77y.
Christian W.,Dec.26,1977,66y.
Christine C.,Sept.8,1970,78y.
Edward W.,Nov.23,1988,84y.
Esterh C.,June 4,1994,77y.
Florence M.,Feb.22,1959,70y.
Gudrun Balsted, May 23,1944,58y.
Hans,Nov.26,1914,35y.
Idella H.,July 16,1987,78y.
infant,Feb.7,1960, s.b.
J. Maynard,Mar.23,1956,63y.
Jeanette Anna,Sept.9,1924,prem.
Jens,Nov.27,1944,79y.
Jens T.,July 2,1958,76y.
Jens T.,Mar.1,1949,62y.
Jessie E.,Oct.11,1952,81y.
Marion E.,Mar.20,1935,18y.

Marion S.,Sept.16,1930,38y.
Marjorie B.,May 18,1989.
Mary N., Sept. 11,1978, 88y.
Nels, bu:May 25,1942.
Nels,June 10,1918,57y.
Ole,May 11,1947,72y.
Peter J.,July 12,1951,62y.
Phyllis C.,July 4,1978,77y.
Reynold B., Apr. 10,1911,2y.
Robert E.,Brig.Gen.,Jan.2,1981,70y
Robert T., Sr.,May 15,1983,44y.
Thomas H.,Feb.4,1947,60y.
JESS
Alexander,Apr.9,1963,79y.
Alice G.,July 2,1946,84y.
Annie P.,Dec.12,1943,78y.
Athea C., Jan.14,1981,86y.
Clifford, Nov.2,1938,43y.
Elizabeth H.,Nov.11,1934,58y.
Eva M.,Jan.19,1927,51y.
John E.,Aug.5,1937,78y.
John William,Jan.18,1953,80y.
Martha I.,Dec.17, 1973,47y,
  rem. from Chabei Cem., East
  Boston, July 1990.
Moreland, July 13,1924,87y.
Ruby C., Sept.26,1991,81y.
Sedgmond L.,Dec.11,1924,23y.
Thomas, Aug.30,1919,51/7y.
William J.,XXXX,19d.
William, Dec. 28,1946,80y.
JESSEN
Christian,July 21,1955,70y.
Harry W.,Nov.24,1994,71y.
Isabel M.,July 4,1959,79y.
Neal A.,Dec.7,1981,66y.
Niels H.,June 27,1939,83y.
JEWELL
Henry S.,Jan.7,1894,58y.
Ira C.,June 12,1991,86y.
Irene S.,Aug.14,1979,66y.
Mary Alma,Mar.15,1948,77y.
Merrill P.,Jan.27,1964,91y.
Nancy M.,Jan.11,1894,56y.
JOHNSON
Alice C.,Nov.1,1985,86y.
Andrew J.,Feb.1,1925,69y.
Anna M.,June 21,1937,65y.
Annie M.,May 24,1942,78y.
Celia B.,Dec.31,1969,92y.
Charles A.,Nov.2,1956,88y.
Clarence F.,Apr.25,1924, s.b.
Clarence S.,Nov.27,1946,69y.
Elinor M.,Mar.6,1911.
Emily A.,Dec.25,1971,41y.
Eva,Nov.6,1892,6y.
Evelyn,1825-1907.
Harland W. Oct.2,1979,52y.
Helen,Nov.25,1991,82y.
infant,Dec.31,1955.
John Milton,Mar.6,1951,82y.
Joshua,May 17,1952,92y.
Margaret A.,June5,1941,92y.
Mary N.,Aug.13,1966,76y.
Mary S.,Aug.6,1950,90y.
Maude I.,Jan.30,1953,79y.
Peter, Sept.26,1933,69y.
Ralph I.,Oct.12,1980,85y.
Ruby F.,Sept.5,1954,25y.
Vesta R.,Mar.3,1947,52y.
William,Nov.30,1921,64y.
William A.,June 26,1993,73y.
William Carl, Jan.15,1982,83y.
JONES
Alexander,July 19,1898.
Arthur F.,Nov.7,1952,8y.
Charles C., Jan.17,1955,67y.
Clinton F.,Dec.11,1986,75y.
Edwin,Nov.26,1908,72y.
Ella G.,Dec.24,1967,80y.
Ernest L.,Dec.15,1962,77y.
George A.,Apr.12,1939,58y.
Hattie L.,Feb.9,1912,29y.
James,Mar.29,1953,83y.
Jane E.,June 29,1899.
Jane J.,Sept.21,1895,60y.
Janet H.,Mar.26,1947,76y.
Jennie P.,Nov.9,1980,78y.
Kathleen T.,June 21,1978,78y.
Mitta V.,May 13,1940,75y.
Perley L.,Mar.31,1981,71y.
Philip, Dec.4,1919,2m.
Velma M.,June 6,1975,86y.
Violette E.,June 12,1962,51y.
JORDAN
Addie G. Oxnard,1876-1900,
  d/o J.W.&D.S.
Alfred H., Aug.21,1938,77y.
Anna B., May 26,1972,102y.
Beatrice E.,Oct.4,1964,66y.
Bernice T.,Jan.22,1976,74y.
Blanch P.,Dec.21,1961,61y.
Charles H.,Mar.31,1962,57y.
Deborah S.,Aug.8,1895,48y.
Ella I.,Feb.28,1922,72y.
Elmer E.,Mar.13,1947,75y.
Eva,Feb.6,1901,25y.
Evelyn M.,Sept.7,1954,58y.
Fannie L.,May 2,1938.
Frank L.,Feb.9,1991,63y.
Frederick V.,May 13,1985,65y.
George K.,June 13,1969,81y.
Harriet E.,Oct.15,1926,85y.
Hildred,1896-1901, d/o J.W.& D.S.

Iva B.,Sept.13,1934,65y.
John W.,Nov.11,1925,85y.
Joyce Ann,June 26,1944,1d.
Leonard B.,Mar.14,1970,67y.
Lucille R.,June 7,1966,42y.
Minnie A.,Sept.26,1957,85y.
Minnie Small,Feb.4,1933,73y.
Mother,1847-1895.
Philip S.,Aug.18,1986,63y.
Raymond M.,Nov.21,1965,64y.
Rufus King,Apr.26,1942,78y.
Rufus N.,June 9,1966,66y.
Terry Scott,Nov.15,1962,2d.
Thelma M.,Apr.21,1972,73y.
Wilma E.,May 2,1975,80y.
W. Scott,May 7,1935,87y.
William A.,Feb.4,197173y.
William R., June 6,1991,66y.
Wilson Everett,1873-1902.
JOY
Edna W.,June 25,1946,89y.
Frances M.,Oct.31,1960,79y.
JOYCE
Annabelle Q.,Sept.20,1946,82y.
Thomas W.,July 7,1939,81y.
JUDKINS
Alice H.,Feb.5,1969,81y.
Joseph,Mar.31,1977,95y.
JUSTESEN
Karen,Mar.31,1938,79y.
Christian,Apr.30,1911,65y.
Jannex,can't read stone.
KAFAES
Tom,Nov.26,1914,19y.
KALIVAS
Nicholas, Nov.23,1955,74y.
KALPERIS
Irene P.,Dec.18,1985,99y.
Thomas D.,July 9,1976,85y.
KARSTENSEN
Carl H.,June 15,1980,78y.
KASKI
Hazel T. Feb.6,1955,63y.
KAUFMANN
Marion D.,Feb.8,1980.
Norman C.,Comdr.,Dec.261980,78y.
KEARY
Alan N., Apr.8,1975,58y.
KEATEN
David Lewis,Oct.10,1938,1y.
Dorothy E.,June 24,1987,68y.
John D.,Mar.26,1986,44y.
Lewis P.,Oct.26,1979,63y.
KEATING
Dennis,May 12,1924,74y.
Minnie L.,Nov.21,1964, s.b.

KEENE
infant,Mar.7,1965, s.b.
infant,Feb.22,1955,prem.
infant,Jan.8,1954, s.b.
KEITH
William R.,Oct.26,1944,45y.
KELLEY
Cole H.,July 13,1985,75y.
Ellard A.,Feb.18,1983,85y.
Evelyn L.,Oct.30,1983,87y.
Francis R.,Aug.27,1931,18y.
Gordan W., Apr.25,1953,78y.
Gordan W.,Jr.,Mar.26,1945,36y.
Lillian P.,Sept.27,1991,89y.
Mildred H.,Nov.22,1986,81y.
Sarah A.,May 8,1929,78y.
William H.,Dec.14,1944,62y.
William H.,1848-1938,
  Westbrook's last Civil War Vet.
KELLY
Alfred C.,Aug.1981.
Andrew C.,June 15,1952,75y.
Ann L.,June 30,1991,90y.
Eva J.,Oct.10,1978,68y.
Howard R.,Oct.21,1971,76y.
infant,Oct.6,1907, s.b.
James M.,Sept.18,1961,86y.
Jennie L.,May 1,1953,80y.
Louise P.,May 22,1945,69y.
Mildred B. Nov.9,1993,86y.
Philip D.,Sept.6,1983,72y.
Sarah E.,Dec.31,1944,61y.
Stewart E.,Nov.21,1991,67y.
William H. Aug.30,1938,90y.
William H.,Jr.,Oct.27,1933,49y.
KELSON
Alice L., Apr.16,1972,67y.
Arthur H.,Jan.11,1953,55y.
Charles,July 19,1893,9m.
Charles H.,May 29,1915,60y.
Charles W.,Mar.13,1962,66y
Emily W.,Oct.25,1974,73y.
Louise A.,Feb.1,1920,65y.
Marie, Apr.30,1919,20y.
Percy,1892-1893,s/o C.H.& L.A.
William A.,Feb.5,1989,61y.
KENDERINE
Dorothy, July 27,1990,72y.
Jesse, Rev.,May 4,1966,81y.
John E.,Sr.,Oct.25,1993,77y.
Maude E., Mar.19,1950,60y.
KENISTON
Arthur S.,Oct.26,1980,86y.
Graham E.,Jan.29,1983,60y.
Wilma Graham,Feb.22,1928,34y.
KENNEDY
Elizabeth M.,Oct. 23,1978.

Emma L.,May 14,1908,33y.
Etta,June 1,1903,29y.
Evelyn M.,Apr.8,1905,1y.
George C.,Nov.30,1945.
George L.,bu:Nov.21,1936,71y.
Mary C.,Nov.14,1945,84y.
Walter Noyes,Apr.4,1937,66y.
William S.,July 23,1961,56y.
William S.,Jan.9,1956,63y.
William,May 27,1940,75y.
KENNEY
Alice L.,Apr.22,1911,5m.
Annie,Jan.25,1941,84y.
David A.,Dec.19,1943,75y.
infant,Nov.7,1959, few hrs.
Joseph F.,Feb.10,1938,59y.
Louisa A.,Jan.13,1929,93y.
Louise C.,Mar.11,1963,58y.
Vivian M.,July 8,1992,77y.
KENNIE
Everett W.,July 17,1990,83y.
Henrietta W.,Mar.2,1967,94y.
James,1806-1892.
James, Feb.28,1987,77y.
James H.,June 6,1942,73y.
Julie C.,Dec.24,1985,75y.
Mary E.,Apr.29,1949,17y.
Shawn C., Dec.22,1968,2m.
William E.,Sr.,Nov.13,1980.
KENNY
Bertram H.,Mar.11,1974,65y.
Mildred H.,Oct.20,1965,81y.
KENT
Alice S.,Dec.2,1988,86y.
John H.,Aug.18,1977,81y.
KERR
Jensine J.,June 9,1941,83y.
Theodore L., Apr.20,1936,78y.
KIERSTEAD
Mae Ellen, June 2,1950,50y.
KIMBALL
Almena, Mar.1,1907,2y.
Almena,1842-1892.
Carl L., Aug.10,1946,59y.
Clara, June 5,1947,76y.
Clarence E.,Jan.5,1982.
Clarence W.,Mar.6,1941,45y.
Dora B.,Nov.25,1946,60y.
Elsie,1896-1896.
Elvin, Apr.11,1909,2m.
Emily,Mar.24,1939,90y.
Emma L.,July 5,1967,74y.
Frank,1879,2y.
Harry B.,Oct.1,1964,79y.
Isaac,Apr.21,1912,69y.
John,1872,4m.
John M.,1874-1895.

Julia Josephine,Mar.7,1929,58y.
Mark F.,Oct 24,1914,64y.
Samuel W.,May 20,1941,54y.
Sarah G., Jan.2,1928,76y.
Sarah S.,Dec.30,1921,78y.
Simon O.,Jan.4,1909,65y.
Walter W.,May 22,1928,2y.
Wilbur E.,May 1,1922,51y.
William E.,Dec.9,1930,59y.
KING
Celia E.,Dec.12,1949,70y.
George M.,Feb.12,1942,42y.
Ovide D.,Dec.16,1951,50y.
Raymond G.,Sr.,Aug.14,1985,77y.
Rene J.,May 27,1957,51y.
Richard O.,Mar.24,1980,51y.
Thomas C.,June 29,1933,55y.
KINMOND
Althea M.,Dec.28,1981,83y.
Annie M.,June 25,1947,80y.
Catherine Y.,Feb.23,1931,86y.
Emma L.,Dec.25,1955,73y.
Ernest F.,Sept.14,1977,80y.
Ernest F.,Sept.17,1904,59y.
Isabella F.,June 12,1923,75y.
James Y.,Mar.22,1971,90y.
John,Apr. 9,1974,90y.
John,July 23,1939,70y.
John M.,Aug.29,1956,61y.
Joseph,July 22,1971,83y.
Lottie H.,Oct.13,1957,77y.
Marjorie A.,Feb.19,1976,86y.
Marjory Milne, Apr.19,1891,75y, w/o John.
Myra E., July 3,1934,29y.
Thelma B., Dec.16,1981,78y.
KIRKPATRICK
Alice C.,Nov.22,1950,81y.
Clyde Victoria,June 14,1931,35y.
Edith O.,Sept.11,1993,85y.
James,Feb.20,1946,88y.
Jean,Dec.3,1929,2d.
Leroy,1896-1896.
Louise,1889-1889.
Nellie,Feb.14,1907,48y.
Percy E.,Nov.15,1993,87y.
Philip,Dec.19,1945,25y.
Walter,1889-1889.
Walter J.,May 1,1971,79y.
William H.,Sept.18,1946,75y.
KIRKWOOD
Mary C.,Sept.4,1910,53y.
Richard,Oct.14,1927,72y.
Roberta Mary, Apr.19,1921,5d.
KLEWIADA
Mildred M.,Jan.2,1970,67y.

KLINKE
Edwin, Aug.13,1984 68y.
Grace E.,Mar.13,1985,60y.
KLOTH
Agnes F.,June 10,1994,94y.
Arndt P., Apr.8,1984,80y.
KLOWAS
Augustine "Gus",Mar.29,1993,86y.
Sarah E."Sadie",Nov.26,1988,74y.
KNEELAND
Lester E.,Sept.9,1916,36y.
KNIGHT
Almon L.,July 14,1913,59y.
Betty Jane,Dec.8,1928,3d.
Cecelia F.,May 18,1988,81y.
Clyde E.,June 11,1994,77y.
David, Apr.16,1940,69y.
Edna M.,Apr.5,1901,9y.
Edwin C.,Mar.26,1957,73y.
Edwin P.,Aug.21,1944,73y.
Elizabeth C.,Oct.9,1939,82y.
Ellen H., Sept.10,1924,60y.
Eva M.,June 6,1964,83y.
Eva May,Sept.8,1935,54y.
Fay A.,July 16,1990,57y.
Forrest L.,June 24,1977,70y.
George S.,Sept.20,1965.
George Sumner,Jr.,Jan.1932, s.b.
Hortense W.,June 2,1984,92y.
infant, Jan.13,1928, s.b.
James Melvin, Aug.18,1915,67y.
John M.,Jan.5,1984,49y.
Kenneth R.,Sept.9,1912, 8y.
Laura E.,1874,9y,rem. from
  Knight's Private Cem. Oct.1921.
Leland W., Feb. 8, 1970, 86y.
Linwood D.Sr.,Sept.6,1958, 50y.
Lovina, 1903, 38y, w/o Moses,rem.
  from Knight's Private Cem. 1921.
Mary A.,Sept.20,1938,91y.
Mary L.,May 4,1905,71y.
Mary L.,Jan.2,1973,64y.
Mary L.,Feb.16,1907,39y, rem.
  from Knight's Priv. Cem.1921.
Merrill B.,June 15,1965,59y.
Mertie S., Apr.4,1962,77y.
Moses,1877,41y,rem. from
  Knight's Private Cem. 1921.
Nellie E., Feb.11,1943,56y.
no name, Oct.22,1909,81y.
Philena M., 1878, 3y, removed
  from Knight's Priv. Cem. 1921.
Raymond,XXXX, 2wks., rem.
  from Saccarappa Cemetery.
Richard L.,Jan.29,1922,5y.
Sarah B.,June 21,1929,80y.
Sarah F.,Sept.12,1945,72y.

Sarah J.,Apr.15,1928,69y.
Walter V.,June 16,1938,81y.
Wilhemina,Feb.15,1907,41y,
  rem. from Knight's Cem.1921.
William E., Nov.19,1969,35y.
KNOWLES
Alice F.,Nov.22,1973,76y.
Charles E.,Sept.28,1970,76y.
Donald P.,Jan.4,1973,74y.
Margaret L.,Aug.15,1993,20y.
KNOWLTON
Agnes B., Aug.25,1967,76y.
Dorothy C.,Oct.18,1968,73y.
Ethel G.,Feb.18,1957.
Florence E.,Oct.6,1908,36y.
George H.,Nov.15,1948,78y.
Guy H.,July 12,1974,71y.
John Dennison,Jan.15,1941.
John G.,Dec.15,1940.
Matilda B.,Feb.16,1960,72y.
Ralph W.,Apr.20,1968,74y.
Sarah L.,June 1,1972,86y.
KNOX
Arthur R.,Feb.3,1994.
Edward J.,Sr.,June 12,1960,77y.
Elmer L., Mar.5,1935,22y,
  rem. from Buxton 1946.
Ethel M., Jan.19,1971,69y.
Ida M., Dec.11,1969,84y.
Irving N.,June 18,1962,48y.
Lorne W.,May 21,1964,78y.
Mary B.,Dec.17,1918,26y.
William D., Jr.,May 4,1972,34y.
KNUDSEN
Bessie H.,Aug.19,1948,50y.
Charles A.,Apr.13,1976,60y.
Madeline J.,Oct.19,1973,68y.
Philip Bortel,June 6,1921,2d.
William, Aug.2,1937,40y.
William G.,Dec.4,1982,64y.
KOMATZ
infant,Mar.29,1939, s.b.
KOURAPIS
Bertha L.,Aug.21,1993.
Lewis O.,July 25,1961,66y.
KOTT
Anton,June 10,1965,73y.
KUBAT
Marion N.,June 12,1976,63y.
Nelson R.,May 5,1938,22d.
William,June 9,1978,62y.
LABBE
Joseph,bu:Oct.24,1991.
Michael D.,June 6,1964,6y.
Michelle,bu: Oct.24,1991.
Russell S.,May 21,1967,s.b.
Steven P.,Apr.5,1982,24y.

LABRECQUE
Edith B.,Oct.9,1981,61y.
Guy L.,Jan.17,1991,80y.
Ina G.,Aug.30,1957,46y.
Kathryn D.,Jan.25,1953,16y.
Lorenzo L.,Aug.24,1982,82y.
LABRIE
Samantha D.,Dec.16,1978,s.b.
LaCHANCE
Fred E.,Nov.21,1943,32y.
Virginia H.,Nov.4,1944,23y.
LADD
Agnes T.,Dec.8,1962,90y.
Blanche M.,July 20,1985,86y.
Clara,1895-1897,d/o E.J.& H.E.
Dana L.,Aug.28,1954,64y.
E.P.,1832-1874.
Enoch E.,Pvt.,1899-Jan.8,1919, in France.
Eugene J.,May 31,1948,82y.
Everett E.,Oct.7,1979.
Hannah M.,1832-1909,w/o Rev.E.P.
Hattie E.,July 27,1915,51y.
Raymond E.,Sept.5,1977,56y.
LAFFIN
Anna M.,Dec.23,1946,66y.
Arthur A.,Mar.1,1953,68y.
Bertha B.,Nov.10,1956,57y.
Clarence, Apr.21,1956,74y.
Emily J.,Mar.26,1945,72y.
Forrest G.,Oct.4,1969,63y.
George Frederick,July 6,1948,75y.
Helen R.,Mar.13,1914,12y.
J. Warren, Aug.13,1986,87y.
James L.,Aug.18,1944,42y.
Lockard L.,Feb.10,1944,69y.
Maggie,1890-1903,d/o M.T.& C.
Mary Edith,July 13,1926,22y.
Mary E.,June 13,1966,77y.
Mary J.,Oct.17,1957,74y.
Victor,Mar.24,1908,21y.
LAGARSON
Hilma E.,July 29,1944,68y.
Victor E.,Nov.5,1927,54y.
Victor Oliver,Oct.5,1918,16y.
LALLY
Francis W.,Nov.24,1985,60y.
LAMB
Arnold A.,Mar.12,1915,2m.
Beryl Estha,July 11,1917,2m.
Cora B.,Dec.25,1938,66y.
Eldon P.,Dec.18,1938,67y.
Frank Wilson,M.D.,Jan.21,1941,68y
Grace B.,Jan.24,1973,97y.
Helen L.,Mar.1,1968,61y.
Henry W.,Dr.,Apr.19,1964,65y.
Jessie K.,1885-1889.

John,1787-1865.
Leslie Alton,Oct.9,1918,2y.
Louise M.,Sept.2,1906,24y,d/o Marrett
Lucy Leighton,1808-1896,w/o John Marrett, Oct.9,1907,64y.
Nellie,1864-1867,d/o W.W. & S.
Olive Binford,Jan.22,1931,81y.
Susan, Feb.11,1907,73y.
Virginia Rachel, Aug.20,1919,3m.
William M., Mar. 3, 1957, 84y.
William W., Sept.25,1910,73y.
LAMBERT
Daniel W.,Jan.16,1957,4m.
LAMPRON
Girard, Jan.3,1992,70y.
LANDRY
Arthur J.,Nov.2,1977,58y.
Bruce J.,May 8,1971,22y.
infant,Dec.13,1935,s.b.
LANE
Eliza B.,Nov.14,1970,86y.
infant,Dec.13,1935, s.b.
Lemuel S.,Dec.23,1921,68y.
Mary Poole,Nov.20,1914,59y.
Robert R.,Oct.19,1974,89y.
Robert Webb, Apr.4,1990,45y.
LANGEVIN
Joseph O.,May 18,1987,66y.
LANGLEY
John, Sept.10,1949,79y.
Laura R.,Aug.24,1967,84y.
LANGSHAW
Hattie,Sept.1,1901,33y.
LANGUET
infant, Apr.7,1944.
LaPLANTE
Edward J.,Aug.9,1993,43y.
Frederick J.,July 23,1982,26y.
George A., Jan. 20,1978, 54y.
Harriet M.,Aug.27,1981,61y.
Laura A.,Jan.27,1977,78y.
Lucien E.,Feb.15,1983,64y.
Medgar C.,Sept.2,1966,76y.
Steven W.,July 22,1982,76y.
LAREEN
infant, May 7,1921, s.b.
LARRABEE
Benjamin T.,Nov.13,1956,76y.
Margaret C.,Jan.3,1986,101y.
Philip E.,Sept.5,1988,73y.
LARSEN
Christian L.,Jan.2,1965,86y.
inf/o Warren,May 10,1921,s.b.
Jens C.,Dec. 28,1914,66y.
John E.,Apr.28,1972,72y.
Lars,Oct.13,1960,84y.
Maren, Oct.8,1921,71y.

Ruth Thompson,Dec.29,1932,17y.
LARSON
Mildred M.,Feb.4,1994,88y.
LASTAGE
Linda Ann H.,Mar.18,1990,38y.
LAUBER
Georgianna, June 9,1990,89y.
LAURITSEN
Anders,Dec.25,1927,70y.
Edward H., Feb.13,1984,57y.
Harry A.,June 21,1958,39y.
Henry P.,Apr.25,1930,36y.
infant,Dec.3,1923, s.b.
Jensine C.,Feb.11,1934,45y.
Johanna Marie, Apr.23,1932,73y
LAVERTY
Abbie May,Jan.12,1907,37y,
w/o E. Allen.
Allen L.,Jan.14,1918, 3y.
Carleton R.,July 7,1936,39y.
Cora B., Sept.19,1961,59y.
E. Allen,Mar.30,1951,89y.
Edwin J.,July 5,1945,85y.
H. Clayton,Feb.8,1955,69y.
Isaac,1817-Mar.14,1892.
Isaac,Nov.16,1918,69y.
infant, Aug.17,1916, s.b.
infant, Feb.22,1915,prem.,
ch/o Harold & Addie.
Jenny L.,Nov.5,1948,81y.
Lucinda C.,Jan.2,1926.
Mabel A.,Oct.3,1978,82y.
Merton E.,Oct.28,1973,76y.
LAVIGNE
Hormida J.,Nov.5,1975,72y.
LAWRENCE
Adeline Elder,Apr.14,1930,50y.
Charles M.,Apr.5,1900,28y.
Charles W.,Capt,Feb.23,1912,77y.
child,1903-1904.
Edith Emma, 4d, d/o Wm. C. &
Emma, rem. from Mt. Rest Cem.,
Brookville,MA, Sept.1919.
Elizabeth S.,Jan.22,1933,93y.
Emma J., 37y, w/o Wm.C.,
removed from Mt. Rest Cem.,
Brookline, MA, Sept.1919.
Lewis H.,1894-1896.
Lorens,1815-1892.
Maria,1825-1926,w/o Lorens.
Mary A.,Oct.1,1910,2y.
Minnie D.,bu:Sept.30,1936,64y.
Percival C.,May 14,1956,76y.
Robert A.,bu:Sept.22,1936,25y.
William C.,Jan.29,1953,94y.
Winfield S.,May 21,1959,82y.

LAWRENSEN
Christine B., Mar.17,1946,79y.
John,Nov.19,1942,76y.
Marie,Jan.1,1926,100y.
Vestae E.,May 4,1904,9m.
LAWSON
infant, Jan.24,1937, prem.
LEAVITT
Ida Cook,Dec.2,1928,67y.
John C.,Nov.8,1937,79y.
Mary Ann,June 5,1951,79y.
LeBEAU
Albert, Nov.23,1955,74y.
Etta Louise,Apr.20,1944,65y.
Julia A., Jan. 6, 1912, 58y.
LEBEL
Rodolphe A.,Jan.9,1983,59y.
LeBROCK
Annie,Dec.10,1938,75y.
Belle,1882-1884.
Eliza,1852-1892,w/o Wm.
Lillian,1885-1886.
Mary,1851-1900,w/o Wm.
William,1842-1913.
LeCONTE
Earl R., Sr.,Aug.22,1985,38y.
Mona L.,Dec.28,1975,62y.
Rudolph,Jan.27,1965,52y.
Velma M.,May 7,1936,32y.
LEEMAN
William E.,Jr.,Jan.10,1990,77y.
LEGENDRE
Elsie R.,Nov.9,1979,77y.
Noe J.,Nov.28,1967,66y.
LEIGHTON
Abbie M.,Dec.17,1910,63y.
Addie M.,June 11,1981,94y.
Arthur E.,Feb.18,1936,60y.
Ashton L.,bu:Apr.30,1930,64y.
B.D.,Aug.9,1901,34y.
Barrett W.,Feb.2,1966,58y.
Benjamin T.,Dec.24,1931,35y.
Charles W.,1863-Feb.1,1909.
Christine W.,Oct.27,1982,85y.
Clifford E.,Nov.22,1933,51y.
Clifford H.,Oct.18,1970,66y.
Cora M.,Nov.14,1967,82y.
Cynthia,Oct.6,1909,newb.
Dana F.,Nov.27,1893,1y.
Dwight W., Dr.,July 6,1987,75y.
Eben,Sept.27,1922,71y.
Edmund,Nov.25,1970,10hrs.
Ella M.,May 27,1960,91y.
Emma E.,1889,16y.
Emma E.,June 26,1905,w/o Henry.
Emma F.,Feb.10,1917,78y.
Ernest A.,Sept.2,1966,69y.

Ernest F.,Oct.8,1967,73y.
Ernestine F.,Mar.6,1976,71y.
Ethel W.,Mar.3,1981,96y.
Frank L.,Sept.26,1915,65y.
Franklin B.,Oct.11,1919,63y.
Fred L.,Sept.17,1954,92y.
George,Feb.4,1913,71y.
George H.,1870-1904.
George W.,Feb.29,1962,69y.
Gertrude,Feb.20,1911,30y.
Gertrude,Mar.23,1926,70y.
Hannah Austin,Oct.1,1933,90y.
Helen M.,Feb.3,1926,38y.
Howard L., Col.,Nov.14,1960,69y.
infant,Oct. 9,1915,ch/o L.P.& M.
infant,Sept.27,1910,prem.
infant,Nov.1,1917,s.b.
infant, Aug.8,1946,1d.
Isaiah,July 9,1925,76y.
James E.,May 30,1991,49y.
Jason, Apr.5,1894,66y.
Jennie A.,Oct.31,1940,70y.
Jennie L,Jan.21,1901,40y,w/o Walt
Jessie M.,Feb.2,1970,72y.
John A.,Nov.22,1949,72y.
Julia A.,July 10,1954,89y.
Keith M.,Oct.25,1984,89y.
Leon P.,May 17,1940,65y.
Leonard,Jan.8,1964,87y.
Leslie S.,July 13,1936,51y.
Lewis L.,Sept.13,1965,80y.
Lloyd Ernest,June 20,1936,9m.
Lloyd S.,Feb.9,1946,51y.
Lloyd S.,Mar.17,1961,38y.
Louisa D.,bu:May 14,1933,58y.
Lydia D. Crockett, Oct.7,1906,58y, w/o Frank L.
Mabel L.,Aug.18,1941,78y.
Mabel L.,Mar.18,1937,58y.
Marcia A. Libby,Aug.3,1910,27y, w/o Arthur.
Margaretta,Nov.29,1990,88y.
Marion H.,Mar.21,1983,77y.
Martha,infant, can't read stone.
Martha H.,Jan.3,1901,66y,w/o Jason.
Martha J.,June 5,1976,76y.
Mary E.,Nov.6,1972,86y.
Mary E.,Feb.24,1938,73y.
Melvin H.,Apr.29,1927,56y.
Nellie M.,May 19,1949,76y.
Oliver H.,July 30,1917,80y.
Paul A.,1897-1898.
Paul R.,Dec.12,1993,65y.
Raymond E.,Apr.17,1973,70y.
Richard A.,Apr.21,1973,41y.
Richard E.,Nov.9,1993,66y.
Roger F.,Feb.5,1933,25y.
Royden R.,Apr.30,1918,39y.
Sewell S.,May 4,1924,85y.
Shirley Merton, Oct. 5,1928,64y.
Shirley M.,Jr.,June 12,1974.
Thomas M.,bu:Oct.7,1928.
Vivian L.,Oct.27,1937,51y.
Walter L.,Apr.13,1926,68y.
William S.,Feb.28,1928,65y.
Winfield L.,Jan.22,1906,16y.
LEKOUSES
Angleo J.,May 4,1973,64y.
John G.,Nov.22,1963,86y.
Katherine,Nov.9,1933,49y,rem.
from Forest City Cem. Nov.1953.
LEMUIX
Eugene,bu:Feb.14,1943,48y.
LEONARD
Carroll E.,June 18,1978,69y.
Frederick M.,Feb.8,1932,61y.
Georgia L.,Mar.11,1987,78y.
Susan M., Nov.26,1955,67y.
LEPENVIN
Homer J.,Apr.21,1957,62y.
LERMOND
George F.,1856-1888.
Ottalie,1887-1888.
LESSOR
Charles,June 1,1908,66y.
LETARTE
Arthur R.,July 10,1922,24y.
LeTOURNEAU
Mildred,Mar.21,1958.
Roland, Apr.3,1971,75y.
LEVESQUE
Alice T.,May 21,1966,68y.
Bernard F.,Mar.16,1967,38y.
J. Albert, May 30,1965,62y.
Michael S.,Jan.4,1981,2 hrs.
Raoul F.,Dec.27,1980,74y.
LEVITCH
Alexander V.,Oct.29,1960,89y.
Ida E.,bu:July 2,1954,82y.
LEWIN
Cora M.,Feb.25,1950,65y.
LEWIS
Alfred F.,Apr.8,1909,74y.
Amy L.,Feb.2,1953,83y.
Anna C.,May 18,1952,92y.
Archelaus,May 26,1956,88y.
Carolyn M., Apr.20,1978,67y.
Charles E.,Apr.10,1901,69y.
Effie M.,Jan.24,1984,72y.
Ellen,Dec.30,1917,81y.
Ellen M.,Apr.26,1944,78y.
Frances,Feb.25,1977.
George P.,1841-1886.
George P.,June 2,1942,68y.

Harold Earle,Nov.13,1951,67y.
Harold L., Apr.24,1993,77y.
Harold M.,Sept.20,1962,74y.
Harvey A.,Nov 4,1964,51y.
Hebert O.,May 4,1901,36y.
Helen Bettes,Nov.16,1940,75y.
Inez M.,Sept.26,1978,92y.
Josiah D,1871-1896.
Lavira J.,Aug.26,1948,80y.
Richard W.,Sept.25,1981,59y.
Roberta M.,Feb.28,1963,74y.
Ruth E.,Oct.2,1981,62y.
Ruth M.,Jan.6,1961,53y.
Susan, Aug.19,1938,103y.
Tennah Rice,Mar.29,1926,90y.
Thalia C., Apr.11,1956,70y.
Thomas M., Apr.7,1940,77y.
Warren C.,May 7,1984,66y.
Wilbur P.,Aug.24,1924,68y.
William B.,1876-1882.

LIBBY

A.Henry,1855-1856.
Abbie T.,Feb.25,1979,63y.
Abbie Warren,June 29,1921,62y.
Abby P.,1833-1898.
Albion D.T.,Aug.21,1963,86y.
Alfred J.,July 19,1915,45y.
Alice A. Boothby,Jan.30,1925,80y, w/o Alonzo
Alice J.,Feb.18,1935,66y.
Alonzo,Jan.14,1904,62y.
Annie L.,Aug.19,1902,41y.
Annie V.,Mar.6,1932,61y.
Arno Dean,Jan.23,1922,s.b.
Bertha F.,Mar.1,1955,83y.
Bessie M.,Apr.17,1899,9m.
Carl V.,Jan.23,1978,80y.
Carlton R.,Nov.21,1954,36y.
Carol Ann,June 19,1951,4m.
Carolyn W.,July 5,1949,77y.
Celia A.,Dec.3,1963,60y.
Charlie W.,1899-1900.
Charles,Nov.20,1900,11m.
Charles C.,May 6,1942,64y.
Charles J.,1859-1859.
Clifford E.,June 15,1979,66y.
Clifford S.,Apr.11,1961,86y.
Dianne Lee,Feb.23,1947,4 hrs.
Dorothy M.,Feb.1,1979,58y.
E.H.,May 17,1908,50y.
Edgar H., Aug.17,1951,56y.
Edward D.,Nov.27,1936,73y.
Edward D.,Mrs., no dates, rem. from another cem., Oct.1918.
Edwin R.,Feb.12,1913,81y, h/o Susan J.
Effie M.,Nov.4,1933,37y.

Eleanor Boynton,Oct.8,1987,87y.
Elizabeth,Dec.4,1938,78y.
Elizabeth B.,Feb.14,1993,75y.
Elsie B.,May 3,1989,78y.
Esther June,Jan.6,1921,2y, d/o Roscoe & Julia.
Ethel M.,Nov.19,1963,56y.
Evans H.,June 13,1966,73y.
Everett A.,Aug.31,1959,61y.
E. Winnifred,Jan.21,1992,93y.
Fannie B., Aug.11,1940,61y.
Florence M.,bu:Feb.27,1943.
Frances Gertrude,June 1917,15y.
Frank E.R.,Jan.16,1933,60y.
Frank L.,June 8,1906,47y.
Frank S.,1880-1889.
Franklin S.,Jan.26,1883.
Franklin S.,1831-1865.
Fred B.,1865-1887,s/o A. & A.B.
Fred,July 19,1924,71y.
Frederick,Sept.7,1925,4m.
Frederick E.,Feb.3,1964,22y.
Freeland E. Oct.21,1971,78y.
George J.,1872-1887,s/o A.& A.B.
George I.,Nov.2,1959,62y.
George,Jan.15,1914,66y.
Georgia A.,Aug.12,1894,19y.
Georgia M.,Jan.6,1945,54y.
Georgia,Sept.3,1900,37y.
Gertrude Ethel,Jan.23,1922,23y.
Gladys,Aug.28,1953,39y.
Guy E.,Oct.7,1969,69y.
Harlan P.,Aug.13,1905,48y.
Harry Paul,Mar.27,1946,1d.
Herbert L.,Sept.9,1982,69y.
Howard,1860-1860.
infant,June 27,1913,1d.
Jane W.,June 30,1932,2d.
Jennie Purington,Sept.27,1909,39y.
John A.,Jan.8,1972,74y.
John W.,May 1,1987,66y.
Josiah E.,Dec.24,1914,56y.
Julia E.,July 27,1955,76y.
June Esther,Jan 2,1921,2d.
Katherine S.,Oct.19,1925,23y.
Keith E.,July 26,1990,72y.
Laura S.,Mar.2,1958,76y.
Lillian E.,Dec.20,1926,72y.
Lillian P.,Apr.20,1946,88y.
Lewis F.,1857-Apr.2,1898.
Lot,Dec.28,1926,73y.
Lottie A.,Apr.21,1918,38y.
Lucy A.,Sept.1,1829-Nov.1,1901, w/o Peter.
Mabel L.,Jan.19,1972,91y.
Marjorie E.,Jan.25,1980,80y.
Mary A.,Mar.25,1955,60y.

Mary E.,Oct.8,1981,76y.
Mary E.,Dec.28,1924,55y.
Mary E.,Oct.25,1957,64y.
Maude B.,Jan.22,1960,84y.
Mildred F.,Feb.11,1963,74y.
Mildred Irene,May 31,1942,42y.
Millard Harmon,Apr.28,1932,40y.
Milton D.,1889-Nov.18,1892.
Nellie G.,Feb.21,1927,40y.
Nellie S.,bu:Sept.30,1966,95y.
Nelson E.,May 27,1949,74y.
Norris L.,Nov.6,1950,70y.
Olin C.,July 20,1945,39y.
P. Libby,Apr.20,1947,88y.
Percy Lawrence,Dec.21,1926,31y.
Peter,1826-June 30,1899.
Philip G.,1905-1905,s/o S.H.&L.S.
Philip H.,Aug.22,1939,44y.
Philip S.,Jan.10,1973,69y.
Raymond E.,bu:June 22,1928,s.b.
Roland,Sept 4,1902,3y.
Roscoe F.,Feb.4,1954,71y.
Rose McGuire,Aug.25,1954,72y.
Ruth S. July 1,1991,73y.
Sarah B.,1880-1885,d/o A.&A.B.
Sarah J. Thomas,Dec.28,1935,55y, w/o E.R.
Stephen H.,July 22,1951,72y.
Stephen I.,Mar4,1909,43y,h/o Eliz.
Susan,1888-1909.
Susan A.,July 23,1925,20y.
Susan J.,Feb.7,1934,83y.
Susan S.,May 18,1991,97y.
Verna, Aug. 2,1903,5y, d/o F.E.R.
Vernon C.,Apr.13,1975,55y.
Viola M.,Nov.19,1982,81y.
Walter F.,Mar.3,1942,66y.
William D.,bu: Oct.23,1927,54y.
William F.,Nov.3,1958,72y.
William F.,Oct.30,1935,73y.
William L.,Nov.23,1993,69y.
William,July 23,1921.
LIBERTY
Sarah A.,Jan.21,1979,2y.
LIND
Adma T.,Oct.17,1992,81y.
Clifford C.,Mar.22,1991,83y.
Helen J.,Feb.15,1981,104y.
Oscar C.,Apr.9,1945,71y.
LINDEMAN
Rudolph"Chet"Jr.,July 26,1991,76y
LINDQUIST
Robert E.,Dec.22,1972,81y.
LINDSTROM
Paul R.,May 7,1923,35y.
LINSKY
John J.,Jr.,Apr.20,1978,58y.

LITTLE
Cynthia M.,Dec.19,1900,74y.
Ella M.,Nov.23,1956,90y.
Frank J.,July 26,1935,68y.
infant, Feb.7,1947,10 min.
Josiah E.,1732-1875.
LITTLEFIELD
Edgar M., Sept.8,1929,49y.
Georgia I.,Feb.6,1989,93y.
John F.,bu:May 3,1930,75y.
John J.,Nov.21,1981,63y.
Ralph L.,Cpl.,Mar. 8,1945,23y, killed in action.
Robert B.,July 17,1971,77y.
LIVINGSTONE
Andrew, Aug.28,1905,72y.
Elizabeth,May 15,1920,84y.
Erva L.,Jan.16,1972,62y.
Esmond C.,Feb.21,1928,31y.
Etta K.,Dec.4,1953,82y.
infant,Dec.16,1973, s.b.
Lillian M.,Dec.26,1993,89y.
Mildred M.,Oct.17,1946,35y.
Myrtle S.,Dec.10,1929,29y.
W. Ronald,Oct.9,1977,81y.
Ruby M.,May 2,1971,75y.
Sterling K.,Aug.14,1961,52y.
Sterling K.,Jr.,Nov.1,1951,17y.
William Armour,Nov.24,1921,52y.
LIVERMORE
Hervey C.,Nov.13,1949 72y.
LOGAN
Nelson A.,Oct.30,1928,46y.
LOMBARD
Eben M.,Dec 21,1922,80y.
Howard C.,Nov.291901,29y.
Leroy F.,Apr.17,1988,73y.
Mary E.,June 12,1902,60y,w/o Eben M
LONDON
Charles L., Apr.4,1910,67y, h/o Cordelia Warren Hanson.
Dana W.,Dec.3,1957,67y.
Margaret C.,July 13,1972,80y.
LONG
Ethelie M.,Feb.26,1939,56y.
James S.,Dec.9,1978,88y.
infant,June 7,1920,prem.
LOOKE
Dorothy H.,Sept.11,1929,20y.
LOPEZ
Bertrand G.,Feb.7,1979,67y.
Reba W.,Dec.24,1954,62y.
Richard D.,Aug.9,1965,53y.
Russell E.,Oct.21,1945,33y.
Walter B.,May 1,1965,73y.
LORD
Alma,Oct.15,1986,79y.

Charles E.,Feb.28,1953.
Charles P.,July 17,1905,69y.
Chester A. ,Apr.9,1957,74y.
Chester E.,Mar.17,1947,52y.
Cornelia A.,Dec.12,1933,81y.
Elbridge,Feb.3,1904,65y.
Ellen,Mar.7,1893,55y.
Elmer E.,Mar.17,1929,66y.
Elnera L.,Oct.5,1972,99y.
Flora J., Apr.1,1939,64y.
Frederick, Aug.30,1898,34y.
George H.,Dec.13,1965,92y.
Harold M.,bu: Sept.9,1950,63y.
Harold N.,Oct.4,1966,77y.
Harold N.,Jr.,Dec.20,1955,43y.
Herbert E.,Jan.19,1956,87y.
Ira N.,June 1,1944,57y.
Irene L.,Jan.28,1989,76y.
Jeanne M.,May 12,1948,73y.
Julia,June 5,1924,57y.
Lucy A.,July 2,1918,75y.
Mabel C.,Apr.5,1935,45y.
Marguerite B.,Oct.6,1977,78y.
Marion E.,Mar.16,1972,80y.
Mary S.,1843-Jan.5,1905.
Nathan,Feb.27,1907,69y.
Norman C.,Oct.7,1974,69y.
Trevor F. Aug.9,1988,87y.
Willard C.,July 15,1943,71y.
LORING
infant,June 10,1920.
Mary Ellen, Oct.4,1983,90y.
LORRAIN
Edward A.,Mar.7,1973,55y.
LOTHROP
Carolyn Ann,Mar.8,1942,2m.
Dora B.,Dec.12,1968,83y.
Edward H.,Feb.27,1971,92y.
LOVEITT
Clyde,Nov.24,1970,76y.
Ruth A.,June 28,1979,83y.
LOVELL
Alfreda F. Crosby,Oct.2,1911,74y, w/o Samuel W.
Henrietta,Feb.11,1901,45y,w/o N.B.
Eliza F.,Jan.28,1897,58y.
Samuel,Oct.14,1913
LOWE
Augustus,July 17,1918,62y.
Marlene W.,Dec.23,1988,53y.
Wilma B.,Jan.29,1991,66y.
LOWELL
Allie L.,Nov.15,1932,77y.
Alice S.,Aug.8,1982,65y.
Eliza F.,Jan.28,1897,58y.
Elmer E.,Feb.13,1953,83y.
Ernestine L.,Mar14,1966,67y.

Florence L., Oct.13,1973,87y.
George E.,Nov.9,1929,56y.
George R.,Apr.9,1977,68y.
Grace C.,Nov.28,1959,83y.
Harriet E.,1816-1892,w/o Thos.
Harry L. Sept.18,1955,77y.
Hartley I.,Aug.30,1919,3y, s/o Elmer & Grace.
Henrietta, Feb.11,1901,45y.
Katherine J.,Mar.15,1991,27y.
Mabel H.,Oct.3,1991,84y.
Myrtle M.,Aug.7,1985,89y.
Newell B.,Dec.9,1938,84y.
Ottalie I.,Nov.11,1943,65y.
Robert R.,May 12,1979,64y.
Stella C., Apr.6,1988,68y.
Stephen S.,Sept.19,1915,78y.
Thomas,1808-1887.
Walter E.,Dr.,June 10,1952,66y.
LUCAS
Anne M.,Feb.26,1976,65y.
Augustus H.,Dec.28,1943,79y.
James C.,Feb.5,1980.
Lily H.,Apr.11,1947,71y.
Margaret C.,May 22,1944,73y.
LUGDON
Lynwood M.,Jr.,Aug.29,1965,21y.
LUKE
Flora B.,June 20,1992,82y.
Francis A.,Feb.25,1994,68y.
Francis E.,July 14,1978, 2y.
LUND
Fred J.,July 20,1964,92y.
Mabel E.,July 4,1953,78y.
LUNT
Walter N.,Jan.28,1964,53y.
LYNCH
Ernest H.,May 22,1944,65y.
Lester R.,Apr.2,1994,89y.
LYNN
Marcia I.,Nov.11,1972,77y.
LYONS
Florence S.,Jan.17,1961,75y.
MAASBYLL
Lillian P.,May 29,1940,64y.
Peter J.,June 14,1941,69y.
MacCORMICK
Agnes H.,Mar.24,1982.
Charles A.,Mar.27,1930,36y.
Margaret, Oct.17,1967,86y.
MacDONALD
A.Joseph,June 6,1988,72y,
Alexander,May 11,1968,61y.
Alice S.,Aug.25,1969,88y.
Angus K.,June 7,1932,64y.
David O.,Oct.8,1987,44y.
Franklin H.,bu:Oct.16,1936,91y.

Helen P.,June 10,1943,7m.
Herbert M.,Jr.,Sept.2,1982.
Mary F.,Oct.15,1933,50y.
Norman A.,Aug.19,1848,68y.
Norwood,July 29,1955,45y.
MACE
Charles W.,Apr.25,1924,83y.
Clementine L. Wells,1820-1878.
Jane Elder,bu:Sept.18,1912,68y.
Timothy H.,1846-1877.
Timothy L.,1809-1876.
MacFARLAND
Charles W.,Apr17,1896,4m.
MacHARDY
John A.,Feb.18,1977,69y.
MacKAY
Virginia Lee,July 22,1951,35y.
MacKENZIE
Mary E.,Dec 7,1978,70y.
Ruel D.,July 1,1981,78y.
MacLEOD
Kenneth L.,Feb.17,1978,70y.
MacMILLAN
Deborah E.,July 15,1973,9y.
Doris E.,Feb.20,1984,63y.
William,Mar.20,1979,76y.
MacPHERSON
Grace C.,Nov.4,1962,75y.
William L., Aug.19,1946,67y.
MacQUARRIE
Alexander,May 4,1929,68y.
Clarence S.,bu:July 11,1941,71y.
MADDOCKS
Dexter H.,Mar.28,1986,82y.
Helen E.,Jan.12,1986,83y.
MADDOX
Alice May,1892-1894.
Ella M.,May 3,1922,55y.
Ethel L.,Oct.5,1916,22y.
Sanford A.,Sept.28,1930,74y.
MADSON
Arthur A.,July 6,1956,66y.
Charles,Feb.2,1937,76y.
Charles A.,Dec.16,1934,47y.
Eva L., child, can't read stone.
Isabelle,Feb.12,1912,57y.
Lena A.,1855-1896.
Mads C.,Dec.20,1929,77y.
MAGILL
Alexander,Aug.7,1966,69y.
Margaret L.,Jan.3,1961,61y.
MAHONEY
Sandra J.,July 31,1981,27y.
MAIN
Charles,July 9,1986,93y.
Eva May,Sept.7,1944,70y.
Florence L.,Oct.16,1975,82y.

Hazel L.,May 25,1979,85y.
Lettie E.,Sept.6,1943,68y.
Mildred T.,July 24, 1957,70y.
MAKOWSKI
Adele M.,May 16,1939,55y.
MALIA
infant,Nov.30,1972,s.b.
Irene,Oct.15,1974,54y.
MALLORY
David W.,Nov.2,1958,63y.
MALNICK
Paul P.,Apr.16,1962.
MALONE
Marshall, Jr.,Aug.30,1984,1m.
MANCHESTER
Agnes D.,June 3,1977,76y.
Anna C.,Jan.20,1975,77y.
Arthur,June 18,1957,94y.
Arthur L.,Sept.25,1957,68y.
Bertrand D.,Feb.11,1951,73y.
Emma M.,June 27,1984,88y.
Harold U.,Jan.24,1981,83y.
Helen Ridley,Mar.13,1942,79y.
Herbert,bu:Aug.9,1941,81y.
Howard,Jan.21,1974,74y.
Julia L.,bu: Jan.2,1960,96y.
Lovisa M.,Sept.18,1931,53y.
Rupert S.,Jan.14,1968,67y.
Stephen W.,July 11,1918,31y.
Violet M.,May 18,1988,96y.
MANNING
infant,Nov.13,1961.
MANSFIELD
Isiah,Jan.25,1913,66y.
Sarah Mason,Feb.18,1913,53y, w/o Isiah.
MAQUIRE
Priscilla M.,July 31,1991,78y.
Stanley O.,Aug.13,1982,64y.
MARABITO
Patricia,Apr.28,1938,1m.
MAREAN
Albert E.,July 20,1957,55y.
Emma L.,Mar.22,1973,74y.
Harold C.,Oct.29,1983,81y.
MARION
Anna T.,Jan.20,1973,85y.
Ned T.,Nov.15,1948,38y.
MARKOS
Calliope,Aug.1,1984,80y.
George,Sept.27,1970,88y.
infant,Mar.11,1936,prem.
MARR
Charles A.,Oct.6,1920,83y.
MARRINER
Mahaloth Ann,June 10,1961,77y.

MARSH
Dorothy Elwell,Feb.26,1936,28y.
William H.,Dec.17,1977,55y.
MARSHALL
Ida E.,July 27,1957,84y.
infant,May 28,1946,5 hrs.
Mary,1884-1911,d/o John & Helen.
MARSTERS
Emma L.,Aug.16,1959,71y.
Errold W.,Nov.12,1987,72y.
Harry L.,July 26,1964,76y.
MARSTON
Anna I.,Sept.14,1988,66y.
David H.,Feb.22,1982,60y.
Edward,Nov.26,1962,71y.
Ernest K.,May 18,1994,44y.
Eva G.,Apr.21,1954,70y.
Grace D.,July 29,1990,86y.
Virginia Alice,Jan.19,1919,4y,
 d/o Eva Bailey Marston.
MARTIN
Alonzo B.,Feb.14,1948,78y.
Cecil,Sept.7,1981,75y.
Doris M.,Nov.28,1977,73y.
Dorothy L.,July 28,1963,52y.
Eben E.,Mar.31,1973,70y.
Elizabeth P.,Jan.13,1953,83y.
John H.,July 23,1955,81y.
Katherine,Sept.27,1975,52y.
Laura J.,May 21,1974,53y.
Maggie,May 10,1970,87y.
Mame C.,Aug.24,1975,92y.
Maud E.,bu:Oct.20,1965,74y.
Nellie Emma,June 26,1940,61y.
Orin R.,Nov.27,1967,87y.
Percy L.,Oct.10,1980,85y.
Roland C.,Feb.22,1983,79y.
Terry Eugene,Jan.3,1952.
Wilbur L.,Dec.22,1963,83y.
MASON
Fred H.,July 12,1961,76y.
Ida M.,Sept.24,1972.
Mattheau D.,Oct.5,1981,1y.
Raymond C.,Mar.10,1950,43y.
MATTHEWS
Alfred J.,Jan.7,1947,63y.
Burt T.,Dec.2,1952,71y.
Ernest L.,Nov.12,1961,76y.
Ethel M.,Mar.22,1972,88y.
Ina E.,Nov.5,1940,53y.
Jane,Nov.22,1934,75y.
Josephine G.,May 4,1955.
Mildred,Aug.17,1911,23y.
Susan,Feb.25,1931,78y.
Thomas,Dec.11,1918,63y.
Walter H.,Oct.30,1922,32y.
William,1843-1897.

MAXIM
Harriet L.,Sept.4,1945,60y.
MAXWELL
Cora B.,Aug.19,1899,33y.
Edward H.,Nov.12,1987,81y.
Elsie M.,Sept.3,1974,87y.
Erving O.,Oct.17,1959,82y.
Phebe,Sept.10,1921,83y.
R. Pauline,Nov.12,1987,82y.
MAY
Amy G.,June 9,1949,49y.
Cecil G.,Feb.21,1968,75y.
Charles S.,May 28,1966,70y.
Dorothy,Nov.13,1994,78y.
Homerine D.,Feb.7,1979,70y.
John H.,May 1,1966,83y.
John H.,July 31,1981,77y.
Libbie K.,Apr.10,1966,80y.
Lilly N.,Dec.29,1942,
Orrin B.,Feb.24,1926,65y.
Roland M.,Apr.23,1920,s.b.
MAYE
Alonzo W.,July 3,1956,56y
infant,Aug.27,1944.
John,Feb.20,1938,1d.
Lois B.,Nov.13,1969,70y.
MAYBERRY
Alice, Apr.2,1992,76y.
Avis M.,July 7,1985,62y.
Earl E.,Aug.28,1971,75y.
Edward L.,Sept.26,1994,93y.
Elizabeth E.,May 9,1916,72y.
Elizabeth,Sept.29,1939,77y.
Florence,1905,d/o Lewis & Elizab.
George,Nov.13,1910,58y.
Hattie L.,Feb.12,1960,66y.
Helen G.,May 26,1916,44y,w/o Edwin.
Isabel Plummer,July 7,1914,50y.
James L.,1846-1869.
James,Jr.,1869-1869.
Lewis A.,bu:Aug.11,1931,71y.
Mary M. Hall,Apr.21,1898,75y,
 w/o Simon.
Nelson,Mar.2,1905,68y.
Orlando,July 12,1942,79y.
Rachael B.,Apr.30,1985,83y.
Simon H.,Oct.8,1902,84y.
Willard,June 15,1925,48y.
Willard,Jr.,Oct.13,1914,5d.
William J.,1897,s/o Lewis & Elizab.
MAYO
Clifford,Apr.22,1936.
Edith L.,bu:Nov.27,1950,87y.
H. Louise,Oct.9,1935,18y.
James E.,June 22,1935,rem.
 from Naples in 1936.

McALLISTER
Gladys,Feb.21,1931,38y.
McALONEY
Antonia Marie,Oct.1,1956,67y.
Cecil G.,July 19,1984,90y.
James H.,1860-1897.
J. Milburn,Sept.9,1923,30y.
John E.,July 7,1916,60y.
Margaret,1857-Aug.30,1898, w/o Jamess H.
Susie S., Aug.14,1957,84y.
McARTHUR
William J.,Mar.25,1929,65y.
McBAIN
infant,Oct.29,1929,prem.
McBRIDE
Charles,Sept.5,1915,prem.
Charles H.,May 5,1962,83y.
child,Sept.7,1915,0y.
Katherine E.,Aug.9,1973,70y.
Nora M.,Aug.27,1965,81y.
Robert H.,Feb.22,1971,64y.
McCANN
Addie M.,1836-1876,w/o David.
Arabelle Hall,July 11,1951,90y.
Carrie A.,May 15,1960,93y.
David N.,1826-Nov.30,1903.
Frank H.,Oct.25,1946,83y.
Sarah J.,1836-1890,w/o David.
McCARNEY
Marion S.,Jan.22,1989,89y.
Thomas,Sept.3,1957.
McCARTHY
Edward Francis,Feb.8,1924,1m.
Ellen,Jan.24,1923, s.b.
Michael E.,Oct.25,1950,66y.
Susan Hooper,Nov.30,1952,70y.
McCLELLAN
Annie,1878-1904.
Charles,1878-1890.s/o J. & M.
George B.,1889-1890,s/o J.& M.
infant,XXXX.
John E.,Feb.23,1952,75y.
James,May 15,1915,71y.
Jospehine E.,Jan.4,1924,39y.
Lucille,Nov.1,1916,51y,w/o Chas.
Lucy W.,1858-Feb.21,1906.
Margaret E.,Nov.18,1993,89y.
Martha,Feb.26,1884,42y,w/o Jas.
Mattie,1873-1891,d/o Jas. & M.
Samuel,1879-1902.
McCLOSKEY
Catherine,Dec.19,1911,76y.
Robert,Jan.7,1901,51y.
McCLURE
Walter T.,May 30,1987,65y.

McCONKEY
Beulah G.,June 14,1993,82y.
Frank L.,Dec.4,1968,60y.
McCORMACK
Archibald F.,Mar.13,1934,62y.
Teresa L.,Feb.7,1965,84y.
Thomas,bu:Dec.7,1956,57y.
McCUBREY
Alice, July 31897,7y.
Arthur L.,Apr.3,1960,82y.
Charlotte C.,Oct.20,1971,76y.
Dale J.,Sept.18,1977,29y.
Frances H.,Jan.22,1987,68y.
Fred S.,Aug.23,1914,11y.
George A.,Mar.7,1983,70y.
infant,Nov.6,1918, s. b.
James Winlsow,Aug.4,1940,69y.
Margaret I.,Jan.6,1988,90y.
Peter L.,Sept.2,1972,23y.
Raymond S.,May 29,1963,66y.
Robert W.,Dec.6,1966,71y.
Sally H.,Dec.18,1962,83y.
Vienna E.,May 31,1948,76y.
Warren,July 28,1896,5m.
McCUE
Sally A,May 27,1994,61y.
McCURDY
Mary S.,June 16,1975,73y.
McDADE
Elizabeth J.,Feb.4,1986,65y.
Roger W., Apr.17,1991,65y.
Susie M.,Nov.2,1980,90y.
William,May 1,1965,85y.
McDONALD
infant,Aug.13,1943.
McDONOUGH
Alice M., Apr.4,1939,58y.
Idella M.,Mar.6,1974,85y.
John J.,Sept.16,1957,68y.
McDOUGALL
Alice C.,May 18,1926,68y.
Arthur,Sept.28,1944,83y.
Charles E.,Feb.7,1934,40y.
infant,Mar.5,1914,s.b.
Lester N.,Jan.19,1987,67y.
Marion B.,June 21,1977,86y.
Martha L.,Nov.23,1985,64y.
Miles N.,Jan.5,1937,42y.
McDUFFIE
George R.,Dec.14,1979,74y.
McENTIE
Alice C.,May 18,1926,68y.
Arthur,Sept.28,1944,83y.
Harlan P.,Apr.17,1918,23y.
infant,Mar.5,1914,1d.
Thomas P.,Apr.3,1937,72y.

McELROY
Barbra I.,July 25,1973,52y.
Frank L.,Aug.1,1956,81y.
Viola B.,May 13,1949,70y.
McFARLAND
Andrew J.,Aug.22,1919,67y.
Arthur P.,June 5,1958,73y.
Bessie J.,Feb.27,1936,69y.
Carrie M.,Dec.30,1963,74y.
Charles M.,Apr.17,1896,4m.
Clara E.,1865-1910,w/o John W.
Clayton E.,Dec.31,1955,54y.
David,Jan.6,1946,49y.
Earl K.,Mar.20,1968,76y.
Fannie E.,May 26,1958,62y.
Harriet L.,Jan.17,1962,72y.
Harry,June 23,1971,82y.
Jennie M.,Jan.20,1923,59y.
John W.,Nov.7,1941,88y.
King S.,May 14,1940,77y.
Mabel A.,Apr.13,1947,48y.
McGAFFEY
Arthur W.,Dec.15,1971,89y.
Coffin Q.,Aug.26,1919,87y.
Lillian A.,Oct.10,1946,86y.
Lillian W.,Jan.28,1977,91y.
Sarah B.,May 26,1899,70y.
William A.,June 4,1935,79y.
McGLINCHEY
Jean L.,Sept.5,1961,35y.
McGOWEN
infant, Apr.16,1924,1d.
McGUIRE
Clara, Mar.1,1937,79y.
McHARDY
infant, Aug.8,1929, s.b.
McINTYRE
Constance A.,Sept.3,1982,38y.
McKAY
Maurice K.,Dec.25,1967,68y.
Peter Edwin,July 24,1925,54y.
Violet M.,May 24,1981,77y.
McKEAGUE
Charles B.,July 14,1953,68y.
Ella F.,Oct.19,1926,56y.
Ella F.,Feb.27,1937,74y.
Harry L.,May 1,1978,79y.
Laura C.,Jan.6,1925,29y.
Mildred,Nov.27,1976,80y.
Paul A.,Apr.19,1991,70y.
Thomas D.,Sept.10,1962,68y.
McKEEN
Frances E.,Apr.27,1977,60y.
Ida B.,Sept.5,1946,81y.
McKENNY
Bion,Sept.23,1915,57y.
Gerald E.,Apr.28,1914,3m.
H. Marie,Dec.22,1986,71y.
John L., Apr.22,1993,58y.
Mary,bu:Feb.18,1931,74y.
infant,Dec.25,1892,1y.
McKENZIE
Doris J. Oct.18,1980,79y.
George J.,removed from
St.Hyacinthe Cem. Dec. 1937.
John S.,Feb. 23,1945,72y.
Mary E.,Mar.26,1941,90y.
Stanley E.,Jan.18,1939,47y.
William Chesley,July 4,1931,46y.
William D.,Sept.6,1914,71y.
McLEAN
Alexander,Dec.26,1914,64y.
Margaret,May 31,1920.
McLEART
Robert Gordon,Jan.16,1919,4y.
McKINLEY
Blair R.,Feb.7,1951,52y.
Frieda B.,Mar.4,1984,73y.
Mildred F.,May 23,1985,76y.
Paul R.,Nov.15,1960,15y.
Philip B.,May 24,1966,28y.
Victor M.,Apr.29,1982,76y.
McLAUGHLIN
Daisey W.,May 5,1963,80y.
John Jenner,Sept.21,1966,80y.
McLEAN
Alexander,Dec.26,1914,64y.
Gordon,Jan.14,1919,34y.
Margaret,May 28,1920,66y.
McLEESE
Woodrow W.,Feb.2,1989,72y.
McLELLAN
Ada May,Jan.31,1928,46y.
Annie S.,Oct.21,1947,75y.
Charles M.,bu:Nov.21,1937,57y.
Lucille W.,Oct.30,1916,51y.
Maude M.,Nov.18,1986,102y.
Maude Swan,Sept.13,1922,46y.
Wesley M.,bu:Apr.11,1937.
McLUCAS
Annie M.,Mar.8,1965,71y.
Preston J.,Feb.17,1962,78y.
McMANUS
Ida M.,June 4,1933,63y.
John,Sept.29,1924,78y.
McMILLAN
Winifred A. Sept.7,1933,38y.
McNAIR
Edith M.,Sept.12,1964,71y.
Elizabeth Scott,Sept.18,1938,75y.
James D.,July 9,1911,25y.
James,July 9,1911,25y.
Jean L.,Mar.26,1978,70y.
William A.,Apr.1,1966,79y.

William A.,Jr.,Aug.9,1964,43y.
William,Oct.7,1929,70y.
McNALLY
Margaret,Sept.2,1927,52y
McNEIL
Bridget A.,Dec.16,1985.
McPAIL
John B.,Aug.31,1994,84y.
McPHAIL
Benjamin,bu:Sept.16,1935,65y.
Bertha,Aug.8,1922,47y.
Irene A.,Apr.24,1975,62y.
Robert James,bu:Feb.28,1937,6m.
McPHEE
Belle M.,May 23,1925,56y.
Clyde H.,Jan.30,1943.
David Meredith,Aug.22,1939,5m.
William B.,Apr.6,1956,47y.
MEADE
Darla S.,May 6,1981,1m.
infant,July 15,1953,21hr.
MEEHANN
Alice E.,Mar.22,1961,80y.
Dennis J.,May 29,1973,21y.
Eliza C.,June 29,1906,54y.
George,Feb.21,1916,68y.
George A.,May 23,1948,69y.
Helen M.,Jan.26,1908,1y,d/o R.L.
Henry W.,Sept.23,1910,27y.
Ida M.,Dec.21,1970,86y.
Robert L.,Mar.23,1958,73y.
Saide A.,Mar.28,1954,74y.
Thomas,Sept.21,1943,66y.
MEGGISON
Alice L.,Feb.2,1947,37y.
Alton"Pat",Dec.17,1989,85y.
Ernest E.,June 15,1990,83y.
Forest L.,Feb.10,1968,70y.
Rachel H.,Dec.23,1993,86y, w/o Alton.
William C.,Nov.4,1951,37y.
MEGOUIER
Etta M. Walker,Aug.5,1925,66y.
MEIKLE
Patricia F.,July 20,1994,46y.
MELCHER
George Ward,Oct.5,1931,60y.
Laithe M.,Sept.3,1964,58y.
Mary A.,Mar.3,1979,55y.
Maud E.,Mar.15,1929,52y.
MELUSCIERWC
Harry,Aug.3,1933,67y.
MERRICK
Adena,Apr.26,1917,10y.
Ethel L.,Apr.13,1967,80y
Frank E.,Dec.23,1971,88y.

MERRILL
Annie Louise,1920,17w,d/o R. C.
Arthur E.,July 21,1935,20y.
Fred W.,Mar.16,1924,42y.
Helen A.,June 18,1987,77y.
infant,May 27,1930,prem.
Irving R.,Oct.21,1960,68y.
Lillian May,May 27,1930,36y.
Llewlyn Henry,June 15,1930,18d.
Mildred Alice,Sept.21,1932,30y.
Nancy Ann,Nov.22,1946,prem.
Nellie D.,Oct.8,1952,67y.
Pearl W.,May 27,1974,86y.
Percy B.,July 10,1993,77y.
Raymond W.,Aug.11,1952,46y.
Ralph C.,Feb.1,1961,67y.
Samuel P.,Feb.9,1898.
Warren P.,Nov.27,1992,73y.
Winifred A.,Nov.13,1959,43y.
MERRIMAN
George C.,Oct.28,1911,68y.
Leland E.,Apr.3,1960,22y.
Sarah G.,July 1,1894,50y.
MERRITT
Helen J.,June 5,1989,72y.
MERSERVE
Bertha E.,Aug.16,1957,69y.
Chester A.,Nov.14,1980,69y.
Irving,Jr.,Nov.18,1942,4m.
Nelson H.,Nov.29,1957,77y.
Richard Irving,Dec.24,1943,3m.
MESERVE
Emma,Aug17,1993,81y.
METCALF
Addie Verrill,Feb.17,1953,85y.
Agnes M.,May 18,1994,97y.
Carlton D.,Mar.18,1901.
George S.,June 30,1958,62y.
Nellie May,Sept.6,1932,57y.
Richard W.,May 7,1983,64y.
Winship B.,Aug.18,1955,81y.
MICHAUD
Rebecca & Tracey, 1962 & 1963, 1y & stillborn, rem. from St. Hyacinth in 1991.
MILES
Eva M.,Mar.27,1927,48y.
Morris B.,Aug.26,1926,48y.
MILLER
Addie B.,June 1,1944,60y.
Andrew,Mar.4,1932,77y.
Andrew J.,June 27,1954,75y.
Betsey,Feb.15,1935,81y.
Cornelius,Mar.31,1933,70y.
David,Feb.28,1958,81y.
Donald J.,Mar.2,1993,61y.
Dora E.,Jan.4,1941,86y.

Harry, H.,Dec.1,1919,40y.
Harvey Merritt,Sept.25,1918,29y
Herbertina W.,July 14,1953,68y.
Jessie E.,June 22,1959,77y.
John H.,June 3,1929,12y.
John J.,Mar.15,1930,83y.
Keith V.,Oct.3,1973,67y.
Lena Mae,1890-1890.
Lewis L.,Mar.14,1952,5m.
Margaret E.,Oct.9,1959,86y.
Margory M.,Mar.12,1916,4m.
Mary L., Apr.2,1977,89y.
Mary Olive Whitney,Aug.5,1913, w/o Noah.
Melony Dawn,Jan.3,1993,21y.
Mila Aug.13,1893,8y.
Mildred L.,Dec.1,1967,85y.
Noah,b.Nova Scotia,d.July 7,1920,72y.
Orrin L. Aug.25,1984,96y.
Phyllis E.,Oct.28,1979,71y.
Ralph "Drag",Jan.27,1988,83y.
Ralph W.,Feb.7,1944,66y.
Rosalie P.,Oct.27,1957,74y.
William T.,Dec.22,1954,79y.
Winnifred F.,Jan.17,1973,56y.
MILLETT
Elizabeth E.,Mar.19,1940,78y.
MILLIGAN
Ellen E.,July 4,1931,45y.
Harriet H.,Feb.24,1978,84y.
John T.,Dec.24,1954,62y.
MILLIONS
Agnes D.,1853-1883.
Arthur G.,1850-1891.
Ella E.,Oct.10,1967,92y.
Ella F.,1853-1868.
Ellen R.,May 15,1902,74y,w/o George.
Frank H.,Jan.20,1923,71y.
George,May 8,1901,79y.
Harry F.,1880-1912.
Jean, Apr.23,1979,87y.
Jennie M.,Jan.10,1939,82y.
Margaret J.,1887-1890.
MILLS
Gerald M.,June 11,1967,27y.
MILSTEAD
Barbara J.,Sept.16,1950,28y.
MILTON
Alice Jane,Dec.25,1928,64y,w/o David.
Catherine,May 14,1928,70y.
Charles R.,Nov.15,1956,65y.
Daisy M.,Sept.1,1979,76y.
David S.,Feb.11,1907,44y.
Edward Melvin,Dec 6,1928,4m.
James H.,Feb.13,1946,53y.
Lewis,Nov.7,1946,56y.
Reuben,May 7,1927,74y.

Robert W.,Jan.8,1970,70y.
Selina A.,Mar.27,1977,86y.
William,Sept.13,1899,4y.
MINA
Anastasia P.,Aug.15,1972,81y.
Thimi,rem. from Worcester 1963.
MINER
Howard A.,June 7,1968,71y.
MINNICK
Elizabeth, Feb. 27, 1908.
John F.,Mar.29,1942,83y.
John F.,Jr.,1899,1y.
Mariette,Oct.8,1923,78y.
Nellie,Nov.15,1892,21y.
Ralph,Jan.26,1901,5y,s/o John.
William,May 4,1904,68y.
Willie J.,July 16,1892,5m.
MITCHELL
Earle L.,Jan.16,1976,80y.
Ella K.,Sept.19,1939,65y.
Frank H.,June 19,1936,42y.
Jasper,June 10,1932, prem.
Jemina E.,Nov.4,1949,78y.
Nathaniel G.,Sept.4,1933, s.b.
Stanley S.,Feb.28,1956,56y.
Susan E.,May 26,1977,78y.
Willis P.,Feb.15,1956,80y.
MINSTER
Daniel L.,Aug.8,1974,80y.
Dorothy K.,Aug.28,1983,62y.
Effie M.,June 18,1983,91y.
MOCKLER
Cheryl A.,Nov.9,1942,6m.
John Lawrence Oct.12,1940,s.b.
MOERTL
Josef, July 25, 1975, 79y.
MOGAN
Arthur W.,Sept.24,1914, 16d.
Clara K.,Sept. 16,1923, 38y.
Harry C.,June 17,1982, 65y.
infant, Sept.1,1917, prem.
infant,Feb.10,1920, s.b.
Matthias F.,Nov.25,1944,57y.
MOODY
Alice M. Feb. 5,1942,67y.
Ann M.,Aug.14,1905,67y.
Arthur B.,Mar.15,1963,89y.
Bertha L.,Apr.9,1989,56y.
Clara E.,1866-1881.
George Allen,Jan.10,1942,78y.
Harris B.,Feb.2,1929,84y.
infant,May 11,1921,s.b.
infant,Nov.19,1936,s.b.
Leander,Aug.8,1901,70y.
MOORE
Almeda E.,Sept.24,1968,93y.
Cedric E.,Sr.,Nov.8,1989,88y.

Charles H.,Sept.16,1934,69y.
Charles R.,Sept.7,1980,80y.
Dorothy M.,Feb.25,1967,71y.
Eva J.,Nov.11,1962,76y.
Guy A.,Jan.22,1940,49y.
Harold C.,Sept.16,1960,61y.
Harry W.,Mar.18,1954,41y.
John C.,Apr.5,1933,61y.
Lois B.,Mar.8,1974,82y.
Margaret A.,Apr.13,1982,78y.
Norman Alva,Sept.15,1927,3m.
Olive T.,Aug.21,1989,91y.
Ruth E.,July 27,1980,58y.
William A.,Feb.26,1938,60y.
William, Jr.,June 5,1981,79y.
MORABITO
Madeline C.,Jan.23,1975,57y.
MORAN
Elizabeth M.,Sept.24,1988,65y.
MORELLI
Lisa,May 1,1980, s.b.
MOREY
Hellen M.S.,Dec.21,1977,86y.
Leonard, Sr.,Mar.15,1974,83y.
MORGAN
Ethel H.,Apr.8,1985,83y.
Jemima Burgh,Sept.8,1931,54y.
Mabel Bessie,Apr.2,1915.
Michael M.,Sept.8,1941,78y.
Sarah J.,Oct.20,1911,64y.
MORIN
J. August,Nov.20,1969,70y.
Katherine L.,Mar.18,1986,82y.
Laurice, Sept.11,1969,60y.
Theodore H.,Aug.18,1973,75y.
MORRELL
J. Lee,Sept.10,1941,54y.
John W.,Feb.12,1966,78y.
Susie H.,Nov 2,1973,96y.
Sylvia M.,Aug.29,1994,47y.
MORRILL
Ralph A., Aug.31,1955,55y.
Rose H.,May 25,1952,43y.
Vivian M.,July 26,1953,64y.
MORRIS
Annie W.,Sept.22,1942,84y.
MORRISON
Sylvia E.,May 8,1969,49y.
MORSE
Anna I.,May 31,1942,81y.
Charles E.,Mar.25,1959,55y.
Eden A.,Oct.8,1994,78y.
Edmund K.,Aug.6,1918,36y.
Edmund K.,July 23,1893,43y.
Ernest C.,Feb.21,1956,79y.
Judith K.,Apr.11,1968,20y.
Marcia,child, can't read stone.

Mary C.,Nov.28,1986,77y.
Merrill Everett,Dec.2,1942,2d.
Merrill L.,Sr.,May 15,1973,71y.
Robert E.,July 14,1985,53y.
Roger Alan,Jan.15,1987, s.b.
Russell K.,May 22,1979,67y.
Zella G.,Feb.5,1994,78y.
MORTON
Annie Stevens,May 20,1920,w/o C.S
Athea S.,June 3,1911,64y.
Edna V.,Oct.13,1983,90y.
Elmira D.,Nov.11,1979,84y.
Frances L.,Nov. 8,1962,67y.
George C.,May 11,1989,100y.
Harry H.,July 14,1964,72y.
Hattie,Sept.6,1903,20d.
infant,Jan.26,1924, s.b.
infant,can't read stone.
John,Mar.12,1993, 56y.
Leslie L.,July 9,1894,16d.
Lottie E.,Aug.1,1899,6m.
no name,Aug.30,1900,s.b.
Norman A.,June 21,1987,61y.
Seth Clark,Dec.19,1940,82y.
MOSHER
Edwin W.,Feb.17,1976,87y.
Florence A.,Sept.29,1974, 81y.
MOULTON
Alden,Jan.25,1880,35y.
Hardy A.,Jan.11,1933,62y.
Jannette,June 29,1911,38y,
during childbirth.
Olin C.,M.D.,Sept.27,1924,46y.
Olin C.,Jr.,M.D.,Feb.9,1985,76y.
Randall,July 10,1910,2m.
Teresa E.,May 2,1959,83y.
MULCAHY
Jessica C.,Oct.12,1985,3m.
MULKERN
Patrick J.,July 13,1981,64y.
MULLIGAN
Almond,1860-1891.
Edward Douglas,1826-1899.
MULLIN
Tena M., Sept.13,1947,44y.
MULVANY
Anna M.,Dec.7,1954,66y.
George A., June 18, 1962, 83y.
MUNRO
George C.,Dr.,Sept.3,1983,77y.
MUNROE
Clara S.,May 28,1983,82y.
MURCH
Charles G.,May 14,1974,71y.
Jeanette A.,Dec.8,1976,76y.
Valmot M.,July 28,1992,55y.

MURPHY
Delmont H.,Jr.,July 22,1987,72y.
Frances M.,July 12,1990,63y.
Helen M.,Aug.22,1969,66y.
Hilda M.,Oct.24,1960,57y.
infant,July 15,1967,s.b.
Johnson H.,June 21,1982.
MURRAY
Annie Marie,May 13,1935,3 hrs.
Bertrice E.,Sept.26,1965,64y.
Emily,Aug.6,1986,88y.
Fannie, Feb.18,1913,51y.
George D.,Sr.,Sept.26,1983,85y.
Hugh,Jan.21,1930,86y.
Irene Beatrice,Nov.30,1932,27y.
Jennie Abbie,Feb.26,1951,84y.
Margaret,Nov.24,1917,73y.
Nancy L.,Dec.10,1993,64y.
Neil,Dec.30,1928,65y.
Theodore F.,rem. from Calvary Cem., Portland, Aug.1933.
NADEAU
Eda F.,Apr.211993,81y.
Hector L., Sr.,Apr.23,1987,83y.
NASH
Morrill J.,Mar.1,1957,44y.
NASON
Annie L.,June 5,1899,28y.
Benjamin,Sept.30,1949,88y.
Frank B.,June 7,1917,31y.
Leo R.,Jan.11,1983,78y.
Lizzie M.,bu: Oct.3,1931,63y.
Paul A.,June 17,1983,70y.
Pearl L.,Feb.25,1991,90y.
William H., Aug.7,1964,91y.
William Huff,Feb.2,1924,60y.
NAUGHRITE
Alexander T.,Jan.24,1948.
Annie M.,July 20,1954,87y.
NAYLOR
Beatrice H.,Feb.9,1973,75y.
Edith Jane,Feb.7,1926,32y.
Fred H.,May 9,1929,60y.
Fred H.,Jr.,Dec.3,1973,76y.
George I.,Apr.8,1957,73y.
Grace E.,Sept.21,1937,45y.
inf/Wm. & Marion,June 12,1915, s.b.
infant,Mar.10,1930 s.b.
Julia G.,Oct.5,1947,81y.
Oden T.,Jr.,Mar.27,1945,26y, killed in action in Germany.
Oden T.,Oct.6,1945,52y.
Rubie E.,June 26,1957,63y.
Thomas,Oct.20,1914,62y.
Thomas J.,Sept.12,1893,7m, s/o Thomas &Julia.
Victoria R.,Apr.3,1913,45y.

Vivian Knipe,Dec.26,1930, rem. to Damascotta.
William R.,Major,May 20,1972, 77y, rem. to Virginia.
William R.,Jr.,Nov.11,1963, 25y, rem. to Virginia.
NEAL
John H.,Sept.6,1930,58y.
Lizzie M.,Feb.25,1929,67y.
Willis Warren,Oct.27,1931,76y.
NEARY
Robert D.,July 13,1977,25y.
NELSON
Amelia A.,Apr.3,1967,75y.
Anna,Sept.11,1985,96y.
Annie,1895-1897,d/o Mads & Maren.
Augusta M. Oct.13,1941,55y.
Bertrand B.,May 20,1978,74y.
Christian,Jan.20,1926,37y.
Clifton Howe,Apr.29,1906,10y, s/o Edwin & Ida.
Edward,Sept.8,1915,s.b.
Edward,Nov.25,1971,87y.
Edward R.,Nov.14,1938,11d.
Edward L.R.,May 26,1940,70y.
Evelyn,Aug.10,1904,6m.
Frank W.,Oct.25,1987,72y.
Frederick B.,Feb.4,1964,68y.
Hans H.,Aug.10,1970,83y.
Ida Dyer,Mar.15,1910,35y,w/o Edwin.
infant,Aug.18,1946,s.b.
James Irving,Jan.7,1914,10y.
John,Nov.24,1949,66y.
Kenneth A.,Aug.11,1975,67y.
Kenneth H.,Dec.10,1992,66y.
Maren, Oct.18,1942,88y.
Mildred S.,Dec.12,1992,70y.
Miriam C.,May 27,1990,74y.
Nels F.,July 1,1947,86y.
Ruby Eunice,May 5,1916,2y, d/o Christian & Sena.
Ruth C.,Mar.8,1969,66y.
NEVERS
Arthur W.,Aug.7,1978,50y.
Donald Staples,Feb.7,1943,4y.
George F.,May 16,1977,73y.
Georgia G.,May 8,1994,89y.
infant, June 17,1953,s.b.
Handy F.,Feb.6,1945,76y.
Handy F.,Mrs., rem. from Forest City Cem. Aug. 1945.
Kathleen D.,Feb.10,1991,59y.
Kenneth W.,June 27,1968,32y.
NEVILS
H.N.,June 3,1900,68y.
Mary R.,June 18,1896,64y.

NEWALL
infant,Mar.16,1930, s.b.
infant,Nov.25,1944.
NEWCOMB
George W.,June 18,1960,23y.
infant,Oct.26,1958.
Henry R.,Apr.2,1955,63y.
Mamie B.,Dec.27,1953,69y.
NEWHALL
Edna I.,Dec.26,1975,73y.
George D.,June 2,1989,91y.
Nettie M.,June 8,1949,79y.
Robert F.,Jan.25,1943,73y.
NEWTON
infant,July 7,1943, s.b.
NIELSEN
Abbie,Apr.11,1963,86y.
Arnold M.,June 5,1965,63y.
Einer,Apr.2,1927, 38y.
Henry Peter,June 29,1923,10y.
Hildur,Feb.5,1959,76y.
Jeanie J.,Oct.9,1981,92y.
Jennie,May 11,1964,86y.
Johanna C.,Mar.7,1949,61y.
Karen Mary,Mar.16,1972,80y.
Lawrence I.,Aug.27,1978,64y.
Lillian S.,July 1,1985,83y.
Mildred C.,Sept.28,1973,65y.
N. Peter,Nov.7,1977,89y.
Mads Nelson,May 27,1922,70y.
Peter M.,Nov.14,1936,58y.
Peter P.,Oct.21,1942,35y.
Rasmus,June 8,1967,86y.
Roland C.,Dec.16,1989,77y.
NIES
Albert B.,Sept.24,1955,64y.
Gladys B.,Apr.31,1989,97y.
NIXON
Inez M.,Mar.12,1978,89y.
Violett E.,Oct.1,1991,76y.
NICHOLAS
James J.,Oct.30,1988,67y.
NICHOLS
Clara E.,July 10,1895,1y.
Clyde H.,June 6,1959,72y.
NOACK
Arno,Oct.6,1993,91y.
NODEN
Catherine E.,May 23,1987,70y.
John R.,Nov.14,1971,84y.
Joseph L.,Aug.29,1965,21y.
Lillian H.,Aug.29,1954,69y.
NORBERG
Ralph L.,Feb.23,1994,53y.
NORBERT
Carl E.,May 8,1971,57y.
Clinton,June 20,1992,72y.

Daniel F.,Dec.2,1970,s.b.
Doris A.,July 20,1987,66y.
Frank J.,Dec.22,1943,59y.
Gladys M.,Oct.17,1986,68y.
infant,May 24,1926, s.b.
Susie E.,Sept.19,1986,85y.
NORDFORS
Scott T.,Feb.17,1993,32y.
NORGARD
infant,May 20,1972,s.b.
Mary,Jan.23,1921,45y.
NORRIS
Beryl A.,Oct.12,1974,38y.
NORTON
Alice F.,Mar.3,1960,86y.
Arthur H.,Jan.5,1943.
Asamath E.,Jan.1,1935,86y.
Francis L.,Nov.4,1962,67y.
Fred A.,Oct.19,1959,79y.
Grace H.,Aug.25,1964,86y.
Henry L.,1868-1891.
Horace F.,Nov.29,1911,68y.
Mary B.,Apr.8,1934,62y.
May,Sept.6,1894,5m.
Ralph H.,Dec.26,1960,85y.
Ruth V.,June 26,1961,69y.
Sophia M.,Mar.21,1926,84y.
Stephen R.,1866-1906.
Zimri D.,1831-1876.
NOYES
Albert S.,Nov.7,1969,68y.
Charles W. Oct.16,1877,41y,
rem. from Saccarappa Cem.1917.
Elma B.,June 16,1986,88y.
George P.,Aug.27,1946,53y.
Helen E.,Sept.29,1922,81y.
NUTE
Helen,Feb.21,1923,80y.
O'BRIEN
Edward,Oct.8,1946,67y.
Edward M. Aug.31,1984,78y.
Geraldine D.,July 18,1994,46y.
Hebert S.,1862-July 10,1892.
Lizzie B.,Dec.31,1963,82y.
Marion,July 25,1985,79y.
Meloney Ann,Oct.20,1961,4m.
William E.,Dec.24,1957,68y.
O'BRION
Rae,Sept.13,1927,42y.
O'CONNOR
Minnie C.,Jan.2,1931,48y.
OHLSTEN
infant,Aug.23,1958,2d.
OLMSTEAD
Mary S.,Dec.13,1939,86y.
OLDREAD
John,1889,39y.

OLSEN
Alice A.,Mar.3,1920,prem.
Bertha G.,Oct.5,1959,59y.
Carl E.,Aug.6,1989,78y.
Louise,Oct.13,1944,45y.
Ralph W.,Apr.23,1964,66y.
Rose M.,Mar.10,1972,85y.
O'NEAL
Helen M.,Apr.10,1933,82y.
Michael,Dec.29,1923,79y.
OSBORNE
Edmond P.,May 12,1921,48y.
Susanne G.,June 9,1963,82y.
OSGOOD
Elizabeth C.,Jan.16,1972,75y.
Maynard L.,Feb.16,1980,88y.
O'SHEI
Sylvia T.,Aug.1,1965,29y.
OSMOND
Oscar L.,Aug.10,1981,57y.
OTIS
Ann F.,July 1,1971,27y.
Harrison M.,Dec.29,1978,89y.
Mary C.,May 28,1983,92y.
OWENS
Helen A.,Oct.31,1980,22y.
OXNARD
Eunice,Mar.16,1923,62y.
William A.,Nov.7,1922,56y.
PACKARD
Edwin R.,Oct.19,1971,73y.
wilma E.,Dec.31,1994,101y.
PAINE
Florence E.,Nov.1,1973,75y.
Leon K.,Nov.3,1950,78y.
Mary E.,Oct.29,1948,78y.
PALMER
Beatrice R.E.,Dec.21,1924,15y.
Daniel Seymore,Jan.19,1933,80y.
Dorothy,Sept.4,1985,80y.
Grace V.,July 9,1964,68y.
John F.,Feb.17,1902,76y.
Kenneth R.,1895,2m,s/o D.& Annie.
Mary C.,Aug.15,1951,74y.
Mary L.M.,July 15,1930,78y.
Miriam C.,July 11,1944,89y.
Nathan,1840-1891.
Rowena M.,1893,3m,ch/o D. & A.
Roy R.,Nov.18,1972,88y.
Sadie Knight,Jan.9,1930,40y.
William H.,July 26,1968,75y.
PAPERDOPOULUS
Kalupe D.(Peters),June 27,1917,26y.
PAPPAS
Lewis N.,Feb.27,1957,70y.
Pota L.,May 21,1932,45y.

PARDI
Anthony S.,Feb.4,1994,50y.
PARENT
Clinton E.,Jan.19,1963,77y.
Marie E.,Sept.29,1953,74y.
PARK
Fred W.,Nov.27,1977.
PARKER
Abbie,M.D.,June 6,1948,91y.
Albert L.,Aug.18,1935,81y.
Alvin L.,Jan.31,1907,67y,
  s/o James & Sally.
Ann D.,Sept.8,1969,69y.
Annie M.,Apr.1,1934,67y.
Annie M.,Feb.20,1994,86y.
Bernice M.,Mar.7,1986,89y.
Carl Rust,Nov.29,1966,84y.
Eliza A.,Oct.31,1945,89y.
Emma D.,1861-Sept.21,1893,w/o W.H.
Ernest H.,Dec.29,1946,53y.
Everett R.,Sept.27,1963,63y.
Florence A.,bu:Apr.6,1962,76y.
Frank H.,Feb.5,1915,56y.
Frank Lester,July 14,1932,72y.
Harriett M.,bu:May 8,1947.
Harry H.,1878-1891,
  s/o Phinias & Dora L.
Howard L.,Feb. 28,1923,4d.
Ida Greenlaw,Oct.31,1928,69y.
Leon V.,M.D.,Dec.11,1922,39y.
Mabel A.,Aug.1,1985,104y.
Mary W.,Dec.5,1963,58y.
Maurice H.,Jan.31,1959,60y.
Nellia A.,July 28,1930,67y.
Nellie D.,Feb.2,1951,83y.
Phineas C.,Sept.15,1892,41y.
Preston C.,July 28,1930,60y.
Sarah Jane Twitchell,Aug.9,1908,
  73y, w/o Alvin L.
Theodore,July 10,1940,79y.
Wesley T.,Jan.7,1972,77y.
William H.,Mar.28,1971,61y.
PARKHURST
Abbie M.,Feb.17,1920,40y.
Charles S.,May 11,1921,41y.
Forrest W.,Mar.6,1992,92y.
Leroy G.,Mar.28,1974,57y.
Marion K.,Nov.29,1931,77y.
Mary,Nov.1,1991,85y.
Mildred L.,July 29,1972,84y.
PARLIN
Scott S.,Sept.3,1972,1y.
Susanne H.,June 14,1960,96y.
PARSONS
Albert H. Oct.5,1935,40y.
Annie J. Sept.7,1931,68y.
Everette W.,Jan.10,1917,15y.

Fay Fuller,Mar.9,1916,24y.
George A.,May 28,1914,57y.
George A.,Jr.,1880-Nov.29,1903.
Harry A.,Feb.1,1933,73y.
Nellie E.,Aug.8,1946,85y.
PARTRIDGE
Hazel A.,July 22,1986,89y.
Seth L. June 21,1983,86y.
PASS
Carrie B.,Nov.2,1969,69y.
Joseph,Mar.31,1945,52y.
PATCH
Annette W.,Mar.13,1933,89y.
PATENAUDE
Clara N. Sept.27,1972,99y.
Nelson A.,Sept.6,1940,83y.
PATRIDGE
James W.,Aug.7,1953,84y.
Josie M.,Dec.22,1963,91y.
PATTERSON
James H.,Sept.11,1954,92y.
Mary E. June 9,1928,56y.
PAUL
Herbert N.,Apr.18,1973,84y.
Margaret A.,Nov.20,1984.
PAULSEN
David L.,Mar.21,1976,22y.
Pauline L.,Sept.15,1992,97y.
Walter,Jan.5,1973,83y.
PAYNE
Alice H.,Oct.13,1981,84y.
Cyrus V.,Mar.3,1946,85y.
Howard F.,1890,infant.
Sarah J.,Mar.31,1926,65y.
PEARSON
Edgar T.,July 7,1981,63y.
Frances M.,Dec.27,1935,69y.
infant,July 29,1943,3 mins.
PEASE
Blanche G. Oct.25,1976,89y.
Everett A.,Sr. Oct.2,1972,78y.
Fred A.,June 3,1955,58y.
George,Sept.3,1915, s.b.
George E.,Mar.20,1946.
Gladys V.,Aug.11,1971,78y.
Rose A.,Oct.22,1956,68y.
PEASLEY
Charles R.,Sept.21,1939,85y.
Elizabeth,Nov.3,1950,72y.
Irving C.,Jr.,Nov.24,1931,8y.
Irving C.,Aug.9,1939,40y.
PECK
Ernest O.,Sept.19,1944.
James S.M.,Dec.31,1975,80y.
Ruby Davis,Dec.2,1981,78y.
PEFFER
Christine L.,Aug.8,1966,81y.

Richard,Sept.19,1990,71y.
PELLERIN
Glena E.,Dec.2,1962,69y.
Joseph L.,Mar.14,1960,84y.
PENDER
Frank, Apr.25,1915,62y.
PENDEXTER
Edward E.,Aug.20,1970,59y.
Guilford F.,Feb.3,1985.
Ingrid,Feb.24,1993,78y.
Myrtle G.,June 1,1969,65y.
PENDLETON
Harriet Shaw,Dec.15,1918,21y.
Mary,Mar.30,1935,prem.
Richard E.,Aug.19,1943,16d.
Richard H.,Dec.14,1976,77y.
PENLEY
Anna J.,July 23,1992,86y.
Dorothy L.,May 12,1993,64y.
Ellery O.,Sept.9,1989,86y.
Lillian M.,May 25,1963,66y.
PENNELL
Adelaide F.,May 30,1937,66y.
Albert G.,Nov.16,1955,46y.
Catherine Martin,1830-1871,w/o Jas.
Clifford B.,Sept.20,1951,66y.
Duisilla T.,Nov.5,1929,81y.
Edward S.,Feb.24,1924,80y.
Ella L.,May 20,1958,70y.
Elmer E.,bu: Oct. 5,1937,77y.
Frank H.,Sept.19,1917,62y.
Irene C.,Nov.14,1923,35y.
Irving R.,Mar.23,1948,71y.
James,Jan.27,1903,84y.
Jane M.,May 17,1907,73y,w/o Jas.
Janice I.,Jan.8,1980,42y.
Jennie F.,June 25,1940,80y.
Margaret R.,July 11,1956,42y.
May Emery,Dec.3,1921,49y.
Merle S.,Oct.31,1964,84y.
Pauline T.,Apr.2,1974,89y.
Pearl C.,May 14,1965,82y.
Richard E.,May 13,1986,77y.
William J.,Oct.4,1926,71y.
William Lewis,July 10,1931,46y.
PERCIVAL
infant,bu: Aug.29,1938, s.b.
Ralph N.,Sept.24,1979,69y.
PERCY
Edith H., Apr.19,1972,87y.
Harold M.,July 8,1958,71y.
William J.,June 27,1895,38y.
PERKINS
Bessie E.,June 2,1957,76y.
Clifford T.,Dec.25,1942,47y.
Elsie P.,Jan.3,1943,49y.
Robert Joseph,Mar.12,1960,2y.

PERRIN
Ina Swan,Oct.12,1973,86y.
PERRY
Alfred K.,Aug.3, 968,60y.
Beatrice M.,bu:May 11,1950,46y.
Elsie G.,Oct.20,1982,86y.
Harry,May 9,1976,90y.
Hazel M.,Aug.31,1964,70y.
infant,Dec.30,1942,s.b.
infant,Feb.13,1962, s.b.
Irene L.,Nov.10,1943,12y.
Mary A.,Aug.13,1958,74y.
Maud M.,June 20,1919,2d.
Melville C.,Aug.6,1966,86y.
Mildred S.,July 15,1962,71y.
Thomas B.,May 5,1991,96y.
Ward M.,June 21,1919,2d.
Warren R.,Feb. 3,1974,82y.
PETERS
Alexandra T.,bu:May 5,1964,9y.
Barbara,Nov.12,1990,73y.
Charles L.,Aug.13,1962,81y.
Chris,July 8,1993,85y.
Christina,May 28,1933,87y.
Evelyn M.,Sept.21,1992,79y.
Harry A.,Oct.27,1964,63y.
Henry J.,Feb.17,1989.
Kaliepe D. Paperdepimlos,
June 27,1917, 26y.
Kostas L.,Feb.21,1921,43y.
Mildred E.,Aug.14,1969,57y.
Mildred R.,Aug.21,1976,87y.
Panoyota L.,Dec.29,1965,73y.
Thomas A.,Feb.19,1943,6m.
Walter N.,Apr.5,1965,72y.
William Timothy,Jan.30,1938,8m.
PETERSEN
Alice G.,June 28,1944,80y.
Anne C.,Dec.1,1954,83y.
Annie G.,Jan.23,1945,50y.
Catherine I.,Mar.31,1992,83y.
Charles A.,1860-June 1907.
Frederick H.,Aug.21,1957,87y.
Hans,1861-1913.
Hans J.,July 10,1962,66y.
Harriet F.,1830-1896,w/o Wm.C.
Jakobine T.,1853-1925,w/o Chas.A.
Kristina,Aug.1,1940,85y.
Lars C.,July 12,1935,85y.
Marie D.,Apr.24,1980,86y.
Marie T.,1876-1913.
Martin,Oct.10,1985,92y.
Mary K.,Apr.9,1963,83y.
Olivia,Sept.17,1938,84y.
Peter H.,June 26,1944,61y.
PETERSON
Adelbert D.,Apr.21,1922,85y.
Andrew M.,June 5,1965,80y.
Arthur C.,Nov.11,1961,76y.
Axel,Mar.8,1958,76y.
babies,1893 & 1897.
Bernice E.,Dec.5,1971,58y.
Carl F.,Mar.22,1905,29y.
Christian,Aug.6,1892,4m.
Clarence O.,1895-1896.
E.Elton,Feb.8,1981,77y.
Ella B.,bu:Apr.7,1950,62y.
Ellsworth C.,Oct.16,1945,44y,
rem. to Pine Grove, Falmouth.
Elmer L.,Oct.9,1905,1m.
Eva M.,Apr.27,1956,70y.
Evelyn,June 15,1991,78y.
Flora M.,June 20,1941,40y.
Freda P.,Mar.26,1906,8y,
d/o Fred & Annie C.
George F.,Dec.26,1927,47y.
Gertrude E.,May 1,1967,60y.
Hans A.,Sept.1,1913,52y.
Hans P., Dec.14,1959,82y.
Harold "Hire" L.,Nov.12,1989,84y.
Harry A., Aug.13,1919,13y,s/o Peter.
Harry,Jan.8,1957,69y.
Hattie,Mar.18,1911,25y,
d/o Neils & Olivia.
Henry H.,Oct.9,1966,66y.
infant,Nov.7,1918, s.b.
infant,June 2,1921,prem.
infant,Feb.18,1896,prem.
Jacobine,Mar.5,1925,72y.
John, Jr.,Jan.1,1980, s.b.
John R.,Nov.30,1925,65y.
Josie M.,June 3,1961,72y.
Karen M.P.,Dec.1,1919,64y.
Katherine,July 6,1957,72y.
Laura A.,Nov.8,1918,20y.
Maria F.,Feb.26,1913,37y.
Marianne,Apr.28,1930,75y.
Martina O.,July 17,1955,77y.
Mary L.,July 27,1919,70y,
w/o W.K. Dana Peterson.
Niels,Nov.9,1916,74y.
Nicholas A.,July 16,1960,69y.
Peter H.,Sept.19,1911,32y,s/o Neils.
Stanley F.,Sr. Oct.30,1985,77y.
Walter A.,Oct.15,1987,78y.
William,June 16,1945,68y,
rem. to Pine Grove,Falmouth.
Woodrow R.,Dec.30,1967,48y.
PETTES
Eva M.,Apr.22,1966.
infant,Apr.26,1973, s.b.
Norman W.,Apr.5,1962,78y.
PETTO
Everett J.,June 28,1988,75y.

PHILBRICK
Hannah B.,Nov.13,1901,64y.
Milton A.,Nov.16,1976,82y.
PHILIPS
Roland Merle,June 30,1913,2y.
PHILLIPS
Angela True.,Oct.19,1920,69y.
Edward L.,Nov.5,1914,68y.
Edward L.,Aug.20,1960,51y.
Emelia B.,Sept.27,1928,57y.
F. Pauline,May 16,1987,90y.
Herman,Oct.22,1914,42y.
Kailah E.,July 25,1990,2m.
Lewis E.,Sept.28,1940,70y.
Mary O.,Oct.14,1956,83y.
Paul E.,Sr.,Sept.26,1986,84y.
Ruth M.,Jan.7,1960,56y.
Stanley G.,July 18,1977,83y.
Winfred W.,Sr.,Feb.20,1968,61y.
PHINNEY
Eva A. May 13,1979,74y.
Harriet F.,1830-1896,w/o Wm.C.
J. Warren,Aug.26,1950.
Lottie F.,July 7,1926,53y.
William C. Apr.9,1913,77y.
PICKARD
John F.,Jan.11,1993,86y.
Mildred L.,Dec. 31,1971,65y.
PICKREIGN
Robert J.,Dec.27,1969,3m.
PIERCE
Sarah A.,1819-1898,w/o Simon D.
Simon D.,1814-1889.
PIKE
Alden,Dec.1,1906,53y,b.Norway.
Blanche L.,July 3,1981,94y.
Ella M.,Feb.25,1935,80y.
Ethel Frances,July 17,1930,37y.
George C.,Jan.8,1942,80y.
Harry L.,Dr.,Oct.23,1949,69y.
James R.,Apr.15,1975,55y.
Josephine Y.,July 13,1978,94y.
Mary Louise,July 3,1925,63y.
Merton L.,Jan.21,1968,77y.
PILLSBURY
Herbert F.,June 6,1966,82y.
Lendall A.,Jr.,Aug.29,1982,59y.
Lendall A.,Sr.,Sept.21,1970,82y.
Lillian E.,May 5,1944,49y.
PINDER
E. Louise,Dec.31,1934,78y.
Frank,Apr.22,19162y.
Rudolph,Oct.19,1931,65y.
PINETTE
Agnes Wilson,Sept.29,1970,85y.
PINKHAM
Beatrice E.,Apr.19,1994,88y.

Bruce E.,Jan.30,1938,3y.
Burt H.,Oct.16,1950.
Chester L.,Sept.16,1990,85y.
Edith J.,July 29,1978,71y.
Gardiner F.,Apr.3,1990,81y.
Irene B.,Jan.8,1985,65y.
Kate,Dec.20,1918,33y.
PITTS
Alice J.,Oct.9,1941,55y.
Herbert,June 13,1969,91y.
PLACE
Leeman A.,Apr.26,1994,83y.
PLACEY
Willard Ernest,Jan.26,1928,40y.
PLAISTED
Albert H.,May 29,1939,4y.
Carl V.,Feb.13,1969,53y.
Carrie E.,July 25,1962,62y.
Jill A.,Jan.31,1955,6m.
John H.,Oct.11,1985,75y.
Margaret E.,Feb.1,1980,60y.
Wesley E.,Jr.,Apr.23,1966,47y.
Wesley E.,Sr.,Dec.29,1953,64y.
PLUMMER
Alice L.,Dec.1,1952,72y.
Alta E.,May 8,1961,85y.
Charlotte R.,June 27,1951,66y.
Cyrus H.,1835-Mar.29,1904.
Daniel E.,Jan.21,1971,65y.
Elizabeth M.,July 23,1921,52y.
Emily J.,Mar.13,1932,81y.
Eugene M.,Oct.17,1950.
Frank,Apr.21,1892,23y.
Hannah C.,1840-Aug.5,1903,w/o Cyrus
Hugh J.,bu:Dec.19,1937.
John Sept.5,1958,78y.
Lucious,bu: Apr.19,1943.
Mabel W.,bu: Dec.7,1950,76y.
Mary E.,Aug.27,1937,44y.
Perley S.,Oct.5,1967,80y.
Scott,bu:Feb.20,1937,76y.
PODAS
George A.,Nov.1,1955,68y.
POITRAS
Henry P.,Aug.6,1908,4m.
POLAND
Erland,Mar.4,1918,1m.
POLLEY
Frances C.,May 1,1977,47y.
Winfield L.,May 1,1977,50y.
POMELOW
David P.,Dec.4,1969,17y.
POMELEAU
Clyde C.,July 22,1991,44y.
Marion R.,Sept.8,1986,81y.
Peter C.,Aug.6,1975,81y.

POOLE
Adeline C.,Dec.17,1964,79y.
Albert H.,Apr.4,1964,77y.
Cora B.,Jan.27,1960,81y.
Cora M.,Feb.18,1994,85y.
Francis Wm.,Jan.10,1934,84y.
Jennie S.,bu:Apr28,1937,80y.
Margaret Parker,Feb.10,1944,55y.
Marjorie S.,Jan.30,1976,77y.
Parker,Nov.20,1965,74y.
Susan Jackson,June 30,1926,67y.
William W. May 30,1937,80y.
POOLER
Audrey E.,Aug.31,1981,65y.
PORTER
Carolyne L.,May 30,1990,80y.
Charles N.,Apr.7,1920,78y.
Charles Omer,Nov.14,1949,72y.
Elizabeth C.,Aug.15,1962,86y.
Ermon R.,Mar.4,1916,1d.
Frank L.,Nov.17,1944,73y.
Gertrude S.,Nov.24,1978,89y.
Helen D.,June 23,1962.
Horace C.,Dr.,June 14,1944.
infant, Jan. 13, 1894, 6m.
Laurence W.,Feb.20,1993,87y.
Mary,Apr.10,1942,72y.
Mary Fitzwilliams,Nov.14,1912, 34y, w/o Frank L.
Mildred J.,Aug. 5,1985,82y.
Ralph C.,Oct.10,1937,46y.
Robert E.,May 19,1913,2y.
Richard D.,Oct.24,1985,42y.
Susan J.,May 11,1921,73y.
Vance L.,Nov.22,1943,75y.
POST
Alice M.,Sept.30,1963,93y.
Erdine C.,Feb.12,1965,70y.
Frank H.,May 20,1940,73y.
Frank W.,Dec.23,1989,65y.
Harold W.,June 24,1987,90y.
Lloyd M.,Mar.6,1983,61y.
Paul B., Aug.26,1979,59y.
POTRIAS
Raymond G.,Oct.19,1988,65y.
POTTER
Clara E.,Dec.23,1977,89y.
Clarence R.,Oct.1,1968,81y.
Mildred B.,bu:May 8,1943,49y.
Theodore E.,Apr.15,1980,68y.
POULIN
Joseph H.,Aug.28,1975,26y.
POWERS
Bessie J.,Sept.5,1959,78y.
Edward M. "Doc",Dec.17,1981,83y.
Lucy S., Sept.20,1957,55y.
Madeline W.,July 6,1991,85y.

PRATT
Annie B.,Oct.21,1937,65y.
Alice M.,Feb.2,1987,95y.
Archie T.,Mar.10,1964,75y.
Belmont H.,July 31,1957,69y.
Bertha A.,June 1,1994,94y.
Charlotte S.,Nov.23,1945,88y.
Cyrus S.,1849-1897.
Earl L.,Aug.2,1950,56y.
Elizabeth S.,Apr.14,1926,68y.
Ethel M.,Apr.16,1981,86y.
George H.,Oct.16,1970,77y.
Harry Burnham, Apr.13,1911, 32y, h/o Emma Girard, s/o Scott.
Hazel A.,Nov.8,1966,73y.
Joseph G.,May 16,1957,83y.
Kenneth,July 20,1924, prem.
Leroy T.,Dec.6,1911,26y.
Lila M.,June 30,1959,70y.
Mae C.,Apr.19,1982,75y.
Marvin A.,Jr.,Aug.7,1924,18d.
Mildred C.,Oct.3,1986,83y.
Milton B.,Dec.16,1989,79y.
Nettie,July 23,1943,61y.
Rahma W.,Nov.7,1969,73y.
Rebecca,Mar.24,1901,81y.
Robert,Jan.13,1992,77y.
Robert M.,Jr.,Apr.10,1988,45y.
Rose A.,Mar.30,1981,90y.
Ross A.,July 13,1966,71y.
Samuel,Sept.24,1943,61y.
Stephen & Rosie,Aug.24,1914,0y.
Susie,Mar.5,1971,80y.
W. Scott,Sept.26,1915,65y.
Walter K.,June 3,1982,78y.
Walter L.,Aug.8,1974,63y.
PRAY
Hannah Fogg,1805-1896,w/o Levi.
PREBLE
Joy Marion,June 9,1954,69y.
K. Mabel,Apr.25,1957,76y.
PRESCOTT
Doris M.,Apr.10,1985,84y.
Michael C.,Feb.24,1958.
Stephen M.,Nov.19,1972,82y.
PRESSEY
Arthur W.,Feb.16,1959,71y.
Charles I.,Sr.,May 20,1981,66y.
Clara U.,Aug.17,1927,57y.
Fred W.,bu:Oct.14,1931,71y.
PRESTON
Bertha B.,July 15,1990,75y.
Clara U.,1871-1927,w/o Fred W.
Gloria J.,July 1,1945,2d.
Wilbur L.,Dec.16,1985,75y.
PREUSSNER
Bruno Otto,Feb.26,1981,d.Ocala,Fl.

PRIDE
Alfred B.,Mar 27,1921,72y.
Aaron G.,Feb.17,1948,54y.
Agnes M.,Nov.20,1968,78y.
Beverly June,Apr.26,1926,4d.
Blanche Libby,Dec.17,1931,44y.
Clarence G.,Aug.1,1968,91y.
Clara J.,Mar.7,1931,70y.
Charles F.,Mar.30,1946,83y.
Charles H.,"Top",Oct.10,1987,74y.
Charles S., rem. from Saccarappa Cemetery Sept. 1928.
Cora P.,Feb.15,1968,98y.
Dwinal,Apr.9,1915,89y.
Dwinal,Oct.23,1938,53y.
Edith H.,Jan.28,1935,50y.
Ella E.,May 19,1958,88y.
Eva W.,May 20,1986,84y.
Everard F.,Nov.26,1943,69y.
Frances W. Harden,Mar.10,1911, 61y, w/o John M.
Frank P.,July 20,1947,73y.
Freeland,Nov.28,1932,82y.
George E.,Dec.27,1919,73y.
Harold G.,Apr.21,1959,67y.
Harry L.,Dec.5,1945,71y.
Henry Bryant, Apr.15,1929,46y.
Henry L.,Aug.17,1959,58y.
Howard S., rem. from Saccarappa Cemetery Sept.1928.
Inez P.,Nov.18,1982,90y.
infant,Apr.9,1935,newb.
infant,Apr.6,1925, s.b.
Jennie M.,Feb.23,1963,89y.
John M.,Jan.26,1918,70y.
Katherine T.,Jan.9,1940,75y.
Leon C.,Apr.19,1979,68y.
Lilla M.,Dec.6,1942,67y.
Marion K.,Feb.1,1984,72y.
Martha Victoria,Mar.28,1954,44y.
Mary F., Dec.26,1915,67y.
Maude A.,Dec.21,1973,96y.
Melville John,Nov.6,1944,71y.
Merritt G.,Aug.17,1969,81y.
Mildred P.,Dec.29,1992,100y.
Millie S., rem. from Saccarappa Cemetery, Sept.1928.
Owen F.,Apr.9,1988,77y.
Phyllis G.,July 13,1915,10y.
Ralph H.,Sept.3,1947,52y.
Richard W.,Nov.25,1987,79y.
Robert E.,Oct.8,1914, 5m.
Roberta Lee,July 24,1939,9m.
Sarah S.,Feb.2,1901,65y.
Stephen K.,Mar.2,1949,3y.
Walter D.,Apr.23,1934,73y.

PRINCE
Alfred S.,Aug.14,1976,67y.
Zenas E.,Dec.8,1909,81y.
PROCTOR
Carroll H.,Apr.5,1964,60y.
Claudia J.,Jan.25,1989,34y.
Ellward, Apr.22,1967,58y.
Eva,June 17,1970,63y.
Gary A.,Jan.10,1955,2y.
Harriett E.,Feb.24,1969,83y.
Henry,June 10,1948,70y.
Herman L.,Apr.7,1985,55y.
infant,Dec.1,1924, s.b.
Lillian F.,Jan.27,1914,7m.
Martha,June 3,1969,85y.
Norman L.,Apr.11,1965,84y.
Ralph J.,July 27,1983,77y.
Raymond L.,July 5,1925,4y.
PROPHET
David, XXXX,s/o W. & M.
Willie,Jan.2,1894,8m,s/o W. & M.
PROULX
Camille P.,Oct.18,1916,2m.
PROUTY
Charles H. Oct.22,1922,60y.
Marion,Feb.3,1906,2m.
PRUE
Grace M.,Nov.6,1967,87y.
PUGH
Ella Petria Yde,Oct.20,1939,31y.
Jane O.,Mar.9,1902,1y.
Jane U.,Aug.26,1932,69y.
Mary V.,July 23,1914,43y.
Norman A.,Aug.7,1970,85y.
William J.,July 6,1947,93y.
PURINGTON
Ellen M.,Aug.1,1928,82y.
infant,Jan.15,1917,s.b.
Moses D.,May 5,1913,72y.
PUTNAM
Abbie A.,Nov.8,1924,78y.
Ira N.,June 8,1914,68y.
PYLES
Henry,bu:Nov.9,1928.
QUIGLEY
Agnes Jane,July 28,1931,65y
John,Dec.22,1929,74y.
Sadie M.,Apr.6,1936,61y.
QUIMBY
Agnes Foster,Dec.18,1953,100y.
Annie,Apr.29,1904,49y.
Bessie N.,June 10,1960,76y.
Charles E.,Sept.12,1911,63y, s/o Aaron & Esther C.
George B.,bu:Apr.21,1941,62y.
Grant Allen,Sept.22,1937,1d.
infant,May 21,1923, s.b.

Preston, July 12,1912,62y.
William Preston,July 12,1912,
  62y, s/o Daniel & Hannah Nason.
QUINBY
Dorcus L.,1819-1901.
George A.,Apr.11,1925,75y.
Ida E.,June 29,1927,72y.
Leonard C.,1817-1887.
Lillian B.,June 6,1928,56y.
Mary Quinby,May 19,1926,76y.
QUINLAN
infant,Aug.20,1988, s.b.
infant,Jan.24,1978, s.b.
QUINN
Frank,Nov.22,1991,70y.
Patrick,Mar.13,1931,75y.
RACKLIFF
Claude,Apr.19,1912,28y.
Dale K.,Apr.4,1910,5m,
  s/o Evan & Olive.
Evan D.,Nov.11,1916,50y.
George, Capt.,Nov.8,1910,45y,
  1st w. Hannah Thompson,
  2nd w. Mrs.Angie L. Ruris.
Jane M.,Aug. 1,1898,52y.
Myrtle R.,June 22,1911,4y.
Nellie M.,Dec.6,1902,32y.
Olive M. Oct.2,1978,90y.
RAMSON
George,Oct.12,1928,77y.
RAND
Abbie M.,June 15,1901,53y.
Charles E.,Nov.17,1904,51y.
Eugene A.,June 11,1901,23y.
Flora M.,Mar.28,1929,71y.
Herbert L.,Nov.28,1967,78y.
Ida L.,Dec.21,1935,82y.
Jennie L.,Aug.9,1933,74y.
Leroy H.,Sept.2,1932,75y.
Loring P.,1846-1905.
RANDALL
Augustus G.,June 19,1993,82y.
Clara L.,Dec.3,1939,86y.
Daniel Walter,July 17,1958,46y.
Elmer W.,July 2,1964,90y.
Gary M.,Mar.10,1965,17y.
infant,June 20,1954,3 hrs.
May Belle,Oct.14,1973,95y.
T. Arlene,July 26,1985,53y.
RANSFORD
Warren R.,Apr.28,1935,32y.
RATHGEB
Anne M.,Dec.23,1941,88y.
Ernest,Mar.2,1930,55y.
Ernest F.,May 22,1909,67y.
RAWDING
Arthur L.,Sept.26,1964,27y.

Gloria D., Sept.26,1964,27y.
Janette,Sept.26,1964,5y.
Roland A.,Jr.,Jan.4,1961,8m.
RAYMOND
Addie G.,Sept.24,1894,8m.
Alice H.,Sept.17,1960,74y.
Agnes Dale,Jan.24,1920,86y,w/o
  John.
Archie,Mar.5,1929,60y.
Bessie,Jan.15,1901,4y.
Beulah F.,June 7,1980,72y.
Ettie B.,Jan.23,1920,73y.
Ettie Louise,Mar.21,1919,45y.
Fanny Boothby,July 10,1918,39y.
Fern,June 22,1993,77y.
Frank E.,Nov.13,1945,71y.
Frederick,Dec.13,1994,82y.
George H.,Mar.3,1906,65y,
  1st w. Lucy Haskell,
  2nd w. Marietta Brackett.
Harlan M.,Feb.7,1916,75y.
Harriet S.,Feb.6,1916,73y,
  w/o Harlan,double funeral,died
  within 16 hrs. of each other.
Hebert Swan,Dec.15,1907,28y.
Jonas,1812-1888.
King S.,July 16,1934,66y.
Lena,1869-1870,d/o G.H.& L.A.
Lillian C.,Dec.1,1961,89y.
Linton M.,June 8,1987,81y.
Louisa T.,Dec.23,1974,60y.
Lucy A.,1843-1875.
Mabelle D.,Feb.7,1931,59y.
Marion Mead,1883-1884.
Mary R.,Dec.31,1896,81y,w/o Jonas.
Mary Read,Apr.18,1942,73y.
Nettie F.,May 13,1974,97y.
Philip S.,July 30,1949,47y.
Richard G.,Nov.9,1929,48y.
S.T.,June 15,1940,71y.
Vera B.,Jan.19,1983,78y.
REAGAN
Joseph L.,Oct.20,1982,79y.
Marjorie,Jan.4,1992,81y.
RECORD
George W., Jr.,Mar.31,1977.
George W.,Sr.,June 13,1952,55y.
infant,July 26,1972,s.b.
REDDEN
Dennis,July 6,1900,67y.
Elizabeth E.,Sept.18,1935,72y.
Frank F.,Dec.11,1942,74y.
James A.,Sept.4,1929,66y.
John T.,May 7,1920,63y.
Louisa J.,Jan.18,1940,87y.
Lydia,July 18,1892,32y.
Margaret I.,May 4,1945,74y.

Mar E.,1832-1889,w/o Dennis.
Mary J.,Jan.6,1928,75y.
Tamsan,1895,inf/o Dennis & M.E.
William H.,Jan.9,1913,58y.
REECE
Annie M.,Feb.3,1950.
Carroll W.,Jan.23,1979,64y.
Emily C.,May 23,1990, rem.
  from Saccarappa Cem.Dec.1993.
George J.,Jr.,May 20,1960,51y.
Greta P.,Mar.26,1964,59y.
Leverett A.,Sept.18,1950.
Louise W.,Dec.2,1938,35y.
William S.,June 3,1945,70y.
REED
Christie D.,Feb.13,1977,86y.
Harry C.,Nov.8,1955,67y.
Nellie R.,Dec.26,1934,76y.
Sumner K.,Apr.20,1915,58y.
REEVES
Geraldine O.,Mar.27,1957,39y.
REID
Mary E.,Mar.17,1962,37y.
William A.,Apr.26,1955,57y.
William A.,Nov.16,1914,39y.
REMSEN
Edna,Oct.29,1928,32y.
RENY
Adele,Jan.28,1946,81y.
Frank J.,June 8,1986,38y.
Fred J.,Nov.17,1973,88y.
Fred W.,"Ted",Oct.27,1990,77y.
Marslean, Jan.31,1916,81y,
  remains brought from New York.
Nora M.,Aug.8,1970,84y.
Richard E.,Feb.13,1955,43y.
Richard E.,Jr.,Jan.16,1931,s.b.
REYNOLDS
Harold R.,Dec.24,1900,11d.
Josiah E.,Nov.8,1910,68y.
Margueretta J.,Dec.15,1893,43y.
RHODES
infant,Feb.17,1917,s.b.
RHOADES
Lester P.,Aug.31,1970,87y.
RICCI
Wilma L.,May 29,1958,53y.
RICE
Addie M.Willard,1861-
  July 6,1897,w/o Howard.
Charles H.,Sept.9,1895,52y.
John B.,Apr.10,1930,39y.
Mae F.,Feb.27,1978,84y.
RICH
Clara J.,Feb.2,1971,71y.
Edmund H.,May 23,1970,74y.
Mary Ann, Nov.24,1918,81y.

Randall B.,Jan.18,1994.
Sadie S.,July 1,1975,69y.
RICHARD
Edward Ricker,Feb.11,1940,6d.
Grace M.,Jan.12,1982,56y.
RICHARDS
A.Grace,1893-Feb.27,1912.
Albert H.,Feb.28,1990,42y.
Albert J.,Nov.12,1955,48y.
Alice,Dec.22,1970,50y.
Bertha H.,Feb.22,1985,69y.
David Arthur,May 19,1948,9y.
Henry E.,Aug.4,1939,83y.
infant,Aug.3,1957,6hrs.
Jennie L.,1890-1906,d/o H.E.&M.L.
Joseph F.,Nov.19,1959,49y.
Louise E.,Feb.22,1985,73y.
Mary L. Berry,Mar.29,1942,78y.
Ronald E.,Dec.19,1980,35y.
William T.,Mar.22,1944,4m.
RICHARDSON
Alma,Feb.4,1992,77y.
Carrie S.,May 30,1974,86y.
Carroll M.,May 28,1942,57y.
Charles Davis,May 30,1944,6d.
Edwin A.,Aug.31,1916,64y.
Hazel,Mar.20,1905,6m.
Kate E.,May 25,1929,75y.
Leonard E.,July 7,1991,78y.
Shirley S.,Feb.15,1988,69y.
RICHTER
Sarah E.,Mar.21,1961,8d.
RICKER
Addie M.,Mar.31,1926,67y.
Bertrand Arthur,1881-1890.
Clarence E.,May 9,1969,68y.
Frank W.,Apr.23,1940,83y.
RIDEOUT
Alice S.,June 7,1960,85y.
Benjamin A., removed from
  Saccarappa Cem. May 1927.
Bessie L.,Sept.29,1961,81y.
Carrie A.,Mar.4,1944,93y.
Emma E.,June 28,1944,90y.
Emma W., rem. from Saccarappa
  Cemetery,May 1927.
Ernest S.,Mar.3,1926,30y.
Josephine B. Dec.16,1956,66y.
Helen L., rem. from Saccarappa
  Cemetery May 1927.
Percy R.,Aug.19,1949,76y.
RIDLEY
Joshua,Mar.4,1906,52y.
RIDLON
David G.,Sept.14,1977,55y.
Florence P.,Nov.15,1985,54y.

RIGGS
Elizabeth F.,Aug.3,1937,74y.
Eva H.,Nov.19,1971,83y.
Elmer L.,Oct.25,1992,44y.
Frank E.,Feb.28,1952,63y.
Frank E.,Sr.,June 19,1943,82y.
RILEY
Robert G.,Dec.3,1987,71y.
RINDY
Gregory A.,Feb.26,1986,2hrs.
RING
Lottie B.,52y, rem. from South Portland July 1926.
RIPLEY
Abbie N.,Apr.7,1991,85y.
RIVERS
Mabel,bu:July 10,1961,77y.
RIZZO
Lorraine V., Sept. 24, 1982, 77y.
Sullivan J.,Sr., Sept.24,1976,72y.
ROBBINS
Clifton W., June 20,1964,49y.
Edythe S.,Jan.6,1971,75y.
Leavitt C.,Apr.6,1979,70y.
Mary A.,Nov.17,1978,83y.
Robbins,Ronald A.,1953,2y, rem. from St. Hyacinthe Cem.1993.
ROBERTS
Alice Jane, Sept.13,1930,2m.
Anna B.,Sept.1,1965,74y.
Arthur L.,May 22,1928,59y.
Benjamin F.,May 15,1898,64y.
Bennie,May 7,1912,18y.
Charles C., Nov. 30, 1975, 91y.
Charles M.,May 25,1892,26y.
Charles M.,Oct.15,1990,81y.
Douglas M.,Mar.14,1914,1y, grandson/o Frank Pender.
Edna May, Aug. 24,1917,14y.
Ellen A.Knight,July 31,1845-Mar.5,1912,66y,w/o Wm.
Elva A., May 7,1964,73y.
Harry F.,Jan.1912, s/o B.Frank & Melvina.
Gary H., Feb. 24, 1937, 2d.
George T., Feb. 28, 1930, 70y.
George W., Dec. 9, 1927, 73y.
Gilbert F., July 28, 1943, 72y.
Hattie Cora, July 23, 1941, 72y.
infant, June 19, 1941, 4hrs.
Iva L., Dec. 20, 1952, 66y.
James, Dec. 31, 1912,83y, s/o Clifford & Ann.
James Clifford,June 27,1916,58y.
James Ernest,Sr.,July17,1958,73y.
Jennie G.,Nov.16,1949,89y.
Lillian J., Mar.30,1919,45y, w/o Gilbert F.
Lillian A., Apr.17,1985,96y.
Louina S.,Mar.27,1934,63y.
Marcia A.,June 18,1923,69y.
Marcia I.,Sept.12,1916,25y.
Marguret,Nov.23,1946,60y.
Marjorie H.,Dec.3,1994,82y.
Mary S.,Nov.12,1917,90y.
Melvina N.,Apr.20,1921,86y.
Merle A.,May 7,1980,59y.
Mildred L.,Oct.24,1933,22y.
Percy L.,Aug.10,1962,73y.
R. Fred,Nov.7,1963,78y.
Royal A.,May 4,1952,65y.
William,Jan.20,1923,79y.
ROBERTSON
Bernard F.,Nov. 23,1960,77y.
Elizabeth C.,July 9,1971,86y.
John W.,Dec.8,1965,68y.
Paul W.,Sept.24,1943.
Thelma E.,Feb.20,1989,95y.
ROBICHAUD
Edmond J.,Apr.5,1975,67y.
ROBIE
C.Maud,Sept.24,1993,103y.
Charles C.,Apr.11,1979,65y.
Frank H.,May 25,1934,45y.
Frank H.,Jr.,Oct.3,1981,69y.
William K.,Jan.31,1988,70y.
ROBINS
Dermont H.,May 30,1959,73y.
ROBINSON
Amelia L.,Jan.12,1972,72y.
Annie E.,Apr.10,1970,73y.
Benjamin W., Aug.20,1988,83y.
Blanche B.,bu:June 7, 1927,42y.
Carrie S.,July 19,1926,60y.
Clara M.,July 28,1993, 87y.
Corrine M., Feb.24,1984,67y.
Edith B.,Jan.14,1965,67y.
Edith L.,Feb.7,1971,72y.
Edward,Dec.17,1991.
Edward J.,Nov.3,1964,68y.
Elizabeth O.,Nov.30,1957,9m.
Frances E.,Apr.17,1968,78y.
Frank I.,June 8,1961,69y.
George C.,Mar.9,1983,88y.
Harley S.,Dec.20,1963,75y.
Harry J.,Oct.1,1979,82y.
infant, Sept. 7, 1900, 10hrs.
infant,Nov.3,1946,2hrs.
Jean A.,Dec.24,1985,22y.
Jean S. Aug.4,1919,7w, d/o Edw.
Jessie S.,Aug.2,1988,88y.
John J.,1816-1888, rem. from Saccarappa Cemetery.

Kathleen H.,Jan.12,1948,1y.
Leroy "Jock",Nov.26,1985,86y.
Lucy P.,Feb.1892,21d.
Marcia A.,1859-1891,removed from Saccarappa Cemetery.
Margaret Isabelle,Aug.18,1930,61y.
Maria D.,1874-1907.
Mary Strain, Oct.21,1933,50y.
Oscar G.K.,Feb.14,1953,82y.
Paul L.,Jr.,June 30,1988,20y.
Robert S.,Dec.5,1919,74y.
Robert S.,Oct.12,1987,90y.
Susie S.,Oct.24,1963,68y.
Trevor W.,Jan.21,1922,11y.
ROBY
Elizabeth G.,June 21,1974,86y.
James,Oct.21,1933,15y.
James E.,Cpl.,Oct.3,1958,21y.
William,Sept.2,1977,65y.
William E.,Nov.10,1971,86y.
ROCK
Helen M.,July 12,1923,40y.
ROCKWELL
Carl E.,June 30,1993,70y.
Clarence E.,Oct.4,1970,89y.
Lillie V.,Feb.26,1970,82y.
ROCKWOOD
Roberta Mary,Apr.20,1921,5d.
ROGERS
Annie K.,Apr.19,1974,73y.
Byron E.,Sr.,June 5,1982,84y.
Clifton K.,Oct.8,1987,63y.
Ida B.,Nov.22,1962,73y.
Josephine A.,Dec.14,1972,35y.
Margaret,July 28,1923,1d.
Marilyn Anne,Feb.6,1930,3m.
Mary L.,Sept.13,1990,55y.
ROLFE
Charles E.,Nov.19,1918,72y.
Emma L.,Oct.17,1938,80y.
George W.,Dec.17,1938,83y.
Martha E.,Apr.8,1930,82y.
ROLLINS
Charles,Nov.22,1918,72y.
ROMA
Colin A.,Nov.19,1986,78y.
Dorothy R.,May 21,1993,83y.
Melvin M.,Feb.28,1994,82y.
ROME
Edward W.,Sept.23,1937,75y.
Etta, Mar. 23, 1948, 88y.
Margaret D.,Jan.19,1993,79y.
ROOD
Edith M.,Feb.23,1937,65y.
George S.,Oct.4,1948,79y.
ROOT
Persis May,1879-1896,d/o S.E.

Stephen E.,Dr.,1834-1904.
ROSENBLAD
Wilfred N.,Aug.4,1974,61y.
ROSS
Carol Ann Kay,Sept.17,1934,1d.
Elizabeth Walker,Feb.2,1911,68y.
John C.,1853-1907.
M. Elizabeth, Feb.2,1911,68y.
ROOT
Almira,May 6,1928,75y.
Bertwell C., Feb 5,1939,70y.
Caroline,bu:May 7,1931,55y.
Eastman S.,Mar.13,1950,52y.
ROPER
Linda C.,May 11,1981,27y.
ROUNDS
infant,July 12,1955, newb.
ROUX
Sibyl B.,June 15,1991.
ROWE
Arthur S.,1864-1897.
Edith M.,Jan.27,1932,65y.
Francis N.,1843-1889, w/o Luther.
Luther,Jan.29,1915,75y.
ROY
Albert L.,Sept.19,1991,72y.
Eugene L.,July 8,1944,60y.
Joseph J.C.,June 28,1977,74y.
infant,Mar.2,1929,1m,inf/o Eugene.
Louis, Dec.6,1934,54y.
Mary L. King, Oct.12,1952,72y.
Ora,Jan.21,1929,30y.
Rita M.,Apr.10,1987,66y.
Wilma,Feb.10,1988,88y.
RUBITO
infant,Dec.17,1955,prem.
RUSSELL
Annie P.,Sept.25,1942,81y.
Calvin, Apr.18,1932,75y.
F. Herman,May 24,1941,28y.
Fred A.,Dec.31,1924,42y.
George F.,Dec.15,1935,76y.
Helen E.,Oct.25,1931,60y.
Marion E.,Dec.12,1993,89y.
Maurice E.,Oct.19,1956,50y.
RUTTER
Bernice H.,June 30,1969,62y.
Doris M.,Jan.10,1981,72y.
Douglas E.,Aug.12,1965,61y.
Harold H.,Sr.,Feb.5,1970,71y.
John C.,Mar.7,1931,63y.
Marion A.,Apr.26,1937,71y.
Marion L.,July 18,1963,37y.
Ralph S.,Aug.26,1983.
Reginald J.,May 13,1975.
Ruth V.,Jan.22,1985,83y.

RYCOSKY
Benjamin J.,June 29,1967,58y.
Doris F.,Aug.7,1968,55y.
SAARINE
S. Alfred,Sept.7,1979,53y.
SAGER
Elton N.,Feb.23,1954,55y.
ST. CLAIR
Austin,Apr.15,1964,81y.
Flora M.,Oct.3,1967,79y.
Preston,July 14,1974, s.b.
ST.PETER
Preston,July 14,1974,s.b.
ST. PIERRE
Alfred J.,Aug.31,1957,43y.
Barbara Rose,Jan.2,1938,prem.
Doris,July 27,1985,83y.
James W.,July 22,1972,59y.
Lewis J.,Jan.11,1966,69y.
Nellie,Nov.25,1983,84y.
Ovide A.,June 28,1972,72y.
Phyllis D.,Apr.2,1966,51y.
SANBORN
Arthur,Dec.5,1939,62y.
Charlotte R.,Jan.5,1942,78y.
SANBORG
Victoria,Dec.24,1972,90y.
SANDERS
Grace L.,Aug.3,1947,56y.
SANDERSON
Edward C.,Dec.21,1966,81y.
Eve C.,Mar.15,1971,68y.
infant,Jan.28,1924,s.b.
Lois Roberts,Jan.22,1928,30y.
Lorraine,Oct.2,1940,14y.
Mabel L.,May 8,1993,92y.
Ralph E.,Sr.,May 15,1972,78y.
SANVILLE
Daphne J.,July 19,1970,54y.
SARGENT
Bertha, July 9,1956,56y.
Betty B.,Dec.9,1993,71y.
Ernest L.,Mar.13,1991,71y.
Shannon Lee,Jan.7,1987,newb.
SARTY
Arline F.,June 15,1977,66y.
Donald A.,May 15,1974,70y.
SAUNDERS
Alice N.,Jan.13,1941,64y.
Arthur L.,bu:Mar.22,1950,74y.
Frank A.,Feb.28,1922,48y.
H. Warren,Aug.15,1960,55y.
Harold A.,Feb.18,1966,79y.
Harry W.,Jan.1,1949,77y.
Helen, Sept.15,1962,85y.
Marion M.,Feb.8,1973,81y.
Mildred T.,Jan.10,1958,67y.

SAWYER
Alverdo,Jan.17,1959,52y.
Angus T.,Mar.26,1940,63y.
Bertha E.,Sept.30,1993,91y.
Bradley, rem. from
St. Hyacinth Nov.1954.
Carrie, Sept.14,1910,35y.
Charles F.,Nov.18,1945,78y.
Charles L.,Oct.3,1959,48y.
Clarence P.,Aug.17,1951,86y.
Edgar F.,1858-1885.
Ernest C.,Feb.19,1941,2d.
Eunice E,Nov.28,1898,78y,w/o W.F
Frances R.,Sept.18,1991,79y.
G. Merrill,Oct.10,1983,74y.
George W.,Dec.8,1917,77y.
Gertrude M.,Jan.20,1959,82y.
Harold A.,Jan.21,1972,71y.
Harry W.,June 18,1984,78y.
Hattie E.,1871-1876,d/o J.P.& L.M.
Hattie G.,Oct.7,1966,89y.
Harvey E.,Oct.10,1963,56y.
Ina E.,Sept.16,1963,85y.
infant,July 31,1982, s.b.
Irving W.,Jan.1,1959,70y.
John P.,Mar.20,1917,77y.
Lawriston W.,Oct.25,1939,62y.
Levi W.,May 10,1932, 5y.
Lois B.,Dec.31,1971.
Louisa M.,June 13,1910,72y.
Louise D.,Feb.3,1954,85y.
Margaret E.,May 1,1987,56y.
Maria C.,Feb.4,1933,90y.
Mark P.,Feb.19,1959,5y.
Martha,June 13,1958,79y.
Melissa J.,Dec.19,1920,73y,w/o Geo W
Olivette M.,Nov.7,1983,87y.
Roger M.,Apr.23,1940,49y.
Stanley D.,May 22,1971,66y.
Walter H.,July 12,1929,66y.
Warren L.,Nov.24,1944,50y.
Wilbur C.,Jan.24,1935,37y.
William F.,Feb.1,1904,80y.
Zelia F.,1852-1860.
SAYLOR
Charlotte A.,Oct.6,1953,66y.
SCATES
Ida L., Feb. 22,1934,75y, rem.
from Evergreen Tomb July 1936.
John C.,May 10,1949,90y.
Karl D.,Feb.18,1969,81y.
Margaret K.,Mar.7,1972,83y.
SCEGGELL
Arthur B., Oct. 15, 1982, 88y.
Ivetta W., Feb. 5, 1987, 77y.
SCHAUER
infant, Apr.9,1944, prem.

SCHERMERDORN
Myra,Oct.3,1984,79y.
SCHLEMBERGER
Curt, Jr.,July 12,1986, s.b.
SCHMIDT
Hans J.J.,Mar.26,1951,76y.
Hans Johnson,Jan.1,1921,71y.
Lavrense K.K.,Apr.6,1940,63y.
Marin Peterson,Apr.13,1919,92y.
SCHNEIDER
Fred J.,July 12,1967,60y.
SCHWARTZ
Caroline R.,Jan.22,1907,77y.
Charles J.,May 4,1854-July 21,1909.
J.C.,Sept.20,1892,70y.
Martha J.,June 1922,73y.
SCOTT
Harry W.,Aug.7,1939,72y.
Hector M.,bu:Feb.1,1950,57y.
Mary,July 22,1922,89y.
Richard A., Jan.13,1976,82y.
Vivian, Nov.6,1992.
SCRIBNER
Emily Ermina,Feb.21,1926,58y.
Ethel L.,Feb.28,1992,78y.
James C.,Jan.20,1945,89y.
Kenneth K.,Sept.3,1990,79y.
William M.,Nov.20,1926,64y.
SEAGERS
James,1890-1890,s/o J.& S.M.
William,1896-1897,s/o J.& S.M.
SEAL
Frederick H.,Jan.9,1892,54y.
SEARWAY
infant,Feb.10,1944, prem.
SEAVEY
Francis P.,Mar.12,1946,31y.
Llewellyn,Sept.18,1925,48y.
Viola C.,Nov.8,1983,67y.
SECORD
Anna E.,Apr.15,1989,58y.
Bertha A.,Aug.30,1983,96y.
Clyde C.,Sr.,Dec.26,1989,82y.
George E.,Mar.13,1973,88y.
George R.,May 5,1989,78y.
Isa M.,Mar.13,1966,67y.
SEGER
Crystal L.,Sept.6,1991,22y.
Hannah A.,Apr.11,1968,82y.
John I.,Apr.16,1953,64y.
Lawrence W.,Nov.6,1943,21y.
SELBY
Edward,Apr.26,1947,10d.
SEMATOWIC
Frank V.,Sept.25,1962,75y.
SENTER
Albion,1839-Apr.14,1908.

Alice M.,Feb.7,1958,87y.
Annette A.,1839-Apr.30,1916.
Edith E.,Oct.2,1961,90y.
Harold L.,1896-1896.
Howard E.,Jan.18,1953.
infant,Mar.4,1916,s.b.
Nettie M.,1890-1901.
Walter H.,Apr.6,1950,81y.
William,July 8,1914,68y.
Willis A.,Oct.25,1944,79y.
SEXTON
Orvilla L.,May 2,1923.
SHANE
Llewellyn Oct.1,1961,70y.
Margaret I.,Feb.4,1991,94y.
Samuel,Feb.20,1917,84y.
Violet R.,Feb.28,1991,63y.
SHANNON
Sarah,Nov.15,1919,63y.
SHARPE
C. Mabel,July 16,1971,91y.
SHAW
Adelbert W.,Nov.22,1920,76y.
Almeda B. Merserve,Feb.25,1910, 70y, w/o Albert W.
Catherine L.,Aug.9,1973.
Charles E.,Dec.5,1966,87y.
Charles R.,Mar.2,1925,77y.
Daisey,July 26,1946,77y.
Earl S.,Aug.15,1971.
Edgar R.,June 23,1953,76y.
Edna Glidden,July 26,1945,21y.
Eliza J.,Nov.25,1962,83y.
Francis,bu:Mar.15,1934.
Gladys L.,Jan.19,1983,84y.
Harriet P.,Sept.27,1916,63y.
infant,Sept.18,1944, prem.
infant,Oct.31,1926,prem.
Irvin S.,Nov.23,1944,67y.
J. Howard,Aug.14,1938,28y.
Jessie M.,Aug.23,1957,80y.
John N.,Jan.13,1927,76y.
Joseph H.,Nov.25,1964,75y.
Lydia E.,Oct.21,1927,62y.
Robert C.,Nov.26,1918,23y.
Rose A.,Apr.17,1957,72y.
Roy E.,Nov.13,1952,56y.
Venerance E.,Jan.26,1989,75y.
Wesley H.,Dec.11,1973,61y.
SHEA
Catherine M.,Mar.19,1969,78y.
Donald H.,Feb.21,1959,69y.
SHEEHAN
Francena,Aug.8,1920,76y.
Samuel M.,June 8,1915,63y.
SHENEFIELD
Arline H.,July 21,1965,41y.

SHERMAN
Hazel,Mar.28,1990,80y.
SHERWOOD
Cecil P.,Aug.20,1962,59y.
Margaret C.,May 9,1964,60y.
SHIBLES
Granville C.,Dr.,Nov.29,1962,68y.
Martha G.,Dec.4,1992,97y.
SHIELDS
Susan,Dec.16,1938,72y.
SHIRLEY
Cecil D.,Dec.7,1976,74y.
Clifford H.,Jan.27,1994.
Eliza M.,July 3,1979,74y.
Ethel L.,May 20,1977,73y.
William A.,May 18,1977,78y.
SHORTELL
Ida May Hussey,May 19,1916,59y.
SIEWERTSON
Catherine M.,Nov.14,1914,36y.
Stewart, Jan.1941,72y.
SILVA
Charles E.,June 21,1964,83y.
Ernest F.,June 14,1959,60y.
Evelyn T.,Dec.2,1967,61y.
SIMMONS
Doris M.,Mar.25,1959,39y.
Elizabeth,Sept.20,1917,47y.
SIMPSON
George W.,Oct.4,1974,88y.
Jennie B.,Jan.9,1968,79y.
SINCLAIR
Andrew,July 19,1938,79y.
David Carlton,Nov.13,1986,47y.
Everett,Nov.7,1947,54y.
Guy V.,Sept.7,1957,79y.
Guy V.,Jan.16,1980,69y.
Hazel B.,Jan.19,1960,64y.
Harold,May 14,1955,64y.
infant,Mar.17,1930, s.b.
Isabelle W.,Sept.23,1937,69y.
James,Aug.2,1975,76y.
James M.,Sept.18,1898,27y.
Laura,Jan.26,1953,67y.
Pearl W.,Jan.11,1989,93y.
Rebecca,1827-Jan.12,1894,w/o Jas M.
Steven M.,Oct.23,1992, 51y.
Wilma B.,July 23,1979,77y.
SKILLINGS
Bertha L.,Apr.9,1954,78y.
Bertha S.,Oct.12,1956,79y.
Earle L.,Dec.9,1984,80y.
Elizabeth Ekkeb,Jan. 25,1930,74y.
Ethelyn M.,Aug.1,1993,88y.
George J. Oct.24,1940,65y.
John F.,Sept.28,1944,70y.
John J.,Mar.15,1911,70y.
Lizzie A.,Apr.28,1875,w/o Allen.
Mary Ellen Trickey,June 2,1903, 57y, w/o John J.
Rachel L.,1812-1895,w/o Tim. A.
Robert L.,Apr.4,1912,2y.
Stephen H.,Dec.30,1945,96y.
Timothy A.,1808-1891.
SKINNER
Daisey Blanche,Oct.25,1927,17y.
SKOLAS
James,June 26,1954,59y.
Linda A.,July 15,1983,45y.
Mary E.,Mar.20,1989,93y.
Thomas,Nov.29,1992,66y.
SKYES
Julia May 1,1987,85y.
Marion M., Mar.17,1988,91y.
SLOAN/E
Alice L.,July 9,1952,72y.
Daniel I.,bu:Sept.20,1937,63y.
George H.,June 27,1894,4m.
James Henry, Apr.4,1937,71y.
John,Oct.10,1920,58y.
Robert,Dec.14,1911,77y.
Sarah Elizabeth, May 11,1919, 87y,w/o Robert.
SLOAT
Harold K.,Sept.18,1980.
Marion H. June 1,1983,69y.
SLOCOMB
Alma G.,Mar.16,1986,45y.
SMALL
Adelbert L.,Sept.16,1929,49y.
Arthur L.,Apr.18,1922,63y.
Ashley II.,Mar.21,1924,71y.
Carrie F.,June 29,1970,78y.
Cora I.,July 21,1961,31y.
Edward Durgin,May 10,1939,58y.
Erland C., Aug.30,1993,88y.
Emma L.,Jan.13,1923,69y.
Eva B.,July 6,1896,10y.
F. Allen,July 21,1971,78y.
Flossie V.,July 5,1976,85y.
Frederick W.,Sept.13,1965,73y.
Grace C.,Mar.11,1948,62y.
Harvey E.,Mar.12,1962,77y.
infant,Mar.29,1929, s.b.
infant,Oct.13,1955, s.b.
Joseph D., Mar. 16, 1959, 73y.
Laura A., Jan. 23, 1975, 84y.
LutherL.,1853-Apr.28,1906.
Marion Lois,Feb.7,1914,6w., rem. from Saccarappa Cem.
Mary Priscella,Aug. 3,1917,4y.
Mary S.,Mar.31,1954,77y.
Myra E.,July 17,1962,81y.
Nellie N.,Mar.17,1927,62y.

Olin C.,Aug.18,1991,82y.
Ralph D.,Nov.5,1931,50y.
Ruby Harriett,Sept.29,1921,7y.
Shirley M.,July 22,1983,66y.
Theresa W.,May 14,1976,88y.
Wayland P., Aug.23,1979,58y.
SMEATON
Mary M., 1902 (?), b. Scotland.
SMIDTH
Hans Johanson, Dec.30, 1920,71y.
SMITH
Ada B.,Aug.31,1942,68y.
Albert J.,Feb.4,1941,75y.
Ann M.,Aug.23,1981,79y.
Anna T.,bu:Dec.30,1959,82y.
Annie Hight,Dec.27,1927,64y.
Annie K.,Nov.15,1940,75y.
Annie M.,Feb.3,1981,92y.
Arnold, Dec.19,1993,72y.
Arthur L., Sept.21,1936,78y.
B. Frank,June 12,1986.
Barbara E.,Feb.19,1986,56y.
Bertha L.,May 28,1928,55y.
Boardman C.,IV,May 27,1987,19y.
Byron Herbert, Apr.18,1943,73y.
Carolyn J.,May 10,1988,96y.
Carrie E.,July 7,1970,84y.
Catherine M., Apr.12,1927,88y.
Cecilia R.,Apr.8,1992,76y.
Charles, rem. from Cemetery in Windham Nov. 1928.
Charles,Feb.26,1932,s.b.
Charles,bu:Oct.17,1927,38y.
Charles D.,Oct.26,1925,55y.
Charles G.,Oct.28,1927,38y.
Charles G.,Nov.23,1949,78y.
Charles G.,Jr.,Apr.15,1912.
Charles L.,Oct.6,1954,72y.
Charles R.,Jan.24,1968,65y.
Cheever S.,Dr.,Dec.9,1962,66y.
Chester N.,Apr.14,1968,68y.
Clara,Mar.2,1902,25y.
Clara G.,Aug.22,1960,80y.
Clarence A.,May 1,1963,62y.
Daniel Q.,Sept.15,1984,56y.
Daniel J.,Mar.16,1992,30y.
Doris F.I.,Oct.8,1988,92y.
Dorothy E.,Dec.2,1985,80y.
Dorothy M.,Jan.14,1979,76y.
Dorothy M.,Nov.4,1921,7m.
Dorothy Q.,Mar.1,1984,74y.
Earl, Mar.30,1917,2d.
Elizabeth,May 12,1921,86y.
Elizabeth E.,Nov.7,1933,67y.
Elizabeth Jane,Sept.27,1926,2m.
Elroy,Aug.30,1928,18y.
Elvira L.,Nov.5,1926,82y.
Ernest A.,May 19,1976,83y.
Ethel F.,Dec.29,1971,88y.
Evelyn M.,May 7,1994,93y.
Evelyn P.,Sept.30,1964,88y.
Fred, Apr.10,1988,85y.
Gary S.,July 11,1971,16y.
Geneva, May 3,1927.
George A.,Oct.21,1968,83y.
George E.,May 8,1973,62y.
George F.,Oct.30,1949.
George M.,Oct.17,1919,86y.
George W.,June 3,1931,57y.
George W.,Dec.3,1939,44y.
Glenna M.,May 7,1983,68y.
Goldie E.,Oct.26,1939,65y.
H.A.,Aug.18,1918, s.b.
Hans N.,Nov.16,1951,70y.
Harriett M.,Nov.18, 1973,74y.
Harry A.,Aug.23,1922,56y.
Hattie M.,Apr.7,1968,88y.
Horace M.,Aug.14,1993,86y.
Howard E.,Jan.4,1972,92y.
Ida E.,bu:Nov.6,1942,56y.
Ida M.,1865-1877,d/o Wm.& Olive.
infant,Aug.24,1918, s.b.
infant,bu:Jan.4,1963.
infant,July 18,1934,prem.
infant,July 19,1937, s.b.
infant,Oct.10,1920.
J. Earl,Aug.17,1939,47y.
J. William,bu: Sept.20,1942,36y.
James D.,Dec.21,1936,76y.
James D.,Jr.,Sept.14,1983,91y.
James K.,June 20,1922,62y.
James,Nov.6,1900,6y.
Jane G.K.,Nov.28,1930,71y.
Janet D.,Mar.3,1924,61y.
Jennie M.,July 21,1930,65y.
Jens H.,May 14,1943,79y.
Joan A.,Aug.23,1990,77y.
John C.,Aug.3,1898,67y.
John W. May 2,1946,61y.
John W.,Feb.19,1942,81y.
John W.,Mar.25,1928,47y.
John William,Sept.16,1942,36y.
John,May 22,1907, prem.
John,Aug.5,1894.
Jorgen H.,Oct.18,1948,60y.
L. Edward,Oct.3,1978,60y.
Larry C.,Aug.14,1992,47y.
Lewis C.,Dec.3,1965,83y.
Lillian M.,Mar.6,1900,24y,w/o B.
Lillian M.,Mar.20,1988,66y.
Lois M.,Aug.24,1990,96y.
Lora F.,Jan.17,1976,86y.
Lottie E.,Sept.23,1963,65y.
Lottie L.,Mar.5,1987,84y.

Lucille,Oct.8,1986,88y.
Lulu A.,Oct.13,1920.
Lydia J.,bu:June 2,1919,69y,w/o Wm.
Madge W.,July 12,1947,63y.
Manilla G.,1886-1891,d/o T.P.& A.H.
Margaret D.,bu:Oct.16,1928,66y.
Margaret D.,1836-1913,w/o Wm.
Margaret G.,July 13,1964,66y.
Marie C.,Mar.19,1970,87y.
Maron, Apr.8,1919,92y.
Martin D.,Jan.8,1910,5y.
Mary A.,Jan.24,1959.
Mary B.,Mar.9,1947,79y.
Mary E.,June 21,1911,54y.
Maude E.,Feb.9,1940,49y.
Michael J.,Sept.18,1989, s.b.
Minnie H.,Apr.22,1967,90y.
Minnie L.,1873-1907,w/o S.W.Jr.
Murial M.,Sept.11,1973,69y.
Myrtle,Dec.12,1991,87y.
Niels H.,Nov.5,1962,93y.
Olive C.,1843-1911,w/o Wm.
Paul H. Aug.12,1958,68y.
Paul J., Col.,May 3,1968 51y.
Rachel Janetta,Mar.28,1949,86y.
Ralph W.,July 15,1935,61y.
Ray A., Mar.19,1989,63y.
Robert A.,Apr.5,1969,73y.
Robert E.,Sr.,Sept.29,1985,57y.
Robert G.,Feb.10,1988,81y.
Reuben O.,Aug.17,1972,76y.
Ruth,Sept.11,1992,99y.
S. Nelson,Jan 5,1914,16y.
Sarah, Apr.16,1892,40y,w/o R.
Selah E.,Sept.25,1956,60y.
Stephen W.,Capt.,Dec.21,1928.
Thomas D.,Mar.11,1964,90y.
Thomas D.,Jr.,Dec.21,1917,6y.
Thomas P.,May 7,1915,62y.
Vena L.,Sept.1,1972,71y.
Vernon T.,Jan.28,1960,47y.
Vivian S.,Feb.5,1898,5m.
W. Kenneth, Aug.15,1974.
Walter E.,bu:Apr.7,1943.
Warren W.,Nov.30,1964,70y.
Wesley H., Feb.7,1978,65y.
Willard, May 12,1911,3y.
William,1831-1903.
William D., July 24,1987, 36y.
William D.,bu: June 14, 1926.
William D., Oct.30,1942,53y.
William J.,July 6,1914,68y.
William D.,1833-June 28,1904,
 b. Scotland,h/o Margaret D.
William Boyd,Mar.22,1907,32y,
 s/o William. B.
William, June 26,1903,72y.

SMYTH
Annie J., Jan 29,1953,59y.
Bryce,June12,1922,s.b.
Bryce Edward,June 12,1918,10m.
Christy, Oct.23,1957,61y.
Elizabeth H.,Feb.25,1981.
infant, Sept.4,1917, s.b.
James,Mar.25,1984,93y.
John E. Apr.1,1979,79y.
Joseph,Feb.4,1918,61y.
Joseph, July 24,1967,79y.
Mary,Jan.25,1947,84y.
Sylvia T.,Jan.8,1990,87y.
Vera B.,Mar.7,1957,60y.
William,Dec.30,1961,68y.
William D.,Nov.3,1972,45y.
SNEDDON
James B.,Mar.21,1963,69y.
Margaret W.,July 25,1989,94y.
SNOW
Horace M., Sept.16,1943,78y.
Lettie E.,1872-1890,
 d/o Capt.J.T.& A.M.
SODERGREN
Ernest, Apr.3,1961,78y.
Grace, Mar.13,1986.
SOLOWAY
Taylor M.,Aug.31,1992,infant.
SOPER
Howard M., Oct.27,1966,70y.
Vernona M.,Aug.8,1994,92y.
SORENSEN
Ernest, Apr.3,1961,78y.
Hilda K., Oct.3,1940,51y.
Kjestina, Apr.22,1905,53y.
Meta,1880-1911.
S. Peter,July 27,1913,62y.
SPARKS
Celicia, Apr.16,1992,38y.
SPAULDING
Leona M.,Apr.4,1986,66y.
SPEAR
Angie L.,Apr.22,1976,89y.
Carroll A.,Nov.8,1903,22y.
Everett H.,July 29, 1978, 68y.
James F.,July 3,1922,75y.
Gilbert I.,June 16,1943,57y.
Helen A.,Feb.27,1924,55y.
Laura E.,Jan.22,1935,79y.
Marion E.,Oct.18,1928,80y.
no name,rem. from Evergreen
 Cemetery, 1920.
Willard W.,Feb.14,1922,67y.
SPEIRS
Alexander,Oct.5,1927,67y.
Archibald,Jan.2,1934,70y.
Bessie E.,Jan.9,1961,88y.

child/o Alex. & Lottie,1888-1889.
Ernest,1882-1905.
Ernest L.,June 30,1955,37y.
Hazel E.,Jan.19,1981.
Henry T.,Oct.19,1979,70y.
infant/o Alex. & Lottie,1892-1892.
Lottie Plummer,1861-1895,
w/o Alexander.
SPELMAN
Ina M.,Feb.7,1921,35y.
Mildred Peterson,Feb.10,1921,35y.
SPENCER
Dorothy Davis,Sept.23,1992,83y.
Edwin Isaac,Oct.28,1930,62y.
Florence C.,July 3,1989,89y.
Franklin H,Lt.Col.,Oct.1,1979,82y.
Ruth A.,July 17,1928,2y.
Sophronia R.,June 12,1945,73y.
SPENCER
Edwin Isaac, Oct.28,1930,62y.
SPENETTA
Evelyn, XXXX, 30y, rem. from
Saccarappa Cemetery June1927.
SPILLER
Alpheus M.,May 9,1957,72y.
Amos Luther,Jan.16,1951,84y.
Arnold, Feb.2,1989,71y.
Arthur C.,Apr.9,1943,48y.
Carroll D., Aug.5,1965,67y.
Cyrus W.,Dec.13,1911,59y,
h/o Susan Edwards.
Daniel A., Nov.10,1969,87y.
Donald Anderson,Mar.29,1922,5d.
Edith W.,Jan.12,1948,77y.
Guy W.,May 17,1964,71y.
infant,July 1,1942, s.b.
infant,Aug.16,1961, sb.
J. Lillian,Nov.5,1993,90y.
Katherine E.,Dec.24,1977,84y.
Lambert,Jan.11,1912.
Maurice R.,June 25,1957,57y.
Mildred L.,July 6,1962,75y.
Nellie Davis,Jan.13,1992,94y.
Susie D.,June 7,1929,69y.
Walter E.,Apr.7,1985,67y.
SPRING
Eliza S. Bean,July 30,1924,71y.
Fred W.,Dec.22,1944,90y.
SPRINGER
Bruce G.,Nov.21,1946, prem.
George T.,bu: Oct.15,1937.
Lida Ellen,bu: Aug.28,1941,84y.
Lizzie E.,June 28,1893,37y.
SPROUL
Elsie L.,Dec.5,1976,75y.
Honoria M.,Aug.14,1983,76y.
James E.,Nov.4,1953,78y.

Matthew C.,Oct.27,1991,81y.
Martha,Nov.27,1947,73y.
Rufus H.,May 5,1991,93y.
SQUIRE
Helen M.,Nov.28,1982,83y.
William H.,Nov.15,1959,60y.
ST.CYR
Omer L. Sept.11,1991,79y.
STACKI
Frank I.,Jan.6,1994.
STACKPOLE
Andrew Jackson,Apr.18,1904,63y.
Isabelle,1843-May 13,1898,
w/o Andrew J.
STANFORD
J.F.,July 29,1909,62y.
Maggie,1887-1900,d/o J.F.& M.A.
Margaret A.,Nov.20,1936,87y.
Paul A.,Sr.,Jan.23,1990,76y.
Rose A., Apr.12,1969,85y.
Walter E.,June 29,1927,44y.
STANLEY
Arthur B.,Mar.23,1962,53y.
Earle E., June 10,1964, 63y.
Frances M., Apr.20,1964, 64y.
STANTON
Hattie E.,Feb.6,1947,69y.
Julia E.,Aug.3,1977,69y.
Lewis G., Sept.7,1947,65y.
Thomas W.,May 31,1919,5d.
Virgil A.,Oct.6,1981,75y.
STAPLES
Almon A.,Dec.13,1976,86y.
Beatrice C.,Nov.17,1975,83y.
Cyrus E.,Feb.6,1924,62y.
Edward C.,Aug.24,1966,77y.
Elsie L.,May 16,1986,70y.
Hattie E.,Apr.24,1960,83y.
Helen, Nov.28,1971.
Henrietta S.,Jan.6,1967,78y.
Henry F.,Mar.20,1957,81y.
infant, Oct.21,1974, s.b.
Jere,189491897,45y.
Joseph W.,Apr.4,1967,65y.
Leonard L.,May 5,1959,48y.
Llewellyn, Aug.4,1926,53y.
Lovina, Sept.15,192X.
Margaret S.,Nov.26,1970,85y.
Maud Linda, Aug.12,1927,45y.
Maurice E.,Mar.29,1967,61y.
Raymond T.,June 27,1961,52y.
STARBIRD
Frances,1795-1877.
Joshua,1787-1879.
STEARNS
Alice M., Nov.26,1978,91y.
Helen,bu:Sept.1,1927,45y.

infant, Dec.13,1940, s.b.
STERLING
Dorothy Wilcox,July 22,1937,20y.
Duane,Jan.24,1952,13hrs.
Malcolm P.,July 6,1966.
Paul,Jan.24,1952,1hr.
Wilma A.,Aug.31,1987,96y.
STEVENS
Aaron W.,Mar.27,1948,78y.
Caroline,Oct.27,1918,84y.
Catherine M.,Feb.16,1938,74y.
Cora B.,Aug.27,1951,82y.
Frances G.,1845-1924,w/o Moses.
George L.,Oct.17,1920,57y.
Hazel W.,July 1,1987,76y.
Horace C.,Nov.4,1935,63y.
Howard M.,Jan.6,1937,71y.
John,Mar.22,1912,82y,
h/o Ann Marie Cram.
Laurel, Sept.1,1933,30y.
Lawrence,1891-1892,s/o W.S.
Moses,Sept.11,1917,rem.from Gray.
Nina C.,Nov.30,1966,84y.
Pauline M.,Sept.14,1990,95y.
Shuyler C.,May 23,1954,81y.
W. Bernard, Sept.6,1957,72y.
Walter S.,Mar.7,1952,90y.
Wesley J.,1885-1908.
STEVENSON
Abbie E.,Dec.29,1915,69y,w/o Alex.
Alexander,1845-1894.
Benjamin D.,Oct.18,1944,70y.
Catherine,Feb.3,1935,85y.
Ernest A.,Mar.16,1991,92y.
Frank A., Apr.25,1933,57y.
Herbert W.,July 4,1940,48y.
Jessie W.,Dec.17,1961,67y.
Marguerite C.,July 7,1988,88y.
Maud L.,Mar.7,1950,68y.
Ora E.,Feb.7,1968,83y.
STEVES
Blanche W. Feb.11,1952,74y.
Lois M. Sept.17,1907,69y,w/o Thos.
May M.,1875-1880.
Thomas A., Sept.17,1898,70y.
STEWART
Anson B., Mar.4,1958,55y.
Melissa,XXXX, rem. from
Buxton Oct.1928.
Nettie A.,Jan.29,1955,84y.
Ruby,Sept.23,1954,56y.
STEWERTSEN
Catherine M.,Nov.16,1914,36y.
STICKNEY
Charles H., Apr.2,1943,41y.
Eva W.,Mar.30,1911,27y,w/o Herb.
Fred W.,July 24,1960,87y.

Herbert H.,Dec.7,1936,62y.
Maude, Mar.4,1972,94y.
STIGMAN
Phyllis R., Jan.17,1990,83y.
William R.,Jr.,Nov.23,1928,
5d.,rem. from Eastern Cem.,
Gorham in 1953.
William R.,Nov.9,1987,88y.
STIMPSON
Charles S., Oct.8,1987,75y.
STIMSON
Carolyn S.,Jan.17,1922,37y.
Mary W., Apr.8,1930,74y.
Virginia W.,Aug.14,1880,10m,
removed from Gray 1924.
STOCKFORD
Hattie I.,Feb.10,1957,83y.
William B.,Apr.24,1955,84y.
STODDARD
Katherine, Feb.22,1981,85y.
Lewis A.,Dec.13,1946,31y.
Michael J.,Apr.24,1969,16d.
William P.,Apr.23,1974,82y.
STOKES
Catherine,June 16,1912,72y.
Charles L.,Oct.23,1954.
Elizabeth,June 15,1914,49y.
Flora J.,Feb.21,1956,78y.
James,July 12,1910,60y.
John P.,Sept.29,1921,62y.
Sarah E.,June 16,1914,49y.
STONE
Edward L.,Feb.26,1926,70y.
Francis E.,Aug.2,1949,82y.
John,1827-1893.
John,June 14,1958,83y.
STROUT
Alonzo T.,June 5,1953,84y.
Betty M.,July 3,1992,62y.
Charles E.,Feb.15,1951,21d.
Dorothy L.,July 1,1957,46y.
Edward J.,Sr.,Dec.15,1972,62y.
Frances E.,July 12,1985,62y.
Glenn R.,Dec.8,1958,20y.
Guy R.,Oct.31,1947,68y.
Harry M.,Dec.28,1944,53y.
infant,Apr.26,1917, s.b.
infant,Jan.25,1951,2 hrs.
Jennie M.,Oct.1,1961,86y.
M. Betty,July 3,1992,62y.
Marcia M.,Apr.3,1957,81y.
Marvin S.,June 5,1958,80y.
Mildred E.,May 2,1970,72y.
Rachel S.,May 2,1943,48y.
Robert,May 1,1928,3d.
Roger C.,Apr.23,1917.
Viola M.,Dec.1,1950,76y.

Willia G.,July 4,1973,80y.
STUART
Etta M.,June 15,1966,83y.
Everett M.,June 12,1980,86y.
Gertrude E.,Oct.23,1958,47y.
J. Warren,Mar.22,1981,88y.
Margaret E.,May 4,1965,67y.
Mary B.,July 11,1989,93y.
Peter L.,Nov.20,1928,83y.
STUBBS
Anna L.,Nov.5,1941,71y.
Emma G.,June 13,1982,87y.
Harold T.,Nov.17,1964,69y.
Madeline I.,May 14,1973,40y.
Wilbur J.,Jan.3,1938,71y.
STULTZ
Charles T.,May 7,1958,47y.
Edith, no dates,80y.
Howard F.,Jr.,June 2,1982,73y.
Howard F.,Sr.,Dec.28,1982,101y.
infant,Feb.12,1974, s.b.
Mary E.,Aug.15,1967,84y.
Pauline R.,May 1,1988,68y.
Richard A.,Nov.21,1974,4y.
STURGIS
Alice Luetta,1862-Aug.13,1899.
Eben H.,1807-Dec.12,1904.
Eben H.,1841-1890,49y (?).
Esther Cannell,1838-Feb.15,1910, w/o Lewis B.
Lewis B.,1838-Dec.7,1911.
Mary A.,1815-1889.
STURTEVANT
Zane L.,June 25,1987,67y.
SULLIVAN
Charles F.,Feb.19,1943,84y.
Francis J.,Aug.8,1988,86y.
George M.,May 2,1954,62y.
Gertrude L.,July 15,1980,86y.
SUTERMEISTER
Bertha B.,Apr.23,1971,92y.
Edwin, July 30,1958,81y.
Margaret,Dec.5,1963,57y.
Pauline H.,Apr.21,1957,48y.
SWAN
Chester D.,July 30,1963,88y.
Clifford L.,Dec.4,1975,76y.
Dudley T., Apr.15,1912,61y, s/o Caleb G. & Abigail H.
Elizabeth Dutch, Jan.7,1930,82y.
Jerainie N.,June 26,1975,65y.
John, Dr.,Nov.17,1900,60y.
Lulu M.,Apr.12,1976,85y.
Mabel E.,June 11,1954,67y.
Mary Lenora,Mar.29,1921,62y.
Maurice R.,July 22,1973,59y.
Percy R.,June 2,1948,69y.

Persis D.,Jan.22,1961,92y.
Ralph Edwin, Apr.17,1924,12d.
Wilson J.,Dec.19,1927,60y.
Winifred, Apr.1,1892,22y.
SWARTZ
infant, Mar.1,1916, s.b.
SWEET
Amanda Jane,Mar.19,1916,63y.
Folmer R.,Feb.6,1982,66y.
Irving J.,Oct.31,1994,78y.
Mary J.,Jan.28,1940,w/o Maurice.
Maurice A.,May 9,1955,72y.
SWEDSEN
E. Gertrude,July 3,1994,95y.
Fred W., Feb.24,1973,81y.
Lorena P., Sept. 4, 1964,74y.
SWENSON
Gustau A.W.,May 15,1906,3m.
Karl E., May 20,1906,1y.
SWERTSEN
infant,Mar.8,1907,2m.
SWETT
Amanda Jane,Mar.22,1916,63y.
Annie R.,Feb.4, 1937, 86y.
Arthur C.,Sr.,Jan. 23,1961,63y.
Charles N.,May 6,1945,44y.
Charles W., Apr.11,1959, 88y.
Ella M. Sawyer,Dec.1,1937,87y.
Elvira K.,Oct.28,1937,89y.
Fred W.,July 30,1955,80y.
George B., Sept.6,1921,74y.
Isabel S,"Queenie",Aug.17,1982,84y.
Leslie B.,May 15,1960,58y.
Lizzie M., Apr.26,1952.
Martin Z., Apr.19,1900,91y.
Nancy, Apr.13,1900,88y.
Sarah W.,May 9,1954,65y.
Winfred Scott, Aug.27,1915,72y.
Walter E.,May 12,1969,90y.
Warren S.,May 17,1959,71y.
SYKES
Clifton E., Sept.15,1992,59y.
SYLVESTER
Alice B.,Nov.24,1899,21y.
Carrie E.,Feb.8,1901,42y.
Charles E.,July 14,1942,87y.
Cora G.,bu:Jan.9,1937,77y.
Emma L.,July 2,1959,73y.
no name,Feb.17,1901,71y.
Richard G.,Oct.14,1919,90y.
SYLVIA
Alton E.,Oct.10,1990,51y.
SZOSTAK
John H., Nov.25,1990,70y.
TAGGERT
Catherine C.,May 20,1928,36y.
Daniel, June 24,1919,78y.

Edel B., Oct.7,1979 76y.
Jennie,1884-1884.
Lawrence B.,June 18,1965,78y.
Leland R., Aug.15,1982,93y.
Mabel Guptill,Mar.31,1913,51y.
Mabel G., Nov.15,1919.
TAPLEY
Ethel M.,Sept.23,1970,74y.
Frederick R.,July 5,1992,79y.
Harriet A.,Dec 8,1954,63y.
Joseph H.,June 18,1961,49y.
Mariam, Apr.7,1892,75y.
Mary I.,June 13,1971,50y.
R. Frederick,July 5,1992,79y.
Scott A.,Sept.2,1936,49y.
Walter C.,Oct.9,1965,71y.
TARDIFF
Leona P.,Mar.5,1988,80y.
Patrick F.,Nov.23,1976,73y.
TAYLOR
Alma I.,Dec.19,1993,84y.
Arthur M.,Mar.11,1886,4y,
rem. from Pine Grove Cem.,
Portland in 1925.
Elizabeth M., June 17,1931,53y.
George A.,Oct.2,1934,73y.
George E.,Mar.14,1973,79y.
Harold Fred,Mar.23,1942.
Herbert W.,Mar.17,1946,68y.
Horace P.,Feb.17,1920,39y.
Howard, June 24,1954,68y.
Jonas, Rev.,June 22,1921,32y.
Laura H.,May 9,1973,80y.
Martella E., Sept.22,1971,56y.
Mary K. Oct.13,1963 83y.
Myrtle E.,Jan.28,1952,59y.
Powell P.,Sr.,Feb.24,1978,81y.
Priscilla E.,Oct.28,1964,77y.
Ralph E.,July 5,1937,62y.
Richard T.,Sept.25,1949,75y.
Sarah E.,Apr.4,1953,85y.
Sarah June, Sept.19,1932,83y.
Thora L.,Mar.6,1950.
William, Jan.14,1925,75y.
Winona E.,Dec.24,1970,64y.
TEAGUE
Gladys M.,Feb.16,1967,60y.
James H.,Dec.29,1947,65y.
Mellcora A.,Jan.1,1970.
TEDFORD
Harry J., Feb.4,1939,70y.
infant, Feb.5,1956, s.b.
Milo Victor, Aug.29,1945,39y.
Nancy J.,Jan.2,1988,41y.
TEMPLE
Charles M.,Nov.18,1967,27y.

TENNY
Elizabeth C.,Dec.6,1988,97y.
TERRIO
Robert T.,May 17,1967,42y.
TETRAULT
Gertrude C.,May 18,1956,35y.
infant, Apr.14,1942, s.b.
Leo J.,Nov.13,1992,79y.
Mildred M., July 18,1983,77y.
THAYER
Beatrice M.,Sept.28,1946,45y.
THEIS
Emma, Sept.8,1943,78y.
Ernest, Sept.8,1960,72y.
Frederick W.,Sept.26,1927,65y.
Marion E.,Nov.5,1934,42y.
Mildred, Nov.18,1991,94y.
THERIAULT
Alice R., May 12,1993,71y.
Arthur H.,May 21,1966,70y.
Arthur H.,bu:Jan.17,1933,14y.
Blanche S., Oct.18,1979,81y.
Henry, Feb.26,1941.
infant, Mar.8,1956,2hrs.
infant, Feb.3,1957,5hrs.
Louisa Ruth,Sept.6,1933,s.b.
Mabel W.,June 28,1990,91y.
Ovide J. Feb.12,1958,59y.
Richarad H.,Jr.,Jan.6,1955,3d.
THIBEAULT
Lea Nicole,Dec.27,1981,3d.
THISLTE
Leah M.,Sept.10,1987,69y.
Roy L.,Feb.21,1987,71y.
THOMAS
Anna E.,Jan.21,1948,75y.
Charles A.,July 5,1976,91y.
Clara M.,May 4,1969,80y.
Edna E.,Sept.3,1985,93y.
infant,May 31,1958, s.b.
Karen I.,Feb.28,1980,93y.
Paul K.,Sept.19,1964,53y.
Roma E.,Nov.7,1940,43y.
Sidney B.,Mar.9,1954,84y.
Thomas S.,Mar.9,1973,84y.
THOMPSON
Alvena F., Apr.19,1971,75y.
Annie E., Feb.28,1984,96y.
Annie S.,Nov.13,1973,65y.
Bennett E.,Sept.18,1974,64y.
Charles C.,Dec.30,1951,60y.
Charles O.,Feb.24,1942,65y.
Clifford N.,July 11,1952,73y.
Clifford R.,Oct.9,1969,67y.
Daisy M., Oct.22,1957,78y.
David Alfred,Nov.9,1920,5y.
Guy E.,Aug.7,1973,80y.

Harland M.,June 12,1970,62y.
Helen B.,Nov.4,1982,84y.
Henry M.,Dec.1,1964,77y.
Herbert Lee,Apr.5,1952,72y.
Herman,Sept.7,1943,77y.
Hovey G.,July 31,1953,69y.
Ida F.,Dec.8,1939,87y.
John D.,Sept.22,1994,85y.
Katherine M.,Feb.22,1959,52y.
Keith J.,May 9,1981,65y.
Lillie Dora,Feb.15,1933,65y.
Lottie M., Oct.22,1943,63y.
Martha M.,Dec.30,1951,70y.
Mary C.,Nov.7,1957,73y.
Mildred M.,Dec.4,1971,78y.
Norma Ann, Oct.9,1932,2d.
Norman, Mar.20,1975,79y.
Ralph B.,Mar.6,1991,79y.
Virginia J.,July 3,1976,41y.
Virginia O.,Nov.27,1981,55y.
THOMSEN
Anna Marie,Feb.23,1931,73y.
Helen,1900-1900.
Martin A.,Nov.14,1937,81y.
THONSEN
Amalie Katrina,Jan.23,1958,73y.
Christian, Aug.27,1937,89y.
Christian H.,Oct.16,1965,79y.
Ida C.,July 4,1919,30y.
Katherine M.,1851-1913.
THORNE
Arthur C.,Aug.7,1968,59y.
Milton,Apr.11,1974,96y.
Winnie A.,Sept.10,1944,63y.
THORNTON
Sewell L.,June 30,1945,58y.
THUOTTE
Josephine,Sept.16,1932, s.b.
THURLOW
Susan A.,Feb.6,1901,78y.
THURSTON
Richard L.,Jr.,Nov.23,1971,9y.
THYGESEN
Nicolay, May 1913.
TIBBETTS
Adrienne,Dec.27,1974,85y.
Charles H.,1866-187X,s/o R.P.& L.A.
Edward H.,1873-74,s/o R.P.& L.A.
Elizabeth M.,June 4,1944,85y.
Florence Fanny,Nov.18,1953,86y.
Lucy A. Holland,May 31,1926,84y.
Robert P.,1833-1902.
Roy H.,Apr.1,1982,73y.
TIEDWELL
Beatrice C.,June 16,1990,80y.
George D.,Sr.,May 18,1969,71y.

TILTON
Burton H., Rev.,July 7,1949,78y.
Edith M.,July 27,1958,79y.
Emma Wright,Oct.6,1933,62y.
Gladys L.,Feb.21,1945,53y.
TIMBERLAKE
Elsie J.,May 13,1987,83y.
Leslie B.,Aug.26,1977,77y.
TIMONEY
Evelyn, Sept.29,1951,47y.
TINGLEY
infant, Nov.15,1939, s.b.
TINKER
Arthur L.,Nov.14,1959,34y.
Florence B.,May 1,1975,78y.
TINKHAM
Caroline May,Nov.9,1936,55y.
Florida L.,June 26,1922,65y.
TINSMAN
John L.,July 20,1954,15y.
Lois B.,Sept.22,1964,53y.
Luther D.,Mar.4,1924,71y.
Norris E.,Dec.5,1959,62y.
Winfield G.,Aug.19,1967,66y.
TITCOMB
Alan W. Aug.29,1972,63y.
Alice L.,Nov.1,1946,77y.
Almira E.,Mar.14,1926,83y.
Charles W.,Mar.12,1921,61y.
Jennie S.,1836-July 11,1897, w/o Charles W.
Wingate C., Aug.6,1933,65y.
TITUS
Grace J.,Mar.21,1967,83y.
TODD
Rufus A.,Feb.23,1924,52y.
TOFT
Edith, Apr.9,1945,54y.
TOHER
Cynthia L., Oct.18,1943.
TOMPSON
Alfretta L.,Apr.5,1961,69y.
Charles,Nov.21,1969,86y.
Edith,1885,3y.
Flossie,1887,child.
Gertrude E.,1877-1896.
John E.,May 19,1928,87y.
Mabel L.,July 1,1937,58y.
Rose L.,Nov.27,1907,56y,w/o John.
TONGE
John, Jan.7,1941,73y.
Margaret E., Apr.18,1941,73y.
TORREY
Alice Q.,July 17,1971,86y.
Bates, Jr.,Dec.17,1978,88y.
Grace B.,Feb.23,1988,90y.
Stephen A., Apr.23,1975,49y.

Wilfred V.,July 1,1964,68y.
TORSEY
Mary A.,Dec.3,1982,84y.
TOWER
Carol A. Lucas,Nov.13,1987,43y.
TOWLE
Jabez O.,Sept.16,1904,65y.
Mary E.,May 8,1898,58y.
TOWNSEND
Arnold R., Jan.4,1986,71y.
Charles W.,Apr.10,1934,43y.
Florence M.,July 25,1982,94y.
Guy A., Dec.28,1944,55y.
Harry E.,June 29,1960,80y.
Herbert A.,Mar.6,1929,51y.
Ida M., Dec.1,1932,80y.
John,XXXX, 61y, rem. from Oak Rd. Cem., Standish Dec.1932.
Lawrence Lee,June 8,1938,1y.
Lawrence L.,Sept.4,1967,69y.
Lena D., bu:Jan. XXXX, 60y.
Nathaniel M. Aug.26,1985,79y.
Philip W., Apr.4,1975,57y.
V.Gladys, Sept.11,1933,37y.
Verna M., Aug.28,1953,44y.
TOWSEY
Edward W.,July 15,1965,57y.
infant,Nov.8,1948, s.b.
TRACEY
E. George, June 24,1992, 66y.
George Wellington,Aug.2,1927,25y.
Martin L.,Jan.4,1964,75y.
Mary B.,Jan.8,1967,85y.
Mary C.,Jan.21,1936,78y.
Oscar L.,Mar.10,1939,57y.
Pearl B.,Aug.3,1961,52y.
Richard J.E.,Sept.29,1969,23y.
TRAFTON
Almira L.,Oct.5,1988,85y,w/o John.
Aramenta E.,Mar.27,1936,79y.
Ella M.,Jan.26,1963,87y.
James A.,May 28,1943,87y.
John E.,1838-1897.
May C.,June 20,1994,95y.
Norman E.,Dec.19,1962,65y.
Otis S.,Jan.12,1947,71y.
Roudolf H.,Mar.30,1980,78y.
TRASK
Anson,1812-1899.
Elizabeth M,1816-1884,w/o Anson.
Ella F.,1859-Dec.18,1944.
Emma Gertrude,1878-1887, d/o J.H.&M.E.
Harriett E.,Sept.24,1932,80y.
James Henry,1840-Dec.20,1916.
John Wesley,1873-1889.
John Wesley,1850-1866.
Mariam E.Wellman,1850-Dec.8,1920.
Mariam Lillian,1872-1892.
Sarah E., Jan.31,1926,75y.
William E.,Oct.1,1920,76y.
TRAVIS
Robert L.,Apr.26,1984,77y.
TRICKEY
Albert A.,Oct.8,1908,68y.
Daniel W.,Feb.2,1905.
Susan Gould,1845-Dec 2,1911, w/o Albert.
TRIPP
Emma A.,Dec.3,1976,92y.
Evelyn S.,Mar.2,1991,87y.
Herman W.,June 24,1976,75y.
Irvin J.,bu:May 2,1950,25y.
Lois H.,July 1,1966,35y.
Sylvia G.,Jan.15,1927,1y.
TRUAX
Raymond,June 21,1944,30y.
TRUE
Mabel H.,June 7,1976,93y.
TRUEWORTHY
Mildred A., Sept.5,1979,82y.
Richard, July 16,1926,9d.
TRUMBALL
Alice T.,Nov.5,1972,83y.
Daniel D.,Oct.25,1943,78y.
Harriet J.,Jan.5,1940,71y.
Ralph J.,May 9,1969,81y.
TRZENSKA
David F.,Dr.,Oct.11,1987,34y.
TUCKER
Agnes L.,bu: Sept.24,1962,80y.
Alma A.,Dec.28,1963,73y.
Amory W.,Dec.14,1967,86y.
Anna M., Apr.10, 1957,73y.
Eva M., Oct.14,1943.
James A.,Apr.25,1948,63y.
John H.,Nov.29,1957,85y.
Inez F.,bu:Apr.18,1963.
Marjorie R.,Jan.3,1994.
Willis A.,Aug.28,1958,75y.
TULLAR
Annie I.,June 27,1938,73y.
TURGEON
Albert E.,bu:Nov.30,1936,7y.
TURNBULL
Isabella R.,1829-May 1,1894, w/o David.
TURNER
Adella N.,Jan.19,1932,81y.
Fred R.,Nov.21,1933,60y.
Fred W.,Sr., Apr.14,1980,74y.
Gladys, May 28,1912,3m.
Isabelle L., Aug.24,1965,82y.
J.Arthur,Jan.17,1944,84y.

Princess H., Aug.1,1966,63y.
Ralph A.,Jr.,Sept.16,1927,s.b.
Walter G.,Mar.21,1981,78y.
TUTTLE
Charles S.,Jan.20,1940,65y.
Charles W.,May 25,1961,58y.
Grace J., Aug.29,1960,83y.
infant, Nov.24,1961, s.b.
Ivory S.,Feb.15,1970,72y.
Mildred A.,May 11,1985,85y.
William S.,Apr.2,1970,34y.
UNTERREINER
Bernard R.,Nov.16,1956,56y.
Cora K., Nov.3,1946,41y.
VALENTINE
Abigail,Oct.8,1774-Jan.27,1861, w/o William.
Leander,July 23,1895,81y.
Marcena A.,May 16,1845-Apr.1,1846,d/o Leander.
Margaret S., May 23,1892,70y.
William,Apr.14,1773-Apr.16,1845.
VALIA
Pauline M., Apr.10,1908,8y.
VALLEY
Frances M., Mar. 3,1980,53y.
VALLIERE
Gertrude W.,Dec.13,1989,72y.
VAN BUSKIRK
Jennie,Oct.20,1937,78y.
John, Apr.30,1931,84y.
VANDERBULCKE
Leopold P.,Dec.14,1977,79y.
VAN TASSEL
Charles W.,June 30,1955,39y.
VAN VLIET
Richard,Mar.29,1936,1d.
VANNAH
Abbie F.,May 12,1973,89y.
Forest H.,Apr.16,1956,72y.
VANNER
Alexander K.,Feb.6,1945,73y.
Caroline B.,Oct.23,1935,55y.
Hazel A.,Jan.15,1927,21y.
VARNEY
Charles W., July 11,1946,74y.
Earl L.,Apr.13,1965,47y.
Mabelle S.,Jan.24,1969,83y.
Paul D.,Oct.31,1974,50y.
William L.,Nov.13,1956,37y.
VAUGHAN
Fred C.,Jan.22,1949,47y.
Joyce A.,Nov.17,1993, 52y.
VENO
Mildred C., Feb.27,1936,39y.
VENTRESCO
Josephine, Oct.27,1984,66y.

VERRILL
Agnes Grant Oct.14,1920,84y.
Albert Jr.,Oct.30,1991,77y.
Albert S.,May 5,1973,84y.
Anna B., Aug.6,1975,69y.
Anna O.,Oct.8,1964,85y.
Charles L.,Dec.25,1898,no body, died on the Steamer Portland.
Charles E.1892-1892,s/o C.L.&A.B.
Charles N., Sept.10,1900,10m, removed from Gray,ME 1942.
Clara E.,Apr.28,1973,85y.
Edith,1871,1y,d/o G.H.&A.
Fred A.,June 4,1934,69y.
Howard S.,Jan.23,1898,32y.
John S.,Dec.13,1946,3m.
Laurence M.,June 5,1975,71y.
Lewis M.,Jan.8,1943.
Martha, Apr.13,1973,22y.
Mary A.,Nov.8,1987,88y.
Mary Davis,Dec.12,1941,53y.
Mary T.,Feb.25,1953,90y.
Philip T.,Oct.6,1962,70y.
VINAL
Nellie L.,Nov.21,1935,68y.
Ora B.,bu:Dec.19,1928,61y.
VIOLETTE
Ludger J.,Dec.24,1978,70y.
WADES
Agnes M.,Sept 6,1986,68y.
Louis J.,Feb.13,1977,64y.
WAITE
Albert E.,Sr.,Mar.28,1971,70y.
Beatrice,Mar.13,1991,78y.
Charles Leo,Aug.29,1954,77y.
Joseph R.,Feb.24,1978,73y.
Lillian P.,June 21,1989,81y.
Mary M.,May 28,1935,58y.
RichardH.,Nov.161,984,64y.
WALKER
Albert Ernest,Oct.12,1918,28y.
Dianne M.,Dec.16,1968,10y.
Forest E.,June 14,1946,68y.
Harry S.,Feb.4,1961,54y.
Helen M., Mar.29,1989,90y.
Jody,June 1,1960, infant.
Kathleen "Kitty",Aug.16,1991,82y.
Kenneth O.,Nov.29,1929,29y.
Kenneth R.,Feb.14,1950,1y.
Lillian M.,Aug.10,1953,79y.
Maud,Nov.25,1956,77y.
WALLACE
James C.,bu:Sept.29,1950,89y.
Harriet,1842-1868.
WALTMAN
children of Raymond,June 1914, s.b.
Clifford M.,Nov.18,1978,85y.

Clifford M.,Jr.,Aug.11,1929,1d.
Horace H.,Feb.28,1932,73y.
Hazel J.,Apr.22,1985,88y.
James R.,Lt.Col.,Feb.5,1970,79y.
Jane A.,Nov.14,1950,81y.
Lois P.,Jan.19,1972,78y.
Mary H.,June 16,1918,56y.
Robert B., Aug.8,1931,66y.
R. Percy, Sept.22,1902,6y,
s/o Robert & Mary.
WALTON
Jane,May 1910,79y,wid/o Jos. H.
Mona H., Sept.28,1989,90y.
WANASKY
Flora B.,July 14,1940,56y.
WARD
Addie F.,Nov.17,1985,99y.
Alfred W.,Jan.19,1959,55y.
Chesley L.,June 17,1965,83y.
Fred,Jan.8,1919.
George L.,May 31,1896,2y.
Ina E., Sept.23,1966,79y.
Mary E.,Sept.9,1947,62y.
Nelson H.,July 18,1975,80y.
Susan J.,Dec.25,1917,76y.
Wilbur C.,Apr.10,1976,87y.
WARDSWORTH
Irene J.,Aug.15,1968,75y.
WARK
Bessie Guptill,Dec.20,1937,76y.
Camilla S.,July 17,1969,76y.
William L.,June 24,1922,29y.
WARMING
Adolf N., May 26,1992,94y.
Ingeborg S.,May 20,1989,84y.
Kristine, Apr.30,1974,82y.
Lauridtz N., Dec.26,1977,86y.
N. Adolf, May 26,1992,94y.
Stanley Carl, May 6,1920,6m.
Ruth L.,Feb.1,1964,47y.
WARNER
Elaine, Nov.18,1942,12y.
Ethel M., Oct.3,1982,83y.
Roy L., May 5,1975,96y.
WARREN
Albert F.,Mar.9,1920,70y.
Edith M.,Mar.12,1959,85y.
George T.,Apr.8,1994.
Harry F.,July 12,1911,31y.
infant,June 23,1937, s.b.
John W.(?), Feb.8,1922,75y.
Lelia A.,June 27,1940,87y.
Lewis P.,June 30,1900,82y.
Martha J.,July 24,1941,90y.
Mother,1818-1896.
Father,1817-1900.
Roscoe G.,1835-1894.

Russell S.,Dec.12,1986,71y.
Sarah,Apr.14,1896,77y.
Sarah Olive,May 12,1926,75y.
Sumner W.,1886-1899.
WASHBURN
Caroline W.,July 11,1930,74y.
Frank J.,Dec.24,1932,81y.
Harry W.,Mar.30,1928,41y.
John H.,Jan.2,1926,85y.
Lucy Jennie, Apr.20,1917,54y.
WATERHOUSE
Almon N.,May 11,1941,79y.
Ann,Dec.22,1988,52y.
Annie L.,May 3,1935,72y.
Charles M.,Jan.10,1928,78y.
Earl R.,Dec.18,1957,62y.
Eleanor R.,July 20,1990,101y.
Ernestine B.,Mar.2,1935,78y.
George Howard,Mar.18,1918,61y.
Grace M.,Apr.23,1953,81y.
Harold, removed from Hillside
Cem., No. Windham Nov.1918.
Howard H.,Aug.23,1923,69y.
Leon E.,Mar.12,1971,81y.
Lewis R.,Nov.8,1931,66y.
Mabel B.,June 10,1989,87y.
Martha A.,May 19,1936,77y.
Melvin H.,Nov.7,1962,84y.
Sarah,Oct.14,1917,39y.
Sarah Emma,Sept.11,1916,66y.
WATERMAN
Charles F.,Aug.7,1938,76y.
Glenna C.,May 7,1964,4m.
Hazel M.,Jan.7,1938,41y.
Nellie M.,Dec.16,1902,36y.
S. Freeman,Feb.12,1943,50y.
Wilton C.,Sr.,July 30,1989,71y.
WATKINS
children,May 7,1927.
Clinton A.,Jan.29,1927,73y.
Howard Clark, Apr.30,1927,1m.
Rebecca E.,Nov.11,1942,87y.
WATSON
Addie M.,1872-1894,w/o Walter J.
Adele,Apr.30,1943.
Albert J.,Dec.31,1929,58y.
Alice I.,Jan.30,1959, 69y.
Alice I., Mar.3,1934, 48y.
Annie May, Nov.24,1942, 64y.
Benjamin,Aug.2,1911,8m.
Bertha L.,Aug.14,1973,72y.
Bertha L.,June 14,1936, 55y.
Bessie L., Sept.25,1922, 40y.
C. Colby, Mar.3,1952,69y.
Clarence H.,Apr.22,1899,17m.
Charles F.,1885,20y,s/o D.& Jane.
Chester E.,Mar.30,1944,53y.

David Hamblen,1829-1882.
Edward B.,July 1, 1974,50y.
Eleanor L.,Feb.22,1985,71y.
Elizabeth,1905-1905.
Erma,1899-1900,d/o W. & A.M.
Eva St.Clair,Jan.5,1959,83y.
Evelyn F.,Mar.16,1991.
Fannie May,Mar.22,1941,59y.
Frederick E.,Jan.29,1965,92y.
George E.,Jan.27,1953,75y.
Harold C., Aug.17,1990,85y.
Harry B.,Sr.,July 14,1974,83y.
Harry F.,Feb.24,1925,69y.
Jane Sanborn1829-1892,w/o David.
John, Aug.16,1918,73y.
Julia M., Nov.25,1976,79y.
Laurence T.,1889-1895.
Lawrence J.,Feb.7,1976,80y.
Leslie L.,Nov.13,1945,46y.
Lewis M.,Sr.,Aug.11,1976,84y.
Mary E.,Dec.13,1912,64y,w/o John.
Matilda M.,Aug.14,1982,100y.
Millard F.,Aug.20,1957,75y.
Phebe B.,Jan.4, 1951,57y.
Ralph K.,Jr.,June 27,1978,39y.
Robert D., uly 18,1968,40y.
Rodine,1903-1903.
Roland,1903-1903.
Roselia,Jan.14,1969,74y.
Royal F.,Nov.20,1942,39y.
Ruth K.,Apr.29,1986.
Sadie May Jamison,Mar.17,1903, 23y, w/o Millard F.
Samuel M.,Oct.7,1950,71y.
Sarah, July 26,1943,87y.
Sarah I.,Mar.28,1922,68y.
Theodore F.,May 30,1964,61y.
Thomas,Aug.2,1929,81y.
Thurston A.,Feb.14,1905,2m.
Virgil L.,Feb.10,1966,84y.
Walter J.,July 15,1936,67y.
William N.,Feb.9,1943,69y.
Wynona A.,Mar.4,1906,3d.
WATT
Alexander,1887-1887.
Angus McMillan,1872-1896.
Belle,bu:June 5,1970.
Bessie,Feb.24,1957,74y.
John, Jan.6,1941,90y.
John,Jr.,1869-1893.
Martha L., Aug.4,1911,63y.
William R.L.,1870-1896.
Woodbury K.D.,1870-1902.
WEBB
Leora E.,May 13,1975,88y.
Michael A.,Feb.7,1991,44y.
Steward, Apr. 1, 1953, 68y.

WEBBER
Annie L.,Jan.21,1928,57y.
Arthur B.,Jan.5,1974,88y.
Beatrice,July 1,1949,76y.
Benjamin,1836-1897.
Edwin E.,May 20,1967,99y.
Eliza W.,Nov.28,1953,79y.
Florence L.,Dec.7,1972,80y.
Harold V.,July 25,1973,72y.
Henry N., Nov.24,1929,52y.
Herbert E.,Apr.27,1957,91y.
Lillian D.,May 25,1959,89y.
Mary R.,Jan.14,1943,102y.
WEBSTER
George A.,Nov.7,1971,62y.
Iva J.,Dec.7,1987,92y.
Thelma Audrey,Apr.24,1923,4m.
WEDGE
Anthony F.,Sr.,Nov.30,1981,74y.
Mildred I.,Aug.12,1959,51y.
WEED
Elizabeth,Dec.4,1969,71y.
Mildred E., Aug.14,1972,79y.
WEEKS
Delia L.,1847-1903,w/o Joseph.
Evelyn S.,Apr.4,1953,84y.
Ira E.,Apr.4,1934,71y.
Joseph E.,1835-1897.
Leon C.,Apr.11,1977,78y.
Lillian M.,Jan.4,1949,74y.
Mary A., Aug.23,1969,70y.
WEEMAN
Daisy M.,May 27,1957,57y.
Raymond E.,Mar.25,1981.
WEIR
Gary C., Nov.20,1979,25y.
Lillian B.,Mar.23,1976,59y.
WEIST
Annie,Jan.17,1937,85y.
WELCH
Agnes H.,Jan.29,1972,81y.
Arthur F.,Nov.2,1929,41y.
Belle H.,Jan.23,1943,75y.
Chester L.,Jan.11,1902,11y.
Edith L.,Jan.10,1964,88y.
Edna Strout,1878-1912, w/o Merton H.
Elias F.,Feb.10,1965,48y.
Gertrude H.,Apr.22,1962,42y.
Gertrude S.,Sept.27,1962,77y.
Gilbert P.,Oct.20,1954,75y.
H. Leroy,Dec.9,1963,70y.
H. Leroy, Nov.8,1980.
Henry L.,Mar.5,1937,70y.
John A.,35y, rem. from Evergreen Cem.,Portland,1898.
Lillian,Feb.1982,80y.

Mary F., Nov.19,1933,86y.
Merton H.,Mar.2,1875-Feb. 26,1905.
Milan O.,Oct.30,1961,62y.
Nellie A.,Sept.23,1988,98y.
Philip G., Apr.8,1964,49y.
William P.,Nov.13,1960,81y.
Winfield S.,Oct.8,1946,72y.
WELLMAN
David P.,Sept.11,1978,64y.
WELLS
Harry C.,Aug.11,1949,58y.
Leah P., Aug.4,1962,65y.
WENTWORTH
Angie B. Mayberry, Jan.21,1909, 28y, w/o William H., removed from North Windham 1916.
Annie L.,May 3,1953,87y.
Arthur,bu: Aug.31,1937,62y.
Augustus S.,Jan.18,1927,65y.
Bessie Whitney,Feb.23,1942,65y.
Blanche E.,Dec.20,1941,52y.
Chester,Oct.7,1916,11y.
Clayton N.,July 16,1969,62y.
Clifford, Aug.12,1968,79y.
Edward R.,1824-Mar.16,1894.
Edward R.,Feb.14,1940,37y.
Eleanor J., Apr.14,1966,64y.
Eliza B.,July 28,1967,95y.
Ella Cobb,Nov.10,1952,74y.
Elvina C.,May 6,1929,70y.
George H.,bu:June 20,1928,70y.
Grace E.,Apr.17,1966,75y.
Harold W.,Aug 21,1913,17y.
Josephine,Oct.21,1925,52y.
Leland N., Sept.17,1983,81y.
Leland Nelson,Jr.,Feb.15,1923,3m.
Leroy L.,Jan.20,1924,44y.
Lincoln,May 4,1985,77y.
Lyman,Dec.21,1934,64y.
Mary S.,1824-Aug.23,1908, wid/o Edward S.
Nettie J.,Mar.4,1954,85y.
Philip L.,Oct.17,1942,32y.
Ray Lyman,Sept.10,1908,7m, s/o Lyman & Eliza E.
Roland Clifford, Aug.28,1916,1y.
Roscoe,bu:Sept.4,1937,64y.
William H., June 4,1952,71y.
WESCOTT
Amanda,June 2,1982, s.b.
Delbert E.,Jr.,Mar.19,1994,77y.
Dorothy O.,Mar.24,1960,48y.
Elizabeth F.,Sept.17,1943.
Fred C.,Mayor,Dec.29,1993,61y.
Harold G.,Mar.23,1990,78y.
Kenneth E.,Dec.29,1974,36y.
Kenneth L.,Mar.20,1983,68y.

Melissa, Oct.4,1993,24y.
Norris A.,May 8,1974,65y.
Norris A.,Jr.,Jan.25,1978,41y.
Travis J.,Dec.21,1988,5y.
WEST
Edwin L.,Mar.12,1919,65y.
Elsie,Jan.31,1950,61y.
Emeline,Feb.8,1899,33y.
Ernestine,1863-1897,w/o Edwin.
James, Jan.1,1939,59y.
Marion F., Apr.23,1976,84y.
Winfred M.,1885-1888.
WESTERBERG
Gustof A.,Jan.28,1944,69y.
WESTON
infant, Sept.3,1928, s.b.
WETMORE
Margaret A.,Dec.22,1944,82y.
Maxwell V.,July 26,1941,41y.
WHARFF
Dorothy M., July 18,1936,37y.
Harold S., Sept.24,1972,75y.
WHEELER
Adelia A., Apr.23,1909, 57y, wid/o George.
Alice O.,Jan.4,1958,79y.
Douglas E.,Oct.17,1989,62y.
Euric W.,July 18,1936,27y.
Florence E.,Nov.18,1969,88y.
Frances E.,Feb.5,1955,61y.
George H.,Sept.4,1906,56y.
George H.,Sept.20,1937,68y.
Harry A.,June 9,1963,73y.
Harry A.,Jr.,Feb.11,1976,59y.
Herbert N.,Jan.21988,57y.
Isabelle W.,Apr.4,1939,65y.
Lloyd W.,Jan.20,1963,79y.
Louis E.1888-1889,s/o G.D.& A.A.H.
Perley W.,Aug.31,1954,33y.
WHEET
Frederick E,M.D.,Jan.16,1952,84y.
Harriet J.,June 13,1945,74y.
WHELDEN
Grace E.,Sept.9,1958,87y.
Lothrop H.,June 11,1931,63y.
WHIDDEN
George H.,Capt.,Aug.29,1924,83y.
Lucy H., Feb.5,1909,56y.
Susan A. Maybury,1841-1911.
WHIPPLE
Blanche A.,Feb.3,1974,76y.
Charles Wesley,1852-1881.
Edith M.,Nov.26,1988,59y.
Frank H.,Oct.22,1947,75y.
Frederick R.,Feb.6,1958,66y.
John,1806-1869.
Lillian G.,Jan.28,1961,78y.

Sally Houston,1809-1888.
Susan A. Mayberry,1841-1911,
  w/o George A.
WHITE
Charles F.,Mar.7,1937,79y.
Charlotte W.,May 8,1986,94y.
George W.,Sept 20,1917,64y.
Harvey A.,Sept.9,1972,73y.
Helen Christine,Dec.6,1930,27y.
infant, Apr.11,1965, s.b.
Jennie, Oct.22,1953, 85y.
Langdon R.,Dr.,Apr.24,1968, 7y.
Richard H.,Nov.16,1984, 64y.
Ricky Dana,Nov.16,1964,8y.
WHITEHEAD
Sarah J.,Mar.28,1939,81y.
WHITEHOUSE
Ella J.,May 21,1935,77y.
WHITING
Edward,June 12,1917,70y.
WHITMAN
Alice Lelia,Feb.11,1929,39y.
Edward C.,Feb.7,1957,60y.
Fred Eugene, Sept.22,1943,74y.
infant, Feb.9,1929, prem.
Joseph E.,Dec.17,1977,86y.
Josephine F.,Aug.28,1961,92y.
Martha V.,Oct.28,1981, 85y.
J.Richard,July 4,1985,64y.
WHITMORE
Dorothy M.,Aug.23,1953,47y.
John D.,Nov.24,1956,63y.
Theresa E.,Apr.3,1935,2m.
WHITNEY
Agnes B.,Dec.3,1974.
B. Ober,Dec.25,1918,73y.
Carrie C.,Jan.1,1915,31y,d/o Iver Holt.
Clara E., Mar.19,1914,57y,w/o James.
Donald E.,Apr.9,1943,1m.
Edward A.,May 9,1917,7Xy.
Etta M.,Mar.8,1905,23y.
Evelyn T.,Oct.3,1966,88y.
Fannie Louise,Mar.26,1944,89y.
Fred E.,bu:Nov.28,1937,80y.
H. Lee,Jan.17,1975,92y.
James A.,May 1,1934,81y.
Linda,May 7,1895,80y.
Madelyn G.,June 13,1948,41y.
Margaret,Oct.5,1928,83y.
Mary A.,Mar.22,1914,57y.
Oral R.,Sept.26,1942,69y.
Roy E.,1884-1893,s/o E.A.&M.
Thurston L.,Mar.24,1926,1d.
Thurston L.,Sept.22,1953,48y.
WHITTAKER
Marion G., Sept.4,1950,54y.

WHITTEN
Martha A.,July 17,1930,78y.
Nathalie E.,Jan.31,1970,81y.
Willard M., Feb.7,1925,70y.
WHITTIER
Helen W.,July 26,1990,65y.
J. Henry,Nov.18,1934,76y.
Maria Louise,Dec.5,1931,70y.
WIDBER
Clarence Dana,Aug.14,1939,s.b.
Frances Louise,June 29,1916,4y.
infant,Mar.23,1938,prem.
WIEMERT
Martin F.,Sept.2,1978,39y.
WIGGIN
Albert F.,May 9,1945,79y.
Herbert E.,Mar.24,1946,83y.
Ida Louise Hatch,Feb.15,1932,35y.
James F.,July 26,1977,82y.
Roy L.,May 24,1991,98y.
Thelma H.,Mar.4,1986,84y.
WIGHT
Donald M.,May 3,1936,70y.
Emmaline L.,Oct.28,1937,73y.
WILDER
Frances Lance,July 2,1916,5m.
WILDES
Brian H.,Oct.16,1976,rem. from
  Highland Mem. Gardns, S.P.,1987.
WILKINS
Edgar P.,Nov.4,1960,72y.
Hattie,Jan.5,1971,83y.
John,Mar.20,1940,75y.
Mary F.,Oct.2,1948,63y.
Nancy A. Smith,Sept.6,1914,64y,
  wid/o Johnson.
infant,Dec.25,1905, newb.
Samuel F.,Oct.16,1939,80y.
Statie E.,bu:Oct.28,1941,76y.
WILKINSON
Leslie P.,Apr.16,1985,63y.
WILLETTE
Claire E., Sept. 26, 1980.
WILLIAMS
Everett M.,Oct.24,1972,79y.
infant,Jan.31,1938, prem.
Richard C.,Feb.25,1967,12y.
Sarah Davis Dec.9,1943,53y.
Shirley H.,Nov.9,1994,69y.
WILLIS
Beatrice I.,Apr.15,1994,92y.
Rufus, Col.,May 5,1964,68y.
WILSON
Allan C.,Feb.24,1961,56y.
Barbara Joan,Nov.3,1930,2d.
Barbara M.,Jan.9,1975,44y.
Bessie M.,July 28,1961,62y.

David W.,Dec.24,1923,2d.
Doris P.,Apr.26,1987,67y.
Dorothea L.,Dec.23,1965,62y.
Earle W.,May 15,1972,64y.
Helen C.,Mar.2,1980,73y.
infant,Mar.12,1981, s.b.
infant,Sept.11,1957, 6hrs.
James D.,Mar.3,1987.
Jason F.,Sept.9,1934,72y.
John C.,May 11,1974,52y.
John M.C.,June 10,1982,84y.
Joy C.,Nov.23,1992,88y.
Katherine P.,Jan.13,1955,92y.
Keith A.,Dec.22,1989,47y.
Lena B.,Oct.5,1968,93y.
Margaret D.,Mar.31,1941,85y.
Richard R.,Sr.,Aug.21,1981,72y.
Roy L.,June 15,1924,44y.
Russell A.,June 6,1901,83y.
Russell O.,Sept.4,1964,19y.
Virginia L.,Sept.27,1974,43y.
Wilber W.,Aug.13,1963,85y.
WING
Margaret I.,July 4,1976,93y.
William W.,Mar.17,1959,76y.
WINSHIP
Addie H. Elder,Oct.7,1842-
  Feb.3,1876,1st w/o John O.
Carroll Warren,July 2,1944,20y.
E. Maude, Sept.19,1944,71y.
Elmer L.,Dec.7,1979,81y.
Gertrude S.,Oct.25,1955,82y.
Harry H.,Mar.23,1992,72y.
Helen A.,Mar.24,1967,72y.
Helen M.,May 14,1952,87y.
infant July 31,1956,1d.
John Oliver,Feb.3,1923,84y.
John Oliver,1838-1929.
Josiah D.,May 5,1959,83y.
Lillian M.,bu:Feb.17,1967,69y.
Paul Wayne,Oct.5,1928, s.b.
Ralph,July 7,1871-Aug.17,1872,
  s/o John & Addie. Addie & Ralph
  rem. from Evergreen, Nov.1920.
WINSLOW
Adelaide G.,Nov.3,1960,95y.
Alfred F.,Jan.15,1948,75y.
Clyde, Sept.28,1945,67y.
Ethel M.,Mar.8,1954,81y.
George H.,Mar.19,1949,95y.
Howell M.,July 18,1940,79y.
Ida E.,Apr.24,1961,90y.
John B.,July 24,1940,71y.
John Clifford, Mar.26,1989,87y.
Julia E.,Jan.15,1966,76y.
Martha,1831-1908,w/o Nathaniel.
Mary E.,Jan.1941.

Nathaniel P.,1831-1880.
Ruth W.,Sept.10,1966,78y.
Sarah G.,Howell,1902,41y.
Sumner P.,Nov.29,1968,79y.
WINTER
John N.,Apr.14,1965,72y.
Walter J.,May 4,1958,65y.
WINTHER
Christian H.,Jan.30,1971,79y.
Christian H.,Jr.,Nov.1,1945,19y.
WISWELL
Charles M.,May 1,1974,51y.
WITHAM
Agnes E.,Nov.24,1979,79y.
Byron C.,Oct.1,1914,59y.
Celia S.,July 3,1973.
Clark B.,June 2,1914,30y.
Florence,Oct.11,1930,46y.
Florence E.,Apr.12,1964,85y.
Leroy C.,Mar.14,1969,85y.
Mary Clark, May 8,1932,72y.
Merrill F.,1894,29y.
Orrin,Oct.13,1955,78y.
WITHEE
infant,Jan.22,1914.
WOGAN
Thomas E.,Jan.19,1955,68y.
Thomas E.,Jr.,May 9,1979,58y.
WOLFE
William L.,"Skip"Nov.26,1989,70y.
WOOD
Arthur,Oct.15,1915, prem.
Alfred W.,Jan.16,1959,55y.
Arthur L.,Sept.18,1963,85y.
Charles, Jan.26,1918,75y.
Constance D.,Apr.12,1985, 69y.
Dora A.,Jan.18,1962,48y.
Freddie,1896-1909.
Howard S.,bu:Nov.17,1941,74y.
Irene L.,Sept.23,1993,72y.
John W., Aug.13,1921,83y.
inf/o Arthur,Oct.16,1915, s.b.
infant, June 6,1941, s.b.
Mary E., Feb.10,1950,62y.
Mary E.,June 9,1957,80y.
Mary Sadler, Apr.29,1910,
  69y, w/o John W.
Nettie S.,July 20,1940,71y.
Owen E.,Dec.24,1913.
Owen E.,Apr.18,1994,80y.
Park, Sept.13,1993,78y.
Willard S., Apr.20,1899,3m.
WOODBURY
Eben R.,Capt.,1844-1909.
Elizabeth,1819-1891,w/o John.
George C.,1885-1888,s/o E.R.&L.E.
John,1816-Aug 6,1896.

John W., Nov.24,1905,34y.
Lutie E.,1848-1897,w/o E.R.
Susanne W.,Nov.30,1933,80y.
WOODIS
Roland A.,Nov.12,1972,57y.
WOODMAN
Ada Ellen,Mar.5,1932,80y.
Addie L.,Aug.12,1907,49y.
Alice Louise,1868-1868.
Ann, Feb.2,1988,55y.
Annie Belle,1866-1894,w/o C. Harold.
B. Frank,Feb.17,1901,48y.
Benjamin J.,July 3,1903,85y, h/o Charlotte Babb.
C. Harold, Feb.8,1902,37y.
Carrie J., Jan.15,1977,93y.
Charles B., Aug.10,1901,60y.
Charles B.,Oct.31,1993,88y.
Charlotte F.,Feb.8,1902,80y.
Clyde W. Spear,Mrs.Jan.9,1910,67y.
Emily D. Merrill, Dec.14,1909,72y, wid/o Sewall.
George M., Jan.27,1944,72y.
George M.,Jr., Nov.3,1988,81y.
George M.,III, Apr.20,1963,18y.
Guy Perley, Nov.11,1944,75y.
Isabel G., July 26,1908,4m., d/o Postmaster Ben.
Mary Ann,1830-1858,w/o Sewall.
Philip E.,1887-1887.
Robert C.,Mar.2,1933,39y.
Russell D., b.Searsmont-1844-Nov.22,1905.
WOODS
Edward A., Apr.9,1954,60y.
Richard W.,June 17,1994,60y.
WOODWARD
Alice G.,May 12,1964,83y.
WORK
Milton W., Apr.15,1992,61y.
WORMWELL
Frederick E.,Jr.,June 30,1989,68y.
twins,Nov.25,1919,prem.
WORTHINGTON
Christina M., June 14,1949,84y.
William,Aug.24,1939,74y.
WORTHLEY
Harold D.,Mar.4,1963,70y.
Lucy H.,Apr.30,1960,61y.
WRIGHT
Cheryl Edith, Feb.6,1948,1m, rem. to Spurwink Cem.1975.
Elaine A.,Sept.23,1992,83y.
infant, July 19,1951,2 hrs., rem. to Spurwink Cem.1975.
Mavis L.,June 23,1983,60y.
Sarah J., Apr.27,1933,71y.

Thomas, June 16,1962,3y.
Virginia I.,Dec.30,1981,63y.
WTERMAN
Nellie M.,Dec.16,1902,36y.
WYER
C. Roy, July 20,1957,82y.
Edwinna R. Oct.1,1941,67y.
Eleanor J.,Dec.12,1977,80y.
Fannie B.,Nov.25,1958,81y.
Gladys M.,Jan.5,1934,42y.
Grace B.,Feb.20,1944,75y.
Hazel C.,Apr.22,1971,71y.
Henry O.,Dec.14,1942,73y.
infant, Aug. 5,1918,s.b.
Marion Louise, Aug.3,1918, s.b.
Otis W.,Aug.16,1990,94y.
Robert Otis,Dec.27,1929,9y.
Susie V.,Mar.4,1929,59y.
Walter H.,June 27,1947,89y.
William T.,Feb.8,1940,74y.
WYNN
Gerard M.,Maj.,Nov.14,1967,38y.
YDE
Louise, Apr.14,1929,24y.
Mathilda, Feb.19,1925,43y.
Otto M.,May 13,1940,67y.
YEATON
Charles H.,Dec.26,1973,84y.
Margurite H.,Feb.22,1968,77y.
YORK
Clinton A.,Nov.16,1915,3m.
Clinton F.,Dec.5,1903,2m.
Donald S.,June 15,1958,59y.
Eleanor M.,Feb.3,1994.
Fred F.,July 19,1962,88y.
George, Apr.25,1914.
George H.,Sr.,Nov.19,1990,88y.
Howard M.,Jr.,May 8,1970,49y, rem.to Chicopee Cem.,Buxton,1974.
Ida, Apr.22,1962,79y.
James E.,Aug.19,1994,87y.
Jessie F.,Jan.26,1951,54y.
Kenneth C.,Dec.21,1967,57y.
Steven L.,Apr.9,1984,36y.
Wilma E.,Mar.7,1994,92y.
YOUNG
Ann H.,1828-1895,w/o Daniel P.
Charles Francis,Mar.26,1934,61y.
Daniel P., June 2,1908,80y.
Eliza M.,Mar.21,1973,75y.
Fred C.M.,Oct.31,1947,79y.
Frederick E.,Apr.3,1926,65y.
Guy A., Apr.3,1945,58y.
infant,Sept.8,1955, prem.
Irene P.,Oct.31,1954,48y.
J.Otis,Nov.29,1926,65y.
Mary Elizabeth,June 17,1953,85y.

Maurice W.,May 1,1938,34y.
Olive A.,Jan.5,1931,82y.
Ralph D.,Oct.13,1972,68y.
Sarah E.,July 31,1934,72y.
. . . . .

Approximately 500 burials were not recorded onto index cards when that system began in 1914. All that was recorded was the deceased name and section and grave numbers. I tracked down about 420 of these missing persons and recorded the information from their gravestones. Some burial cards did not show the death date, just the burial date, that has been noted by the notation of bu: then the date.

Woodlawn Cemetery

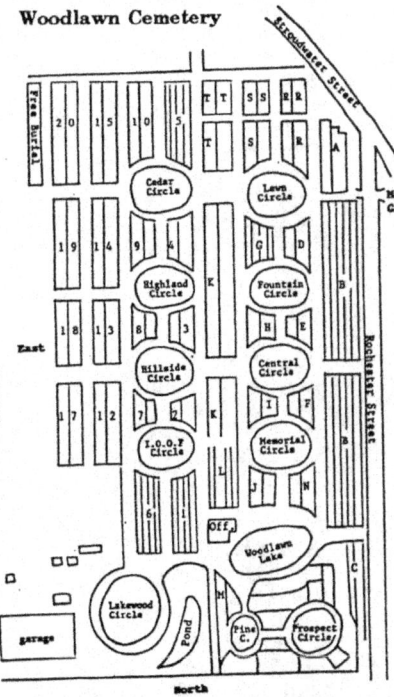

✢ **LEIGHTON TOMB** ✢
Off Hardy Road, Falmouth. Remains removed c.1957.

LEIGHTON
Dorcus (Dolly) Wilson,Nov.22,1778-Nov.22,1866,w/o Nathaniel.
Nathaniel,July 21,1779-Aug.29,1849

✢ **GRANT FAMILY** ✢
Cumberland Street, almost to the Windham line. Behind golf course buried in weeds. Located by Ray Ridge while golfing.

GRANT
Frank,1860-1863,s/o S.& S.
Sarah,1820-1864,w/o Stephen.
Stephen,1816-1897.

✢ **PROCTOR GRAVEYARD** ✢
Approx. 684 East Bridge St., Westbrook. Several burial prior to 1838.

PROCTOR
John,c.1823,80y,his grave lies at the base of a lone tree on a high knoll. (At the time of burial).

✢ **LEIGHTON-STAPLES** ✢
Hardy Road, Falmouth. 6 stones in old enclosure. 2 sides of stone wall remaining.

LEIGHTON
Georgianna,Apr.15,1853-May 26,1861,d/o Levi E. & Martha.
Lucy C.,Sept.10,XXXX,9m.
Stephen,1765-July 2,1847,83y.
Ruth,1759-Nov.4,1843,85y,w/o Step.
STAPLES
Jeremiah,1794-May 2,1840,46y.
Jeremiah,Jan.29,1872,33y.
Lydia,1799-Apr.10,1880, w/o Jeremiah (1794).

✢ **ALLEN FAMILY** ✢
Winn Rd.,off Rte.9, near the Falmouth town line, Cumberland. Old list not checked.

ALLEN
Clarissa I.,1824-1891,w/o Peter L.
Daniel R.1815-1890.
Florence E.,Sept.22,1859,4y, d/o P.L.& C.I.
Ida Florence,Aug.21,1861,5m, d/o P.L.& C.I.
Marianne,1815-1891,w/o Daniel R.
Peter L.,1822-1897.

✥ SACCARAPPA CEMETERY ✥
✥ VETERAN BURIALS ✥

From an old map given to me in 1995 by Phil LaViolette.

Revolutionary War:

Haskell, Nathaniel.
Hatch, Nathaniel.
Quinby, Joseph.

War of 1812:

Babb, Alexander.
Babb, Col. Henry.
Chesley, Isaac,.
Clements, Jeremiah.
Conant, Daniel,Jr.
Plummer, Major.
Proctor, James.
Quimby, Benjamin.
Quimby, Charles.
Small, Joseph.
Towle, Levi.
Valentine, Capt. Joseph.
Wallace, John.
Warren, Nathaniel.
Winslow, David.

Spanish American War:

Merrill, Marshall.
Sloan, William.
Webb, William F.

Civil War:

Adams, Frank.
Anderson, Charles.
Babb, J.D.
Babb, Joseph H.
Babb, Marshall
Babb, Northman L.
Bachelder, Henry.
Barbour, Amandel.
Bixby, George.
Blatchford, Henry.
Boyd, John.
Britten, Edward.
Brock, Albert.
Brown, William C.
Bryant, John.
Clement, Nathaniel.
Cloudman, Capt. Andrew.
Cook, Randall.
Cousens, Harry.
Hanson, Elbridge.
Harmon, John.

Hayes, Marshall.
Hodgkins, Maurice.
Hodsdon, Andrew.
Hodson, Charles.
Horr, Daniel P.
Hunt, James.
Hurd, Washborn.
Huston, Ithamar.
Kollock, Edward.
Kollock, Royal.
Maffitt, George.
Marriner, George.
Mayberry, George.
Mayhewm Hebron.
Meserve, John.
Morris, James.
Pennell, George.
Phinney,E.B.
Pratt, William.
Proctor, George.
Proctor, James.
Quimby, Isaac
Quinby, M.H.
Quinby, Orrin.
Rice, Daniel.
Riley, Charles.
Roberts, John.
Scott, John G.
Smith, Edsel.
Smith,John.
Spear, Lt. Fred B.
Sproul, H.B.
Stearns, J.E.
Stiles, Albion.
Stiles, M.W.
Sweetser, Augusta.
Swett, Alphonse.
Swett, John.
Swett, Samuel.
Swett, William M.
Tole, Joseph H.
Totman, W.H.
Tyler, Abram.
Verrill,Daniel.
Webb, James.
Welch, Alvin F.
Wescott, Enoch.
Wheeler, Henry.
Willis, Charles E.
Wood, Philander.
Woodbury, George.
Woodsum, E.S.
Wormwood, John P.
Wyer, Otis.

World War I:

Adams, Hebron.

✤ **SACCARAPPA CEMETERY** ✤
Church Street, Westbrook.

The Deering News,
July 26-19,1899, "Grandpa's Scrapbook", column written by Leonard B. Chapman:

The growth of Saccarappa village, situated within the territorial limits of the City of Westbrook, was exceedingly slow the first hundred years of its existence which commenced in 1729. Wages were low, rum was cheap, residences small and in inferior quality. A century after the settlement a part of what is now called Main street was known as "Slab City" and derisively alluded to as "holy ground". The change for the better is great.

In a land conveyance record of 1762 a fourth acre reservation "where some children are buried" was made for a burying place, that is located on the northerly side of the village, which was publicly used many years and which to the discredit of the city may now be seen in a fearfully neglected condition.

April 3, 1827, the following persons for $200 purchased of Nathaniel and Sarah Haskell, of Saccarappa, a "parcle of land located near Saccarappa village" for a burying lot, commencing bounds at the north east corner of the "Haskell (family) burying ground, so-called-" "one acre and eighteen squarerods, "excepting from the northeast corner, 4 1/2 rods, with right of way to and from the lot from the public highway leading through said village." "Said piece of land being in common and undivided and is for a burying ground."

Susanna Partridge, widow,Westbrook
Levi Towle
Benjamin B. Foster
Noah Nason
Henry Babb
Aaron Winslow
Nathaniel Warren
Moody F. Walker
Archelous Lewis
Major Plummer
Samuel Longfellow
William Akers
William Roberts,Jr.
Josiah Pierce, Esq.,Baldwin.
Simon Gilman
David Hayes
John Stiles
Daniel Tomson
John Warren
Daniel T. Pierce
Wm. Valentine
Lewis Pease
Henry Plummer
Charles Pratt
Joseph Partridge
Otis Valentine ----

P. Lary
Isaac Walker
David Winslow
Mark Babb
Ezekial Crague
Moses Stiles
Solomon Babb
Nathaniel Babb
Nathaniel Murch
Solomon Conant
George Haskell
Montgomery Anderson
Samuel Babb
Ebenzer Haskell
Nathaniel Haskell
Nathan Harris
Isaac G. Walker
Moses Quinby,3rd
Edmond Woodbury
Stephen Barow
Levi Bailey
George D. Jorden
Benjamin Roberts,Jr.
Isaac W. Bailey
Nathan Baker
Joseph Babb
Benjamin Foster
Robert Warren
William Small
Samuel Bailey
Stephen Longfellow
Peter Pride
Nathan Libby
Abiel Cutter
John Pride,Jr.
Daniel Babb.
Jeremiah Clement
Simeon Quinby
Dennis H. Angers
Simeon Mabery
James Baker
Nathaniel Wakefield
Edmund Haskell
Henry C. Babb
Simon Davis
Alexander Babb
Josiah Woodbury
David Winslow
Solomon Babb
Joseph Haskell
William Baker
Frederick Haskell
William Moulton
Moses Quinby
Thomas H. Howe
Stephen Babb
Gardner Bacon
Joseph Libby
William Babb,Jr.
Nelson Babb
William Mabury
Henry Adams
Joshua Kellock
Daniel Stevens
Simeon Carter
Sargent S. Freeman
Charles Quinby
John Proctor
Luther Fitch
George Pride
James Brown

The foregoing list contains seventy-five names.

In 1914 Saccarappa Cemetery was placed in the hands of the Woodlawn Cemetery Trustees by an act of the legislature. Burials obtained from city records unless marked with [GS], these were obtained from gravestones.

ADAMS
Albert H.,Feb.9,1939,1m.
Charles F.,Mar.3,1854, 26y.
Frank,1839 -1903.
Fred W.,Mar.1,1868-Apr.4,1903, s/o John & Louisa.
Hebron M.,XXXX,53y.
Jason L.,1864 -1920,[GS]
John,Aug.13,1831-Nov.6,1905.
Kittie W.,1872,1y.
L.Herbert, Aug.16,1875,23y.
Lillian L.,1871-1888,w/o A.H.

Lizzie Trask Rand,1849-Aug.1915,
  wid/o Frank.
Louisa S,Aug.3,1837-Oct.5,1910,
  w/o John.
Mary Ann P.,Dec.27,1852,21y,
  w/o Charles F.
Sarah J. Winslow,Nov.1,1899,64y,
  w/o David Adams.
AKERS
Benjamin M.,June 25,1891,75y
George W., Aug. 30,XXXX,6m,
  s/o B.M. & L.F.
John A. Aug.30,XXXX,4m,s/o B.&L
Lucy A.,Oct.5,XXXX,4m,d/o B.& L.
Lucy F. Moulton, Apr.17,1890,76y,
  w/o Benjamin M.
Mary M.,Nov. 4,1862,23y,
  d/o B.M.& L.F.
ALBERTO
John,1867-1870 [GS].
ALDEN
daughter, b.&d.July 10,1821,
  d/o Capt. Charles & Nancy.
ALEXANDER
Louisa Barbour,Sept.1938,74y,
  w/o Warren J.
Warren J.,1860 -1939.
ALLEN
Blanche,1884 -1888,
  d/o Walter & Clara.
Carrie,1861-1863,
  d/o Walter C. & Clara A.
Charles,1815 -1878.
Clara,1846 -1849.
Clara A.,1860 -1915,w/o Walter,[GS].
Flora C.,1850-1916,[GS].
Frances B.,Apr.25,1936,67y.
Frank E.,1880 -1885,s/o G. & M.
George,1811-1882,h/o Martha.
George C.,1853-1870.
Harriet C.,1819 -1878, w/o Chas.
Martha A.,1824-1890.
Walter C.,1862-1918.
William C.,1845-1921,[GS].
ANDERSON
Charles A.,May 15,1917,81y.
Emma E.,Nov. 4,1893,4y,
  d/o J.P.& M.T.
Eunice,Feb.4,1854,37y,w/o Abram B.
George,Aug.14,1954, 88y.
John G.,Sept.14,1849,10m,
  s/o Joseph & Lucy.
Lucy, Dec.5,1848,28y, w/o Jos.
Maud May,Jan.31,1872,5m,
  d/o Charles & Sarah.
Sally Babb,May 1,1853,44y,
  w/o Montgomery.

Virgeanna, Dec.17,1915,75y.
ANDREWS
Charles I., Mar.4,1841,
  s/o E.R. & Mary Ann [GS].
Charles L.,Mar.4,1846,4y,
  s/o J.R. & Mary Ann.
ATWOOD
Levi, Dec.7,1837,42y.
Lydia Jane, Sept.18,1837,7m,
  d/o Levi & Sarah.
Nathaniel Hyram,Feb.27,1836,4y.
Sarah B.,Apr.20,1838,37y,w/o Levi.
AUSTIN
Abbie,Mar.1906 [GS].
AYER
Abigail W. Sargent,1802-1883,
  w/o Jacob.
Jacob,Jan.15,1801-Aug.2,1865.
Jacob, Jr.,May 13,1832-Oct.1,1849,
  s/o Jacob & A.W.
James F.,1838 -1882.
BABB
Alexander,1780-1862.
Ann Maria M.,1839-1842.
Betsey,1809 -1843,
  d/o Soloman & Joanna [GS].
Chandler P.,1832-1853,
  s/o John & Mary.
Charles, Oct. 21,1793-May 20,1821.
Charles E.,1856-XXXX.
  s/o E.R. & M.P [GS].
Charles W.,1847-1855,s/o E.R.& M.P.
Daniel,1810-1872.
David W.,1825 -1896.
Deborah Thompson,Mar.1832,5y,
  d/o Henry & Harriot.
Edward A.,1851,1y,s/o E.R. & M.P.
Edward A., Aug.28,1854, 1y,
  s/o Luther L. & Lorania S.
Edward R.,1816-1894.
Eliza Jones,1799-Aug.2,1865,
  w/o Lemuel.
Elizabeth,XXXX,w/o Capt.Henry.
Elizabeth A. Irish,1836-1907,
  w/o Marshall L.
Elizabeth L. Newcomb,
  Sept.24,1849,42y,w/o Peter.
Emily E.,Apr.19,1850,4y,
  d/o Stephen & Emily.
Emily E.,Dec.9,1896,89y,w/o Stephen.
Emma Larrabee,Dec.1848,5y,
  d/o Henry & Harriot.
Esther A.,1839-1869,
  2nd w/o David W.
Esther Wescott,1785-1881,w/o Alex.
Frank L., Nov. 5,1853,17m,
  s/o Joseph & Tabitha.

Fred W.,1859-Oct.13,1885.
Freeman F.,Nov.1861,60y [GS].
George,1800-1836,s/o S. & J.
George G.,Apr.12,1865,21y,
  s/o E.R. & M.P.
George R.,Aug.30,1857,1y,
  s/o J.R. & M.E.
George R.,May 16,1847,16m,
  s/o J.R. & M.E.
George W.,Aug.17,1920,62y.
Greengrover M.,July 30,1842,
  2y, s/o E.R. & M.P.
Harriet Jane Wood,Oct.11,1904,
  73y,w/o Joseph H.
Harriot Farmer,Aug.11,1852,53y,
  w/o Henry C.
Harry E.,Oct. 22,1863,2y,
  s/o Marshall L.
Harry J.,Oct. 8,1862,20d,
  s/o Cyrus & Mary
Henry C.,Nov.16,1864,69y.
Henry C., Jr.,July 15,1838,2y,
  s/o Henry & Harriot.
Henry,Jan.15,1822, 8m,
  s/o Henry C. & Harriot.
Henry, Capt.,Feb. 1,1834,49y,
  h/o Elizabeth.
inf/s/o E.R.& M.D.,Jan.3,1851 [GS].
Isaac W.,Sept.20,1848,24y.
J.H.,Dec.29,1872,50y.
James L.,July 11,1937,76y.
Jennie,185X-1873,d/o David & Lucy
Jennie L.,1861-1937 [GS].
Joanna Libby,Mar.16,1844,72y,
  w/o Nathaniel.
Joanna Roberts,1778-1850,
  w/o Solomon,Sr.
John,XXXX,h/o Mary Winslow.
John, Apr.9,1873,72y,h/o Rhoda.
John R.,1824 -1884.
Joseph,Apr.5,1819,47y,h/o Margaret.
Joseph,July 1,1803-Mar.4,1884,
  h/o Tabitha.
Joseph A.,Sept.13,1846,1y,
  s/o E.R. & M.P.
Joseph F.,Apr.2,1849,14m,
  s/o Joseph & Tabitha
Joseph H.,1822 -1886 [GS].
Joseph H.,1829-1897,
  h/o Harriet Jane [GS].
Joseph Henry,Oct.25,1829,68y.
Leander V.,Sept.18,1843,18m,
  s/o J. W. & Maria A.
Lemuel, May 2,1869,71y,
  h/o Eliza Jones.
Lewis, 1816 -1837,s/o Sol. & Joanna.

Lizzie M.,Nov.28,1857,3y,
  d/o J.R.& M.E.
Louisa D.,Mar.22,1866,27y,
  d/o Joseph & Tabitha.
Louisa T.,Dec.11,1915,74y.
Lucy A.,July 26,1856,32y,
  1st w/o David W.
Lucy Libby,July 16,1806-
  Oct.13,1890, w/o Samuel S.
Luther F.,Oct.12,1843,10m,
  s/o John & Rhoda
Malcolm J.,Aug.2,1909,54y.
Margaret Bayley,Sept.8,1841,65y,
  w/o Joseph.
Marshall,Dec.6,1826, 8y.
Marshall L.,Nov.19,1902,68y.
Marshall,Mar.30,1818,6m.
Martha C.,Oct.4,1891,71y.
Martha E. George,1889,69y,
  w/o John R.
Mary E. Haskell,1883 -1909,
  3rd w/o David W.
Mary Winslow,1813-1848,w/o John.
Melinda P.Dolley,Jan.29,1899,79y,
  w/o Edward R.
Nathaniel,Aug.6,1812,31y.
Northman L.,Feb.29,1912,67y.
Olive C.,Sept.1,1842 [GS].
Porter,Sept.24,1819,42y [GS].
Rebecca Proctor,Jan.7,1798 -
  Apr.4,1882, w/o Charles.
Rhoda P. Quimby,Jan.16,1860,36y,
  w/o John.
Samuel,1886,73y.
Samuel S.,Aug.30,1882,70y
Sarah B. Jordan, May 4,1847,22y,
  w/o Isaac W.
Smith, May 19,1902,78y,
  s/o Alexander & Esther.
Soloman,1770 -1854.
Soloman, Jr.,Jan.1,1829,31y,
  died at sea, s/o S. & J.R.
Stephen,1802-1881.
Susan C., Aug.23,1842,1y [GS].
Susie J., Dec.24,1924,87y,
  w/o Malcolm J.
Tabitha L. Darling,Mar.19,1866,
  56y,w/o Jos.
William H.,Mar.24,1852,34y,
  s/o Mary S. Elizabeth.
Willie, XXXX [GS].
BACHELDER
Elizabeth M.,Feb.25,1919,71y [GS].
Henry A.1848-Jan.2,1919.
Isaac,Oct.20,1897,77y.
Sarah A.,Dec.17,1927,88y,w/o Henry .

BACON
Gardner,1858,54y,h/o Jane.
Jane W. Plummer,1876,69y
Lucy E.,1873, 26y.
BAGLEY
Mary J.G.,1817-1886,w/o V.
BAILEY
Bethia W. Small,1796-Oct.4,1890, w/o Isaac W.
Caroline,May 9,1851,29y.
Frederick A.,Nov.1901,71y.
George G.,May 26,1849,22y.
Isaac W.,1798-May 1872.
James A.,Dec.1901,s/o Isaac [GS].
Joseph,Jan.15,1833,1m,s/o I.W.& B.
Nathaniel E.,Dec.24,1849,19y, s/o Isaac & Sara.
Wendell S.,Oct.5,1838-Jan.22,1911, 72y,s/o Geo. & Sarah Barbour Bailey.
BARBOUR
Amandall,Sept.25,1903,64y.
Calvin H., Mar.1906,74y [GS].
Caroline Stearns,1838-1872, w/o Amandall.
Celia, July 25,1938,75y, d/o Calvin H. & Christina.
Christina Cutter,1834-1897, w/o Calvin H [GS].
Ella Clough, Aug.26,1940,74y.
Emma Winslow,1808-1884, w/o Hiram [GS].
Ethlyn A.,1902 -1904,d/o Mel. & Mary.
Florence Lillian,Jan.20,1890- Nov.28,1902, d/o G.W. & M.F.
Frank,1862 -Nov.16,1935,h/o Sadie E.
George, Apr.13,1922,73y,h/o Nellie.
George E.,1849 -1922 [GS].
George W.,1871-1940 [GS].
George W.,Dec.12,1946,68y.
Hiram,1871,64y.
James I.,1874-1884 [GS].
Mae C.,1890-1940, w/o Geo.W.
Mary, June 9,1950,73y,w/o Melville
Melville L., Sept.3,1939,61y.
Nellie,Jan.26,1934,81y,w/o George.
Nellie, Oct.14,1943,78y.
Rose Clark,1852-1934,w/o Geo.E. [GS]
Sadie E.,1865-1940,w/o Frank [GS].
William E.,1858-1893 [GS].
BARKER
Ann W. Haskell,May 21,1803- Nov.29,1886,w/o William [GS].
Anna F.,Oct.27,1937, 79y.
Charles W.,Apr.9,1830-Jan.19,1876.
David G.,Dr.,Apr.15,1830,44y.
Deborah B. Joslyn,Apr.11,1846,64y, w/o David.
James,Mar.25,1846,64y.
Jeremiah G.,July 25,1881,67y.
Loeann Harmond, Apr.30,1826- Mar.18,1884,w/o Charles W.
Mary Haskell,Oct.24,1828,9m.
Mary C.,May 1,1872, 34y,w/o William.
Mary G.,June 12,1837,28y.
Sarah Emery Morrill, May 11,1854,39y, w/o J.G.
William W.,Dec.20,1883,81y.
Ann M.,Feb.27,1885, 68y, d/o John & Ann Shaw.
BATCHELDER
Henry,1843 -1918,s/o Ira & Sally [GS].
Ira,Dec.17,1806 -Dec.1,1882.
Sally Robertson,July 28,1813- Aug.2,1883, w/o Ira.
Sarah A.,1839-1927,d/o Ira & S. [GS].
BEAN
David M.,Sept.12,1825-May 26,1897, h/o Mary A.
Diantha A.Small,May 21,1899,67y, 1st hus. Joseph Small, 2nd hus. L.O.Bean.
Mary A. Cloudman,June 1,1823- Sept.4,1910,w/o David M.
BELLE
C.,1886-1894 [GS].
BENNETT
Fred J., XXXX [GS].
Mabel A. Kimball,1876-1917, w/o Fred J. [GS].
BERBASKY
Carl E.,May 28,1934,62y.
Ella M.,Jan.21,1904,70y,w/o Carl A.
Nellie Louisa,May 19,1876,3y, d/o Carl E. & Ellen M.
BERRY
Earl C.,Oct.1920,64y [GS].
Lizzie S.,May 13,1862,17y, d/o Elias & Nancy.
Rena Maud, May 2,1934,57y.
BERRYMAN
Hannah J.Putnam,Dec.2,1862 - June 1947, wid/o William J.
William James,Jan.16,1942,83y.
BEST
Ella,Dec.30,1863 [GS].
Florence,Sept.20,1865,2y, d/o John L. & Mary E.
Julia A.,Dec.30,1865,19y.
Mariam J.Babb.,Dec.16,1811- Nov. 22,1865, w/o Tritten.
Tritten,Apr.14,1804-Dec.6,1865.
BETTIS
Adeline,1847-1885,w/o Chas. W.
Marcena A.,Mar.15,1924,70y.

William F.,Aug.15,1933,80y.
BETTS
Fisher,1812-1890 [GS].
Joseph A.,1869-1879 [GS].
Lester C.,1872-1902 [GS].
Margaret A.,1831-1904,w/o Fisher.
BICKFORD
Abner G.,Jan.6,1912,80y,
h/o Salome & s/o Alex.&Mary.
Fred L.,Dec. 31,1864,3y.
Jane M. July 2,1960,84y.
Joanna,Mar.1903,wid/o Chas.S. [GS].
Mabelle G.,Oct.3,1899,27y.
Salome H. Rice,Nov.6,1909,72y,
w/o Abner G.,[GS].
BIRTNELL
Ethel Maude,XXXX,5y [GS].
BIXBY
G. Ellie,Aug.23,1894-Aug.27,1954.
Elizabeth C.,Oct.27,1894,73y.
George E., Sept.10,1954,50y.
George F.,Sept.10,1866,1y.
George Lewis,Nov.1,1930,85y,
h/o Hattie E.,s/o J.W. & L.P.
Hattie E. Mittsmen,
Mar.12,1908, 57y,w/o Geo. L.
John W.,July 28,1901,83y,s/o John &
Margaret Vaugh Wise Bixby.
Lydia P. Rand,Dec.17,1874,57y,
w/o John B.
BLAISDELL
Almira Y.,June 28,1844,37y,w/o Levi.
Alphonso, XXXX [GS].
Olive C., Sept.4,1842,3y.
Susan C.,Aug.23,1842,1y.
BLAKE
Bessie,Sept.14,1885,6w,&
Jessie, Aug.24,1885,3w,
twins of Silas & Olive.
Olive Gray,July 10,1907,wid/o Silas A.
Silas A.,Dec.12,1889,38y.
BLATCHFORD
Annie L.,Mar.26,1873,17y,
d/o H.& H.M
Harriet M. Evans,Mar.17,1896,70y,
w/o Henry.
Henry, Jan. 4,1907,84y.
Henry A.,1848-Jan.2,1918 [GS].
BOHNSON
Frederick L.,July 11,1886,7m
John L.,June 10,1854-Apr.19,1911.
P.Frederick,July4,1884.
BOND
Harriet,Mar.3,1860, 65y,w/o L.
Leonard,May 19,1870,77y.

BOODY
Frederic E.W.,Jan.8,1856,34y.
Mary S. Roberts,Mar.1,1857,31y,
w/o F.E.W.
BOOTHBY
A.L.,1820-June 27,1898,h/o Ruth C.
Alfred R.,Feb.10,1937, 53y.
Asa, Prof.,Apr.23,1843 -May 2,1912,
78y,s/o Asa & Abigail Small Boothby.
Elizabeth A.,Mar.27,1951,61y,
w/o Alfred.
Elizabeth M.,Aug.6,1945,85y,
w/o Willard B.
Emma B.,Dec.18,1918,82y,
w/o Richard.
Richard,Feb.26,1871,37y.
Ruth C.,1820-1886,w/o A.L.
Willard B.,Nov.19,1937,78y.
Willard B.,Mar.4,1944,25y.
BORUP
Annie E.,Nov.4,1880,24y,
w/o H.W. Olesen Borup.
H.W. Olesen, Jr.,XXXX,1y.
BOYD
John C.,XXXX,35y,h/o Belle.
Belle Dearborn,1899,52y.
BOYINGTON
Lydia,Mar.19,1879,80y.
BRACKETT
Charles H.,June 21,1874,43y.
Charlie,XXXX inf. s/o Charles
& Sarah L. [GS].
Cornelius T.,June 29,1859,22y,
s/o C.T.S. & M.A.
Dorcas,XXXX,75y.
Jane E. Hilton,Sept. 14,1862,25y,
1st w/o Charles H.
Johnnie S.,Sept.18,1860,10m.
Leon H., Mar.2,1933, 66y.
Melinda,Apr.19,1818-Mar.16,1879.
Samuel R., Feb.2,1848,16y,
s/o C.T.S.& M.A.
Sarah L., May 26,1914,81y,
2nd w/o Charles H.
Sewall,Feb.9,1819-Apr.21,1880.
Solomon S.,1827-1859 [GS].
BRADBURY
Horace J.,Rev.,Oct.9,1880,65y,
Lucy F.,Feb.6,1863,41y,w/o H. J.
BRADLEY
Susanna P.,Nov.3,1844,62y,
1st hus. Nathaniel Partridge,
2nd h. Rev.Caleb Bradley.
BRAGDON
Clara Davis,1854 -1887,1st w/o J.W.
Ida Swett,1866 -1897,2nd w/o J.W.
John W.,Jan.20,1907,56y.

BRIGHAM
Mary Etta Hazelton,1856-1932,
w/o J.D.
BRITTON
Uyilda E.,Oct.26,1914,73y.
BROCK
Albert S.,Aug. 3,1911,68y,s/o Daniel
& Hulda Washburn Brock.
Inez,Mar.17,1917.
BROWN
Angie M. Jordan,1885,1m,
d/o J.L.& A.J. [GS].
Angie Jordan,1862-1885,w/o J.L.
Carrie H.Jordan,1883-1885,
d/o James & Angie.
Charles W.,1887,41y,s/o W.C. & H.N.
Dorcas Jordan b.Windham,ME,
Dec.3,1794 -Nov.12,1866,w/o Sam'l.
Ernesteen C.,1853-1854 [GS].
Flora,1861-1870 [GS].
Frances E.,Aug.27,1849,18m,
d/o Otis & Harriet.
Frank Leslie,Mar.2,1859,
s/o John & Mary.
Franklin C.,1854,4y,s/o W.C.& H.N.
Freddie,1862 -1863,s/o John.
Harriet H. Roberts,Oct.8,1848,35y,
w/o Otis.
Harriet N. Chase,1822-1855,
1st w/o William C.
Huldah Copp,1864, 73y,w/o Jas.
James Luther,1783-1840,
h/o Huldah,s/o W.C. & H.N.
James,July 9,1911,55y,h/o Angie
John, Oct. 24,1899,76y.
Mary F. Libby,1888,59y,w/o John.
Otis,Apr.1,1896,h/o Harriet H. R.
Samuel, b. Boscawen, NH ,
June 6,1787-Apr.23,1856.
Sarah, 1818-1891,2nd w/o Wm.
William C.,1816-1889,
1st w. Harriet N.Chase,
2nd w. Sarah.
William H.,1858-1896 [GS].
BROWNE
George S.,Aug.11,1842-Nov.29,1872.
Harriet P.,Oct.6,1837-June 19,1870.
BRYAM
Nathaniel,Feb.17,1836,4y.
BRYANT
Haliburton,1858-1924,h/o Nellie W.
John W., Dec.7,1897.
Lewis C.1883-1891,s/o H.A.&N.
Mary A. Quinby,May 17,1928,76y,
h/o John W.
Nellie W.,1853 -1918.

BRYSON
Donald,1848-1891,h/o Annie.
Annie McNair,Dec.14,1917,76y.
BUNNELL
Alice W., Sept.1902 [GS].
Mabel Louise,Nov.1906,6y,
d/o Fred J.& Mabel E.
Margaret E.,Jan.26,1900,
6m, d/o F.J.& M.A.
BURNELL
Charles E.,Apr.21,1928,71y.
Ethel Maud,Oct.23,1897,5m,
d/o Charles & Nellie.
Harry,July 12,1924,46y.
Nellie,Dec.29,1924, 63y.
BURNHAM
Caroline,Aug.15,1860,35y,w/o Paul D.
James W.,Dec.31,1858,6m,s/o A.H.& S
Sophronia, Oct.21,1858,26y,
w/o Albion H.
CALDWELL
Agnes M.,July 25,1930,55y.
CARY
Mary Ann,Nov.27,1837,25y,
w/o Benjamin W.
Corrilla P.,Aug.28,1845,10m,
d/o Benj. W. & Mary Ann.
CARMICHAEL
Donald,Oct.2,1955,34y.
CASH
Harriet R. Hawkes,Jan.26,1899,76y,
w/o James P.
James P.,Aug.15,1901,80y.
CHASE
Albert,May 28,1913,78y,h/o Sarah M.
Albert Burleigh,1871-1895.
Amos A., Capt.,Feb.26,1915,86y.
Annie May, 1869-1870,
d/o Albert & Sarah.
Eleazer Oct.1812-July 3,1902.
infant,1874-1876 [GS].
John Alberto,1867 -1870,
s/o Albert & Sarah.
Louise D. Brown,Jan.20,1910,
72y,w/o Amos A.
Mary Ann Dearborn,Jan.1817 -
May 23,1881,w/o Eleazer.
Sarah M. Gould,Dec.6,1922,85y,
w/o Albert.
CHESLEY
Fanny,Sept.5,1856,70y,w/o Isaac.
Isaac,Feb.5,1857,84y.
Joseph,1815-1883 [GS].
Nehemiah,June 9,1867,46y.
William, Sept.12,1860,31y.

CHRITCHETT
John Hobart,Sept.21,1855,1y,
  s/o Nathaniel & Sarah.
CLAYTON
James H., Oct.10,XXXX,92y.
CLEMENTS
Caroline,Oct.26,1846,4m,
  d/o Samuel & Eliza.
Charles, XXXX, 1y.
Edward,May 19,1855,6y.
Eliza Moulton,July 17,1893,81y,
  w/o Samuel.
Elizabeth Conant,Jan.11,1879,88y,
  w/o Jeremiah, Jr.
Ella,Aug.13,1947,91y.
George,XXXX,1y.
Hannah Barbour,Oct.17,1917,92y,
  wid/o Nathaniel.
Jeremiah,June 2,1866,86y,
  War of 1812.
Jeremiah Jr.,July 6,1882,65y.
John M., Nov.10,1844, 6y,
  s/o Samuel & Eliza.
Leander, Sept.12,1848-Sept.11,1911,
  h/o Mary A.L.
Leander, Jan.6,1846, 31y.
Lillian,Oct.1873,4m,d/o L.& M.A.
Marthenia,XXXX,3y.
Mary A.L.,Jan.7,1901,53y,
  w/o Leander.
Mary E. Gould,1857-1913.
Nathaniel, Nov.1903,83y,
  s/o Jeremiah & Betsey.
Samuel,June 17,1877,65y.
CLOUDMAN
Angeline,Aug.20,1839,
  d/o Josiah & Susan.
Charles W.,June 21,1844,15y,
  s/o J.T. & M.A.
Andrew, Capt.,Aug.9,1862,28y,
  10th ME Regt.,Killed in battle of
  Cedar Mountain.
Eliza B.,June 6,1888,75y [GS].
Freeman C.,May 12,1849,7m,
  s/o Josiah & Huldah.
Hattie F.,Dec.11,1860,23y,
  s/o Josiah & Susan.
Huldah Estes,Aug.12,1896,78y,
  2nd w/o Josiah.
Josephine L.,July 10,1928,78y,
  w/o J. Dana.
Josiah, Dec.15,1893,84y,
Mayberry,Dec.17,1858,34y,w/o Andw.
Paul L., Apr.23,1864,57y
Susan Babb,Sept.10,1839,26y,
  1st w/o Josiah.
John T.S.,Jan.15,1852,46y.

CLOUGH
Charles I.,Aug.7,1882-Dec.20,1904.
COBB
Abbe Ann, Apr.19,1935,87y.
Augusta,Mar.22,1922,69y.
Claraett, Feb.7,1848,3y,
  d/o Lydia & Amos.
Daniel,1810-1872 [GS].
Edward F.,Oct.14,1895,77y.
Elijah, Dec.19,1855,56y.
Elizabeth A.,Dec.5,1860,18y.
Elizabeth A.W.,Feb.8,1899,77y,
  w/o Edward F.
Ellen T.,Nov.23,1844,d/o C.P&R. [GS].
Harriet M.,Oct.9,1846,14y.
Henry C., Aug.10,1850,1y,
  s/o Amos & Lydia.
Pamela K.,Aug.14,1863,35y.
Samuel C.1813-1886 [GS].
Sarah E.,1833-1860,w/o Enoch B
6 children of E.F. & E.A.W.:
Dorcus M.,Dec.16,1861,5w &
Edwin E., Feb.12,1856,5y
Henry F.,Feb. 2,1869,16y &
James, Sept.23,1863,6m &
Lewis R., Nov.4,1868,8y &
Lizzie L.,Jan.10,1858,6m.
Lydia Ann, July 19,1857,26y,
  w/o Amos H.
Sarah J. Bailey Sept.28,1884,62y,
  w/o Elijah.
COFFIN
Frederick E., July 27,1856,2y,
  s/o John E. & Sophia S.
COLE
Mary,1800-1888,w/o Stephen.
Stephen, 1890, 88y.
CONANT
Ann, Sept.21,1844,79y,w/o Daniel.
Anna S.,Oct.18,1945,65y.
Daniel,Dec.16,1853,92y,h/o Ann.
Daniel, Jr.,July 16,1874,80y.
Mary, Feb.9,1881,84y.
Nathaniel,Oct.2,1871,72y.
Solomon,Mar.30,1801-Sept.4,1869.
Susan S. Libby,Mar.11,1913,89y,
  w/o Solomon.
Daniel,Jan.12,1932,75y,
  s/o Solomon & Susan.
Willie A.,Dec.24,1862,14m,
  s/o Solomon & Susan.
CONNELL
Elizabeth,Aug.11,1884-May 16,1963,
  d/o John & Catherine Flint McNair.
John F.,Sept.29,1876-Feb.17,1954.
COOK
Carrie L.,Apr.5,1883,19y .

Carrie L.,Aug.20,1861-Jan.5,18XX,
d/o Ernest [GS].
Elizabeth M.,Dec.3,1921,83y,w/o G.H.
Ernest H., Dr.,1860-1893.
George Frederick,June 30,1926,70y.
George H.,1832-1889,h/o Eliz.M.
Hannah C. Foster,Sept.1,1837,27y,
w/o Mark H.
Lillian J. Haskell,Jan.31,1956,88y,
w/o George F.
Laura M.,July 17,1898,38y,w/o Geo.F.
R.R.,Sept.15,1905, 64y.
COOPER
Sarah L.,June 27,1977,90y.
COUSINS
Abbie Hodsdon,Dec.12,1916,69y,
w/o H. S.
Ebenezer,Nov.19,1876,79y.
Harrison S.,Oct.30,1904,61y,
COX
Frances H.,1850,1m, &
Franklin H.,1859,1y,2 s/o Wm.& Mary.
George,1859, 5y, s/o Sam & Sarah.
George C.,July 1857,5y,s/o Wm.& M.
George E.,Sept.1844,8d,s/o Wm.& M.
Mary A. Kennard,1817-1885,w/o Wm.
Samuel,1815,26y.
Sarah,Mar.13,1845, 50y,w/o Samuel.
William,1813-1862.
CRAGUE
Charles H.,Feb.13,1893,72y.
Ella M.,1878-1886,d/o W.L.& L.M.
Ezekiel,Jan.21,1852,55y.
Hannah Stone,Oct.13,1876,76y,
w/o Ezekiel.
Harry L.,1885,1m,s/o W.L.& L.M.
Lewis H.,1884-1892,s/o W.L.& L.M.
Lucy M.,Dec.12,1949,88y,w/o Wm. L.
Martha A. Knight,1824-1892,w/o Chas
William L.,Feb.7,1912,53y.
CRAWFORD
Margaret M.,Sept.16,1964,88y,
h/o Walter.
Walter J.,June 8,1876-
Dec.28,1967,91y.
CROCKETT
Flora Merrill,Sept.19,1916,61y,
w/o Oscar.
James,Elder,Jan.16,1854,36y.
Lucy C., Apr.16,1877,63y,w/o Nelson.
Mary P.,Nov.14,1880,59y.
Nelson,Sept.2,1875, 64y.
Oscar S.,May 18,1911,58y.
CROSBY
Antoinette P.,Nov.23,1855,18y,
d/o Zina & Deborah.
Deborah,1870,63y,w/o Zina.

Joshua B.,Feb.24,1854,18y,
s/o Zina F. & Deborah.
Maud Debeck,XXXX,1y.
Zina F.,1887,77y.
CROWTHER
Carrie W.,May 12,1865-Feb.2,1877.
Mary Ann,Sept.1,1880,1m.
Timothy,Mar.19,1871-Apr.21,1880.
CUMMINGS
Herman L.,Sept.16,1945,63y,h/o Lulu.
Lulu B. McCann,Apr.5,1957,76y.
CURRIE
Larry,Feb.9,1848, s.b.
CUTTER
Abial A.,Mar.7,1872,47y,h/o Louisa H.
Benjamin F.,Jan.16,1819-May 2,1908.
Benjamin F.,Apr.19,1822-
Apr.24,1891,h/o Zilpha A.
Charlie,Feb.21,1879,8y,
s/o Simon & Jospehine
Christiana,b. Steuben,Me.,
Mar.25,1782-Apr.6,1852,
w/o Col. Simon.
Freddie,Feb.21,1879,4y,
s/o Simon & Jospehine.
Frederick,Aug.28,1847,2y,
s/o Fred & Martha.
George H.,Sept.19,1848,2y,
s/o Simon & Nancy.
Harlan W.,May 3,1940,79y.
Hattie E. Elwell,1857-1896,
w/o Herbert H.
Herbert H.,July 24,1916,67y.
Josephine Kimball,May 19,1922,80y,
w/o Simon.
Louisa Hale,Oct.21,1864,40y,
w/o Abial A.
Sarah F., Mar.11,1852,1y,
d/o Simon H. & Nancy M. [GS].
Simon, b. West Cambridge,MA -
d. Apr.4,1899,57y
Simon, Col.,Apr.17,1788-
Sept.20,1842.
Zilpha A. Whitney,Jan.16,1819-
May 2,1908,w/o Benj.F. [GS]
DALE
Elizabeth Morton,1799-1875,w/o Jos.
Frances,1836-1855,
d/o Joseph & Elizabeth.
Joseph,1799-1869,h/o Elizabeth
Josey P.,XXXX [GS].
Martha,1831-1866,d/o Jos.& Elz.
DAVIS
Charles,Feb.26,1923.
Horace Oscar,Aug.27,1940,88y,
h/o Lula F. Small.
Julia Stanley,May 17,1939,78y.

Lula F. Small,XXXX,66y.
DAY
Martha E. Bixby,Mar.12,1894.38y.
Matilda,Nov.27,1947,32y,w/o Orville.
Sophia,Mar.8,1847,40y.
DEARBORN
Adelaide F.,July 8,1851,2y,
George W.,June 30,1842,8y,
d/o & s/o Otis R. & Abba C.
DEBECK
John,Sept.13,1818-May 14,1900
Harriet E. Crosby,Feb.27,1816-
June 18,1886, w/o John.
Lydia H.,Aug.29,1890,48y [GS]
Phebe A.,1849-1897,d/o John & H.E.
Mary S.,Apr.4,1935,89y.
DILLINGHAM
Lizzie,1831-1905.
Sarah H.,1807-1881,w/o Wm.
Sarah Hall,1800-1846,w/o Wm.
William,1797-1860,h/o Sarah Hall.
DIXON
Hattie A., June 30,1871,5y.
James E.,June 12,1855,1y &
Mary E.,Dec.16,1861,2y,
s/o & d/o Alanson & Maria.
DOOLAN
Thomas,Jan.1898,65y [GS].
DOUGLAS
Arveller,Dec.19,1851,7y,
d/o Gardner & Asenath.
DRAPER
Mrs. George,Dec.1910 [GS].
Sarah A. Stiles,1827-1911,w/o Geo.E.
DRINKWATER
Adella Scott,Mar.11,1867,7m &
Sarah Leoline,June 5,1859,5y,
2 d/o L.A. & S.L.
Sarah B.,Apr.12,1867,45y,
w/o Capt. Leoline A.
DUCKER
Jane Richardson,1800-1880,
d/o J. & E. Richardson [GS].
John,1793-1880,
h/o Jane Richardson [GS].
John R.,Jan.22,1857,17y,s/o J.& J.
DYER
Charles H.,Aug.30,1851,14y,
s/o David & Mary.
David,Aug.20,1872,74y,War of 1812.
David, Jr.,1840-1889,s/o Dav.& Mary.
Edmond M.,Oct 5,1825,1y,
s/o David & Mary
Frances B.,May 1,1852,15y,d/o Eliza I.
George W.,1811-1843,s/o Eliza I.

Hannah B. Dorr,1810-1892,
w/o Geo.W.
Harriet A.F.,Nov.1,1846,1y,
d/o W.W. & E.A.
Henry,Nov.1832,7y,s/o D.& M.
Levia,July 1845,1y,d/o D.& M.
Louisa F.,1835-1895,w/o David, Jr.
Mary Babb,1801-1880,w/o David
Sarah B.,Oct.17,1945,93y.
William W.,Feb.25,1855,47y.
EDGERLY
Frank N.,Oct.1,1932,84y.
EDWARDS
Bryce McLellan,Mar.23,1800-
Apr.15,1871.
Martha Irish,July 15,1808-
July 22,1884,w/o Bryce.
Martha McLellan,May 2,1846,1y,
d/o Bryce & Martha [GS].
ELDER
Josiah,Feb.8,1848,37y.
Mary S.,June 12,1812-Oct.26,1901,
w/o Josiah L.
Mehitable Sands,Oct.23,1877,62y,
w/o S.L.
S.L.,Jan.22,1873,60y.
ELWELL
Benjamin,1825-1890.
Charlotte A.,July 12,1881,51y,
d/o R. & H. Hanson.
Lavina Allen,1821-1883,w/o Benj.
EMERSON
Wiliam Granville,May 18,1832,
4y,s/o Myrick & Deborah H.
EMERY
Maria Dillingham,1837-1913.
EMMONS
William A.,1849, at sea,44y,
h/o Elizabeth T. Hinds.
ESTY
Charlie H.,1872-1880,s/o D.F. & M.H.
D. Franklin,Nov.24,1921,84y.
FAUGHT
Frank H.,Mar.8,1950,77y,
h/o Georgie M.
FENTON
Cornelia,1878-1880,
d/o Charles & Cornellia.
Cornellia J.,1842-1880,w/o Chas
Fannie C.,1871-1882, &
Helena M.,1876-1882,
2 - d/o Charles & Cornellia.
FIELD
Amos L.,Oct.18,1908,65y.
Charles W.,July 6,1896,16y.
Georgia E.,May 25,1891,40y.

Georgie M.,Jan.30,1975,94y,
w/o Frank H.
James E.,Feb.14,1956,71y.
Laura L.,Dec.20,1964,90y.
Margena B.,Feb.11,1905,50y,
w/o Amos L.
FLINN
William H.,June 5,1855,31y.
FOREST
Edward W.,Apr.21,1908,33y.
Herbert W.,July 13,1903,1m.
Josie M.,Feb.10,1910,31y,w/o E.W.
FOSS
Elroy,Oct.23,1845,s/o S.W. & F.
Frances H.,July 4,1853,51y,w/o S.H.
FOSTER
B.B.,Sept.1,1832,21y,died at sea [GS]
Benjamin B.July 22,1857,78y,
Bessie Valentine,1881-1914,
w/o Oscar.
C.L.,Oct.13,1853,26y,at sea [GS]
Elizabeth S.,Feb.4,1925,52y,w/o Robt.
Helena R.,Jan.3,1947,49y,w/o Oscar.
John A.,Nov.8,1856,32y.
Oscar,Apr.9,1962,78y.
Rebecca,Dec.19,1850,64y,w/o Benj.
Robert L.,1866-1927 [GS].
Sarah,July 17,1850,22y [GS].
Susan F.,May 13,1818,11m,
d/o Benjamin & Rebecca.
FOUGHT
Georgia M.,Jan.30,1975,94y,
w/o Frank H.
FRACKER
Harry,1878 -XXXX.
Martha,1797-1881,w/o Harry.
FREEMAN
Lydia,1775-1841.
Mary,Apr.27,1851,74y,w/o Eben.
Nathaniel,Capt.,XXXX,lost at sea,
h/o Lydia.
FURLONG
Abba Quimby,Mar.15,1849,21y,
w/o Thomas T.
GERHARDT
Cora,May 3,1888,1y.
Emma,Apr.21,1923,66y.
Ernest,Sept.30,1941,73y,s/o Friedich
W. & Kristine Kroner Gerhardt.
Willie G.,May 29,1886,14y.
GIPSON
Emma H.,Feb.15,1845,2y,
d/o Tobias & Sarah.
Mary P. Freeman,Apr.22,1857,40y,
w/o Timothy.
Sarah,May 27,1847,26y,w/o Tobias.
Timothy,Apr.22,1857,41y [GS]

GILBERT
Olive J.,1849-1930 [GS]
GILE
John H.,June 23,1870.
Margaret J.B.,July 30,1842,7y,
d/o J.H. & M.E.
Matilda E.,Apr.2,1848,43y,w/o J.H.
Ruth,no date,23y,sis/o John.
GILMORE
Hugh,Apr.17,1903,47y.
GILPATRICK
Caroline I. Lewis,Sept.15,1926,74y,
w/o George W. [GS]
George W.,Sept.8,1907,58y.
GLADHILL
Benjamin,Sept.8,1866,28y.
GOODING
Charles H.,May 19,1856,28y,
Mary Ann,Mar.25,1853,24y,w/o C.H.
GOODRIDGE
Eliza A.,Apr.5,1823-Dec.29,1871,
d/o George W.
GOOLD
Annie Blanchard,1870,24y,
Josiah,May 26,1822,38y,
Lucinda Burleigh,1804-1873,w/o Thos.
Mary Frances,1841-1869.
Mary M.,July 4,1829,40y,w/o Josiah.
Sarah M.,Feb.24,1838,25y.
Thomas,1809-1853,h/o Lucinda.
GORE
Addie L. Proctor,1886,39y,w/o I.D.
Isaiah D.,Mar.21,1899,59y.
GRAFF
Emma,Mar.12,1988,94y.
Walter,Mar.16,1976.
GRAHAM
Ann C.,1812-1856,w/o Wm.
Benjamin ,Sept.8,1866,28y [GS]
William,1812-1866,h/o Ann C.
GRANT
Charles,1859-1887 [GS].
GREEN
Callie M.,1864 -1890
GenevieveBatchelder,Nov.13,1885,
22y,w/o Adelb. E.
Jane C. McKenney,1829-1889,
1st w/o Nelson.
Lizzie,Feb.21,1897,26y.
Lydia Porter,Mar.20,1909,78y,
2nd w/o Nelson.
Nelson,Feb.8,1909,78y.
GUSTIN
Daniel Franklin,1859-Dec.1917.
Ellie F.,1882-1883,d/o D.F.& F.H.[GS]

Everett E.,Apr.22,1948,57y,
  s/o D.F. & F.H.
Flora H. Wescott,Jan.19,1921,64y,
  2nd w/o Daniel F.
Lillian F. Caswell,June 9,1883,20y,
  1st w/o Daniel F.
Lillian F.,Aug.17,1883,10m.
HAGGETT
Earle L.,Aug.25,1937,49y.
Nellie Lillian Cash,May 1,1940,75y,
  w/o Will C.
Will C.,Dec.4,1944,85y.
HAINES
Sarah M.,Oct.30,1896,65y,w/o Chas.C.
HALE
Cora H.,May 2,1859-June 5,1888,
  d/o J. & H.
Della H.,Jan.21,1884-July 6,1888,
  d/o J.& H.
Harriet N.,1832-1888,w/o Josiah.
Josiah,Jan.26,1905,78y.
Lydia M.Debeck,Aug.29,1890,48y.
HALL
John L.B.,1916 (?),70y, s/o
  Silas & Rebecca Best Hall [GS].
Lizzie S.,1853-1874 [GS].
Silas,1806-1890,h/o R.B.
Silas M.,Jan.31,1932,76y [GS]
Rebecca Best,1819-1888,w/o Silas[GS].
William M.,Jan.11,1923,73y.
HANSON
Benaiah,Dec.8,1851,17y,s/o Robt & H.
Clara,Mar.20,1913,67y.
Elbridge,Dec.21,1881,46y,
  s/o Robert and Harriet.
Harriet,May 7,1887,82y,w/o Robert.
Harriet M.,July 7,1851,19y.
Juliette M.,Jan.28,1854,13y,
  d/o Robert & Harriet.
Oliver A.,Dec.26,1920,73y.
Robert,Deacon,Aug.6,1865,67y,
  h/o Harriet.
HARDING
George W.,1895-1954.
Helen Louise,June 11,1843,22y,
  d/o Robert & Sarah.
Olive V.,June 17,1895-Feb.1947,
  w/o George W.,
  d/o Wm.& Nellie Phinney Vanner.
HARMON
Aseneth,1823-1864,w/o W.V.
Edwin A.1850-1880,s/o J.O. &S.S
John O.,1822-Jan.15,1909.
Llewellyn,1891,1y,s/o J.O. & S.S.
Llewellyn V.,1853-1883,s/o J.O.& S.S.
Sarah E.,Aug.23,1862,21y.

Sophia S. Graffam,Aug.10,1911,87y,
  w/o John O.
William V.,Aug.25,1896,76y.
HARRIS
Adeline Louise,Sept.16,1832,2y,
  d/o Nathan & Rebecca.
Annie Kimball Totman & a child,
  XXXX,1st hus. Capt.W.H.Totman.
Nathan,Nov.1,1847,47y.
Rebecca H. Foster,Oct.7,1835,28y,
  w/o Nathan.
HARRISON
Joseph,Dec.1943,99y.
HASEY
Annie Frances Hurd,Oct.22,1862-
  Jan.20,1911,w/o John F.
Ernest L.,June 6,1965,68y.
Fred W.,Dec.12,1936,54y.
John F.,Oct.11,1857-Aug.12,1897.
HASKELL
Adeline Hatch,Mar.22,1835-
  Nov.6,1916,w/o Solomon.
Albion,Mar.24,1825,2m,
  s/o Dexter & Caroline [GS].
Angier M.,Feb.12,1847,23y.
Ann W.,Nov.29,1886,83y.
Annie M.,Mar.28,1885,23y,
  d/o Dexter & Caroline.
Caroline A.,Sept.23,1883,50y,
  w/o Dexter V.
Charles,Dec.22,1921,63y.
Charles,Mar. 5, 1848,23y.
Cora May,Sept.6,1860.
Dellie M.,1861-1878,d/o Sol.& Adeline.
Dexter V.,Apr.24,1866,36y.
Ebenezer,July 25,1839,40y.
Edmund,Sept.28,1852,52y.
Elizabeth,Dec.23,1850,85y,w/o Mark.
Frankie,May 2,1863,3y &
Freddie,Aug.11,1866,2y,
  2 s/o Dexter & Caroline.
Frederick,Oct.14,1845,41y.
Helen,Mar.23,1832,19m,
  d/o Joseph & Lydia.
infant,Dec.2,1834,3y,
  s/o Nathaniel & Sarah.
infant,Mar.28,1822.
Joseph W.,July 1,1835,36y
Lydia Jordan,Mar.8,1832,
  32y, w/o Joseph W.
Mark,Feb.20,1827,65y,h/o Elizabeth.
Mark,Mar.23,1832,26d,
  s/o Joseph & Lydia.
Mary,Apr.27,1801,77y,w/o Sol.
Mary,May 8,1821,27y,
  d/o Mark & Elizabeth.
Nathaniel,Nov.16,1856,65y.

Nattie J.,Sept.18,1860, 1y,
  s/o Solomon & Adeline.
Pamela,Dec.5,1844,2y.
Sally,Oct.2,1846,42y,w/o Ebenzer.
Sarah Caroline,Dec.2,1834,3y,
  d/o Nathaniel & Sarah [GS].
Sarah,May 18,1860,70y,
  w/o Nathaniel.
Sarah C.,Mar.2,1836-Aug.19,1866[GS]
Sarah Marsh,May 17,1805,40y,
  w/o Solomon,Jr. [GS].
Solomon,May 22,1816,92y,h/o Mary.
Solomon,Sept.18,1826-Sept.29,1901,
  h/o Adeline H.
Solomon, Jr.,Dec.26,1816,40y,
  h/o Sarah.
XXXX,1871,d/o Edmund &Sarah.
XXXX,Mar.5,1848,23y [GS].
XXXX,Oct.14,1813,41y [GS].
HATCH
Abigail,1772-1854.
Arthur,1877,1m.
Carrie Merrill,XXXX,77y,
  w/o Nathaniel.
Elizabeth,1758-1812.
Emily Higgins,1862,52y,w/o Geo.
Estella,1874,1m.
George,1870,73y.
Harriet,1794-1811.
Harriet,1837-1923.
Helenah Amanda,May 1,1846,9m,
  d/o Hiram & Nancy.
John W.,1853,23y.
Mary E.,1831-1854.
Melvina,Aug.22,1916,70y,d/o G.&E.
Nathaniel H.,June 6,1915,64y.
Nathaniel, Capt.,1750-1832,
  Revoluntionar War Soldier.
HAWES
Alice May,Apr.12,1894,2d,
  d/o H.H.R & Ella.
Cathie M.,1884,inf/o H.H.R. & Ella.
Eunice,May 27,1874,87y,w/o Joseph.
Frederick,XXXX [GS].
Joseph,Dec.2,1806.
HAYES
Augustus,Nov.19,1834,3d.
David,Apr.26,1831-Mar.12,1899.
David,Mar.26,1870,74y.
David G.,Mar.12,1890,68y [GS].
Fannie A.,Feb.17,1861,27y,
  d/o David & Nancy.
infant son,Nov.19,1831,3d [GS]
Marshall,Jan.23,1872,44y.
Nancy Webb,Jan.25,1889,83y,
  w/o David.
Willie,XXXX [GS].

HENDRICKSON
Hans,1887,34y.
Joanna,XXXX,11m,d/o John &Maria.
HERLYCK
Christiana Chromes,1832-1905,
  w/o Laust [GS].
Laust C., Apr.17,1882,52y.
HEZELTON
Albert H.,May 11,1875,9y,
  s/o Moses L. & Mattie A.
Almery,1834-1905,s/o Ivory & Hannah
Edwd. Augustine,Sept.1,1878,26y.
Hannah Thompson, Oct.19,1798-
  Oct.20,1884,w/o Ivory.
Ivory,Aug.15,1804-Nov.17,1884.
Ivory, Jr.,Oct.2,1829-May 8,1900,
  s/o Ivory & Hannah.
Jane Richards,June 18,1830-
  Nov.12,1859,w/o Ivory,Jr.
Moses Q.,July 2,1895,62y [GS].
HIGGINS
Ellen J. Phinney,Oct.4,1876,45y,
  w/o Freeman.
Freeman,Oct.12,1895,70y.
Josey P.,Aug.1,1861,2y,
  s/o Freeman & Ellen.
HODGES
James G.,June 6,1895,26y.
Jason G.,June 6,1875,5y [GS].
HODGKINS
Abbie F. Cloudman,Feb.28,1926,
  80y,2nd w/o Morris.
Morris,1820-1887.
Sarah E. Knowlton,1824-1873,
  1st w/o Morris.
HODSDON
2 children,no names or dates.
Andrew P.,July 18,192X,77y.
Charles A.,Dec.1,1915,73y,
  h/o Mary E.
Frank B.,1869-1877 [GS].
Lottie B.,1865-1880 [GS].
Mary A. Stevens,May 7,1900,88y.
Mary E. Johnson,Dec.17,1906,60y,
  w/o Charles A.
Minnie I.,Aug.25,1928,61y.
William P.,Feb.23,1924,87y.
HOLMES
Joseph Waldo,June 29,1838,4y,
Mary Waldo,June 29,1838,3y,
Sumner,Jr.,May 10,1838, 2y,
  3 ch/o Sumner & Sarah [GS].
Sumner Smith,Apr.20,1839,31y,
  h/o Sarah.
HOLT
Abbie E.,Aug.24,1900,50y,w/o Chas E.

Charles E.,Nov.27,1911,65y.
HOPKINS
Annie L. Towle,1860-1922,w/o W.J.
Marius,Nov.1,1922,60y.
Warren J.,1862-1922 [GS].
HORR
Daniel P.,July 14,1841Jan.21,1920,
  h/o Lydia A.S.
Genie E.,Dec.12,1882,26y,w/o R.C.
Harlan P.,July 7,1880,inf/o R.C.
Irving,Aug.16,1947,76y.
Rensselaer C.,1852-1889 [GS].
HOUSTON
Ithamar,Jan.15,1841-Sept.19,1917,
  h/o Rebecca.
Rebecca Augusta Wilbur,
  July 28,1845-Aug.15,1915.
HOWE
Abba Cutter,May 7,1865,55y,
  d/o Col.Simon & Christiana Cutter
Calvin, Dr.,Aug.26,1815,65y.
P.Osborne,Feb.24,1870,28y.
HUGHES
Anna,May 16,1947,84y.
Anna,Dec.30,1862-May 16,1947,
  d/o Peter & Catherine [GS].
Catherine Brown,Apr.27,1900,63y,
  w/o Peter.
HUNT
Elizabeth,Feb.1910,62y,w/o Chas.H.
James E.,Apr.8,1881,32y.
HURD
Adelaide Maria,May 8,1893,51y,
  w/o Washburn.
Eva Marion,Feb.1893,1m,d/o Chas.
Tristram,July 15,1812,37y.
Washburn,Dec.1,1871,32y.
IDIORNE
Althesta W.,Sept.18,1840,5y,
  d/o Wm. & Jane L. [GS].
IRISH
Angeline,1886,60y.
JACKMAN
Betty S.,July 1,1958,102y.
David,Feb.6,1831,75y.
Georgia A.,Nov.19,1914,65y,w/o I.B.
Ingalls B.,1848-1888.
Ernest W.,June 13,1956,77y.
Henrietta L.,June 11,1958,82y.
Louise Ayer,1876-1958,w/o Ernest.
JEWETT
Belinda,1806-1886 [GS].
Paul,1798-1864 [GS].
Samuel H.,1859 [GS].
JOHNSON
(Father),1771-1847.
(Mother),1780-1865.

XXXX,Sept.8,1866,28y.
Abbie,1813-1865 [GS].
Daniel Trickey, Capt.,Dec.27,1845,
  34y,in Boston.
Edwin,Mar.11,1831,1m,
  s/o Bartholowmew & Susan.
Gardner,1805-1883.
Harriet,1858,32y.
Harry,1826-1853.
Jesse,June 11,1849,3y, s/o
  Bartholowmew & Susan [GS].
Josephine,1841-1923 [GS].
Mary,1811-1845,w/o Gardner.
Rufus,1815-1891.
JORDAN
Aurelia Bodge,1850-1932,
  w/o Mahlon [GS].
Elizabeth,Oct.27,1894,73y,
  w/o George D. [GS].
Ella S.,Apr.21,1877,
  d/o Ephraim T. & Sarah M.
Ezekiel,Mar.29,1854,42y,
  h/o Susan [GS].
Fred L.,1867-1884,s/o G.A. & M.J.
Frederick A.,Nov.11,1901,71y,
  s/o Joseph W.
George A.,Apr.16,1906,67y.
George D.,Aug.26,1882,77y.
George S.,Mar.26,1851,11y,
  h/o Margaret.
Henrietta,Oct.30,1847,8m.
Mahlon A.,1857-1903 [GS].
Margaret,Mar.23,1833,w/o Jos. [GS].
Mildred J. Partridge,July 30,1899,
  61y,w/o Geo. A.
Sarah M.,July 4, 1814,w/o E.T. [GS].
Sarah M. Hurd,Oct.29,1877,63y,
  w/o Ephraim T.Hurd.
Sarah Tower,Oct.28,1858,48y,
  w/o George D.
Sumner W.,Oct.7,1844,2y,
  s/o Ezekiel & Susan.
JOSEPH
Frederick A.,Nov.11,1901,71y,
  s/o Joseph W.Joseph [GS].
KELLEY
Inez,1858-1907 [GS].
KENNARD
Betsey Chase,Apr.14,1878,89y,
  w/o Edward.
Edward,Sept.2,1878,89y.
KERR
Jane,1850-1906,w/o William D. [GS].
William D.,1847-1890 [GS].
Willie,May 29,1882,13y,
  s/o Wm. & Jane [GS].

KIMBALL
Clark N.,1839-1853.
Evelyn M.,July 27,1915,1d.
James D.,1849-1851.
Jona,1813-1865.
Mary B.,1845-1886.
Nellie M.,1847-1865.
Patience Knight,1812-1876,w/o Jona.
KING
Marietta,May 14,1875,21y.
KNIGHT
A.Eugenia,Aug.24,1911,62y,
  w/o John C.
Adelbert S.,Apr.18,1963,79y.
Arthur L.,1878-1967.
Bertha W.,Feb.16,1926,
  d/o Joseph & Esther.
Betsey E. Crockett,
  July 27,1804-July 27,1891.
Betsey W. Morse,May 3,1895,
  w/o Ephram.
Diantha M.Plummer,
  1834-1889,w/o Mark.
Edith W.,Mar.7,1959,72y.
Elizabeth S. Sawyer,1881,47y,
  w/o John
Ephram,1809-1854.
Ester J. Babb,Mar.23,1899,62y,
  w/o Joseph.
Freddie W.,Nov.2,1862,3y,
  s/o Joseph & Esther.
Gertrude,Jan.31,1875-July 1,1884,
  d/o J.M.& M.A.
John,1834-1881 [GS].
John C.,Feb.26,1831-June 19,1902.
Joseph,1833-1924.
Mark,Feb.25,1913.
Mattie M.,Mar.7,1961,72y.
Rebecca K. Gilpatrick,Aug.24,1914,
  66y,w/o Mark.
Samuel,Aug.17,1863,67y,h/o Betsey E.
KNOWLTON
Daniel W.,June 5,1897,66y.
John J.,July 16,1826-Jan.17,1911.
Lizzie Maud,Oct.24,1866Oct.15,1867,
  d/o J.J. & S.
Martha L. Allen,Dec.31,1929,71y,
  w/o William E.
Ralph,XXXX,inf./o Wm.& M.
Susan A.F.Denison,Aug.30,1832-
  Sept.11,1896,w/o John J.
William E.,Aug.10,1936,77y.
KNOX
Archie O.,Nov.16,1879-
  Aug.12,1957,77y.
Bertha L.,July 9,1942,60y.

Margaret J. McDonald,
  May 28,1936,78y,w/o Wm. B.
William B.,Apr.16,1928,80y.
KOLLACK
Ann,1876,74y,w/o Joshua.
Charles H.,1855,1m,s/o J. & A.
Eben,Feb.10,1871,63y.
Edward K.,1865,27y,s/o J. & A.
Emma M.,Nov.1900,48y,
  w/o Horace [GS].
Horace T.,1849-1920 [GS].
Irene,Dec.2,1852,14m [GS].
Irene Davis,Jan.15,1900,79y,
  w/o Royal T.
John T.,1867,24y,s/o J.& A.
Joshua,Oct.6,1844,42y.
Leo Percy,June 10,1876,3y,
  s/o H.T. & E.M.
Lucy H.,Jan.9,1866,28y,
  d/o Eben & Sarah.
Margaret A.,May 7,1947,97y,
  w/o Horace T.
Mary E.,1837,8y,d/o J. & A.
Royal T.,Aug.31,1865,40y.
Sarah,1866,43y,d/o Josh. & Ann.
Sarah P. Babb,May 25,1876,70y,
  w/o Eben.
Winfield S.,Dec.2,1852,14m,
  s/o R.T. & Irene.
Zebiah,1899,62y,s/o J. & A.
LAGHY
Michall,Mar.10,1864,75y [GS].
Michael,Mrs.,Jan.21,1870,83y
LAMB
Mary A.,May 24,1861-Sept.18,1908.
Samuel,Mar.28,1865,68y.
Sarah Larrabee,Sept.16,1875,75y,
  w/o Samuel.
LAMBERT
Rose,Feb.14,1923,73y,w/o Wm.
William,Feb.8,1918,41y.
LANE
Charles W.,1830-1888.
Emma W.,1830-1902.
Eva,Feb.5,1853-Feb.20,1870.
John W.,May 15,1963,97y.
LaPOINTE
A.Robert,June 17,1988,79y.
LARRABEE
Adeline,Aug.12,1845,22y, w/o Sam.
Adeline,Apr.21,1846,1y,d/o S.& A.
Samuel,1819-1852.
LARY
Elizabeth W.,Oct.18,1852,75y,
  w/o Samuel.
Jane Wise,1803-1889 [GS].
Margaret B.,Sept.22,1844,26y.

Mary A.,May 1,1869,57y.
Moses P.,June 9,1871,71y.
Samuel,Nov.2,1838,65y.
LEARY
Jane,June 19,1889,86y.
LEAVITT
Asa,Nov.17,1857,47y.
Emily F.,XXXX,3y,d/o Asa & Emeline.
LEIGHTON
Alvin,Feb.14,1884,74y,
Amanda Adams,Feb.27,1867,55y,
w/o Henry H.
Caroline I.,Sept.15,1926,74y.
Charles H.,Nov.20,1858-Mar.1950,
s/o Alvin & Hannah
Hannah Sawyer,Jan.5,1892,86y,
w/o Alvin [GS].
Henry H.,Nov.25,1852,26y.
Lucy B. Vanner,June 24,1948,82y,
w/o Charles H.
Mary E.,Apr.21,1855,21y,
d/o Amanda A.
Mary L.,1855-1855,
d/o Alvin & Hannah [GS].
Maud Woodbury Sweetser,
Nov.1910, w/o George E. [GS].
LEONARD
James R.,Feb.1924,87y, s/o
Thomas & Mary Goff Leonard [GS]
LEWIS
Ann E. Hurd,Jan.2,1894,61y,
w/o William H.
Eugene,Aug.26,1854,1y &
Freddie,June 4,1864,2y,
2 s/o Wm.H. & Ann E.
George S.,Rev.,XXXX.
Harriet M. Cushing,1827-1904,
w/o John M.
Helen A.,Feb.25,1851,14m.
Ida Brackett,Aug.10,1913,52y,
w/o William.
Jennie May,Apr.25,1978,93y.
John M.,1822-1885 [GS].
William Henry,Nov.19,1899,71y.
William,Jan.18,1917,57y.
LIBBY
Addie M.,Sept.27,1851,17m,
d/o Solomon & Mary J.
Albert,1840-1896 [GS].
Albert M.,Dec.2,1883,53y.
Algie V.,1889-19XX,
ch/o Albert & Mary E. [GS].
Alonzo,July1838-Apr.1840,
s/o Andrew & Sophronia.
Andrew,Apr.2,1800-May 7,1848.
Ann J.,Mar.1,1864,33y,w/o Cyrus E.
Annie Cora,XXXX,2y, d/o C.E. & L.

Arthur F.,July 12,1948,79y,
s/o Albert & Mary E.
Caroline P.,June 1908,
w/o Jacob Warren Libby [GS].
Charles D.,1854-1904.
Charles W.,Aug.1910,45y,
s/o Jacob Warren Libby [GS].
Charles W.,June 10,1845,12y,
s/o Peter & Tamson .
Clara E.,Nov.16,1947,82y,
d/o Albert & Mary E.
David B.,Sept.7,1888,65y,
h/o Sarah Maria.
Ellen M. Field Rich,1912,65y.
Emma A.,June 10,1912,40y.
Eunice H.,1858-1899 [GS].
Father,1796-1855.
Mother,1801-1876.
Frank J.,July 11,1888-Nov.11,1954.
George A.,Sept.29,1852,19y,
s/o Peter and Tamson.
George L.,1902,6y,s/o C.D.& M.C.
George R.,Sept.1905 [GS].
Herbert L.,1879-1882,
s/o Albert & Mary E. [GS].
infant,XXXX,ch/o A. & M.E. [GS].
Leo D.,Dec.6,1892-Aug.21,1958.
Lester Grover,Oct.21,1890-
Sept.24,1955.
Lucy J.,Dec.23,1899,51y,
d/o D.B. & S.M.
Mary C.,Oct.11,1924,61y,w/o Chas D.
Mary E.,1877, w/o Frank.
Mary E.,June 20,1926,81y,w/o Albert.
Sarah Maria,Nov.1902,74y,w/o David.
Sophia Newcomb,Feb.2,1937,76y,
2nd w/o Stephen H.
Sophronia,June 6,1834-Nov.2,1836,
s/o Andrew & Soph.
Sophronia,Nov.8,1811-Oct.12,1868,
w/o Andrew.
Stephen H.,Nov.21,1927,93y.
Willis E.,1867-1913 [GS].
LINDETTE
A.,1873-1952,
d/o Abbie B. Stackpole [GS].
LONGFELLOW
Leander,Sept.4,1813,1y,
s/o Moses & Marcy.
Marcy,Sept.7,1817,37y,w/o Moses.
Moses,Sept.24,1816,45y.
LONGLEY
Anna B.,1836-1866,w/o David.
LORING
Georgiana H.,Dec.8,1956,89y.
Greely,Mar.22,1918,55y.
Louisa B.,Sept.28,1917,78y.

Perley V.,Apr.17,1954,63y.
LOVEJOY
Georgianna Kollack,XXXX,
w/o G.H. [GS].
LOW
Ann,Aug.2,1869,87y,w/o Benj.
Benjamin,Sept.17,1826,46y.
John A.,Sept.21,1810-Oct.2,1885.
Lois,July 5,1802-May 27,1893,
w/o John.
LOWE
Susan M.,1824-1893,w/o James.
LUCAS
Helen L.,June 9,1986,48y.
LYNCH
Laura C.,May 19,1975.
Zeldeme P.,Dec.10,1944,42y.
MABURY
John,June 12,1810,80y [GS].
Johnson,Jan.16,1827,20y [GS].
MAFFIT
Mary E.,Apr.1909,62y [GS].
MAHAR
William E.,Feb.29,1931,52y.
MANCHESTER
Benjamin B.,Jan.1909,76y [GS].
Charlotte A.,Jan.11,1915,66y [GS].
MAREAN
Celia C.,1889,17y,d/o Frank & Mary.
Della May,July 1,1864-
Apr.1947,82y,d/o Frank & Mary
Francis (Frank) July 30,1906,73y,
h/o Mary, s/o Col.Wm.& Charity Davis.
Mary L. Goodwin,Nov.6,1912,80y.
MARINER
Abigail Moore,1868,57y.
George F.,Apr.28,1911,73y.
Mary E. Haskell,Feb.16,1921,
82y,w/o George.
MARRETT
Adeline Irish,1901,90y,w/o Wm.
William,M.D.,1859,59y.
MARSHALL
Emily L. Graves,Dec.2,1919,57y,
w/o William J.
William J.,May 29,1938,81y.
MARTIN
Deantha A.,Oct.2,1828-
Mar.14,1879,2nd w/o Noah R.
Noah R.,Dr.,Mar.28,1820-Oct.1911.
Elizabeth Bangs,June 9,1873,52y,
w/o Noah R.
MASON
Alden P.,1853-1891 [GS].
Anna,Mar.22,1859,74y,w/o John.
Susie E.,1858-1932,
w/o Alden P. [GS].

MAW
Annie W.,1880,28y,w/o Chas.P.
Charles P.,Nov.12,1895,46y.
Lena C.,1877-1926,w/o P.E.
MAY
Hattie,XXXX,9y [GS].
MAYBERRY
Elizabeth,1885,83y.
Frank W.,1888, 29y
George C.,Sept.2,1905,76y.
Hannah R. Strout,1889,62y,
w/o Andrew D.
Johnson,Jan.6,1827,20y.
Katie C.,1861-1896,w/o Lewis M.
L.R.,1908,73y.
Mark,Feb.19,1924,71y.
Martha Proctor,Feb.25,1917,w/o L.R.
Philema B.,May 11,1897,91y,w/o Wm.
Sarah,Dec.1,1855,83y.
Thomas,June 12,1810,80y.
William G.,Apr.24,1870,69y.
MAYHEW
Eliza,1811-1870.
Ellen,Dec.27,1927,82y,wid/o Hebron.
Hebron,Apr.21,1927,86y.
Helen F.,1836-1873.
Pamelia,May 7,1838-Oct.30,1917.
Thomas,May 3,1898,94y.
MacKENZIE
Charles F.,Sept.8,1941,62y.
Elmer H.,1888-1916,lost at sea [GS].
Lena Hasey,Apr.11,1974,85y,w/o C.F.
McCANN
Caroline E.,Sept.12,1856,27y,
w/o David N.
Elizabeth A. Cobb,Dec.5,1860,18y.
Ella M. Bean,Nov.21,1855-
Mar.7,1885,w/o Joseph H. &
d/o D.M. & M.A. Bean.
Joseph H.,Oct.27,1844-Dec.26,1943.
Nellie L.,Jan.26,1958,80y.
McCARTY
Affie M. Libby,July 19,1823,76y,
w/o Oliver P.
Harry Clinton,Mar.20,1876-
Dec.7,1935, h/o Agnes &
only s/o Oliver & Affie.
Oliver P.,Mar.21,1899,54y.
McCORSON
Mary P. McNair,Sept.6,1901,
w/o Dennis [GS].
McCREADY
Evelyn F.,July 14,1953,46y.
McDONALD
Martha,1878,33y,w/o Stephen.

McFARLAND
Patrick,Mar.21,1885,23y.
McKELLAR
Donald,1888,3y.
Donald,1891,79y.
Janet,July 28,1937,85y.
Margaret,1857-1922 [GS].
Mary Russell,May 1924,73y [GS].
Robert,1857-1922 [GS].
McLELLAN
Annie P. Chandler,Dec.19,1930,77y, wid/o William.
Ella,Oct.31,1854,3y.
Henry S.,Sept.4,1892,43y.
James W.,Oct.8,1856,32y.
Marie Louise,Nov.14,1922,42y, w/o Winfield.
Martha,May 2,1846,1y.
Mary F. Conant,Jan.19,1892,41y, w/o Henry S.
Rosabell H.,Feb.19,1915,73y, 2nd w/o Samuel E.
Samuel E.,Mar.17,1887,65y.
Sarah E. Babb,Jan.18,1864, 36y,1st w/o Samuel E.
William Edward,Feb.2,1937,84y.
Winfield S.,Feb.17,1935,67y.
McMASTER
Caroline,June 24,1861,25y,w/o Sam'l.
McNAIR
Emma L.,Aug.28,1982,92y
James,1819-1886.
John L.,Nov.5,1942,53y.
John,Dec.18,1917,62y.
John,Jan.7,1949,72y.
Julia M.,May 4,1961,83y.
Katherine Flint,1854 -1908, w/o John [GS].
Marion F.,May 27,1973,90y.
Mary P.,1888, died in England, w/o John.
MEGGISON
Annie B.,Oct.5,1984,83y.
Cephas W.,Nov.27,1935,68y, h/o Gertrude A.
Gertrude A. Jackman,Jan.1,1945, 54y,w/o Cephas.
MERRELL
Caroline T. Haley,May 17,1865, 51y, w/o Sewell T.
Dolly W.,May 10,1875,89y, w/o James W. [GS].
Harriet T.,June 20,1851,27y, w/o Charles H. [GS].
James W.Mar.4,1842,63y [GS]
Mary H.,XXXX, d/o C.H. & H.T. [GS].

Mother,Jan.21,1870,82y [GS].
William,Aug.1869,1m, s/o Sewell T. & Caroline.
MERRILL
Albert G.,Mar.26,1950, 65y [GS].
Albion,Apr.2,1863,25y.
Charlotte,Jan.11,1915,66y,w/o Edw.
James H.,June 26,1836,3w, s/o John & Jane.
Jane E.,June 25,1888,80y, in Camden, ME.,wid/o John
John, Sept.29,1875,88y.
Marshall H.,Oct.10,1880-Feb.25,1948.
Martha T.,Apr.2,1863,25y,w/o Albion.
Mary C.,Aug.30,1867,11m, d/o Sewell T. & Caroline.
Mary Jane,June 23,1846,5y, d/o John & Jane.
MERSERVE
Albert G.,Aug.4,1884-Mar.1950, s/o A.M.& Sarah.
Albert M.,Nov.14,1903,48y
Ella F.,1883,1m,d/o A. & S.
Ella Frances,Nov.23,1875,22y, w/o Henry L.
Isa Maude,Nov.29,1955,79y.
Jonathan,Mar.10,1903,77y.
Sarah A. Haines,Apr.25,1857- Feb.26,1944, wid/o A.M. & d/o Charles & Sarah Furlong Haines.
MILLIONS
Deborah Newcomb,Aug.27,1857,73y, w/o Ebenezer.
Ebenezer,Mar.26,1865,75y.
Hannah,Sept.20,1830,20y, d/o Ebenezer & Deborah.
Hezekiah B.,May 15,1917,79y.
Mary L.,Sept.20,1856,36y, d/o Ebenezer & Deborah.
MITCHELL
Almeda Hanson,Sept.28,1913,55y, w/o Daniel H.
Daniel H.,Apr.17,1916,57y.
Elmer M.,June 25,1866-Apr.22,1898, s/o Andrew & Sophia.
Martha P.,1836-1894,w/o Rev. H.B.
MITSMEN
George U.,Jan.28,1896,30y.
Mattie A.,Apr.9,1926,54y, d/o John & Caroline.
MITSMENN
Albert L.,May 16,1916,52y.
Alice,1892,1y,d/o Albert L. & Amy.
Catherine,Nov.5,1875,49y,w/o John.
Helen A. Gore,Apr.X,1880,23y, d/o John & Catherine.

John,Aug.17,1886,61y,h/o Catherine.
MOFFITT
J.W.,XXXX,Co.G.,12th Maine Inf.
MORRIS
George A.,Oct.16,1917,72y.
George,XXXX,101y.
Harry F.,Dec.22,1939,68y.
James W.,1847-1929.
James W.,XXXX,64y.
Jane,XXXX,70y,w/o George.
Joseph J.,May 1915,62y.
Mattie,Apr.16,1874,27y,
d/o George & Jane.
Olive J.,c.1930,81y,wid/o J.W.
MORTON
John P.,Nov.1909,23y [GS].
MOULTON
Abbie,May 24,1903,92y.
Jennie R.S.,Sept.14,1872,
w/o Charles,d/o Simon Cutter.
Joseph,Dec.28,1883,69y.
MURCH
Addie L.,Oct.7,1833,12y.
Byron A.,1857,7w,s/o Joshua & Lydia.
Edward P.,1838-1839,
s/o Nathaniel & Mercy.
Edward P.,1844,1m,s/o Nath'l & M.
George G.,June 14,1875,56y.
s/o Nathaniel & Mercy.
Harlan P.,Sept.2,1923,84y.
Loretta T.,1836-Jan.19,1922,
w/o Harlan.
Lydia A.Cloudman,Oct.29,1865,31y,
w/o Joshua.
Lydia J.,1842-1898,
d/o Nathaniel & Mercy.
Lydia P.,Nov.17,1840,27y,
d/o Nathaniel & Mercy.
Mary W.,1807-1890 [GS].
Mercy Sawyer,1807-1887,
w/o Nathaniel.
Nancy W.,Jan.24,1864,76y,
w/o Nathaniel.
Nathaniel,July 28,1838,50y,
h/o Nancy W.
Nathaniel,1811-1870,
h/o Mercy Sawyer.
Oscar,July 21,1857,10y.
Philip G.,1871-1872,
s/o Harlan & Loretta [GS].
NASH
Enoch G.,Feb.2,1908,43y,
s/o F.M. & J.W. [GS].
Francis M.,1832-1920,
h/o Juliet W. [GS].
Juliet Wescott,Apr.10,1896,61y,
w/o Francis M.

Louise May 1892,4y,d/o O.&Myra.
Myra B. Wyer,1862-1892,w/o Oliver B.
Percy R.,1884,1m,s/o O.& M.
NASON
Charles L.,Jan.31,1849,19y,
s/o Noah & Susan.
Clara S.,Sept.6,1848,2y,
d/o Noah & Susan.
Elizabeth L.,July 27,1919,80y,
d/o Noah & Susan.
Martin Van Buren,Feb.11,1836,
4y,s/o Noah & Susan.
Noah,Apr.21,1848,47y.
Sarah S.,Jan.27,1878,63y.
Susan S.,Oct.20,1892,64y,
d/o Noah & Susan
NAYLOR
Edward A.1873-1930,h/o Eva.
Eleanor L.,1911, d/o Edw. & Eva [GS].
Eva E. Herrick,Feb.19,1943,68y,
w/o Edward A.
Marie E. Tefft,Jan.22,1913,72y,
w/o William H.
William H.,Dec.28,1925.
NEAL
Elizabeth Lamb,1832-Dec.6,1919,
w/o William H.
Harriet F.,1843-1860 [GS].
Harriet H.,1815-1864.
John H.,1846-1849.
Sarah,1787-1887.
Sarah E.,1850-1854.
William H.,Jan.4,1894,78y.
Willie T.,1857-1863.
NELSON
Jonathan,May 25,1852,70y,h/o Lydia.
Jonathan W.,Aug.15,1846,22y.
Lydia W.,Apr.3,1856,70y.
NEWCOMB
Celia M.,Apr.8,1845,1m,
d/o Lowell & Huldah.
Elizabeth L.,Nov.15,1853,4y,
d/o Lowell & Huldah.
Elizabeth L.,XXXX,31y [GS].
Ellen J.,Jan.27,1845,18m,
d/o Lowell & Huldah
Hannah M.,Oct.26,1872,82y.
Lowell V.,Mar.19,1849,31y,
h/o Huldah.
Sarah A.,May 16,1853,5y,
d/o Lowell & Huldah.
NOBLE
Harry E.,July 29,1929,50y.
Henrietta C.,Mar.5,1919,66y,
w/o Herman H.

NOYES
Charles W.,1877,41y.
O'BRION
Thomas,Aug.7,1857,4y,
s/o Patrick & Catherine.
O'REILLY
Charles J.,Dec.11,1939,62y.
Jane,Aug.12,1957,81y.
ORDIORNE
Atlhesta W.,Sept.18,1840,5y,
d/o William & Jane.
ORDWAY
John N.,Aug.4,1851,5y,
s/o Moses & Irena B.
PAINE
Almira,Jan.25,1839,2y,
d/o Solomon & Nancy.
PALMER
Clara May,Aug.18,1935,79y.
Angie L.,Oct.20,1950,72y.
PARKER
Angeline Irish,1826-1886,
w/o Joshua G. [GS].
Eva Grant,1866-1892 [GS].
Joshua G.,1825-1883.
Mary E.,May 29,1850,28y,
w/o Abraham.
Sarah L.,1912,82y.
PARSONS
Almeda,May 31,1852,6m,
d/o Thaddeus S. & Betsey.
PARTRIDGE
Adeline M.,Sept.24,1834-
Apr.21,1863,1st w/o John W.
Charles F., 1854-1934,
h/o S.Everetta [GS].
Charles H.,Nov.4,1934,80y.
Clara,Apr.22,1846,3y,
d/o G.W. & Nancy.
Flora Angie,Aug.12,1866,
8m,d/o N. & S.B.
Franklin,June 24,1821-
July 24,1865,h/o Susan F.
Franklin S.,1848-1920 [GS].
Fred A.,Mar.26,1863-
Oct.25,1949,s/o J.W.& A.M.
G.W.,1884,39y.
George H.,May 14,1840,9m,
s/o G.W. & N.S.
Hannah,Oct.14,1834-Mar.26,1923,
2nd w/o John W.
Henry J.,June 14,1841,2y.
Isabella,Mar.9,1864,38y,2nd w/o G.W.
John W.,Aug.12,1831-May 28,1911.
John W.,Feb.11,1872,75y.
Joseph H.,Apr.21,1851,10m,
s/o J. & Mary [GS].
Joseph, Capt.,Sept.27,1856,71y,
h/o Lydia Quimby.
Katherine,May 3,1944,85y [GS].
Lizzie E. Nellie,Apr.3,1934,76y [GS]
Lydia Quimby,Sept.29,1882,93y,
w/o Joseph.
Nancy S.,Aug.11,1847 ?,31y,
1st w/o G.W.
Nathaniel,Sept.15,1826,44y,
h/o Susanna P. Bradley.
S.Everetta Knowlton,Mar.9,1936,78y,
w/o Charles F.
Sarah B. Ayer,Jan.26,1885,49y,
w/o Nathan.
Susan F.,Mar.21,1823-Jan.24,1897,
w/o Franklin.
PAULSEN
Christine M. Herlyck,
July 26,1860-Mar.7,1946,
w/o Jess P. [GS].
Jess P.,Oct.12,1861-Apr.15,1921 [GS].
Kristine M.,Mar.10,1946,85y.
PEARSON
Annie T.,Oct.26,1940,82y.
Henry,Apr.14,1826-May 1914 [GS].
James H.,1826-1904 [GS].
PENNELL
Almena S.,Feb.22,1861,22y.
Catherine Bragdon1859-1944,
w/o Charles R. [GS].
Charles,no date, Civil War [GS].
Charles R.,May 3,1922,69y.
Clemonchia,Apr.25,1914,25y.
Elizabeth A.,Nov.14,1916,79y.
Everett L.,July 18,1970,90y.
FlorenceM.,June14,1951,72y.
George A.,Mar.12,1894,74y.
Hannah W.,Nov.8,1852,40y.
Hattie J.,June 22,1863,5y,
d/o Wm.L. & J.
James ,July 4,1818-Jan.1903,
h/o Jane M. Haskell, s/o Joseph
& Elizabeth Stone Pennell [GS].
Joseph Henry,1852-1870 [GS]
Joseph H.,Apr.21,1851,10m,
s/o James & Mary.
Katherine,Nov.10,1858-May 1944,
wid/o Charles R., d/o Timothy & Ruth
Richards Bragdon.
Nellie,Apr.3,1939,76y.
S.J.,1821-1891, w/o Wm. L.
Sarah B.,Jan.1907,
wid/o Ephraim J. [GS].
Sarah F.,June 21,1853,4y,
d/o Wm. L. & Sophia S.
Sarah,Nov.30,1862,81y,w/o Thos
Susan A.,Miss,Sept.3,1962,92y.

Susan,Sept.8,1846,2y,
  d/o James& Mary.
Thomas,Mar.2,1848,81y.
William L.,1821-1886.
Wm.L.,Mrs.,1821-July 25,1891.
PERKINS
Ellen T.,Nov.23,1844,4y,
  d/o C.A.& P.R.
PERRIN
Elinor B.,1913-XXXX [GS].
Herbert A.,Apr.29,1974,62y.
PERRY
Malphus,1855-XXXX.
Susan E.,1862-1894,w/o Malph.
PETERSON
Carl C.,1884-1885,s/o Christian.
Charles,Apr.7,1958,71y.
Chris,1873-1930 [GS].
Christian,Oct.28,1847-June 19,1908.
Marie,Dec.16,1960,85y.
PHILLIPS
Lillian M. Hasey,1892-19XX,
  w/o Willard T. [GS].
Willard True,Apr.29,1941,88y,
  h/o Lillian M.
PHINNEY
Anna Davis Mariner,
  Sept.21,1921,73y ,wid/o Edw.
Caroline McLucas,Apr.15,1863,
  35y, w/o Sargent.
Carrie M.,1969.
Edmund,Mar.1,1868,68y.
Edward B.,Oct.7,1898,70y,
  h/o Anna Davis, s/o Edmund.
Elizabeth,June 4,1870,70y,
  w/o Edmund.
George F.,1837-Apr.1911 [GS].
Harriet J.,July 27,1857,8y,
  d/o Sargent & Caroline.
Mary C.,Mar.1858,1y,
  d/o Sargent & Caroline.
Mary E. Haskell,Feb.16,1921,
  82y, w/o George F. [GS].
Mother,1811-1868 [GS].
Sargent,Dec.23,1867,45y.
PIERCE
Frances L.1828,1d,d/o D.T.& F.E.L
PIKE
Elizabeth P.,1796-1887,w/o Robert.
Nancy J.,Nov.1920.
PLAISTED
Carrie,XXXX [GS].
Eugene,Sept.27,1854,1y,
  s/o Joseph & Rosilla.
Margaret,Nov.18,1863,86y,w/o Roger.
Rosilla,1826-1894,w/o Jos.M.
Sarah,Aug.26,1787-Oct.13,18XX.

Simon,May 25,1777-Sept.25,1841,
  h/o Sarah.
PLUMMER
Charles H.,Aug.20,1830,11d,
  s/o Major & Mary.
Elizabeth W.,1922.
Elizabeth W.,Aug.24,1921,78y,
  w/o A.J.
George H.,Aug.16,1948,81y.
George W.,May 10,1833,1m,
  s/o Major & Mary.
infant,Apr.7,1898,1d.
Major,Oct.6,1836,40y,h/o Mary.
Marshall H.,Jan.20,1830,
  2y,s/o Major & Mary.
Melvel C.,Jan.14,1836,2m,
  s/o Major & Mary.
Nellie F.,1870-1927 [GS].
POTTER
Flora Martin,June 5,1859-
  June 1,1922,1st w/o GE.
George E.,M.D.,XXXX,67y.
Olive B.,Dec.4,1871,77y.
Sarah,July 17,1850,22y.
PRATT
Alice M.,Sept.28,1937,62y [GS].
Almena L.,Apr.1,1842-
  June 14,1912, d/o Cushing & E.
Annie M.,Apr.,1942,69y.
Asa W.,Sept.15,1835-Dec.29,1912,
  h/o Harriet A.,s/o Cushing & Elizabeth.
Carrie M.,1872-1942 [GS].
Cathie,Oct.27,1863,6y,
  d/o Joseph P. & Elizabeth M.
Charles W.,Dec.18,1825-Jan.2,1883.
Cushing,Apr.3,1870,76y.
Elizabeth J. Vaughn,
  Mar.20,1802-Aug.4,1881,w/o
Cushing
Elizabeth M. Cousins,Dec.17,1916,
  93y, w/o Capt. Joseph.
Frances A.,Sept.16,1830-Dec.15,1891.
Harriet A.,May 11,1923,89y,w/o Asa.
Harriet J.,Jan.11,1826-May 26,1903.
infant,Sept.3,1956,2d.
John Cushing,1874-1874 [GS].
Joseph P., Capt.,Aug. 24,1868,
  50y,h/o Elizabeth M.
Katie,Oct.27,1863,6y,
  d/o Capt. J.P.& E.M. [GS].
Lydia S. Pride,Feb.20,1829-
  Dec.10,1910,bu. Brockton,MA. [GS].
Loria E.,May 8,1915,71y,w/o Wm. H.
Mary J.,Dec.29,1871,50y.
Sarah V.,Aug.30,1875,43y,
  d/o Cushing & Elizabeth.
William H.,Apr.2,1894,78y.

PRIDE
Alice M. Holt,1875-XXXX,w/o And.M.
Andrew M.,Aug.17,1930,67y.
Ann Bennett,Mar.21,1939,87y,
  w/o Willard R.
Arthur W.,1875-1889,s/o J. & M.
Asa H.,1854,1m, s/o John & Mary.
Charles Apr. 1909.
Ethel D.,1877,1m,d/o John & M.
Frank,Apr.3,1886,74y.
Gertrude E.,1872-1877,d/o John &M.
Howard,May 4,1919,27y.
John,1864,61y, h/o Mary.
Mary Hunnewell,1815-1875.
Sabra,Sept.1,1863,33y,w/o Horace.
Scottie,XXXX,3y.
Sidney,Nov.18,1956,76y.
Willard R.,Aug.20,1938,84y.
William E.,Feb.14,1913,61y.

PROCTOR
Adeline E.,1830-Nov.1920 [GS].
Elizabeth Quimby,Mar.2,1844,
  42y,1st w/o James.
Elizabeth S. March,
  Dec.13,1860,59y,2nd w/o Jas.
Frank,Nov.1912,s/o Wm. H. [GS].
Franklin L.,July 16,1848,24y.
George,Nov.27,1916,73y,
  s/o Jas. & Eliza. Quinby Proctor.
George W.,Sept.22,1862,32y.
Harriet,Oct.13,1872,55y.
James H.,Jan.12,1832-
  Jan.23,1886.
James,Mar.8,1870,73y.
John,Nov.4,1866,63y.
John,Sept.22,1860,21y.
Lucy E. Crockett,Sept.5,1916,
  70y, w/o George .
Lydia S.,July 12,1830-
  Sept.8,1898,w/o James H.
Mary A.,Mar.3,1931,96y.
Mary E.,Feb.8,1908,76y,w/o Royal B.
Mary W. Babb,July 25,1881,76y.
Royal B.,Lt.,Apr.4,1865,28y.
Samuel A.,July 6,1855,73y.
William,Mar.28,1871,63y.

PUTNAM
Euphemia,Feb.25,1886,25y,
  d/o Robert H. & Elizabeth.

QUIMBY
(this is the spelling on
  City burial cards)
Aaron,1810-1872,h/o Esther.
Abigail March,1770-1818,
  1st w/o Moses.
Benjamin,Nov.6,1810,64y,h/o Eliz.

Benjamin,b. Somersworth, NH,
  July 13,1786-Apr.19,1854,
  68y, s/o Benj. & Anne Plummer.
Betsey Walker,1770-1849,
  2nd w/o Moses.
Cathie Ella,1876,1y,d/o Chas.& Mary.
Catherine Brown,Feb.2,1822-
  June 19,1896,w/o Isaac F.
Charles,May 18,1874,80y,
  1st w. Mary D.,
  2nd w. Joanna Libby.
Daniel T.,1822-1888.
Edwin M.,July 1,1842,4y,
  s/o Aaron & Esther.
Eliza Bailey,Oct.17,1791-
  May 5,1874, w/o Joseph Jr.
Elizabeth,,Oct.27,1821,34y,
  w/o Benjamin III.
Esther Cloudman,Apr.2,1893,
  84y,w/o Aaron.
George A.,Sept.21,1851,4y.
Hannah Nason,June 20,1820-
  Oct.1902,82y,w/o Daniel,
  d/o Solomon & Lydia Gilman.
Isaac F.,Capt.,May 26,1818-
  Apr.1898.
Joanna Libby,May 29,1874,
  71y, 2nd w/o Charles.
Joseph, Jr.,Mar.12,1791-Apr.28,1838,
  h/o Eliza.
Lucretia,Nov.20,1822,8y,
  3rd d/o Benjamin & Elizabeth.
Lydia E.,Aug.21,1851,2y, d/o
  Geo. & Roxanne Emerson,[GS]
Marshall H.,July 12,1862,27y,
  at Ship's Island.
Mary Ann,Feb.26,1831,14y,
  d/o Simeon & Mary.
Mary A.,Mar.7,1852-
  May 15,1928, d/o Dan. & Han.
Mary D.,Nov.10,1844,50y,
  1st w/o Charles [GS].
Mary,Dec.12,1822,14y,
  1st d/o Benj. & Elizabeth.
Mary W.,Nov.10,1844,50y,
  1st w/o Charles.
Moses,June 21,1759-
  Mar.20,1840,h/o 1st Abigail,
  2nd Betsey.
Moses,Aug.10,1879,74y,
  h/o Reliance Cloudman.
Orrin W.,June 14,1863,22y,
  s/o George W. & Roxanna.
Reliance Cloudman,Feb.4,1892,88y,
  w/o Moses.
Sarah,Aug.2,1850,58y,
  2nd w/o Benjamin III.

Sarah E.,July 1846,4y,d/o M. & R.
Sarah/Sally,Feb.11,1842,53y,
  w/o Simeon.
QUINBY
Azubah Partridge,1744-1829,
  w/o Joseph,
  s/o Daniel & Hannah [GS].
Eliza Ann,Mar.17,1831,1y.
Joseph,1742-1806,R.S.1775 [GS].
Sarah Frances,Apr.1831,3y [GS]
QUINN
Glenna R.,May 4,1972,38y.
RACKLIFF
Ernest B.,1862-1925.
Ida V.,Jan. 30,1865 -
  Apr.4,1891,w/o Ernest B.
Nettie B.,XXXX,96y.
RANEY
Alice J.,1864-1920,
  w/o Charles E. [GS].
Charles E.,1880-1940 [GS].
Harry S.,1891-1950 [GS].
Mildred L.,1893-1965 [GS].
William A.1882-1903 [GS].
RASMUSSEN
Carrie M.,1881-1946.
Jorgen,Apr.12,1963.
RAWDING
Clarence B.,Jr.May 10,1972,22y.
RAWDINGS
Glena G.,Feb.5,1965,62y.
Howard B.,Sept.28,1964,69y.
Howard M.,Sr.1923-1975,
  buried at sea [GS].
Victoria A.,June 30,1964,8y.
RAY
Mary M.,Jan.27,1877,42y,
  w/o F.M.,& d/o Wm. &
  Adeline Marrett [GS].
RENY
Charles Edward,June 1,1940,79y.
Harry S.,Jan.30,1950,58y.
Mildred L.,Apr.16,1965,72y.
Sarah J.,Jan.2,1921,57y,s/o C.E.
William A.June 28,1903,20y.
RICE
Daniel,Mar.9,1891,77y.
Salome H.,Nov.6,1909,72y.
Sarah P.,Oct.12,1885,88y,w/o Daniel.
RICH
Edmund H.,1829-1928.
Ellen M. Field Libby,1847-1912,
  wid/o A.M.Libby,
  w/o George W. Rich [GS].
Howard H.,Jan.19,1892,1y,s/o Edm.
Lydia F.,July 8,1873,16y,
  d/o Edmund & Tryphena.
Mary E.,Mar.2,1871,10y.
Nellie J.,May 28,1865,2m,
  d/o Edmund & Tryphena.
Tryphena T. Mitchell,
  1836-1899,w/o Edmund.
RICHARDS
Percy,1884,1m [GS].
RICHARDSON
Ellen P.,Feb.7,1838,68y,w/o John.
John,June 19,1838,70y.
Margaret C.,Aug.19,1838,45y.
Mary P.,Feb.15,1836,33y.
RICHIE
Charles S.,1823-1886.
Hattie May,XXXX,9y.
RICKER
Alice M.,1863-1866,
  d/o Joseph P. & Mary.
Annie L. Morris,1874-1938,
  w/o Arthur.
Arthur W.,1861-1940 [GS].
George C.,June 16,1926,75y,
  s/o J. & M.
Henrietta F. Sands,1854-19XX,
  w/o Geo. C. [GS].
Joseph P.,June 28,1910,85y
Lucy H. Penniman,Sept.1976,
  77y,w/o Arthur.
Mary E. Goold,Jan.25,1911,
  83y,wid/o Joseph P. [GS].
RIDEOUT
Benjamin A.,June 20,1900,54y.
Emma W.,Feb.8,1918,24y, d/o
  Benj.& Emma Merrill Rideout.
RIGGS
Albert B.,Mar.17,1869,5y,
  s/o Augustus & Martha.
Augustus W.,Oct.15,1922,88y.
Eveline Pike,Nov.14,1851,48y,
  1st w/o George.
George Francis,Oct.4,1844,18y.
George,May 22,1872,72y.
Grace,Nov.15,1894,76y,
  2nd w/o George.
Martha J. Merserve,
  Apr.17,1914,72y,w/o Augustus.
Will E.,Feb.8,1888,32y.
RILEY
Charle H.,M.D.,Nov.27,1868,34y
  adopted s/o N.R. & E.B.Martin.
Rena May,Dec.18,1882,1y,
  d/o C.E. & S.A.
ROBERTS
Abba Webb,Feb.7,1834,19y,
  w/o Capt. Joseph [GS].
Adelaide,Apr.11,1848,15y,
  d/o Benjamin & Mary.

Amelia H. Grover,Aug.18,1899,
  68y,2nd w/o Joshua D. Roberts.
Anna Blanche Swett,Feb.14,1880-
  Oct.15,1945,w/o Perley C. [GS].
Arthur W.,May 4,1857,15y,
  s/o Benjamin & Mary.
Arthur Wellington,Sept.14,1839,1y.
Benjamin,Aug.17,1857,89y,
  h/o Rebecca Dyer.
Benjamin, Jr.,Nov.1,1855,
  57y,h/o Mary.
Betsy Hatch,Dec.7,1816,39y,
  1st w/o William.
Charles,Mar.18,1896,92y.
David W.,May 11,1943,9y.
Dorcus Johnson,Dec.6,1864,
  84y,2nd w/o William.
Eddie,Dec.3,1858,5y,
  s/o Charles & Eleanor.
Eleanor J. Cheney,June 21,1896,
  86y,w/o Charles.
Ellen Babb,1818-1870,
  1st w/o Joshua D.
Emilia H.,1831-1899,
  2nd w/o Joshua D. [GS].
Eva M.,Apr.28,1959,88y.
Evelyn,Mar.9,1992,88y.
Florence E. Dec.21,1860 -
  May 31,1943,d/o John & M.E.
John,1837-June 22,1917.
Joshua D.,Mar.16,1904,89y,
  h/o Ellen Babb & Emilia H.
Marietta B.,1872-1941.
Marietta,May 17,1871,36y,
  d/o Eleanor J.
Martha E.,Aug.14,1897,54y,
  w/o John.
Martha,Feb.7,1837,37y,
  d/o Benj. & Rebecca.
Mary Kollack June 23, 1873,
  69y,w/o Benjamin.
Perley C. May 19,1978,72y.
Perley Cheney,Nov.1,1878 -
  Jan.22,1906,h/o Anna Blanche.
RebeccaDyer,Jan.25,1837,
  62y,w/o Benjamin.
William,Nov.17,1867,93y.
ROBERTSON
Margaret,Mar.15,1886,66y,
  w/o John [GS].
ROBINSON
John J.,1886.
Lemuel,1881.
Marcia A. Mitsmenn,Oct.21,1891,
  32y,w/o R.S.
ROUNDS
Annie L.,May 17,1925,65y.

Elizabeth Babb,Oct.16,1873,47y,
  w/o David.
George B.,1882-1891 [GS].
Henry E.,Oct.31,1850,7m,
  s/o Daniel & Elizabeth.
Sarah J.,July 6,1849,
  inf. d/o Daniel & Elizabeth.
RUSHA
E. Mary,June 20,1917,42y.
RUSSELL
Martha A.,June 6,1847,17y,
  d/o John S. & Martha.
Martha ,Aug.1,1833,40y,w/o John S.
Mary,May 1924,73y.
Mary Ann,Aug.18,1842,20y,
  d/o John S. & Martha.
SANDS
Henry F.,Jan.27,1902,83y.
Jane L.,Nov.10,1839,
  d/o James & Nancy A. Sands.
Mabel,May 10,1830,12y,
  d/o Isaac & Nancy [GS].
Maria W. Babb Aug.29,1896,
  80y,w/o Henry F.
SAWYER
Abigail M. Huston,1902,86y,
  w/o Nelson.
Betsey,June 25,1861,80y,w/o Robert.
Carroll N.,May 4,1941,20y,s/o Ella M.
Ella Mayberry,Feb.15,1939,48y.
Hannah L.,Jan.5,1893,86y.
Lettice P.,1825-1885,w/o Jos.
Martin LaForest,Aug.30,1885,
  3w, d/o Joseph & Lettice.
Nelson,1813-1864.
Robert,Dec.29,1831,50y.
SCOTT
Charity,1832-1877,
  w/o John W. [GS].
Elleura M.,Aug.25,1915,78y.
Flora B.,1859-1863.
John G.,Oct.16,1897,74y,h/o Elleura.
John W.,1829-1894 [GS].
Meldon M.,1857-Dec.20,1919.
SENATE
Joseph,Aug.13,1938,74y
Lily May Bachelder,1919,w/o Jos.
SHACKFORD
Marietta R.,Jan.3,1847,8y,
  d/o Daniel & Joanna.
SHACKLEY
Caroline P.,May 22,1817-Oct.11,1867.
SHAW
Mary M.,Dec.26,1967,83y.
S. Abba,Feb.12,1861,3y,
  d/o Sam & Sarah.

Sarah R.,May 21,1863,28y,w/o Sam'l.
Whitefield E.,Feb.6,1889-
June 10,1972,83y.
SHORT
Edward Augustine,May 18,1852-
Sept.1,1878,s/o J.S. & S.C. [GS].
Sophronia C. Hezelton,
Oct.18,1863,32y,w/o Jos.S.
SIMONTON
Andrew,1805-1873,h/o Dolly.
Dolly Stinson,1884,79y.
SKILLINGS
Elizabeth Boyd,1890,66y.
Ellenor B.,Oct.15,1860,69y,w/o John.
Ellen J.,1821-1836.
James W.,July 25,1851,20y,
killed by lightening.
John B.,July 14,1861,72y.
Mary,1819-1871,d/o J.B. & E.B.
SLOAN
William W.,Apr.22,1945,s/o Zachariah
& Augusta Walton Small.
SMALL
Abbie M. Copps,Mar.1909,77y,
w/o John W. [GS].
Albion W.,1836-1915.
Alphonso,Oct.6,1849,2w.
Benjamin W.,Nov.2,1841,5m.
Caroline W.,July 3,1848,16y,
d/o Wm. & Harriet.
Charles,Mar.7,1880,70y.
Clara,Sept.23,1859,3m.
Daniel,1888-1901 [GS].
Daniel,Capt.,Dec.28,1813,48y.
Daniel W.,1807-1881.
Eddie,Apr.14,1880,4y,s/o W.& M.
Edward W.,Jan.14,1913,63y.
Edwin,Sept.23,1921,75y.
Elmer F.,Sept.4,1873-July 1949,
h/o Lillian M. & s/o Zachariah &
Augusta Walton Small.
Georgie W.,Sept.27,1885,9m,
s/o J.R. & Mary Smith.
Harriet N.,1826-1904.
Herbert A.,Sept.10,1943,65y.
J.Hacker,May 17,1904,54y.
Jennie M.,Apr.30,1924,72y.
Joseph L.,Feb.28,1873,54y.
Joseph N.,Feb.4,1919,72y.
Joseph,Nov.10,1859,82y.
Lillian,Mar.22,1861,6y,
d/o J.W. & M.A.
Lillian M.,May 16,1924,51y,
w/o Elmer F.
Lois,Dec.27,1906,90y,w/o Chas.
Lucy C.,Aug.4,1857,87y,
w/o Capt.Daniel.

Lucy E.,Apr.12,1857,23y.
Lydia A.,Aug.9,1916,83y,w/o Zachar.
Marion Lois,Oct.1907,6w,d/o Ralph B.
& Myra Pride Small [GS].
Martha A.,Jan.24,1937,83y.
Martha V.,XXXX,1d,d/o H.& R.
Mary A.,Aug.30,1847,32y,
1st w/o Samuel.
Mary,Dec.31,1918,69y.
Mary M.,1840-1904,w/o Albion.
Mary,Mar.11,1843,58y,w/o Jos.
Mattie,Oct.22,1872,22y.
Nellie W.,Oct.10,1879,21y,
d/o Joseph & Diantha.
Richard C.,Apr.12,1928,3y,
s/o J.W. & H.L.
Samuel,June 21,1866,55y,
Sarah G.,May 22,1895,74y,
2nd w/o Samuel
Sarah J.,Nov.8,1853,22y.
Sarah Webb,Feb.27,1893,86y,
w/o Daniel W.
Sylvia,May 19,1923,w/o J.R.
William,Dec.19,1847,48y.
Zachariah,Mar.23,1899,74y.
SMITH
Arixine Southgate,Dec.6,1820,
27y,1st w/o Henry.
Arthur L.,Feb.6,1929,38y.
Edith L.,Aug.26,1895,28y.
Elizabeth McNair,Oct.25,1917,78y.
Ella,Feb.27,1933,73y.
Etril G.,1815-1882,47y.
Frederick Southgate,Feb.11,1811,
2m, s/o Henry & Arixine.
Henry,July 20,1853,70y,
1st w Arixine,2nd w Sally N.
infant,July 21,1924, s.b.,
ch/o George & Mary
John Coit,Feb.1,1820,17m,
s/o Henry & Arixine.
Jonathan,1826-1885.
Lovina,1892,69y.
M.Evelyn,Sept.1950,48y,
d/o Walter & Marguerite.
Marguerite E. Griffiths,
Apr.30,1927,47y,w/o Walter.
Merrill W.,Oct.7,1920,64y.
Minnie A.,Apr.16,1947,56y.
Sally M.,Mar.6,1887,92y,
2nd w/o Henry.
Susan M.,Feb.1906,wid/o John.
Walter W.,Nov.21,1959,87y.
SNOW
Daniel W.,Nov.14,1904,69y.
Edward Harmon,July 2,1894-
Sept.12,1901,s/o T.H. & E.A.

Ellen A. Mariner,June 11,1901,
67y,w/o Temple.
Temple H.Nov.29,1915,81y.
SNOWDEAL
Nettie B.,1871-1967 [GS].
SPEAR
Connie M.,Feb.6,1864,23y,
w/o Rev. D.D.
SPEARS
Fred B.,May 4,1942,72y.
Mary F. Barbour,Sept.19,1939,
w/o Fred B.
SPILLER
Alice M. Batchelder,Aug.11,1870-
Sept.24,1911,w/o William B.
William B.,Sept.8,1867-
Oct.27,1946.
SPINETTA
Evelyn M.,Apr.1902 [GS].
SPROUL
Arthur H.,May 24,1937,55y.
Hattie M.,Mar.31,1947,84y.
Helen M.Blatchford,Apr.18,1904,
57y,w/o Hiram [GS].
Hiram B.,July 15,1839-Oct.29,1892.
James,by 1920.
Sophie Baker,Mar.2,1920,
85y,wid/o James.
STACKPOLE
Abbie E.B.,June 5,1926,81y,
Abbie Lindette,Oct.1,1952,79y,
d/o Abbie B.
Alice D.,Feb.23,1954,82y,
d/o Abbie B.
STAPLES
Frances B.,Apr.25,1936 [GS].
George W.,1829-1830.
Harriet E.,1822-1854.
John M.,1836-1868.
Lydia J.,1825-1878.
Father,1789-1842.
Mother,1795-1875
and their 5 children.
Statira C.,1831-1832.
STARBIRD
Sumner F.,Aug.27,1858-
May 3,1927 [GS].
STERNS
Albert J.,Feb.6,1920,55y.
Cora M.,June 17,1943,77y,
w/o Albert J.
Elva O.,July 28,1894-May 10,1897,
d/o A.J. & C.M.
Joseph E.,May 23,1885,43y.
STEVENS
Mary,June 24,1918.

William Boutell,Oct.3,1835,
s/o Wm. & Mersylvia.
William H.H.,Apr.26,1841,
10m,s/o Wm. & Mersylvia.
STILES
Albion P.,1824-Oct.1903,
1st w. Ellen Brackett,
2nd w. Emma Ward.
Almira Starbird,Apr.6,1826,
29y,1st w/o Moses.
Annie M. Quincy,Mar.1922,
80y ,wid/o Wm. Merritt Stiles.
Eliza A.,1827-1911,w/o M.C.
Elmer E.,1866-1867.
Hannah Freeman,1809-1864,
w/o John.
John,1798-1866 [GS].
Moses C.,1827-1895,
s/o Moses & Sarah.
Moses,Nov.14,1861,65y,h/o Almira.
Sarah S. Cloudman,Mar.10,1859,
56y,2nd w/o Moses.
Sarah Frances,Apr.6,1834,3y,
d/o Moses & Sarah.
William Merritt,Jan.28,1912,79y,
h/o Annie M.
STROUT
Charles H.,June 1908,61y,
s/o Albert & Fannie [GS].
STURGIS
Lottie May,1870-1872,
d/o Melville & Sarah J.
Melville C.,Aug.6,1893,58y.
Sarah J. Cannell,Jan.30,1905,68y,
w/o Melville C.
SULLIVAN
Raymond F.,Sept.1938,31y [GS].
SWEET
Ellen Frances Knight,June 17,1849-
Apr.1911,w/o Alphinso M. [GS].
SWEETSER
Alfred S.,Nov. 6,1844-Aug. 20,1931,
h/o Donzetta.
Donzetta A. Woodbury,
Aug.12,1847-Nov.18,1910.
SWETT
A.D.,July 24,1904,70y.
Abbie L.,Mar.26,1912,73y.
Alfred W.,Apr.30,1955,85y.
Alphonso M.,Mar.18,1924,76y.
Augustus B.,1890-1918.
Catherine B.,Oct.3,1874 -
Oct.15,1947,w/o Alfred.
Charles,1864.
Charles S.,Mar.10,1934,64y,
h/o Ruth M.
Ellen F.,Feb.27,1897,2y,d/o Alfred W.

Ellen F. Knight,Aug.17,1849-
Apr.1911,w/o Alphonso.
Everett Bertram,Aug.13,1917,
s/o Augustus.
Fred Merrett,1867-1868,
s/o Alphonso & Ellen.
George H.,July 10,1874,32y,
s/o Samuel & Hannah.
Hannah B.,June 15,1865,63y.
Helen L.,1835-Dec.1910,
d/o Samuel & Hannah.
Kate Louise,Sept.12,1871,5m,
d/o Nathaniel & Abbey.
Katherine M.,Jan.13,1958,91y,
sis/o Charles M.
Leona R.,June 9,1979,76y.
Lydia,1859.
Margaret Cloudman,1838-
Sept.1905,w/o Wm. H. [GS].
Olive M.,1897-1973,w/o Augustus [GS]
Robert A.,June 1,1889-May 5,1968.
Ruth M.,Nov.3,1933,60y.
Samuel W.,June 12,1866,57y,
h/o Hannah.
William Henry,1831-1900 [GS].
TEFFT
Hannah C.,Feb.2,1921,74y.
TEWKSBURY
Sophia L.,Jan.29,1930,96y.
THOMPSON
Alice E.,Apr.16,1949,68y.
Elinor I.,1852-1925 [GS].
Elizabeth A.,Nov.19,1939,85y.
Elizabeth Boyd Skillings,1824-
1890, w/o James B. [GS].
Elizabeth J.,Jan.7,1837,15m,
d/o Robert & Esabella.
Frank Skillings,1898,34y.
Frederick Arthur,July 6,1882-
Oct.17,1960.
George B.,Aug.25,1908,40y.
James B.,1822-1904.
TOLE
J.W.,XXXX.
Mary Quimby,June 15,1842,
w/o Levi.
TOTMAN
Capt. W.H.,Feb.5,1874,41y,
h/o Annie Kimball.
Willie Kimball,XXXX,2y,
s/o Capt. W.H. & Annie K.
TOWER
Joseph,Apr.15,1822,43y.
Margaret,Mar.23,1833,49y,
w/o Joseph.

TOWLE
Charles H.,Apr.15,1906,71y,
h/o Harriet N.
Clara F.,1839,1y,
d/o Lorenzo & Harriet.
Clarence,1877,11y.
Ellen C.,1833-1844,
d/o Lorenzo & Harriet
Gardner M.,1837-1838,
s/o Lorenzo & Harriet.
Harriet M.,Jan.17,1918,78y,
d/o Lorenzo & Harriet.
Harriet Merrill,1876,71y,
w/o Lorenzo.
Harriet N. Libby,Apr.20,1897,59y,
w/o Charles.
Levi,Sept.7,1840,58y,
h/o Mary Quimby.
Lorenzo,1881,73y.
Martha M.,1835-1910,
d/o Lorenzo & Harriet [GS].
TRICKEY
Daniel,Apr.26,1863,92y.
Eleanor Johnson,1815-1854,
1st w/o John.
Jane Johnson,1817-1902,
2nd w/o John.
John,Jan.24,1892,84y.
Sarah Johnson Nov.8,1857,82y,
w/o Daniel.
TUFTS
Frances Esther,May 1910,62y,
1st w/o S. F.
Harlan,1884,5y,s/o S.F. & F.E.
Samuel F.,1864 -1912 [GS].
Samuel F.,July 1927,77y,
h/o Frances E. & h/o Susan H.
Susan H. Smith Cutter,
Mar.1912,48y,2nd w/o S.F.
Walter E.,June 18,1928,50y.
TYLER
Abram,1840-1921 [GS].
Charles L.,June 29,1944,68y.
Charlie,Aug.27,1875,
d/o Freida Hanson Tyler [GS].
Fred,July 28,1945,74y.
Freda H.,Jan.13,1950,76y.
Lizzie S.1840-1882,1st w/o Abram.
Sue H. Barbour,June 3,1908,
64y,2nd w/o Abram.
VALENTINE
Alice M.Aug.27,1945,74y.
Caroline,May 7,1888,72y.
Foster,185X-1935 [GS].
Grover C.,Oct.30,1883-
Dec.3,1884, s/o L. & L.J.

Hazel M.,June 18,1890-July 1,1963,
  d/o Leonard & Laura .
Laura J. Paine,Sept.24,1935,83y,
  w/o Leonard, d/o C.& J. Paine.
Leonard,Apr.5,1919,79y.
VANNER
Nellie Phinney,Sept.2,1941,85y.
William C.,Jan.16,1935,70y.
VARNEY
Alice M.,June 8,1941,79y [GS].
Frank J.,Mar.7,1950,66y.
Gertrude B.,Sept.6,1948,71y.
VARNUM
Alice Scott,1861-June 8,1941.
Inez French,June 13,1918,25y.
VERRILL
Daniel L.,1830-1897.
Elizabeth,1802-1885 [GS].
Lewis,1805-1870.
WAKEFIELD
Gibson,June 12,1851,90y [GS].
Nancy,Jan.12,1854,90y,
  w/o Gibson.
Nathaniel,Nov.7,1833,30y.
Stephen,Oct.4,1880,76y.
WALKER
Albion,Mar.25,1825,2m,
  s/o Capt. Isaac & C.H.
Albion,Sept.5,1821,15m,
  s/o Isaac & C.H.
Isaac,Capt.,Dec.26,1833,35y.
Caroline Haskell,Apr.5,1836,
  39y,w/o Isaac.
Caroline Valentine,Aug.3,1816-
  May 7,1888,w/o Moses B. [GS]
Elizabeth,Apr.13,1832,10y,
  s/o Isaac & C.H.
Eunice G.,couldn't read [GS].
Hannah Webb,Feb.28,1878,88y,
  w/o Isaac G.
Harold R.,Apr.8,1980,77y.
Isaac Gibbs,Sept.6,1863,77y.
James,Mar.20,1846,6y,
  s/o Wm. & Ann [GS].
James B.,Deacon,Jan.2,1848,45y,
  h/o Laurinda.
Laurinda,Aug.30,1881,76y.
Lowell V.,Jan.6,1818-Aug.22,1882.
Mahlon L.,Apr.3,1853,4y.
Marion L., couldn't read [GS].
Mary Haskell,Oct.24,1828,
  9m,d/o Wm & Ann [GS].
Moses Bryson,June 30,1902,
  h/o Caroline Valentine,
  s/o Isaac & Hannah.
Ornville Stone,July 31,1843,3m.

Ornville Stone,May 19,1846,2y.
Robert E.,Mar.12,1948.
Sarah Elizabeth,Jan.20,1842,1d.
Sarah,Jan.12,1821,20d,
  d/o Isaac & Caroline.
WALLACE
Dolly Hamblen,1782-1840,w/o John.
Elizabeth Collins,1809-1868,
  w/o George W.
George H.,1845-1847,
  s/o George & Elizabeth.
George,July 20,1923,76y.
George W.,1812-1883.
Henry,1842-1847,
  s/o George & Elizabeth.
James A.,July 3,1857,24y.
John,1780-1859.
Lewis P.,1814-1890 [GS].
Lewis P.,1843-1844,
  s/o George & Elizabeth.
Mary E.,1840-1847,
  d/o George & Elizabeth.
Sarah B. Robinson,
  Nov.13,1910,82y,w/o Wm.
William,Dec.11,1873, 53y.
WALTON
Farwell,Nov.1,1846,44y.
Jane H.,Mar.18,1910,79y,w/o Jerem.
Jeremiah H.,Jan.9,1897,69y,
  s/o Farwell & Mary.
Mary Hall,Apr.30,1896,89y,
  w/o Farwell.
WARD
Eunice Libby,Nov.5,1899,43y,
  w/o Valette D.
Valette D.,Feb.1920,63y.
WARREN
Caroline A.,Apr.3,1806,
  Watertown, MA.-Dec.20,1869.
Daniel S.,July 1,1837,17y,
  s/o Nathaniel & Ann.
Eleanor Lamb,Jan.13,1835,
  50y,w/o Capt. John.
Ellen L.,Dec.27,1927,82y [GS].
George,July 29,1876,65y.
George,Sept.16,1856,11d,
  s/o George & Catherine.
Jane Johnson,June 15,1740-
  Nov.25,1809,69y, w/o John.
John,Mar.5,1731-Jan.30,1807.
John, Capt.,Sept.10,1845,69y,
  h/o Eleanor Lamb Warren.
Kittie W.,1871-1872 [GS].
Lillian L.,1867-1888 [GS].
Robert,Apr.19,1835,58y,
  s/o John & Jane.

Rufus King,May 31,1858,3y,
s/o George & Catherine.
William L.,Apr.11,1855,20y,
s/o Capt. John & Eleanor.
WATERHOUSE
Eliza B.,June 6,1888,75y.
WATERMAN
Martha,Oct.18,1846,23y,w/o Moses.
WATSON
Benjamin L.,May 11,1876,44y.
Bethia,Nov.26,1859,66y,
w/o Nathaniel.
Nathaniel,Mar.7,1857,80y.
Sarah W.,Apr.28,1842,4y,
d/o Joseph H. & Maria H.
Sophronia,Mar.26,1846,4y,
d/o Joseph H. & Maria H.
WAY
John N.,XXXX,s/o O.R.D.Way [GS].
O.A.,Aug.4,1851,5y [GS].
WEBB
Alice,1894,[GS].
Cathie Ella,1875-1876 [GS].
Cathy May,1884 [GS].
Charles H.,Oct.26,1859,15y,
s/o Charles & Lucretia.
James M.,Jan.24,1892, 56y.
Jane Bailey,1784-1848, w/o Dan.
William W.,Feb.22,1926,58y,
Spanish American War.
WEBBER
Evelyn R.,1856-1928 [GS].
WELCH
Alvin F.,June 5,1838-Mar.23,1894,
Pvt.,Civil War,h/o Mary Bailey.
WESCOTT
Elizabeth W. Babb,1822-1894,
w/o Levi,
Enoch,Aug.12,1861,22y,
s/o John & Charity.
John Jr.,July 16,1847,46y.
John Lendell,Aug.7,1872,20y,
s/o Eliot & Huldah.
John W.,July 11,1817,10y [GS].
Levi,1821-1894.
WEYMOUTH
Alice M.,Jan.31,1958.
Fred W.,1863-1888.
Mabel Babb,Feb.6,1944,84y,
w/o Fred.
WHEELER
Abbie M.,1852-1929,w/o Henry.
Emma Estella Kent,1867-1955.
Freddie H.,1870-1876.
Gilman Grover,1873-1943.
Henry M.,1842-1904.

WHITNEY
Aaron,Feb.15,1847,74y.
Ann,May 9,1799-Feb.26,1881.
Cynthia Smith,Dec.17,1833,27y,
w/o Luke.
Olive S.,Dec.10,1844,75y,w/o Aaron.
Zilpha A.,May 2,1908,89y.
WHITTEN
Joseph,June 5,1873,61y.
WIGGINS
Isaac,Feb.26,1915,69y,h/o Mary
Mary F.,June 18,1929,89y.
WILBUR
Orin,Mar.20,1821-Apr.3,1880.
Rebecca K.,May 10,1818-
Apr.10,1876,w/o Orin.
WILLIAMS
Sarah,June 26,1841,41y,
d/o Isaac & Caroline Walker.
WILLIAMSON
Olive L.,June 6,1973,76y,
WILLIS
Adelia M.,1855-1929,w/o C.E. [GS].
C.E.,1839-1920 [GS].
WILSON
Betsey C.,Mar.13,1890, 83y.
Francis,Nov.27,1855,57y,
h/o Betsey C.
Joseph H.,Nov.23,1894, 62y,
s/o F. & B.C.
WINSLOW
Alfred B.,1858-1933 [GS].
Amasa,1806-1885.
Caroline Gower,1814-1861.
David,Dec.12,1830,58y.
Emma,1884,76y.
Everett O.,Aug. 22,1979 58y.
George,May 20,1832,19y,
s/o David & Olive.
Hattie M.,1860-1922,w/o Alfred B.[GS]
Hilda G.,Apr.23,1993,75y.
Jane,Apr.1832,8y,d/o D. & Olive.
Louisa Foster,Feb.1,1847,31y,
w/o Capt. Peter G.
Olive W.,May 20,1832,19y,
w/o David [GS].
Sarah D.,Sept.30,1872,19y,
d/o W.S. & M.A.
WINTERS
Rebecca M. Wallace,
1838-1867,w/o Richard,
d/o George & Elizabeth Wallace.
WOOD
Mary E.,Aug.27,1925,88y,
wid/o Philander.
2 children of Philander & Mary.

WOODBURY
Betsey,Mar.9,1847,26y,
w/o Hugh [GS].
Betsey Atkinson,Mar.9,1863,92y,
w/o Hugh.
E.M.,1806-1886,80y.
George A.,1845-1890.
Helen I.,Sept.21,1857,24y,
d/o E.M. & J.W.
Hugh,Dec.23,1816,50y.
Jane W. Murch,Jan.18,1896,86y,
w/o E.M.
John R.,Sept.15,1843,11m,
s/o Hugh & Betsey.
Nancy,Apr.12,1837,40y,
d/o Hugh & Elizabeth.
Rhomena F.,Nov.20,1931,78y.
William,June 7,1825,33y.
William M.,Apr.4,1841,9m,
s/o Hugh & Betsey.
WOODMAN
Charlotte,Aug.8,1863 [GS].
Mary,Aug.8,1863,1d,
d/o B.J. & Charlotte.
WOODSOME
Lois C.,Mar.24,1897,45y.
WOODSUM
Freitty,Mar.23,1921.
WORMWOOD
Abbie D.,1881-1922,w/o George.
Edwin F.,Aug.26,1968,61y,
s/o George & Abbie.

✦ **ST.HYACINTH CEMETERY** ✦
300 Stroudwater Street.
At least 25% of the burials were
not recorded by the Church. Many
burials were obtained from
obituaries,marked {O}. I also went
stone by stone to find the missing
burials, but there were so many
missing that I did about 75% before
winter set in.

ABBIOG
Patricia,May 1958,(III-L-12).
ABBOTT
Doris,1898-1971,(II*).
ACKER
William,June 1992,(III-Q-237).
ADAMS
Charles A.,Dec.1954,(III-G-15).
AFTHIM
Gloria,Aug.1989,54y,(III-N-103).
Margaret,July 1980,(III-N-103).
William,June 1980,(III-N-103).

AKERLY
Claudia,Mar.1957,(III-N-2).
ALBERT
August,Nov.1982,(III-L-68).
Ferdinand,1864-1929,(II-82).
Georgienne H.,1863-1911,
w/o Ferdinand,(II-82).
J.Wilfrid,Rev.,1903-1972,(II*).
Yvonne,1896-1926,(II-82).
ALLARD
Frances,Feb.1968,(III-N-114).
Peter,Feb.1968,(III-N-114).
Roger,Feb.1968,(III-N-114).
Susan,Feb.1968,(III-N-114).
XX, 1969,(III-N-114).
ALLEN
Agnes J.,Apr.1944,73y,
(III-H-22).
ANDERSON
Joseph,1891-1962,(III-G-16).
Laura E.,1894-1985,(II*).
Lydia L.,1892-1985,w/o Joseph.
Rudolph J.,Jr.,1913-1993,
h/o Ruth Jordan,(III-G-15).
Ruth,1918- 1993,(III-G-16).
Walter R.,1895-1961,(II*).
Walter,1941-1961,(II-189).
ANNIS
Harlie,Mar.1977,(III-Q-146).
ARCHAMBAULT
Alphonse,1850-1911 (II*).
Anglique Pinaux,1887,83y,
w/o Joseph,(II*).
Arthur,1947,(I-E-16E).
Cleophas,May 1888,(II-5).
Eva,1891-1967,(I-E-16E).
infant,Apr.1959,inf/o Philippe,
(I-E-16E).
Joseph,1873,70y.
Selanire,1847-1930,w/o Alph.
(I-E-16E).
Thomas,1947,(I-E-16E).
XX,1887,w/o Cleophas,(II-5).
ARMENTINO
Marie,1900-1918,w/o Ralph.
Ralph,1893-XXXX.
ARNOLD
Saundra Ann,1964,(III-L-62).
ARSENAULT
Adolphe,1861-1928,(I-C-11E).
Aime,Mar.1958,(III-H-1).
Albert A.,1916-1989,(I-F-3A).
Albert,1943,(III-H-1).
Andre,1893-XXXX,(II*).
Andrew,1859-1933,(II-B).
Andrew,1893-1972,(II*).

Arthur,1937,(III-B-6).
Arthur,1965,(III-N-97).
Bessie,1983,(II-209).
Bridget McRoy,1849-1926,
  w/o Andrew,(II-B).
Callixte,1916,(II-157).
child/o Roland,1961,(I-A-3E).
Clovis,Nov.1969,(III-H-1).
Elizabeth,1903-1983,(II*).
Elzeline M.,1897-1928,w/o A.J.,(I*).
Emile,Dec.1957,(III-N-46).
Evangeline,1924-1932,(III*).
Exeline Gallant,1948,(III-G-11).
Francois,1869-1950,
  h/o Mary Jane,(III-H-1).
Ida M.,1902-1968,(II*).
Jeannette,1990,(III-N-137).
Joseph O.,1891-1937,(III-A-8).
Joseph,1885-1950,(II*).
Joseph,1940,(I-E-11W).
Joseph,Jan.1989,(III-H-1).
Joseph,July 1960,(III-N-62).
Josephine,1976,(I-D-9W).
Leo,1910-1988,(II*).
Leona Theriault,1897-1918,
  w/o Andre,(II-209).
Louise,Mar.1984,(III-B-6).
Martin,Aug.1956,(III-L-25).
Mary,1866-1941,(II*).
Mary,1969,w/o Jos.,(III-N-62).
Octave,Mar.1960,(III-N-63).
Patrick,1884-1938,(II*).
Raymond,Dec.1991,(III-N-63).
Rita,Jan.1966,(III-N-111).
Robert P.,1925-1944,(III-A-8).
Sara,1930,(II-147).
Thomas L.,1882-1946,(II*).
Thomas J.,1912-1968,(II*).
XX, 1937,w/o Adolphe,(I-C-11E).
XX,1956,w/o Jos.,(I-E-11W).
XX,1941,w/o John,(II-215).
AUBE
Alice,1899-1980,(II-162A).
Aurele,1918,(I-D-13W).
Barbara,Oct.1973,(III-G-21A).
Bernadette Giordis,1887-1922,
  w/o Wm.,(II-162).
Cleophas,1871-1932,(II-13).
Delvina D.,1879-1918,
  w/o Aurele,(I*).
Eugene,1901-1969,(III-G-49).
Eva M.,1904-1985,(*)
Eva,1881-1929,w/o Ernest,
  (I-C-7E).
George J.,1885-1926,(I-D-8W).
George W.,1922,(II-13).
Gloria,May 1981,(III-G-21A).

Hermine Caron,1880-1969,
  w/o George J.,(I-D-8W).
Irene Provost,1903-1993,
  w/o Philip,d.1991,(III-L-84S).
Janita,1937,(I-C-7E).
Joseph,May 1902,65y.
Josephine,1880,(II*).
Josephine,1965,(III-N-85).
Lena,May 1982,(III-Q-175).
Malvina Pomerleau,1864-1917,
  w/o Pierre Anselme,(II-162).
Marie Leclair,1962,(II-13).
Ovide,1989,(III-H-24A)
Philip,1991,(III-L-84S)
Pierre Anselme,1856-1909,(II-162).
Rene,1931,(I-C-7E).
Rosida,1901-1978,(I*).
Simone,1918,(II-162).
Victor,1927,(II-13).
William,1881-1960,(II-162).
AUBIN
Rose,Nov.1964,(III-M-15).
William,1964,(III-M-15).
AUCLAIR
Achille,1882-1952,(II-218).
Joseph Paul,1979,(III-M-23).
Marie Anne Lebel,1887-1960,
  w/o Achille,(II-218).
AUCOIN
Delphine,Oct.1956,(III-L-32).
George, Oct.1957,(III-L-32).
Georges,Nov.1968,(III-L-32).
AUDET
AgnesMar.1965,(III-Q-11).
Bella,July 15,1987,(III-Q-70).
Joseph,1951,(II-64).
Joseph,Apr.1991,(III-Q-11).
Marcel,June 1970,(III-Q-70).
Marie Gravel,J1947,(II-64).
BABB
Hattie,1880-1891,(II*).
BABINEAU
Alice,1918-1988,(III-G-34).
Eugenie,1895-1987,(III-G-34).
BACHOFEN
Ernest,1894-1959,(II-153).
Rose,1900-1988,(II*).
BAILLARGEON
Adelard,June 1958,(II-178).
Anna,Aug.1969,(I-B-6E).
Anysie,1893-,1919,
  w/o Edouard,(II-236).
Benjamin,1969,(I-B-6E).
Edouard,1858-1916,(II-178).
Edouard,1896-Mar.1963,(II-236).
Irene,1923-Jan.1925,(II-236).
Melande,May 1963,(I-B-6E).

Oscar,Jan.27,1987,(I-B-6E).
Rose,1903-Dec.1964,w/o Edw.,
(II-236).
BAIN
Percilla M.,1965,(III-N-40).
BAKER
Robert,1976,(III-N-156).
BALCOURT
Hermaine B.,Apr.24,1882,(II*).
BARD
Antonio,1991,(III-M-33N).
Roger A.,1950-1994,
h/o Priscilla LeBlanc,(III-M-33N).
Ronald,1918-1987,(II*).
BARIL
Emile,1883-1934,(II*).
inf/o H.,June 1937,(II-3).
Lucien,Jan.1974,(III-J-13).
BARR/E
Aime A.,1910-1993,
h/o Rosalie Boivin, (III-N-186).
Andrew,1986,(III-D-6).
Bertha,1981-1985,w/o D.L.(III*).
Charles,Mar.1945,(III-H-11).
Emilia Thibault,1949,(III-H-11).
Emily Irish,1914-1994,w/o Rene,(III*).
Joseph,1881-1940,(II-158).
Josephine,1886-1975,w/o Joseph,
(II-158*).
Lucien,Dec.1917,(II-158).
Paul G.,May.1931,(II-158).
Ruth,1984,(III-D-6).
BARROWS
Katherine,1922-1990,
w/o Leslie,d.1983,(III-Q-172).
BEATTY
Minnie F.,1877-1926,w/o Thos,(II-96).
Raymond W.,Sept.1975,(III-K-4).
Irene J.,1908-July 1957,
w/o Raymond,(III-K-4).
BEAUCHAMP
Alfred,1900-1949,(III-G-20).
Joseph R.,1864-1940,(III*).
Regis,June 1940,(III-G-20).
BEAUDETTE
Armand T.,1987,(III-M-15).
BEAUDOIN
Albert,Aug.1924,(II-178).
Alice,Apr.1981,(III-N-195).
Benjamin Hebert,1869-1917,(III*)
Eleus--,1977,(III-N-91).
Ernest C.,1987,(III-N-194).
Felanise,1857-1921,w/o Gracia.
Gracia,XXXX,(III*).
Joseph C.,1963,(III-N-91).
Phelanise,1952,(III-C-1W).
Rose,July 1980,(III-N-91).

Theresa B.,1903-1985,(II*).
Treffle Noel,1926,(III-C-1W).
XX,1921,w/o Treffle,(III-C-1W).
BEAUMIER
Adrien,Jan.1958,(III-H-44).
Albertine,Aug.1988,(III-H-51).
Amelia,1886-1912,ch/o F.& C.
Celina,1853-1926,w/o Francois,
(I-D-3W).
Emile,1890-1912, ch/o F.& C.
Florestine,1899-1964,w/o Maurice,(I*).
Francois,1847-1929,(I-D-3E).
Gertrude,Apr.1984,(III-H-44).
Henri, Feb.1929,(I-D-3W).
Louise Gladu,1962,(III-H-44).
Maurice,1891-1966,(I*).
Philippe,Apr.1946,(III-H-44)
BEAUPRE
Jean P.,Sr.,1921-1982,(I*).
BECKER
Alice Casey,1893-1933,(III-A-2).
BEGIN
Anastasie,1864-1916,w/o Louis,
(II-26).
Anne Marie,1931-1942,(II-305S).
Camille Beaudry,1843-1917,
w/o Louis.,(II-81).
Camille J.,1887-1975,(II-301).
Celestine,1878-1957,(II*).
Cesarie,1897,w/o Frank C.,(O/F*).
Clement G.,1914-1970,(II*).
Doris L.,Mar.1929,(II-26).
Emile,Jan.1963,(III-L-41).
Francois-Xavier,1962,(II-81).
Francois,1885-1962,(II-301).
Frank G.,1901-1964,(II*).
George,1879-Mar.1931,(II-305S).
Germaine,1911-1978,(II-305S).
inf/o Clement,1943,(II-301).
Joseph,1887-1951,(II-81).
Leo P.,Aug.19,1987,(III-Q-127).
Louis P.,1865-1933,(II-26).
Louis,1841-1912,(II-81).
Louisa B.,1893-1991,(II-81).
Marie,1892-1906,(II*).
Philias,1893-1953,(II-26).
Philip,Dec.1985,(III-Q-209).
XX,1959,w/o Geo.,(II-305S).
BELANGER
Aime,1938-1991,
h/o Doris Jennings,(III-M-44).
Albert,1898-1972,(II*).
Alexina,Jan.1961,(III-L-62).
Alphonse,Apr.1916,(II-26).
Alphonse,1866-1946,,(II*).
Alphonse,1977,(II-195).

Alphonsine,1886-1977,
　w/o Ephraim,(II*).
Alphonsine,1859-1935,
　w/o Auguste,(II-F-5N).
Agnes M.,1904-XXXX,
　2nd w/o Joseph .
Asaie J.,1860-1946,h/o Henedine L.
Auguste,1857-1927,(II-F-5N).
Bernadette H.,1903-1929,
　1st w/o Joseph A.,(*).
Blanche,1909-1927,(I-C-10W).
Catherine,1897-1932,
　w/o Philippe,(I-A-8E).
Cyprien,1891,63y,(II)
Desire,1875-1952,(II-163A).
Emile,Apr.1966 ?,(III-L-62).
Emilia,1870-Aug.1921,
　d/o Valier & Helene,(II-195).
Emma,Feb.1896,(II-26).
Ephrem,1872-Aug.1962,
　s/o Valier & Helene, (II-195).
Eugene,1888-1952,(III-G-47).
Fabien,1857-1943,(I-C-10W).
George,Nov.1987,(III-N-2).
Helene,1836-1930,w/o Valier,
　(II-195).
Henedine Lecomte,1947,
　wid/o Isaac J.,(III-H-37).
Hormidas,1905-1960,(III-G-47).
Hormidas,Mar.1967,(III-Q-22).
J. Amedee,1895-1966,(III-G-47).
Jerome,Feb.1935,(I-A-8E).
Joseph A.,1895-1966,(*).
Laurent,Sept.1973,(III-Q-116).
Leon J.,1922,(II-F-12N).
Leon,1864-1921,(I-C-10W)
Leopoldine,1880-1951,(II-163A).
Marie Louise,1902-1979,
　w/o Albert,(II-254).
Marie Rioux,1864-1927,
　w/o Fabien,(I*).
Marion G.,1915-1994,
　d/o Emile & Alexina Blanchette {O}.
Napoleon,June 1959,(III-H-15).
Napoleon,July 1990,(III-H-15)
Philias,July 1895,25y,(II-26).
Philip,1991,(III-L-79).
Philip,1887-1977,(I-A-8E).
Philomen,1865-1935,
　d/o Valier & Helene,(II*).
Robert L.,1929-1937,(II*).
Rose de Lima,1950,(I-C-10W).
Rose Lefebvre,Jan.1967,
　w/o Leon J.,(II-F-12N).
Valier,1832-Dec.1916,(II-195).
Wilfrid,May 1955,(III-H-10).
XX,1946,w/o Napol.,(III-H-15).

Yoland,July 1965,(III-N-54).
BELLEFEUILLE
Clovis,1849-Feb.1920,(II-241).
David,1879-Oct.1956,(II-247).
Delaney D.,1846-1927,
　w/o Clovis,(II-241).
Florida Belanger,Apr.1948,
　(III-H-62).
Oscar,1883-July 1952,(III-K-4).
Ovide,July 1977,(III-H-62).
Thomas,1884-Dec.1947,(II-247).
Wilfrid,June 1954,(III-H-62).
BENNETT
Robert S.,1952-1990,
　h/o Christine Segar, {O}.
BENOIT
Annie Broduer,1908,w/o A.H.
BERG
Eugene,1920-1993,h/o Virginia
　DeNormandie,(III-L-97).
BERGERON
Anna B.,1896-1938,(II*).
Armandina B.,1877-1964,(II-241).
Cecile D.,1800-Jan.1929,
　w/o Alfred,(1-B-5E).
Elzear,1854-1939,(II*).
Joseph,1863-1933,(II*).
Margaret C.,1907-1980,(III*).
M. Clara,1892-1983,(II*).
Oscar,Mar.7,1902,17y,(O/F*).
Rosa M.,1883-1927,w/o Joseph,
　(I-E-18-E).
Virginie,1861-1952,(II*).
Yvon,1901-Aug.1979,(III-K-30).
BERNARD
Anna,July 1919,(II-157).
Edward,Apr.1960,(III-L-22).
Joachim,Feb.1946,(I-D-9W).
Joseph E.,1883-1970,(II*).
Joshua J.,1871-1946,{O}.
Leda, 1893-1955,(III-B-10).
Marguerite,Aug.1926,(II-157).
XX, Dec.1925,w/o Philom.,(II-157).
XX,Apr.1926,w/o Joachim,(I-D-9W
XX,1952,w/o Edw.,(III-L-22).
BERNIER
Alfred,June 1953,(III-H-8).
Alphonsine Landry,1862-1935,
　w/o Louis(1865),(I-B-2W).
Alvine,1886-1958,w/o Louis,(I-B-2W).
Amedee,May 1962,(III-N-87).
Anna Morin,1887-1950,
　wid/o Joseph,(III-D-5).
Armand,Jan.1960,(III-H-34).
Arthur,Jan.1976,(III-H-8).

Bertha,1912-1993,1st hus.
Raymond Belanger,d.1972,
w/o John J.,III, (III-H-33).
Cecile E.,Aug.1988,(III-N-159).
Elmire Laberge,May 1962,(III-H-34).
Fernande Fortin,1911-1993,
w/o Odilon J.,{O}.
Florence,1982,(III-Q-123).
George E.,1977,(III-Q-123).
Ida,June 1993,(III-J-S-9).
infs/o Joseph,1923,1924,
1925,1928,(II-222).
inf/o Philip,1959,(I-E-16E).
Isabelle,Feb.1988,(III-L-1).
Jeannette E.,1935-1935,(II*)
Joseph,Dec.1943,(III-D-5).
Joseph,July 1980,(III-N-87).
Jules,Sept.1951,(III-L-1).
Lena Fecteau,1907-1993,
w/o Albert,(III-D-5).
Leoni,1887-1947,(III-H-8).
Leopold,Jan.1970,(III-N-89).
Lionel J.,1987,(III-H-34).
Lionel,1987,(III-N-159).
Ludger,Apr.1959,(III-N-61).
Louis,1865-1937,(I-B-2W)
Louis,1886-1930,(I-B-2W)
Marc,Nov.1958,(III-L-1).
Philip,June 1981,(III-N-183).
Rene,July 1945,(III-D-5).
Rhea Girardin,1920-1990,
w/o Arthur P.,d.1975,(III-K-8).
Rita,May 1938,(I-B-2W).
Rolland,Feb.1937,(II-179).
Ronald A.,Aug.1962,(III-N-100).
Ronald,June 1969,(III-N-84).
Susan,Sept.1965,(III-N-84).
Theodose,Sept.1930,(II-231).
Wilbrod,Oct.1918,(III-D-3W).
XX,1957,w/o Geo.,(III-G-52).
BERRY
Blanche B.,1906-1945,(III-G-37).
Carl,1905-1947,(III-G-37).
All in (II-132).
Arthur N.,June 1887.
Demerise,Aug.1888.
Elzear,June 1913.
Eugenie,Apr.1893.
Exilia,Aug.1890.
Marie V., Sept.1885
Peter E.,Apr.1961.
XX, Apr.1937, w/o Elzear.
BERTIN
Amedee,May 1975,(III-N-144).
Germain,Apr.1988,(III-N-144).
Henry S.,Apr.1977,(III-N-81).

Joseph N.,May 1964,(III-N-81).
Joseph,1867-1942,(III-G-62).
Rose Anne,1878-1947,(III-G-62).
BERUBE
Alexina Goozie,1875-1945,(I-E-8E).
Almira Fournier,1865-
Jan.1931,w/o Arthur,(I-E-5E).
Alphonse,Nov.1961,(I-E-8E).
Aime H.,1937,40y,h/o Vernie Smith.
ch/o Susan, Feb.1960,(I-E-5E).
Edward,1894-1968,(I-E-5W).
Emma J.,1895-1965,w/o Edw,(I-E-5W)
Ernest,1890-1959,(I-E-5E).
Eugene,Feb.1955,(III-H-59).
J. Arthur,1864-1938,(I-E-5E).
James,Oct.1980,14y,(III-M-20).
John B.1869-1932,(I-E-8E).
Lea,1861-1925,w/o J.B.,(I-E-8E).
Louise,Jan.1988,(III-M-6).
Margaret G.,1887-1964,(II*).
Robert,Feb.1960, infant,(I-E-5E).
XX, Gouzie,Jan.1962,(I-E-8E).
BETTEZ
Arthur Louis,1907-1912,(II*).
Ernestine,1867-1891,(II*).
J. Onezime,1869-1949,(III-G-24).
Joepsh E.,1917-1981,(II*).
Louis Joseph,Mar.1936,(III-G-24).
Louis,1827-1916,(II-135).
Mary Lucia Letarte,1942,
w/o Joseph,(III-G-24).
Marie Ann Corneault,1834-1917,
w/o Louis,(II-135).
Pierre A.,1868-1959,(III-G-24).
Robert E.,Aug.1987,(III-QS-32).
BIBEAU/BIBAULT
Louis,Aug.1928,h/o Marie,(I-E-7E).
Marie Daniel,1860-1946,(I-E-7E).
BILODEAU
Eva,Aug.1982,(III-N-1970).
BINETTE
George,1952,(II-40A).
John,Feb.1978,(III-Q-154).
Thomas,Oct.1954,(II-40A).
Theresa M.,1918-1992,
w/o Geroge, d.1981,(II-40A).
XX, 1958,w/o Geo.,(II-40A).
BLAIS
Alphonse,1964,(III-F-2W).
BLAKE
Celia A.,1893-1971,(II*).
Joseph L.,1892-1961,(II-203).
BLANCHARD
baby,Oct.1970,(III-N-115).
Chritsina,1876-1919,w/o P.O.,
(II-174).
Ephrem,1910-1956,(II-174).

Eva,1908-1925,(II-174).
Marie,Sept.1970,(II-224A).
Mary A.,1895-1970,(II*).
Mary A.,Apr.16,1894,32y,(O/F*)
Mathilda Arsenault,1894-1991,
   w/o Elzie, d.1972,{O}.
Pierre O.,1870-1947,(II-174).
Sophie,May 1936,(I-D-9W).
BLANCHET/TE
Alphonsine LIzotte,1860-1945,
   w/o Joseph,(II-158).
Anaice M.,1859-1940,(II*).
Arthur J.,1898-1931,(II-309S).
Benoit,1922-June 1931,(II-309S).
Emile A.,1922-1987,(II*).
Ernest,1906-1920,(II-158).
inf/o Arthur,1923,(II-158).
inf/o Arthur,1928,(II-158).
Joseph,1861-1939,(II-158).
Josephine,1862-1917,w/o Jos.,
   (II-158).
Justine O.,1884-1980,(II-309S).
Maria B.,1894-1989,(II*).
Michael,Nov.1974,(III-M-23).
Peter M.,1979,2w.,(III-N-30).
Pierre J.,1861-1939,(II-309S).
Servule J.,1874-1938,(II-309S).
XX,Feb.1957,w/o Philippe,(III-N-30).
XX, Feb.1918,w/o P.O.,(II-174)
XX, June 1940,s/o P.,(II-309S).
BLOCK
William,Aug.1925,Spanish War,
   (I-D-13E).
BLOUIN
Alphionsine,1868-1934,w/o Jos.,(III*).
Joseph,1870-1947,(III-G-9).
BOGDHAN
Frank,1991,(III-Q-242).
BOIS
David,Sept.1960,(III-N-64).
BOISSONNEAU
Alexandre,1904-1943,(II-151).
Alphonsine,1878-1908,(II*).
Aime J.,1886-1954,(III-A-9).
Arthur,Sept.1980,(III-H-41).
Celina,1882-1908,(II*).
Claire,Aug.1981,(III-H-41).
Edmond,June 1959,(III-L-7).
Edna,1898-1923,(II-151).
Ernest,Feb.1969,(III-H-41).
Flora Mason,1889-1935,
   w/o Aime,(III-A-9).
inf/o A.,Aug.1928,(II-151).
J. Ovila,1896-1972,(II-151).
Sophranie,1857-1946,
   w/o Telesphore,(II-151).
Telesphore,Sept.1928,(II-151).

XX,1960,w/o Edmond,(III-L-7)
BOISVERT
Blanche,1898-1984,(III*).
Daniel M.,1954-1993,
   h/o Catherine Fraser,(III-Q-281).
Exilia M.,1867-1954,
   w/o Napoleon,(III-G-39).
Napoleon,May 1937,(III-G-39).
Napoleon,1902-1992,(III-G-39).
Raoul,1892-1986,(III*).
Rose,1898-1978,(III-G-39).
XX, June 1939,w/o Alf.,(II-41).
BOIVIN
Arthur,Apr.1963,(III-H-57).
ch/o John,Feb.1956,(III-H-57).
Emma,Mar.1977,(III-H-57).
Hilda,May 1992,(III-L-76).
Joseph E.,Feb.1953,(III-H-57).
Romeo,Mar.1946,(III-H-57).
BOLDUC
Alexander,Mar.1992,(III-Q-71).
BONA
Earl,1906,(II-B).
Emma,Mar.1905,(II-B).
BONIN
Bernadette L.,1894-1989,(III-K-35).
Donald C.,1925-1981,(III*).
Lorina,Nov.1988,(III-M-27).
Pauline,Dec.1990,(III-M-5).
BOUCHARD
Ernest,Mar.1962,(III-N-85).
BOUCHER
Albert,1877-1898,(II-103).
Alphonsine,1853-1909,
   w/o Cleophas,(II-103)
Anna,1875-1937,(II-79).
Antoinette,1921-1937,(II-103).
Cleophas,1853-1929,(II-103).
Demerise R.,1861-1954,(II*).
Ernest,May.1962,(III-N-85).
Eugene W.,1890-1963,(II-228).
George C.,1914-1914,(II*).
inf/o Eugene,1924,(II-228)
Irene Croteau,1971,(III-L-9).
Irene G. Senechal,1930- 1991,
   w/o Maurice,(III-L-9).
M.A.Laura,Dec.1887,(II-103).
Marceline,1831-1910,
   w/o Narcisse,(II-79).
Margaret G. Powers,1892-1919,
   w/o Eugene,(II-228).
Mildred M. Babkirk,1931-1992,
   w/o Robert (III-Q-265).
Narcisse,1835-1907,(II-79).
Peter,1869-1928,(II*).
Philip,1913-1928,(II*)
Philippe A.,1925-1944,(II*).

Philippe,Nov.1947,(II-228).
Raoul,Dec.1953,(III-L-9).
Rose M.,1892-1969,(II*).
Sabine,Apr.1890,(II-103).
XX,1954,w/o Cleophas,(II-103).
BOUDREAU
Rickey D.,1979-1980,(II*).
BOULANGER
Alfred J.,1878-1960,(II-305N).
Antoinette,1968,(II-F-13S).
inf/o Em.,June 1933,(II-305N).
Nova G.,1916-1985,(II*).
Paul J.,1892-1944,(II-306N).
Rachel,May 3,1982,(III-Q-45).
Roland,1916-May 1936,(II-305N).
Romeo,Apr.1981,(III-Q-45).
Wilfrid,1894-1972,(II*).
XX, July 1956,w/o Alf.,(II-305N).
XX, Jan.1965,w/o Alf.,(II-305N).
BOURASSA
Armand,May 6,1986,(III-L-82S).
Pierre G.,Mar.1959,(III-N-75).
Rachel Briard,1916-1993,
  w/o Armand,(III-L-82S).
BOUSSANNEAU
Aime J.,1886-1954,(II*).
Flora M. Mason,1889-1935,w/o A.J.
BOURGEOUS
Albani,1861-1922,(II-141).
Albani,July 1949,(III-H-32).
Delia,1889-1924,(II*).
Edmund,Mar.1959,(III-H-19E).
Edouard O.,Rev.,1948,(III-H-32).
Elizabeth,1892-1907,(II*).
Leona,Nov.1977,(III-H-32).
Lydia,1918-1918,(II*).
Margueritte,1867-1926,
  w/o Albani,(II-141).
Marie E. Comeau,1890-1991,d/o
  Albenie &Marguerite,(III-H-32).
May,1913-1913,(II*).
Richard,Mar.1952,(III-H-19E).
XX,1954,w/o Albani,(III-H-32)
BOURQUE
Alice Larriviere,1871-1944,
  wid/o John,(II-204).
Roland,1929-1936,(III*).
BOUTHILLETTE
David,Nov.1965,(III-H-47).
Euclide,Dec.1952,(III-H-47).
Leopold,Jan.1978,(III-H-47).
Lionel,Apr.1971,(III-Q-74).
Marie Leclair,1947,(III-H-47).
BRADBURY
Chrystela,1908-1926,(II*).
Julia Quinn,1883-1910,(II*).

BRAGDON
child,1958,s.b.,(II).
Eva,1957-1957,(III-G-2).
Lisa Lynn,child,1967,(*).
Michael Todd,child,1977,(*).
BRASSARD
Albert,1950-1950,(I-D-8E).
Alma,Apr.1926,(I-D-8E).
Angeline Eno,1899-1941,(I-D-8E).
inf/o Romeo,Apr.1926,(I-D-8E).
Joseph A.,Oct.1953,(I-D-8E).
Romeo,Mar.1948,(I-D-8E).
Wilbrod,Oct.10,1935,(I-D-8E).
Virginia,1865-1945,
  w/o Ferdinand,(I-D-8E).
BRAULT
Benjamin,Oct.1931,(III-B-C).
XX,1943,w/o Benj.,(III-B-C).
BREAULT
Blanche,1929-1993, d/o John &
  Irena Smith,(III-J-S-19).
Julia H.,1896-1984,(*).
Lea,1888-1952,w/o Alf.,(II-52A)
Rene J.,1899-1982,(*).
BRETON
Aime,Dec.1976,(III-N-154).
child,June 1974,(III-Q-69).
Floranda,Feb.1970,(III-Q-69).
Nancy,May 1993,(III-N-7).
Napoleon,1866-1955,(II*).
BRIARD
Anna,Feb.1961,(III-L-8).
Arthur,Feb.1981,(III-L-8).
Ferdinand,Mar.1924,(II-168).
Ferdinand,July 1950,(III-L-8).
Rosette,Sept.1980,(III-L-8).
XX,Dec.1912,w/o Ferdinand.
BRIDGES
XX,June 1954,w/o Lewellyn,
  (III-H-61).
BRIGHAM
Alice J.,1901,d/o Jesse D.& Catherine.
Cedric W.,1889-1972,(III*).
Evelyn L.,1902-1921,(II-126).
Marie L. Pomerleay,1890-1972,
  w/o Cedric,(III*).
Mildred M.,1897-1912,
  d/o Jesse D.&Catherine,(II*).
BRIM
child/o John,1944,(II-67).
Robert B.,1923-1985,(II*).
BRISSETTE
Walter,Sept.1991,(III-QS-31).
BRITTON
W.,1907-1970,(II*).
BROCHU
Albert J.,1898-1947,(II*).

Anna Morin,1887-1973,(II*).
Cecile,Aug.1988,(III-N-150).
John Rene,1925-1987,(II*).
Joseph N.,1885-1937,(II*).
BROOKS
Agnes Robichaud,Mar.1970,(II-198)
XX,Sept.1957,w/o Geo.,(III-N-33).
BROWN
Daniel,Apr.1986,2m.(I-F-4A).
Marie,Mar.1979,(III-M-7).
BRUCE
Carole Lynda,1943-1994,
d/o Wallace & Rita, {O}.
BRUNELLE
Alfred,Dec.1965,(III-N-109).
BRYAN
Elizabeth A.Welch,1877-1954,
w/o Harry, (II).
Harry,1875-Jan.1962,(II-6).
BRYMER
Arthur J.,1911-1989,(II-F-4N).
Arthur J.,1873-1931,(II*)
Cora A.,1909-1985,w/o A.J.,(II*).
Louise,Oct.1952,(II-F-4N).
Marie L.,1870-1952,(II*).
BRYSON
Donald,1921-1953,(I-E-3E).
Richard A.,1924-1990,
s/o Wm. & Rose McHugh, {O}.
Rose,1892-1970,(I-E-3E).
BUOTE/BUOTTE
Delima,1870-1941,(II*).
Dominic,1863-1945,
h/o Delima Fournier.
Florence,1884-1959,(III-D-1).
Frank J.,1879-1950,(II-136A).
Georgianna Pomerleau,1902-1977,
w/o Stan,(II).
Irene,1930-1939,(III-G-19).
Judith,1940,(III-D-1).
Marceline,1862-1937,(I*).
Mary J.,1881-1965,(II*).
Mary J.,1881-1940,(III*).
Napoleon,1892-1921,(III-D-1).
Paul,1928-Sept.1992, s/o Stanley &
Georgianna Pomerleau, (III-G-19).
Roach,1851-Jan.1923,(III-D-1).
Stanley J.,1889-1941,(III-G-19)
Theresa,1854-1922,
w/o Roach,(III-D-1).
XX, 1927,w/o Pierre,(III-D-1).
XX,s/o J.F.& M.J.,1906-1913,(I*).
BURCHILL
Marie LaPlante,1923-1993,{O}.
BURGOYNE
Dorothy Thorne,1931-1994,
w/o Robert, {O}.

BURKE
Arthur A.,1906-1947,(II-17).
Catherine Murphy,1867-1947,
(III-G-14S).
Elizabeth C.,1866-1937,(II*).
John J.,1862-1936,(II-17).
John P.,1889-1971,(III*).
Julia M.,1893-1953,(III-G-14).
Julia K.,1835-1893,w/o Steph.,(II-17).
Katherine Murphy,1867-1947,
w/o Patirck,(III*).
Mary M.,1868-1945,(II-17).
Nellie Atherley,1872-1909,
w/o John,(II*).
Odile M.,1894-1972,(III*).
Patrick,1864-1939,
h/o Katherine Murphy,(III-G-14).
Stephen T.,1890-1957,(III-G-14).
Stephen,1832-1922,(II-17).
Stephen,Jr.,July 1942,(II-17).
BURNS
Andrew,1872-1893,(II*).
Margaret W.,1906-1986,(II*).
Mary,1865-1883,(II*).
Mary,1832-1901,w/o Patrick,(II*).
Patrick,1831-1889,(II*).
BURRILL
Julia C.,Sept.1994,78y,
w/o Carl, d.1989.
BURTON
Cheryl A.,1960,7y,(III-G-50).
BUTEAU
Adrien,Oct.1979,(III-QS-5).
BYRNE
Agnes,1890-1965,(I-E-16W).
Antoinette L.,1892-1952,
w/o William,(I-E-16W).
John,1848-1935,(I-E-16W).
Joseph A.,1888-1955,(I-E-16W).
Mary S.,1881-1962,(I-E-16W).
Mary W.,1852-1932,(II*).
Rosetta,1893-1940,w/o Joseph,
(I-E-16W)
William T.,1891-1953,(I-E-16W).
CABRAL
Kathleen O. Burke,1918-1991,
w/o Edward,(III-K-14).
CAISSY
XX,Feb.1957,w/o Pierre,(III-L-39).
CALANTONIO
Rebecca L.,1975,1m,(III-L-23).
CAMERON
Lorraine Aubin,1924-1992,
w/o James (III-M-15).
CAMPBELL
Bessie M.,1863-1954,w/o Jas.,
(I-D-12E).

James,Oct.1925,(I-D-12E).
Leo A.,1907-1966,(I*).
Rebecca,1874-1922,(II*).
William V.,May 1942,(I-D-12E).
CANTARA
Alma,1914-1989,(II*).
CANTON/CANTIN
Eva,Oct.1946,w/o Ludger,(II-F-14).
Henry,Jan.1974,(II-F-1N).
Honore,1855-1934,(II-F-1N).
J. Ovila,1899-1920,(II-F-1N).
Ludger,Nov.1947,(II-F-14).
Margurite M.,1857-1928,
  w/o Honore,(II-F-1N).
Mary,1909-1987,(II).
Philip,1905-1975,(II).
XX, Oct.1950,w/o Henry,(II-F-1N)
XX, May 1934,w/o Art.,(II-158).
CARDWELL
Yvonne,Dec.1981,(II-314).
CARLIN
Tracy,Feb.1991,(III-M-44N).
CARMEAN
Cheryl,1953-1960,(III*).
CARON
Adele R.,1897-1985,(III*).
Alfred,Sept.1984,(III-J-16).
Amedie Joseph,1897-1970,(II*)
Arlene Goodman,1916-1993,
  w/o Raymond,d.1991,(III-Q-184).
Arthur,May 1919,(II-233).
Blanche,Nov.1965,(III-N-108).
Diana Belanger,1865-1924,
  w/o Honore(II-F-4S).
Donald P.,1929-1993,
  h/o Harriet LeClair,{O}.
Hermenegilde,Sept.1945,(II-233).
Honore,1853-1923,(II-F-4S).
inf/o Ludger,June 1923,(II-240).
Joseph A.,1902-XXXX.
Joseph,Jan.1965,(III-N-19).
Lena D.,1896-1925,(III*).
Ludger,1892-May 1948,(II-240).
Marie,July 1979,(III-N-47).
Ovide,1893-1981,(III-B-3E).
Paul,Feb.1975,(III-N-143).
Raymond Ludger,1915-1991,
  h/o Arlene Goodman,{O}.
Raymond W.,XXXX,(II*).
Ronald,Mar.1975,(III-J-16).
Rose Anna,1891-1979,(II-240).
Simeone P.,Feb.1940,(II-F-5N).
Victor,1889-1959,(II-F-4S).
XX,1957,w/o Jos.,(III-N-19).
XX,Oct.1923,w/o Herman,(II-233).
XX,1855-1945,w/o Alphons.O.,
  (I-D-8W).

CARRIER
Arthur,Nov.1960,(III-N-72).
ch/o Robert,1961,(III-N-72).
Donald,June 1990,(III-Q-46).
Eugene,Aug.1924,(II-190).
Flavien,1848-1923,(I-E-18E).
Frank,Apr.1937,(III-G-37).
Helene Ouellette,June 1948,(II-190).
Joseph,Jan.1935,(II-190).
Melanie,Dec.1961,(III-G-37).
Odile M. Joyal,1850-1932,
  w/o Flavien,(I-E-18E).
XX,Aug.1945,w/o Edmond,(III-H-50)
CARRIGNAN/CARIGNAN
Albany L.,1903-1976,(I-B-3W).
Emelie Beaudette,1865-June 1925,
  w/o Onesime,(II-223).
Laurent C.,1917-1930,(I-B-3W).
Marguerite L.,1907-1987,(I-B-3W).
M. Antoinette,1912-XXXX,(I*).
Onesine,1862-1915,(II*).
Phelanise Mullaire,1875-1946,
  w/o Victor,(I-B-3W).
Theodore,1871-Jan.1958,(II-223).
Victor,1874-1951,(I-B-3W).
CARROLL
William,1921,70y.
CARTER
XX, June 1955,w/o Edw.,(III-J-6).
CARVER
Cecil F.,1902-1991,
  h/o Rene Phaneuf,(III-L-29).
CASEY
George,July 1910,(*).
Gerard,May 1927,(II-177).
Urbain,1853-1938,(III-A-2).
CASTONGUAY
Alphonsine,1862-1941,w/o Amable,
  (III-G-27).
Marie B.,1897-1960,(III-G-27).
Rita,Mar.1984,(III-N-57).
CHAILLER
Alexandre,Oct.1967,(II-58A).
Gustave,Oct.1953,(II-58A).
Lucie,June 1952,(II-58A).
M.Philomene.Sept.1890,(II-139).
Phydime,Sept.1887,(II-139).
XX, Oct.1954,w/o Alexander,(II-58A).
XX,Feb.1935,w/o Phydime,(II-139)
CHAISSON
Alexis,Aug.1955,(III-L-24).
Mary Judith,Feb.1965,(II-136A)
Mildred,Aug.1987,(III-L-24).
CHAMARD
Louis J.,Sr.,1901-1966,(I*).
CHAMBERLAND
Eloi,Feb.7,1962,(I-B-1E).

James,Sept.1947,(I-B-1E).
Joseph A.,1876-1929,(I-B-1E).
Martha,Mar.1931,(I-B-1).
Rene,Apr.1956,(I-B-1E).
Sylvia,1905-1977,(I*).
Theodorine Gilbert,1880-1955,
  w/o Joseph A.,(I-B-1E).
CHAMPAGNE
Agnes, 1885-1911,w/o Alb.,(II-D).
Charles,1882-1944,h/o Elizabeth
  Carney,(III-H-36).
Elizabeth,1855-1919,w/o Ls.,(II*).
Emery,1902-1912,s/o Amanda,(II).
Francois X.,Oct.1956,(III-N-18).
Henry,1884-1914,(II-D).
Joseph,Mar.1988,(III-N-159).
Louis,1850-1905,(II-D).
Mary Eslie,Oct.1990,(III-H-36).
Ralph 1933-1992,
  h/o Delores Gagne,(III-L-83S).
Roland,Apr.21,1987,(III-L-83S).
Rose,Apr.1979,(III-N-18).
XX,Nov.1918,w/o Louis,(II-D).
CHAPMAN
Josephine Patenaude,Aug.1889-
  May 1965,w/o Huston E.B.,Sr.,
  (I-C-4W).
CHAREST
Bernadette E.,1916-1977,
  w/o Germain,(II*).
Lisa,1968-1970,inf/o David &
  Janice,(II*).
Omer,1909-Oct.1980,(III-G-60).
Roger,1951-1951,inf/o G.J.&B.E.,
  (I-E-11E).
CHARETTE
Conrad G.,May 1988,(III-Q-193).
Henry,Jan.1965,(III-Q-9).
infant/o Leo,1943,(II-71).
Leo J.,1909-1993,
  h/o Mabel,d.1992,(III-H-51).
Leopold,Apr.1969,(III-N-127).
Mabel Gegne,1915-1992,w/o Leo,
  (III-H-51).
Victor,Aug.1946,(III-H-51).
CHARLAND
Emma Huneau,1885-1963,
  (II-148).
George,1885-1906,s/o F.& Tali(II)
Henry,1882-1953,(II-148).
Marie Rosabba,XXXX, (O/F*).
Tali,1863-1905,w/o Frances(O/F*).
William,1883-1951,
  h/o Exilda Huneau, {O}.
CHARON
4 inf/o Alph.,XXXX,(II-9).
Jean,1935,(II-156).

Maria Leah,June 1933,75y,(II-9).
Maria,1882,9y,(II-9).
XX,Oct.1918,w/o Jos.,(II-9).
CHARTIER
Edmond,Jan.1978,(III-N-28).
CHASE
Timothy,Dec.1969,(III-N-130).
CHASSE/CHESSEY
Alexander,1890-1963,(II-61).
Delima,1849-1903,w/o Samuel,
  (II-61).
Ephrem,1880-1955,(II-61).
Louis J.,1888-1961,(II-61).
Rosalie,May 1965,(III-N-55).
Samuel,1835-1903,(II-61).
Samuel,1880-1960,(II-61).
CHAYER
Alexander L.,1903-1967,(II*).
Andrew,1928-1985,(*).
Anita R.,Dec.1987,(III-N-193).
Claurice,Sept.24,1896,?(II*).
Gustave P.,1871-1953,(II*).
Helen F.,1902-1954,w/o A.L.(II*).
Lucie G.,1877-1952,(II*).
Phidime,1887,48y,(II*).
Ulric,Jan.1980,(III-N-193).
XX,1890,2m.,(II*).
CHICHESTER
Denise Jeanne,1956-1984,(II-F-4N).
CHILDS
Leon,Apr.1968,(III-H-1).
CHRETIEN
Aurore H.,1897-1966,w/o Oscar,(II*).
Clara,Dec.1896,(II-111).
Clara Boucher,1901,w/o Louis.,
  (II-111).
Clara Fournier1857-1931,
  w/o Hosanna,(II-150).
Henry,1888-1967,(II-150).
Joseph,1883-1938,(III-G-7).
Jospehine,1884-1972,w/o Jos.,(*).
L. Hosanna,1856-1931,(II-150).
Leo,1905.(II-111).
Louis,1861-1934,h/o Edisse Girard,
  (II-111).
Louis,1890,(II-111).
Louis,Nov.1909,(II-111).
Lucia C.,1886-1895,(II*).
Maria C.,1885-1945,(II*).
Maurice,Sept.1907,(II-111).
Oscar,1893-1966,(II*).
Oscar,Oct.1892,(II-111).
Ovilda,Dec.1953,(III-L-2).
Robert,Jan.1918,(II-150).
Wilfred,July 1992,(III-L-64W).
XX, Sept.1936,w/o Ls.,(II-115).

CHRISTIAN
Wilfred,1908-1992,
h/o Irene Ferron.{O}.
CHRISTIE
Marie,Dec.1988,(III-N-138).
CHRISTMAN
Amedee,Dec.1953,(III-G-10).
Elizabeth,1876-1958,
w/o Amedee,(III-G-10).
Lucienne,Mar.1973,(III-Q-105).
Mederigue,1898-1901,(II*).
Napoleon,1902-1993,h/o Lucienne
Melanson,d.1973,(III-Q-105).
Yvonne,1907-1911,(*).
CLARK
Mary A.Lampron,Dec.1946,
w/o Edward E.,(III-B-2).
CLEARY
James,May 1938,(III-A-4).
Janet,Feb.1935,(III-A-4).
CLEMENT
Jacques,Oct.1960,(III-H-13).
Jean,1823-1909,(II*).
Shirley Gallant,Sept.1960,
(III-H-13).
CLEMONS
Beatrice,1981,(III-J-14).
CLIFFORD
Leslie W.,1912-19XX,(II*).
Margaret M.,1916-1977,w/o L.W.(II*).
COBB
all in (III-G-54):
Helene Burke,1898-1963.
Lincoln B.,1895-May 1963.
Maxine M.,1927-Mar.1943.
COLBY
Beatrice Buotte,1903-1983,(II*).
COLLINS
Annie McMahon,1884,61y,
w/o Thomas, (II*).
Arthur R.,1918-1994,
h/o R. Alma Landry, {O}.
Bridget J.,1878,20y,d/o Thos.(II*).
Mary,Oct.1930,(II-2).
XX, 1969,(II-2).
COMEAU
Christine,1858-1917,w/o Jos.,(II-50).
Delores,1906-1917,d/o J.& C.(II*).
Jacques,1839-1920,(II*).
Joseph,1867-1957,(II-F-4N).
Henrietta,1841-1923,(II*).
Marie,1890-1991,(II*).
Clara Swisko,1884-July 1920,
w/o Carl,(II-141).
CONANT
Carl A.,Nov.1960,(III-H-14).
Lydia,1885-1917,(II*).

XX, Feb.1953,(III-H-14).
CONDON
John N.,Nov.1894,(II-51).
CONNELLY
Edward,June 1953,(III-H-3).
Erin,May 1982,(III-L-75).
CONNOR/S
Anita Delcourt,Nov.1994,70y.
Bertha J. Phaneuf,1969,(III-L-29).
Clara B.,1916-1990,
1st hus.Edw. J. Bishop,
2nd hus.Thomas R. Jones,
3rd hus. Nehemiah, d.1980,{O}.
Harold, Nov.1967,(III-L-29).
Mary J.O.,1887,26y,d/o P.&B.J.O.
Vincent,Jan.1987,(III-L-86S).
COOK
Anthony,Nov.1988,(III-Q-229).
Mary,Feb.1952,(I-C-1W).
Mary A. Peterson,1881-1982,(I*).
COOPER
Marie,July 1983,(III-L-97N).
Mary,Feb.1971,(I-D-9W).
COPPOCK
Edward,1861-1941,(II*).
Marion B.,1855-1915,
w/o Edw.,(II-184).
Marion,1891-1981,(II*).
CORBIN
Clifford,May 1993,(III-Q-282).
CORMIER
Mary,June 1967,(III-N-Single).
COTE
Edouard,May 1907,(II-139).
EuphemieRousseau,1874-
May 1960,w/o Wilfrid,(III-G-55).
Evanie,1887-Jan.1965,(III-G-55).
Helen Doiron,Jan.1962,(III-N-43).
Henri T.,1916-1994,
h/o Anita Jalbert, {O}.
Jeremie,May 1959,(III-N-44).
Laurie,Oct.1963,child,(III-N-43).
Leo,May 1980,(III-Q-168).
Marie Reine,1906-1942,(III-G-55).
Wilfrid,1877-1958,(III-G-55).
XX, Nov.1907,w/o Ed.,(II-139).
COULOMBE
Alva B.,1900-1984,(*).
COUTURE
Alcide,Apr.1993,(III-Q-186)..
COUTURIER
Adelina,1868-1940, w/o Adjutor,
(I-D-9E).
Adjutor,1865-1926,(I-D-9W).
Adjutor,Jr.,Nov.1946,(I-D-9E).
Joshua J.,1873-19XX,(I*).
Julia,1863-1926, w/o Joshua T.,(I*).

Laurent R.,1903-1962,(I-D-9E)
COYNE
John J.,May 1939,(III-D-3W).
COX
Robert J.,1970,(III-N-129).
COXON
Frank E.,Jr.,1931-1994,
  s/o Frank & Deneige St.Cyr,{O}.
CRAW
Janet T. McLaughlin,1908-1991,
  w/o Romeo,{O}.
Romeo,Nov.1993,(III-Q-261).
CRAWFORD
Lorraine T.,1927-1979,w/o Geo.,Jr.,(*).
CROCKETT
Gloria T.,Oct.1989,58y,
  w/o Harry, (III-N-133).
Harry,June 1982,(III-N-133).
CROZIER
Sylvia Roy,1915-July 1993,
  w/o Ashley, (I-A-6 E).
CULLINAN
Dolores O.,1922-1980,(III-K-1).
Paul E.,1914-1971,(III*).
CURRAN
Eliza A.,1866-1931,w/o Martin,
  (I-D-13E).
Martin,Sept.1905,(II-136).
Martin,Jr.,May 1913,(II-136).
XX,Sept.1893,w/o Martin,(II-136).
CURRIER
Eugene,1899-1924,(II*).
Flora Marie Buotte,1898-1945,(III*).
Frank P.,1885-1937,(III*).
Helen Ouellete,1870-1948,
  w/o Joseph,(II*).
Joseph,1854-1935,(II*).
Melanie R.,1889-1961,
  w/o Frank,(III*).
CURRY
Yvonne Fecteau,1920-1992,(III-J-52).
CYR
Marie Louise,1894-1990,(III*).
Robert Andrew,1989,8y,(III-L-94).
Wildfred,June 1992,(III-L-94).
DAIGLE
Claude,Mar.1988,(III-H-43).
Delina,Mar.1974,(III-H-43).
George,Feb.1955,(II-150).
Ida Chartrand,1885-1945,
  w/o George,(II-150).
Maria Christian,1885-1945.
Sophia,Sept.1949,(III-H-43).
DALPEE
Blanche,Oct.1988,(III-Q-119).
Joseph,June 1974,(III-Q-119).

DALY/DALEY
Charles C.,1927-1993,(III-N-12).
Delima Martin,May 1962,(III-N-86).
Henry, Mar.XXXX,(III-N-132).
Kathleen,1963,child,(III-N-86).
DAME
Alfred J.,1902-1950,(II*).
Alphonse,1918,(II-10).
Alphonse,1866-1943,(I-B-4W).
Amie W.,1930-1974,(I-B-4W).
Arthur,1891-1961,(I-B-7).
Domitilde,1881,21m,(II*).
Ellen Niles,1897-XXXX,w/o Arthur,(I*).
Elmire,1886,infant,(II*).
Emelia A.,1907-1965,(I-B-4W)
F.X.,Sept.1916,(II-10).
Henry,1969,(III-L-21).
Lucy Sharon,1865-1930,
  w/o Alphonse,(I-B-4W).
M.A.,Feb.5,1888,6m,(O/F*).
M. Adeline,13m,(O/F*).
Melglorre,1835-1891,(II*).
Richard Earle,1928-1929,(I-B-7).
Romeo,June 1960,(III-L-21).
Rosalie,1837-1921,w/o Melg.,(II-10).
Rose,Mar.1974,(III-L-21).
William A.,Apr.1943,(I-B-4W).
William A.,1901-1974,(I*).
DANA
Catherine M.,1900-1978,(I*).
DANCAUSE
Alphonse J.,1896-1926,(I-D-10W).
Georgianne,1858-1930,
  w/o Ludger,(I-D-10W).
Joseph,May 1945,(I-D-10-W).
Ludger,Dec.1937,(I-D-10W).
DANDENEAU
Leo,Sept.1967,(III-N-126).
DANDONNEAU
Genevieve Larivee,1914,(II*).
inf/o Ernest,Aug.1926,(II-208)
Marie Clarence Hebert,
  1846-1907,(II*).
DANFORTH
Mauro,June 1991,(I-E-5E).
Myrtle,Nov.1979,(I-E-5E).
DANIEL/DANIELS
A. Rosie,1905,10m,(II*).
Adeline,June 1965,(III-N-70).
Adora,Nov.1953,(III-J-7).
Aime,Sept.1982,(III-N-174).
Alphonse A.,1909-1952,(I-E-7E).
Andrew H.,1896-1981(II*).
Arthur,1873-1927,(II-91).
Beatrice Duchesneau,1872-1927,
  w/o Theodule,(I-D7W).
Bertha,1899-1977, d/o T.

B. Conrad,Mar.1934,(I-E-7E).
Carmen,Sept.1994,80y,
 w/o Gerald, d.1991.
Claudia,Oct.1993,(III-N-174).
Gerald C.,1916-1991,(II-306S).
Helen Letarte,1909-1952,
 w/o Andrew,(II-64A)
Joseph,1871-Mar.1924,(I-E-7E).
Joseph,1896-1891,s/o T.& B.,(II*)
Olympia,Apr.1976,(III-J-7).
Palmyre Caron,1868-1912,
 w/o Arthur,(II*).
Philias,Nov.1937,(II-72).
Rosilda,Jan.1961,(III-L-5).
Ruth,Mar.1921.
Theodule,1869-1948,(I-D-7W).
XX,1901,w/o Francois,(O).
XX,1838-1910,(II*).
XX,Feb.1933,w/o Philias,(II-72).
DANIS
Delphis,Feb.1955,(III-J-2).
Robert G.,July 1990,74y,
 h/o Simone,{O}.
XX,July 1952,w/o Delph.,(III-J-2)
DANONNEAU
Clar,1907,w/o Norbert,(O).
Dora,Oct.1916,(II-73).
Norbert,Jan.1917,(II-73).
Olida,Aug.1924,(II-73).
D'ARCHE
Albert,Dr.,1895-1959,(III-G-20).
Orianne Beauchamp,Jan.1985,
 (III-G-20).
DARLING
Steven E.,Sept.1993,(I-A-4E).
DAVAN
Benedict M.,1946-1969,(III*).
Diane Lefebvre,1934-1992,
 w/o John,Jr.,d.1978,(III-K-11).
John R.,1940-1978,(III*).
DAVIDSON
Olivia Langlois,1877-May 1962,
 w/o William,(II-310N).
William,1891-1973,(II*).
DAVIO
Alfred,June 1969,(III-Q-57).
DAVIS
Deborah A.,Jan.1992,(III-Q-264).
Harold,1891-1948,(III-G-33).
DeBOYES
Albert,Jan.1948,(III-H-12).
Aldano,Oct.1971,(III-H-12).
Virginie Rancourt,Dec.1960,(III-H-12).
DECELLES
Marie S.,1885,24y,(II*).
DECORMIER
Albert,1889-1940,(II*).

Alice M.,1875-1931,(*).
Bibiane,1850-1935,(II*).
Clotilde,1872-1923,(II-21).
Cora,1887-1942,(II-21).
Flora,1882-1904,(II-21).
Francois Saul,1845-1906,(II-21).
Gracia,1894-1968,(II-21).
Ida O.,1879-1937,(II-21).
Lucilda E.,1895-1984,(II*).
Mary,Jan.1990,(II-28A).
Rosana,1878-1881,(II-21).
Regina Tanguay,1855-1936,
 w/o Saul,(II-21).
XX,1938,w/o Alfred,(I-E-15W).
DELCOURT
Albert,1897-1971,(III*).
Antoinette,June 1988,(III-L-28).
Bertrand,1989,(III-Q-239).
Herve J.,1904-1918,(II-208).
inf/o Antoine,1948,(II-202)
Louis J.,1889-Oct.1940,(II-35).
Louise M. Harvey,1867-1939,
 w/o Marville,(II-202).
Marie A. Fournier,1879-1968,
 w/o Simon,(II*).
Marville,1928,(II-202).
Marvin,1861-1928,(II*).
Maurice,May 1925,(II-208).
Merilda,1897-1971,w/o Albert(*).
Notalie,1918,(II*).
OscarJ.,1896-1970,(III-L-28).
Raymond,Mar.1965,(III-L-28).
Rene W.,1918-1991,s/o Simeon &
 Marie Anna Fournier,(II-191).
Robert,1906-Jan.1988,(II-191).
Roger,1912-Oct.1917,(II-191).
Roland O.J.,1914-1990,(II-202).
Romeo,1908-1949,
 h/o Bertha Belanger,(II-191).
Rosanna,1895-1939,(II*).
Simeon,1878-May 1956,(II-191).
XX,1939,w/o Oscar,(II-202).
DELIMA
Rose,1868-1950,(I*).
DELISLE
Camille J.,1914-1975,(I-D-8W)
Noella M.Aube,1913-XXXX,
 w/o Camille,(I*).
DEMERS
Alice,1884-1945,(III*).
Alphonse,Sept.1960,(III-H-22).
Anna,XXXX,(O/F*).
Arthur,Aug.1988,(III-G-19A).
Celina,1850-1920,(III*).
Cleophas,Nov.1960,(III-J-12).
Ida,Sept.1945,(II-194).
Joseph,Sept.1959,(III-C-2E).

Josephine,1885-1953,(III*).
Philomene,1859-1923,(II-194).
Raymond,Sept.1973,(III-Q-111).
XX,1921,w/o Antoine,(III-C-2E).
XX,Apr.1945,w/o Jos.,(III-C-2E).
XX,June 1958,w/o Alph.,(III-H-22)
DEMONTIGNY
Joseph,1853-1937,(II*).
Julie,1853-1935,(II*).
Rose,1882-1964,(II*).
DENEAULT
Emma R.,1930?,21y, w/o Victor,{O}
DENIS
Robert,Nov.1975,(III-N-165).
Wilfred,Sept.1967,(III-Q-42).
DEROCHE
Benjamin,1877-1946,{O}.
Frank E.,1933-1948,(II*).
Lisa Anne,1970-1970,(*).
Wilfred J.,1910-1994,
  h/o Gloria Dwyer,d.1984,{O}.
DERRAH
Eva,1904-Jan.1980,(III-G-37).
George T,1905-1966,h/o Eva,(III*)
DESCHAMPS
Blanche,July 13,1987,(III-N-95).
Fernand,Nov.1964,(III-N-95).
Joseph,June 1928,(I-E-4E).
Timothee,Sept.1927,(I-E-4E).
XX, Nov.1924,w/o Jos.,(I-E-4E).
DESALLE
infant,Dec.1962,(II-64A).
DESFOSSES
Ovide,1870-1936,(II*).
DESFRESNE
Helen,July 1964,(III-H-60).
DESHAIES
Delima,1856-1939, w/o Joseph.
Eugene,1891-1946,(I-C-10E).
Joseph,1852-1927,(I*& w/o).
Joseph,Oct.1927,(I-C-10E).
Maurice,Jan.1950,(I-C-10E).
Olive,Feb.1964,(I-C-10E).
XX,Mar.1939,w/o Jos.,(I-C-10E).
DESJARDINS
Claude,Nov.1994,77y,
  h/o Pauline Leblanc.
Philippe,Msgr.,Mar.1969,92y,
  (III-H-22).
Vernon,Nov.1964,(III-N-94).
DEROCHES
Benoit,Jan.1946,(III-H-30).
Celina Doucet,1886-1950,
  (III-H-30)
Daniel,1927,(III-E-2W).
Mary Doucet,1922,w/o Daniel,
  (III-E-2W).

DIMINO
Stephen A.,1945-1985,(III*).
DINARDO
Ethel Charette,Jan.1992,(III-Q-9).
DION
Benjamin,1982-1982,(II*).
Catherine,1899-1987,(II-164A).
Joseph,1897-1989,(II-164A).
Maria Leda Aube,Oct.1949,(III-H-41).
DIONNE
Josephine Caouette,1963,(II-91).
DOHERTY
James,1863-1955,(III-G-23).
Margaret C.W.,1866-1936,w/o Jas.
DOIRON
Fred D.,1896-1981,(III-G-18).
Homere,Sept.1916,(II-24).
Joseph,Oct.1973,(III-N-43).
Leocade,1899-1938,w/o F.D.,(III*).
Olivier,June 1965,(III-N-6).
Sophie,May 1961,(III-N-6).
Victor,Feb.1943,(I-E-10E).
XX, July 1940,w/o Victor,(I-E-10E).
XX,1938,w/o Alfred,(III-G-18).
DOIRONT
Adelaide,1865-1941,(II*).
August J.,1899-1924,(II*).
Victor,1854-1941,(II*).
DOLAN
Edward J.,May 1963,(III-N-37).
DONOVAN
John H.,1880-1933,(II*).
Lydia Guimond,1882-1952,
  w/o John H.,(II-104).
Mary E.,1879-1880,d/o M.& M.E.
Mary Eagan,1850-1925,w/o Mich.,(II*).
Michael.1853-1916,(II*).
DOOLEN
Hannah,Sept.1921,(II-138).
Mary Quinn,May 1919,(II-128).
Minnie,Apr.1931,(II-138).
Thomas,1833-1898,(II*).
DOOLEY
Bridget H.,1873-1909,(II*).
John,1846-1925,(II*).
Mary Donahue,1844-1910,
  w/o John,(II*).
DORAN
Hilda F.,Apr.1959,(II-314B).
Thomas,1880-Jan.1956,
  h/o Catherine F.,(II-314B).
DOSTIE
Joseph A.,1895-1927,(I*).
DOUCETT/E
Albert,1900-1961,(II-186).
Dumas,1892-1914,(II*).
Edmund,1908-1977,(II*).

Elizabeth,1869-1946,
  w/o Moses,(II-186).
Frank,Oct.1978,(III-Q-158).
George M.,1990,54y,
  h/o Priscilla Harvey,{O}.
Ida,1904-Dec.1980,(III-K-33).
Jeremie,Sept.1942,(II-1).
John,Nov.1955,(III-L-38).
Joseph A.,1890-1959,(II-186).
Laurent,May 1946,(III-H-38).
Louise A.,1989,81y,(III-Q-158).
Marie,1888-1970,(II-186).
Marie Gallant,Feb.1917,(II-211).
Maxime J.,June 21,1896,26y,(O/F*).
Moise,May 1947,(II-186).
Moses,1868-1963,(III-H-38).
Napoleon,June 1931,(II-186).
Napoleon,1896-1957,(II-186).
Philip,July 1976,(III-H-38).
XX, Aug.1952,w/o Jeremie,(II-1).
XX,1958,w/o John,(III-L-38).
XX,1957,w/o Moise,(III-H-38).
DOUGHERTY
  Raymond,1909-1952,(II-36A).
DOYLE
  Albert T.,Oct.1967,(III-J-3).
  Edmund,1842-1929,(II*).
  Julia A.,1869-Feb.1949,(II-229).
  Maria,Aug.1953,(III-J-3).
  Mary E.,1875-Dec.1935,(II-229).
  Mary O'Meara,1845-1919,(II*).
DRAKE
  J.,Oct.1978,(III-N-40).
  Priscilla Marcous,Nov,1994,90y,
    w/o Joseph B.
DRISCOLL
  Arthur,1891-1944,
    h/o Mila Powers,(III-G-38).
DROBISH
  Leon,Dec.1987,(III-L-46N).
DROUIN
  Blanche,July 1979,(III-N-29).
  Emile C.,Nov.1994,84y,h/o Jeanne.
  Emile P.,1905-1947,(I-B-5E).
  Gedeon,Nov.1956,(III-N-29).
  Jeanne,June 1983,(III-Q-162).
  Joseph,1867-1945,(I-B-5E).
DUBOIS
  David D.,1876-1943,(II-F-8A).
  Joseph,1842-1878,(II*).
  Mary,1874-1921,(II-F-8A).
  Regina Rioux,1884-1963,
    w/o David,(II-F-8A).
  Souphrine,1850-1935,
    w/o Jos,(II-F-8A)
DUBREUIL
  George,1879-1923,(I-E-18W).

DUCHAINE
  Albertine Porell,1900-1973,(III*).
  Alice McHugh,1911-1991,w/o Emil,
    (I-E-3E).
  Cardine Trembley,1844-1918,(II*).
  Diana M.,July 1937,w/o Joseph,
    (III-B-1).
  Elzear J.,1861-1943,(III-B-1).
  Emile,1902-1988,(II*).
  Jean M.,May 1,1962,(*).
  Jennevieve M.,1868-1920,(*).
  Joseph,Jan.1963,(III-B-1).
  Leo A.,1920-1990,{O}.
  Medora,June 1974,(III-B-1).
  Xavier F.,1836-1912,(II*).
DUCHESNE
  Adelard,1883-1956,(I-B-3E).
  Aime,June 1967,(III-M-22).
  Alfred,Mar.1970,(III-M-22).
  Arthemise,Dec.11,1884,15y,(O/F*)
  Aurore,Oct.1971,(III-M-22).
  Delphine,Apr.1,1885,19y,(O/F*).
  F.X.,Jan.31,1890,17y,(O/F*).
  F.X.,Jr.,Aug.1916,(II-154).
  Julie,1874-1922,(II-154).
  Leo A.,1920-1990,(I-B-3E).
  Margaret,Aug.1963,(III-M-22).
  Marie Lebrun,July 19,1885,
    20y,w/o Exeas,(O/F*).
  Regina,1892-1976(I*).
  Rose,1887-1938,(II-154).
  Ulric,May 1963,(I-C-2W).
DUCLOS
  Alaric,1852-Aug.1918,(II-213).
  Albert,Mar.1961,(III-N-79).
  Alma,1787-Sept.1945,(II-213).
  Anna,1876-Aug.1949,(II-219).
  Azilda,1853- Sept.1942,w/o Alaric,
    (II-219).
  Delia Tourangeau,Dec.1963,(III-N-79).
  Georgiana,June 1993,(III-N-76).
  Hormidas J.,1892-1950,(II-219).
  Josephine G.,1889-1963,w/o Ovila,
    (II-213).
  Ovila,1894-Apr.1949,(II-213).
  XX,May 1959,w/o Alida,(III-N-76).
DUFOUR
  Alfred,1879-Dec.1953,(III-G-13).
  Charles,1895,32y,(II*).
  Eugene,1886,18y,(II*).
  Joseph,18XX-XXXX,(II*).
  Joseph Paul,Apr.1948,(III-G-13).
  Louise Debien,1890,53y,
    w/o Joseph,(II*).
  Sophie L.,1891-1940,
    w/o Victor,(III-G-13).
  Victor J.,1893-1973,(III*).

Victor,1925-Dec.1969,(III-K-13).
DUGAS
Andre G.,1943-1993,
 1st w. Dorothy Kaler,d.1977,
 2nd w. Penny Pooler,{O}.
DUMAS
Antoinette Bourque,1947,(II-206).
DUNN/E
Dorila E.,1896-1981,(III*).
Elizabeth A. Powers,1879-1949,
 (III-G-16).
John,1873-1936,(III-G-16).
Thomas J.,1906-1960,(III-G-16).
Wm.,1881, inf/o Thos.& Mary,(II*).
DUPUIS
Adeline,1861-Dec.1935,(III-A-9).
DUVAL
Delvina,Apr.10,1880,18y,(O/F*).
Ferdinand,Feb.19,1899,66y,(O/F*).
Samuel,Mar.1929.,(I-C-12W).
XX,1943,w/o Samuel,(I-C-12W).
DYER
Emma,Apr.1924,(II-193).
DZIALA
Edward,1918-1989,
 h/o Josephine Yanaskevic, {O}.
EDSTROM
Simone Doiron,1990,
 1st hus.Wm.Sparks,
 2nd hus. Albert,(III-G-18).
ELDRIDGE
Rose,1876-1954,(II*).
Sanford E.,1870-1942,
 h/o Rose Elaine Benoit, {O}.
ELLIOTT
Wilfred,Apr.1965,(III-M-5).
ELSINGER
Marie Arsenau,1912,w/o Wm,(II*).
EMMONS
Annette Rioux Cox,1906-1993,
 1st hus. Robert James,d.1970,
 2nd hus.Rodney Emmons,d.1989,
 (III-N-129)
ESTY
Blanche L.,1898-1970,(III-G-2).
Richard L.,1925-1933,(III-G-2).
Sheila Gallagher,1936-1993,
 w/o Donald,Sr.,(III-M-49N).
ETHERLEY
Ellen B.,May 1909,(II-17).
EUGLEY
Dolores B.,June 1975,(II-151).
Fred M.,Aug.1952,(II-151).
EXCHANGE
Donald R.,1931-1992,h/o Veronica
 Dandeneau,(III-M-18S).
Ernest,July 1956,(III-N-1).

FARLEY
Charles W.,Oct.1952,(I-E-5W).
Margaret R.,1894-1979,(II*).
William P.,1897-1966,(II*).
FARRELL
Margaret Hebert,1898-1947,(II-113).
FECTEAU
Agnes Pitre,1882-1962,w/o Arsene,(I*).
Albert,1889-Oct.1942,(III-G-60).
Alphonse,June 1989,83y,h/o Irene
 Gagnon,(III-Q-238).
Arsaria Bergeron,Jan.2,1919,35y,
 w/o Henry.
Arsene,1876-1938,(I-A-1)
Arthemise Fortin,1849-1913,(II*).
Cecile M.,1942-XXXX,(I*).
Elizabeth Poirier,1887-1920,
 w/o Arthur,(II-83)
Emile,Feb.1990,(III-N-181).
Ezalia B.,1884-1919,
 w/o Honore,d.1919,(II*).
Gaston V.,Oct.1989,80y,(III-L-13).
Henry, Jan.1,1919,{O}.
Honore,1873-1919,(II*).
Honore,1848-1910,(II*).
J. Robert,Sept.1927,(II-83)
Joseph A.,1877-1949,
 h/o Amanda Lafraniere.
Joseph O.,1880-1942,(II-248).
Leo J.,1910-1993,w/o Mabel,(I*).
Mabel Bastien,1912-1992,
 w/o Leo J.,(I*).
Maria,1904-XXXX,(I*).
Marie Landry,1890-1963,(III-G-60).
Mary M.,1883-Dec.1958,
 w/o Jos.O.,(II-248).
Philip J.,Mar.3,1924-Sept.11,1991,(I*)
Wilfrid,Mar.1983,(III-L-72).
FEENEY
Annie,1868-1931,w/o Thos,(II-114)
Daniel,1813-1897,(II-114).
J.,Aug.1990,(III-J-10).
James,1899,(II-114).
James,Mar.1983,(III-M-16).
Pearl H.,1895-1896,(II-114).
Katherine McDonough,1835-1916,
 w/o Daniel, (II-114).
Thomas,1870-1941,(II-114).
FENDERSON
Ronald,1929-1944,
 s/o Willard M. & Mary,(III-H-9).
FENEUF
Josephine,Dec.18,1882,3y,(O/F*).
FERNANDEZ
Joseph,1921-1991,
 h/o Shirley Gallant,(III-L-39).

FERRIS
David W.,Dec.1994,58y,
 h/o Daine Gregoire.
FERRON
Ernest,Aug.1983,(III-N-189).
Virginie,Aug.1932,(II-253).
Elmina,1836-1924,w/o Jos.,(II-253).
Vina M.,1942-1942,(II*).
FICKETT
Donald E.,Apr.1958,(III-N-71).
Irene King,1918-1992,w/o Geo. H.,
 (III-Q-122).
FIELD
Wilma R.,1896-1973,(III*).
FILES
Fedora,Mar.1978,(III-L-65).
Raymond,Feb.1973,(III-L-65).
FILION
Roland C.,1927-1992, h/o Eva
 Martin Fredettte,(III-QS-18).
FINN
Agnes Frances,1948,(III-G-51).
Margaret L.,Oct.1943,
 wid/o Cornelius,{O}.
FISHER
Everett C.,May 1970,(III-H-48).
Margaret,Nov.1980,(III-Q-178).
FLAHERTY
Albina,Nov.1955,(II-F-5N).
Alice,Dec.1959,(III-L-18).
Hazel,Apr.1954,(II-152).
John W.,XXXX,(I*).
Lucienne Caron,1918-1991,
 w/o Edward,(II-25).
Michael A.,1858-1931,(II*).
Mary E.Mc Callion,Mar.1936,
 w/o Michael,(II-152).
Veronica Hebert,June 1994,
 w/o John W. {O}.
FLUETT
Gerald C., 1920-Mar.1988,
 s/o Marie Levesque,(I-C-1E).
FOLEY
Daniel W.,1890-1943,s/o P. & M.
Ellen,Nov.1956,(III-G-40).
Helen T. Mahoney,1894-1957,
 w/o Daniel W.,(III*).
Margaret Sullivan,1860-1946,
 wid/o Patrick, (III*).
Martin T.,1897-1945,s/o P. & M.
Patrick,1858-1936,(III*).
Rachel,1948-Nov.1992,(III-G-60).
Thomas,Dec.1968,(III-Q-51).
XX, June 1958,w/o John,(II-174).
XX,Apr.1946,w/o Thos.,(III-G-40).
FORGET
Rosanna,1881,(II*).

FORTIER
Alfred,Aug.1978,(III-N-17).
FORTIN
Alexina G.,1868-1942,
 w/o Ovide J.,(II-117).
Anna,Jan.1976,(I-E-4E).
Auguste,Oct.1968,(I-E-4E).
Caroline P.,1851-1930,(II*).
Germain F.,1904-1907,
 d/o O.J.& A.M.,(II*).
Jean A.,1849-1913,(III*).
Leo,1903-1958,(II-117).
Leonce,June 1938,(III-G-6).
Lucien,1901-1901,s/o O.J.&A.M.,(II*).
Ovide J.,1872-1923,(II-117).
Vitaline Sirois,Mar.1949,(III-G-6).
Yvonne M.,1899-1982,w/o Leo A.,(II*).
XX,July 1930,w/o Jean,(II-117).
FOSS
Mae E.,1892-May 1973,(II-253).
FOSTER
Shawn,Jan.1992,(III-Q-221).
Bertha J,1907-1958,w/o John,(II-148)
FOUGERE
Arthur J.,1900-1960,(III-A-4).
Celina,1872-1933,(III*)
Emma Rose Vachon,1903-1992,
 w/o Arthur,d.1960,(III-A-4).
Edna Joan,1921-1991,
 w/o Wm.d.1988, (III*).
William,1873-1954,(III-A-4).
William,1915-1988,(III*)
Celina,1872-1933,w/o Wm.,(III-A-4).
FOURNELL
Catherine C. Barieau,Feb.1920,
 w/o Charles, Sr.,(II-149).
Charles, 1874-1952,(II-149).
Charles J.1902-1966,(II-149).
Marie,1872-1956,(II-149).
Mary Huneau,1875-1926,
 w/o Charles.Jr.,(II-149).
FOURNELLE
Catherine Barieau,1837-1920,(II*).
Charles J.,1846-1890,(II*).
Dorothy A.,1928-Dec.1977,
 w/o Joseph G.,(II-222A).
Exilia,Oct.1953,(I-E-11W).
Emma Harnois,1880-1963,
 w/o William,(II-222A).
Joseph Gerard,1922-1987,
 (II-222A).
William,1876-1953,(II-222A).
FOURNIER
Achille J.,1890-1982,(II*).
Aime Napoleon,1881-1963,(I-D-11E).
Alexander,1902-1990,
 h/o Alice Sauve,(III-N-93).

Anna T.,1889-Jan.1966,
  w/o Wildrod L.,(II-235).
Antoine,1840-1901,(II-47).
Archelas,Apr.1942,(II-252).
Archie,Mar.1982,(II-226).
Arthur,Oct.1889,(II-53).
Arthur J.,1895-1948,
  h/o Laura Theriault,(II-189).
Atilla Christman,1864-1950,
  (II-252).
Bernadette,1920-1925,(I-D-11E).
Demerese,Oct.28,1887,23y.
Edna McFarland,1919-1994,
  w/o Aime J.,{O}.
Euphemie,June 1901,(II-53).
Georgianna Rousseau,1867-1952,
  w/o Joseph,(II-53).
Georgiana Joncas,1842-1916,
  (II-191).
infant,1932,inf/o Nap,(I-D-11E)
Joseph,Apr.1893,(II-53).
Joseph,1866-Oct.1960,(II-53).
Josphine Charland,Oct.1959,(II-252).
Judith G.,1890-1933,w/o Napoleon,
  (I-D-11E).
Lena,Aug.1973,(III-L-71).
Louis W.,1865-Aug.1949,(II-235).
Louis,Sept.1979,(III-N-53).
Louisa M. Powers,1890-Oct.1918,
  w/o Archille,(II-226).
Lucy M. Burgess,1892-Aug.1963,
  w/o Achille,(II-226).
Marie,1868-Feb.1920,w/o Louis,
  (II-235).
Marie Paule Fournier,1918-1994,
  d/o Napoleon & Etiennette Samson.
Napoleon,1894-1910,(II-53).
Napoleon,Apr.1963,(I-D-IIE).
Napoleon,Feb.1978,(III-L-71).
Noelia,Feb.1918,(II-53).
Octavia Blanchette,1844-1938,
  w/o Antoine,(II-47).
Philip,Mar.1974,(III-N-182).
Philomene,Sept.26,1880,34y,(I*).
Philomaine L.,1850-1920,(II*).
Rebecca,Dec.1927,(I-D-11E).
Rene J.,July 22,1987,(III-N-182).
Robert,Oct.1964,(III-N-93).
Wilbrod,1893-June 1957,(II-235).
William,Jr.,1897-1920,(II-252).
William,Sr.,1850-1928,(II-252).
  XX,June 1924,w/o Arthur,(II-226).
FOYE
Agnes Sullivan,1894-1951,(II-129).

Constance,1920-July 1992,
  w/o Wm.J.,Jr.,(III-K-26).
W.J. Arthur,1913-1974,(III*).
William ,July 1957,(III-E-1E).
William J.,Jr.,1923-1988,(III*).
FRANCOEUR
Alexina,Jan.1953,(III-A-8).
Alida Guimond,1887-1966,
  w/o William,(III*).
Andre G.,Jan.1946,(II-314).
Aurele,Feb.1959,(III-N-74).
Chrysologue,1866-1914,(II-171).
Georgianna,1851-1917,(III*).
Jean P.,Jan.1946,(II-314).
Jeannette,July 1978,(III-H-8).
Joseph,1889-Apr.1931,(II-314).
Leda G.,1888-Aug.1976,
  w/o Joseph,(II-314).
Ovide J.,1914-June 1973,(II-314).
Raymond C.,1923-1973,(II-314).
Rita,Dec.1918,(II-29).
Roland,1906-1979,(III-L-73).
Pamela Duval,1870-1929,
  w/o Chrys.(II-171)
Paula Vaillancourt,1908-1942,
  w/o Roland,(III-G-48).
William,1881-1927,(III*).
XX,Oct.1969,h/o Rose,(III-L-73).
Yvonne C.,1911-1981,(II*).
FRANK
Herman,May 1991,(III-N-176).
FRASIER
Felix J.,1902-1993,
  h/o Bertha Auclair,(III-M-29N).
XX Begin,1889-1946,w/o Donald,(II*).
FREDETTE
Albert O.,1914-1949,(II-239).
Alfred,1911-Nov.1918,
  s/o O. & Dorilla,(II-237).
Alfred,1876-1945,h/o Elmire Caron,
  (II-243).
Belzemine,1883-1918,w/o Alfred.
Dorilla,1882-1944,w/o Odilon,(II-237).
Elmire Caron,1880-1945,w/o Alfred,
  (II-243).
Elmire M.,1895-1992,(I-E-11E).
Eugene,Mar.1990,73y,
  h/o Gabrielle Gouzie,(III-Q-173).
Eva,1922-XXXX,w/o Albert O.,(II*).
Joseph,1871-1914,(II*).
Hanriette Bernier,1889,51y,
  w/o Octave,(O/F*).
Henri,Apr.1990,(III-N-192).
Leda,1890-1968,(II*).
Leon,Nov.1964,(III-D-5).

Maria,1871-1916,w/o Joseph,
  (II-223)
Odilon,1874-June 1940,(II-237).
Ovide,1890-1971,(II).
Philip J.,1888-1981,(II*).
Raymond,Dec.1917,5m,(II-37).
Robert,June 1980,.(III-N-192).
Simone,1906-1912,(II*).
Marier Belzemire,1883-1918,
  w/o Alfred,(II-243).
FURLOTTE
David J.,Jr.,1930-1970,{O}.
GAGNE
Anna Rousseau,1889-1963,(II-71).
Aurele,Dec.1954,(II-77).
Blanche M.,Jan.1987,(III-K-23).
Gerald,May 1982,(III-Q-176).
Henry A.,1910-Apr.1990.
  h/o Bernadette St.Pierre O}.
Herminie,1915-1925,(II-71).
Hormidas L.,1911-1963,(II-71).
Josephine,1888-1970,w/o Oral,(II-77).
Louis O.,1919-1964,(II-77).
Ludovic .,1914-1992,
  h/o Doris LeBreton,(III-Q-40).
Marie B.,1889-1963,(II*).
Oral W.,1884-1954,(II*).
Oral,Sept.1985,(III-K-23).
Oscar J.,1881-1928,(II-71).
Pierre,Sept.1962,(III-N-47).
Raoul H.,May 1918,(II-77).
Rose A.,1886-1905,(II*).
Theresa E. Bernier,Sept.1990,75y,{O}.
GAGNON
Aime W.,1911-1991,(III-J-8).
Alberic,May 22,1908-Dec.4,1927,(I*).
Albina M. Tanguay,1892-1966,(II*).
Alexina,1896-1924,(I-E-1E).
Alexandrine,1861-1869,
  w/o Thomas,(I-E-1E).
Alfred,July 1958,(III-L-55).
Altheol,Mar.1956,(III-J-8).
Claire,May 2,1912-XXXX,(I*).
Cleophas,1870-1953,(III-B-8).
Cleophas,1834-1924,(II-177).
Delphine,1865-1881,(II*).
Dianna,1865-1941,w/o Pierre,(II-177).
Elie,1863-Jan.1933,
  w/o Herminie,(II-29).
Elzear,1870-1944,(II*).
Emile,Aug.1963,(III-J-8).
Emilie (Nellie),1907-1989,(I-E-1E).
Eva Dandeneau,1893-194X,(II*)
Francis,May 1934,(I-E-1E).
Herminie,1867-1956,(II-29).
Hubert,Dec.1962,(III-J-8).

Ida Langlois, Sept.1941,59y,
  w/o Joseph,(II-310).
Imelda Tremblay,June 1959,(III-L-14).
inf/o Ed.,Aug.1920,(II-177).
Joseph,June 1931,(II-310N).
Joseph R.,1917-1976,(II*).
Joseph,1892-1982,(III*).
Laurent,Oct.28,1958,(I-E-1E).
Lionel,1911-Jan.1989,
  h/o Theresa,(II-309N).
Louise C.,June 1990,95y,
  w/o Joseph, (III-G-26).
Louis,Jan.1976,(III-J-8).
Madolyn M.,Dec.1994,80y,w/o Roger
Marie,Jan.1926,(II-29).
Marie,1872-1955,(II*).
Napoleon,1889-1980,(II*).
Pierre,1863-1961,(II-177).
Philibert,1829-1885,(II*).
Odile Bernier,1872-1948,(III-B-8).
Oscar J.,1881-1928,(II*).
Osias,1896-1912,(II-177).
Raymond Richard,1865-1945,(II*).
Robert,1905-1990,
  h/o Yvonne Lepenven,(III-L-43).
Roger,Mar.1919,(II-29).
Roger J.,1920-1994,
  h/o Madalyn M. Porello,(III*).
Rolland,Feb.1932,(II-238).
Sophie E. Tremblay,1833-1904,
  w/o Philibert,(II*).
Susan A.,1946-1978,(III-K-28).
Thomas,1861-1946,(I-1-1E).
William,1858-1876,(II*).
XX,1958,w/o Hubert,(III-J-8).
XX,Mar.1940,w/o Jos.,(III-G-26).
Yvonne,1906-1994,w/o Robt. T.,
  d.1990,(III-L-43).
GALIPEAU
Albert,Aug.1947,(III-H-25).
Celestine,Feb.1949,(III-H-21).
Flore,Mar.1962,(III-H-21).
Georgianna,Nov.1974,(III-H-35).
Gerard L.,1919-1994,
  h/o Yvette Francoeur, {O}.
Horace,Oct.1976,(III-H-35).
Laurent,Dec.1955,(III-L-4).
Leonidas,Apr.1963,(III-L-4).
Maurice,Mar.1989,(III-L-17).
Ovila,Sept.1963,(III-H-21).
Raoul P.,1901-1991,(III-H-21).
Rosario L.,Apr.30,1917-
  Nov.11,1971(I-B-2W).
Rose Delima,Sept.1970,(III-L-4).
Ruth,July 1976,(III-N-157).
Yvonne Brassard,Mar.1949,(III-H-35).

GALLAGHER
M. Norah,1907-1971,(III*).
Owen F.,Sr.,1907-1967,(III*).
GALLANT
Adeline B.,1896-1966,(I*).
Adolphe G.,1865-1930,(I-D-6W).
Albert,July 1963,(III-H-6).
Albina R.,1907-June1932,
 w/o Geo.A.,(I-A-7E).
Alice St.Pierre,1869-1936,
 w/o Adolphe,(I-D-6W).
Alphonse,1897-1985,(III*).
Angus,Aug.1,1934, 79y,(I*).
Angus,1877-1948,(I*).
Arline F.,1935-1943,(II*).
Arsene,Oct.1948,(I-D-1W).
Arthur J.,June 1981,(III-L-34).
Auguste,1924,(I-E-10E).
Benjamin J.,1881-1946,{O}.
Bernadette,1906-1939,(I-B-4W).
Bertha Bernier,1976,(III-H-34)
Catherine,1884-1969,
 w/o John D.,(I-D-1W).
Edmond F.,1905-1927,(I-D-6W).
Edouard,Aug.1948,(I-A-7E).
Edward,July 1906-May 15,1914,(I*).
Eugene L.,Aug.1986,(III-Q-30).
Eugene,1859-1940,(III-B-6).
Evelyn,1906-1920,(I*).
Evevlyn F. Rousseau,1918-1982,
 w/o Alphonse,(III*).
Flora V.,1908-1985,w/o Edm.F.,(I*).
Francois,Oct.1956,(III-B-6).
Frank J.,1895-1918,(II*).
George A.,1905-1939,(I-A-7E).
Germaine,Mar.1961,(III-B-7).
Germaine,Aug.1979,(III-L-34).
Henriette,Mar.1922,w/o Thomas,
 (II-F-12S).
Henry J.,Nov.9,1942,(I-A-7E).
Hyacinth,Aug.1934,(I-C-6).
Jean,May 1949,(I-D-1W).
Jean C.,Nov.1957,(III-L-34).
Jean F.,June 1918,(II-215).
Jerome,1853-1935,(I*).
John D.,1885-1945,(I-D-1W).
John,Jr.,1917-1949,(I*).
Joseph A.,May 1961,(III-B-7).
Joseph H.,1894-1937,
 h/o Julia B,(III-G-11).
Joseph, can't read dates.??
Joseph,1890-1928,(I-E-4E).
Joseph,Apr.1961,(I-E-10E).
Joseph,May 1980,(III-H-35).
Josephine,1894-1985,w/o Joseph,(II*).
Judith Gaudet,Mar.27,1899,53y,
 w/o Antoine,(O/F).

Julia B.,1896-1983,w/o Jos.H.,(III*).
Leonard A.,1919-1944 in Germ.,{O}.
Leonard A.,Mar.1950,(III-H-6).
Lionel J.,June 1987,(III-H-34).
Mary C. Cousins,1900-1937,
 w/o Alph.,(III-G-44).
Mary,Nov.26,1932,72y,(II*).
Modeste Gaudet,Feb.1949,(II-196).
Norman J.,May 6,1895-Mar.8,1970,
 (I-D-6W).
Priscilla,1859-1942,(II*).
Prospere,Nov.8,1957,(III-B-7).
Robert,XXXX, inf.
Thomas,Aug.1927,(II-196).
Thomas A.,Jan.1937,(II-F-12S).
Urban F.,Mar.11,1901-Mar.8,1970,(I*)
XX,June 1933,w/o Euge.,(III-B-6).
XX,Mar.1970,w/o John C.,(III-L-34).
GARDNER
David R.,1948-1994,
 w/o Doris LeBorgne,{O}.
GARNEAU
Felix,1865-1944,(II-242).
Malvina Ste Croix,1870-1950,
 w/o Felix,(II-242).
Ovide,XXXX,(II*).
GARRISON
Yvonne E. Smith,1937-May 1990,
 (III-K-27).
GATO
Harold F.,1923-1994,
 h/o Theresa Gouzie, {O}.
GAUDET
Agnes Gallant,1893-1963,(III-G-44).
Beatrice E.,1888-1971,w/o Eman.,(I*).
Emanuel J.,1886-1925,(I-D-13W),(I*).
Isadore,1882-Mar.1945,(II-215).
John N.,1900,34y,(I*).
Richard,1887-1946,(III-G-44).
Rita,Apr.1925,(II-F-12S).
GAUDREAU
Agnes,1881-May 1956,
 w/o Joseph,(I-A-8W).
Aime,1899-1981,(II*).
Aldire Boucher,1859-1892,w/o Philias,
 (II-181).
Anne,June 1955,(II-63).
Arthur,1884-1913,(II-181).
Augustin L.,1857-Oct.1928,(I-C-2W).
Belzemire G.Perry,1872-1923,(II-181).
Clara,1896-1914,
 d/o Zephirin & Emma,(II*).
Conrad G.,1919-1920,(II*).
Denis,Oct.1965,(II-181).
Edesse,1882-1908,w/o Henry,(II*)
Edna Marie,1918-1992,{O}.

Emma B.,1867-Dec.1945,
  w/o Zeph.,(II-254).
Emma,Mar.1953,(I-C-2W).
Ernestine,June 1970,w/o Paul,
  (III-N-118).
Florentine Landry, Apr.1896,25y,
  w/o Napol.,(II-63).
infant,Dec.1891,(II-63).
inf/o Jesse,May 1918,(II-181).
inf/o Camille,1920,(II-254).
Jean B.,1838-1914,(II-181).
John B.,1854-1934,(II*).
Joseph,Sept.1929,(II-30).
Joseph,1889-1957,(I-A-8W).
Joseph Ovid,1898-Apr.1930,(I-B-2E).
Joseph,Jr.,July 1907,(II-30).
Laure,Nov.1968,(III-Q-49).
Louis,May 1905,(II-30).
Marie E.,Oct.6,1880,1y,(O/F*).
Muriel I.,1931-1932,(II-254).
Napoleon,1866-1949,(II-63).
Philias,1855-1935,(II*).
Philias,1887-1902,(II-181).
Pierre Z.,1902-1964,(II-63).
Rachel C.,1923-1926,(II-254).
Rose Anna,1892-1893,(II-181).
Sizaire Carleau1834-1918,
  w/o J.B.,(II-181).
Ulderic,1892-1929,(I-C-2W).
Wildred,1877-1903,(II*).
Yvonne,1896-1946,{O}.
Zephirin,1864-1934,(II-254).
XX, Aug.1919,w/o Jos.,(II-30).
XX, Feb.1918,w/o Phil.,(II-30).
XX, Mar.1926,w/o Napol.,(II-63).
XX, Feb.1946,w/o Ernest,(III-H-25)
GELINAS
Anna,Mar.1923,(II-59).
GENEST
Alice D.,Aug.1965,(II-F-8).
XX, Jan.1940,w/o Arthur,(II-F-8).
GEOFFROY
Regina,Oct.1918,(II-83).
GERVAIS
Elsie,Aug.1969,(III-N-110).
Joseph Alfred,1890-1950,(II-67).
Patricia,Dec.1965,(III-N-110).
Rose D.,1894-1986,w/o J.A.,(II*).
GIGUERE
Agnes,Oct.1990,(III-Q-235).
Alice,Mar.1975,(III-N-9).
Alice Bellefeuillem,1906-1991,
  d/o David & Mary (III-G-5).
Eliza,Oct.1967,(III-G-4).
Gerard,Jan.1990,(III-Q-235).
Jeanne P.,1943,(III-G-4).
L. Thomas,1937-1993,(III-N-9).

Laurent,Oct.1963,(III-N-9).
Lucien,1937,(III-G-4).
Philip,Jr.,1903-1971,h/o Alice,(III*).
Philippe,1875-1942,
  h/o Eliza Lebrecque,(III-G-4).
Robert L.,1930-1987,(III-G-4).
GILBERT
Eli,1881,(O/F*).
GILLESPIE
Pauline M. Dame,1924-1969,
  d/o Richard Earle Dame.
GILLIGAN
Lila Buotte,1906-1994,
  w/o Joseph P.,d.1959,(II*)
GILMAN
Irene,1930-1967,(III-G-30).
XX,Sept.1958,w/o John J.,(III-L-6)
GIRARD
Alfred,Aug.1887,(II-116).
Ann M.LaValle,1897-1982,(II).
Anna,1870-1921,w/o F.X.(II-250).
Annette,1899-1983,(II*).
Annie E.,1880-1943,w/o John B.,(II*).
child,Jan.1888,(II-101).
Elouise E.,1907-1928,(II*).
Eugene,1901-1979,(II*).
Francois X.,Jr.,1872-1923,(I-E-14W).
Francois X.,1846-1919,(II-101).
Henry J.,1914-1964,(II-116).
Henry X.,1894-1968,(II-101).
John B.,1875-1922,(II).
Louis,1926,(II-115).
Louisa Mae Filmore,1897-1962,
  w/o H.X.,(II-102).
Marie,1885-1971,w/o Wm.,(III*).
Napoleon,Aug.1900,(II-116).
Olive E.,1900-1985,(II*).
Priscilla,1924-1987,d/o Louisa M,(II*)
Wilfred,1876-1932,(I-A-8W).
William,1864-1935,(III*).
Xavier,June 1886,(II-116).
XX, Aug.1893,w/o Nap.,(II-116).
XX, Nov.1943,w/o John,(I-E-14E).
XX, Mar.1936,w/o Wilfrid,(I-E-14W).
XX, Aug.1887,w/o F.X.,(II-101).
GIRARDIN
Ilda Talon,1912,21y,w/o Lucien,(II*).
GIROUARD
Phauline,1885,1m,(O/F*).
Hector,June 1980,(III-N-191).
GLADU
Isaie,Nov.1957,(III-L-39).
Mary Ann,Aug.1968,(III-Q-49).
GLEASON
XX, Jan.1940,w/o Leo,(II-32).
XX, Jan.1926,w/o Philom.,(II-156).

GOAN
John E.,Mar.1953,(III-H-37).
GODIN
Arthur,1907-1986,(II*).
Augustin,Nov.1961,(III-J-6).
Frederic,Mar.1960,(III-N-77).
Germaine,1909-1937,(II*).
Henrietta,1874-1951,w/o Jules,(II*).
Jules,1861-1941,(II*).
Leo J.,1908-1993,
 h/o Cecile Chaisson, {O}.
GOFF
Nellie,1883-1963,(I-A-4E).
GOODY
Avie,Aug.1968,(III-N-69).
J.F.,July 1965,(III-N-69).
Peter,1869-1950,
 h/o Annie Richard {O}.
GOREY
Barbra,June 1952,(III-G-5).
John,Jan.1939,(III-G-5).
GOSSELIN
inf/o Joseph,Oct.1921,(II-169).
Joseph,May 1974,(III-N-155).
Leo A.,1940-1993,h/o Margaret
 Coulombe,(III-M-45).
Marie Antoinette,1991,(III-N-155).
GOTHRO
Annie,1889,38y,w/o Philip,(II*).
Mary E.,1892,11y,d/o P. & A.,(II*).
Philip,1908,59y,(II*).
GOUZIE/GOOZEY
Albert,1885-Apr.1968,(I-E-18W).
Ambrose,Feb.1962,(II-112A).
Ambrose,Nov.1969,(III-N-90).
Ambrose,Sr.,May 1921,
 Civil War Veteran,(II-220).
Blanche,Jan.1961,(II-112A).
Celine Pelletier,1864-Nov.1917,
 w/o Ambrose,(II-220).
Cleophine Hudon,1882-1963,
 w/o W.M.,(I-C-4E).
Francoise,1916-1928,
 d/o Wilfrid & Cleo.,(I-C-4E).
Henry L.,Nov.1993,(III-Q-288).
inf/o Tancred,1917,(II-24).
Mary P.,1875-1959,
 w/o Albert,(I-E-18W).
Mederic,July 1954,(I-C-4E).
Olivine,Mar.1979,(III-N-90).
Philippe,Jan.1983,(III-N-152).
Robert,1916-1991,
 h/o Theresa Martin,(III-Q-169).
Tancrede,May 1962,(III-N-90).
Theodore,Oct.1916,(II-24).
Wilfrid M.,1877-1954,(I*).
XX,Mar.1965,w/o August,(III-H-45).
XX, Feb.1919,w/o Ambrose,Sr.,
 (II-220).
3 infants,XXXX:
 Thomas C.Landry,
 Dianne M.Winslow, and
 Michael R. Taggert.
GOYETTE
Alfred,1866-1947,(III-H-7).
Almina Nadeau,1864-1950,
 w/o August {O}.
Anna,Feb.1955,(III-H-7).
Elmina Nadeau,Nov.1950,(II-200).
Fred Emile,Jan.1950,(III-H-7).
Georgiana,Sept.1954,(III-H-7).
Ludger,1921-1952,(II-112A).
GRADY
M. Louise,Jan.20,1898
 Mar.16,1980,w/o M.J.,(I*).
Michael J.,Sept.20,1892-
 Sept.2,1959,(I-A-7E).
GRAFFAM
Mary Kennie,1881-1933,
 d/o Mary A.,(II*).
GRAHAM
David,1859-1937,(II*).
Evelyn,Feb.11,1985,(III-M-8).
GRANT
Bertrand,1909-1950,(II-162A).
Blanche Girardin,1918-1991,
 w/o Bertrand,(II-162A).
Flora Harnois,Nov.1976,(II-173)
GRAVEL
Guillaume,1842-1922,(II-64).
Henry,1894-1970,(II*).
Joseph,1952,(II-F-1S).
Mary A.,1960-XXXX,(II*).
Obeline M.,1890-1950,(II*).
Rose E.,1866-1952,w/o Jos.,(II-F-1S).
GREEN
Alice Quinn,1881-1916,(II-144).
Christopher R.,1978,(I*).
inf/o Hubert,no dates,(III-N-38).
John J.,Aug.1968,(III-Q-34).
GREGOIRE
Alice Toussaint,1875-1964,(III-A-1).
Alma G. Morgan,1910-1967,(II*).
Bella Lapierre,1903-1960,(I-E-2W).
Delina,July 1941,(III-G-59).
Peter Edward,1889-1948,
 h/o Dora Cormier, {O}.
Pierre,Mar.1948,(III-G-59).
Philippe,1903-1957,(III-A-1).
Wilfrid,1874-1920,(III-A-1).
Wilfrid,1901-Mar.5,1951,(I-E-2W).
William,Dec.1930,(I-E-2W).
XX,Oct.1964,w/o Peter,(III-G-59).

GRENIER
Blanche G.,1903-1980,
w/o Archie E.,(II*).
Pauline,1941-1941,(II-F-9S).
GRESLEY
Michael,1871-Dec.1957,(II-301A).
Mina,1895-Sept.1961,
w/o Michael,(II-301A).
GREY
Julia Susan,1902,41y,w/o Jos.,{O}.
GRIFFITHS
ch/o Albert,Nov.1920,(II-145).
Elmer,1896-May 1941,(III-B-6).
Mary L.,1900-1994,w/o Elmer,(III*).
Nellie,1890-1910,(II*).
Sarah V.,1862-1910,(II*).
William J.,1860-1917,(II*).
GRIMARD
Joseph,Oct.1987,(III-Q-171)
Samuel,Apr.1984,(III-Q-171).
GRONDIN
Alberta C. Sampson,1902-Oct.1951,
w/o Simon,(III-K-2).
Anna E.,Boucher,Mar.14,1885-
Aug.26,1959,w/o J.Ernest,(I-A-4W).
Anna M.,1875-1938,w/o Herman,
(I-C-4E).
Emmanuel R.,Msgr.,1898-1973.
Ernest,Feb.1933,(I-A-4W).
Herman,1874-1934,(I-C-3E).
J. Ernest,May 21,1878-
Feb.1,1988,(I*).
Simone A.,1896-1971,(III*).
GUEVIN
Irene,July 1973,(III-Q-36).
Roger,Aug.1964,(III-Q-1).
GUILBAULT
Celina Letendre,1845-1919,
w/o Hubert,(II*).
GUILMETTE
Alphonse,1915-1992,
h/o Rita Deroche,(III-N-164).
Leo,1889-1959,(II-101).
GUIMOND
Alfred J.,1874-1952,(II-219A).
Amanda Bernier,1903-1993,
w/o Jos. O.,(1987),(III-K-33).
Anna M.,1878-1972,(III*).
Anne,Dec.1961,(III-L-62).
Arthur,1897-1934,(II-F-9S).
Blanche Lavoie,1917-1991,
w/o Robert,(III-L-44S).
Celina,1875-Sept.1951,w/o Joseph,
(II-F-9S).
Claudia D.,1873-Feb.1960,
w/o Alfred,(II-219A).
Joseph,1870-1949,(II-F-9S).

Martha,Nov.1984,(III-G-31).
Philip,1903-Sept.1966,(II-120A).
Ovide J.,1901-1987,(III*).
Robert,June 1985,(III-L-44S).
Romeo,1936,(III-G-31).
Rose Cote,Oct.1970,(III-N-38).
Samuel,Apr.1958,(III-G-31).
Valmont,Nov.1962,(III-N-38).
XX, Apr.1946,w/o Sam,(III-G-31).
GUITARD
Charles,1895-1965,(III-G-58).
Elizabeth,Jan.28,1933,(I-A-3E).
Frank,1881-1947,(III-G-58).
George,Oct.1972,(III-N-134).
J. Victor,1912-1991,
h/o Dorothy ,(III-Q-127).
Philomene Bouley,1871-1946,
wid/o Edward,{O}.
Regina,1891-1987,(III-G-59).
Stephen,Feb.6,1987,(III-Q-117).
HADDON
Dorothy,July 1989,(III-L-46N).
HAENSEL
Adrienne,Mar.1983,(III-H-37).
HAFNER
Charles J.,Nov.16,1889-
Apr.10,1965 (I*)
Elizabeth Burke,1937,54y,
w/o Charles,{O}.
Elizabeth S.,1890-1945,(II*).
HAGAN
Corinne B.,1898-1990,w/o Geo.,
(I-B-2E).
George,1900-1984,(I*).
William M.,Capt.1841-1906,{O}.
HALE
Florence R.,1920-1969,(III*).
HAM
John E.,1884-1979,(II*).
Katherine T. Doyle,1880-
Sept.1954,w/o John,(II-229)
HAMEL
Julian N.,1910-1986,(III*).
HAMILTON
Georgianna St.Cyr,1887-1947,{O}.
Pauline,Sept.1989,(III-H-24A).
XX,May 1947,w/o Dexter,(III-H-5).
HAND
Richard J.,1929-1993,h/o Phyllis
J. Pride, (III-J-1).
Theodore,May 1950,(III-J-1).
Winnifred,Dec.1959,(III-J-1).
HANDLEY
Emma Letarte,1900-1947,(II-49).
HANDLON
Adolphe,1891-1976,(III*).
Catherine,1951-1951,(III-A-10).

Edward R.,1923-1973,(III-A-10).
Flora L.,1893-1971,w/o John J.,(III*).
John J.,1896-1936,(III-A-10).
Robert J.,1916-1972,(III*).
HANLEY
Sonya Briton,1931-1971,(I*).
HANNA
XX,Feb.1942,w/o Theo.,(III-G-45).
HARNOIS
Agnes,Dec.1956,(II-173).
Dellerise,1888-1931,(I-E-17E).
Elise H.,1856-1936,w/o J.B.,(II-173).
Elizabeth J,.1929-1988,w/o Leo. P.
Elizabeth,Sept.1967,(III-N-113).
Flora,1886-1976,(II*).
Fredde,1891-1892,(II*).
Francoise,1905-1929,
  w/o Eugene, (I-C-3W).
Henry,Oct.1938,(II-173).
J. Baptiste,1851-1904,(II*).
John,1969,(III-N-113).
Leonard P.,1926-XXXX,(I*).
Mary,Sept.1984,(II-173).
Noe,May 1975,(III-L-40).
Philippe,Aug.1959,(II-173).
Raymond H.,1898-1971,(II*).
Theophile,1861-June 1947,(I-E-17E).
Mathilda S.,1859-1923,
  w/o Theoph.(I-E-17E).
HARRIMAN
Louis,1911-July 1984,
  h/o Germaine S. Caron,(III-K-25).
HARVE
Hubert,Aug.18,1882,62y,(O/F*).
Marie Aug.12,1880,15y,(O/F*).
HARVEY
Albertine,Mar.1981,(III-L-3).
Arthur J.,1898-1984,(II*).
Berndette,Sept.1990,(III-J-12).
ch/o Roger,May 1949,(II-177).
Caroline Delcourt,1858-1936,(II*)
Doris,1917-1990,(III-K-1).
Elie,June 1905,(II-32).
Elise,1867-1943,(III*).
Elmire T.,1860-1938,(I*).
George M.,1935-1989,
  h/o Priscilla C.,(III*).
Georgette,1911-1971,(III*).
Henri,1855-1927,(I*).
inf/o Romeo,June 1938,(II-F-10S).
James,1856-July 1934,(II-230).
Jane,1905-Feb.1990,(III-G-61).
Joseph,Nov.1942,(II-F-10S).
Lenore DeBrin,Mar.1902,
  w/o Elie,(II-32).
Ludger J.,July 4,1895-
  May 30,1966,(I*).

Mederic,1890-1955,(III-K-1).
Odon,1901-Aug.1960,(III-G-61).
Ovide,Mar.1955,(III-L-3).
Romeo,July 1973,(III-Q-108).
Rosanna,1890-Aug.1965,(III-K-1)
Thomas,May 1965,(III-J-12).
Valdor,1913-1993, w/o Doris
  Mason, d.1990, (III-K-1).
Wilda Morais,Feb.1948,(II-43).
William,Dec.1953,(III-J-12).
Wilphide E.,1878-1948,w/o Wm {O}.
XX,Mar.1957,w/o Thos.,(III-J-12).
XX, July 1939,w/o Henry,(I-B-3E).
XX,Aug.1936,w/o Jos.(II-F-10S)
XX,1943,w/o George,(III-G-61).
HAUGHNEY
Hannah,1821-1916,(II-184).
HAUSEMANN
XX,Mar.1968,w/o Alphonsine,
  (III-N-115).
HAWKES
Cecil,Sept.1962,(III-N-20).
HAYER
Blanche L.,1894-1981,(I*).
Lawrence,Jan.1986,(II-Q-182).
William A.,1894-1958,(I*).
HAYES
Margaret,1902,(II*).
Michael,Apr.1935,(II-120).
HEAD
Charles A.,1859-1938,(III-B-4).
Mary E.,1860-Apr.1939,
  w/o Charles,(III-B-4).
HEALY
Florence M.,1990,(III-N-115).
HEATHER
Malcolm,Apr.1916,(II-190).
HEBERT
Adeline Huard,1864-1907,
  w/o Elie,(II-143).
Adjutor,Feb.1969,(III-N-168).
Albert,Aug.1988,(III-N-31).
Alvina Rodrigue,1882-1962,(I-C-11W).
Anna H.,Mar.1966,(I-C-11W).
Arthur,1898-1916,(II-146).
Arthur,Nov.1956,(III-N-31).
Basilice,1895-Sept.1991,
  w/o Henry,(III-K-5).
Bessy Legere,1895-1991,{O}.
Damase,July 1933,(I-D-5W).
Edna,1901-1917,(II-146).
Edward,1875-1942,(III-G-53W).
Edward B.,1880-1964,(I*).
Elie,1865-1945,(II-143).
Elisa Duchesne,1863-1950,
  wid/o Philip,(II-146).

Elizabeth H.,1883-1925,
  w/o Edward B.,(I*).
Eugene,Jan.1970,(II-241).
Eugene J.,1902-1980,(II*).
Evelyn,1903-1993,(II-146).
Georgianna,1880-1987,(III*).
Gerald,Oct.1976,(III-Q-75).
Henry,Aug.1953,(III-K-5).
Henry,1896-1953,(III*).
Homere V.,1895-1950,(II-143).
Joseph A.,1871-1949,(II-113).
Joseph,1866-1946.
Katherine,1884-1943,(I-D-5W).
Louise,1991,w/o Leo H.,(III*).
Maryjane,XXXX,
  d/o John W.& Veronica,(I*).
Mary Alice,1864-1908,w/o Philip,(II*).
Mary J.,1873-1938,(II*).
Mary,Dec.1967,(I-D-5W).
Mary Mogan,1852-1928,
  w/o Damase,(I-D-5W).
Mathilde N.,Mar.1913,(II-143).
Ovide,Aug.1974,(III-Q-26).
Philippe,1870-1946,(II-146).
Philippe,Jr.,1902-1959,(II-146).
Poline,XXXX, inf.,(*).
Thomas J.,1849-1933.
Thomas J.,1892-1959,(I-C-11W).
Veronica, XXXX,w/o John W.,(I*).
William,1877-1944,
  h/o Georgianna, (III*).
XX, June 1947,(II-113).
XX,Mar.1938,w/o Joseph,(II*).
HEFNER
Charles,Apr.1965,(I-D-4W).
HELD
Albert F.,1905-1957,(I-A-4E).
Estella M.,1905-1961,(I-A-4E).
HENDRICKSON
Dorothy,XXXX,5m,(*)
HENRY
Ralph,Feb.1980,(III-N-173).
HERBERT
Dorothy M.,Feb.1922,(III*).
Earl K.,1920-1986,(III*).
Edward J.,1875-1942,(III*).
Jessie M.,1892-1979,(III*).
HERRICK
Robert N.,1929-1987,(II*).
HEYDRIE
Augustus,1868-1950,(II-128).
Mary Jane Graham,1863-1935,
  w/o Augustus,(II*).
HILL
Irma E.,1897-1924,(I-E-7W)
K.Lorraine,1931-1982,(I*).
Merle C.,1899-1985,(I*).

Nora F.,1875-1951,(I-E-7W).
Norman M.,1895-1952,(II-250).
Richard A.,1929-1929,(I*).
Ronald,June 1949,(II-250).
HODGSON
Ethel,Sept.1977,(III-Q-152).
HOLT
Eva Gallant,1904-1926,(I-D-1W).
Margaret A.,1884-1911,w/o Archie,(II*)
HOUDE
Gerard,Oct.1994,85y,
  h/o Jeanne Beaudoin.
HOULE
Clara,Sept.1937,(III-D-3E).
Delana,Mar.19,1882,21y,
  w/o Abraham A.,(O/F*).
XX,1921,w/o Abraham,(III-D-3E).
HOWARD
Denis T.,Sept.1954,(III-J-15).
Mary,Dec.1962,(III-H-30).
HUARD/E
Alex S.,1888-1928,(I*).
Barthelemy,1858-1918,(II-214).
Clara R. Labonte,1865- Feb.1942,
  w/o Barth.,(II-214).
Emile P.,1893-1937,(II-245).
Eva,1903,20y,w/o Bartholomew {O}.
Mabel E. Sinclair,1880-1956,
  w/o Alex,(I-B-7W).
Marie Maurice,Mar.20,1901,45y,
  w/o Bartholomew, (O/F).
Marie Anna,1889-1949,
  w/o Emilie,(II-245).
HUNEAU
Delima,1847-1924,w/o Francis,(II*).
Franc.,Dec.1923,(II-148).
Francis,1852-1909,(II*).
HUNT
Angelina G.,1895-1952,w/o A.C.,
  (I-D-11E).
Arthur C.,1888-1946,(I-D-11E).
HUNTER
Flora,July 1985,(III-N-42).
Guy,May 1983,(III-N-42).
infant,Aug.1930,(I-E-1E).
HUNTRESS
Frederick J.,1913-1992,
  h/o Margaret Larrivee,(III-N-78).
IRELAND
Lena,1898-XXXX,(III*).
JACKSON
Stanley P.,1933-1993,
  h/o Elizabeth,{O}.
JACQUES
Alma,Oct.1961,(III-N-66).
Beverly O.,1925-1993,(III-K-14).
Joseph,Feb.1980,(III-N-66).

Richard J.,1946-1984,(III*).
Thomas J.,1944-1989,(III-K-14).
JEAN
Delphine Arsenault,Mar.1962,
(III-N-21).
Felix,Aug.1960,(III-N-21).
JEFFERDS
Gertrude M. Gallant,1892-1993,
w/o George,d.1952,(II-F-12S).
Leonara M.,June 1955,w/o Lionel,
(II-F-12S).
Lionel,1909-1960,(II-120A).
Warren A.,Aug.1933,(II-F-12S).
JEFFREY
Madeline M.,1862-1943,(II*).
William,1859-1940,(II*).
JEROME
William,June 1974,(II-N-166).
JOHN
Catherine,Jan.1952,(III-H-42).
JOHNELEY
inf/o Joseph,1948,(II-82).
Lorraine Albert,May 1970,(III-L-68).
JOHNSON
Emilia,1897-1970,(I-E-4W).
Gerald B.,Apr.1958,(III-L-24).
Harry F.,1883-1948,
h/o Etta Morrisey,(II-F-3S).
Harry W.,1907-1982,(II*).
Marie Morrisey,May 1970,(III-E-3W).
Mary L. McEntee,1869-1938,
w/o Robert, (II-201).
JOLETTE
Andre M.,Sept.1989,64y,
h/o Claire Turgeon,(III-Q-240).
Henri,1879-Jan.1958,(III-K-4).
Antoina B.,1881-May 1955,
w/o Henry,(III-K-4).
JONES
Blanche Thibeault,1911-1992,
w/o Ellis,d.1982,{O}.
Bridget Mogan,1855-1912,
w/o W.H.,(II-113).
Henry (Joncas),1963,(III-H-45).
Joan R.,1942-1947,d/o Jos. & Ruth.
Joseph,Apr.1948,(III-H-19W).
William H.1850-1896,(II-113).
XX,Mar.1958,w/o Henry (Joncas),
(III-H-45).
JORDAN
Sarah J.,1889-1957,(I*).
JUTRAS
Belzemire,1874-1952,w/o Edm.,
(I-E-6W).
Bernadette,1903-1924,(I-E-6W).
Edmond,1868-1916,(I*).
Romeo,1898-1897,(I*).

Rudolph A.,1900-1974,(I-E-6W).
KEEFE
John,Apr.1957,(III-L-19).
KELLEY
Lawrence,May 1963,(III-N-104).
KENNEY
Elizabeth,Aug.1903,(II-126).
James,Mar.1952,(III-G-40).
John William,1915,(II-126).
Joseph,1871-1947,(II-144).
William C.,Aug.1914,(II-126).
Mary Ellen,1876-1957,
w/o Joseph,(II-144).
KENNIE
James,1877-1952,(III*).
Joseph,Apr.1989,(I-D-4W).
Mary A.,1845-1927,w/o Wm. J.,(II*).
Perley C.,Aug.1966,52y,
h/o Lillian Lampron,{O}.
S.Elizabeth,1882-1903,
ch/o Mary A.,(II*).
William C.,1885-1914,
ch/o Mary C.,(II*).
William J.,1836-1915,(II*).
KICHEN
Peter,1895-1930,(II*).
KIMBALL
Gladys,1922,(I-E-15E).
Mary,1967,(I-E-15E).
Wilbur,1943,(I-E-15E).
KINMOND
Bridget H.,1842-1920,
w/o George T.,(II-128).
John D.,Nov.1965,(III-J-9).
Nellie,Sept.1952,(III-J-9).
KING
Albert J.,1906-1959,(I*).
Jennie Roma,1912-1993,
w/o Raymond F.,d.1967,{O}.
John D.,1878-1944,
h/o Virginia Rioux, {O}.
Leo Felix,Feb.1920,16y,
s/o John & Virginia, {O}.
Mary,1894-1963,(I*).
Ovide,1915-1964,(I*).
Roland,1917-1972,(I*).
Vernon R.,Jr.,1926-1978,
h/o Theresa C.,(III*).
Virginia,1883-1953,(I*).
KIRKPATRICK
Nancy Lea,1951,d/o Geo.,(II-26).
KLUCHNIK
Eva,Apr.1967,(III-J-14).
KNEELEN
Clara,1888-1949,(II*).
KNIGHT
Lawrence,1983,(III-N-195).

Rachel,July 1988,(III-N-195).
KOON
William,Jan.1952,(I-C-6).
LaBARRE
John B.,1861-1929(I-B-6E).
LABBE
Francois,Oct.1933,(I-E-12W).
Ludovic J.,1895-1964,(I-E-12W).
Mildred,July 1982,(III-J-7).
S.Laforest,Oct.6,1902,47y,
  w/o Eugene,(O/F*).
XX, June 1923,w/o Francois,(I-E-12W).
LABERGE
Emma,June 6,1898,19y,(I*).
Charles,1855-May 1926,(II-3).
Heloise Francoeur,1864-1936,(II).
Joseph Noe,1865-1895,(I*).
Josephine,1881-1972,(II*).
Napoleon,1862-1918,(II-44).
Napoleon,Jr.,Mar.1936,(II-44).
Eliza Mailly,1859-1931,
  w/o Charles,(II-3).
XX, Nov.1936,w/o Nap.,(II-44).
LaBONTE/LeBONTE
Agnes,Aug.1962,(I-B-5W).
Melvina,1850-1929,(I*).
William D.,Jr.,1879-1902,(I*).
LABRECQUE
Albertha A.,Sept.4,1987,(III-Q-29).
Alma,Aug.1973,(I-C-5E).
Amanda Christmane,1882-Dec.1918,
  w/o Regis,(II-227).
Antonio,July 1957,(III-N-4).
Douglas C.,1977-1991,(III-N-8).
Eleonore Lemieux,1855-1904,
  w/o J.B.,w/o J.B.,(II-25).
Elizabeth Conant,Sept.1962,(III-N-8).
Eugenie,June 1981,(III-N-80).
Henry G.,1870-1947,(II*).
inf/o Edmond,Jan.1962,(III-N-4)
J.B.,May 1903,(II-25).
Jean B.,Jr.,1846-1938,(II-25).
Jeannette,1929-1994,w/o Emil,{O}.
Joseph,June 1975,(III-N-80).
Josephine,Sept.1891,(II-25).
Leo,July 1924,(I-E-9).
Lumina,Aug.1956,(I-C-5E).
Mae,Feb.1961,(III-N-4).
Marie Theriault,1869-1947,
  w/o Henry G.,(II*).
Myrtle,Jan.16,1988,(I-A-3E).
Phillippe,Jan.1992,(III-J-S-4).
Regis,1879-Mar.1958,(II-227).
Regis,May 1928,(II*).
Remi J.,1892-1984,(III*).
XX, Feb.1933,w/o J.B.,(II-33).
XX,Mar.1931,w/o Regis,(I-C-5E).

Yvonne Picher,1885-1959,
  w/o Regis, (II*).
LABRIE
Alfred,1990,(III-M-28S).
Margaret,July 1985,(III-M-28S).
LACHANCE
Adelard,Dec.1959,(III-N-48).
Armand,Dec.1961,(III-M-2).
Elizabeth,June 1991,(III-L-91N).
Oliva,June 1964,(III-M-2).
Romeo,1994,74y,h/o Stella Jalbert.
LACOMTE
Gedeon,Feb.1926,(II-5).
XX,w/o Gedeon,June 1922,(II-5).
LAFERRIERE
Delima,Oct.1952,(III-H-43).
LAFFIN
Eugene,June 1969,(III-Q-19).
LAFFY
Agathe,July 1904,(II-E).
Claude,July 1904,(II-E).
LAFLAMME
Antonio,1890-1962,(II-306S).
Ernest,Oct.1987,(III-N-162).
Evarist T.,1916-1969,(II-306S).
Margaret A.,1908-1992,(II-306S).
Zelia,1889-1964,w/o Antonio,(II*)
LAFOND
Agnes,1876-1962,(I*).
Arcade,1908,33y, (II*).
Arthur A.,1879-1966,(II*).
Georgina L.LaBonte,1882-1959,
  w/o Damese,(I-B-5W).
Joseph,1877-1926,(II*).
Katherine Dolan,1879-1960,(II-142).
Mary G.,Nov.1965,(III-G-17).
Maxine E.,1892,11m,(II*).
Rosalie Marguerite Decelles,1907,
  57y,w/o Sifroy,(II*).
Sifroy,1849-1909,(II*).
LAFRANCE
Albert,Apr.28,1987,(III-Q-218).
Alfred,1894-1945, {O}.
Alfred,1893-1949,(I-E-13E).
Alice LeBourgne1888-1976,(I-E-13E).
Edouard,Feb.1931,(II-110).
Raymond,Apr.1923,(I-E-13E).
XX, June 1935,w/o Ed.,(II-110).
XX, Feb.1957,w/o Aime,(II-110).
LAFRENIERE
Zephirain,Dec.20,1893,71y,(O/F*).
LALIBERTE
John F.,Nov.1957,(III-N-45).
LAMARRE
Irene R.,1905-1982,(I*).
Leo R.,1904-May 17,1987,(I-C-12E).

LAMBERT
Robert,July 1980,(III-Q-63).
Rose,June 1991,(III-Q-63).
LAMERANDE
Malvina,1862-1928,(II*).
LAMONTAGNE
Alfred Jos.,1887-1947,(I-D-4E).
Clara Toussaint,1876- 1946, (III-H-45).
Emma Gaudreau,1865-Mar.1928, w/o Jean B.,(I-D-4E).
Eugene,Jan.3,1899-Feb.6,1950, (I-D-4E).
Jean B.,1862-1930,(I-D-4E).
Mary,1893-Dec.1959,(I-E-3E).
Robert,Oct.30,1986,(III-Q-217).
LAMPRON
Albert,Dec.1950,(I-E-11E).
Avelena Brisson,1870-1921, w/o Emile,(III-B-2).
Edmond R.,1920-1992, h/o Theresa,d.1974,{O}.
Emilie B.,1865-1942,(III*)
Eugenie Lebron,1858-1921, w/o Luc.,(II*).
Joseph,Feb.1938,(III-B-2).
Lewis J.,1889-1972,(II*).
Mary,Aug.1976,(III-B-2).
Theodore J.,1944,(II-3).
Theresa Vincent,Nov.1994,70y.
Therese,Jan.1974,(III-N-142).
Mary H.,1887-1957,w/o Louis, (II-4-A).
LANDRY
Agnes Albert,1892-1951,(II-20A).
Alexander J.,1902-1971,(I*).
Alfred,Dec.1960,(III-N-60).
Alfred J.,Mar.1969,(III-H-19W).
Alfred,Nov.1949,(II-160A).
Alphonse,1896-1969,(III-A-12).
Amanda Guimond,1862-1930,(II*).
Amedee,1888-1968,(II-128A).
Amedee,July 1949,(II-249).
Anna Bretton,1890-1974, w/o Amedee,(II*).
Archie J.,1866-1930,(II*).
Arthur B.,1892-1940,s/o Clara, (II*).
Barbara Small,1917-1978, w/o Raymond,(II*).
Bernadette,1907-1967,(III*).
Blanche Brosseau,1883-1934, w/o J.C.,(III-B-9).
Carl,1908-1932, h/o Alice Aube Pellern,(I-C-7E).
Cecile,1920-1956,(II-160A).
Cedulie Lemieux,Apr.1947,(III-A-12).
Charles J.,1870-1940,{O}.
Charles,1867-1937,(III-A-12).
Charles,May 1933,(I-C-5W).
child/o Robert,1956,(I-E-13W).
Clara,1868-1949,(II*).
Daniel,1860-1956,(I-E-13W).
Delphine,Mar.19,1883,22y,(O/F*).
Delphine Gloutier,Mar.26,1909, 72y,w/o Jos.D.,(O/F*).
Edward,1895-1971,(III-A-12).
Elizabeth,June 1958,(III-H-4).
Ellen,190X-1944,(II*).
Elmire G.,1865-1944,w/o Jos.,(III-B-9).
Elyear,Dec.10,1873-May 12,1898, (O/F*).
Eugene,Dec.1961,(III-H-27).
Eva,May 1965,(III-N-96).
Florence M.,1919-1968,(II*).
Florence R.R.,1924-1983,(II).
Fred,1877-1949,(II*).
Frederic,Dec.18,1962,(III-B-9).
Georgianna,Feb.1978,(III-N-85).
Gertrude Couturier,Sept.1949, (III-H-27).
Helen,1901-1947,(III*).
Irene Lampron,1911-1993, w/o Leo, (III-M-26N).
J. Camille,Jan.1958,(III-B-9).
J. Jeremiah,Feb.18,1913- May 12,1961,(I-A-4W).
James,Sept.1908,(II-32).
Jeannette,1897-1969,(II-52A).
Josaphat,Feb.1950,(II-249).
Joseph C.,1886-1957,(III*).
Joseph C.,1898-1961,(II-A-12).
Joseph D.,Mar.17,1902,68y,(O/F).
Joseph,1892-1950,(II*).
Joseph,Dec.1937,(III-B-9).
Joseph,July 1,1893,58y,(O/F*).
Josephine,1877-1958,w/o Louis, (II-148).
Josephine,1905-1985,(III*).
Laurent,1960,child,(III-N-22).
Leona,Oct.1982,(III-J-10).
Linda,no date,sis/o Denise Welch.
Louis,Apr.1923,(I-E-13W).
Louis,1878-1964,(II-148).
Louis B.,1892-1975,(II-20A).
Margaret Milan,1902-1962, w/o Alexander J.,(I-C-5W).
Marguerite M. Grondin,Oct.17,1912- July 4,1983,w/o J. Jeremiah,(I*).
Maria,1884-1981,(II-104A).
Marie,Mar.1981,(II-160A).
Marie P.,1865-1938,(II*).
Mark,XXXX,(II*).
Martin,Mary A.,1893,36y,(I*).
Mary,1883-1981,w/o Fred,(II*).

Mary Celina Mason,1866-1908,
  wid/o George {O}.
Michael Joseph,Aug.1961,(II*).
Narcisse,June 1930,(I-E-13W).
Narcisse,1886-Nov.1935,(II-249).
Narcisse,Sept.1963,(III-H-27).
Noel, Apr.1911,(II-32).
Octiavie,Jan.1919,19y,(II-249).
Oliver J.,Dec.1994,79y,
  h/o Mildred Perkins.
Ovide,Oct.20,1891-Jan.20,1966,
  (I-B-6W).
Patrick,XXXX,(II*).
Raymond,Jan.1993,(III-L-69).
Robert Y.,1927-1959,(II-52A).
Robert,Dec.1959,(III-L-26).
Samuel,May 1923,(II-249).
Sedulie Lemieux,1866-1947,
  wid/o Charles, {O}.
Severine,1935,w/o Noel,(II-32).
Susan Blanchard,1887-1963,
  (I-E-13W).
Vincent, Arsene,Aug.21,1898,26y,(I*).
William,Oct.1946,(III-H-4).
Zephirin,Mar.3,1898,15y,(O/F).
Zephirin,1862-Feb.1936,(II-249).
XX,June 1944,w/o Leon,(III-A-12).
XX,1944,w/o Edouard,(III-A-12).
XX, Jan.1929,w/o Ovid,(I-B-6W).
XX, Mar.1938,w/o Daniel,(I-E-13W).
XX, May 1930,w/o Zephirin,(II-249).
XX,Mar.1945,w/o Wm.,(III-H-4).
LANGEVIN
Henry,1895-1974,(II-F-1N).
Medora,1916-1971,(II*).
Obeline "Minnie",1890-1950,
  w/o Henry S.,(II*).
LANGIS
Eudore,1966,(III-G-52).
Jeannine Landry,1931-1993,
  w/o Robert,d.1982,(III-M-14).
Jessica O.,Nov.1989,66y, {O}.
Josephine,Apr.1969,(III-G-52).
Robert,July 1982,(III-G-52).
Rose Belanger,1900-1994,
  w/o Germain {O}.
LANGLOIS
Augustin,1887-1894,(II*).
Clara,1872-1911,(II*).
Dalima,1851-1937,w/o J.B.,
  (II-147).
Frederic,1879-1911,(II*).
Jean B.,1846-1928,(II-147).
Jessica O.,Nov.1989,(III-L-48S).
Mederic,1886-1919,(II-147).
Walter,1879-1901,(II*).

LAPIERRE
Ambroise,1880-1925,(I-E-2W).
Isaac,Nov.20,1901,33y,(II*).
William,1869-Dec.15,1930,(I-E-2W).
Philomene,1873-1927,w/o Wm.,
  (I-E-2W).
LAPOINTE
Anatole,Oct.1901,(II-193).
Anne Marie,1878-1964,(II*).
Arthur David,1882-1952,(II-99).
Cecile M.,1916-1917,(II-99).
Christine,1846-1941,w/o David,(II*).
David, 1841-1907,(II*).
Dellerise,Sept.1907,(II-193).
Ernest,1863- 1948,(II-193).
J.A.Mederic,1903,(II-193).
Joseph Arthur,1877-1878,(II*).
Joseph Henry,1909,
  inf/o Henri & Ernestine,{O}.
Juliette,1904-July 1914,(II-193).
Romeo,1893-1935,(II-193).
Seneville,1868- Aug.1938,
  w/o Ernest,(II-193).
XX, Oct.1941,w/o David,(II-99).
XX, Dec.1964,(II-99).
XX, Oct.1918,w/o Barthel,(II-193).
LARIVIERE/LARREVERE
Alice Bourque,1864-1944,
  w/o J.B.,(II*).
Alice V.,1916-1984,w/o Eugene.
Cleophas,1849-1929,(II-204).
Frederic,Sept.1952,(II-204).
J.B.,1796-1894,(II*).
Marie Decormier,1843-1903,
  w/o Cleophas,(II*).
XX, Feb.1940,w/o Frederic,(II-204).
LARRABEE
Westley,1902-1962,(III-G-35).
LARRIVEE
Anne,Dec.1952,(II-F-7).
August M.,Apr.1945,(II-F-7).
Augustin,1864-1934,(II-205).
Aureli,1868-1917,
  w/o Augustin,(II-205).
Bertha W.,1905-XXXX,w/o Geo. R.,(I*)
Blanche,1900-1912,
  d/o A.M.& S.G., (II-F-7).
Delia,Sept.1981,(II-F-7).
Delia,1854-1898,(II).
Edgar,Oct.1905,(II-F-7).
Edouard,Oct.1918,(II-41).
Eugene J.,Oct.1977,(II-12A).
Eugene P.,Aug.1946,(III-G-29).
Elizad,1855-1934,w/o Augustin,
  (II-205).
Flora,Aug.1919,(II-233).
Gabrielle,Aug.1991,(III-Q-159).

George R.,1906-Sept.22,1986,
  (I-E-6W).
George Ls.,Sept.1989,(II-F-7).
Henry,Feb.1955,(III-H-51)
Henry Aime,Oct.1968,(II-F-7).
infants(6),XXXX,(II-11).
infant/o Leo,May 15,1919,(II-41).
Joseph,1868-June 1914,(II-41).
Joseph,Apr.1915,(II-11).
Joseph Paul,1946-1946,(II*).
Leda,Dec.1967,(III-N-154).
Lucie,Mar.1911,(II-156).
Marie A.,Sept.1988,(II-F-7).
Mary,1870-1929,w/o Albert O.,(II*).
Mary Jane Welch,1888-1976,
  w/o Oliva P.,(II*).
Olive,June 1990,(III-M-37S).
Ovila P.,1886-1971,(II*).
Robert,Aug.1982,(III-Q-180).
Roger,Feb.1979,(III-Q-159).
Ruth McFarland,1923-1992,
  w/o Eugene,(III-L-92N).
Thomas A.,Oct.1911,(II-156).
Virginia Laberge,May 1951,(II-12A).
Wilfrid,May 1961,(II-F-7).
Sisarie Gaudreau,1861-1923,
  w/o Auguste M.,(II-F-7).
XX, Aug.1907,w/o Jos.,(II-11).
XX, Feb.1898,w/o Jos.,(II-41).
LARRIVIER
Joseph,193X,67y,{O}.
LASHER
Irene,Oct.1992,(III-H-10).
LAUZON
Adelard,1902-1946,
  h/o Martha,(III-H-31).
LAVANGIE
Leroy,May 1953,(III-H-63).
Paul,1991,(III-H-63).
Robert,Apr.1948,(III-H-63).
LAVIGNE
Albert H.,1918-1992,
  h/o Gladys,d.1969,(III-K-37).
Aline,1904-1945,(II*).
Alma B.,1887-1916,(II*).
Arthur,May 1964,(III-N-67).
Bernadette Gladu Davis,1906-1991,
  (III-Q-81).
Gladys M.,1917-1969,w/o Alb.H.,(III*).
Henry,May 1980,(III-QS-(0.
Irene,Aug.1973,(III-N-148).
J. Gilbert,1889-1958,(II-223A).
Joseph,1865-1946,(III-H-53).
Josephine,Sept.1965,(III-N-67).
Ludger P.,1869-1954,(II*).
Mary Ann D.,1889-Mar.1958,
  w/o Wm.,(II-301B).

Mary Gertrude,1892-1972,
  w/o J.G.,(II*).
Mary L.,1875-1938,
  w/o Ludger P.,(II*).
Robert O.,1990,76y,(III-N-148).
Wilfred,May 1970,(III-Q-136).
William J.,1888-1964,(II-301B).
LAVIOLETTE
Berndaette Barr,1900-1956,
  w/o William.,(II-123).
Fabiola,1897-Dec.20,1986,(II-309B).
Georgiana,1860-1941,
  w/o Benj.,(II-123).
Joseph Adelard,1896-Aug.1965,
  (II-309B).
Leo,1922-Dec.1960,(II-309B).
Peter,1895-XXXX,(II*).
William,1893-1977,(II-123).
LAVOIE
Alexandre,Aug.1965,(III-H-28).
Honora G.,Sept.1994,90y,
  w/o Alexander.
Melande B.,1885-1963,(I*).
Phidime,1944,(III-H-23).
Philip,Nov.1988,(III-Q-228).
Raymond,1950,(III-H-28).
XX,Oct.1961,w/o Azelia,(III-H-23).
LAWRENCE
O. George,Dec.1991,(III-Q-225).
LEADBETTER
Claude,Jan.1956,(III-L-11).
LEAVITT
Francis,1919-1964,(III-G-63).
Julia G.,1893-1971,(II-215).
LEBEAU
Adelia Paquet,1880-1918,
  w/o Alfred,(II*).
Clifford,1900-1963,(II-F-11N).
Ellen M.,1879-1889,(II*).
Irene M.,1905-1982,(II*).
Julia A. Naylor,1854-1912,
  w/o Martin,(II*).
Lilly M.,1890-1891,(II*).
Martin,1951,(II-F-11N).
Martin,1848-1913,(II*).
ValerieSicard Martin,Dec.1921,
  44y,(II-F-11N).
XX,Aug.1918,w/o Alfred,(II-197)
LEBEL
Anne M.,1873-1961,(II-185).
Anne-Marie,July 1953,(II-82).
Bernadette,Jan.1990,(II-14-A).
Bernadette,Nov.1985,(III-N-187).
Eugenie,Dec.1970,(III-L-15).
Georgette F.,1914-1992,(II*).
Germaine,1904-1953,(II-185).
Hermaine,1853-1921,(III*).

Joseph E.,1864-1915,(II*).
Joseph,1900-1980,(II-185).
Lucien,Apr.1983,(III-N-187).
Machilda,Apr.1973,(III-L-41).
Marie Rouleau,1840-1928,(II-185).
Marie Pomerleau,1890-1947,
 w/o Stanilas,(III-G-25).
Paul E.,1908- 1992,
 h/o Alice Barr,(II-H-11).
Peter,1963,ch/o Ray.,(III-L-68).
Robert,1922-1938,(III-G-25).
Stanislas,1886-1949,(III-G-25).
Victoria,1858-1939,(III-C-2W).
Victorine,1885-1983,(III*).
Walter,July 1967,(III-L-15).
Willie,June 1974,(III-G-25).
LEBERGE
4 ch/o Napol. & Heloise, all (II*):
J.Eduoard,1888-1893.
Marie A.,1900-1901.
Paul C.,1883-1936.
R. Anna,1895-1897.
LEBLANC
Clara,1888-1972,w/o Ray,(III*).
Delphine Richard,1866-1948,
 (II-212).
Elizabeth,Sept.1987,(III-Q-200).
Eugene Pete,July 1989,73y,
 h/o Marguerite Galipeau, {O}.
Jean,Dec.1925,(II-169).
John,1925,(II*).
Raymond,1885-1933,(III-B-5).
Raymond H.,Apr.1990,47y,
 h/o Sandra Allen,(III-Q-199).
Rita O. Varney,1921-1983,
 ch/o Ray & Clara,(III*).
Roger,1922-1935,(III-B-5).
XX, Dec.1918,w/o Jean,(II-169).
LEBORGNE
Albert J.,1890-1950,(II-134).
Alexandre,Sept.1939,(II-134).
Alphonse,Sept.1952,(II-FA).
Aristide,1949,(III-D-9).
ch/o Charles,1961,(III-D-9).
ch/o Raymond,Apr.1959,(III-H-32)
Edmond,1860-1936,(I-E-13E).
Exsefe (?),1855-1939,
 w/o Edmond,(I-E-13E).
inf/Leon,1957,,s.b.,(II-FA).
Jean Charles,1921-1990,69y,
 h/o Yvoette,(III-D-9).
Joseph N.,1894-1971,(II*).
Joseph Oliver,1928-1938,(II*).
Marie Ann,1896-1978,
 w/o Joseph N.,(II*).
Mary Potvin,1880,21y,
 w/o Alexandre,(II*).

Michael,Mar.1957,(II*).
Offalline,Oct.1979,(III-D-9).
XX,1943, w/o Alexandre,(II-134).
LEBOUVIER
Felix,1889,(II-127).
LEBRUN
Emma,1860-19XX,w/o A.L.,(I*).
LECARREE
Joseph T.,1895-1944,(II*).
LECLAIR
Albertine,1902-1969,(III*).
baby,Aug.1966,(III-G-22).
Elizabeth,1863-1942,w/o Stan.,
 (II-315).
Eugenie,1898-June 1990,92y,
 w/o Harry,{O}.
Harry R.,1920-1932,(III*).
Harry,1897-Feb.1970,(II-180).
Leo F.,1894-1928,(I*).
Stanislaus,1856-1937,(II*).
William L.,1892-1951,(II-315).
LECLERC
Alcide,1906-May 1961,(III-G-56).
Bertha,Oct.1988,(III-H-42).
Darilos ?, Feb.1974,(III-H-42).
Jos. L.?, Oct.1970,(III-Q-28).
Roland,May 1949,(III-H-42).
LECOMTE/LECONTE
Augustin,1858-1913,(II-175).
Octavie L.,1859-, Sept.1933,
 w/o Augustin,(II-175).
LeCONTE
Adrian T.,1908-1986,(II*).
Arthur,1899-1937,(II*).
Eugene F. Sr.,1897-1971,(II).
Gedeon,1896-1913,(II*).
Hazel C.,1895-1970,(II*).
Leona M.,1916-1979,(II*).
Lionel,1902-1966,(II*).
Napoleon,Jr.,1888-1931,(II-310S)
Napoleon Sr.,1860-1945,(II-310S).
Olumine M.,1866-1932,
 w/o Napoleon,Sr.,(II-310S)
XX,Jan.1917,w/o Eugene,(II-172).
LEDOUX
Ann Egan,1850-1924,w/o Marcel,
 (I-E-6E).
Charles J.,1888-1964,(I-E-6E).
Charles J.Jr.,Rev.,1913-1969.(I*)
Flora D.,Feb.1960,(III-L-30).
Linda A.,July 1949,(I-E-6E).
Marcel,1846-1929,(I-E-6E).
Ovila,Feb.1955,(III-L-30).
Sabine M.,1890-1972,(I*).
Vincent A.,Dec.1928,(I-E-6E).
LEDUC
Eva Arsenault,Apr.1951,(III-G-5).

LEE
Rosie Woods,1921-1991,
 w/o John G.,(III-M-38N).
LeFAY
Claude,July 1904, {O}.
LEFEBVRE
Antoine,1882,59y,(II*).
Bertha T.,Aug.1989,74y,(III-N-140).
Olumina Olympe,1890-1946,{O}.
Grace Rioux,Nov.1989,92y,
 w/o Philip E.,(III-G-63).
Hormisdas,Nov.1954,(III-J-18).
Joseph F.,1887-1967,(II-180).
Joseph M.,1860-1929,(II-180).
Lumina,1890-1946,(II-180).
Leonise Lamontagne,1869-1927,
 w/o Jos.M.,(II-180).
Marcella,1927-1992,(III-N-140).
Napoleon,Mar.1968,(III-N-140).
Philip E.,1897-1991,
 h/o Grace Phaneuf,(III-G-63).
LEGARRE
Joseph,Feb.1944,{O}.
LEGERE
Edmund J.,Jr.,1914-1993,
 h/o Laura Poirier,d.1985,(III-G-12).
Laura,1985,(III-G-12).
Leah,1897-Sept.1965,(III-K-5).
Matthias,Mar.1955,(III-L-37).
Valeda,July 1981,(III-L-37).
LEIGHTON
Arthur L.,1892-1956,(III-G-2).
Elvin Alexander,1872-1951,(II-52).
Gladys B. Graffam,1893-1969,(III-G).
Maria Beniot,1868-1939,(II*).
Paul E.,Dec.1932,(II-59).
J. Percy,1872-1939,
 h/o Phoebe Fournier,(III-G-2).
Philomina,1875-1956,(III-G-2).
Priscella,Oct.1975,(III-N-161).
Robert,June 1949,(III-H-49).
Roland B.,1903-1984,(II*).
Royden,1990,74y, h/o Simone
 Belanger,(III-N-161).
LEMAY
Francois,July 1973,(III-L-67).
Marie,Aug.1976,(III-L-67).
Mark,Aug.1974,(III-L-67).
Raymond,July 1958,(III-L-67).
LEMIEUX
Aime,1896-1964,(II-171).
Cyprien,Sept.XXXX ,(II-246).
Delia Gagnon,Apr.5,1883-
 Aug.30,1921,w/o Wilfrid.
Elizabeth,Nov.1975,(III-Q-89).
George P.,1940-1950,(II-94).
2 inf/o Eugene,1920,(II-246).
Laura,1896-1960,w/o Aime,(II-171).
Leo,Dr.,1900-1971,(II-94).
Marguerite,June1904,73y,
 w/o Victor,(II-25).
Roland A.,May 1988,(III-N-163).
Sedulie,1866-1947,(II*).
Victor,Mar.1898,(II-25).
Wilfrid,Dec.8,1875-
 Sept.23,1930,(I-C-12E).
XX, Aug.1919,w/o Cyprien,(II-246).
LENNEVILLE
Adjutor J.,1894-1974,(III-G-35).
Aglaee,1864-1943,w/o J.W.,(III*).
Joseph W.,1866-1941,(III-G-35).
Kathleen Vallee,1897-1971,
 w/o Prospere,(III*).
Prospere,1897-1952,(III-G-8).
LEPENVEN
Adeline,1902-1963,(III-G-57).
Albert,Oct.1954,(III-J-17).
Arthur O.,1911-1993,h/o Viola
 McKenney,(III-G-57).
Charles J.,1855-1935,(III-G-57).
Joseph A.,1896-1952,(II-205).
Virginia LePage,1870-1944,
 w/o Charles,(III-G-57).
LEROUX
Amedee,1870-1904,(II*).
Gerald,Sept.1969,(III-N-116).
Julia Garneau,1898-1960,
 w/o Wilfrid,(II-68).
Wilfrid,1898-1970,(II-68).
LESSARD
Amanda,June 1970,(III-N-131).
Leo,Mar.1961,(III-N-65).
Theodore,Oct.1972,(III-N-131).
LESTAGE
Melanie,Mar.1960,(III-N-73).
Zephirin,Aug.1969,(III-N-73).
LETARTE
Arthemise,1888-1903,(II-49).
Arthur G.,1884-1953,(II-221A).
Elise,1885-Jan.1955,(II-221A).
Helen,Feb.1964,(III-N-25).
Henriette Perroult,Sept.1923,
 w/o Pierre,(II-36)
Joseph Cleon,1922-1993,
 h/o Rose Fecteau,(III-L-52S).
Josephine,1888-1974,(II-221A).
Lucienne,1897-1992,(III-G-9).
Marie,May 1927,w/o Paul,(II-49).
Marie Yvonne,1897-1935,(III*).
J. Ovide,1894-1980,(III-G-9).
Paul,1859-1934,(II-49).
Pierre,1855-1912,(II).
Valmont,Nov.1987,(III-Q-163).

LEVESQUE
Amable,1891-1950,(I-C-1E).
Anthime,Mar.1961,(III-N-51).
Bruno,1826-Sept.1916,(II-4).
ch/o Robert,Feb.1956,(III-H-54).
Christina.1900-1969,(III-G-50).
Damase,Mar.1934,(II-F-8A).
Euphemia,1867-Apr.1941,
 w/o F.X.,(I-C-1E).
F. Xavier,1865-1928,(I-C-1E).
Georgiana,Nov.1988,(III-N-51).
Gerald C. Fluett, 1920-1988,
 s/o Marie Levesque,(I*).
Henri T.,,Sept.1976,(I-E-14W).
Marie,1880,29y,(II*).
Marie,1856-1927,w/o Michel,(II-102).
Marie,1888-1984,(I*).
Marie Houle,1866-1948,(III-G-43).
Michel,1854-1937,(II-102).
Napoleon,1900-1947,(III-H-54).
Philomine,Mar.1924,(II-4).
Theophile,1889-1932,(III-G-43).
Theophile,1899-1951,(III-G-50).
Yvette,1907-Nov.1977,(II-193).
LEWIS
Arthur,June 1963,(III-N-105).
LINSCOTT
infant,Apr.1962,(III-A-5).
LIBBY
David Clifton,1953-1954,(*).
LIRETTE
Benjamin Wood,Mar.1950,(II-65).
Marie-Jeanne,1875-1956,(III-A-9).
LITTLE
Cynthia,Dec.1900,73y.
LIZOTTE
Adeloza,Dec.1994,89y,
 w/o Bruno,d.1982.
Bruno J.,1903-1982,
 h/o Adelaza C.,(*).
Conrad G.,1931-1933,
 s/o B.J.& A.D.,(*).
Lucille,May 1987,(III-Q-216).
Paula,Nov.1976,(III-K-21).
Ronald,1948-1976,
 h/o Paula W.,(III*).
LOCKE
Stephen,May 1967,(III-Q-67).
LONG
Aurore Gaudreau,1963,(I-C-2W).
Catherine,Aug.1951,(I-D-15)
LORING
Katherine L.,1884-1951,(I*).
William L.,1894-1924,(I*).
LOYAL
Cecile,Nov.25,1882,68y,
 w/o Louis,(O/F*).

LUSSIER
Exilia Leclerc,May 1941,(II-58).
Philias,Feb.1903,(II-58).
LYDEN
James,Aug.1962,(III-M-9).
Mary Joyce,Oct.11,1933-
 Feb.28,1935,(I-D-10).
MAHER
Ernest,XXXX,Canadian Soldier,(II*).
MAHONEY
Ellen T.,Jan.1957,(III-G-40).
MAILHOT
Alice,1900-1933,(II*).
Jeremie,1843-1917,(II-8).
Joseph,1896-1977,(II-16).
Mary,Sept.1969,(II-8).
Mederic,Jan.1903,28y.(II-8).
XX,July 1923,w/o Mederic,(II-8)
XX, Nov.1923,w/o Jeremie,(II-16).
XX,Feb.1945,w/o Joseph,(III-B-8).
MAILLET
Emile,Nov.1976,(III-N-123).
Eva, June 1931,(II-188).
Flora,Jan.1970,(III-N-123).
Frank,May 3,1939,(II-27).
Theodore,Aug.30,1986,(III-J-2).
Valerie"Blanche" Danis,1910-1991,
 w/o Theodore,(III-J-2).
MAILLY
Dominic,Dec.1891,(II-109).
Ludger,1899-1975,(II-167).
Robert,June 1970,(III-Q-71).
XX, Jan.1908,w/o Dominic,(II-1909).
XX, Nov.1940,w/o Dominic,(II-167).
XX, Jan.1955,w/o Ludger,(II-167).
MALACHOWSKI
Edward,1991,(III-Q-279).
MALLIA
May Anna,1960,(I*).
Mildred L.,1925-1989,(I*).
MALLOY
Angela,Nov.1982,(III-Q-182).
XX,grd/o Lawrence Hayer,
 Jan.1986,(III-Q-182).
MANNION
Mary,1874-1901,(O/F*).
MARCOUX
Alma Payer,1899-1939,
 w/o Pierre,Jr.,(II-182).
Delia Pomerleau,1862-1934,
 w/o Pierre (II-182).
Edouard,1891-1891.
Gideon,1889-1897,(II*).
Pierre,1861-XXXX,(II*).
Pierre,1888-1956,(II-182).
MARIER
Joseph,1880-1972,(O).

Leo J.,1910-1993,
  h/o Sarah,(III-K-3W).
Marie,1871-1951,w/o Joseph,
  (III-K-3E)
Roland A.,1906-1983,{O}.
MARION
Ls.Phil,1944,(I-C-9W).
Robert J.,1944,(I-C-9W).
Robert,Jan.1928,(I-C-9W).
XX,Feb.1937,w/o L.Phil,(I-C-9W).
MARROTTE
Louise Racicot,1923-1993,
  w/o Rodolphe,(III-M-48).
MARTEL/L
Agnes,May 1968,(III-M-8).
Albaney,Feb.1975,(III-Q-8).
Delvina Ouellette,1855-July 1916,
  (II-190).
Honore,1847-Nov.1927,(II-190).
James,Aug.1960,(III-M-8).
James,Nov.1,1986,(III-M-8).
Yvonne Rose,Sept.1966?,(III-Q-8).
MARTIN
Alphee,Nov.1977,(III-N-102).
Amanda,June 1988,(III-N-111).
Amanda Duval,1864-1902,
  w/o Joseph,(II*).
Amanda,1888-1906,
  d/o J.&A.M.,(II*).
Anna,1889-1961,(II-22).
Archie,Oct.1962,(III-N-102).
Celina,June 1968,(III-N-102).
Delia,1863-1939,(II-F-11N).
Edmond,June 1956,(III-L-25).
Elise L.,1885-1974,(II*).
Ephrem,1862-1921,(III-E-1W).
Jessie M.,1887-1956,(II*).
Joseph,1882-1907,s/o J.& A.M.,(II*).
Joseph N.,1867-1942,(II-239).
Joseph,1858-1917,(II-22).
Joseph L.,1894-1964,(II-305S).
J.Robert,1928-1946,(I-D-4W).
Laurent,1859-Jan.1947,(II-211).
Lauretta,1896-1973,(II*).
Marguerite,1896-XXXX<(II*).
Mary A.,1893,(O/F*).
Marie,1982,(III-QS-18).
Mary Bernadette,July 1989,90y,
  w/o John,(III-L-25).
Ovide J.,1895-1979,(II*).
Philip L.,1918-1983,(II*).
Robert F.,1920-Mar.1990,
  h/o Victoria Kumore,(III-Q-246).
Romuald,Apr.1959,(III-E-1W)
Simonne Jolette,1909-1949,(III-A-5).
Suzanne,1865-1944,
  w/o Laurent,(II-211).

Sylvere,Mar.1931,(II-196).
Theodore,Mar.1974,(III-Q-114).
William B.,Oct.1956,(II-309A).
Yvonne,1900-1976,w/o Ovide,(II*)
Marie Louse Truedill,1864-1934,
  w/o Ephrem,(III-E-1W)
XX, Mar.1956,w/o Jesse,(II-309A).
MARTINEAU
Alfred,1891-1920,(II-179).
Arthur,Aug.1963,(III-43).
Elise,1866-1944,w/o Marc,(II-179*).
Eugenie,1889-1915,w/o Alf.,(II-179*).
Georgianna,1909,w/o Napoleon.
Irene,1914-1933,(II-179).
Marc,1867-1945,(II-179).
Mark,Jr.,July 1951,(II-179).
Olive Albert,July 1951,
  w/o Mark,Jr.,(II-179).
Raymond,Dec.1926,(II-179).
Rebecca Hebert,1900-1943,
  w/o Arthur,(II-43).
Wilfrid,1893-1916,(II-179).
MARZUL
Stanely,Nov.1990,(III-QS-35).
MASKIEWICZ
Charles,1886-1965,(I*).
MASON
Fred,1887-1945.
Mary, 1910, 23,{O}.
MASSON
Jean,Dec.1917,(II-98).
MATHEWS
Edward,1880,9y,s/o Geo.,(II*).
George,1838-1907,(II*).
Mary Ann,1832-1917,w/o George,(II*).
MAUK
Louise P.,Mar.1979,(III-Q-161).
MAURICE
Laurent,1825-1908,(II-68*).
MAVODONES
Janes M.,1942-1971,(II*).
MAXWELL
Sara Quinn,Nov.1947,(III-H-40).
MAY
Daniel,Dec.31,1899,{O}.
MAYO
Scott,Apr.1963, ?.
McCANN
John F.,Apr.17,1947,(I-D-9E).
McCLELLAN
Evelyn W.,1908-1977,(II*).
McCORMICK
Charles A.,III,1941-1941,(III-G-34).
McCROARY
John P.,Aug.1954,(III-Q-3).
McCULLOUGH
Alice E.,1908-1987,(I*).

Henry F.,Jr.,1902-1963,(I-D-10E).
Henry F.,Sr.,1861-1925,(I*).
Lillian L.,1904-1974,
  w/o Henry J.,Jr.,(I*).
M. Thomas,Sept.1994,57y,
  h/o Claire LaChance.
Martin,Dec.1957,(III-L-27).
Mary Joyce,1868-1955,
  w/o Henry J.,Sr.,(I-D-10E).
Michael J.,Mar.31,1896-
  May 7,1966,(I*).
MacDONALD
Florence L.,1914-1981,(II*).
Herbert,1900-1986,(II*).
Lester E.,1941-1966,(II*).
McDONOUGH
Barbara,Jan.1939,(II-106).
Bartholomew,1868-1895,(II-106)
John A.,Sept.1966,(III-Q-6).
Katherine,1878-1898,(II-106).
Mary E.,1874-1920,(II*).
Mary,1839-1907,w/o Thos.,(II-106).
Sarah,1870-1905,(II-106).
Thomas,1843-1915,(II-106).
William,1866-1923,(II-106).
McENTEE
Rose A. Trayner,1846-1918,
  w/o James,(II*).
McFARLAND
Alice M.,1887-1977,(III*).
Esther J.,1920-1932,(III*).
McGEE
John,Mar.1974,(III-Q-113).
McGUIRE
Bernard,Dec.1963,(II-C).
Ellen Welch,1864-1950,(II-C).
Helen M.,1896-1904,(II-C).
Thomas,1856-1937,h/o Ellen,(II).
William B.,1891-1963,(II).
McHUGH
Bridgette,Feb.1925,w/o Patrick,
  (I-E-3E).
Patrick,1871-1913,(I-E-3E).
McINNIS
Ann,Nov.1963,(III-H-16).
McINTEE
Mary T.,Sept.1918,(II-201).
McKENZIE
Howard A.,1893-1957,(II-193).
Olive,1896-1978,(III*).
McLAUGHLIN
Blanche,June 1953,(III-H-39).
Lazare A.,1867-1947,(III-H-39).
Louis,Aug.1964,(III-N-68).
Warren,Oct.1959,(III-H-39).

MELANCON
Emilienne Arsenault,Aug.1948,
  (I-C-11E).
Francois, 1915, {O}.
McLEOD
Patricia,1927-1933,(III*).
MERCIER
Alphonse,1875-1933,(II*).
Cecilia,Jan.1975,(III-Q-112).
Joseph,Aug.1976,(III-Q-112).
Lawrence A.,Sr.,1910-1990,79y,
  h/o Sylvia,d.1962, (III-G-32).
Norman,Jan.1990,(III-G-32).
Sylvia Turgeon,Feb.1962,w/o L.A.,
  (III-G-32).
METCALF
Pauline,Aug.1956,(III-N-15).
METHOT
Albert L.,Oct.1930,(I-C-8W).
Alice M.,1901-1937, w/o O.J.,(I*).
Alice M.,1921-1944,
  d/o O.J.& A.M.,(I-C-8W).
Homere J.,1893-1958(I-C-8W).
Irene R.,1932-XXXX,d/o O.J.&A.M.,(I*)
XX Nadeau,1937,36y,w/o Homere,
  (I-C-8W).
METIVIER
Alfred,Feb.1920,(I-E-17W).
Alfred,June 1932,(I-E-17W).
Conrad G.,1919-1991,
  h/o Rene Tardiff,(III-Q-262).
Emma Auclair,Dec.1950,
  wid/o Alfred,(I-E-17W).
George,July 1978,(I-E-17W).
MEYLEN
XX, 1944, w/o Albertine,(II-F-11S).
MICHAUD
Leo,May 1970,(III-N-11).
Louis,Sept.1964,(III-Q-5).
Rudolph L.,1926- 1991,
  h/o Beatrice Harnois,(III-Q-259).
Severine A.,1880-1939,w/o Ths F,(III*)
Thomas F.,1944,(III-G-13).
MICHEL
Lucien,June 1966,(III-Q-38).
MICHIELETTE
Gayle,1991,(III-L-97N).
MINERVINO
Martin M.,1915-1994,
  h/o Rita Richards,{O}
MITCHELL
Clara McFarland,XXXX,(II*).
MOGAN
Bridget,1828-1902,w/o Mathias,(II*).
George R.,1926-1986,(I*).
Mathias,1817-1899,(II*).
Michael F.,1885-1933,(I-A-4E).

Sarah, Nov.1957,(I-A-4E).
MOLINSKEY
Frank,1888-1942,(II*).
MONDOR
Bernadette,June 1989,(III-L-95S).
Edward W.,1920-1976,(III-K-20).
Gabriel,Apr.1988,(III-L-95S).
Irene A.,Mar.12,1982,(III-L-88).
Lucien,Sept.1980,(III-L-88).
Viriginia,Sept.1967,(III-L-23).
MONGEAU
Moise,Mar.1929,(I-B-8W).
Moise,Mar.1976,(I-B-8W).
MONTDOR
Joseph,Mar.1957,(III-L-5)
Isidore,Apr.1954,(III-J-13).
Theresa,Apr.1983,(III-L-5).
XX Bouthillette, July 1962,
  w/o Albina, (III-L-5).
MORABITO
Hilda F.,1913-1959,w/o Fred,(II*).
MOREAU
Aime,July 1971,(III-L-33).
Aime,Dec.1979,(III-Q-166).
Alda,1918-Feb.1927,s/o P.& E.,
  (I-D-6E).
Anglea,Mar.1919,(II-134).
Anna H.,1892-1972,
  w/o Geo.E.,(III*).
Arthur,1932-1944,s/o P.J.,(III-D-3E).
Arthur J.,1915-1985,(II).
Arthur R.,1990,75y,
  h/o Marie Swim,(III-Q-150).
Elise Tessler,1885-1950,
  w/o Philip,(I-D-6E).
Ernest Eli,1893-Jan.1945,(II-221).
George Edward,1890-1971,(III*).
George,1884-1946,(III-H-3).
Henry J.,Mar.1965,(III-L-37).
Iolande,Apr.1924,(II-134).
inf/o Rene,Dec.1948,(II-134).
Malvina,Sept.1964,(III-L-37).
Olivine Clement,1863-Apr.1940,
  w/o Victor,(II-221).
Peter Michael,1942-1977,(II).
Philip,1882-1965,(I-D-6E).
Philip,1975,(III-D-6).
Realde,Oct.1919,(II-134).
Victor,1859-June 1917,(II-221).
XX,1944,w/o George,(III-H-3).
XX,May 1957,w/o Aime,(III-L-33).
XX,Sept.1955,w/o Edm.,(III-L-31).
MORENCY
Alice,1890-Mar.1929,(II-252).
Pierre,Aug.1934,(III-E-3E).
MORGAN
Alma G.,Sept.1967,(III-A-1).

MORIN
Albert,Jan.1968,(III-H-50).
Alice H.,1889-Mar.1980,(II-232).
Arthur C.,Jan.1922,(II-232).
Arthur,Dec.1957,(III-N-58).
Clementine,Mar.1970,(III-Q-56).
Ethel Raymond,Mar.1973,(III-Q-102).
Helene,1858-1925,w/o Theod.ore,
  (I-E-4W).
inf/o Leopold,1957,s.b.,(II-232).
Joseph,1859-1928,(II-222).
Joseph Louis,1884-1930,(II-216).
Lina G.,1891-July 1977,(II-232).
Marie Louise Laberge,1885-
  Aug.1959,w/o Jos.L.,(II-216).
Noel D.,1885-1983,(II*).
Paul,Feb.1969,(III-Q-56).
Paul Eugene,1915-1916,(II*).
Philippe A.,1916-1917,(II-216).
Rachel,Dec.1918,(II-232).
Roseanna,1887-1919,(II*).
Rosilda,Apr.1918,(II-210).
Theodore,1858-1928,(I-E-4W).
Victoria,1859-1916,w/o Jos.,(II-222).
MORRILL
Marie Poule,Aug.1974,(III-L-56).
Michael,Oct.1960,(III-L-56).
MORRIS
Alfreda,Apr.1986,(III-H-33).
William,1889-1948,
  h/o Elfrida Belanger,(III-H-33).
XX, 1858-1907, w/o Chas.F.(II).
MORTON
Eben,1867-1934,(II*).
E. Barrett,1897-1918,
  s/o Eben & Mary (II*).
Mary A.,1862-1904,w/o Eben,
  (II-A).
MOSKEIWIZ
Kazinez,May 1965,(I-D-2E).
MULHERN
Harry,Feb.1971,(III-Q-75).
MULLIGAN
John,1872-1959,(III-G-14).
Mary Barry,1877-Sept.1959,
  w/o John,(III-G-14).
MULLIN
Anna H.,1898-1935,(II-173).
MUNROE
Diane Gosselin,1965- 1992,
  w/o Terrance,(III-M-45S).
MURPHY
Alice N.,1886-1961,(II*).
Annie Louise McDonough,1876-
  1907,w/o John,(II-106).
Anne,July 1948,(II-130).

Annie J. Kane,1844-1918,
  w/o Stephen,(II*).
Delia,1872-1927,(II*).
John,1874-1947,(II-122).
Josephine Sirois,1875-1950,(II-162).
Nora,Nov.1958,(II-130).
Octavie Lecomte,1880-1959,(II-175).
Robert J.,1882-1973,(II*).
Stephen,1840-1903,(II*).
Thomas,1914-1917,
  s/o J.J. & Octavia,(II-175).
MURRAY
Anna Frances,May 1909,
  d/o Daniel & Catherine,{O}.
Marie Mabel Swyer,1910,4m,
  d/o Felix & Ida,{O}.
MUSHREAU
Lititia,Mar.1966,(III-Q-16).
NADEAU
Auguste,1865-July 1945,(II-200).
Barbara,1963,(*).
Cymodocee,1862-1944,(II-37).
Damase,1838-June 1920,(II-200).
Emile J.,1885-1976,(I-C-5W).
Emilina Goyette,1864-1950,(II*).
Ferdinand,1893,63y,(II).
Freeman,Aug.1977,(III-N-179).
George,1918-1941,(III-G-28).
Helene,1929-1961,(III-G-28).
Joseph,July 1946,(I-C-8W).
Leon,1884-Sept.1962,(III-G-28).
Lillian N.,1897-1973,
  w/o Emile J.,(I-C-5W).
Maria L.,1888-1953,w/o Leon
  (III-G-28).
Marie Belanger,1840-1929,
  w/o Damase,(II*).
Mathilda,1883-1961,d/o T.&P.,
  (I-C-5W).
Octavie,1900,{O}.
Philomen,1857-1930,w/o Thos.,
  (I-C-5W).
Robert J.,1949-1969,(III*).
Robert,1915-Aug.1936,(I-C-5W).
Sarah Morin,1900,70y,
  w/o Ferdinand,(II*).
Theresa M. Small,1913-1966,(III*)
Thomas,1854-1928,(I-C-5W).
XX, Nov.1927,w/o Jos.,(I-C-8W).
XX,1929,w/o Damase,(II-200).
NASH
Alice Cecelia,1921-1941,(II*).
Mary T.,1881-1967,(II*).
NAYER
Allan,Jan.1993,(III-J-S).
NAYLOR
George,1861-1943,(I-D-13E).

John,May 1910,(III*).
Lynnie A.,1889-1984,(I*).
Mary A.,1823-1903,w/o Jos.,(II-136).
Mary J.Black,1867-Aug.1936,
  w/o George,(I-D-13E).
Peter, 1864-1930,
  h/o Katherine Smith, {O}.
NELSON
Emma V.,1896-Dec.1979,
  w/o George A.,(I-D-3E).
George A.,1894-Aug.1951,(I-D-3E).
George A.,1914-1993,
  h/o Delma R.,(III-J-S6).
Lydia M.,1894-1976,w/o W.C.,(II*).
Walter C.,1881-Nov.28,1951,(II-253).
NEWMAN
Eugene Wood,1891-1917,(II*).
NICHOLAS
Louis,May 1976,(III-N-35).
Rose G.,June 1960,(III-N-49).
NICHOLS
Melanie,Sept.1968,s.b.(II-227).
NILES
Delia B.,1864-1925,w/o Jacob,(I*).
Jacob L.,1867-1956,(I-D-14W).
NOEL
Rose,Dec.1909,(II-143).
NORMAND
Adelaid J.,1880-1948,(I-D-1E).
Annie M.,1903-1911,(*).
Caroline Couillard,1853-1905,(II*).
Joseph A.,1887-1946,(II*).
Mary D.,1987-1957,w/o A.J.,(I-D-1E).
Phydime,1853-1913,w/o P.,(II*).
Theodore J.,1905-1926,
  s/o A.J.& M.D.,(I-D-1E).
Theresa,May 1979,(III-QS-3).
NORTON
Beatrice,Dec.1990,(III-H-6).
O'BRIEN
Bridie M. Foley,1881-Oct.1965,
  w/o James D.,(III-G-40).
Catherine,1835-1904,w/o Pat.,(II*).
inf/o Francis,1942,(II-F-2S)
James D.,1878-1946,(III-G-40).
John,1854-1885,(II*).
Louis,Aug.1935,(II-170).
Nellie T.,1864-1902,(II*).
Patrick,1830-1906 ?,(II*).
O'CLAIR
Freddie,1912-1979,(II*).
O'DONNELL
Thomas B.,1919-1985,(II*).
O'GARA
Catherine,1892-1910,(II-159).
John,1856-1949,(II-159).

John Lawrence,Sr.,1897-1963,(II-159).
Margaret C. Wilson,1899-1987,(II*).
Maria,1861-1934,w/o John,(II-159).
OLSSON
Georgianna M.,1950,69y,
 w/o Charles H.,{O}.
Joseph,Aug.1973,(III-N-141).
Lillian,Apr.1989,(III-N-141).
OLZAK
Edward,June 1993,(III-M-49S)
Wanda,1982,(III-M-49S).
OUELLETTE
Alex,July 1991,(III-L-85N).
Alfred,1875-July 1934,(III-A-6).
Alphonse,1847-1918,(II-18).
Arthur,Jan.1953,(II-250).
Catherine,Jan.1920,
 w/o Alphonse,(II-18).
Clara,Sept.19,1889,(O/F).
Desire,1859-1936,(II-47).
Edward,1880-1965,(II-314A).
Florence,1874-1976,w/o Alfred,(III*).
Frank,Jan.1931,(II-250).
George,1841-Nov.1919,(II-250).
Godile,1871-1951,w/o John,(II-18).
John W.,1873-1951,(II-18).
Joseph T.,1871-1947,(II-250).
Lillian Dugay,1899-1938,
 w/o Alfred Jr.,(III-A-6)
Marcella Guimond,1904-1992,
 d/o John & Godilie Guimond,(II-18)
Mary G.,1879-1955,
 w/o Edward,(II-313A*).
Natalie1867-Sept.1916,
 w/o Desire,(II-47).
Philomene,1844-1917,(II*).
XX,1884,21y,(O/F).
XX,Aug.1958,w/o Emile,(III-N-60).
PAILLER
Albina,Apr.1965,(II-F-2S).
Donat J.,Feb.1950,(II-F-2S).
Ernest,Apr.1921,(II-F-2S).
Eva,Nov.1965,(III-Q-13).
Joseph,Dec.1933,(II-F-2S).
Lea,June 1959,(II-F-2S).
XX, June 1935,w/o Donat,(II-F-2S)
XX, Oct.1937,w/o Ernest,(II-F-2S).
PALMIERI
Daniel L.,1918-1986,(III*).
PAQUETTE
Adelia,Nov.1970,(III-J-13).
PATENAUDE
Selim,Mar.27,1933,(I-C-4W).
PATRY
Thomas,Oct.1969,(III-N-117).
PAULIN
Alma,1889-1933,w/o Isaic,(I*).

Anthony,1900-1986,h/o Rose,(II*).
Corinne,1875-1949,(II-33).
David L.,1881- 1948,(II-33).
Edgar,1923-July 1929,s/o Isaic,
 (I-E-8W).
Isaie,1895-1980,(I-E-8W).
Marie,1888-1933,w/o Isaic,(I-E-8W).
Roland A.,1940-1956,(II*).
William,1933,(II-115).
XX, July 1964,w/o Isaic,(I-E-8W).
PAULUS
Anthony,Nov.14,1986,(II-305A).
Roland,May 1956,(II-305A).
PAYNE
Gerald,Nov.1963,(III-N-11).
Sharon,May 1989,(III-N-11).
PEACHWALL
Mary A.,1891-1961,(I-E-6E).
Vincent,Oct.20,1986,(III-G-46).
PEASE
inf/o George,Apr.1919,(II-150).
PECORARO
Philip L.,1963-1991,(III-M-34N).
PEDNAULT
Almaise,Feb.1953,w/o George,
 (II-F-11S).
Cecile C.,1899-May 1981,
 w/o H.J.,(II-314A).
Charles,1861-1943,(II-172).
Emile J.,1909-1977,(II*).
George,Jan.1922,(II-F-11S).
Hormidas J.,1901-1975,(II-314A).
Irene Gosselin,1918-1944,
 w/o Emile,(II-172).
2 infant,1955 & 1969,(II-F-11S).
Lionel,1911-1952,(II-120A).
Lottie,June 30,1986,(III-N-50).
Louise M. Brown,1869-1940,
 w/o Charles,(II-172).
Mary,1912-1973,w/o Emile J.
Raymond C.,1941-Aug.1977,
 (III-K-22).
Robert,Dec.1980,(III-K-22).
Valida Lecount,1896-1917,(II*).
PELLERIN
2 ch/o Onesime,no dates,(III-L-16)
Ernest,1873-1964,(I*).
Ernest,1894-1927,(I-C-7W).
Monique,May 1954,(III-L-16).
Onesime,May 1977,(III-L-16).
Rene,1914-1931,(I*).
XX,Dec.1953,w/o Onesime,(III-L-16).
PELLETIER
Anna M.,July 1921,(II-158).
Conrad J.P.,1925-1944,(II*).
Conrad,1948,(II-302E).
Damien F.,1888-1932,(II-302E).

Ernest A.1906-1994,
  h/o Elva Pomerleau, {O}.
Georgianna,1905-1992,w/o Joseph,
  d.1966, (III-Q-27).
Laurent,Nov.1924,(II-158).
Marguerite,Dec.1988,(III-Q-207).
Omer,July 1989,75y,(III-N-148).
Phil. A.,Feb.1920,(II-158).
Celestine M.,1882-1960,
  w/o Damien,(II-302E).
PENNELL
W.Lawrence,1914-1992,
  1st w. Margaret Roberts,d.1956,
  2nd w. Edna Marcoux,(III-M-20).
PERIAULT
Alexander,1926,86y,Civil War Vet,{O}.
PERKINS
ch/o Calvin,1963,(III-H-19E).
PERRIN
Alphonse,Nov.1906,(II-38).
Clara I.,Oct.1896,(II-38).
Julie,Feb.1933,(II-38).
XX, Oct.1925,w/o Odile,(II-38).
PERRON
Philippe,May 195,(III-F-2W).
PERRY
Robert,Dec.1976,(II-220).
Romeo Joseph,1919-1976,
  h/o Mary Ledoux,(II*).
PESCE
Marie,1960,(*).
PETERS
Benjamin H.,1898-1943,(II*).
Dominique,1887-1937,(II*).
Estelle R.,1897-1972,(II*).
Manuel,Mar.1977,(III-Q-20).
Mary,Dec.1976,(III-Q-20).
Stella Tardiff,1972,(II-215)
Susan E.,1947-1952,(II*).
PETERSEN
Carl M.,1935-1937,s/o C. & L.,(III*).
PETERSON
John H.,1908-1929.
PHANEUF
Adele Lebrun,1917 ?,
  w/o Emanuel,(II*).
Alector,Mar.1937,(II-88).
Elise St.Pierre,1867-1946 ?,{O}.
Godfey,1891-Oct.1964,(III-G-63).
Irene Gagnon,1909-1993,
  w/o Romulus,d.1982,(III-M-14).
Japhet,1863-Nov.1955,(III-G-33).
Joseph P.,1849-1944,(III-G-63).
Josephine,1887-XXXX,(III*).
Leona Langlois,1959,(III-L-29).
Noel,1937,(II-87).

Parmilie Paulhus,1868-1946,
  wid/o Alector, {O}.
Romulus,Apr.1982,(III-M-14).
Ulric,May 1953,(III-L-29).
XX, 1946,w/o Tarnelie,(II-88).
Elise St.Pierre,1867-1946,
  w/o Japhet,(III-G-33)
Soufrenie Rioux,1858-1939,
  w/o J.Phil.,(III-G-63)
PHILLIPS
Anna,1868-1945,w/o John,(I-D-2E).
John,1868-1938,(I-D-2E).
Joseph,July 3,1900-
  June 24,1962,(I-D-2E).
Maria,1903-1981,(I*).
Peter,1917-1926,s/o J.& A.,(I-D-2E).
PINEAU
Alice Huard,1891-1975,w/o G.C.,(I*).
George C.,1891-1980,(I*).
PINETTE
Albert,1900-1927,(I-E-12E).
Arthur,1877-1965,(III*).
Arthur,June 1957,(III-G-42).
Bridgette,1896-1966,(II*).
Elie,1944,(III-H-52).
Francois,July 1959,(III-H-52).
inf/o Camille,1944,(III-G-42).
Joseph,June 1992,(III-J-3S).
Lena Gagnon,1879-1946,
  w/o Frank,(III-H-52)
Leo P.,1919-1921,(II*).
Marcel L.,1865-1931,(I-E-12E).
Odile Theriault,1878-1957,(III*).
Pamela LaMarre,1873-1932,
  w/o Marcel,(I-E-12E).
Paula A.,1944-1944,(III*).
XX,June 1957,w/o Art.,(III-G-42).
PINKHAM
Albert,1909-1986,(III*).
Flora M. Campbell,1906-1988,
  w/o Albert,(III*).
PITRE
Emeline Gallant,July 24,1914,
  45y,w/o Henri,(III*).
Henry,Jan.1954,(III-H-51).
Marie Parent,Feb.1962,(III-H-51).
Michael,May 1962,(III-N-88).
Shirley,Mar.1932,(II-215).
PIZZO
Alphonse,Jr.,1930-1993,
  h/o Frances Griffin,{O}.
PLAISTED
Albena L.,1888-1930,
  w/o Harry,(II-25)
PLANTE
Francois,1876-1965,(I-D-7W).

Marie Dansreau,1870-1944,
 w/o Francois,(I-D-7W).
PLOUDE
Joseph,1863-1936,(II-F-9N).
Odina Breault,1871 1950,
 w/o Joseph,(II-F-9N).
Philip J.,Sr.,1901-1993, h/o
 Theresa Beaudoin,d.1985,(II-F-9N)
Philip J.,Jr.,1927-1977,(II*).
POIRIER
Alfred J.(Perry),1895-1951,(I-D-11W).
Antoinette Bourque,1884-1947,
 w/o Michel,(II*).
Arthur J.,1898-1984,(III*).
Bella,Mar.1987,(III-Q-109).
Benjamin,1865-1926,(I*).
Camille J.,1901-1973,(II*).
Cornelia,Mar.1932,(I-D-11W).
Eugenie,1855-1888,(O/F*).
Eva Fecteau,1923-1994,
 w/o Paul, d.1981,{O}.
Flora O.,1902-1971,(II*).
Francis X.,1903-1992,
 h/o Bella,d.1987,(III-Q-109).
Joseph,Feb.1920,(II-248).
Louie,1852-1924,(I*).
Marie,Dec.1925,(I-D-11W).
Michel,1875-1915,(II*).
Narcisse,Dec.1957,(III-G-12).
Ovide,1894-Dec.1948,(III-H-13).
Rose C.,1902-1986,w/o Arthur J.,(III*).
Roseanna,1868-1956,w/o Benjamin,
 (I-D-11W).
POISSON
Anna,Dec.1955,(II-79).
Eugene,Aug.1934,(II-79).
George Fisher,June 1949,(III-H-48).
XX,Oct.1955,w/o Geo.,(III-H-48)
POITRAS
Alfred,Apr.1949,(III-H-55).
Bertrand,July 1930,(II-108).
Conrad,July 1991,(III-Q-258).
Delia,May 1953,(III-J-6).
Elizabeth Francouer,1849-1894,
 w/o F.X.,(II*).
Ernest,June 1958,(III-J-6).
F.X.,Mar.1926,(II-108).
Henri,1853-Oct.1923,(II-244).
Joseph,1885-1926,(I-E-18w).
Joseph R.,II, July 1990,28y,{O}.
Julienne Francoeur,1852-
 May.1919,w/o Henri,(II-244).
Lewis Chas.,1885-1924,(II-244).
Leon,Mar.1977,(III-J-6).
Marie A. Godin,1911-1992,
 w/o Leon,d.1977,(III-Q-153).
Olive,June 1972,(III-Q-87).

Paul,May 1989,(III-M-24N).
Philip R.,1943,(II-108).
Nora,1889-1937,w/o Jos.,(II-18).
Robert J.,1918-1993,
 h/o Fernande Lebel, {O}.
Roland J.,1912-1945,(III-H-10).
Ulric,Dec.1956,(III-H-10).
XX,1944,w/o Ulric,(III-H-10).
POMERLEAU
Adeline Trembley,1856-1946,
 w/o Anthime,(II-187).
Ambroise,Aug.1916,(II-187).
Anne,Feb.1919,(II-187).
Anthime,1857-1914,(II-187).
Aurore M.,1903-XXXX,
 w/o Rosaire,(III*).
Damase,1875-Dec.1914,(II-125).
Damese,1888-1960,(II-183).
Delia Berry,1871-1931,
 w/o Leonidas,(II-153).
Donat,Feb.1946,(II-125).
Donat,1899-1976,(II-155).
Elsie M.,1911-XXXX,
 w/o Wilfred H.,(II*).
Eva,1901-1930,w/o Wm.,(II-155).
Florida,1884-1902,d/o Timothy,(II-1).
Frederick,1912-1934,(II-187).
Gedeon,Feb.1957,(II-187).
George,1898-1945,(II-183).
George R.,Dec.1932,(II-183).
Grace,1878-1959, w/o Nap.,(II-1).
inf/o Wilfrid,1929,(II-1).
Jane Buotte,1880-1950,(II-125).
Joseph G.,1885-1957,(II*).
Joseph Leo,Aug.1922,(II-155).
Leonidas,1870-1916,(II-153).
Leontine Valliere,1888-1947,
 w/o Philias,(II-183).
Louise M.,1867-1929,
 w/o Louis D.,(II-183).
Louis Arthur, 1897-1920,(II-183).
Louis D.,1853-1938,(II-183).
Lucie Ridley,1870-1911,w/o Nap.,(II*).
Napoleon,1881-1942,(II-1).
Napoleon,1858-1912,(II*).
Paul J.,Dec.1946,(II-205).
Philias,1893-1937,(II*).
Roland,Dec.1943,(II-153).
Ronald,Feb.1933,(II-1).
Rosaire L.,1907-1982,(III*).
Rose Dostie,1876-1954,(I-D-7E).
Ruth Beaumier,1899-1979,
 w/o Donat,(II-155).
Sylvia,Sept.1929,(II-183).
Tancred,Mar.1932,(II-187).
Timothy M.,1907-1991,
 h/o Theresa Lepenven,(II*).

Veronica Rajotte,1926,w/o Jos,(II*).
Wilfred H.,1905-1949,(II*).
Wilfrid,1896-1942,(II-155).
William,1895-1951,(II-155).
Willie,1927-1974,(III-G-25).
XX, 1904,w/o Damase,(II-125).
XX, Jan.1926,w/o Gedeon,(II-187).
POOLER
Alice M.,1882-1977,(I*).
PORELL
Bernadette Lebebvre,1911-1992,
 w/o John P.,d.1982,(III-M-21).
Ernest,Feb.1978,(III-L-36).
Gregory M.,Aug.1953,(II*).
Gregory S.,1948,(II*).
Laurette A.,1912-1981,(II-220A).
Leonard L.,1912-1974,(II-220A).
Margaret M.,1886-Jan.1953,(II).
PORELLO
Josephine Manganillo,1878-1918,
 w/o Pasquale,(II*).
Nancy,1901-Mar.1980,(II-251).
Pasquale,1875-Aug.1941,(II-251).
POULIN
Albert,Oct.1980,(III-Q-161).
Corinne,Mar.1949,(II-33).
David L.,1899-July 1948,(II-33).
Joseph Camille,1928-1990,
 h/o Shirley Field,{O}.
M.,1901,w/o John, (O).
William,1869-1933,(II-115).
POUTRE
Sister Carmelle,Mar.1990,58y,{O}.
POWELL
Jeanne A.,1912-1984,(III*).
POWERS
Anne G.,Aug.1897,(II-226).
Antoinette,Mar.1937,(III-G-38).
Celilia E.,1880-1966,(II*).
Edward,1859-1924,(II*).
Florence,July 1993,(III-D-8).
George H.,1914-1980,(III-A-1).
Grace,May 1958,w/o Martin,(III-G-38).
Irene G.,1912-XXXX.
J.Everett,Feb.1908,(II-226).
Joseph,May 1955,(II-88).
Julia C.,1821-1902,
 w/o Michael,Sr.,(II*).
Katherine Cisco,1864-1894,(II*).
Martin,1860-1944,(III-G-38).
Marie,1905- 942,(II*)
Mary P.,1855-1898,
 d/o M.S.&J.C.,(II*).
Michael,Sr.,1821-1898,(II*).
Michael,Jr.,1857-1939,(II*).
Nancy Jess,1846-1911,(II*).
Oswald,Apr.1900,(II-226).

Patrick J.,May 1950,(III-D-8).
Robert,1978,(III-D-8).
Robert S.,July 1952,(II-15).
Thomas,1843-1898,(II*).
Vera Bolster,Mar.1944,(III-D-8).
XX, July 1942,w/o Axina,(II-252).
XX,June 1958,w/o Pat.,(III-D-8).
PRATT/E
Anita,Nov.1954,(III-J-19).
Louise Grondin,no dates,(I*).
Olianna B.,1923-1943,(II*).
XX, Jan.1929,w/o Thare,(I-C-3E)
PRINCE
Benjamin,1861-1944,(III-C-1&2).
Joseph A.,Dec.1957,(III-N-57).
Rosilda,1862-1932,(III*).
Theodore,1905-1937,(III-C-2W).
Victoria,Apr.1983,(III-C-1&2).
PRIOR
Cleveland,June 1965,(III-N-101).
PROULX
Alfred,1862-1934,(III-B-10).
Gabrielle,1943,(III-N-106).
Gerard,Sept.1983,(III-N-106).
Roland O.,1906-1992, 1st wife
Gabrille Gagen,1943,h/o Doris,(III*).
Howard Warren, (III-N-106).
Leonide,1868-1935,w/o Alf.,(III-B-10).
Roland O.,1906-1992,
 h/o Doris Howard Warren, {O}.
Rosario,Apr.1955,(III-L-10).
PROVENCHER
Laurette E.,May 4,1987,(III-L-8).
PROVOST
Elise,Dec.1945,(I-C-12W).
QUINLAR
Marie A.,1902-1987,(II*).
Milton A.,XXXX, WWII.(II*).
QUINN
Bridgit,Sept.1901,63y,w/o Pat.,(II-67).
John,1857-1954,(II-144).
John J.,1871-Jan.1909,(II-76).
Mary,Dec.1917,(II-76).
Mary Ann Joyce,1859-1924,
 w/o John,(II*).
Susan M.,1822-1906,w/o John,(II-76).
Thomas P.,Mar.1901,(II-67).
XX,Dec.1936,w/o Patrick,(II-67).
RADLEY
Alice,July 1976,(III-L-11).
RANCOURT
Arthur J.,1904-1968,(II-231).
Bernadette O.,1909-1941,
 w/o A.J.,(II-231).
Reina,June 1956,(III-N-3).
REDDEN
Florence,Apr.1964,(III-G-46).

Harry,Sept.1965,(III-G-46).
REDLON
Elizabeth,1892-1924,d/o E. &M.,(I*).
Eugene D.,1880-1930,(I*).
J.J,Apr.1929,(I-E-2E).
John Joseph,1928-1955,(II*).
John T.,1898-1949,s/o E.& M.,(I*).
Margaret,May 1959,(I-E-2E).
Margaret C.Earls,1901-1953,
w/o John T.,(I*).
Margaret R. Coughlin,1860-1930,
w/o Eugene,(I*).
REECE
Emily C.,June 1990,(III-N-32).
REED
Elizabeth,1886-1910,
w/o James N.,(II-113).
RENNA
Mark,Oct.1989,(III-Q-S-13).
RENY
Edward A.,July 1953,(III-H-16).
Laura,Oct.1967,(III-H-16).
REYNOLDS
Catherine,Aug.1889,(II-12).
Janis Hebert,1978,(III-Q-95).
John,May 1940,96y,(II-12).
Nicolas,1887,(II-12).
Bridget S., Aug.1906,58y,
w/o John,(II-12).
RICARD
Alina,Feb.1917,(II-24).
RICHARD/S
Alfred,1882-Feb.1949,(III-H-20).
Arthur,Oct.1976,(III-L-79).
Beatrice,Oct.1978,(III-Q-157).
Celia,1868-May 1940,
w/o Napoleon,(II-306S).
Celina,1867-1944,w/o Richard,
(II-234).
Delma M.,Mar.1989,(I-D-4W).
Delphine,1865-1948,(II*).
Delvina Martin,1884-Jan.1949,
w/o Alfred,(III-H-20).
Edward,Apr.1989,(III-Q-157).
Elize,1851-1940,(II*).
Emile,1899-1919,(II*).
George,1845-1933,(I-E-11W).
Joseph A.,1891-1966,(II*).
Joseph Emile,Aug. 1919,(II-234).
Louise L.,1893-1945,(II*).
Marie,Oct.1970,(III-N-128).
Marie,Mar.1955,(II-F).
Mary A.,1889-1971,w/o Jos.A.,(II*).
Patrick,1868-1944,(II-234).
Philippe,1892-1949,(II-306S).

RIDLEY
Alfred Ovila,1927-1927,
s/o O.F. & A.M.,(III*).
Annette, May 1919,(II-188).
Antoinette Martin,1898-1968,(III*).
Ovila F.,1892-Jan.1934,(III-A-5).
XX, Oct.1919,w/o Joshua,(II-188).
RIOPEL
Arthur,May 1968,(III-M-3).
RIOUX
Amanda,1881-1971,(II*).
Amedie,1886-1928,(I-C-2E).
Delia Lebel,Jan.1973,(III-L-42).
Edesse Larivee,1837-1905,
w/o Oliver, (II).
Emma G.,1860-1939,w/o Philias,
(I-C-2E).
Eugene Joseph1886-July 1956,
(II-170).
Fabien,1893-1946,(I-C-2E).
Flora,1896-1934,(III*).
Frank L.,1890-1946, {O}.
Georgette,June 1968,(III-L-42).
Georgianne Delcourt,1856-1920,
w/o Severin,(II*).
Hector,Mar.23,1972,(III-L-42).
Jacob,1857-1913,(II*).
Laura,Aug.1934,(III-G-3)
Marie,1860-1924,w/o Jacob,(II*).
Mary,Nov.1963,(I-C-2E).
Napoleon,1872-1945,(III-G-3).
Noel,Oct.1959,(III-L-42).
Oliver,1843-1914,(II*).
Ovide Joseph,July 25,1915-
Oct.13,1964,(I-C-2E).
Robert,1921-1990,(I*).
Robert A.,1921-1990,(I*).
Roland Frank,June 25,1917-
June 16,1972,(I*).
Severin,1850-1912,(II-169).
XX,Dec.1920,w/o Severin,(II-169).
Elisc,1875-1934,w/o Napoleon,
(III-G-3)
ROBERGE
Alfred,1905-1906,(II*).
Anna Marie,1908-1910,(II*).
Aurore,1904-1905,(II*).
Flora,1898-1976,w/o J.A.,(II-153).
George W.,Dec.1986,(III-N-188).
infant, ch/o Olivier & Matilda,
1890,(O/F*).
Joseph A.,1891-1979,(II-153).
Josephine,Sept.1917,(II-127).
Marie E.,1956,w/o Maurice,(II*).
Matilda Loyal,Dec.5,1890,40y,
w/o Olivier,(O/F*).
Oliver,1911,(II-127).

Philippe,1895-1896,(II*).
Roland,1907-1943,(II*).
Wilfred,1880-1943,(II*).
ROBICHAUD
Albert,1903-1904,(II*).
Alfred J.,1905-1922,(II-198).
Alfred,Apr.1874-1954,(II-97).
Angeline Gaudet,Apr.1963,
  w/o Reuben J.,(II-89).
Anthony P.,1886-1947,(II*).
Arthemise,1900-1918,(II-198).
Camille,1912-1912,(II*).
Ephraim J.,1879-1909,(II*).
Eugene,Jan.1978,(III-H-17).
Evangline,Dec.1935,(I-C-IIE).
Eveline,1908-1910,(II*).
Evelyn,Sept.1992,(III-Q-214).
Felix,Apr.1945,(III-H-17).
Helene,1904-1926,(II-89).
Jerome,1839-1923,(II-97).
John C.,1872-Oct.1937,(II-198).
Josephine,July 1990,84y,
  (III-H-17).
Margaret E. Guitard,1882-1955,
  w/o Alfred,(II-97).
Marie Buote,1876-1947,
  w/o John C.,(II-198).
Marie Louise,July 1979,(III-H-23).
Oliva R.,1915-1990,(III-H-17).
Paul Clement,1919-1920,(II-198).
Reuben J.,1877-1964,(II*).
Sophie,1841-1925,(II*).
Stanley,1912-Nov.1953,(II-198).
Susan,1847-Jan.1919,
  w/o Jerome,(II-96).
XX,Dec.1951,w/o Felix,(III-H-17).
XX, Dec.1935,w/o John P.,(I-C-11W).
XX,Jan.1925,w/o J.Urbain,(II-89).
ROBICHEAW
Albert A.,1911-1992,(I-D-6E).
John,Oct.1971,(III-Q_78).
ROBINSON
Elaine F.,1916-1979,(II*).
Karen,1946-1950,(*).
ROCHELEAU
Ann L.,Aug.1983,(III-L-78).
Dora J. Goyette,1893-June 1975,
  2nd w/o William,(III-A-7).
Elmire H.,1870- Mar.1939,
  w/o H.G.,(II-230).
Florida E.,1896-1906,(II*).
Henry G.,1867-Dec.1950,(II-230).
Honorine Lauzon,1899-1935,
  w/o William,(III-A-7).
infs/o Oscar,1924 & 1925,(II-230).
Jeannette,1906-1946,(II-230).

Jospehine, Gagnon,1899-Dec.1991,
  (III-A-7).
Oscar R.,1893-1952,(III-A-7).
Ovide J.,1892-July 1920,(II-230).
Wilfred,Jan.14,1895,22y,(O/F).
William,1894-Dec.1961,(III-A-7).
ROGAN
Loretta Dilworth,1940-1993,{O}.
ROGERS
Scott A.,June 1956,(III*).
ROMA
Catherine,Aug.1953,(III-J-4).
Charles,Dec.1955,(III-J-4).
Francis,Aug.1965,(III-N-83).
Francis L.,1907-1990,{O}.
Laurette Roy,1919-1993,
  w/o Francis,d.1965,(III-N-83).
RONDEAU
Alfred,1897-1959,(II*).
Arthur,Dec.1976,(III-N-160).
Delima Lapointe,1871-1947,{O}.
John B.,1894-1948,(III-H-26).
Mary Ann,Sept.1966,?,(III-H-26).
Rita,Nov.1980,(II-F-7).
ROSS
Marion,1911-Mar.1980,(II-251).
ROSVALLY
Arthur R.,1907-1978,(II*).
Doris,1903-1988,w/o A.R.,(II*).
ROUNDS
Mary Murphy,Jan.1962,(II-130).
ROUSSEAU
Alfred,1888-Oct.1954,(I-E1W).
Alfred,Apr.1959,(II-F-7).
Anastasie Morin,XXXX,w/o Jos.,(III*)
Clareece E.,1920-1994,(III*).
Delia,1893-1974,w/o Wilfr.,(III*)
Eugene,1912, (II-176).
Eva, July 1920,(II-176).
Joseph,1881-1962,(II-176).
Louis J.,1892-1950,(III-G-44).
Louise A.,Mar.1959,(III-K-9W).
Phelanise Gaudreau,1881-1955,
  w/o Joseph,(II-176).
Robert,Mar.1968,(III-K-9E).
Roland A.,1913-1968,(III*).
Rose,1892-Dec.1990,
  w/o Alfred (1954),(III-K-8).
Sylvia,1923-Sept.1927,(I-E-1W).
Telesphore,1898-1985,(II*).
Wilfrid,1890-1953,(III-K-7).
ROUTHIER
XX, Aug.1920,w/o Philom.,(II-180).
ROY
Albert,Sept.1959,(I-C-2E).
Anna Buteau,Dec.1962,(III-H-29).
Armand A.,Dec.21,1944,23y.

Armand,Apr.1949,(III-H-29).
Denis,Dec.1959,(III-N-5).
Donald E.,1927-1993,
  h/o Theresa Tardiff,(III-N-13).
Edmond,June 1963,(III-H-29).
Emile Joseph,1877-1944,
  h/o Mary Louise Lanfevin,(II*).
George J.,1885-1940,(I-A-6E).
inf/o Eugene,1928,(II-217).
Irenee,Dec.1961,(III-L-66).
Laura F. King,1891-1970,
  w/o G.J.,(I-A-6E).
Leandre,Sept.1980,(III-H-29).
Leo Paul,Sept.1982,(III-N-13).
Lucien,Sept.1948,(III-H-29).
Marie,Aug.1974,(III-N-5).
Napoleon,Nov.1994,77y.
Norman,Nov.1994,70y,
  h/o Alda Moreau.
Ovide,Apr.1955,(III-B-2).
Palmyra,Oct.1969,(III-N-13)
Robert G.,1930-1994,
  h/o Laurette Delcourt,(I-A-6E).
Simone,Mar.8,1982,(III-L-66).
Theresa Rita,Aug.1990,61y,
  w/o Donald E.,{O}.
Virginie,Jan.1953,(I-C-2E).
XX, 1924, w/o Thomas,(I-A-6E).
RUDBALL
Anthony,Sept.1989,(III-Q-244).
SAINDON
Irma,1905-Apr.1976,(II-254).
SAMPSON
Eleanore,Jan.1972,(III-Q-79).
Frederick,Aug.1972,(III-Q-79).
Genevieve Gariepy,1873-1958,
  w/o Joseph E.,(III*).
Joseph E.,1874-1959,(III*).
SAMSON
Herthemise Begin,1870-1939,(II-23).
inf/o George,1936,(II-23).
Joseph,Jan.1959,(III-K-2).
L. Etienne,1866-1934,(II-23).
Evelyn J.,1899-Jan.1955,
  w/o George,(II-23).
Marie,July 1977,(III-L-12).
Philippe,Mar.1957,(III-L-12).
XX,Feb.1958,w/o Jos.,(III-K-2).
SARRASIN
Emile A.,1898-1968,(II*).
Florine Baillergeon,1898-1981,
  w/o Emile A.,(II*).
SAUCIER
Rita,Oct.1994,67y,w/o George.
SCRIBNER
Michael C.,1968-1992,(III-L-93N).

SCRUTON
Joseph,Jan.1972,(III-Q-82).
SEGER
Walter E.,1944-1953,(II*).
SEMPLE
Fernande B.,1917-Oct.1956,
  w/o Arthur T.,(I-B-6E).
SENECHAL
Raymond,Feb.1966,(III-N-112).
Telesphore,Dec.1967,(III-N-112).
SEVIGNY
Deborah,Dec.1958,(I-A-5).
SHEEHAN
Eva,Apr.1994,(III-N-12).
SHEEHY
Mary Caravasio,1990,73y,
  w/o Maurice,(III-Q-247).
SICARD/SECARD
A. Eulalie Landry,1868-July 1936,
  w/o Augustin,(1952),(III-A-11).
Aldea,Feb.1979,(III-N-52).
Adolph,1892-1976.(III*).
Adolphe,1836-1903,(II-60).
Alice,1899-1988,(III-A-3).
Alfred,1906-1944,(III-A-11).
Augustin,1866-1950,(III-A-11).
Augustin,Jan.1962,(III-N-52).
Carmine ?, May 197X,(III-N-52).
Cedulie,1841-1903,w/o Adolphe,
  (II-60).
Cleophas,1859-1912,(II-60).
Dellerise,1868-1947,(II-60).
Emma,1904-1933,w/o Oril,(III-A-3).
Esdras,1885-1915,(II-19).
Felix,1879-1935,(II*).
Jean B.,July 1907,(II-19).
Joseph A.,1900-1973,(III*).
Laurent,May 1901,(II-19).
Loda,1907-1907,(II*).
Louise,1904-1958,(III-A-11).
Ludovic,1887-1887,(II-19).
Lumina Bella,July 30,1987,(II-F-7).
Maria L.,1883-1884,(II*).
Marie A.,1897-1989,(III-A-11).
Melvina L.,1865-1948,w/o Philias.
Malvina Larivee,1865-1948,(II).
Mildred E.,1904-1984,
  w/o Joseph A.,(III*).
Oril,1902-1974,(III-A-3).
Philias,1862-July 1933,(II-19).
Philias,May 1935,(III-A-3).
Rosalia,1883-1964,(III-A-3).
Roy,1912-1990, (III-A-11).
XX,Jan.1884,(II-19).
XX,1901,w/o Onizime, (O).
SIDEBOTTOM
Arthur,Feb.6,1987,(III-Q-213).

SIMON
Herve,1903-1962,(I-D-9E).
John,XXXX,(III-G-52).
Ruth Couturier,1894-Mar.1963,
 w/o Herve,(I-D-9E).
SIMONEAU
Arthur,Mar.1955,(III-G-52).
XX,Mar.1955,w/o Art.,(III-G-52).
SINCLAIR
XX,May 1944,w/o Guy V.,(III-H-16).
SIROIS
Alice,Mar.1981,(III-M-14)
Ann Chisholm,1869-1939.
Annie Morissette,1878-July 1940,
 w/o Charles S.,(III-G-21).
Armand J.,Oct.1989,81y,
 h/o Mary Stockwell, {O}.
Armand,1880-1901,(II*).
Charles,1877-1959,(III-G-21).
Delia Pitre,1909-1984,
 w/o Joseph Albert,(III*).
Emilie T.,1848-1906,
 w/o Julian S.,(II*).
Florent,1866-1945(I-B-8W).
inf/o Alf.,Apr.1942,(III-G-21).
inf/o Ovide,Apr.1921,(II-217).
Jean,June 1968,(III-Q-44).
Jeanne,1898-1993,(I-B-8W).
Joseph J.,1873-1916,(II-217).
Joseph Albert,1902-July 1987,
 (III-G-21).
Joseph G.,1942-42,s/o J.A.& Delia,
 (III*).
Julian S.,1848-1906,(II*).
Velena,1879-Feb.1942,
 w/o Joseph J.,(II-217).
SMALL
Rose Nicolas,Jan.1959,(III-H-26).
SMITH
Arthur,Apr.20,1972,(III-Q-83).
Donald L.,1941-Jan.1951,(II-231).
Emma,1923,1st w/o Frank,(I-A-6W).
Flora M.,1893-1979,(II-30).
Floyd L.,Jr.,1925-1942,(II*).
George A.,Dec.1960,(III-N-36).
James H.,1872-1944,(II*).
John M.,1894-1950,(I-A-6W).
Laurette,Feb.5,1987,(III-Q-83).
Lulu G.,1871-1970,(II*).
Margaret M.,1897-1965,(I-E-3E).
Mary Smith,1884-1979,(II).
Patricia,1942-1946,(III-B-C).
Rose L.,1900-1965,(I-E-10E).
Rose Helen,1933-1975,(III*).
Winfred L.,Dec.1955,(II-30).
XX, Sept.4,1930,2nd w/o Frank,
 (I-A-6W).
XX, Oct.1918,w/o J.W.,(II-231).
SODERBERG
Natalie Landry,Oct.1969,(II-249).
SPARKS
Simone E.,1923-1990,
 w/o Wm.R.,(III*).
William R.,1923-1983,(III*).
SPILLER
Lloyd Raymond,1917-Jan.1947.
Lucy,Aug.1969,(both III-H-46).
SPRAGUE
Lorette J.,1913-1977,(I*).
SPRINGER
Charlotte,1906,d/o J.W.& S.A.(II*).
Sarah W.,1869-1956,(II-A).
ST. CROIX
Marie,XXXX,(II*).
ST.CYR
Beatrice Arsenault,1920-1994,
 w/o Armand,(III-H-5).
Edward,June 1961,(III-L-63).
Joseph,May 1948,(III-H-5).
Lea,May 1961,(III-L-63).
XX,Sept.1956,w/o Jos.,(III-H-5).
ST.HILAIRE
Rene,1926,(II-72).
ST.PIERRE
Aime,July 1956,(III-G-33).
Albert J.,1903-1969,(II-159A).
Alfred T.,1877-1957,(II-163).
Alfred,June 1976,(III-Q-94).
Anne Marie,Jan.1988,(III-L-70).
Clephas,Jan.1953,(III-B-8).
Conrad,Dec.1936,(II-163).
David J.,1938-1991,
 h/o Priscilla Gervais,(III-L-70).
Ernest,1904-1960,(II-159A)
Fedelise,1882-1976,(II-163).
Ferdinand,1882-1947,(II*).
Jean,1845-1923,(II-160).
Joseph,May 1951,(III-L-15).
Josephine,1865-1950,(III-B-8)
Josephine,Nov.1961,(III-N-80).
Josephine Gagnon,1865-Nov.1950,
 wid/o Mark,(III-B-8).
Laurette,1907,(II-163).
Louis,1864-Sept.1938,(II-27).
Marc,1861-Oct.1947,(III-B-8).
Marguerite Chiasson,1879-1949,
 w/o Ferdinand,(II-159A).
Mary Barbe,1876-1933,(II*).
Nere Fournier,1844-1910,
 w/o Jean,(II*).
Rosanna,Sept.1949,(II-160).
Sylvia,Apr.1973,(III-L-15).
Venerante Belangers,Aug.4,
 1889,48y,w/o Frederic,(O/F*).

Virginia,1924,(II-27).
Wildred,Feb.1987,(III-L-70).
XX,Nov.1933,w/o Louis,Sr.(II-27).
STACK
Abby,1860-1888,w/o Thos,(II-F-10N)
David W.,Nov.1931,(II-F-10N).
Ernest J.,1896-1916,(II-F-10N).
Margaret,1868-1954,w/o David, (II-F-10N).
Thomas,May 1899,79y,(II-F-10N).
Thomas,1888-1932,(II-F-10N).
Ursula T.,1894-1967,(II*).
STANWOOD
Amelia A.,1906,w/o Arthur H,(O).
STERLING
Ruth I.,1915-1985,(III*).
Chartley,1918-1981,(III*).
STICKNEY
XX, Feb.1925,w/o Fred,(III-E-1W).
STIRLING
Catherine,Nov.1964,(III-N-92).
STONE
Annie,1889-1961,(II*).
STREET
Rosana, 1881,(O/F*).
STROUT
Georgette,Apr.1922,(II-34).
SULLIVAN
Alice,June 1961,(II-122).
Angelina,Jan.1961,(III-H-56).
Anna G.,1834-1901,w/o Mortimer, (II-137).
Catherine,1861-1908,w/o James,(II*).
James,1861-1901,(II*).
John,Oct.1918,(II-184).
John F.,1865-1907,(II-127).
John H.,June 1949,(III-H-56).
John Murphy,Jan.1947,(II-122).
Mortimer O.,1840-1910,(II-137).
Raymond F.,1906-1938,(II*).
Thedora,1897-1960,(II-129).
XX,Jan.1910,w/o Wm.,(II-137).
SWEENEY
Martha,1890-1902, d/o C.H.& I.N.,(II*).
SWETT
Alfred,Oct.1993,(III-M-39S).
SWISKO
Joseph Harold,1948,(III-H-14).
SYLVESTER
Raymond,1917-1923,(*).
TAGGART
Michael,Oct.1952,(I-C-5W).
TANGUAY
Albert,May 1914,(II-54).
Albert J.,1897-1960,(III-K-8).
Alexina,May 1956,(III-H-20).

Augustin,Aug.1980,(III-M-13)
Azilda,1865-1933,w/o Remi,(I-A-3W).
Blanche,1900-Oct.1990,(II-54).
Cecile M.,Aug.12,1904,(*).
Delrice Archambeault,1911,62y,(II*).
Edmond G. Tanguay,1918-1967, h/o Phyllis A. Brigham,(III*).
Edward,Apr.1967 ?,(III-C-3).
Elmire Marie,Sister,Jan.13,1892- May 16,1970,(I-A-3W).
Eugene,1889-Feb.1970,(II-48).
Eugene Joseph,Oct.1994,81y, h/o Jeannette LeBrecque.
Florence J.,1936-1953(I-A-3W)
Francois,1825-1883,(III*).
George,Sept.1913,(II-54).
Gerard A.,1938-1944,(I-A-3W)
Germaine,1903-1982,(II).
Ida Bouillon,1894-Nov.1948, w/o Eugene,(II-54)
Lucrenne,1906-1988,(II-48).
Ludivine Marie,Oct.27,1902- Mar.23,1973,(I*).
Philomene,1915,w/o Geo.,(II-54).
Remi,1858-Jan.1951,(I-A-3W)
Rose Marie,1866-1949,(III-G-36).
Rose M.,Nov.13,1887- Nov.13,1966,(I-A-3W).
Virginia Archambeault, 1828-1900,w/o Francois,(III*).
XX, July 1911,w/o Ludger,(II-5).
XX,Apr.1979,w/o Augustin, (III-M-13).
TARDIFF
Alice,1888-Apr.1980,(II-244).
Cleon,Aug.1939,(I-B-8E).
Fred D.,1902-1969,(I*).
Henry T.,1907-1993, s/o Joseph & Almina Gregoire,(I-B-8E).
Joseph A.,1876-1958,(I-B-8E).
Melina Grigoire,1888-1933, w/o Joseph,(I-B-8E).
Rose Eva,Apr.1917,(II-108).
Ruby A.,Apr.29,1910-Apr.20,1985,(I*).
Theodore,1889-Dec.1954,(II-244).
Wilfrid,June 1969,(I-B-8E).
TETRAULT
Abraham,1853-1898,(II-115).
Albert L.,1907-1975,(III*).
Edisse Girard,1862-1936,(II*).
Louis,1888-Apr.1988,(III-G-28).
M. Eulalie,1890-July 1,1986,(III-G-28).
Napoleon,1877-1956,(III-G-49).
Elizabeth L.,1913-1941, w/o Albert L.,(III-G-49)

Julie,1877-July 1956,
  w/o Napoleon, (III-G-49)
THERIAULT
Alfred J.,1898-1968,(II*).
Belonie,July 6,1853-Dec.1,1927,
  (I-C-9E).
Christine,Nov.29,1860-Aug.27,
  1929,w/o Belonie,(I-C-9E).
Ella Landry,1894- 1992,
  w/o Alfred,d. 1968,(I-E-13W).
Frank,Apr.10,1887-Dec.13,1966,(I*).
Fred,Apr.1968,(I-E-13W).
Herbert,1939,58y,{O}.
Hubert C.,1881-1941,(II*).
Leo Paul,1920-1988,(I*).
Patric,Apr.1962,(III-H-4).
William,Jan.1946,(III-H-4).
XX,Mar.1916,w/o Gervais,(II-189).
THIBEAULT
Aime L.,Jul 1976,(III-L-10).
Amelia R.,1898-1942-Sept.1942,
  w/o Geo.,(III-G-41).
Arthur,1943,(III-L-10).
Emilien,Nov.1949,(III-E-10).
Eva M. Gaudreau,1900-1992,
  w/o Willie,d.1979,(III-K-10).
George A.,1898-1962,(III-G-41).
Joseph,1868-Nov.1952,(III-G-41).
Ludger,1905-1951,(II-104A).
Marie Blanche,1973,(III-L-10).
Michael,Sept.1964,child,(III-G-41)
Regina,1906-1970,w/o Ludger,(II*).
Sara,Apr.1989,(III-M-44S).
Willie,1899-1979,(III-K-10).
THOMAS
Mary Stack,Oct.1941,(III-J-11).
THOMPSON
Charles H.,1868-1947,(II-138).
THORNDIKE
Mary,1882-1967,(II-175).
THUOTTE
Adeline J. Kerwin,1897-1929,
  w/o Emile,(I*).
Albertine,July 1969,(III-G-56).
Alphonsine Chretien,1878-1908,(II*).
Amanda,1875-1919,(II*).
Amedee,July1950,(II-42).
Agnes,1908-1971,w/o Rene,(II*).
Archer,Jan.1965,(III-L-66).
Augustin,1868-1951,(III-G-56).
Blanche M. Tourangeau,1897-
  Feb.1933,w/o Emile,(I*).
Delia,1893-July 1961,
  w/o Ludger,(I-C-8E).
Delvina Lemieux,Mar.1947,
  w/o Augustin, (III-G-56).

Emile J.,June 20,1894-
  Mar.12,1971,(I*).
Ernestine Lapointe,1865-Aug.1949,
  (III-G-50).
Gerard R.,1943-1968,(I-C-8E).
Henry,1870-Apr.1933,(III-G-50).
Honora,1905-1955,(II-150).
John,Jan.1936,(II-150).
John,1899-Feb.1958,(III-G-57).
Joseph,1864-Feb.1939,(III-G-36).
Josephine,1899-1978,(III-G-57).
Ludger,1893-1969,(I-C-8E).
Napoleon,1873-Apr.1932,(II-238).
Odiana M. Tanguay,1865-
  July 1932,w/o Jos.,(III-G-36).
Ovide,June 1965,(III-N-41).
Raymond,Sept.1989,(III-Q-53).
Rene,Dec.1928,(II-152).
Rene,1905-1956,(II*).
Rita,1920-Jan.1928,(I-C-8E).
Thelma S.Lemay,1917-1960,(I-C-8E).
Verna L. Bryan,1895-1971,
  w/o Emile,(I-B-1W).
XX, Aug.1954,w/o Amedee,(II-42).
XX, Feb.1939,w/o John,(II-96).
XX, Feb.1919,w/o Napol.(II-238).
Yvonne,1894-Oct.1959,(III-G-36).
TITCOMB
Ethel,Dec.1968,(III-Q-52).
TOBIN
Annie B.,1868-June 1938,
  w/o Jas.,(III-G-52).
James P.,1866-1954,(III-G-51).
TONDREAU
Adelard,Sept.1950,(I-A-8W).
Delvina G.,1878-Sept.1931,
  w/o Adelard,(I-A-7W).
Emma Lemieux,1863- Feb.1939,
  w/o Joseph,(III-G-12).
Emelia 1892-1971,(III*).
Ernest,1894-1940,(III*).
Garnet,Apr.23,1973,(III-L-13).
Henry,May 1959,(III-L-13).
Joseph,1861-1940,(III-G-12).
Lydia,Oct.1967,(III-L-13).
Narcisse Poirer,1885-1957,(III*).
Sylva,1910-June 1947,(I-A-7W).
TOURANGEAU
Alice B.,Nov.1989,(III-Q-7).
Arthur,Sept.1964,(III-Q-7)
Catherine Gallant,Aug.1962,(III-J-5).
Dolores,Mar.1917,(II-50).
Dominic,1886-1891,(II-109).
Emma,1862-1922,w/o Ludger,(II-109).
Lily,Oct.1994,79y,w/o Roland D.,Sr.
Ludger,1861-1910,(II-109).
Ludger,Oct.1953,(III-J-5).

Marie Emma,1884-1985,(II*).
Marie Virginia,1888-1967,(II-109).
Regina,June 1890,s.b.,(II-109).
Theodore,1900-1953,(II-109).
TOWNSEND
Francie J.,1896-1983(II*).
George J.,1918-1918,(II*).
Henry N.,1915-1918,(II*).
Raymond J.,1918-1927,(II*).
Suzan Marie,1958-1961,(II*).
TREMBLAY
Alice E.,1891-1923,(II*).
C.Elise,1889-1901,(II*).
Ellen Welch,1859-1940,
  w/o Gideon,(II*).
Gideon,1857-1911,(II*).
Hyacinthe,1830-1881,(II-1).
Rebecca D.,Oct.1989,88y,(II-18).
Romeo T.,Sept.1979,(III-QS-4).
Lucie Lavigne,1832-1913,
  w/o Hyacinthe,(II-1).
Mary L.,1886-1889,(II*).
TREPANIER
Adele Desrosiers,1862-1950,(II-164A).
Alfred,Apr.1969,(III-N-128).
Ferdinand,1857-1932,(II*).
Oneil,1925-Aug.1991,(III-N-128).
TRINE
Patrick L.,1947-1947,(*).
TRZENSKA
Mary G.,1891-1945,(II*).
TURGEON
Adelard,1884-1955,(II-118).
Albert E.,1880-1938,(II-118).
Aldea Aube,1899-1973,
  w/o Ovide J.,(III*).
Alfred V.,1878-1960,(II-305N).
Alma Gagne,July 1989,(II-71).
Alphonse,1872-1937,(III-G-32).
Anna B.,1897-1964,w/o L. Armand,
  (II-188).
Arthur,1866-1913,(II-118).
Armand F.,Feb.1964,(III-H-52).
Bertrand,Sept.1957,(III-H-52).
Eugenie Caron,1875-Nov.1946,
  w/o Alph.,(III-G-32).
Hermine Begin,1845-1920,
  w/o P.,(II-118).
inf/o L.A.,Apr.1916,(II-118).
inf/o L.A.,Oct.1918,(II-118).
infant,Apr.1916,(II-188).
Joseph,Apr.1957,(III-H-52).
Leo,1923-Sept.1979,(II-71).
Louis Armand,1888-1948,(II-188).
Lydia M. Deshaines,1880-1965,(II*).
Marie,1867-1950,82y.,(II-118).
Marie Anna,Mar.1968,(II-118).

Ovide,1898-Jan.1959,(III-G-32).
Pierre,Mar.1907,63y,(II-118).
Roland,July 1993,(III-Q-59).
XX,July 1919,w/o Armand(II-188).
XX, Oct.1919,w/o Joshua,(II-188).
TWOMBLY
Albert,Mar.1962,(III-H-2).
Elsie,1901,13y, (O).
George H.,1893-1967,(II*).
Ina B.,1892-1975,w/o Geo.H.,(II*).
Mary E.,1927-Dec.1943,(III-H-2).
UNO
Frank, Apr. 1909,{O}.
USHER
Harry E.,1907-1985,(III-G-12A).
Irene M. Delcourt,
  1906-Oct.1969,(III-G-12A).
VACHON
Aime,Nov.1961,(III-N-23).
Alphonse,1940,56y,(I-E-11W).
Emma Richards,1875-1957,
  w/o Evangeliste,(II*).
Evangeliste,1936,65y,(I-E-11W).
Emma,Dec.1957,Evang.,(I-E-11W).
Florence C.,July 1964,(III-G-59).
Fleride ?,1887 ?, (O/F*).
Herode,Nov.25,1883,21y,(I*).
Ludger,1908-1973,h/o Blanche,(III*).
Rodolphe,July 1920,(II-84).
XX, Jan.1937,w/o Beloni,(I-E-11W).
VAIL
Bernadette A.,1910-1982,(I*).
VAILLANCOURT
A.E.,1895,31y,(II*).
Amedee,Feb.1929,(II-192).
Charles,1841-1922,(II-192).
Dina L.,1870- 1944,w/o Amede,
  (II-192).
Kenneth,May 1974,(III-Q-118).
Laurette,Mar.1973,(II-192).
Laurette Chayer,Oct.1994,54y,
  w/o Roger.
Odilon,Apr.1928,(II-192).
Philomene St. Pierre,1842-1915,
  w/o Charles, (II*).
Rose,Dec.1958,(II-192).
XX, 1935,w/o Alf.,(II-40).
VALIDA
inf/o Isaic,Feb.26,1884,(O/F*).
VALLE
all in section III,
info. taken from newspaper articles.
Charles A.,Feb.1868-May 1949.
Katherine Lynch,1869-1931,w/o Chas.
Rudy,1901-1986.
William Lynch,XXXX.

VICTOR
Gladys Dufour ?,Dec.1969,(III-K-13).
VIGEANT/VEGEANT
Agnes D.,1886-1947,w/o Ulderic,(1*).
Alfred J.,1890-1973,(I*).
Agnes Dame,June 1947,(I-D-3E).
Amanda J.,1902-1980,(III*).
Elmire Richard,1867-1945,55y,
  w/o Uldric,{O}.
Ulderic,1859-1946,(I*)
Ulderic J.,1889-1959. (I-D-3E).
Wilfred J.,1898-1980,(III*).
XX, July 1945,w/o Jos.(I-D-3E).
VINCENT
Adoloza?, July 1978,(III-N-163).
Arsene,1898,26y,(II*).
Blanche,1897-1971,2nd w/o
  Donat,(II).
Clarinda,1893-Feb.1924,
  w/o Donat,(I-E-11E).
Donat,1889-July 1973,(I-E-11E).
Emma Lussier,May 1947,(III-H-61).
Hormisdas,May 1960,(III-H-61).
infant/o Phil.,Mar.1923,(II-26).
Marie D.,1884-1947.
Philip,Sept.1976,(III-N-163).
Roland A.,1919-1991,(III-H-61).
XX,Mar.1953,w/o Hormisdas,
  (III-H-61).
VIOLETTE
Emma D.,1881-1972,w/o Henry,(II*).
Henry A.,1882-1967,(II*).
J. Armand,1917-XXXX,(II*).
Jeanette I.,1908-XXXX,(II*).
Sanford J.,1910-1930,(II*).
Syr X.,1906-1975,(II*).
VOKEY
Mark C.,1953-1994, {O}.
VORONEKE
Mary,1916-1921,(III*).
WADLEIGH
Nellie,1870-1938,(II*).
WALDRON
Rose Anna Gouzie, Oct.12,1907-
  Jan.5,1993,w/o Royal Harrison,
  (I-C-4E).
Royal Harrison, Oct.30,1903-
  Feb.5,1935,(I*).
WALLACE
William,Aug.1895,(II-46).
WARD
Aubrey,Apr.1969,(III-H-15).
Cyrus K.,1835-1901,h/o Susan J.,(O).
Emma,June 1974,(III-Q-120).
WATERS
Hugh M.,1924-1957,(II*).
Irene W.Jordan,1927-1988,(II*).

Rose Anna Martineau,1903-1992,
  w/o Frank,d.1983,(III-Q-143).
WEED
Raymond,May XXXX,(III-N-122).
WELCH
Alice Lapointe,1899-1962,
  w/o Leo J.,(III-K-6).
Arthur,Dec.1965,(III-H-60).
Catherine,1944,(II-6).
Charlotte Gallant,June 1948,(III-H-58)
Coralena,1890-1896,5m,(II-9).
Dannie,1883-1897,
  s/o D.F.& M.A.,(O/F*).
David,Apr.1937,(II-6).
Dennis,1875-Apr.1946,
  h/o Charlotte Gallant,(III-H-58).
Elizabeth,1841-1912,w/o Wm.,(II).
Elizabeth,Jan.1954,(II-6).
Elizabeth Blanchard,Feb.1946,(II-57).
George,1869-Jan.1887,(II-6).
Harold,Nov.1962,(III-N-34).
James H.,Dec.1895,(II-57).
James M.,Dec.1940,16y,(III-H-24)
John E.,May 1957,(III-H-24).
Laura E.,Sept.1895,(II-6).
Laurette Phillips,May 1990,
  w/o J. Edmond,(III-L-20).
Leo J.,1899-Dec.1962,(III-K-6).
Madeline R.,1904-1988,
  d/o P.H. & R.B.,(II*).
Mary,Feb.1896,(II-57).
Mary J.,1872-1942,(II*).
no name,1883-1897,
  s/o D.F. & M.A.,(O/F*).
Patrick H.,1871-1954,(II-225).
Robert,Jan.1907,s/o Wm.,(II-74).
Roland,1914-Apr.1990,{O}.
Rose,1917-1918,(II*).
Rose Richard,1870-Feb.1949,
  w/o Patrick H.,(II-225).
Thomas W.,1866-1916,(II-156).
Walter,1886-1934,(II-6).
William,1836-Mar.1898,(II-6).
William A.,1867-1947,(II-74).
William J.,Mar.1949,(III-H-60).
XX, Jan.1942,w/o Wm.,(II-74).
XX, Mar.1912,w/o Wm.,(II-6).
XX, Dec.1925,w/o Thos.,(II-156).
WELLINGTON
Jeffrey E.,1969-1992,(III-K-31).
Jerry E.,1945-1979,(III-K-31).
WENTWORTH
Josephine,Sept.1953,(III-C-2E).
Rose D.,1879-1949,(II*).
WHITE
Anna,Sept.1971,(III-Q-77).

Nellie Guilford,1908-1992,(III-J-X).
William,Apr.1992,(III-Q-77).
WHITLOCK
Delia B.,1900-1986,(I*).
WILKINS
James,1860-1930,(II*).
Thercile,1857-Sept.1916,
w/o James,(II-39)
WILLIAMS
Agatha Cryer,Aug.1962,(II-F-13N).
George,1858-1912,(II-69).
John F.,Mar.1946,(II-F-13N).
John S.,1825-1904,(II-69).
Lily Smyth,July 1970,(II-F-13N).
Mary Ann,1895-1917,w/o Chas.J.,(II*).
Susan M.,Mar.1948,(II-39).
Susannah,1829-1896,w/o J.S.,(II-69).
XX, Apr.1917,w/o Chas.,(II-196)
WILSON
Alex.G.,1863-1943,(II-137).
Elizabeth,1870-1952,w/o A.G.,(II-137).
Francis C.,1949,(II-137).
Julia M.,1825-1910,w/o Wm.,(II-137).
WING
Deborah Ann,1954-1966,
d/o H.C. & D.L.,(II-123).
WINKPAW
Robert,1985,(III-N-101).
WINSLOW
Agnes M.,1886-1952,(I-D-14E).
Diana,June 1947,(I-C-5W).
Edwin A.,1874-1925,(I*).
Evelyn Nadeau,1917-1993,
w/o Henry, d.1982,(III-M-11).
Sophia,Feb.1994,(III-M-11).
WITZEL
James,July 1958,(III-D-2).
John,Aug.1935,(III-D-2).
Raymond H.,July 1936,(III-D-2).
XX, May 1956,w/o Exilia,(III-D-2).
WOOD
Agnes,Sept.1976,(III-L-72).
Amanda Gravel,1872-1903,(II*).
Benjamin,1864-1950,(II*).
Lawrence,Sept.1973,(III-L-72).
Norman,Dec.1964,(III-N-82).
WORONECKE
Amelia,Aug.1971,(III-H-18)
John,Fan.1951,(III-H-18).
WRIGHT
Shannon,Dec.1982,(III-N-73).
YALE
Evelyn Levesque,1895-1972,
w/o William,(III*).
William Wooster,1895-1944,(III-G-43).

YAMBANIS
Anthony,Feb.1979,(III-Q-50).
Juliette,Dec.1968,(III-Q-50).
YEAGER
Edgar J.,1885-1949,(II*).
Edouard,1885-Apr.1949,(I-E-7E).
Josephine B.,1885-1968,w/o E.J.,
& Joseph Daniel, (II*).
Josephine,Jan.1968,(I-E-7E)
YORK
Ulysses A.,1905-1946,(I*).
XX, Oct.1946,w/o Ulysses,(I-D-11W).
YOUNG
Cecilia,Apr.8,1987,(III-N-134).
George,Mar.1979,(III-N-134).
ZAHARES
Anna M.T.,Jan.1927,(II-226).
Aurore F.,1898-1981,(III*).
Donald J.,Nov.1993,
h/o Hazel E. Spaulding,(III-J-19).
George,July 1952,(III-J-10).
Louis J.,1892-1968,(III*).
Therese,1925-1927,(III*).
ZELENSKY
John,1892-1962,(II*).
Margaret,1904-1942,(II*).

Bits & Pieces of old or damaged stones:

Valida,1881-Feb.26,XXXX,inf/o Isaie.
XX,Aime,1897-1937,(II*).
XX, Georgette, 1918-1922,(II*).
XX, Maurice,1896-XXXX,(II*).
XX,Ellen M.,1879-1889,(II*).
XX, Ernest H.,1894-1945,(II*).

Many of the women were not addressed by their first names, only Mrs. so and so. I tried to locate their gravestones and give these women an identity.
I apologize for any spelling errors, I am not French. I transcribed as well as I could from both the gravestones and the Church records.

XX=No information available.
XXXX, no year available.
( ) information from Church records.
(I*), (II*),(III*) = information from gravestone, not in Church records.
(O/F)= taken from gravestones in section II, which were mostly in French.

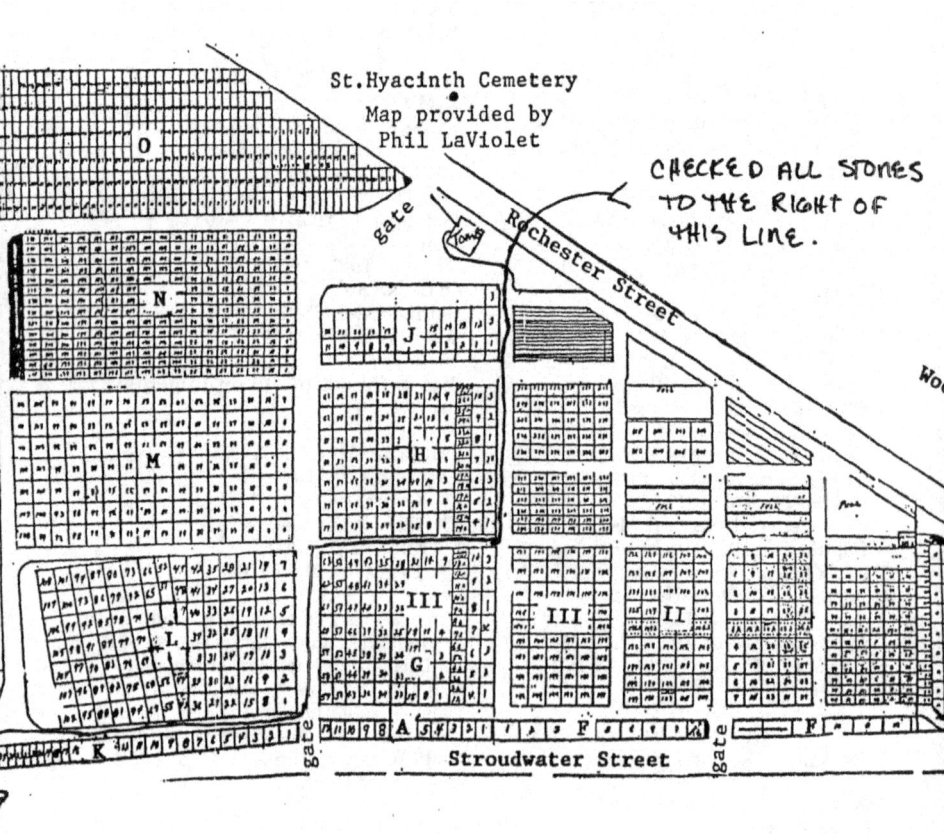

✤ **SOUTH STREET** ✤
17 South Street, Gorham. Also known as the "Old Village Cemetery" and as "The Old Yard". In 1770 Jacob Hamblin presented this burial ground to Gorham,it was originally a part of lot 16, his homestead. All gravestones checked, additional burials from Isaac Cobb's records. * no gravestone found.

ALDEN
Austin,Deacon,Mar.25,1729-Mar.23,1804,1st w. Salome Lomard, bu.:Ft.Hill Cemetery,
2nd w. Hannah Battles (1784).
Josiah,1760-1834.
Sarah Robinson,1757-1820, w/o Josiah.
AYER
Sarah,Apr.9,1828,80y,w/o Peter & w/o Capt. Paul Junkins.
BACON
*Lydia Gorham,Apr.14,1803,62y, w/o Edward,sis/o Hon. William.
Mary,Mar.6,1846,79y,w/o Timothy.
Timothy,Oct.28,1849,87y.
BLAKE
Sally,Nov.8,1846,69y.
BOWMAN
Nathaniel,Dr.,June 8,1797,30y, "killed by the falling of the meetinhouse steeple on the 1st Parish in Gorham.", h/o Sally Johnson.
BRADBURY
John,Dec.31,1822,5w.,s/o J.& M.
Marsha,Nov.26,1822,36,w/o John.
BRIGGS
Lucy Perkins,June 10,1783,19y, 1st w/o Abiel.
BUTTERICK
John,Jan.3,1813,88y.
CHADBOURN/E
Abigail,Aug.15,1813,65y,w/o Silas.
Silas, Lt.,Aug.8,1752-June 15,1823, 1st w. Abigail Crockett, 2nd w. Lucy Seiver Crockett, s/o Humphrey & Phebe,Officier in the Revolution.
CLARK
James L.,Mar.10,1846,11y.
Leonard,Aug.22,1808,4y,s/o M. & M.
Leonard,July 22,1804,5y,s/o M. & M.
Martha,Nov.12,1829,67y.
Moses,Jan.2,1824,60y.
COBB
*Chipman and his 2nd w.Mary Bloom Green Hall, both by 1798.

Priscilla Brossard,Sept.14,1808, 50y,w/o James.
Olive,May 15,1830,77y,w/o Nathaniel.
Susannah Bacon,Dec.24,1718-July 6,1807,wid/o Nathaniel.
CRENY
Louis A.,Nov.24,1818,33y.
CROCKETT
Elizabeth,Mar.6,1845,88y, w/o Samuel (1830).
*Mary Whitney,1794,w/o Samuel.
Priscilla,Nov.5,1822,28y,w/o Samuel.
Samuel,Dec.19,1798,82y ?.
Samuel,Mar.15,1830,77y.
Thomas H.,Oct.27,1839,21y.
ch/o William & Mary:
Marsha Ann,July 2,1842,1y;
Sarah Ann,Sept.14,1838,18m;
Silas B.,May 20,1840,7y.
CROSS
Charlotte T.S.,Aug.25,1843,w/o Dr.E. E.,Dr.,probably here,a broken stone next to her leaning on tree.
Harriet,Oct.20,1790-Mar.11,1798, d/o Thos. & Lucy.
Lucy,Mar.16,1748-May 21,1821,w/o T.
Rebekah,Jan.20,1774-Apr.11,1794, d/o Thomas & Lucy.
Thomas,Nov.18,1741-Feb.15,1819.
William,Capt.,Aug.21,1779-Feb.14,1819,s/o thos. & Lucy.
DAVIS
Salome Alden,Feb.3,1816,29y, w/o Solomon.
DIX
Mary B.,Oct.3,1820,39y,w/o John, d/o Wm. Williams of Boston.
EDWARDS
Clark Swett,1838-1842.
Dorothy Hill,1795-1827.
Eliza Rolf,1801-1841.
James Lawrence,1827-1828.
James M.,1793-1859.
Martha Jane,1823-1823.
Martha McLellan,July 20,1842,68y, w/o Samuel.
Melville Cox,1834-1835.
Samuel,Feb.23,1847,7y.
ELDER
Hannah Freeman,1755-Apr.22,1786, 1st w/o Samuel.
Isaac,Jan.19,1739-July 15,1795, h/o Mary H.,s/o Samuel.
Mary Graffam,1748-1829, 2nd w/o Samuel.
Mary Hatch,1796-1820,w/o Simon.

Mary Hunnewell,Sept.14,1804,
60y,w/o Isaac.
Mary Jane,1820-1828,d/o Simon & M.
Samuel,Aug.29,1748-May 10,1819.
ch/o Isaac & Mary;
Hannah,Oct.10,1801,15y;
William,Jan.15,1782,76y.
ch/o Samuel & Hannah:
Ruth,1789-1865;
Lois,1797-1798;
ch/o Samuel & Mary:
*Peter,Oct.5,1787-Jan.29,1815,
Ruth Huston,1776-Feb.10,1786.
FENNO
Temperance Harding,Dec.8,1789-
Mar.24,1816,w/o Capt.John.,
T.H. was a Pilgrim descendent of
Mayflower (on gravestone).
FILES
George,Feb.3,1766-Jan.1,XXXX.
Temperance,Sept.19,1824,55y,w/o G.
FREEMAN
Hannah,Feb.21,1823,18y,
d/o Nathaniel & Elizabeth Mosher.
FROST
Benjamin,Mar.8,1833,58y.
Benjamin,Jr.,Feb.7,1836,23y.
Betsey,Mar.9,1835,61y.
Margaret,Nov.12,1842,22y,
d/o Benjamin & Mary.
Mercy,Nov.23,1824,41y,
Randall H.,May 13,1840,25y.
GORHAM
*Temperance,Apr.14,1788,43y.
William,Hon.,July 12,1743-
July 22,1804,1st w. Temperance
White, 2nd w. Temperance Garrett.
GOULD
Elizabeth,Oct.2,1794,26y,
w/o Nathaniel,d/o Rev.P. Coffin.
HAMLIN / HAMBLEN
Content,1707-c.1790,1st h.Jacob,
2nd h. James Miller (1787).
Elizabeth,Sept.7,1838,84y,
w/o Jacob (1826).
Franklin,Nov.6,1917.
Hannah,Apr.14,1797,77y,
w/o Gershom of Barnstable.
Jacob,1702-June 3,1774,
h/o Sarah Hopkinson.
Jacob,Oct.15,1826,70y.
Jacob,Capt.,Dec.18,1874,82y.
Sarah Lombard,Dec.3,1893,93y.
HAMLEN
Clara Evelyn,1854-1917.
Fannie H.,1885,61y,w/o Francis.
Francis Asbury,1823-190X.

Franklin,1865,5m,s/o F.& F.
HARDING
David,b.Wellfleet,MA,Mar.14,1762-
Jan.10,1831.
Jeruihah,May 27,1774,30y,w/o Jesse.
Mary,1770,30y,w/o Zephaniah.
Mary,Apr.9,17X2,7m,d/o Zeph.
Mary,Nov.7,1778,1y,d/o Z. & Mary.
Temperance,b.Barnstable,MA,-
d.Aug.29,1810,w/o David.
David & Temperance were Pilgrim
descendents of Mayflower (on stone).
HIGHT
s/o George & Mary:
George A.,Aug.25,18X9-July 1,1820;
William H.,Dec.1,1821-Nov.25,1824.
HUNT
Abner,Jan.8,1798,10y,
s/o Capt. Oliver & Sarah.
Daniel,Apr.19,1816,6y,
s/o Daniel & Angelina.
Daniel,Capt.,June 28,1775-Apr.20,
1833,h/o Angelina Griffin Hastee.
Mary L. Fogg,Oct.31,1805-
Apr.19,1893,w/o Charles.
Oliver,Capt.,Mar.2,1822,67y.
Sarah,Jan.1,1810,47y,w/o Oliver.
HUNTING
Mary Lord,Jan.3,1852,26y,
w/o Rev.John P.
IRISH
James,Jr.,Apr.1,1816,80y,
s/o James & Elizabeth.
Mary Deane,1766-1853,w/o Obadiah.
Mary Gorham,Aug.1736-May 13,1825,
w/o Jas.Jr.,d/o of Capt.John Phinney,
the 1st white child born in Gorham.
Obadiah,1765-1852,s/o Jas.& M.C.P.
JACKSON
Sarah Louisa,July 20,1843,10w,
d/o E.W. & S.McL.
Sarah McLellan,Mar.18,1844,30y,
w/o Rev. Eliphalet.
JEWETT
*Caleb,Rev.,Apr.16,1802,49y.
Martha,Mar.16,1801,84y,w/o Jas.
JONES
Martha,Feb.10,1801,18y,
d/o Ephraim & Mary.
LARRY
*Abigail,Mar.1844,83y,w/o Stephen.
*Dennis,1796,102y.
Stephen,Apr.1838,77y,s/o Dennis.
LEWIS
Desire Parker,May 19,1815,79y,
2nd w/o George.

George,July 24,1819,78y,Rev. Soldier,
1st w. Mary Davis (1782).
*Lothrop,Feb.13,1764-Oct.9,1822,
s/o George & Mary.
*Margaret,Sept.26,1807,25y,d/o Geo.
Mary,Sept.29,1779-Sept.27,1804,
d/o George & Mary.
*Mary Ware,July 9, 1925,16m,
d/o Stephen L.
Stephen L.,Mar.4,1825,30y.
*Tabitha,Oct.9,1774-Apr.15,1807,
w/o Lothrop,ch/o Stephen Longfellow.
LIBBY
Rhoda M.,Aug.8,1824,29y,w/o Jos.,
d/o Allen & Martha Davis.
LITTLE
*John P.,Mar.26,1809,36y.
LONGFELLOW
*Ann,Miss,Nov.26,1781-Dec.7,1817,
d/o Stephen & Patience.
*Catherine,Aug.20,1786-July 5,1804,
d/o Stephen.
*Patience Young,Dec.5,1745-
Aug.12,1830,w/o Stephen.
Samuel, Col.,July 30,1789-
Oct.13,1818,h/o Sophia Storer.
Stephen,Hon.,Aug.13,1750-
May 28,1824,h/o Patience Young.
LORD
Diantha Angeline,Nov.27,1831,1Xy,
d/o Rev.John & Mary.
Mary,Sept.23,1853,w/o Rev.John.
McDUGALL
Anna Elder,July 5,1791,26y,
w/o David,d/o Isaac & Mary.
Mary,Sept.8,1803-July 26,1805,
d/o David & Phebe.
McLELLAN
Abigail,May 11,1821,83y,
w/o James (1792).
Anne,Nov.22,1773,2y,d/o Cary & E.
B.,Miss,Sept.12,1810,25y.
Elder Hugh,Jan.2,1787,77y
Elizabeth McLellan (nee)
July 16,1802,96y,w/o Elder Hugh.
Elizabeth Staples,July 12,1831,24y.
Eunice,AUg.18,1784,39y,w/o Cary.
Eunice,July 24,1773,4y,d/o Cary & E.
James,Dea.,Jan.15,1792,56y.
James,Dea.,Aug.10,1845,69y.
Lois,Nov.20,1859,80y,w/o Dea.Jas.
R.,Miss,Sept.23,1812,25y.
Samuel,July 22,1825,54y.
MARCH
James,Col.,Mar.29,1823,53y.
Sarah J.,Aug.22,1863,83y,w/o James.

MOSHER
Abigail,Oct.23,1815,74y,w/o James.
*James,Oct.2,1834,99y.
NOYES
Jeremiah,Rev.,Jan.15,1807,28y.
PAINE
Lucy,Jan.18,1861,76y,w/o Samuel.
Samuel,Dea.,XXXX.
Sarah,Nov.2,1817,w/o William.
William,Jan.19,1827,83y.
PARKER
Mary,1745,stone broken.
PHINNEY
Abigail,Mar.19,1822,16y,
d/o James & Abigail.
David,Oct.22,1801,9y,
s/o Stephen & Anna.
Edmund,July 23,1723-Dec.15,1808,
h/o Elizabeth Meserve, Col. in Rev.
Eliza,Aug.19,1800,5y,
d/o James & Abigail Mosher.
Elizabeth,Aug.1,1795,65y,w/o Edm.
Heman,Oct.5,1793,11m,
s/o Nathaniel & Mary.
*James,Oct.18,1834,93y,s/o John.
John,Capt.,Apr.8,1693-Dec.29,1780,
1st settler in the town of Gorham,
h/o Martha Colman, s/o John.
*Lucy,Dec.29,1863,82y,2nd w/o Jas.
Martha Colman,Dec.16,1784,86y,
w/o John.
*Martha,Sept.3,1816,76y,1st w/o Jas.
Stephen,Nov.27,1800,38y.
PRATT
Benjamin,Mar.17,1812-Oct.21,1821.
Elizabeth,1819,w/o Benjamin.
PRENTISS
Dolly,1795,35y,w/o Samuel.
Mary Caroline,Mar.8,1815,2y,d/o Wm.
Samuel,Apr.19,1815,62y.
William,Capt.,Feb.23,1826,47y.
RAND
Clarissa,July 7,1825,32y,w/o Rev.Asa.
Grata,Apr.29,1818,33y,w/o Rev.Asa.
REYNOLDS
Sylvester,Sept.4,1826,29y,
s/o Soloman & Joana,of Southport,
Tioga County, New York.
ROLFE
Nancy,Nov.6,1821,37y.
Rebecca,May 26,1816,32y,w/o Benj.
SHAW
Betsey,Oct.15,1806,21y,w/o Enoch,
d/o George King Rainham.
SMITH
*Mary Longfellow Lewis,Feb.15,1820,
23y,1st w/o Jacob Sheaff,d/o Lothrop.

Nancy McLellan,Oct.23,1839,25y,
w/o Stevens,d/o Sam.& Nancy Staples.
STAPLES
Mary Adeline Burnham,Feb.12,1834,
34y,w/o Samuel.
Nancy,June 15,1839,65y.
Samuel,Feb.4,1837,71y,h/o Nancy.
Stephen McLellan,Feb.17,1832,31y.
ch/o Samuel & Mary:
Thomas H.,Dec.25,1832,4y;
XX, Jan.1,1824,2y,d/o.
STEPHENON (on stone)
Neptune,Aug.6,1824,44y,
"he was a colored man who lived with
Col. William Tyng".
STURGIS
David,Dec.6,1828,47y.
Jonathan,May 11,1833,92y,h/o Tem.
Temperance,Mar.26,1824,82y.
THACHER (family tomb built 1810)
*Apphia T. Nason,1808-1839,
grandchild of Josiah is buried in the
family tomb,along with the rest of
the family.
Josiah,Dec.25,1799,h/o Apphia Mayo.
TOWLE
Mary L.,July 22,1850,64y,w/o Abner.
Serena,June 20,1840,22y,d/o A.&M.
WARREN
Ezekial,July 8,1813,12y,
s/o Hugh & Polly.
James,Apr.12,1821,69y.
Martha,Mar.17,18XX,w/o James.
WATTS
David,Aug.1776,11m,
s/o David & Mary.
David,Aug.30,1804,12th ME, Rev.War.
Sarah,Jan.11,1784,20y,
w/o Capt.David,d/o Joseph Davis.
WHITMORE
Samuel,Col.,Aug.28,1808,28y,
s/o Samuel & Mary Whitney.
WHITNEY
Marsha,Nov.10,1886,75y,w/o Steph.

✤ **FARMER FAMILY** ✤
From Gorham Town Clerk. No location.

FARMER
Stanley,Jan.23,1978.

✤ **NORTH GORHAM** ✤
North Gorham Road. Gorham.List
obtained from Gorham Town Clerk.
Managed by a private association.
Gravestones not checked.

ABBOTT
Charles H.,July 18,1871,38y.
ANDERSON
Albert,1989,54y.
Anna P.,1857-1934.
Cynthia Blake,1827-1860.
Huldah Potter,June 21,1874,56y.
Moses,1811-1863.
BACON
Addie Johnson,1867-1952.
Albion,1874-1954.
Leroy C.,Dec.16,1899-Jan.10,1984.
Leroy,Jr.,1926-Aug.25,1973.
Marion S.,1903-1949.
Mary Ann C.,1899-1986.
BARSTOW
Burton A.,1912-Feb.18,1973.
Mary L. Moses,1877-1927.
BEAN
Maria S.,June 8,1875,30y.
BENNETT
Margaret Cannell,Aug.1,1808-
May 13,1882.
BENSON
Ann M.,May 16,1864,35y.
Benjamin F.,May 25,1885,32y.
Benjamin S.,Sept.14,1897,72y.
Charles H.,Apr.27,1874,23y.
BERRY
Glennie Marshall,Dec.12,1886-
Oct.24,1967.
Lewis Ray,Aug.13,1890-June 25,1977.
BIRRELL
Michael Scott,Oct.1964-June 12,1965.
BLAKE
Mary Elwell,1862-1945.
Mehitable,XXXX.
Walter P.,1851-1923.
BOYD
Agnes H. Boyd,Apr.17,1860-
Mar.29,1932.
William H.,Fb.12,1860-Jne 30,1892.
BUHELT
Marshall N.,Apr.27,1984,28y.
BUMPUS
infant,XXXX.
CANNELL
Barnabas,1816-1900.
Clark,Jan.1815-Feb.1900,
3rd w. Elsie Wood.

Dorcas M. Plaisted,Jan.1,1877,57y,
2nd w/o Clark.
Erenac,1883-1907.
Eva M.,XXXX.
Francis,Jan.30,1841,27yw/o Wyer.
George C.,Aug.12,1848,4y.
George C.,Sept.13,1854,1y.
Heman,1821-1895,h/o Lucy A.G.
infant,XXXX.
John J.,1840-1906.
Joseph,Oct.22,1873,73y.
Lorana,1824-1915,w/o Barnabas.
Lucy A. Gilman,1821-1868.
Margaret Nason,Dec.28,1855,77y.
Marshall,July 1832,11y.
Marshall,XXXX.
Mary J.,1859-19XX,
Sarah A. Harmon,Sept.1,1845,25y,
1st w/o Clark.
Temperance G. Sturgis,
Dec.26,1887,89y,w/o Joseph.
Thomas,Mar.12,1854,86y,h/o Marg.,
s/o Philip & Jane.
William,July 1,1863,30y.
William M.,1883-1950.
Wyer,Mar.8,1848,45y,1st w. Francis
Plaisted,2nd w. Sarah Harmon.
CARLETON
Carroll Edward,1891-1961.
Edward Carroll,Sept.8,1913-
Apr.24,1974.
CARVER
Emma C.,1859-1860.
Granville,1830-1901.
Lizzie M.,1860-1860.
Margaret S. Moses,1832-1912.
CHAPMAN
Louise G. Catlin,1931-May 9,1986.
CHARLES
Eliza J.,1845-1901.
Geneva R.,1898-Mar.13,1983.
Hattie M.,1884-1944.
Oswell,1847-1928.
Rodney E.,1905-1983.
Weston O.,1876-1937.
COLE
Everett,Aug.19,1860,42y.
Flora,Dec.12,1858,2y.
COLLEY
Emily F.,Feb.7,1864,14y.
Eunice,Dec.11,1877,85y.
Jane P.,July 26,1868,42y.
John,Apr.2,1823,38y.
Mary Ann,Feb.2,1831-12y.
Mary Ann,Aug.18,1854,2y.
Samuel,Oct.15,1841,25y.
Samuel,June 9,1878,31y.

Sarah S.,July 31,1839,16y.
William W.,Oct.9,1820-Dec.11,1870.
Winnie J.,Aug.22,1864,6y.
CONANT
Arthur R.,1918-1938.
Romayne Larkin,1899-1983.
Russell Lee,1900-June 2,1970.
COOK
Eliza,1821-1888.
Sylvanus B.,1821-1889.
William C.,June 22,1863,13y.
CROCKETT
Addie H. Parker,1850-1889.
Elsie,1891-Aug.22,1973.
Horace M.,1847-1909.
Ralph P.,1877-1939.
DAGGETT
Marie Louise,Mar.27,1899-
Oct.13,1969.
DEAN
Jules,July 16,1978.
DELMONT
Florence Cannell,1885-Apr.1910,
d/o John & Mary Ward Cannell.
Trevor J.,1879-19XX.
DYER
Anna L.,1913-1988.
Elizabeth L.,Nov.18,1891-XXXX.
G. Manning,1883-1958.
George G.,Nov.19,1853-Mar.20,1926.
infant,Sept.6,1889,6d.
Jennie Welch,June 25,1877,18y.
Lizzie E.,Sept.2,1864-Oct.10,1943.
Velma G.,Jan.26,1903,2y.
William M.,1915-1985.
EMERY
Carl Eugene,1897-Oct.14,1969.
Clara A. Jaques,1894-Nov.7,1979.
Russell E.,1948-May 13,1968.
EVANS
Thomas H.,1950-1952.
FILES
Frank H.,1882-1955.
Gertrude Jaques,1882-1941.
FOGG
Almon L.,July 18,1865-May 7,1891.
Almon L.,1895-1912.
Daniel W.,1871-1955.
Dora Frost,Sept.15,1857-Jan.2,1944.
Dorcus Libby,XXXX.
Hannah M.,Jne 5,1830-Aug.29,1895.
Horace H.,June 4,1855-Dec.2,1929.
Joseph F.,Aug.9,1830-Oct.2,1908.
Mary Parker,1870-1954.
Milton H.,1897-1972.
FOSTER
XX, c.1880,12y.

FOYE
Eric Mark,July 15-19,1983.
FREYER
Eleonore G.,1881-Mar.15,1968.
GARDINER
Bessie B. Clifford,1895-1986.
Clarence W.,1887-Apr.21,1966.
GERRISH
Hannah,Dec.13,1876,75y.
GERRY
Maud E.,Feb.14,1908,21y.
GIBBS
Agnes Freyer,1905-1991.
GILMAN
Albion,1857-1862.
Annie Warren,Mar.26,1865-Jan.4,1951.
Bertrand Ward,Oct.24,1890-Oct.22,1977.
Carrol Warren,1888-Mar.26,1909.
Charles H.,1860-1862.
Daniel S.,Feb.2,1859.
Ebenezer,Jr.,1796-1868.
Edward G.,1832-1904.
Effie Josephine Hurd,Dec.21,1889-Apr.6,1969.
Elvira M.Blake,1837-1868.
Frances T. Cobb,1834-1874.
Hannah Cannell,1798-1877.
Hannah E. Waterhouse,1831-1898.
Ithiel Blake,1862-1935.
William Cannell,June 11,1892,67y.
Zachariah S.,1821-1901.
GLADU
Jennie Howard,1872-Dec.3,1968.
GOODRICH
Samuel B.,Jan.1,1933.
GOUDY
Velma Plaisted,Dec.4,1897-Sept.8,1970.
GRAVES
Frederic A.,1880-1946,h/o Annie.
GUPTILL
Arthur W.,July 9,1904-Apr.10,1964.
HALE
Charlotte J.Chase,Aug.19,1893,54y.
Lydia B.,Oct.10,1827-Apr.20,1858.
Washington,XXXX.
HALL
Abigail H.,Aug.18,1841,17y,
d/o Daniel & Mary.
Annie Cummings,June 18,1862-July 31,1863,1st w/o Benaiah.
Aubrey E.,Oct.12,1869.
Augusta Elnora,1858-1864,s/o Joshua
Benaiah H.,Apr.21,1825-June 8,1872.
Clara W.,Dec.6,1862,11y.
Commie P.,Dec.19,1862,4y.
Daniel,Jan.9,1864,74y.
Ellen Jane,1826-1828,d/o Levi & J.
Emeline Tapley,1858-1859.
Emeline,1821-1828.
Frankie P.,June 19,1864,1y.
Hannah Harmon,1786-1813.
Harry H.,Oct.4,1858.
Hattie T.,Oct.31,1863-Apr.7,1865.
Hattie W.,1833-1858.
Helen M.,Nov.23,1852,18y,
d/o Daniel & Mary.
Horace Greeley,1862-1865,s/o Joshua.
infant son,July 7-Aug.14,1867.
infant twin,Oct.31,1868.
Jane Emery,1795-1845,2nd w/o Levi.
Joshua Emery,1823-1864,s/o Levi.
Julia Richards,1861-1898.
Leslie,1986.
Levi,1787-1851,1st w. Hannah H.
J. Lewis,1832-1884.
Lucy Ann Kilborn,1825-1910,
w/o Joshua E.
Margaret,July 31,1860,68y,w/o Dan.
Margaret,June 3,1915-Jan.12,1982.
Mary Nason,1831-1902.
Peter R.,July 28,1869,42y,s/o Daniel.
Preble C.,1822-1896.
Sarah Hawkes,Feb.16,1827-May 31,1884,2nd w/o Benaiah.
Stewart,July 4,1851,22y.
Stewart C.,1855-1911.
Valentine M.,Aug.22,1841,20y,
s/o Daniel & Mary.
HARLOW
Mildred Francesca,1880-Nov.24,1971.
Walter N.,1875-1956.
HASKELL
Effelyn C.,Apr.28,1875-Jan.30,1948.
HAWKES
Albert R.,1833-1908.
Emily W.,1862-1940.
Hannah Morrell,1806-1882.
Harry H.,1859-1910.
Huldah W.,1844-1929.
Lydia T.,1836-1901.
Samuel R.,1799-1847.
Sarah Maria Whipple,1839-1916.
HEATH
Berthena M.,Aug.8,1822-Dec.12,1904.
George W.,Sept.28,1821-Sept.8,1918.
Martha E.,Dec.15,1851-May 31,1853.
Winnie G.,Aug.3,1862-May 19,1876.
HICKS
Clinton,Nov.6,1851,8y.
Ebeneber,May 21,1844,39y.

Ephraim,Mar.23,1783-Dec.14,1835,
h/o Rachel Morton.
Herba H.,Sept.10,1859.
Maranda,June 19,1844,18y.
Mark,XXXX,h/o Sarah Hooper.
Sarah Hooper,July 27,1895,71y.
Susan Parker,1803-1873,w/o Ebene.
HIGGINS
Lydia P. Parker,Aug.21,1902,35y.
HILL
Clifford M.,May 3,1906-Apr.27,1967.
HOWARD
Charles A.,1862-1862.
Elias R.,1835-1923.
Fred H.,1877-1914.
Harry,1864-1864.
Mary A.,1839-1907.
Parker,1860-1860.
HOWE
Alice J.,Aug.18,1965.
Bernard Randolph,Apr.30,1971.
Dorothy Frances Whipple,
Jan.22,1907-Sept.2,1976.
HUBBARD
Harriett M.,1850-1922.
HUNNEWELL
James R.,Jan.1,1866.
HUNTT
Jennie L. Carver,1876-1916.
HURD
Ellen J. Blake,1848-1930.
John Albert,1862-1938.
Olive Nason,1841-1897.
HUTCHINS
Joseph A.,Nov.17,1857,1y.
Simeon N.,Sept.16,1858,52y.
IRISH
Eva M.,1883-1886.
Fred C.,Oct.14,1988,81y.
George H.,1876-1958.
Henry M.,1853-1923.
Lydia M. Moses,1854-1937.
Nellie Plaisted,1879-1934.
JAQUES
Arthur H.,1856-Mar.15,1902.
Charlie A.,1881-1900.
Frederick J.,1878-1899.
Georgia L.,1858-1931.
Philip M.,1898-Oct.29,1966.
Tracy W.,1888-1918.
JENKINS
Sophia W. Hunnewell,1833-1918.
KELLEY
Louise Emery,1923-Aug.20,1977.
LABRECQUE
Harriett E.,1888-1980.
John L.,1881-1944.

John N.,Sr.,May 4,1908-1987.
John Steven,1955-1983.
LARKIN
Arthur D.,1869-1918.
LATHAM
Levi B.,1878-1961.
Olive E. Mann,1881-May 26,1975.
LEBRECQUE
John L.,1945,63y,h/o Harriet Nason.
LESTAGE
Dennis P.,1960-Mar.19,1976.
LETOURNEAU
Denis A.,Jr.,Oct.26,1990,43y.
Nicholas,Aug.20,1982,s.b.
LIBBY
Abigail,July 28,1838,38y.
Alfred,Dec.4,1811-Feb.20,1902.
Arthur Jackson,1879-1961.
Bert,XXXX.
Bertie J.,Jan.19,1875.
Clara,XXXX.
Esther H. Libby,Oct.11,1814-
July 3,1895.
Frederick A.,Feb.3,1851-Aug.30,1925.
Lizzie W.,May 30,1847-June 22,1887.
Lottie M.,1894-XXXX.
Louisa M.,May 28,1853,6y.
Margarite,XXXX.
Marshall F.,May 9,1912.
Sarah A. Knight,Apr.24,1849-
June 12,1931.
Sarah Moses,XXXX.
Woodbury S.,May 19,1816-XXXX,
h/o Apphia T. Moody.
LOMARD
William D.,Sr.,1912-June 24,1982.
LOW
J. Everett,1888-1956.
Rose W. Madden,1889-1938.
LUBEE
Annie L.,June 18,1854-Aug.20,1932.
Harold S.,June 30,1880-Aug.15,1946.
Rosamond E.,Dec.1,1877-Apr.23,1901.
Thomas W.,May 5,1854-May 3,1917.
Vance P.,July 26,1885-May 9,1902.
MABRY
Augusta E. Sprague,Mar.15,1853-
May 8,1889.
Bertrand D.,1882-1904.
Charles Howard,Sept.13,1845-XXXX.
Ella Frances,June 14,1854-
July 29,1855.
Enoch,Aug.17,1849-1926.
Georgeana,Aug.14,1847-Apr.23,1875.
Harland J.,Jan.17,1880-Nov.23,1881.
Jefferson,Jan.30,1814-Dec.12,1871.
Lillian M.,1866-1937.

Lucretia Ann,Oct.22,1819-July 3,1885.
Martha Ellen,Nov.11,1843-XXXX.
Susan Dole,May 20,1854-Dec.26,1882.
Virginia V.,1890-1924.
MacDONALD
Mary A. Walker Larkin,1870-1957.
MADSON
Eva Louise Mabry,Sept.24,1975.
MANCHESTER
Addie M.,1872-1958.
Almon,Sept.2,1839-Jan.23,1859.
Benjamin,Feb.13,1803-Apr.1,1881.
Charles Nahum,1900-Feb.6,1971.
Eben F.,1832-1911.
Elmer E.,1862-XXXX.
Gracie M.,1871-XXXX.
Harlan F.,1873-XXXX.
Howard C.,1873-1913.
Idella M.,1867-1868.
infant,Jan.30,1914,newb.
Joseph B.,1870-1938.
Madeleine I.,1906-
Maria L.Varney,1841-1912.
Polly/Mary,June 3,1829,24y.
Susan,May 18,1808-June 6,1894.
Warren P.,1880-XXXX.
H. Wyman,1859-1902.
MANSON
Donald E.,1906-1987.
Gertrude A. Stewart,1919-Oct.1978.
MARSH
Forest J.,1915-1983.
MARSTON
Herbert A.,1881-Jan.22,1964.
Lena Agnes Boyd,1885-Aug.31,1972.
MARTIN
Almeda F.,1849-1876.
MAYBERRY
George Willard,Mar.4,1868,5y, s/o Henry.
Cora Jane,May 8,1876,18y,d/o H.
Elizabeth A. Bennett,Apr.19,1820-Nov.21,1907,w/o Henry.
Henry,Sept.8,1828-Jan.4,1904.
Laurence Fred,Aug.-Sept.1883.
Mark L.,Aug.23,1881,58y.
Mary,Nov.27,1856,35y.
Nellie M.,1847-1907.
MAYBERY
Alfred,Mar.8,1810-Aug.20,1882.
Lucretia,Jan.16,1818-Nov.7,1896.
McNUTT
Alex,1837-1900.
MITCHELL
Eben,1810-1890.
Emeline,1818-1898.
Georgia Mabry,1877-1958.
MORTON
Martha,1853-1895.
MOSES
Adeline Higgins,1829-1925.
Alice M. Johnson,1865-1895.
Alonzo J.,1835-1917.
Annie E.,1852-1889.
Annie Strout,1857-1880.
Celia M. Bradeen,1858-1925.
Charles Alvin,1854-1925.
Edward Marshall,1861-1958.
Eva M. Barbor,1885-1931.
Fannie A. Mabry,1863-1902.
Frances,Mar.17,1922-Nov.25,1958.
Frank A.,1885-XXXX.
George H.,1851-1926.
Harry E.,1895-1896.
Josiah,1799-Feb.22,1860.
Lillian M.,1868-1907.
Lulu Belle Smith,June 9,1889-Nov.25,1958.
Lydia,June 30,1879,81y.
Marshall Henry,1824-1906.
Mina A.,1886-1922.
Orrin P.,1822-1891.
Russell Wolcott,July 22,1893-Dec.12,1975.
Sadie F. Leslie,1856-1877.
Sarah A.,1829-1888.
Susan Q.,1835-1884.
William,Jan.15,1858,29y.
Wolcott Newman,Jan.23,1928-Jan.3,1943.
MUEHLE
Mary R.,1906-1986.
Paul Victor,1904-1980.
NASH
Hazel,Dec.2,1892-Sept.27,1940.
William,1895-after 1940.
William Melvin,Feb.9,1964,
Lena,Feb.16,1968.
NASON
Abbie J.,May 6,1928.
Augusta M.,1859-1879.
Almira,Jan.1,1891,86y,unm.d/o Jos.
Charles A.,Mar.17,1888,39y.
Charles Earl,Sept.6,1807.
Comfort Manchester,1812-1855, w/o Ebenezer.
Earl,Apr.19,1875,67y,w/o Elmira.
Ebeneber L.,1810-1894.
Elizabeth Waterhouse,Aug.6,1863, 81y,w/o Joseph.
Elmira Morton,Feb.22,1849,38y
Emily Z. Parker,Feb.22,1893,36y.
Georgia,Apr.23,1875,27y.
Guy,1921?.

Harriet,Jan.20,1895,76y,w/o Isaiah.
Hattie J.,1862-1942.
Isaiah,Dec.13,1881,64y,s/o Uriah Jr.
James,Capt.,May 23,1847,53y.
James,Oct.22,1862,38y.
Jemima Snow,1786-Feb.6,1868.
Joseph,Apr.8,11860,77y.
Lena A.,1888-1968.
Lewis E.,1866-1936.
Lot,Aug.7,1840,65y,h/o Betsey Lord.
Mary A.,1832-1897.
Rebecca,1825-1911.
Rebecca Jane,1828-1918.
Ruth Ann,May 12,1840,25y,
d/o Lot & Betsey.
Samuel E.,XXXX.
Susan Proctor,Nov.15,1861,68y,
w/o James (1847).
Uriah,Jr.,1785-Feb.6,1863,h/o Jemi.
William P.,May 23,1871,56y.
NOURSE
Albert H.,1870-1957.
NUGENT
Brian E.,Aug.4,1853-May 4,1970.
Dennis,June 21-22,1949.
Melville Arthur,1919-July 1,1982.
OSGOOD
Nelson,Nov.21,1860,26y.
PARKER
Albert J.,1864-1864,s/o Joseph W.
Albion,Mar.22,1850,1y,s/o Jere & S.
Amanda S.,May 10,1909,66y.
Eleazer H.,Jan.28,1814,43y.
Elizabeth Rand,Apr.4,1858,83y,
w/o Eleazer H.
Ellen A. Plummer,Apr.29,1833-
Apr.20,1898,2nd w/o Jeremiah.
Emily,1854-1854,d/o Jos. W.
Emily L.,1855-1925,d/o Jos.W.
Esther,Mar.30,1813,17y.
Frances Swazey,1866-19XX,
w/o Wendell P.
Horace Greeley,1860-1925,
h/o Mary Elwell.
infant,1845-1845.
Irving,Sept.7,1911,74y,s/o Jere & S.
Jeremiah,Sept.20,1807-
Nov.12,1890,s/o Eleazer.
Joseph W.,1813-1901,s/o Eleazer.
Kate,1852-1912,d/o Jos.W.
Lizzie,1859-1859,d/o Jos.W.
Maria Cook,Dec.16,1882,30y,
w/o Winfield (1910).
Mary P. Lombard,1826-1891,
Neal Dow,May 11,1861,8y.
Sally P. Nason,Mar.19,1850,32y,
1st w/o Jere..

Winfield S.,Sept.5,1844,2y,s/o Jere.
Winfield Scott,Jan.19,1847-
May 20,1910,s/o Joseph W.
Wendell P.,1863-1942,s/o Jos.W.
PEARSON
Charles Albert,1871-1943.
Clara Louise,1886-Dec.17,1966.
PERHAM
Florence,1921-July 4,1987.
PLAISTED
Althea B.,1857-1928.
Fred S,XXXX.
Harris M.,1881-1949.
Henry F.,1852-1935.
Huldah A.,Apr.19,1894,68y.
Minnie R.,Feb.24,1882,17y.
Trafton E.,1930-1986.
Trafton S.,1845-1934.
Virgil W.,1893-1893.
PORTER
Florence M.,1903-1965.
Frank E.,Sr.,1899-1971.
RICE
Betsey S.,Mar.7,1880,77y.
Lucy Ann W.,Feb.22,1834,3y.
Mary C.,June 16,1852,17y.
William A.,Oct.25,1871,68y.
RICHARDSON
Doris E. Manchester,Nov.27,1988,
91y.
ROLFE
Byron G.,Sept.6,1896-July 3,1970.
Emery,Nov.2,1862,19y.
L. Katherine Moses,Sept.20,1893-
Mar.14,1986.
SALISBURY
Elbridge G.,Jan.25,1892,80y.
Mehitable E.,Dec.22,1985,70y.
SAWYER
Emeline A.,1842-1937.
George F.,Dec.18,1902,71y.
SCHOLL
Josephine Manchester,Oct.20,1991,
85y.
SHAW
Beatrice Batty,1885-1917.
Benjamin,June 27,1859,56y.
Carlyle W.,1842-1923.
Chester B.,July 18,1863,24y,
Civil War Vet.,s/o Josiah.
Clara Parker,1848-1930,w/o Carlyle.
Clinton D.W.,Aug.6,1839-XXXX,
Josiah B.,Apr.22,1883,75y.
Polly Haskell,1802-1894,w/o Josiah.
Scott P.,1878-1954.
Willie A.,Mar.1,1860,1y.

SMITH
Edward O.,1881-1961.
Ernest R.,1884-1956.
H. CLiffford,1898-1917.
Harry W.,1870-1937.
J. Hamilton,1893-1958.
Marion Reid,1893-Nov.21,1988.
Mary D.,1857-1941.
Ruby F.Higgins,1890-1974.
Walter A.,1857-1907.
SPINK
Arthur M.,Sr.,Feb.23,1897-
  Apr.3,1981.
Robert S.,Aug.20,1961-Apr.29,1981.
STILES
Wayne W.,1936-1975.
STROUT
Daniel W.,Feb.9,1872,13y.
Dora B.,Sept.27,1862,2y.
A. Eugene,Apr.17,1881,3y.
Horace J.,Sept.24,1888,15y.
infants,July 20,1863.
Rachel,May 21,1889,52y.
Rachel,May 21,1889,52y.
Thomas,Rev.,Jan.9,1904,73y.
SUTKOVOY
Alex,1896-1977.
STAPLES
Celia Rena,Mar.21,1909,25y,
  w/o Wm.M.Cannell.
SWETT
Charles C.,Sept.8,1854,30y.
Clark,May 5,1839,48y.
Martha,Jan.22,1843,45y.
THOMAS
George M.,Mar.11,1874-Apr.5,1874.
Howard G.,Sept.23,1895,24y.
Jennie N.,Apr.30,1889,17y.
Joseph Willard,1867-1956.
Julia E. Blake,July 10,1896,54y.
Maitland D.,Jan.19-Apr.11,1877.
Manuel,May 19,1919,77y.
Sarah Beatrice Smith,1867-1953.
TOFT
Bodil J.,1817-1887.
George T.,1896-1930.
Henrik M.,1855-1942.
Howard W.,1894-1967.
Jacob J.,1816-1899.
Marie J.,1852-1924.
TOMLINSON
Clifford,1904-1982.
Delphine C.,1902-1990.
Florence B. Woodworth,1879-1941.
Fred A.,1876-1937.
TRICKEY
Albert,May 29,1835-July 13,1851.

Albert F.,Feb.22-Sept.11,1855.
Charles S.,Apr.1847-June 19,1917.
Edward H.,Sept.29,1837-May 1880.
Harriet H.,Feb.10,1814-Oct.5,1889.
Ida A. Brown,1860-1930.
infant,Jan.22,1905.
Jennie Mayberry,Aug.20,1864-
  Jan.5,1949.
John,1845-1916.
Lydia M. Gilman,Dec.22,1849-
  May 16,1891.
Otis,May 26,1849-July 20,1907.
Peter,Jan.31,1804-Apr.25,1892.
Peter,1859-1922.
TURNER
Evangeline,XXXX.
Samuel,Sr.,XXXX.
Clara M.,1855-1887.
George S.,Jan.6,1858-Dec.12,1933.
Leslie Pearl,Nov.28,1887-
  Oct.13,1897.
Rose Milligan,Dec.14,1858-
  Oct.12,1923.
Samuel G.,1847-June 21,1882.
TURTLOTT
Bessie J.Atherton,1881-19622.
VARNEY
Alice J.,June 26,1861,2y.
Edwin R.,June 24,1884,51y.
Janette L.Rice,Mar.24,1930,91y.
VERRILL
Emma A. Parker,Dec.22,1851-
  Feb.23,1898.
WARD
Annie M. Turner,1870-1945.
Charles M.,1840-1864,s/o John & M.
Eleanor Webb,1802-1883.
Frank W.,1863-1935.
Hannah Mitchell,1773-1856.
Jesse,1771-1845,h/o Hannah.
Lewis B.,Oct.1853,18y,s/o John & M.
Lucy A.,Apr.26,1855,22y.
Mehitable Nason,Nov.18,1806-
  Mar.9,1864,w/o Joseph.
Roswell Nason,Arp.5,1898,64y,
  h/o Sarah Jane Warren.
Sarah J. Warren,Jan.4,1891,48y.
William W.,Dec.1844-Oct.20,1863.
ch/o Jesse & Hannnah:
  Abigial,1829-1830.
  Abigail,1830-1830.
  John,1801-1801.
  John,1805-1861,h/o Mary Gerrish.
  Joseph,Sept.24,1865,58y.
  Solomon,1816-XXXX,unm.
WARREN
Etta A.,1849-XXXX.

William M.,1840-1912.
WEBB
Eli,Aug.13,1883,57y.
WEBSTER
Alice V.,1894-1968.
Ellen J.,1833-1892.
Elwood W.,1924-1981.
Frank E.,1860-1935.
Harold B.,1892-1972.
Josie S. Bassford,1862-1950.
Lydia Ann,1856-1857.
William C.,1820-1895.
WENTWORTH
George H.,June 10,1911,63y.
WESCOTT
Caroline H. Sturgis,1802-1882.
Harvey,1806-1890,h/o Caroline H.
William T.C.,1841-1888.
WHEELER
Elizabeth,May 24,1852,30y.
Jonathan,XXXX.
Sarah,XXXX,10d.
WHIPPLE
Bertha Frances,1875-1947.
Carl L.,1875-1964.
Caroline A.,Sept.13,1849,3y.
Charles A.,1842-1915.
Charlotte E.,Sept.3,1838,2y.
Elizabeth P.,1881-1968.
Ella M.,Sept.17,1859,6y.
Emily,1806-1875.
James,1801-1855.
Jane Parker,1846-1928.
William A.,1867-1936.
WHITE
Enoch,May 2,1866,63y.
Mary Ann,Mar.11,1877,76y.
William H.,July 27,1869,33y.
WHITTIER
Ruth A.,1843-1915.
WIGNOT
Albert A.,1863-1927.
Teresa J.,1874-1932.
WILLIAMS
Catherine,Dec.5,1883,3m.
Eddie,Apr.22,1891-Aug.11,1900.
Leslie,XXXX.
Mary,XXXX.
Nellie,Nov.27,1882,7m.
WILSON
Ellen Louise,May 17,1911-
Jan.20,1972.
WYMAN
Marion,July 26,1890-Sept.24,1982.
Thomas C.,Apr.2,1890-Nov.14,1964.
YERXA
Hazen I. Trickey,1895-1929.

✦ **HILLSIDE CEMETERY** ✦
Huston Road, Gorham.
Managed by Association.A list of early
burials was given to me, burials after
1985 were obtained from the Gorham
Town Clerk. This is not a complete list.

ADJUTANT
Frank W.,1945.
Winifred May,Feb.7,1967.
ALLEN
Beatrice Helen,Nov.10,1975.
Dorothy C.,Mar.20,1980.
Luella H.,Apr.26,1990.
ARMSTRONG
Florence A.,Aug.29,1970.
AUSTIN
Eunice,June 15,1992,rem. from
a Windham cemetery
Philip,Sr.,May 16,1992.
BACON
Jane W. Marston,1814-1890,
w/o Dea. William.
William,Deacon,1811-Dec.23,1892.
BAGLIVO
Vincent,Nov.1,1985.
BAILEY
Cedric Arnold,Sept.3,1975.
Emma F.,Feb.16,1865,10y,
d/o J.P.& M.E.
Raymond Jr.,Dec.4,1982.
Stella,Sept.9,1971.
BALLARD
C. Sanderson,Nov.15,1981,32y.
BATCHELOR
Estella Abiah Nichols,Apr.4,1964.
Henry,Oct.29,1973.
BEAUMIER
Robert H.,Jan.2,1973.
BECKWITH
Alice Christine,Jan.16,1974.
Harvey D.,Jan.30,1982.
Jayne,May 20,1987.
Lillian,May 20,1987.
BELANGER
Joseph Alex,Nov.25,1992.
BENNETT
Howard Collins,Sept.10,1982.
John,Apr.23,1988.
Marion C.,Aug.10,1965.
BENSON
Helen N.,July 31,1980.
Leslie A.,Apr.18,1966.
Peter Bruce,Aug.30,1984.
Robert J.,Oct.1982.
BERRY
Charles J.,1841-1900.

Dorothy M.,Sept.29,1992.
Gertrude,Dec.2,1980.
Lousia A.,Jan.4,1890,54y,d/o N.&L.
Lydia Anderson,Aug.7,1891,81y,
w/o Nathaniel W.
Nathaniel W.,Feb.17,1872,64y.
Robert P.,Dec.7,1842,4y,s/o N.W.&L.
Sarah Crockett,1844-XXXX,
w/o Charles J.
BICKFORD
Beaulah,Apr.30,1987.
child,Apr.5,1972.
BILLINGS
Ralph B.,May 11,1992,84y,
h/o Flavilla Knight..
BLAKE
Mildred,Apr.24,1982.
Theodore,May 30,1980.
BODGE
Lawrence,May 15,1989.
BOLTON
Albert,Aug.27,1994.
Isabelle Ellen,Aug.19,1986.
BRACKETT
Charles H.B.,1941.
Drusilla,1927.
Edmund,1951.
Hattie Jordan,1890.
Harriet,May 5,1987.
Gertie H.,1865-1867.
Guy Leland,Dec.21,1967.
Iva Knight,1963.
Jessie,1927.
Lewis Edmund,Nov.17,1969.
Lewis W.,1861-1868.
Lewis,1867-1877.
Lewis,1920.
Mary,1944.
Mary Edna,Aug.14,1975.
Samuel Lord,1844-1911,
h/o Esther Hanson.
Winnie,1858-1866.
Woodbury,1855-1857.
BRAGDON
Inez Thompson,Feb.8,1971.
BRIDGE
child,XXXX.
Harriet Rebecca,Oct.2,1977.
BROCHE
Florence Hattie,June 10,1970.
BROOKES
Bertha Acker,Jan.10,1971.
Mark,May 16,1986.
BROOKS
Miles,Apr.30,1987.
BROWN
Alfred,1893.

Amos,June 30,1868,60y,
s/o Joseph & Betsey Thomes.
Annie,1931.
Asa P.,Nov.2,1882,24y.
Bertha,1886.
Betsey Hawkes,1803-1879,
w/o Joshua S.
Bertrand,1967.
Colby,1939.
Ella M.,Jan.16,1966.
Frank F.,1888-1962,
h/o Lilliam Hamblen.
Hattie, May 14,1992.
Joshua L.,1803-1882,s/o Ezra & S.
Lendall,June 23,1893,62y,
h/o Evelyn C. Hamblen,
s/o Joshua & Betsey.
Mehitable Wing,Feb.17,1872,66y,
w/o Amos.
Willis,Mar.14,1983,60y.
BUOGIRNO
Ruth Margaret,July 23,1966.
BURKE
Mary E.,(Betty) July 15,1988.
Raymond,May 24,1968.
BURROWS
newb.,Dec.27,1978.
BURTON
Edwin M.,Feb.14,1826-Dec.3,1855,
h/o Lucy Ford.s/o Wm. & Mary.
Mary Berry,Mar.23,1876,82y,
w/o Wm. Jr.
Mary Ross,Apr.11,1830,72y,w/o Wm.
William,b. Gloucester Co.,VA.,
d.Sept.23,1841,82y.
William,Jr.,June 9,1882,84y,
s/o Wm.& Mary.
BYRNE
Annie,May 19,1990.
CARVER
Anna M.,Dec.4,1968.
CHABOT
Antoine,Apr.15,1964.
CHAMBERS
Albert,June 29,1978.
Beatrice E.,Feb.29,1972.
Harris Miles,July 4,1965.
Mamie Mae,Mar.3,1970.
CHANDLER
Alice Hooper,192X.
Grace L.,1944.
William Parron,Jan.9,1968.
William,Jr.,Aug.14,1990.
CHAPLIN
Dorothy,June 17,1993.
CHARLES
Steven Theodore,Dec.8,1967.

CHRISTENSEN
Harold,June 11,1994.
CILLEY
David,Oct.27,1872,82y.
Hannah,Apr.21,1872,86y,w/o David.
CIZEK
James,May 8,1989.
CLARK
Joan Audrey,Oct.4,1978.
Theresa,Feb.12,1979.
CLEMENT
James Henry,Oct.15,1986.
XX,May 4,1981.
CLIFFORD
Everett M.,Apr.1,1969.
CLOSSON
Harry,1960.
Mary E.,1961.
CLOUDMAN
Emma C. Clay,Jan.13,1911,
w/o Horace.
Eunice,July 7,1801-Feb.27,1885.
Jesse,Jan.25,1848,79y,1st w.Hannah
Swett (1815), s/o Timothy & Cath.
Partridge Cloudman.
Helen P.,July 17,1868,24y.
Horace,Feb.15,1893,s/o Sewell.
Lester,May 9,1890,21y.
Lucy A. Sweetser,Apr.7,1830-
Oct.17,1880,1st w/o Solomon B.
Maebelle Burnell,July 31,1969.
Mark,Mar.5,1811-Sept.13,1892,
h/o Susan Burnett.
Nathan,Nov.24,1895,58y,h/o Helen P.
Austin,s/o Mark & Susan.
Rebecca,June 17,1989.
Ruth Kimball,June 24,1987.
Sarah Bacon (Sally),
Mar.23,1869,82y,2nd w/o Jes.
William,1826-1909,h/o Emily J. Dunn
(1876,39y), s/o Wm.& Sarah Haskell
COBB
Chester,1936.
Elizabeth,Feb.23,1971.
Emma Ida,July 15,1968.
Florence Willis,June 2,1965.
Mildred F.,Aug.28,1990.
Levi Randall,Aug.16,1967.
COCHRAN
Esther,Apr.1,1851,1y,d/o Thomas &
Margaret.
COMA
John,Mar.25,1968.
CONLEY
David R.,Jr.,Feb.14,1970.
COOK
Clifton,July 31,1985.

COOTE
Frances,May 26,1994.
COPERTHWAITE
Lillian S.,Feb.28,1975.
CORKUM
Burton J.,June 1987.
Gordon J.,Feb.,1977.
Lena A.,Oct.14,1965.
COUSINS
Daniel,May 8,1992.
Doris A.,Apr.29,1994.
CROCKER
Hattie Bertha,Dec.27,1965.
CROCKETT
George,Apr.21,1948.
John F.,Dec.31,1861-Jan.25,1862,
s/o L.S. & M.J.
Lathrop S.,Dc.10,1815-June 28,1885.
Mary J. Libby,Nov.17,1822-
uly 1,1882,w/o Lathrop.
Mary,Apr.24,1990.
Oscar S.,Feb.6,1849-Aug.6,1868,
s/o L.S. & M.J.
CUSHING
Eugene Ellsworth,Nov.14,1971.
DAICY
Annie K.,Mar.11,1968.
DAVIS
Charles,Sept.23,1989.
George C.,July 1911,72y,
h/o Ardella Parker, in Civil War.
Gladys,Nov.25,1980.
Harlan,July 5,1984.
Marjorie,May 18,1990.
Philip,Aug.31,1993.
DAY
Cecil,Oct.10,1985.
Elsie Naomi,Sept.1,1969.
DEGUIO
Mary,Mar.3,1896,74y,2nd w/o Jos.
DIONNE
Raymond J.,Aug.10,1979.
DIX
Alice Elizabeth,Feb.27,1982.
John,Jr.,1962.
DOLLOFF
Irene Mary,Jan.10,1982.
DOUGLASS
Amanda Lee,Nov.8,1980,newb.
Charles W.,Sept.10,1973.
Margaret,Oct.30,1987.
DOW
Charles,May 18,1992.
Emily,Sept.13,1979.

DOXEY
John,June 15,1887,an Englishman died very suddenly at Mallison Falls. He was a union soldier & buried by the G.A.R.
DUBAY
Alma,June 26,1968.
DUFORD
Eugene,May 10,1993.
DUMBROCYO
Fred,1976.
DURANT
Alice G.,Oct.19,1988.
Carroll H.,Dec.22,1979.
DWYER
Margaret,Oct.3,1974.
DYER
Dorothy,May 12,1993.
Harold Leroy,Nov.17,1974.
DYKE
Herbert Willis,May 3,1970.
DYWER
Albert,Apr.24,1979.
EDDY
Joanna,Dec.10,1976.
EDWARDS
Myrtle H.,July 1,1972.
EMERSON
Harold,May 8,1991.
EMMONS
Alta,Sept.24,1986.
ENNIS
Fred,1962.
Mildred Ward,Dec.16,1966.
ERICKSON
Beaulah,Oct.21,1991.
Edith,1962.
Rudolph,June 26,1987.
Ryner,Apr.24,1990.
ESTES
Dorcus Chesley,1781-1867.
James,XXXX,child.
Levi,1820-1907,h/o Hannah Cloudman(1897,73y).
Nabby,1803-1805.
Rachel,1815-1891.
Ralph Brown,Jan.10,1978.
Robert,1777-1872,h/o Dorcus.
Effie L.,Jan.30,1968.
ch/o Robert & Dorcus:
Abigail,1810-1846,
Charles H.,1827-1873.
ESTEY
James,Sr.,XXXX.
EVANS
Beverly,Apr.27,1992.

FEARON
Clyde Milton,July 4,1975.
Elizabeth,Aug.7,1969.
FICKETT
Margaret,May 2,1988.
Stanley,May 27,1987.
FLANDERS
Jotham,Capt.,Nov.12,1887,78y.
FLEET
Marcia,Jan.13,1911,w/o Hale.
FLYNN
William J.,1870-1893.
FOGG
Harvey Andrew,Jr,Sept.8,1967,inf.
Joseph Parker,Jan.30,1970.
Madelyn,Apr.16,1988.
FOLEY
Agnes L.,July 24,1966.
Thomas,May 14,1969.
FOREHAND
Charles E.,May 2,1974.
FOSTER
Ralph,June 13,1992.
Wilfred Laurier,Sr.,Feb.17,1978.
FREEMAN
Clifford,1988.
Harlan,Apr.22,1965.
Lawrence J.,July 11,1991.
Lorette E.,Apr.23,1977.
Mildred,June 15,1992.
FRENCH
Bertrand H.,Apr.5,1966.
Clyde V.,Nov.24,1973.
Florence,Feb.1966.
Gladys E.,Aug.22,1972.
Stanley,July 15,1975.
Wilbur V.,Nov.10,1967.
FRINK
Emily,1843-XXXX,w/o John P.
John P.,1845-1898,Co.F,17th Me Vols.
John,Col.,1812-1890,s/o Sam.& Mary.
GALE
Mary A.,Feb.18,1981.
Vincent,Oct.31,1981,62y.
GARLAND
Cecil,Feb.21,1983,70y.
Eleanor,May 8,1976.
GASTON
Amy,June 12,1979,4m.
Evelyn,Oct.22,1992.
Larry Alfred,Sept.12,1974.
GILMAN
Alan L.,June 8,1982.
GILPATRIC
Daniel H.,Feb.2,1960.
Daniel Oscar,Sept.22,1975.
Gladys Violet,Aug.3,1976.

Nellie M.,Dec.14,1987.
Oscar E.,Aug.18,1968.
GIROUX
Scott,Aug.20,1991,3y.
GRADY
Alfred Joseph,Sept.16,1980.
GRAY
Charles E.,June 19,1980.
Sherman,June 11,1992.
GREENE
Bruce,1970.
Ellsworth J.,Aug.25,1986.
Mary V.,June 27,1965.
William James,Jan.22,1964.
GUIMOND
Chad Philip,Nov.13,1975,4m.
GUPTILL
Freeman,Nov.26,1965.
HALE
Delia,1856-1899,w/o J.W.
HALL
Clara M.,May 7,1965.
Donald Cleaves,Jan.17,1964.
Philip T.,Nov.5,1969.
HAMBLEN
Albert,Apr.2,1890,70y,
 h/o Cynthia W. Silla (1889).
Dave,1980.
George W.,Sept.8,1893,74y,
 s/o Allen & Lydia Winslow.
Joseph,May 1,1985.
Joseph H.,Jr.,Aug.9,1993.
Laureta Anderson,1831-1893,
 w/o Edwin R.
Mary J. Hanson,1819-1888,w/o G.W.
Marion E.,Jan.19,1976.
Nellie F.,May 15,1964.
HAMEL
Dana H.,Sept.7,1978.
Eva,Sept.26,1973.
HAMLIN
Arleen T.,Jan.20,1980.
HANSON
Emily,1814-1884,d/o Tim.& Rebecca.
Eric,1961,newb.
Eugene,June 13,1992.
Fanny,1804-1882,d/o Tim.& Rebecca.
Frank D.,May 10,1991.
Isaac Aaron,July 24,1990,newb.
Jean,Aug.1,1994.
Juanita M.,Mar.19,1966.
Mark Allen,1957, newb.
Rebecca Hawkes,1775-1858,w/o Tim.
Timothy,1776-1855.
HARDING
C. Wesley,Mar.22,1856,37y.
Frances,Aug.3,1852,52y,w/o Freeman.

Jane Hanson,Oct.25,1886,76y,
 w/o C.Wesley.
HARLOW
Margaret Marion,Feb.7,1977.
HARMON
Arlene M.,Oct.15,1978.
Mehitable,Mar.1,1865,79y.
William,Dec.13,1848,87y,
 Soldier in Rev.,h/o Mehitable.
HASKELL
Jessie,1927.
HAWKES
E. Stanley,Aug.29,1985.
Edwin Percy,Oct.26,1968.
Edwin,May 1,1985.
Elijah,1819-1888,
 s/o Benjamin & Ruth Roberts.
Mary,May 1,1984.
Ruth,1818-1899,w/o Elijah.
Tom,Nov.16,1984.
HAWXWELL
Clara,Sept.19,1988.
William,Aug.17,1988.
HAYES
Ruth Russell,Nov.26,1969.
HICKEY
s.b. infant,Feb.4,1970.
HODGKIN
Emma Elizabeth,Feb.17,1967.
Eva M.,May 12,1993.
Everettt Merle,Mar.6,1966.
Hazel Marie,Sept.5,1966.
HODGMAN
Ada M.,July 29,1968.
John William,Mar.1,1969.
HOMAN
Arthur,July 1,1986.
HOPKINS
Norris Stanley,June 14,1964.
Viola,Aug.14,1987.
HORR
Vesta,May 4,1984.
HOWARD
XX,1976.
HUFF
Nelson Henry,June 7,1965.
HUGHEY
Pearl,Nov.12,1990.
Robert K.,Apr.25,1987.
INGALLS
Harry,Sept.2,1982.
JAMES
Clarence W.,May 8,1989.
Edward A.,June 28,1979.
JAMESON
Alice M.,Feb.9,1982.
Frederick L.,Mar.16,1966.

JEMERY
Medas,Oct.17,1985.
Mildred,May 29,1991.
JENSEN
Marion G.,Mar.4,1980.
JOHNSON
Alice Rand,Feb.24,1983.
Beulah A.,Jan.2,1970.
Dorothy,May 1,1984.
Francis,May 1,1984.
Harriette W.,Apr.29,1979.
Helen,Sept.29,1987.
Irene Glynn,June 30,1975.
John E.,Jan.17,1964.
John R.,1957.
John,Apr.27,1988.
Lawrence,May 5,1985.
JONES
Annie L.,Jan.15,1965.
KELLER
Mary Smith,1883-1946.
Millard,July 20,1988.
KETECK
John,Jan.10,1963.
KIDDER
Florence A.,June 3,1965.
KIMBALL
James,Apr.26,1985.
Leslie,Mar.8,1979.
Mora June,Feb.8,1969.
XX, 1980.
KNIGHT
Charles D.,1984.
Charles Waldo,Aug.5,1973.
Conrad Eugene,July 21,1973.
Edward,1959.
Eugene,June 13,1991.
Evelyn Hawkes,1914-1950,w/o Philip.
Frank E.,1957.
Frank,June 29,1984.
Jeannette,Dec.3,1994.
Mattie,Aug.27,1981.
Nina,Mar.28,1978.
Roy,1944.
Ruby,Sept.12,1987.
Warren,Oct.21,1989.
KNOWLES
Robert,Oct.28,1980.
KUUSELA
Arvo M.,1981.
Ida,Sept.6,1976.
Laura J.,Jan.21,1967.
Manda,Oct.22,1992.
KYLE
James Alexander,Feb.23,1979.
Sadie Frances,June 8,1973.

LACHANCE
Mary,May 22,1989.
LAGASSE
Roland Paul,Oct.8,1980.
LAMB
Richard,Feb.9,1971.
LAMONTAGNE
Dennis,Sept.29,1964.
LANPHIER
Helen,Aug.11,1992.
LARRIVEE
Emeline C.,Nov.5,1971.
Eugene Joseph,Jan.14,1965.
James David,Oct.31,1974.
James David,Jan.8,1966.
LARRY
Hattie E.,Oct.7,1862,3y,
d/o Daniel P. & Abigail Hicks.
Joseph C.,Sept.8,1888,84y.
Mary Isabel,Jan.31,1860,2y,
d/o Daniel P.& Abigail.
Mary Purinton,May 13,1885,79y,
w/o Joseph.
Meshach P.,May 6,1864,32y,
killed in the battle of the Wilderness,Co.H,17th Me Reg,s/o J.&M.
LASKEY
Michelina,Nov.1,1991.
Milford Leroy,Jr.,June 9,1966.
LATHAM
Dorothy B.,Jan.21,1967.
LEPAGE
Albert,1976.
Albert,July 3,1966.
LEWIS
Tremblaky,June 17,1985.
LIBBY
Daniel,June 2,1893,75y,s/o Jos.& M.
Joseph,Jr.,Apr.2,1843,62y.
Mary,May 14,1993.
Mercy Whitney,May 21,1860,80y,
w/o Joseph,Jr.
Parmelia,1822-1899,w/o Daniel.
Stephen,1804-1881,h/o Mary W.Lowe.
s/o Joseph & Mercy.
Tyng W.,May 1921,86y,h/o Catherine
Meserve Brackett (1898).
LITTLE
William,May 15,1989.
LOCHLIN
Frank,1913.
Mary A. Pretty,1913.
Onsville,1959.
LOCK
Arthur,Apr.30,1988.
LOCKE
infant,1975.

LONG
June G.,Mar.14,1981.
Kenneth,Aug.16,1981.
LOVEITT
Richard G.,Feb.27,1976.
MacDONALD
Arthur,May 20,1994.
Donna,July 7,1976.
Vivian S.,Jan.24,1977.
MAGNUSSON
Ada K.,1852-1924.
Carl Jr.,May 1,1986.
Carrie Elizabeth,May 2,1975.
J.A.,1846-1927.
Paul,July 13,1992.
Victoria A.,1894-1951.
MAINS
Clifford,July 14,1993.
Elsie E.,Sept.20,1984.
infant,Sept.24,1964.
Raymond,May 29,1984.
MANCHESTER
Frank,Sept.8,1993.
LaForest Arnold,Apr.26,1969.
MANNETTE
Grace,May 11,1992.
Harry,1969.
MARSHALL
Bertrand F.,Dr.,1866-1945,
h/o Eva Smith (1936).
MASON
Chester Albert,Aug.23,1969.
Edna Mae,Jan.31,1969.
Philip Harold,Mar.31,1969.
MAXFIELD
Christie,Aug.7,1894,11m,d/o Geo.
MAYBERRY
Annie,1926.
Ansel L.,1919.
Benjamin B.,My 16,1825-Jn.3,1892.
Doris,1909.
George,1953.
Kimberly Paul,XXXX.
Mary Huston,Nov.7,1826,55y,
 1st w/o Richard.
Mary,Aug.1827,21y,d/o Rich.& Mary.
Nellie May,June 18,1972.
Richard,Jan.13,1853,87y,
 2nd w.Betsey Brackett,
 s/o William & Jane Miller.
Stephen P.,June 10,1824,20y,
 Accidentally drowned in Little River
 at a place called "Harding's Bridge".
McELROY
Earl Harry,July 23,1978.
Lee Donald,Nov.10,1975.

MEGGISON
Percy W.,May 22,1980.
MENEZES
Joseph,Oct.26,1994.
MESERVE
Ada E.,Jan.8,1967.
MESSENGER
Mace Willis,June 25,1994,
 h/o Jane Flint,
 s/o Carl H. & Emma Willis.
METAYER
Arthur J.,Mar.23,1964.
MICHAUD
Laversa,May 20,1989.
MITCHELL
Edith M.,Jan.21,1965.
MORRILL
Everett,May 7,1988.
MORRISSETTE
Jennie,June 19,1968.
MORSE
Flossie L.,Apr.27,1968.
Harold,June 4,1993.
Kenneth,Oct.28,1989.
Mary Jane,Oct.13,1968.
MORTON
Aurilla Saunders,Sept.8,1969.
Birdie,July 20,1993.
Frank Stuart,Apr.1,1964.
George,Sr.,Aug.28,1984.
Katherine,Mar.21,1977.
Rachel Helen,May 19,1976.
MOULTON
Clara H.,1882,6m.
Mary,1817-1890.
MOXCEY
Joanne L.,Feb.24,1982.
John Nichols,Dec.1,1971.
Kenneth,Sept.3,1993.
Richard D.,June 29,1992.
NASON
Clyde Everett,Nov.16,1974.
NAY
Edson O.,Apr.6,1908,
 h/o Flora Douglass.
NEALY
Chelsea,Sept.26,1989,s.b.
NEWCOMB
John Everett,June 14,1968.
Marie Melanson,Oct.21,1968.
NEWHALL
Isabel Julia,Feb.1,1895,15y,
 at Newhall,d/o Ezra F. & Julia F.
 Taylor Newhall.
NICHOLAS
Donna Louise,Jan.24,1969.
Eva C.,Aug.18,1973.

Granton,Oct.25,1990.
Robert J.,Aug.20,1987.
NICHOLS
Donald,Apr.28,1987.
Robert J.,Aug.20,1987.
NODINE
Ruth,Jan.2,1977.
PAINE
Sarah J.,1825-1859,w/o Freeman.
ch/o Freeman & Sarah J.:
Albert L.,1870;
Almira,Apr.29,1849,1y;
Freeman Alroy,Aug.8,1853,8m.
PALOZZI
Diane Lee,Aug.17,1974.
PARADY
Elizabeth,July 15,1994.
George A.,XXXX.
PARKER
Clyde R.,May 9,1975.
Dana Milton,Sept.22,1965.
Gladys,June 20,1985.
Harvey,Aug.9,1965.
Norman L.,May 8,1989.
Philip Reginald,Oct.25,1980.
PARKHURST
Frederick,Oct.22,1992.
PARSONS
Elizabeth P.,Nov.7,1984.
Ellen Catherine, Jan.10,1968.
Herbert C.,Oct.10,1978.
PAUL
George Dowling,Sept.19,1971.
PEARSON
Harriett,Sept.8,1975.
Lawrence B.,Dec.29,1972.
PEDERSEN
Alan P.,Mar.28,1975.
PENEK
Merrill,Mar.26,1964.
PENIUK
Annastozia E.,Nov.11,1976.
PETTO
Marion Evelyn,Feb.12,1981.
PERKINS
Lester Daniel,July 8,1985.
PETERSEN
Carl,June 17,1991.
PETERSON
Reginald James,Oct.10,1971.
PIERCE
Everett,Jan.12,1983,69y.
Timothy,Apr.26,1985.
PLUMMER
Lester,Oct.22,1992.
Walter,Nov.8,1981,4y.

POIRER
David A.,May 5,1994,56y,
h/o Shirley Manzer.
POULIOT
Francis,Sept.23,1992.
POWELL
Mary Ann,Dec.20,1982.
POWERS
Joseph Cephas,Oct.14,1989.
PRATT
Alexander T.,Sr.,Sept.21,1993,91y,
h/o Ruby Chambers (1974).
Annie,June 3,1992.
Clements,May 4,1981.
Electa Monty,1943.
Horace,1929.
Mary Smith,1907.
PRINCE
James,July 27,1992.
PUDVAH
Edith,June 3,1987.
QUINT
Erdine,Aug.30,1988.
RAMSEY
Harry E.,July 14,1987.
Jeffrey,Apr.21,1988.
Roxie A.,1978.
RAND
Samuel M.,1821-1887.
REEF
Robert,1980.
REYNOLDS
Audrey,May 1,1986.
Gary,1974.
RILEY
Martin,Sept.4,1984.
Timothy,Aug.25,1992.
RIVINIUS
Abby Albertina,Aug.7,1865,6m,
d/o Wm. & Abby.
ROBBINS
Helen Anna,Nov.26,1984.
ROBERTS
Maria,Nov.13,1984.
ROBINSON
Joseph L.,Feb.1,1911,44y,
s/o Thomas & Louisa Weeks.
Stanley,July 27,1991.
Thomas L.,1840-June 22,1890.
RUSSELL
Edith,1949.
John,1943.
Marjorie,1958.
Norman,1965.
Otis,Rev.,1901,h/o Susan M.
Susan M. Sawyer,Jan.24,1907,78y.

SANVILLE
Altie,Oct.15,1981,72y.
Mary,May 7,1988,w/o Altie.
SARGENT
Alice,Jan.14,1982.
June,Nov.25,1991.
Vaughn,Nov.13,1991.
SAUNDERS
Charles L.,1976.
Kilton L.,Oct.19,1993.
Margery,May 3,1990.
SAWYER
Beverly,July 27,1992.
Lorraine,May 15,1993.
SAYWARD
Ted,1974.
SEVERY
Marie,May 30,1992.
SEWELL
Evelyn,May 8,1989.
SHAW
Ella Phinney,Nov.23,1994,w/o F.A.
F. Alden,July 4,1982.
Howard,1980.
Irving,Nov.13,1986.
SHOLTS
Eva Lou,June 25,1990.
Lloyd,Apr.27,1990.
SICILIANO
Arnold,July 9,1987.
Arnold.May 7,1991.
Joseph M.,July 9,1987.
Julia,May 7,1991.
SKILLINGS
Stephen H.,1866-1945.
SMALL
Annie,June 22,1878,22y,
d/o Francis & Ruth.
Benjamin D.,1824-1885.
Daniel B.,Mar.29,1872,24y,
only s/o Benj. & Mary.
Herman D.,Dec.7,1877,26y.
Mary B.,1825-XXXX,w/o Benj.
Ruth W.,Mar.18,1811-June 26,1897,
w/o Francis,Jr.
SMEARER
George,May 1983.
SMITH
Alice B.,Nov.19,1877,19y,
d/o John F.& Mary A.Thomas.
Clyde,May 1,1984.
Ernest,June 23,1981.
Francis,Nov.18,1981,51y.
George,1963.
Georgie,Apr.26,1990.
Laura,July 27,1991.
Lawrence,1937.
Louella,Nov.16,1990.
Paul,1975.
Sophroni,1963.
Timothy C.,Nov.6,1987.
Wendall,1971.
SNOW
Lester,Apr.27,1992.
SPEARIN
Thomas N.,Sept.30,1981.
SPRING
Angie,Nov.18,1987.
Francis,Nov.9,1989.
STARBUCK
Rachel,1958.
STEVENS
Charles,1826-Feb.1,1909.
John G.,July 4,1879,36y,
accidentally killed while firing a
salute at Newhall.
Susan Irish,1828-Nov.24,1908,
w/o Charles.
STEWART
Agnes,1982.
STILES
Dorothy,Apr.30,1985.
STROUT
Alfreda,June 26,1990.
Edwin,May 1,1985.
Howard,Sept.8,1982.
Irene,May 1,1985.
June,Nov.25,1991.
Rodney,May 7,1991.
Wilton,Aug.21,1991.
STULTZ
Pearl,May 8,1992.
STURGIS
Benjamin R.,Apr.30,1896,85y,
h/o Keziah Elder (1889).
SWENDSEN
Charles,1980.
THOMAS
Anna Ross,Oct.11,1836,56y,w/o Wm.
Charlotte L., Knight,1803-
July 8,1895,w/o Merrill.
Merrill,1801-1885,s/o Wm.& Anna.
William,Mar.14,1774-Feb.25,1860.
THOMPSON
Martin A.,1890-1948,h/o Edna Smith.
TOOTHAKER
Elizabeth,May 21,1988.
George,1981.
TRACEY
Carole,May 3,1990.
TREMBLAY
Beatrice,Spr.28,1986.
Louis,June 15,1985.

TRIPP
Clyde Revere,Sr.,Nov.3,1982.
TRUE
Kenneth,Nov.6,1982.
TWITCHELL
Hilery H.,Aug.10,1984.
USHER
Mary S. Lord,Feb.1917,84y.
Sidney,Feb.9,1872,46y,h/o Mary S.
USTIC
Dora,c.1950.
Procup,1932.
VAN TASSEL
Mary E.,Apr.24,1961.
Sumner,Apr.24,1961.
VERRILL
Andrew,1980.
Earl F.,July 7,1994.
Harold,Oct.18,1983.
Margaret,Nov.10,1994.
Paul E.,Mar.21,1982,58y.
WAIG
Justin S.,Nov.5,1986,2m.
WAITT
Louis Albert,Apr.29,1991.
WALES
Arline R.,Aug.26,1993.
WALTMAN
Frances,Sept.21,1991.
Henry,Sept.11,1992.
WARMING
Alvin,1975.
WARREN
Ada Hawkes,May 26,1992.
WEBB
Charles,1923.
Emma L.,1957.
George,1937.
Hannah,1889.
Hazel,May 7,1991.
John M.,1890.
Lida,1918.
Lucius,1887.
Mary Jordan,1940.
Rufus,1929.
WELCH
Joseph,Apr.27,1987.
WESCOTT
Dorothy,July 13,1984.
Hannah Hanson,1800-1886,
  2nd w/o James.
James,1794-1870,1st w.Dorcus
  Libby (1849).
Kenneth,Apr.29,1986.
Lillian,1884-1897,d/o W.H.& Lizzie.
Ruth M.,Jan.31,1983.
WIDGER
Myrtle,Oct.21,1985.
WIGGIN
Clyde,1980.
WILLETTE
Celia,May 14,1987.
Roger,Sept.1,1982.
WILLIAMS
Celia,May 14,1987.
Deborah Whitney,Oct.27,1851,92y.
Hadley,May 24,1986.
Hannah,Jan.26,1853,59y,d/o P.&S.
Harriet,Apr.12,1869,40y,unm,
  d/o Peter & Salome.
Jeremiah,May 3,1823,68y,h/o Debor.
John J.,Feb.12,1898,67y,
  s/o Peter & Salome Elwell.
Joseph,Oct.7,1869,78y,unm.
Lydia,Apr.19,1865,77y,unm.
Mary,Nov.29,1873,91y,
  w/o James Ridlon.
Mary Ann,Jan.15,1856,38y.
Peter,Oct.29,1784-Jan.25,1856,
  h/o Salome Elwell (c.1866).
Sarah,Apr.22,1837,10m.
Susan,May 7,1863,77y,unm.
WILLIS
Elsie,June 2,1985.
Lois D.,June 5,1985.
Ralph M.,Sept.26,1992.
Richard,July 19,1994.
Robert,May 8,1993.
WOOD
Robert,1981.
WOODIS
Lewis,Feb.2,1982.
WORD
Henry A.,1981.
WRIGHT
Charles E.,1980.
YERRINGTON
Gladys,May 19,1993.
Raymond,Sept.1,1992.

✤ **CLAY CEMETERY** ✤
Near White Rock School House on the old Wescott farm. Only 3 stones had inscriptions in 1900.

CLAY
Anna Young,Mar.14,1879,79y
William,May 3,1871,80y,h/o Anna Y.
McDONALD
Joseph,Sr.,1815,no marker.
Sarah Towel,1828.
YOUNG
Joseph,1810,h/o Lydia.
Lydia Snow,July 9,1850,74y.

✣ FORT HILL CEMETERY ✣
Fort Hill Road, Gorham. List from Gorham Town Clerk, records were taken from stones in 1982.

ADAMS
Sarah/Susan,Mar.13,1859,55y,
d/o Joseph & Mercy.
ALDEN
Hezekiah,Nov.27,1768,16m,s/o Austin.
Salome Lombard,May 18,1780,44y,
1st w/o Austin.
BAKER
Betsey Clement,Aug.17,1859,
83y,w/o Daniel.
Daniel,June 9,1856,90y,bro/o Moses.
Sarah,Oct.25,1820,20y,d/o Dan. & B.
BANGS
Lydia,Sept.18,1923,85y.
COCHRAN
Esther,Apr.1,1851,19y.
DORSETT
Susan,July 18,1784.
ELWELL
George,Jan.10,1810-1896,
h/o Nancy,s/o Geo. & Mehitable.
Mehitable Cain,July 17,1852,76y,
w/o George (1775-1810,at sea).
Nancy Smith,1882,72y,w/o Geo.
Sallie,1883,84y,d/o Geo.& Mehitable.
FILES
Ann Berry,June 1,1871,71y,
1st h. Stephen Thomes,
2nd h. Robert Files.
Esther Thomes,Mar.1,1844,81y,
w/o Samuel.
Samuel,Aug.4,1759-Apr.7,1835,75y,
s/o Wm.& Joanna, Rev.War Soldier.
HAMBLEN
Cyrus,Oct.5,1789-Dec.25,1853,
1st w. Elizabeth Freeman,
2nd w. Martha Thomes.
Eleanor,Aug.14,1814,1y,
d/o Joseph & Polly.
Elizabeth Freeman,Nov.30,1844,
52y,1st w/o Cyrus.
Grata,Nov.17,1816-Dec.23,1853.
Hannah,Sept.13,1877,72y.
Hannah,Dec.13,1879,72y.
John,May 7,1781-Feb.28,1842,
h/o Olive.
Joseph,June 17,1763.
Joseph,Oct.21,1832,69y.
Martha Thomes,Feb.13,1872,77y,
2nd w/o Cyrus.
Olive Murch,Mar.17,1845,55y,
w/o John.

Polly Frost,Apr.18,1767-
Mar.5,1860,w/o Jos.
Timothy,1775-1857,s/o Timothy &
Anna Harding.
Timothy,Dec.20,1820-Nov.17,1861,
s/o John & Olive.
HARRIET
Ann,Mar.27,1844,41y.
HIGGINS
Barnabas,Feb.16,1816,33y,
s/o Joseph & Mercy Cook..
JORDAN
Charles,Mar.30,1795-Nov.15,1857,
h/o Sally Brown.
Statira F.,Nov.6,1816,17y,
d/o Charles & Rebecca.
LOMBARD
Jedediah,Apr.8,1728-Jan.24,1820,
1st w. Susan Dorsett,
2nd w. Susanna Libby,
s/o Soloman & Sarah Purrinton.
Lydia Bangs,Sept.18,1823,83y.
Richard,Feb.23,1741-Oct.21,1825,
h/o Lydia Bangs.
Soloman,1763,1y.
Soloman,Apr.5,1702-1781,s/o
Jedediah,Jr.,& Hannah Barnstable.
MARBLE
Ann,Jan.17,1830,86y,w/o Daniel.
MOTLEY
Ann Harriet,Mar.25,1844,41y,
d/o Robert & Nancy.
Ellen Waite,Sept.7,1855,40y,
d/o Robert & Mary Ann.
Mary,Feb.18,1856,41y.
Mary Ann,Oct.25,1775-Sept.13,1871,
w/o Robert.
Mary Storer,Feb.18,1858,11m.
Richard,Nov.19,1848,73y,bro/o Robt.
Robert,Capt.,Feb.27,1848,75y.
MURCH
Henry,May 11,1864 ?,38y.
Martha A.,Aug.19,1865,38y.
Olive A.,Feb.22,1876,22y,d/o H.& M.
PALMER
Adelaide,July 21,1850,17y,w/o Edw.
Maria H.,Nov.22,1841,10y,
d/o Asa & Maria.
PHINNEY
Rebecca,1795-1848.
PURRITON
Humphrey,Deacon,June 27,1758,56y.
ROBERTS
Charles,1843-1886.
Joshua,Mar.8,1783-Sept.16,1855,
s/o Joseph & Hannah Freeman.
Mary Thomes,Aug.25,1869,79y.

Mehitable C.,Sept.4,1854,28y,
w/o Leonard C.
STUART
Soloman Lombard,Feb.12,1762-
Dec.29,1763,s/o W.& S.
Susannah,1756-Jan.4,1758,2y,
d/o Wentworth & Susannah.
Susannah,Jan.4,1758,56y.
THOMES
Abagail,Dec.24,1882,91y,w/o James.
Abigail,Feb.4,1838,43y,w/o Stephen.
Ann Gray,July 14,1824,63y,
w/o Chas.T.
Charles T.,Nov.25,1833,83y.
Comfort,Feb.7,1857,71y.
Eleanor C.,Nov.19,1830,18y,
d/o Nathaniel & Mary.
Ezra,June 16,1818,36y,
s/o George & Lydia.
George,Apr.28,1821,76y,
s/o Thomas & Mary.
Hannah,Apr.20,1874,71y.
James,Nov.9,1865,78y,
s/o Charles & Anne.
Job,Dec.7,1843,51y.
Lydia Brown,May 13,1822,77y,
w/o George.
Miranda,Oct.25,1818-Nov.22,1895
d/o William & Sarah.
Nathaniel,Aug.3,1850,66y,
h/o Mary Higgins (1874).
Samuel,Mar.3,1798,51y,
s/o Thomas & Mary.
Sarah,Oct.8,183X,78y.
Sarah,May 20,1846,83y,w/o Samuel.
Sarah ,Apr.7,1852,64y,1st w/o Sam.
Stephen,Apr.13,1847,50y,
1st w. Abigail Twombley,
2nd w. Ann Berry.
Susan,Sept.13,1835,47y,
d/o Charles & Anna.
William,Sept.3,1861,74y,s/o Geo.& L.,
1st w. Salley Plaisted,
2nd w. Hannah Plaisted.
TOBBETTS
Sarah,Oct.8,1831,78y.

✣ **NONESUCH CEMETERY** ✣
Rolling Acres Farm on Nonesuch Road.

WATERHOUSE
Janet Marie,Oct.4,1989.

✣ **SAPLING HILL CEMETERY** ✣
1793 Route 237, Gorham.
Obtained from Gorham Town Clerk,
and is not complete. Managed by
Association.

BAILEY
Ada White,July 1994,89y,
w/o Henry P. (1959).
Edith E.,Feb.7,1972.
BAKER
Ann,May 2,1845,w/o Livy.
Susan R.,June 13,1985.
ch/o Livy & Ann:
Caroline F.,Sept.29,1829,2y;
George,Feb.20,1821-Aug.11,1842.
Mary,Apr.23,1820.
BARBOUR
Mary Ann,July 19,1852,25y,w/o Rich.
BETTES
Charles,Apr.11,1838,23y,
s/o Capt. Jacob & Hannah.
BODGE
Donald H.,Dec.25,1971.
BOLTON
Abigail,Jan.14,1872,67y,d/o W.& E.
Eunice,Apr.8,1862,77y,w/o Wm.
Hannah,Dec.28,1843,83y,w/o Thos.
Katherine F.,July 9,1976.
Thomas,Aug.29,1851,36y,s/o W.& E
Thomas,June 18,1793,35y.
William,July 10,1856,73y.
BRACKETT
Alton L.,Feb.26,1975.
Lettie Ann,June 29,1971.
BRAGDON
Lizzie Brown,Dec.28,1912,
w/o Edgar P.M.
BROWN
Jerry L.,June 23,1982.
BUNKER
Rodney D.,Feb.1994,91y,h/o Helen
Noiles,s/o Delmont & Estella Dickson.
BUTTERFIELD
Vena Louise,Dec.19,1969.
Willard Dana,Jr.,Aug.16,1979.
CARLL
Clarence E.,June 1,1971.
Lillian R.,Feb.1,1977.
CARR
Richard,Nov.23,1896,63y.
CASH
Dorothy Isabelle Lopez,Nov.18,1972.
COOK
Solomon C.,July 31,1855,27y.
CROCKETT
John C.F.,Jan.8,1986.

Mary,Jan.11,1875,87y,w/o Solomon.
Solomon,Jan.22,1825,44y.
DELORY
Francena H.,Mar.11,1978.
Richard Oliver,Dec.18,1979.
DOUGHERTY
Elizabeth,Dec.28,1964.
DOUGHTY
Ernest E.,Apr.3,1970.
DOUGLAS
Edith W.,Oct.30,1969.
ELDRIDGE
Etta M.,Apr.16,1986.
EVANS
Marguerite A.,Dec.3,1986.
FARLEY
Maude Lois,Jan.8,1973.
FLOOD
Olive M.,Apr.30,1848,18y.
GREEN
Elizabeth S.,Feb.3,1977.
GREENE
James E.,Aug.22,1982.
Maurice Luther,Apr.27,1966.
Ralph Edward,Dec.17,1968.
GRENDELL
Earl,May 7,1978.
John L.,May 20,1968.
Kenneth Malcolm,Apr.5,1986.
GUERIN
Susie May,Apr.9,1983.
HALL
Sarah Maria,Nov.13,1854,32y,
w/o Otis T.
William Harris,July 5,185X,7m,
s/o O.T. & S.M.
HARDING
David,Mar.1,1828,96y,h/o Sarah.
Elkanah,Aug.27,1850,91y,
s/o David & Sarah.
Hannah Elder Brown,
July 19,1828,50y,2nd w/o Elkanah.
Lucy Bacon,1838-1913,w/o Chas.B.
Martha Knight,May 30,1801,
32y,w/o Elkanah.
Sarah Brown,June 4,1804,69y.
HARRIS
Anna,Jan.191,839,39y,w/o Wm.
Morna Louise,Jan.22,1977.
William,June 25,1845,57y.
HOWE
Ina May,Feb.25,1979.
HUBBARD
Samantha,Nov.26,1979.
HYMAN
Donald H.,Aug.28,1980.
Helen Crockett,Dec.25,1973.

IRISH
Clyde,Mar.3,1975.
Daniel F.,May 10,1824-Nov.28,1887.
Margaret,Jan.31,1834-Oct.9,1881.
JOHNSON
Alice Rand,Feb.24,1983.
George W.,Apr.7,1870,42y.
JORDAN
Esther,Sept.15,1878,71y,w/o Levi.
KEMP
Lydia Elder,Dec.17,1745-
Apr.19,1825,w/o Ebenezer,Jr (1833).
KIMBALL
Ella Marion,Dec.1,1967.
KNIGHT
Maude Cressey,Oct.1,1977.
LANDRY
Annette Marie,Jan.7,1971.
Laurence,Sept.11,1991.
LARRIVEE
Theodore,Dec.19,1979.
LEIPOLD
Irene Louise,Apr.16,1979.
LIBBY
Betsey Haskell,Nov.30,1839,42y,
1st w/o Cary.
Cary,1854,59y,2nd w.Eliz. Chase.
Henry E.,Sept.18,1969.
Prentiss Thayer,Dec.30,1964.
Sally T. Sanborn,Nov.27,1867,70y,
w/o Daniel (1857).
Viola,Aug.14,1972.
LORD
Ivory,May 3,1891,80y.
Mary J.,Jan.26,1851,45y,w/o Ivory.
LOURA
Abbie Ann,Sept.2,1964.
David H.,Apr.14,1967.
MAY
Myron Herbert,Mar.13,1986.
MAYE
Chester Harold,June 21,1971.
McCAULEY
Hattie Rose,Mar.23,1974.
McLELLAN
Karen Dawn,Aug.12,1969.
MORTON
Albert,Sept.1912.
Eli,Nov.8,1896,76y,
h/o Louisa Rounds.
Helen A.,Apr.5,1982.
Howard,Jan.19,1890,22y,
s/o Wm.& Mary.
Willard Leroy,Jan.8,1975.
MUSSEY
Esther,May 20,1855,68y,w/o Joseph.
Joseph,Aug.15,1842,76y.

NADEAU
Haidee L.,Jan.18,1969.
O'TOOLE
Lillian Eldora,Dec.26,1964.
Peter John,Apr.20,1968.
PALMER
Herbert Wallace,June 17,1966.
PATTERSON
Annie Eleanor,Feb.24,1976.
Richard L.,Sr.,Dec.6,1981.
PURINTON
Lorenzo,Jan.10,1881,80y,h/o Sarah.
Lydia Small,Dec.13,1894,75y,w/o Otis.
Otis,Feb.2,1899,79y.
Sarah Gerrish,Jan.10,1881,79y.
William G.,Jan.1913.
SAWYER
Charles H.,June,XXXX,21y,s/o H.& M.
Henry,Aug.1,1840,64y.
Louisa,Feb.1,1889.
Mary,July 14,1860,78y,w/o Henry.
SMITH
ch/o Ephraim,Jr.:
Albion,Sept.25,1851,37y;
Samuel,July 20,1850,36y,unm.
SULLIVAN
Linda J.,July 3,1987.
WALKER
Emery O.,Nov.13,1844-Mar.15,1887,
Co.F.,30th Me.Regiment.
WARD
Elizabeth Walker,Nov.1,1869,80y.
Ezekiel,Mar.25,1857,70y,h/o Eliza.
WATERHOUSE
Ann Bolton,Oct.24,1859,42y,w/o Sam.
Elizabeth Jane,Dec.18,1853,34y,
unm.,d/o Wm.H. & Sarah.
Samuel S.,Capt.,Aug.15,1887,76y,
2nd w. Eleanor Small.
Sally B. Smith,Oct.10,1843,63y,
w/o Wm.H.
William H.,Nov.4,1867,88y,
2nd w. Sarah Donnell.
WEBB
Edward,Nov.18,1846,86y,s/o E.& S.
Eli,Nov.7,1837-Oct.20,1826.
Horace,Sept.13,1828,2y,
s/o Seth & Mary.
Lydia,Aug.11,1877-Jan.1,1790,
d/o Edward & Sarah.
Sarah,Feb.28,1826,84y,w/o Eli.
Sarah Bolton,Aug.28,1850,89y,
w/o Eli.
WIGHT
Alzina Hawkes,Oct.13,1984.
WINSHIP
Sadie V.,Aug.31,1982.

✤ **SWETT GRAVEYARD** ✤
792 rear Route 202,Gorham.
Checked all stones.Managed by Town.

ABBOTT
Mary,Oct.2,1853,67y,w/o Wm.
William,Oct.10,1852,77y.
ALLEN
Laura,Aug.1,1858,1y,d/o Wm.& M.F.
Mary F.,May 6,1839,19y,w/o Wm.
William,Aug.23,1865,31y,Union Sold.
ATKINSON
Nancy Trueworthy,Dec.10,1875,
69y,w/o Theodore.
Harriet F.,June 11,1846,5y,
d/o Theodore & Nancy.
Stephen P.,Oct.20,1854,22y,
s/o Theodore & Nancy.
Theodore,Nov.10,1884,79y.
BANGS
Ebenezer,June 11,1807,41y.
BEAN
inf/o David M. & Mary A.,Nov.26,1852.
BERRY
Robert P.?,Oct.7,1842,4y,
s/o Nathaniel IV & Lydia.
BLAKE
Mariam Knight,Feb.14,1880,80y,
w/o Freeman.
CLOUDMAN
John,Aug.9,1850,74y.
Sarah,Aug.5,1870,86y,w./o John.
CLOUTMAN
Catharine Partridge,Mar.24,1832,
91y,w/o Timothy.
Timothy,Oct.22,1829,92y,
s/o Edward who was taken prisoner
by the Indians in their attack on
Gorham, Apr.19,1745.
CROCKETT
James,June 10,1846,77y,
1st w. Sarah Sanborn,
2nd w.Ruth Lord.
DINSMORE
John,Apr.15,1862,24y.
DORSETT
Edmund,Capt.,Dec.14,1876,77y.
Sophia Swett,Jan.17,1864,61y,
w/o Edmund.
ch/o Edmund & Sophia:
Almira,Jan.5,1851,16y,
Edmund G.,May 5,1851,11y,
Folsom,Aug.25,1854,25y,
Simon,Oct.12,1855,19y.
ELLIS
Inez,Mar.19,1860,ch/o C.B.& E.B.

FRINK
Charles M.,July 21,1849,1y,
 s/o John & Hannah.
Mary,Sept.24,1849,77y,w/o Sam.
Samuel,May 16,1860,84y.
GILMAN
Eugene,Apr.18,1874,18y.
GOOLD
George,Aug.25,1809-Dec.26,1895.
Mary Ann Rounds,Nov.15,1849,
 40y,1st w/o George.
ch/o George & Mary Ann:
Albert A.,Oct.23,1842,3y;
Mahala R.,Oct.19,1842,7y;
Oliver,Nov.3,1812,7y.
GRAFFAM
Ellen I.,Dec.26,1854,25y,w/o John N
Joseph F.,Dec.9,1850,6m,s/o J.& E.I.
Mary B. Swett,July 9,1860,61y,
 4th w/o Caleb,d/o Joshua & M.
HANSON
Lewis,July 24,1874,67y.
Rebecca Swett,July 3,1880,71y,
 w/o Lewis.
HODSDON
George W.,Apr.9,1853,47y.
JOHNSON
Mary J.,Sept.12,1849,29y,w/o Wm.H.
KALLOCK
Salome G. Dorsett,Mar.15,1870,
 25y,w/o Marshall,d/o Edm. & S.
Susie,XXXX.
KNIGHT
Charlotte,Mar.23,1854,54y.
Joseph,Sept.22,1734-Sept.9,1799,
 Mass Militia,Rev. War.
Joseph,July 14,1829,52y,
 s/o Joseph who was twice captured by Indians,and like him was accidentally drowned in the Presumpscot Riv. at Little Falls.
Mariam,Feb.14,1880,80y.
Mary Loveitt,June 9,1852,83y,
 w/o Joseph.
LIBBY
Appleton,Mar.15,1843,1y,
 s/o Simon & Rebecca.
RICHARDSON
Rebekah,Nov.17,1870,68y.
SMALL
Ann Bailey,Sept.20,1853,63y,
 w/o James (1858).
James,Jan.31,1858,76y.
James Lewis,Mar.13,1873,44y,
 Co. K. 9, Me Volunteers.
Frances,Apr.25,1852,31y,w/o Joseph.
Mary B.,June 1901,75y,wid/o Benj.

Nathan M.,Aug.10,1842,30y.
ch/o Joseph L., & Frances:
Frances H.,Oct.23,1849,3w;
Harriet F.,Feb.16,1846,6w.
SWETT
Clark,Col.,May 5,1839,48y.
Hale,Elder,Aug.8,1834,34y.
Joseph,July 14,1829,52y.
Joshua,Capt.,Apr.20,1851,89y,
 Rev. Soldier.
Martha Edwards,Jan.22,1843,
 44y,w/o Clark.
Mary,June 9,1852,83y,w/o Joseph.
Mary Bailey,Aug.22,1849,80y,
 w/o Joshua.
William,Dec.29,1830,26y.
TRUEWORTHY
Catharine Harriet,May 12,1841,22y.
WALKER
Eliza A. Dorsett,Jan.22,1851,25y,
 w/o Henry,d/o Edm.& Sophia.
WATERHOUSE
Charles E.,Sept.11,1849,1y,
 s/o Gardner & Jane W.B.
Jane W. Babb,Dec.6,1849,35y,
 1st w/o Gardner.
WEED
John H.,May 21,1844,8m,
 s/o Alvah S. & Louisa.

✦ **DYER FAMILY CEMETERY** ✦
Straw Road, South Gorham. All gravestones copied in 1995 by Gary Wilson.

DYER
Helen L.,June 9,1886,21y,
 d/o Wm.& Sarah.
Nathan,May 8,1853,57y.
Polly Grant,Jan.22,1859,61y,
 w/o Nathan.
Rebecca Huston,Oct.17,1823,59y,
 w/o Wm.(1832).
Ruth H.,Feb.3,1866,67y.
Sarah A.,Feb.11,1878,48y,w/o Wm.M.
Susan Jane,Oct.9,1854,20y,d/o N.&P.
William M.,Feb.8,1900,66y.
William,Sept.22,1832,62y.
GRANT
Susan,Feb.3,1862,73y.
HODSDON
Nancy,1873,w/o Timothy.
Timothy,XXXX.
VARNEY
Cora,Sept.8,1887,4m,
 d/o Fred & Cora E. Dyer.

✤ HAMBLEN CEMETERY ✤
1 1/2 miles south of Little Falls, on the farm first settled by George Hamblen and still lived on by the Hamblen Family. Private property. All stones checked.

COBURN
Eveline,Apr.19,1837,28y,
w/o Jacob,Jr.
ELKINS
Charles,Mar.11,1924-Dec.7,1982.
GOOLD
Sarah B.,July 3,1853,33y,w/o Geo.
HAMBLEN
Adeline M.,Dec.15,1834,18y,
d/o Joseph & Esther.
Albert,1818-1890,h/o Cynthia.
Allen,Aug.21,1853,65y,s/o Geo.& S.
Almery T.,Feb.26,1862,51y,
h/o Elizabeth Butterfield.
Andrew R.,Oct.4,1831,3y,
s/o Joseph & Esther.
Charles,Jan.12,1845,28y.
Cynthia Silla,Nov.19,1823-
May 14,1889,w/o Albert.
Decker P.,July 16,1828,22y,
s/o John & Hannah.
Elias S.,Mar.24,1838,26y,s/o J.& H.
Esther Bangs,Apr.12,1867,80y,
w/o Joseph.
George,Dec.18,1834,85y.
Hannah Bangs,July 2,1847,65y,
w/o John.
Howard,Feb.18,1871,1y,unm.,
s/o Byron & Mary.
Joseph,Sept.20,1851,68y,s/o Geo.
Lydia Winslow,Mar.26,1872,80y,
w/o Allen.
Lydia,Oct.8,1843,3y,
d/o Charles & Content.
Ruth,Oct.9,1850,32y,d/o John & H.
Sarah Jane,Jan.4,1854,37y.
Sally Clark,May 19,1822,42y,
w/o Almery.
Sarah Rich,Sept.2,1830,74y,w/o Geo.
ch/o Albert & Cynthia:
Eliza J.,Nov.23,1844-Mar.19,1845;
Hannah M.,1846-1847;
Henrich,Sept.23,1843-1843;
inf/s,May 3,1856-May 7,1856;
Joseph E.,Feb.17,1863-Mar.24,1864;
Marcena,Nov.18,1850-Apr.23,1857.
TRUE
Eve M.,Dec.25,1852-Nov.11,1906,
w/o E.B.

✤ SOUTH GORHAM ✤
Burnham Road. Records obtained from Gorham Town Clerk. List is not complete.

AHLQUIST
Marjorie E.,Nov.26,1978.
Martin A.B.,Sr.,Mar.18,1973,78y.
Rudolph E.,May 27,1979.
Sophie May,June 17,1975,77y.
Winonah Alberta,June 12,1965.
ALDRICH
Martha A.,Jan.12,1941.
AYER
Carrie L.,July 16,1943.
BAILEY
Charles W,XXXX.
Nettie C.,May 16,1946,w/o Chas.
BANKS
Carl,Oct.31,1988.
BENT
Harold,Oct.23,1993.
BERRY
Abram,May 19,1854,70y.
Amanda M.,Dec.23,1876,44y,
d.o Abram.
Ancil,Dec.29,1898,71y,
s/o Abram.
Francis A.,Sept.8,1909,72,
s/o Abram.
Henry N.,June 18,1895,65y,
s/o Abram.
Jane M.,Apr.13,1890,56y,
d/o Abram..
Mehitable,Nov.15,1871,76y,
w/o Abram.
BICKFORD
Abram,May 19,1871,69y.
Abram,Jr.,Aug.26,1913,73y,
s/o Abram & Mary J. Bickford.
Amanda T.,1935,w/o Abram,Jr..
Charles W.,Jan.14,1916,64y,
s/o Abram & Mary J.
Charlotte L.,Oct.27,1859,25y,
d/o Abram & Mary J.
Jennie F.,Jan.22,1964,w/o Percy.
Jesse Loring,Sept.15,1971.
M. Elizabeth,1859,d/o Abrm & Mary.
Mary J.,Sept.15,1877,71y,w/o Abram.
Olive J.,1873,37y,d/o Abram & Mary.
Percy L.,Apr.19,1963,
s/o Abram,Jr. & Amanda.
BONNEY
Paul,May 18,1989.
BRAGDON
C. Philip,1907-1972.
Carrie R.,1889-1970.

Philip,Jan.4,1972.
BRIGHTON
Anna K. Lane,Nov.5,1912,80y,
w/o John H.
John H.,May 24,1890,67y.
BRINKERHOFF
Gladys E.,May 16,1956,
w/o Harold E.R.
BROWN
Benjamin,May 24,1938.
Clarasa,Oct.12,1882,81y.
Earl,XXXX,inf/o Benj. & Mattie..
John E.,Nov.15,1883,75y.
Mattie E.,Mar.27,1968,w/o Benj.
BURDWOOD
Alfred,1922.
Joseph,Sept.9,1909,
s/o Alfred & Josephine.
BURGOYNE
Lindsay J.,1931.
BURNHAM
Alice,May 19,1992.
Asa,1923.
Carrie F.Tapley,1929,w/o Asa.
Fred A.,Nov.24,1953,s/o Asa & Carrie.
Hannah,Feb.28,1887,74y,w/o N.D.
Ida,Nov.17,1936,w/o Nicholas.
Nicholas,Sept.7,1913,55y.
Virginia A.,Oct.23,1958,d/o Asa & C.
BUTLER
Esther M.,Dec.7,1976.
Francis W.,1831-1909.
inf/o F.W. & Mary.,Mar.7,1875,3d.
Mary B.,1835-1890,w/o F.W.
Perley C.,Nov.26,1884,3y,
s/o F.W.& M.B.
William France,1866-1937.
BRYANT
Cornelia,May 8,1990.
Gordon S.,Mar.18,1971,58y.
CAPEN
Pauline,Apr.30,1986.
CAREY
Ellen H.,Aug.9,1898,66y,w/o O.A.
Oliver A.,July 15,1912,67y.
CARTER
Marjorie C.,Mar.14,1971,57y.
CHAPLES
Ruth Merserve,Apr.28,1994.
CORNISH
James Otis,Sept.12,1936.
Mabelle,June 12,1964,w/o James.
COSTALES
Matilda,May 6,1967.
CURLEW
Alfred,Sept.27,1967.
Fred,Aug.10,1991.

George,May 2,1980.
Robert,Oct.2,1984.
Scott Everett,Jan.21,1969,newb.
Thomas L.,Jr.,Dec.9,1992.
CURRIE
Alfred,Sept.27,1967.
Doris Mitchell,May 2,1980.
DEERING
Albert Leroy,Feb.7,1941,
s/o Albert & Clara.
Albion L.,Oct.8,1977.
Andrew J.,Nov.5,1922,46y.
Charles W.,1932.
Clara,Oct.10,1987.
Eddie S.,Feb.5,1880,s/o C.W. & Z.B.
Emma,Aug.22,1945,w/o Willis D.,
d/o C.W.& Z.B.Deering.
Esther B.,Nov.25,1967,w/o Albion.
Ethel,May 17,1985.
Frank S.,Nov.23,1917,s/o C.W.& Z.
George A.,Sept.16,1985.
George A.,May 17,1985.
Irene H.,1903/09,85y,w/o James L.
James L.,1901,90y.
Jennie E.,1950,w/o Louville W.
Jennie Smith,Oct.8,1883,36y,
w/o Reuben..
Jeremiah,Jr.,Sept.1,1877.
Louisa L.,1901?,90y,w/o Jas.L.
Louville W.,1929,s/o Jas.L.& Irene.
Martin,1913,s/o Jas.L. & Louisa.
Rena E.,Aug.26,1886,18y,
d/o Jas.L. & Irene.
Ruben,Mar.9,1902,63y.
Sarah,Dec.24,1884.
Willis F.,Feb.17,1940.
Zilpah B.,June 14,1909,w/o C.W.
DOUGHTY
Jean Ellen,Nov.14,1971,38y.
DUNN
Eugene,Sept.10,1876,3y,s/o J.L.
Susan,Dec.6,1915,65y,w/o J.L.
DUNNING
Clement Everett,Mar.23,1966.
Marion Tasca,Oct.3,1966,w/o C.E.
DYER
Linwood,Oct.15,1958,s/o William.
Patricia Ann,May 7,1857,inf/o Wm.
ENGHART
Mrs. David,XXXX.
FAULKNER
Abram,1931.
FISHER
William Patrick,Sept.5,1974,78y.
FOYE
Dana,Dec.5,1953.
Ora M.,Jan.1973,w/o Dana.

GORMAN
infant,May 18,1991,s.b.
Steven,Aug.14,1990.
GOULD
Frank,Nov.21,1980.
GRAY
Constance Ruth,1922-1973.
Gladys,May 1,1987.
Minard L.,June 15,1967.
GREEN
Dennis L.,1895.
Ellen M.,May 26,1950,w/o James W.
Grover C.,Nov.11,1966,s/o Jas.& E.
James W.,Oct.6,1943.
Lydia E.,1902,w/o Dennis L.
Polly,1900,w/o Thomas.
Robert Clark,Apr.23,1970,
   s/o James & Ellen.
Thomas,Oct.13,1860,53y.
GRENIER
Amos,May 24,1993.
Lulu,Sept.19,1986.
GUPTILL
Sarah J.,1902,82y,w/o Wm.
William,Dec.18,1881,73y.
GUSTIN
Alphonso,XXXX.
Annie L.,Apr.18,1948,w/o Alphonso.
Charles W.,Oct.9,1961,s/o Alp. & A.L.
Ezra C.,Dec.5,1872,6y.
Frank,XXXX.
George B.,Feb.1902,75y.
Hepsabeth,1922,85y,w/o George B.
Jennie R.,Feb.15,1886,17y,
   d/o Geo.B. & H.R.
Joseph,Mar.15,1888,27y.
Sarah A. Knight,Apr.25,1867,26y,
   w/o Hiram.
HALL
Albert H.,May 7,1954.
Jason H.,Sept.28,1850,1y,
   s/o Timothy & Lovesah.
Lovesah M.,Nov.20,1859,25y,w/o Tim.
Timothy M.,Nov.10,1855,40y
HANSCOM
Clyde,Apr.12,1985.
Hortense,June 1,1941,w/o Walter.
Leslie L.,Jan.1,1919,ch/o W.A.& H.
Walter A.,Oct.5,1961.
Warren,Feb.5,1968,inf/o Warren A.
HANSON
Francis H.,XXXX,10m,d/o Nicholas.
Nicholas,Jan.18,1887,65y.
Oloff N.,Feb.24,1864,5y,s/o Nicholas.
Sarah,Dec.3,1880,51y,w/o Nicholas.
HARDING
Lydia M.,June 8,1899,w/o Joseph H.

HARMON
Ann H.,May 26,1897,69y,w/o Joseph.
Ernest D.,1923,s/o Lewis L. & Lucille.
John,May 19,1899,44y,s/o Jos. & Ann.
Joseph,Mar.18,1891,67y.
Lawrence,XXXX,s/o Lewis & Luella.
Lewis L.,1926,s/o Jos.& Ann.
Lucille M.,Mar.30,1938,71y,w/o Lewis.
Ralph,Sept.28,1981.
Mildred,May 3,1985.
HARRIMAN
Alta Hayes,Apr.20,1965,w/o Jesse.
Jesse,Aug.5,1968.
HAYDEN
Hermon,Apr.30,1970,9y,
   s/o Elden & Nellie.
HICKS
Harry,1906-1906.
Harry,July 10,1972.
HIGGINS
Arthur Thomas,Apr.25,1987.
Carrie A.,Nov.26,1979.
HILLOCK
Adrian Guy,Oct.4,1962,
   s/o John & Martha.
Arnold F.,Apr.14,1958,
   s/o Arnold & Irene..
Arnold S.,Oct.2,1936.
Donald R.,Oct.18,1960,
   s/o John E. & Martha.
Frederick,Oct.2,1936.
John E.,June 26,1953.
Martha,Feb.24,1945,w/o John E.
Mertie Ella,June 8,1971,69y, w/o
   Perley Merserve & Donald Hillock..
Stanley William,Dec.6,1957,
   inf/o Wm. & Virginia..
Stanley,Apr.28,1990.
HUNTLEY
Bertha G.,Apr.24,1963.
HURD
Lena May,1913-Jan.3,1948,
   d/o Geo. & Lucy Johnson..
HUTCHINS
Glendon O.,1937.
JACQUES
Laurie Ann,Feb.24,1969,2m.
JOHNSON
Adelaide,May 24,1989.
Ernest,Apr.26,1990.
Ethel,Mar.3,1972,58y.
Flora,XXXX,w/o William.
George,XXXX,bro/o William.
George,Apr.19,1955.
Lucy S.,Mar.29,1975.
Perley S.,Jan.1905,inf/o Geo. & Lucy.
Ramona,Oct.22,1985.

William Almon,Mar.25,1969.
William,XXXX.
JORDON
Albert W.,Nov.8,1936.
Melinda,XXXX,w/o Albert.
Rufus,XXXX,s/o Albert W.
JOSE
Lena H.,Aug.23,1887,5y.
Mary E.,July 14,1924,w/o Wm. W.
William W.,June 14,1902,71y.
KEMP
Andrew A.,Oct.10,1832,21y.
KIMBALL
Amos,Sept.9,1827,53y.
KNIGHT
Adra A.,Jan.1905,50y,w/o Samuel.
Amos,1893,17y,s/o Turner & Mary.
Benjamin F.,1939,
  s/o Lewis & Sophia.
Bertha H.,Sept.7,1896,
  inf/o Benjamin F. & Eva.
Blanch E. Stone,Mar.29,1947,51y,
  w/o Percy.
Eva,Dec.22,1918,59y,w/o Benj. F.
George W.,Mar.16,1921,
  s/o James & Mary.
Ina Saunders,Sept.12,1966,
  w/o George W..
infant,July 15,1851,
  inf/o Isaac & Lucy.
Isaac,Dec.14,1884,75y.
James,May 7,1883,70y.
Jennie W.,Sept.24,1937,
  w/o John O.
John O.,Oct.18,1924,77y.
Lewis P.,1909.
Lucy S.B.,Aug.4,1882,69y,
  w/o Isaac.
Marion,XXXX,w/o Roscoe L.
Mary E.,1899,50y,w/o Turner H.
Mary E.,Nov.26,1913,90y,
  w/o James.
Mattie A.,1883,inf/o Samuel & Adra.
Percy C.,Mar.4,1972,84y.
Perley C.,May 27,1945.
Ralph,1906,28y,s/o Turner & Mary.
Roscoe Libby,Aug.14,1965,
  s/o Benjamin & Eva..
Samuel B.,1926.
Sarah A.,May 25,1867.
Sherman,Jan.4,1958.
Sophia P.,1885,w/o Lewis P.
Turner,1927.
Vesta F.,1914,d/o Benj. & Eva.
Vesta S.,1881,d/o Lewis & Sophia.
Winifred E.,May 4,1866,9y,
  d/o Lewis & Sophia.

LAKIN
Charlotte Lee,June 13,1958,inf.
LARRABEE
Betsey Hodsdon,1878,51y,w/o Ivory.
Elizabeth S.,1892,62y.w/o Jas. G.
Ivory K.,July 13,1859,36y,
  s/o Phillip & Polly Grant.
James G.,1898,80y..
James F.,1850,3y,s/o Ivory & Betsy.
Mary (Polly),1844,58y,1st w/o Philip.
Philip,Sept.7,1872,89y,
  2nd w. Nabby Hall (1849).
LEARY
Eliza Jane,June 21,1908,76y.
Patrick,Oct.26,1869,56y.
LEATHERBERRY
Annie,Oct.1,1982.
LIBBY
Abigail,Apr.23,1831,22y,w/o Joseph.
Abigail,July 28,1838,38y.
Abigail,XXXX,w/o Roscoe.
Alvin,Feb.1,1853,51y.
Ann H.,Apr.16,1893,77y,w/o Wm.
Anna Louise,Apr.19,1882,4m,
  d/o J.Augustus & Louise L.
Annie A.,1935,w/o J.Augustus.
Ansel,1897,s/o J.A. & Annie A.
Asbury F.,May 14,1911,74y.
Bertha,May 2,1884,5m,
  d/o Henry & Mary.
Charles,May 14,1850,83y.
Charles,Nov.23,1826,8y.
Charles,Sept.15,1829,1y.
Charles,Sept.6,1906,50y.
Charles,Jan.1,1925.
Clara M.,1890,28y.
Daniel C.,Nov.11,1945,s/o Wm & Ann.
Dominicus,Dec.18,1822,71y.
Dominicus,Feb.19,1901,75y.
Dominicus,May 18,1820,26y.
Dorothy,Oct.13,1846,85y,w/o Domin.
Edith Knight,Jan.14,1959,
  w/o Lester,d/o Samuel & Adra.
Elilleen K.,June 9,1918,5y,
  d/o Lester & Edith.
Elizabeth Morris,Aug.28,1856,
  30y,w/o Isaac.
Ellen E.,Apr.25,1910,62y,
  w/o Asbury F.
Elvin,XXXX,s/o Lewis & Lydia.
Enoch,Sept.25,1843,77y.
Everett F.,Aug.25,1955.
Florence Day,XXXX.
Florence E.,1901,31y,
  d/o Lewis & Lydia.
Frances E.,Jan.6,1942,w/o Charles.
Grace E.,Dec.5,1977.

Hannah,Sept.2,1841,41y,
 1st w/o Luther.
Hattie M.,July 29,1881,24y,
 d/o John IV.
Helen Maude,Nov.24,1971,81y,
 w/o Joseph.
Henry D.,1919.
Henry,Dec.1911.
Herbert E.,June 10,1961,
 s/o Lewis & Lydia.
infant,1816.
Ivory F.,Aug.8,1941.
J. Augustus,Jan.27,1912,62y,
 s/o William & Ann H..
James W.,July 23,1913,71y.
Jennie W. Riggs,July 15,1885,34y,
 w/o Charles F.
John M.,Mar.27,1947.
John,May 19,1869,74y.
John,IV,Sept.25,1879,53y.
Joseph A.,Apr.18,1964,
 s/o James & Mary.
Lemuel,1829,80y.
Lemuel,Jr.,1854,70y.
Lester,1923.
Lettice A.,Apr.21,1858,6y,
 s/o Wm.& Ann H.
Lettice,Mar.6,1873,80y.
Levi,XXXX.
Lewis B.,Oct.2,1915.
Lewis J.,Dec.1917,87y.
Louise L.,Mar.7,1883,31y,
 w/o J.Augustus.
Lucretia Libby,1901,68y,w/o John IV.
Lucretia,Jan.1901,wid/o Woodbury,?.
Lucy E.,1882,18y,d/o Lewis & Lydia.
Luther,1886,92y.
Lydia,Dec.1924,83y,w/o Lewis J.
Mammie C.,1893,19y,d/o Lewis.
Martha C.,Jan.18,1872,10y,
 d/o John IV.
Martha H.,Aug.21,1826,6y.
Martha W.,Nov.17,1885,59y,w/o Levi.
Martha,Aug.1860,20y,d/o Luther.
Mary A.,1922.
Mary,1869,93y,w/o David Waterhouse.
Mary,1926,w/o Henry D.
Mary J.,1929,w/o James W.
Mary,Feb.1924,w/o John M.
Mary Fogg,Feb.23,1839,79y,
 w/o William (1838).
Mehitable Bragdon,1817,63y,
 w/o Lemuel (1829).
Narcissa Harmon,1869,78y,
 w/o Lemuel.
Norman L.,Feb.24,1918,40y.
Polly,Oct.22,1837,69y,w/o Charles.

Rebekah,Oct.15,1816,w/o Enoch.
Roscoe,June 25,1880.
Sarah E., Apr.20,1961,
 d/o Lewis & Lydia.
Sarah P.Files,Aug.24,1878,75y,
 2nd w/o Luther.
Sarah,1872,100y.
Stephen W.,Mar.20,1946.
Susan Hustin,June 18,1892,
 29y,w/o Charles.
Tabitha,Mar.16,1893.
William A.,Apr.20,1950,
 s/o James & Mary J..
William H.,Sept.22,1826,4y.
William J.,Apr.29,1960,
 s/o George H. & Bessie E.Rhodes.
William,1881,s/o Henry & Mary A.
William,1937,bro/o John M.
William,Nov.7,1886,21y,s/o Lewis.
William,Oct.1,1838,75y.
William,Oct.31,1883,70y.
LLOYD
Forrest T.,Sept.16,1945.
LOMBARD
Ephraim,July 23,1843,70y,
 1st w.Polly Perkins (1803,29y).
Jane Norton Larrabee,Mar.23,1859,
 82y,2nd w/o Ephraim.
LOWE
Addie E.,Apr.11,1955,w/o Geo.W.
Ammon L.,1890.
Charles J.,1890,s/o Chas.& Eliza A.
Charles,1867.
Eliza A.,1924,w/o Charles.
George W.,Mar.28,1949,s/o Sidney N.
Mary P.,1852,w/o Charles.
Sydney N.,1885.
Tristram M.,1927,s/o Chas. & Eliza.
LUND
Frances L.,May 14,1962,w/o Russell,
 d/o Warren N. & Phyllis Washburn.
LUNT
Eugene,Feb.4,1958.
Morris A.,Oct.12,1965,
 s/o Eugene & Nellie.
Nellie G.,Dec.28,1962,w/o Eugene.
MADDIX
Agnes,June 2,XXXX,w/o Merrill.
Merrill,Nov.26,1955.
Timothy Merrill,May 2,1959,inf.
MAHER
George Franklin,Nov.29,1966.
MARSH
child,Mar.1889,5wks.
Fannie G.,Aug.23,1964w/o Linwood.
George H.,July 10,1898,42y.
James R.,Mar.19,1906,44y.

Linwood,Mar.20,1972,82y.
Lottie Riggs,July 23,1946,w/o David.
Sarah M.,July 27,1887,39y,
  w/o George H.
MAYHEW
Alfred,1905.
Margaret,1911,w/o Alfred.
McELROY
Norman,May 11,1987.
twins,May 1968.
McKENNEY
Agnes,1914.
Delia W.,XXXX.
Laura D.,1891,92y.
Lucy A.,1936,w/o W.W.
Mahala A.,Sept.18,1913,75y.
Moses M.,XXXX.
Moses,Mar.24,1828.
Salome,July 3,1842,w/o Moses.
Sophronia,XXXX,w/o Moses.
Washington,June 12,1932.
William Henry,XXXX,s/o W.W.
William,XXXX.
Willie H.,1889,s/o W.W. & Lucy A.
McLELLAN
Charles,Apr.5,1951.
Clara,Oct.7,1897,d/o C.A. & Lois.
Eva,Jan.7,1895,d/o C.A. & Lois.
Howard,Oct.15,1897,s/o C.A. & Lois.
Lotie E. Knight,1894,w/o Charles.
MELLEN
George S.,May 17,1941.
Rose Ellen,Sept.4,1975.
MERCIER
Ardine,Aug.9,1968,w/o Paul.
Lionel Henry,July 9,1977.
Mary Marie,Dec.12,1975,91y.
MERRILL
Brian Donald,Oct.17,1970,newb.
Mary Crockett,July 28,1872,80y,
  2nd w/o Seward..
Nelson H.G.,July 31,1857,24y,
  h/o Mary E. Merserve, s/o Sew.& Mary.
Olive R.,July 26,1843,
  d/o Ephraim & Jane Lombard.
Seward,Col.,Jan.7,1863,70y,
  1st w. Joanna Day (1828), s/o Dan.
MERRY
Lawrence,Dec.20,1972,73y.
Shirley E.,Aug.10,1958,w/o Lawrence.
MESERVE
Addie A.,Aug.21,1893,15y,
  d/o William & Mary J.
Addie H.,Sept.13,1905,70y,w/o Robt.
Agnes,1923-1970,d/o Irma.
Albert,Mar.9,1942.
Alice A.,Apr.7,1880,23y.
Alonzo J.,Mar.14,1942.
Arthur L.,Dec.3,1967,s/o Freedom.
Blanche,Dec.1967,w/o Melville.
Charles E.,1927.
Charles,XXXX.
Charles,XXXX,s/o Robt. & Ida.
Clifford,Aug.5,1987
Cora Evangeline,Nov.3,19XX.
Dale,Sept.9,1985.
Edward A.,1927.
Edwin,Sept.18,1943.
Ella M.,Apr.1903,35y,w/o Edw.A.
Emery Charles,Apr.19,1972,62y.
Emily F.,July 12,1963,w/o Walter.
Esther R.,Dec.17,1845-Jan.9,1871,
  d/o Samuel.
Esther,Sept.27,1927,w/o James G.
Eva,May 24,1986.
Everett L.,Feb.1916,27y.
Everett,May 15,1993.
Florence M. Allen,Apr.28,1959,
  w/o Charles.
Fred E.,Aug.28,1892,29y,
  s/o Robert & Addie..
Freedom,1898,47y.
Geneva,1899,12y,d/o Robt. & Ida.
Geraldine,Nov.4,1992
Hannah M. Allen,Jan.11,1916,
  83y,w/o Hiram.
Harry C.,Apr.26,1976.
Helen M.,1896,1y.
Henrietta,Mar.31,1871,20y,
  d/o William & Mary.
Hiram,Apr.8,1894,70y.
Ida,1896,39y,w/o Robert.
infant,XXXX,d/o Phinias & M.E.
Irma E.,May 6,1967,w/o Edwin.
Irving,Sept.24,1986.
J. Sumner,1905,61y.
James G.,Nov.19,1923.
John A.L.,July 13,1938.
Leon H.,1898-1935.
Lucy,June 5,1971,w/o Wendell.
Lewellyn,1884,8y.
Margaret,June 16,1967,w/o Albert.
Mary J.,May 17,1894,73y,w/o Wm.
Mary T. Owen,1935,w/o Charles.
Melville Jeremiah,Apr.5,1965.
Melville L.,1897,24y.
Mildred F.,July 9,1941,w/o John A.L.
Minnie M.,Oct.12,1943,w/o Nelson C.
Minnie,June 23,1903,22y,
  d/o James G. & Esther.
Myra,Apr.24,1955,w/o Robert B.
Nelson C.,1925,s/o Robt. & Addie.
Norine,Nov.24,1954,
  d/o Edwin J. & Doris Silver.

Perley H.,Aug.16,1943.
Philip L.,Sept.9,1909.
Phineas,Sept.6,1994.
Ralph E.,Sept.14,1978.
Robert,June 15,1903,74y.
Robert,XXXX.
Roy,Sept.14,1966,s/o Robt. & Ida.
Samuel,Jan.30,1870,65y,h/o Hannah Green (1894,90y).
Tristram,Mar.10,1960,
 s/o Nelson & Winnie.
Walter S.,Dec.11,1947,
 s/o Hiram & Hannah.
Wendell,Sept.4,1985.
Willard,June 10,1879,1m,
 s/o James G. & Esther.
William,Jan.10,1892,74y.
Willis M.,May 1,1962,s/o Jas. & Est.
Willis,May 19,1989.
MILLIGAN
Eula H.,1920.
MITCHELL
Agnes M. McKenney,Apr.1914, 39y,w/o Wm.A.
Carl H.,Oct.1918,29y,
 s/o Chas.H. & Mayvilla.
Charles P.,Feb.22,1950,s/o C.H. & M.
Charles H.,1930,
 s/o Wm.H. & Mary A. Libby Mitchell.
infant,May 13,1882, d/o Charles & Mayvilla Waterman Mitchell.
Mabel Lillian,Sept.10,1970,w/o Carl.
Mary A.,1922,w/o William H.
Mayvilla N. Waterman,1928,w/o C.H.
William A.,1932,s/o Wm.H. & M. L.
William H.,Oct.1900,77y.
MITSMENN
George,May 10,1974.
Velma,Feb.1972,80y,w/o George.
MOORE
Mary,1855,27y,d/o David & Sophia Waterhouse..
MORRELL
Guy L.,Aug.11,1945.
Lena Knight,Sept.19,1964,w/o Guy.
MORRIS
Abigail Burnham,Dec.29,1867,82y.
Ann Louisa,Mar.8,1821,33y,
 d/o Charles & Rhoda.
Charles,in Wales 1749-Feb.6,1818.
Charles,Mar.29,1840,47y.
Eliza Emerson,Sept.5,1855,64y,
 w/o Charles.
George W.,Sept.30,1871,24y.
James H.,Dec.30,1830,52y,
 s/o Charles & Rhoda.

Harriett N.,Apr.19,1865,29y,
 d/o William T. & Sarah.
Rhoda Libby,Feb.16,1821,75y,
 w/o Charles.
Rhoda Caroline,June 17,1845,20y.
Sarah A.Harding,Aug.15,1903,90y,
 w/o William T.
William T.,Dec.29,1888,76y.
MORSE
Frank O.,Apr.2,1872,18y.
Willie A.,Apr.2,1977,18d.
MOSES
Adeline,Oct.13,1841,37y,w/o Wm.
Ann L., Mar.10,1876,57y,w/o Wm.
Joseph A.,1882,54y.
Mary L.,Nov.26,1829,22y,w/o Wm.
William A.,1882.
William,Capt.,Aug.7,1880,76y.
MOULTON
Emery L.,Dec.7,1960,s/o Freedom & Mary McLellan.
infant,June 27,1940.
Zora,Nov.1957,w/o Emery.
NELSON
Henry,Sr.,Jan.2,1972.
NEWCOMB
Harriet Ella,May 20,1949,w/o Sam.
Samuel,May 3,1951.
William Patrick,Sept.5,1974.
NEWELL
Harriett,Aug.4,1833,18y.
NICKERSON
Avis,May 1,1987.
NORWOOD
Abraham,1923.
Fannie L.,1922,w/o Abraham.
O'CONNER
Addie M.,Sept.26,1963,w/o Cecil.
Cecil E.,Sept.17,1964.
PARLIN
Emery W.,Apr.29,1969.
Helen S.,May 8,1980.
PENNY
Ivory,1855
Nancy,1961,w/o Ivory.
PERHAM
Mary Frances,June 27,1953.
PETERSON
Ruth Ella,Sept.4,1984.
PIKE
Eunice,1867,69y,w/o Humphrey.
Humphrey,1835,33y.
PILLSBURY
George J.,1923,s/o Wm. & Martha.
Martha,1920,w/o William.
William F.,1928.

PRESCOTT
H. Scott,Nov.14,1965.
Helen E.,1918,inf/o H.Scott
Jennie D.,July 3,1975.
Marion L.,May 8,1987,w/o H. Scott.
REED
Allen G.,Aug.2,1916,79y.
Emily T.,Oct.1905,64y,w/o A.G.
RIGGS
Albert,1906,54y.
Clara,1937,w/o Albert.
Evie,1883,infant.
Lydia A. Bickford,1926,w/o Charles.
Mattie L.,1891,10y.
ROBERTS
Betsey Huston,Nov.4,1873,86y, w/o Samuel.
Clifford A.,Dec.3,1958,s/o Albert L. & Eva M. Deering Roberts.
Ella O.,1848,1y.
Francis,June 22,1850,22y,s/o S.&B.
infant,Jan.15,1942,s.b./o A.L.& E.
Lester W.,1936.
Olive Stevenson,1907.
Samuel,Aug.5,1849,70y, 1st w.Elizabeth Staples (1811,29y).
Samuel,1887,71y.
ROBINSON
Oscar,July 25,1984.
SANBORN
Anna Louise,Dec.20,1955,w/o O.P.
Etta L.,1939,w/o T.C.
John,Apr.24,1915,80y.
Nellie M.,July 18,1955.
Ormond Prescott,Feb.29,1962, s/o John W. & Ruth Libby.
Orville W.,Apr.11,1923, s/o Wm.L. & Nellie M.
Ruth A.,XXXX.
T.C.,July 28,1955,s/o John W.
William,Apr.17,1968.
SANVILLE
John Harold,1943.
SAUNDERS
Arthur R.,1935.
Ethel M.,Aug.23,1955.
Rupert A.,May 27,1958.
Winona,Aug.27,1938.
SCOTT
Helen E.,1918.
SHERMAN
Geneva M.,June 18,1893,27y, d/o J.B. & S.R.
Gerogia Mitchell,Oct.31,1948,w/o O.C.
Harry L.,May 3,1953,s/o Jos.B.
Jennie,XXXX,infant.
Joseph B.,Oct.13,1890,51y.
Nellie J.Vaillancourt,June 18,1933, w/o Harry L.
Orra C.,Apr.30,1959,s/o Jos.B.
Sarah R.,Aug.28,1875,33y,w/o Jos.B.
SKINNER
J.F.,Dec.25,1912,73y.
SMITH
Charles,Mar.4,1853,43y.
Sarah,Dec.12,1856,39y.
Wilbur,Apr.19,1986.
SPEAR
Florence,1928,w/o W.E., d/o Wm. & Flora Johnson.
Wright Elmer,May 2,1963.
STEEVES
Dennis,July 3,1985.
STEVENSON
Vevie ?, 1877,26y,d/o Chas.& Mary.
STOREY
Bertha,May 11,1987.
Clara E.,Jan.1,1892,40y,w/o Jas.F.
Eva M.,1881,1y,d/o Jas. & Clara.
infant,Apr.29,1964,s/o Richard.
James F.,Feb.13,1918,64y,s/o Jas.& Nancy Meserve.
James,Aug.16,1888,64y.
Louise M.,Dec.22,1955,w/o Philip.
Mabel F.,Dec.30,1966,d/o J.F.& M.E.
Mary E.,1934,w/o James T.
Nancy Larrabee,Dec.12,1866,73y, w/o James.
Philip Larrabee,Dec.10,1966,s/o J.F.
STRAW
Arthur J.,Feb.27,1940.
Jennie D.,July 3,1975.
Mary,1922,w/o Arthur J.
Robert A.,Mar.12,1978.
STROUT
Comfort Emery,Apr.25,1839,52y, w/o Geo.Jr.
Dora,Apr.3,1883,46y,w/o Wm.E.
Franklin,July 1,1847,25y,s/o G.&C.
George,Jr.,Sept.10,1837,57y.
Mary E.,Mar.12,1832,28y,w/o Wm.
Mary,Nov.19,1832.
Sarah,Jan.15,1864,58y,w/o Wm.
William E.,Dec.18,1915,76y.
SYMONDS
Esther Maud,1892-1976.
TAPLEY
Ann,Apr.9,1915,81y,w/o Jas.F.
Arthur W.,June 11,1965.
Beulah L.,Jan.26,1975.
Collins M.,Nov.13,1914,81y.
Edwin,Jan.24,1864,3y,s/o Jas.
Elijah D.,Dec.5,1868,67y.
Eliza S.,Aug.29,1889,88y,w/o Elijah.

Elizabeth Eleanor,Sept.20,1950,
d/o Howard & Dorothy.
Frank,May 21,1946.
Harriet Susan,Dec.18,1977.
Howard,Jr.,May 25,1991.
James F., Sept.1900,69y.
Jesse H.,XXXX.
Leora,Apr.22,1986.
Mary Ella,Jan.20,1965.
Melissa C.,Aug.1917,79y.
Willard,Apr.21,1888,11y,s/o Jas.
THOMPSON
Lena M.,Nov.26,1962,ex-wife/o Orrin,
d/o James & Ellen Green.
Mary A.,1920,w/o Walter P.
Orrin,Dec.5,1955,s/o W.P. & M.A.
Ralph Leslie,Jan.27,1973.
Walter A.,Oct.2,1918,31y,
s/o W.P.& M.A.
Walter P.,XXXX.
TOUTLOFF
Blanch Libby,1959,w/o Wm.C.,
d/o Henry D. & Mary A..
William C.,1921.
TRIPP
2 infants,XXXX.
Addie L.,1920,w/o Moses B.
Arthur,Sept.20,1951,
s/o Harry & Sarah.
Caroline,Sept.1917,61y.
Cornelia E.,1920,w/o Fred.
Eliza E.,1876,54y.
Emma E.,Oct.31,1976.
Ernest Gray,Oct.16,1977.
Ernest,Jan.16,1949,s/o Harry & S.
Francis B.,Oct.29,1916,8y,
s/o Roscoe G. & Emma.
Fred,1927.
George B.,1901,79y.
George,Jr.,Oct.7,1877,25y.
Gordon R.,1922,s/o Roscoe & Emma.
Harold,June 29,1984.
Harry,Mar.15,1945.
Howard L.,Jan.8,1943.
Isabelle,XXXXd/o Roscoe & Emma.
Laura W.,May 18,1961,w/o Ernest.
Moses B.,1910.
Roscoe G.,Mar.14,1936.
Sarah E., Mar.31,1946,w/o Harry.
Zachariah,1903.
VARNEY
Marcia Reed,Feb.13,1969,2d.
WASHBURN
Ethel,Dec.7,1969.
Nathan,1891-Aug.12,1970.
WATERHOUSE
Benjamin,Sept.1,1893,75y.

David,1793-1867,h/o Sophia..
Dorcus Libby,1836,77y,w/o George.
Dorothy,June 1,1982.
George,Oct.9,1835,87y.
Irene,May 14,1985.
Martha,1908,81y,w/o Benjamin.
Mary Roundy,1869,93y,w/o David.
Sophia Coolbroth,July 3,1853,57y.
WATERMAN
Mayville,1928.
WELCH
Roland,July 3,1993.
WHEELER
Jennie Belle,Apr.20,1883,7m,d/o Z.J.
Lucy P.,Apr.16,1879,42y,w/o Z.J.
Margaret,Oct.1916,72y,w/o Z.J.
Z.J.,Rev.,Aug.21,1914,77y.
WISWELL
Joseph,1869,78y.
WRIGHT
Margaret Ann,Dec.20,1943.
William J.,Sept.4,1955.

✦ **WHITE ROCK CEMETERY** ✦
North Gorham Road. Established in
about 1791. Managed by Association.
List not complete.

BUXTON
Malcolm H.,May 16,1978.
CHASE
Todd Allen,Nov.28,1965.
DAVIS
Rebecca P.,1904,65y,w/o Wm.Wiley.
GREEN
Cyril K.,Dec.13,1976.
JEWELL
Helen Wilma,Feb.3,1980.
KIMBALL
Ethel Lombard,May 1908,29y,
w/o John A.
LAMB
Annie Haskell,Aug.12,1984.
MARSTON
Lena Agnes,Aug.31,1972.
McGOWEN
Lida Gertrude,Jan.1,1984.
MERSERVE
Mary Louise,Feb.20,1973.
NUGENT
Brian E.,May 4,1970.
Dennis,June 22,1949.
Melville Arthur,July 1,1982.
PHINNEY
Lillian Ethel,Oct.30,1974.
WESCOTT
Hannah Frost,1813-1907,w/o Abner.

✧ WEST GORHAM CEMETERY ✧
Dow Road, West Gorham. Managed by Association.Checked all gravestones.

BACON
Isaac E.,July 16,1874,51y,s/o Nathaniel & Nicy,Civil War Vet.
Mariam H.,Nov.18,1890,67y,w/o I.E., d/o Richard & Lucy Ayers Bacon.
Nycia Emery ,Feb.23,1844,55y, w/o Nathaniel,Jr.
BEANE
Daniel F.,1890-19XX.
Delia E.,1890-1924,w/o Daniel.
E. Everett,1859-1927.
Sarah W.,1861-1944.
BLAKE
Hannah Hopkins,Jan.27,1842, 78y,w/o Joseph (1840).
Joseph,July 13,1835,32y, h/o Elizabeth Moody.
Joseph,Jan.28,1840,82y,Rev.War Vet.
Susannah Higgins,Apr.12,1862, w/o Timothy,73y.
Timothy,Jan.7,1883,93y,War 1812.
CALDWELL
Mary,Aug.1,1844-Feb.3,1904.
Sanford P.,May 2,1854-June 7,1936.
CLAY
George,May 8,1987.
Lillie M.,Oct.23,1988,w/o George.
CLEMENT
Dolly Tappan,Apr.17,1893,81y.
George T.,Oct.26,1857,42y,h/o D.T. s/o Geo.T. & Dolly.
Henry George,Oct.21,1857,14y,
Lizzie M.,Oct.8,1857,11y;
Luther T.,June 16,1854,6m.
CLEMENTS
Jacob H.,1798-1860.
Moses B.,1827-1904.
Sally C.,1800-1880,w/o Jacob.
COREY
Sarah,May 3,1826-Jan.12,1900, w/o W.B.
DROWN
Arthur M.,Aug.12,1877,55y.
Eliza A.,Jan.21,1856,30y,w/o A.M.
Hannah,Dec.3,1875,83y,w/o Solomon.
Luther A.,Oct.8,1855,19d,s/o A.&E.
EASTMAN
Jacob Herbert,Mar.18,1863-Sept.14,1865,s/o J.& Ruth.
Ruth L.,Sept.22,1935-Sept.11,1863, w/o Jonathan.

FILES
Abbie S.,Aug.1,1863,41y, d/o Wm.& Abigail.
Abigail,Mar.13,1819,39y,w/o Wm.E.
Addie,Sept.29,1870,19y,d/o Edward & Jane H.
Cyrus,Aug.11,1903,71y,s/o Wm. & E.
Ebenezer,Feb.24,1758-Sept.30,1833.
Ebenezer,Jr.,May 3,1872,88y.
Edward,Oct.26,1874,49y,s/o Eben.& S.
Edward Everett,1859-1927.
Elizabeth Moulton,Feb.25,1857,62y, 2nd w/o William E.
Francis,Nov.26,1880,63y.
Frank Augustus,1846-1909, h/o Cornelia Watson.
Hannah W.,Oct.17,1860,42y, w/o Francis.
Harriet C.,Aug.31,1849,2y, d/o wm. & Elizabeth.
Harriet H.,Nov.12,1837-Nov.28,1921, w/o Francis.
Henry B.,Mar.12,1876,24y.
Lorenzo D.,Sept.14,1871,51y, 2nd w. Etta Flood.
Mary,Feb.30,1833,75y, w/o Ebenezer (1833).
Salome S. Foss,Sept.25,1869,58y, d/o William & Abigail.
Sarah Sturgis,Jan.22,1863,36y, w/o Lorenzo D.
Sarah Stuart,Apr.8,1873,78y, w/o Ebenezer,Jr.
Sarah Whitney,1861-1944.
William E.,Dec.24,1843,63y.
FOLEY
Edward J.,Aug.31,1993,72y, h/o Eleanor Jones,s/o Daniel & Helen Mahoney Foley.
FROST
Dominious,Dec.6,1862,69y,War 1812, s/o Moses..
Henry,July 13,1826,28y,h/o Sophronia Irish,s/o Moses & Sarah.
Justin,June 6,1849,10m,s/o D.& S.
Moses,Sept.20,1850,84y.
Sarah McKenney,Nov.10,1839,73y, w/o Moses.
Susan Parker,1814-1897,w/o Dom.
GILKEY
Reuben,Capt.,1789-1868,s/o James & Polly Marr.
Phebe Marr,1805-1867,w/o Reuben.
GOODWIN
Mary E.Scammon,1851-Dec.1911, w/o Joseph.

GUSTIN
Marion E.,1911,3m,d/o George.
HARDING
Martha Ann Brown,Jan.20,1826, 82y,w/o Capt. Samuel,d. at sea 1789.
HASTY
Maria L.,Jan.6,1875,4y, s/o Thomos,Jr.& Edith.
Sarah D.(Sally),Sept.7,1883, 79y,w/o Thomas J.
Thomas J.,Mar.1,1873,68y.
ThomasJ.,Jr.,Oct.12,1876,40y, h/o Edith Lombard.
HIGGINS
Fannie Blake,June 22,1878,85y, w/o Saul.
Isaac,Dec.19,1855,75y,1st w.Esther Parker,2nd w.Ruth Kent
Joseph,Capt.,Jan.1804,54y,at sea, h/o Elizabeth Files.
Mercy,Dec.19,1843,88y,w/o Capt.Jos.
Saul Cook,Fb.16,1895,100y,Civil War.
Ruth Kent,Feb.12,1861,71y,w/o Isaac.
HUNTLEY
Mary E.,Nov.10,1972.
IRISH
Abigail F. Rounds,Mar.3,1865,79y, w/o Daniel (1829).
Adaline,Nov.7,1874,52y,w/o A.P.
Albion P.,Oct.3,1819-Aug.23,1893.
Caroline H.,Jan.9,1848,23y,w/o A.P.
Stephen,Apr.6.1841,84y, h/o Anna,(1846,86y).
JACKSON
Margaret,Jan.17,1864,87y,w/o Zeb.
Zebediah F.,Jan.14,1862,87y.
JORDAN
Caroline M.,1832-1895.
Charles E.,1829-1908.
Desire P. Lewis,May 12,1796-Mar.14,1880,w/o Nathaniel.
James L.,June 14,1824-Jan.13,1884.
Lewis,July 21,1874-Aug.22,1880, s/o J.D.? & Lucy.
Mary J.Martin,Mar.10,1840-Dec.22,1870,w/o James L.
Nathaniel,May 11,1790-Sept.11,1882,War of 1812.
ch/o C.E.& C.M.:
Henry,Mar.14,1863,4y:
Mary T.,1873-1888.
KINSMAN
Susan Frost,May 7,1842,38y,w/o C.
LEED/SEED ?
Francis,XXXX, Co.P.,10th ME Inf.
LEWIS
Achsah J.,Nov.29,1846,8y,d/o G.& M.

Amanda J.,June 3,1914,81y, 2nd w/o Simon.
Eliza Frost,Aug.26,1851,33y, 1st w/o Simon J.
George,Apr.14,1844,45y.
Hannah Harding,May 3,1848,73y, w/o Rev.James.
James,Aug.20,1855,85y,War of 1812.
Mary S.,Mar.11,1851,45y,w/o Geo.
Simon J.,June 13,1884,62y.
ch/o Elder James & Hannah:
Elijah P.,June 20,1831,26y;
James,May 1814,12y;
Josiah,May 9,1842,31y,in Iowa;
Samuel H.B.,Oct.16,1816,23y, in Port au Prince;
Samuel H.B.,Sept.19,1843,29y, in GA.,h/o Dolly Lunt;
Timothy,May 1802,2y.
MASSUERE
Nevens,July 26,1838,4m, s/o Rev.Francis & Almira.
PARKER
Polly,Dec.4,1993.
PICKERING
Abigail O.,Aug.18,1838,23y, d/o Anthony & Mary D.
Sarah E.,Mar.23,1842,24y,d/o ?.
RICHARDSON
Almira W.,Feb.25,1831,3m,d/o A.& D.
Dorcus,Sept.28,1853,50y,w/o Artemas.
SAWYER
Albion P.,Dec.18,1825-Aug.20,1912, Civil War Soldier.
Eliza Gilkey,June 17,1833-Nov.7,1913,w/o Albion P.
Isaac M.,1856-1862.
Phoebe,1861-1870.
Reuben,1855-1855.
SHAW
Dewayn,Ma.24,1962-May 22,1965.
Timothy,XXXX.
SNOW
Thankful,Feb.15,1837,75y.
SPINNEY
Charlotte M.,July 18,1864,16y, d/o John D. & Dorcas.
Dorcus E. Redlon,Jan.13,1827-May 22,1909,w/o John D.
George R.,Jan.5,1858-Jan.24,1929.
John D.,Mar.21,1819-Mar.11,1904, Co.K.,5th Me Vol.
John M.,Mar.22,1873,22y.
Willie V.,July 14,1864,4y,w/o J.& D.
STEVENS
Walter,Feb.20,1935-May 5,1991.

STROUT
Lizzie E.,Oct.9,1857,8y,d/o Micajah C.
 & Olive F.
STUART
Hannah,Oct.5,1848,56y.
TIBBETTS
Lewis,Sept.4,1924-Sept.3,1993.
TOPPING
Mary M.,Dec.5,1808-Mar.5,1896.
Sybel,Mar.2,1824-Feb.6,1899.
WASS
Charles Henry,Sept.9,1886-
 June 18,1920,WWI.
Eulalia F.,1884-1934,w/o C.H.
ch/o Charles H. & Eulalia:
 Harold E.,1907-1915;
 Grace E. Dolloff,1909-XXXX;
 Beryl J.,1911-Mar.17,1912,1y;
 Loring J.,1914-1944,bu.in France.
WATSON
John,Mar.12,1878,74y,s/o Edmund
 & Betsey.
Luther D.,Aug.14,1852,s/o J.& M.
Martha A.,July 23,1876,59y,w/o John.
Maud,Nov.20,1877,6y,
 twin d/o Oliver C.& Kate E.
WOOD
Marjorie E.,Sept.14,1920-
 June 22,1990,1st w/o Frank.

✦ **SMITH PRIVATE GROUND** ✦
Wilson Road. Managed by Town.
Originally the property of Capt.
Ephraim Smith,born in Barnstable,
Mass. and a member of the
Boston Tea Party.

BETTIS
Hannah,Nov.18,1837,53y,w/o Jacob P.
Thomas,June 20,1831,
 s/o Capt.Jacob & Hannah.
SMITH
Ephraim,Jan.1751-Jan.13,1835.
Elizabeth Harding,Dec.8,1834,78y,
 w/o Ephraim.
S.,Sept.17,1821,30y.
C.D.,May 1818,13y.

✦ **NORTH STREET CEMETERY** ✦
North Street, Gorham. Managed by a
private association. Not checked.
Many burials not listed.

AMES
Isaac,Aug.14,1813,33y.
BACHELDER
Clara,1849-XXXX,w/o Henry L.
Henry L.,1828-1898.
Rae E.,Mar.20,1990.
BANGS
Elizabeth N.,Nov.18,1826-
 Dec.21,1891
Eva Adalaide,June 21,1851,6w.,
 d/o Reuben & Elizabeth.
G.E.,XXXX,29th Unass'd Co.Me.Inf.
Joseph,Mar.18,1853,83y.
Mary,Oct.5,1857,79y,w/o Joseph.
Reuben W.,Aug.11,1820-Apr.26,1893.
BATCHELDER
Edwin A.,1884-1915.
BEAUTTE
M. Ethel,Sept.28,1978.
BENNETT
Abbie F.Blake,1836-1899,w/o Geo.T.
Athru T.,Feb.4,1895,2m,
 s/o Frank W., & Jennie.
Calvin M.,1855-1916.
Charles K.,1853-1923.
Frances,1830-1862.
George T.,1829-1916.
BENSON
Everett D.,Aug.14,1981.
BLAIR
Abigail M.Elder,Aug.31,1854,35y,
 w/o John.
Ann Wood,1872,w/o Peter.
John,Nov.27,1848,32y.
Peter,b.Scotland-d.Mar.6,1848,84y.
Samuel E.,1846-XXXX,Civil War
 Soldier,diedat Fortress Monroe.
BLAKE
Deborah,Jan.15,1850,94y,w/o John.
James C.,Oct.10,1874,74y.
John,Mar.21,1826,66y.
John,Jr.,July 15,1818,26y,
 s/o John & Deborah.
Lillian J.,Feb.17,1881,2y,
 d/o Charles H. & Abbie.
Nathaniel,Feb.28,1843,90y.
BOOTHBY
Emeline Irish,XXXX,w/o Leonard.
Leonard M.,Jan.31,1903,38y.
BRAGDON
Dolly C.,May 18,1809,58y,w/o Wm.

BRYANT
Frank Eugene,July 10,1981.
John C.,1831-1915.
Scot,July 12,1984.
Tryphena,1826-1919,w/o John/
BURNELL
Susan,Aug.28,1857,47y.
BURNS
Hughey M.,Oct.13,1883,50y.
Wallis M.,XXXX,6m.
BUTTERFIELD
Abby W.,Sept.9,1871,51y,w/o Moses.
Mary A.,Mar.4,1866,44y,w/o Moses.
Moses,Dec.28,1889,74y.
CARTIER
Troy Aaron,Apr.13,1973.
CHARTIER
Dana Scott,Apr.13,1973.
COBB
Abra A.,1850-1912,w/o Isaac H.
Amos,1837-1898.
Comfort M.,Dec.28,1886,70y,w/o R.H.
Ethel M.,1876-1937,w/o Melville.
Eudocia Chaplin,1856-1929,w/o Amos.
Geneva E.,1879-1882.
George L.,1838-1887.
Isaac H.,1843-1926.
Lula M.,1876-1891.
Melville A.,1873-XXXX.
Robert H.,Aug.24,1901,88y.
Robert O.,1878-1943.
S. Marion,Aug.12XXXX,6m &
Susie,Mar.7,1872,1m,
d/o Amos & Juliette.
Velma E.,1910-1910.
COTTON
Carrie M.,Oct.27,1886,22y,d/o W.&M.
Maria Sturgis,1805-1885,w/o Wm.
William,1801-1876,s/o Ebenezer.
COUSINS
Sarah J.,Apr.10,1845-Nov.25,1902.
CRABTREE
Evelyn A.,May 17,1964.
CROCKETT
Almon,Jan.13,1856,10m,s/o G.& E.J.
Eliza J.,May 28,1855,24y,w/o Geo.W.
George W.,Dec.22,1832,62y.
DORRELL
Susan,w/o Isaiah,stone buried.
DOUGLASS
Alice W.,1901-1901.
Alverde L.,May 24,1884-XXXX.
Annie N.,1875-XXXX,w/o Orman L.
Bert E.,Jan.7,1881-Dec.13,1945.
Carrie E. Gile,Sept.11,1886,w/o A.L.
Clifford L.,Dec.2,1881-Dec.14,1946.

Edward K.,Oct.14,1842-Nov.25,1901,
Co.K.25th Regt.Me Vol.
Elizabeth A. Knight,Apr.12,1816-
Aug.12,1885.
Freedom,Mar.2,1818-Oct.24,1886.
George M.,Mar.15,1846-Aug.11,1912.
James E.,Dec.22,1877-Dec.3,1934.
Josephine Chick,Nov.26,1829-
Dec.14,1850,w/o Edward K.
Lyndon,1905-1988.
Nellie M.,Apr.23,1970.
Olive E.,1902-1988,w/o Lyndon L..
Orman L.,1872-1927.
Winnifred McLellan,May 21,1849-
June 26,1904,w/o Geo. M.
DUDLEY
Hannah A.,Oct.11,1901,87y,w/o Wm.
Horatio,Aug.3,1843,7y,s/o Wm.& H.A.
William,Mar.25,1852,48y.
DURGIN
Ada Amanda,June 21,1971.
Helen,Oct.23,1989.
James A.,Aug.3,1988.
ELLIOTT
Clara M.,June 18,18411-
May 31,1866,w/o E.F.
ELWELL
Alice F.,June 15,1805-Apr.6,1874.
Hariet,Sept.20,1837-Oct.3,1865.
Henry W.,Feb.24,1809-Mar.30,1863.
FARRIS
Rita Dawn,Feb.4,1979.
FAULKNER
Ella Maria,Oct.1,1857,1y,
d/o Edward Y.& Harriet.
Harriet M.,July 20,1858,36y,
w/o Edward Y.
FELCH
Conrad Charles,1956.
Harry,1959.
FILES
Ann L. Strout,1815-1887.
Ebeneber,1810-1842,
h/o Bethiah Bangs.
Edna S.,1895-1895,gr/d/o Edw.& H.
Edward,1786-1887.
Edward,1818-1906,h/o Hannah.
Hannah Shaw,1789-1878,
w/o Edward (1887).
Hannah Crockett,1822-1891,
w/o Edward
J.Wesley,Sept.23,1837-Feb.17,1911.
Jonathan S.,Oct.9,1890,79y.
Julia M.Shaw,1838-1903,w/o Wm.E.
Levisa Ann,Mar.20,1877,66y,w/o Jon.
Louisa R.,Mar.2,1896,89y.
Lucie E.,Feb.25,1891,23y,w/o Geo.E.

Mary Susan Whitney,Feb.23,1840-
Jan.25,1902,w/o J.Wesley.
S.M.,1830-1908.
Sally,Jan.9,1886,82y.
William E.,1832-1909.
ch/o Edward & Hannah:
Atwood W.,1855-1856;
Horace W.,1854-1900;
Joseph S.,1822-1846.
Rose D.,1846-1889;
Sargent S.,1861-XXXX;
Sophia J.,1857-1895.
FITZ
George T.,Oct.5,1861,1y,s/o J.S.& M
John T.,Oct.5,1861,1y,
s/o John S. & Maria M.
FOSTER
James A.,1844-1916.
Rensford,May 23,1964.
Sarah A. Bennett,1838-1919,w/o Jas.
FREEMAN
Robert L.,Nov.6,1846,1m,
s/o Wm.B.& Mary J.
GETCHELL
Daniel P.,1856-1925.
Gertrude L.,1865-1918,w/o Daniel.
Isaac,1821-1917.
Mary E.,1821-1917,w/o Isaac.
Wilder Leon,Aug.22,1970.
GILKEY
Catherine Staples,Nov.17,1845,75y.
Charles,Nov.12,1827,29y,h/o Cather.
Frederick,May 22,1808-May 10,1877.
Hattie E.,Nov.7,1885,40y,unm.
Isaac,Dec.21,1905,75y.
Lydia Bangs,Apr.6,1851,45y,
w/o Frederick.
GLOVER
Ornan Loring,May 28,1969.
GORDON
Edith H.,Apr.23,1981.
George K.,June 18,1965.
Joseph R.,1949,s/o Robert.
Mary,Dec.31,1982.
Phyllis,1988.
Robert C.,Oct.13,1980.
Seth L.,June 18,1965.
GRANT
Virginia,May 19,1990.
Wendel,Oct.18,1993.
GRAVES
Annie Bachelder,Jan.19,1968.
Annie L.,1888-XXXX,w/o Fred.A.
Frederick A.,1880-1916.
John,Nov.23,1991.
GRONLUND
Carla Jean,May 9,1966,11m.

HALL
Abigail,1845,68y,w/o Daniel.
Christiana,1851,44y,w/o Ebenezer.
ch/o Ebenezer & Christiana:
Harriett S.,1842,3y;
Daniel R.,1851,6m.
HAMBLEN
Allen,Feb.4,1888,81y.
Enoch,Nov.28,1843,70y.
Happy,July 20,1852,74y,w/o Enoch.
HAMBLIN
Arthur,1822-1895.
Eliza A.,1832-XXXX,w/o Arthur.
John,1886-1887.
HANSCOME
John Carleton,July 17,1979.
Richard,Sept.19,1988.
Robert Lee,Apr.19,1971.
HARMON
Caroline,Feb.10,1876,28y,w/o Benj.L.
ch/o Naphthalia & Hannah:
Lydia A.,Aug.25,1848,6y;
Roscoe,Dec.26,1850,7y.
HAYNES
Horace M.,1820-1897.
Ida M.,1861-1938.
James L.,Dec.31,1849-Mar.5,1921.
Leslie A.,1868-XXXX.
Mary E.,1831-1910.
Mary,Sept.1910,79y.
Olive A. Libby,Sept.8,1852-
May 24,1931,w/o James L.
HEATH
Heidi Elizabeth,Apr.9,1967,s.b.
HILL
Marvin E.,Jr.,1988.
HUNT
Elizabeth Ellen,July 15,1854,
19y,d/o George & Miriam.
George,June 27,1860,58y.
Louisa V.,Jan.15,1861,24y,
d/o George & Miriam.
Miriam,Nov.14,1799-Feb.18,1873,
w/o George.
HUTCHINSON
George,Nov.18,1972.
INGALLS
Donald W.,Dec.28,1982.
Harry C.,Aug.30,1982.
INGRAHAM
Louise E.,Oct.8,1974.
IRISH
Abigail,Apr.14,1856,84y.
Abigail,Sept.23,1869,75y.
Benjamin,Aug.31,1899,81y.
Benjamin,Nov.25,1839,74y.
Delilah,June 3,1859,80y.

Deliverance Skillings,1741-1821,
w/o Thomas T.
Elisha,May,7,1876,84y.
Eunice T.,Mar.7,1896,84y,w/o Jacob.
Harriet,June 12,1898,77y,w/o John H.
Jacob,Jan.9,1884,79y.
Jacob,1879,85y.
Jane,Apr.23,1828,61y,w/o Benj (1839)
Jane,Feb.6,1876,56y.
Jane,1851,56y,w/o Jacob.
John H.,Nov.29,1890,68y.
John M.,1872-1945.
Julia A.,Mar.19,1905,74y.
Lucy R.,Oct.1,1907,87y,w/o Benj.
Mabel Newcomb,1877-XXXX,
w/o John M.
Mary L.,Oct.14,1871,9y,
d/o Joshua & Ellen A.
Mary,May 2,1980,d/o Mary,
sis/o Myrtle Sanborn.
Mary,Apr.12,1825,20y,
d/o Reuben & Abigail.
Mary,Dec.29,1861,70y,w/o Elisha.
Mary,Sept.19,1870,88y.
Morris,1878,48y.
Reuben,Oct.15,1807,44y.
Thomas T.,Jan.29,1737-
Aug.14,1832,Rev.War Soldier.
Thomas,Sept.1,1908,79y.
Wilbur,Oct.4,1854,5y,
s/o Benj.Jr.& Lucy R.
JOHNSON
Abigail,Sept.2,1817-Jan.3,1841,
w/o Matthew (1858).
Ada L.,Jan.4,1874-Dec.24,1911,
w/o Almon.
Albion Francis,Feb.13,1837-
Dec.6,1898.
Almon,Oct.31,1870-Jan.3,1918.
Charles,1824-1895.
Cora A.,1863-1865,d/o I.L.& H.F.
Daniel,May 16,1829,5m,s/o Wm.& M.
Daniel,1829-1910.
David,June 22,1859,31y,
s/o Wm.& Mary.
Dorothy,Sept.4,1794-Dec.12,1864,
70y,2nd w/o Thomas.
Edward R.,Dec.24,1854,11m,
s/o Wm.L. & Nancy T.
Edward,Feb.15,1850,23y,
s/o Samuel & Jane.
Edwin C.,May 24,1878,29y,s/o Chas.
Elizabeth,1905-1906,d/o John & Lena.
Eliza Libby,May 5,1804-
Apr.12,1882,w/o John.
Ella P.,1866-XXXX,d/o I.L.& H.F.
Ellen E.,1850-1920,w/o Phineas.
Ellen M.,June 18,1842-Sept.11,1919,
w/o Lewis (1912).
Freeman W.,Nov.3,1853-Aug.7,1883,
s/o Daniel & Maria.
Hannah F. Abbott,1842-1921,
w/o Isaac L.
Hannah Johnson (nee),
Nov.14,1842,73y,w/o Matthew.
Harold,1877-1898,21y,s/o Melville.
Harold,XXXX,3y,s/o E.M.& A.L.
Hattie M.,Sept.26,1881-Mar.16,1882,
d/o Freeman & Nellie.
Helen Whitney,Aug.3,1840-
Dec.21,1911,w/o Albion.
Herb<u>u</u>t,1855-1877.
infant,Feb.12,1864,4w,d/o P.I.& E.
infant,Mar.23,1901,s/o E.L.& B.
Isaac L.,1836-1901.
Jane,Aug.5,1834,9y,d/o Wm.& Mary.
Jane Trickey,June 28,1853,48y,
w/o Samuel.
Jennie B.,1846-1935,w/o Melville C.
John E.,1872-XXXX.
John,May 8,1800-Sept.3,1856.
Lena Thomes,1869-XXXX,w/o John E.
Lewis,Jan.11,1844-May 24,1912..
Lottie F. Cote,1881-1925.
Mabel F.,June 23,1880,12y,d/o P.I.
Margaret,Nov.23,1993.
Margaret,Mar.14,1856,11d,
d/o Wm.L. & Nancy T.
Maria,1837-1922,d/o Daniel
Martha Libby,1834-1912,wid/o Chas.
Martha,1834-1912,w/o Charles.
Mary Ann Small,1825-1900,
w/o Matthew (1858).
Mary Chamberlain,Apr.2,1835,
86y,w/o Robert.
Mary Eliza,Jan.10,1845,5y,d/o S.& J.
Mary Sawyer,1851-1936,w/o Herb<u>u</u>t.
Mary,Sept.5,1796-Apr.18,1830,
1st w/o Thomas.
Mary,Dec.5,1858,55y,w/o Wm(1876).
Matthew,Mar.27,1846,81y.
Matthew,Dec.26,1816-Feb.2,1858.
Matthew,Apr.18,1829-Oct.2,1914.
Melville C.,1843-1913.
Nellie A.,July 22,1880,6y,d/o P.I.& E.
Nellie E.,XXXX,w/o Freeman W.
Olive M.,1863-1865,d/o I.L.& H.A.
Phineas I.,1839-1911.
Robert J.,Nov.6,1846,4y,s/o Wm.B.
Robert,July 13,1834,72y.
Robie K.,1908-1930,s/o John & Lena.
Rose Ann,Mar.6,1836-May 15,1878,
w/o Matthew (1914).

Samuel,Oct.9,1861,56y,
  2nd w. Elizabeth Libby.
Sarah J.,1831-1895,w/o Wm.H.
Thomas,Oct.5,1790-Apr.29,1869.
William,Capt.,May 28,1876,78y.
William H.,1821-1890.
ch/o Matthew & Rose Ann:
Charles H.,Feb.6,1863-Oct.27,1902;
Jennis E.,Feb.28,1861-Mar.1,1862;
Lizzie,Mar.6,1856-Sept.5,1857;
Merrill F.,Apr.1,1859-Mar.20,1862;
twin dau.,May 14,1878.
JONES
Doris Ellen,Aug.24,1969.
KENISON
George L.,July 30,1975.
Levi,Mar.9,1981.
LAMONT
Clifford L.,1883-1947.
Margie,1887-1936.
Nellie M.,1899-XXXX,w/o Clifford.
Oscar,1895-1932.
LIBBY
Abigail,May 8,1802,39y,w/o Simeon.
Abigail,Apr.14,1856,83y,w/o Reuben.
Ai S.,Aug.8,1843,10m,s/o Benj.& B.
Ai,June 22,1837,37y.
Albert F.,1858-1919.
Albert F.,Jan.14,1845,15m,s/o Sam.
Albert W.,Feb.13,1974.
Alice A.,Nov.5,1971.
Alice I.,1869-1935,d/o Wilder & B.C.
Albion K.P.,1837-1915.
Allison,Dec.9,1891,75y.
Allison,Aug.10,1860,82y.
Allison,May 14,1816,59y.
Asa,Co.K.25th Me.Inf.
Benjamin,May 8,1843,82y.
Benjamin,Mar.24,1871,75y,
  1st w.Ann Wescott, Civil War Soldier.
Betsey Wescott,July 16,1866,
  2nd w/o Benjamin.
Betsey C.,Aug.29,1917,88y,w/o Wilder.
Betsey,Apr.27,1853,84y,
  w/o Edward (1848).
Caroline M.,1841-1917,w/o Albion.
Charles E.,1853-1915.
Charles M.,Dec.10,1870-Nov.19,1948.
Daniel,May 11,1826,34y.
Darius,July 1,1873,76y.
Ebenezer,Feb.15,1833,22y.
Edward,1829-1907.
Edward,Mar.15,1848,87y.
Elizabeth Johnson,Jan.17,1887,
  80y,2nd w/o Ai (1837).
Elmer H.,1874-1953.
Ephraim,Oct.6,1866,83y.

George M.,May 21,1894,29y.
Gordan P.,Sept.1,1846,16y,s/o Benj.
Harold S.,1877-1898.
Harriet O.,Mar.25,1879,44y,w/o Asa.
Howard C.,Feb.18,1964.
Ida L.,Oct.1,1855,3m,d/o S.& R.
Jane Cannell,Feb.10,1805-
  May 2,1872,w/o William (1881).
Jennie B.,1846-1935,w/o Mellville.
Jeremiah N.,Mar.25,1887,79y.
Jethro,Feb.6,1849,86y.
John J.,May 14,1842,5m,s/o M.& M.
John,Mar.10,1826,55y.
Jordan F.,Sept.4,1846,16y,s/o B.& B.
Lee A.,July 5,1888,23y,s/o John & Z.B.
Lena L.,July 9,1972.
Lettice,May 3,1852,84y,w/o Jethro.
Lewis,Feb.21,1901,72y.
Lois,Mar.25,1860,76y,
  w/o Allison (1869).
Louisa R.,Apr.4,1849,1m,d/o S.& R.
Lucy A.,Apr.15,1862,48y,w/o Jeremiah
Mabel A.,June 20,1964.
Mabel A.,1874-XXXX,w/o Elmer H.
Madge C.,1866-1910.
Maria,Oct.10,1832,19y,d/p Edw.& B.
Mariam P.,Dec.27,1854,22y,
  w/o Frank O.
Marrett,Sept.25,1885,83y,
Martha,Dec.31,1822,26y,w/o Daniel
Martha,Apr.24,1821,1m,d/o Benj.& B.
Martha Skillings,Oct.11,1831,27y,
  1st w/o Ai (1837).
Mary J.,Feb.7,1967.
Mary J.,Mar.28,1877,35y,w/o N.P.
Mary P.,Oct.26,1904,79y,w/o Allison.
Mary,Apr.18,1866,82y,w/o Ephraim.
Mary,Nov.7,1876,80y,w/o Marritt.
Mary,Apr.1825,20y,d/o Reuben.
Mellville C.,1843-1913.
Merrill,Oct.28,1989.
Merton P.,1909-1909,s/o E.H.& M.A.
Merwin C.,Aug.11,1964.
Nelson P.,Mar.2,1906,58y.
Pearl Viola,May 23,1968.
Phebe,Aug.15,1840,75y,w/o Benj.
Phebe,May 18,1885,81y,w/o Darius.
Rebecca A.,Dec.16,1872,56y,
  w/o Simon (1864).
Robie,May 23,1992.
Roy A.,1897-1897,s/o E.H.& M.A.
Rosalia B.,May 30,1858,34y,
  w/o Samuel (1878).
Reuben,Oct.15,1807,44y.
S.Emily Mitchell,1839-1907,
  w/o Edward.
Sally,Nov.22,1898,84y,w/o Samuel.

Samuel,Apr.18,1822,25y.
Samuel,Sept.20,1878,58y.
Samuel,Apr.18,1875,75y.
Sarah,XXXX,w/o Allison (1816).
Sarah,July 18,1870,81y,w/o Simeon.
Simeon,Dec.14,1870,86y.
Simeon,Mar.11,1930,31st Mass.Regt.
Simon,Sept.15,1864,52y.
Susan,Feb.1,1854,31y,w/o Thomas.
Thomas,July 8,1807,18y,s/o Alli.& S.
Wilder M.,Sept.1,1902,75y.
Wilder M.,Sept.1826,1y,s/o Ai & M.
William F.,July 9,1862,16y,
s/o Samuel K.& Sally.
William H.P.,Apr.1840,6y,s/o S.& S.
William,Sept.1,1804-Mar.22,1881.
Zilpha B.,Sept.17,1896,61y,
w/o John F.
ch/o Jeremiah & Lucy:
Anna Maria,Sept.24,1856,16y;
Daniel S.,Sept.21,1851,7y;
Mary B.,July 18,1844,3d;
Royal T.,July 25,1836,3m.
d/o Edward & S. Emily:
Albert W.,July 12,1880,5y;
Cora May,May 6,1870,17m;
John J.,May 14,1842,5m;
Margaret,Sept.23,1885,83y;
Mary W.,Nov.7,1879,80y.
ch/o Asa & Harriet O.:
Leslie F.,Apr.5,1880,5y,son;
Hattie,Mar.29,1880,11y;
Charlie F.,Mar.20,1871,29y.
Charlie L.,Oct.3,1863,4y.
LOMBARD
Simeon,May 9,1843,58y..
LUCE
Jennie A.,1849-1907,w/o Albert E.
MARTIN
David E.,June 22,1817,60y.
Eva L.,Mar.6,1975.
Hazel E.,July 22,1916,23y,w/o Albert.
infant,XXXX.
infant,Dec.29,1978.
Lizzie P.,Sept.8,1879,35y,w/o Wm.
Mary,Jan.20,1841,74y,w/o David.
Ora,Aug.30,1867,1y,d/o J.H.& L.P.
william,May 7,1891,50y.
MASON
Ora Anna,Sept.20,1852,1y,
d/o Almon & Margaret.
MAYE
Richard D.,Mar.19,1973.
McLELLAN
Elva,June 4,1990.
Louis S.,Oct.5,1965.

McLUCAS
Bertha E.,June 2,1979.
MERRIFIELD
Alice L. Miller,Oct.10,1885-
Dec.10,1907,w/o Geo.B.
Chester,1959.
George B.,Co.F.Coast Guard Me.Inf.
Gladys,Oct.24,1994.
MERRILL
Lula M.,July 17,1919,43y,w/o Arthur.
MERRITHEW
Arnold G.,Aug.8,1980.
Viola S.,Dec.26,1978.
METCALF
Benjamin E.,July 24,1863,20y.
Eunice,Dec.11,1851,53y.
Irene B.,Apr.7,1811,81y,w/o Wm.
William,Jr.,Jan.26,1899,68y.
William,Sept.29,1879,92y,h/o Eunice.
MITCHELL
Anna,1879-1921,w/o W.A.
Asa,July 30,1868,58y.
Martha L.,Jan.5,1968,14yd/o A.& M.
Mary,Feb.2,1850,27y,w/o Asa.
MORSE
C.,1857-1908.
Dorothy,1898-1908,d/o C.& S.A.
Sarah A.,XXXX,w/o C.
MORTON
Hannah,July 1,1866,54y,w/o Isaac.
Isaac,Jan.28,1834,28y.
Reuben,June 13,1817,31y.
MOULTON
John W.,Aug.19,1849,2y,
s/o Jonathan & Lucy.
Levi,Mar.1,1886,54y.
NEVENS
Robert,Mar.26,1838,50y.
NEWCOMB
Alice M.,Oct.27,183X,70y,w/o Enos.
Ara Maria,1885-May 4,1972.
Charles F.,1857-1922,s/o M.T.& S.E.
Cynthia L.,1906-1912.
Delilah,Mar.4,1892,84y,w/o Hanson.
Edith & Edna,1886-1886,sis/o Elizab.
Elizabeth,1865-1880.
Emily Frances,Jan.112,1851,15y,
d/o Isaac & Martha.
Emules,Nov.20,1839,1y,ch/o H.& D.
Enos,Apr.10,1848.
Hanson,Aug.1,1872,70y.
2 infants,XXXX.
Isaac,Feb.5,1858,48y.
Isaac B.,1869-19XX.
John Nelson,1832-1912,h/o Mary.
Kenneth I.,1907-1908.
Lloyd E.,1941-1942.

Lloyd I.,1919-1944.
Mark T.,Oct.7,1832-Oct.20,1907.
Martha,Nov.22,1857,43y,w/o Isaac.
Mary Ann,Nov.9,1835,1m,d/o H.&D.
Mary Ellen Wescott,1837-1918.
Mary G.,Mar.28,1853,7y,d/o I.& M.
Sarah E.,May 16,1840-June 30,1884,
w/o Mark T.
William,Mar.13,1819,21y.
NICELY
Charles Cairns,Nov.22,1965.
NORTON
Hannah,July 17,1866,54y,w/o Isaac.
Isaac,Jan.28,1834,28y.
Major,May 13,1825,28y.
Mary,Feb.14,1864,67y,w/o Major.
O'BRIEN
Gordan,May 25,1990.
Lucille,1985.
PAINE
Abner,1829-1898.
Anna,Nov.13,1831,77y,w/o John.
Eunice,Jan.27,1871,83y,w/o Richard.
John,Mar.22,1826,1y,s/o R.& E.
Mary E.,Jan.28,1828-Oct.8,1906,
w/o William E.
Richard,May 29,1859,71y.
William H.,Apr.7,1822-Jan.23,1907.
ch/o William & Mary E:
Ellyn Mary,Aug.30,1853,4y;
Llewella,Dec.1865,7w,dau;
Llewellyn W.,June 24,1864,9y,dau.
Llewellyn V,Aug.1,1850,3y.
PARSONS
Arthur,Apr.1,1971.
Howard W.,1861-1905.
Howard,May 12,1993.
Louise M.,Oct.10,1981.
PHINNEY
Alexander,1791-1866.
Charlie E.,Feb.20,1864,10m,
d/o Stephen & Almira.
Ellen Johnson,Apr.28,1841-
Dec.19,1929,w/o F.C.
Frederick C.,June 21,1832-
June 18,1916.
John,Oct.10,1844,82y.
John,Apr.22,1826,s/o John & Susan.
Raymond,May 4,1991.
Stephen,May 16,1886,57y.
Susan,Dec.20,1840,74y,w/o John
Taphenes Files,1796-1864,w/o Alex.
ch/o Alexander & Taphenes:
Ann Maria Rounds,1831-1905;
Louisa,1836-1939;
Samuel,1830-1855;
Temperance,1826-1846.

PLAISTED
Abigail T.,July 3,1883,85y,
w/o Andrew,Jr.
Abigail,Jr.,Aug.27,1873,79y.
Andrew,Nov.27,1855,92y.
Major,Mar.27,1887,88y.
Mary,Nov.6,1839,79y,w/o Andrew.
Mary L.,Nov.14,1901,74y,w/o Major.
RAND
Abigail,Nov.15,1832,11y,
d/o John B.& Ruth.
Ann,Sept.7,1881,68y,w/o Noles.
Ephraim,Dec.18,1848,4y,s/o N.H.&A.
Leah B.,Mar.11,1845,39y.
Noles H.,Jan.3,1872,62y.
RANDALL
Sadianna W.,May 1,1984.
REED
Clara L.,June 21,1859-Feb.1,1922,
d/o Chas.S. & Emeline D.
Emeline D.,Mar.23,1902,73y,
w/o Charles S.
ROBERTS
Frank D.,June 24,1852-XXXX.
Nellie E.,Jan.26,1859-Dec.27,1918,
w/o Frank.
ROUNDS
Ann Marie,1831-1905,d/o Alexander
& Taphenes Phinney.
SANDS
John,Mar.1876,24y.
SAWYER
Elizabeth B.,Jan.2,11893,70y,w/o S.B.
Fannie E.,Sept.20,1895,21y,
d/o S.B. & E.B.
inf/o,May 23,1850,5w,s/o S.B.& E.B.
Richard,1985.
S.B.,Rev.,Dec.3,1910,82y.
SHAW
Abigail,July 11,1850,75y,w/o Caleb.
Caleb,Capt.,May 10,1845,72y.
SKILLINGS
Abigail K.,June 3,1862,41y,w/o Thos.
Anna,Dec.31,1851,68y,w/o Benjamin.
Benjamin,Jan.28,1856,73y.
Gershom,Feb.19,1873,57y.
Patience,Dec.17,1890,73y,w/o Gersh.
Thomas,Oct.1,1850,36y.
s/o Thomas & Abigail:
Barnabus,Mar.7,1826,14y;
Benjamin F.,Nov.15,1829,4y.
SPILLER
Amos F.,1878-1947.
Elizabeth D.,1879-1949.
Frank A.,1915-1915.
infant,June-Nov.1915,s/o A.F.& E.D.

STONE
Damarias,Feb.28,1836,85y,
w/o Jonathan.
Eunice,May 1,1859,59y.
Fanny,Apr.22,1847,37y,w/o Rev.Jesse.
Jonathan,Apr.19,1834,79y.
Mary,Oct.6,1833,32y,d/o Jon.& D.
STRUMPH
Edith,1977.
STURGIS
Hannah,Feb.3,1857,71y,w/o Joseph.
Joseph,Jan.1842,60y.
THOMAS
Charles B.,Mar.7,1872,31y.
TRACY
Elbrdige M.,Feb.1973.
WENTWORTH
Daniel,XXXX,Civl War Soldier.
Esther H.,May 30,1891,77y,w/o Dan.
WESCOTT
Abigail,June 30,1843,81y,w/o Reuben.
Alice E.,1888-19XX,w/o Elmer.
Alvin S.,Oct.4,1857,22y.
Anna H.,Dec.25,1875,26y,w/o Reuben.
Calvin C.,1854-1903.
Calvin C.,1904.
Clarence M.,1869-1898.
Darah H.,1856-1921,w/o Norris.
Elmer W.,1896-XXXX.
Emeline C.,1827-1900,w/o Stephen.
Everett R.,1965.
Harriet M.,Mar.8,1854,25y.
infant,1964.
Mabel H.,1874-XXXX,w/o Clarence M.
Martha A. Libby,1825-1910,w/o Wm.
Mary Ann,Oct.10,1884,78y,
w/o William (1875).
Mary E.,July 8,1907,63y,
2nd w/o Reuben.
Melinda,May 1850,11m,d/o Wm.& M.
Norris D.,Feb.21,1854,1y,s/o Wm.& S.
Norris N.,1855-1921.
R. Edgar,1896-1910.
Reuben,Dec.7,1841,80y.
Ruth A.Deering,Nov.9,1993,77y,
w/o Everett (1965).
Sarah,Dc.19,1900,72y,w/o Wm.(1905)
Stephen,1822-1886.
William,Feb.13,1905,80y.
William,May 21,1875,73y.
William,M.D.,1818-1877,Civil War.
WHEELAND
Amy,1961.
WHITESIDE
Elizabeth,1843-1918.
Thomas,Rev.,Sept.19,1839-
Mar.25,1911,h/o Elizabeth Laney.

WHITNEY
Abigail,June 1,1841,79y,w/o Daniel.
Abigial N.,1823-1895,w/o Wm.S.
Alston V.,Oct.2,1858-Mar.24,1908.
Betsey,Jan.23,1853,70y.
Catherine,Sept.15,1847,23y,
d/o Samuel & Dorcus.
Charlotte,1848-1850.
Cora Belle,Aug.28,1862-Jan.15,1928,
w/o Frank L.
Damaris,Nov.11,1848,20yd/o P.& E.
Daniel,Dec.13,1834,80y.
Dorcus,May 30,1863,84y.
Ella H.,1854-1872.
Emily F.,Apr.5,1844,3y,d/o Z.& H.
Eunice,Dec.25,1869,81y,w/o Peter.
Eva Ladora,Sept.16,1853-
Mar.8,1926,w/o Frederick E.
Flavilla B.,1850-1873.
Forrest,Dec.20,1858-Jan.16,1859.
Frank I.,Dec.13,1859-May 13,1933.
Frank Leslie,Apr.11,1858-
Jan.10,1928.
Frederick E.,Aug.7,1851-Feb.28,1926.
Freeman,July 19,1855,49y.
Hannah,Dec.10,1824,69y,w/o Zeb.
Hannah,Aug.28,1833,44y,
d/o Zebulon & Hannah.
Helen A.,1852-1927,w/o Flavilla.
Herman S.,1847-1908.
John,Oct.31,1877,85y.
Jonathan S.,July 13,1906,82y.
Katie C.,Feb.17,1867-Aug.28,1886.
Louisa,Sept.3,1834,28y,d/o D.& A.
Lydia A.,Aug.20,1869,58y,w/o Freem.
Marshall,July 11,1821-July 18,1884.
Martha,Apr.14,1865,83y.
Mary J.,Jan.20,1862-Dec.4,1921.
Mary Lula,Aug.7,1865-Apr.15,1948.
Mary,Dec.28,1824-Oct.7,1891,
w/o Robie.
Peter,Mar.15,1842,54y.
Rachel A. Hopkinson,May 29,1835-
July 13,1919,w/o Jonathan.
Robie,Feb.10,1818-Dec.28,1893.
Rufus,Feb.24,1817,32y.
Samuel,Sept.9,1864,90y.
Sarah A.,Feb.7,1830-Apr.29,1910,
s/o Marshall.
Susan,Apr.16,1878,57y,w/o Zeb (1877)
Tabitha,Aug.15,1860,63y.
Thaddeus P.,Sept.26,1847-
Oct.10,1909.
William E.,1841-1844,s/o Wm.S.& A
William S.,1814-1900.
Willie F.,June 16,1863,5y,s/o Z.& H.
Zebulon,Sept.11,1833,86y.

Zebulon,Sept.24,1877,65y.
WILBAND
Cecil R.,Mar.13,1940.
WING
Randall,May 6,1991.
XX
Ann Wiggin,Feb.22,1841-Apr.11,1920,
w/o Gorham L.
Gorham L.,Oct.23,1837-Apr.3,1926.
XX
Mirah,Jan.15,1864,75y,stone broken.

✤ **SHAWS MILL CEMETERY** ✤
Shaws Mill Road near Kathryn, many
broken stones,checked them all.
Managed by Town.

EDWARDS
Deborah,1824-1908,w/o Marcus.
Marcus M.,1816-1900.
children/o Marcus & Deborah:
Hannah J.,1854-1869;
Sarah F.,1859-1877.
EMERY
Ella J.,June 26,1870,14y,
d/o Warren & Julia.
Julia,Mar.21,1887,49y,w/o Warren.
Warren G.,Dec.28,1910,80y.
MORTON
David,Mar.25,1883,91y.
Salome,Aug.4,1857,61y,w/o David.
MOULTON
Alonzo,Aug.7,1838,4y,
s/o David & Salome.
Anna,Jan.8,1861,73y,w/o Daniel.
Daniel,XX 30,1855,73y.
Daniel,Feb.28,1820,26d,
s/o David & Anna.
Joanna,Jan.15,1834,91y,w/o Peter.
John,Sept.19,1821,19y,
s/o Simon & Abigail.
Jonathan,Oct.6,1852,44y.
Mary,June 23,1808,37y,w/o Josiah.
Peter,June 2,1812,70y.
Theodore H.,Sept.21,1854,1y,
s/o Jonathan & Lucy.
--ny H.,stone broken,ch/o Dan.& Anna
RAND
Anna M.,Dec.11,1883,82y,w/o Edm.
Edmund,Apr.26,1875,74y.
Elmer A.,1873-1892.
infant,XXXX.
Statira M.,Jan.18,1842,d/o Edm.& A.
Wilson S.,Oct.5,1898,55y.
SHAW
Albion P.,1828-1891.
Anna,Feb.16,18X7,70y,w/o Sargent.

Lydia,Jan.27,1872,74y,w/o Peter.
Peter,July 2,1866,72y.
Phebe,1802-1880,d/o Sargent & A.
Sarah J. Strout,1840-1913,w/o A.P.
Sargent,Oct.23,1745-Dec.3,1823,
Rev. War Soldier.
children/o Albion & Sarah J.:
Lizzie May,1870-1913.
Ralph W.E.,1863-1940.
William A.,1867-1890.
WIGGIN/S
Comfort,Mar.23,1860,63y,w/o Sam.
Harriet C.,July 27,1850,17y,
d/o Samuel & Comfort.
Lavina E.,Mar.11,1847,3m,
d/o Andrew & Charlotte.
Samuel,Jan.12,1882,86y.
William M.,Feb.2,1850,27y,s/o S& C.
--ew,XXXX, stone broken.

✤ **HUSTON CEMETERY** ✤
Didn't locate. Managed by Town.

HUSTON
Elizabeth,July 5,1808,31y,w/o Simon.
Hannah,May 10,1835,57y,w/o Wm.
Lydia,July 13,1806,29y,d/o Wm.& E.
Simon,Jan.6,1817,38y.
William,Dec.25,1814,40y.

✤ **ALLEN FAMILY CEMETERY** ✤
Winn Rd.,off Rte.9, near the
Falmouth town line, Cumberland.
Old list was not checked.

ALLEN
Clarissa I.,1824-1891,w/o Peter L.
Daniel R.1815-1890.
Florence E.,Sept.22,1859,4y,
d/o P.L.& C.I.
Ida Florence,Aug.21,1861,5m,
d/o P.L.& C.I.
Marianne,1815-1891,w/o Daniel R.
Peter L.,1822-1897.

✧ EASTERN CEMETERY ✧

231 Main Street, Gorham. Also called "The New Yard". Land was purchased around 1830. Good records from Town Clerk after 1909, prior burials I obtained from gravestones. Many stones were very difficult to read. Complete to May 1995.

ABBOTT
Cyrus,1836-July 15,1910,
h/o Elizabeth Richardson.
Elizabeth C. Richardson,Apr.2,1932.
Ernest,1872-1878,s/o Cyrus & E.
Freddie J.,1874-1878,s/o Cyrus & E.
infant,Apr.12,1937,s.b.

ADAMS
Abbie L.,1855-1908.
Anna L.,June 14,1858,32y.
Edmond,Dec.16,1992.
George S.,May 13,1927.
Mary S.,July 11,1929.
Ruth Ethel,1889-1900,d/o W.L.& S.A.
Sarah E.,July 22,1945.
Walter S.,Mar.4,1926.
Walter,1894-1894,s/o W.L.& S.A.

ALDEN
Ada D. Douglass,Mar.28,1866-
  Mar.8,1942,w/o George.
Austin,June 28,1978.
Beatrice,Feb.26,1955.
Carl H.,Jan.29,1964.
Charles,Jan.20,1789-June 6,1866.
Charles Gardner,1854-Dec.24,1911,
  s/o Henry & Rachel Carll.
Clarissa,May 20,1823-Sept.13,1853,
  d/o Gardner & Martha.
Edith Salome Harlow,Aug.14,1909,
  w/o Carl H.
Emma L.,Dec.28,1949.
Gardner,Jan.13,1795-Sept.8,1831.
George,Jan.21,1864-May 27,1949.
Gladys Wood,July 27,1943.
Grace B.,Aug.24,1967.
Henry,May 20,1823-Sept.30,1871.
Ira C.,Jan.28,1959.
John L., Jan.30,1918.
John Fremont,Sept.1857-June 1865.
Lewis Linclon,Feb.2,1889-
  Sept.27,1918.
Martha Hicks,1785-Feb.11,1849,
  w/o Gardner.
Mary E.,Nov.30,1855-Aug.19,1938.
Nancy Quimby,1791-1873,w/o Charles.
R. Ann Carll,Nov.1829-Jan.1888,
  w/o Henry.
Rena D.,Apr.18,1973.

ALEXANDER
Bertie A.,1883-1884.
Charles,Aug.1910,74y.
Emma Louise Cole,1862-1904.
George William,1870-1870,s/o J.& M
infant,Aug.28,1950.
James C.,1838-Aug.26,1910.
Linda,1838-Mar.29,1911.
Margaret S. Lombard,1843-1888,
  w/o James C.
Minnie May,1874-1882,d/o J.C.& M.

ALLEN
Alex M.,Feb.12,1919.
Almira E.,Oct.31,855,19y,d/o S.& M.
Amanda Small,Apr.19,1926.
Anna M.,Oct.15,1929.
Annette M.,Dec.7,1917.
Charles H.,June 16,1934.
Emma M.,Apr.17,1973.
Eunice S.,Aug.31,1856,2y,d/o S.&M.C.
Eva F.,Dec.18,1933.
Frank A.,Dec.19,1949.
George A.,Dec.10,1918.
George F.B.,XXXX,s/o Samuel & Mary.
George S.,bet.1914 & 1917 ?.
George S.,Sept.21,1934.
Hilda Mae,Aug.2,1993.
James,1886-1886.
John M.,May 27,1914.
Lillian M.,Mar.25,1963.
Mark B.,Aug.13,1984.
Mary C.,Nov.14,1884,94,w/o Samuel.
Mary Emma,Feb.19,1973.
Mary W.,Sept.14,1921.
Samuel,Sept.1869,62y.
Susie Maud,Sept.30,1946.
William M.,July 18,1839-Feb.11,1896.
Win M.,Feb.4,1923.

ANDERSON
Ada,Apr.23,1975.
Frederick,1891-May 27,1908,
  s/o Stephen B.& Mary A.
Laura E.,1877-1950,w/o W.J.
Leon,Oct.2,1981.
Mary A.,May 14,1953.
Paul L.,Sept.3,1954.
Rose,Apr.25,1990.
Stephen B.,Mar.11,1923.

ANDREWS
Addie,Aug.20,1921.
Ava Crockett,Mar.17,1976.
Walter J.,1879-Sept.19,1945.

ARCHER
Doris,Nov.20,1992.

ARMSTRONG
Arthru M.,Sept.6,1961.
Kate T.,Nov.14,1960.

ARNOLD
Florence,Oct.2,1980.
Herbert F.,May 21,1959.
ASHWORTH
infant,Oct.7,1946.
ATKINSON
Charles,1910.
AUSTIN
Albert,Aug.12,1964.
Alice,Aug.22,1972.
Delia A.,Sept.23,1950.
Eunice,June 15,1992, remov. from Windham.
Everett,Aug.17,1992.
Gladys,Aug.23,1967.
Harry W.,Sept.22,1958.
William H.,Nov.19,1957.
AVERY
Mary Hersey,Nov.8,1927.
AYER
George F.,Apr.1,1918.
Harriet Estes,1851-July 4,1912, d/o Jos. & Maria Edwards Estes.
BABB
Daniel,Dec.13,1866,85y.
Hiram,1823-1884.
Jane,Sept.19,1852,70y,w/o Daniel.
BABCOCK
Elsie,May 3,1986.
Richard B.,Nov.16,1940.
BABKIRK
Clifford,Apr.30,1982.
BACHELDER
Henry L.,Nov.14,1985.
Richard F.,May 25,1944.
BACON
Cornelia Maynard,Dec.1,1912, wid/o Samuel F.
Richard Orrin,May 19,1928.
BAILEY
Alfred,Nov.7,1829-Apr.16,1904.
Elizabeth T.,Sept.1,1942.
Elizabeth V.,Mar.26,1826-Apr.21,1914.
Francis,Apr.24,1981.
Jane,Aug.8,1886,84y,w/o Capt.Sam.
Samuel,XX,18,18XX,67y.
BAKER
Arvilla B.,Apr.29,1970.
Betsey Hill Hanscom,Sept.26,1795-Apr.3,1840,1st w/o Ira.
Cynthia Towle,Oct.18,1884,78y, 2nd w/o Ira.
Daniel H.,1826-1904.
Flora A.,Feb.5,1931.
Frank M.,Feb.6,1912.
Hannah E.,Mar.8,1845,16y.
Ira,Sept.23,1796-July 8,1861.
Jacob C.,Feb.3,1888,79y,h/o Ruth.
Mary Ann,Jan.1847,10m.
Mary Ann,Feb.7,1849,40y,w/o S.W.
Moses,Mar.25,1847.81y.
Octavius B.,May 2,1845,3y.
Ruth H.,Aug.23,1900,85y.
Sarah M. Hall,1826-1882,w/o D.H.
Sarah,Mar.1,1853,71y,w/o Moses.
William,Aug.18,1947.
William G.,June 1,1944.
Winnie M.,1866-1905.
BANCROFT
Lucius,Sept.15,1860,43y.
BANGS
Alice D.,Sept.14,1849,14m, d/o C.C.&E.A.
Charles C.,1814-1869.
Eliza A.,1821-1852.
Emily A.,1815-1899.
Nathan B.,Sept.16,1881.
Statira,Aug.3,1862,52y,w/o Nath.B.
Willie,1849-1850.
BARBRICK
Ruth,Oct.1977.
BARKER
Susan Viola,May 17,1927.
BARNES
Ellen S.,Sept.24,1932.
Sarah,1841-1897,w/o Willard F.
Willard F.,1838-May 20,1920.
BARROWS
Marietta L.,July 22,1956.
Roland,Feb.13,1955.
BARTLETT
Alice H.,June 25,1929.
Edna Dudley,May 18,1943.
Elmer F.,Dec.8,1872-Dec.21,1928.
Emma W.,July 21,1977.
Ferdinand,Oct.3,1914.
Mrs. Ferdinand,May 28,1925.
Fred E.,Apr.24,1938.
George A.,Nov.10,1919.
George E.,1842-1906.
George H.,Dec.20,1950.
Hannah F.,Apr.23,1949.
Harry O.,1887-1888,s/o G.E.& M.J.
Katherine M.,July 2,1970.
Lizzie,Apr.3,1913.
Martha Jane,Dec.13,1938.
Susan G.,1819-1894.
Susan M.,Sept.21,1872-XXXX.
Willis A.,1883-Sept.26,1967, h/o Emma Wilkins.
BASSETT
Alfred,1837-1901.

Georgianna Bradbury1841-
Nov.7,1930,w/o Alfred.
BEAMAN
Emma P.,Dec.19,1914.
BEAN
infant,Mar.12,1929.
Edward Everett (Tink),Oct.3,1993.
Elizabeth E.,Apr.16,1969.
Emma Higgins,1845-Oct.18,1933.
Frank L.,Nov.13,1966.
Levi H.,1844-1887.
Mary Elaine,Aug.7,1952.
Nina,July 16,1964.
Richard H.,1823-1869.
Richard Stanley,Oct.18,1926.
Robert,May 24,1994.
Roland E.,Dec.13,1915.
Roland E.,XXXX,6m,s/o F.L.& E.
Sarah E.,Aug.10,1920.
Shirley,Sept.23,1994.
Sophia,Sept.10,1848,w/o Jonathan.
T.M.,Aug.3,1920.
Ulitta,1813-1888,w/o Richard H.
Vina,July 16,1964.
BECKWITH
Charles,Nov.13,1946.
Elizabeth A.,Feb.28,1942.
Lizzie B.,Aug.11,1929.
BEEDE
Linwood C.,Oct.22,1957.
Madelyn,Apr.2,1981.
BEMAN
Charlie H.,1861-1881,s/o G.N.& E.P.
E.Patience,1914,76y,w/o George.
George N.,Dec.7,1927.
BENNETT
infant,July 29,1992.
BENSON
Abigail S. Dow,June 9,1852,
68y,w/o James.
Alton,Nov.26,1994,h/o Kay.
Arthur M.,1821-1905,s/o Jas.& Abig.
Elizabeth Lowell,1819-Oct.8,1909,
w/o Arthur M.
James,May 10,1832,60y.
Laura J.,Sept.28,1850,1y,
d/o Arthur & Elizabeth.
Mary H.,1811-1882,d/o Jas.& Abig.
BERGEN
P.B.,Apr.30,1942.
BERRY
Emily P.,May 19,1971.
Ethel,May 7,1985.
George W.,Mar.13,1940.
Grace W.,Apr.28,1931.
Herbert,Jan.5,1953.
James Morris,Sept.17,1983.

John W.,Feb.20,1944.
Mabel E.,Apr.23,1957.
Phebe E.,Feb.4,1917.
Priscilla,Nov.12,1986.
BICKFORD
Bion W.,Sept.14,1937.
Eliza J.,Sept.2,1918.
Eva P.,June 24,1962.
George I.,1824-1903,h/o Eliza.
Gertrude H.,1873-1874,d/o W.I.& H.J.
Hannah J.,Sept.29,1926.
Willis D.,1902-1902,s/o B.W.& Eva.
Willis W.,Dec.19,1941.
BILLINGS
Aveline Davis,1827-1893,w/o Daniel.
Charles L.,1841-1863.
Daniel,1812-1883.
Evelyn M.,Sept.3,1919.
Gertrude M.,Mar.3,1972.
Grace A.,July 23,1955.
Herbert,1869-1882.
Horatio S.,Feb.6,1926.
John C.,1849-1867.
John F.,Apr.23,1950.
Miriam A.,1865-1896.
Miriam F. Watson,1808-1863,
w/o Daniel.
BIRNIE
Robert S.,Oct.3,1933.
BLAKE
Adam M.,Sept.29,1973,infant.
Clarence W.,Apr.21,1915.
Ebenezer H.,Jan.2,1879,64y.
Elizabeth E.,Aug.3,1940.
Harold E.,Jr.,July 10,1935.
Harry N.,Feb.18,1932.
Horatio S.,Feb.9,1914.
Mehitable I.,July 7,1873,56y,
w/o Capt.E.H.
BLOOD
George L.,Mar.7,1916.
BOLTON
Frank O.,May 24,1924.
Grace,May 5,1921.
Lottie S.,Apr.30,1938.
Thomas E.,May 22,1934.
Walter S.,Jan.12,1910.
BOND
Agnes,Nov.8,1933.
Esther,XXXX.
Mary E.,Aug.28,1932.
Otis,Sept.7,1915.
Phineas M.,XXXX.
BONNEY
Ada,May 1,1979.
infant,Feb.26,1957.
Janice F.,May 11,1975.

Muriel,May 14,1986.
Roscoe L.,May 1,1978.
BOOKER
Maud E.,Aug.22,1947.
BOOTE
George,Apr.28,1982.
Maude A.,Apr.21,1972.
BOOTHBY
Alpheus,Dec.28,1925.
Carrie Norton,Aug.5,1940.
Charles E.,July 20,1925.
Charles E., 1917/18 ?.
Charlotte M.,Sept.6,1934.
Chase A.,July 21,1927.
Clinton,XXXX,1y.
Ethel,May 5,1970.
Ethel H.,Dec.14,1959.
Grace L.,May 10,1967.
Hannah B. Johnson,Aug.24,1851, 24y,w/o Ansel L.,d/o Wm.& Nancy.
Harriet A.,Oct.27,1923.
Israel,Nov.17,1936.
Jennie S.,Dec.28,1921.
Leander,Apr.13,1948.
Leon E.,Jan.14,1961.
Salome E.,Oct.27,1952.
Thomas R.,Aug.24,1983.
children/o Alpheus & Jennie.
Anna M.,1877-1877;
Hattie A.,1885-1888;
L.May,1879-1896.
BOREK
Cara Susan,Oct.11,1984.
BOTTON
Fannie,Jan.4,1915.
BOWDOIN
Abbie T.,Jan.22,1972.
Emery R.,Apr.7,1966.
BRACKETT
Arthur F.,Apr.14,1965.
Edward E.,Jan.21,1940.
Elizabeth C.,Jan.29,1923.
Frances W.,Jan.25,1919.
Hazel N.,May 2,1937.
Lewellyn E.,Apr.23,1924.
Lizzie,Apr.12,1968.
BRADBURY
Albert G.,1808-1875.
Alice W.,June 20,1848,29y,w/o E.W.
Charles H.,1835-1885,Co.K,3rd Me.Inf.
Clarissa Warren,1808-1876,w/o A.G.
Frank M.,1845-1875.
Mary E.,1843-1866.
BRADDOCK
Winnie,1865.
BRAGDON
Annette W.,Aug.17,1969.

Ernest J.,May 17,1961.
Ernest J.,1910/11 ?.
Francis S.,1904-Nov.11,1911 d/o E.J. & J.F.
Fred L.,Nov.14,1923.
Jennie F.,Sept.13,1939.
Maud S.,Sept.25,1944.
Maurice,June 8,1976.
Stacy,Sept.20,1993.
Warren,July 16,1981.
BRANSCOMBE
James,May 6,1991.
BRIDGES
infant,May 2,1949.
Dianne,May 5,1979.
BROADHURST
Arthur G.,June 30,1976.
Lillian,July 19,1985.
BROAD
Caleb,Oct.23,1846,27y.
Daniel,Sept.30,1846,63y.
Elizabeth J.,Apr.7,1854,23y.
Elizabeth,Apr.27,1838,17y,w/o David.
Henry,Jan.10,1872,43y.
BROCATO
Evelyn M.,May 27,1961.
Samuel,June 21,1972.
BROCK
infant,June 12,1956.
BROFEE
Linwood,July 28,1980.
BROOKS
George W.H.,July 27,1906,76y, h/o Emily Patrick.
Uldena,Apr.13,1983.
BROW
Ruth S.,May 13,1983.
BROWN
Abbie A.,Sept.1,1940.
Abigail D. Babb,1820-1895.
Abigail Stevens,Jan.12,1827-Oct.26,1905,w/o Nathaniel.
Ada Storer,Apr.1909.
Ann Maria,June 10,1929.
Anna M.,1830-Dec.11,1930.
Anna,Dec.14,1871,80y,w/o Isaac.
Appleton,1862-Jan.17,1950.
Bertha,July 7,1966.
Clayton,Mar.5,1969.
Elinor,Apr.13,1880,66y,w/o Soloman.
Elizabeth F.,1807-1869,w/o Wm.E.
Ellen R.,June 11,1930.
Ernest C.,May 17,1939.
Ethel,May 8,1991.
Evelyn,June 1,1994.
Francena Boyton,1848-1934,w/o O.D.
Freeman J.,Nov.26,1946.

Freeman,Co.K,17th Me. Inf.
George A.,1920.
George A.,Aug.31,1957.
Harold C.,May 2,1961.
Harriett F.,1836-1837.
Ida A. Babb,1849-1873.
Ina N.,May 26,1965.
infant,Nov.5,1976,s.b.
James Wm.,1852-1853.
John E.,1849-1894.
John J.,Apr.14,1915.
L.W.,Jan.29,1923.
Lelia W.,Apr.24,1968.
Mary A.,Mar.14,1879,63y,w/o Stephen.
Mary D.,Apr.28,1877,70y,w/o Stephen.
Mary Grace,May 2,1980.
Mary Jennie,1856-1860.
Mary,Oct.25,1848,40y,w/o Stephen.
Mary,Mar.25,1850,48y,w/o Nathaniel.
Nappi E.,Jan.14,1957.
Nathaniel,Mar.16,1800-Aug.31,1879.
Othello D.,1851-1899.
Philip A.,May 14,1982.
Ralph H.,May 14,1949.
Raymond E.,July 8,1970.
Rosina May,May 22,1977.
Royce,July 9,1983.
Sabra,1921.
Sabra H.,Nov.6,1927.
Simeon,1815-1861.
Stephen,Oct.19,1881,74y.
Susan D.,Apr.20,1976.
Thomas W.,Oct.16,1920.
William E.,1806-1851.
William H.,July 23,1935.
William S.,1813-1881.
BRUNT
June K.,Feb.8,1972.
BRYANT
Jesse G.,Aug.26,1955.
Marion H.,Dec.6,1974.
Ruth E.,Mar.22,1874,39y,w/o F.A.W.
Walter L.,June 22,1949.
BUCK
Julia Celeste,Mar.26,1840-
Sept.26,1924,d/o S.T. & M.B.
Miriam B.,Oct.8,1812-Nov.11,1890,
w/o Samuel T.
BUMPS
Evelyn F.,July 22,1942.
Michael,May 24,1988.
William C.,Oct.20,1969.
BURBANK
Emily Wood,June 5,1932.
BURNELL
infant,Sept.22,1973,s.b.
Elvira F.,May 30,1920.

George S.,Jan.26,1955.
Lila D.,Feb.14,1965.
M.C.,Aug.15,1915.
Martha May,May 10,1955.
Susan A.,Mar.31,1877,52y.
BURNHAM
Alonzo,May 1,1959.
Avis P.,Oct.21,1922.
Charles E.,Jan.15,1944.
Durwood,Apr.23,1982.
Edna L.,Dec.10,1963.
Everett,Apr.21,1973.
May E.,Apr.27,1948.
Raymond S.,Sept.20,1943,inf.
Rebecca,Oct.20,1863,47y,
  d/o Thomas G., & Priscilla.
Velva,Oct.23,1990.
BURROWS
Frank W.,Nov.8,1956.
Helen,Apr.18,1980.
Nellie F.,Feb.26,1919.
BURT
Arthur P.,Apr.17,1939.
infant,Aug.31,1913.
Maude E.,May 17,1956.
BUSHLEY
Donald M.,Oct.20,1958.
Marion,Apr.27,1978.
BUTLER
Charles A.,Oct.15,1930.
Delia,Oct.11,1866,11y,d/o G.S.& S.S.
Fannie,June 23,1921.
George W.,Dec.221903,81y.
Horace F.,Dec.2,1958.
Lillian T.,Apr.15,1983.
Louise M.,Feb.26,1959.
Raymond W.,June 10,1970.
Sarah S.,July 22,1875,51y,w/o Geo.
BUZZELL
Rebecca A.1816-1899.
BYRON
Parker D.,May 5,1980.
CALDWELL
Addie F.,June 18,1930.
Josiah,Jan.1,1954.
CAMPBELL
Fred W.,June 23,1964.
CANNON
Robert C.,Mar.6,1959.
CARD
D. Maria Usher,1829-1893.
J. Lillian,Nov.9,1856,2y,s/o J.C.& D.
James Usher,Aug.28,1852,10m,s/o J.C
John C.,1816-1885.
Lucy E.,Oct.1,1853,6m,d/o J.C.& D.M.
Stephen S.,Apr.1861,1y,s/o J.C.& D.M.

CAREY
Earl,May 28,1991.
Virginia,May 1,1978.
CARGILL
Alberta,Aug.10,1944.
Arthur,Apr.30,1988.
Carl D.,July 28,1961.
Carroll D.,Apr.12,1936.
Chancil E.,Nov.11,1966.
Dorothy,Nov.15,1916.
James,Dec.27,1994.
CARLL
Inez F.M.,Jan.22,1955.
Willis,Apr.21,1980.
CARNE
Florence,Aug.2,1983.
W. Stanley,Rev.,May 21,1952.
CARPENTER
Dorothy,June 29,1989.
CARR
Leroy,Oct.7,1988.
CARRIGAN
Laura Etta,Dec.18,1950.
CARSON
Annie,Apr.2,1981.
Clayton M.,Apr.14,1953.
George W.,Sept.9,1959.
Hazen,July 9,1850-Sept.23,1944.
James F.,Apr.30,1952.
Lillian F.,Aug.16,1951.
Marion F.,Feb.14,1968.
Solomon J.,Oct.1,1977.
Tryphosa A.,1850-Sept.4,1927.
CARSWELL
Mary F.,June 24,1988.
CARTER
Eliza E.,Feb.18,1856,21y,d/o E.&M.
Harriet D.,July 24,1856,17y,
  d/o Enos & Martha.
Martha H. Vine,1851,40y,w/o Enos.
CARUSO
Joseph,Aug.8,1988.
CARUTHERS
Dale E.,May 15,1973.
Glayds,Oct.21,1973.
CASHMAN
Susie E., 1941.
Timothy W.,June 1,1926.
CATES
James P.,Sept.23,1838,27y.
Mary E.,July 2,1843,8y,
  d/o J.P. & Margaret.
CATON
Ann S.,Aug.28,1921.
CAVALUZZI
Carl,Sept.15,1987.
John,May 18,1984.

CHADBORNE
Augustus,1853,2y,s/o G.& H.O.
Cordelia Edwards,Apr.1910,90y,
  w/o George.
Desire Watson,Aug.11,1858,69y,
  w/o Nahum.
Elizabeth,Apr.3,1959.
Ethel,Mar.1,1972.
Florence Fogg,Dec.29,1943.
Frederick,June 14,1831-Mar.9,1828,
  s/o Nahum & Desire.
Frederick,Dec.25,1825-XXXX,d.young.
George,Apr.23,1824,4y,s/o G.& H.O.
George,1821-Mar.27,1914.
Harriet O, Boynton,1825-Apr.30,1891,
  1st w/o George.
Milton W.,Aug.18,1937.
Nahum,Dea.,Aug.6,1857,73y.
P. Cordelia,Apr.13,1910.
Samuel Longfellow,Nov.2,1818-
  May 1,1829,s/o Nahum & Desire.
Warren,May 17,1975.
CHANDLER
Doris,June 30,1988.
Eliza A.,Sept.10,1961.
Preston,Apr.11,1956.
Sharon J.,June 8,1975.
Wiley P.,Nov.27,1967.
CHAPLIN
Geoergia B.,Oct.14,1927.
Harry W.,III,May 21,1961.
CHARLTON
Beatrice,Nov.22,1991,w/o Arnold.
Harold H.,Apr.17,1973.
Henry S.,July 14,1949.
Lulu M.,Nov.3,1946.
CHARRIER
Norman,Apr.30,1994.
CHASE
Thomas,Feb.14,1874,43y.
CHELLIS
Edith H.,Mar.1,1922.
Eugene D.,1909.
Eugene D.,Feb.3,1912.
George,Jan.18,1910.
Mrs. George,May 14,1921.
Robert D.,Oct.28,1970.
CHURCHILL
George N.,Oct.19,1953.
Seliva B.,Apr.13,1935.
CHUTE
Mary Elizabeth,May 26,1981.
CIZEK
stillborn,Apr.19,1962.
CLARK
infant,Dec.29,1943.
Bealey W.,Apr.13,1910.

Bealey W.,Oct.31,1944.
Carrie,Oct.2,1991.
Charles,July 28,1856.
David Lester,Mar.12,1937.
Dora B.,Aug.30,1937.
Edward,XXXX
Emma Louise,Aug.20,1979.
Ernest T.,Sr.,Apr.16,1974.
Evalina D. McLellan,June 11,1819-
Mar.1910,d/o Alexander & Belinda.
Ida M.,Oct.7,1974.
Ila,Oct.1,1977.
Ira V.,Oct.11,1918.
Ida D.,May 1,1970.
Isabel R.,Aug.30,1927.
Mary Gladys,May 10,1993.
Milton,Mar.25,1952.
Perley,June 5,1923,s.b.
Perley H.,May 4,1931.
Raymond G.,May 10,1976.
Robert A.,Sept.17,1952.
Susan Fogg,Sept.27,1950.
CLAY
Almira,Mar.1,1906,82y.
Catherine,1814-1895,w/o James.
Charles C.,Dec.26,1937.
Cora L.,Dec.9,1862,9y,d/o J.& C.
Eli,Nov.5,1891,74y.
Flora M.,July 2,1948.
Helen M.B.,Oct.17,1957.
James,1814-1885.
Minna,Apr.17,1980.
CLEAVES
Frank H.,1851-1902,h/o Harriett.
Grace M.,May 1,1976.
Harriet N.,1860-Mar.14,1947.
Lincoln Lewis,Aug.8,1940.
CLEMENT
Charles Fred,1849-Nov.13,1909,
h/o Julia Cressey.
Charles J.,Nov.28,1924.
Edith,Jan.7,1974.
Edmund T.,1830-July 27, 1910.
Elizabeth C.,May 12,1928.
Ellen HIgginsm1837-1904,w/o E.T.
Emma S.,Sept.13,1928.
Fred,Apr.24,1954.
George C.,May 2,1970.
George M.,July 7,1942.
Hannah Fogg,1813-1882,w/o Sam.R.
J. Granville,Jan.1,1921.
Jacob,1849-1855,s/o S.R.& H.F.
John P.,Feb.17,1921.
Julie F.,1858-1905,w/o Chas.F.
Lou M.,1854-1907,w/o J. Granville.
Mary H.,1842-1857,d/o S.R.& H.F.
Minnie,Jan.31,1956.

Moses B.,Apr.22,1971.
Samuel R.,1810-1897.
Verne M.,June 30,1970.
Walter C.,Feb.25,1926.
CLIFFORD
Jerome J.,May 1,1991.
Kimberlay L.,Apr.5,1965,inf.
CLINCH
Olive,Aug.2,1982.
Nancy,Aug.21,1986.
Walter,Apr.22,1971.
CLOUGH
Albert,Aug.13,1990.
Berton,Apr.13,1944.
Blanche E.C.,Apr.22,1958.
Edward E.,Apr.28,1928.
Gertrude M.T.,Apr.19,1932.
Mrs.Hartley,Jan.3,1912.
Hartley,1846-Oct.24,1915.
Melissa McKenney,1845-1903,
w/o Hartley
Nellie,Apr.16,1975.
COBB
Charles E.,July 15,1921.
David,Sept.27,1837,59y,
s/o David & Lucy.
Ebenezer,Oct.4,1768-Dec.23,1840,
1st w. Sarah Hanscom.
Gershom F.,Rev.,1833-Mar.7,1909.
Mary E.,July 29,1922.
Mary L.,Mar.23,1914.
Mary Larrabee,Dec.23,1786-
Sept.8,1859,2nd w/o Ebenezer.
Maud,Apr.26,1978.
Moses,Apr.23,1846,19y.
Myrtle,Jan.31,1941.
Sally Watson,Oct.7,1847,
65y,w/o David.
Samuel,Oct.15,1773-Oct.15,1839.
Tabitha Elwell,Oct.14,1839,69y,
w/o Samuel.
Walter W.,Feb.8,1958.
COBURN
Byron G.,1941.
Byron G.,Dec.23,1835-Dec.13,1894.
Edwin,Dec.5,1813-Oct.23,1891.
Elizabeth,Aug.19,1813-May 20,1884,
w/o Edwin.
Eliza J.,1837-Apr.11,1916,w/o J.H.
Frank E.,Nov.18,1948.
Frankie,1832,child.
Jacob,Mar.29,1808-Sept.11,1882.
Jacob,Aug.2,1855,76y,h/o Mary.
Joseph H.,1827-1901.
Laura J.,Feb.21,1940.
Mary,Oct.30,1856,76y,w/o Jacob.

Theano J.,Sept.10,1813-July 28,1880,
w/o Bryon G.
Tryphena S. Hancock,Sept.9,1805-
Oct.4,1899,w/o Jacob.
children/o Joseph H.& Eliza J.:
Byron G.,1869-1941;
Harry H.,1874-1878;
John E.,1864-1890;
Wilbur J.,1860-1894.
CODMAN TOMB:
Abigail Loring,Aug.16,1855,75y,
2nd w/o James.
Elizabeth Waite,Jan.1797,31y,
1st w/o James.
James,1763-Jan.3,1840.
James,Capt.,1825,(small stone at
base of tomb).
COFFIN
Anna P.,July 3,1923.
Earle P.,Jan.8,1940.
Leila E.,Apr.2,1909.
William P.,1847-1902.
COLBY
Almeda Lane,May 5,1956.
E.K.,Rev.,1812-1902.
Georgianna J.,Jan.3,1927.
William,May 10,1993.
COLE
Doris Evelyn,Nov.29,1926.
Elsa May,Feb.3,1924,infant.
CONNER
Alvira,Apr.20,1982.
CONNERS
Charles W.,May 26,1988.
Herbert,Sept.13,1945.
CONNORS
Adeline A.,July 1,1946.
Doris,July 7,1994.
CONWAY
Doris,May 1,1979.
Erlin,May 5,1993,s/o Doris.
James,Aug.20,1973.
COOK
Belinda E.,Nov.1925, &
Charles W.,Nov.1925,both
rem. from Waterboro.
Charles,June 14,1945.
Chester,Apr.30,1988.
ch/o Charles,June 6,1925.
Gustave,May 2,1984.
Lizzie M.,June 2,1924.
COOMBS
Dorothy Ann,Mar.17,1938.
Freeland N.,Dec.24,1931.
COREY
Mildred,Nov.1,1986.
Ralph,Nov.1,1986.

S. Peter,Apr.4,1937.
COTTON
Elmer S.,1940.
Mary Toppan,Nov.1,1927.
William,May 6,1862,26y,
h/o Mary E. Emery.
COUSINS
Elizabeth A.,Jan.18,1943.
Evelyn R.,Mar.6,1932.
Perley C.,May 27,1949.
Scott Winfield,July 18,1968.
Willis,Nov.6,1979.
Wright H.,May 3,1947.
COYNE
Edward,Jan.12,1956.
Florence,Oct.19,1980.
CRESSEY
Albert,1820-1905.
Alvin,1806-1858.
Annie B.,Feb.16,1934.
Annie C.,Oct.10,1921.
Barbara Ann,June 14,1926,
inf/o Raymond J.
Carrie D.,May 3,1947.
Charles H.,1817-1872.
Charles H.,July 9,1919.
Charles R.,Jan.22,1929.
Daniel,Aug.21,1848.
Doris E.,July 31,1909-Apr.16,1916,
d/o Alvin & Irene.
Doris L.,Apr.8,1916.
Dwight S.,1891-1893,s/o Melville W.
E.G.,Mar.24,1923.
Ebenezer,1779-1829.
Elizabeth D.,Feb.17,1932.
Elizabeth Patrick,1827-1882,
2nd w/o Albert.
Ella C.,Sept.30,1919.
Ella,1851-1920.
Emeline,June 14,1923.
Emily A. Hobson,1830-1853,
1st w/o Albert.
Emma H.,1855-Apr.10,1916,
d/o Albert & Emma H.
Ernest A.,May 24,1946.
Florence,July 29,1988.
Frances E.,Apr.30,1922.
Frances May,Apr.23,1948.
Francis O.,Feb.9,1864,5y,d/o Jos.& R.
George A.,1887-1887,s/o Edw.& Nellie.
George A.,July 21,1962.
Ginger L.,Feb.4,1946.
Grace,Apr.27,1987.
Guy R.,1862-1905.
Hannah,Dec.27,1847,89y,w/o Joseph.
Hattie P.,Aug.18,1942.
Hattie W.,1869-1907,w/o Guy R.

Henry S.,1855-Feb.15,1931.
Herbert B.,Jan.27,1911.
Horace,Oct.12,1911,70y,
 h/o Lorantha Elwell.
Isabella M.,Mar.7,1864,9y,d/o J.& R.
John H.,Jan.19,1930.
Joseph,Feb.8,1858,70y,h/o Sarah.
Joseph,July 22,1832,79y,h/o Hannah.
Joseph,Aug.29,1898,77y.
Laura C.,Feb.10,1864,d/o Jos.& R.
Lavantia,Feb.8,1916.
Martha Ann,1822-1903,
 d/o John & Martha.
Mary E.,1835-1866,d/o Jas.,2nd.
Mary L.,1861-1864,d/o Wm.
Melville W.,1867-1905.
Nellie E.,1861-Jan.26,1918,
 d/o Albert & Emma H.
Nellie M.,Feb.14,1922.
Philo B.,Oct.7,1988.
Rebecca Harding,1822-1896.
Rhoda,Sept.20,1868,36y,w/o Joseph.
Sally C.,May 14,1975.
Samuel,1817-1893.
Sarah J.,1823-1906,w/o Joseph.
Sarah W.,1822-1851,w/o Chas.H.
Sarah Chick,Feb.14,1863,w/o Eben.
Sarah Flagg,1810-1888,w/o Alvin.
Sarah Watts,Sept.29,1847,53y,
 1st w/o Joseph,d/o David Watts.
Susan B.,1845-1903,1st w/o Chas.H.
Villa,1855-1909.
Willie,Feb.2,1922.
William A.,Dec.6,1959.
William W.,1828-1892,s/o Jas.,2nd.
children/o Alvin & Sarah:
Caroline A.,1843-1869.
Eben F.,1841-1866;
Eliza A.1839-1869;
Elizabeth,1845-1850;
Harriet E.,1851-1888.
children/o Ebenezer & Sarah:
Eliza A.,1820-1831;
John,1814-1892,unm.;
Joseph,1812-1858;
Martha,1810-1851, see "McCorrison".
CRISSIKOS
Louis,Oct.29,1951.
CRITCHLEY
Edward,July 8,1986.
Hilda,June 14,1983.
Jan,May 25,1983.
CROCKETT
Ava,Apr.21,1976.
Betsey Hunt,Dec.30,1851,73y,w/o John
Charles E.,Sept.19,1937.
Edward C.,1828-1896.

Ella F.,Dec.9,1915.
George W.,Apr.16,1826-May 26,1906.
Harriet Folsom,Mar.23,1851,50y,
 2nd w/o Samuel.
Harriet G.,Sept.12,1947.
Howard,Oct.29,1966.
John,Mar.7,1776-Aug.8,1843.
Martha Philbrick,1830-1905.
Mary,1804-1888,w/o William.
Nancy F. Tappan,1828-Apr.14,1910.
Nelson M.,Feb.13,1933.
Priscilla,Aug.2,1853,22y,d/o S.& H.
Robert,July 13,1970.
Sadie,June 22,1967.
Samuel,Feb.20,1790-Sept.15,1855.
William,1806-1859.
XX,July 10,1923,ch/o Howard.
CRONKITE
Clayton,Oct.5,1990.
CRONEY
Florence E.,Sept.29,1940.
CROSSMAN
George W.,Sept.14,1982.
CROWE
Irene,Dec.15,1990.
CROWELL
Marion B.,Man.7,1974.
CUMMINGS
Aaron,Dea.,Aug.30,1854,68y.
Mary Susan,May 28,1928.
Nancy R.,Mar.19,1862,65y,
 w/o Dea. Aaron.
CURTIS
Arthur & Hattie,infants,XXXX.
John,Aug.11,1879,26y.
John,Capt.,Jan.7,1869,69y.
Johnnie,Sept.3,1881,2y,s/o J.& S.E.
Mary P.,1806,1y,d/o John & Mercy.
Mercy,June 1867,89y,
 1st h. Capt. John Curtis,Sr.,
 2nd h. Thomas Burnham.
Statira Staples,1802-1883,w/o John.
CUSHMAN
Charles M.,Aug.3,1932,60y.
Elizabeth E.,Oct.8,1914,68y,w/o S.B.
Simeon B.,Apr.22,1893,56y.
XX,May 29,1864,3y,ch/o S.B.& E.E.
CYR
Annie F. & baby,May 30,1938.
DAICY
Chester W.,Apr.6,1949.
Flora,Aug.9,1967.
Samuel,May 5,1989.
Vondella Sawyer,May 21,1985.
DAME
Mary Ann,Dec.24,1878,74y.
Moses B.,Feb.29,1868,41y.

Susan M.,Feb.28,1869,35y,w/o Moses.
Theophilus,Jan.29,1875,74y.
DARLING
George L.,June 13,1865,73y.
John,Apr.6,1832,74y.
Mahala,July 29,1856,53y,w/o Geo.L.
DAVIS
Allen,May 22,1818,48y.
Amelia Decker,Feb.13,1912,63y,
  w/o Caleb.
Charles,Sept.25,1989.
Clifford,May 24,1941.
Cornelia W.,Mar.5,1886,5y,
  d/o D.H.& M.E.
Daniel W.,July 10,1917.
Daniel,Jan.2,1873,72y,h/o Miriam.
Edith Marie,Aug.10,1984,w/o Elton.
Elisha,1824-1907.
Eliza M. Davis,Nov.26,1885,73y.
Ellen E. Patrick,1831-1909,w/o Elisha.
Ellen,1890-1892.
Elton,July 24,1981.
Eunice Frost,July 19,1861,
  58y,w/o Josiah.
Everett,June 18,1935.
Frances M.,Dec.20,1859,26y,
  d/o Josiah & Elizabeth.
Frederica,May 13,1963.
Hannah P. Patrick,1833-1874,
  w/o Lewis.
James L.,June 20,1857,9y.
James L.,Dec.16,1882,76y.
James S.,Mar.4,1924.
James W.,May 18,1824-Feb.14,1885.
Jevoe ? D.,May 24,1916.
Joseph,May 17,1921,rem. from
  Limington.
Josiah,Aug.5,1843,49y,s/o James.
Julia Elizabeth,Oct.22,1841,4m,
  d/o Josiah & Elizabeth.
Lewis,1829-1902.
Lydia M.,Dec.7,1907.
Martha Morris,Jan.7,1847,
  75y,w/o Allen.
Mary A.,May 25,1886,57y,d/o D.& M.
Mary E.,June 6,1916.
Maud D.,Aug.12,1935.
Mildred,Mar.7,1945.
Miriam Stone,May 24,1876,78y,
  w/o Daniel.
Naomi,Apr.2,1981.
Priscilla,May 17,1921,rem. from
  Limington.
Roy,May 2,1992.
Ruvian,Mar.14,1953.
Sarah E.,May 9,1932.
William T.,Apr.28,1951.

DAY
Celinda Brown,1815-1910,
  w/o Lewis Kent,d/o James Reynolds.
Edith P.,July 10,1957.
Eva K.,Dec.6,1970.
Gloria,Aug.6,1987.
George S.,Jan.11,1926.
Harley M.,1881-July 1,1945.
Harry,Dec.23,1945.
Jennie S.,June 30,1942.
Kenneth,Oct.21,1987.
Lena McConkey,Aug.1980,w/o Harley
Lewis E.,Sept.12,1983.
Lewis K.,1811-1901,h/o Celinda.
Muriel,Nov.9,1920.
Selina B.,Feb.3,1910.
DEARBORN
Geneva,Dec.24,1938.
Thomas F.,May 10,1938.
DEAS
Gabrielle,Apr.25,1986,child.
DEERING
Cora M.,1878-1894,d/o G.E.& R.
Fred W.,1850-1892.
Frederick S.,Feb.27,1876,61y.
George E.,1852-1890,h/o Rebecca.
Lawrence,1895-Apr.20,1983.
Lucy F.Knight,1854-May 26,1919,
  w/o Reuben.
Lucy M.,Sept.15,1869,54y,w/o Fred S.
DELANEY
John S.,Apr.18,1974.
DEMASS
William J.,June 26,1956.
DEMERILL
Lottie A.,1844-1890,w/o Frank E.
DEMERS
William J.,June 26,1956.
DENNETT
Ethel,Apr.14,1980.
George L.,Oct.20,1918.
DIKE
John S.,Mar.17,1936.
Lillian Hobsen,Feb.24,1927.
DOBLE
Annie S.,Jan.26,1929.
Leonard F.,Mar.26,1929.
DODGE
John W.,Apr.21,1984.
DOLLEY
Eliza H. Cumming,1840-May 10,1911,
  w/o Samuel F.
Grace L.,Nov.15,1956.
Mary C. Watson,1871-1906,w/o Walt.
Samuel F.,1839-1906.
Samuel F.,May 1911.
Walter,Jan.27,1878-XXXX.

DONHAM
Joseph N.,Apr.20,1920.
Oriella,Aug.10,1934.
DOUCETTE
Raymond,July 3,1982.
DOUGLASS
Alonzo B.,Jan.28,1918.
Asa W.,Mar.3,1940.
Daniel,1825-1901.
Dexter O.,Oct.24,1956.
Elizabeth,Nov.1,1961.
Ellen E.,Sept.6,1909.
Elisha,Mar.1907.
Emily B.,1864-1868,d/o D.&M.A.L.
Geneva M.,Nov.1,1943.
Mary A. Lowell,1824-1900,w/o Danl.
Ruth G.,Feb.18,1936.
William R.,Dec.2,1940,infant.
DOW
Abraham,May 12,1850,53y.
Donald O.,June 7,1993.
Emma E.,Apr.20,1974.
Grace W.,Dec.13,1951.
DOWNS
Ida Bell,May 11,1984.
DOYLE
Donald,July 21,1979.
DREW
Elsie,Apr.19,1962.
DROWN
Alonzo,1844-Feb.8,1918.
Edgar F.,Oct.16,1941.
Edna,1883-1884,d/o Alonzo & E.J.
Eliza J.,1846-Mar.1906,w/o Alonzo.
Ernest H.,1881-1900,s/o Al. & E.J.
Etta,Feb.2,1920.
Fannie B.,1866-1885.
James L.,1820-1898.
Lucinda A.,1821-1896,w/o Jas. L.
Mabel F.,May 17,1959.
Melvina F.,Feb.8,1954.
Roscoe G.,Aug.7,1922.
Viola J.,June 4,1922.
Oscar L.,May 24,1945.
unnamed,Apr.4,1921.
DUBBS
Harrison,May 9,1981.
Helen,May 10,1993.
DUDLEY
Emily D.Libbey,1844-Aug.13,1918, w/o Woodbury J.
Jean,Sept.9,1978.
DUNHAM
Charles N.,Jan.9,1940.
DUNN
Joan Roberts,Apr.25,1833, 31y,1st w/o Samuel.
Martha Roberts,Apr.9,1893, 79y,2nd w/o Samuel.
Sarah,Jan.10,1832,6y,d/o S.& Joan.
children of Samuel & Martha:
Eveline,May 27,1866,5y;
Mary E.,July 25,1874,16y;
Melville,Apr.15,1864,18y;
Samuel,Aug.12,1871,70y.
Samuel,Jr.,July 23,1872,22y,unm.
William F.,II,Apr.14,1865,19y.
William,Jan.24,1832,4y.
DURGAN
Barber,XXXX,Co.K.,12th Me Inf.
Carl,May 11,1991.
Virginia,May 19,1990.
DURGIN
Barber B.,Mar.25,1925.
Fred L.,July 13,1960.
John E.,Sept.2,1961.
Lillian,Jan.20,1941.
Marion,July 26,1993.
Marion G.,Dec.11,1969.
Ronald (George R.) Nov.9,1990.
Wilbur L.,July 30,1975.
DURKEE
E.Leslie,1897-1899.
Edmund L.,1870-June 4,1922.
Nellie F.,1873-1900,w/o Edm.L.
DYER
Annie E. Johnson,June 14,1907, w/o Clark.
Charles, 1814 ?-Nov.26,1847.
Clark C.,Oct.21,1815-Jan.2,1894.
Clark,Sr.,Feb.3,1910.
Frank E.,Apr.25,1942.
Hazel M.,XXXX,14d,d/o H.H& L.M.
Jennie,1846-1889,w/o Charles E.
Lydia Clemons,May 29,1888,75y, 1sth. Charles Dyer,
2nd h.Capt. Nathan Winslow.
Marilla S.,Jan.11,1918.
Mary A.,Apr.20,1918.
Mary G.,Oct.29,1912.
Randolph C.,Oct.30,1939.
Sara Louise,June 1,1991.
EASTERN
Clinton S.,Apr.6,1922.
Donald,Mar.15,1962.
Katherine Shute,Oct.25,1929.
Phoebe C.,Jan.19,1923.
EASTMAN
Kimball,1839-1904.
Percy K.,1872-1884,s/o K.& P.C.
Phebe C. Clement,1839-1923.
EATON
Amanda,Oct.31,1981,newb.
Charles P.,1843-1882,s/o S.W.& M.B.

Eddie,Jan.21,1854-Sept.17,1870.
Miranda B. Knox,Aug.15,1811-
Aug.19,1888,w/o Stephen.
Sophia,Sept.10,1908,67y,
d/o Clark & Eunice McLellan Perry.
Stephen W.,Mar.12,1808-Mar.5,1877.
EDDY
Timothy,July 12,1976.
EDMONDS
Daniel,Jan.28,1929.
Ernest H.,Oct.6,1877,4wks.
John H.,1827-Aug.27,1913.
Lena M.,May 26,1917.
Lucy A.,1826-1907,w/o John H.
Mabel R.,Apr.10,1887,22y,d/o J.& L.
Myrtie L.,May 5,1884,1y.
Ralph E.,Nov.30,1892,7y,
s/o Daniel & Louise.
EDWARDS
Abba F.,Oct.3,1896,64y,w/o J.H.R.
Annie Proctor,1836-1870,w/o Paul R.
Arthur L.,July 29,1866,1y,s/o T.B.
Bessie M.,1883-July 13,1926.
Catherine,Oct.19,1874,92y.
Charles M.,Co., Co.A.,5th ME Inf.
Elizabeth B. Woodman,Sept.22,1888,
w/o Josiah (1859).
Emeline McLellan,Aug.25,1846,
37y,1st w/o James H.R.
Frank B.,III,Aug.15,1948,inf.
George Calvin,Aug.28,1832,9m,
s/o Calvin & Susan.
Harriet M.,1829-Apr.3,1910,
w/o James H.R.
James H.R.,May 26,1890,82y.
Lavina A.,Aug.13,1902,61y,w/o T.B.
Maria A.,Dec.31,1887.
Mary E.,1847-Oct.26,1922,w/o Paul R.
Mary,Dec.1835-Feb.4,1879.
Paul Richmond,1836-1907.
Ralph B.,Apr.16,1873-Mar.9,1903.
T.B.,1815-1900.
W.M.G.,Oct.4,1853,s/o T.B.& M.R.
William C.,June 9,1874-Sept.1,1912.
ELDEN
John M.,July 9,1836-May 20,1892.
Patience,Dec.4,1856,70y,
w/o Capt.Silas C.
XX,Oct.4,1837,w/o Gideon. ?
ELDER
Abigail O.,May 16,1852,65y.
Bethiah,1816-1886,w/o Wm.
David,Dec.23,1869,84yh/o Abigail.
Edward T.,July 24,1949.
Elizabeth Johnson,Jan.5,1804-
Jan.24,1889,2nd w/o Simon.

Everett,June 2,1850-Aug.19,1867,
s/o Wm. & Bethiah.
Florence M.,July 15,1941.
Frances E. Roberts,1833-May 20,1911.
George J.,Nov.7,1929.
Lizzie,Aug.8,1845-Dec.1,1874.
Randall J.,1833-June 6,1906,
h/o Frances.
Ruth,Feb.27,1951.
Simon,Dec.4,1791-May 4,1862,
1st w.Mary Hatch.
Stuart R.,Nov.26,1957.
William S.,1819-1887.
children/o Simon & Elizabeth J.:
 Catherine S.,1825-1845;
 Edward,1839-1840;
 Eunice,1832-1832;
 George L.,1841-1845;
 Henry,1829-1829;
 Martha,1827-1851;
 Miraim,1823-1823;
 Sarah J.,1830-1854.
ELFSTROM
Carl A.,June 28,1947.
ELKINS
Charles,Feb.25,1940.
Levi,Nov.3,1961.
Lillian H.,Dec.13,1926.
ELIOT
Charles A.,June 27,.1923.
Merton,Apr.10,1923.
ELLIOTT
Alice H.,June 20,1958.
Annie,Sept.14,1984.
Arthur C.,Mar.31,1950.
Charles D.,Oct.12,1928.
Clifford E.,June 20,1958.
Dana C.,July 20,1976.
Jean,May 2,1985.
Judith Ann,Nov.23,1958.
Ralph,May 26,1972.
Ruth C.,June 20,1958.
ELLIS
Carlton,Aug.30,1990.
Gray,Jr.,Aug.11,1987.
Kenneth W.,Oct.9,1971.
William F.,Feb.6,1934.
Will Warren,1853-1905,
h/o Harriett Hanson
ELLSWORTH
Joseph,June 22,1859,30y.
Mary A.,Sept.2,1870,41y,w/o Josiah.
Mary Annis,May 15,1942.
ELWELL
Blanch,July 18,1948.
Frank M.,Aug.1,1957.
Gardner,Dec.1,1851,23y.

Mary Ann,Sept.17,1983.
Susan,Apr.4,1839,41y,w/o John S.
Washburn C.,June 1916.
EMERSON
Hannah,Sept.25,1840,68y,w/o Bulkley.
EMERY
Albion,Oct.27,1952,rem. from
  Shaw Mills Cemetery.
Bryanne E.,Dec.30,1979,infant.
Caroline,Oct.27,1952,rem.from
  Shaw Mills Cemetery.
Daniel,1754-1825.
Delia A.,Dec.27,1958.
Eliza B.,Jan.28,1923.
Elizabeth,1790-1869,2nd w/o Jonath.
Flora E.,Mar.6,1946.
Fred P.,Oct.10,1960.
Frederick D.,1834-1903.
George,XXXX,s/o J.& J.
Harriet,Oct.27,1952,rem.from
  Shaw Mills Cemetery.
infant,July 10,1963,s.b.
Jane,1800-1886,w/o Josiah.
Jane,1773-1839,1st w/o Jonathan.
Jonathan,1780-1845.
Josiah,1800-1853.
Mark P.,Feb.14,1986.
Martha F.,Apr.30,1943.
Mary A.,1820-1861.
Reuben M.,Dec.3,1953.
Sarah J.,1828-1831.
Sarah,1756-1846,w/o Daniel.
Stephen A.,June 23,1916,72y,
  h/o Mattie Sawyer.
Sueia Anna,Feb.20,1936.
Virginia Lidback,July 3,1992.
Walter E.,Apr.15,1952.
Wilmot W.,May 4,1954.
EMMONS
Ida May,1876-1900,w/o Albry P.
ERNEST
Mary,May 1,1985.
ERSKINE
Albert,Aug.20,1985.
Elizabeth,Oct.19,1839,19y,
  d/o Asa & Mary M.
ESTES
Abba A.,June 13,1842-July 16,1862.
Albert Smith,July 10,1837-
  Aug.30,1862,killed at the 2nd batttle
  of Bull Run.
Edward A.,1847-1892.
Edward B.,1873-1876,s/o E.A. & M.H.
Ellen M.,Feb.7,1912.
George H.,July 10,1847-Aug.6,1848.
Joseph,Feb.3,1805-May 30,1892.

Maria Edwards,June 8,1809-
  Apr.21,1893.
Mary Hersey,1844-1927,wid/o Edward,
  w/o Solomon D. Avery.
EVANS
Phillips B.,1895-1898,s/o E.W. & E.F.
EVELETH
Fannie B. Lord,1872-1954 ?.
Samuel A.,1826-1856.
FAIRBANKS
Annie,Jan.7,1953.
George L.,Nov.3,1883,28y.
FANJOY
Ellen I.,Dec.16,1971.
Leroy,Aug.18,1970.
FARDON
Mary Katherine,Nov.29,1895,17y,
  d/o Thomas & Bertha.
FARNHAM
Ann Maria,1835-1905,d/o John & A.
Annie M.,1801-1892.
George,1826-1863.
John,Capt.,1790-1868.
Sarah E.,1832-1846,d/o John & Ann.
FARR
David M.,1840-1895.
Flora E.,Nov.9,1921.
Ivory C.,June 11,1936.
Mary O.,1852-Aug.18,1910,w/o D.M.
Webster,1872-1888,s/o D.M.& M.O.
FARRIN
Edna G.,Apr.15,1981.
William G.,June 24,1987.
FEEN
Emma M.,Dec.1910,wid/o John.
FEENEY
Charlotte W.,Mar.31,1958.
Daniel,Nov.4,1930.
Edith,Sept.29,1972.
Emma L.,1877-Dec.25,1910.
Gertrude H.,May 3,1957.
Harry,Aug.25,1961.
John W.,1876-1904,h/o Emma L.
Justina,June 7,1947.
Mary M.,July 23,1932.
Patterson G.,Sept.4,1928.
childern/o John W.& Emma L.:
  Albert Stanley,1904-1904;
  Catherine,1900-1900.
FELCH
Betsey,Oct.3,1841,56y,w/o Isaac.
Isaac,June 14,1841,59y.
Lydia C.,Oct.24,1841,18y.
Sarah P.,Apr.23,1841,23y,d/o I.& B.
FENDERSON
Fred,Aug.31,1946.
Mary Etta,Dec.6,1962.

FENLASON
Blanche,Nov.3,1951.
Elbert,May 6,1975.
Henrietta,Sept.25,1942.
Mary W.,Jan.12,1984.
Mary,May 2,1984.
Waldo G.,Nov.28,1979.
Waldo,Nov.28,1979.
Waldo,Sept.25,1942.
FERGUSON
Carole M.,Apr.26,1975.
FERRIS
Hannah,June 5,1846-Nov.23,1924,
w/o Leonard Z.
FIELD
Larry E.,Apr.27,1957.
Thomas J.,Aug.29,1953.
FIFIELD
Alice A.,July 18,1966.
Harry H.,Apr.18,1958.
Imogene H.,Dec.13,1938.
infant,Sept.10,1941,s.b.
James J.,Sept.8,1938.
Walter V.,July 3,1933.
FILES
Albion P.,1824-1872.
Almon L.,Jr.,1874-July 24,1923.
Almon L.,1840-1904,s/o Wm.E.& A.
Amey G.,May 17,1972.
Anita S.,May 9,1964.
Annie L.,Sept.26,1882,5m,
d/o Lothrop L. & Mary E.
Apphia Blake,1818-1897,w/o Wm.E.
Augustus F.,Mar.25,1909.
Bertha,Nov.14,1972.
Blanche B.,Feb.15,1958.
Carrie W.,June 11,1931.
Cecil W.,June 10,1962.
Charles E.,Nov.20,1914.
Charlotte Martha,1874-1880,
Cornelia Watson,1847-May 24,1922,
w/o Frank A.
David F.,1830-1905,1st w. Fannie
Curtis,2nd w.Morgie Eastman.
Earle,Jan.5,1983.
Eliza A.,May 11,1924.
Eliza Lombard,1843-1924,
w/o Almon L.
Ellen C.,Apr.23,1975.
Elvon,June 14,1947.
Ernest W.,Apr.12,1958.
Etta N. Hayes,1941.
Eunice B. Freeman,1808-1885,
w/o Stephen (1882).
Fannie P.,1862-1863,d/o D.F.& M.E.
F.Christenze,1877-1897,d/o H.G.& N.
Frank Augustus,1846-1909,
h/o Cornelia Watson.
George E.,Mar.31,1949.
Hattie M.,Dec.16,1910.
Herbert G.,1850-Mar.14,1917.
Ida M.Root,1867-1946.
Hattie M.,1856-1910.
Inez G.,Mar.19,1972.
Lewis L.,May 20,1938.
Lizzie S.,1865-1882.
Lothrop L.,Aug.25,1892,41y.
Lothrop L.,Sept.27,1870,62y.
Lottie M.,Mar.25,1909.
Mabel B.,Jan.2,1969.
Margie S.,Feb.24,1933.
Mary E.,Oct.16,1889,35y,w/o Lothrop.
Mary L.,1858-1872.
Mary P.,July 19,1909,93y,
w/o Lothrop L. (1909).
Merle,Nov.20,1982.
Minnie G.,1875-1898,d/o H.G. & N.D.
Mirilla M. Spear,1831-1918.
Morton C.,Aug.6,1986.
Nellie D.,1850-1896,w/o Herbert G.
Nellie J.,June 23,1935.
Philip,May 10,1983.
R.Earle,June 23,1957.
Rae E.,May 19,1923,w/o Earle.
Salome M.,Mar.16,1978.
Stepehn C.,Jr.,1901-1901,s/o S.& E.
Stephen C.,Dec.23,1941.
Stephen,1800-1882.
Vane E.,May 7,1950.
William E.,1815-1884.
Willie E.,Aug.1872,5m,s/o L.L.&M.E.
FINNEY
Alberta M.,Apr.8,1939.
Edwin L.,June 21,1948.
Estella H.,Sept.29,1958.
James E. & Heris,Mar.16,1916.
FISK
Mary D.,Jan.2,1850,49y,
w/o Rev. A.Wm.
FISKE
James,Dec.25,1910.
FITZMORRIS
Agnes L.,Apr.23,1976.
FLIGHT
Evelyn,May 17,1988.
John,Apr.17,1974.
Howard F.,June 14,1934.
FLINT
Annie W.,Apr.23,1957.
FLOYD
Everett A.,1891-1893,s/o F.E.& J.M.
Frank E.,Jan.28,1957.
George M.,1840-1904.

Herbert F.,June 16,1943.
Lena M.,May 22,1946.
Myra M.,1846-1893,w/o G.M.
FLY
Eunice,1802-1878.
FLYNN
Emma,1862.
FOGEL
Barbara,Feb.26,1952.
FOGG
Agnes E.,Dec.19,1962.
Arthur J.,1842-1908.
Asa R.,Dec.22,1929.
Barbara,May 4,1920.
Benjamin C.,Dec.30,1913.
Blanche M.,1876-1892.
Carrie Watson,Aug.28,1849-Sept.6,1888,w/o Dr.Wm.P.
Celia,Apr.6,1964.
Christiana O. Baker,1812-1865, w/o Moses.
Clara Ellen,Sept.13,1935.
Daniel,Apr.14,1773-Oct.23,1829.
Edna E.,Sept.15,1973.
Edna Merrill,Nov.25,1952.
Edward D.,May 13,1964.
Eleanor W.,Jan.16,1919.
Eliza A.,1821-1855,unm.d/o Geo.& J.
Eliza S. Sawyer,1826-1905,w/o Benj.C.
Elizabeth B.,Aug.21,1849,6y, d/o Moses & C.O.B.
Elizabeth H. Babb,July 25,1842,26y, w/o Asa Rand.
George,1784-1868.
Grata Rand,1819-1847,unm., d/o George & Joanna.
Hannah Clement,Feb.10,1842,65y.
Helen,June 3,1923.
Horatio,1833-1862.
Howard B.,1885-1892.
Howard J.,Mar.7,1946.
Howard,Apr.18,1977.
James P.,Mar.6,1914.
James Roy,Aug.14,1963.
Joanna Fogg,1786-1861,w/o George.
Leon,Apr.23,1982.
Marjorie,Nov.3,1980.
Mary Jane Bray,1825-Oct.10,1909, w/o Deacon Rufus A.
Mary Eliza,Mar.23,1831,10m, d/o Wm. & Mary Ann.
Moses,1809-1892.
Nettie,June 20,1925.
Nellie M.,Feb.8,1941.
Peter S.,Dec.7,1951.
Raymon E.,Aug.3,1916.
Rufus A.,Dea.,1828-Dec.14,1909.
Samuel,1826-1850,s/o Geo. & Joanna.
Susan A.,1846-1907,w/o Arthur J.
Susan A.,1838-1906,w/o Horatio.
William M.,Apr.10,1851-July 19,1884.
William,Jan.28,1831,27y, h/o Mary A. Barrett.
FOLSOM
Dudley,Dr.,Nov.20,1886,68y.
Lucretia Swazey,Sept.27,1837,65y.
FORD
Emma,Apr.2,1981.
John A.,Rev.,Apr.14,1938.
Katie F.,Mar.16,1938.
Robert P.,Mar.24,1931.
Theodore,Feb.6,1962.
FOREST
Clifford,May 1,1989.
Russell,Dec.15,1946.
FORREST
James L.,Sept.2,1980.
Russell,May 20,1986
FOSS
George,Feb.10,1932.
Rufus A.,Dec.16,1909.
FOSTER
Alfred G.,Feb.17,1943.
Arvner L.,Oct.16,1948.
Betsey,Apr.24,1839,52y,w/o Wm.H.
Edwin,June 20,1984.
Ernest,June 4,1965.
Ervette M.,May 17,1929.
Hazel A.,Oct.23,1964.
Sadie A.,Oct.12,1962.
William Hart,Sept.22,1838,5Xy.
Willie R.,Sept.2,1958.
XX,Mar.1,1881,72y.
FOX
Eleanor M.,Nov.13,1918.
Daniel W.,Feb.9,1919.
Elizabeth,Oct.16,1981.
FRASER
Thomas,Sept.20,1978.
FREEMAN
Charlotte F.,1837-XXXX,w/o Cyrus.
Cyrus M.,1820-1900.
FRENCH
Albert P.,1833-1905.
Albert,Apr.23,1923.
Mary E.,1832-1905,w/o A.P.
FRITZ
Charles W.,May 6,1966.
Ruth A.,Oct.5,1976.
FROST
Almira,June 16,1817-Mar.25,1898.
Annie A.,Jan.26,1845-Mar.23,1886.
Benjamin,1777-1779,twin to Nathan.
Caroline C.,Aug.17,1824-Apr.19,1914.

Charles,Capt.,May 29,1859,39y.
Charles Fred,July 12,1871,20y,
  d/o Charles & E.J.
Charles H.,Oct.29,1855,29y,
  s/o Jeremiah & Hannah.
Content Hamblen,Dec.4,1845,67y,
  w/o Capt. Nathaniel.
David,Apr.8,1859,38y.
Deborah,XXXX.
Eunice J. Staples,May 9,1820-
  Feb.22,1903,w/o Charles.
Frances,XXXX.
Francina P. Jackson,Mar.25,1847,
  29y,w/o Joseph H.
George Ai,Feb.2,1873,20y,s/o C.&E.J.
Hannah Higgins,Sept.28,1856,74y,
  w/o Jeremiah, (d.1845).
Jacob,Apr.4,1867,57y.
Joseph H.,June 12,1818-July 12,1845.
Martha M.,Dec.25,1844,8y,d/o J. & R.
Nathaniel,Capt.,June 24,1777-
  Feb.9,1830,twin to Benjamin.
Nelly,XXXX.
Sunie F.,May 3,1854,4y,
  d/o Jacob & Ruth.
Susan F.,July 10,1848,2y,d/o J.& R.
Susan,w/o Capt.Jacob,stone broken.
FULLER
Eliot W.,Aug.14,1962.
Mabel F.L.,Sept.6,1956.
GAGNE
Joseph,May 3,1985.
Mary L.,Sept.8,1965.
GALLISON
Frances E.,Apr.3,1919.
GAMMON
Edmon/Edmund,Aug.4,1841,63y.
Elden,1811-1884.
Elizabeth P.,Feb.28,1917,93y.
Helen M.,Aug.25,1849,16y,
  d/o Elden & Mariam.
Miriam,Feb.10,1895,87y,w/o Elden.
Sarah,Mar.19,1875,86y,w/o Edm.
GARLAND
Catherine Wiggin,Aug.19,1825-
  Sept.15,1901,w/o Samuel.
Mary K.,Jan.3,18611-Aug.8,1891,
  d/o S. & C.
Samuel,May 1824-Nov.1898.
GARON
Alec J.,Mar.9,1959.
Luela M.,Sept.26,1980.
GATCHELL
Elton Elroy,Sept.13,1974.
Georgie,May 19,1990.
William E.,May 26,1951.

GAVETT
Charles J.,Jan.1,1969.
Eva,Jan.6,1969.
George E.,Feb.12,1951,infant.
GAYNE
Mary L.,Sept.10,1965.
GETCHELL
Elton,Sept.13,1974.
Fred,Nov.28,1972.
Hattie E.,Nov.24,1935.
Ida E.,Dec.11,1969.
John H.,Mar.10.1940.
GIBBS
Bernice R.,Nov.27,1948.
Shirley Marie,Mar.17,1943.
Stanley George,July 13,1950.
GIDDENS
Ellen,Feb.17,1942.
Fred A.,May 28,1917.
GIDDINGS (on stone)
Sarah E. Cressey,1853-1942,
  w/o Fred A. (see Giddens).
GILBERT
George A.,Dec.8,1951.
Martha,Apr.31,1848,39y.
Sarah,Feb.1,1849,63y.
GINN
Chester M.,May 15,1967.
Eugenia M.,Apr.14,1964.
Irving,Dec.30,1994.
GOACH
Ira,Nov.6,1958.
GOLDBERG
Livinghton,Apr.10,1933,s.b.
GOODRICH
Alice,Oct.27,1989.
Ralph,Oct.27,1989.
GOODWIN
Alice Louise,Mar.8,1924.
Claarinda Buzzell,1809-1898.
Jane Rounds,1818-1903,w/o Moses.
Moses,1808-1872.
children/o Moses & Jane R.:
  Mary Abbie,1843-1851;
  Philena,1841-1863;
  Alice Louisa,1848-1924;
  Charlotte Rounds,1844-May 2,1928.
GORDON
child/o Irving,Nov.15,1923.
Grace,Oct.15,1979.
Hamilton,Oct.14,1930.
Helen M.,Apr.18,1911.
Irvin H.,Feb.17,1947.
Irving D.,Nov.10,1910.
Lyman,Sept.25,1922.
Marion L.,July 27,1939.
Mary B.,Sept.4,1965.

Matilda Miles,Apr.26,1945.
Robert,May 3,1986.
William F.,June 4,1945.
GORHAM
Frederick H.,1858-1858.
Frederick,1821-1878,s/o Wm.
Sarah C. King,1827-1899,w/o Fred.
William F.,1864-1945.
GOSS
Harriett H.,Nov.14,1946.
GOULD
Clarence F.,Sept.17,1955.
Sarah M.,Oct.7,1974.
GRAFFAM
Alice M.,July 5,1938.
Charlie W.,Feb.23,1920.
Clifford A.,Aug.1884,4m,s/o T.S.& L.M.
Clifford,July 6,1913.
Delbert,Nov.10,1910.
Ferdinard,June 13,1960.
Ida M.,1856-1899,w/o J.W.
XX,1882-1882,inf/o C.W.& A.M.
Johana,XXXX.
John W.,Nov.23,1914.
Lucille,May 13,1981.
Lucy J.,Feb.23,1959.
Lydia,XXXX.
Melville D.,May 17,1956.
Minnie G.,May 21,1985.
Nelson H.,Apr.30,1975.
Nelson W.,July 21,1961.
Samuel, Feb.28,1900,67y.
GRANT
Charles Robert,May 18,1981.
David,Oct.15,1986.
Herbert N.1844-Sept.22,1909.
GREENE
Bethiah T. Lincoln Staples,1803-1896,
1st w/o Alexander Staples,
2nd w/o Samuel Greene.
GREENLEAF
Ernest,Oct.15,1986.
Ethel A.,Apr.26,1967.
GREENOUGH
Roland,Oct.4,1965.
Roland,Dec.15,1975.
Barbara,Jan.22,1953.
Railton,Aug.19,1959.
GREY
Annie L.,July 20,1965.
Harold F.,Nov.29,1960.
GRIFFIN
Drusilla B.,Aug.8,1921.
George H.,Oct.11,1922.
GROUARD
Charles S.,Aug.24,1933.
Fannie I.,Feb.5,1957.

Leonard C.,1821-1905.
Mary W.,1830-1908,w/o L.C.
Walter A.,1854-1856.
GROVER
Almon,Apr.21,1948.
Carrie B.,Jan.26,1959.
GUPTILL
Arthur L.,Mar.3,1956.
Edward W.,Mar.29,1910.
Edward A.,1920-May 4,1942,
s/o Wm.S. & Ruth.
Ethel W.,July 21,1982.
Joel E.,1844-1905.
Lucy E.,1847-Feb.12,1916.
Mary C.,1821-1893,w/o Wm.(1895).
Nellie A.,Dec.2,1934.
Ruth Louise,May 1978.
Vernon C.,June 1,1984.
William,1825-1895.
children/o Edward W. & Nellie A.:
Edward W.,1895-1897;
William S.,1888-1926.
GUSTIN
Darius,1836-1914.
Edith M.,XXX.
Elmer E.,Feb.7,1950.
Grace D.,Apr.23,1975,w/o Henry O.
Helena,Oct.13,1953.
Henry O.,Oct.13,1953.
Lena,XXXX.
Lizzie Chase,1838-1864,w/o Darius.
Lyman,May 13,1932.
Myrtle,Oct.13,1953.
Nancy A.,Aug.21,1942.
Susan Foss,1840-1884,w/o Darius.
children/o Darius & Lizzie:
Daniel Chase,1844-1884;
Lizzie,1869-1869;
Rose,1857-1881.
HADLOCK
XX,Apr.29.1944.
Guy F.,Jr.,Apr.24,1953.
Vera L.,May 18,1944.
HAGNE
Mary Russell,Oct.30,1944.
HAGUE
Abbie B.S.,Jan.18,1929.
Albert H.,Sept.15,1975.
Marjorie Abbott,Aug.1,1987.
William B.,Oct.7,1923.
HALE
Charles,May 2,1978.
Ella Rebecca,Apr.5,1926.
infant,Nov.16,1961.
HALL
Addie R.,Apr.28,1946.
Caroline H.Mar.19,1909.

Carrie B.,Nov.22,1844-Mar.16,1909,
w/o Levi.
Emma E.,June 19,1873-Apr.1,1894.
George C.,Nov.24,1885-June 2,1872.
Leonard F.,July 16,1914.
Leonard F.,Aug.8,1933.
Leonard F.,Nov.20,1987.
Levi,Apr.20,1832-Dec.24,1895.
Stanley F.,June 17,1966.
HAM
s.b. infant,Mar.17,1965.
HAMBLEN
A. Raymond,1881-1898.
Albert M.,Feb.22,1943.
Allen,1789-1853,h/o Lydia Winslow.
Archelaus L.,1831-1904.
Byron,1831-1893.
Cyrus,1827-1895,s/o Nath.& Sarah.
Earl W.,1877-1882.
Esther,May 26,1818-Aug.5,1891,
w/o William M.
Hattie E. Carll,1842-1889,w/o A.L.
Howard,1871,1y,s/o Bryon & Mary.
inf/twins,1951.
infant,July 15,1952.
Levi,1828-1871.
Lydia Winslow,Mar.28,1872,80y.
Mary,1839-1906,w/o Byron.
Nathaniel,1794-1867.
Sarah J. Carll,1834-1896,w/o Levi.
Sarah H. Shane,1800-1880,w/o Nath.
William M.,Dec.8,1812-Aug.26,1866.
children/o Joseph & Mary:
XX,1830;
Emeline L.,Nov.6,1840,12y;
Mary E.,May 30,1845,20y.
children/o Levi & Sarah:
George N.,1856-1894;
Henry A.,1869-1897;
Maria C.,1858-1933.
HAMBLIN
Allen,Mar.10,1916.
Almeny,Oct.24,1911.
Arthur T.,June 24,1938.
Charles L.,Apr.16,1944.
Clara E.,June 19,1917.
Clinton J.,Jan.28,1951.
Clyde S.,Feb.4,1969.
E.C.,Sept.24,1918.
Effie May,Aug.8,1943.
Fannie H.,Nov.6,1917.
Forrest B.,Aug.4,1975.
Franklin,Nov.6,1917.
Fred L.,June 1,1935.
Howard,Mar.10,1916.
Howard,Dr.,Feb.4,1941.
Ida Octavia Mosher,Apr.24,1941.

infant,1950.
Jessie,Aug.27,1957.
Lewis A.,Aug.2,1930.
Lydia,Mar.10,1916.
Maria C.,July 30,1933.
Mary E.,Mar.10,1909.
Mora F.,Jan.7,1957.
Robert C.,Nov.25,1970.
Ruth W.,Apr.28,1967.
Stewart B.,Nov.6,1976.
Susie C.,May 21,1959.
HAMBURY
Benjamin,1795-1886.
Caroline E.,1836-1890,d/o B.& E.
Eunice,1803-1888,w/o Benjamin.
HAMLEN
Arthur M.,Dec.113,1845,25y.
Joseph,Jan.30,1849.
Sewall,Mar.21,1846,30y.
XX,Apr.23,1843,49y.
HANAS
infant,Sept.28,1949.
HANAFORD
Carroll,Apr.12,1973.
HANNAFORD
Charles B.,Jr.,May 1,1967.
Charles B.,Jan.4,1952.
Charlie G.,Dec.1906,6y,s/o Harry H.
Eugene F.,1899-1900.
Hattie J.,Oct.7,1924.
John,Apr.5,1968.
Marguerite,Sept.2,1987.
HANSCOM
Abbie H. Strout,1838-1895,
w/o Almon W. (b.1831).
Ada,Sept.2,1965.
Almon,Sept.28,1868,69y.
Charles,1860-1905.
Charlotte A.,1897.
Charlotte,Apr.7,1921.
Daniel,Esq.,June 15,1799-
Mar.18,1833,h/o Mahala Virgin.
Ella E.,July 3,1944.
Esther Libby,July 3,1830,72y,
w/o Humphrey.
Eunice Sloane,June 27,1860,
69y,2nd w/o John H.
Eunice,1854.
Flossie E.,Nov.2,1946.
Frances Jane,Jan.24,1832,6m,
d/o Dan & Mahala.
Gertrude,May 3,1988.
Gertrude,May 11,1947.
Humphrey,1905.
Humphrey,Jan.28,1754-Sept.19,1836.
Isabella Deering,May 17,1870,60y,
2nd w/o Almon.

John H.,Nov.27,1880,89y,
1st w. Fanny Riggs,d.1823.
John,May 19,1763-May 10,1836.
John,July 15,1953.
Joshua,1886.
Luther,June 26,1930.
Mary,Feb.20,1830,56y,w/o John.
Myrtle,Nov.11,1917.
Rebeckah Hanscom,1797-
July 11,1835,37y,w/o Almon.
Rufus,Dec.23,1801-Nov.20,1873.
Sabra,1846.
William,1900.
HANSCOMB
Charlotte,Nov.7,1921.
Frank E.,1844-1893.
Walter G.,June 10,1910.
Walter S.,Btry.E,2 Arty,Span.Am.War.
HANSCOME
Ernest M.,Oct.7,1934.
Flossie E.,Mar.26,1946.
Luther,June 26,1930.
Myrtle E.,Nov.11,1917.
inf/twins,Sept.27,1957.
HANSON
Charles,1806-1908.
Clara B.,Nov.15,1956.
Frank R.,1896-1897.
Fred,May 5,1947.
Georgia Davis,1854-1927,wo Jos.B.
Hattie M.,1867-1867.
Isaac A.,1862-Apr.12,1933,h/o Nettie.
Joseph B.,1846-1899.
Luther F.,1872-1872,s/o Chas.& R.M.
Marion,1899-1902.
Mary Bean,1809-1885,w/o Oliver.
Nellie W.,June 18,1963.
Nettie Maria,1866-May 8,1927,w/o I.
Oliver,1806-1855.
Rancyanna Mayo,1837-Aug.31,1915,
w/o Charles.
Rosie M.,1871-1872.
HARDING
Alexander,Oct.8,1862,72y.
Angeline T.,Dec.27,1811-Aug.6,1900,
w/o Colman.
Annah Bacon,Feb.1861,93y,
2nd w/o Nicholas.
Annie,July 15,1925.
Charles Gorham,1838-1854?,
s/o Chas. & Eliza A.
Charles W.,1854-Aug.13,1918.
Charles,Capt.,1805-1886.
Clara B. Garland,1854-Oct.5,1927.
Colman,Col.,Dec.11,1813-
July 15,1885.
David,Feb.4,1854,57y.

Edward,Dec.24,1837-May 6,1842.
Edward,May 25,1929.
Edward Carlton,1869-1871,
s/o Edward & Iza C.
Edwin L.,May 27,1914.
Eliza A. Bailey,1812-1884,w/o Chas.
Emma,June 9,1927.
Etta Low,Feb.19,1931.
Frank C.,Nov.10,1915.
Fred A.,Nov.27,1936.
Fred C.,Mar.10,1916.
Fred W.,Aug.20,1922.
Frederick C.,June 25,1955.
Frederic,May 6,1842,2y,
d/o Joseph & Louisa.
George B.,Jan.22,1846-Nov.9,1895.
Grace L.,Dec.1,1935.
Harry L.,1869-Nov.11,1935.
Iza C. Carlton,1836-1872,w/o Edward
Joseph,Dec.18,1785-Feb.8,1845,
s/o Zephaniah.
Josephine,Apr.7,1934.
Josiah,July 16,1920.
Josiah,Sept.25,1835-May 6,1842.
Josiah,XXXX,Co.C.,104 Ill. Inf.
Julia H.,Sept.21,1948.
Louisa Bryant,June 4,1875,70y,
w/o Joseph.
Mary A.,Mar.3,1925.
Mary A. Edwards,1807-1881,
w/o William B.
Mary C.,1867-July 30,1957,
d/o Roscoe & M.E.
Mary E. Higgins,1835-May 25,1918,
w/o Roscoe.
May E.,1853-1853,d/o Chas.& Eliza A.
Miriam Bacon,July 24,1818,53y,
1st w/o Nicholas.
Nancy,Nov.9,1868,31y,w/o Robert.
Nicholas,Mar.16,1838,72y,
s/o Zephaniah.
Roscoe G.,1834-Nov.16,1910,
h/o M.E.Higgins.
Ross H.,1882-1904.
Roxana V.,Jan.20,1873,69y,w/o Alex.
Ruth Etta,Apr.26,1928.
Sarah I.,Apr.25,1953.
Walter,Nov.10,1924.
William B.,Col.,1802-1859.
William P.,July 9,1962.
HARIUSH
Sylvia,May 14,1954.
HARLOW
Charles F.,July 13,1973.
Frank L.,Mar.17,1938.
Grace,Aug.13,1964.
Ida A.,May 29,1963.

Mary H.,July 21,1920.
HARMAN
Adalbert,Oct.8,1945.
Albert,May 7,1950.
Benjamin L.,May 6,1919.
Charlotte A.,May 1,1948.
Delia A.,May 17,1951.
Dwight L.,May 1,1964.
Ellen H.,Aug.3,1916.
Lucy L.,May 12,1942.
HARMON
Delphina P.,Jan.2,1882,59y.
G. Howard,Apr.11,1961.
Joseph,Oct.13,1848,50y.
Mary J.,Sept.18,1969.
Mildred E.,Apr.18,1975.
Mellon K.,Mar.2,1926.
Russell,May 2,1984.
Shirley,Feb.21,1895,72y.
Shirley,Jr.,Oct.28,1864.
children/o Mellon & Delia:
Cecil M.,1888-1894;
Neal S.,1895-1895;
Ruth,1905-1905.
HARRIMAN
Cynthia,Mar.5,1882,76y.
HARRINTON
Ellen,May 4,1979.
Kathryn Dal,Apr.18,1953,infant.
William A.,May 8,1959.
HARRIS
Morgan,1825-1904.
HARRISON
Arthur A.,Apr.25,1962.
child/o Herb,Apr.29,1923.
Herbert W.,Apr.23,1935.
Joseph W.,Aug.3,1935.
Viola C.,July 28,1918.
Wendall,Nov.9,1978.
HASKELL
Arthur,Dec.15,1932.
Bertha,May 10,1979.
HASKEY
Clayton J.,Sept.22,1975.
Shirley J.,Apr.23,1976.
HASSETT
Henry,May 9,1987.
HASTY
Annie L.,Dec.9,1931.
John A.,Dec.16,1931.
HATCH
Jane McIntosh,June 5,1844,85y,
 2nd w/o Asa.
Jane,Dec.16,1834,36y,
 d/o Asa & Rebecca.
HATTENBURG
C.E.,Apr.21,1948.

Elizabeth,Aug.15,1960.
Lola I.,Apr.28,1966.
John,May 23,1986.
HAWKES
Arnold R.,July 2,1976.
Dennie,Dec.12,1990.
Derna,Aug.1,1979.
George,Oct.31,1985.
Josiah,May 20,1985.
Hattie E. Rounds,Nov.13,1886,
 42y,w/o Geo.F.,& d/o Robt.& Harriet.
Kenneth,Apr.30,1989.
Lincoln F.,Mar.31,1987.
Raymond,Nov.9,1988.
HAWKINS
Charles,Feb.17,1955,h/o Clara M.
Clara M. Coburn,1869-July 16,1945.
Sarah Lane,Dec.8,1840,50y.
HAYES
Cornelius,Oct.31,1946.
Elijah,Dec.22,1847,42y.
Eliza G.,Nov.10,1848,34y,w/o Elijah.
Georgiana,Dec.4,1980.
Jennie C.,June 24,1939.
John F.,Feb.28,1959.
Sarah S.,Nov.28,1839,3y,
 d/o Erastus & Mary.
HEATH
A.G.,1861-1900.
E.I.,1838-1905,w/o Giles.
F.L.,1859-1900.
infant,Nov.17,1942.
HEDGES
Helen P.,June 7,1969.
Mary Louise,May 18,1926.
HEMSCHEMEYER
Mary,1846-July 1,1926,w/o Henry.
HENKEL
Eleanor,May 5,1979.
John E.,Apr.17,1981.
M.Katherine,Sept.16,1942.
Lula,May 31,1990.
Ove,May 10,1972.
HERRICK
Abbott L.,Apr.22,1955.
Florence,Apr.22,1985.
Fred,June 6,1984.
Georgia A.,Jan.11,1920.
Melville W.,Sept.7,1918.
Nellie,Jan.5,1924.
HERSEY
Clarissa A.,Feb.17,1850,2y,d/o S.& N.
Ida M.,1936.
Lydia M. Fuller,1838-1895,w/o Wm.P.
Nancy,1812-1893,w/o Seth,Jr.
Rebecca,Feb.18,1850,7y,d/o S.& N.

Seth,Dec.5,1853,78y, 2nd w.
Rebecca Whitten,d.Jan.12,1853.
Seth,May 28,1842,4y,s/o Seth & N.
Seth,Jr.,Aug.18,1857,50y.
Tamsin Cushing,Dec.28,1839,60y,
  1st w/o Seth.
Thomas,Apr.11,1841,24y,
  s/o Seth & Tamsin.
William P.,1834-Sept.21,1910.
HEWES
Searles,May 16,1987.
Marjorie,May 25,1991.
Vyndel A.,Apr.27,1968.
HICKS
G.H.,1865-1930 ?.
HIGGINS
Affie R.,Mar.28,1963.
Ellen,Apr.25,1990.
George F.,Mar.28,1944.
John Lowell,Sept.16,1909.
John, 1803-1885.
Julia Maria,June 9,1925.
Martha Topping,1814-1880.
Sarah A.,Dec.16,1909.
Sybil,June 1,1933.
HILL
Alfred,May 8,1990.
Andrew W.,Oct.12,1963.
Frances Plaisted,July 28,1975.
Hannah W.,Feb.9,1945.
Maud Coffin,May 14,1982.
Robert,Oct.11,1979.
Virginia,Nov.14,1994,w/o Alfred.
William B.,June 10,1962.
HILLIARD
Eliza Heddle,July 15,1837,62y,
  w/o Rev. Timothy.
Harriet Sarah Waldo,Aug.1811,22m.
Timothy,Jan.2,1842,65y,
  s/o Timothy & Mary.
HINKLEY
Charles K.,1843-July 11,1924.
Elizabeth B.,1880-Oct.30,1954.
John A.,1848-Dec.17,1915.
John Toldord,1896-1897,
  s/o J.A. & M.E.T.
Maria Paine,Jan.8,1926,81y,
  w/o Stepehn (1898)..
Mary Carter,Feb.17,1877,36y,
  w/o Stephen (1898).
Mary C.,1881-Sept.19,1962.
Mary C.,Jan.20,1833-Feb.1,1903.
Mary E. Tolford,1861-1900,
  w/o John A.
Robert L.,1882-May 19,1946.
Sophronia Shedd,Jan.5,1890,
  85y,w/o Stephen.

Stephen,Apr.19,1867,68y.
Stephen,Jan.4,1898,59y.
Susan S.,1835-Sept.12,1911.
William H.,July 8,1842,2y.
HOAG
Frances F.,June 1993.
HOADLEY
Fannie A.Libby,Jan.3,1847-
  Dec.28,1911,w/o Lawrence.
HOBBS
Rose E.,1846-Mar.10,1916.
HOBSON
Betsey Hancock,1792-1866.
Eliza Jane,Apr.27,1927.
Jabez, Capt.,1790-1874.
children/o Jabez & Betsey:
  Elizabeth J.,1837-1927;
  Jabez,1837-1905.
HODGDON
Alvah T.,Sept.1,1943.
John Charles,Mar.9,1950.
Matha E.,Apr.24,1969.
HODGKINS
Benjamin P.,Aug.1,1937.
Winfred F.,June 22,1957.
HOIT
Frances E.,Dec.24,1849,7y,
  d/o Wm.& Martha.
William,June 15,1812-Mar.31,1888.
HOLDEN
Gertrude W.,Feb.12,1959.
Jennie Libby,1944,
Leverett C.,Sept.17,1941.
Minnie A.,Feb.4,1917.
Minnie A.,June 28,1927.
HOLMES
Ruth M.,1925.
HOOPER
Edward A.,1838-May 3,1910,
  h/o Nellie Estes.
Edward A.,2nd.,1891-1918,in France.
Ellen M. Estes,1849-July 14,1932.
Eva L.,May 19,1935.
Gary,Nov.11,1970.
Graver C.,May 24,1964.
Mable,1960 ?.
Ray H.,May 7,1946.
Ruth C.,Apr.21,1976.
HOPKINS
Herbert S.,Sept.25,1963.
Nellie,Jan.7,1954.
HOPKINSON
Abbie L.,1858-Feb.13,1935,
  d/o John B. & Sarah F.
Frank,Jan.13,1932.
John B.,1824-1898.
Rebecca,Dec.11,1874,90y,w/o Steph.

Sarah F.,1829-1903,w/o John B.
Stephen,Mar.7,1855,83y.
Susan W.,Jan.11,1957.
William,Aug.3,1843.
HOSKIN
Barbara,Apr.15,1983.
Imogene,July 31,1957.
HOVEY
H.M.,Sept.15,1913.
Minnie Eaton,Apr.11,1873,w/o M.M.
Myron M.,1913.
HOWARD
Melissa F.,June 24,1969.
Todd,Oct.5,1982.
HOWE
Elizabeth,June 30,1994.
Elwood,July 3,1987.
Sarah H.,Nov.29,1956.
Lincoln H.,May 25,1964.
W.H.,May 9,1946.
HOYT
Alice D.,Aug.9,1956.
Bonnie,Sept.13,1984.
Esta Louise,Feb.9,1936.
Florence N.,Oct.12,1925.
Frank E.,July 20,1972.
Harold,Aug.10,1972.
Harry,Jr.,May 31,1990.
Harry A.,Sr.,June 7,1962.
Katherine S.,Apr.29,1951.
Lucy E.,1847-1903,w/o S.C.(1915).
Lydia,July 4,1964.
Samuel,Nov.4,1989.
Samuel C.,Aug.14,1914.
Samuel C.,1837-1915.
Sarah Hamilton,Sept.17,1953,inf.
HUFF
Clinton A.,Nov.4,1918.
Clifton Aubren,Feb..28,1927.
Esther,May 8,1991,w/o Clinton.
Fred W.,Oct.14,1951.
Howard A.,Sept.25,1967.
Irving H.,Apr.21,1965.
John S.,Mar.6,1943.
Lila,May 6,1994.
Lois F.,Aug.23,1941.
infant,Dec.2,1956.
infant,Jan.6,1938.
infant,Oct.11,1955.
Richard F.,Apr.30,1962.
XX, May 26,1911.
HUGHES
Caroline,Apr.23,1990.
William,May 13,1992.
HUNT
Gregory,Oct.11,1955,infant.

Joseph,Apr.14,1867,83y,
Mary,Oct.6,1865,81y,w/o Joseph.
HUNTER
infant,Dec.8,1941.
Andrea S.,Dec.20,1965.
HUSE
Marion,May 25,1988.
Oscar E.,Dec.1,1959.
HUSSEY
Albert,Aug.28,1888,4d,s/o Alb.& C.F.
Albert F.,1839-1890.
Carrie Fogg,Feb.14,1846-
Feb. 26,1926,w/o Albert F.
HUTCHERSON
Alice,Mar.8,1951.
Annnie F.,Sept.6,1943.
Augustus S.,1839-Mar.31,1925.
Blanche M.,July 16,1914.
George,July 28,1980.
Jason,Jan.13,1951.
Louise C.,Feb.18,1893,15y.
Lucius,Oct.15,1966.
Olive A. Smith,1848-Sept.22,1920,
w/o Augustus S.
Sadie F.,July 10,1892,10y.
Susan,Aug.2,1960.
Syrene Emma,June 26,1925.
HUTCHINSON
Arthur,Aug.18,1953.
Florence E.,Sept.21,1965.
HUTT
Ethel,July 11,1955.
George,Apr.21,1970.
HUTTON
Alexis Marie,June 4,1986.
HYBERTS
Doreen Ray,Aug.14,1952.
Philip,May 5,1993.
Rowena,Apr.23,1976.
Roxanne,Jan.6,1959.
HYMAN
Hazel,Apr.30,1992.
INGALLS
Joseph P.,July 16,1922.
Phineas,Feb.21,1858,60y.
IRISH
Elizabeth Roulliet,1849-1865,
d/o Thaddius & Ellen A.
Ellen A. Davis,1827-1869,
1st w/o Thaddius P.
Fred D.,July 16,1923.
Hazel M.,July 28,1970.
Isaac C.,1803-1887.
James H.,Oct.29,1919.
James Henry,1823-1846,
s/o James & Rebecca.

James,Gen.,Aug.18,1776-
June 30,1863.
Junia,May 2,1973.
Junia H.,Apr.22,1947.
Lester,Sept.14,1989.
Louisa Mason,1789-1881,2nd w/o Jas.
Lucy J. Rice,1830-1900,2nd w/o Thad.
Maria M. Murch,1809-1846,w/o I.C.
Maria,Oct.11,1924.
Marshall,1814-1885,h/o Mary T.
Mary T. McLellan,1832-1894.
Philip J.,July 5,1934.
Rebecca Chadbourn,Apr.9,1780-
Oct.5,1831,1st w/o James.
Thaddeus Pomeroy,1824-Oct.19,1912.
William M.,1855-1885.
IRVING
David,May 1,1982.
JACKSON
Eliphalet W.,Mar.25,1924.
JAMES
Cyrus D.,1844-1862.
Joseph,1818-1893.
Sarah,1817-1890,w/o Joseph.
JAQUES
Leroy & Merle,XXXX,ch/o P.& L.W.
JARVIS
Theodore,Sept.16,1959.
JENSEN
Mark Christian,May 17,1969.
JEWELL
Edwin S.,July 7,1930.
Hannah F.,Sept.17,1925.
Morrill,Nov.1,1915.
Morrill,Dec.26,1936.
Nathan,May 5,1990.
Mark,May 21,1969.
James C.,Feb.21,1928.
JEWETT
Fannie A.,1836-1883,w/o George H.
George H.,1827-1888.
James C.,1928.
Joseph S.,Mar.22,1867-Mar.22,1898.
Joseph S.,1863-1864.
Lizzie,1856-1886,w/o Jas.C.
Martha,Nov.2,1850,64y,
d/o Caleb & Betsey Bacon Jewett.
JOHNSON
Albert A.,Mar.9,1888,in Chicago.
Augustus,May 6,1870,62y.
Caroline,b.Limington,May 6,1831-
Dec.30,1875,w/o Thomas A.
Catherine,1831-1889,w/o Henry (1915)
Emily,Feb.10,1918.
Ernest,Nov.1,1969.
F.Ada Chase,1859-1883,w/o Fred H.
Fanny A.,Nov.1,1915.
Francis A.,XXXX.
Frank P.,Aug.9,1918.
Fred H.,Apr.23,1934.
George C.,Sept.24,1833-Mar.28,1892.
Georgia M.,Nov.6,1930.
Helen C.,Oct.23,1946.
Helen M.,Oct.31,1969.
Henry B.,Mar.4,1915.
infant,Jan.31,1950.
Lewis R.,Feb.28,1919.
Lucy A.,June 16,1950.
Martha E.,June 4,1916.
Mary H.,Apr.20,1875,70y,
w/o Augustus.
Mary N. Meserve,1814-1888.
Mary,July 25,1880,77y,w/o Robt.R.
Melville,Oct.20,1941.
Nancy T.,Aug.5,1805-Aug.27,1882,
w/o Wm.
Nathaniel,1807-1891,h/o Mary N.M.
Robert R.,Sept.15,1874,75y.
Rose Chute,Apr.30,1920.
Ruth R.,Oct.21,1925.
Thomas A.,b.Cornish,Mar.5,1830-
Apr.14,1873.
Walter H.,Dec.7,1969.
William,Apr.24,1803-Aug.18,1877.
William,1786-1883.
XX,July 1854,4y,s/o Randall & Eliza.
JONES
Alice F.,Apr.26,1921.
Amy,1862-1887,w/o Thomas.
Charles H.,May 28,1927.
Charles W.,Mar.18,1920.
Eliza W.,1825-Sept.29,1914,
w/o Freeman L.
Embert S.,Oct.25,1930.
Fannie,May 30,1920.
Freeman L.,Mar.31,1863,40y.
Martha M. Estes,June 19,1835-
Dec.16,1921.
Thomas,1856-1907.
Warren H.D.,Aug.15,1972.
William H.,May 17,1834-Mar.28,1903.
JORDAN
Abby F.,1836-1892.Edwin W.,1828-
1856.
Elinor Tate,1800-1886,w/o Nathaniel.
Hattie M.,Dec.23,1912.
Henery N.,1832-1882.
John W.,Apr.14,1924.
Lydia A.,1838-May 2,1920,w/o H.N.
Martha E.,Aug.11,1833-June 1,1916,
w/o George C.
Mellen D.,1872-1906.
Nathaniel,1793-1872.

JOSE
Almira,Dec.4,1919.
Charles A.,1847-1918,Civil War.
Henry R.,Feb.14,1915.
Sarah J.,1848-1905,w/o Chas.A.
JOY
Harold,Apr.25,1990.
Marion,July 28,1987.
KANE
Cornelia B.,June 14,1954.
John P.,Jan.31,1925.
KEATING
James S.,Oct.26,1937.
Nellie F.,May 7,1954.
KEENE
Arthur,Jr.,July 18,1974.
KELLEY
Charles,Jan.31,1958.
E.M.M.,June 23,1918.
KELLOGG
Elizabeth,1805-1870,w/o Gardiner.
Gardiner,1802-1841.
Mary F.,Dec.7,1916.
children/o Gardiner & Elizabeth:
Charles F.,1841-1885;
Gardiner,1829-1900;
Louisa T.,1834-1893;
Lucy E.,1837-1906;
Mary Elizabeth,1831-1831.
KELLY
Annie M.,May 11,1971.
KELSEY
Mary L.,Aug.12,1835-Sept.8,1908.
KENDALL
Elizabeth Robie,Oct.28,1987.
KENNIE
Gladys M.,Jan.23,1944.
Jeremiah,Nov.26,1957.
Malcolm,May 9/23,1993.
KEY
Joseph,Feb.24,1977.
KIMBALL
Blanche,Aug.30,1982.
Carrie T.,June 11,1954.
Charles H.,Apr.16,1931.
Clinton,Sept.17,1982.
Dorothy,July 18,1986.
Earl T.,Feb.18,1960.
Ephraim,Nov.17,1955.
Florence A.,Nov.2,1916,w/o Wm.P.
George,Feb.17,1896,7m,s/o J.& M.A.
John F.,Apr.12,1877,57y.
Marcena J.,1819-1905,w/o Melville.
Mary Ann,May 15,1902,85y, w/o John F.
Melville C.,1824-Jan.3,1911, h/o Jane Bacon.

infant,Apr.26,1935,s.b.
Philip H.,Dr.,July 7,1942.
William H.,July 11,1925.
William P.,Dec.27,1932.
William Alfred,1879-1892,s/o W.P.& F
KING
Ann W. Bixby,1816-1889,w/o Rufus.
Chester,1887-1887.
Esther Kennard,1814-1898,w/o Cyrus.
James,1774-1847,h/o Sarah T.
Susanna Thompson,1704-1874.
William B.,June 2,1814-June 17,1907.
children of James & Susanna:
Charles,1823-1884,unm. s/o J.& S.
Cyrus,1809-1898,s/o J.& S.
James T.,1821-1878,unm. s/o J.& S.
James,1811-1814,s/o Jas.& S.T.
Joseph,1813-1892,unm. s/o J.& S.
Rufus,1807-1889,s/o J.& S.
Susan A.,1817-1898,d/o J.& S.
KINNIE
Myrtle V.,May 17,1967.
Roy W.,June 11,1961.
KIRBY
Wilma,Apr.23,1982.
KNAPTON
Alice Moody,Jan.6,1945.
Anna M.,18822-1907.
Annie M.,Aug.25,1911.
Donald B.,May 23,1957.
Earle,Oct.23,1984.
Ernest F.,Dec.16,1950.
Eva M.,June 14,1966.
Fred,Sept.12,1944.
infant,June 25,1915.
Mary E.,1868-Dec.1906,w/o Wm.B.
Robert,Feb.24,1977.
William B.,1858-Apr.19,1952.
KNEELAND
Cornelius,Apr.6,1925.
Eunice A.,July 13,1973.
Fannie S.,Oct.30,1933.
Henry W.,Feb.15,1957.
Ira,June 7,1909.
Ira Staples,1893-1903.
KNIGHT
Ella F.,Feb.21,1940.
John W.,Feb.7,1949,80y.
Katherine E.,July 11,1960,infant.
Mildred,May 4,1992.
Willard M.,Aug.22,1975.
KNOWLES
Mildred Sotter,Aug.11,1929,infant.
KRAMLICH
infant,Aug.13,1959,s.b.
KYTE
Margaret,1986.

Robert L.,Sept.28,1967.
LABRANCHE
Joseph Roger,Dec.16,1987.
LACHANCE
Todd Lee,July 19,1968,infant.
LaFONTAINE
Joseph,Jan.31,1933.
LaFOUNTAIN
Lizzy A.,Feb.21,1956.
LAMPRON
Theodore,May 22,1992.
LANDRY
Annabel,Nov.1979.
Annie M.,Nov.22,1948.
George A.,Feb.1,1948.
Robert J.,June 15,1926.
LANE
Cylence,Nov.6,1984.
Ernest A.,Mar.3,1963.
George Wm.,Feb.26,1840,3y,
 s/o Wm.A. & Ann N.
Sabrina J.,July 10,1925.
William H.,June 18,1915.
LAROCHELLE
Ann,Nov.8,1977.
Arthur E.,Apr.3,1950.
Betty Lou,Feb.8,1956.
Larochelle Harry,May 13,1921,s.b.
Harry,Sr.,May 27,1967.
Joan L.,Feb.8,1956.
Patricia A.,Feb.8,1956.
Sarah E.,June 21,1944.
William G.,Apr.5,1939.
LARRABEE
Annie,Apr.18,1977.
George M.,Nov.16,1965.
LARRY
Eunice,Dec.31,1910.
Isabelle S.,Jan.17,1915.
John,Apr.23,1872,77y.
Lucy,Mar.12,1876,79y,w/o John.
LAWRENCE
Alice E.,Oct.3,1923.
Charles,June 27,1959.
LEATHERS
Bernard I.,June 19,1958.
LEAVITT
Asa,1810-1857.
Asa,June 17,1921.
Bertha L.,Oct.11,1930.
Clara E.,Apr.11,1914.
Eliza A.,Dec.23,1811-May 19,1888.
Elizabeth B. Moore,1856-1899,
 w/o J.Samuel.
Elizabeth E. Wescott,1843-
 Oct.18,1917,w/o George B.

Emeline Frost,1819-1900,
 w/o Asa (1857).
Emilie,May 15,1918.
Emily F.,1847-1850.
Emily,June 17,1921.
Eva L.,Hooper,1872-1935.
George B.,1844-Feb.23,1922.
Ida M.,1878-Apr.20,1941,
 d/o G.B.&E.E.W.
J. Samuel,May 16,1923.
John S.,Sr.,1830-Nov.28,1909.
Joseph,Feb.16,1904-Feb.1,1886.
Henry J.,Mar.9,1838-Mar.1907,
 h/o Mary Harriman,s/o Joseph &
 Eliza A. Jackson Leavitt.
John S.,Deacon,Dec.1909,79y.
Lydia French,1820-Mar.28,1907,
 w/o Deacon John.
Mary Harriman,Jan.25,1921.
Mary R.,Apr.26,1935.
William B.,June 17,1921.
William P.,1853-1907.
LEBER
Emil,Sept.9,1983.
LEE
Mary E.,1824-1867.
LEHOUX
Susan,Sept.6,1979.
LEIGHTON
Adelonz,Aug.15,1988.
Jessee,Oct.8,1981.
Raymond E.,Apr.4,1966.
LERMOND
Etta E.,June 9,1940.
Leonard J.,Nov.28,1943.
Marcia L.,Oct.2,1915.
Gertrude M.,June 6,1920.
LEWIS
Catherine,1813-Mar.19,1825,
 d/o Lothrop & M.J.P.
Celia L.,July 4,1944.
Florence,May 20,1972.
George L.,May 11,1933.
George,Rev.,Feb.26,1910.
Hugh M.,Apr.4,1939.
Lothrop,Oct.9,1822,58y.
Katherine B.,Apr.3,1913.
Mary McLellan,June 21,1938.
Mary Jasckson Prescott Little,
 May 30,1863,88y,w/o Lotthrop.
Mary Payne Files,July 17,1909,
 93y,wid/o Lothrop.
Percy R.,Feb.10,1946.
Philip P.,Dr.,Dec.3,1926.
Robert V.,Sept.12,1969.
Ruth B.,July 5,1979.

LIBBEY
Charles O.,1811-1876.
Hannah McDougall,1809-1897,
  w/o Charles O.
inf/o Joshua,Mar.11,1938,s.b.
inf/o Joshua,Oct.31,1927.
children/o Charles & Hannah:
Curtis S.,1850-1850;
Emily D.,1844-1918,
  w/o Woodbury J. Dudley;
Mary E.,1839-1841;
Mary E.,Sept.4,1933;
Oliver,1835-1904.
LIBBY
Agnes M.,Aug.24,1974.
Andrew C.M.,1858-1863.
Ann S.,Jan.29,1870,49y,w/o David.
Anna Huston Phinney,Jan.9,1849,
  81y,w/o Simeon,d.1830.
Caroline E.,Apr.21,1941.
Catherine L.,Jan.10,1843,32y.
Charles,1841,s/o Joseph.
Clarissa H.,Mar.12,1925.
Clinton A.,June 11,1909.
Clinton A.,Jan.11,1929.
Cora E.,1867-1900,d/o C.S.& M.E.
Cyrus S.,1842-May 2,1907,
  h/o Martha.
Daniel B.,Feb.23,1823,7m,
  s/o Jacob & Mary.
Daniel C.,1816-1897.
Daniel,1784-1839.
Damaris,1822-1896.
David P.,Mar.5,1864,55y.
Delbert,1875-19XX.
Ed,May 18,1923.
Elaine J.,Oct.6,1984.
Eliza M.,Oct.13,1918.
Elizabeth Phinney,Mar.7,1824,
  35y,1w/o Joseph.
Elizabeth Warren,1791-1878,
  w/o Daniel (1839).
Ella W.,1857-1885.
Ellen Bragdon,Feb.19,1927.
Eugene H.,June 21,1931.
Evelyn B.,Nov.2,1972.
Frances I.,1854-Aug.31,1930.
Freeman,Oct.1,1987.
Hannah,Mar.2,1797-Sept.6,1881,
  d/o Wm.T. Riggs, 1st h.David Burnell,
  2nd h.John Libby.
Harriet Weeks,May 1,1932.
Harriet R.,July 29,1841,29y,
  d/o Isaac & Susan.
Harry M.,June 3,1965.
Isaac,June 24,1851,63y.
Iva J.,June 16,1942.
Jennie D.,Oct.13,1918.
Jennie M.,Sept.23,1883,20y,
  d/o M.P. & Mary.
Joseph,Sept.6,1835,49y.
Joshua,Sept.24,1981.
L.A.,Feb.16,1846-July 19,1899.
Leon M.,July 11,1955.
Lewis B.,1848-Oct.2,1915.
Lorinda,Mar.23,1955.
Love Phinney,May 22,1851,53y,
  2nd w/o Joseph.
Lula M.,June 30,1946.
Lydia E.,May 10,1930.
Martha Eastman,1840-Oct.19,1916.
Mary A.,June 16,1812-May 22,1897.
Mary B.,Oct.28,1872,61y,w/o Jacob.
Mary P. Thompson,Mar.20,1834-
  July 2,1915,w/o Milton P.
Mary (Polly),Aug.1993,68y,
  d/o Jeremiah & Gladys Wilson Libby.
Melissa S.,Oct.7,1956.
Merton,Aug.23,1974.
Milton P.,Oct.31,1872,35y.
Nellie B.,Aug.16,1957.
Pauline,Oct.3,1984.
Ruth W.M.,1820-1897,w/o D.C.
Stephen,Apr.14,1924.
Susan,Apr.27,1871,83y,w/o Isaac.
Susan,Jan.14,1839,21y,d/o I.& S.
sons/o E.G.& E.M.:
Adrian Keith,1903-1903;
XX,1895-1895.
children/o Joseph V.& Mary:
Katie,Sept.17,1850,3y,?:
XX,Sept.22,1852,2y;
Lulu ? M.,1856.
LIDBACK
Elizabeth Doughty,Nov.10,1987.
George M.,Nov.20,1946.
LINCOLN
Albert W.,June 27,1915.
Eliza Fogg,Dec.15,1828,27y,w/o Sam'l.
Eliza,Oct.18,1833,d/o Sam'l & Jane R.
Emma E.,May 7,1939.
Hattie L.,Sept.29,1932.
Hilda,May 11,1991.
LINNELL
Elisabeth,1811-1872,w/o Russell.
Russell,1808-1854.
children/o Russell & Elisabeth:
Thomas H.,1840-1842;
Emmaetta,1849-1850;
Charles R.,1836-1865;
John W.,1847-1862;
Frances E.,1834-1869;
Edward H.,1838-1888.

LITTLE
Allien K.,1859-1896.
Clara E.,May 29,1936.
Earle M.,1890-1893.
Edward S.,Feb.9,1920.
infant dau.,XXXX.
John O.,Sept.18,1809,17m,
s/o John P. & Mary J.
John P.,Mar.26,1809,36y.
Mildred E.,May 25,1948.
Moses E.,1852-1902.
Paul A.,Dec.12,1910.
Paul E.,July 24,1863,35y.
Rhoda T.,June 10,1890,60y,w/o P.E.
children/o Paul E. & Rhoda T.:
Frank H.,XXXX;
Herbert,XXXX;
LITTLEFIELD
Addie F.,1854-1930.
George E.,May 7,1959.
infant,May 14,1934,s.b.
Louise,Jan.15,1929.
Vestavious,1847-June 11,1909.
LOMBARD
Addie M.,Mar.18,1841-May 14,1935,
w/o William H.
Adeline,May 17,1935.
Albert,Mar.26,1887,60y.
Annie Eugenia,Nov.8,1944.
Bertie A.,Aug.1871,3wks,s/oW.H.&L.A.
Charity Merrill,Jan.13,1830,39y,
w/o Samuel.
Charles O.,July 14,1880,19y,
s/o Albert & Sarah.
XX,ch/o Charles,Nov.11,1922.
Clarence A.,July 15,1976.
E.L.,Jan.9,1915.
Ernest,May 7,1992.
Eunice F.,July 7,1924.
Hellen,Nov.184X,2y,d/o W.H. & Mary.
Herbert J.,Sept.9,1959.
James,Dec.18,1920.
James G.,Nov.11,1922.
Jesse A.,Jan.28,1941.
Jessie & Georgie,XXX,ch/o Albert & S.
Lucina W.,May 15,1950.
Lydia Ann,1856-May 1935,w/o Wm.
Mary R.,July 19,1862,39y,w/o Wm.H.
Richard,Sept.30,1880,85y.
Ruth,Oct.18,1987.
Sarah L. Silla,Mar.29,1887,60y,
w/o Albert.
Temperance,Nov.21,1864,69y,
w/o Richard.
Theodore,Aug.13,1988.
William H.,Apr.8,1819-June 7,1903.
William H.,Mar.5,1909.

William H.,Jr.,1852-1909,h/o Lydia.
LONG
Anson A.,Oct.9,1939.
June G.,Mar.14,1981.
Rebekah J. Frye, Oct.18,1858-
June 26,1932,w/o Anson A.
Stacia,May 31,1940
LORD
Annie B.,July 20,1972.
Ann White,1820-Nov.26,1929,w/o S.W.
Eben C.,June 21,1921.
Edward A.,1855-1856.
Fannie B.,June 29,1954.
Helen A.,1847-1850.
Henry R.,1851-Sept.24,1920.
Harry,Oct.24,1934.
Isaac,Apr.21,1837,53y.
Jennie L.,Dec.1,1941.
Samuel W.,1814-1887.
Samuel,Nov.26,1929.
Susie R.,1847-July 30,1925,w/o Henry.
L.Violette,Mar.30,1951.
Wilmot Perkins,Rev.,Feb.14,1941.
Winnie W.,June 8,1921.
LOVE
Nellie,Apr.28,1982.
Robert,Nov.23,1984.
LOVEITT
S. Louise,Mar.17,1961.
Ulysses G.,May 15,1918.
Ulysses G.,June 14,1937.
LOVENDALE
Christine,Nov.8,1924.
Helen A.,1880-1894,d/o J.E.& C.
John,Oct.22,1964.
John E.,Oct.11,1917.
Olga,June 18,1958.
LOW
Abbie C.,May 7,1877,53y,w/o Amon.
Amon,Nov.27,1852,32y.
LOWE
Esther Fogg,Dec.2,1934.
Harold,Aug.1,1993.
Lillian L.,1874-1875.
Lizzie,1891-1893.
Martha E.,Oct.13,1917.
Wilbur H.,Nov.20,1936.
William W.,Nov.24,1914.
LOWELL
Abbie P. Watson,1816-1896,
w/o Reuben.
Alice K.,June 10,1957.
Annie L.,June 11,1939.
Betsey Rice,1820-1889,w/o Henry.
Charles,Jan.26,1960.
Charles H.,1849-Feb.25,1909.
Clayton,July 27,1979.

Clifford E.,1874-1902.
Elizabeth S.,Nov.19,1918.
Elizabeth Bean,1849-1919,w/o Chas.H
Ephraim Morse,Jan.17,1965.
Ernest E.,Apr.22,1946.
Eva,Apr.13,1966.
Eva,Dec.22,1965.
Frances,May 11,1985.
George Philip,June 12,1973.
George W.,1822-1897.
Harriet L.,May 4,1959.
Harry H.,Apr.21,1970.
Henry,1819-1862.
Idella M.,1878-XXXX,w/o C.E.
John Richard,Sept.9,1929.
Leonara I.,June 25,1960.
Lewis H.,Jan.28,1940.
Lucy J.,1825-1849.
Reuben,1816-1882.
Richard P.,Jr.,Aug.13,1981.
Richard S.,Apr.21,1973.
Roland E.,Aug.28,1969.
Sarah J.,1827-Feb.12,1912.
Shirley,July 27,1979.
Stephen,1781-1848.
Wealthy,1788-1859,w/o Stephen.
infant,Aug.16,1957.
children/o George W.& Lucy J.:
  Julia E.,1847-1881;
  Lucy,1845-1846.
children/o George W. & Sarah J.:
  Lucy E.,1852-1887;
  Edwin H.,1855;
  Carrie F.,1859-1865;
  George,1867;.
children/o Henry & Betsey:
  Arthur,1859-1859;
  Fred E.,1861-1880;
  Herbert H.,1857-1863;
  John R.,1842-1905;
  Mary L.,1854-1860;
  Oscar A.,1847-1847.
children/o Reuben & Abbie P.W.:
  Abbie A.,1854-1857;
  Edward G.,1850-1863;
  Ellen A.,1845-1848;
  Greenlief M.,1848-1848.
LOWERY
Ellen Jennie,June 18,1842-
  July 9,1868,d/o Robt. & Mary Ann.
James,Aug.8,1841,11y,s/o R.& M.A.
Jane,Mar.7,1842,1y,d/o R. & M.A.
John N.,1846-1847,s/o Robt. & M.A.
Mary Ann Neil,Mar.4,1854,48y,
  w/o Robert.
Robert B.,Sept.17,1856,23y,
  in St.Louis,s/o Robt. & Mary Ann.

LUCE
Heidi,June 3,1983.
infant,July 24,1944,prem.
LUKE
Harrison R.,May 26,1973.
John R.,July 28,1972.
LURVEY
Michael,Dec.15,1987.
Florence Verrill,Mar.11,1945.
LUTHE
Harry H.,Oct.15,1973.
Jane B.,Sept.12,1992.
LYNCH
Eunice M.,Sept.30,1916.
MABERY
Charles Frederic,June 30,1927.
Emma,Mar.23,1925.
Frances Lewis,Nov.19,1926.
Lawrence Frederic,1882-1882,
  s/o Charles & Frances.
MacDOUGALL
H.G.,May 14,1949.
Ruth L.,Oct.14,1948.
MacKENZIE
John,Apr.28,1990.
MacLEOD
Clarence,Oct.7,1957.
MAGRATH
Elizabeth,1840-1875.
Mary Davis,July 25,1809-
  Oct.19,1875,w/o Thomas.
Thomas,Jan.24,1866,65y.
MAILMAN
Nicole,May 16,1977.
MALCHON
Georgia F.,Sept.5,1950.
MANCHESTER
Charles A.,Mar.29,1963.
Ella,Sept.17,1980.
MANKIN
Henry,Dec.25,1850 ?.
MANN
Almeda F.,July 10,1969.
Edmund,Mar.8,1862,70y.
Eugene Williard,1867-1886.
Florence,July 10,1969.
Helen Maria,Sept.7,1841-
  May 13,1924.
Horace Preble,Oct.23,1843-
  Nov.15,1923.
James, Hon.,June 22,1822-
  Aug.26,1868.
Miriam F.,Oct.19,1821-
  Jan.8,1902,w/o James.
Sarah,July 5,1868,79y,w/o Edmund.
MANNING
John E.,June 24,1924.

MARCHI
Francis V.,Nov.19,1924.
MAREAN
Gladys Rankin,Sept.13,1929.
MARR
Maria W.,Sept.6,1894,70y,
  w/o John W.
MARSTON
Emma,Oct.21,1926.
Florence E.,May 4,1977.
Harriet,J.R.,May 1,1855,21y,w/o O.
Maybelle H.,July 30,1924.
Orrin,June 18,1856,26y.
Percival F.,Feb.23,1916.
MARTIN
Charles F.,Oct.24,1958.
Frank J.,1953/54.
Jennie P.,Oct.23,1955.
Mildred,May 15,1992.
Nellie N.,Dec.16,1917.
Norman A.,Dec.8,1936.
Owen L.,Apr.15,1975.
Sylvia,Aug.7,1994.
Yula,May 14,1986.
MATTA
William,Apr.26,1960.
MAXELL
Ethel,May 28,1983.
MAYBERRY
Frank Howard,1934?.
Richard Edward,May 11,1965.
MAYO
Anne B.,1882-1973.
Edmund F.,1836-1904.
Elizabeth Brown,June 2,1910,65y,
  wid/o Edmund F.
Jennie,1873-1878.
John F.,1840-1907.
L.E.,Mrs.,May 31,1910. ?.
Lydia Brown,1845-1910,w/o Edm.F.
McALLISTER
Ed. C.,Oct.18,1947.
Jo B.,Apr.9,1947.
McBRIDE
Nora H.,Aug.27,1965.
McCAUSLAND
Virginia,May 19,1992.
McCLELLAN
Lewis,Oct.2,1912.
S.E.,Jan.18,1909.
McCLURE
Esther M.,June 14,1967.
McCONKEY
Alice,Nov.8,1980.
Frances D.,1933, ?.
William H.,Dec.14,1942.

McCORRISON
Martha Cressey,1810-1851,w/o Daniel.
McCURRY
John,May 27,1987.
McDANIELS
Fannie O.,July 1,1949.
Ivory S., 1932.
McDONALD
David R.,Dec.6,1935.
Vivian S.,Jan.24,1977.
McDOUGALL
David,1764-1849,1st w. Anna Elder.
Phebe Freeman Paine,1771-1839,
  2nd w/o David.
McINTOSH
Harold F.,July 5,1970.
Minnie B.,May 1,1973.
McKENNEY
Alice I. West,Feb.27,1918,w/o Howard.
David Hasty,1815-1893,h/o Rebecca.
Howard Augustus,1848-Oct.5,1908.
Rebecca McLellan,1816-1892.
Sarah Louise,1846-1849,d/o D.H.& R.
McKEVITT
Cora S.,Dec.28,1956.
Joseph,1933.
McLELLAN
Acton Patten,Dec.28,1813-
  Dec.10,1903,s/o Robt.& Rebecca.
Adrieane,Dec.4,1936.
Albert E.,May 10,1965.
alexander Prescott,Feb.23,1835,
  3m,s/o Hugh & Elizabeth.
Betsey Phinney,Apr.21,1865,78y,
  w/o David,(1860).
Binnie D.,1841-1905,niece & adopted
  d/o Hugh D.
Charles A.,Apr.5,1951.
Charles Ishmael,Apr.25,1929.
Charles,1811 ?, his wife,1873 ? -
  stone badly worn.
Charlie,XXXX.
Cynthia,1858-1868.
Daniel,Feb.11,1813,18y.
David,Mar.13,1844,27y.
David,Jan.26,1870,64y,twin to Wm.
David,June 21,1786-Mar.3,1860.
Eliza A. Cross,1804-1883,w/o John.
Eliza J.,1834-Feb.24,1913,w/o Jos.T.
Elizabeth P. Lewis Staples,
  Sept.1,1838,22y,w/o Hugh,
  d/o Lothrop & Mary Lewis.
Ellen,Jan.24,1840,3m,d/o Wm.& M.J.
Evelina D.,Jan.27,1960.
Francis A.,Jan.1,1913.
Francis H.,Jr.,June 9,1854,
  s/o F.H.& Almira.

Francis,Aug.27,1821-Oct.31,1853.
Fred,Apr.19,1926.
Goldie L.,Oct.9,1949.
Harriett L.,Nov.3,1857,10y,
 d/o Wm.& M.J.
Hugh D.,1805-1878.
Jane Harding,Sept.1,1845,
 81y,w/o William (1843).
John,1799-1858.
Josiah T.,May 17,1825-May 3,1897.
Martha A.,Aug.13,1822-Sept.7,1867.
Mary J.,b. Ireland,d.Apr.25,1873,35y,
 w/o John.
Mary J. Storer,1828-Feb.6,1909,
 w/o Simon E.
Mary J. Merserve,Dec.20,1861,
 41y,w/o Wm.
Mary Larrabee,1913,wid/o Lewis.
Mary Libby,Mar.17,1886,68y.
Mary,XXXX.
Mehitable Harmon,Mar.28,1870,
 w/o William.
Myra,XXXX.
Paulina P.,Sept.12,1847-Feb.28,1904,
 d/o Robt. & Rebecca.
Pauline Atkinson,18335-1881,
 w/o Arthur.
Prince,1829,100y,a slave,whom the
 first William McClellan of Gorham,
 bought in Portland,ME,and paid for
 in shooks. Prince drove the team to
 draw them. He ran away and enlisted
 on Capt.Manley's Privateer,was
 discharged in Boston,came back,was
 freed, given 10 acres of land and a
 pension. His wives,Dinah,d.1800 &
 Chloe,d.1827. This was on his grave-
 stone,it is badly worn,Prince,in 1829
 could still be made out.
Rebecca Patten,Jan.20,1861,75y,
 w/o Capt. Robert.
Rebekah Hersey,1803-1833,w/o John.
Robert, Capt.,Nov.23,1830,48y.
Samuel E.,1855-1881,s/o S.E.&M.J.S.
Samuel,Oct.20,1853,69y.
Simon E.,1824-1909.
Tabitha,Mar.21,1857,63y.
Theophilus C.,1833,s/o J.& R.H.
William,Aug.13,1833,51y.
William,May 13,1843,84y,
 twin to David.
William,Sept.1,1850,37y,
 s/o Wm.& Mehitable.
William,Aug.21,1920.
McLEOD
infant,1931,s.b.

McMACKIN
Hattie Libby,June 1906,28y,
 w/o Clarence A.
infant,Feb.13,1910.
McPHAIL
infant,Jan.13,1948.
McPHERSON
Margaret,Oct.29,1962.
McQUILLAN
Elizabeth,1820-1850,d/o J.& J.
Elmira Lombard,1826-1866.
Jael,1791-1875,w/o John.
Jeremaih T.,1822-1863.
John,1784-1841.
Mary F.,May 2,1916.
Rebecca,1860-Apr.22,1925,d/o J.T.& E
MELLIN
Ada M.,Dec.11,1951.
MELLOR
Mary H.,Sept.1,1919.
MERRILL
Almond,Aug.7,1832,20m,s/o Gardner.
Carrie E. Bacon,1844-1872,w/o E.C.
Charles F.,1841-Oct.28,1910,
 h/o Emily Whitney.
D.F.,May 2,1916.
Daniel,Aug.112,1745-July 11,1830.
Dorcus Crockett,June 22,1830,75y,
 w/o Daniel.
Edwin C.,1842-1881.
Edwin D.,Aug.6,1964.
Elizabeth F.,1810-1896,w/o Nelson.
Emily C.,Nov.26,1924.
Frank W.,Feb.24,1925.
Gardner,Apr.21,1798-Feb.18,1835.
Harriet Sahw,Jan.3,1867,16y.
Horatio,1819-1901.
Joanna,Feb.24,1828,30y,w/o Seward.
Josephine McGraw,Sept.1859,4y.
Julia Ann,1929.
Lewis F.,Jan.4,1951.
Lina E.,1906,w/o Wm.
Mariam F.,Mar.11,1859,43y,w/o Wm.
Nelson,Oct.27,1877,67y.
Nora L.,Feb.25,1949.
Olive A.,1830-Nov.20,1913.
Rebecca Julia,Jan.1860,11y,
Samuel C.,Nov.26,1833,3y,
 s/o Seward & Marry.
Stephen,Oct.10,1846,22y,
 s/o Gardner & Clarissa.
William,Lt.,1833-Aug.19,1918.
XX-berilla,1866,43y,w/o Horatio.
MERRIMAN
Dana R.,May 4,1976.
Dorothy,May 1978.
infant,Dec.13,1911,s.b.

Robert,Apr.22,1994.
MERRITT
Darius F.,1830-May 10,1916.
Frank L.,Mar.26,1947.
Matilda A. Chandler,1844-
June 25,1908,w/o Darius.
Susie W.,Mar.5,1926.
MESERVE
Amy E. Barnes,1861-Oct.7,1908.
Cora Bell,Sept.187X,8y.
Dorothy E.,1909-1913,d/o G.H.& P.H.
Eben R.,July 27,1916.
Eliza E.,Feb.5,1924.
Esther,1814-1887,w/o Horace.
Franklin O.,Dec.11,1968.
Fred E.,Oct.1,1947.
George H.,Nov.24,1948.
Harriet,May 24,1857,21y,d/o H. & E.
Horace,1811-1885.
Jennie D.,Dec.19,1911.
John E.,1839-1908.
Mary C.,1929.
Mildred,May 5,1979.
Roger Emery,May 21,1985.
METCALF
Ida,Oct.15,1863,5wk.,d/o B.F.& M.E.
MICHAUD
infant,May 12,1982.
MILLETT
Charlotte A.,Oct.11,1972.
Jennie A.,Sept.20,1927.
Thomas F,Rev.,Apr.2,1927.
MILLIGAN
Edward,Dec.14,1946.
Martha E.,Aug.26,1968.
MILLS
James,1909.
Marietta Weeks,Oct.1,1943.
MITCHELL
Alice M. Cliff,1864-1906,d/o Edw.A.
Edwin A.,1834-Oct.6,1919.
Harold M.,Sept.8,1920.
Mark R.,1905-Oct.20,1913.
Mary A.,1840-Aug.30,1920,w/o E.A.
Richard,Nov.30,1978.
MOLASKY
Myrtle H.,1932.
MONAGHETTI
Electis,July 9,1967.
Peter,Sept.20,1978.
MONAHAN
J.A.,Sept.29,1879-Aug.31,1913.
MONKS
Julia,May 21,1980.
MOODY
Albert,Nov.9,1928.
Bernard,Jan.21,1918.

Blanche S.,1932.
Cordelia,1934.
Ethelyn,May 15,1984.
Eugene,Jan.13,1945.
Herbert,Aug.19,1950.
infant,Mar.24,1915.
James L.,Aug.13,1985.
James M.,1821-1891,h/o Lydia L.W.
James W.,May 6,1965.
Lydia L. Weatherbee,1824-1887.
Melvin,July 19,1941.
Rosco G.,June 27,1935.
Roy,May 2,1986.
ch/o James M. & Lydia L.W.:
Andrew W.,1851-1856;
Charles S.,1860-1862;
Jane,1850-1856;
L. Freddie,1863-1865.
S.Lizzie,1857-1862;
MOORE
Charles S.,1843-1863.
David,1812-1876.
Elizabeth Small,1817-1865,
w/o David.
Ella F. Robinson,1847-1853.
Henry W.,1841-1846.
Isaac W.,1845-1846.
Lillian,Dec.7,1968.
MOREY
Dorothy Ellen,1930.
Harry W.,Oct.12,1960.
Sadie F.,Jan.19,1952.
MORRELL
Elizabeth A.,Oct.1,1968.
Guy L.,Aug.11,1945.
Louisa D.,Mar.31,1911,79y,
w/o Lemuel R.
MORRILL
Clara,Dec.7,1922.
Donald G.,Apr.23,1940.
Ernest F.,Mar.28,1956.
Harry,Sept.17,1882,8m,s/o H.L.& C.
Helen,July 11,1985.
Henry L.,Jan.3,1929.
Lemuel R.,1825-1893.
Lovisa D. Mason,1881-1911,w/o Lem.
Minnie,May 8,1869,7y,d/o L.R.& L.D.
MORSE
Ernest H.,1898-1899,s/o Frank & Flo.
Florence O.,July 7,1918.
Mary Russell,June 2,1853,13y,
d/o C.D. & H.D.
MOSES
Eva,Oct.18,1980.
Wilbur M.,Aug.13,1975.
William W.,Apr.10,1838-Jan.22,1884.

MOSHER
Abbie H.,1873-1874.
Albert E.,Sept.30,1992.
Albert H.,Apr.2,1929.
Anna M.,1869-Feb.10,1919.
Annie E.,1851-Feb.2,1927.
Augustus,Oct.20,1818-Mar.29,1895.
Benjamin,Mar.31,1863,89y.
Clifford,1867-1901,murdered,
s/o Rufus & M.F.W.
Clinton,1856-Oct.26,1926.
Daniel,Sept.8,1848,64y.
Dolly F. Richardson,Jan.25,184X,
w/o Rufus.
Eddie F.,Nov.1874,1y,s/o R. & M.H.
Edward,Dec.12,1837,29y.
Edward,1845-1846,s/o Rufus & Dolly.
Effie C.,1864-Mar.14,1923.
Emma,May 10,1983.
Eunice Elder,July 29,1852,78y.
Frederick C.,Aug.26,1831,7y,
s/o Nathaniel & Susan.
Frederick N.,1860-1890,
s/o Rufus & M.F.W.
Hugh W.,Apr.20,1847,s/o Ben.& Polly.
inf/o C. & E.C.,1888.
James H.,1834-Oct.5,1910.
Lydia McN.,1827-1887,w/o Mark.
Marion S.,Nov.15,1919.
Mark,1818-1901.
Marshal M.,Apr.7,1863,25y,
s/o Hugh W. & Jane M.
Marshal,Nov.8,1863,7m.
Martha F. Woodman,1827-
July 11,1914,w/o Rufus.
Mary E.,Apr.5,1943.
Mary H.,Nov.8,1878,33y,w/o Rufus.
Mary H.,Feb.9,1949.
Merrill,Oct.10,1816-Mar.23,1880.
Nathaniel,Nov.26,1830,27y,
h/o Susan Barker.
Nathaniel,May 5,1769-May 29,1848,
h/o Eunice.
Octavia,Jan.3,1853,59y,w/o Daniel.
Polly,Nov.24,1850,68y,w/o Benjamin.
Rufus,1815-1889.
Rufus,Oct.6,1876,29t.
Sarah M. Mosier (on stone),
Aug.22,1846,23y,d/o Benj. & Polly.
Sophia C. Burbank,Sept.18,1863,21y,
w/o Marshal M.,d/o Joseph & Susan.
Willard J.,1871-1989.
children/o Daniel & Octavia:
Abigail P.,May 12,1836,12y.
Abagail,1823,8m;
Stephen W.,1832,1y.

children/o Mark & Lydia McN.:
Clara,1856-1885;
Thomas S.,1868-1869;
Wilhelmena,1853-1863;
Foster,1851-1862;
Sarah E.,1849-1850;
Mary B.,1864-1865.
MOSHIER
Clifford,July 1901.
MOTLEY
George H.,1826-1906,h/o Emma A.
MOTTERSHEAD
infant,Dec.20,1965,s.b.
Joseph H.,Apr.26,1975.
Pauline B.,Apr.26,1975.
MOULTON
Almeda,Aug.26,1876,64y,w/o Zetotes ?
Charles F.,Oct.24,1876,6y.
Daisy B.,Nov.21,1966.
Earl Lindon,June 27,1940.
Ellen,July 31,1920.
Fannie,1934.
Freedom,1922.
Harry,Aug.6,1876,4y.
Ida Quimby,Mar.18,1937.
James L.Apr.11,1915.
James W.,Rev.,Apr.9,1928.
John S.,June 23,1806,47y.
Liberty,June 29,1923.
Martha,Sept.26,1917.
Mary L.,Sept.2,1941.
Nellie/Nettie C.,Nov.8,1927,72y.
Orrin,Jan.12,1949.
Paul Phillip Servy,June 27,1940.
XX,ch/o Emery,Apr.23,1923.
MUNROE
Mary,July 11,1880-Dec.12,1878.
MUNSON
Alta Edith,1930.
Catherine S. Smith,1855-1926.
Elizabeth F. South,1825-1863.
George J.,1873-1874.
Harry S.,1877-1879.
MURCH
Abbie Harriet Baker,June 8,1906,
47y,w/o Charles H.
Charles H.,1858-June 2,1922.
Charles W.,Mar.16,1953.
Hattie A. Blake,1859-1908,w/o C.H.
Jane Blake,1818-1884,s/o Samuel.
Laura J.,1848-Feb.1924,w/o Wesley.
Nellie J.,1858-July 1940,2nd w/o C.H.
Samuel,1805-1876.
Wesley,1839-Jan.18,1917.
MURCHIE
George H.,Mar.26,1973.

MURRAY
Alta,Apr.12,1990.
Frederick H.,1888-XXXX.
Harriet Lombard,Nov.19,1906,86y.
John,b.in Ireland-d.1898,71y.
Marian,May 21,1990.
Mildred J.,1889-1933,w/o F.H.
Millie E.,Jan.23,1916.
Oren H.,Oct.17,1940.
child/o Philip H.,Dec.14,1943.
Richard W.,Apr.12,1990.
Richard,Apr.27,1987.
MURRY (on gravestone)
Eliza J.,Dec.6,1850,9m,
d/o John & Harriet.
MYERS
Elizabeth G.,1824-1897.
NASH
Clara P.,1863-1886.
Juliette J.,1835-1903,w/o O.C.
Orrin C.,1835-1881.
NASON
Annette,1844-1865.
Elisha F.,1835-1877.
Ernest E.,Dec.28,1927.
Frances E.,Feb.1,1926.
Greta Ellen,Aug.7,1934.
Josie,1862-1874,d/o E.F.& M.A.W.
Kenneth,May 9,1992.
Martha A. Watson,1839-1879,
w/o E.F.
Nellie,Mar.18,1957.
Winnie A.,Mar.4,1934.
NEAL
Charles S.,Aug.6,1947.
Doris,June 1,1986.
Elwood,May 11,1985.
Gertrude,July 6,1974.
Hazel,May 11,1985.
Ralph,July 2,1990.
Zulah M.,Dec.14,1939.
NELSON
Aaron,Dec.9,1975.
Harriet,Apr.23,1990.
Nathalie T.,June 19,1940.
Thelma,May 16,1986.
NEWCOMB
Alice M.,1859-1896,w/o Gardner M.
Gardner M.,1859-1896.
Humphrey H.,Oct.13,1950.
Jessie W.,Dec.8,1963.
Leonard,1835-1875,
h/o Julia A. Hanson.
Louisa Mary,Oct.10,1926.
NEWMAN
John C.,May 15,1919.

NICHOLS
Mildred L.,Aug.23,1959.
NICKERSON
Annie M.,Apr.14,1912.
NIELSON
Carl,May 10,1989.
Johanne A.,Aug.20,1990.
Minnie J.,Dec.1,1937.
Peter,Jan.19,1940.
Verna,Oct.15,1990.
NOONAN
Grace,Apr.30,1992.
John J.,Oct.5,1960.
NORTHRUP
Brantford,Aug.3,1985.
NORTON
Eugene,Jan.21,1964.
Georgia,Aug.31,1952.
NOYCE
Frank C.,May 9,1959,infant.
Susan,Nov.18,1957,infant.
O'BRIEN
Catherine,Feb.7,1953.
child,Aug.1,1945.
Edward,Apr.22,1981.
Herbert,Dec.21,1963.
Margurite,May 19,1971.
Raymond,Aug.1,1945.
ODIORNE
Charles E.,Jan.15,1901,81y.
Dorothy,June 7,1928.
Frank W.,Oct.31,1922.
Freddie & Mamie,XXXX.
Lydia L.,May 10,1893,70y,
w/o Charles E.
Roseanne,July 2,1946.
O'DONAL
Charles,July 15,1982.
OLSON
Andrew J.,Nov.29,1958.
Charles,Nov.1983.
David G.,Sept.30,1960.
Elinor Paine,Aug.18,1986.
Hansine G.,Sept.25,1973.
John G.,Oct.22,1971.
OSBORNE
Annie R.,Oct.11,1949.
Charles D.,Aug.12,1968.
Charles H.,May 14,1917.
Charles S.,Dec.26,1939.
Francis M.,Oct.21,1926.
Francis M.,Oct.9,1877,22y,
s/o J.J.& E.L.
Frank W.,Nov.29,1958.
George,Aug.28,1979.
Georgia A.,1864-1883,1st w/o Wm.H.
Isable,July 10,1938.

Lillian,July 29,1962.
Mary G.,Nov.20,1935.
Mary M.,Nov.30,1994.
Sarah E.,Aug.24,1924.
Stacy,May 6,1987.
Summer L.,Sept.2,1959.
William Henry,1859-Mar.29,1936.
PACKARD
Dorothy,May 10,1993.
Everett S.,June 8,1954.
John W.,Apr.29,1934.
Mercy,May 22,1991.
Sarah J.,Nov.13,1948.
Myrton B.,July 18,1980.
Walter C.,Oct.28,1957.
PAGE
Hattie,May 26,1978.
Isabel,Sept.27,1941.
John,June 14,1989.
Pitt M.,Apr.5,1938.
PAIGE
Myrle L.,Nov.16,1971.
Robert P.,July 12,1986.
PAINE
BelindaW. McLellan,June 7,1822-Nov.22,1909,2nd w/o James.
Charles,Apr.8,1874,68y.
Eddie,1872-11875.
Ellen F.,Sept.7,1920.
Ellen F.H.,1834-Feb.1924,w/o P.I.
Hannah Lowell,July 8,1891,80y, w/o Charles.
Hannah Cressey,Nov.22,1846,70y, w/o William.
James,Apr.15,1868,65y.
Mary Frost,Apr.12,1853,48y,w/o Jas. P. Ingalls,1834-1911.
Phineas Q.,Aug.26,1911.
William H.,Feb.27,1856,15y,s/o J.&M.
William,Jan.31,1852,82y.
children/o Charles & Hannah S.:
Abbie L.,Oct.20,1861,24y;
C. Henry,May 25,1866,23y;
Ella Susan,Oct.8,1853,3y;
Fred L.,Apr.28,1880,32y;
William,Jan.20,1899,47y,
PALMER
Alice M.,Mar.13,1952,infant.
Edward S.,1827-Aug.23,1908.
Harry H.,Dec.2,1943.
Henrietta R.,Oct.17,1940.
Maria B. Starbird,1834-1894, w/o Edward S.
Martha,July 20,1948.
PARKER
Alice,May 13,1988.
Betsey,Mar.13,1869,73y.

Charles Lothrop,Mar.15,1851,14y, s/o John & Louisa.
Dana,Jan.3,1870,9m,s/o G.M.& Sarah
Edith G.,May 15,1967.
Eliphalet,Sept.30,1840,76y.
Eliza A.,July 8,1960.
Elizabeth,1816-1868,w/o Loammi.
Elizabeth,Oct.29,1913.
Gardner M.,Apr.21,1920.
Mrs.Gardner,Mar.20,1925.
Gardner M.,Jr.,Mar.23,1936.
H.Greeley,July 9,1925.
James L.,Sept.13,1851,1y,s/o Geo.M.
Jane,Oct.5,1849,82y,w/o Eliphalet.
John M.,Aug.15,1799-July 31,1873, s/o Moses & Mary.
Joseph E.,Apr.21,1977.
Joseph E.,Mar.13,1921.
Linnie M.,1861-Jan.26,1933,w/o P.Y.
Loammi,1806-1893,h/o Elizabeth.
Loammi,Oct.29,1913.
Louisa,Apr.17,1885,80y,w/o John M.
Mahlon Hasty,May 31,1863,22y, s/o John & Louisa.
Mary E.,Mar.13,1921.
Mary L.,May 19,1923.
Mary,Feb.24,1851,95y,w/o Moses.
May F.E.,Apr.16,1947.
Moses,Oct.28,1809,69y.
N.Greely,Mar.13,1921.
Percy R.,Sept.17,1974.
Phineas Y.,1851-May 11,1923.
Robert C.,May 26,1926.
Samuel,Aug.8,1815,22y,s/o Eli & Jane.
William,Aug.10,1972.
PARKHURST
Alpheus C.,July 29,1839-June 21,1880
Arthur D.,Apr.14,1954.
Edna A.Sleeper,June 3,1848-July 9,1911,w/o Alpheus C.
Freddie H.,Dec.1875,1y,s/o A.C.&E.A.
John F.,Apr.17,1914.
John L.,May 20,1850,60y.
Leonard Woods,June 26,1900,64y.
Leonard,May 18,1923.
Lila C.,June 26,1946.
Lillian L.,Apr.23,1968.
Marsha C/G.,Feb.6,1891,86y, w/o John L.
Mary P. Knapp,Apr.2,1911,69y, w/o Leonard Woods.
Sarah E.,Mar.26,1885,54y, d/o John L. & Marsha C/G.
children/o Leonard Woods & Mary:
Allie C.,Aug.12,1869,11m;
Shirley L.,July 29,1866,2y.

PARLIN
Jennie D.,Apr.30,1945.
Seth S.,Nov.28,1925.
PARRINGTON
Ann,Sept.28,1861,70y,w/o John.
John, b.Yorkshire,Eng.-
d.Feb.7,1836,37y.
William,Jan.13,XXXX, &
Sarah,1836?, 2 ch/o John & Ann.
PASSAGE
Marcia Cressey,May 16,1937.
PATRICK
Abbie F.,Mar.8,1916.
Alma F.,Nov.21,1927.
Charles P.,Sept.20,1910,
h/o Elizabeth Emery.
Charles P.,1839-1910.
Charles,b.Stroudwater 1745-1830.
Charles,Aug.27,1887,78y.
David,Sept.1,1776-Sept.4,1838.
David,May 16,1917.
Deborah B.,Feb.16,1863,36y,
w/o George.
Edward K.,1838-1843.
Effie,Oct.2,1947.
Eliza Harding,1800-1847,w/o Step.A.
Elizabeth Jordan,Jan.15,1850,
67y,w/o Daniel.
Frank,July 12,1913.
Fred W.,Feb,19,1909.
Fred W.,Aug.18,1954.
George,1822-1903.
Gladys S.,Apr.9,1973.
Lewis J.,Dec.19,1941.
Lizzie C.,June 29,1923.
Lucy Paine,Jan.22,1891,75y,
w/o Charles (1887).
Maria,1858-1879.
Marion C.,Feb.20,1935.
Martha D. Watts,1821-1864,
2nd w/o Stephen A.
Mary E.,1839-Feb.25,1910,w/o George.
Mary E.,Oct.28,1878,36y,w/o Chas.P.
Mary Fickett,Oct.15,1788-
Mar.23,1864,w/o Thomas.
Oliver W.,June 2,1913.
Orin A.,1909.
Samuel,Oct.27,1913.
Sarah,Oct.26,1838,18y,
d/o Charles & Susan.
Sarah,Aug.7,1929.
Stephen A.,1803-1874.
Stephen E.,Apr.9,1973.
Thomas,Nov.24,1782-Dec.9,1857.
William,July 11,1856,2m,
s/o George & Deborah.

PEABODY
Elizabeth R.,Mar.10,1834,18m;
Emily E.,Feb.20,1847,12y;
William Henry,July 7,1832,
ch/o Wm. H.
William H.,Mar.2,1842,42y,
h/o Hannah March.
PEAVEY
Edna,July 6,1970.
PELLETIER
Jeannette A.,Jan.21,1969.
Reed,May 17,1985.
Vincent,May 23,1992.
PELLEY
infant,Dec.20,1947,s.b.
PENFIELD
Almira Strout,Aug.19,1868,53y.
Charles R.,Mar.7,1851,14y,s/o C.&A.
Charles,Capt.,Jan.20,1814-
Apr.18,1868,h/o Almira.
PERCY
Fannie E.,Apr.18,1930.
Gardner A.,Oct.1,1949.
Gardner A.,Jr.,Dec.3,1934.
Lache H.,Jan.1,1916.
Lisle C.,July 15,1968.
Mildred M.,Feb.17,1934.
PERKINS
inf/o Ernest,Aug.14,1920,s.b.
James A.,Feb.24,1925.
Jennie,Oct.21,1935.
Julia,May 28,1925.
Phillip S.,Dec.13,1962.
Sella L.,Mar.8,1915.
Wendell H.,Sept.29,1885,42y.
William N.,Feb.17,1958.
PERRY
Abby,1804-1887,bu. in Jackson,NH.
Clark,Rev.,July 22,1843,43y.
Edward J.,July 8,1933.
Eunice McLellan,Dec.17,1891,
84y,w/o Clark.
Frank H.,1867-1893,
only ch/o J.J.& M.S.
Mrs.James,June 1909.
James J.,1836-1901.
James,1811-1853,bu.in Jackson,NH.
John C.,Mar.10,18XX.
John S.,Apr.26,1913.
Mary E.,XXXX,w/o John C.
Mary S.,1846-June 1,1909,w/o Jas.J.
Sophia E.,Sept.10,1908.
PETERS
Charles,Sept.15,1986.
Fred,May 14,1952.
Margaret W.,May 31,1975.

PETERSON
John,Nov.6,1979.
PHILLIPS
Caroline S.,1835-Feb.11,1920.
D.M.,Sept.19,1864,28y,killed in battle.
Elizabeth,Jan.13,1877,73y,w/o Oliver.
Oliver,Apr.8,1891,84y.
W.Willard,Nov.4,1865,28y.
PHINNEY
Abigail,Oc.t26,1840,39y,w/o James.
Angelina Crockett,Mar.19,1888,
    82y,wid/o Eli,2nd w/o Benjamin.
Benjamin,July 19,1841,44y,
    s/o Nathaniel.
Betsey Sloper,Mar.18,1833,32y,
    1st w/o Benjamin.
Cynthia M.,Mar.20,1869,32y,w/o Jas.
Eli,Nov.30,1833,32y.
Elizabeth,1781-1864.
James,Sept.27,1876,73y.
James,Oct.18,1834 ?,93y ?
James,Jan.13,1860,93y.
James E.,Mar.20,1916.
Lucy,Dec.29,1863 ?,82y, ?,w/o James.
Martha Colman,Mar.13,1837,6y,
    d/o James & Cynthia.
Martha,Sept.3,1816,76y,w/o James.
Mary J.,May 29,1872,37y,w/o Frank.
Mildred Martin,XXXX,96y,
    w/o Norman A.,d/o Samuel & Eva
    Haynes Phinney. Oldest direct
    descendant of Capt. John Phinney,
    Gorham's 1st settler.
Mary J.,1823-1888.
Mary Bangs,Aug.17,1821,50y,
    1st w/o Nathaniel.
Nathaniel,Nov.14,1850,79y,
    2nd w. Betsey Hatch (1864).
Oliver Pierce,Sept.20,1833,1m,
    s/o James & Cynthia.
Thomas W. McLellan,
    Jan. 27,1910,83y.
PHIPPS
Ai,Feb.22,1835,58y,s/o Jeremiah.
Eunice McLellen,Sept.28,1844,
    63y,w/o Ai.
Joshua,Col.,Aug.20,1866,85y.
PIERCE
Guy,May 20,1992.
Virginia S.,Dec.13,1930.
PIKE
Emeline C.,May 4,1835,25y,
    w/o Humphrey.
PILLSBURY
George,1929.
James H.,Apr.24,1974.
Madeline,May 26,1978.

PINKHAM
Magaret A.,Oct.24,1938.
PIPINIAS
infant,Nov.29,1966.
PLAISTED
Edna,May 19,1952.
Edward W.,June 16,1926.
Elma R.,Dec.18,1929.
George P.,Aug.3,1935.
John Milton,1888-1907.
Laurence,Oct.11,1966.
Louise M.,Sept.21,1972.
Maria Young,Oct.15,1955.
Walter Lee,Jan.31,1962.
PLUMMER
A.Dana,Apr.13,1918.
Alvin B.,1807-1886.
Alvin B.,Nov.30,1912.
Carrie B.,Mar.15,1915.
Etta,June 28,1991.
Flora B.,Feb.8,1944.
Fred,Aug.18,1993.
John D.,Nov.16,1864,13y,
    s/o Alvin & Sarah.
Sarah,June 27,1879,62y,
    w/o Alvin B.(1886).
Susan,Dec.5,1874,36y,
    d/o Alvin & Sarah.
POMEROY
Catherine Montgomery,May 15,1831,
    10m,d/o Thad. & Catherine.
Catherine Pearson,Sept.11,1831,37y,
    1st w/o Rev. Thaddeus.
Edward P.,June 4,1888,61y,
    s/o Rev. Thaddeus.
Harrietta Rubery,b. Charleston,S.C.,
    Jan.17,1808-Dec.27,1833,
    2nd w/o Thaddeus.
John P.,Sept.26,1826,1y,s/o T.& C.
Mary H.,Feb.7,1825,10m,d/o T.& C.
Thaddeus,Jan.14,1831,8y,s/o T.& C.
Thaddeus Rubery,Oct.27,1833,5m,
    s/o Thad. & Harrietta.
ch/o Thad.& 3rd w. Emily Sweetsir:
Charles,Mar.1839-Apr.1839 &
Thomas R.,Mar.1839-Sept.1839.
PORTER
David L.,June 1986.
Kenneth C.,Jr.,Mar.2,1937.
Noble,May 25,1988.
Ruth,July 21,1989.
POULE
Elizabeth H.,Apr.1,1787-July 29,1875,
    w/o Richard.
PRATT
Georgianna,Sept.6,1873,1y,
    d/o Alexander & Catherine.

Kasey,June 30,1984,1y.
Leroy,Apr.29,1991.
PRESCOTT
Gladys,Apr.23,1982.
John Edwin,Feb.4,1935.
Myron M.,Apr.29,1969.
PRIDE
Annie E.,Apr.17,1947.
Frank B.,Aug.6,1948.
XX,1829,100y, stone unreadable.
PROUDFOOT
Rose,Dec.6,1952.
QUINN
Edith W.,Aug.23,1967.
Pearl,Apr.20,1983.
RACKLEFF
Mabel,Mar.13,1961.
RAMSAY
Kenneth,Oct.30,1981.
RAND
E. Sherman,May 12,1945.
Elizabeth H. Babb,July 25,1842, w/o Asa Rand.
Flora M.,Mar.16,1933.
RANDALL
Alton John,Apr.24,1928.
Benjamin,July 17,1906.
Ellen C.,Oct.4,1933.
Ervie E.,Sept.6,1947.
Eula G.,May 3,1939.
Gilberta H.,July 29,1946.
Harry,Mar.30,1935.
infant,Oct.4,1946,1d.
James A.,May 31,1936.
John Richard,Oct.1924,infant.
Lee A.,Dec.28,1952.
Lee,Dec.15,1918.
Leon,May 16,1969.
Lizzie Libby,1869-1904,w/o Wm.N.
Marie,Nov.12,1987.
Mary J.,June 14,1969.
Mary L.,Nov.25,1923.
Maurice J.,July 1,1974.
Rowena G.,Nov.6,1942.
Ruth,Sept.23,1973.
Walter D.,Feb.2,1946,s/o Art. F.
William N.,1862-Dec.30,1928.
RANKIN
E. Wilma,Sept.29,1944.
Edith L.,1880-1891.
Frank,Sept.16,1932.
infant,1889.
May ..,1858-1884.
Ralph B.,May 2,1930.
Sumner R.,1891-1902.
RAWSON
Maude Frances,Apr.29,1977.

Samuel H.,May 26,1946.
REDLON
Abbie Frost,Nov.9,1874,21y, w/o Wm. A.
REED
Aaron,Feb.5,1947.
Anna Shackford,Apr.16,1929.
Blanche Evelyn,Oct.28,1977.
Clara E.,Aug.21,1915.
Elbridge A.,Apr.9,1957.
Gracie,Feb.16,1825,2y,d/o L.& E.
Jennie F.,Apr.2,1946.
Lemuel A.,Dec.9,1926.
REICHENKNOCH
infant,Oct.11,1945.
Mrs.XX.,June 7,1925.
RICE
Ada C.,Feb.10,1938.
Ann,Jan.24,1827,4y,d/o John & Mary.
Anna,Aug.8,1836,80y,w/o Lemuel.
Betsey,June 4,1818,5y,d/o J.& M.
John,Oct.7,1784-May 24,1863, 1st w.Mary, 2nd w.Salome, 3rd w.
Mary Kilbourn,d.1880,95y.
Leo H.,1967.
Mary Hanscom,Apr.26,1827,56y, 1st w/o John.
Sarah Alden,Sept.23,1869,49y, w/o Simeon.
Salome Hanson,Nov.9,1852,63y, 2nd w/o John.
RICH
Adoniram J.,Mar.8,1932.
Frances,July 23,1940.
Genista Alberta,Nov.30,1977.
Horace T.,Jan.14,1972.
J. Rich,Aug.25,1921.
Judith C.,Sept.23,1946.
Lemuel,Oct.15,1908.
Minnie M.,May 3,1947.
RICHARDS
Melville W.,Oct.7,1911.
Thomas,Jan.13,1863,22y.
RICHARDSON
Abbie J.,1855-1881,w/o Geo.A.
Abigail F.,Apr.26,1828-Feb.6,1901, w/o Freeman H.
Abigail,Jan.18,1875,79y,w/o Isaac.
Alpheus,Jan.24,1939.
Arthur F.,June 6,1954.
Arthur,Jan.28,1862,s/o F.H.& A.F.
Charles E.,Apr.4,1934.
Dolly F.,Dec.19,1921.
Dorcus Freeman,1835-1895.
Ezra,1822-1905.
Freeman H.,July 28,1828-Apr.11,1902
Freeman,Apr.24,1981.

Freeman,Jr.,May 15,1990.
George A.,Jan.3,1919.
Gladys,Apr.27,1978.
Hannah A.,1837-Feb.1920,w/o Ezra.
Isaac,Oct.4,1872,78y.
Isaac,Jr.,1826-1888.
J.I.,May 18,1946.
James F.,Sept.9,1951.
John M.,1830-1903,h/o Dorcus F.
Keith,Sept.21,1980.
Lydia,Apr.12,1824-July 19,1898.
Marshall L.,Feb.28,1960.
Martha E.,Jan.17,1926.
Merton,Sept.7,1988.
Norma Edith,Apr.24,1927.
Norman L.,Nov.18,1962.
Olive,1874-1878,d/o G.A.& A.J.
Sadie,Nov.18,1936.
Sarah,May 20,1833,48y,w/o Benj.
Virginia A.,Mar.4,1974.
Vyra,Apr.24,1986.
Wilma L.,June 5,1948.
RICHMOND
Donald,Oct.20,1984.
RICKER
David L.,Aug.8,1972.
RIDGWAY
Alice Culm,1840-,Dec.1,1925.
Benjamin S.,1873-1901.
Carrie S.,1870-1896.
Edith,Feb.20,1949.
Frances E.S.,1871-1898.
James B.,1959.
Samuel,1835-Sept.23,1908.
RIDLON
Agnes E.,May 19,1973.
Elmer,Nov.2,1959.
Eveyln Mary,Jan.29,1942.
Francis A.,Mar.31,1927.
J. Frank,Sept.22,1935.
Joseph R.,June 5,1973.
Lizzie M.,May 7,1932.
Sarah Evelyn,Mar.14,1940.
RIGGS
Eliza R.,Aug.10,1864,18y,d/o Wm.& L.
Lucinda,Feb.6,1878,53y,2nd w/o Wm
Mary,Oct.18,1772-Mar.1,1827,w/o Wm
Rebecca H.McQuillan,1818-1842,
  d/o John & Jael McQuillan.
William,May 2,1769-July 14,1840.
William,Jan.22,1810-Nov.13,1861,
  1st w. Rebecca McQuillan,2nd w.Luc.
ROBERTS
Charles J.,Oct.15,1908.
Charles T.,1817-1900,
  s/o Joshua & Mary.
Charlie,Jan.2,1898,50y.

Doris,May 11,1987.
Dottie,May 30,1915.
Edward A.,June 2,1936.
Eleanor,Sept.7,1978.
Elizabeth P.,May 19,1934.
Eugenia Ayer,Jan.21,1943.
Florence N.,Dec.24,1899,36y,
  w/o J.D.,d/o Clark & Annie Dyer.
George F.F.,Mar.15,1942.
Hattie C.,Mar.14,1958.
Harriet Mulloy McIntosh,1825-
  1891,w/o C.T.
John,July 25,1914.
L. Wilbur,June 14,1945.
Leonard C.,1821-1892.
Lester,Jan.9,1913.
Lettie,Jan.28,1954.
Lydia A.,Nov.25,1920.
Mabelle S. Cousins,Aug.15,1930.
Margaret,June 24,1896,47y,w/o Chas.
Maria L. Hamblen,1836-1903,w/o L.C.
Mehtiable C. Waterhouse,1826-1854,
  w/o Leonard C.
Willard A.,Sr.,Apr.16,1969.
children/o Leonard & Maria L.:
George T.F.,1863-1943;
Hattie C.,1870-1958;
infant,1857;
Mary T.,1858-1863;
Nellie M.,1866-1891,w/o E.I.Talbot.
ROBIE
Alice,June 1979.
Amy T.,Dec.26,1967.
Clarissa Adams,July 27,1860,68y,
  w/o Dea. Thomas S.
Eliza,Mar.29,1916.
Eliza,1856-1863,d/o F.& M.O.P.
Eliza,Nov.2,1865,w/o Toppan.
Flora Barton,Apr.22,1942.
Francis B.,Oct.8,1876,67y.
Franics,July 1,1864,31y.
Fred K.,Feb.5,1912.
Frederick,Governor, 1822-1912.
Frederick,June 7,1964.
G.P.,Nov.9,1921.
Harriet M.,May 23,1878,40y,
  w/o Francis (1864).
Inez A. Gardiner,1843-1916,
  w/o Toppan (1875).
John W.,Feb.28,1958.
Lena M. Smith,1855-Mar.29,1916,
  w/o S.P.
Lydia,Feb.23,1811,29y,w/o Toppan.
Martha E.,Sept.3,1915.
Martha L.,Jan.12,1886,73y,w/o F.B.
Mary F.,Aug.6,1962.

Mary Oliver Priest,1828-1893,
w/o Frederick.
Sarah,Apr.23,1828,35y,w/o Toppan.
Silvanus Prince,1848-1921,s/o F.B& M
Susan E.Farwell,1848-1904,w/o Geo.
Thomas,Dea.,Jan.14,1791-
Oct.22,1838.
Toppan,Jan.14,1871,88y.
Toppan,Jan.30,1875,35y.
Walter H.,Apr.27,1859-June 7,1888.
William P.F.,Nov.9,1937.
children/o Charles & Emily P.:
Charles Toppan,1836-1853;
Charles,July 30,1812-Dec.21,1886;
Eliza,1841-1852;
Emily P.,Nov.6,1814-Oct.11,1893;
Frances Maria,Oct.8,1818-
Jan.22,1854.
George,Oct.1,1816-Dec.2,1856;
Lincoln,1842-1867;
children/o George & Francis M.:
Chester,1850-1893;
George Thaxter,1848-1849;
Georgia Anna,1842-1859;
Prescott,1846-1862;
Sarah L.,1843-1908.
children/o Thomas S. & Clarissa A.:
Catherine Emerson,Dec.11,1834,3y;
Benjamin Adams,Sept.13,1832,4y;
Joseph Adams,1830-1832;
Lucinda Adams,Jan.13,1832,9y;
Thomas Sargeant,1826-July 31,1832.
ROBINSON
Annie M.,Jun e 17,1931.
Christy,Oct.12,1975.
Egar R.,Nov.23,1945.
Ella M.,Sept.9,1919.
George E.,May 26,1992.
George W.,Apr.17,1940.
George,Aug.23,1993.
Grace L.,Nov.18,1949.
James S.,1868,10y,s/o John & K.S.
James S.,Mar.29,1916.
Janet,Apr.20,1983.
John,Aug.1,1826-Apr.15,1899.
Joseph L.,Feb.1911,44y.
Kate,Jan.15,1919.
Katherine,June 4,1983.
Katherine Shaw,1840-Sept.9,1912.
Laurence B.,Mar.19,1920.
Mildred B.,June 8,1951.
Minnie W.,186-1894.
Robert,1965.
ROGERS
Charles A.,Mar.18,1929.
Charles A.,1844-1944,h/o Emily C.
Emily C.,1843-1894.
Emily W.,July 13,1967.
Florence A.,June 9,1971.
William Wells,June 12,1982.
ROLFE
Catherine B.,Aug.19,1911.
Charles E.,Oct.19,1940.
David F.,1817-1903.
Dorothy E.,Jan.9,1974.
Elizabeth,May 5,1952.
Hattie M.,APr.14,1944.
Martha B.C.,July 14,1920.
W.T.,1882-1882.
ROOT
Ida May,Aug.19,1946.
ROSS
Bessie F.,July 12,1935.
ROSSIGNOL
Nelson W.,Nov.13,1959.
ROUNDS
Abial,Feb.11,1924.
Carrie C.,May 16,1924.
Elizabeth,Sept.21,1893,58y.
Harriett Sturgis,Feb.20,1889,
82y,w/o Capt.Robert.
Mary E.,Dec.16,1816,16y.
Robert B.,May 1,1897,88y.
Robert,Capt.,Mar.6,1860,60y.
Sarah Lunt,Jan.26,1838-Feb.2,1924.
ROWE
Albion W.,Feb.27,1935.
Clara E.,1934.
Clinton,Jan.27,1918.
Edgar D.,Dec.11,1937.
Erlon M.,Aug.14,1917.
Etta,Oct.15,1908.
Harry K.,1965.
Howard F.,1877-1899.
L. Edith W.,Apr.26,1955.
Lovina A.,1895-1903.
Mabel M.,1875-1875.
Mary S.,1851-1891.
Miriam Bernice,May 13,1977.
Roscoe G.,1843-1896.
Sarah Paine,1820-1896,w/o Wm.
Stanley,May 25,1993.
William,1817-1859.
ROWELL
Edgar,Aug.3,1933,infant.
RUSSELL
Helen,Oct.27,1968.
Muriel L.,1904-1905.
Robert,May 8,1980.
Walter E.,1869-July 8,1948,h/o W.P.S.
Winifred Parker Stone,May 6,1970.
RUST
Charles,Jan.19,1843,5y,
s/o Meschach & Sally.

Charlotte Susan,Jan.9,1992.
Martha Ann,1832,6y,
d/o Meshach & Martha.
Martha Frost,Mar.25,1835,32y,
w/o Meshach.
Meshach,Aug.5,1874,78y,s/o Wm.,
Meshach was a triplet.
Sarah (Sally) Waterhouse,
Feb.23,1881,80y,w/o Meshach.
Sarah,Apr.2,1981.
Susan Maria,Sept.15,1832,2y,
d/o Meshach & Martha.
Warren D.,May 29,1976.
SALLEY
Kenneth,July 26,1984.
Marian,Oct.21,1988.
SAMPSON
Albert H.,July 13,1935.
Alfred J.,July 18,1994.
Arthur J.,Jr.,June 29,1959.
Arthur H.,Apr.11,1963.
Dottie M.,Oct.30,1913.
Lucy J.,June 9,1940.
Pearl B.,May 19,1962.
SANBORN
Cora H.,Jan.4,1932.
D.W.,May 17,1948.
Eleanor R.,Dec.5,1956.
Fred E.,Dec.26,1926.
SAMPSON
Frederick B.,1874-Oct.5,1906.
Hattie,1849-1874.
SANDS
Douglas,June 15,1992.
SANFORD
Fred A.,1867-Apr.23,1942.
James S.,1854-June 21,1938.
Nathan J.,1826-1900.
Sarah M.,1826-Aug.17,1900.
SANTORO
John H.,Dec.4,1874,46y.
SANVILLE
Frank Ivory,May 1,1978.
Frank J.,Jr.,Jan.17,1943.
SARGENT
Clara A.,Apr.27,1966.
inf/o Louis,Feb.2,1920.
SAUNDERS
George G.,Mar.21,1909.
SAWTELLE
ch/o John,May 15,1919.
Barbara,Mar.29,1919.
John S.,Sept.7,1943.
Maud L.,June 17,1972.
SAWYER
Alice L.C.,May 15,1965.
Annie E.,Mar.1,1922.

Everett W.,May 15,1965.
Joseph W.,June 21,1924.
Martha A. McQuillan,1828-Nov.1910.
Richard,May 6,1991.
Martha McQuillan,1910.
SCAMMAN
Annah Davis,June 4,1875,76y,
2nd w/o Edward.
Anna Maria,Sept.22,1851-
Dec.20,1917,d/o Edw.& Sarah P.
Annie,May 16,1918.
Arzilla Whitney,1843-May 9,1914,
w/o Fred D.
Edward,Apr.30,1790-Dec.29,1869.
Edward Allen,Mar.14,1858-Dec.1,1883
s/o Edw.& Sarah.
Frederick D.,1838-July 3,1915.
Henry G.,Jr.,July 25,1967.
Polly Davis,Oct.3,1825,33y,1st w/o Ed.
Sarah P. Wingate,Nov.26,1867,42y,
w/o Edward.
SCOTT
Eva C.,Dec.10,1959.
SCRIBNER
Ernest F.,1977.
Olive,May 1,1989.
SEGER
Doris,Sept.26,1980.
Emma W.,Oct.14,1957.
James A.,Jan.10,1963.
John,Sept.12,1940.
SHACKFORD
Bessie C.,Jan.4,1924,w/o Theo.
Elizabeth O.Wood,1837-1896,w/o J.F.
Joseph F.,1839-1903.
M.T.,1897-1902.
Sarah D. Bradbury,1839-1907,
w/o Theo.
Stephen W.,Mar.25,1928.
Theodore,Dec.2,1920.
SHAW
Charles C.,Jan.29,1955.
Esther P.,July 28,1951.
Eugene K.,July 7,1942.
F.Alden,July 4,1982.
Herbert,Oct.22,1986.
Hubert Alden,Jan.3,1956.
Josiah,Nov.7,1852,78y.
Margaret,Nov.1986.
Tabitha Watson,Mar.27,1868,91y,
w/o Josiah.
Timothy D.,May 24,1965,infant.
SHEDD
Lucy,Dec.17,1793-Aug.8,1862,
d/o Eben & Lucy ?.
SHELDON
Ella,Apr.7,1918.

SHEPARD
Ethel A.,July 20,1976.
SHEPHERD
Esther,May 27,1982.
SHERMAN
Carrie L.,Nov.28,1959.
Ernest B.,Sept.27,1957.
Henrietta,Nov.25,1950.
Stella I.,July 6,1940.
William G.,Aug.27,1944.
SHIRLEY
Charlotte R.Knight,1838-
Sept.15,1928,w/o Josiah C.
Edna A.,June 1,1968.
Josiah Chase,1825-1895.
Philip E.,June 22,1955.
SHOREY
John,1826-July 20,1909.
Rebecca S.,1828-1894.
SHUGARS
Charles,Apr.14,1981.
SILVER
Gertrude E.,Apr.22,1954,w/o John.
John H.,1877-Nov.2,1947.
SIMMONS
Ellen Murch,Aug.20,1930.
John S.,1828-1902.
SKILLIN
Clara J.,Mar.8,1928.
Edna B.,Apr.6,1965.
Eleanor E.,Oct.24,1914.
Edward H.,Oct.5,1936.
George,Aug.17,1908.
George E.,Nov.4,1942.
Hazel M.,May 24,1947.
SKILLING
Frank,Nov.13,1893,39y.
Joseph,June 1888,74y.
Mary Nason,June 16,1894,72y, w/o Joseph.
SKILLINGS
Albert C.,Apr.16,1873,33y.
Edward A.,Nov.10,1887,19y, s/o Albert C., & Sarah J.
George,Sept.22,1826-Aug.15,1908.
Herbert N,.Dec.28,1936.
Horatio C.,June 8,1917.
Joseph,Apr.6,1853,74y.
Mary A. Hill,Sept.12,1832-Apr.30,1893,w/o George.
Mary E.,Oct.14,1932.
Mary L.,Sept.11,1857,41y, d/o Joseph & Susan.
Samuel M.,Sept.13,1941.
Sarah J. Buck,Dec.25,1846-May 9,1930.

Sussan Clark,Mar.2,1834,44y, w/o Joseph.
children/o George & Mary:
Delia J.,1892,4m;
George E.,1863-1942;
Herbert N.,1867-1936;
Martha J.,1883,18y;
Mary.1890,1y.
SLOMAN
Edith,Jan.13,1948.
SMALL
Clarence A.,Feb.8,1977.
SMART
Ernest,Apr.18,1977.
Frances A.,Jan.27,1969.
Lucy,Apr.25,1980.
Marion,Oct.22,1957.
SMILEY
Sarah J.,Mar.3,1877,82y,w/o Samuel.
SMITH
Almira,Jan.12,1867,73y,w/o Ebenez.
Benjamin R.,May 7,1971.
Caroline Fox,Nov.4,1890,75y, w/o H.P.A.
Catherine,Mar.22,1913.
Charles A.,Aug.9,1973.
Charles,Oct.6,1954.
child/o Robert,Nov.8,1913.
Charles Llewellyn,Sept.9,1840, 17m,s/o Stevens & Sophia.
David,Aug.14,1982.
Deborah Annie,Oct.8,1926.
E.H.F.,1844-1905.
Edgar H.,July 11,1949.
Edward T.,Gen.,1807-1885.
Edwin R.,1838-1892.
Ellen M.,Dec.31,1912.
Esther H.,Dec.8,1954.
Fanny,1844-Apr.1931,d/o W.P.& M.J.
Frank W.,Sept.18,1969.
Geneva,Aug.7,1979.
Grace,May 28,1982.
H.P.A.,Nov.20,1870,50y.
Helen H.,July 19,1975.
Helen,Aug.1977.
Henry W.,Jul 19,1918.
Horatio Fox,Aug.28,1864,19y, s/o H.P.A. & Caroline.
Howard,Sept.19,1988.
infant,Dec.27,1972.
Jacob Sheafe,Apr.28,1786-May 1,1880
James E.,June 29,1966.
John & Mary,XXXX,can't read.
Katherine S.,Apr.20,1926.
Katherine Towle,1825-1913, wid/o J.Howe.
Laura Ann,May 21,1951.

Leslie,Sept.18,1956.
Lucy Ann,Nov.22,1846,18y,
    d/o Ebenezer & Almira.
Mabel M.,Nov.21,1945.
Malcolm,May 5,1985.
Margaret,1814-1897,w/o Gen.Edw.T.
Martha L.,Oct.31,1861,20y,
    d/o Stevens & Sophia C.
Mary A.,Nov.1,1923.
Mary J.,1806-1892,w/o W.P.
Mary,Oct.16,1891,80y,w/o Wm.
Marylin D.,Sept.27,1976.
Mildred (Lulu),Sept.19,1986.
Myrtle E.,Apr.23,1958.
Oliver,Apr.12,1910.
Oliver,Dec.13,1922.
Philip,July 5,1949.
Ronald H.,Oct.31,1954.
Robert H.,July 23,1921.
Samuel,Nov.6,1839,21y,s/o Jacob &
    Mary L. Lewis Smith.
Sarah A,.Apr.1,1910.
Silas M.,XXXX,Co.A.,5th Me Inf.
Sophia C.,Oct.8,1859,51y,w/o Stevens.
Stevens,Sept.13,1876.
Tabitha Stephenson,Dec.1,1857,69y,
    2nd w/o Jacob S.
Wendell P.,1805-1862.
William,Jan.15,1891,84y.
SNOW
Christine L.,Apr.21,1971.
Donald F.,July 27,1971.
SOULE
Benjamin,Dec.22,1968.
Mary,1849-1890,w/o Charles B.
Mildred M.,Jan.20,1942.
Theodora,May 4,1990.
SOUTH
James W.,Apr.29,1926.
Myra B.,Aug.24,1918.
SOUTHARD
Kenneth R.,Oct.23,1987.
SPENCE
Doris D.,June 21,1954.
Fred W.,Apr.7,1972.
SPURR
Frank,May 18,1984.
STACKPOLE
Jennie E.,Jan.12,1937.
STALL
J.A.,Dec.31,1920.
STANDLEY
Angela,Sept.15,1989,infant.
STANTON
Isabelle,Jan.10,1926.
STANWOOD
Amelia A.,Oct.1906,w/o Arthur H.

Arthur H.,July 2,1936.
Caroline,Apr.13,1915.
Edith H.,Mar.14,1926.
STAPLES
Ai,Feb.22,1835,58y,s/o Jeremiah.
Alexander McLellan,Sept.10,1844,
    41y,at St.Mary's Geo.
Bethiah T. Lincoln,1803-1896,
    1st h. Alexander Staples,
    2nd h.Samuel Greene.
Ellen R.,1823-Nov.1846,23y,
    d/o Ai & Eunice.
Eunice McLellan,Sept.28,1844,63y,
    w/o Ai.
Jeremiah,May 19,1868,58y,
    1st w. Ann Murray,
    2nd w. Sarah Emery.
Mary Elizabeth,July 18,1874,36y,
    d/o Wm. & Mary.
Mary McLellan,July 16,1852,
    56y,w/o William.
Nancy M.,Mar.7,1851,23y,
    d/o William & Mary.
William,July 28,1838,41y,s/o Samuel.
children/o Alexander & Bethiah:
    J. Alexander,1833-1842;
    Lincoln Thaxter,1843-1872;
    Lydia A.T.,1828-1833.
    Statira,1830-1832.
STEVENS
Ansel,1836-Nov.10,1911.
Benjamin,Nov.29,1843,83y,
    h/o Amy Webb.
Charlotte,Nov.11,1844,56y.
Charlotte Ann,Jan.20,1840,21y,
    d/o Henry & Hannah.
Cora M.,Sept.16,1864,5m,
    d/o Parker & Laura F.
Elizabeth Davis,1833-1902,w/o Ansel.
Elizabeth Wescott Chadbourne,
    Mar.23,1820-Apr.21,1889,w/o J.I.
Evelyn,July 9,1985.
Farnum,Feb.25,1887,85y.
Fred S.,Apr.27,1927.
Hannah,Aug.7,1877,73,w/o Farnum.
Hannah Libby,Oct.21,1866,75y,
    w/o Henry.
Henry,Aug.11,1835,51y,s/o Ben.Jr.
John M.,1844-1865,s/i J.I.& Sarah.
Jonathan Ignatius,Jan.6,1812-
    July 26,1867.
Madeline,Sept.30,1850,23m,
    d/o J.I.& Sarah.
Maud C.,May 6,1974.
Nellie P.,Jan.29,1947.
Parker,Sept.30,1864,31y.
Rebecca,May 29,1873,87y.

Roy,May 18,1959.
Sarah Pitts,Mar.15,1855,38y,w/o J.I.
Zilmorah,Jan.30,1853,23m.
children/o Farnum & Hannah:
Almon,July 28,1863,16y,
Eliphalet I.,Dec.17,1832,1y,
Olive M.,June 20,1878,36y,
STEPHENSON
Almira S.,Mar.31,1809-Dec.21,1836,
d/o Samul & Abigail.
Anne L.,Jan.1,1814-Apr.21,1861,
d/o Samuel & Abigail.
Frederick,May 10,1813-Apr.29,1887,
s/o Stephen & Harriet.
Harriet Storer,Feb.9,1838,52y,
w/o Capt.Stephen.
Mary L.,Mar.1,1816-Apr.18,1857,
d/o Samuel & Abigail.
Stephen,Capt.,Mar.10,1831,52y,
s/o Capt. John.
Stephen,Feb.12,1846,37y,
s/o Capt.Stephen.
William Henry,Oct.31,1850,40y,
in Singapore,s/o Stephen & Harriet.
STEWART
Elizabeth S.,Jan.21,1938.
Herbert,June 9,1986.
Robert,Oct.27,1994.
Lois,Feb.3,1951,w/o William.
William H.,Rev.,May 9,1955.
Winifred H.,Oct.15,1982.
STICKNEY
Abbie F.,Mar.18,1899,79y,w/o John F.
Bertie,XXXX,7m.
Charles A.,Mar.8,1882,35y.
Fred A.,Nov.20,1886,35y.
John F.,Sept.5,1887,66y.
STIEHL
Ralph,Oct.27,1978.
Geneva M.,June 4,1976.
Ann McDaniel,Mar.25,1937.
STIGMAN
Alicia,July 17,1989.
Henry,Apr.24,1974.
Irene,July 1,1979.
James H.,Aug.15,1965.
Jennie Newcomb,1872-1904.
Solon,June 2,1982.
Willaim T.,Nov.28,1910.
William R.,Jr.,Nov.25,1928.
William T.,1865-Dec.27,1923.
STILPHEN
L.H.,Sept.26,1922.
Rosa D.,Dec.14,1923.
STONE
Archelaus,1791-1865,s/o Jonathan.
Betsey Emery,1793-1879,w/o Arch.

Elizabeth H. Bangs,1819-Mar.11,1911.
Gertrude L.,July 5,1960.
Ralph C.,July 10,1966.
Samuel E.,1817-July 1906,h/o E.H.B.
children/o Samuel F.& Elizabeth:
Mary E.,1845-1878;
Willie R.,1851-1876.
STORER
Caroline,Mar.1,1848,39y,d/o E.& C.
Catherine,June 3,1774-Feb.26,1840,
w/o Ebenezer.
Catherine,Jan.7,1887,78y,
d/o Ebenezer & Catherine.
Ebenezer,b.Wells,July 98,1758-
Jan.20,1846,s/o John,Jr.
Elizabeth Lake,May 23,1840,12y,
d/o Eben. & Eunice.
Ellen,1812-May 19,1857,d/o E.& C.
George L.,Nov.1,1854,64y,
s/o Ebenezer & Eunice.
Louisa C.,Nov.23,1854,12y,d/o E.& C.
Mary Ann,Mar.5,1844,55y,d/o E.& E.
William H.,1810-1878,s/o Eben. &
Catherine,h/o Harriett Rolette.
STROUT
Daniel S.,Mar.10,1870,71y.
George E.,Dec.31,1937.
George H.,Mar.29,1946.
George,1828-1889.
Georgia E.,Oct.30,1975.
Harry O.,Aug.4,1910.
Henrietta C.,Mar.19,1932.
Isaac H.,1861-1901.
Lydia W.,Aug.14,1926.
Phebe L. Meserve,July 1,1880,
58y,2nd w/o Wm.
Rebecca A.,Sept.17,1926.
Rebecca B.,Mar.13,1867,69y,
w/o Daniel S.
Sarah E.,July 26,1936.
William E.,July 5,1916.
William D.,Jan.4,1951.
STURGIS
Alonzo,May 3,1961.
David,1817-1882.
David,Jr.,Nov.5,1981.
Dorothy,Nov.7,1979.
Fred O.,1862-1899.
Harriett Paine,1830-1881.
Kezia H.,1871-1895,d/o M.C.& M.L.
Marshall C.,Apr.3,1925.
Mary L.,Mar.12,1934,w/o Marshall.
Nellie Jane Tripp,June 26,1928.
William L.,Oct.25,1968.
SUMMERSIDES
Annie J.,1870-Sept.9,1939.
Charles H.,1858-1875.

Effie J.,Oct.15,1950.
Frederick R.,Apr.16,1960.
John C.,Capt.,1832-1902,h/o Miriam.
John L.,1860-1862.
Miriam R.,1836-Mar.21,1909.
Marion,Aug.30,1963.
SWEETSER
Henry,Apr.8,1925,h/o Mary.
Mary E.Elder,Apr.3,1915.
SWETT
Barbara,May 1,1978.
Caroline A.,Jan.5,1956.
Caroline,Apr.28,1990.
Eddie M.,1883-1894,s/o H.F.& C.A.
infant,1894.
Mabel J.,Dec.7,1962.
Maynard L.,Jan.1,1963.
Timothy,July 17,1979.
William H.,Dec.3,1983.
SYKES
Ruth L.,Feb.8,1972.
SYLVESTER
Mamie,May 4,1956.
Warren C.,Nov.9,1946.
SYMES
Ella F.,Dec.25,1885,24y,w/o Frank S.
Harry,1828,4y.
SYPHERS
Leroy,Sept.22,1990.
Marjorie,July 27,1989.
TALBOT
Nellie M. Roberts,1866-1891,w/o E.I.
TANDBERG
Charles,Mar.1955.
Karen,1845-1908,w/o Thomas.
S.Thomas,1843-1903.
TAPLEY
ch/o Melville,June 10,1909.
Melvin E.,Apr.8,1930.
Nellie H.,Apr.8,1942.
TARBOX
Frank,Nov.18,1930.
Frank,1858-1878, W.H.F.& B.F.(back)
Hannah,XXXX, M.D.S.(on back)
Samuel,Nov.18,1930.
TARR
Edith L.,May 31,1974.
TAYLOR
Aldana,July 10,1910,wid/o Horace.
Horace P.,Nov.22,1887,59y.
Lona May,Mar.29,1948.
Lori,Oct.30,1976.
TEMM
Edwin C.,Mar.19,1964.
TEMPLETON
Lee W.,Dec.21,1961.

THESTRUP
George J.,Mar.11,1824-July 3,1908.
Mary Ellen,May 16,1848-
Nov.25,1922,w/o Geo. J.
Nancy,June 12,1826-Nov.1884,
w/o George J.
THOMAS
James G.,XXXX,16th Me Inf.
William E.,1829-Mar.23,1909.
THOMBS
George F.,July 4,1943.
Irene M.,June 1,1952.
THOMES
Alisha,Nov.22,1953.
L.T.,1847-1918.
Llewellyn True,Sept.12,1988.
Rebecca E.,1848-Apr.10,1911,
w/o L.T.
children/o L.T. & Rebecca:
Hollis E.,1872-1873;
Ezra H.,1873-1887;
Hattie J.,1880-1895;
Hattie M.,1885-1885;
Elizabeth F.,1880-1899.
THOMPSON
Charles,Sept.17,1922.
Clara J.,1854-1886.
George M.,1849-1898.
Grace Ellen,Sept.2,1937.
Henry A., Co.L. 1st ME.Inf.
Walter M.,1872-1895.
TIBBETTS
Annie L.,July 20,1868,26y,w/o John F.
TODD
Charles W.,Apr.22,1949.
Lydia A.,Mar.1,1911.
Minnie B.,Nov.5,1940.
TOKARSKI
Jospehine D.,July 1,1940.
TOMLINSON
Bertha,Oct.22,1952.
TOWLE
Jeremiah,1770-1846.
Ralph L.,Aug.101,964.
TRACY
Bertha W.,Dec.23,1943.
George B.,Mar.30,1936.
Sidney S.,Aug.27,1927.
TRAVERS
Clifton C.,Feb.24,1955.
John R.,Nov.5,1930.
TREWORGY
Edith N.,Nov.2,1956.
Leon M.,May 22,1946.
Paul W.,July 28,1972.
TRIPP
Pheba Ann,Jan.31,1927.

TUPPER
Ralph L.,Mar.19,1944.
TURNER
Elizabeth C.,Oct.18,1950.
Elizabeth W.,July 29,1917.
James B.,Apr.10,1911.
Lincoln,Oct.5,1982.
Marjorie,Dec.1,1993.
TUTTLE
William,May 17,1985.
TWADDEL
Caitlin Ann,May 19,1983,newb.
TWOMBLEY
Alice M.,1886-1895.
Charles M.,1877-1896.
Frank W.,1875-Apr.30,1950.
George,1880-1884.
Harry N.,Dec.10,1943.
Jennie W.,Feb.2,1931.
Nellie M.,June 9,1970.
Ruth G.,Mar.6,1935.
Wilson M.,Mar.4,1928.
TYLER
Allen,1814-1896.
Daniel,Mar.3,1860,59y.
Mary H.,Feb.1,1888,69y,w/o Daniel.
TYNG
Elizabeth Ross,Oct.25,1831,80y,
  w/o Wm,bu:Eastern Cem.,Portland.
UMPHREY
Louise,Sept.7,1988.
USHER
Carl,Nov.7,1984.
Charles E.,1848-Dec.26,1880,
  h/o Susan Benson,s/o G.W.& L.M.
Ella W.,Sept.26,1947.
Ethel W.,Aug.30,1967.
Henrietta,Nov.28,1941.
Henry A.,1827-1872,h/o Olive.
Henry A.,Apr.8,1972.
Henry William,Aug.31,1943.
Laura D.,May 11,1972.
Olive J.,1827-May 11,1884.
Sarah B.,June 5,1919.
William H.,Nov.28,1939.
VAN BLAREOM
infant,Apr.4,1954.
VAUGHN
Irving,Aug.21,1989.
VERRILL
Norman L.,May 1,1962.
Norman,Oct.29,1934,infant.
Paul E.,Mar.21,1983,58y.
VINE
John D.,Nov.2,1884,h/o Sarah.
John,Jr.,Sept.19,1868,36y.
Sarah Jane,May 30,1870,60y.

WADSWORTH
Gladys S.,Dec.15,1930.
WAGG
Charlotte Hobbs,Feb.2,1907,
  81y,2nd w/o James.
Edward A.,1861-1886,s/o Jas.& C.H.
Frances L.,Mar.5,1854,37y,w/o Jas.
Freddie,XXXX.
James,Apr.24,1814-Dec.21,1890.
James Henry,1886-1886,s/o J.& C.H.
WAGNER
female,July 23,1970.
Lena R.,June 17,1964.
Ruth G.,Oct.14,1950.
Winifield S.,Apr.16,1963.
WALKER
A.E.,Dec.18,1908.
Albert E.,Oct.1,1939.
Albert L.,May 11,1893,30y,
  s/o Ivory & Sarah.
Albert R.,Dec.16,1948.
Charles A.,July 9,1921.
Elizabeth G.,Oct.31,1970.
Ellen G.,July 8,1957.
Eugene,July 28,1948.
Francis,Nov.5,1958.
Frank H.,Jan.19,1946.
Gladys M.,Mar.14,1945.
Humphrey M.,Aug.21,1829-1909.
Ivory,Oct.31,1906,81y.
John R.,Mar.4,1940,infant.
Lawrence S.,Oct.12,1930.
Lloyd,Aug.1978.
Mary S.,May 11,1939.
Ralph,Apr.17,1980.
Ruth,May 16,1987.
Sarah A.,Dec.31,1913.
Sarah A.,Nov.6,1894,59y,w/o Ivory.
W.L.,Dec.18,1908.
Willard L.,Feb.9,1914.
XX,May 12,1942.
WALLACE
Angelina T.,Sept.20,1926.
Homer,Dec.18,1908.
John C.,Feb.23,1912,Co.K.,25th Me.In
Sarah C.,Apr.26,1918.
William,Sept.8,1918.
WARD
Alphia,May 24,1915.
Philip H.,Dec.23,1940.
WARREN
Albert F.,Sept.14,1862,19y.
Barry Eugene,Feb.4,1935.
C.Elmer,Apr.9,1947.
Carrie,May 3,1938.
David,1794-1866.
David,1857-1894.

George W.,Jan.4,1853,22y.
J. Frank,Nov.7,1919.
Mrs J.F.,June 1,1909.
James,Rev.,Feb.2,1858,53y.
James,Feb.6,1905,82y.
Julia J.,Dec.28,1916.
Mary H.,1808-1891,w/o Wm.
Mary J.,Aug.26,1861,13y.
Mary M.,1849-1896.
Mary R.,Apr.19,1900,76y,w/o James.
Rebecca,1824-1903.
Rhoda Day,1851-1878.
Sabra Hill,1821-Jan.28,1919,
   w/o David (1866).
Sally J. Googins,Aug.4,1873,70y,
   w/o Maj. William.
Samuel,Jan.17,1837,81y.
Sarah A.,Mar.7,1913.
Sarah Gray,Mar.1840,79y,w/o Samuel.
Sarah Hubbard,Feb.28,1931.
Sarah,June 14,1836,46y,w/o James.
William,Mar.9,1879,83y,s/o Jas.
William,Rev.,Jan.28,1879,72y.
WASGATT
Ellen,Aug.10,1909.
WASS
Harry S.,Oct.7,1935.
Mable W.,Dec.2,1958.
WATERHOUSE
Ai,1792-1867.
Hannah Goodwin,1754-1842,w/o Theo.
Hattie M.,Nov.11,1872,w/o Cyrus T.,
   d/o Charles Dyer.
Olive,1793-1892,w/o Ai.
Theophilus,1751-1826.
WATERMAN
Aaron,Oct.10,1844,23y,s/o John & L.
Anna Anderson,Sept.7,1871,
   w/o Dr.John (1865).
Caroline F.,1888-Apr.4,1948,
   d/o John A. & M.E.S.
Charles W.,Aug.21,1930.
Charles,Oct.10,1837,10y,s/o J.& L.
Emma C.,Sept.19,1930.
Evelina L.,1830-1881.
John A.,1827-1893,w/o Evelina.
John A.,Apr.13,1938.
John,1865,76y.
Lauriette L.,Nov.17,1945.
Lucy D.,July 11,1931.
Margaret Payson,July 14,1926.
Mary E. Smith,1849-Apr.5,1936,
   w/o John A. (1893).
Meranda,Nov.4,1844,3y,d/o John &
   Lydia Hamilton Waterman.
Octavia M.,1953.
XX,1866-1931.

children/o John A. & Eveline L.:
Fanny,Mar.18,1859-Nov.28,1862;
XX,Jan.24,1837-Jan.7,1878.
WATERS
Abbie C.,1837-1877.
Abigail I.,1806-1873.
Cornelius,1795-1880.
James C.,1840-1870.
Rebecca I.,1831-1892.
children/o Geo.W. & Sarah Forbes.
Charles H.,May 12,1845,2y;
Harriett,May 24,1841,10m.
WATSON
Abbie A.,Apr.12,1966.
Ann Hopkinson,Nov.30,1882,79y,
   w/o Naaman.
Anna M.,1941.
Annie Louise,Nov.6,1975.
Aaron W.,1847-1870.
Charles H.,Dec.26,1826-Sept.19,1904,
   2nd w. Lydia Gage Rounds.
Clarinda F. Rand,1842-Nov.9,1913,
   w/o John G.
Clarence E.,May 10,1953.
Dorothy,Aug.17,1987.
Earl R.,Apr.25,1973.
Edmund,Dec.13,1847,76y.
Elizabeth,Apr.8,1882,66y,
   d/o Edmund.
Elizabeth Cressey,Jan.1,1838,
   63y,w/o Edmund.
Etta B.,Nov.18,1924.
Frank Lewis,Nov.20,1935.
Greenlief C.,Dec.18,1863,77y.
Henry H.,May 29,1946.
Henry L.,Apr.20,1977.
Jane,Sept.23,1940.
John,Oct.26,1834,93y.
John G.,1837-Feb.23,1917.
John S.,Feb.8,1945.
Katherine S.,Mar.18,1937.
Leonard,1824-1904.
Lillian Florence,Oct.23,1977.
Lydia Sands Tompson,Jan.22,1884,
   92y,w/o Greenlief C.
Lydia,May 27,1925.
Mary A.,1816-1887,w/o N.M.
Mary Small,June 25,1868,38y,
   1st w/o Charles.
Major R.,1814-Apr.1,1845,
   h/o Caroline McArthur.
Maud,1871-1877.
Mildred,Jan.26,1959.
Naaman C.,June 28,1886,81y.
Nathaniel M.,1813-1896.
Oliver C.,Feb.3,1917.

Robert Nathaniel,1893-1894,
  s/o Wm.& Etta.
Susannah,July 3,1858,59y,
  d/o Edmund.
Tabitha Whitney,Sept.13,1831,
  86y,w/o John.
Tabitha,Oct.28,1829,22y,
  d/o Edmund & Elizabeth.
Tabitha,May 24,1905,68y,d/o N.& Ann
William P.,M.D.,1852-Sept.14,1933.
William P.,Jr.,June 9,1951.
3 wives of William P.,M.D.:
  Annie Clement,1854-1883;
  Caroline Fogg,1849-1888/9;
  Etta Bachelder,1860-1924.
WATTS
Harry H.,Feb.20,1956.
Harry H.,Jan.21,1929,s.b.
John,Mar.1,1948.
Louise,May 25,1989.
May H.,May 25,1950.
WAY
Frances H.,Mar.24,1914,76y.
George H.,1839-Mar.2,1912,
  h/o Lucy A. Patrick.
Lucy A. Patrick,Jan.8,1891,52y.
Susan Shedd,Aug.1885,86y,
  w/o Christopher.
WEBB
Almarine J.,May 1912.
Alviavia,May 16,1912.
Lawrence E.,June 28,1954.
Lizzie A.,Aug.1,1914.
Sarah B.,July 25,1938.
WEEMAN
Ella Rankin,Jan.6,1951.
WEEKS
Alonzo,1836-1907.
Alvah,1810-1887.
Angelina H.,1813-1892,w/o Alvah.
Angelina R.,May 18,1954.
Barbara,Dec.29,1921.
Edna,Apr.9,1955.
Edward J.,184X-1905,
  h/o Marietta P.,s/o Robert & Harriet.
Gardiner D.,1834-1893.
Harriet A.,June 5,1947.
Harriet Huston Lomard,1811-1885.
infant,Mar.15,1912.
infants,1858 & 1877,2 s/o G.D.& N.J.
Julia F.,1829-1868.
Kenis,Nov.28,1984.
Marietta Plummer,1855-1943,
  w/o Edward J.
Mary E.,Oct.26,1925.
Mary Grace,Aug.21,1944.
Narcessa J.,1838-1895.

Percy T.,July17,1956.
Randall C.,1822-1907.
Robert,1818-1897.
Susan L.,1835-1891.
Wilhelmina A.,Sept.17,1957.
WELCH
L. James,June 24,1993.
WENTWORTH
Addie S.,Apr.19,1926.
Annie C.,June 14,1933.
Edith Ethelyn,188-1908.
George H.,1848-1911.
John G.,Sept.7,1916.
John R.,July 18,1941.
Lottie,XXXX.
Lucy A.T.,Apr.24,1973.
Lucy E.,Feb.10,1842-Oct.2,1859,
  d/o Thos. & Martha.
Margaret,1940.
Mary L. Wilson,1851-June 27,1921,
  w/o George H.
Mildred S.,July 12,1972.
Ralph M.,Aug.26,1983.
Ruth H.,Apr.29,1961.
T.Edward,June 3,1850-Feb.14,1860,
  s/o Thos. E. & Martha.
T.E.,Sept.13,1814-Nov.3,1882.
W.H.,May 28,1946.
Willard,Aug.30,1983.
WESCOTT
Alvin,Sept.17,1862,2m.
Eliza R.,May 28,1844,1y,
  d/o John & Eliza.
Eliza N. Riggs,Jna.30,1886,70y.
Emolis Weston,Dec.13,1835,9y,
  s/o Moriah & Reuben,Jr.
Frances Ann,1848-1858,d/o R.& M.A.
Jennie L.,Aug.2,1861,4y,
  d/o John & Eliza.
John E.,Sept.11,1846 ?,s/o John & E.
John,Nov.14,1892,77y,h/o Eliza N.R.
Lawrence J.,Mar.30,1964.
Lendall,1829-1907,s/o R.,Jr.& Maria.
Maria Gurney,Apr.18,1860,68y,
  w/o Reuben.
Martha A. Lombard,1823-Dec.5,1909.
Martha,Oct.27,1876,29y.
Reuben,Jr.,Aug.2,1838,50y.
Reuben III,1819-1899,h/o Martha A.L.
Willie J.,June 31,1881,20y,
  s/o John & Eliza.
WEST
Agnes B.,May 14,1940.
Chester Howard,Apr.29,1977.
Florence L.,Nov.30,1949.
WESTON
Edward P.,Oct.14,1879,60y.

Edward,Apr.18-June 25,1875 ?.
Mary Eliza,Sept.18,1868,51y,w/o Edw.
WETHERBEE
Andrew,Dec.21,1861,64y.
Susan,June 7,1880,86y,w/o Andrew.
WETSELL
George F.,Feb.11,1947.
Virginia,July 21,1981.
Jeanette E.,Jan.9,1919.
WEYMOUTH
William E.,Dec.7,1922.
WHEELER
Evelyn C.,Apr.18,1967.
William A.,Sept.24,1958.
WHITCOMB
Dorothy.Dec.18,1969.
Myron L.,III,Oct.26,1967.
WHITE
Frances A.,Apr.23,1971.
Huldah,17X8-187X,w/o John (18XX)
Huldah,Nov.26,1929.
John M.,1828-1892.
John,1784-18XX.
John,Nov.26,1929.
Reuben W.,Nov.23,1963.
WHITMAN
Alice P.,Sept.22,1968.
Frank B.,Mar.12,1949.
Perry F.,June 30,1916.
R. Berkeley,Nov.6,1993.
WHITMORE
Alice P.,Sept.25,1968.
George,1941.
WHITNEY
Alfred M.,1828-1899.
Benjamin F.,Jan.3,1928.
Charles,May 22,1875,60y.
Clarence E.,Aug.9,1941.
Eli J.,Oct.3,1912,86y,
h/o Sarah E. Brown.
Elizabeth P.,1826-1887,w/o A.M.
Eunice,May 17,1875,w/o Chas.
Frank A.,Mar.15,1912.
Frank E.,June 28,1962.
Fred F.,Nov.5,1919,47y.
Geneva F.,Apr.10,1962.
Ida F.,Nov.6,1917.
Jennie Pierce,June 29,1939.
Martha R.,June 1,1854,1y.
Mildred S.,Apr.17,1981.
Mildred W.,Mar.12,1959.
Ralph,Apr.11,1956.
Robie,Aug.21,1948.
Rozanna,June 3,1879,71y.
WHITTE
Edward E.,Sept.23,1879,
s/o Wm.H.&Mary D.S.

Dary Duguid Smith,July 30,1869,
30y,w/o Wm.H.
WHITTER
Daniel Francis,1851-1907,h/o Nancy.
Elizabeth M.,1885-Feb.19,1947.
Helen Mary,1881-1882.
Nancy Frye,1853-Feb.17,1926.
WIEDIEN
Carlton Davis,Jan.11932.
Marguerite H.,June 12,1985.
WIGGIN
Ernest,May 24,1972.
John A.,Rev.,July 20,1930.
Laura R.,Jan.23,1935.
Lewis E.,1940.
Lola E.,Dec.4,1938.
Mary A. Elliot,1815-1904,w/o David.
Naomi F.,Apr.10,1938.
Simeon R.,Oct.22,1916.
WILCOX
Theodore,May 27,1988.
WILDER
Alfred E.,Dec.10,1959.
Amanda,July 6,1921.
Henry,Sept.30,1985.
Marion,Aug.15,1954.
Walter,Mar.10,1914.
William W.,Feb.26,1942.
WILLIAMS
George H.,Mar.27,1926,Co.C,12th Me.
Jennie M.,1862-1897,w/o Geo.H.
WINCHESTER
Frederick B.,Feb.19,1932.
Georgia A.,Jan.1,1928.
Guy W.,June 3,1971.
WINGATE
Ellen G.,Jan.8,1922.
Henry F.,Feb.28,1835-Nov.28,1865,
bu: Gold Hill, Nevada.
John,Apr.28,1799-Sept.21,1858.
Mary E.,June 29,1924.
Rebecca I.,Oct.30,1830-Aug.14,1853.
Sophronia I.,Sept.5,1799-
Mar.31,1886,w/o John.
WOOD
Albion P.,1820-Feb.4,1883,
h/o Jane B. Wales.
Anthony,Apr.20,1963.
Elsie V.,Dec.10,1950.
George A.,Sept.27,1983.
George L.,1882-1956.
George R.,Oct.30,1956.
George W.May 16,1859-
Oct.23,1860,s/o Albion.
Harry E.,Apr.18,1968.
Jane B.,Dec.24,1915.
Josephine,Sept.7,1947.

Mary,May 16,1859-Mar.20,1866,
    d/o A.P.& J.P.
Nanette K.,May 29,1901-
    Sept.12,1967.
Olive,Oct.19,1856-Mar.21,1866,
    d/o A.P.& J.B.
WOODMAN
Alice Lena,1865-Feb.25,1928.
Jane,May 16,1912.
Martha B.,May 13,1848,25y,w/o M.H.
Olive B.,1823-1895.
Willard W.,Sept.5,1944.
WOODS
Wesley,May 24,1922.
WOODWARD
Edna J.,May 20,1992,101y,
    w/o Louis B.,d/o Wm.& Mary Ellen
    Sturgis Leavitt.
Lewis B.,Feb.10,1965.
WORCHESTER
Susan Edwards,Sept.14,1874,92y,
    w/o Thomas.
Thomas,Mar.1845,72y,s/o George &
    Margaret.
WORDEN
Annie L.,Dec.23,1923.
Joseph E.,Jan.16,1934.
WORTHLEY
Mary J. Allen,1863-Aug.10,1909,
    w/o N.T.,Jr.
Nathaniel J.,Jr.,Nov.21,1940.
WRIGHT
Alvin W.,Sept.6,1972.
Charles E.,Sept.8,1936.
Fletcher,June 8,1988.
Irvin P.,Jan.26,1950.
Marie,June 8,1988,w/o Fletcher.
Mary Elizabeth,Aug.18,1934.
YORK
Abbie R.Stickney,1895,30y,w/o Geo.
YOUNG
infant,Nov.2,1973.
Annette,May 2,1985.
Beulah E.,Dec.1,1975.
Chester L.,Apr.15,1966.
Edna W.,Apr.26,1967.
Edward L.,Mar.19,1965.
Elizabeth,Dec.23,1923.
Ernest S.,Dec.4,1972.
Frank O.,1895.
Frank D.,Apr.22,1977.
Gary A.,May 26,1955.
George F.,Feb.27,1937.
Lilliam L.,Aug.19,1954.
Lucy Harmon,1898-July 6,1919,
    w/o Frank O.
Mary Baker,Aug.6,1975.

Mary Belle,July 3,1934.
Phylis A.,Oct.19,1918.
Ruth,Nov.5,1986.
Walter Earl,Apr.28,1993.
Walter T.,Aug.12.1973.
William Edward,Jan.25,1930.
XX
Orrin A.,Mar.9,1858,5y.

Monument:

**Dedicated to the Memory of
Comrades of John R. Adams
Post No.101 Organized
June 16,1884,
Department of Maine G.A.R.**
(their order)

Bragdon, Edward P.M.
Berry, Hiram
Bartlett, George E.
Burnell, Melville C.
Billings, Horatio
Burnell, Nathaniel A.
Brackett, George A.
Colby, Joseph
Day,George L.
Davis, Charles
Douglass,Elisha
Davis,Daniel W.
Demerritt, Frank E.
Freeman, James E.
French, George
Forbes, Darwin A.
Floyd, George M.
Goff, Elias F.
Gustin, George B.
Harding, Edward
Harding, Josiah
Harding, Walter
Harding, Coleman
Harding, Edwin S.
Harding, Frank C.
Hale, Henry W.
Hague, William B.
Haines, Charles F.
Hall, Stillman
Hanson, Joseph B.
Hoyt, Samuel C.
Huston, John
Hasty, WIlliam
James, Joseph
Kane, Andrew C.
Lincoln, Albert W.
Lord, John A.
Little, James W.
Libby, Steven P.

Lane, Nathan
Libby, Lendall A.
McLellan, Acton P.
McLellan, Josiah S.
Maryfield, Moses B.
Merrill, William
Motley, George H.
Millett, Henry R.
McDonough, Thomas
Marston, Albion K.P.
Pillsbury, George W.
Patrick, Albert
Pierce, Levi L.
Robie, Frederick
Ridlon, Lorenzo E.
Sturgis, Marshall C.
Sanborn, John W.
Strout, William E.
Summerside, John C.
Small, George F.
Sweetser, Henry N.
Spinney, John D.
Shackford, Theodore
Small,Benjamin
Shaw, Carlile W.
Thomas, Manuel
Thomas, James S.
Whitney,Benjamin F.
Winslow, Levi H.
Wallace, John C.
Whitney, Frank C.
    end

C. T. AMES,

DEALER IN

Granite AND

Marble

Monuments.

Cemetery Work of all Kinds.
Office—15 Main St.. West End.   House—92 Church St.
WESTBROOK, MAINE.
(1897)

"Oh! friends of mortal years,
The trusted and the true;
Ye are watching still in the
"vale of tears",
But I wait to welcome you."

✦ **SMITH STREET CEMETERY** ✦
18 Smith Street, South Portland.
  On behalf of the Independent Order B'nai B'rith, Barnard Aaronson, Morris Stearns and Samuel C. Abrahams purchased a sixty-five by one hundred foot lot from John Woodbury in May 1875. This was Portland's first Jewish Cemetery. The stones in Hebrew are marked with an [H]. Some stones were in poor condition making translations into English difficult. What could not be translated very well is at the end. Many thanks to Rabbi & Mrs. Wilensky for translating 40 stones into English and to Jill Ketover for double checking these translations.

ABRAHAMSON
Rose,Mar.18,1936.
ABRAMS
Abraham Sol,1889-1916.
Abram,1877-1938.
Bertha,1883-1945,w/o Abram.
Dora,1840-1910, w/o Isaac.
Etta Shalit, Apr.14,1865-
  June 12,1941.
Hiram,Feb.22,1878-
  Nov.15,1926,s/o Isaac & Dora.
Isaac,1844-1922.
Louis H.,Aug.27,1889,80y.
William,Mar.12,1870-
  Sept.16,1895,s/o Isaac & Dora.
ALBERT
David,1847-1922.
Reisel,1866-1916.
ALPAROWITZ
Fannie,1889-1902,
  d/o Simon & Mary E.
BERENSON
Hyman H.,May 1880-May 1892.
BERENSTEIN
Chaim Tsvi,6th of Kislev XXXX [H].
BERLINER
Ida,1927.
Louis (Yehudah),Jan.13,1912,
  s/o Tsvi Dov.
BERMAN
Aaron Z.,1869-1922.
Toubie,Dec.4,1897,72y.
  w/o Shia, [H].
Tserna Glika Yudelson,
  May 26,1915,d/o Yeshayahu [H]
S. (Yeshayahu),5675-1914,
  s/o Yosef [H].

BERNSTEIN
Bernard S.,Apr.6,1910-
July 17,1920, s/o J.S.
Hyman Leo,Apr.25,1890-
Dec.13,1900.
Joseph S.,Oct.13,1935,67y.
Leonard H.,Dec.3,1911-
July 22,1919,s/o J.S.
Thressa Levin,Sept.20,1876-
Oct.26,1958,w/o Joseph.
BOAS
Isaac,Dec.27,1881,75y.
BRENTON
Yisrael Yitzchak [H].
BRIGGS
Cyrus K.,Nov.1,1976.
Josiah [H].
Sara Devorah,10th of Tamuz,
d/o Yitzchak.
Teibe,Apr.10,1920 [H].
Yitshak,6th of Cheshvan 5670-1909,
s/o Yeshaya [H].
CAPLAN
L.,1855-1923.
Ray, Mrs.,XXXX [H].
CHACHAM
David 14th day of Kislev-5659.
COBERMAN
Simon,Feb.12,1921,
s/o Avraham Azev Chain [H].
COHEN
Aida Helen,Oct.7,1924,17y,
d/o Herman & Rose.
Bernard,1870-1946.
Esther Judelshon,1878-1953,
w/o Bernard.
Naftoli,1913.
Nathan,1899-1907,
s/o Bernard & Dora.
Rose,1884-1929.
Rosie,June 24,1892,22y.
Zalman,26th of Cheshvan XXXX,12y,
s/o Naftoli & Fagie Yudis Cohen [H].
COOK
Abram,Oct.8,1935,h/o Minnie.
Bessie M.,Oct.30,1919.
Minnie,Jan.6,1941,48y.
Max L.,XXXX.
Yenke,Dec.23,1925,w/o Shmuel,
d/o Avraham Tsvi [H].
Shmuel,Sept.24,1924,
s/o Yechiel Mechel (Kuk) [H].
CUMMINGS
Frank,July 31-Aug.28,1923.
Herman G.,June 14,1888-
Feb.15,1949.

Marion,Apr.20,1888-
Apr.24,1950,w/o Herman.
DALTON
Rebecca,Nov.15,1931.
DAVIS
Alfred D.,Oct.23,1923,23y.,
s/o Harmon & Anna Briggs Davis.
Anna C.,Feb.20,1962.
Harmon,1870-1935,
Jennie,1870-1946.
DION
Mary,1855-1934.
Simon,1851-1908.
DORFMAN
Rachel S.,Sept.13,1923.
Simon,Mar.30,1916.
DRUKER
Annie,Oct.8,1893,35y,w/o Nathan.
DVILINSKY
Israel, XXXX [H].
EPSTEIN
Esther,1894.
Nahum,1914.
ERLICK
Philip,1853-1908,b.Austria.
EVANS
Rassia,1864-1922.
FRANK
Abraham Louis,July 4,1891-
Oct.17,1931.
Frances Rose,Oct.18,1892-
Dec.31,1975.
GINSBURG
Annie (Henna),Jan.11,1919,
w/o Berry,d/o Yehuda.
Berry,XXXX [H]
GOLDBERG
Jennie,1864-1915.
Max,1862-1940.
Yaba Rivka,6th of Tammuz 5679-
1919,d/o Betzalel [H].
GOLDBLATT
Ada L.,Oct.7,1863-July 22,1941.
Hilton M.,July 24,1894-June 8,1981.
Marckus S.,Dec.15,1856-
Mar.25,1926.
GOLDSTEIN
Rachel Leah,1852-July 4,1876.
Rosa,July 13,1920,35y.
GOODKOWSKY
Mark,Feb.25,1919,41y.
GOODSIDE
Abraham,1876-1940.
Jane,1876-1950.
GORDON
Henry R.,1874-1943.

GRAFF
David S.,Dec.25,1911,s/o Ar [H].
GREENBERG
Silas,Oct.24,1877-Nov.26,1884,
  s/o N. & T.
JUDELSHON
Birdie,1899-1979,w/o Harry S.
Harry S.,1895-1983.
Isaac,XXXX [H].
Jacob,1850-1942.
Eva Gertrude,Mar.25,1885,36y,
  w/o Isaac.
Rachel,Apr.9,1898,53y.
KALIN
Eli Zelig,July 14,1912,
  s/o Meir Klein.
Shprintza,Oct.24,1913,
  d/o Ben Tsion.
KAMBER
Bernard,1882-1954,h/o Ida.
Ida S.Briggs,May 11,1963.
KAPLAN
Rochel Leah,Mar.20,1920,
  d/o Yehuda Ezba.
KATZ
Yitshak,Oct.3,1910,s/o Tsvi [H].
LANSKY
Annie Dorfman,1890-1941.
LERMAN
Breindel Zeisel [H].
Kalman,6th of Tishrei 1920,
  s/o Shimon [H].
LEVINE
Dina,1901-1908 [H].
Jeneva M.,Nov.1882-July 1972.
Mark,1878-1925.
LEVINSKY
Harry,1893-1918.
Mordechau Shual,26th of Tamuz
  1902, s/o Yaakov Nisan.
Moshe,XXXX,s/o Yaakov Nisan.
Philip S.,June 16,1923,55y.
Sarah Leah,1872-1934 [H].
LEVINSON
Rachel (Rochel Hinda),no dates [H].
LUBIN
Simon,July 26,1898,78y.
LUBLINSKY
no name or dates,11m.
MARKSON
Ethel,1857-1924,w/o Nathan.
Jennie I.,(Shaina Chaya)
  Mar.7,1928,d/o Dovber [H]
Nathan,1857-1948.
MEYERS
Edith L. Briggs,June 21,1965.

Harold A.,Feb.7,1888-June 1,1934.
Herbert F.,July 20,1920-
  June 26,1943.
MICHAELSON
Max,1891-1919.
Morris,1910-1926.
Nettie,Jan.19,1940.
MILLER
Tevia,Jan.28,1931,52y.
MOORGOFSKY
Abraham,1842-1928.
Jennie,1848-Feb.16,1920.
MORRISON
Sprinze,b.1858-Nov.1893.
NATHAN
Gdalie,1862-1897.
NELSON
Chaya Toyba,(Toby),Nov.4,1932,
  d/o Yitzchak [H].
NOSON
R' Chaim Noson,June 13,1921,
  69y,s/o Moshe.
ORANSKY
Rebecca,June 9,1882-
  Feb.18,1931,d/o Yaakov.
PINK
Miriam Gertrude,1856-1935,
  m/o Bertha Pink Wolf.
ROBINSON
Abraham,Aug.18,1942.
Bessie,Dec.30,1902,34y.
David,Aug.4,1914,s/o Yitzak [H]
Etta,Nov.19,1946.
Max,1868-1938.
Mollie,Jan.24,1930.
Nechoma,1882-1925.
ROSENBERG
Albert,Aug.27,1895-
  Jan.21,1926,s/o Simon & Sarah.
Helen,Feb.14,1854-Nov.5,1886.
Judah,June 8,1825-Dec.13,1885.
Rebecca,Jan.15,1823- Mar.23,
  1906,b.Horszell,Russia Poland.
Simon,Mar.1852-June 3,1922.
ROSENBLOOM
Israel,June 23,1892,52y.
ROSENTHAL
Bertina Wolf,1891-1956,
  w/o George J.
George J.,1888-1940.
Harry,1890-1942,h/o Henrietta W.
Henrietta Wolf,1883-1962.
RUBBINS
Barnett,May 15,1925,72y,
  both died in Waterville,ME.
Bessie L.,Jan.14,1915,57y,
  w/o Barnett.

Israel,July 28,1919,28y.
RUBIN
Hannah H.,of Jerusalem,
Oct.18,1890.
RUBINSKY
Eva,1864-1908.
Milton W.,1921-1930.
SANFORD
Benjamin B.,Dr.,Nov.2,1899-
May 25,1959.
SANTOSKY
Bessie,Sept.18,1946.
Isaac,Feb.8,1904-Sept.30,1973.
Isaac S.,Mar.22,1941.
Joseph,Aug.21,1912-July 20,1972.
Louis,Jan.6,1896-Oct.4,1964.
Max,Aug.24,1942.
Simon,1833-Dec.16,1933.
Rebecca,Mar.4,1888,45y.
Reuben,July 13,1908-June 27,1974.
SCHIFF
Mulka Sima,Jan.31,1931.
SCHWEBE ?
Iky,Jan.14,1891-Sept.20,1891.
SHACHLACH
Mori Yitzchak ben chaim [H].
SHALIT
Annie R. Abrams,1873-1966.
Barnard L.,1869-1915.
David Harold,June 20,1858-
Nov.20,1927.
Harold M.,Dr.,Feb.11,1893-
Jan.4,1953.
Mae,Apr.18,1906-Apr.23,1949.
SHINE
Harry H.,July 25,1887-Aug.24,
1892,s/o Solomon & Emma.
Rebecca,Mar.29,1881-Sept.20,
1883,d/o Simon & Rosa.
William M.,1850-1895,
b. Kempen,Russia.
SILVERMAN
Anna L.,1894-1947.
Bessie Abrams,1906-1935,
w/o Samuel.
Chaya Rivka,Jan.2,1924,
d/o Yaakos Elazar [H].
Harry,1871-1909.
Isadore,1887-1906.
Liba Lea,Mar.21,1920,d/o Leib [H]
Samuel,1906-1935.
SIMANSKY
Abraham,1878-1921.
Chaya Rivka,Mar.26,1925,
d/o Aharon.
Harry S.,1882-1916.
Hyman,1866-1943.

Ida R.,Mar.26,1925,d/o Aharon [H].
William,1884-1936.
SIMAVLOS
David,Sept.8,1889.
SIMIANSKY
Jacob,1836-1916.
SIVOVLOS
Fannie,1860-1937.
Simon,1863-1908.
SLOSBERG
Lotta,1836-1918.
Maurice,1842-1922.
P.,1805-1912.
STAHL
Solomon C.,b.Germany,Jan.5,1846-
d.Groveton,NH,Sept.8,1878.
STAR
Ida,Feb.22,1936,49y,w/o Max.
Max,Dec.28,1953,67y.
Minnie,1847-1933.
TAYLOR
Esther,1863-1926,w/o Jason.
Isabella,Feb.3,1903,18y,
d/o Jason & Ester.
Jacob,Dec.25,1873-Jan.1,1934.
Jason,1862-1936.
Myer Benny,1895-1929.
THORNER
Abraham,Mar.13,1941,54y.
Rebecca,Jan.24,1945,54y.
UDEL (JUDELSON)
Ira,1890-1935.
WARSASKI
Allen H.L.,XXXX.
Eli Chaim Leib,Feb.15,1919,
s/o Avraham.
WATERMAN
Bernard S.,June18,1908,62y.
David Chanuch
ben R.Yedudah Levi [H].
Joseph B.,Mar.5,1922-
Feb.7,1923,s/o Ellis & Bella.
Sarah G.,1851-1926.
WEBBER
Abraham,July 3,1923,54y.
Elizabeth,Mar.22,1931,54y,
w/o Abraham.
Lillian H.,Feb.26,1967.
Max,1898-1976.
Rebecca,1900-1983,w/o Max.
Sarah,5601-5669/1841-1909 ?
William,1938.
WINAT
Sophie,1877-1959.
WOLF
Annie A.,Nov.9,1931,w/o Joseph.
Benjamin,1878-1954.

Bertha P.,1883-1965,w/o Benj.
Hiram,Dec.12,1876-Oct.2,1916,
  h/o Ida T.,s/o Jos. & Annie.
Hiram B.,1850-1925.
Ida T.,1878-Sept.17,1929,w/o Hiram.
infant,Sept.23,1906,s/o Hiram & I.T.
Jennie F.,1847-1899.
Joseph H.,Dec.13,1921.
Martie L.,Oct.7,1887,13y,
  s/o Joseph H.& Annie.
Sarah,June 6,1892,11y.
Zvi & Chana [H].
WOLMAN
Edward M.,June 19,1914-
  July 10,1923,s/o Frank.
Louis M.,1860-1932.
Mary,1860-1917,w/o Louis.
Yechiel Michel,Father,1834-1911,
  s/o Betzalel Tsiv, [H].
Chana Gittel,Mother,1837-1910,
  d/o Teshlam Eliezer [H].

Partial translations as follows:

Risha ?, 9th of Adar 5669-1909,
  70y,d/o Moshe [H].
Malka ? ,5666-1906,d/o Avraham.
Beila,June 16,1924,21y,
  d/o Chanoch Meyvosh.
Ettel Henna,6th of Iyar XXXX,
  d/o Avraham Shlomo.
Roder Dovber,Dec.3,1921,
  s/o Yaakov Ezro.
Eli Zelig,July 14,1912,
  s/o Meir Klein (Kalin).
Yitzchak,22 Cheshvan,s/o Chaim.
Shlomo Zalman,s/o Nafrali.
Yitshak,Oct.3,1910,s/o Tsvi.
Avraham,XXXX,s/o Yitschak Tsvi.
Yaakov,12th of Nisan XXXX,35y,
  s/o Moshe.
Chaim Tsvi,XXXX,s/o Shlomo.

Please feel free to contact Jewish Federation of any additions or corrections to this list. We would like it to be a correct as possible.

Blais Funeral Home
ROBERT E. BLAIS, Director

AMBULANCE SERVICE — MONUMENTS

Tel. 854-2341
35 CHURCH STREET (1963) WESTBROOK

J. F. SPEAR,
Furnishing Undertaker.

Coffins, Caskets and Robes of every kind desired.
FLOWERS AND WREATHS FURNISHED.
Hearse and Carriages Furnished at Reasonable Rates for any part of the Town.

111 MAIN STREET, - SACCARAPPA.
(1888)

ALBERT BOUCHER,
UNDERTAKER and
FUNERAL DIRECTOR

Graduate Massachusetts College of Embalming. Arterial Embalming.

10 RIVER ST. WESTBROOK.
(1904)

1904

C. T. AMES,
MANUFACTURER OF
Granite and Marble
MONUMENTS
and Tablets.

937 Main Street,
WESTBROOK, - ME.

JOHN W. HAY
Funeral Director

AMBULANCE SERVICE
795 MAIN STREET   WESTBROOK
          Telephone 854-2581 (1963)

Aaskov,15,153
Abbiog,168
Abbott,15,25,33,58,119,148,153,
  268,322,342,364
Abrahamson,413
Abrams,413
Acker,268
Adair,153
Adams,1,3,5,17,25,58,100,119,139,
  148,153,240,240a,268,339,364
Adde,153
Additon,153
Adjutant,78,329
Adkins,153
Afthim,268
Aherns,153
Ahlquist,344
Aho,153
Aikens,83
Akerly,268
Akers,72,139,241
Albee,153
Albert,268,413
Alberto,241
Alcorn,153
Alcott,119
Alden,87,119,153,241,364
Aldrich,25,53,74,87,344
Alewine,58
Alexander,87,153,241,364
Allan,153
Allard,268
Allen,1,6,8,15,17,25,41,44,49,
  51,53,58,71,74,76,87,119,148,
  153,241,268,319,329,339,342,
  363,364
Alore,152
Alparpwitz,413
Amato,87
Ames,87,119,154,355
Anagnestepoules,154
Andersen,153
Anderson,1,6,8,17,33,39,49,77,
  78,83,87,119,240a,241,268,
  322,364
Andren,154
Andrew,36,41,59
Andrews,59,154,241,364
Annis,155,268
Anthoine,41,59,70,83,148,155
Anthony,155
Anzelc,87
Appleby,155
Archambault,268
Archambeau,155
Archer,364
Arenovsky,155

Arey,155
Armentino,268
Armstrong,119,155,329,364
Arnold,268,365
Arntz,87
Arsenault,87,120,155,268
Ashby,155
Ashley,155
Ashworth,365
Asker,155
Asquith,6
Athas,155
Athearn,155
Atherton,18,59,87
Atkins,120
Atkinson,37,53,87,342,365
Atwater,41,155
Atwood,45,241
Aube,148,155,269
Aubin,155,269
Auclair,269
Aucoin,269
Audet,269
Auger,59
Auld,155
Austin,53,59,60,72,120,155,
  241,329,365
Averill,152
Avery,365
Axelson,155
Ayer,155,241,319,344,365
Babb,25,59,78,87,107,145,
  152,155,240a,241,269,365
Babbidge,25,120,148,156
Babcock,120,365
Babineau,269
Babkirk,365
Bachelder,1,6,53,78,120,156,
  240a,242,355,365
Bachofen,156,269
Bacon,53,78,139,156,243,
  319,322,329,353,365
Badger,87
Bagdahn,156
Bagley,25,243
Baglivo,329
Bahnert,156
Bailey,6,41,49,53,78,87,107,
  109,120,148,156,243,329,
  340,344,365
Baillargeon,269
Bain,270
Baird,156
Baker,25,39,41,51,53,59,72,87,156,
  243,270, 339,340,365
Balcourt,270
Baldwin,120

Balk,25
Ball,157
Ballard,120,157,329
Bamberg,157
Bancroft,157,365
Bangs,87,327,339,342,355,365
Banks,53,120,157,344
Barber,1
Barbour,1,110,120,146,157,
 240a,243,330
Barbrick,365
Bard,270
Barden,59
Baril,270
Barker,78,100,157,243,365
Barnes,157,365
Barney,157
Barr/e,270
Barrett,157
Barrows,120,157,270,365
Barry,157
Barstow,322
Barter,157
Bartlett,100,365
Bartol,139
Barton,44,157
Bassett,158,365
Baston,158
Batchelder,1,45,53,158,243,355
Batchelor,329
Bateman,139,
Bates,101
Bauer,49,59
Baxter,158
Bayliss,158
Beal/e,53,83,139,158
Beals,33,100
Beaman,366
Bean,23,120,148,158,243,322,
 342,366
Beane,59,353
Bearce,158
Beatty,158,270
Beauchamp,270
Beaudette,270
Beaudoin,270
Beaulec,158
Beaumier,158,270,329
Beaupre,270
Beautte,355
Beaver,158
Becker,270
Beckett,139
Beckwith,329 ,366
Bedell,120
Bedigan,87
Beede,366

Beels,100
Beem,18
Beers,59
Beesley,158
Begin,158,270
Belanger,270,329
Bell/e,45,87,158,243
Bellefeuille,271
Belyea,59
Beman,366
Bennett,59,83,120,158,243,271,
 322,329,366
Benoit,88,271
Benson,322,329,355,366
Bent,344
Berbasky,243
Berenson,413
Berenstain,413
Berg,120,271
Bergen,366
Bergeron,1,152,271
Berliner,413
Berman,413
Bernard,271
Bernier,158,271
Bernstein,414
Berry,49,59,78,100,120,158,
 243,272,322,329,342,344,366
Berryman,243
Berryment,159
Bertin,272
Berube,272
Bessley,59
Best,243
Bettez,272
Bettis,243,355
Bettney,159
Betts,244,340
Beverage,159
Bibeau/Bibault,272
Bickford,25,37,53,78,244,330,
 344,366
Bicknell,120
Billings,159,330,366
Billington,159
Bilodeau,159,272
Binette,272
Bird,159
Birnie,366
Birrell,322
Birtnell,244
Bisbee,159
Bishop,59,111,120,159
Bixby,145,159,240a,244
Black,25,59,88,159
Blackwood,159
Blair,355

Blais,272
Blaisdell,159,244
Blake,26,45,53,88,107,110,120,
 152,159,244,272,319,322,
Blake,342,353,355,366
Blanchard,4,6,15,18,33,121,148,
 160,272
Blanchet/te,160,273
Blasland,160
Blatchford,240a,244
Blemis,160
Blenis,160
Blenkhorn,160
Bliven,160
Block,273
Blood,366
Blouin,273
Boas,414
Bodge,36,53,59,88,121,160,
 330,340
Boe,160
Boff,160
Bogdahn,160,273
Bohnsen,160
Bohnson,244
Bois,273
Boissoneau,160,273
Boisvert,273
Boivin,273
Bolduc,160,273
Bolles,160
Bolster,59
Bolton,83,121,330,340,366
Bolus,88
Bona,273
Bond,101,244,366
Bondarko,160
Bonin,273
Bonnell,160
Bonney,121,344,366
Boody,41,88,121,160,244
Booker,367
Boomer,160
Boote,367
Booth,160
Boothby,110,121,160,244,355,367
Borek,367
Bortell,49,59
Borup,244
Bothwick,59
Botton,321,367
Bouchard,273
Boucher,88,273
Boudreau,88,273
Boulanger,274
Boulier,160
Boullie,148,161

Bourassa,274
Bourdage,160
Boure,160
Bourgeous,27
Bourque,274
Boussanneau,284
Boutelle,160
Bouthellette,161,274
Bowden,26,45,49,148
Bowdoin,367
Bowen,121
Bowers,161
Bowes,161
Bowie,8
Bowman,319
Boyce,161
Boyd,148,161,240a,244,322
Boyington,244
Boyle,161
Boynton,152,161
Brace,161
Brackett, 330,340,367
Brackett,15,16,17,18,23,42,59,
 71,78,107,121,148,161,244
Bracy,161
Bradbury,83,163,244,274,319,367
Braddock,367
Bradley,83,112,121,161,244
Brady,59
Bragdon,39,78,88,148,161,244,
 274,330,340,344,355,367
Braley,162
Brannigan,162
Branscombe,367
Branson,59
Brassard,162,274
Brazier,88,162
Breault,274
Breedlove,162
Breen,162
Breil,26
Brenton,414
Breton,274
Brewer,101,121
Briard,274
Bridge,330
Bridges,34,162,274,367
Bridgham,162
Briggs,319,414
Brigham,245,274
Brightman,162
Brighton,345
Brillingham,26
Brim,274
Brink,6
Brinkerhoff,345
Brisco,107

Brissette,274
Britt,49
Britton,240a,245,274
Brix,162
Broad,101,367
Broadhurst,367
Brocato,367
Broche,274,330
Brock,240a,245,367
Brockelbank,162
Brofee,367
Bromley,83
Brookes/s,49,70,162,275,330,367
Broome,59
Brow,367
Brown/e,8,18,26,36,42,44,45,
  49,54,59,78,83,88,101,111,
  121,145,148,152,162,240a,
  245,275, 330,340,345,367
Brownlee,162
Bruce,18,275
Brueck,162
Brume,88
Brunelle,275
Bruni,88
Bruns,8,88,101,162
Brunt,368
Brush,162
Bruton,45
Bryam,245
Bryan,275
Bryant,121,162,240a,245,345,
  356,368
Bryden,163
Brymer,275
Bryson,163,245,275
Bubar,54
Buchard,163
Buck,107,121,163,368
Buckland,88
Buckley,121,163
Buckman,8
Bucknam,8,18
Bugbee,163
Buhelt,322
Bumps,368
Bumpus,322
Bunker,340
Bunnell,163,245
Bunyan,163
Buogirno,330
Buote/Buotte,275
Burbank,368
Burchill,88,121,275
Burdwood,163,345
Burgess,163
Burgh,163

Burgin,163
Burgoyne,275,345
Burke,88,163,275,330
Burnell,34,49,163,245,356,368
Burnham,34,78,88,121,163,245,
  345,368
Burns,88,163,275,356
Burpee,164
Burrell,59
Burrill,275
Burroughs,159
Burrows,164,330,368
Burt,368
Burton,148,164,275,330
Busby,164
Bush,49,88
Bushley,88,368
Bushway,26
Bustin,59
Buteau,275
Butler,88,107,164,345,368
Butterfield,3,164,340,356
Butterick,319
Butts,54,164
Buxton,18,26,352
Buzen,54
Buzzell,164,368
Bye,164
Byrne,275,330
Byron,368
Cabana,164
Cabral,164,275
Caccia,164
Cahill,18
Cairns,164
Caissy,275
Calantonio,275
Calder,6,88
Caldwell,121,139,245,353,368
Calkins,49
Callahan,164
Callamore,164
Calnan,164
Cameron,164,275
Camire,164
Campbell,45,59,121,148,164,
  275,368
Canfield,164
Cannell,71,164,322
Canning,165
Cannon,368
Cantara,276
Canton,/Cantin,276
Cape,165
Caplan,414
Capon,345
Card,368

Cardwell,276
Carey,345,369
Cargill,369
Carle,88
Carleton,323
Carlin,276
Carll,49,340,369
Carlson,165
Carlton,88
Carmean,276
Carmichael,165,245
Carne,369
Caron,88,165,276
Carpenter,139,165,369
Carr,49,165,340,369
Carras,165
Carrier,26,276
Carrigan,369
Carrignan/Carignan,276
Carroll,45,149,152,165,276
Carson,369
Carswell,369
Carter,122,165,276,345,369
Cartier,356
Cartland,88,109,165
Cartoni,37
Cartret,165
Caruso,369
Caruthers,369
Carver,165,276,323,330
Cary,122,165,245
Casey,88,165,276
Cash,36,78,165,245,340
Cashman,369
Cassanos,165
Cassia,165
Castella,45
Castle,165
Castonguay,276
Caswell,54,78
Cater,165
Cates,165,369
Catlin,165
Caton,369
Cavaluzzi,369
Cedebjer,18
Cellamore,49
Center,26
Cererra,49
Chabot,330
Chacham,414
Chadborne,369
Chadbourne,165,319
Chadburn,166
Chadsey,122
Chadwick,166
Chaffin,88

Chailler,276
Chaisson,88,276
Chamard,166,276
Chamberlain,1,101,122
Chamberland,276
Chambers,122,166,330
Champagne,277
Champaine166
Chandler,34,51,59,88,149,166,
  330,369
Chaples,345
Chaplin,88,166,330,369
Chapman,101,152,166,277,323
Charest,277
Charette,277
Charland,277
Charles,323,330
Charlton,369
Charmard,166
Charon/Charron,122,277
Charpentier,59
Charrier,369
Chartier,277,356
Chas,122
Chase,18,34,45,54,89,122,151,
  166,245,277,352,369
Chasse/Chessey,277
Chayer,277
Chellis,369
Chenery,8,18,122
Cheney,18,59,122
Chesley,36,60,101,166,240a,245
Chichester,277
Chick/o,166
Chicohnee,152
Childs,122,277
Chin,166
Chipman,166
Choate,122
Chretien,277
Chrichett,246
Christe,122
Christensen,166,331
Christian,45,278
Christie,89,167,278
Christman,278
Chubbuck,122
Churchill,139,369
Chute,40,74,89,167,369
Cilley,122,167,331
Cizek,331,369
Clapp,122
Clapper,167
Clark/e,8,18,54,60,70,89,101,107,
  122,139,149,167,278,319,331,369
Claussen,167
Clay,78,167,338,353,370

Clayton,246
Cleary,278
Cleaves,26,370
Cleeves,167
Clement,26,122,167,240a,278,
 331,370
Clements,89,240a,246,353
Clemons,89,278
Cleveland,8
Clifford,26,139,278,331,370
Clinch,370
Clish,167
Closson,331
Cloudman,1,79,167,240a,246,
 331,342
Clough,8,34,122,167,246,370
Cloutier,167
Cloutman,79,342
Coalfleet,167,169
Cobb,1,8,23,40,41,42,54,60,70,
 72,74,76,79,83,109,111,122
Cobb,145,148,149,152,167,246,
 278,319,331,356,370
Cobbey,147
Cobby,79
Coberman,414
Coburn,152,344,370
Cochran,331,339
Cochrane,168
Codman,79,371
Coe,18
Coffin,371
Coffin,72,168,246
Cohen,414
Colburn,168
Colby,45,89,123,278,371
Colcord,60
Cole,60,83,123,168,246,323,371
Coleman,168
Colesworthy,18
Colley,1,4,8,123,168,323
Collins,18,74,107,168,278
Collis,168
Colpritt,168
Coma,331
Comeau,278
Conant,145,168,240a,246,278,323
Conary,123
Condon 169,278
Conklin,169
Conley,331
Connell,169,246
Connelly,278
Conner/s,169,371
Connor/s,89,169,278,371
Conway,324,371

Cook/e 44,74,76,89,123,169,240a,
 246,278,323,331,340,371,414
Cookson,123
Coolbroth,169
Coolfleet,169
Coolong,169
Coombs,101,123,169,371
Cooper,169,247,278
Coote,331
Copeland,169
Coperthwaite,331
Coppock,169,278
Copps,101
Corbett,169
Corbin,169,278
Cordwell,79,169
Corey,123,353,371
Corkery,123
Corkum,331
Cormier,278
Corning,139
Cornish,345
Coro,169
Costa,169
Costales,345
Costello,123
Cote,169,278
Cotton,45,123,169,356,371
Coulombe,278
Courndyer,170
Couses,139
Cousins/Cousens,170,240a,247,
 331,356,371
Couture,27
Couturier,278
Covell,139
Cowan,170
Cox,123,139,170,247,279
Coxon,279
Coyne,152,279,371
Crabtree,16,170,356
Craft,170
Cragin,170
Crague 36,39,170,247
Craig,152
Craigie,170
Cram 8,18,36,89,123,139,170
Crandall,123,170
Cranton,149
Craw,279
Crawford,170,247,279
Crawley,170
Creelman 42
Creny,319
Cressy,170,371
Cribb,123
Crissikos,372

Critchett,1
Critchley,372
Crocker,26,89,170,331
Crockett 26,51,60,89,170,247,279,
　319,323,331,356,340,342,372
Crommie 45,89
Croney,372
Cronkite,372
Crooker,170
Crosby,170,247
Cross,8,60,123,170,319
Crossman,372
Croto 89
Crowe,170,372
Crowell,170,372
Crowley,170
Crowther,247
Crozier,171,279
Culleton,89
Cullinan,279
Cumberland,171
Cummings 8,60,89,101,139,171,
　247,372,414
Cunningham,89,171
Curan/Curran,171,279
Curit,89,171
Curlew,345
Curneil,26
Currie,60,247,345
Currier,60,171,279
Curry,279
Curtis 42,45,54,123,171,372
Cushing,89,171,331
Cushman 89,139,372
Cutter,171,152,247
Cyr,171,279,372
Daggett,323
Dahms,171
D'Darche,280
Daicy,331,372
Daigle,279
Dailey,60
Daisey,171
Dale,247
Daley/Daly,171,279
Dall,171
Dallen,171
Dalpee,279
Dalton,102,414
Dame,279,372
Damon,171
Dana,139,171,279
Dancause,279
Danforth,171,279
Danie,172
Daniels,72,123,152,172,279
Danis,280

Danonneau,280
Darker,123
Darkis,172
Darling,123,172,280,373
Dauphinee,172
Davan,280
Davenport,172
Davidson,111,172,280
Davio,280
Davis,8,26,54,60,75,79,83,89,
　110,123,139,172,247,280,
　319,331,352,373,414
Day 37,60,84,89,123,172,248,373
Deake,139
Deakin,172
Dean/e,140,172,323
Dearborn,54,123,149,248,373
Deas,373
Debeck,172,248
Deboyes,280
Decelles,280
Decker,173
Decormier,124,280
Decosta,173
Decoster,18
Decreny,15
Deering,70,345,373
Degrasse,60,124,331
Delaney,373
Delcourt,173,280
Delima,280
Delisle,280
DeLong,173
DeLorme,173
Delory,341
Demass,373
Demerill,373
Demers,173,280,373
Demontigny,280
Deneault,280
Denis/Dennis,124,280,281
Dennett,373
Dennison,173
Densmore,173
Deragon,173
Derice,173
Deroche,173,280,281
Derocher,173
Deroches,280
Derosier,173
Derrah,280
Desalle,280
Deschamps,280
Desfosses,280
Deshaies,280
Deshon,60,
Desjardins,280

Devery,75
Devine,89
Dewey,89,173
Dewitt,124
Dexter,173
DiBiase,173
Dickey,173
Dickinson,54
Dietz,89
Diffin,173
Dike,373
Dill,102,173
Dillingham,152,248
Dimick,124
Dimino,281
Dinardo,281
Dineen,173
Dingley,124
Dinsmore,173,342
Dion/Dionne,173,281,331,414
Dix,173,319,331
Dixon,9,248
Doak,173
Dobbin,1
Doble,373
Dobson,173
Dodge,84,373
Doherty,49,281
Doiron,281
Doiront,281
Dolan,281
Dolby,60
Dole,54,79,102,109,111
Dolley,37,42,49,71,75,331,373
Dolloff,49,173
Donahue,89
Donham,374
Donovan,173,281
Doolan/Doolen,248,281
Dooley,281
Doran,281
Dorfman,414
Dority,173
Dorrell,356
Dorsett,339,342
Dostie,281
Doucette,173,281,373
Dougherty,173,282,341
Doughty,1,18,26,84,111,173,345
Douglas,60,173,248,341
Douglass,45,79,331,356,374
Dow,60,124,174,331,374
Dowling,174
Downs,174,374
Doxey,332
Doyle,89,174,282,
Draper,248

Dresser,124,140,174
Drew,45,149,374
Drinkwater,19,174,248
Driscoll,174,282
Drisko,174
Drost,45
Drown,353,374
Drowne,140
Druin,174
Druker,414
Dubay,174,332
Dubbs,374
Dubois,84,282
Duchaine,174,282
Duchaineau,174
Duchesne,174,282
Ducker,248
Duclos,174,282
Dudley,174,356,374
Due,174
Duffill,174
Duford,332
Dufour,282
Dugas,174,283
Duke,152
Dumas,283
Dumbrocyo,332
Dumont,60
Dunbar,6,9,54,174
Duncan,140,174
Dunfield174
Dunham,6,60,84,124,374
Dunlap,9,60,174
Dunn/e,26,174,283,345,374
Dunnell,175
Dunning,345
Dunsmore,89
Dunton,60,175
Dupuis,283
Duran,19,175
Durant,60,175,332
Durell/Durrell,175
Durgan,374
Durgin,102,356,374
Durkee,374
Duval,283
Dvilinsky,414
Dwyer,175,332
Dyer,26,54,60,89,124,140,152,175
  248,283,323,332,343,345,374
Dyke,107,332
Dyson,175
Dziala,283
Eager,149
Ealy,175
Earl,175
Eastern,374

Eastman,175,353,374
Eastup,175
Eaton,175,374
Eaxon,140
Ebbeson,9
Eddy,175,332,375
Edes,89
Edgerly,175,248
Edmonds,375
Edstrom,283
Edwards,19,89,124,175,248,319,
332,363,375
Ekberg,34
Eklof,89
Elden,375
Elder,39,45,60,70,73,79,89,124,
175,319,375
Eldridge,124,175,283,341
Elfstrom,375
Eliot,375
Elkins,45,175,344,375
Ellinwood 89
Elliot/t,26,51,54,60,79,124,283,
356,375
Ellis,50,342,375
Ellsworth,375
Elmer,124
Eloartoka,176
Elsinger,283
Elwell,70,84,176,248,339,356,375
Emerson,54,89,140,176,248,
332,376
Emery,23,36,84,90,124,176,248,
323,363,376
Emmons,60,176,248,283,332,376
Enghart,345
Ennis,54,332
Epes,102
Epstein,414
Erickson,332
Erkelens,176
Erlick,414
Ernest,376
Erskine,176,376
Espeaignette,45
Estabrooks,124
Estes,45,54,60,176,332,376
Estey/Esty,84,177,248,283,332
Etherley,283
Eugley,283
Eustis,124
Evans,34,61,177,323,332,341,
376,414
Eveleth,84,376
Ewing,50
Exchange,283
Fabricius,177

Fairbanks,177,327,376
Fairservice,177
Falt,177
Fanjoy,376
Fardon,376
Farley,177,283,341
Farmer,26,322
Farnham,376
Farnsworth,34,177
Farquarhasen,177
Farr,61,177,376
Farrar,177
Farrell,283
Farrin,376
Farris,34,356
Farrow,77
Farwell,26,34,73,102,177
Faught,248
Faulkner,50,177,345,356
Fawcett,177
Faye,149
Fearon,332
Fecteau,90,177,283
Feen,376
Feener,177
Feeney,283,376
Felch,356,376
Felker,84
Fellows,61,177
Fenderson,283,376
Feneuf,283
Fenlason,177,377
Fenno,320
Fenton,71,248
Ferguson,90,377
Fernald,90,177
Fernandez,283
Ferren,178
Ferris,124,178,284,377
Ferron,284
Fessenden,19,140
Fick,178
Fickett,34,61,102,284,332
Field/s,3,6,9,17,27,42,46,61,73,
152,178,248,284,377
Fielding,125,149
Fifield,178,377
Fifion,284
Files,178,284,320,323,339,353,
356,377
Filiault,178
Final,178
Finn,284
Finnerty,178
Finney,178,377
Fiorillo,61
Fish,61,178

Fisher,9178,284,345
Fisk/e,178,377
Fitts,178
Fitz,178,357
Fitzgerald,90,102
Fitzmorris,377
Flaherty,90,284
Flanders,332
Fleet,332
Fleming,90
Fletcher,111,178
Flick,178
Flight,377
Flinn,249
Flint,23,125,178,377
Flood,341
Floyd,377
Fluent,125
Fluett,284
Fly/e,90,178,378
Flynn,9,378
Fobes,178
Fogel,378
Fogg,55,61,102125,178,323,332,378
Foley,178,284,332,353
Folsom,378
Foote,178
Forbes,50,125
Ford,61,178,378
Forehand,332
Forest,249,378
Forget,284
Forrest,178,378
Fortier,284
Fortin,90,284
Foss,61,79,179,249,284,378
Foster,1,3,27,46,50,51,55,61,73,90,179,249,284,323,332,357,378
Fougere,284
Fought,249
Fournell/e,284
Fournier,179,284
Fowler,55,125,149
Fowles,61
Fox,378
Foy/e,61,73,125,179,284,324,345
Foyette,179
Fracker,249
Francoeur,285
Frank,27,34,55,61,70,149,179,285,414
Fraser,179,378
Frasier,285
Fraster,102
Frates,140
Frederick,179

Fredette,285
Freeman,79,90,145,152,179,249,332,378
Freemen,320,357
French,36,107,179,332,378
Freyer,324
Frink,332,343
Fritz,378
Frost,9,55,84,102,109,179,320,353,378
Fry,27
Frye,61,70,109,179
Fuller,61,179,379
Fullerton,179
Fulton,9
Furlong,249
Furlotte,286
Furnell,152
Gaffney,179
Gagne,286,379
Gagnon,179,286
Gale,179,332
Galipeau,286
Gallagher,287
Gallagher,61,287
Gallant,61,287
Gallison,6,17,36,109,378
Gallop,50,180
Galvin,110
Gammon,1,61,107,180,379
Ganeua,149
Gardiner,125,180,324
Gardner,34,287
Garfield,90
Garland,152,180,332,379
Garneau,287
Garner,180
Garon,379
Garrey,145
Garrison,287
Garvey,180
Gassett,180
Gaston,332
Gatchell,379
Gates,90
Gathercole,180
Gato,287
Gaudet,61,90,287
Gaudreau,287
Gavett,379
Gay,180
Gayne,379
Gayton,180
Geer,180
Gelinas,180,288
Gemmell,180
Genest,288

Geoffroy,288
George,180
Gerdes,90
Gerey,180
Gerhardt,249
Gerrish,27,324
Gerry,90,149,180,324
Gervais,287
Getchell,180,357,379
Gibbin,61
Gibbs,27,324 ,379
Giddens,379
Giddings,379
Giddy,180
Giguere,287
Gilbert,152,180,249,288,379
Gildart,180
Gile,249
Gilkey,353,357
Gillelan,19
Gillespie,288
Gilliam
Gilligan,288
Gilman,46,51,61,73,140,180, 288,324,343,332
Gilmore,180,249
Gilpatric/k,61,180,249,332
Gilpin,181
Gilson,90,249
Ginn,379
Ginsburg,414
Girard,181,288
Girardin,288
Girouard,288
Giroux,333
Given,125,149
Gladhill,249
Gladu,288,324
Glantz,51
Gleason,61,181,288
Glencross,125
Glendenning 79
Glidden,181
Glover,357
Goach,379
Goan,289
Goddard,125,181
Godin,289
Goff,181,289
Going,125
Goldberg,379,414
Goldblatt,414
Golden,181
Golder,181
Goldstein,414
Goodall,181
Goodell,39,80

Goodenow,19
Goodhue,125
Gooding,249
Goodkowsky,414
Goodnough,181
Goodnow,181
Goodrich,19,84,125,324,379
Goodridge,181
Goodside,414
Goodwin,55,90,102,125,181,353, 379
Goody,289
Googins,181
Goold,37,44,125,249,343,344
Goozey/Gouzie,289
Gordan,149,152
Gordon,90,146,181,357,379,414
Gore,140,249
Gorey,289
Gorham,320,346,380
Gorrie,181
Gorrivan 61
Goss,182,380
Gosselin,289
Gothro,289
Goudy,324
Gould,19,77,125,320,346,380
Gouzie/Goozey,289
Gow 9
Gowen,61,146,149,182
Gower,125,182
Goyette,152,289
Grace,182
Grady,46,182,289,333
Graff,249,415
Graffam,27,36,50,80,90,125,182, 289,343 ,380
Graham,15,51,61,90,182,249,289
Granger,80
Grant,46,55,80,107,182,239,249, 289,357,343,380
Gravel,289
Graves,46,90,110,183,324,357
Gray,55,61,80,90,102,140,183, 333,346
Greeley,19,34,183
Green,90,125,140,149,183,249, 289,341,346,352
Greenberg,415
Greene,1,90,183,333,341,380
Greenlaw,61,71,183
Greenleaf,125,183,380
Greenough,183,380
Greenwood,183
Greep,183
Gregg,27,140
Gregoire,289

Grendell,183,341
Grenier,183,290,346
Gresley,290
Grey,290,380
Gribben,61
Grier,183
Griffin,61,90,183,380
Griffiths,183,290
Griggs,183
Grimard,290
Grimes,183
Griswold,140
Grondin,290
Gronlund,357
Grose,183
Grouard,380
Grover,50,183,380
Grows,125
Guerin,341
Guernsey,183
Guevin,290
Guilbault,290
Guilman 90
Guilmette,290
Guimond,183,290,333
Guinard,183
Guitard,290
Gunn,27,183
Guptill,62,73,183,324,333, 346,380
Gurney,6,27,34,125,184
Gushga,184
Gustin,27,184,249,346,354,380
Guthrie,184
Guyer,184
Haase,184
Hacker,109
Hackett,62,75,125,184
Haddock,62,184,
Haddon,290
Hadlock,6,184,380
Haenesel,184,290
Hafner,62,290
Hagan,184,290
Hagberg,90,125
Hagen,62
Hagerman,184
Haggett,250
Haggman,70
Hagne,380
Hague,184,380
Hahn,184
Haines,51,126,250
Hale,50,84,140,145,149,184,250, 290,324,333,380 324,333,341, 346,357,380

Hall,6,9,17,19,24,27,42,52,62,73, 75,80,84,107,112,140,184,250
Hallett,126
Halloran,184
Hallowell,184,
Ham,24,185,290,381
Hamblen/Hamlin,9,19,100,185, 320,333,339,344,357,381
Hamblet 41
Hamblin,357,381
Hambury,381
Hamel,185,290,333
Hamilton 19,55,77,102,140,185, 290
Hamlen,320
Hamm,185
Hammond,90,140
Hanaford,381
Hanaford/Hannaford,381
Hanas,381
Hancock,102,126
Hand,290
Handley,290
Handlon,290
Handy,185
Hanes,185
Hanley,291
Hanlon,185
Hanna,291
Hanscom,62,185,
Hanscom/e 55,102,346,357,381,382
Hanscomb,382
Hanscombe,185,
Hansen ,7,34,62,185
Hansley 46
Hanson,109,126,140,185,240a, 250, 333,343,346,382
Hanson,9,36,37,42,46,62,70,75, 77,84,90,102
Harding,44,55,84,185,250,320, 333,341,346,354,382
Hardy,15,80,145,149,185
Hariush,382
Harlow,324,333,382
Harman,383
Harmon,27,52,55,62,90,149,185, 240a,250, 333,346,357,383
Harnden 62
Harnois,291
Harper,111
Harriet,339
Harrigan,186
Harriman,46,91,186,291,346,383
Harrington,152,186,383

Harris,19,34,50,62,80,84,91,
  126,140,186,250,383
Harrison,186,250,383
Hart,90,186
Hartford,186
Harthorn,186
Hartley,186
Hartshorn,140
Harve,291
Harvey,27,91,186,291
Harvie,186
Haselton,186
Hasey,250
Haskell,24,46,62,77,84,91,102,
  107,126,186,240a,250,
Haskell,324,333,383
Haskey,383
Hassett,383
Hasty,354,383
Hatch,62,126,186,240a,251,383
Hathaway,91,186
Hatt 62
Hattenburg,383
Haughney,291
Hausemann,291
Haven,147
Hawes,104,145,186,251
Hawkes,36,41,42,46,52,55,62,75,
  77,80,84,91,103,109,126,187,
  291, 324,333,383
Hawkins,149,383
Hawks,27,41
Hawxwell,80,333
Hay,187
Hayden,62,346
Haydt,62
Hayer,291
Hayes,46,187,240a,251,291,333,383
Haynes,357
Hayward,187
Hazelton,187
Hazlett,187
Head,291
Heal,91
Healy,291
Heath,187,324,357,383
Heather,291
Hebeler 84
Hebenstreit,187
Hebert,187,291
Hedges,383
Heel,188
Hefner,292
Held,292
Helming,188
Helmold,188
Hemingway,188

Hemschemeyer,383
Henderson,188
Hendrickson,188,251,292
Henkel,383
Hennessy,50
Henry,188,292
Herbert,292
Herlyck,251
Herman,188
Herrick,91,103,126,149,188,
  292,383
Herring,50
Hersey,91,125,288,383
Hethcoat,34
Hewes,188,384
Hey,188
Heydrie,292
Heywood,140
Hezelton,251
Hibbard,46
Hickey,188,333
Hicks,3,9,24,27,34,107,188,324,
  346,384
Higgins,9,46,91,100,126,188,
  251,325,339,346,354,384
Hight,320
Hill,17,27,62,91,103,126,140,
  152,188,292,325,357,384
Hilliard,384
Hillock,188,346
Hills,189
Hilton,189
Hindle,84
Hinds,103,126
Hinkley,384
Hinks,9
Hinkson,91
Hitchings,19,126
Hoadley,126,384
Hoag,75,384
Hobb,63
Hobbs,9,15,16,17,384
Hobson,63,129,384
Hodgdon,63,384
Hodge,75
Hodges,251
Hodgkin/s,151,189,240a,251,
  333,384
Hodgson,292
Hodsdon,9,84,91,240a,251,343
Hoegg,126
Hoffman,189
Hogan,189
Hoit,384
Holbrook,141
Holden,384
Hollis,189

Holm,189
Holmes,27,103,111,123,251,384
Holston,127,189
Holt,189,251,292
Homan,333
Hood,127,189
Hooker,189
Hooper,37,50,55,91,189,384
Hopkins,127,189,252,333,384
Hopkinson,189,384
Horn,103
Horne,127
Horr,19,63,189,240a,252,333
Hoskin,385
Houde,292
Houghton,84
Houle,292
Houston,252
Hovey,385
Howard,46,91,103,107,127,189, 292,325,333,385
Howe,75,190,252,325,341,385
Howell,127
Howley 63
Hoy,190
Hoyt,24,63,190,385
Huard/e,292
Hubbard,152,190,325,341
Huckins,152
Hudson,127,190
Hueston,190
Huff,52,190,333,385
Hughes,19,190,252,385
Hughey,333
Hulbert,190
Hulit,24,27,190
Humphrey,24
Huneau,292
Hunewell,73
Hunewill,73,190
Hunnewell,39,77,80,127,190,325
Hunt,320,357,385
Hunt,46,63,71,73,91,103,109, 127,152,190,240a,252,292,
Hunter,190,292,385
Hunting,320
Huntington,127
Huntley,149,190,346,354
Huntress,292
Huntt,325
Hurd,190,240a,252,325,346
Hurley,190
Huse,190,385
Hussey,43,63,84,190
Hussy,75,90,385
Huston,1,6,9,27,52,111,127,149, 152,191,240a,363

Hutcherson,385
Hutchins,28,103,191,325,346
Hutchinson,91,191,357,385
Hutt,385
Hutto,191
Hutton,385
Hyberts,385
Hyde,191
Hyman,341
Hynes 34
Idiorne,252
Ilsley,5,127
Ingalls,46,333,357,385
Ingersol,70,80
Ingersoll,28,191
Ingraham,127,141,191,357
Ireland,292
Irish,46,50,55,91,191, 320, 325,341,354,357,385
Irving,191,386
Irwin,80,84,252
Iverson,191
Jackman,252
Jackson,9,41,63,75,80,103,127, 141,191,292,320,354,386
Jacob,46
Jacobs,19,34,50,127
Jacobsen,80,191
Jacques,91,292,346
Jacquis,63
James,43,191,333,386
Jameson,55,80,150,151,333
Jaques,191,325,386
Jaquis,44,63
Jarmon,191
Jarrett,127
Jarvis,386
Jaynes,91
Jean,63,293
Jefferds,293
Jeffords,63,191
Jeffrey,293
Jemery,334
Jenkins,191,325
Jenks,191
Jennette,191
Jennings,191
Jennison,191
Jensen,191,334,386
Jenson,9,80,91
Jepson,91,108
Jerome,293
Jerris,127
Jess,192
Jessen,192
Jewell,192,352,386
Jewett,50,141,252,320,386

Jimino,56
John,293
Johneley,293
Johnson,9,36,56,63,80,84,91,
　103,110,127,146,150,152
Kendall,387
Kenderine,193
Kenison,358
Keniston,193
Kennard 75,77,92,252
Kennedy,19,193,293
Kenney,108,128,194,293
Kennie,92,103,194,293,387
Kenniston 92
Kenny,194
Kent,63,128,194
Keonig,92
Kerr,194,252
Keteck,334
Key,387
Kichen,293
Kidder,141,334
Kiestead,194
Kilborn 19,92
Kimball,10,63,73,92,128,194,
　253,293,334,341,347,352,387
Kincaid 92
King,28,64,112,150,194,253,
　293,387
Kinghorn 56
Kingman 85
Kingsbury 40
Kinmond,194,293
Kinney,28,35,50
Kinnie,387
Kinsman,354
Kirby,387
Kirk,46
Kirkpatrick,194,293
Kirkwood,194
Klewiada,194
Klinger,103
Klinke,195
Kloth,195
Klowas,195
Kluchnik,293
Knapp 19
Knapton,387
Knaut,128
Kneeland,195,293,387
Knight,1,3,10,16,19,41,43,64,
　72,77,81,92,108,112,141,145,
　146,147,150,152,,195,253,
　293,334,343,347,387
Knouse,46
Knowles,128,195,334,387
Knowlton,195,253

Knox,195,253
Knudsen,56,195
Koljonen,92
Kollack,253,343
Kollock,240a
Komatz,195
Koon,294
Kourapis,195
Kramlich,387
Kubat,195
Kuusela,334
Kyle,334
Kyte,387
Labarre,294
Labbe,195,294
Labonte/Lebonte,294
Labranche,388
Labrecque,196,294,325
Labrie,196,294
Lachance,194,294,334,388
Lacomte,294
Ladd,196
Laferriere,294
Laffin,64,196,294
Laffy,294
Laflamme,294
Lafond,294
Lafontaine,388
Lafountain,388
Lafrance,294
Lafreniere,294
Lagarson,196
Lagasse,334
Laghy,253
Lailer,50,92
Lakin,92,347
Laliberte,294
Lally,196
Lamarre,294
Lamb,46,50,56,64,72,92,196,
　253,334,352
Lambert,196,253,295
Lamerande,295
Lamont,10,359
Lamontagne,295,334
Lampron,196,295388
Lancaster,81
Landersheim,28
Landry,46,50,196,295,341,388
Lane,92,196,253,388
Langevin,196,296
Langille,92
Langis,296
Langley
Langlois,296
Langshaw,196
Languet,196

Lanphaier,334
Lansky,415
Lapierre,296
Laplante,196
Lapointe,253,296
Lareen,196
Larhette 92
Lariviere/Larrevere,296
Larkin,325
Larochelle,388
Larrabee,64,128,147,196,253,
296,347,388
Larrivee,46,64,296,334,341
Larrivier,297
Larry,81,320,334,388
Larsen,64,196
Larson,197
Lary,253
Lasher,297
Laskey,197,334
Latham,28,129
Latham,325,334
Lauber,197
Laughton,28
Lauritsen,197
Lauzon,297
Lavangie,297
Laverty,197
Lavigne,197,297
Laviolette,297
Lavoie,297
Lawrence,19,92,129,197,297,388
Lawrensen,197
Lawson,10,197
Leach,129
Leadbetter,297
Leary,254,347
Leatherberry,347
Leathers,388
Leavitt,28,37,92,129,197,254,
297,388
LeBeau,197,297
LeBel/l,197,297
Leber,388
Leberge,294,298
Leblanc,298
Leborgne,298
Lebouvier,298
Lebrecque,325
Lebrock,197
Lebruin,298
Lecarree,298
Leclair,298
Leclerc,298
Lecomte/Lenonte,197,298
Ledoux,298
Leduc,298

Lee,103,299,388
Leed,354
Leeman,92,197
Leeper,19
Lefay,299
Lefebvre,299
Legarre,299
Legendre,197
Legere,92,299
Legrow 35,50,52,64,73,92
Lehoux,388
Leighton,3,5,6,10,15,24,28,46,
52,56,92,109,129,141,147,
150,197,254,299,388
Leipold,341
Lekouses,198
Leland,29
Lemay,299
Lemontague,152
Lemuix,198,299
Lennan,64
Lenneville,299
Leonard,64,85,198,254
Lepage,334
Lepenvin,198,299
Lerman,415
Lermond,198,388
Leroux,299
Leslie,19
Lessard,299
Lessor,198
Lestage,299,325
Lester,150
Letarte,198,299
Letourneau,198,325
Levesque,198,300
Levine,415
Levinsky,415
Levinson,415
Levitch,198
Lewin,198
Lewis,29,92,103,141,198,254,
300,354,388
Libbey,389
Libby 10,16,24,29,38,43,50,52,
56,64,71,72,73,75,77,85,92,
103,108,129,146,152,199,254,
300,321,325,334,341,343,347,
359,389
Liberty,200
Lidback,389
Lincoln,6,389
Lind,200
Lindeman,200
Lindette,254
Lindquist,200
Lindstrom,200

Linneken,16,29
Linnell,389
Linscott,300
Linsky,200
Lirette,300
Little,36,64,85,129,141,200,
 300,321,334,390
Littlefield,71,200,390
Littlejohn,10,19
Livermore,200
Livingstone,200
Lizotte,300
Lloyd,348
Lobdell,104
Lochlin,334
Locke,5,10,20,300,334
Logan,29,200
Logue,93
Lomard,325
Lombard,64,93,200,339,348,
 359,390
London,200
Long,93,200,300,335,390
Longfellow,254,321
Longley,254
Looke,200
Lopes 47
Lopez,200
Lord,2,3,6,10,24,38,43,64,72,81,
 93,129,152,147,200,321,341,390
Lorenzen,81,85
Loring,10,93,201,254,300
Lorrain,201
Lothrop,201
Loughran,43
Loura,341
Love,390
Loveitt,38,73,201,335,390
Lovejoy,148,255
Lovell,129,201
Lovendale,390
Lovett 64
Lovis,38,390
Low,129,255,325
Lowe,20,29,201,255,348,390
Lowell,10,16,43,47,56,64,71,73,
 75,85,93,109,129,150,152,201
Lowell,390
Lowery,391
Loyal,300
Lubee,325
Lubin,415
Lublinsky,415
Lucas,129,201,255
Luce,111,360,391
Lucey,47
Lufkin,7,24,29

Lugdon,201
Luke,201,391
Lund,7,201,348
Lundberg 75
Lunt,10,17,64,108,110,130,
 147,201,348
Lurvey,391
Lussier,300
Luthe,391
Lyden,300
Lydstone,130
Lyford,29
Lynch,20,56,130,201,255,391
Lynn,201
Lyons,201
Maasbyll,201
Maber,81
Mabery,255,391
Mabry,325
MacCormick,201
MacDonald,326,335
MacDonald,64,201,302
MacDougall,
MacDougall,391
Mace,130,202
MacFarland,202
MacHardy,202
MacKay,202
MacKenzie,202,255,391
Mackey,152
MacLeod,93,202,391
MacMillan,202
Macomber,93,150
MacPherson,202
MacQuarrie,202
Maddix,348
Maddocks,202
Maddox,202
Madson,202,326
Maffitt,240a,255
Magill,130,202
Magnusson,335
Magrath,391
Maguire,29
Mahar,255,300
Maher,348
Mahoney,64,152,202,300
Maillet,300
Mailly,300
Mailman,391
Main,29,202
Maines,93,335
Mains,47,64,85,93
Makowski,202
Malachowski,300
Malchon,391
Malia,202

Maling 29
Mallia,300
Mallory,202,300
Malloy,300
Malnick,202
Malone,29,202
Manchester,50,64,72,77,93,150,
 202,255,326,335,391
Manfield
Mank,50,150
Mankin,391
Mann,64,93,391
Mannette,47,335
Manning,202,391
Mannion,300
Mansfield,108,130,202
Mansise,29
Manson,326
Maquire,202
Marabito,202
Marble,339
March,85,321
Marchi,392
Marcoux,300
Marean,202,255,392
Mariah,2
Marier,300
Marinelli,56
Mariner,20,255
Marion,202,301
Markos,202
Marks,130
Markson,415
Marr,202,392
Marrett,255
Marriner,202,240a
Marrotte,301
Marsden,130
Marsh,203,326,348
Marshall,94,130,203,255,335
Marsters,203
Marston,2,4,7,10,29,75,108,130,
 203,326,352,392
Martel/l,301
Martin ,64,130,141,152,203,255,
 301,326,360,392
Martineau,301
Marton,326
Marzul,301
Maskierwicz,301
Mason,10,20,35,43,56,85,94,
 104,130,203,255,301
Mason,152,335,360
Masson,301
Massuere,354
Mathews,10
Mathews,301

Matta,392
Matthews,203
Mauk,301
Maurice,301
Mavaodones,301
Maw,152,255
Maxell,392
Maxfield,38,52,75,94,104,130,335
Maxim,203
Maxwell,41,52,69,94,130,141,
 203,301
May/e,203,255,301,341,360
Mayberry,47,65,77,81,85,94,
 110,203,240a,255,326,335,392
Maybery,326
Mayhew,255,349
Mayhewn,240a
Maynard,38,56
Mayo,20,94,203,301,392
McAllister,204,391
McAloney,204
McArthur,204
McBain,204
McBride,392
McCann,204,255,301
McCarney,204
McCarthy,204
McCarty,255
McCatherin,94
McCauley,341
McCausland,392
McClellan,204,301,392
McClosky,204
McClure,204,392
McCollough,152
McConkey,204,392
McCormack/McCormick,301
McCorrison,392
McCorson,255
McCready,255
McCroary,301
McCubrey,204
McCullough,81,301
McCurdy,204
McCurry,392
McDade,204
McDaniels,392
McDevitt,94
McDonald,41,85,94,111,130,204,
 255,338,392
McDonough,204,302
McDougall,204,392
McDowell,141
McDuffie,204
McDugall,321
McElroy,56,205,335,349
McEntee,302

McEntie,204,
McFarland,205,256,302
McGaffey,205
McGarth,93,130
McGee,302
McGinty,65
McGlinchey,205
McGoldrick,94
McGowen,205,352
McGregor,3
McGuire,205,302
McHardy,205
McHugh,302
McInnis,302
McIntee,302
McIntire,130
McIntosh,71,94,130,392
McKay,205
McKeague,205
McKeen,130,205
McKellar,256
McKenney/McKenny,130,205,
 349,392
McKenzie,93,205,302
McKevitt,392
McKinley,205
McKnight,47
McLaughlin,29,205,302
McLean,130,205
McLeart,205
McLeese,205
McLellan,20,30,56,65,73,152,
 205,256,321,341,349,360,392
McLeod,302,393
McLucas,94,205,360
McMackin,56,393
McMahon,104
McManus,205
McMaster,256
McMillan,81,205
McMillin,47,205
McNair,205,256
McNally,206
McNamara,50
McNeil,48,206
McNutt,326
McPail/McPhail,206,393
McPhee,94,206
McPherson,94,130,393
McQuillan,393
Meade,206
Meader,30
Means,104
Meehan,65
Meehann,206
Meg-quier,48
Meggison,56,206,256,335

Megouier,206
Megquire,141
Meikle,206
Melancon,302
Melanson,48
Melcher,11,130,206
Mellen,349
Mellin,393
Mellor,393
Meluscierwc,206
Menezes,335
Mercier,302,349
Mermelstein
Merrell,256
Merrick,43,206
Merrifield,360
Merrill,2,3,4,5,11,17,20,35,48,65,
 71,81,85,104,108,110,130,141,
 152,206,240a,256,349,360,393
Merriman,206,393
Merrithew,360
Merritt,206,394
Merry,349
Mersereau,81
Merserve,206,256,352
Meserve,240a,335,349,394
Messenger,335
Messier,50
Metayer,335
Metcalf,20,206,302,360,394
Methot,302
Metivier,302
Meyer/s,94,415
Meylen,302
Michaelson,415
Michaud,65,206,302,335,394
Michel,302
Michielette,302
Miele,65
Miles,72,206
Miller,11,81,94,206,415
Millett,56,207,394
Milligan,207,350,394
Milliken,20
Millions,36,207,256
Mills,48,56,94,207,394
Milstead,207
Miltimore,4
Milton,207
Mina,207
Miner,207
Minervino,50,302
Minnick,207
Minot,110
Minster,207
Misenor,131

Mitchell,5,20,56,81,94,104,207,
　256,302,326,335,350,360,394
Mitsmen/n,256,350
Mockler,207
Modoc,110
Moertl,207
Moffett,94
Moffitt,152,257
Mogan,207,302
Molasky,394
Molinskey,303
Molzen,43
Monaghetti,394
Monahan,394
Mondor,303
Mongeau,303
Monks,394
Montdor,303
Montgomery,56,81
Moody,12,20,43,94,131,207,394
Moon,104
Moore,30,65,75,110,131,207,
　350,394
Moorgofsky,415
Morabito,208,303
Moran,208
Moreau,65,303
Morelli,208
Morency,303
Morey,94,208,394
Morgan,208,303
Morin,208,303
Morong,50
Morrell,41,50,52,65,73,85,94,
　208,350,394
Morrill,30,48,56,94,131,208,
　303,335,394
Morris,44,65,131,208,240a,257,
　303,350
Morrison,7,20,24,30,94,208,415
Morrissette,335
Morse,2,48,85,94,112,131,141,
　146,208,335,350,360,394
Morton,38,44,48,50,75,94,104,
　208,257,303,335,341,360,363
Mosely,110
Moses,73,95,131,326,350,394
Mosher,131,208,321,395
Moshier,395
Moskeiwiz,303
Motley,95,336,395
Mottershead,395
Moulton,208,257,335,350,360,
　363,395
Mountfort,7,24,30,131
Moxcey,335
Moyer,95

Muehle,326
Mugford,39,111
Mulcahy,208
Mulhern,303
Mulkeron,208
Mulligan,208,303
Mullin,208,303
Mulvany,208
Mundy,95
Munroe,72,208,303,395
Munson,395
Murch,150,208,257,339,395
Murchie,395
Murdock,131
Murphy,20,209,303
Murray,108,209,304,396
Murry,7,396
Mushreau,304
Mussey,341
Myers,396
Nadeau,209,304,342
Nash,65,150,209,257,304,326,396
Nason,95,108,209,257,326,
　335,396
Nathan,415
Naughrite,209
Nay,335
Nayer,304
Naylor,104,209,257,304
Neal,131,209,257,396
Nealy,335
Neary,209
Neeley,65
Nelson,20,38,56,65,95,209,257,
　304,350,396,415
Nevens,360
Nevers,209
Nevils,209
Newall,24,210,350
Newbegin,7,20
Newcomb,48,69,95,99,131,152,
　210,257,335,350,360,396
Newell 44
Newhall,210,335
Newman,17,20,108,304,396
Newton,131,141,210
Nicely,361
Nicholas,210,304,335
Nichols,16,75,95,131,210,304,
　336,396
Nickerson,20,350,396
Nickols,131
Nielson,210,396
Nies,210
Niles,304
Nixon,210
Noack,210

Noble,257
Noden,210
Nodine,336
Noel,304
Noonan,65,396
Noone,95
Norberg,210
Norcross,35,210
Nordfors,210
Norgard,210
Normand,304
Norris,210
North,108
Northup,396
Norton,12,20,30,210,304,361,396
Norwood,350
Noson,415
Nourse,327
Nowak,95
Noyce,396
Noyes,5,7,12,17,20,30,131,150,
 210,258,321
Nugent,327,352
Nute,131,210
Nutter,108,131
Nutting
O'Brien,7,30,38,131,210,304,
 361,396
O'Brion,95,210,258
O'Clair,304
O'Connel,65
O'Conner,210,361
O'Donal,396
O'Donnell,304
O'Gara,304
O'Neal,152,211
O'Reilly,258
O'Shei,211
O'Toole,342
Oaksmith,131
Odgen,131
Odiorne,396
Ohlsten,210
Oldread,210
Oleson,75
Oliver,35,132
Olmstead,210
Olsen,16,211
Olson/Ollson,20,305,396
Olzak,305
Oransky,415
Ordiorne,258
Ordway,258
Orton,132
Osborne,211,396
Osgood,104,211,327
Osmond,211

Otis,211
Ouellette,305
Ovington,150
Owens,211
Oxnard,211
Packard,16,56,132,211,397
Paddon,81
Page,12,95,397
Paige,12,397
Pailler,305
Paine,39,81,108,,211,258,321,
 336,361,397
Palmer,20,52,65,95,211,258,
 339,342,397
Palmieri,305
Palozzi,336
Pane,56
Paperdopoulus,211
Pappas,211
Parady,336
Pardi,211
Parent,211
Park,211
Parker,8,81,95,,105,110,141,
 146,211,258,327,336,354,397
Parkhurst,211,336,397
Parkinson,50
Parlin,211,350,398
Parquette,305
Parrington,398
Parris,141
Parry,50
Parsley,150
Parson,361
Parsons,17,65,85,141,211,
 258,336
Partridge,21,52,65,105,132
 ,212,258
Pass,212
Passage,398
Patch,212
Patenaude,212,305
Patrick,5,12,398
Patridge,105,212
Patry,305
Patte,141
Patterson,212,342
Paul,95,212,336
Paulin,305
Paulsen,212,258
Paulus,305
Payne,95,150,212,305
Payson,141
Peabody,398
Peachwall,305
Pearson,16,30,95,132,141,212,
 258,327,336

Peary,95
Pease,86,212,305
Peasley,110,212
Peavey,95,398
Peck,12,212
Pecoraro,65,305
Pedersen,336
Pednault,305
Peffer,212
Pellerin,212,305
Pelletier,305,398
Pelley,398
Pelton,132
Pender,56,212
Pendexter,56,212
Pendleton,51,212
Penek,336
Penfield,398
Penfold,132
Peniuk,336
Penley
Pennell,86,141,212,240a,258,306
Penney,132
Penny,350
Percival,212
Percy,212,398
Perham,327,350
Periault,306
Perkins,95,212,259,306,336,398
Perrin,213,259,306
Perron,48,306
Perry,66,95,152,213,259,306,398
Pesce,306
Petee,21
Peters,141,213,306,398
Petersen,213,306,336
Peterson,2,12,21,31,35,48,57,
    132,213,259,306,336,350,399
Pettes,213
Pettingill,4,12,31,51
Petto,66,213,336
Phaneuf,306
Phelps,108,150
Philbrick,214
Phillips,12,214,259,306,399
Philpot,81,95
Phinney,95,141,214,240a,259,
    321,339,352,361,399
Phipps,399
Pickard,214
Pickering,96,354
Pickreign,214
Pierce,21,105,132,214,259,
    336,399
Pike,31,214,350,399
Pillsbury,214,350,399
Pinder,214

Pine,57
Pineau,306
Pinette,214,306
Pink,415
Pinkham,204,306,399
Pipinias,399
Pitre,306
Pitt,96,214
Pizzo,306
Place,96,214
Placey,214,259,306
Plaisted,86,306,327,361,399
Plante,306
Plimpton,31
Ploude,307
Plummer,57,66,96,141,214,240a,
    259,336,399
Podas,214
Pode,215
Poirer,307,336
Poisson,307
Poitras,214,307
Poland,21,96,214
Polley,132,214
Pollock,132
Pomeleau,214,307
Pomelow,214
Pomeroy,399
Pool,12
Pooler,215,308
Pope,4,75,77
Porell,48,308
Porello,308
Porter,86,132,152,215,327,399
Porterfield,96,105
Post,66,215
Pote,12,21
Potrias,215
Potter,48,66,96,152,215,259
Pottle,150
Poule,399
Poulin,215,308
Pouliot,336
Poutre,308
Powell,308,336
Powers,44,96,132,215,308,336
Pratt,51,57,66,86,132,215,240a,
    259,308,321,336,399
Pray,96,215
Preble,142,215
Prentiss,321
Prescott,215,351,400
Pressey,215
Preston,215
Preussner,215
Price,48

Pride ,3,16,24,35,44,57,66,81,96,
  108,110,132,147
Pride,150,216,260,400
Prince,5,12,21,35,96,132,142,
  216,308,336
Prior,66,308
Proctor,51,66,96,132,216,239,
  240a,260
Prophet,216
Proudfoot,400
Proulx,216,308
Prouty,216
Provencher,308
Provost,308
Prue,216
Pudvah,336
Pugh,216
Pulieris,66
Pulkkinen,96
Pumroy,13
Purington,110,216
Purinton,52,77,86,132
Purrington 7,31
Purrinton,
Purriton,339,342
Purvis,31
Putnam,216,260
Pyles,216
Quigley,216
Quimby,81,86,216,240a,260
Quinby,105,133,145,217,240a,261
Quinlan,66,217
Quinlar,308
Quinn,133,217,261,308,400
Quint,48
Quirion,31
Rackleff,133,400
Rackley,21,96
Rackliff,48,133,217,261
Radley,308
Ramsay,400
Ramsdell,13
Ramsey,31,133,336
Ramson,217
Rancourt,308
Rand,36,38,86,96,133,217,321,
  336,361,363,400
Randall,48,217,361,400
Raney,261
Rankin,400
Ranks,21
Ransford,217
Rasmussen,261
Rathgeb,217
Rawding/s,217,261
Rawson,400
Ray,261

Raymond,133,217
Raynes,57
Rea,36
Read,73,76,108,133
Reagan,217
Record,133,217
Redden,217,308
Redding,21
Redlon,309,400
Reece,218,309
Reed,31,66,76,96,218,309,351,
  361,400
Reef,336
Reeves,76,218
Reichenknoch,400
Reid,218,105
Rempher,133
Remsen,218
Rendall,44,
Renna,309
Reny,218,261,309
Reynolds,57,66,96,133,218,309,
  321,336
Rhoades,96,218
Rhodes,218
Ricard,309
Ricci,133,218
Rice,13,86,96,112,142,218,
  240a,261,327,400
Rich,48,110,218,261,400
Richard/s
  5,7,13,48,96,105,142,218,261,
  309,400
Richardson,13,96,133,218,261,
  327,343,354,400
Richie,261
Richmond,401
Richter,218
Ricker,13,108,152,218,261,401
Rideout,25,31,35,74,218,261
Ridgway,401
Ridley,218,309
Ridlon,96,218,401
Rieser,66
Riggs,21,81,105,133,219,261,
  351,401
Riley,48,57,133,152,219,240a,
  261,336
Rindy,219
Ring,219
Riopel,309
Rioux,309
Ripley,219
Rivers,66,219
Rivinius,336
Rizzo,219
Robbins,13,57,66,133,219,336

Roberge,309
Roberts,16,31,44,66,72,133,142,
 219,240a,261,336,351,361,401
Robertson,96,219,262
Robichaud,219,310
Robicheaw,310
Robie,219,401
Robins,219
Robinson,13,38,66,76,77,86,105,
 134,142,219,262,310,336,351
Robinson,402,415
Roby,220
Roche,31
Rocheleau,310
Rock,220
Rockwell,220
Rockwood,220
Rodgers,96,110
Rogan,310
Rogers,57,66,86,96,134,220,
 310,402
Rolfe,97,220,321,327,402
Rolillard,66
Rollins,48,220
Roma,220,310
Rome,220
Romer,97
Rondeau,310
Rood,220
Root,7220,402
Roper,220
Rose,13
Rosenberg,415
Rosenblad,220
Rosenbloom,415
Rosenthal,415
Ross,134,142,220,310,402
Rossignol,402
Rosvally,310
Roth,97
Round/s,105,220,262,310,361,402
Rousseau,310
Routhier,310
Roux,220
Rowe,66,134,220,402
Rowell,402
Roy,220,310,
Rubbins,415
Rubin,416
Rubinsky,416
Rubito,220
Rudball,311
Rumery/Rumroy,21
Rusha,262
Russell,31,57,134,150,220,262,
 336,402
Rust,402

Rutherford,57
Rutter,220
Ryall,66,105
Rycosky,221
Ryder,134
Saarine,221
Sager,221
Saindon,311
Salisbury,327
Salley,403
Sampson,21,134,142,311,403
Samson,311
Sanborg,221
Sanborn,17,66,69,97,134,142,
 221,351,403
Sanders,72,221
Sanderson,221
Sands,134,262,361,403
Sanford,403,416
Santoro,403
Santosky,416
Sanville,221,351,337,403
Sardy,21
Sargent,134,221,337,403
Sarrasin,311
Sarty,221
Saucier,311
Saul,86
Saunders,134,145,221,337,351,
 403
Sawtelle,403
Sawyer,5,13,44,48,57,66,74,81,
 97,100,108,110,112,134,142,
 150,152,221,262,327,337,342,
 354,361,403
Saylor,221
Sayward,67,74,337
Scales,21
Scamman,134,403
Scandalios,97
Scates,221
Sceggell,221
Schauer,221
Schellinger,97
Schermerdorn,222
Schiff,416
Schlemberger,222
Schmidt,222
Schmitz,134
Schneider,222
Scholl,16,327
Schreiber,81
Schwartz,222
Schwebe,416
Scolley,105
Scott,35,48,67,135,222,240a,
 262,351,403

Scribner,135,222,311,403
Scruton,311
Seabury,81
Seagers,222
Seal,135,222
Seamans,82
Searway,222
Seavey,21,31,67,135
Secard/Sicard,311
Secord,222
Sedgley 57
Seed,354
Seeley,53,97
Seger,222,311,403
Selby,222
Sellers,48
Sematowic,222
Semple,311
Senate,262
Senecal,31
Senechal,311
Senter,48,67,86,97,222
Severy,337
Sevigny,311
Sewell,337
Sexton,222
Shachlach,416
Shackford,222,403
Shackley,262
Shalit,416
Shane,222
Shannon,222
Sharpe,222
Shaw,13,21,31,35,57,67,82,86,
    97,150,222,262,321,327,
Shaw,337,354,361,363,403
Shea ,57,222
Shedd,403
Sheehan,135,222,311
Sheehy,311
Sheil,57
Sheldon,403
Shenault,150
Shenefield,222
Shepard,404
Shepherd,404
Sheppard,135
Sherman,16,223,351,404
Sherwood,16,97,223
Shibles,223
Shields,223
Shine,416
Shinn,135
Shirley,135,223,404
Sholes,7
Sholts, 337
Shorey,404

Short,263
Shortell,223
Shugars,404
Shute,2
Sicard/Secard,311
Siciliano,337
Sidebottom,311
Siewertson,82,223
Silla 53
Silva,223
Silver,150,404
Silverman,416
Simansky,416
Simavlos,416
Simiansky,416
Simmonds,150
Simmons,21,97,404
Simon,312
Simoneau,312
Simonton,21,263
Simpson,223
Sinclair,97,223,312
Sirois,312
Sivovlos,416
Skillin,2,31,51,97,404
Skilling/s,97,135,223,263,337,
    361,404
Skinner,97,223,351
Skolas,223
Skyes,223
Slemons,105
Sloan,105
Sloane,223,240a,263
Sloat,31,223
Slocomb,223
Sloman,404
Slosberg,416
Small,13,32,48,51,53,97,108,110,
    111,135,147,150,223,240a,263,
Small,312,337,343,404
Smallwood 21
Smart,404
Smearer,337
Smeaton,224
Smidth,224
Smiley,404
Smith,2,13,44,48,57,67,72,76,82,
    86,97,105,110,135,142,224,
    240a,263,312,321,327,342,351,
    355,404
Smithson,51
Smyth,225
Sneddon,225
Snell,16,25,32
Snow,76,97,225,263,337,354,405
Snowdeal,264
Soderberg,312

Sodergren,225
Soloway,225
Somes,97
Soper,225
Sorensen,225
Soule,7,13,32,44,135,405
South,225,312,405
Southard,405
Sparks,312
Sparrow,105
Spaulding,225
Spear/s,58,225,240a,264,351
Spearin,337
Speirs,225
Spelman,226
Spence,135,226,405
Spenetta,226
Spiers,97
Spiller,57,151,226,264,312,361
Spinetta,264
Spink,328
Spinney,57,354
Splar,142
Spofford,97
Sposedo,98
Sprague,51,98,312
Spring,82,226,337
Springer,226,312
Springfield,32
Sproul,226,240a,264
Spurr,405
Squire,226
St.Clair,13,21,221
St.Croix,312
St.Cyr,226,312
St.Hilaire,312
St.Peter,221
St.Pierre,221,312
Stack,313
Stacki,226
Stackpole,226,264,405
Stahl,416
Stall,405
Standley,98,226
Stanley,82,405
Stanton,98,226,405
Stanwood,313,405
Staples,67,69,74,82,98,108,147,
  226,264,322,328,405
Star,416
Starbird,16,77,135,226,264
Starbuck,337
Starling,21,77
Starr,142
Stearns,226,240a
Steeves,58,67,351
Stein,98

Steinman,135
Stephenson,322
Sterling,227,313
Sterns,264
Stetson,142
Stevens,32,58,67,69,82,86,98,
  99,100,106,108,135,142,227,
  264,337,354,405
Stevenson,227,351,406
Steves,227
Stewart,7,22,71,86,227,337,406
Stewertsen,227
Stickney,227,313,406
Stiehl,406
Stigman,227,406
Stiles,67,152,240a,264,328,337
Stilphen,406
Stimpson,67,227
Stimson,106,227
Stinson,32,67
Stirling,313
Stocker,7
Stockford,227
Stoddard,32,227
Stokes,227
Stone,13,67,136,227,313,362,406
Storer,142,406
Storey,
Stowell,22
Straw,341,351
Street,313
Striker,67
Strout,14,48,51,98,142,227,
  264,313,328,351,355,406
Strumph,362
Stuart,71,98,228,340,355
Stubbs,228
Studley,35
Stults,67
Stultz,228,337
Sturdivant,14,22,142
Sturgis,67,228,264,322,337,
  362,406
Sturtevant,228
Sullivan,35,228,264,313,342
Summersides,406
Sumner,142
Sutermeister,228
Sutherland,58
Sutkovoy,328
Swallow,136
Swan,67,98,151,228
Swartz,228
Swedsen,228
Sweeney,313
Sweet,136,228,264
Sweetland,48

Sweetser,136,240a,264,407
Swendsen,337
Swendsen,58
Swenson,82,228
Swertsen,228
Swett,2,4,14,17,40,74,77,82,228,
 240a,264,313,328,343,407
Swisko,313
Sykes,228,407
Sylvester,48,76,136,228,313,407
Sylvia,228
Symes,407
Symonds,351
Syphers,407
Szostak,58,228
Taber,98
Taggert,228,313
Tailor/Taylor,22,35,67,86,98,
 136,151,229
Tait,98
Talbot,407
Talfer,98
Tame,25
Tandberg,98,407
Tanguay,313
Tanner,142
Tapley,48,229,351,407
Taplin,22
Tappan,142
Tarbox,407
Tardiff,229,313
Tarr,407
Tate,106,142
Taylor,407,416
Teague,229
Tebbetts,151
Tedford,229
Teel,98
Tefft,265
Telle,58
Temm,407
Temple,229
Templeton,407
Tenney,136
Tenny,229
Terrio,229
Terrison,7
Tetrault,229,313
Tewskbury,265
Thacher,322
Thayer,38,67,74,109,142,229
Theis,229
Theot,152
Theriault,229,314
Thestrup,407
Thibeault,229,314
Thibideau,98

Thistle,229
Thoits,35,71
Thomas,98,106,151,229,314,
 328,362,407
Thombs,407
Thomes,17,32,67,106,340,407
Thompson,22,38,51,67,86,98,
 136,229,265,314,337,352,407
Thomsen,230
Thomson,142
Thonsen,230
Thoresen,32
Thorn/e,109,136,152
Thorndike,314
Thorne,137,230,230
Thorner,416
Thrasher,14
Thunborg,106
Thuotte,230,314
Thurlow,14,69,99,230
Thurston,25,35
Thygesen,230
Tibbetts,48,98,137,230,355,407
Tiedwell,230
Tillson,32
Tilton,230
Timberlake,230
Timmons,67
Timoney,230
Tingley,230
Tinker,230
Tinkham,106,230
Tinsman,230
Titcomb,14,23,230,314
Titus,230
Tobie,98
Tobin,314
Todd,143,230,407
Toft,230,328
Toher,230
Tokasksi,407
Tole,240a,265
Tomlinson,328,407
Tompkins,137
Tompson,23,230
Toms,68
Tondreau,314
Toner,86
Tonge,230
Toothaker,337
Topping,355
Torrey,68,111,137,230
Torsey,231
Totman,240a,265
Tournageau,314
Toutloff,352
Tower,231,265

Towle,68,152,231,240a,265,
　322,407
Townsend,58,68,231,315
Towsey,231
Tracey,231,337
Tracy,362,407
Trafton,231
Trask,231
Travers,407
Travis,231
Treen,23
Tremblay,315,337
Trepanier,315
Treworgy,407
Trickey,106,147,231,265,328
Trine,315
Tripp,68,77,231,338,352,407
Trott,68,82
Trowbridge,143
Troy,137
Truax,231
True,17,32,82,98,231,344
Trueworthy,231,343
Trumball,98,231,
Tryon,137
Trzenska,231,315
Tucker,231
Tuero,71,86
Tufts,265
Tukesbury,14,137
Tukey,53,68,74,86
Tullar,231
Tupper,408
Turgeon,231,315
Turkington,98
Turlott,328
Turnball,231
Turner,2,14,51,98,231,328,408
Tuttle,137,232,408
Twaddel,408
Twitchell,338
Twombley,137,315,408
Tyler,240a,265,408
Tyng,408
Udel (Judelson),416
Ullrich,32
Umphrey,408
Underwood,23,143
Uno,315
Unterreiner,232
Upton,98
Usher,86,315,408
Ustic,338
Vachon,315
Vail,106,315
Vaillancourt,315
Valentine,232,240a,265

Valia,232
Valida,315
Valle,315
Valley,232
Valliere,232
Van Blareom,408
Van Tassell,338
VanBuskirk,232
Vanderbuclcke,232
Vannah,232
Vanner,232,266
VanTassel,232
VanVliet,151,232
Varney,51,53,68,70,71,74,76,
　77,86,98,232,266,328,343,352
Varnum,266
Vaughan,68,232
Vaughn,408
Veno,232
Ventresc,232
Ventresca,98
Verrill,32,48,58,232,240a,266,
　328,338,408
Victor,316
Vigeant,316
Vigue,23
Vinal,48,232
Vincent,99,316
Vine,408
Violette,58,232,316
Vokey,316
Voris,137
Voroneke,316
Vose,137
Vosmus,99
Wades,232
Wadleigh,316
Wadsworth,408
Wagg,109,408
Wagner,408
Waig,32,338
Waite,14,68,232
Waitt,2,338
Wakefield,99,137,266
Walden,16,44
Waldron,151,316
Wales,58,338
Walker,35,38,68,74,82,106,137,
　147,151,232,266,342,343,408
Wall,48
Wallace,74,100,137,152,232,
　240a,266,316,408
Walls,23
Walsh,99
Waltman,232,338
Walton,32,87,137,233,266
Wanasky,233

Ward,14,58,106,233,266,316,
 328,342,408
Wardsworth,233
Wark,58,82,233
Warming,233,338
Warner,32,68,233
Warren,48,76,233,240a,266,
 322,328,408
Warsaski,416
Wasgatt,409
Washburn,14,25,32,233,352
Wass,355,409
Waterhouse,3,23,44,70,99,106,
 233,267,340,342,352,409
Waterman,137,233,267,352,
 409,416
Waters,316,409
Watkins,233
Watson,35,82,143,233,267,
 355,409
Watt/s,5,7,234,328,410
Way,267,410
Webb,37,38,49,76,77,82,87,
 99,107,109,145,152,235,240a,
 267,329,338,342,410
Webber,4,68,234,267,416
Weber,83
Webster,14,23,234
Wedge,68,234
Weed,234,316,343
Weeks,58,234,410
Weeman,72,234,410
Weir,234
Weist,234
Welch,14,234,240a,267,316,
 352,338,410
Weld,137
Wellington,316
Wellman,235
Wells,235
Wentworth,58,69,99152,,235,
 316,329,362,410
Wescott,352,362,410
Wescott,58,69,83,99,148,151,
 235,240a,267,329,338,
West,32,58,235,410
Westbrook,146
Westerberg,146,235
Weston,137,235,410
Wetherbee,72,411
Wetmore,235
Wetsell,411
Weymouth,2,137,267,411
Wharff,235
Wheeland,362
Wheeler,235,240a,267,329,411
Wheet,235

Whelden,235
Whidden,69,235
Whipple,235,329
Whitcomb,35,411
WhiteWhitte,14,49,69,87,137,236,
 316,329,411
Whitehead,87,236
Whitehouse,7,137
Whiteside,362
Whiting,236
Whitlock,317
Whitman,14,236,411
Whitmore,23,236,322,411
Whitney,23,25,32,71,99,143,
 236,267,322,362,411
Whittaker,236
Whitten,112,236,267
Whitter,411
Whittier,37,236,329
Widber,236
Widger,99,338
Wiedien,411
Wiemert,236
Wier,83
Wiggin/s,14,87,137,236,267,
 338,363,411
Wight,77,83,236,342
Wightman,151
Wignot,329
Wilbanddd,362
Wilber,23
Wilbur,23,99,267
Wilcox,110,411
Wilder,2,14,236,411
Wildes,151
Wiley/Willey,53,69,99
Wilies,151
Wilkins,236,317
Wilkinson,236
Willard,137
Willette,236,338
Williams,14,38,49,51,69,99,143,
 236,267,317,329,338,411
Williamson,267
Willis,143,236,240a,267,338
Wilson,15,25,32,36,69,83,100,
 111,138,236,267,317,329
Winat,416
Winch,17,25
Winchester,411
Wing,69,237,317,362
Wingate,411
Winkpaw,317
Winship,77,83,99,237,342
Winslow,7,15,16,33,36,49,69,76,
 77,83,99,110,111,138143,152,
 237,240a,267,317

Winter,237
Winters,87,267
Winther,237
Wise,145
Wisewell,33
Wiswell,87,237,352
Witham,36,58,138,143,237
Withee,237
Witzel,317
Wogan,237
Wolf,416
Wolfe,237
Wolman,416
Wolstenhulme,99
Wood,237,240a,267,317,355,411
Woodbury,99,138,147,151,237,
  240a,268
Woodford,109,138
Woodis,58,238,338
Woodman,23,44,138,238,268,412
Woods,69,238,412
Woodsome,268
Woodsum,240a,268
Woodward,238,412
Woodworth,49
Worchester,412
Word,338
Worden,412
Woritny 69
Work,238
Wormwell,238
Wormwood,240a,268
Woronecke,317
Worrey,69
Worth,99
Worthing,99
Worthington,238
Worthley,238,412
Wright,44,76,99,138,238,317,
  338,352,412
Wterman,238
Wyer,138,238,240a
Wyeth,138
Wyman,2,15,69,329
Wynn,238
Yale,317
Yambanis,317
Yates,69,99
Yde,238
Yeager,317
Yeaton,143
Yerrington,338
York,15,23,33,39,49,69,99,
  138,238,317,412
Young,5,49,99,238,317,338,412
Zahares,317
Zelensky,317

www.ingramcontent.com/pod-product-compliance
Lightning Source LLC
Chambersburg PA
CBHW060910300426
44112CB00011B/1413